JUSTICE SYSTEM

CORRECTIONS

SENTENCING & SANCTIONS | PROBATION | PRISON | PAROLE

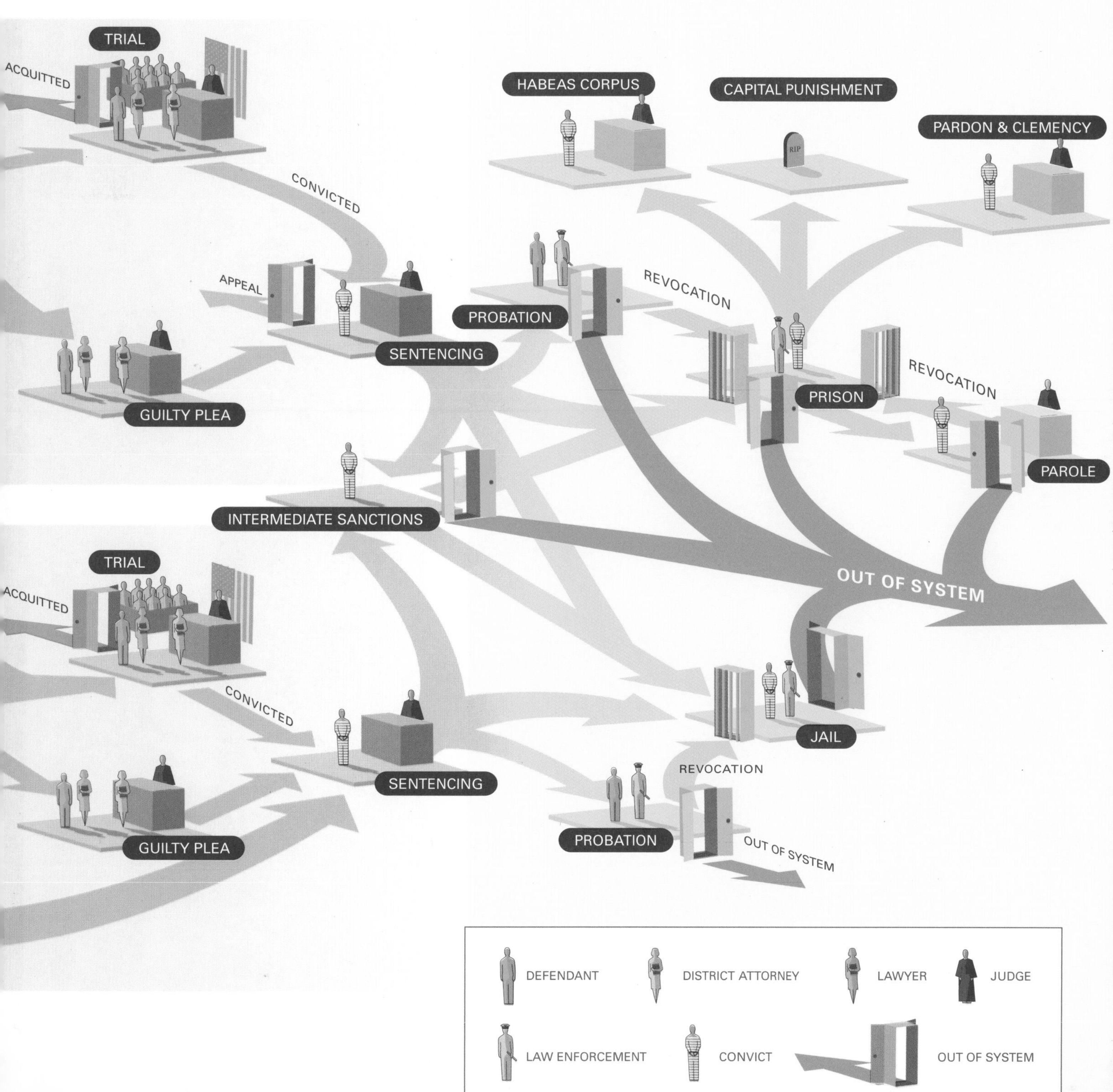

Welcome to Criminal Justice

Mainstream and Crosscurrents

At the heart of this textbook are the **Crosscurrents**, which contrast the successes and reforms of the criminal justice system by emphasizing contemporary cases as well as the unpopular laws, ill-funded agencies, and honest mistakes that impact the quality of American justice. Linked closely to the theme of each chapter, the Crosscurrents feature reveals the multiple facets of crime and the solutions we are searching for.

About the Author

John Randolph Fuller has been a professor of criminology at the University of West Georgia for more than 24 years. He brings both an applied and a theoretical background to his scholarship and has been recognized by his students as an outstanding teacher. Fuller was voted the 1991 Arts and Sciences Faculty Member of the Year and the 2001 Honors Professor of the Year. His love of teaching and his commitment to helping his students understand the real world of criminal justice are what motivated him to develop this book.

Fuller served as a probation and parole officer for the Florida Probation and Parole Commission. He worked in Broward County, Florida, where he managed a caseload of more than 100 felons. In addition, he served as a criminal justice planner for the Palm Beach Metropolitan Criminal Justice Planning Unit. In this capacity he worked with every criminal justice agency in a three-county area and wrote grants for the Law Enforcement Assistance Administration that funneled more than $1 million into local criminal justice agencies.

Fuller is the author of numerous journal articles and book chapters and has authored and edited books on criminal justice, criminology, and corrections.

Features

FOCUS ON ETHICS

Righteous Vengeance?

As a police officer you have been on the trail of a serial child molester who frequents the city's parks. You have a good idea of who it is, but this suspect has been smart enough to elude arrest and conviction for over 10 years. This morning you found your suspect dead, lying in a pool of blood with his skull crushed. Close to the body you discover a baseball bat with the name of the son of a prominent politician printed on the bat handle. You know that this 17-year-old boy was a victim of molestation 10 years ago when this problem first surfaced in the community. Your suspicion is that the boy killed the molester, but you also believe that the suspect needed killing and that the boy did the community a great service. If you hide the bat, there will be no way to trace the crime to this young man who you think had a good reason to commit this act. If you enter the bat into evidence, the boy could be convicted of murder and sent to prison for a long time. Because you have twin eight-year-old sons, you are happy this perpetrator will no longer prowl the city parks. Can you turn a blind eye to this crime? Can you protect this otherwise good boy? If you do hide the bat, should you tell his father so that he could protect you if you are found out, or maybe because you think he could help get you promoted? You know the correct procedure would be to arrest the boy, but a little voice inside your head is whispering something about a "greater justice," and you are tempted to hide the bat. What do you do?

QUESTIONS

1. Arrest the boy and let the criminal justice system take its course?
2. Hide the bat, and protect the boy?
3. Hide the bat, protect the boy, and tell his father the truth?

CROSSCURRENTS

Life in a Police State

Courtesy of CORBIS-NY.

Our procedural law dictates the rules that the criminal justice system must adhere to in arresting, prosecuting, and imprisoning suspects. Given that some of the inefficiencies of the system allow some criminals to escape punishment, it is sometimes tempting to relax the constraints we place on law enforcement and allow the police and judges unbridled freedom in fighting crime. However, there could be negative unintended consequences to such a policy. Without any constraints on the criminal justice system, we would have a police state. What would it be like to live under such a system?

Aleksandr Solzhenitsyn gave us a good idea in his book, *The Gulag Archipelago*, in which he recounted life in the former Soviet Union where the rights of the individual were sacrificed to the unfettered discretion of the government. The result was a system of state-sponsored terror in which the criminal justice system was a tool of internal repression. Of particular interest for the study of law enforcement is Solzhenitsyn's first chapter on arrest, in which he provided multiple examples of how law enforcement, without laws for the enforcers, makes arrests in a police state.

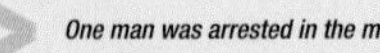

- ***One man was arrested in the middle of an operation on his stomach ulcer.***
- ***A man was with his wife at a train station when an unidentified man asked to talk to him in private. The two men stepped into an adjoining room. The woman did not see or hear from her husband again for 10 years.***
- ***After a neighbor was arrested, a woman went to the police station to inquire what she should do about the neighbor's daughter who was left behind. The police told her to sit down. They arrested her a couple of hours later solely to meet their arrest quota.***

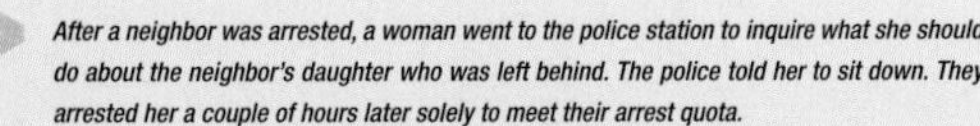

The police do not identify themselves. According to Solzhenitsyn, "You are arrested by a meterman who has come to read your meter. You are arrested by a bicyclist who has run into you on the street, by a railway conductor, a taxi driver, a savings bank teller, the manager of a movie theater. Any one of them can arrest you, and you notice the concealed maroon-colored identification card only when it is too late" (p. 10). Solzhenitsyn, who called the police the "organs," contended that they operated with absolute authority and virtually no oversight. The criminal justice system was not only corrupt, it was surreal. There was neither rhyme nor reason to who was arrested and punished, and the courts were as ruthless and unprincipled as the police. Without the checks and balances found in democracies, a government could easily become a police state. The men who crafted the Constitution of the United States were well aware of these dangers.

QUESTIONS

1. Could the United States ever become a police state?
2. Was the Soviet Union police state a government run amok, or had there possibly been good reasons for it? What do you think?

Source: Aleksandr I. Solzhenitsyn, *The Gulag Archipelago 1918–1956* (New York: Harper and Row, 1973), 3–23.

Ethics & Criminal Justice

▲ **Focus on Ethics** boxes appear in every chapter and provide the student with ethical dilemmas that are routinely faced by criminal justice practitioners. These dilemmas are complex and require the student to consider the balancing of values, procedures, and the law in arriving at solutions.

Theory & Practice

▲ **Crosscurrents** boxes appear in every chapter and provide the student with concrete, real-life examples of how justice is administered in the United States.

NEWS FLASH

Rodney King and Double Jeopardy

Courtesy of CORBIS-NY.

The concept of double jeopardy is easily misunderstood. Although basically it refers to the prohibition of a defendant being tried twice for the same crime, the full definition is a bit more complicated. Take, for example, the two trials of the police officers who participated in the 1991 beating of motorist Rodney King.

On March 3, 1991, Los Angeles police officers stopped Rodney King's car after a high-speed chase and ordered him to exit the car and lie on the ground. His two passengers, both adult males, complied, but King did not leave the car immediately. King, who had been drinking, resisted arrest, behaving erratically and aggressively. Four officers, Laurence Powell, Timothy Wind, Theodore Briseno, and Stacey Koon, began beating King with their batons, fracturing his skull and causing internal injuries.

Unknown to the police, plumbing company manager George Holliday was videotaping the incident from his nearby apartment. The next day he released the tape to the media. On March 7 the Los Angeles County district attorney dismissed the charges against King. On March 15 the four officers were charged with assault.

The case went to trial in a state court, and on April 29, 1992, the officers were cleared of assault. Riots ensued and continued across Los Angeles for several days. In the end, 55 people were killed, about 2,000 were injured, and over 7,000 were arrested. The National Guard was eventually sent in to help restore order.

By February 1993 the four officers were on trial again, this time on federal charges of violating King's constitutional rights. Officers Timothy Wind and Theodore Briseno were acquitted, but the jury found Stacey Koon and Laurence Powell guilty. Koon and Powell received 30-month prison terms.

Although, at first glance, the two trials appear to violate the double jeopardy prohibition, the trials had enough differences to steer clear of double jeopardy (see table).

	First Trial	Second Trial
Jurisdiction	State	Federal
Offense	Assault	Violation of constitutional rights
Type of suit	Criminal	Criminal

The primary issue involves the concept of "dual sovereignty." In *U.S. v. Lanza* (1922), the Supreme Court decided that dual sovereignty permits successive state and federal prosecutions for the same crime, stating that, "an act denounced as a crime by both national and state sovereignties is an offense against the peace and dignity of both and may be punished by each." Therefore, the first trial was conducted by the State of California and the second by the federal government, each concerning a different offense. Because both cases were tried in criminal courts, the officers were eligible for incarceration in both trials.

Sources: BBC, "Flashback: Rodney King and the LA Riots," July 10, 2002, http://news.bbc.co.uk/1/hi/world/americas/2119943.stm. The Rodney King Beating Trials, *Jurist*, http://jurist.law.pitt.edu/trials24.htm. *U.S. v. Lanza*, 260 U.S. 377 (1922).

Current Events

▶ **News Flash** boxes appear in every chapter and present current and interesting events that highlight and reinforce the important characteristics of offenders, workings of the criminal justice system, and criminal justice policy issues.

CASE IN POINT

Gideon v. Wainwright

The Case	**The Point**
Gideon v. Wainwright 372 U.S. 335, 83 S. Ct. 792 (1963)	Indigent defendants have the right to court-appointed attorneys in felony cases.

Clarence Gideon, an impoverished drifter, was charged in 1961 with breaking and entering a poolroom with the intent to commit a misdemeanor, a felony under Florida law. Gideon went to court without money or a lawyer and asked the court to appoint counsel for him. The judge told him that counsel was appointed only if the punishment for the offense involved the death penalty. The case went to a jury trial in which Gideon defended himself. He was found guilty and sentenced to five years in prison. On appeal, the Supreme Court overturned his conviction and established that indigent defendants have the right to court-appointed attorneys in felony cases.

Wrote Justice Hugo Black, "In our adversary system of criminal justice, any person hauled into court, who is too poor to hire a lawyer, cannot be assured a fair trial unless counsel is provided for him."

▼ **Chapter Objectives** Each chapter begins with a list of objectives that tells the student the important issues covered in the chapter.

Legal Themes

▲ **Case in Point** boxes present major court cases in every chapter. These cases are the bedrock of the criminal justice system and are summarized with an eye toward understanding by someone who does not have a legal education.

CHAPTER

8

History and Organization of Courts

COURTS PLAY A PIVOTAL ROLE IN THE U.S. CRIMINAL JUSTICE system. They are responsible for both determining the guilt or innocence of the defendant and deciding on the disposition or sentence for defendants who are found guilty. This all must be done according to a complex and ever-changing network of laws, personnel, and political pressures. The courts are besieged on all sides by those who observe an institution in crisis, such as the following:

> Law enforcement officers, who complain that offenders are treated too leniently[1]

> Corrections officials, who have no room in their prisons for new inmates and are concerned about the severe sentences that keep inmates incarcerated for many, many years[2]

> ... court as an unfathomable machine that fails ... iminals are released because of

objectives

After reading this chapter the student should be able to:

1. Explain why some observers see U.S. courts as "an institution in crisis."
2. Discuss how courts are subject to outside influences.
3. Outline the history of courts.
4. Discuss trial by ordeal and trial by battle.
5. Discuss the Assize of Clarendon.
6. Discuss the beginnings of the jury trial.
7. Discuss the Magna Carta.
8. Explain the problems of early American courts.
9. Discuss U.S. slave courts.
10. Draw a connection between England's legal treatment of early American colonists and the Revolution.
11. Discuss the cases, historical events, and individuals that have affected the way the courts have evolved.
12. Explain court organization; include the federal court system and courts of appeals.
13. Discuss the role of the Supreme Court.
14. Discuss specialized federal courts and the types of cases they handle.

▼ **Review Questions** At the end of each chapter are open-ended questions that help the student review the major ideas in the chapter.

REVIEW QUESTIONS

1. What two problems affect the image and functioning of the court?
2. Are courts purely a feature of European societies?
3. What system did Europeans use in lieu of violence to settle wrongs and disputes?
4. What was the first type of jury?
5. Why were the first grand juries and trial juries flawed?
6. What was the Court of the Star Chamber?
7. What served as the foundation for U.S. courts?

Glossary

Actual-seizure stop An incident in which police officers physically restrain a person and restrict his or her freedom.

Actus reus "Guilty deed." The physical action of a crime.

Adjudicatory hearing The process in which a juvenile court determines whether the allegations in a petition are supported by evidence.

Adversarial process A term describing the manner in which U.S. criminal trial courts operate; a system that requires two sides, a prosecution and a defense.

Alibi A defense that involves the defendant(s) claiming not to have been at the scene of a crime when that crime was committed.

Amicus curiae Someone who is not a part of a case who gives advice or testimony. Also called "friend of the court."

Anomie A condition in which a people or society undergoes a breakdown of social norms and values.

Argot roles Specific patterns of behavior that inmates develop in prison to adjust to the environment.

Arraignment A court appearance in which the defendant is formally charged with a crime and asked to respond by pleading guilty, not guilty, or *nolo contendere*.

Arson The act of intentionally burning a building. Any death that results from arson is murder, regardless of the arsonist's intention.

Ascertainable criteria A peacemaking criminology term that states that everyone involved in a criminal justice process should understand the rules and procedures employed by the system.

Assize of Clarendon A 12th-century English law that established judicial procedure and the grand jury system. It also took power from the local courts and returned it to the English crown.

Atavism The appearance in a person of features thought to be from earlier stages of human evolution. Popularized by Cesare Lombroso.

Authority The right and the power to commit an act or order others to commit an act. Permission.

Bail agent An employee of a private, for-profit company that provides money for suspects to be released from jail. Bail companies usually charge the suspect a fee of 10 percent of the amount of the bond. Also called a bondsman.

Bailiff An officer of the court responsible for executing writs and processes, making arrests, and keeping order in the court.

Behaviorism The assessment of human psychology via the examination of objectively observable and quantifiable actions, as opposed to subjective mental states.

Bench trial A trial ... without a jury, in whi... Sometimes called a co...

Beyond a reasonabl... proof required to win ... criminal cases to proc...

Bill of Indictment ... accused person that i... whether enough evide...

Bill of Rights The f... Constitution that gua... to citizens.

Blood feud A disag... on personal vengeanc...

Bobbies A popular ... 1829 by Sir Robert Pe... derived from the short...

Boot camp prison ... boot camp training an... offenders. Often used ...

Bow Street Runners ... 1748 by magistrates H... Fielding whose memb... a designated post.

Broken windows th... or deviant behavior w... a justification for clea... drunks, and unruly te... committed.

Bureau of Alcohol, T... enforcement organiza... that enforces federal l... tobacco, firearms, exp...

Burglary The act of ... other structure or veh... not required and burg... committed, such as as...

Glosario de español

Actual-seizure stop
Aprehensión y captura Situación en la que oficiales policíacos restringen físicamente a una persona limitando así su libertad.

***Actus reus* "Guilty deed"**
***Actus reus* "conducta delictiva"** La acción por la cual se comete el delito.

Adjudicatory hearing
Vista adjudicatoria Procedimiento, en el tribunal de menores, donde se determina si hay pruebas para los cargos descritos en la petición.

Adversarial process
Sistema acusatorio Término que describe el sistema de justicia criminal de los Estados Unidos, está basado en el litigio entre dos partes, un abogado defensor (representa al acusado) y un fiscal (representa al estado).

Alibi
Coartada Defensa en la que el acusado reclama no haber estado presente en la escena del delito cuando éste ocurrió.

Amicus curiae
Amicus curiae Persona que a pesar de no ser parte del litigio ofrece consejo o testimonio. También es conocido como "amigo del tribunal."

Anomia
Anomia Condici Condición o situación en la que una persona o sociedad pierden sus valores y normas sociales.

Argot roles
Jerga carcelaria Patrón de conducta, comportamiento, y lenguaje desarrollado por los confinados para adaptarse al ambiente carcelario.

Arraignment
Acusación Vista en la que el acusado es formalmente informado de los cargos en su contra y donde se exige se declare culpable, inocente, o que no se opone a la acusación.

Arson
Incendio provocado Acción intencional por la cual se incendia un edificio o estructura. Si alguien muere durante esta acción, el cargo criminal será homicidio, independientemente de la intención del acusado.

Ascertainable criteria
Criterios afirmables Termino usado en Criminología de la Paz, que establece que toda persona envuelta en el proceso de justicia criminal debe entender las reglas y procedimientos usados en este sistema.

Assize of Clarendon
Sesión de Clarendon Durante el siglo 12 en Inglaterra, ley que estableció el procedimiento jurídico y el sistema del gran jurado. Además removió algunos poderes de los tribunales locales y los otorgó a la corona inglesa.

Atavism
Atavismo En una persona, la apariencia de rasgos físicos que se creen son rezagos de una etapa evolucionaria anterior. Popularizado por Cesare Lombroso.

Authority
Autoridad Poder, autoridad y legitimación para realizar un acto u ordenar a otros realizar un acto. Permiso.

Bail agent
Fiador Empleado de una compañía privada (a comisión, con fines de lucro) la cual provee los medios económicos que permite que los sospechosos de actos criminales puedan ser puestos en libertad. Usualmente estas compañías recargan un 10 porciento del monto de la fianza.

Bailiff
Guardia, alguacil Oficial del tribunal responsable de ejecutar órdenes judiciales y otros procedimientos, pueden arrestar y mantienen el orden público en el tribunal.

Behaviorism
Estudio psicológico de la conducta Evaluación psicológica que usa medios objetivamente observables y acciones cuantificables, es lo opuesto al estado mental subjetivo.

Bench trial
Juicio de derecho Juicio frente a un juez, sin jurado, donde el juez hace la determinación. También se conoce como juicio.

Beyond a reasonable doubt
Mas allá de toda duda razonable Se refiere al nivel de prueba requerido para ganar un caso en un tribunal. Este nivel de prueba es necesario en casos criminales para asegurar un veredicto de culpabilidad.

Bill of Indictment
Auto de acusación Declaratoria sobre los cargos acusatorios en contra del acusado que es presentada al gran jurado para que éstos decidan si hay evidencia suficiente para la acusación.

Bill of Rights
Carta de derechos Las primeras 10 enmiendas a la Constitución de los Estados Unidos que garantizan los privilegios y derechos fundamentales de los ciudadanos.

Spanish translation by
Dr. Myrna Cintrón
Prairie View A&M University

◀ **Glossary** Key words identified in each chapter are defined in the text margin where the word appears and then at the end of the book in its extensive glossary. This helps students identify the important terms and phrases used in the criminal justice system.

◀ **Spanish Glossary** The glossary is repeated in Spanish to allow native Spanish-speaking students to better comprehend the exact technical or legal meaning of important terms. This is the only introduction to criminal justice text that provides a Spanish glossary.

Eye on Criminology

Policing in the U.S.

◀ ▼ The history of law enforcement is presented with an eye toward the important issues and problems that have resulted in the present-day system of policing with all its accomplishments, shortcomings, and challenges for the future.

History and Organization of Law Enforcement CHAPTER 5 149

Figure 5.1 The Nine Principles of Policing

The following principles appear in the appendix of Charles Reith's *A New Study of Police History* (1956). Although popularly attributed to Sir Robert Peel, the principles were probably written by Charles Rowan and Richard Mayne, whom Peel appointed to direct and organize the newly created Metropolitan Police.

1. To prevent crime and disorder, as an alternative to their repression by military force and severity of legal punishment.
2. To recognize always that the power of the police to fulfill their functions and duties is dependent on public approval of their existence, actions, and behavior and on their ability to secure and maintain public respect.
3. To recognize always that to secure and maintain the respect and approval of the public means also the securing of the willing cooperation of the public in the task of securing observance of laws.
4. To recognize always that the extent to which the cooperation of the public can be secured diminishes proportionately the necessity of the use of physical force and compulsion for achieving police objectives.
5. To seek and preserve public favor, not by pandering to public opinion, but by constantly demonstrating absolutely impartial service to law, in complete independence of policy, and without regard to the justice or injustice of the substance of individual laws; by ready offering of individual service and friendship to all members of the public without regard to their wealth or social standing; by ready exercise of courtesy and friendly good humor; and by ready offering of individual sacrifice in protecting and preserving life.
6. To use physical force only when the exercise of persuasion, advice, and warning is found to be insufficient to obtain public cooperation to an extent necessary to secure observance of law or to restore order; and to use only the minimum degree of physical force which is necessary on any particular occasion for achieving a police objective.
7. To maintain at all times a relationship with the public that gives reality to the historic tradition that the police are the public and that the public are the police; the police being only members of the public who are paid to give full time attention to duties which are incumbent on every citizen in the interests of community welfare and existence.
8. To recognize always the need for strict adherence to police-executive functions, and to refrain from even seeming to usurp the powers of the judiciary of avenging individuals or the State, and of authoritatively judging guilt and punishing the guilt.
9. To recognize always that the test of police efficiency is the absence of crime and disorder, and not the visible evidence of police action in dealing with them.

Sources: Charles Reith, *A New Study of Police History* (Edinburgh: Oliver and Boyd, 1956), 121–142, 287–288; Civitas: The Institute for the Study of Civil Society, *Principles of Good Policing*, http://www.civitas.org.uk/pubs/policeNine.php.

their founder's nickname of Bob, were expected to adhere to a strict military-type discipline based on Peel's nine principles of policing (see Figure 5.1). The bobbies set a new standard of police professionalism; however, their jurisdiction was limited to the city of London. It was not until 1856 that the rural provinces were required to establish police forces.

Policing in the United States

Like many aspects of American culture, policing has its roots in English tradition. Although the police developed differently in England than they have here, some commonalities are worth examining. According to Samuel Walker and Charles Katz, "the English heritage contributed three enduring features to American policing":[8]

1. **Limited police authority.** As opposed to other countries in Europe, the Anglo-American tradition of policing places a good deal of emphasis on the rights and liberties of the individual.
2. **Local control.** Law enforcement agencies are, for the most part, local, city, or ... l police force. We ... ey are not like the ... control is highly

Sentencing

▼ The courts deal with a wide variety of crimes, and the sentencing patterns of those sent to prison are the subject of great debate in the criminal justice system.

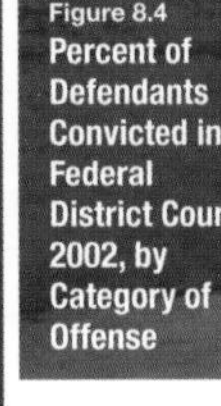

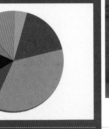

Figure 8.4 Percent of Defendants Convicted in Federal District Courts, 2002, by Category of Offense

Source: Federal Justice Statistics Resource Center, http://fjsrc.urban.org/noframe/dist/d2002/cat/s2_t3.cfm.

150 PART 2 Enforcing the Law

"Peel Fights Night Watchmen." A satirical English cartoon depicts Sir Robert Peel fighting a group of night watchmen.
Courtesy of CORBIS-NY.

3. **Fragmented system.** There are over 18,000 separate law enforcement agencies in the United States that range from federal (FBI, Secret Service), to state (highway patrol), to local (city police, county sheriff). These agencies are only loosely coordinated and have little oversight from the federal level.[9]

Many differences between the United States and England affected the development of their respective policing styles. One was the lack of a single, coherent philosophy. Whereas the English police were unified under the vision of Sir Robert Peel, local police organizations in the United States formed their own policies and procedures. Another factor was the large and ever-expanding political geography of the United States. As stakes were claimed and territories formed, government and law enforcement followed slowly. This led to the phenomenon of the "Wild West." The further the country developed from the cities and seats of government on the East Coast, the less controllable it became. A third factor was immigration. The constituency of the United States was (and is to this day) in constant flux, resulting in cities, states, and territories filled with people representing a vast array of cultures and languages. Conversely, the English police of the day were responsible for a static political and physical geography that had a homogeneous culture and language.

THE 19TH CENTURY. Jurisdictional difficulties and labor troubles gave rise to some of the nation's most famous private police. Laws were passed that allowed companies to maintain or contract with their own police forces and agencies. Pennsylvania's Coal and Iron Police became famous for its strong-arm antilabor activities. The Pinkerton National Detective Agency, founded in 1850 by Scottish political refugee Allan Pinkerton, was used for protection against thieves and labor activists by railroad companies and coal companies.

As the century waned, urban police became an integral part of their communities—so integral, in fact, that many police officers began to work for the political bosses of their communities. For example, officers would, through various measures, help ensure the election of "their" candidates. Or they would accept money in return for not enforcing certain laws. Two of the most important cities in which this type of activity—and its reform—occurred were New York and Chicago.

488 PART 5 Problems in the Crosscurrents

Boot camp institutions are patterned after military basic training. Critics claim that these programs are no more effective than traditional methods of reforming juvenile offenders.
Courtesy of CORBIS-NY.

obedience. They are physically and mentally rigorous and relatively inexpensive when compared with a training school. Although these programs are popular, critics point out the high potential for abuse and that the programs are no more effective in preventing recidivism than traditional programs.[54]

> **Traditional training schools.** These often overcrowded and understaffed programs are where the more serious offenders are incarcerated. Some training schools physically resemble adult prisons; and others may have the appearance of a college campus.[55]

In addition to these four types of public institutions are a number of public and private residential placement facilities, with juveniles in their mid to late teens comprising most of these placements (see Figure 14.5). These programs offer the court, the parents, and the youth an alternative to traditional types of confinement. Although the private programs can be very expensive, some can offer exceptional educational and counseling opportunities. However, some of the private programs are extremely controversial; at those located in other countries, the legal rights of young offenders can be extremely limited.

Treating Children as Adults

One of the outgrowths of the get-tough-on-crime approach has been to treat serious juvenile delinquents as adult criminals. Rather than handling these cases in juvenile courts, which are geared toward the needs of the child, these cases are waived to the criminal court where the protection of society is paramount. It is argued that the most serious juvenile offenders require a minimum criminal sentence that is not available in juvenile court. Critics of the waiver process point out that sending a juvenile to adult court does not always ensure the protection of the public because the child may serve only a fraction of the sentence imposed by the criminal court. Additionally, the criminal court may not have the treatment alternatives for young offenders that are available in juvenile court. Finally, there is evidence of a racial bias in who gets waived to criminal court, with young, black males being disproportionately selected.[56]

What is the right balance between protecting children and holding them accountable for their actions? To answer this question, we need to consider the presumed advantages

Treating Children as Adults

◀ Consideration of the problems must include the issues of youth crime and the juvenile justice system. This text devotes a whole chapter to deal with these concerns and fully covers some of the suggestions for reforming how young criminals are processed.

Criminal Justice Policy

Restorative Justice

▶ Restorative justice programs are emerging as a new method to deal with the problems of crime and delinquency. This text develops the links between the theory of peacemaking criminology and the practice of restorative justice.

logic to it that would allow that decision to be applied to other cases at other times. This, of course, means that racial or sexist bias should be eliminated, but it does not mean that justice need be mechanical or absolutely uniform. Individualized justice allows for discretion, but the categorical imperative dictates that decisions should have a defensible reason that promotes an overarching goal of not only justice, but social justice arrived at by correct means.

Is the peacemaking perspective simply a warmed-over version of liberal philosophies? Is it unrealistic, utopian, and naive? Is it the equivalent of giving in to the criminal element and turning the asylum over to the lunatics? Actually, no. The peacemaking perspective does not excuse crime or erase the culpability of offenders. Rather, it aims to craft institutions and policies that repair the harm caused by crime and reduce the suffering of victims, families, offenders, and the greater community.

Much of what the peacemaking perspective advocates is already ingrained in the criminal justice system. What the peacemaking perspective does is to provide a philosophical foundation for practices that recognize the promise of believing that people are basically good and that our institutions can achieve better results by modeling the types of behavior we demand of our offenders. For instance, when the state kills through capital punishment, it has a brutalizing effect on society according to the peacemaking perspective. Abusive behavior by the police alienates not only the victim, but also those who witness the event. Programs that promote the rehabilitation of offenders have been a consistent feature in the criminal justice system for decades, but because of the drain of resources caused by the war on crime, they have been neglected, underfunded, and made politically unpopular. But just how has the peacemaking perspective been implemented in the criminal justice system? One major strategy for injecting the principles of peacemaking is the restorative justice movement.

Restorative Justice

Restorative justice is a way to apply peacemaking criminology to the criminal justice system and to the community.[19] Whereas peacemaking may seem theoretically vague or idealistic, restorative justice has concrete evidence that its philosophy is workable in the real world. By highlighting the principles of restorative justice and reviewing some of the types of programs in which it has been effective, our goal here is to demonstrate that restorative justice and peacemaking are serious endeavors that deserve consideration as alternatives to the war-on-crime perspective.

Restorative justice forces us to consider the problems of crime in a different manner than do the traditional methods.[20] According to the principles of restorative justice, the criminal justice system is just a small part of society's response to crime. The possibility of making substantive changes in our crime picture is limited if we depend primarily on the formal criminal justice system. Restorative justice practices involve the community and, most important, establish and strengthen programs within the community to respond not only to crime, but also to some of the underlying conditions that contribute to crime.[21] The principles of restorative justice were aptly delineated by Ron Claassen from the Center for Peacemaking and Conflict Studies at Fresno Pacific University:[22]

1. Crime is primarily an offense against human relationships and secondarily a violation of the law (since laws are written to protect public safety and fairness in human relationships).
2. Restorative justice recognizes that crime (violations of persons and relationships) is wrong and should not occur, and also recognizes that after it does, there are dangers and opportunities. The danger is that the community, victim(s), and/or offender(s) emerge from the response further alienated, more damaged, disrespected, disempowered, feeling less safe and less cooperative with society. The opportunity is that injustice is recognized; equity is restored (restitution and grace); and the future is clarified so that participants are safer, more respectful, and more empowered and cooperative with society.

The USA Patriot Act

◀ Terrorism is having a major impact on the criminal justice system. Our police and courts are being called upon to perform new duties and to face an uncertain threat, and these issues are causing fundamental changes in the way we think about crime and the expectations we have of our criminal justice personnel.

A third and longer-term impact of the war on terrorism is that the criminal justice tem is experiencing an influx of new and talented personnel at all levels. As an empl the criminal justice system competes with other employers for the best talent. Pri September 11, criminal justice salaries often were not competitive, although the work was dangerous. Now, criminal justice programs at many universities are experiencing an influx of students. There is a new urgency and status associated with serving and protecting the public, with nothing but solid support for the mission of the domestic police and fire personnel.

THE PATRIOT ACT. The response of Congress to the terrorist attacks of September 11 was to pass the Patriot Act. Officially titled "Uniting and Strengthening America by Providing Appropriate Tools Required to Intercept and Obstruct Terrorism Act," the Patriot Act gives the government greater latitude over a broad range of concerns that specify the rights of citizens, aliens, and government agents.[11] Moreover, the act toughens penalties for those who assist terrorists and provides financial relief for victims of terrorism, including public safety officers and their families. Two particularly sweeping and controversial components of the Patriot Act are of concern to students of the criminal justice system: the reorganization and retasking of federal law enforcement and the implications for civil liberties and legal rights.

Department of Homeland Security. There has been a great deal of speculation that the September 11 terrorist attacks could have been prevented if our criminal justice system had communicated more efficiently. Some people believe that enough information was in the hands of officers from different agencies and that a coordinated and centralized command structure could have collated this information and prevented the attacks. Whether this is true is not of concern here because the mere suggestion that the attacks were preventable moved the president and Congress to restructure the federal government by creating the cabinet-level Department of Homeland Security. The intent of this action was to ensure that these agencies were organizationally allied in the most efficient and productive manner to combat terrorism.

The overall impact of the creation of the Department of Homeland Security will not be known for several years, but it is interesting to observe which agencies managed to retain their independence and which ones were brought under the auspices of the new department. For instance, the two agencies that seemed to be the most likely candidates to be brought into the Department of Homeland Security were the Federal Bureau of Investigation (FBI) and the Central Intelligence Agency (CIA). Each has a mandate to protect the United States from terrorism, with the FBI being responsible for activities within our borders and the CIA being responsible for activities in other countries that may threaten the United States. Of course, the nature of the threats often overlap, and there has been considerable friction between the FBI and CIA over the years as to which agency is responsible for which threats. However, it has been suggested that these two agencies did not share vital information that could have prevented the events of September 11. Curiously, neither of these agencies was included in the reorganization. Why? There are two plausible answers, and the truth may contain elements of each. The first lies within the nature of the agencies' basic missions. Preventing terrorism is only a small (albeit significant) part of what the FBI and CIA are mandated to do. By being under the Department of Homeland Security, they could lose their authority to decide how best to deploy their resources. This is a reasonable explanation for allowing these agencies to retain their independence and their current organizational placement; however, over the next few years, it will be crucial to monitor how well each agency works with the Department of Homeland Security. The second reason the CIA and FBI have remained independent of the Department of Homeland Security is political. These are each mature agencies that, over the years, have developed networks with politicians, a large number of loyal alumni, and their own organizational culture. Placing them under the Department of Homeland Security would have required more of a political battle than was desired after September 11.

Intermediate Sanctions

▶ Because of prison overcrowding, the criminal justice system is devising new ways to monitor offenders outside of incarceration. Intermediate sanctions have been developed that attempt to balance the demands of cost effectiveness, safety of the community, and offender rehabilitation. This text reviews and evaluates these initiatives with an eye toward their efficacy, cost effectiveness, and political feasibility.

Intermediate Sanctions

Intermediate sanctions are sentencing alternatives available to the judge who finds regular probation too lenient and prison too severe.[29] If prisons were not so crowded, many offenders who receive intermediate sanctions may actually be incarcerated. With the pressures for parole boards to release inmates early to make room for new offenders, some of these intermediate sanctions are also employed at the parole stage of the criminal justice process.

Intermediate sanctions give the criminal justice system a broader range of mechanisms of social control and enhance the public's perception that crime does not pay. Although some of these newer intermediate sanctions are problematic, the critics' concerns are being addressed, and the courts are becoming cognizant of the issues that must be resolved. Here are some of the more notable intermediate sanctions.

Intensive Supervision Probation

Intensive supervision probation is simply what probation used to be before the advent of unreasonably high caseloads for probation officers.[30] Intensive supervision probation is actually a form of triage, whereby those offenders deemed the most problematic are allocated extra supervision. Probation officers assigned to these troublesome offenders are given small caseloads and are expected to have more frequent contact with clients. It is believed that if probation officers can concentrate on those who actually need help or really pose a threat to society, then they can recognize emerging problems and intervene quickly. A number of tools are available to the intensive supervision probation officer to aid in detecting wrongdoing. One of the most controversial of these tools is drug testing.

Drug Testing

Testing probationers or parolees for illegal drug use is a technological solution to a human problem. Rather than relying on behavioral cues or lifestyle changes to detect drug use, the officer can require that clients, either on a routine or random basis, submit a sample of urine for analysis. Because one of the conditions of freedom is to refrain from the use of illegal drugs, and because probation and parole are conditional-release practices, the client has a choice of cooperating or going to prison. Most offenders cooperate and are able to retain their liberty, live with their families, hold down a job, and escape the pains of imprisonment. Submitting a urine sample, while humiliating and insulting, seems like a small price to pay for staying out of prison. This is not to say, however, that offenders do not attempt to frustrate the system by masking their drug use. Probationers use a range of techniques to deceive authorities. These techniques include submitting someone else's urine, eating or drinking various items that mask the presence of drugs, and missing or delaying tests until drugs have been diluted in the body. Probation and parole authorities counter these deceptions by increasing the sophistication of the drug tests (for example, using hair strands instead of urine), surprising the clients with random tests, and closely monitoring the administration of the tests.

House Arrest and Electronic Monitoring

House arrest is a very old concept that has appeal today because it allows offenders to maintain family ties, work to support themselves and pay taxes, take advantage of community resources such as school and counseling services, and save the state the cost of incarceration.[31] Typically, offenders are required to stay home except when they are attending approved activities such as employment, school, treatment programs, or religious services. They are especially restricted during the evening hours when most crimes take place and when they can expect unannounced calls or visits from their probation officer. Although some citizens may be concerned about some home-confined offenders being a danger to the community, for the most part, these probationers are selected because they are low-risk and have relatively stable residences in which to be confined. Electric monitoring is often used to supplement house arrest but is also used with other programs.

Criminal Justice
Mainstream and Crosscurrents

John Randolph Fuller, Ph.D.
State University of West Georgia

Upper Saddle River, New Jersey 07458

Library of Congress Cataloging-in-Publication Data
Fuller, John R.
Criminal justice : mainstream and crosscurrents / John Randolph Fuller.
p. cm.
Includes bibliographical references and index.
ISBN 0-13-112255-X
1. Criminal justice, Administration of—United States. 2. Crime—United States. I. Title.

HV9950.F85 2005
364.973–dc22

2004056099

Executive Editor: Frank Mortimer, Jr.
Development Editor: Susan Beauchamp
Assistant Editor: Mayda Bosco
Production Editor: Ann Mohan/WordCrafters Editorial Services, Inc.
Production Liaison: Barbara Marttine Cappuccio
Director of Manufacturing and Production: Bruce Johnson
Managing Editor: Mary Carnis
Manufacturing Buyer: Cathleen Petersen
Marketing Manager: Tim Peyton
Editorial Assistant: Kelly Krug
Creative Director: Cheryl Asherman
Design Coordinator: Mary Siener
Cover Designer: Michael L. Ginsberg
Cover Image: Getty Images
Interior Designer: Amanda Kavanagh
Director, Image Resource Center: Melinda Reo
Manager, Rights and Permissions: Zina Arabia
Interior Image Specialist: Beth Brenzel
Cover Image Specialist: Karen Sanatar
Image Permission Coordinator: Joanne Dippel
Photo Researcher: Kathy Ringrose
Composition: Carlisle Communications, Ltd.
Printing and Binding: Courier/Kendallville
Cover Printer: Coral Graphics

Photo Credits: pp. 1, 2, 3, 40, 41, 74, 75, 106, 145, 179, 213, 251, 283, 355, 395, 427, 463, 499 courtesy of CORBIS-NY; p. 107 courtesy of Corbis/Bettmann; pp. 143, 144, 178, 212, 249, 250, 282, 320, 321, 353, 354, 392, 426, 461, 462, 498, 536 courtesy of Getty Images; p. 537 photo by Richard T. Nowitz, courtesy of Corbis/Bettmann. Other photo credits and credits and acknowledgments for material borrowed from other sources and reproduced, with permission, in this textbook appear on appropriate pages within the text.

Pearson Education LTD.
Pearson Education Singapore, Pte. Ltd
Pearson Education, Canada, Ltd
Pearson Education–Japan
Pearson Education Australia PTY, Limited
Pearson Education North Asia Ltd
Pearson Educaçión de Mexico, S.A. de C.V.
Pearson Education Malaysia, Pte. Ltd

10 9 8 7 6 5 4 3 2 1
ISBN 0-13-112255-X
ISBN 0-13-192656-X

Dedication

For Amy

Who made me rewrite everything. Several times.

Lupus grex grex lupus est.

Brief Contents

Contents

Preface

Having taught the introduction to criminal justice course for many years using many books, I embarked on the journey to tell the story of criminal justice in a way that will help students grasp both the excitement of the field and the immense responsibility of serving the country and community. Although several fine books are already on the market, I have sought to provide a fresh approach to the teaching of the class, one that my students have found to be particularly relevant and interesting. To that end, I have written this book to reflect a theme that captures the excitement and potential of studying crime and the criminal justice system: the mainstream and crosscurrents.

The field of criminal justice is not a deep, still pond where one can see the bottom through crystal clear water. Rather, it is like a fast-moving stream with currents, crosscurrents, eddies, rapids, and hydraulics. Heraclitus' observation that one cannot step into the same stream twice is also true of the field of criminal justice, which can change just as dramatically. This book is intended to reflect those changes. Since the terrorist attacks of September 11, 2001, the field of criminal justice has become even more complex and challenging to study and to write about. The basic mission of some criminal justice agencies, such as the FBI, have been altered; a new cabinet-level department in the federal government, the Department of Homeland Security, has been created; and state and local criminal justice agencies now have the additional duties of being the first responders to terrorist attacks. Yet, in spite of this new and unprecedented threat, the fundamental job of the criminal justice system remains. Protecting individuals and property within the rule of law has always been a difficult mission. The delicate balance between public safety and individual rights and liberties is being stretched anew by the additional requirements of terrorist threats; the laws designed to address those threats, such as the USA Patriot Act; and the emotions of citizens, which range from legitimate concern to paranoia.

To develop a healthy perspective on the field of criminal justice, the student must have an appreciation for the history of social control, an understanding of the limits of science and the government, and a willingness to think critically about how the system might be reformed. It has been my experience that those who work in the criminal justice system often have practical ideas for its improvement. Many of my students and former students have been law enforcement officers, probation or parole officers, corrections workers, and rape crisis center employees. I continually learn from them about their successes, concerns, and frustrations of working in the criminal justice system. Having been there myself, I know that practical experience gives one a perspective that cannot be duplicated in the classroom. Therefore, this book is written with the view that the criminal justice system is not as neat and orderly as is often portrayed in textbooks. There are crosscurrents, if you will allow me to extend the analogy, that must be put in context if we are to understand the reasons people commit crimes and how the criminal justice system responds to violations of the law.

I hope that this fresh approach to criminal justice will find a space in criminal justice education. The book is designed to be, first and foremost, a mainstream text that covers the canon required in the first course that most criminal justice majors are exposed to. Additionally, the book serves as an introduction to the discipline for those students who have not yet chosen a major. In addition to these goals, the book offers a crosscurrents theme that extends the student's critical thinking skills beyond the memorization of dry facts and figures. The history and contemporary concerns of the discipline of criminal justice are among the most interesting and necessary fields of study offered at universities. It is somewhat regrettable that the employment opportunities in criminal justice are so plentiful because it would be better for us all if crime were less prevalent. Nevertheless, good people are needed to fill the many positions in the criminal justice system that require workers who can solve problems, act ethically, and be trusted to use power responsibly. To the extent that this book facilitates the development of those types of individuals, it will be judged a success. I remain committed to improving the integrated educational package that accompanies the book, and I eagerly solicit suggestions for improvement from both instructors and students. You can contact me at crosscurrent@comcast.net.

Organization of the Book

The book is organized in a manner that introduces the student to the field of criminal justice, follows cases through the criminal justice process, and highlights some of the pressing unresolved issues and concerns that continue to challenge criminal justice practitioners. Part One features four chapters. The first chapter identifies some of the ways we understand crime, highlights the structure of the criminal justice system, and relates the system to other institutions that affect criminal justice. Chapter 2 deals with the history and issues concerning the measurement of crime and why this is such an important task. Chapter 3 reviews the major schools of criminology and the important biological, psychological, and sociological theories that attempt to explain crime. Chapter 4 provides an introduction to criminal law and identifies the different types of laws, sources of law, and features of what constitutes a crime.

Part Two is concerned with enforcing the law. Chapter 5 presents the history and organization of law enforcement. Chapter 6 highlights some of the issues and problems with controlling the police, and Chapter 7 considers some of the pressing issues facing contemporary law enforcement.

Part Three deals with the court system. Chapter 8 provides a history of how courts were developed and how they are currently organized. Chapter 9 covers the courtroom work group and explains the roles of the prosecutor, defense attorney, and judge. Chapter 10 covers plea bargaining, the trial, and sentencing.

Part Four deals with the correctional system. Chapter 11 covers the history of social control and capital punishment, and Chapter 12 deals with life in the contemporary prison. Chapter 13 explains how corrections are used in the community setting by covering probation, parole, and intermediate sanctions.

Finally, Part Five highlights some of the pressing problems that continue to challenge the criminal justice system. Chapter 14 deals with the special issues of juveniles who break the law and differentiates between the adult and juvenile criminal justice systems. Chapter 15 covers how personal and public values affect the criminal justice system, exploring how drug abuse, gambling, and sex work are sometimes considered crimes and sometimes considered legitimate enterprises. Chapter 16 explores the future of criminal justice by contrasting the war-on-crime metaphor with the growing movement toward peacemaking criminology and restorative justice.

Acknowledgments

A book of this size and scope is not written without the assistance of many people. I wish to acknowledge those who helped in both small and substantial ways to make this book a reality and who offered many suggestions that allowed me to produce a much better book than I would have if left to my own limited skills and insights. First, I was fortunate to have a wonderful set of outside reviewers who provided both conceptual and technical advice:

- Frank Afflito, The University of Memphis, Memphis, TN
- Jerry Armor, Calhoun County Community College, Decatur, AL
- Beth Bailey, Charleston Southern University, Charleston, NC
- Paul Becker, University of Dayton, Dayton, OH
- Robert Bing, University of Texas-Arlington, Arlington, TX
- James Black, University of Tennessee, Knoxville, TN
- Steve Brandl, University of Wisconsin–Milwaukee
- Susan Brinkley, The University of Tampa, Tampa, FL
- Steve Brodt, Ball State, Muncie, IN
- Ronald Burns, Texas Christian University, Ft. Worth, TX
- Kim Davies, Augusta State University, Augusta, GA
- Alex delCarmen, University of Texas-Arlington, Arlington, TX
- Holly Dersham-Bruce, Dawson Community College, Glendive, MT
- Dana DeWitt, Chadron State College, Chadron, NE
- John Doherty, Marist College, Poughkeepsie, NY
- Vicky Dorworth, Montgomery College, Rockville, MD
- Dave Graff, Kent State University-Tuscarawas Campus, New Philadelphia, OH
- Robert Griffiths, Suffolk County Community College, Selden, NY
- Doris Hall, California State University–Bakersfield, Bakersfield, CA
- William Harver, Widener University, Chester, PA
- Bill Head, Indiana University, Bloomington, IN
- Chris Hertig, York College, York, PA
- Denise Huggins, University of Arkansas–Fayetteville, Fayetteville, AR
- Art Jipson, University of Dayton, Dayton, OH
- Paul Katsampes, Metropolitan State College of Denver, Denver, CO
- Bill Kelly, Auburn University, Auburn, AL
- Curt Kuball, Reedley College, Reedley, CA
- Steve Light, SUNY, Plattsburgh, Plattsburgh, NY
- Vivian Lord, University of North Carolina, Charlotte, NC
- Jeff Magers, Stephen F. Austin State University, Nacogdoches, TX
- A.L. Marstellar, Drury College, Springfield, MO
- William McCamey, Western Illinois University, Macomb, IL

- Dave McElreath, Washburn University, Topeka, KS
- Susan McGuire, San Jacinto College, Houston, TX
- Kevin Meehan, California State University–Fullerton, Fullerton, CA
- Kenneth Mentor, New Mexico State University, Las Cruces, NM
- Patrick Mueller, Stephen F. Austin State University, Nacogdoches, TX
- Donna Nicholson, Manchester Community College, Manchester, CT
- Emmanuel Onyeozili, University of Maryland, Eastern Shore, Princess Anne, MD
- Michael Polakowski, University of Arizona, Tucson, AZ
- John Race, University of Pittsburgh, Pittsburgh, PA
- Jeff Ross, University of Baltimore, Baltimore, MD
- Joe Schafer, Southern Illinois University Carbondale, Carbondale, IL
- Barbara Sims, Penn State University, University Park, PA
- Jeffrey Spears, University of North Carolina at Wilmington, Wilmington, NC
- David Streater, Catawba Valley Community College, Hickory, NC
- Susette Talarico, University of Georgia, Athens, GA
- Carol Thompson, Texas Christian University, Ft. Worth, TX
- Kim Tobin, Westfield State College, Westfield, MA
- Kevin Walsh, Texas A&M University, College Station, TX
- Jeremy Wilson, Catawba Valley Community College, Hickory, NC
- Dawn Young, Bossier Parish Community College, Bossier, LA

The people at Prentice Hall deserve special recognition for all the work and insights they applied to this project. Robin Baliszewski has put together the best criminal justice publishing team in the business. Ken Wiklendt, the Prentice Hall sales representative for West Georgia, for many years encouraged me to write for his company, and I am happy that I took his advice. I have been impressed with the dedication and professionalism of everyone with whom I worked. The book was first envisioned by Kim Davies and brought to completion by Frank Mortimer. This book happened because of the vision of these two accomplished editors. Susan Beauchamp served as the development editor and provided sage advice and copious amounts of encouragement. Marketing editor Tim Peyton, as well as Barbara Rosenberg and Robert Mutchnick, all provided useful suggestions for the improvement of the book. The Prentice Hall production team was invaluable in providing their professional expertise. Mary Carnis, Barbara Cappuccio, Cathleen Petersen, Mary Siener, and Amanda Kavanagh were all instrumental in keeping the project moving forward. I would also like to thank Ann Mohan and the wonderful people at WordCrafters.

I wish to thank my colleagues at the University of West Georgia. They were generous in allowing me to scavenge their bookshelves, availed me of their expertise on criminal justice and sociological issues, and were extremely encouraging at every phase of the project. These supportive colleagues include Chris Williams, Florence Ferguson, Ron Hunter, N. Jane McCandless, Marc LaFountain, Sandra Stone, Marjorie Snipes, and Don Wagner. Friends and family members who helped include Katie Fuller, Melanie Hembree, Myrna Cintron, and Eric Hickey.

Finally, I wish to thank my wife, Amy Hembree, to whom this book is dedicated. She has been instrumental in every part of the writing process. Without her editing, research, and critical reading skills, this book would be the poorer.

About the Author

John Randolph Fuller has been a professor of criminology at the University of West Georgia for more than 24 years. He brings both an applied and a theoretical background to his scholarship and has been recognized by his students as an outstanding teacher. In 1991, the Student Government Association at West Georgia voted him the Arts and Sciences Faculty Member of the Year. In 2001, the Student Honors Council recognized him as the Honors Professor of the Year. His love of teaching and his commitment to helping his students understand the real world of criminal justice are what motivated him to develop this book.

He served as a probation and parole officer for the Florida Probation and Parole Commission, working in Broward County, Florida, where he managed a caseload of more than 100 felons. In addition, he served as a criminal justice planner for the Palm Beach Metropolitan Criminal Justice Planning Unit. In this capacity he worked with every criminal justice agency in a three-county area and wrote grants for the Law Enforcement Assistance Administration that funneled more than a million dollars into local criminal justice agencies. By working directly with offenders as a probation and parole officer and with criminal justice administrators as a criminal justice planner, Dr. Fuller has gained significant insights that inform his writing about the criminal justice system and have aided him in identifying both the mainstream practices and the crosscurrents of problems that continue to prevent the achievement of justice for all.

Dr. Fuller has authored and edited numerous journal articles, chapters, and books on criminal justice, criminology, and corrections. He regularly presents his writings at the annual meetings of both the American Society of Criminology and the Academy of Criminal Justice Sciences.

PART **one**

CRIME Problems, Measurement, Theories, and Law

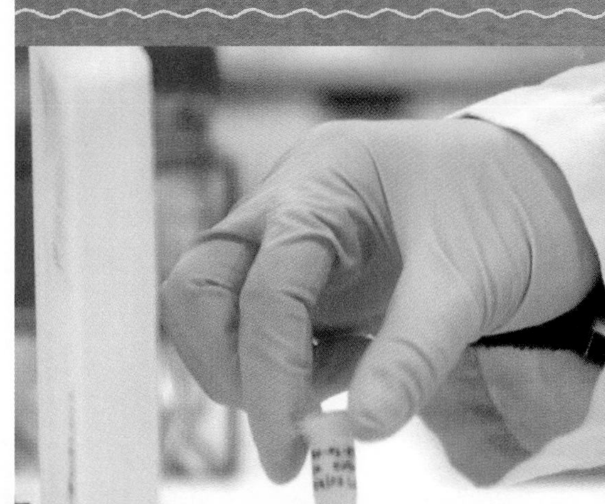

outline

CHAPTER 1

The Problem of Social Control

THE ACADEMIC DISCIPLINE OF CRIMINAL JUSTICE IS A particularly pertinent area of study in the contemporary world. The terrorist events of September 11, 2001, made all of us aware of the fragility of life and the importance of the missions of those criminal justice practitioners who are responsible for protecting citizens from crime and terror. Although the terrorist events at the World Trade Center in New York City and the Pentagon in Washington, D.C., represent an extreme end of the crime continuum, they also illustrate how everyone is dependent on the brave men and women whose jobs are to maintain the social order. September 11 raised the visibility of the criminal justice system, which will continue to receive scrutiny, criticism, and great credit for working to accomplish the maintenance of order under difficult circumstances.

The amazing feature that sets the U.S. criminal justice system apart from those of many other countries is the way individual rights are protected as an integral part of the functioning of law enforcement. In the short run, it might be a lot easier, considerably more efficient, and a good bit less expensive to allow the criminal justice system to enforce the laws without the

objectives

After reading this chapter, the student should be able to:

1. Appreciate the level and quality of the information concerning ideas about the criminal justice system.
2. Understand how the criminal justice system works with other institutions to control the behavior of individuals.
3. Look at the criminal justice system and ask whether the system metaphor is illustrative or misleading.
4. Discuss the picture of crime presented by the media and suggest ways it might be improved.
5. Explain how the number of cases decreases as we trace their movement through the criminal justice system.
6. List and discuss the multiple goals of the criminal justice system.
7. Explain why the criminal justice system is the system of last resort.

restraints imposed by constitutional rights. Yet, these restraints are precisely what make the United States such a beacon of freedom around the world. By protecting the rights of marginal individuals such as aliens, the impoverished, criminals, and even terrorists, the United States demonstrates a high level of respect for both people and laws. In the long run, this example of democracy in action serves to show the world that the response of a government to the problems of crime can be both forceful and compassionate.

The criminal justice system is faced with the prospect of maintaining a delicate balance between imposing order and preserving individual rights. This is an extremely difficult task in the best of times and becomes even more problematic in times of terrorism. Yet, it would be a grave mistake to think of these issues as mutually exclusive. In other words, keeping citizens safe does not require that they lose their constitutional rights. The successful creation and nurturing of meaningful communities require that the government serve the citizens' interests by finding methods to address crime without allowing law enforcement agencies to turn the country into a police state that relies on its own brand of terror to maintain order. Achieving this delicate balance is part of the Herculean task of the criminal justice system. As we construct new responses to the threats of terrorism, this task will challenge lawmakers, police officers, judges, correctional officials, and the rest of us to develop a new appreciation for the complexities and ambiguities of crime control in the 21st century. The primary purpose of this textbook is to illustrate these complexities and ambiguities by explaining the workings of the mainstream criminal justice system, as well as the crosscurrents that run through it.

Those who work in the criminal justice system are able to see through the romantic and frivolous veneer of pundits who contend that getting tough on crime is the only way to ensure our safety. Although criminal behavior must be addressed within the rule of law, many practitioners recognize that more fundamental questions need to be considered. These questions about the nature of justice in the United States include concerns of racial prejudice, economic inequality, and differential access to the decision-making processes in all realms of society. This text offers a substantially mainstream approach to the field of criminal justice while also introducing some of the crosscurrents of injustice, inefficiency, and insensitivity that all too often plague our society. It is hoped that this balanced approach to the study of criminal justice will inspire students with the idea that the future will require the best and brightest citizens to take a real interest in ensuring that justice is meted out within a system that respects individual rights.

What Is Crime?

Crime can be described as an action taken by a person or a group of people that violates the rules of a given society to the point that someone is harmed or the interests of that society are harmed. Most people envision crimes as fairly straightforward, often sordid affairs, such as robbery, rape, and murder. A measure of this can be seen in the FBI's Crime Clock in Figure 1.1.

- On July 22, 1991, police in Milwaukee, Wisconsin, found a man in handcuffs wandering on the street. The man claimed that he had escaped from another man

Figure 1.1
Crime Clock 2002

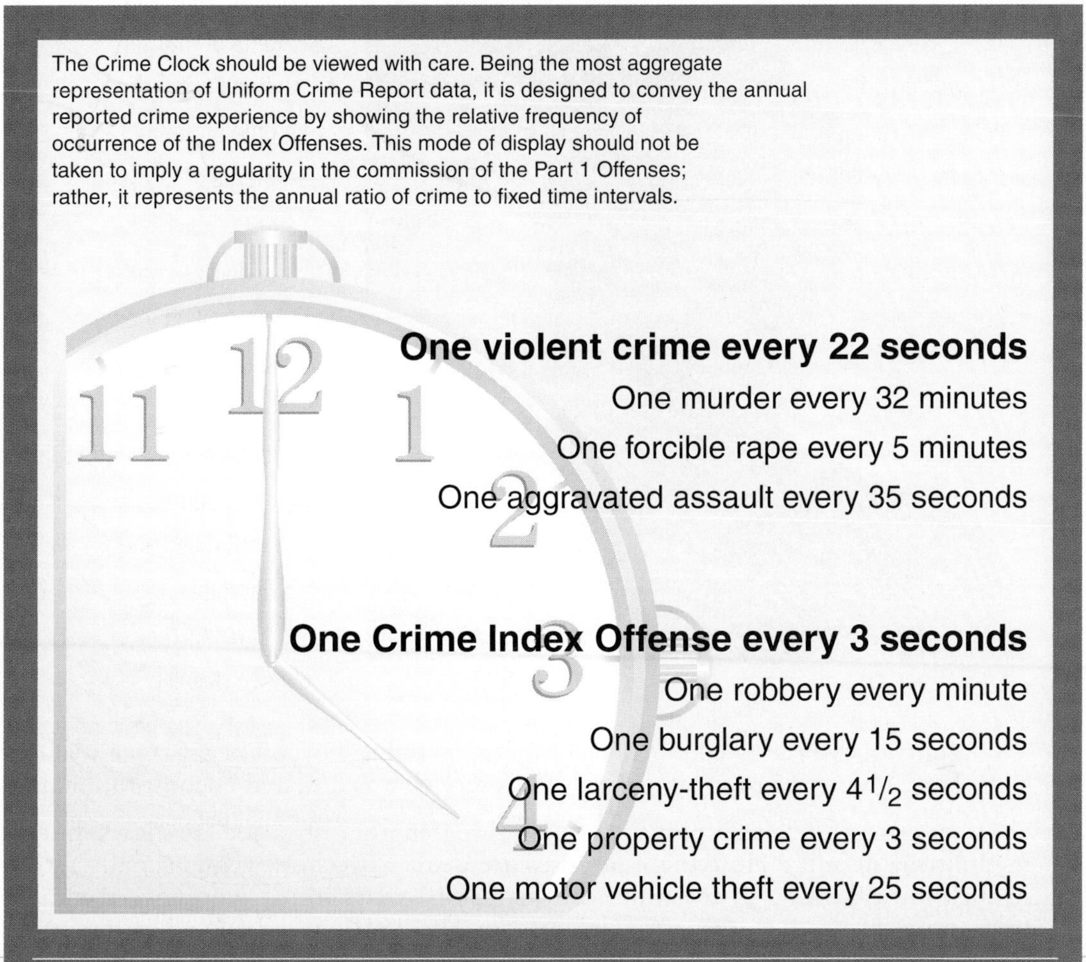

The Crime Clock should be viewed with care. Being the most aggregate representation of Uniform Crime Report data, it is designed to convey the annual reported crime experience by showing the relative frequency of occurrence of the Index Offenses. This mode of display should not be taken to imply a regularity in the commission of the Part 1 Offenses; rather, it represents the annual ratio of crime to fixed time intervals.

One violent crime every 22 seconds
One murder every 32 minutes
One forcible rape every 5 minutes
One aggravated assault every 35 seconds

One Crime Index Offense every 3 seconds
One robbery every minute
One burglary every 15 seconds
One larceny-theft every 4 1/2 seconds
One property crime every 3 seconds
One motor vehicle theft every 25 seconds

Source: http://www.fbi.gov/ucr/cius_02/html/web/offreported/crimeclock.html.

who was trying to kill him, and he led the officers to an apartment littered with bones. Police arrested the apartment's owner, Jeffrey Dahmer, and began an investigation the next day. Clad in hazardous waste suits, officers removed evidence from the dwelling, including skulls found in the refrigerator, the freezer, and a filing cabinet; three headless torsos stashed in a 55-gallon drum; miscellaneous entrails and decomposing limbs; and photos of decaying corpses. The various body parts amounted to the remains of 11 people. It was later determined that Dahmer had killed 17 men and boys in a spree that had begun in 1978, during his first summer out of high school, with the murder of a young male hitchhiker.[1]

Many crimes do not involve the harming of other people, but the breaking of laws set up to keep a society in a certain order. Although order is a good thing to have in a society, sometimes the order itself is questionable.

- In December 1955, a young, black seamstress for a Montgomery, Alabama, department store got on a city bus and sat down in the "colored" section. When the "whites only" section filled up, a white man was left standing. The bus driver demanded that the woman, Rosa Parks, and three other patrons in the colored section, give up their seats for the white man. Of the four blacks, Parks was the only one who would not move. She was arrested and, four days later, found

Rosa Parks is a hero of the civil rights movement. She showed that unjust laws can be changed by principled nonviolent protest.

Courtesy of Corbis/Bettmann.

> guilty of disorderly conduct. The Montgomery bus boycott began. One year later, Montgomery's segregation of bus service was declared unconstitutional.[2]

Other crimes, such as espionage crimes, threaten not only a society's laws, but also its political stability. How these offenses are dealt with, however, is usually a result of the political mood of the times. In the last 10 years, those who have committed treasonous crimes have been sent to prison. The 1950s were a much different era, however.

> In 1950 the FBI arrested Julius Rosenberg, an electrical engineer who had worked for the U.S. Army during World War II, and his wife, Ethel. The couple was indicted for conspiracy to provide classified military information to the Soviet Union. In their 1951 trial, the government charged that, in 1944 and 1945, the Rosenbergs had persuaded Ethel's brother, an employee at the Los Alamos atomic bomb project, to provide them and another person with top-secret data on nuclear weapons. The primary evidence against the Rosenbergs came from Ethel's brother and his wife. Both Julius and Ethel were found guilty and sentenced to death; their codefendants received prison terms. Many people complained that the fervently anti-Communist political climate of the day made a fair trial impossible, and the Rosenbergs claimed innocence throughout the whole ordeal. Despite many appeals and pleas for clemency, the Rosenbergs were executed on June 19, 1953, becoming the first U.S. civilians to suffer the death penalty for espionage.[3]

Is crime the breaking of a moral principle? If so, whose morals? Is crime the breaking of a societal law? What if the societal law is immoral? Is crime the breaking of political laws or mores? What if those laws result in large numbers of people being imprisoned or even executed? Questions such as these make talking rationally about crime difficult. The personal nature of crime compounds this problem. Crime can be scary. Crime can hurt people. And in a heterogeneous society such as the 21st-century United States, even the concept of "rational" is up for grabs. What is rational to one person may not be rational to another, and everyone has his or her own solution to crime based on what he or she considers to be rational.

Taking these factors into account, a student of criminal justice can begin to understand how the outwardly simple progression of crime → arrest → trial → punishment really represents a myriad of subtleties and complications. Still, as individuals, we hold tightly to the perspectives that support our personal notions of fairness, justice, and goodness, even when we know those notions might be grounded in the privilege of middle-class values concerning race, class, and gender. However, crime is a messy, human problem that does not respond to simple, mechanical, or straightforward solutions.

By way of example, let me tell you about my neighbor, who is a pilot for a major airline. When he is at a gathering and someone becomes aware of his occupation, he seldom has to defend his area of expertise. No one tells him how to land his 747 at New York City's JFK International Airport; they do not offer advice on what to do in the event of a water landing, nor do they attempt to explain how to properly adjust the wing flaps. For the most part, they talk about how fascinating it must be to fly for a living and then try to find another topic of conversation. By contrast, when I am at such gatherings and people find out that I am a criminal justice professor, I get an earful of opinions about how to deal with criminals. Unfortunately, these opinions are uninformed by the research done in criminology, and often reflect personal biases and ideas borrowed from talk radio and cable television programs that spin news to support political agendas. I smile politely when individuals say we should "cut off thieves' hands like they do in the Mideast," or "we should lock drug users up for the rest of their lives." I used to argue with them, but I seldom changed anyone's point of view.

To be fair, whereas flying a 747 is beyond the experience of most individuals, being a victim of a crime is not. Therefore, almost everyone has passionate opinions about what to do with the criminal justice system. Although I envy my neighbor the pilot for his unchallenged expertise, I would not trade occupations. Twenty-five years of studying crime and working with the criminal justice system has taught me one important lesson: The truth is not always clear. Truth is a shade of gray. So even though people may have opinions about crime that I find ridiculous, I treat them with respect because I am uncertain about my own conclusions. I have strong opinions about crime and justice, but I try to keep an open mind because new research, changing political atmospheres, or my own personal experiences may affect the way I understand criminal justice issues.

The study of crime and the criminal justice system is not an exact science. No one has a lock on the truth, and each of us needs to be humble in how we assert our views. We need to use what C. Wright Mills called the **sociological imagination.**[4] Mills encouraged us to take a step back from the personal experiences of our lives and examine issues while divorced from our social location. For example, could a father of a murdered daughter reasonably sit on a jury of the accused killer? Of course not. Likewise, according to Mills, each of us should attempt to look at crime and criminal justice policy from a neutral and objective position. The key word here is *attempt.* It can be argued that no one can truly be neutral and objective when considering social issues. We must be honest and acknowledge that our social class, race, gender, age, and other personal attributes affect our thinking. Only by explicitly stating our social location can we, and those we seek to convince, put our opinions in context and evaluate them.

sociological imagination Refers to the idea that we must look beyond the obvious to evaluate how our social location influences how we see society. One's race, age, gender, and socioeconomic status are thought to influence values and perspectives.

Objectivity and neutrality are worthy goals, but beware of those who claim to have achieved them. Often these individuals represent the status quo. Their unexamined views may reflect the conventional wisdom of their particular occupation, religion, or social class.

It is fair to ask exactly what perspective this book takes. What political and social values underlie its attempts at neutrality and objectivity? How does the author envision the criminal justice system, and what attempts does he make to temper his views by presenting alternative explanations? It is with a healthy regard for these questions that this book is designed. The subtitle, "Mainstream and Crosscurrents," illustrates how consensus about crime and criminal justice is lacking. Any intellectually honest criminologist must recognize that the criminal justice system has some issues and problems that require critical review. Therefore, this book presents both the conventional practices of the system and alternative methods, ideas, and practices that may improve the way we dispense justice in the United States. The intent is not to foster the ideas of the author, but rather to present different lines of thinking about important issues and to suggest that rigorous examination of the criminal justice system informed by research is the best way to understand and improve it.

One of the themes of this book is that what we know about crime is often based on incomplete and inaccurate information. This is the case for several reasons:

1. **We tend to personalize.** We have experiences that are real and immediate, and we expect everyone else to be as concerned as we are. When crime affects us, we want others to be just as outraged and insulted. Relatively minor offenses against us are serious matters in our lives and inform our opinions. Nevertheless, the experiences of crimes done to us cannot reliably be extrapolated to all others.
2. **All crime is local crime.** One of the by-products of improved communications has been the perceived immediacy of crime.[5] In the past, we learned of crime from the newspaper and our local television stations. Now with cable television and the Internet, we are all connected in such a way that incidents that happen thousands of miles away are envisioned as having a local danger. For example, the school violence that happened in Jonesboro, Arkansas, and Littleton, Colorado, was so thoroughly covered in the media that the tragedies began to seem like a local danger. Now, many schools have emergency plans to respond to violent situations, and they are practiced much like fire drills. Although the threat of school violence may be real, the likelihood of the threat is often exaggerated.
3. **Crime statistics do not tell the whole story.** Measuring crime is a tricky business. Applying those measurements to our own situations can be even trickier. Crime is not evenly distributed over time and across jurisdictions. Not all of us are equally susceptible to crime or equally affected by it. We sometimes inform our fears on a misreading of the actual threat of crime.
4. **We sometimes let our prejudices affect our thinking.** There is a long history of how social class and racism have influenced our thinking about crime. Control of the "dangerous classes" has sometimes created more injustices than it has solved.[6]
5. **We have a too-limited idea of the dangers to our health and safety.** The barely visible crimes of corporations and governments often are not considered to be as serious as street crimes, even though they may do more actual harm to society and individuals.[7]

Social Control

Imagine how chaotic society would be if there were no rules and everyone did whatever they wanted. Meaningful communities would be impossible. To live with other people, individuals must curb their appetites, ambitions, and desires. The problems of maintaining individual freedoms within a group setting are the concerns of our systems of social control. The institutions in our society—religion, family, school, and community—all have, among other missions, the goals of socializing individuals into the group.

socialization
A process by which individuals acquire a personal identity and learn the norms, values, behavior, and social skills appropriate to their society.

Socialization is an imperfect process. Not all of us are socialized to the same degree, and in many societies, especially democracies, social value is attributed to being a maverick, rebel, or outsider.[8] These themes or roles often are played out in external deviant behavior such as wild dress, tattoos, body piercing, or to a more extreme extent, crime. More than a simple quest for identity, crime is often a calculated method to gain material possessions or demonstrate one's dominance.[9] Making broad general statements about crime is difficult because so many behaviors are considered to be crimes. It is useful then to make some distinctions about general types of crime that excite popular imagination. In the next chapter, we will consider types of crime in a more detailed and legalistic manner. Keep in mind that the categories here are intended as a brief and introductory overview with the goal of showing that crime is a complex and confusing term and that specification of types of crime is required in order to consider the topic.

Crime in the United States

All crime is not created equal. Many crimes go undetected, and their harm to society is not generally perceived. Some crimes are just a step across the line of good and effective business practices and are considered the price we pay for a market economy. An example of this would be insider trading. Other crimes are sensationalized by the media and given such vast resources in their detection and prosecution that they distort the perception of the amount and seriousness of crime in society. Finally, there is the problem of street crime, of which everyone is afraid. These broad categories of crime illustrate how complex and differentiated the crime issue really is.

SENSATIONAL CRIME. Much of what we think we know about crime comes to us from the media. Television news programs and dramas, newspapers, and reality-based television programs such as *COPS* tend to distort and sensationalize the picture of crime in the United States. There is an old newsroom saying: "If it bleeds, it leads." On one hand, we depend on the media to give us the truth in the news, but we must realize that the media have an agenda of their own that is concerned with selling newspapers and commercials.[10] Selling the product of news is how careers are made in media. Although many journalists try to report the news fairly, the decision of exactly what is newsworthy is made at an executive level and often on grounds having to do with sensationalism.

Cases such as the O. J. Simpson trial and the JonBenet Ramsey murder have received an excessive amount of coverage far beyond their real news value to most people. In many ways, cases such as these have transcended being news to become entertainment. These cases actually affected only a few individuals in a direct manner and normally would have been reported only in the local media, but because of some sensational or unusual feature, they became national news. At issue here is what this treatment of a few high-profile crimes does to our perception of crime in our country. When some local crimes become nationally reported to such an extreme extent, they take on the appearance that everyone, everywhere, should be concerned about their safety. For example, the school shootings in Colorado, Tennessee, Oregon, and Mississippi, have caused schools across the nation to prepare for potential violence. Schools across the nation now have lockdown drills in which classrooms are locked so angry, gun-bearing parents, children, or teacher's spouses are kept from getting inside. Much like fire drills or the old "duck and cover" nuclear war drills of two generations ago, the new school safety drills are measures that will never be needed in most jurisdictions. They are required as a result of the public perception that school violence is at an epidemic level. Another crime-related fad is so-called "zero-tolerance" policies: Many of these policies punish children with suspension or expulsion for even the slightest infraction of rules that bar drugs or weapons. However, the truth is that the children are safer in school than in their homes and always have been.

We must be careful when considering how the media report crime. The good news is that media outlets report the truth. The bad news is that, often, they do not report the whole truth. They do not put the news of crime in context for the viewer. In many ways, the media distort the context to make the news more immediate and personal. Certain crimes are selected for their sensational nature and made into national issues. Why was the JonBenet Ramsey case so widely and intensely reported? When we consider the thousands of other cases each year in which children are killed, we must ask why this case in Colorado interests the media so much? The answer is probably connected to the parents' upper-class status and the fact that, because JonBenet was a beauty pageant contestant, there are a lot of

Tweety Bird Is a Thug: Zero Tolerance and the School

In an effort to make our society safe from the ravages of drugs and violence, many schools, businesses, and organizations have developed "zero-tolerance" policies that treat any degree of deviant behavior with severe penalties. Although these policies are attractive to many, there are some inherent problems when officials are allowed no discretion in deciding whether the offense truly warrants attention.

An example of how zero-tolerance policies can be taken to ridiculous extremes took place in suburban Atlanta in September 2000, when Ashley Smith, an 11-year-old student at Garrett Middle School, was suspended for 10 days because the chain on her Tweety Bird wallet violated the school district's zero-tolerance weapons policy. When school administrators do not make a distinction between a weapon and a wallet chain, it suggests that they are willing to sacrifice the well-being of their students for the symbolic message of the war on crime. Ashley's father, Raymond Smith, said, [the policy] "lacks common sense. A little piece of chain is not a deadly weapon." The school later lifted the suspension amid media attention.

QUESTIONS

1. Was Smith's suspension just?
2. Do you generally agree with school zero-tolerance policies?
3. Have you ever been punished as a result of a school zero-tolerance policy?

Source: CNN, "Georgia Girl's Tweety Bird Chain Runs Afoul of Weapons Policy," September 28, 2000, http://www.cnn.com/2000/US/09/28/wallet.suspension.02/.

photographs and videos portraying the five-year-old child in "grown-up" makeup and clothing. The ability of the media to print these photographs and play the videos repeatedly helped to keep this case in the spotlight. How much would we have cared about the beating of Rodney King in Los Angeles if not for the videotape of that event?[11]

STREET CRIME. Sensationalized crimes may fascinate us, but our fears are mostly focused on street crime.[12] The fear of rape, assault, or robbery is a real fear for many individuals, and most people take precautions to limit their chances of being victimized. However, street crime includes a wide variety of acts both in public and private spaces, including interpersonal violence and property crime (see Figure 1.2). These are the offenses most often included in measurements of crime. Homicide, rape, assault, larceny, arson, breaking-and-entering, and motor vehicle theft are offenses measured by the Uniform Crime Reports and the ones that are envisioned in discussions about the crime rate.

A healthy fear of street crime is wise. The impact of a rape, assault, and especially a homicide can alter how a person and his or her loved ones think about relating to others and can require many years of recovery. However, we should not overdo our fear of street crime because it is still a relatively rare event. The vast majority of us are able to go about our daily lives without encountering danger. It is not necessary to carry a weapon or to distrust people most of the time. In fact, most people feel safe most of the time.[13]

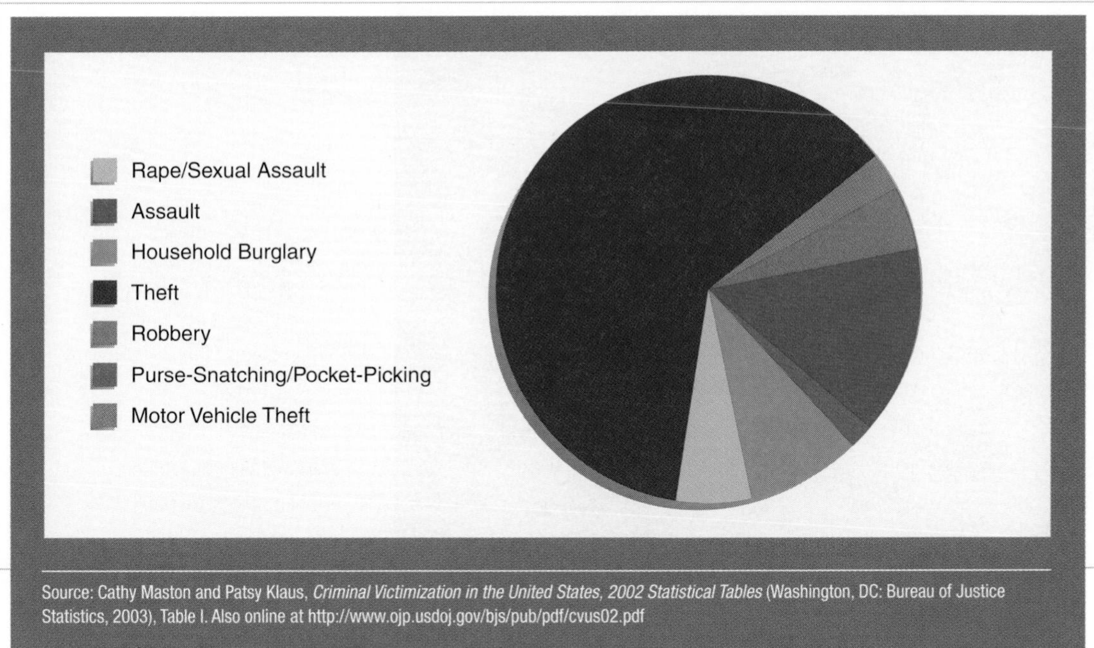

Source: Cathy Maston and Patsy Klaus, *Criminal Victimization in the United States, 2002 Statistical Tables* (Washington, DC: Bureau of Justice Statistics, 2003), Table I. Also online at http://www.ojp.usdoj.gov/bjs/pub/pdf/cvus02.pdf

Figure 1.2 Percentage of Victimizations by Type of Crime, 2002

Some studies have found that those with the least likelihood of being victimized fear crime the most. Elderly citizens demonstrate the greatest fear of street crime, yet they are the least likely to encounter it. Conversely, young males are the most victimized, yet they do not have a great fear of crime. In some ways, this disjuncture is understandable, but it is also illustrative of just how distorted our conception of crime has become.

It is interesting to note that the crime rate is not always correlated with the public perception of the level of crime. During the 1990s the crime rate went down while the concern about crime as a political issue continued to stay high. People felt that crime was one of the most important problems faced by society even as the rate of crime declined.

Because the public is so concerned about street crime, many of our criminal justice resources are devoted to its prevention and prosecution. This emphasis on street crime is both understandable and problematic. It is understandable because citizens need to feel that the criminal justice system is doing all that can be done to protect innocent people from predatory criminals. To have communities in which individuals feel safe in public spaces, the police must engage in preventive patrol and make arrests when laws are violated. Although the merits of the symbolic reassurance can be argued, clearly the public demands that the police "do something" to prevent crime and apprehend criminals.[14] According to some criminologists, the aggressive control of street people is necessary to have meaningful communities. People who feel safe on the streets are engaged in public interaction to a greater degree, and this, in turn, means that the streets are populated by more and more lawful citizens. When people do not feel safe on the street and stay behind locked doors, the criminals and street people take over the public places and crime results.[15]

The emphasis on street crime is also problematic in that resources are not allocated toward the prevention of other types of crime. Jeffrey Reiman contended that corporate crime is really much more harmful to society than street crime. He added that the preoccupation the criminal justice system has with street crime is fueled by a racist and class-conscious society. Although the impact of street crime may be significant to individuals, the impact of corporate crime is much more damaging to everyone. Reiman argued that

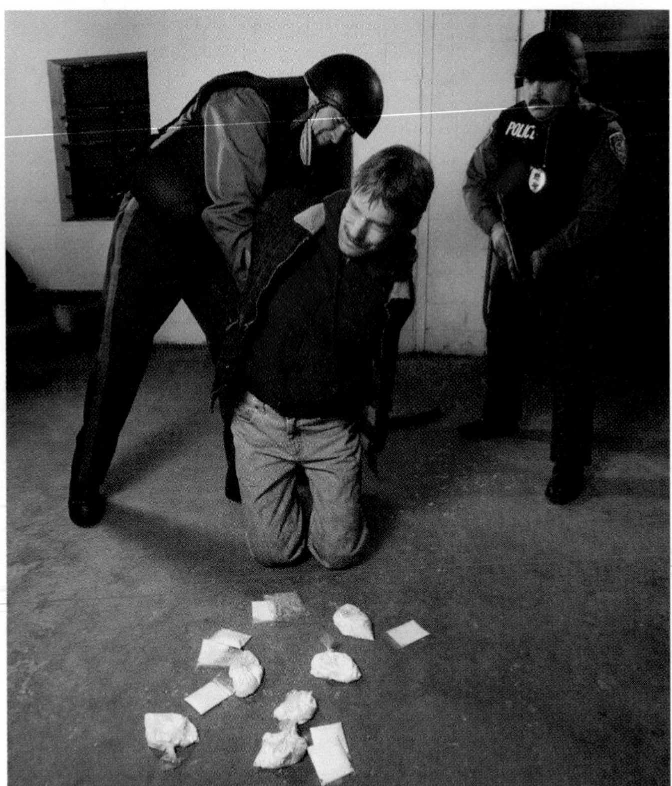

Because drug users often commit crimes to support their addictions, the government has declared a "war on drugs." Law enforcement officers arrest drug dealers in an effort to reduce the number of other crimes including assault, homicide, and breaking-and-entering.

Courtesy of Corbis Royalty Free.

individuals with the most money and power define crime and use the criminal justice system to protect their own interests.[16]

CORPORATE CRIME, WHITE COLLAR CRIME, AND ORGANIZED CRIME. Criminals come in all sizes and shapes. Sometimes they are packaged to look like ordinary citizens. Sometimes they are conventional in all the other aspects of their lives, and it is difficult to envision them as criminals. Because harmful behaviors are not always defined as crimes, envisioning how otherwise honorable citizens can be considered criminals is sometimes difficult. So-called pillars of society known for their charity, public service, and conventional behavior occasionally are the biggest crooks. Some criminals manage to do a great deal of harm to others even while they appear to be doing good deeds.

Corporate crime involves the breaking of laws in an otherwise lawful pursuit of profit. For example, an industrial company that does not follow safety standards in disposing of its industrial waste material can do irreparable harm to the environment and to the health of thousands of people. Although the intent of the company's officers may be simply to maximize profits and not hurt anyone, the result can be devastating. What is good for the company's shareholders may be harmful to those who live in the community where the factory operates. The company's officers did not go out and physically rob or mug the citizens, but the damage done to the community water supply can be immensely more harmful. Corporations can hurt individuals in an infinite variety of ways. Yet, when we look at the law and the response by the criminal justice system, we see that street crime is treated with greater penalties.[17]

Sometimes the terms *corporate crime* and *white collar crime* are used interchangeably, but there are important distinctions between them.[18] Corporate crime involves the purposeful commission or omission of acts on the part of individuals acting in their capacity as representatives of a business. Their goal is to make money for the business, and the

CROSSCURRENTS

American Kids Are All Right

The press and the politicians would have us all believe that juvenile crime problems in the United States are worse than ever. In an effort to get elected or sell newspapers, the message given to the public has been distorted and overly negative. Although the United States faces significant problems, some encouraging trends speak to the welfare of the country and the concerns of those interested in the causes of juvenile crime:

- Poverty. *Since 1993 the child poverty rate has dropped by 17 percent, according to the National Center for Children in Poverty at Columbia University in New York. This reversed a 15-year trend during which child poverty had increased nearly 40 percent.*
- Teen births. *Teen birth rates are the lowest ever recorded (in 60 years). However, the United States still has the highest teen birth rate of any industrialized nation.*
- Child deaths. *Infant, child, and adolescent mortalities have been declining for the last two decades and are at historic lows. Among teenagers, motor vehicle deaths have dropped by 36 percent over the past 20 years, and deaths by firearms have decreased by nearly 28 percent.*
- Juvenile crime. *Whether kids are victims or perpetrators of serious violent crime, both categories have fallen steadily since 1993.*

QUESTIONS

1. Is juvenile crime really as bad as the media report?
2. Can government crime statistics be trusted?
3. Are children more poorly behaved now than they were when you were a child?

Source: Francine Kiefer, "U.S. Children Near Records for Well-Being," *The Christian Science Monitor,* August 18, 2000, http://www.csmonitor.com/durable/2000/08/18/f-p1s3.html.

crimes they commit are related to their pursuing the profit motive of the corporation. White collar crime, by contrast, is not necessarily aimed at the consumer. White collar crime can involve employees harming the corporation. The treasurer who embezzles money or the office manager who makes excessive long-distance phone calls are harming their company and not the public.

Organized crime is committed by individuals working together systematically to break the law. Organized crime in the United States can bring to mind Italian Americans involved in the Mafia or La Cosa Nostra. These organizations, which first gained notoriety during the **Prohibition** years, have been made famous in books, movies, and television programs. However, many groups of people are engaged in organized crime.[19] Asian, Hispanic, and Russian peoples, former prison inmates, and a host of other groups engage in organized crime activities. Like Prohibition, the **war on drugs** has provided opportunities and incentives for a wide variety of criminal organizations. Organized crime is different from corporate and white collar crime in the way it interacts with the criminal justice system and the harm it does to society. Typical activities of organized crime groups include narcotics trafficking, prostitution rings, and murders for hire.

Prohibition
The period from January 29, 1920, to December 5, 1933, during which the manufacture, transportation, and sale of alcoholic beverages was made illegal in the United States by the Eighteenth Amendment. Enforcement legislation was entitled the National Prohibition Act or Volstead Act.

war on drugs
A policy aimed at reducing the sale and use of illegal drugs. The war metaphor is used to illustrate how serious the drug problem has become in the United States. The war on drugs is fought on many levels, but the criminal justice system spends enormous resources on this problem.

Corporate crime costs the country billions of dollars each year. The victims are the corporation's employees and shareholders. One of the most high-profile cases was the Enron scandal in which top executives engaged in deception about the company's financial condition. Here, handcuffed former Enron executives are shown entering the Houston federal courthouse in May 2003.
Courtesy of CORBIS-NY.

In 2001, Martha Stewart was found guilty of lying to investigators about a stock trade. The government has a duty to ensure that the stock market is operated fairly and that those who cheat are punished.
Courtesy of CORBIS-NY.

NEWS FLASH

White Collar Crime

Two of the best-known white collar criminals of recent memory are Ivan F. Boesky and Michael Milken. Both worked for respected investment firms and engaged in insider trading on the stock market. They cheated by using illegally obtained secrets about impending mergers to buy and sell stock before the mergers became public knowledge. Boesky was sentenced to pay $100 million in fines and served 22 months in prison and another four months in a halfway house. Milken paid over $1 billion in fines and restitution and served two years in prison. These are extreme examples of the types of punishments meted out to white collar criminals, but what is important to remember is that these men had that much money to pay their fines. It gives us some idea of the profitability of their wrongdoing. Today, Boesky lives a quiet life outside the limelight, and Milken does philanthropic work, maintains a Web page, and has a new cookbook.

Sources: Milken Home Page, http://www.mikemilken.com/biography.taf. "Boesky Now a Cult Figure," *Augusta Chronicle*/Associated Press, November 16, 1996, http://www.augustachronicle.com/stories/111696/boesky.html.

The Criminal Justice System

When crimes are committed, the role of the criminal justice system is to respond in the name of society. As citizens in a democratic government, we elect officials to provide services to all of us. The criminal justice system comprises a variety of agencies from different levels of government, each with a mission to deal with some aspect of crime. Although some of these agencies appear to overlap in duties, and the system appears to be inefficient and cumbersome, the system chugs along with an internal logic and processes a vast number of cases.

However, the criminal justice system is criticized for being ineffective and failing to produce the justice that many people expect. To understand the system's inefficiencies, we must first realize that it is not exactly a system.

First, the system is not confined to one level of government. The criminal justice system spans the range from local governments to the federal government. The lines of authority and distinction between agencies is not always clear, and in some cases may need to be negotiated according to the politics of the case. For example, tension exists between federal agencies such as the **Federal Bureau of Investigation (FBI)** and local law enforcement agencies. Depending on the circumstances of the case, it must be decided if federal or state laws have been violated and which agency has the primary responsibility for investigation. Although interagency cooperation is the norm, conflict may arise on occasion. Additionally, problems between different components of the criminal justice system may exist. The goals and missions of law enforcement are not always viewed as identical to those of the judicial system or the prison. Individual criminal justice practitioners may believe that other agencies are working against them rather than with them. For example, the police may feel that district attorneys and judges are working against them by procuring probation and light sentences for offenders. Or prison officials may believe that lawmakers who legislate tougher, longer sentencing are overcrowding the prisons.

Federal Bureau of Investigation (FBI) The principal investigative arm of the Department of Justice. It investigates the crimes assigned to it and provides cooperative services to other law enforcement agencies.

It is useful at this point to specify what levels of government and which components make up the criminal justice system.

Levels of Government

One of the most perplexing features of the criminal justice system is how responsibilities are spread unevenly across different levels of government.[20] Law enforcement, courts, and corrections tasks are divided differently across the local, state, and federal branches

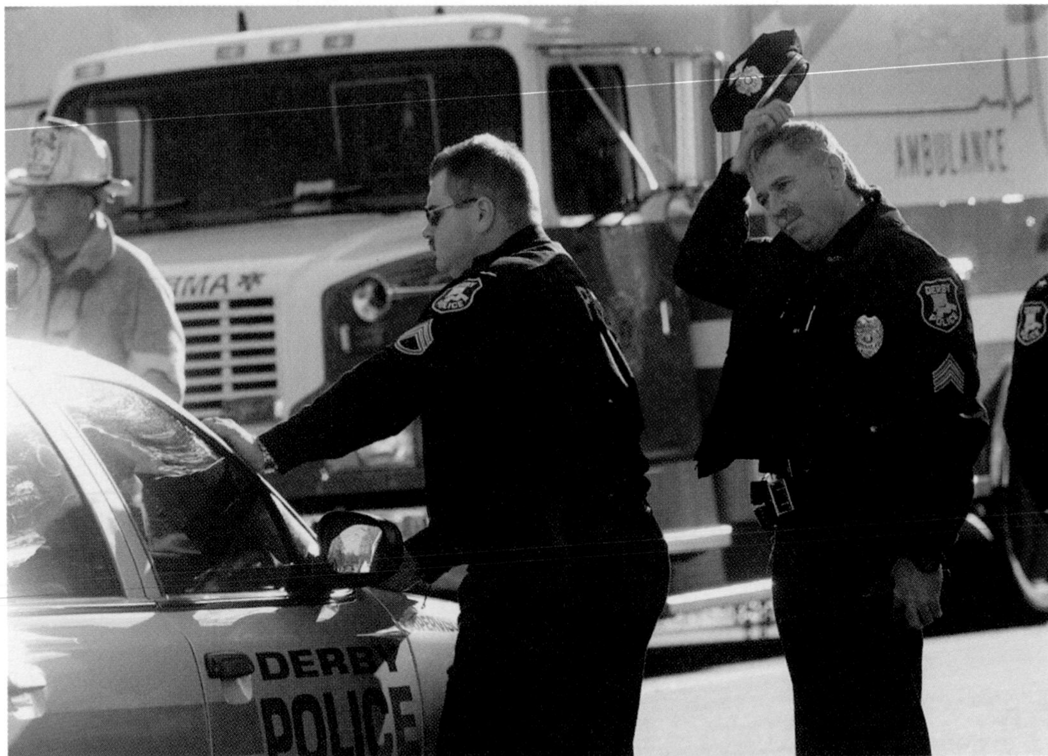

Local law enforcement officers have a great deal of authority in enforcing the law. They are responsible for handling most street-crime violations and are also first responders to emergencies.
Courtesy of CORBIS-NY.

sheriff
From the English words *shire* and *reeve* (king's agent). An official of a county or parish who primarily carries out judicial duties.

warrant
A writ issued by a judicial official that authorizes an officer to perform a specified act required for the administration of justice, such as an arrest or search.

bailiff
An officer of the court responsible for executing writs and processes, making arrests, and keeping order in the court.

misdemeanor
A crime considered less serious than a felony. Usually tried in the lowest local courts and punishable by no more than one year in jail.

felony
A crime punishable by a term in state or federal prison and sometimes by death. In some instances, a sentence for a felony conviction may be less than one year. Felonies are sometimes called "high crimes."

of government. Additionally, an inherent overlap exists between jurisdictions in terms of appeal and oversight functions. This overlap is inevitable given the checks-and-balances aspect of the Constitution. Although this redundancy makes the criminal justice system inefficient, the goal is to protect citizens against overzealous police officers and prosecutors.[21]

LOCAL-LEVEL CRIMINAL JUSTICE. Each state has a different configuration of political jurisdictions. Cities, counties (or parishes), and multijurisdictional agencies are vested with responsibility in varying ways depending on the state law. What is most striking about how the criminal justice system is organized is the fact that most of the authority for law enforcement lies at the local level. Many people misunderstand the relationship among the three levels of police, believing that local police answer to state police, who, in turn, answer to federal police. This is not true. Generally, police departments answer to themselves, their communities, and the courts.[22]

The chief law enforcement officer for each county is the locally elected **sheriff.** There are more than 3,000 sheriff's departments in the United States.[23] The sheriff's office is responsible for a variety of functions that go beyond traditional law enforcement. Serving **warrants**, providing **bailiffs** to the courts, and administering the local jail are all responsibilities of the sheriff's office. In addition, the sheriff provides law enforcement to the unincorporated areas of the county or parish.

Incorporated cities usually have their own police departments. The city police are responsible only for the jurisdiction of the city and do not provide the range of services that the sheriff's office does. Because their jurisdictions overlap to a large degree, the municipal police and the sheriff's office cooperate at many levels. In some large metropolitan areas, the law enforcement functions of the city and county are combined to save the costs of duplicate services.

Some court functions are vested at the local level and will vary widely according to how each state organizes its governmental functions. For the most part, the city and county deal with **misdemeanor** violations of the law. As opposed to **felony** cases that are punishable by more than one year in a state prison, misdemeanor cases are punishable by up to one year in a local jail. County jails serve an important and underappreciated function.

Jails have two types of inmates.[24] The first consists of those who are awaiting trial and unable to make bond or get released on their own recognizance. These inmates include

Sheriffs' departments are responsible for a variety of law enforcement functions. They perform many of the same functions as the police; the one important distinction is jurisdiction. The police patrol the incorporated areas of a city while the sheriff's office patrols the unincorporated areas of the county.
Courtesy of CORBIS-NY.

both those who have committed very minor offenses and some very dangerous individuals who are rapists and murderers. This makes the job of the local jail extremely difficult. Jails seldom have the resources to provide protection to both the public and all of the inmates. Many jails are overcrowded and can be dangerous places, even though most of the inmates are not violent people.[25]

The second type of inmate represents those who have been sentenced to a year or less of incarceration. Often, these inmates are transferred to a **county stockade** to separate them from those awaiting trial. Often, they are put to work. In many counties, these inmates can be seen on work crews picking up trash on the highways.

county stockade
A component of a county corrections system. The stockade usually holds offenders who have already been sentenced. Because of overcrowding in state systems, many county stockades hold state felony offenders on a contract basis.

One distressing aspect of the local jail in many jurisdictions is the number of state prisoners who serve all or part of their sentences in local jails. Because of overcrowding in many state prison systems, the flow of inmates is backed up into the local jails where individuals must serve their time while waiting for bed space in a state prison.[26] Although local jails are paid by the state for housing the sentenced inmates, this situation causes security problems for the jail and limits the opportunities to provide any sort of rehabilitative programs at the local level.

STATE-LEVEL CRIMINAL JUSTICE. Law enforcement functions at the state level usually are confined to specialized missions. State highway patrol units are responsible for maintaining safety on the state roads and interstate highways and also may issue driver's licenses. Most states also have an agency responsible for investigating crimes that transcend the local level of jurisdiction. For example, the Georgia Bureau of Investigation (GBI) investigates accusations of political corruption and assists local law enforcement agencies with cross-jurisdictional issues. States also have crime laboratories that examine evidence from local cases across the state. Each state has its own criminal code that defines state crimes. Additionally, in some states, statewide agencies deal with violations of alcoholic beverage or fish and wildlife laws.

Although most law enforcement in the criminal justice system is done at the local level, most of the action for the courts is at the state level. Most states divide their courts into multicounty judicial circuits that rule on state law. Homicide, rape, robbery, and most other crimes, unless committed under special circumstances (for instance, on federal land or when perpetrators cross state lines), are tried in the state court system.[27] The court

U.S. Secret Service
A federal investigative law enforcement agency authorized to protect the president and other U.S. government officials and visiting officials. The agency also investigates financial fraud and counterfeiting.

U.S. Border Patrol
The mobile uniformed law enforcement arm of the Immigration and Naturalization Service. Its primary mission is to detect and prevent the illegal entry of foreign-born persons into the United States.

Immigration and Naturalization Service (INS)
An agency of the Department of Justice responsible for enforcing the laws regulating the admission of foreigners to the United States and for administering immigration benefits, including the naturalization of applicants for U.S. citizenship.

U.S. Marshals Service (Federal Marshals)
Created in 1789, the agency protects federal courts and ensures the effective operation of the judicial system. The agency also carries out fugitive investigations, custody and transportation of federal prisoners, security for government witnesses, and asset seizure in federal forfeitures.

U.S. Customs Service
The primary enforcement agency protecting U.S. borders and dealing with smuggling, imports, and exports.

Drug Enforcement Administration (DEA)
Enforces U.S. controlled substances laws and regulations. Also brings to the U.S. criminal system organizations involved in the growing, manufacture, and/or distribution of controlled substances to be trafficked in the United States.

function at the state level is a very important part of the criminal justice process. Judges, prosecutors, and public defenders are paid by state budgets and answer to voters at the circuit level rather than at the city or county level. Some court officials, such as attorneys general and state supreme court judges, answer to voters in statewide elections.

States are also responsible for most of the inmates in prison. Each state, depending on size, has an extended prison system that can house thousands of inmates. Still, overcrowding in many state prison systems has resulted in a backup of inmates in local facilities and also in pressure for parole boards to release more inmates to make room in the system for more recent offenders.[28] States also have extensive probation and parole agencies to deal with many thousands more offenders.

FEDERAL-LEVEL CRIMINAL JUSTICE. Law enforcement functions at the federal level include a wide range of agencies responsible for enforcing federal laws and assisting state and local governments (see Figure 1.3). The best-known federal agency is the Federal Bureau of Investigation (FBI), followed closely by the **U.S. Secret Service.** However, the work of these agencies is often at odds with public perception. The romanticized popular conception of the FBI and the Secret Service leads many criminal justice students to desire a career in federal law enforcement. In truth, the work of these agencies is often not as exciting as that of local law enforcement agencies. Much of the work of federal law enforcement is concerned with white collar crime. Thus, the tasks of investigation often are more suited to the accountant than the detective. As part of the Department of the Treasury, the Secret Service spends more time and resources dealing with counterfeiting than protecting the president.

Other law enforcement agencies of the federal government include the **U.S. Border Patrol**, the **Immigration and Naturalization Service** (INS), the **U.S. Marshals Service**, the **U.S. Customs Service**, the **Drug Enforcement Administration** (DEA), and the **Bureau of Alcohol, Tobacco, Firearms, and Explosives** (ATFE).

The federal system of courts parallels the state system and handles offenders who commit federal crimes. In addition, there is a system of appellate courts at which cases from either the state or federal courts can be appealed. The United States Supreme Court is the final court of appeal, but it deals with only a few cases.

The federal government has its own prison system for those convicted of federal crimes. In the past, federal prisons were considered safer than many state systems because they housed mainly white collar offenders. However, with the war on drugs in recent decades, the federal prison system now receives many inmates with extensive histories of drug-related crimes, some of which are connected to the violent drug trade. The federal government also has probation and parole agencies that supervise federal offenders in the community.

The picture of the criminal justice system that emerges is one that is complex, overlapping, and difficult to predict. Each level of government has carved out for itself a piece of the law enforcement, courts, and corrections pies. Each level of government is authorized to enforce and apply the law within narrow, but often unclear parameters. Criminal justice agencies at each level of government answer to the public through different and unequal voting pressures. For example, voting your local sheriff out of office is much easier than getting rid of an FBI director whose agency has blown a case in your community.

Criminal Justice Process

With an appreciation of how complex the criminal justice system is, we now turn to a discussion of how cases are processed. It is clear to most observers of the system that only a very small percentage of the crimes committed result in someone going to prison.

The criminal justice system is frustrating not only for the general public, but also for those who work in the system, as well as for victims, offenders, and their respective families. By examining the process that cases undergo in the criminal justice system and identifying why cases exit the system before they reach what the public believes is the desired result, we can see why the system generates so much annoyance. The system is close to being overloaded. An even slightly larger percentage of cases would be nearly impossible for the system to process in a fair and legal manner given the resources currently available.

Figure 1.3
Department of Justice Organization as of March 1, 2003

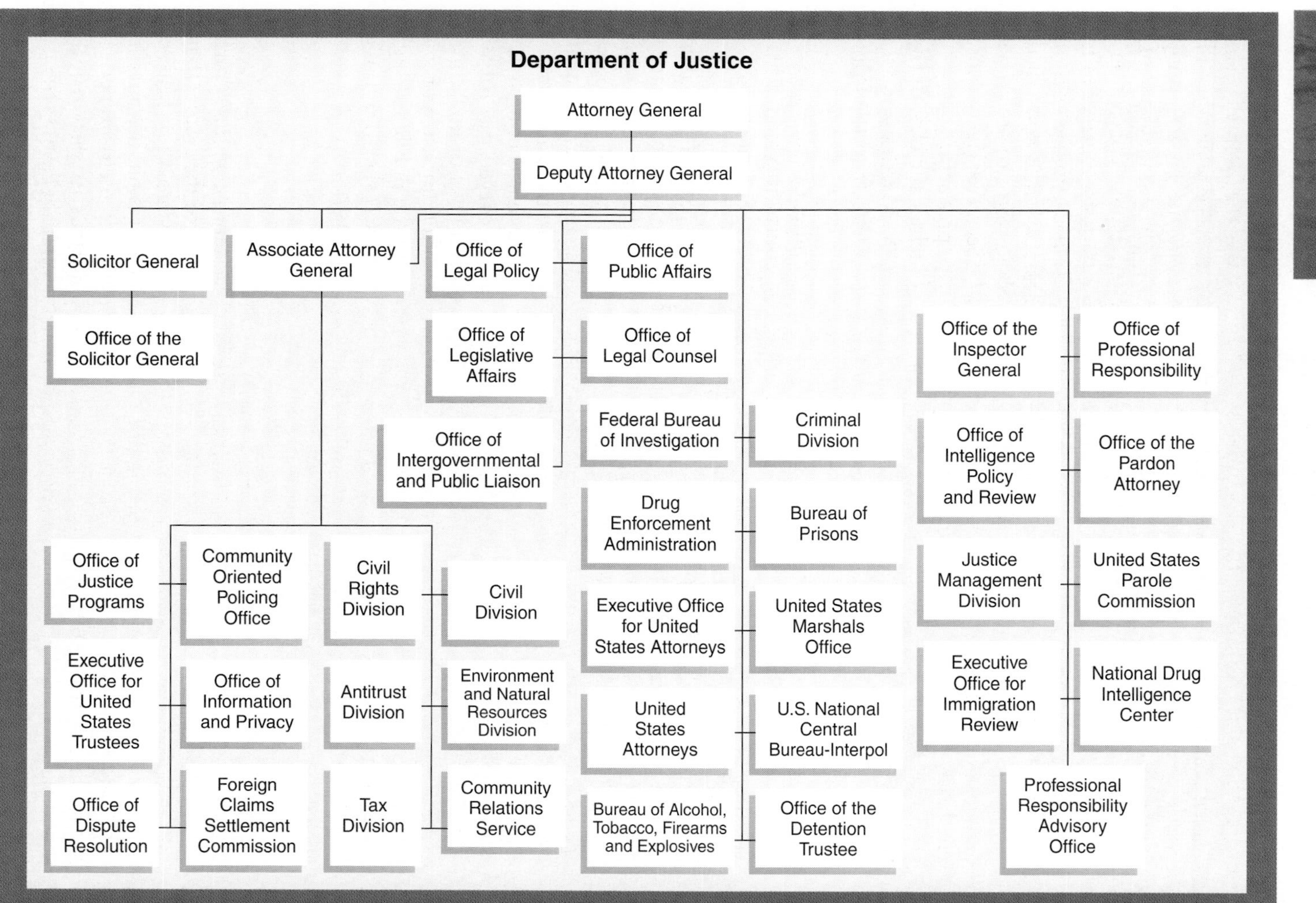

Department of Justice
Attorney General
Deputy Attorney General
Solicitor General
Office of the Solicitor General
Associate Attorney General
Office of Legal Policy
Office of Legislative Affairs
Office of Intergovernmental and Public Liaison
Office of Public Affairs
Office of Legal Counsel
Federal Bureau of Investigation
Drug Enforcement Administration
Executive Office for United States Attorneys
United States Attorneys
Bureau of Alcohol, Tobacco, Firearms and Explosives
Criminal Division
Bureau of Prisons
United States Marshals Office
U.S. National Central Bureau-Interpol
Office of the Detention Trustee
Office of the Inspector General
Office of Intelligence Policy and Review
Justice Management Division
Executive Office for Immigration Review
Office of Professional Responsibility
Office of the Pardon Attorney
United States Parole Commission
National Drug Intelligence Center
Professional Responsibility Advisory Office
Office of Justice Programs
Executive Office for United States Trustees
Office of Dispute Resolution
Community Oriented Policing Office
Office of Information and Privacy
Foreign Claims Settlement Commission
Civil Rights Division
Antitrust Division
Tax Division
Civil Division
Environment and Natural Resources Division
Community Relations Service

Source: U.S. Department of Justice, http://www.usdoj.gov/dojorg.gif.

The Federal Bureau of Investigation is responsible for enforcing the federal law. The FBI is a high-profile law enforcement agency that many students of criminal justice hope to join upon graduation.
Courtesy of CORBIS-NY.

Bureau of Alcohol, Tobacco, Firearms, and Explosives (ATFE)
A law enforcement organization within the United States Treasury that enforces federal laws and regulations relating to alcohol, tobacco, firearms, explosives, and arson.

The Secret Service is responsible for protecting the president and other officials. Here, the Secret Service arrests John Hinckley after his 1981 assassination attempt on Ronald Reagan.
Courtesy of CORBIS-NY.

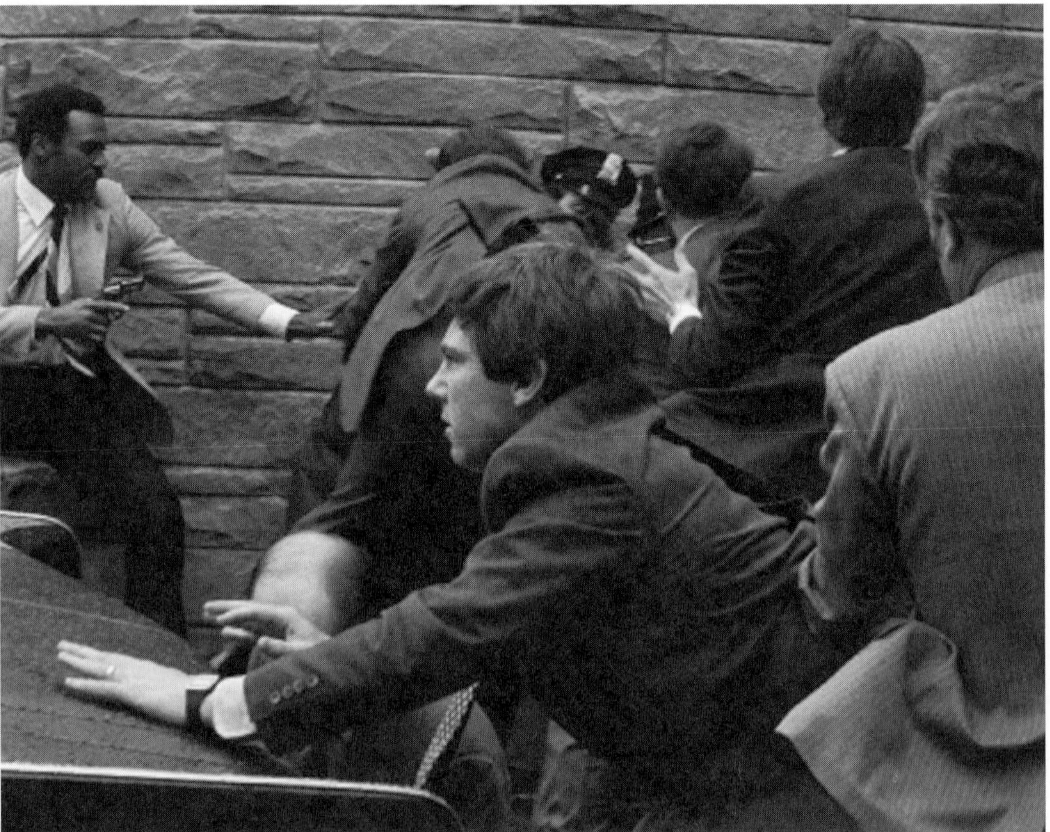

NEWS FLASH

Secret Service Finds Children

In 1994 Congress expanded the mission of the Secret Service to help law enforcement locate missing children. Working with the National Center for Missing and Exploited Children, the forensic experts of the Secret Service have used their skills in dissecting documents, creating composites, and analyzing handwriting to help develop evidence that is beyond the capabilities of local law enforcement agencies. The Secret Service has helped investigate over 700 crimes of child abuse, abduction, and homicide. In one particularly gruesome case, the agency was able to match the writing carved into a girl's abdomen with the handwriting of a suspect who was later convicted of multiple counts of criminal sexual assault, aggravated kidnapping, and attempted murder. The suspect was sentenced to 120 years in prison for his crimes.

Source: Chitra Ragavan, "Protecting Presidents—and Children," *U.S. News & World Report*, August 13, 2001.

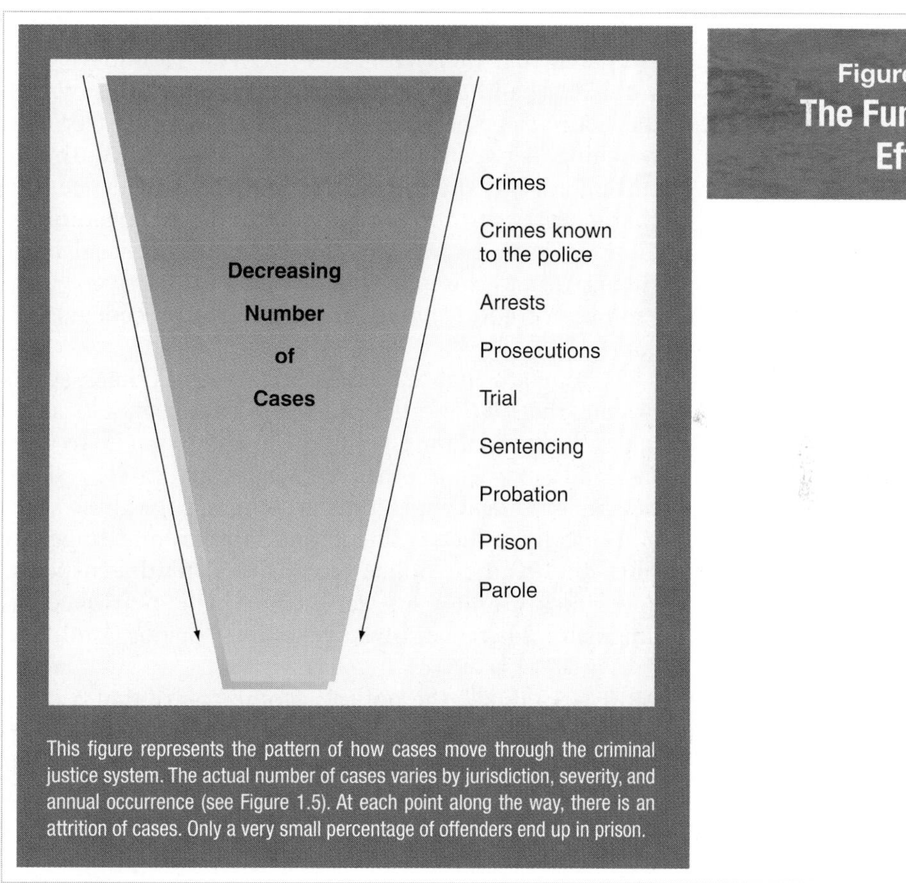

This figure represents the pattern of how cases move through the criminal justice system. The actual number of cases varies by jurisdiction, severity, and annual occurrence (see Figure 1.5). At each point along the way, there is an attrition of cases. Only a very small percentage of offenders end up in prison.

Figure 1.4 **The Funnel Effect**

discretion
The power of a judge, public official, or law enforcement officer to make decisions on issues within legal guidelines. For example, a prosecutor exercises discretion about which cases are inserted into the criminal justice system.

Therefore, police officers, prosecutors, judges, and corrections officials use **discretion** to decide which cases are pushed further into the criminal justice system and which ones are kicked out.

It is useful to envision the criminal justice system as a large funnel in which cases move downward toward their final disposition (See Figure 1.4). The problem with the funnel is that it is too small to hold all the cases, and so a considerable amount of leakage occurs.

CRIMES. At the wide mouth of the funnel are all the crimes committed in society. This includes every murder, rape, burglary, insurance fraud, shoplifting, and car theft. It includes all the harms done to society and individuals that are covered by the criminal law. It includes all the acts that can be defined as crime whether they have been reported or not. We have no idea of the total number of crimes. Many, maybe even most, crimes are never reported, or if they are, they get handled informally and never make it into the official crime reporting systems. Criminologists call these unreported acts *the dark figure of crime*. We know it is large but have no idea exactly how many or what percentage of criminal behavior it actually constitutes.

CRIMES KNOWN TO THE POLICE. A bit lower and at a point narrower in the funnel are crimes known to the police. This is the first real, and somewhat imperfect, measure of crime. These are the behaviors that the police include in their reports and are officially measured. However, individual police officers or police administrators can exercise considerable discretion in determining just how a behavior will be categorized for reporting purposes. Because we have no idea what percentage of actual crime ends up as crimes known to the police, this measure may be a better indication of what the police do with the crimes they know of than it is of the risk of crime.

INVESTIGATION. In April 1983 the pelvic portion of a female torso was found on the banks of the Mississippi River near Davenport, Iowa. In an autopsy, the pathologist estimated that the victim was between 18 and 40 years old, had probably given birth, and likely had been dismembered with a chainsaw. A forensic anthropologist estimated the victim to be between 4 feet, 7 inches and 5 feet, 9 inches tall, 27 to 49 years old, and weighing between 125 and 145 pounds.[29] With the help of techniques considered cutting-edge at the time, including DNA evidence, investigators matched the woman's characteristics to those of Joyce Klindt, a Davenport woman who had gone missing the month before. Eventually, her husband admitted murdering her, cutting her up with a chainsaw, and dumping her remains in the river.[30] The case has been cited as a classic example of good investigation and set precedents for the use of scientific evidence in court.[31]

Although the police do their best to solve crimes, such success stories are not the norm. In probing the 1996 murder of JonBenet Ramsey, a local police detective was accused of making several crucial mistakes in the investigation.[32] To this day, no one has been charged with the child's murder. In other, less sensational cases, police investigate to the best of their abilities, but must deal with limited resources, poor physical evidence, a cold trail, or just bad luck.

Typically, police gather tissue samples and fingerprints, talk with witnesses and victims, and examine police records of potential suspects. Sometimes the evidence is gathered quickly, and a suspect is apprehended at once. A large number of cases, however, languish, only to be solved years later or not at all.

ARRESTS. Once the police become aware that a crime has been committed, they look for the person(s) responsible, and if they have enough evidence, they make an arrest. It should come as no surprise that the police do not make an arrest for every crime they detect. In fact, **clearance rates** can vary widely depending on the type of crime and the priorities of the law enforcement agency. For instance, most Driving Under the Influence (DUI) offenses go undetected, but proactive police practices such as sobriety checkpoints can greatly increase the arrest statistics for a police agency. Arrests represent only a small picture of what the police do, but they are an important measure in our crime funnel because they provide a good indication of what will happen in the rest of the criminal justice system. Arrests provide the rest of the system with the cases it must handle.

clearance rates
The number of crimes that have been solved by the police. Often, offenders who are arrested for a crime will give information about other crimes they have committed. This allows police to "clear" those cases.

BOOKING. Booking occurs at the police station, where a suspect's name, age, and address are recorded, as well as information on the time, place, and reason for arrest. Usually, a photograph and fingerprints are taken, and the suspect's clothing and personal effects are stored. The suspect usually is placed in a holding cell until he or she can be questioned further.

CASE IN POINT

Mapp v. Ohio

The Case

Mapp v. Ohio 367 U.S. 1081, 81 S.Ct. 1684 (1961)

The Point

Illegally seized evidence is inadmissible in state criminal courts.

In 1957, Cleveland, Ohio, police suspected that a person who was wanted for questioning in a bombing was at the home of a woman, Dollree Mapp. When police went to the home, Mapp wouldn't let them in and requested that the officers get a warrant. While the officers were gone, Mapp called her attorney over. When the officers returned, they waved a piece of paper saying that it was a warrant, but wouldn't show it to either Mapp or her attorney. Mapp grabbed the paper and shoved it into her clothing from where it was retrieved by an officer who then handcuffed Mapp. The officers found no bomb materials in the house, but did find a trunk in the basement full of what the officers said was pornographic materials. Mapp was arrested and later convicted of possessing pornography and sentenced to seven years in prison. Mapp appealed to the Supreme Court, claiming that the police had no right to search her house because no warrant was ever issued. The decision established that the exclusionary rule, in which illegally seized evidence is inadmissible in court, is extended to state criminal cases.

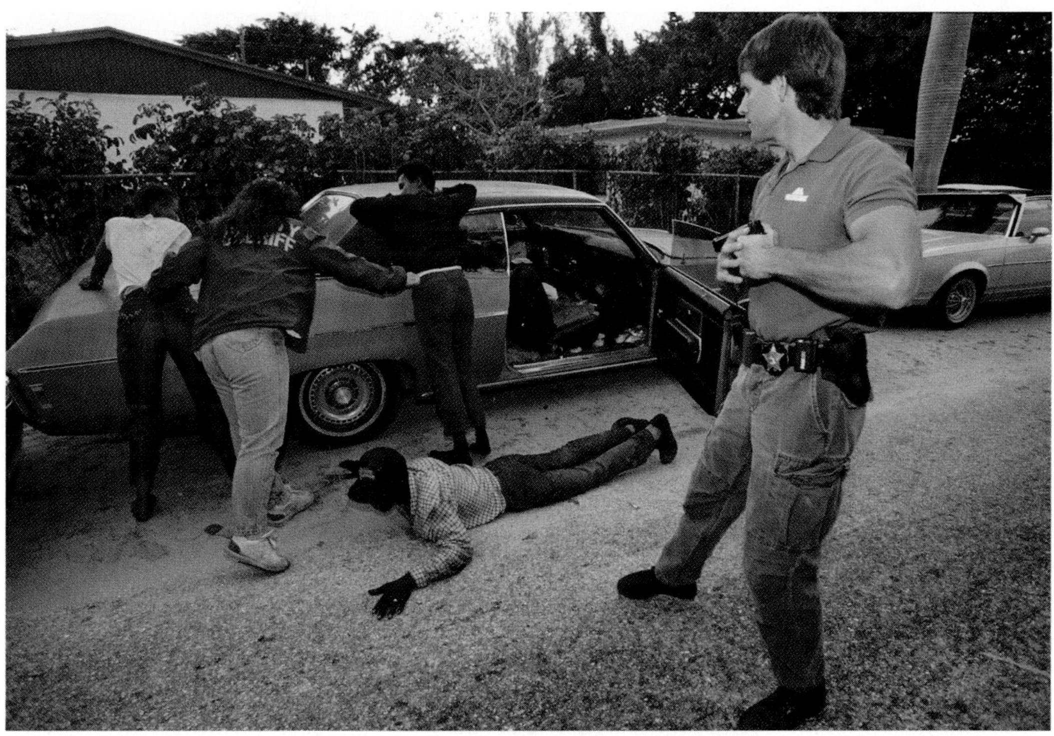

Arresting suspects can be dangerous for law enforcement officers. Until the situation is brought under control, the officers are prepared to use force.
Courtesy of CORBIS-NY.

CHARGES FILED BY THE PROSECUTOR. Of all the arrests made by the police, only a percentage result in a person being charged with a crime by the prosecutor and funneled deeper into the criminal justice system. The discretion used by the prosecutor to decide which cases to eliminate from the criminal justice system is dependent on a number of factors. The first factor is resources. As at every other point in the criminal justice system, the decision to prosecute is dependent on personnel, budget, space, and agency priorities.

CASE IN POINT

Escobedo v. Illinois

The Case

Escobedo v. Illinois 378 U.S. 478, 84 S.Ct. 1758 (1964)

The Point

Upon being accused of murder, a suspect is entitled to counsel and the right to remain silent.

On the night of January 19, 1960, the brother-in-law of Michael Escobedo was shot and killed. Police arrested Escobedo at 2:30 A.M. without a warrant. Escobedo was interrogated, but did not make a statement, and was released that afternoon after his lawyer obtained a state court writ of habeas corpus. Eleven days later, Escobedo was arrested again after an acquaintance (who was also later indicted for the murder) told police that it was Escobedo who shot the man. At the police station, Escobedo asked several times to see his lawyer, who was in the building and was being refused access to his client. Escobedo was not advised of his right to remain silent and after a lengthy interrogation gave a damaging statement that was admitted at the trial. Escobedo was convicted and appealed to the state supreme court, which affirmed the conviction. The U.S. Supreme Court reversed the decision on the grounds that Escobedo had been denied counsel, even after repeatedly requesting it. The court also made the distinction between police investigation and police accusation. When Escobedo was arrested, police were merely investigating a murder. This later shifted to the police accusing Escobedo of committing the murder, a situation in which a suspect is entitled to counsel and the right to remain silent.

The prosecutor may have too many other cases that are deemed more important and so will simply decline to pursue certain ones. The prosecutor may decide that the police have not presented sufficient evidence to ensure successful prosecution of the case. Additionally, the prosecutor may discover that the police made procedural errors in the arrest that would be brought out by the defense attorney and result in a dismissal. Finally, the prosecutor may have personal or agency priorities concerning what types of cases will be pressed. Political corruption cases may be encouraged or discouraged depending on the party affiliation of the state attorney versus the defendant.

bill of indictment
A declaration of the charges against an accused person that is presented to a grand jury to determine whether enough evidence exists for an indictment.

true bill
The decision of a grand jury that sufficient evidence exists to indict an accused person.

no-bill
The decision of a grand jury not to indict an accused person as a result of insufficient evidence. Also called "no true bill."

nolo contendere
Latin for "I do not wish to contend." The defendant neither admits nor denies committing the crime, but agrees to be punished as if guilty. This type of plea cannot be used as an admission of guilt if a civil case is held after the criminal trial.

GRAND JURY. Grand juries are formed to decide whether enough evidence exists to justify an indictment and trial. Grand jurors usually are selected from the same pool of people that provides trial jurors, and are sworn in by a court. The prosecutor bringing the case presents the jurors with the charges or a **bill of indictment** and introduces the evidence. Grand jury proceedings are secret, and witnesses can be called to testify against the suspect without the suspect or the suspect's witnesses being present. Indicted suspects can sometimes later obtain transcripts of grand jury proceedings.

A grand jury returns a **true bill** if it decides to indict. If not, a **no-bill** is returned. A prosecutor may still file charges against a suspect in the event of a no-bill. Prosecutors can bring further evidence to the same jury or present the original evidence to a second jury. In some jurisdictions, prosecutors may choose not to use a grand jury, and instead file a criminal complaint.

Grand juries usually sit for longer than trial juries. Federal grand juries sit about 18 months, but can have their terms extended in six-month increments up to 36 months. State grand juries sit for shorter terms, from a month up to a year. Unlike trial jurors, grand jurors do not convene daily, but may meet once a week or once a month.

INITIAL APPEARANCE, PRELIMINARY HEARING, AND ARRAIGNMENT. After arrest, suspects must be brought before a judge within a reasonable time for an initial appearance. Here, the defendant is formally charged with a crime and will respond by pleading guilty, not guilty, or ***nolo contendere*** (no contest). Defendants also are informed of their rights to bail and to an attorney. Those charged with a misdemeanor may enter a plea immediately. If the plea is *guilty,* the judge may impose the sentence. However, defendants charged with felonies, which are more serious, usually do not enter pleas at this time. Also, they probably have not been able to consult an attorney prior to the hearing. At this point, the defendant is scheduled for a preliminary hearing, also known as the preliminary examination or probable cause hearing. Here, the prosecutor presents enough evidence to establish probable cause, or a ***prima facie*** case. The exception is when defendants have been indicted by grand juries, in which probable cause already has been established. In this case, the defendant's first court appearance is at an **arraignment** similar to the initial appearance.

***prima facie* case**
A case established by evidence sufficient enough to establish the fact in question unless it is rebutted.

arraignment
A court appearance in which the defendant is formally charged with a crime and asked to respond by pleading guilty, not guilty, or *nolo contendere.*

BAIL/BAIL BONDING. The word *bail* comes from an Old French word *bailler,* which means "to hand over" or "to entrust." Bail is money paid to the court to ensure that a suspect who is released from jail will appear in court. The amount of bail is based on the gravity of the offense and how likely or unlikely the defendant is to flee. One alternative to bail is release on one's own recognizance, in which the defendant pays no money and promises to appear in court when required. Defendants with strong community ties, such as a steady job and family, may qualify for such release. Defendants who do not qualify for release on their own recognizance or cannot pay the bail amount are held in jail. Other defendants who are believed to be serious threats to the community or to an individual (such as a witness) or are very likely to flee are held in **preventive detention.**

preventive detention
The jailing of a defendant awaiting trial, usually in order to protect an individual or the public.

Bail bonding refers to the money posted by a bonding company for a defendant who cannot afford bail. The defendant pays a percentage of the bail amount to the bonding company as a fee, and the company agrees to be responsible to the court for the entire amount of the defendant's bail. If the defendant does not show up for court, the judge can issue a warrant for his or her arrest and threaten to keep the money. The bonding company then will track down the defendant and bring him or her back, by force if necessary.

PLEA BARGAINING. One of the points in the criminal justice system that results in the most attrition of cases is the plea bargaining stage. There are many reasons for plea bargaining, and they are not all for the benefit of the defendant.[33] The state has a lot to gain by disposing of cases quickly and efficiently. Prosecutors may decide that the case is weak, and rather than risking dismissal, opt for a negotiated plea that results in some type of punishment. It is recognized in the criminal justice system that plea bargaining is a necessary and often desirable practice. If law enforcement is doing a good job, then the vast majority of defendants are actually guilty of their crimes, and the prosecutors have reliable evidence that is likely to stand up in court. Defense attorneys, seeing no realistic hope of having their clients acquitted of the offenses, are keenly interested in limiting the sentenced imposed by the court. There is no need for a trial, and by plea bargaining, the defense can strike a deal for a less-than-maximum sentence for the offender. Although plea bargaining is not popular with the public, for the criminal justice system (and maybe less so for some defendants), it is a reasonable and inevitable practice.

TRIAL. Few cases actually make it to the trial phase of the criminal justice process. Of the cases that go to trial, only a small percentage end up in guilty verdicts that allow further processing of the case. Some defendants are acquitted or found not guilty. Sometimes the case is dismissed because the prosecution was unable to present a viable case against the defendant. Sometimes the case is dismissed because of prosecutorial misconduct in which the rights of the defendant were violated. The trial is what most people think about when they imagine justice in the United States. However, the media image of life in U.S. courtrooms is highly distorted. Last-minute confessions on the witness stand by distraught individuals who are pressured or tricked by a crafty lawyer do not represent what actually happens in the courtroom. Most of the decisions are made behind the scenes, and excitement and drama in the courtroom are actually quite rare.

SENTENCING. Once a defendant has been determined to be guilty either by plea or by verdict, he or she is sentenced by the judge at a sentencing hearing. When the judge has

Jury duty is a responsibility of citizens. Jurors are charged with listening to the evidence and making a fair and impartial judgment.
Courtesy of Corbis Royalty Free.

presentence report
An account prepared by a probation officer that assists the sentencing court in deciding an appropriate sentence for a convicted defendant. The report includes the defendant's prior, if any, criminal history; relevant personal circumstances; the appropriate classification of the defendant and the offense under the established system; the variety of sentences and programs available; and the offense's impact on the victim.

discretion, he or she considers the circumstances of the crime and the attitude of the offender, as well as the prosecutor's recommendation and the probation office's **presentence report.** Depending on the crime, a sentence can range from a fine and community service to several years in prison to life imprisonment to death. Usually, the law limits the judge to a few options.

Sentencing guidelines are rules for deciding sentences and are set down by a commission. The guidelines classify offenses and offenders and prescribe punishments. According to the United States Sentencing Commission, the sentencing guidelines for federal crimes were created to ensure that "similar offenders of similar crimes would receive similar sentences."[34] Determinate or fixed sentencing limits the judge's discretion in much the same way and also is intended to limit sentencing disparity.

Indeterminate sentencing specifies a range of time that the offender must serve before parole can be granted (for example, a sentence of "10 years to life" for first-degree murder). This shifts the discretion for determining the offender's release from the judge to the parole board.

In a capital case, in which the choice for the offender is either life in prison without parole or the death penalty, a jury chooses the sentence.

PROBATION. Probation is a common disposition for criminal cases. It occurs either after the trial as part of the sentence handed down by the judge to offenders who were found guilty by a jury, or instead of a trial as part of a plea bargaining agreement. Probation is a form of social control in the community and is appropriate for offenders who do not present an immediate risk to the community. However, it should be noted that because of prison overcrowding, many offenders who might otherwise have been incarcerated are being placed on probation.[35]

electronic monitoring
A form of intermediate punishment in which an offender is allowed to remain in the community but must wear an electronic device that allows the authorities to monitor his or her whereabouts. Electronic monitoring may also be done via telephone.

The main advantage of probation to the criminal justice system is cost. Probationers live at home, work at their jobs, support their families, and pay taxes. The state pays probation officers to supervise the offenders, but with caseloads of between 100 and 400, depending on the jurisdiction and level of supervision, the cost is a great saving over that of incarceration. Additionally, many communities now charge cost-of-supervision fees to the offenders that help pay for this expense. The actual level of supervision can vary widely, from reporting once a month to the probation officer all the way up to taking weekly drug tests, participating in **electronic monitoring**, and reporting on a daily basis.

FOCUS ON ETHICS

A Balance of Interests

In your job as a probation officer you are assigned a case of a rich and successful accountant who has been placed on probation for driving under the influence of alcohol. As part of her community service, the accountant has been spending each Saturday morning at a local nursing home where she has been helping the residents fill out their tax forms. This accountant has been able to secure thousands of dollars in tax refunds for these elderly citizens, who have no idea how the tax laws work. In fact, one of the residents, who also happens to be your grandmother, reports that not only is this accountant helping the residents save money, but she also has been coming to the nursing home during the middle of the week, on her own time, and spending hours talking to the lonely and the depressed.

You feel a little guilty that this accountant has developed a close relationship with your grandmother and that you have not been to the nursing home in months. Being suspicious, you investigate to see if the accountant knows that you have a relative in the home, and you discover that not only does she not know, but she has volunteered to serve as a member of the board of directors of the home and help the residents deal with the confusing social service agencies such as Medicare and Social Security.

Late one night you get a call from the accountant. She is obviously drunk and informs you she has just crashed her car into a tree and that she needs a ride home before the police come and arrest her. You know that if she gets another DUI, she will not only lose her license, but also will have to spend 90 days in jail and may well be disciplined by her professional accounting association and could lose her job. Although you have little sympathy for people who cannot control their drinking, this young woman has been turning her life around and doing good works, especially for the elderly. You see potential in this client.

WHAT DO YOU DO?

1. Go help her. You owe her for helping your grandmother, and this is one of the few things you can do to repay the help and kindness that she has shown.
2. Call the police and report her. You are an officer of the court, and you cannot ethically do anything else. Also, you might get in trouble if you do not call.
3. Help her but make a deal stipulating that she will check herself into a clinic and get help for her drinking problem. Use this last incident as leverage to force her to confront her drinking. She is too talented and accomplished to give up on now. She is worth trying to save one last time.
4. Call your supervisor and ask to be relieved of the case because you can no longer be objective.

APPEAL. A written request to a higher court to modify or reverse the judgment of a trial court or intermediate-level appellate court is called an appeal. The process begins when the defendant who loses a trial files a notice of appeal, which usually must be filed within 30 days from the judgment date. The appellate court does not retry the case. Rather, the defendant, now known as the appellant, and the trial's winner, or appellee, submit written arguments, or briefs, and sometimes make oral arguments addressing why the decision should be upheld or overturned. When appellate courts reverse lower-court judgments, it is usually because of **prejudicial error**, and the case is returned to a lower court for retrial. There is no constitutional right to appeal; however, some states have established the right to appeal by statute, whereas others have established it by custom.

prejudicial error
An error affecting the outcome of a trial.

PRISON. Relatively few of the people that the police arrest end up in prison (See Figure 1.5). Prison is an extremely costly option that, in theory, should be reserved for those

Figure 1.5
Decreasing Number of Cases

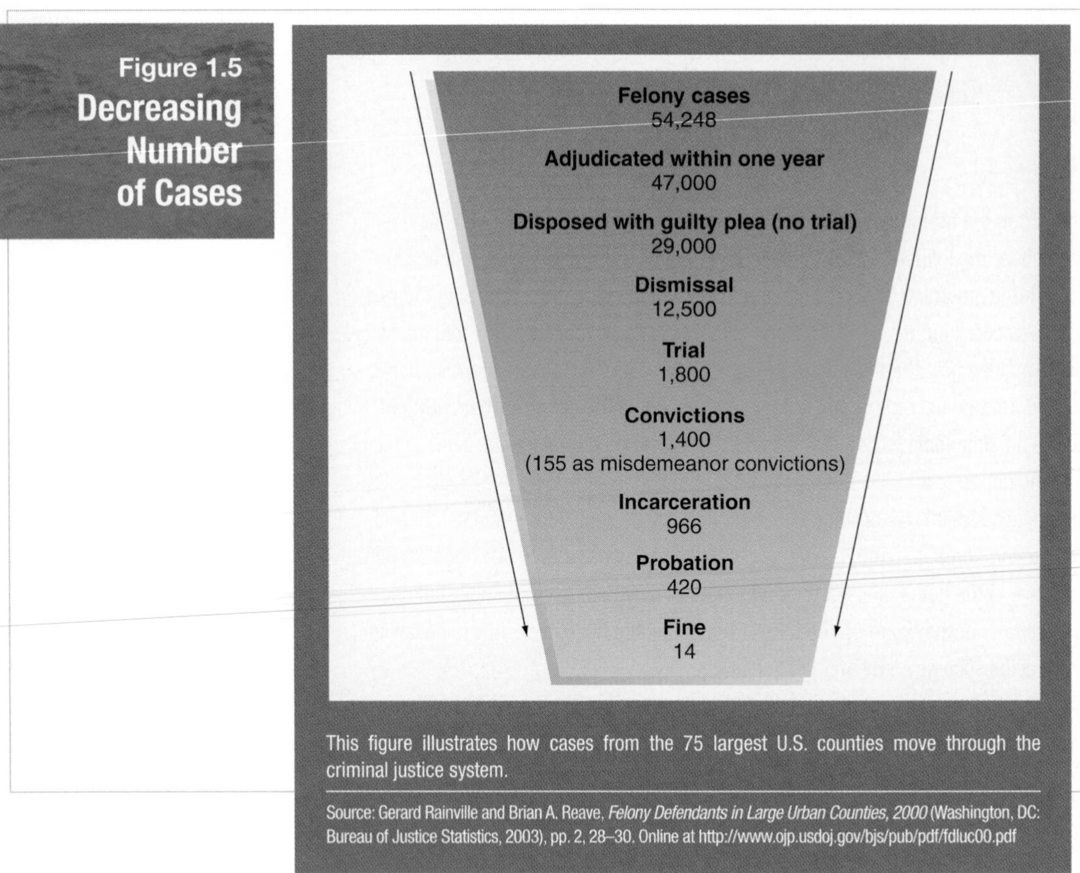

This figure illustrates how cases from the 75 largest U.S. counties move through the criminal justice system.

Source: Gerard Rainville and Brian A. Reave, *Felony Defendants in Large Urban Counties, 2000* (Washington, DC: Bureau of Justice Statistics, 2003), pp. 2, 28–30. Online at http://www.ojp.usdoj.gov/bjs/pub/pdf/fdluc00.pdf

offenders who are a threat to the community. Many individuals are so dangerous that incarcerating them is the only way to ensure that they do not continue to kill, rob, and rape in the community. Other individuals have committed serious offenses such as embezzlement, and although not an immediate threat to the community, are incarcerated to show the rest of us that serious crimes can lead to serious consequences. Ideally, prison should help change the individual and help him or her prepare for life as a free person. However, because of prison overcrowding, the rehabilitative function of the institution has been all but abandoned.[36] Many states are finding the cost of maintaining extensive prison systems to be prohibitive, and are looking for new ways of dealing with offenders, including turning to prisons run by for-profit private corporations. Boot camp prisons for young offenders typically have 90-day programs that employ a paramilitary culture to emphasize order and discipline. These types of programs have their critics, but they are a good deal less expensive than traditional prisons.[37]

PAROLE. Parole is very similar to, and sometimes confused with, probation. Probation occurs instead of prison, whereas parole occurs after prison. Inmates who show successful adjustment to prison life may be given the opportunity for an early release in which a parole officer supervises them.[38] The theory behind parole is to aid the offender in returning to the community. Providing help with finding a place to live, obtaining employment, and dealing with personal issues such as drug and alcohol abuse is encompassed by the parole mission. Today, parole has evolved into a surveillance role in which the officers act more as police officers than as social workers.[39] Some states have abolished parole altogether in lieu of making the offender serve almost the entire sentence.

CAPITAL PUNISHMENT. Capital punishment is a relatively rare event and one for which only a small proportion of offenders are even eligible. Many states do not employ this sentence, and some that do, such as Illinois, have suspended it because of the appearance of discriminatory use and errors.[40] According to Amnesty International, the United States is one of only five stable, industrialized countries to use capital punishment (the others are China, Japan, Russia, Singapore, and Taiwan).[41] Even though there is strong public support for it, there is also very vocal opposition.[42] It is a controversial practice that is sure to be contested in the courts over the next decade. One clear trend is the move by many states to change their method of capital punishment from electrocution to lethal injection. However, critics contend that it is impossible to deliberately kill a person in a humane way.

The criminal justice system is much more complex than suggested by the funnel analogy, and this complexity will be revealed in subsequent chapters that deal in greater detail with components of the system. The analogy's goal has been to indicate how the numbers dwindle drastically when we move down the funnel from crimes that are committed to prison and capital punishment. This funnel analogy illustrates the low number of crimes that catch the full implications of the public's perception of justice. Many of the crimes that do enter the system are systematically excluded for a variety of reasons. In review, these reasons include but are not limited to the following:

1. **Cost.** As a society, we simply cannot afford to spend the money and resources necessary to have a totally crime-free society. Although crime is a serious social problem, many other worthy items compete for our tax dollars. Increased spending on crime means that health care, national defense, education, highways, and a host of other legitimate and desirable services do not get enough of the resources they require to function effectively. For example, decisions have to be made on which military aircraft get built because we cannot afford all of them. Similarly, most students must take out loans to pay for a college education because the government can fund only so many scholarships. The criminal justice system, by some estimates, could bankrupt the nation if funded for all its legitimate needs. Therefore, only a percentage of crimes ever receives what the public believes to be "full justice" (see Figure 1.6).
2. **Discretion.** Criminal justice practitioners exercise a considerable amount of discretion in deciding what happens to individual cases. Although this discretion is constrained

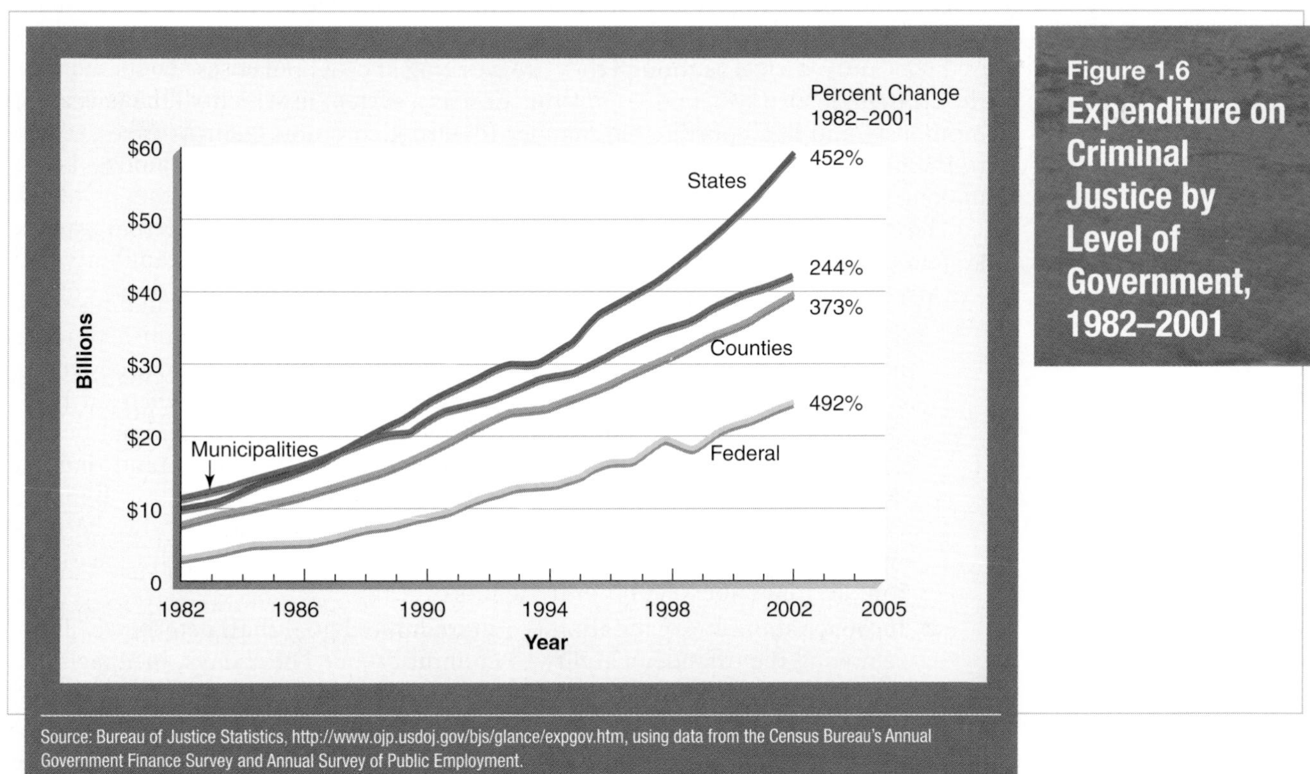

Source: Bureau of Justice Statistics, http://www.ojp.usdoj.gov/bjs/glance/expgov.htm, using data from the Census Bureau's Annual Government Finance Survey and Annual Survey of Public Employment.

Figure 1.6 Expenditure on Criminal Justice by Level of Government, 1982–2001

by resources, a good amount of personal philosophy and judgment also goes into deciding what happens to cases. This discretion is sometimes deemed problematic, and efforts are taken to curb the influence of individual decision makers. For example there can be wide disparity in sentencing across jurisdictions or even between judges in the same city. In an effort to ensure that similar cases are treated more equally, legislatures have passed laws calling for fixed sentences. Mandatory minimum statutes and three-strikes laws greatly limit the discretion judges have in sentencing offenders. Similarly, some law enforcement agencies are mandated to make arrests in domestic assault cases in which there is clear evidence of physical abuse. The use of some discretion is inherent in the criminal justice system, but its use is a contested practice.

3. **Errors.** Sometimes cases simply fall through the cracks. Criminal justice practitioners are human and can make mistakes. They are often overworked and underpaid and experience a considerable amount of stress in doing a difficult job. Most jurisdictions do not have the sophisticated computer systems that link all the components of the criminal justice system that would help ensure that cases are handled efficiently. Also, criminal justice practitioners may make errors in judgment. The police officer who gives a criminal a second chance or the judge who places the sex offender on probation can find himself or herself betrayed by offenders who do not or cannot appreciate the break they have been given.

Problem with the System Metaphor

Can the criminal justice system accurately be envisioned as a system at all? On one hand, the components share an overall common goal of providing justice, but each agency may define that goal in a slightly different way. For example, a police chief may view his or her role as taking dangerous offenders off the street and locking them behind bars for a long time so they cannot further victimize citizens. The counselor in the prison may see his or her role as helping the inmate adjust to prison life and gain the necessary skills to achieve parole and live successfully in the outside world. These goals are not mutually exclusive. If the counselor is successful in rehabilitating the offender, then the police chief's goal of making the community safe is also realized. However, in the actual execution of their everyday jobs, the police chief and the counselor see their goals in a limited way and may feel as though they are working at cross purposes. To these individuals, the criminal justice system does not function as a system in which all the parts work harmoniously and in a coordinated manner toward a common goal. At times, it may seem to them, rather, as though they are competing with one another to find the best way of making society safer.

The criminal justice system has multiple goals (see Figure 1.7). Different aspects of the system emphasize different goals.

1. **Deterrence.** Two types of deterrence are important to the criminal justice system. Specific deterrence occurs when an offender is caught and punished and decides not to engage in further criminal behavior because he or she now understands the consequences of that behavior. General deterrence occurs when an offender is caught and punished, and the rest of us do not engage in criminal behavior because we saw what happened to the offender and we understand that the same consequences would befall us if we were caught breaking the law. By far, general deterrence is the more important of these two types. Imagine how chaotic society would be if each of us had to be caught and punished for each type of crime before deciding not to commit it anymore.
2. **Incapacitation.** Incapacitation is a more limited goal than deterrence. This entails removing the offender's ability to commit crime. These days, incapacitation usually means incarceration. An offender who is behind bars cannot harm citizens in a free society. Historically, incapacitation included exile and the use of such devices as the **pillory**. Today, some believe that **chemical castration** of sex offenders would prevent them from committing rape.

pillory
A wooden frame with holes for securing the head and hands that was used to secure and expose an offender to public derision.

chemical castration
Anti-androgen drugs, usually administered by injection, that have the effect of lowering the testosterone level and blunting the sex drive in males.

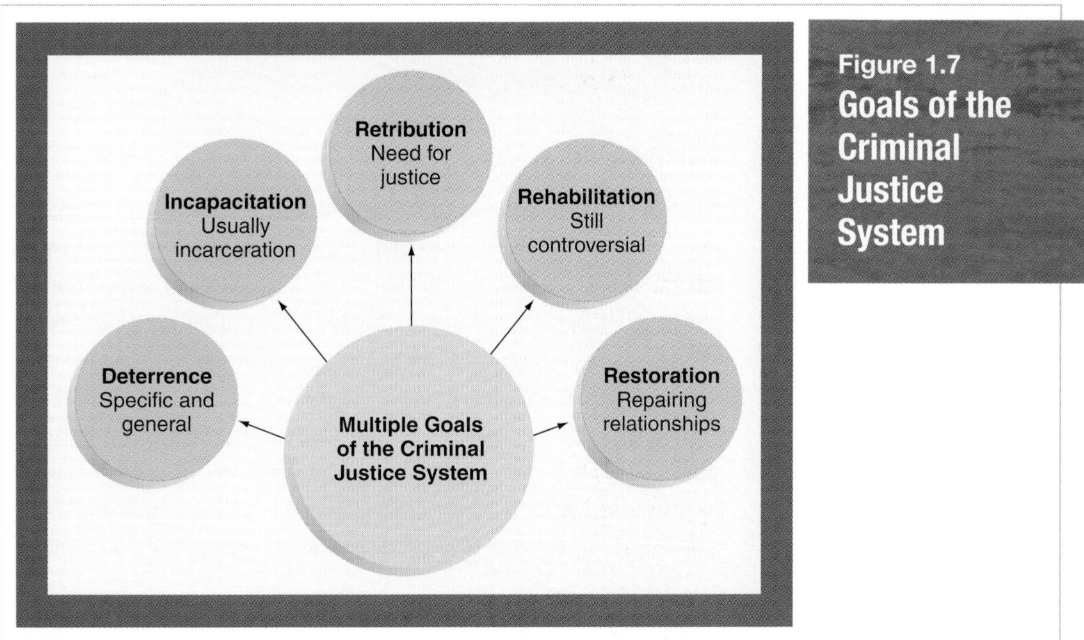

Figure 1.7
Goals of the Criminal Justice System

3. **Retribution.** Many people believe that justice prevails when an offender is punished. If people are going to cede to the criminal justice system the authority to capture, prosecute, and sentence offenders, then they need to feel that their values are taken into account. If offenders do not "get what they deserve" in the eyes of citizens, then the criminal justice system loses credibility, and citizens may take the law into their own hands. Retribution is an ancient motive with religious connotations, and for many people it is one of the most important goals of the criminal justice system.
4. **Rehabilitation.** One of the most controversial goals of the criminal justice system—and one that has fallen on hard times recently—is rehabilitation. This involves correcting the behavior of the offender and giving him or her the skills and emotional strength to survive in society without violating the law. Some corrections practitioners say "habilitation" would more accurately describe this goal because many offenders never had these social and emotional skills to begin with. The debate as to whether rehabilitation works and whether the criminal justice system allocates suitable resources toward this goal is ongoing.
5. **Restoration.** One of the most promising philosophies emerging in the criminal justice literature over recent years is that of restorative justice. The goal of restorative justice is to repair the harm crime has done to the relationship between the offender and victim and between the offender and the community. Because many crimes involve relationships between individuals who will continue to interact after the criminal case has been settled, it is advisable to settle the case with the input of the participants so that they have a sense of commitment to the judgment. Empowering family members, neighbors, and coworkers to help solve disputes allows them to repair the harm done by the crime and to live and work with each other in the future. Restorative justice will be covered in greater detail in Chapter 16.

When considering these multiple goals, we can see why the criminal justice system does not always work as a smooth-functioning and well-coordinated mechanism. With criminal justice agencies spanning different levels of government and contrasting and overlapping jurisdictions, the responsibility for crime is not always clear and agreed upon. With each level of government and each individual agency having its own goals and pressures, the overall accountability for crime is fragmented and disputed. Depending solely on the criminal justice system to maintain social control could lead to even bigger problems. Fortunately, other institutions help to maintain civil behavior and make the job of the criminal justice system easier.

FOCUS ON ETHICS

A Kid in Trouble

While working at the big bookstore in the mall, you see the 12-year-old who lives across the street enter the store and head for the magazine section. As you approach the youth to say hello, you notice him slipping some magazines under his shirt. Although his mother is a good friend of your parents, and he is in the same classroom as your little sister, you know he has had a troubled life. His father, a police officer, was killed in the line of duty only three years ago, and the boy has been in trouble ever since. When the youth realizes you saw him steal the magazines, he offers them back to you with the plea that you don't tell anyone because his mother's new boyfriend, also a police officer, will beat him. You suspect this is true because your parents have expressed concern about his mother's new relationship. You feel conflicted because your boss has been very good to you and has allowed you to work many overtime hours while you go to college. Additionally, she has been accommodating to how your class schedule changes each semester and always finds a way to keep you on the job.

WHAT DO YOU DO?

1. Help the boy.
2. Follow store procedure and alert the security guard.

It All Begins with the Family

The primary institution of socialization in society is the family. The tasks of families are great in terms of transmitting the expectations of behavior in society and providing an emotionally secure and supportive environment. Although we hear a lot about "family values" from politicians, this term is loaded with the political and social expectations of one way of thinking about the family. In actuality, although the ideal of the nuclear family is laudable and still the social norm, it is not the statistical norm. Other configurations of families and other worthy values also exist.

Whether the living arrangement of the family comprises an intact nuclear family with two parents and their children, or divorced and remarried parents with children from prior marriages, the task of the family is still the same. The intact nuclear family is not always the best arrangement for some children. If one parent is abusive or neglectful, or both parents are in conflict over money and family power, the best solution might be for the family to dissolve.[43] The important issues for the student of the criminal justice system are how the norms and rules of society are transmitted to the children and how well the children, in turn, transmit values to their children.

An emerging feature of some families is the use of "tough love" discipline to try to make children conform. In an age when parents are too busy with careers, relationships, and recreation to spend time to know their children's friends and activities, some parents have turned to drug-testing their own children. This tough love aspect of dealing with children is mirrored in the criminal justice system with its "get tough on crime" approach.

RELIGION. Religion is a powerful institution. Although many people do not attend any type of religious service, most people in the United States have been exposed to some sort of religious instruction that has influenced the way they think about dealing with others. Émile Durkheim detailed how religion provides important and positive functions in society by strengthening our sense of community, providing answers about the ultimate meaning of life, providing emotional comfort in times of loss and stress, providing guidelines for everyday life, exerting social control, and sometimes acting as a vehicle for social change.[44]

Of importance to the study of crime is how religion plays a part in exerting social control. By providing rules to guide individuals in the practice of their faith, religion supports many of the laws of civil society. In many ways, societies enact laws that reinforce the religious beliefs of their citizens. Rules about adultery, gambling, child rearing, and observance of religious holidays have all made the transition from religious rules to civil law or practice.

How much should we look to religion in developing secular laws to be enforced by the criminal justice system? The founders of the United States, in an effort to guard against religious persecution, made a clear distinction between church and state. Coming from countries where there were national religions and persecution of people who believed differently, the founders established the United States as a country in which all people would be free to follow their own hearts in religious matters. This freedom to believe has been tested repeatedly over the last two centuries as people arrived from many other parts of the world to become U.S. citizens. Although a change has occurred in the overall pattern of religious practices in the United States (from European Protestantism to all the varied religions found today), it is fair to say that religion has exerted a consistent, and for the most part positive, form of social control.[45]

Like the family, the institution of religion provides people with internal controls over their behavior, which allows them to interact with others without breaking the law. Polite and civil society is only possible when people behave themselves without the supervision of the criminal justice system. If the criminal justice system had to socialize and supervise everyone, the United States would be a police state.

SCHOOLS. As institutions, schools do more than teach children how to read and write. They are also a powerful force in socializing them into the culturally approved ways of interacting with other people. In his 1975 article "Learning the Student Role: Kindergarten as Academic Boot Camp," Harry L. Gracey detailed how five-year-olds are taught to take turns, be quiet, share, and raise their hands and be recognized before speaking.[46] These lessons are reinforced throughout their school years and, from the point of social control, make the job of the teacher much easier. As children internalize these behaviors and learn to conduct themselves in a law-abiding way, the job of the criminal justice system is made much easier also.

However, the job of the school as a socializing institution is sometimes difficult, and it is not always done well. At times, schools have overreacted to the deviant activities of young people and have enacted overly punitive policies. Some of the zero-tolerance policies of recent years have been so draconian as to invite the ridicule of the public.

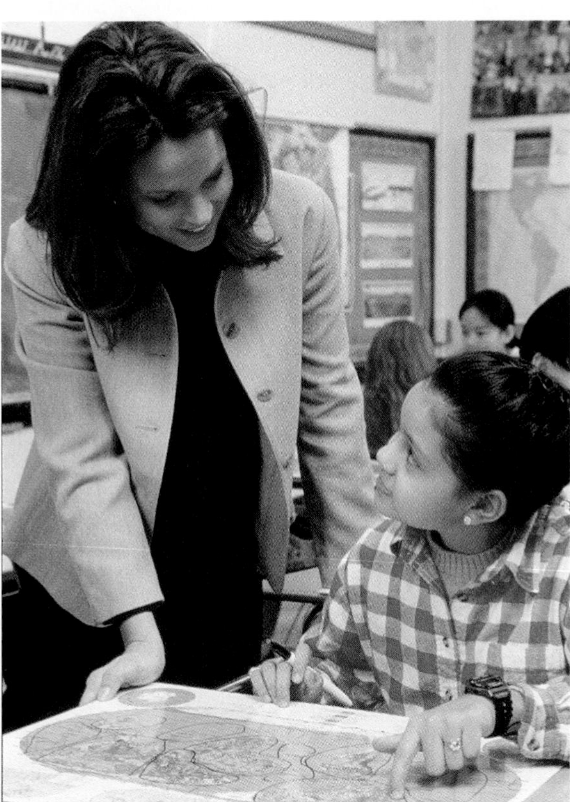

Schools serve multiple functions. In addition to teaching academic subjects, they teach children appropriate behavior.
Courtesy of CORBIS-NY.

Pass or Fail

In 1999 the students of Lockney Junior High School in Lockney, Texas, found themselves embroiled in a controversy involving the rights of individuals and the school board's responsibility to provide education in a safe, disciplined environment. After 12 adults of the town's 2,300 residents were indicted on drug-related felonies, the seven-member school board instituted a policy that required all students to have their parents sign consent forms for random drug testing. If the parents refused to sign the consent form, the student would be subjected to the same punishments as students who failed the drug test: a 21-day suspension from extracurricular activities, three days of in-school suspension, and three sessions of substance abuse counseling.

One student's father, Larry Tannahill, refused to give consent for testing for his son, Brady, then age 12. With the help of the ACLU's Drug Policy Litigation Project, Tannahill challenged the policy in a lawsuit. Critics of the policy pointed out that because there was no indication of drug use by the school's 400 students, random drug testing violated constitutional freedoms from unreasonable searches. Complicating the issue was the status of children as minors and the power of parents to give consent for the tests. In 2001 the school district chose to stop defending the policy by not appealing a federal district judge's ruling that its testing program was unconstitutional. A lawyer for the school district said the appeal was dropped because of its potential cost and the fact that Mr. Tannahill was the only parent who refused to consent to the drug test.

School boards across the country are looking for guidance from cases such as this one, because many board members and school officials consider drug testing the best way to ensure that students do not become involved in drug culture.

QUESTIONS

1. What do you think about random drug testing of students?
2. Are drugs such a significant problem in your school that you would submit to having your body tested for illegal drugs or underage drinking?
3. Was Mr. Tannahill right to sue?

Sources: Anna Belli Gesalman, "Texas Duel: Drug Tests versus Student Rights," *The Christian Science Monitor*, April 18, 2000, http://www.csmonitor.com/durable/2000/04/18/f-p1s4.html. Mark Walsh, "Texas District Drops Defense of Blanket Drug Tests," *Education Week*, May 9, 2001.

THE MEDIA. The media are also agents of social control. There is a risk in thinking of the media as a single entity because it comprises so many aspects, and its components pursue different goals. It is easy to be critical of the media as socializing agents when we treat them as institutions that have an exact goal or purpose. It is useful for our purposes here to select aspects of the media that affect the criminal justice system and suggest how they exert a direct and/or indirect influence on social control.

- **The news.** The way crime is reported exerts a great influence on how we envision and react to it.[47] Although the media should give us an accurate and unbiased picture of the nature of crime, we are also aware that some news programs have as one of their primary goals an entertainment function to attract more viewers to their station. To a large degree, the same can be said of the print media. Even more problematic are some of the quasi-news programs such as *20/20*, *48 Hours*, and *Unsolved Mysteries*. These shows use the facts of the cases they cover, but they highlight the more sensational aspects and fail to provide a balanced picture of crime.[48] Given the decreasing crime rates of the last decade, it would seem that the media would present an improving picture of the crime situation in the United States.

- **Hollywood.** How much is the crime and violence that is depicted on television a reflection of society, and how much distorts the problems and possibly even contributes to them? That is, do individuals filter the imaginary violence that is shown by Hollywood and recognize it for its entertainment value, or do some people go out into society and mimic what they have viewed?[49] Movies, television, and popular music all have come under attack by concerned citizens for messages of sex and violence portrayed in a positive light.[50] What are realistic expectations of the entertainment industry in a country that values free speech and expression? We will not, and cannot, answer this question here. It is raised solely to emphasize how institutions other than the criminal justice system influence social control.
- **The Internet.** An emerging part of the media that affects social control is the Internet. The problems of sex offenders recruiting young people for illicit sexual purposes, online stalkers, and the proliferation of all types of pornography have been well documented and lamented by the media. The Internet is a wonderful tool in many ways, but it does present new challenges for the social control of citizens. While empowering all of us with access to unlimited sources of information, the Internet also has allowed criminals from sexual deviants to international terrorists to communicate in pursuit of their criminal activities. Although some would allow the government to exert greater control over the Internet, this is not really a viable option. The genie is out of the bottle, and we must accept that with the empowerment of the Internet comes new opportunities for criminals and new ways for all of us to be victimized.

The family, religion, school, and media all have positive functions in society. Although their main job may not be to exert social control on citizens, they all do to a certain extent. Only by recognizing that institutions in addition to the criminal justice system perform social control can we appreciate just how massive and difficult this job is. When all these other institutions fail to fully socialize youth or do not satisfy citizens' needs, the criminal justice system must deal with the consequences.

System of Last Resort

As we will see in later chapters, there are many explanations for the causes of crime. Many of the reasons that individuals violate the law are outside the scope and responsibility of the criminal justice system. The criminal justice system has a difficult mission for several reasons. These reasons include, but are not limited to, the following:

- **The offender.** Criminal offenders can be unpleasant. In fact, they often are under the influence of alcohol or drugs, armed and dangerous, and in a really bad mood. Regardless of the reasons, they have already committed acts that have hurt others either financially or physically, and they are resistant to the idea of being held accountable for their actions. Criminal offenders often have convinced themselves that they have legitimate reasons for their transgressions and picture themselves as victims of circumstance and an overzealous criminal justice system. They are arrested, prosecuted, and incarcerated involuntarily. Unlike the school or the church, the criminal justice system cannot expect much cooperation from its charges. In short, the criminal justice system must deal with some of the most disagreeable people in society, often at great risk to its practitioners.
- **Resources.** Despite the fact that crime consistently rates as one of society's major problems, the criminal justice system is not high on the list of things for which citizens want their tax money used. Schools, roads, parks, national defense, and health care all are more popular destinations for public resources. Within the criminal justice system, the law enforcement role is deemed more worthy than corrections, and within corrections, locking up criminals is viewed as a better use of resources than attempting to rehabilitate them. The criminal justice system will most likely always be underfunded, and those who work in it will do so for reasons of

service, dedication, and excitement rather than money. Many good employees will move on to other, more lucrative professions, and the criminal justice system will struggle to attract the best and the brightest young people entering the workforce.

- **Structure.** As we have already discussed, the criminal justice system is not really a system. This is partly intentional and partly because of poor funding. It is intentional to the degree that checks and balances are built into our democracy. The inefficiencies built into the system ensure that in addition to being slow, the process allows for justice to be pursued through due process and oversight. Only in a police state could a criminal justice system give the appearance of abolishing crime. Along with our freedoms, a certain amount of crime and inefficiency in the criminal justice system is inherent in a free society.

Social control in a democratic society is complicated. The place of the criminal justice system in providing this social control is problematic. It is, for all intents and purposes, the institution of last resort. The family, religion, school, and the media exert a tremendous amount of influence over the behavior of individuals. When these institutions individually or collectively fail to develop law-abiding citizens, the criminal justice system must deal with the consequences. It is unrealistic to expect the criminal justice system to be fully successful where these other institutions have failed. Those who end up in prison are not randomly selected from a representative cross section of the population. Rather, a pronounced selection bias results in the most dangerous and disagreeable people tending to be the ones who enter the criminal justice system.

INDIVIDUAL VS. SOCIETAL RESPONSIBILITY FOR CRIME. Most of our discussion up to this point has focused on the idea that crime is a deviant behavior committed by individuals who have not been properly socialized into mainstream society. In keeping with the subtitle of this book, "Mainstream and Crosscurrents," we now introduce a competing idea that argues that crime is a natural result of a flawed cultural and economic system. A body of criminological theory (to be covered in detail in Chapter 3) contends that the individual offender is not solely to blame for crime. Critical criminology theories look at issues such as racism, sexism, ageism, and the vast disparities in wealth in the United States and suggest that this arrangement continues to be maintained because it works well for those in power.[51] In these critical theories, the criminal justice system is considered one of the tools that the rich and powerful use to enhance their privileged position in society. This is evidenced by the observations that the rich are able to hire private security firms to protect themselves and their property, by how the wealthy can hire private attorneys to represent them in court, and by how the powerful can get their concerns encoded into the law. Any balanced discussion of the discipline of criminal justice requires that this critical perspective be examined. It challenges our conception of what justice is in the United States and forces us to look at how individuals benefit or are victimized by such a criminal justice system.

In reviewing such critical issues, the intent of this book is not to engage in trashing capitalism or the practitioners of the criminal justice system. Rather, these important and legitimate concerns are offered as opportunities for reflection and reform. As students and practitioners of criminal justice, we all have the responsibility to honestly and thoughtfully evaluate how justice is dispensed in this country and to do whatever we can not only to fight crime, but also to improve the criminal justice system. Unless and until the issues raised by these critical criminologists are addressed by society, the criminal justice system will continue to be viewed by many as a repressive system of social control designed to keep the powerful in their positions of privilege.

Summary

The distinguishing feature of the U.S. criminal justice system is the way individual rights are protected as a part of the law enforcement function. The criminal justice system must balance the imposition of order and the preservation of individual rights. Crime can be described as an action that violates the rules of society to the point of harming citizens or the society itself. Other crimes, such as espionage crimes, threaten a society's political stability. In any case, crime is a difficult problem that does not respond to simple solutions. When crimes are committed, it is the role of the criminal justice system to respond in the name of society.

The actual crime rate does not always accurately reflect the public's perception of the crime rate. Many crimes go undetected and their harm is not generally perceived. Other crimes are sensationalized and their cases given such vast resources the public's perception of the amount and seriousness of crime is distorted. However, the public's fears are primarily focused on street crime. Other types of crime include corporate crime and organized crime.

Law enforcement, courts, and corrections tasks are divided differently across the local, state, and federal branches of government. Law enforcement functions at the state level are usually confined to specialized missions. At the federal level, law enforcement functions include a range of agencies that enforce federal laws and assist state and local governments. Police officers, prosecutors, judges, and corrections officials use discretion to decide which cases proceed further into the criminal justice system and which do not. Many of the crimes that do enter the system may be eventually excluded as well. For those cases that continue into the system, the criminal justice system has multiple goals, including deterrence, incapacitation, retribution, rehabilitation, and restoration. However, the criminal justice system is not the only means of social control. Other means of social control include the family, religion, schools, and the media. The criminal justice system is therefore the institution of last resort.

KEY TERMS

arraignment p. 25
bailiff p. 16
bill of indictment p. 24
Bureau of Alcohol, Tobacco, Firearms, and Explosives (ATFE) p. 20
chemical castration p. 30
clearance rates p. 22
county stockade p. 17
discretion p. 21
Drug Enforcement Administration (DEA) p. 18
electronic monitoring p. 26
Federal Bureau of Investigation (FBI) p. 15
felony p. 16
Immigration and Naturalization Service (INS) p. 18
misdemeanor p. 16
no-bill p. 24
nolo contendere p. 24
pillory p. 30
prejudicial error p. 27
presentence report p. 26
preventive detention p. 25
***prima facie* case** p. 25
Prohibition p. 13
sheriff p. 16
socialization p. 8
sociological imagination p. 7
true bill p. 24
U.S. Border Patrol p. 18
U.S. Customs Service p. 18
U.S. Marshals Service p. 18
U.S. Secret Service p. 18
war on drugs p. 13
warrant p. 16

REVIEW QUESTIONS

1. Why do we sometimes have a faulty idea of the nature of crime in the United States?
2. In addition to the criminal justice system, which institutions participate in exerting social control?
3. Can the criminal justice system be made more efficient?
4. In what way is the criminal justice process like a funnel?
5. What are the goals of the criminal justice system? Which of these goals is most important? What should be done when these goals are in conflict?
6. Why is the criminal justice system considered the system of last resort?

7. Explain the difference between white collar crime and corporate crime. Should the penalties for both types of crime be more harsh?
8. Why are sensationalized crime cases not representative of most crime cases?

SUGGESTED FURTHER READING

Arrigo, Bruce A., ed. *Social Justice/Criminal Justice: The Maturation of Critical Theory in Law, Crime, and Justice.* Belmont, CA: West/Wadsworth, 1999.

Barak, Gregg, Jeanne M. Flavin, and Paul S. Leighton. *Class, Race, Gender, and Crime: Social Realities of Justice in America.* Los Angeles: Roxbury, 2001.

Donziger, Steven R., ed. *The Real War On Crime: The Report of the National Criminal Justice Commission.* New York: HarperPerennial, 1996.

Meadows, Robert J. *Understanding Violence and Victimization*, 2nd ed. Upper Saddle River, NJ: Prentice Hall, 2001.

Reiman, Jeffery. *The Rich Get Richer and the Poor Get Prison,* 7th ed. Boston: Allyn and Bacon, 2004.

Walker, Samuel. *Sense and Nonsense About Crime: A Policy Guide,* 4th ed. Belmont, CA: West/Wadsworth, 2001.

ENDNOTES

1. Kenneth Pringle, "Inside the Mind of Jeffrey Dahmer," APBNews.com, August 10, 2000, http://www.apbnews.com/media/gfiles/dahmer/dahmer0814.html. At his 1992 trial, Jeffrey Dahmer was determined to be sane and sentenced to 16 consecutive life terms. Inmates beat him to death in a prison bathroom in November 1994. In 1996 a man offered to buy the tools he used to torture, kill, and dismember his victims for more than $400,000, but they were secretly buried.
2. The Troy State University Montgomery Rosa Parks Library and Museum, http://www.tsum.edu/museum/parksbio.htm.
3. Infoplease, "Rosenberg Case," http://www.infoplease.com/ce6/history/A0842422.html. Several screenwriters and actors lost their careers and went to prison after being investigated by the House Un-American Activities Committee in 1947 and 1951. In 1950 Senator Joseph McCarthy announced his famous list of Communist Party members and charged that the State Department had been infiltrated by Communists.
4. C. Wright Mills, *The Sociological Imagination* (New York: Oxford University Press, 1959).
5. Ray Surette, ed., *Media, Crime, and Criminal Justice: Images and Realities,* 2nd ed. (Belmont, CA: West/Wadsworth, 1998). See especially Chapter 3, "The Construction of Crime and Justice in the News Media," for an enlightening analysis of how news is socially constructed.
6. Randall G. Sheldon, *Controlling the Dangerous Classes: A Critical Introduction to the History of Criminal Justice* (Boston: Allyn and Bacon, 2001).
7. Jeffrey Reiman, *The Rich Get Richer and the Poor Get Prison: Ideology, Class and Criminal Justice,* 6th ed. (Boston: Allyn and Bacon, 2001).
8. Stuart L. Hills, *Demystifying Social Deviance* (New York: McGraw-Hill, 1980). See Chapter 2, "The Politics of Social Deviance."
9. Diana Scully and Joseph Marolla, "Riding the Bull at Gilley's: Convicted Rapists Describe the Rewards of Rape," *Social Problems,* February 1985: 251–263.
10. Neil Websdale and Alexander Alvarez, "Forensic Journalism as Patriarchal Ideology: The Newspaper Constructions of Homicide-Suicide," in *Popular Culture, Crime, and Justice,* eds. Frankie Bailey and Donna Hale (Belmont, CA: West/Wadsworth, 1998), 123–141. This is an interesting study of how a newspaper in Arizona in its reporting of 153 homicide-suicide cases stresses the sensational crime scene minutiae over the social structural context.
11. For a fascinating explanation of how videos of crime not only extend the story, but also distort it, see Peter K. Manning, "Media Loops," in *Popular Culture, Crime, and Justice,* eds. Frankie Bailey and Donna Hale (Belmont, CA: West/Wadsworth, 1998), 25–39.
12. See Reiman, *Rich Get Richer,* for a discussion on how we treat street crime more seriously than corporate crime.
13. Each year the government publishes the Uniform Crime Report, which includes the Crime Clock.
14. Ronald D. Hunter and Mark L. Dantzker, *Crime and Criminality: Causes and Consequences* (Upper Saddle River, NJ: Prentice Hall, 2002).
15. James Q. Wilson and George L. Kelling, "Broken Windows," in *Critical Issues in Policing: Contemporary Issues,* 2nd ed., eds. Roger G. Durham and Geoffrey P. Alpert, (Prospect Heights, IL: Waveland, 1993).
16. Reiman, *Rich Get Richer.*
17. Ibid.
18. Lewis R. Mizell, *Masters of Deception: The White Collar Crime Crisis and Ways to Protect Yourself* (New York: Wiley, 1996).

19. Jay S. Albanese, *Organized Crime in America,* 3rd ed. (Cincinnati: Anderson 1996).
20. Daniel L. Skoler, *Organizing the Non-System: Governmental Structuring of Criminal Justice Systems* (Lanham, MD: Lexington Books, 1977).
21. Abraham S. Blumberg, *Criminal Justice: Issues and Ironies,* 2nd ed. (New York: New Viewpoints, 1979).
22. Randy L. LaGrange, *Policing American Society* (Chicago: Nelson-Hall, 1993), 54.
23. Matthew J. Hickman and Brian A. Reaves, *Sheriffs' Offices, 2000* (Washington, DC: Bureau of Justice Statistics, 2003), 1. Online at http://www.ojp.usdoj.gov/bjs/pub/pdf/so00.pdf.
24. Michael Welsh, *Corrections: A Critical Approach* (New York: McGraw-Hill, 1996). Chapter 7 provides a very good analysis of jails and detention.
25. John Irwin, *The Jail: Managing the Underclass in American Society* (Berkeley: University of California Press, 1985).
26. Bureau of Justice Statistics, *Prisoners in 1998* (Washington, DC: U.S. Department of Justice, 1999).
27. Patrick Langan, *State Felony Courts and Felony Laws* 1987 (Washington, DC: Bureau of Justice Statistics).
28. James Austin and John Irvin, *It's About Time: America's Imprisonment Binge,* 3rd ed. (Belmont, CA: Wadsworth, 2001).
29. United States District Court for the Northern District of Iowa Central Division, Report and Recommendation, No. C96-3011-MWB, Decision, Judge Zoss, April 29, 1998; state habeas, http://www.iand.uscourts.gov/iand/decisions.nsf/274509d70785a9eb8625693e005be79c/c68c627c75bbc256862569690052534f.
30. "Disposing of Body Was Desperate Act, Husband Recalls," *Omaha World-Herald,* July 15, 1992.
31. "Evidence in Case Set Precedent, Experts Say," *Des Moines Register,* June 1, 1999.
32. "Ramsey Detective 'Made Mistakes,' Chief Testifies," TheDenverChannel.com/Associated Press, June 12, 2001, http://www.thedenverchannel.com/den/news/stories/news-81537020010612-060634.html.
33. Arthur Rosett and Donald R. Cressey, *Justice by Concert: Plea Bargains in the American Courthouse* (New York: JB Lippincott, 1976).
34. United States Sentencing Commission, Overview of the Federal Sentencing Guidelines, November 1998, http://www.ussc.gov.
35. Welch, *Corrections.*
36. Austin and Irwin, *It's About Time.*
37. Doris Layton Mackenzie and Alex Piquero, "The Impact of Shock Incarceration Programs on Prison Overcrowding," *Crime and Delinquency,* April 1994, pp. 222–249.
38. Richard McCleary, *Dangerous Men: The Sociology of Parole,* 2nd ed. (Albany, NY: Harrow and Heston, 1992).
39. Todd R. Clear and Edward E. Latessa, "Surveillance vs. Control: Probation Officers' Roles in Intensive Supervision," *Justice Quarterly,* 10(3)(1993): 441–462.
40. Hugo Adam Bedau, *Death Is Different* (Boston: Northeastern University Press, 1987).
41. Amensty International, Website Against the Death Penalty, Abolitionist and Retentionist Countries, http://www.web.amnesty.org/rmp/dplibrary.nsf/ff6dd728f6268d0480256aab003d14a8/daa2b602299dded0802568810050f6b1!OpenDocument.
42. Hugo Adam Bedau, William Lofquist, and Michael L. Radelet, "Miscarriages of Justice in Potentially Capital Cases," *Stanford Law Review,* November 1987: 21–179.
43. Murry A. Strauss, Richard J. Gelles, and Suzanne K. Steinmetz, *Behind Closed Doors: Violence in the American Family* (New York: Anchor/Doubleday, 1980).
44. Emile Durkheim, *The Elementary Forms of Religious Life* (New York: Free Press, 1965, first published in 1912).
45. Roger Finke and Roger Starke, *The Churching of America, 1776–1990: Winners and Losers in Our Religious Economy* (New Brunswick, NJ: Rutgers University Press, 1992).
46. Harry L. Gracey, "Learning the Student Role: Kindergarten as Academic Boot Camp," in *Down to Earth Sociology: Introductory Readings,* 9th ed., ed. James M. Henslin, (New York: Free Press, 1997), 376–388.
47. Surette, *Media, Crime, and Criminal Justice.*
48. Kenneth D. Tunnell, "Reflections on Crime, Criminals, and Control in News Magazines and Television Programs," in *Popular Culture, Crime, and Justice,* eds. Frankie Bailey and Donna Hale (Belmont, CA: West Wadsworth, 1998), 111–122.
49. Will Wright, *Six Guns and Society* (Berkeley: University of California Press, 1975).
50. National Research Council, *Understanding Violence* (Washington, DC: National Research Council, 1992).
51. Bruce Arrigo, *Social Justice/ Criminal Justice: The Maturization of Critical Theory in Law, Crime, and Deviance* (Belmont, CA: Wadsworth, 1998).

outline

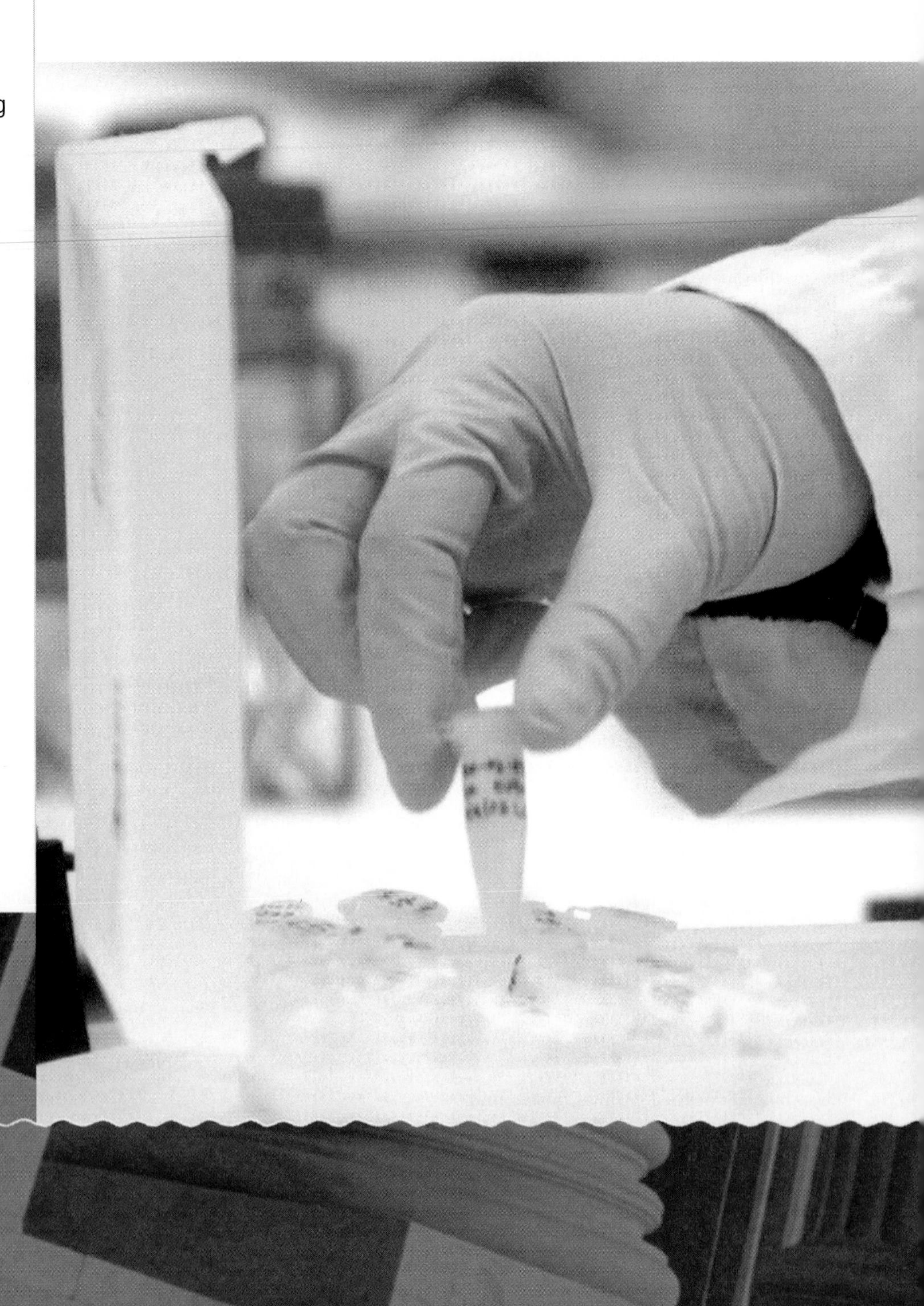

CHAPTER 2

The Nature and Measurement of Crime

objectives

After reading this chapter, the student should be able to:

1. Understand how crime is categorized and measured.
2. Discuss crimes against the person.
3. Discuss what should be taken into consideration when measuring property crime.
4. Discuss the relationship of victimless crimes with crimes against the public order.
5. Discuss some of the problems in measuring crime.
6. Discuss the dark figure of crime.
7. Discuss sources of error in the Uniform Crime Reports.
8. Calculate a crime rate.
9. Compare and contrast the UCR, the NIBRS, victimization surveys, and self-report studies.
10. Compare and contrast the effect of crime-measuring efforts on the general public with how the general public affects crime-measuring efforts.

TO UNDERSTAND CRIME'S EFFECT ON INDIVIDUALS AND society, we need to understand how crime is conceptualized and measured. There is a big difference between a homicide and some children throwing rocks though the windows of an abandoned house. Similarly, there is a big difference between the massive fraud of companies such as Enron and the motorist whose license is suspended after three drunken-driving convictions. Crime can affect individuals or an entire society, and crime can be a minor irritant or a catastrophic blow from which one may never recover. In short, not all crimes are the same.[1] The total numbers of crime, or even the crime rate, fails to capture the variability and deleterious effects of crime. Although crime measures are useful when attempting to compare the relative safety of cities, states, or regions, the way crime is measured can provide misleading and inaccurate pictures of how crime is distributed and how it affects citizens.[2]

This chapter will review the various ways crime has been categorized and measured. By considering the problems of differentiating among different types and levels of crime, and appreciating how crime statistics are gathered and reported, we will see how social, economic, and political factors shape the way we comprehend and ultimately respond to crime.

Categories of Crime and Criminals

We have many ways of categorizing behaviors that offend our sensibilities. We have rules, regulations, norms, folkways, and laws that dictate what is acceptable and what will be sanctioned. Laws attempt to define crime in a comprehensible manner, the most basic distinction being between misdemeanors and felonies. This distinction is a rather crude way to distinguish the seriousness of actions, and it is not made until a law enforcement officer decides what law was violated by the action. Also, the distinction between a misdemeanor and a felony may be blurred when the prosecutor decides what the formal charge will be, and the process becomes even more complicated when, as a result of plea negotiations, the judge passes sentence.[3] Therefore, a man who gets into a fistfight may believe he is acting in self-defense, but may find that because he severely hurt his opponent, a police officer charges him with misdemeanor assault. The prosecutor may decide to kick the charge up to a felony because of the use of a baseball bat, and after the plea negotiation, the charge may once again become a misdemeanor. The relationship between a behavior and the legal designations that are ultimately attached to it is sometimes difficult to justify. Therefore, the legal categorizations of crimes are not the best indicators of the nature of the crime problem.

Another way to understand crime is to consider the victimization. Focusing on the victim or object of harm instead of the charge can provide a better measure of the level of crime. The following three-group typology elucidates the similarities and differences among the general classes of crime:

1. **Crimes against the person.** These crimes include the violent personal crimes of homicide, sexual assault, robbery, and assault.
2. **Crimes against property.** These crimes include burglary, arson, embezzlement, larceny/theft, and auto theft.
3. **Crimes against the public order.** These crimes include drug use, disturbing the peace, drunkenness, and prostitution.

Considering crime in this manner gives a better idea of the harm caused by unlawful actions than does the simple misdemeanor/felony dichotomy. Although each of these categories spans the range of seriousness from minor irritation to extremely disruptive, they group crimes in terms of who or what is harmed. Exploring this typology in greater detail is useful because it reflects the type of harm done to victims. Each of these categories includes a continuum of crimes that differ in degree and may be either stringently punished or relatively neglected by the criminal justice system.

Crimes against the Person

The most severe penalties, including capital punishment, are reserved for violators of crimes against the person. Personal violent crimes such as murder and rape are the most devastating and the most feared of all unlawful actions and garner the majority of press coverage.[4] These serious crimes occur much less frequently than do crimes against property, but they are of the most concern to law enforcement officials and victims. When considering homicide and assault cases, we can discern certain motivations that apparently compel offenders to engage in this serious unlawful behavior.

INTERPERSONAL DISPUTES. Violence is all too often not the means of last resort to settle disputes. Some people use violence as a negotiating tool, and sometimes, when negotiations break down, they employ lethal violence. Sources of dispute can include disagreements over money, charges of infidelity, challenges to masculinity, or insults to moral character. Often, the difference between offender and victim is who is fastest on the draw; that is, there is sometimes no clear relationship between who is responsible for starting the dispute and who emerges the winner. Criminologists use the term **victim precipitation** to refer to instances when the victim plays an active role in initiating the conflict or escalating it to the point of violence.[5] In some segments of society, a subculture of violence emerges in which assault or murder is expected as a way of resolving conflict.[6]

victim precipitation
A situation in which a crime victim plays an active role in initiating a crime or escalating it.

INSTRUMENTAL VIOLENCE. Violence is sometimes used as a means to another criminal end. Drug dealers may kill competitors, robbers may shoot convenience store clerks, and carjackers may assault drivers to steal automobiles. The violence in these cases is used as a tool to accomplish another crime. Killing a witness or a prison guard during an escape is an unfortunate by-product of an offender's greater goal and may have been avoided under different circumstances. Other forms of instrumental violence, however, are premeditated. Intimidating witnesses or "teaching a lesson" to an informant employs violence as an extreme form of communication when "a message" needs to be sent.[7] Often, the motivation or message of instrumental violence is difficult to discern, such as when a robber successfully commits the crime and then shoots the clerk on the way out of the bank.

GROUP VIOLENCE. Another source of motivation to commit acts of violence can be found in the dynamics of certain groups. Assaults or homicides often occur in situations in which groups of young people come into conflict. Violence is often used in instrumental ways when youth gangs clash over territory or symbolic concerns such as colors of clothing or other displays of gang affiliation. Youths may feel a greater sense of bravado when surrounded by friends, and they may feel a greater need to demonstrate their courage and rebellion. Group dynamics may encourage and facilitate, and in some cases even demand, members' use of violence to redress some real or imagined insult. When alcohol or drugs enter the equation, gang violence is even more likely.[8]

Gang violence is a perplexing problem that continues to plague the United States. Often, the gangs are territorially based, and trespassing on another gang's territory can bring a swift and even deadly response.
Photo by Douglas Burrows, courtesy of Getty Images, Inc.-Liaison.

serial murder
Homicides of a sequence of victims committed by an offender in three or more separate events occurring over a period of time.

CHRONIC VIOLENT OFFENDERS. Some offenders commit numerous acts of violence for a variety of reasons. Sometimes the violence is instrumental as a part of a larger pattern of crime, and sometimes it is random and indiscriminate. Often, this type of offender is the hardest to understand because there is no apparent motivation. Although **serial murderers** are extremely rare, they usually have some underlying personal logic regarding the targets they select. Some might kill young women with a certain hair color, such as the case of Ted Bundy. Others might kill exclusively young men, as was the case with John Wayne Gacy. Even though the motivation may be the result some deep-seated psychological problem, the serial murderer is capable of committing many crimes and eluding detection and arrest. If the serial murderer moves from state to state, linking the cases to discern any type of pattern is often difficult.[9]

terrorism
The use or threat of violence against a state or other political entity in order to coerce.

POLITICAL VIOLENCE. Some crimes are committed to send a message. This is the case with political violence, of which the most well-known type is terrorism. **Terrorism** can be domestic, as in the case of the bombing of the Murrah Federal Building in Oklahoma City, or it can be of the international variety, as in the suicide plane hijackings of September 11, 2001. The subject of terrorism will be covered in greater detail in Chapter 16, but it is important to stress here that the political nature of this type of violence sets it apart from other types of crime. Terrorism is often committed by intelligent, sincere people who believe violence is necessary to have their voices heard.[10]

rape
Sexual activity, usually sexual intercourse, that is forced on another person without his or her consent, usually under threat of harm. Sexual activity conducted with a person who is younger than a specified age or incapable of valid consent because of mental illness, mental handicap, intoxication, unconsciousness, or deception is called statutory rape.

sexual assault
Sexual contact that is committed without the other party's consent or with a party who is not capable of giving consent (such as a child or mentally handicapped individual).

RAPE AND SEXUAL ASSAULT. Because the motivations for committing **rape** and other crimes of **sexual assault** are often very different from the motivations for committing other types of personal violent crimes, and because the impact on the victims can be so devastating, these crimes will be considered as unique forms of violence. Although rape has been a consistent occurrence throughout recorded history, the past 40 years have seen a raised awareness of both the definition of what types of behavior constitute sexual assault and greater protections in the law for victims. Women and children, once considered as not having individual rights when the perpetrator was a husband or father, are now protected by the criminal justice system.[11] Child molestation, date and acquaintance rape, and sexual harassment are now recognized as serious types of criminal

The crimes of serial killer Ted Bundy ranged from Washington to Florida. He was eventually executed by the state of Florida. He unsuccessfully acted as his own attorney in his trial.

Courtesy of Corbis/Bettmann.

In April 1995, a truck bomb exploded in front of the Alfred P. Murrah Federal Building in Oklahoma City, Oklahoma, killing 168 people in an act of domestic terrorism. Timothy McVeigh was executed for this crime in June 2001.

Courtesy of CORBIS-NY.

behavior and are dealt with in a more humane and serious manner by law enforcement and the courts.[12]

ROBBERY. **Robbery** can be defined as "the taking or attempting to take anything of value from the care, custody, or control of a person or persons by force or threat of force or violence and/or putting the victim in fear."[13] Robberies vary by location, whether on the street (such as a mugging) or within an institution (such as a bank or a convenience store). Sometimes robbery, such as a purse-snatching or pocket-picking, is classified as a felony when a certain level of force or fear is exerted on the victim. Finally, even though carjackings involve the theft of a motor vehicle, they are considered robberies because of the force involved. (See Figure 2.1 for a graph of selected violent crime victimization rates in 2001 and 2002.)

robbery
The removal of property from a person by violence or by threat of violence.

Crimes against Property

Not all societies have the same attitude about property as modern Western-style democracies.[14] The accumulation of wealth and possessions is an important cornerstone of individual and group well-being in the United States, and laws have been constructed to protect the rights of those who own and control property. These laws range from prohibitions against theft to the copyright procedures that protect intellectual and creative endeavors. The types of property crime that are best measured by the criminal justice system are those in which the offender is a stranger to the victim. Although many laws address differences in opinion while transacting business, these conflicts are usually covered by tort law. Burglary, larceny/theft, and motor vehicle theft are crimes dealt with by the criminal law. Following are several points of interest when considering the measurement of property crime.

larceny
A form of theft in which an offender takes possessions that do not belong to him or her with the intent of keeping them. Some jurisdictions specify "grand larceny" or "petty larceny" based on the value of the stolen items.

burglary
The act of breaking into and entering a building or other structure or vehicle to commit a crime. Extreme force is not required, and burglary is not restricted to theft. Any crime committed, such as assault, is considered to be burglary.

- **Burglary is different from larceny/theft.** When we classify the taking of another person's property, several distinctions determine whether the crime is **larceny/theft** or **burglary**. Burglary involves the unlawful entry of a structure to commit a felony or theft. Larceny/theft involves the unlawful taking of another person's property. Larceny/theft includes theft from a person by stealth such as pocket-picking, purse-snatching (when only minimal force is used), shoplifting, thefts of articles from motor vehicles, and thefts from coin-operated machines.

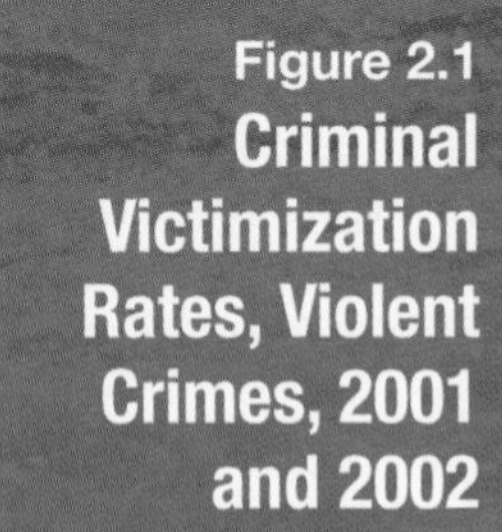

Figure 2.1 **Criminal Victimization Rates, Violent Crimes, 2001 and 2002**

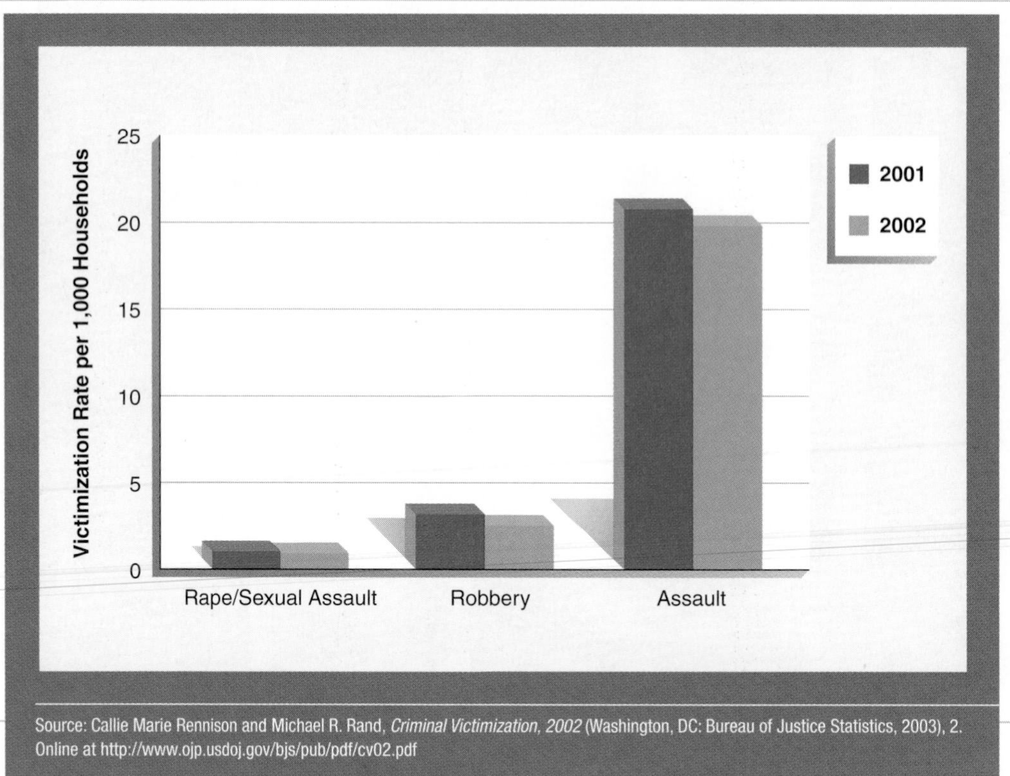

Source: Callie Marie Rennison and Michael R. Rand, *Criminal Victimization, 2002* (Washington, DC: Bureau of Justice Statistics, 2003), 2. Online at http://www.ojp.usdoj.gov/bjs/pub/pdf/cv02.pdf

The difference between robbery and burglary involves a face-to-face confrontation between the suspect and the victim. Here an offender robs a bank.

Photo by LiHua Lan/*Syracuse Newspaper*, courtesy of The Image Works.

- **Motor vehicle theft involves only automobiles and trucks.** The theft of motorboats, construction equipment, airplanes, and farming equipment is classified as larceny rather than motor vehicle theft.
- **Arson involves fires that are purposely set.** It does not matter whether the fire was started with the intent to defraud, only that it was willfully or maliciously set. Fires of suspicious or unknown origin are not treated as **arson.**[15]

arson
The act of intentionally burning a building. Any death that results from arson is murder, regardless of the arsonist's intention.

See Figure 2.2 for a graph of selected property crime victimization rates in 2001 and 2002.

Burglary involves the unlawful entry of another person's property. Often, this includes breaking a window or door or picking a lock. Typically, burglars like to strike when no one is home.
Courtesy of CORBIS-NY.

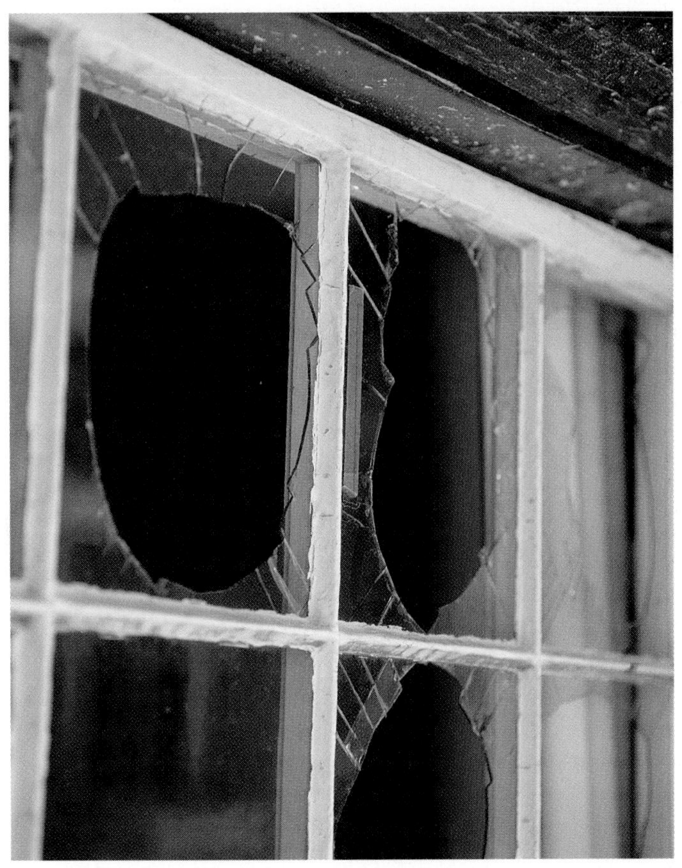

Vandalism involves the destruction or defacement of property. Youths will often break the windows of abandoned buildings for entertainment. Vandalism can cost millions of dollars each year.
Courtesy of CORBIS-NY.

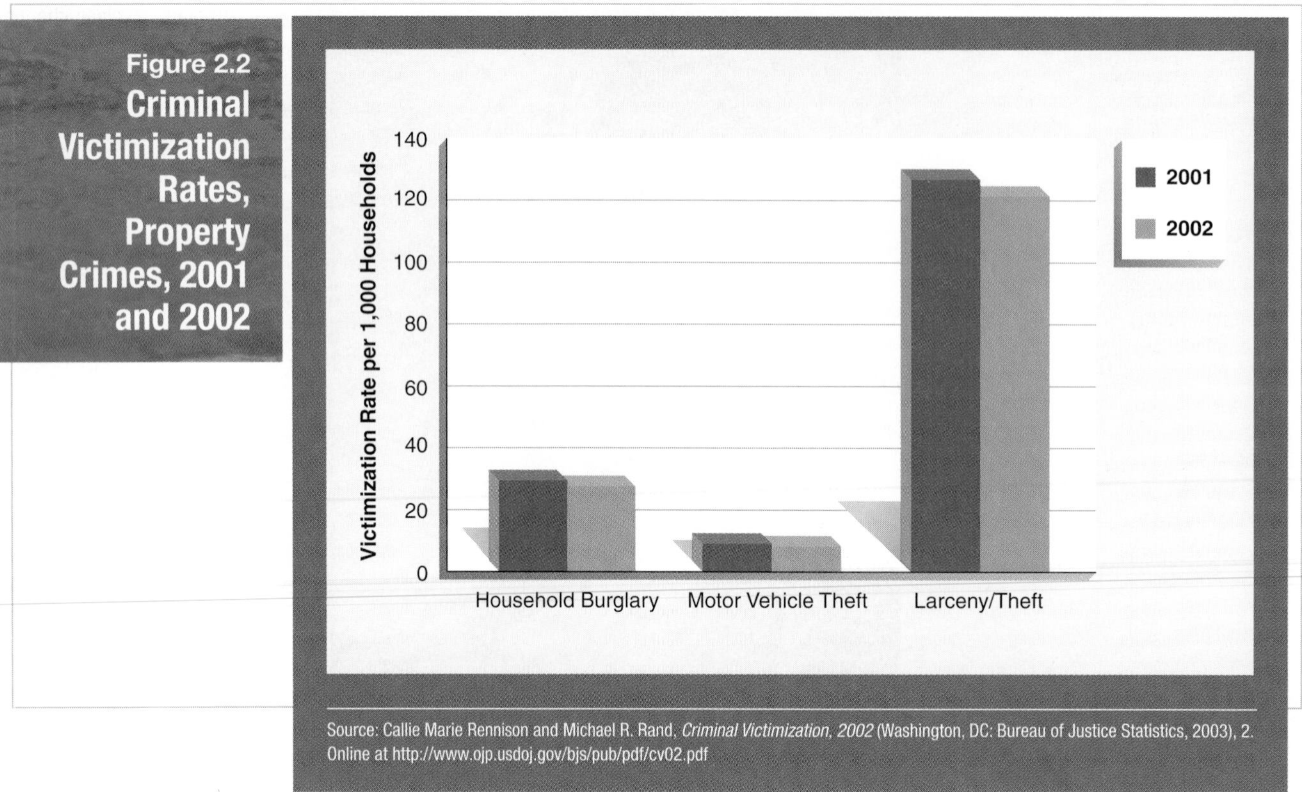

Figure 2.2 Criminal Victimization Rates, Property Crimes, 2001 and 2002

Source: Callie Marie Rennison and Michael R. Rand, *Criminal Victimization, 2002* (Washington, DC: Bureau of Justice Statistics, 2003), 2. Online at http://www.ojp.usdoj.gov/bjs/pub/pdf/cv02.pdf

Crimes against the Public Order

Some crimes involve no discernable victim. Victimless crimes involve consensual interactions or behaviors that offend the sense of propriety of the powerful groups of society who have succeeded in having their concerns and sensibilities elevated to the level of the criminal law. Although broad consensus may exist on some of these behaviors, there is also a good deal of controversy about crimes that are a matter of values.[16] (Chapter 15 deals in greater detail with drug use, gambling, and sex work.) Behaviors that fit into the category of crimes against the public order include vagrancy, disorderly conduct, and liquor law violations. These types of crimes are often considered to be nuisance-type crimes, reflecting quality-of-life concerns for many people, yet they are vigorously enforced in some places and almost completely ignored in others. For instance, when vagrants, street people, and the homeless are considered to be interfering with the tourism trade, shopkeepers, hotel owners, and restaurant managers may ask the police to clear the streets of the "riff-raff and rabble."[17] It is worth noting that the police have broad discretion in deciding how to enforce these public-order crimes. They may overlook the possession of small amounts of marijuana in one instance and decide to make an arrest in another if the offender does not show respect.[18]

Measurement of Crime

Measuring crime is a tricky business. Besides definitional problems as to how to classify certain behaviors, there may also be perceptual problems about just when a behavior rises to the level of a crime. To kids who are fistfighting, their blows might mean they are "just horsing around," but to the parent of the child with the bloody nose, it looks like an assault. To be included in the measurement of crime, the incident must be reported to authorities or researchers who are concerned with determining the level and frequency of unlawful actions.

A riot is classified as a crime against the public order. Often, riots occur after a sports team wins (or loses) a championship game. Destruction of property, drunkenness, and personal injury are often features of riots.

Courtesy of CORBIS-NY.

Primarily, this means that the crime must be reported to the police, who will enter it into the Uniform Crime Reports system and, in certain circumstances, to the National Incident-Based Reporting System. This section will review other ways of measuring crime: victimization surveys and self-report studies.

One of the problems of attempting to measure crime is that not all crimes are reported. If a crime is not reported to the police, it will not get counted in the indices that comprise the official measures of crime rates. The crimes that actually occur but that do not get reported are known to criminologists as the "**dark figure of crime**" (See Figure 2.3). According to noted criminologists Paul and Patricia Brantingham, a victim might not want to report a crime to the police for several reasons.

dark figure of crime
A metaphor that describes crime that goes unreported to police and criminal justice officials and is never quantified.

- A crime may be so subtle that it is never known to have happened. Suppose that while the owner was out, a person used a passkey to break into an apartment with the intent to steal the television, then changed his mind and left, disturbing nothing. This action constitutes a breaking and entering, but no one save the offender would ever know it happened.
- A crime may not be perceived as such. Suppose, in the course of a championship playoff game, a defenseman for the Philadelphia Flyers were to slash a star center of the Montreal Canadiens with his hockey stick, causing a cut requiring six stitches to close. Such incidents do occur in the heat of competition and are defined as major penalties within the context of the game. The incident described, of course, also constitutes a crime that might be classified as an aggravated assault under the U.S. Uniform Crime Reports, or as a wounding in the Canadian Crime Statistics. However, the event is unlikely to be perceived as a crime by either player, by either team, by the referees, or by the fans, and it is unlikely to be reported to the police. In the sport of boxing, a fighter who is abiding by the sport's rules may cause the death of the other fighter and face no sanctions from the criminal justice system, the referee, or the sport's ruling body.
- A crime might not be reported because the offender is a family member, a friend, or an acquaintance.
- A crime might not be reported because the victim believes that it was trivial, or that the potential penalty is too grave for the harm done.

FOCUS ON ETHICS

To Report or Not to Report

You are a married man, and you have made your share of mistakes in life, but now you have placed yourself in a dilemma that threatens to ruin your reputation, your career, and your marriage. If you do nothing, all will be saved in your life, but it will be at the expense of public safety and may result in a life-or-death situation.

While your wife went to Des Moines to take care of her ailing grandmother, you strayed off the path of monogamy, fidelity, and loyalty. You met a young girl who was walking her dog in the park, and after some shameless flirting, you accepted her invitation to meet her at a downtown bar that night. Because this bar was a place you would never have gone to on your own, you were unconcerned that your friends might see you out with another woman. The time at the bar was a blur of drinking, flirting, and suggestive dancing. At 2:00 A.M. you drove her back to her apartment, and after having a nightcap, agreed to go to her upstairs bedroom. After much soul-searching, you decided that you could not violate your marriage vows. Unfortunately, the girl was mad and demanded the $200 that she said you agreed to pay her at the bar. You were shocked by her accusation. When you tried to leave, her boyfriend jumped out of the closet with a baseball bat and beat you senseless. After waking up in the hospital, you claimed that you were mugged in the park and did not get a good look at your assailant. Your wife flew home to take care of you and as you began to heal, you renewed your determination to never again do anything that would hurt your wife.

As the months pass, your unfortunate experience has faded into ancient history, and you believe that no one will ever discover your dalliance. One day, however, as you are watching the local news, you see an exposé about how a number of men have been beaten with a baseball bat and dumped in the park. One of these men was beaten so badly that he had permanent brain damage. The police chief tells the newscaster that it will be only a matter of time before someone is killed by the man with the bat.

You remember the exact location of the apartment and the name of the girl, and you can describe her boyfriend. You know you should tell the police what you know but realize that if you pursue this course, your unfaithful behavior will be revealed. Because you are the vice president of your father-in-law's construction company, you are afraid that you will lose your wife and your job. You are experiencing tremendous stress worrying that someone will be killed by this couple and that it is your moral responsibility to do something about it.

WHAT DO YOU DO?

1. Tell your wife the truth and hope she does not demand a divorce.
2. Go to the police and tell them what you know and beg them not to drag you into the case.
3. Write an anonymous letter to the police telling them what you know but protecting your identity.
4. Keep your mouth shut and let others worry about themselves.

- A crime might not be reported because the victim fears reprisal.
- A crime might not be reported because the victim feels antipathy toward the police. Sometimes the victim is a criminal as well, or is embarrassed by the circumstances under which the crime occurred.[19]

Given these reasons for not reporting crime, does it make any sense to try to measure crime and then base criminal justice system policy on these flawed numbers? The answer is yes, but with caution. Although the dark figure of crime will always be unknown, an idea of the extent of crime can be surmised with the development of precise definitions and uniform reporting standards. Because crime rates are calculated every year and show a pattern of stability, criminal justice experts can assume that unreported crime varies at

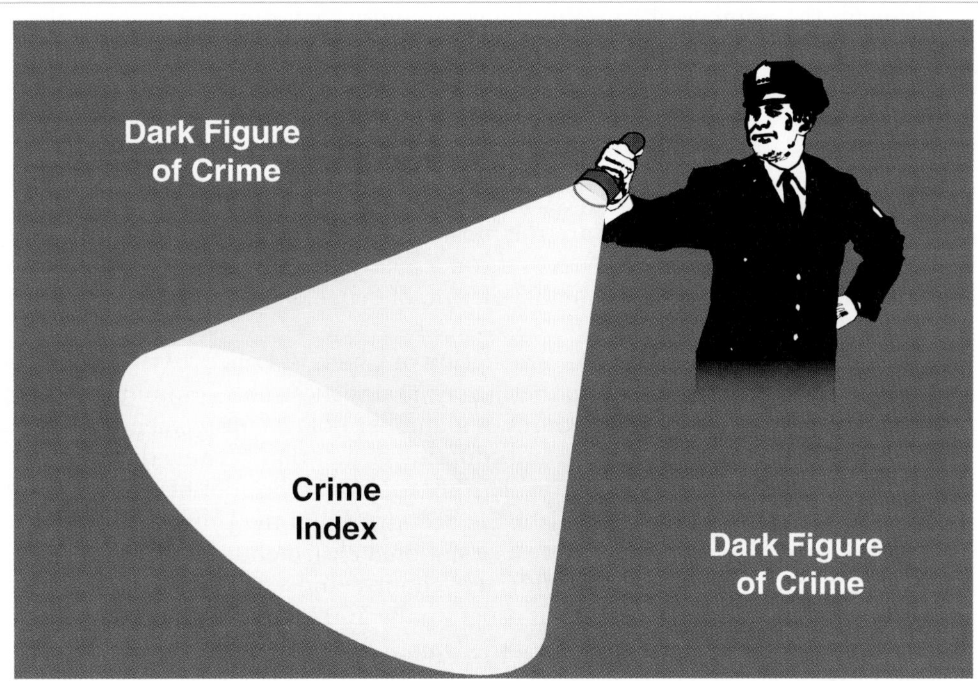

Figure 2.3
Dark Figure of Crime

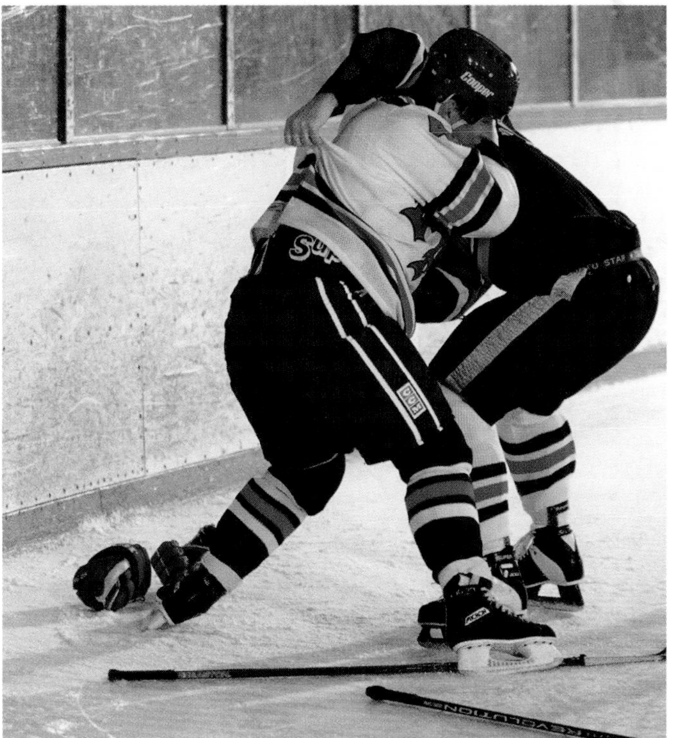

Fights during hockey games are considered part of the game and are punished by time in the penalty box. Sometimes, the violence becomes so extreme that the criminal justice system is used to punish those who go too far.
Courtesy of CORBIS-NY.

about the same rates.[20] That is, an unknown but consistent ratio exists between reported and unreported crime. However, this assumption can be misleading when a change in reporting behavior is interpreted as a change in the level of crime. For example, suppose a community establishes a new rape crisis center. As part of their duties, the center's staff members begin an educational prevention and awareness project in which they visit schools and community groups and encourage women to report sexual assaults. The staff members also support victims in the ordeal of reporting the crimes to the police.

Although the number of rapes in the community may remain constant, the rape crisis center has stimulated an increase in victim reporting that has resulted in more arrests, prosecutions, and imprisonments. Rape appears to be on the rise in the community, when in reality, more of the dark figure of crime is becoming known to the police, and the crime rate has become more accurate.

Uniform Crime Reports (UCR)

Uniform Crime Reports (UCR)
An annual publication by the Federal Bureau of Investigation that uses data from all participating law enforcement agencies in the United States to summarize the incidence and rate of reported crime.

The **Uniform Crime Reports** are the most extensive and useful measure of crime available. Despite the numerous issues and concerns with how these records are compiled and used, they remain the best available picture of crime, even though that picture tends to be out of focus at times.[21]

In the 1920s the International Association of Chiefs of Police (IACP) established a committee to develop a system for gathering crime statistics. This committee studied criminal codes and record-keeping procedures of a number of law enforcement agencies and came up with a model for categorizing and counting crimes that became the foundation for the Uniform Crime Reporting program. The FBI took over the administration of the program in 1930 when Congress enacted Title 28, Section 534 of the United States Code authorizing the Justice Department to serve as a national clearinghouse for the massive data collection effort. Today, over 17,000 city, county, and state law enforcement agencies voluntarily report crime data to this program. By 2002 the program collected data on over 93 percent of the total population of the United States. The UCR is used by scholars, legislators, planners, and the media for research and decision making, and to keep Americans informed about the level and seriousness of crime. For examples, see Figures 2.4 and 2.5.

Although the UCR provides a useful picture of crime in the United States, some sources of error must be considered.[22] The sources of error are of two types: unintentional and intentional.

- **Unintentional sources of error.** The UCR reporting system represents a massive collection effort. Literally tens of thousands of law enforcement officers and recording clerks enter data into the system, and each interpretation by each

Figure 2.4
Crime Index

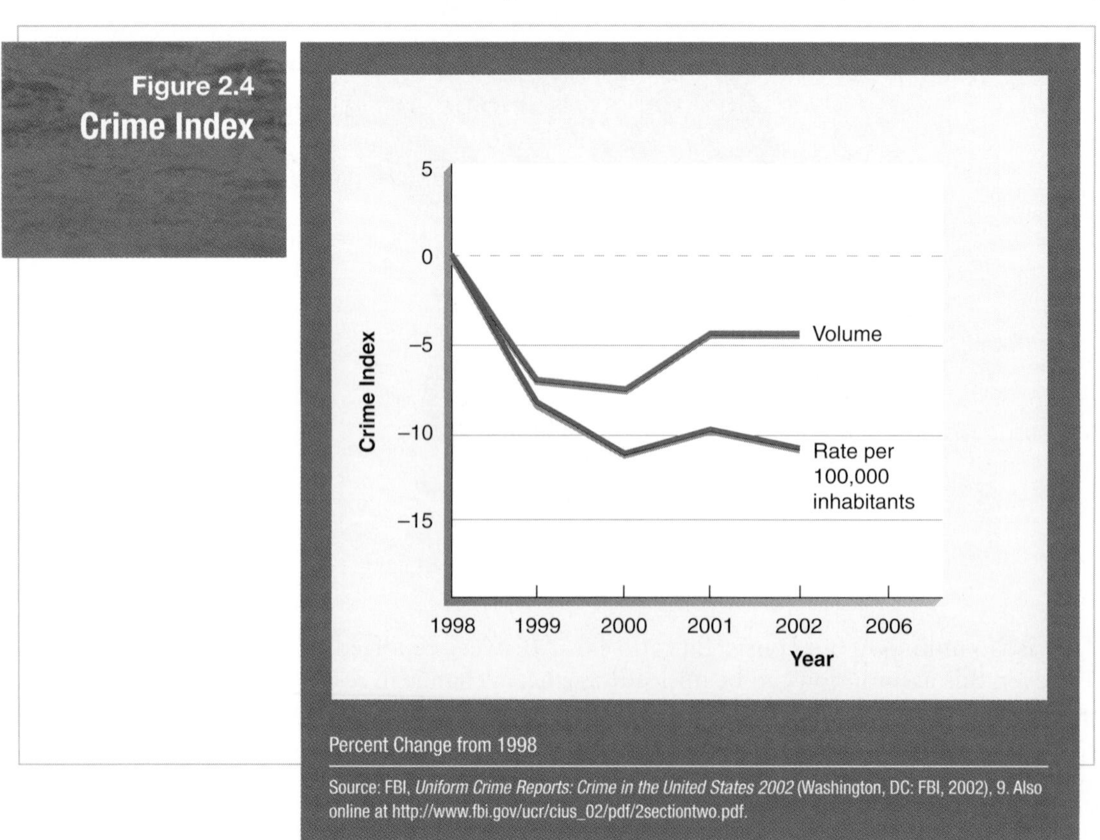

Percent Change from 1998

Source: FBI, *Uniform Crime Reports: Crime in the United States 2002* (Washington, DC: FBI, 2002), 9. Also online at http://www.fbi.gov/ucr/cius_02/pdf/2sectiontwo.pdf.

Figure 2.5
Crime Index Offenses

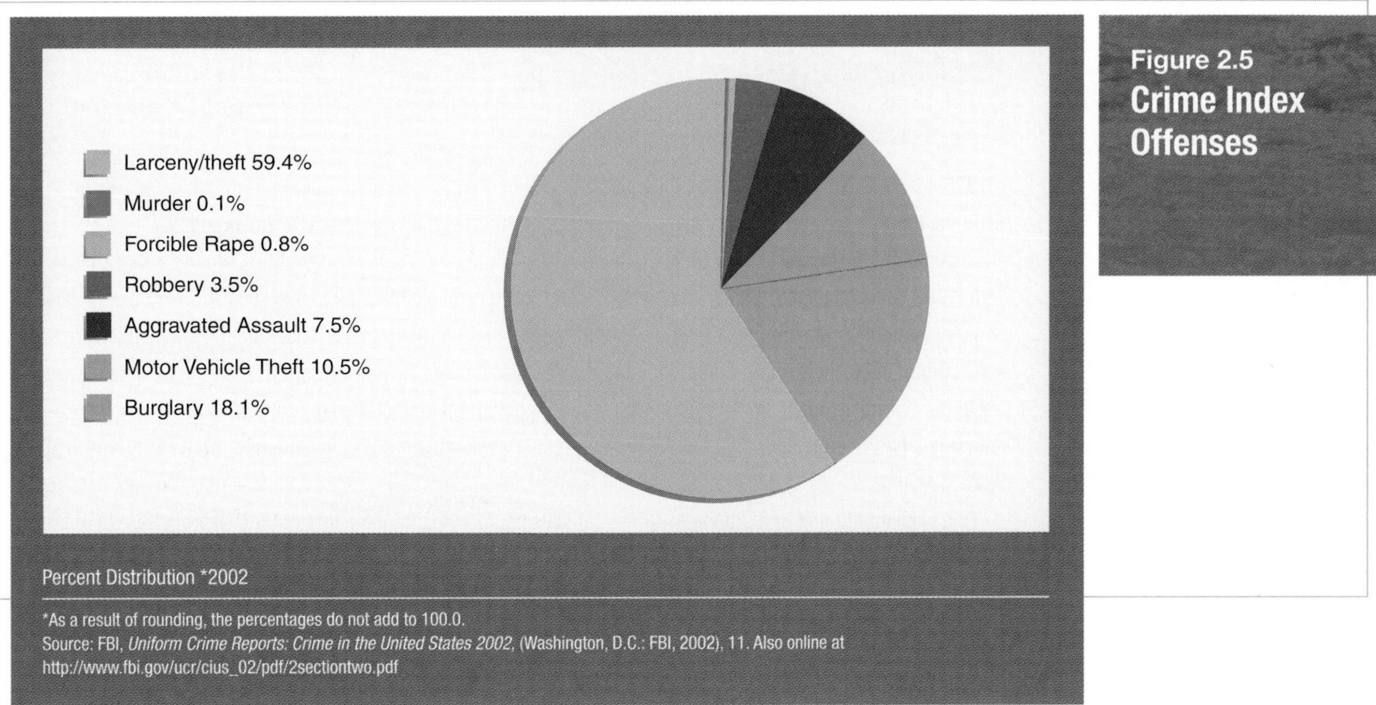

*As a result of rounding, the percentages do not add to 100.0.
Source: FBI, *Uniform Crime Reports: Crime in the United States 2002,* (Washington, D.C.: FBI, 2002), 11. Also online at http://www.fbi.gov/ucr/cius_02/pdf/2sectiontwo.pdf

individual is an opportunity for errors to be made in good faith. For instance, homicide would seem to be the category of crime in which little ambiguity exists. Someone is dead, and this fact means the crime will be reported and coded as such. Yet, in some cases of assault the victim dies in the hospital weeks after the case has been entered into the system. Some jurisdictions are better than others at the follow-up reporting of the subsequent death and the new homicide charge. Additionally, police officers may view crimes differently depending on their own philosophies about gender roles. Variations exist within and across jurisdictions in the categorization of rape if the parties involved are spouses or intimate partners.

- **Intentional sources of error.** The UCR is an important social indicator that reflects the quality of life in a jurisdiction. Police chiefs, sheriffs, mayors, and other public officials are judged by the efficacy of their policies, and the UCR presents objective criteria on which to base pay raises, promotions, and firings. Because careers are based on these numbers, and the opportunity exists to influence these numbers, it is not surprising that sometimes "the books get cooked."[23] This can happen in two directions. For example, a sheriff may want to modernize the fleet of squad cars and so instructs the deputies to change their crime reporting behavior by counting every trivial infraction, inflating the level of crime and bringing in more money. By contrast, a police chief who is worried about reappointment might instruct officers to overlook crime so that the reported crime rate seems to indicate that the chief's policies have been effective in reducing crime.

These examples should not be interpreted to suggest that law enforcement officials are corrupt or that their staffs are incompetent when assigned to participate in the UCR program. Rather, these examples are provided to demonstrate that many possible sources of error exist in the reporting of crime and that this error is unknowable.

crime rate The number of Crime Index offenses divided by the population of an area, usually given as a rate of crimes per 100,000 people.

CRIME RATE. What is meant by the term **crime rate**? The UCR shows the actual number of crimes in each jurisdiction, but jurisdictions with more people will always have more crime. Consequently, to compare the crime level across jurisdictions, we must calculate the crime rate (see Figure 2.6). To compare jurisdictions, the UCR lists eight crimes as "Part I Offenses." These crimes are murder and non-negligent manslaughter, forcible

! NEWS FLASH

Lies, Damn Lies, and Statistics

In 1996, just in time for the Summer Olympics, the city of Atlanta, Georgia, dropped from being the second to being the third most violent city thanks to statistics that reported a sharp decline in violent crime.

Good policing? Or something else?

In 1997 Louis Arcangeli, who was then the deputy police chief, pointed out to then-Police Chief Beverly Harvard that something was odd about the number of "unfounded" crimes (crimes discarded for some serious reason). Before 1996 there were fewer than 300 unfounded crimes a month. During 1996 that number rose precipitously, until it was up to over 600 by May 1996. Arcangeli's memos to Harvard also stated that some violent crimes had been misclassified as nonviolent. In all, these numbers greatly softened the picture of violent crime in Atlanta.

This was not the first time Atlanta's crime statistics had drawn attention. In 1994 the Georgia Bureau of Investigation looked into allegations that the police had treated unsolvable cases as though they had never happened to lower the previous year's crime rate. In investigating the 1996 incident, the GBI discovered 498 robberies and 56 rapes that had never made it to the reported statistics. According to a report in *Creative Loafing,* statistics showed a 2 percent increase in rapes that was somehow reported as an 11 percent decline. Statistically, robberies increased 1 percent, but these were reported as dropping 9 percent.

Police officials claimed sloppy reporting and stated that the numbers the GBI came up with were statistically insignificant. A 2004 audit commissioned by the Atlanta Police Foundation and conducted by a New York consulting firm confirmed that not only did Atlanta underreport crimes for several years in an effort to acquire the Olympics, but also the practice continued until 2002, when Atlanta received a new police chief and a new mayor. The audit found that for 2002 alone, more than 22,000 police reports were missing, and more than 4,000 offenses that could have been counted as violent offenses were not.

In the end, it is important to understand that, for many reasons, crime statistics do not paint an exact picture of crime and are not expected to do so. Even the best-reported statistics will not match reality. Crime is defined by society and, therefore, is subjective to some degree. This means that statistics collected about crime can be just as subjective, if not downright slippery.

Although it is often said that numbers never lie, plenty of evidence exists that they can be made to bend the truth. The same is true for crime statistics, which can be skewed by sloppy or false reporting. Bad reporting is understandable, but false reporting can be a crime on its own. The problem is that it is sometimes difficult to tell the difference.

Sources: John Sugg, "Atlanta's Chief Angel," *Creative Loafing,* January 29, 2003, http://atlanta.creativeloafing.com/2003-01-29/cover.html. Mark Niesse, "Audit: Atlanta Hedged Crimes in '96 Bid," *The Washington Post*/Associated Press, February 20, 2004, http://www.washingtonpost.com/wp-dyn/articles/A58356-2004Feb20.html. "Memos Allege that Atlanta Crime Statistics Manipulated," Online Athens/AP, May 22, 1998, http://www.onlineathens.com/1998/052298/0522.a2crime.html

rape, robbery, aggravated assault, burglary, larceny/theft, motor vehicle theft, and arson. These crimes were selected because they are serious offenses, are widely identified by victims and witnesses as criminal incidents, and are the ones most likely to be reported to the police. A number of other crimes, called "Part II Offenses," are less serious, and reporting of these is not mandatory for participation in the UCR program (see Figure 2.7).

When considering the categories the UCR uses to conceptualize types of crime, we must remember that these categories do not reflect the actual criminal statutes in each jurisdiction. For instance, a misdemeanor drug possession in Keokuk, Iowa, may qualify as a felony possession in the UCR. The reporting system collects data from thousands of

$$\frac{\text{number of crimes}}{\text{(population/number of people)}}$$

or

$$\frac{\text{number of crimes}}{\text{population}} * \text{number of people}$$

For example, in the U.S. in 2002 . . .

$$\frac{\text{11,877,218 reported crimes}}{\text{288,368,698 total U.S. population}} * 100{,}000 = \text{4118.8 crimes per 100,000 people}$$

and

$$\frac{\text{420,637 reported robberies}}{\text{288,368,698 total U.S. population}} * 100{,}000 = \text{145.9 robberies per 100,000 people}$$

Source: Federal Bureau of Investigation, *Uniform Crime Reports, 2002*, http://www.fbi.gov/ucr/02cius.htm.

Figure 2.6
How to Calculate Crime Rates

Part I Offenses

Violent crimes

Murder and non-negligent manslaughter
Forcible rape
Robbery
Aggravated assault

Property crimes

Burglary
Larceny/theft
Motor vehicle theft
Arson (included in the modified crime index, added in 1979)

Part II Offenses

Curfew and loitering laws (juveniles only)
Disorderly conduct
Driving under the influence
Drug abuse violations
Drunkenness
Embezzlement
Forgery and counterfeiting
Fraud
Gambling
Liquor law offenses
Offenses against the family and children
Prostitution and commercialized vice
Runaways (juveniles only)
Sex offenses (except rape and prostitution)
Simple assaults
Stolen property offenses
Vagrancy
Vandalism
Weapons offenses
All other offenses (except traffic)

Figure 2.7
Uniform Crime Report Part I and Part II Offenses

jurisdictions, and the categories of crime are designed to quantify the criminal behavior and social deviance in each jurisdiction, not to reflect which actual criminal laws have been violated. Because the UCR represents a limited agenda of counting crimes and comparing crime rates, it distorts the crime picture in the way it defines wrongdoing. This problem is most apparent when several crimes are committed in one incident.

Suppose someone breaks into your home, beats you up, steals your television set, kicks your dog, and smokes a marijuana cigarette while spray painting obscene graffiti on your living room walls. You report the crime to the police, and after making the arrest, they charge the offender with the multiple crimes. What gets reported to the UCR system, however, is another matter. Because the UCR uses a hierarchy rule when dealing with multiple offenses, only the most serious offense is reported and the rest are ignored.[24] In this case, your assault would be entered into the system, and the vandalism, drug use, theft, and abuse of your dog would not be counted. The offender may be prosecuted for each of the crimes (well, maybe not for kicking the dog), but only the assault will be included in the official crime statistics.

Given the strengths and weaknesses of the UCR system, it should be evident that although the UCR provides a reasonably good picture of crime, it does not tell the whole crime story.[25] Fortunately, other measures supplement the UCR.

National Incident-Based Reporting System (NIBRS)

The UCR system is over six decades old, and although it has been improved greatly, its basic structure still has some problems that make it deficient in providing the types of information necessary for a clear picture of the modern crime situation. Therefore, the government has embarked on a new and more comprehensive crime-reporting system designed to rectify some of the UCR's shortcomings. The **National Incident-Based Reporting System (NIBRS)** is constructed to gather data on each criminal act even if several acts are committed within the same complex of behavior. That is, an incident that includes several different crimes will have each crime enumerated in the statistics rather than only the most serious crime. This new system is a big improvement over the UCR because it compensates for the hierarchal rule by which only the most serious crime is reported.[26]

National Incident-Based Reporting System (NIBRS) A crime-reporting system in which each separate offense in a crime is described, including data describing the offender(s), victim(s), and property.

As one might imagine, the development of a new crime-reporting system is an immense undertaking. Abt Associates of Cambridge, Massachusetts, was contracted to study the

The Uniform Crime Report system requires someone at each law enforcement agency to enter the crimes into the computer system. Extensive training is required to ensure that each jurisdiction defines the criminal behaviors in the same manner.
Courtesy of CORBIS-NY.

Uniform Crime Reports and suggest how a new system might improve the collection of crime data. Abt Associates worked with an oversight panel of personnel from the FBI and the Bureau of Justice Statistics, as well as academics, experts, and personnel from a variety of federal, state, and local agencies. Presented in 1985, the NIBRS collects data on each single incident and arrest for 22 offense categories comprising 46 specific crimes in its Group A offenses. Additionally, only arrest data are reported in 11 Group B offense categories (see Figure 2.8). The advantage of the NIBRS over the UCR is that it allows law enforcement officials to precisely identify when and where crime takes place, its form, and the characteristics of its victims and perpetrators. According to the FBI, "NIBRS has the capability of furnishing information on nearly every major criminal justice issue facing law enforcement today, including terrorism, white collar crime, weapons offenses, missing children, where criminality is involved, drug/narcotic offenses, drug involvement in all offenses, hate crimes, spouse abuse, abuse of the elderly, child abuse, domestic violence, juvenile crime/gangs, parental kidnapping, organized crime, pornography/child pornography, driving under the influence, and alcohol-related offenses."[27]

Participation in the NIBRS system requires that a state overhaul the way it collects and reports crime data. As of July 1999, 18 states were NIBRS-certified, 18 states were in the process of testing NIBRS, and another six states were working with NIBRS to develop

Figure 2.8
The National Incident-Based Reporting System

Group A Offenses

Extensive crime data for these are collected in the National Incident-Based Reporting System.

- Arson
- Assault offenses (aggravated assault, simple assault, intimidation)
- Bribery
- Burglary/breaking and entering
- Counterfeiting/forgery
- Destruction/damage/vandalism of property
- Drug/narcotic offenses (drug/narcotic violations, drug equipment violations)
- Embezzlement
- Extortion/blackmail
- Fraud offenses (false pretenses/swindle/confidence game, credit card/automatic teller machine fraud, impersonation, welfare fraud, wire fraud)
- Gambling offenses (betting/wagering, operating/promoting/assisting gambling, gambling equipment violations, sports tampering)
- Homicide offenses (murder and non-negligent manslaughter, negligent manslaughter, justifiable homicide)
- Kidnapping/abduction
- Larceny/theft offenses (pocket-picking, purse-snatching, shoplifting, theft from building, theft from coin-operated machine or device, theft from motor vehicle, theft of motor vehicle parts or accessories, all other larceny)
- Motor vehicle theft
- Pornography/obscene material
- Prostitution offenses (prostitution, assisting or promoting prostitution)
- Robbery
- Sex offenses, forcible (rape, sodomy, sexual assault with an object, fondling)
- Sex offenses, nonforcible (incest, statutory rape)
- Stolen property offenses (receiving, etc.)
- Weapon law violations

Group B Offenses

Only arrest data are reported.

- Bad checks
- Curfew/loitering/vagrancy violations
- Disorderly conduct
- Driving under the influence
- Drunkenness
- Family offenses, nonviolent
- Liquor law violations
- Peeping Tom
- Runaway
- Trespass of real property
- All other offenses

plans to test the procedure. It will be some years yet before the NIBRS system is used nationwide and can produce the detailed information required by law enforcement agencies in the 21st century.[28]

Moving to this new system of recording crime may produce some unintended consequences. One issue concerning NIBRS is the complexity of the reporting and coding procedures. Law enforcement agencies will be required to invest increased resources and personnel in crime-data collection efforts. In the past, the job of collecting and analyzing data has been done by police administrators, but NIBRS may require highly skilled civilians to make the program work. Another issue of concern is the impact that NIBRS will have on the duties of street-level officers. NIBRS requires a much greater level of detail in the reporting of crime than does the UCR, and some critics are concerned that street-level officers will consider this as interfering with "real" police work. Street-level officers may believe the NIBRS program to be more useful to researchers than to themselves. Finally, law enforcement officials may be concerned with what may appear to be an increase in crime because the NIBRS reports each crime separately, rather than reporting only one crime as does the UCR. The media and the public may not understand how changing the way crime is reported may result in the appearance of more crime, which could be a public relations problem for police executives who are evaluated on how well they control crime in their jurisdictions.[29]

Victimization Surveys

Previous discussions of the UCR and the NIBRS highlighted flaws and issues that each has in developing an accurate picture of the nature and extent of crime in the United States. Because both reporting systems require citizens to report criminal behavior to law enforcement officials, they fail to account for the large, unknown percentage of crime that is the "dark figure of crime." As suggested earlier, citizens might not report a crime to the police for several reasons, but to truly comprehend and respond to unlawful behavior, law enforcement personnel must find other ways to persuade people to assist in measuring the real level of criminal activity.

victimization surveys Surveys that attempt to measure the extent of crime by interviewing people who have suffered crime.

One such method for trying to get at the level of unreported crime is **victimization surveys**. Victimization surveys differ from the previously mentioned ways of reporting crime in many important ways. As the name implies, victimization surveys ask victims of crime about their experiences. They are essentially self-report studies that are done as part of survey research efforts. As such, they do not attempt to create a comprehensive account of crimes, as in the UCR program, but rather, usually use random samples of the general public and focus on specific types of crime. Additionally, a number of crimes are not measured because the parties act in a consensual manner, and there is no reporting victim. For instance, whereas the UCR will measure arrests for drug sales, victimization surveys will miss the successfully completed drug transactions because buyers consider themselves satisfied customers and not crime victims. The same could be said of gambling and prostitution.[30] Although there may be some indirect victims of these crimes (such as the government not receiving taxes on these business transactions), the participants do not view themselves as victims and do not report these crimes in victimization surveys.

Other crimes are more accurately measured by the UCR than by victimization surveys. Perhaps the most obvious is homicide. Although nearly every homicide is reported by the UCR because of the presence of a dead body, homicide victims cannot respond to a victimization survey. Additionally, white collar and corporate crimes are difficult to measure using victimization surveys because people often are unaware that they have been victims of subtle and widespread corruption or fraud. Because of these differences in the types of crimes that are measured, comparing the crime picture of the UCR with victimization surveys is problematic.[31] Rather than attempting to decide which method most accurately reports crime, it is more useful to think of them as measuring different aspects of crime. Used in conjunction, rather than in competition, these measures foster the development of a deeper appreciation of the types of crime in a jurisdiction and how they affect the community.

Like other methods of measuring crime, victimization surveys have evolved from rather crude devices with glaring shortcomings to extremely sophisticated instruments that attempt to account for a variety of confounding variables. As such, victimization surveys have earned a place in the kit of tools that criminologists use to measure crime. The study of how victimization surveys have evolved is interesting. There have been four generations of victimization surveys since their inception in the late 1960s.

FIRST-GENERATION VICTIMIZATION SURVEYS. One of the concerns of the 1968 President's Crime Commission was the inaccurate and biased picture of crime derived from the UCR. As a result, the government attempted to get a clearer picture of the crime problem by asking victims about their experiences. The first national victimization survey, from the National Opinion Research Center (NORC), collected information from 10,000 households across the United States. The most significant conclusion reached by the NORC survey was that the UCR underreported crime by about 50 percent. The way the NORC survey defined crime and gathered its data raised a number of methodological concerns. Still, this first generation of surveys demonstrated that victims were willing to talk about their experiences with researchers and encouraged criminologists to develop more sophisticated surveys.

SECOND-GENERATION VICTIMIZATION SURVEYS. A second, and improved, generation of victimization surveys was created in 1970 and 1971. These surveys attempted to gauge the amount of error incurred by the methodological problems identified in the first generation of studies. One way to measure this perceived error was to survey victims who had reported crime to the police to see if they had problems with memory decay, telescoping, or categorizing the type of crime. Some of these studies attempted a forward records check in which they checked if information provided by the victim was also reported in the UCR. Also, commercial establishments were added to the survey to attempt to measure crime not connected to a single household. One problem with comparing victimization surveys with the UCR is the difficulty of matching the initial crime report with the victim after months or years. This is especially true for commercial establishments that have a high turnover in staff. For example, if a restaurant was robbed last year, the manager and employees surveyed in the victimization survey done this year may be new and thus unable to provide useful information about the robbery.

THIRD-GENERATION VICTIMIZATION SURVEYS. In 1972 a third generation of victimization surveys was done, and although some of the components of the surveys were short-lived because of the exorbitant cost, these surveys provided an outline for ambitious data-gathering efforts that has informed future research efforts. The National Crime Survey (NCS) used an interesting and sophisticated panel method in which roughly 12,000 households were surveyed each month on a rotating basis to correct for some of the concerns of the methodological problems of previous surveys. One improvement made in the NCS was that the researchers talked to more than just one member of the household. Rather than questioning just the head of the household, the researchers talked to everyone in the household, unless the parents objected to their talking to a minor or repeated attempts to contact other family members failed. In addition to the survey of households, the NCS included efforts to gather data on commercial establishments and 26 city surveys in which both residences and businesses were contacted. Unfortunately, both the business victimization surveys and the city surveys were discontinued after a few years because they were deemed too expensive to conduct.

FOURTH-GENERATION VICTIMIZATION SURVEYS. The fourth and current generation of surveys has continued to improve. Although not error-free, they are more sophisticated and have addressed somewhat successfully many of the problems of former surveys. The National Crime Survey, (NCS) under its new name, the National Crime Victimization Survey (NCVS), gathers data on subgroups of victims, seeks to determine what can be done to aid victims after crimes, and attempts to provide empirical information that assists both households and individuals in avoiding victimization. One of the most significant improvements of the NCVS is the use of better screening questions. These questions allow researchers to identify those who are victims of certain offenses and then ask detailed follow-up questions of only those respondents. The surveys are also increasingly using technology,

Some Problems with Victimization Surveys

Although asking crime victims about their experiences shines a small light on the dark figure of crime, these data collection efforts have some limitations that must be considered before we can fully appreciate the contribution they make to the understanding of crime. According to criminologists William Doerner and Steven Lab, the first generation of National Opinion Research Center victimization surveys suffered from the following shortcomings:

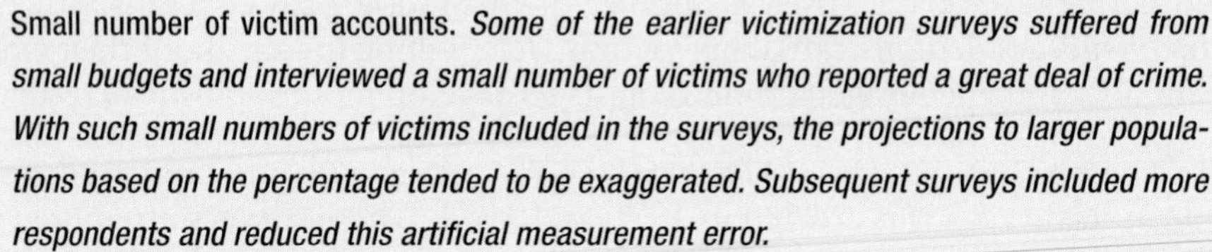

- Small number of victim accounts. *Some of the earlier victimization surveys suffered from small budgets and interviewed a small number of victims who reported a great deal of crime. With such small numbers of victims included in the surveys, the projections to larger populations based on the percentage tended to be exaggerated. Subsequent surveys included more respondents and reduced this artificial measurement error.*
- Major flaws in the wording of questions. *In the first generation of victim surveys, a panel of experts reviewed victims' accounts to determine whether a real crime had been committed. Over one-third of the reports were tossed out because either they contained no real crime or the crime was misclassified.*

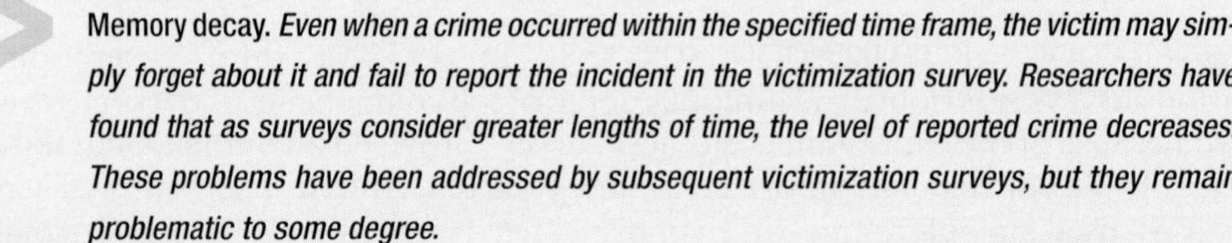

- Telescoping. *Sometimes victims make mistakes in placing the time of the crime within the study period. They misjudge how long ago the incident took place and report crimes for the past year that, in reality, happened long before. This is a common mistake that happens when respondents do not consult calendars, court records, or police reports when they respond to questions about victimization.*
- Memory decay. *Even when a crime occurred within the specified time frame, the victim may simply forget about it and fail to report the incident in the victimization survey. Researchers have found that as surveys consider greater lengths of time, the level of reported crime decreases. These problems have been addressed by subsequent victimization surveys, but they remain problematic to some degree.*

If you were to design a victim survey, how would you deal with the following issues?

QUESTIONS

1. What is the best time frame to ask victims to consider? Six months? One year? Five years? Ten years?
2. How do you stimulate the memories of victims to remember minor crimes? Is there a danger of encouraging victims to define behaviors as crimes when they normally would not do so?
3. Is there a danger in dredging up bad memories for the victims of violent crime? Would your victimization survey be better off not being done?

Source: William G. Doerner and Steven P. Lab, *Victimology,* 2nd ed. (Cincinnati, OH: Anderson, 1998), 30–31.

such as Computer-Assisted Telephone Interviews (CATI). Approximately 30 percent of the surveys use this method, and this practice can be expected to increase. The advantages of CATI are reduced personnel costs and uniformity in questioning and coding. These improvements have resulted in an increase in victimization reporting. Researchers believe that improved surveys stimulate the respondents' memories and enable respondents to better define their types of victimization and more precisely place the time of their victimization within the temporal scope of the survey.[32]

What is the crime picture according to the recent victimization studies? According to the NCVS for 2002, both violent victimizations and property victimizations continued to decrease and were at their lowest rate since 1973 (see Figures 2.9 and 2.10). Since 1999 violent crimes significantly decreased for both males and females as well as individuals of different races (See Figure 2.11).

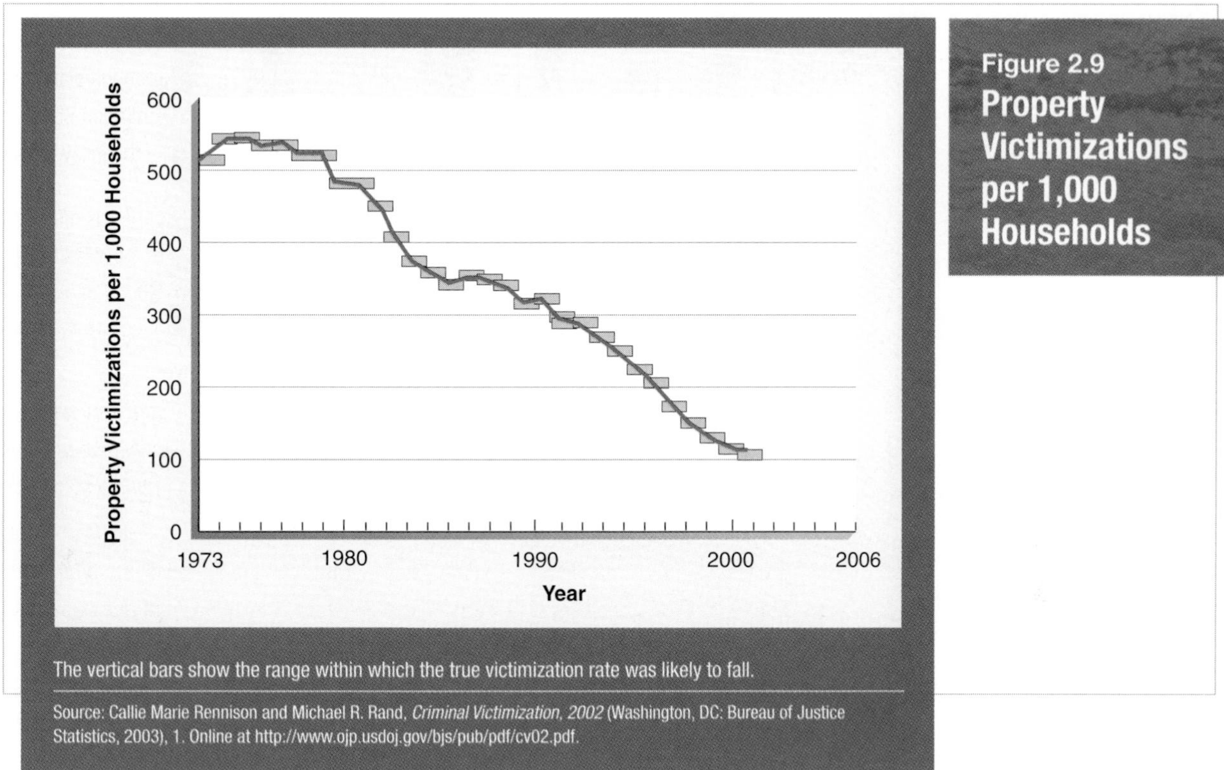

Figure 2.9 Property Victimizations per 1,000 Households

The vertical bars show the range within which the true victimization rate was likely to fall.

Source: Callie Marie Rennison and Michael R. Rand, *Criminal Victimization, 2002* (Washington, DC: Bureau of Justice Statistics, 2003), 1. Online at http://www.ojp.usdoj.gov/bjs/pub/pdf/cv02.pdf.

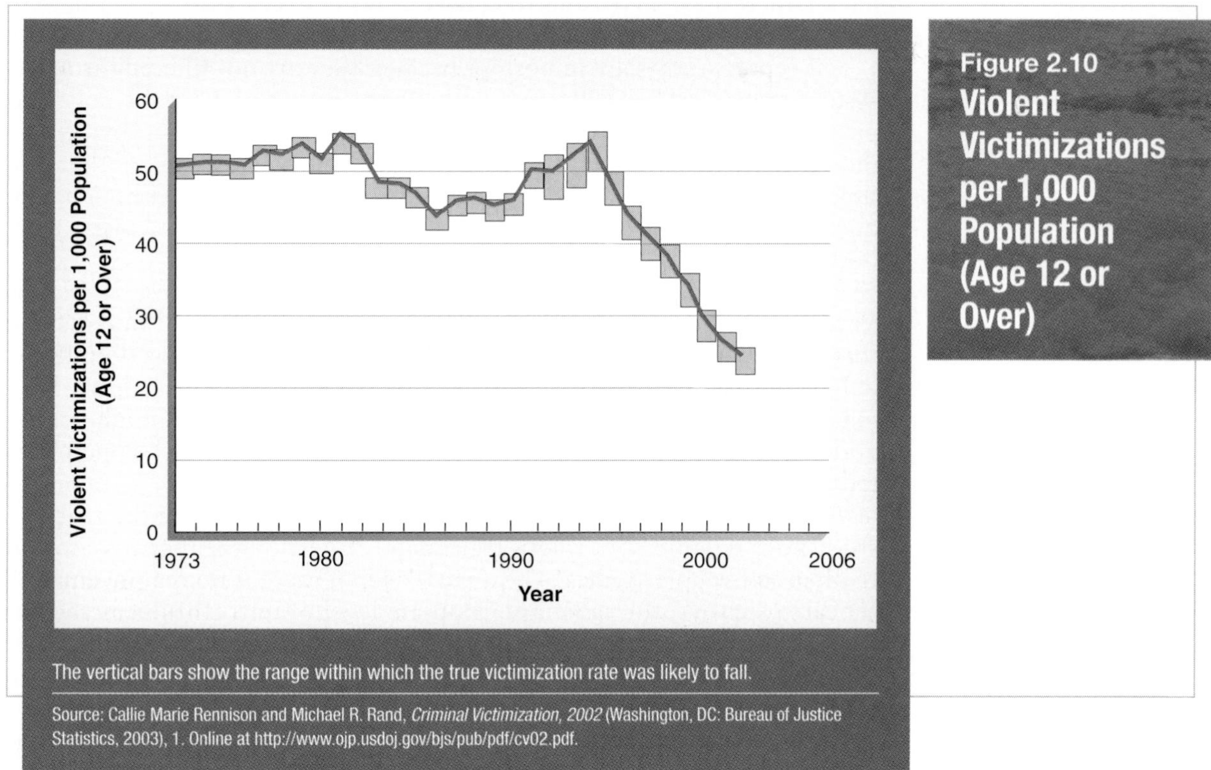

Figure 2.10 Violent Victimizations per 1,000 Population (Age 12 or Over)

The vertical bars show the range within which the true victimization rate was likely to fall.

Source: Callie Marie Rennison and Michael R. Rand, *Criminal Victimization, 2002* (Washington, DC: Bureau of Justice Statistics, 2003), 1. Online at http://www.ojp.usdoj.gov/bjs/pub/pdf/cv02.pdf.

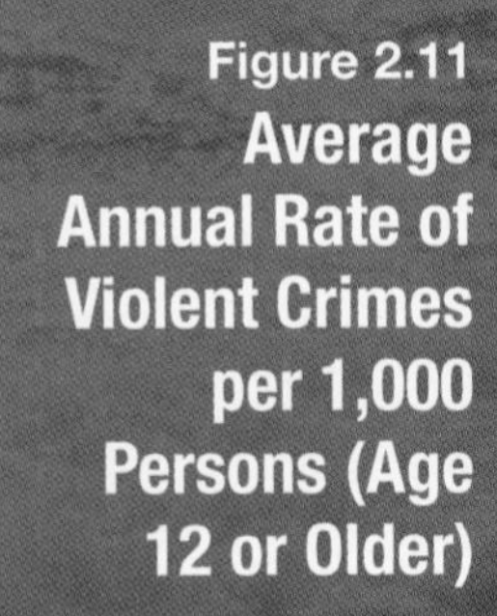

Figure 2.11 Average Annual Rate of Violent Crimes per 1,000 Persons (Age 12 or Older)

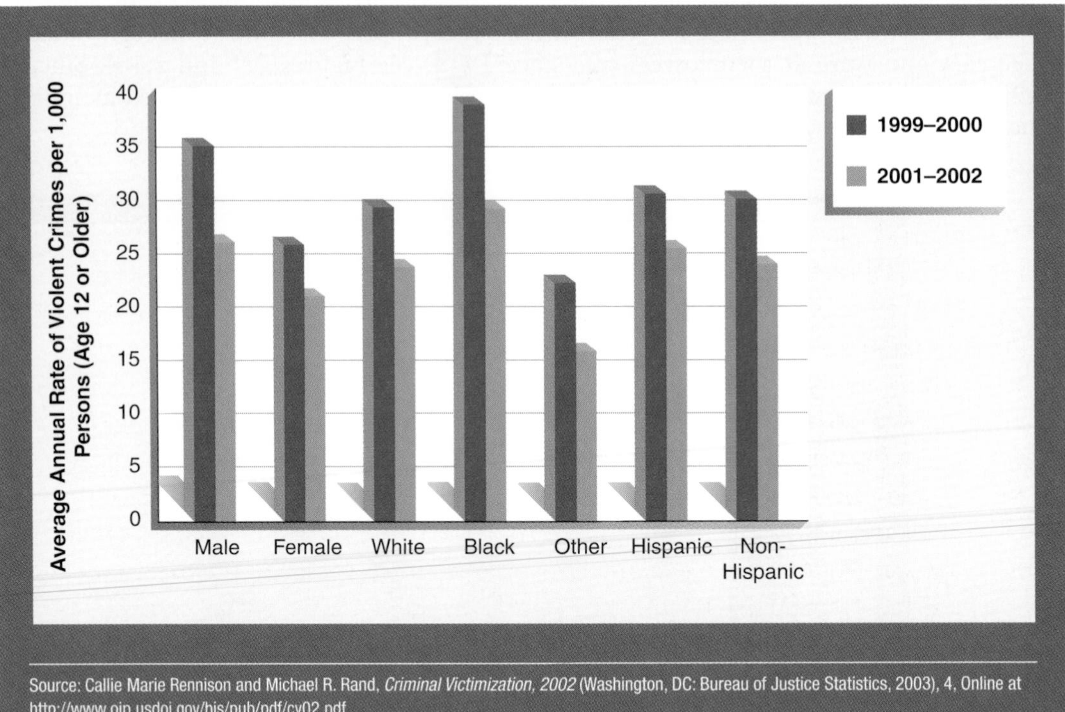

Source: Callie Marie Rennison and Michael R. Rand, *Criminal Victimization, 2002* (Washington, DC: Bureau of Justice Statistics, 2003), 4, Online at http://www.ojp.usdoj.gov/bjs/pub/pdf/cv02.pdf

Self-Report Studies

The third major technique for collecting data on delinquency and criminal behavior is the use of self-report studies. In self-report studies, individuals are asked to identify the types of crimes they have committed over the study period. Although there are some significant concerns about truthfulness when individuals are asked to admit to criminal behavior, there are also reasons to believe that these data provide a different and important picture of crime that is not supplied in studies done by government officials.[33]

Self-report studies are important because they are not filtered through criminal justice system agencies. The UCR provides better measures of what the police do than what the picture of crime actually looks like. Victimization surveys provide the perspective of those who have suffered some loss, but they fail to record crimes that have no direct victim. Self-report studies provide an accurate picture of crime without having to view delinquency and criminal behavior through the lens of law enforcement agencies or victims, both of whom may introduce bias.

Researchers were initially concerned about the willingness of respondents to admit to delinquent or criminal behavior in self-report studies.[34] Surprisingly, people were forthcoming in these studies about many behaviors that they would not admit to publicly. Questions about the underreporting of criminal behavior were eventually matched with questions about overreporting. That is, although some people may lie and not admit to crimes they have committed, others may lie and claim they committed violations that they did not. Because of the anonymity of many self-report studies, it is impossible to determine whether people are telling the truth and whether the studies are reliable. One might legitimately question the incentive for people to tell the truth in self-report studies. The answer is that there is no real incentive. However, over repeated surveys, the same approximate level of untruthfulness can be expected, and researchers can thus assume that the measures are comparable and valid. For instance, if I give a self-report study to my students in Georgia and another professor gives the same survey in Texas or California, researchers would assume that there is a constant percentage of respondents who will over-self-report or under-self-report crimes. If responses are consistent over repeated surveys, researchers assume that any differences

FOCUS ON ETHICS

Crime Wave

Your criminal justice professor is working on a pilot project that, if successful, may help her obtain a large federal grant to study self-reported crime. She asks your class to help her field-test her survey questionnaire. The entire class readily agrees because testing the survey will take up the entire class period next week and there will not be any lectures. Over the weekend, you go to a party on campus and run into several of your classmates who, after a couple of beers, come up with the idea of exaggerating the amount of crime they report. Specifically, your classmates decide to answer all the questions about drug use in the affirmative.

On the day of the survey, you find out that it is not only the students you met at the party who plan to overreport drug use but also just about all the students in the class. No one takes the survey seriously, thinking it quite funny to exaggerate their answers. You are caught up in the atmosphere. Even though you rarely drink alcohol and have never used illegal drugs, you admit to using marijuana daily, crack-cocaine weekly, and ecstasy whenever you can get it. After class, everyone is snickering about greatly overreporting their criminal behavior.

At the next class period, your professor is ecstatic. She says her questionnaire was able to uncover a great deal more self-reported crime than previous surveys have been able to detect. She is confident that because of the pilot project's results, she will secure a federal grant for $500,000 for a nationwide study using her groundbreaking questionnaire. She thanks the class for their cooperation and for answering the questions with such honesty and candor. She is so happy that she lets the class out an hour early.

Now you feel really bad. Your professor is a decent person who has a reputation for caring about her students, working hard to prepare her lectures, and grading fairly. The grapevine says she needs to land this grant to secure tenure, but you worry that her getting this big grant under false pretenses could damage her career in the long run.

WHAT DO YOU DO?

1. Go to the professor's office and tell her that the entire class lied about their criminal activities.
2. Go to the department chair and tell her that the class has been dishonest with the professor and that you are afraid to tell her. Maybe the chair can find a way to break the news to the professor and protect her from making a mistake by pursuing the grant.
3. Do nothing and let the professor apply for the grant. Even though everyone lied on the questionnaire, it still might be an accurate data collection instrument and might be very successful in a nationwide survey.

in self-reported crime measure actual offenses rather than signify errors that have been introduced by lying respondents. Critics question whether these assumptions are warranted.[35]

Researchers have attempted to determine whether respondents tell the truth in self-report studies. For example, in one study of drug use, the researchers gave the subjects a urinalysis test to determine whether their answers to questions about drug use were accurate. Over two-thirds of those who used marijuana lied about it to the researchers, and over 85 percent of those who used cocaine lied.[36]

Another concern about using self-report studies to examine the amount and degree of crime has to do with the issue of representiveness. Many of the early self-report studies were done with samples of convenience. That is, the researchers simply asked students in their classrooms to answer questionnaires. Generalizing to larger populations is difficult when the sample is constructed according to who shows up to class on a particular day. To correct for such a biased sample, researchers use probability theory to draw a sample that reflects the relevant characteristics of the population from which it is drawn. In this way, the researchers can be reasonably confident that the findings derived from their study of a small number of respondents are applicable to the larger population.[37]

Finally, self-reported crime can give an inaccurate picture of the overall crime situation because of the way studies are administered. Basically, two types of techniques are used in self-report studies. The first is a questionnaire that subjects complete. Questionnaires have the advantage of being relatively inexpensive, standardized, and not requiring personal contact. Questionnaires can be mailed, so information can be collected from subjects from many different locations. The disadvantages of questionnaires include there being little opportunity for researchers to clarify the meanings of questions when respondents are confused. Also, the researcher can do little to ensure that the intended respondent is the one actually answering the questions. The response rate can be very low when respondents decide not to participate and throw the questionnaire away.[38]

Self-report studies and victimization surveys are powerful techniques for getting at the dark figure of crime. However, these measures are not substitutes for the UCR. They provide another view of the crime picture, but they are not as comprehensive as the UCR, and each has its limitations.[39] Taken together, these three methods of collecting crime data give us as good a picture as we have ever had of crime, but there are still issues that keep the picture of crime out of focus. Like the proverbial blind men trying to describe an elephant by touch, each of these measures of crime concentrates on a different aspect of the problem and none sees the whole picture. The logical question to ask at this point remains, What part of the crime picture do these three measures miss or obscure?

1. **Corporate crime.** The three measures of crime that we have discussed are not very good at detecting the types of crime that may be committed by corporations in their business pursuits. Price fixing, insider stock trading, and bribery are all crimes that are unlikely to be detected by any of these measures.[40]
2. **Organized crime.** Those involved in ongoing organized criminal activities are unlikely to self-report their unlawful behaviors. Additionally, victims of threats and extortion are often afraid to identify their persecutors and are unlikely to respond truthfully to victimization surveys.[41]
3. **Drug sales.** Although self-report studies have been successful in getting individuals to talk about their drug-taking behaviors, uncovering drug sales has been less successful. The larger the drug dealer's business, the less likely the dealer is to self-identify as such for fear that a response could lead to eventual arrest.[42]
4. **Prostitution and gambling.** Those who engage in prostitution and gambling do not always think a crime has been committed. When there is a satisfied service provider and a satisfied customer, both think of the behavior as a successful business transaction and do not consider themselves to be either criminal or victim.[43]

One might reasonably ask why we even bother trying to measure crime when the data collection methods are so limited. The answer is that we have no choice in the matter. Legislators, criminal justice administrators, law enforcement officers, and the public all make decisions based on their perceptions of how much crime there is and how it affects victims. It is best that they are able to base their decisions on as accurate a picture as possible. Although the crime picture that scholars and government officials provide is limited, the quality of this picture is constantly improving, and it is better than relying on the media or public opinion for the information on which public policy is made and criminal justice system budgets are based. By employing the systematically gathered UCR data with the snapshots provided by victimization surveys and self-report studies, we are able to get a reasonable idea of the scope and severity of the crime problem. Because crime is a socially constructed concept, some ambiguity will always exist about what behaviors constitute crime and whether particular incidents fit those definitions. Additionally, even when we might agree on the definitions of crime, there will always be incentives and motivations for individuals not to report.

Fear of Crime

Only the direct consumers of crime statistics are affected by the limitations of crime-measuring efforts. Government funding agencies, law enforcement departments, and the media are concerned with discovering the overall crime picture so they can decide where to allocate resources or how to enlighten the public. However, most of us know little about these elaborate and expensive ways to measure crime and make our daily decisions to prevent, avoid, or respond to crime based on our perceptions of danger and assumed likelihood of victimization. Despite our relative lack of knowledge of the actual level and seriousness of crime in our communities, we have a healthy respect for the potential impact of crime on our lives, and we take measures to reduce the chances of becoming crime victims.[44] In this way, a realistic fear of crime is a useful attitude. The questions to be addressed here concern where our fear of crime comes from and whether the fear is justified.

For many people, the fear of crime is a constant feature that dictates how they conduct their daily lives. While waxing poetically about the "good old days" when they could leave their homes for an afternoon of shopping and not bother to lock their doors, they spend considerable amounts of money on deadbolt locks, security systems, cameras, and noise machines that sound like big, barking dogs. More generally, we isolate ourselves in gated communities, are suspicious of delivery people, and to a large degree, surrender public spaces to street people at night. The fear of crime, although healthy to some degree, has also diminished our sense of community and has developed into a self-fulfilling prophecy that stimulates crime by reducing the interconnectedness of people. How justified is this fear?[45]

In his book, *Random Violence,* sociologist Joel Best addressed the perception of many people that crime is a significant problem that will soon affect their lives unless they take steps to avoid it. Best contended that perceptions of violence are constructed not by official measures of crime, but by the media, which can distort and sensationalize particular incidents. Isolated violent events can appear to be a threat to everyone.[46] One of the first issues that Best confronted was the notion of random violence, pointing out three problems with this popular conception.

1. **Patternlessness.** The term *random violence* implies that anyone could be a victim at any time. In fact, crime is highly patterned. That is, certain people are more likely to be victims than are other people. When we examine homicide rates (for which we have the most reliable statistics), we see that age, race, and gender clearly affect the probability of victimization. For example, Best argued that homicide rates for white males peak for those between the ages of 20 and 24, then gradually decline as the men grow older. Crime can be examined for patterns, and according to Best, the patterns are so clear and distinct that the term *random violence* is inaccurate.
2. **Pointlessness.** Sensational incidents of crime can appear to be pointless. When the car driven by Susan Smith in South Carolina was allegedly hijacked and found at the bottom of a lake with her two small children still strapped into their car seats, people were at a loss to explain such a senseless and pointless act of cruelty. It was later discovered that Smith drowned her children because she had an affair with a man who did not want a long-term relationship with her because of her children. Smith then killed her children to get them out of the way of her quest to maintain her relationship with her boyfriend. Most crimes have a motive. Violence can be instrumental, but even when it seems random, upon further examination it is often found to have a purpose.
3. **Deterioration.** When the media report a number of sensational crimes, random violence can appear to be epidemic. Because of the national and international scope of the media, all news can be perceived as local news. Widely scattered occurrences of firearm violence in schools can appear to constitute a wave of school shootings that makes all teenagers seem violent.[47]

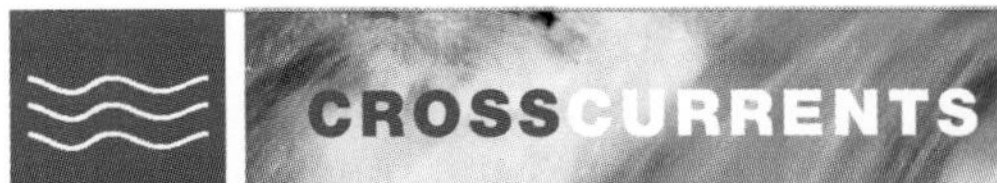

Elderly Crime Victims

Elderly people typically suffer the least victimization but express the highest level of fear. However, the elderly are sometimes at increased risk of victimization for the following reasons:

- *They may be less aware of their surroundings and may neither hear nor see approaching or present danger.*
- *They may be unable to identify the offender.*
- *They may be unable to read or understand the terms of a fraudulent contract.*
- *They have slower reaction times and may not have the physical ability to defend themselves or their property if attacked.*
- *They may live in cities that are generally high crime areas with less than adequate police protection, and as their neighborhoods change, they may be removed from the mainstream.*
- *They may have to rely on public transportation that may take them through areas they would otherwise avoid.*
- *Often, no one is present to protect their home or property while they are away, even for a short period.*
- *Many older people pursue daily activities, such as grocery buying and check cashing, with regularity.*

High-risk groups within the elderly include the following:

- *Elderly males, who are typically at greater risk for violent crime and robbery than elderly females.*
- *Elderly females, who typically are at greater risk for personal larceny with contact, such as purse-snatching, than elderly males.*

QUESTIONS

1. Should the elderly be more afraid of crime? Less afraid?
2. What can be done to make the elderly feel safer?

Source: Office of the Attorney General: Jerry Kilgore, *Street Crime and the Elderly,* http://www.oag.state.va.us/protecting/triad/eldercrime.htm.

Violent crime is usually not random. Crime has clear patterns, and it almost always is purposive despite initial appearances. Unrelated crimes distributed over large geographic areas do not constitute an epidemic and do not signal the deterioration of the social order and a rapid descent into chaos. Yet the public's fear of crime suggests that crime is such a serious problem that society has lost its cohesion and that the old processes of social control are no longer effective.[48] It is enlightening to look at some of the crimes that have fueled the public's perception of random violence.

WILDING. One evening in April 1989, a young woman was attacked in New York City's Central Park while she was jogging. A number of young men were accused and ultimately convicted of the sexual assault, and the term *wilding* entered the crime

FOCUS ON ETHICS

If It Bleeds, It Leads

You are a new producer for a major network's local television news program in a large metropolitan city. This program has trailed its rivals for the past seven years and holds a paltry market share for its time slot. Your predecessor was fired because she failed to produce sensational, lurid, and sex-related news segments. Although you understand the need to be flashy, you trained at a good journalism school in which the professional ethic was deeply ingrained in the curriculum. After several newscasts, your segments have been nominated for regional awards, but the number of viewers has not increased significantly. Your network bosses are pressuring you to deliver the goods or get canned.

Your sports reporter has alerted you to several fights after football games at local high schools. After some initial investigation, you decide the fights are unrelated and that it is not much of a story. However, with a bit of hyperbole and exaggeration, you could portray these fights as a youth gang problem. Never mind that your city has no history of youth gangs and that the police chief and head of the school board will not go on camera because they know the fights are not gang related. However, being under pressure, you instruct one of your news crews to selectively film graffiti, look for stereotypical gang symbols, and find some youths who will claim to be afraid of gang activity in the schools. After several stories about these "gangs," the ratings for your newscast rocket. Because of your newscasts, concerned parents have been meeting with school officials, tensions have increased among the city's high schools, and police officials are concerned that your stories about the nonexistent gang problem may inspire kids to actually start gangs. In an almost comical way, young people have started to adopt the accoutrements of gang culture: wearing red or blue bandanas, flashing gang signs, and even carrying weapons.

The police chief asks for an off-camera meeting with you. At the meeting she requests that your network stop doing stories about the gang problem. She is convinced that your stories about gangs are creating a problem rather than reflecting reality. Your bosses at the station take the opposite view. You are instructed to start laying the groundwork for a new series of programs about the gang problem that is set to air in two months during sweeps week, when the ratings for television advertising are pegged to the number of viewers for each program. Your bosses and the network promise you raises and promotions if you can produce a hard-hitting series that can link the high school fights to dangerous gangs, drug dealing, and violence. You know this would be a real stretch and that it would violate all the bounds of journalist integrity. Recalling a Criminal Justice 101 class from college, you realize that your news programs about gang-related crime have caused people to become afraid of crime that really does not exist.

WHAT DO YOU DO?

1. Hype the gang story and reap all the benefits.
2. Try to do a fair and balanced story about the high school fights and downplay the whole issues of gangs and forfeit the raises, Emmy nominations, promotions, and possibly your job.
3. Get out of journalism because you have lost your way and can no longer see the forest for the trees.

news lexicon to refer to gangs of young men going on crime sprees in which they rob, assault, and rape at random in public spaces.[49] According to Best, the term *wilding,* essentially constructed by the media, finally fell out of favor after two years of heavy usage and dozens of stories in the *New York Times.* The term is used only sporadically today. Perhaps the most revealing aspect of this incident as it pertains to the fear of crime is the later confession to the crime by another man. Those who were convicted of the crime turned out to be innocent, and their wilding behavior may not even have occurred. Repairing the social fabric after such a high level of publicity is difficult. Even after the confession, which was corroborated by DNA evidence, some law enforcement officers continue to believe that the youths were involved.

FREEWAY VIOLENCE. According to Best, journalists have a rule of thumb that states that the third time something happens constitutes a trend. After some apparently unrelated acts of firearm violence on the Los Angeles freeways, the media began to report stories about the new problem of freeway violence.[50] Despite the fact that official data collections did not separate freeway violence from other types of violence, the media started listing all previous incidents of freeway violence to make it appear as though a new phenomenon were afoot.[51] Best contended that other jurisdictions began reporting such incidents of freeway violence, but the term soon faded from the media even though it continues in the popular culture. It has taken on a life of its own to the point where many motorists keep firearms in their cars for self-defense. Although it can be argued that the vast majority of these weapons are never used, many motorists feel a sense of comfort from having a handgun within reach as they travel.

STALKING. Stalking emerged as a social problem at about the same time as wilding and freeway violence, but took an entirely different trajectory as a media concern and became established as a distinct and important issue for the criminal justice system. Stalking refers to the activity in which someone is repeatedly followed, harassed, or physically threatened by another person.[52] The stalker may be a stranger with a romantic fixation on the victim or an ex-lover or estranged spouse who does not want to end the relationship. Because of the links that researchers and law enforcement officials have made between stalking and domestic violence, the issue has gained traction as a social problem. Most states, as well as the federal government, have established antistalking laws to protect victims. Although stalkers certainly existed before the recent interest in stalking, the efforts of the media reporting cases of celebrity

NEWS FLASH

Fear

Surveys conducted in Britain have found that a tenuous relationship exists between crime and the fear of crime. British national crime statistics for 2002 and 2003 found that although the number of crimes committed fell by 2 percent, people were more afraid of crime than ever.

According to the survey, 38 percent of participants thought that crime had risen greatly in the past two years, compared to 25 percent who believed the same thing in 2001. The survey also uncovered another phenomenon: Those who fear crime the most are often the least affected by it, especially the elderly. For example, 16 percent of women over the age of 60 thought they were likely to be victims of mugging, a crime that actually happens to fewer than one woman in 200. On the other hand, young men, who become crime victims at more than three times the national rate, tended to fear crime less.

Researchers also found that even asking survey participants in a certain way about crime could raise their level of fear. By rewording questions, researchers found that participants' level of fear fell by about half, and it fell even more for elderly participants.

Source: *The Economist,* "Fear Itself," July 19, 2003, 45. Also online at http://www.economist.com/world/europe/displayStory.cfm?story_id=1927126.

stalking and the persistent problems of domestic violence have elevated this behavior to a category of crime in its own right.[53]

Each of these new types of crime that has been discovered by the media competes for a place in the public's collective imagination. Although their actual incidence may not legitimately be cause for concern, the media have been successful in portraying the appearance of a crime trend for each. What is most interesting to the student of the criminal justice system, however, is the way wilding and freeway shootings have almost disappeared as criminal justice concerns, whereas stalking has been institutionalized by states that have passed specific laws to protect victims. Once stalking was linked to domestic violence, women's groups were successful in forcing state and federal legislators to enact laws making stalking a new category of crime.

Researchers have spent a good deal of time attempting to measure citizens' fear of crime. Both government agencies and national polling firms have conducted surveys focused on issues from neighborhood safety to whether citizens believe that crime rates are rising or falling. Until about 1965, fear of crime was not rated high on the list of citizens' concerns. Now, although it seldom ranks as high as the economy, taxes, or education, fear of crime is a consistent worry among many Americans.

After a decade of declining crime rates, people still believe that crime has been consistently rising. Although crime has risen slightly for the past couple of years, the national homicide rate dropped 33 percent between 1990 and 1998. The news coverage on homicide, however, increased by 473 percent.[54] It is not difficult to appreciate why the fear of crime is a slippery concept to measure when the actual incidence of illegal behavior is so distorted.

Summary

This chapter has reviewed the way crime is measured and how the level of crime affects the criminal justice system and the public's fear of crime. One major point that the reader should take from this chapter is the fact that not all crimes are equal. Crime is a concept that varies greatly across a host of issues. The first distinctions made about types of crime was among crimes against the person, crimes against property, and crimes against the public order. This simple typology reflects important concerns and values on the part of the public. Crimes against the person are the infractions that can most disrupt the lives of citizens and so, accordingly, carry the most severe penalties. Homicide, rape, and robbery are catastrophic events for victims and require separation from other types of crime in discussion of the crime rate.

Crimes against property range from minor pocket-picking to grand theft, and, although disruptive to people's lives, do not usually carry the same impact as crimes against persons. Larceny/theft, burglary, automobile theft, and arson are each measured by criminal justice data-gathering efforts to ascertain their levels of seriousness and frequency. Finally, crimes against the public order do not enjoy the consensus that the other two categories of crime have. Crimes against the public order offend the sensibilities of some groups of people who have been successful in getting their values encoded into the criminal law. A great deal of variation exists regarding the efficacy of many of the laws that govern the social order, and we find movement to change some of those laws. Gambling and drug laws are consistently being modified to reflect the changing values of society.

Crime is measured in three major ways. The Uniform Crime Reports are the largest, most expensive, most comprehensive, and oldest method used to get an accurate picture of the incidence and seriousness of crime. Although critics have identified many sources of intentional and unintentional errors in the UCR, this method continues to be used to allocate resources, deploy police officers, and inform the media and the public about crime levels. An improved method for gathering national crime statistics currently being developed is the National Incident-Based Reporting System, which is designed to correct some of the more egregious flaws of the UCR. The primary improvement made by

NIBRS is that it collects data on all criminal behaviors that take place in a given incident, not only on the most serious crime.

In an attempt to study the types of crime missed by the UCR and the NIBRS, researchers have developed two alternative methods for measuring crime. Victimization surveys ask victims of crime about their experiences. Victimization surveys are not nearly as comprehensive as the UCR and can only provide a snapshot of the actual incidences of crime. Furthermore, victimization surveys are not immediately comparable to the UCR because they gauge crime according to different time frames, crime categories, and geographic locations than does the UCR. Nevertheless, even though we cannot use victimization surveys to precisely fill in the gaps of official crime statistics, they do provide an alternative picture of crime and highlight some of the issues that escape the UCR.

Self-report studies ask offenders to identify the types of crimes they have committed over the past six months or year. Although we are justifiably suspicious of the validity of these self-reports, in truth, researchers have been surprised at just how much deviance people will admit to when they are assured that their names will not be attached to the reports. Like victimization surveys, self-reports provide an alternative picture of the level and frequency of crime. Because of a number of differences in the way these measures are constructed, they cannot be readily compared and considered to have captured the entire spectrum of crime in a given jurisdiction, but the combined measures do give us an idea of just how complicated measuring crime is. Furthermore, as more resources are expended in money, training, and data-gathering efforts, we can expect our picture of the true nature of crime to come into clearer focus.

Finally, the influence of the media on the public's fear of crime is of concern. Although efforts to determine exactly how much the public knows about the level and frequency of crime are ongoing, a gap clearly exists between fear and actual danger. Those who have the least to fear are often those who go to the greatest extremes to avoid dangerous situations, and those who are victimized the most are the ones who engage in high-risk behavior. The media have elevated isolated incidents of wilding and freeway shootings to the level of crime trends and have also facilitated the institutionalization of categories of newly discovered crimes such as stalking.

As students progress though their study of crime and the criminal justice system, they should remember that the understanding of the level and frequency of crime is imperfect. Knowledge of criminal behavior and victimization should be used with caution because the data-gathering instruments have their limitations and flaws. Also, and maybe even more important, students should realize that crime data are not collected in a vacuum. Those who are concerned with crime rates (law enforcement executives, politicians, and the media) all have vested interests in seeing the numbers reflect their concerns. Although crime statistics are valuable, consumers of those statistics, including criminal justice students, should keep in mind that they should be viewed with a critical eye.

KEY TERMS

arson p. 46
burglary p. 45
crime rate p. 53
dark figure of crime p. 49
larceny p. 45
National Incident-Based Reporting System (NIBRS) p. 56
rape p. 44
robbery p. 45
serial murder p. 44
sexual assault p. 44
terrorism p. 44
Uniform Crime Reports (UCR) p. 52
victim precipitation p. 58
victimization surveys p. 43

REVIEW QUESTIONS

1. One way of understanding crime is by its legal categorizations (misdemeanors, felonies, etc.). What is another good way of understanding crime?
2. What is the three-group typology that elucidates the similarities and differences among general classes of crime?
3. What is the relationship between victim precipitation and crimes against the person?
4. List several reasons for a victim not to report a crime.
5. What are the Uniform Crime Reports?
6. What is a crime rate?
7. What is the National Incident-Based Reporting System?
8. How did victimization surveys evolve?
9. What part of the crime picture do crime measures typically miss or obscure?
10. How often is violent crime random? What crimes have fueled the public's perception of random violence?

SUGGESTED FURTHER READING

Dykema, Jennifer, and Nora Cate Schaeffer. "Events, Instruments, and Reporting Errors." *American Sociological Review* 65 (2000): 619–629.

Hagan, John. *Crime and Disrepute*. Thousand Oaks, CA: Pine Forge, 1994.

Jenkins, Philip. *Using Murder: The Social Construction of Serial Homicide*. New York: Aldine de Gruyter, 1994.

Lab, Steven P., ed. *Crime Prevention at a Crossroads*. Cincinnati, OH: Anderson, 1997.

McCleary, Richard, Barbara Nienstedt, and James Even. "Uniform Crime Reports as Organizational Outcomes: Three Time Series Experiments." *Social Problems* 29 (1982): 361–372.

Miethe, Terence, and Richard C. McCorkle. *Crime Profiles: The Anatomy of Dangerous Persons, Places, and Situations*, 2nd ed. Los Angeles: Roxbury, 2001.

ENDNOTES

1. Scott H. Decker, "Deviant Homicide: A New Look at the Role of Motives and Victim-Offender Relationships," in *Victims and Victimization: Essential Readings*, eds. David Shichor and Stephen G. Tibbetts (Prospect Heights, IL: Waveland Press, 2002), 170–190.
2. Harvey Wallace, *Victimology: Legal, Psychological, and Social Perspectives* (Boston: Allyn and Bacon, 1998).
3. Ellen Hochstedler Steury and Nancy Frank, *Criminal Court Process* (Minneapolis/St. Paul, MN: West, 1996).
4. Chris McCormick, ed., *Constructing Danger: The Mis/Representation of Crime in the News* (Halifax, NS: Fernwood, 1995).
5. Marvin E. Wolfgang, *Patterns in Criminal Homicide* (Montclair, NJ: Patterson Smith, 1958/1975).
6. Albert K. Cohen, *Delinquent Boys: The Culture of the Gang* (New York: The Free Press, 1955).
7. Frederic G. Reamer, *Criminal Lessons: Case Studies and Commentary on Crime and Justice* (New York: Columbia University Press, 2003). See especially Chapter 5, "Crimes of Revenge and Retribution," 97–119.
8. Malcolm Klein, *The American Street Gang: Its Nature, Prevalence, and Control* (New York: Oxford University Press, 1997).
9. Steven A. Egger, *The Killers Among Us: An Examination of Serial Murder and Its Investigation* (Upper Saddle River, NJ: Prentice Hall, 1998).
10. Alex Schmid and Janny de Graaf, *Violence as Communication: Insurgent Terrorism and the Western News Media* (Newbury Park, CA: Sage, 1982).
11. David Finkelhor and Kersti Yllo, *License to Rape: Sexual Abuse of Wives* (New York: Holt, Rinehart, and Winston, 1985).
12. Dean G. Kilpatrick, David Beatty, and Susan Smith Hawley, "The Rights of Crime Victims: Does Legal Protection Make a Difference?" in *Victims and Victimization: Essential Readings*, eds. David Shichor and Stephen G. Tibbetts (Prospect Heights, IL: Waveland Press, 2000), 287–304.

13. *Uniform Crime Reports,* 1998. Available online at http://www.fbi.gov/ucr/ucr.htm.
14. Colin M. Turnbull, *The Forest People: A Study of the Pygmies of the Congo* (New York: Simon and Schuster, 1961).
15. Terence D. Miethe and Richard C. McCorkle, *Crime Profiles: The Anatomy of Dangerous Persons, Places, and Situations* (Los Angeles: Roxbury, 2001).
16. Robert F. Meier and Gilbert Geis, *Victimless Crime? Prostitution, Drugs, Homosexuality, Abortion* (Los Angeles: Roxbury, 1997).
17. John A. Backstand, Don Gibbons, and Joseph F. Jones, "Who's in Jail? An Examination of the Rabble Hypothesis," *Crime and Delinquency* 38 (1992): 219–229.
18. Joseph Goldstein, "Police Discretion Not to Invoke the Criminal Process," in *The Invisible Justice System: Discretion and the Law,* eds. Burton Atkins and Mark Pogrebin (Cincinnati, OH: Anderson, 1978), 65–81.
19. Paul Brantingham and Patricia Brantingham, *Patterns in Crime* (New York: Macmillan, 1984), 49.
20. William A. Bonger, *Criminality and Economic Conditions* (Boston: Little, Brown, 1916).
21. J. Kitsuse and A. V. Cicourel, "A Note on the Uses of Official Statistics," *Social Problems* 11 (1963): 131–139.
22. Michael D. Maltz, "Crime Statistics: A Historical Perspective," *Crime and Delinquency* 23 (1977): 32–40.
23. Ron Martin, "Crime Stats: Questions Linger After Atlanta Audit," *Atlanta Journal-Constitution,* January 28, 1999.
24. Clayton J. Mosher, Terence D. Miethe, and Dretha M. Phillips, *The Mismeasure of Crime* (Thousand Oaks, CA: Sage, 2002).
25. David Seidman and Michael Couzens, "Getting the Crime Rate Down: Political Pressure and Crime Reporting," *Law and Society Review* 8 (1974): 457–493.
26. Michael Maxfield, "The National Incident-Based Reporting System: Research and Policy Applications," *Journal of Quantitative Criminology* 15 (1999): 119–149.
27. FBI, National Incident-Based Reporting System, http://www.fbi.gov/ucr/faqs.htm.
28. David J. Roberts, *Implementing the National Incident-Based Reporting System: A Project Status Report* (Washington, DC: U.S. Department of Justice, 1977).
29. Mosher, Miethe, and Phillips, *Mismeasure,* 72.
30. Meier and Geis, *Victimless Crime?*
31. Brantingham and Brantingham, *Patterns in Crime,* 76–79.
32. William G. Doerner and Steven Lab, *Victimology,* 2nd ed. (Cincinnati: Anderson, 1998), 28–40.
33. Terence Thornberry and Marvin D. Krohn, "The Self-Report Method for Measuring Delinquency and Crime," in *Criminal Justice 2000: Measurement and Analysis of Crime and Justice* (Washington, DC: U.S. Department of Justice, 2000), 33–83.
34. Gordon Waldo and Theodore G. Chiricos, "Perceived Penal Sanction and Self-Reported Criminality: A Neglected Approach to Deterrence Research," *Social Problems* 19 (1972): 522–540.
35. Gary Kleck, "On the Use of Self-Report Data to Determine the Class Distribution of Criminal and Delinquent Behavior," *American Sociological Review* (1982): 427–433.
36. Thomas Gray and Eric Walsh, *Maryland Youth at Risk: A Study of Drug Use in Juvenile Detainees* (College Park, MD: Center for Substance Abuse Research, 1993).
37. Delbert Elliott, David Huizinga, and Barbara Morse, "Self-Reported Violent Offending: A Descriptive Analysis of Juvenile Violent Offenders and Their Offending Careers," *Journal of Interpersonal Violence* 1 (1986): 472–514.
38. William S. Aquilino, "Interview Mode Effects in Surveys of Drug and Alcohol Use," *Public Opinion Quarterly* 58 (1994): 210–240.
39. David Huizinga and Delbert S. Elliot, "Reassessing the Reliability and Validity of Self-Report Delinquency Measures," *Journal of Quantitative Criminology* 2 (1986): 293–327.
40. Elizabeth Moore and Michael Mills, "The Neglected Victims and Unexplained Costs of White-Collar Crime," in *Readings in White-Collar Crime,* eds. David Shichor, Larry Gaines, and Richard Ball (Prospect Heights, IL: Waveland Press, 2002), 49–59.
41. Gary Potter and Larry Gaines, "Underworlds and Upperworlds: The Convergence of Organized and White Collar Crime," in *Readings in White-Collar Crime,* eds. David Shichor, Larry Gaines, and Richard Ball (Prospect Heights, IL: Waveland Press, 2002), 60–90.
42. Tom Mieczkowski, "Crack Dealing on the Street: Crew System and the Crack House," in *Drugs, Crime, and Justice: Contemporary Readings,* eds. Larry K. Gaines and Peter B. Kraska (Prospect Heights, IL: Waveland Press, 1997), 193–204.
43. Robert McNamara, *The Times-Square Hustler: Male Prostitution in New York City* (Westport, CT: Praeger, 1994).

44. Ronald V. Clarke, *Situational Crime Prevention: Successful Case Studies* (New York: Harrow and Heston, 1992).
45. Paul. J. Brantingham and Patricia L. Brantingham, "Understanding and Controlling Crime and the Fear of Crime: Conflicts and Trade-Offs in Crime Prevention Planning," in *Crime Prevention at a Crossroads,* ed. Steven Lab (Cincinnati, OH: Anderson, 1997), 43–60.
46. Joel Best, *Random Violence: How We Talk About New Crimes and New Victims* (Berkeley: University of California Press, 1999).
47. Best, *Random Violence,* 7–21.
48. Ray Surette, *Media, Crime, and Criminal Justice: Images and Realities,* 2nd ed. (Belmont, CA: West/Wadsworth, 1998).
49. Charles Derber, *The Wilding of America: How Greed and Violence Are Eroding Our Nation's Character* (New York: St. Martin's Press, 1996).
50. Van Gordon Sauter, "No Shelter from Freeway Violence," *Los Angeles Times,* June 26, 1987, V-I.
51. Bill Billiter, "Traffic Dispute Results in Third Freeway Shooting," *Los Angeles Times,* July 20, 1987, I-3.
52. Matthew J. Gilligan, "Stalking the Stalker," *Georgia Law Review,* Vol. 27 (1992), 285–342.
53. Valerie Jenness and Kendal Broad, *Hate Crimes: New Social Movements and the Politics of Violence* (Hawthorne, NY: Aldine de Gruyter, 1997).
54. "Scary News, Soothing Numbers," *U.S. News & World Report,* April 23, 2001.

outline

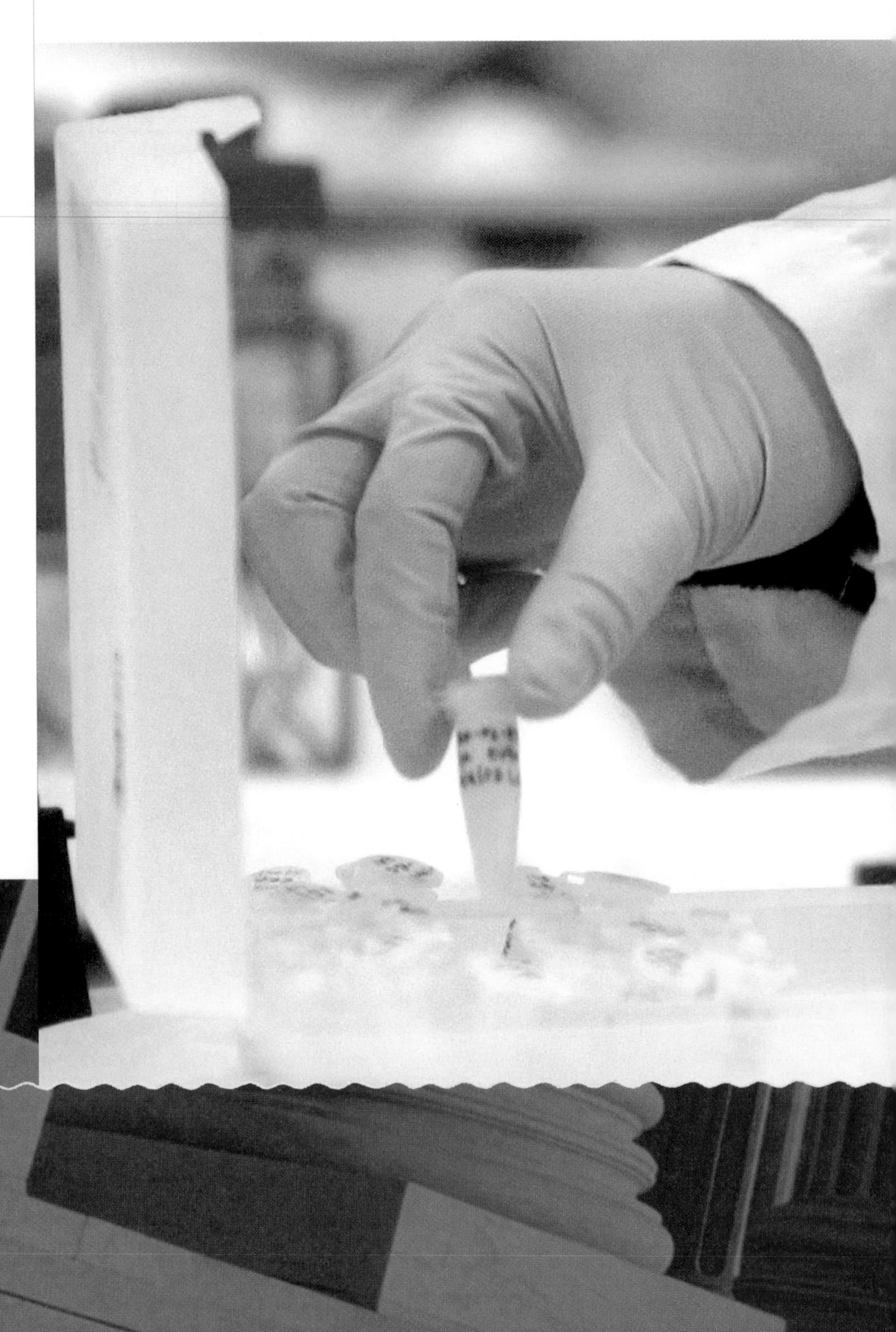

CHAPTER 3

Theories of Crime

Objectives

After reading this chapter, the student should be able to:

1. Discuss the role of demonology in early explanations of crime.
2. Discuss the strengths and weaknesses of the classical school of criminology.
3. Describe Cesare Beccaria's nine principles that should guide our thinking about crime and society.
4. Discuss the role of Charles Darwin in the positivist school of criminology.
5. Discuss early biological theories of crime versus modern biological theories of crime.
6. Describe Sigmund Freud's impact on criminological thought.
7. Discuss the Chicago school of thought.
8. Describe Merton's adaptations to blocked means of achieving cultural goals.
9. Explain Sykes' and Matza's five techniques of neutralization.
10. Discuss the importance of Karl Marx's ideas in criminological theory.

IF THE JOB OF THE CRIMINAL JUSTICE SYSTEM IS TO PREVENT crime and punish or treat the criminal offender, then those vested with these responsibilities should have some idea about why people commit crimes. And they do. We all do. Whether one is a law enforcement officer, a judge, a prison warden, or a citizen, we all have ideas and beliefs about why people rob, rape, embezzle, and kill. However, these ideas and beliefs may not be well formulated, and may be the result of our parents' teachings, media influence, or biases developed from our personal experiences. Still, we not only believe in these ideas about the causes of crime, we also act on them. We lock our doors at night, warn our children about associating with certain friends, wage campaigns against drug and alcohol abuse, and condone the use of capital punishment, all based on our personal ideas about the causes of crime. Whether we realize it or not, each of us, to some extent, uses theories of crime in our everyday life.

This chapter will help us understand the variety and complexity of criminological theories. By looking at the explanations of crime that have guided the actions of people and the criminal justice system, we can better understand why and how crime remains a significant social problem and continues to demand serious study in the 21st century. By understanding the history of how our ideas about the causes of crime have evolved, we can learn to appreciate the fascinating complexity of the law, the criminal justice system, and other methods of social control.

Demonology

The earliest explanations for deviant behavior attributed crime to supernatural forces. In an age in which religion was a powerful force for social control, the actions of wayward people were blamed on the influence of the devil. Powerful rulers invoked the church to legitimize their control of wealth and power, and the church answered by claiming that deviant behavior was not only unlawful, but also sinful. Minor transgressions were therefore violations of God's rules, as well as punishable by the law. The church and state worked together to control the populace.[1]

trial by ordeal
An ancient custom found in many cultures in which the accused was required to perform a test to prove guilt or innocence. The outcome of the test was considered to be decided by a divine authority.

One of the methods used to determine guilt or innocence in earlier times was **trial by ordeal**, in which it was believed that God would intervene and save the innocent. Representatives of the law might place heavy stones on suspects or throw them into deep water based on the idea that God would let only a guilty person die under such circumstances. People who were crushed by tons of stone or disappeared into the swirling waters of a river were "proven" guilty by their inability to summon aid from God.[2]

Trial by ordeal was one method of investigation. It depended on the supernatural to provide evidence of guilt or innocence.
Courtesy of CORBIS-NY.

Sometimes, this supernatural explanation created an unwinnable situation. During the Salem witch trials, women were subjected to the dunking pond and held under water during trials of ordeal. Those who did not drown were considered witches who had invoked the aid of Satan and were killed anyway. Those who drowned were considered to have been innocent.[3]

Religion is a powerful social institution. Often, it can motivate people to commit crimes because of their perceptions of what God or Satan command them to do.
Courtesy of CORBIS-NY.

It is not uncommon even today to hear people claim that either God or the devil instructed them to commit crimes. Often, we think that those who use such an argument are insane. For example, in Texas in 2002 Andrea Yates said she drowned her five small children because she believed it was the only way to save them from going to hell. Although we are shocked by her crime, we also consider her to be a victim of mental illness, but this was not the finding of her jury.[4] Yet, others who "kill for God" are not viewed with the same compassion. Those who have assassinated abortion providers are viewed as rational and responsible people who possess the ability to control their behavior but choose to kill as a political and moral statement. Likewise, many acts of terrorism are attributed to religious or supernatural explanations, but the secular courts deem these to be acts of premeditated homicide.[5]

Some people may still use supernatural explanations for crime, but the criminal justice system has moved on to other theories that lend themselves to empirical testing (see Table 3.1). It is impossible for the court to determine whether God or the devil instructed someone to commit a crime, and in a secular society such as the United States, such religious explanations cannot be considered by the criminal justice system.

Classical School of Criminology

Unlike early theories of crime that used supernatural forces to explain criminal behavior, the **classical school of criminology** argues that people freely choose to engage in crime. The principle of "free will" allows us to consider various courses of action and then select the one we believe is most desirable. If we structure the criminal justice system in such a way that penalties for committing crimes are sufficiently severe, swift, and certain, then people will rationally choose not to commit crimes.[6]

classical school of criminology
A set of criminological theories that uses the idea of free will to explain criminal behavior.

The classical school of criminology is embodied primarily in the works of Cesare Beccaria and Jeremy Bentham. Both of these men were concerned more with reforming the criminal justice system than in finding the causes of crime. The philosophy behind the classical school had implications for how the criminal justice system was organized and how it responded to crime. In a time when many viewed criminal justice as arbitrary, cruel, and inefficient, leading scholars such as Beccaria and Bentham sought to inject rationality and humaneness.[7]

Cesare Beccaria (1738–1794)

Beccaria's ideas about reforming the way society dealt with crime are found in his seminal work *On Crimes and Punishment,* published in 1764.[8] In this work he presented

TABLE 3.1

Criminological Theories

Name/Class of Theory	Theory	Practice	Theorists
Classical School			
Nine Principles	Free will and punishment based on humane principles.	Deterrence through social contract, public education, and legal clarity and equity. Punish proportionally. Eliminate systemic corruption.	Beccaria
Utilitarianism	People are guided by desire for pleasure and aversion to pain.		Bentham
Positivist School			
Biological Theories			
Phrenology	Criminality can be determined by the shape of the skull.	Alter, isolate, sterilize, or eliminate the body. Brain surgery, execution, imprisonment, medication. Also, improvements in diet and health care. These theories have fallen out of favor.	Gall
Atavisms	Criminals have measurable physical differences from non-criminals.		Lombroso
Body measurements			Hooton
Somatotyping			Sheldon, Kretschmer
XYY syndrome	Males born with an extra chromosome tend toward criminal behavior.		
Biochemistry	Hormones, brain structure, and/or brain chemistry may cause criminal behavior.	Medication, diet changes.	
Psychological Theories			
Psychoanalytic theory	Focused on unconscious forces and drives.	Counseling.	Freud
Behaviorism (operant conditioning)	Behavior is determined by rewards and punishments.	Reward reform, punish continued offensive behavior.	Skinner
Sociological Theories			
Chicago school	Social disorganization causes criminal behavior in individuals.	Social reform, ensure equal access to societal incentives and norms.	Shaw, McKay
Differential association theory	Crime is learned.		Sutherland
Strain theory	Unequal access to societal norms.		Merton
Social control theory	Questions why people do not commit crimes.		Hirschi
Neutralization theory	Offenders "neutralize" blame and feelings of shame.		Sykes, Matza
Labeling theory	Deviants conform to the "deviant" label.		Lemert
Critical Sociological Theories			
Marxism	Those in power make laws to favor themselves.	Social reform, providing minority groups access to more power and decision making, recognizing oppression, allocating group-specific research.	Marx
Feminism (gender)	Crime study and the criminal justice system is male dominated, and male oriented.		
Critical race theory	The criminal justice system targets and oppresses people of color.		

Cesare Beccaria's ideas about crime and punishment have provided inspiration for the values of the criminal justice system.
Courtesy of Corbis/Bettmann.

Figure 3.1 Cesare Beccaria's Nine Principles from *On Crimes and Punishment*

1. Social action should be based on the utilitarian principle of "the greatest happiness for the greatest number."
2. The sovereign's right to punish is founded on the necessity of defending public liberty, and the punishments are to be just in proportion, and liberty is to be preserved by the sovereign and considered sacred and valuable.
3. Punishments are set by the legislator by the making of penal laws, and the magistrate cannot increase the punishment already determined by law.
4. Obscurity in the law is evil. Crimes will be less frequent if the code of laws is more universally read and understood. A scale of crimes should be formed where the most serious consist of those which immediately tend to the dissolution of society, and the last of the smallest possible injustice done to a private member of that society.
5. The intent of punishment is to prevent the criminal from doing future injury to society and to prevent others from committing similar offenses. Punishments and the mode of inflicting them ought to make the strongest and most long lasting impressions on the minds of others while inflicting the least torment to the body of the criminal.
6. Secret accusations are a manifest abuse.
7. Torture during the criminal trial is a cruelty consecrated by custom in most nations and should be abolished. No man is judged a criminal until he has been found guilty and is entitled to the public protection. Torture is a flawed tool of investigation where the strong go free and the feeble are convicted.
8. There are advantages to immediate punishment. The smaller the interval of time between the punishment and the crime, the stronger and more lasting will be the association.
9. Crimes are more effectually prevented by certainty of punishment than by the severity. Furthermore, if punishments are very severe, men are likely to commit further crimes to avoid punishment.

Source: Cesare Beccaria, *On Crimes and Punishment* (Indianapolis: Bobbs-Merrill, 1963).

nine principles that should guide our thinking about crime and the way society responds to lawbreakers (see Figure 3.1). These and other ideas formulated by Beccaria have found their way into many of the principles that guide our criminal justice system today. Beccaria suggested that punishment should only be stringent enough to deter crime. He also advocated the abolition of physical punishment and the death penalty. The presumption of innocence, the right to confront accusers, the right to a speedy trial, and the right not to be required to testify against oneself are all traceable to this important thinker.[9]

Jeremy Bentham (1748–1832)

utilitarianism
A theory associated with Jeremy Bentham that states that people will choose not to commit crime when the pain of punishment outweighs the benefit derived from the crime.

Jeremy Bentham is the other major thinker associated with the classical school of criminology. According to Bentham's **utilitarianism** theory, people are guided by their desire for pleasure and aversion to pain. As he said so elegantly:

> *Nature has placed mankind under the governance of two sovereign masters,* pain *and* pleasure. *It is for them alone to point out what we ought to do, as well as to determine what we shall do. On the one hand the standard of right and wrong, on the other the chain of causes and effects, are fastened to their throne. They govern us in all we do, in all we say, in all we think: every effort we can make to throw off our subjection, will serve but to demonstrate and confirm it.*[10]

To understand the actions of people, we need only understand how they comprehend pleasure and pain. According to Bentham, we perform a mental calculus when we consider our behavior. We attempt to weigh the pleasures we would accrue from committing a crime and the pain that would result if we were caught. In considering pleasure or pain, we consider the following:

1. Intensity
2. Duration
3. Certainty or uncertainty
4. Propinquity or remoteness

It is in this consideration of the balance between pleasure and pain that Bentham believed society could affect criminal behavior.[11] Crime can be prevented by structuring the criminal justice system and the law in such a way that potential offenders can calculate that the pains of crime outweigh the pleasures. Bentham's idea is why mod-

Jeremy Bentham's ideas are part of the reasoning behind the classical school of criminology. He believed criminals do a mental calculus weighing the benefits of committing a crime against the costs of getting caught. Courtesy of Corbis/Bettmann.

ern sentencing patterns have a high degree of proportionality. Murder can get the offender the death penalty, but stealing a car will not. When Bentham lived, there were over 200 offenses for which one could be put to death. His work focused on reforming the system by introducing some logic into how, and how much, punishment was meted out.[12]

Bentham's moral calculus is also apparent in the attempt to increase the certainty of punishment. More police officers, better crime-fighting technology, more efficient court systems, and other reforms are aimed at influencing the calculations made by potential offenders. By making prison sentences of longer duration (such as life imprisonment), certain types of severe crime are discouraged. However, some people do not make rational decisions when calculating the rewards versus the risks of crime. Why do offenders rob convenience stores when the potential for reward is so small? Why not rob a bank where there is so much more to gain? Bentham would answer that even though the potential gain is greater in robbing the bank, the potential pain is also greater when one factors in the uncertainty of success. Banks are more carefully guarded and have better technology (vaults, multiple cameras) than convenience stores. Additionally, the uncertainty of robbing a bank is increased when one considers that this constitutes a federal crime and would involve such federal agencies as the FBI.

Neither Bentham nor Beccaria was concerned with why people committed crimes. Motivation was assumed. Particularly for Bentham, criminals acted to increase pleasure. The work of these two theorists is relevant to the legal and administrative functions of the criminal justice system. Later, when we deal with some of the sociological and economic theories of crime, such as **rational choice theory**, we will see how the classical school provides insights.

rational choice theory
A theory that states that people choose criminal behavior consciously. The theory also states that people may choose to commit crime upon realizing that the crime's benefits probably outweigh the consequences of breaking the law.

Positivist School of Criminology

One of the reasons the classical school lost its influence is that it assumed motivation and treated all offenders equally. But not all offenders are equal. They commit crimes for different reasons and are not affected by punishment in the same way. The idea that free will determines when and how people commit crimes fails to appreciate the complex nature of crime and the vast differences among people. Although some of the neoclassical theories attempted to measure free will in a scientific way, one of the weaknesses of the classical theories was that, like demonology, they really were not subject to empirical analysis. There was no way to determine how one exercised free will in deciding to commit a crime.[13]

The **positivist school of criminology** is a natural outgrowth of the rise of the scientific method, which began to develop in the 19th century. By applying the emerging scientific disciplines that were building on the work of Charles Darwin, criminologists shifted the focus of criminology away from the law and the criminal justice system and toward the offender.[14] The question now became: What factors influence people to commit crimes? If Darwin is correct in his theory of natural selection, then what biological mechanisms cause people to commit crimes? Even more interesting to later theorists was the possibility that social behavior was simply part of a biological imperative that could explain human interactions.[15] That is, do people behave in groups according to some survival-of-the-fittest urge that is deeply embedded in their genes? Can science help us to understand the patterns of crime that affect society? The positivist school offers us a two-century adventure as we seek to understand criminal behavior.

positivist school of criminology
A set of criminological theories that uses scientific techniques to study crime and criminals.

Biological Theories of Crime

We are all familiar with how our moods and behaviors are influenced by how we feel. When we are tired, we get cranky. When we go to the supermarket hungry, we come

Charles Whitman, The Texas Tower Sniper

Courtesy of AP Wide World Photos.

On the morning of August 1, 1966, in Austin, Texas, Charles Whitman killed his mother, Elizabeth, and his wife, Kathleen. Then he headed up to the observation deck of the University of Texas Tower with enough guns, ammunition, and food and water to last several days. From there, he killed 14 people and wounded 31 more. Police officers eventually managed to climb the tower and shoot and kill Whitman.

After the attack, many of Whitman's friends were shocked, describing him in interviews as "normal" and "average." However, Whitman had suffered a long series of troubled relationships and failed occupations, and others who knew Whitman said he had confided to them his pent-up rage and frustration. Some said Whitman had described to them how the tower would make a good point from which to shoot people. In a March 1966 report, a Texas University staff psychiatrist to whom Whitman was referred noted that Whitman was very specific about his tower fantasy. Still, Whitman did not snap suddenly. He had a troubled relationship with his father, whom he described as demanding and physically abusive to both himself and his mother. Although Whitman was honorably discharged from the marines in 1964, he had been court-martialed in 1963 for acting as a loan shark to his fellow soldiers. He also wrote extensively about his crimes before he committed them and seemed to have no plans to survive his shooting spree. He wrote instructions for the care of his dog, for his insurance company to cover the bad checks he used to buy his guns, and for any remaining money to be donated to a mental health foundation. He described having intense headaches and requested an autopsy to check for physical causes of his homicidal urges.

The exact cause of Whitman's rampage continues to inspire debate. Although the most obvious clues lie in his troubled personal life, some experts believe that the small tumor found in his brain may have played a role. The tumor was found in a region that is thought to be responsible for emotion, but opinion is split on whether it could have influenced his behavior in such a manner.

Was Whitman insane? Although his actions were thoroughly premeditated, they were certainly affected by difficult personal circumstances and possibly by physical illness. Charles Whitman was not a happy, successful person who woke up one morning and decided to commit mass murder. Whitman himself knew that something was wrong, but he did not know what or why. In one of his final notes, he wrote, "I don't really understand myself these days."

QUESTIONS

1. Was Whitman responsible for his actions?
2. Does the possibility that Whitman's brain tumor made him commit murder excuse his actions? Would his personal problems provide the same excuse?
3. If Whitman had lived and been found guilty at trial, what should his sentence have been?

Source: Mark Lisheron, "A Killer's Conscience," *Austin American-Statesman,* December 9, 2001, http://www.austin360.com/aas/specialreports/whitman/.

home with cookies and ice cream. When we have the flu, we neglect our homework. To argue that the body affects behavior is easy. But does the body influence criminal behavior? Additionally, can science shed light on how this might work? Would it not be useful if we could examine the body for clues of a propensity toward criminality? Scientists have long attempted to find such a relationship. Here we will briefly review some of the better known theories that sought to cast light on heredity, hormones, blood chemistry, and environmental problems such as alcohol and drug use.

Phrenology was accepted as reliable science. It was believed that a trained phrenologist could discern a person's character from bumps on the skull.

Courtesy of CORBIS-NY.

PHRENOLOGY Franz Joseph Gall (1758–1828) is considered to have invented the "science" of phrenology. Phrenology was a technique in which a practitioner assessed a subject's personality by measuring the size and pattern of the bumps on a subject's skull. The term *science* is used advisedly because phrenology is not considered a real science. However, it was once all the rage in medical science, and like many forms of quackery, had just enough scientific trappings to sound plausible. Physicians knew that certain parts of the brain were responsible for certain conditions, problems, and activities. For example, they noticed that the location of a head injury could have much to do with how the patient acted or recovered. Phrenologists, however, theorized that the shape, size, and features of the brain exerted pressures on the skull, which showed up as bumps that could be deciphered by someone with the proper training.[16]

Phrenology was the beginning of a long and fascinating history of scientists' attempts to understand human behavior by looking for physical markers in or on the body. Phrenologists theorized that proclivities for things such as destructiveness, secretiveness, and philoprogenitiveness (love of offspring) could be uncovered by massaging the skull. Although some relationship may exist between the body and behavior, phrenology did not prove to be a realistic method with which to assess this connection. It eventually fell into disrepute because of the political and religious differences among some of the major practitioners and because it was hijacked by outright charlatans. It should be noted, however, that it is still possible, even today, to find adherents of this technique.[17]

ATAVISMS Cesare Lombroso (1835–1909), an Italian physician, believed that criminals were physically different from the rest of the population. Lombroso looked closely at the anatomical features of people, measuring very precisely several points on the face and body. Lombroso's theory claimed that "born" criminals were not as physically evolved as people who obeyed the law, and he compared the born criminal to what he called "savage people."[18] The physical differences of the born criminal were called **atavisms**. These included low cranial capacity, retreating forehead, highly developed frontal sinuses, greater pigmentation of the skin, tufted and crispy hair, and large ears. Other atavisms included dullness of the sense of touch, great agility, relative insensitivity to pain, ability to recover quickly from wounds, precocity for sexual pleasures, laziness, absence of remorse, and impulsiveness. Clearly, it is easier to observe physical characteristics than behavioral characteristics, but regardless of the type of characteristic,

atavism
The appearance in a person of features thought to be from earlier stages of human evolution. Popularized by Cesare Lombroso.

The Skull of the Marquis de Sade

A few years after the death of Donatien Alphonse François, marquis de Sade, the cemetery in which he was buried was excavated and de Sade's body exhumed. A doctor who had been de Sade's physician at Charenton, the asylum that was de Sade's final prison, asked to examine his skull. The doctor, a "fervent adept" of phrenology, had this to say about the infamous libertine and author whose novels had been banned for obscenity:

> *Excellent development of the top of the cranium (theosophy, benevolence); no exaggerated prominences behind and above the ears (no combativeness . . .); cerebellum of moderate size, no exaggerated distance from one mastoid process to the other (no excess in physical love). In a word, if nothing made me suspect Sade . . . of being the author of "Justine" and "Juliette," the inspection of his head would have caused me to absolve him of responsibility for such works. His skull was in all respects similar to that of a Father of the Church.*

Source: L. J. Ramon, "Notes sur M. de Sade," in D.A.F. de Sade, "Oeuvres complètes" (Paris: Cercle du livre précieux, 1966–1967), vol. 15, p. 43. Quoted in Maurice Lever, *Sade*, trans. Arthur Goldhammer (New York: Farrar, Straus and Giroux, 1993), 566–567.

all of Lombroso's atavisms were judged against the standard of what he considered the average law-abiding 19th-century Italian to look like.

Lombroso's work is widely acknowledged because it was one of the first attempts to use the scientific method to examine criminals. Although his science was greatly flawed and riddled with many of the prejudices and biases of his society, he laid the groundwork for using science to find differences between criminals and the general population.[19] In some ways, variations of his work go on today as we deconstruct the human genetic code and gain a better understanding of how brain chemistry works. However, the tools used by Lombroso were so crude and so lacking in the requirements of good scientific method that we are amused today to see what passed for cutting-edge science over a century ago. Lombroso's theory was dealt a major setback in 1913 when Sir Charles Goring published the results of a study of 3,000 English convicts who were compared with a large group of noncriminals. Goring did not find significant differences between the groups in terms of physical measurements or the presence of Lombroso's atavisms. Goring concluded that there was no such thing as a criminal type, putting an end to the argument that criminals are physically different from noncriminals.[20]

PHYSIOLOGY Earnest Hooton (1887–1954) was a Harvard anthropologist who studied the relationship between physiology and crime. He used many of the same concepts as Lombroso in studying 14,000 male inmates and a control group of over 3,000 civilians. Hooton claimed to have found differences between criminals and noncriminals across a wide range of physical features. His findings were criticized by other scholars who objected to his sampling technique, his labeling of inmates as being certain types of criminals, and his racially prejudiced conclusions.[21]

Hooton believed that incarcerated criminals were representative of all criminals. Furthermore, he placed labels on the inmates, such as "murderer" or "robber," based on the crime for which they were incarcerated. Further examination revealed that many of these inmates had prior records for different types of crimes and therefore could have had different labels applied to them. Hooton's claimed relationship between physical characteristics and crime could not stand up under such nebulous labeling. An additional problem concerned the control group of ordinary citizens used by Hooton. A large number of

FOCUS ON ETHICS

Physical Graffiti

Your roommate is a real trip. Like a first-year medical student who thinks she has the symptoms of each disease that she studies, your roommate has started to judge all your friends by the physical characteristics she has learned in her introductory criminological theory class. First, she contends that your boyfriend has so many atavisms that he is a throwback to an early type of an arrested-evolved man. According to her, he has beady eyes, a sloping forehead, an insincere mouth, and deviant ears. Although she has never read the writings of Cesare Lombroso, she is convinced that she can judge a person's character by their physical appearance. For instance, your little brother is tall and skinny. According to your roommate's interpretation of Sheldon's body types, he is an ectomorph and likely to become a check forger or counterfeiter. As a result, she treats your brother poorly because of his build. At a party you found your roommate running her hands through the hair of each young man who asked her to dance. You found out later that she thought she was practicing phrenology. You would not be surprised to find her asking for tissue samples from her dates to check for extra Y chromosomes.

After you confront her about the shallowness of her judgments of others and suggest there is more to a person's character than can be revealed by his or her physical makeup, she starts reading pop psychology books and decides she can psychoanalyze everyone. She studies astrology, Chinese placemats, enneagrams, archetypes, Tarot cards, and the I Ching. She understands none of them and misuses each as she tries to understand people's personalities and motivations.

Here is the problem. Your roommate is in love with the idea of theory. She is looking for a system or explanation that will help her appreciate how people develop character. She adopts every psychological and criminological theory she can lay her hands on, and after they fail to explain everything about everyone, she discards them and moves on to the next theory. She has no tolerance for ambiguity, partial truths, or contrary facts. Her ideal theory must be mutually exclusive and exhaustive, and as each theory fails to neatly order her world, she goes off in search of another. You want to explain to her that there is no perfect theory and that searching for one is not only useless, but also counterproductive.

WHAT DO YOU DO?

1. Tell her that theories are only tools to aid in understanding.
2. Tell her that theories are social constructions and not objective realities.
3. Tell her that instead of demanding one theory, she would be better off trying to integrate several theories.
4. Get a new roommate.

them were firefighters or militiamen, occupations that required certain physical qualifications, and therefore were not representative of the general population.

One example of Hooton's cultural prejudices was that, like Lombroso, he believed that tattooing was the mark of an inferior person. Cultural prejudices against tattooing are now waning as we see a wide variety of people using tattooing as a means of self-expression. Also, tattooing is an important and respected part of many cultures throughout the world. So, the argument can be made today that tattooing is not a sign of degeneracy or criminality, but simply a fashion statement or cultural rite of passage.

somatotyping The use of body types and physical characteristics to classify human personalities.

SOMATOTYPING Another interesting idea that links behavior to physical differences is the concept of body-typing. Developed first by the German psychiatrist Ernst Kretschmer, it was refined and popularized in the United States by William Sheldon (1898–1977). Sheldon used the term ***somatotyping*** to describe his three variations of the body: endomorph, mesomorph, and ectomorph. According to Sheldon, everyone's body

TABLE 3.2

Sheldon's Components of Somatotyping

Body Type	Temperament
Endomorph: Soft, round, pudgy, possibly obese	Viscerotonic: Relaxed, sociable, loves physical comfort, food, affection, approval, and the company of others.
Mesomorph: Muscular, strong	Somatic: Active, assertive, aggressive, noisy. Loves power and to dominate others.
Ectomorph: Thin, fragile	Cerebrotonic: Private, restrained, inhibited, and hyperattentive.

Source: William H. Sheldon, *Varieties of Delinquent Youth: An Introduction to Constitutional Psychiatry* (New York: Harper and Row, 1949).

has these components in some ratio, and they can be measured on a seven-point scale. For example, someone scoring a 1-7-1 would be considered an extreme mesomorph. Although it is easy to see how people could be given scores for how their bodies look, Sheldon claimed that body type was an indication of one's constitutional psychology. The argument that structure equaled behavior was a simple claim dressed up in the jargon of somatotyping science. Sheldon's characterization of the extreme types can be seen in Table 3.2.

Most interesting about Sheldon's work are the policy implications he advocated. If discerning behavior from body type is really possible, then why not control who can and cannot reproduce? If we could simply prevent "inferior" types from reproducing and encourage good stock, we could breed a better class of society. After all, selective breeding had produced beautiful roses and fast racehorses, so why not employ this method to improve society? Luckily, other criminologists, legislators, and the general public did not take Sheldon's ideas seriously. His terminology of endomorph, mesomorph, and ectomorph has remained in the literature, but for the most part, no one believes that body type determines behavior.[22]

XYY SYNDROME In the search for physical differences between criminals and the rest of the population, science has gotten a lot better at using sophisticated techniques. From the rather gross methods of atavisms and bumps on the head, researchers have moved to examining chromosomes.

Each of us is born with two sex chromosomes. Typically, females have two X chromosomes and males have an X and a Y chromosome. A small percentage of males are born with an extra Y chromosome. About one in 1,000 to 2,000 males is an XYY. Typically, these men are not much physically different from XY males besides being a bit above average in height and sometimes having severe acne. Some studies claim that XYY males tend to possess a slightly lower IQ, but this has been disputed. The theoretical link between **XYY syndrome** and crime is attributed to several studies that found that males with XYY syndrome were overrepresented in the populations of correctional institutions. But what could be the theoretical basis for this observation? What is it about the extra Y chromosome that could lead one to commit crimes? At first it was thought that the extra Y chromosome was responsible for more testosterone in the body, which led to more aggression. However, it has been conclusively shown that XYY males are actually somewhat less aggressive than XY males. Lacking a physical explanation for why the

XYY syndrome
A condition in which a male is born with an extra Y chromosome. Such males tend to be tall, have difficulties with language, and have relatively low IQs. The condition was once thought to cause criminal behavior.

studies found more XYY males in prison populations, criminologists have suggested three social explanations:

1. Because XYY offenders are tall, it could be that the criminal justice system practitioners arrest, convict, and sentence them to prison at a greater rate because they look more menacing.
2. The institutionalization rate of XYY males simply mirrors their percentage in lower-income populations.
3. Because they tend to be slightly less intelligent than the normal population, they are less able to compete in legitimate enterprises and turn to crime more often.

The extra-Y-chromosome theory can account for only a small proportion of crime because most crime is still committed by XY males.[23] The interesting policy implication of the XYY controversy is the idea that it could be predicted which men would be crime prone by looking at their chromosomes. As with all the biological theories of crime, the policy implications suggest that by identifying the crime prone early, we can intervene in the life of the individual and prevent crime. The potential for abuse here is significant.

BIOCHEMISTRY As science allows us to better understand the relationship between the body and behavior, researchers are examining three areas to determine whether some people commit crimes for physical reasons. Hormones, brain structure, and brain chemistry all appear to affect behavior. However, isolating an actual, identifiable physical influence on crime is problematic. At best, we hope to understand the interaction physical factors may have with social and psychological influences and pressures related to criminal behavior.[24]

- **Hormones** The body secretes hormones for a number of reasons, but one of the by-products of this activity appears to be alterations in mood and behavior. For instance, a relationship exists between the release of testosterone in males and aggression. The question that scientists and criminologists ask, however, is which one comes first? Because testosterone levels respond to competitive challenges, the relationship between testosterone and aggression may be a by-product rather than the cause of aggression. That is, as men engage in activities such as sports or crime, the level of testosterone rises as a result of the activity instead of causing

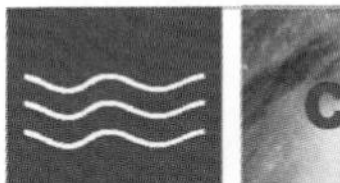

CROSSCURRENTS

The Jukes and Richard Dugdale

In 1877 social investigator Richard Dugdale published *The Jukes: A Study in Crime, Pauperism, and Heredity,* a famous study of an Ulster County, New York, family, a large number of whom were social deviants and criminals.

Dugdale, who developed his theories and gathered data while inspecting prisons for the Prison Association of New York, followed seven generations of a family whose name he changed to "Jukes." Starting with Dutch forebear "Max," who was born in the 1700s, Dugdale traced the line descended from Max's legitimate and illegitimate children. The study made quite a splash. Although Dugdale appeared to credit the Jukes' "degeneracy" as much to nurture as nature, the public seized on what seemed to be the hereditary source of the Jukes' criminality. As a result, Dugdale's study was cited for decades afterward, and still is today by some sources, as proof of how "bad genes make bad people." This interpretation of Dugdale's work was bolstered in 1915 by Arthur Estabrook, who worked for the Eugenics Record Office, a private research organization connected to the then-booming organized eugenics movement. In his study, "The Jukes," Estabrook, not surprisingly, described hundreds more "bad" Jukes.

Sources: Henry Goddard, *The Kallikak Family: A Study in the Heredity of Feeble-Mindedness* (1912), http://psychclassics.yorku.ca/Goddard/index.htm. Richard Louis Dugdale, *The Jukes: A Study in Crime, Pauperism, Disease, and Heredity,* 3rd ed. (New York: G.P. Putnam's Sons, 1985).

it. Hormones affect women's behavior, as well. A popular conception is that premenstrual syndrome (PMS) causes women to act differently than they normally would.[25] Because of a few high-profile cases in which women have used PMS as a criminal defense, the woman suffering from PMS has become a stereotype of a person who is depressed, hysterical, and out of control. A great deal of anecdotal evidence exists that PMS can affect a woman's behavior, but its relationship to crime remains uncertain at best. Although PMS has been used in some cases as a mitigating circumstance to reduce a woman's sentence, studies do not give us a clear and convincing picture of how this natural condition could cause or influence women to commit crime.

- **Brain structure and brain chemistry.** Since the heyday of phrenology, researchers have learned a great deal about the brain. To be sure, the brain is a complex organ that we still know relatively little about. Especially humbling is the sparse knowledge about the links between the brain and behaviors such as crime. However, there are tools to examine how different parts of the brain are responsible for different activities. Techniques such as computed tomography (CT scans), magnetic resonance imaging (MRI), position emission tomography (PET scans), and single photon emission computed tomography (SPECT scans) allow researchers to observe how the brain is influenced by injury. Although there is no consensus about exactly how the brain influences behavior, we must remember that this research is still in its early stages. Some critics would liken this research to phrenology, albeit with more sophisticated tools, but some evidence suggests that it may eventually prove to be fruitful. Brain chemistry is another area in which researchers are looking for causes of crime. Such hormones as norepinephrine, dopamine, and serotonin are of particular interest to criminologists because they regulate behaviors such as impulsivity, feelings of pleasure, and response to danger. Clearly, drug therapy is both promising and subject to abuse. Given the way people use recreational drugs, it is important to pursue research on the relationship between crime and brain chemistry.[26]

All of these biological theories of crime demonstrate a continuing and restless search for the physical reasons that people commit crimes. Although some of the older theories may be amusing, we should bear in mind that they once represented the conventional

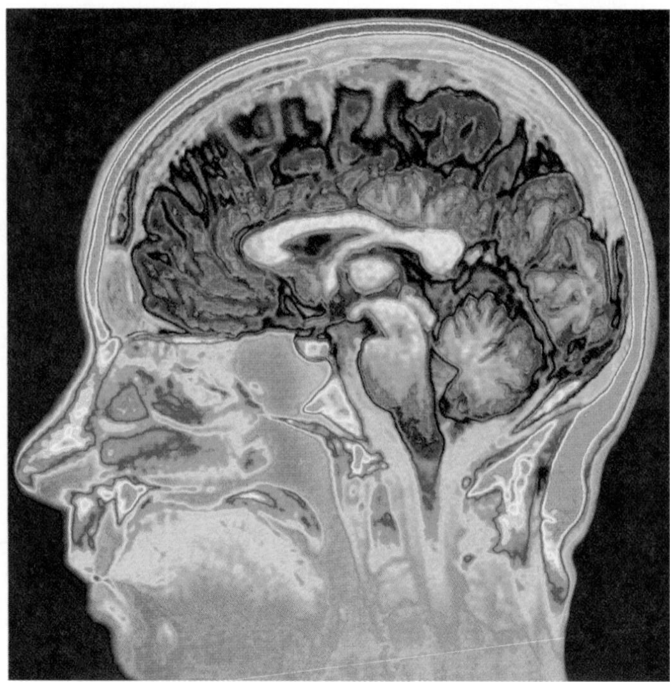

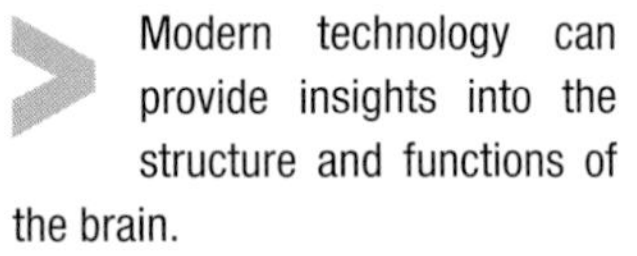

Modern technology can provide insights into the structure and functions of the brain.

Courtesy of CORBIS-NY.

CASE IN POINT

Robinson v. California

The Case

Robinson v. California 370 U.S. 660, 82 S.Ct. 1417 (1962)

The Point

The Supreme Court holds that drug addiction is a disease, not a crime.

A Los Angeles police officer arrested Lawrence Robinson upon noticing on Robinson's arm what appeared to be scars and scabs from narcotics use. At his trial four months later, Robinson was convicted under a California law that made it a misdemeanor to be addicted to narcotics. At the trial, the examining officer said Robinson was neither under the influence of narcotics nor suffering withdrawal symptoms at the time of arrest, and that the scabs on Robinson's arms had been several days old.

On appeal, the Supreme Court held that narcotics addiction is a disease and that people afflicted with disease should not be treated as criminals and imprisoned. Therefore, imprisoning a narcotics addict "inflicts a cruel and unusual punishment in violation of the Fourteenth Amendment." The California law was declared unconstitutional, and Robinson's conviction was reversed.

wisdom of society. These theories often had direct or indirect effects on who was arrested and convicted of crimes. Furthermore, these theories dictated the kinds of punishments or treatments that were applied. Although many criminologists and criminal justice practitioners find biological theories problematic, they may well ultimately provide us with not only a clear understanding of the motivations and causes of criminal behavior, but also effective methods of intervention. However, we should be aware that, as in the past, some severe ethical issues will have to be considered.

Psychological Theories of Crime

Although it is inadvisable, and maybe impossible, to separate the influence of the body and brain on behavior, criminologists make a distinction between biological and psychological theories. With this in mind, we now turn to the psychological explanations of criminal behavior. Sometimes when people commit irrational acts of crime and violence, we think of them as crazy. But what does "crazy" mean? The argument can easily loop back on itself. Crazy people do crazy things, so anyone whose behavior we cannot understand must be crazy. This line of thinking is a dead end in the understanding of criminal behavior. Therefore, notions such as "crazy" have been discarded in favor of more logical explanations of criminal behavior.

PSYCHOANALYTIC THEORY Many scholars contend that all modern psychology began with Sigmund Freud (1859–1939). If a school of psychology is not descended from Freud's psychoanalytic theory, then it was developed in opposition to Freud's ideas. Freud's major contribution was to take the study of the mind from the medical paradigm of considering brain structure and chemistry and to develop a psychological paradigm that focuses on unconscious forces and drives. Freud was trained as a physician and neurologist, so this was a major break with his training and profession. He opened up entirely new ways to think about behavior, and although he is held in some disrepute now for many of his ideas, his terminology has worked its way into our language and, to a large extent, how we think about the mind as opposed to the brain.

Freud contended that the personality is composed of three parts: the id, ego, and superego.

- **Id** The id is like a small child. It comprises our instincts and unsocialized biological drives. It pursues what it wants and has to be controlled, or we cannot operate in society. At an early age, the ego and superego start controlling the id.

Sigmund Freud is considered the father of psychology. His ideas about personality and behavior have influenced how we have come to think about criminal behavior.
Courtesy of National Library of Medicine.

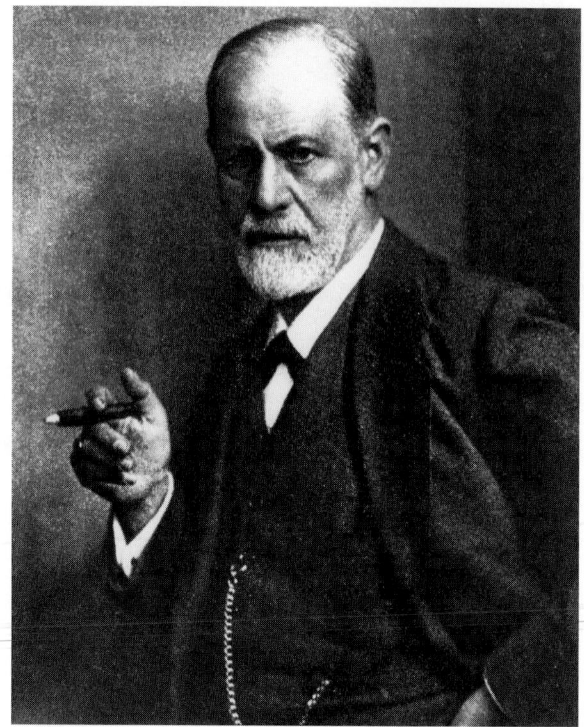

- **Ego** The ego is the part of the personality that learns to solve problems and acts as a brake on the id. The ego deals with reality and analyzes situations so that the id does not cause trouble.
- **Superego** The superego is the conscience. It can be likened to that little voice that tells us what is right and what is wrong.[27]

According to Freud, healthy people have the proper balance of these three components. (For example, an underdeveloped ego will let the id run amok and engage in all kinds of mischief in fulfilling its desires.) This coverage of Freud's ideas is greatly oversimplified. A true understanding of the many facets and nuances of his theory can take years of study.[28]

behaviorism The assessment of human psychology via the examination of objectively observable and quantifiable actions, as opposed to subjective mental states.

operant conditioning The alteration of behavior by giving a subject rewards or punishments for a specified action until the subject associates the action with pleasure or pain.

BEHAVIORISM B. F. Skinner (1904–1990) was an interesting man who theorized that behavior is determined by rewards and punishments. His theory, known as **behaviorism**, is based on the psychological principle of **operant conditioning**. That is, behavior is more likely to occur when it is rewarded and less likely to occur when it is punished or not rewarded. Operant conditioning is more complicated than it first appears. For example, slot machines are set up to pay off on an intermittent schedule. They dispense coins just often enough to keep gamblers pulling the lever. Slot machine designers calculate payoff intervals to encourage more gambling. If the schedule of reinforcement is too long—that is, if the machine does not pay off often enough—then gamblers will stop inserting coins. Like slot-machine designers, behaviorists study how people deal with events of rewards and punishments to see how good behavior can be encouraged and bad behavior eliminated.[29] In the criminal justice system, behaviorism is used extensively in therapeutic communities in which residents are placed on token economies that reward appropriate behavior.[30]

Some issues of behaviorism concern criminologists. First, rewards and punishments in the real world are not given according to predictable or dependable schedules. That is, hard work does not guarantee rewards. Often, the real world favors the strong, the lucky, the well connected, and those who cheat. Behaviorism works best in the artificial environment of the laboratory, the classroom, and the therapeutic community. Offenders can get frustrated quickly when they experience the inequities of the real world. Behaviorism is undependable as a guide for criminological policy because rewards come in many forms. What the middle-class, middle-age criminologist may think is a deterrent to inap-

NEWS FLASH

Lies, Lies, Lies

The question that lies at the basis of all criminal investigation and many, if not most, human interactions is: How can you tell when someone is lying?

The question is distressing for anyone involved in a relationship, especially an emotional one, but it is a crucial issue in law enforcement. An offender who is a really good liar may be able to slip past police questioning. An innocent person who is really nervous may not. Although many procedures, informal tests, and machines have been developed to detect lies, none of these is perfect. The most popular and most reliable method, the polygraph test, is not that reliable, and its results are not allowed in court. Polygraph machines measure changes in heart rate, respiration, and perspiration as a subject answers a series of yes/no questions. According to noted behavioral expert Dr. Paul Ekman, polygraphs may be useful in limited situations if certain questions are asked by examiners with specific knowledge. For instance, a guilty subject may show physical changes in response to the question, Did the stolen Mercedes have a CD player or a tape deck? However, polygraphs may also give false positives and false negatives, resulting in showing innocent respondents as guilty and vice versa.

Until relatively recently, the most popular customers of the polygraph industry were fast-food chains who tested employees in order to pick out those who might steal. Now that such use by private corporations is illegal, polygraphs are most used to screen those working in positions involving national security. However a National Academy of Sciences report, *The Polygraph and Lie Detection,* states that polygraphs are of little use in national security employee screening because of the high number of false responses it gives.

Given the polygraph's questionable reliability, Ekman trains police officers to look for small signs on the faces of suspects. Small movements signifying emotion may "leak" onto the face, such as twitches around the mouth, cheeks, and eyes, even before the subject is conscious of the emotion. According to Ekman, a trained interviewer can pick up these signs quite readily.

Meanwhile, the criminal justice system awaits a foolproof method of detecting lies. Currently, the FBI is testing a new technique. Called "brain fingerprinting," it relies on what Ekman calls "leakage," except that it uses a machine to measure the "leaks" in the brain before they travel to the face or hands. Developed by Dr. Larry Farwell, brain fingerprinting measures the brain's involuntary electrical signals, called p300 responses, while images relating to the crime are shown to the subject. The brain produces the signal so quickly, within 300 milliseconds of processing information, that the subject has no time to alter it. The CIA has given Farwell's company, Brain Fingerprinting, Inc., more than $1 million in research funding.

Sources: Becky McCall, "Brain Fingerprints Under Scrutiny," *BBC,* February 17, 2004. Board on Behavioral, Cognitive, and Sensory Sciences and Education, Committee on National Statistics, *The Polygraph and Lie Detection,* 2003, http://www.nap.edu/execsumm/0309084369.html. http://news.bbc.co.uk/go/pr/fr/-/2/hi/science/nature/3495433.stm. Paul Ekman, "Would You Lie to Me?" *The Observer,* April 27, 2003, http://observer.guardian.co.uk/crime/_story/0,13260,942101,00.html. Tom Paulson, "Seattle-Bound Company Uses Brain Waves to Detect Lies," *Seattle Post-Intelligencer,* January 29, 2004, http://seattlepi.nwsource.com/local/158464_brain29.html.

propriate behavior may be seen by the poor, immigrant, and/or young gang member as a reward. For instance, going to jail evokes fear in most of us, but for some gang members it is seen as a necessary step in the development of a gang identity.[31]

Sociological Theories of Crime

The biological and psychological theories of crime focus on the mind and body to determine why crimes are committed. In short, they argue that something is wrong with the offender, either physically or mentally. Consequently, the policy implications of these types of theories revolve around incapacitating or treating the offender. Another type of criminological theory finds problems not so much with the individual, but with the social situation or environment. A variety of sociological theories consider social structure and social processes as explanations for crime.

Chicago school
Criminological theories that rely, in part, on individuals' demographics and geographic location to explain criminal behavior.

THE CHICAGO SCHOOL The University of Chicago instituted the first sociology department in the United States. The early scholars there developed not only several theories of crime, but also a method for examining crime. Basically, Chicago school criminologists rejected the idea that crime is individual in nature, as the biological and psychological theories suggested, and turned to examining external factors. Two researchers connected to the **Chicago school**, Clifford Shaw and Henry McKay, studied the social disorganization of the neighborhoods of delinquent youths and concluded that something about bad neighborhoods caused crime.[32] Curran and Renzetti summarize this finding as follows:

> *They concluded that in terms of such characteristics as personality, intelligence, and physical condition, delinquents, for the most part were no different from nondelinquents. Of equal significance was their finding that crime and delinquency were not dominated by any particular ethnic or racial groups. This could be seen in the fact that while the racial and ethnic composition of certain neighborhoods changed over the years, the rates of delinquency remained fairly constant. . . . Shaw and McKay reported that neighborhoods with the worst delinquency problems also had the highest rates of other social problems, including deteriorated housing, infant mortality, and tuberculosis. The residents of these neighborhoods were the most economically disadvantaged in the city.*[33]

What was it about these communities that contributed to crime? Poverty was not the only issue. A breakdown in the traditional bonds of social control was caused by these unstable neighborhoods. With families moving in and out of the neighborhood, children were exposed to many different influences. The normal social ties were weakened and new norms emerged. Without the traditional family and community life that immigrants had in the "old country," their children were forced to blend the old ways of doing things with the street

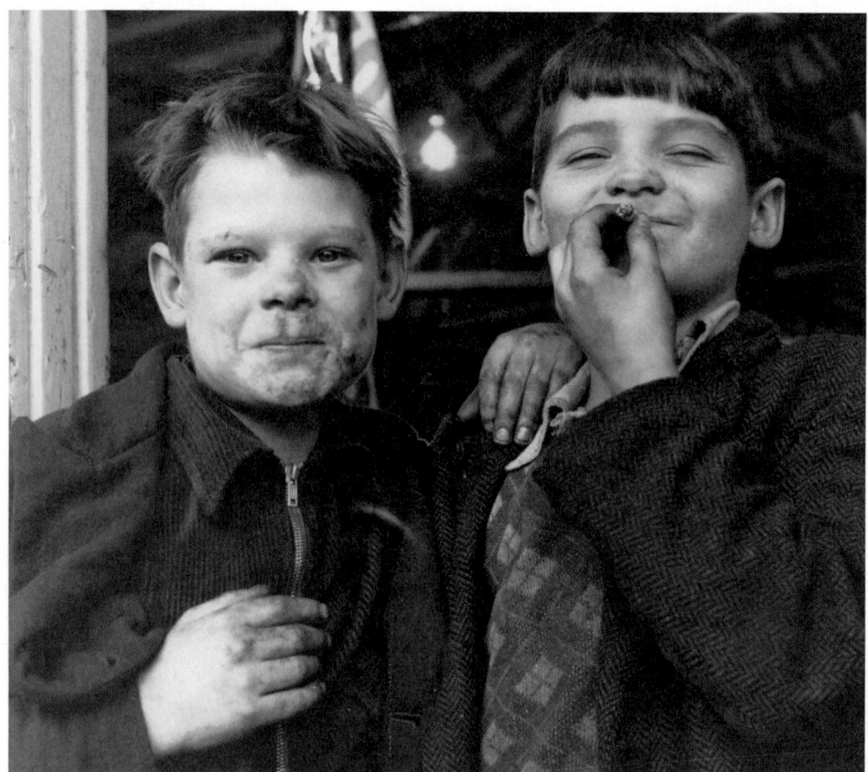

Children can engage in deviant acts at a very early age. Poverty, parental supervision, and peer pressure all influence why young people rebel against society.
Courtesy of CORBIS-NY.

culture of the new country. As families gained economic power and moved out of these socially disorganized neighborhoods, their children committed fewer delinquent acts.

DIFFERENTIAL ASSOCIATION THEORY Edwin Sutherland (1883–1950) developed **differential association theory**, one of the most popular theories of delinquency. Sutherland's theory claims that crime is learned. Young people learn crime in intimate play groups (friends and family) rather than from the media.[34] Sutherland presented his theory in nine propositions (see Figure 3.2). What Sutherland's theory does not do is explain how this learning takes place. In fact, one could question whether learning is really taking place in these groups, or whether it is simply a case of "birds of a feather flock together." If we accept that one's chances of being a delinquent are greater when one's friends are also delinquent, this still does not prove that delinquency is learned in intimate groups. Still, Sutherland's work has stimulated other theorists to pursue the idea that criminal behavior is learned.[35]

differential association theory
States that crime is learned. Children learn crime from other children. Developed by Edwin Sutherland.

DIFFERENTIAL ASSOCIATION AND BEHAVIORISM Ronald Akers took Sutherland's differential association and incorporated it with behaviorism. He contended that crime is learned according to the principles of operant conditioning. Behaviors are conditioned by environmental feedback. Behaviors are likely to increase when they are given positive reinforcement (reward received) or negative reinforcement (punishment removed or avoided).[36] Behaviors are likely to decrease when they are given positive punishment (punishment received) or negative punishment (reward removed or lost). Akers also included the process of modeling in his theory. Modeling involves imitating the behavior of someone respected and admired especially if that person's behavior is being rewarded. Modeling is a complex process that is difficult to test, especially for more serious forms of behavior.[37]

STRAIN THEORY Robert Merton is a famous sociologist who has made many contributions to the field, including the **strain theory** of delinquency. Merton was influenced by French sociologist Émile Durkheim's theory of **anomie** or "normlessness." In times of rapid social change, Durkheim contended that the old norms break down and people lack controls on their behavior. Before new norms can be established, people experience a sense of normlessness and are more likely to engage in criminal behavior. Merton looked at norms and recognized that society holds out the same norms for everybody. The problem arises when there is unequal access to these norms. Those who share the goals promoted by society, but find their means to attain these goals

strain theory
The hypothesis that the causes of crime can be connected to the pressure on culturally or materially disadvantaged groups or individuals to achieve the goals held by society, even if the means to those goals require the breaking of laws. Based on Émile Durkheim's theory of anomie.

anomie
A condition in which a people or society undergoes a breakdown of social norms and values.

Figure 3.2 Edwin Sutherland's Nine Principles of Differential Association

1. Criminal behavior is learned.
2. Criminal behavior is learned in interaction with other persons in a process of communication.
3. The principal part of the learning of criminal behavior occurs within intimate personal groups.
4. When criminal behavior is learned, the learning includes (a) techniques of committing crime, which are sometimes very complicated and sometimes very simple; and (b) the specific directions of motives, drives, rationalizations and attitudes.
5. The specific direction of motives and drives is learned from definitions of legal codes as favorable and unfavorable.
6. A person becomes delinquent because of an excess of definitions favorable to violation of law over definitions unfavorable to violation of law.
7. Differential association may vary in frequency, duration, priority and intensity.
8. The process of learning criminal behavior by association with criminal and anti-criminal patterns incorporates all the mechanisms that are involved in any other learning.
9. Although criminal behavior is an expression of general needs and values, it is not explained by those general needs and values since non-criminal behavior is an expression of the same needs and values.

Source: Edwin Sutherland, *Principles of Criminology*, 4th ed. (Chicago: J.B. Lippincott, 1947), 6–7. Reprinted with permission.

FOCUS ON ETHICS

With Friends Like These

You are a good parent. You love your kids, provide them with all that they need, and are constantly finding ways to give them new growth experiences. You have taken them to Europe, taught them to play chess, allowed them to drink your fine wines with dinner from the time they turned 12, and turned a blind eye to their occasional marijuana use when they went to college. You pride yourself on raising two wonderful, successful, and accomplished children, one a lawyer and the other now in dental school. However, your third child is somewhat different. Your 16-year-old daughter has not taken the same route as your older children. While they were "A" students, officers in their class, and star athletes, your youngest daughter has gone Goth. Her entire wardrobe is black; she wants to get a tattoo of a bat (the kind that flies), and she wears a safety pin in her ear. Recently, she has taken to wearing a dog collar and changes her hair color with her mood. You are afraid to even ask her about body piercing.

All these issues are of little concern to you because she is a bright girl with a good sense of values who is just going though her rebellion phase. What is troubling you are her friends. They are older, not ambitious, parasitic, unclean, and uncouth high school dropouts who spend their time hanging out at the town's punk dive, the Corner Grill. Try as you might, you fail to detect any social redeeming qualities in them whatsoever. You are afraid her new friends will influence your daughter in negative ways. You do not want her using drugs, experimenting with intimacy, or adopting the nihilistic philosophy that denigrates all that you hold precious about the American culture.

Now you have a decision to make. Your daughter has announced that she is leaving home to live with her friends, dropping out of school, renouncing the religion of her childhood, and becoming a vegetarian.

WHAT DO YOU DO?

1. Trust that your daughter will not make any disastrous decisions and allow her to work out her own relationships.
2. Forbid your daughter to move out, make her cease seeing her friends, and insist that she return to school.
3. Pack her off to a boarding school where she will be forced to make new friends, get an expensive but excellent education, and learn some social skills, such as ballroom dancing.

systematically blocked, experience anomie. This anomie is translated into deviant behavior or crime when the person attempts to adapt to the barriers to the goal.[38] For example, American society has a cultural goal of acquiring wealth. The goal of financial independence is pushed by our families, the schools, and the media. It is such a pervasive goal that we tend to take it for granted and assume that it is appropriate for everyone. As we attempt to reach this goal, some of us encounter obstacles. Sexism, racism, class bias, and age restrictions can frustrate our desires to become wealthy. For many people, simply working hard and saving money does not guarantee success. Does one disregard the goal when the means are lacking? According to Merton, the answer is no. One finds other ways of addressing the goal and adapts to the lack of means (see Table 3.3).

Merton's strain theory is easy to understand and seems to have positive policy implications. If people commit crimes because they find their means to compete in legitimate society blocked by poverty and inequality, then all that needs to be done is to remove those blockages. The theory has its critics, however. For instance, is it accurate to say that drug addicts withdraw from society? Many of those who use drugs are able to maintain very conventional lifestyles. Their drug use is not a retreat from society but an effort to engage in society in a more meaningful way. For some people, drugs enhance

TABLE 3.3

Robert Merton's Strain Theory

Adaptive Type	Goals	Means
Conformist. Most people fit this adaptation, accepting the goal of having money and adopting the culturally approved way to achieve get it: hard work and deferred gratification. Most university students would be considered conformists. They work hard, defer gratification, and prepare for legitimate occupations.	Accepted +	Accepted +
Innovator. One accepts the goal of having money but rejects the culturally approved means to obtain it, finding alternative methods instead. Innovations can include crime or legal ways to make money, but the key is that this adaptation does not fall within societal norms. It is legal and possibly lucrative to work as a dancer in a strip club, but generally it is not a socially respected method of obtaining wealth.	Accepted +	Rejected or is blocked —
Ritualist. The goal is rejected, but the means are still accepted. Ritualists are not usually deviant, but they no longer have the goal of achieving wealth and success. Ritualists tend to go through the motions without really hoping to make an impact. For example, some professors deliver the same lecture term after term and seem not to care if the lecture is current or if the students learn.	Rejected —	Accepted +
Retreatist. Both the goals and the means are rejected (or blocked), and nothing is substituted. Examples of retreatists would be drug addicts, alcoholics, hermits, and outcasts. Many of these people will end up as clients of the criminal justice system.	Rejected —	Rejected or is blocked —
Rebel. Rebellious people reject culturally approved means and goals and substitute new ones. Some domestic terrorist groups would fit into this category, as well as hippies of the 1960s who dropped out of conventional society and established communes based on shared resources and responsibilities. Although some of these communes violated the popular sense of appropriate living arrangements, they seemed to meet the residents' needs.	Rejected (substitute) —	Rejected (substitute) —

experiences of dancing, viewing concerts, and relating to others and do not cause them to become stereotypical stoned-out drug addicts. Also, it may be unfair to claim that Americans are primarily materialistic. Other culturally approved, nonmaterialistic goals drive Americans, such as the quest to get an education, the desire to feel like a part of a community, and the wish to help and serve family, church, and country. Merton's theory assumes that having money is the overriding cultural goal. For many people, this may not be the case.[39]

SOCIAL CONTROL THEORY Travis Hirschi's **social control theory** is interesting because it approaches crime from a different angle than other theories do. Most theories assume that people are good and turn to crime only when something is wrong with them or their environment. Hirschi's social control theory, however, does not ask why some people commit crimes. It questions why most people do not. Instead of seeking to explain the relatively infrequent event of crime, social control theory explores the pervasive conforming behavior that makes meaningful communities possible. Hirschi speculated that the mechanism that accomplishes this is a social bond that links us to conventional

social control theory
A theory that seeks not to explain why people break the law, but instead explores what keeps most people from breaking the law. Associated with Travis Hirschi.

society.[40] Only when this social bond is weakened is crime likely to occur. Hirschi contended that this social bond has four elements:

1. **Attachment.** When people are concerned with the feelings of other people, they are less likely to do things that are wrong. A child who values his parent's approval and affection will engage in behavior designed to maintain that good relationship. Hirschi believed that one's attachments to parents, schools, and peers help to form the social bond that keeps one from engaging in criminal behavior.
2. **Commitment.** People are committed to a society when they are successful in it. There is an old saying, "When you ain't got nothing, you ain't got nothing to lose." People who have money, property, and good reputations are committed to the social system that allowed them the opportunities for that success. A frequent mistake in the study of criminal behavior is the assumption that most criminals are committed to conventional society when, in fact, they have not been able to realize their needs in that society. In a sense, then, most criminals have little or nothing to lose.
3. **Involvement.** People involved in conventional activities have less time and energy to engage in crime. "Involvement" is the idea behind a vast array of programs designed to keep young people occupied. Although ballet lessons, Little League baseball, police athletic league programs, after-school day care, and parks and recreation areas for children may have a number of positive features, one of the primary benefits is that they keep children busy.
4. **Beliefs.** Children who believe in the conventional value system of society are less likely to commit crimes. According to Hirschi, children who commit delinquent acts have weakened beliefs in the conventional moral code. Unlike other theories that speculate about deviant subcultures that supply contrasting codes of conduct, Hirschi's theory considers only the dominant culture and envisions that everyone is bonded to it to some degree. The strength of that bond is what determines whether one will become delinquent.

NEUTRALIZATION THEORY Most people do not commit crimes most of the time. Just about everyone seems to be able to get through each day without causing harm to others or stealing property. Most people, therefore, are committed to a law-abiding lifestyle and commit crimes only sporadically. How, then, do these occasional criminals justify their behavior? How do they account for the harm they do to others and still think of themselves as essentially good and decent people? Gresham Sykes and David Matza developed **neutralization theory** to explain how delinquents drift between conventional lifestyles and delinquent ones. The theory states that offenders use techniques of neutralization to deflect feelings of blame and shame.[41] These neutralization techniques are rationalizations, justifications, and accounts of how the offending behavior can be excused or explained away. Sykes and Matza identified five techniques of neutralization:

neutralization theory
A perspective that states that juvenile delinquents have feelings of guilt when involved in illegal activities. Illegal behavior is episodic, and delinquents drift between legal and illegal activities. The delinquent sets aside his or her own legal and moral values in order to drift into illegal activities.

1. **Denial of responsibility.** Offenders deny that the crime was their fault. They may blame the influence of drugs or alcohol for "not being myself." This way they can live with their deviant acts without thinking of themselves as bad people.
2. **Denial of injury.** Offenders can claim that no one actually got hurt. If a male batterer "just slaps his wife around a little," he may try to minimize his actions by saying, "If I really wanted to hurt her, I would have used my fist." Also, drug users will say that drugs affect only themselves, so the law should not be concerned with their drug use.
3. **Denial of victim.** Thieves will contend that the property they steal is insured, so the victim is not really harmed at all. Steroid-using athletes claim that everyone does it, so using illegal performance-enhancing drugs is not bad. A rapist may contend that the victim was "asking for it."
4. **Condemnation of condemners.** Here, the offenders claim that the criminal justice system or society is corrupt and unfair. Illegal drug users point to the harm done by legal drugs, such as tobacco and alcohol, and claim that marijuana is illegal be-

cause the alcohol industry is afraid of competition. The offenders claim a morally superior position from which they reject the legitimacy of those judging them.

5. **Appeal to higher loyalty.** Offenders take responsibility for their actions but claim they were acting to satisfy a higher calling. Those who get arrested for protesting at abortion clinics, and even those who kill abortion providers, contend that they are fully aware that they are violating laws but believe they are upholding a higher law. They view themselves as "following God's law" when they commit murder. In this way, these otherwise conforming people can commit acts of violence that they would never commit under other circumstances.

According to Curran and Renzetti, there are two major issues concerning deviants' use of neutralization techniques. First, even though these appear to be after-the-fact justifications, they can also occur before the misbehavior. One may facilitate one's behavior by loosening one's moral bonds. Second, these techniques of neutralization act as mitigating circumstances in the eyes of offenders. They understand that the law excuses self-defense, accident, and insanity, and they justify their own behavior by claiming that these neutralizations constitute extenuating circumstances.[42]

LABELING THEORY Edwin Lemert (1912–1996) is one of the sociologists responsible for the development of **labeling theory**. Labeling theory contends that people commit deviant behavior because they see themselves as "outsiders" and therefore attempt to live up to that label. Society defines some actions as deviant or unlawful and contends that anyone who engages in these behaviors is a criminal, prostitute, drug addict, thief, sexual pervert, and so on. People who do not get caught escape these labels and find it much easier to exist in society. Therefore, according to labeling theorists such as Howard Becker, "deviance is not a quality of the act the person commits, but rather a consequence of the application by others of rules or sanctions to an 'offender.' The deviant is one to whom that label has been successfully applied; deviant behavior is behavior that people so label."[43]

labeling theory
A perspective that considers recidivism to be a consequence, in part, of the negative labels applied to offenders.

Labeling does not happen accidentally. We go to great lengths to apply positive and negative labels that can greatly affect people's lives. On the positive side, consider the elaborate ceremonies surrounding graduations and weddings. People dress up in elaborate costumes suitable for only this type of occasion, invitations are sent out to friends and relatives, respected officials read sacred documents to apply legitimacy to the event, and then there is a party so that everyone can celebrate the labeled person's change in social status. On the negative side, there are public status-degradation ceremonies in which people are stripped of their positive statuses and labeled with deviant tags. Think about the old movies in which a soldier is court-martialed and has his stripes and insignia ripped from his uniform in a public ceremony. The intent is to shame him and to send a signal to others that bad behavior has negative consequences. By doing this in such a public way, the system influences more than just the individual offender. The courtroom is just such a public stage where a predictable drama is played out so that an offender can be labeled for all to see. The judge sits in an elevated position and wears an imposing costume. The judge looks down on the defendant, who sits with the defense attorney at a table that is physically separated from the others in the courtroom. When the sentence is announced, the defendant is required to stand so that all can witness the reaction. This could all be done in a much less elaborate manner, but the ceremony is designed to accomplish two goals: to impress on the defendant the disapproval of society and to impress on the rest of us that there are consequences to unlawful behavior.[44]

In his theory, Lemert made a distinction between primary deviation and secondary deviation, which is important to appreciating just how powerful the labeling process is in shaping unlawful behavior. Primary deviation is the initial lawbreaking. This can occur for any number of reasons and is of little concern to the labeling perspective. Once someone is caught by the criminal justice system, processed through the court, and successfully labeled, secondary deviation sets in. The offender comes to believe that the label actually is an appropriate one and starts to act according to what he or she perceives is the proper role. The offender thinks, "If they are going to treat me like a criminal, then

I must be one, and I will act like one." The offender internalizes the criminal label and acts accordingly.[45] The policy implications of the labeling theory focus on keeping the offender from internalizing the deviant label. First-offender programs that divert offenders from the traditional criminal justice system are based, in part, on labeling theory. By allowing offenders to escape the criminal label, it is hoped that they will revert to a more conventional lifestyle.[46]

Labeling theory has implications for more than just the criminal justice system. Families and schools are also venues in which children can be affected by positive or negative labels.[47] It is a heavy burden to go through school thinking that you are stupid, slow, ugly, a nerd, a geek, or unpopular. To the extent that secondary deviance sets in, this negative label can become a self-fulfilling prophecy. The child stops trying to succeed in school because he or she believes that he or she is not as smart as the others.

Critical Sociological Theories of Crime

We turn now to another set of theories of crime that, although sociological in nature, must be examined separately because they represent a distinct type of theory with far-reaching implications for understanding the causes of crime and for enacting policies to address crime. *Critical theory* is an umbrella term that encompasses a range of perspectives that consider social justice as a legitimate end. The following theories examine how power is distributed in society and how the criminal justice system often is simply a reflection of power and sometimes a tool of power. Criminologists have developed a number of theories that can be considered critical. These theories are also called "conflict" or "radical" theories. Although there are major distinctions among these terms, we group all these theories under the term *critical* with the caveat that the interested student will find much to explore in researching the different types of theories that concern power.[48]

MARXISM Karl Marx (1818–1883) is an important social theorist whose name is linked with communism. Although the idea of communism reflects his ideas, it is important to note that Marx died before the modern communist states in the former Soviet Union, China, North Korea, Vietnam, and Cuba were established. Because these countries and their economic systems have been historically viewed as problematic by the United States, Marx and the term *Marxism* are not popular. In academic circles, however, Marx is given credit for his unique perspective. It is possible to agree with Marx's critique of capitalism

CASE IN POINT

Gideon v. Wainwright

The Case

Gideon v. Wainwright 372 U.S. 335, 83 S. Ct. 792 (1963)

The Point

Indigent defendants have the right to court-appointed attorneys in felony cases.

Clarence Gideon, an impoverished drifter, was charged in 1961 with breaking and entering a poolroom with the intent to commit a misdemeanor, a felony under Florida law. Gideon went to court without money or a lawyer and asked the court to appoint counsel for him. The judge told him that counsel was appointed only if the punishment for the offense involved the death penalty. The case went to a jury trial in which Gideon defended himself. He was found guilty and sentenced to five years in prison. On appeal, the Supreme Court overturned his conviction and established that indigent defendants have the right to court-appointed attorneys in felony cases.

Wrote Justice Hugo Black, "In our adversary system of criminal justice, any person hauled into court, who is too poor to hire a lawyer, cannot be assured a fair trial unless counsel is provided for him."

and its impact on social justice without embracing communism. Therefore, we consider Marx and his ideas in the spirit that there is much here that is important to the understanding of crime.

Marx studied the 19th-century capitalist system in Europe and found it wanting. Specifically, he said the owners of the means of production (factories and such) paid their workers poorly and used government to pass laws that prevented reform. Those with economic power, then, controlled the system, and they used that power to make sure things did not change. Churches, schools, the economy, and other institutions were all under the control of the owner class. Marx said that the workers put up with this inequitable arrangement because they suffered from **false consciousness**. Because the owners controlled the opinion makers (newspapers, churches, and schools), they were able to make the workers believe they were lucky just to have a job and that they should be grateful. The solution to this state of affairs, according to Marx, was for the workers to rise up and grab the means of production for themselves, through violence if necessary.[49]

false consciousness
An attitude held by members of a class that does not accurately reflect the reality of that class's existence. A term associated with Karl Marx.

Could the workers develop a society that was better than the one they overthrew? Or were they just exchanging one set of exploitive masters for another? George Orwell wrote a scathing satire of Marx's ideas in his novel, *Animal Farm,* in which the ruling pigs said, "All are equal, but some are more equal than others." This is, of course, the critical issue with communism.[50] How is power to be evenly distributed across society? Is it just human nature for those with power to use that power to benefit themselves? In the end, pitting capitalism against communism is a false dichotomy. There are plenty of variations between these extremes, such as labor unions, employee stock ownership plans, Social Security, and owner-financed health plans that 19th-century capitalists would have rejected.

Although Marx actually said very little about crime and the criminal justice system, the criminologists who study his tradition point out that those in power control the making and the enforcement of the law.[51] One need only look at how political campaigns are financed to see how big money influences the making of laws. There is a continuing struggle to balance the rights of people to talk to their legislative representatives on one hand, and to ensure that those representatives are not unduly influenced by gifts, favors, and money on the other hand. When we consider the disparities between how street crimes and corporate crimes are dealt with by the criminal justice system, we can appreciate why

Karl Marx's ideas about the effect of class on society and justice continue to inform critical criminologists.
Courtesy of Corbis/Bettmann.

! NEWS FLASH

Crime and the Economy

Crime is cyclical, and its causes are numerous. No one knows exactly what makes the crime rate rise and fall, but theories abound. One theory is that the crime rate is attached to the economy and jobs. When people have jobs and plenty of money, the theory goes, they have less incentive or need to commit crimes and more to lose if they do commit crimes.

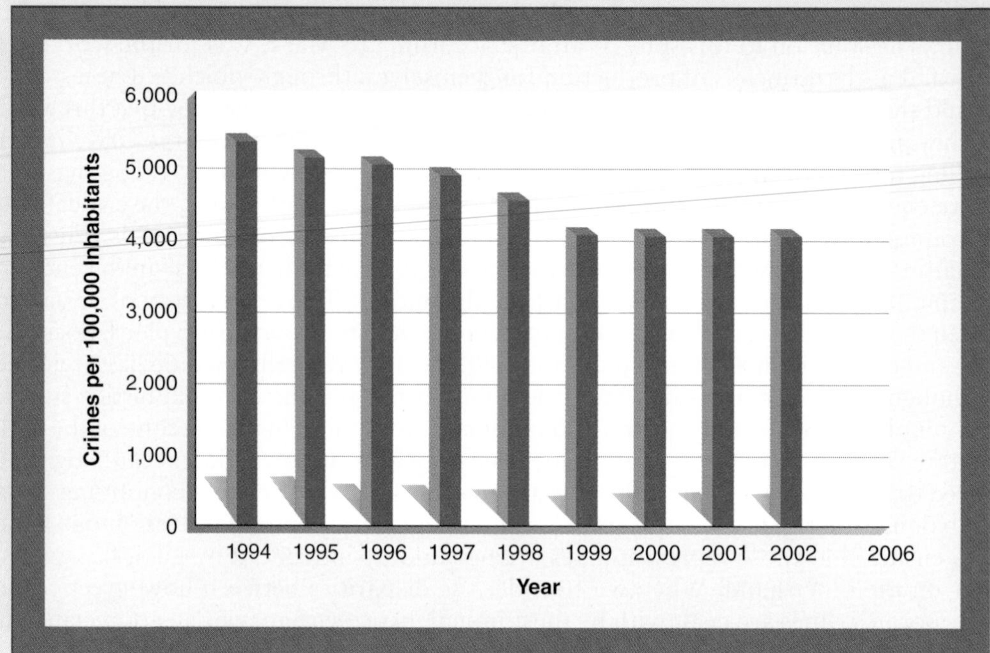

As illustrated in the above figure, crime dropped during the second half of the 1990s and early 2000s. Adherents to the economic theory of crime would point to the booming economy of this period as the primary cause. As the Internet bubble began to swell, creating jobs and sparking record stock prices, the crime rate steadily dropped from 5,375 offenses per 100,000 inhabitants in 1994 to 4,124 in 2000. As the bubble deflated, taking the economy with it, the crime rate rose, dipping only slightly in 2002. However, in the first half of 2002, more major crimes were committed, with slight increases in murder, burglary, and car theft. The year 2002 also represented the second consecutive year that crime had risen.

Sources: Federal Bureau of Investigation, *Uniform Crime Reports, 1995–2002,* http://www.fbi.gov/ucr/ucr.htm. Kevin Johnson, "Analysts Say Economy Is Fueling Crime Hike," *USA Today,* December 16, 2002, http://www.usatoday.com/news/nation/2002-12-16-crime-usat_x.htm.

critical criminologists continue the tradition of studying Marx and considering the role of social class and power in society.[52]

GENDER AND JUSTICE One of the historical defects of criminological theory has been the reliance on male subjects. Like research in education, health, and business, crime research has always assumed that women are just a subset of men and that research findings about men could be readily transferred to women. With the rise of the modern feminist movement in the 1960s, this problem in the research on crime has been addressed with productive results.[53]

Feminism examines how women are treated differently from men in a society dominated by male power structures. As a starting point in addressing the social condition of women, feminists employ the concept of gender, which argues that society has different expectations of females and males. In addition to the obvious physical differences between men and women, gender asserts that there are also different rules, opportunities, and consequences that are automatically distributed according to sex. Sexism is a way the contributions of males and females are valued according to different standards. (For example, a sexually adventurous boy may be called a "stud" or a "player," whereas the same behavior in a girl elicits a less positive label.) Because men have historically dominated our social system, women have been excluded from many occupations, including roles of leadership in the criminal justice system. Consequently, much of what we think we know about female offenders and female criminal justice system practitioners has been based on the study of males. Feminist criminologists (both female and male) have begun to correct this gap in our knowledge about crime.[54]

Feminist theory has many variations. Each has its own perspective and critiques the way women are treated. Curran and Renzetti provided a valuable analysis of the state of feminist criminology in which they highlighted three ways crime can be appreciated from feminist perspectives:

1. **Liberal feminism and criminology.** Liberal feminists consider two features of society as being in need of attention. First, women's opportunities are blocked by a social system controlled by men who reserve most of the power for themselves. Power should be distributed according to accomplishment rather than gender. The second issue for liberal feminists is the way girls are socialized differently from boys. Women are systematically taught to be passive, nurturing, and dependent, whereas men are taught to be assertive, competitive, and aggressive. By changing the way women are socialized and removing barriers to power, women will be able to fully realize their talents and not be limited by a patriarchal, sexist system. As these goals are accomplished, however, women also have opportunities to engage in deviant behavior. As women become more equal, they will also find more opportunities to engage in illegitimate activities and be treated more like males by the criminal justice system.
2. **Radical feminist criminology.** The radical feminist contends that sexism is not so much a product of class relations than it is of the patriarchal structure that places all women at a severe disadvantage, regardless of their social class or race. Radical feminists point to how women are victims of rape, acquaintance rape, pornography, and spousal abuse as evidence that the criminal justice system does not seriously address the concerns of women. Traditional criminology has focused primarily on male street crime and neglected the types of personal violent crimes that affect women. This is true even in the case of rape, in which stranger rape is considered easier to prosecute and more serious than that of acquaintance rape. Radical feminists call for a fundamental overhaul of patriarchal systems rather than the less ambitious legal changes advocated by the liberal feminists.
3. **Socialist feminist criminology.** Socialist feminists use the combined effects of social class and gender to explain women's disadvantaged status in society and in the criminal justice system. Women's opportunities for crime are influenced by the greater controls they experience in society. They are more closely supervised by their parents, husbands, boyfriends, and authorities for what is believed to be "their own good." This greater surveillance both limits their opportunities and increases the chances that their deviant behavior will be detected. Additionally, women are underrepresented in official positions of power and responsibility. If the disadvantages of race are added to the disadvantages of social class and gender, the combined effects produce even greater marginalization.[55]

Feminist theories of criminology also have relevance for men. By looking at how power is concentrated in the privileged male sex role, we can begin to understand how race, sexual orientation, and gender are factors that determine how the criminal justice system treats practitioners, offenders, and victims. Feminist theories also have policy implications. Changes in the way rape victims are treated by police officers and prosecutors are one example of how a feminist perspective can introduce some social justice into legal proceedings. Feminism is more than just a theory. Its various forms also constitute a social movement that forces us to reexamine how people are treated by society's institutions.[56] In the criminal justice system, we can expect to see feminists continue to push for reforms in the treatment of women.

CRITICAL RACE THEORY Critical theories of crime and justice also consider other aspects of both criminal behavior and the reaction of agencies of social control to explain why people commit crime, how crime is defined, and how the criminal justice system operates. One theory that is attracting a good deal of attention is critical race theory.[57] This theory starts with the observation that people of color are overrepresented at every decision point of the criminal justice system and suggests that race is a crucial variable for scholars to examine when attempting to explain the dynamics of the justice system in the United States and, to varying degrees, in other countries. In its starkest form, critical race theory asserts that the concept that "we are a nation of laws and not of men" masks the function of the criminal justice system to legitimize white supremacy and oppress people of color.[58] As a theoretical perspective, critical race theory focuses on inequality, discrimination, prejudice, and differential law enforcement and explains issues such as racial profiling, interracial crime, and racial hoaxes. For example, in the case of Susan Smith, who was found guilty of drowning her two children, the initial search was for a black man whom Smith claimed hijacked her car. Smith provided a detailed description to the police and helped a police artist compose a sketch of the alleged perpetrator. As the case unfolded, it became clear that Smith was lying and that there was no black male suspect. Critical race theory would stipulate that white people were willing to believe that a black man was the likely suspect and that numerous similar miscarriages of justice have been accomplished because of the criminal justice system's racial bias. To understand the experiences of people of color and their treatment by the criminal justice system, we must conduct research based on personalized accounts of harm. Traditional criminal justice research methods do not uncover the types of injustices that are the focus of critical race theory.

INTEGRATED THEORIES A number of criminologists have attempted to develop integrated theories of crime. Recognizing that traditional biological, psychological, and sociological theories are of limited utility, these integrationists have attempted to link theories either in an end-to-end approach to demonstrate where one theory's dependent variable might be used as another theory's independent variable, or by looking for central processes that run through several theories.[59] What the integrationists have not attempted is to link the biological, psychological, and sociological families of theories. This monumental task of creating a grand theory may not be possible given our limitations in designing research methods, our lack of understanding of the human brain, and the ethical issues that apply to human subject research.

Summary

Criminological theory is a lively and ever-changing endeavor that keeps scholars busy refining age-old perspectives and creating new ones that can account for the variety of deviant and criminal behavior. This is a difficult task for at least two reasons. The first obstacle in developing criminological theory is the fact that crime is socially defined. That is, what is considered a crime in one context may be considered normal or even heroic behavior in another context. Killing someone in a war may mean getting promoted and decorated, but the same behavior during peacetime may result in a long prison sentence or the death penalty. When we look for the biological conditions of homicide, we fail to take into consideration the social context surrounding the action. Similarly, sociological and psychological theories of crime are unable to account for many of the conditions that drive people to commit horrendous acts because they cannot fully appreciate the hormonal or biochemical reactions in the human body.

Although we must admit that our theories of crime causation and the workings of the legal and criminal justice systems are of limited utility, we must also recognize that some well-developed and well-tested theories can explain some crime. What is most fascinating to the criminal justice student, however, is the history of attempts to theorize about crime. It would be nice to say that this history has been progressive and that bad ideas have been examined and discarded, but that is not the case. In fact, we might even go so far as to say there are no bad ideas, simply ones that have failed to provide reasonable explanations because of our limited methods of analysis. For instance, the search for physical causes for crime that are exemplified by Lombroso's atavisms and Sheldon's body types have found new impetus in genetic research. Much remains to be discovered about how the body interacts with the environment to produce illegal behavior. Criminologists of many intellectual persuasions continue to delve into the biological, psychological, sociological, economic, political, and historical realms to better explain criminal behavior and society's reaction to crime.

KEY TERMS

anomie p. 93
atavism p. 83
behaviorism p. 90
Chicago school p. 92
classical school of criminology p. 77
differential association theory p. 93
false consciousness p. 99
labeling theory p. 97
neutralization theory p. 96
operant conditioning p. 90
positivist school of criminology p. 81
rational choice theory p. 81
social control theory p. 95
somatotyping p. 85
strain theory p. 93
trial by ordeal p. 76
utilitarianism p. 80
XYY syndrome p. 86

REVIEW QUESTIONS

1. Why are religious or supernatural explanations for crime not considered by the criminal justice system?
2. What is the classical school of criminology's main argument?
3. What modern rights are traceable to Cesare Beccaria?
4. How are individuals guided, according to Jeremy Bentham?
5. What effect did Bentham's philosophy have on modern sentencing patterns?
6. What factors gave rise to the positivist school of criminology?
7. What is phrenology?
8. What is strain theory?
9. What makes Travis Hirschi's social control theory different?
10. Why is labeling theory important?
11. What are the three ways crime can be appreciated from a feminist perspective?

SUGGESTED FURTHER READING

Akers, Ronald. *Criminological Theories: Introduction, Evaluation, and Applications.* 3rd ed. Los Angeles: Roxbury, 2000.

Bernard, Thomas J. "Twenty Years of Testing Theories: What Have We Learned and Why?" *Journal of Research in Crime and Delinquency* 27 (1990): 324–347.

Mann, Coramae Richey, and Marjorie S. Zatz, eds. *Images of Color, Images of Crime.* Los Angeles: Roxbury, 1998.

Schwartz, Martin D., and David O. Friedrichs. "Postmodern Thought and Criminological Discontent: New Metaphors for Understanding Violence." *Criminology* 32 (1994): 221–246.

Taylor, Ian, Paul Walton, and Jack Young. *The New Criminology: For a Social Theory of Deviance.* New York: Harper and Row, 1973.

Williams, Frank P., and Marilyn D. McShane. *Criminological Theory.* 4th ed. Upper Saddle River, NJ: Prentice Hall, 2004.

ENDNOTES

1. Israel Dropkin, *Crime and Punishment in the Ancient World* (Lexington: DC Heath, 1989).
2. Randall McGowan, "The Changing Face of God's Justice: The Debates Over Divine and Human Punishment in Eighteenth-Century England," *Criminal Justice History* 9 (1988): 63–98.
3. Frances Hill, *A Delusion of Satan: The Full Story of the Salem Witch Trials* (New York: Doubleday, 1995).
4. Douglas Cruickshank, "The Andrea Yates Verdict Is Insane," *Salon,* March 14, 2002, http://www.salon.com/mwt/feature/2002/03/14/yates_verdict/.
5. "Minister Who Killed Abortion Doctor Awaits Execution," AP/*USA Today,* September 3, 2003, http://www.usatoday.com/news/nation/2003-09-03-hill_x.htm.
6. Erline Eide, *Economic of Crime: Deterrence and the Rational Offender* (North Holland, Netherlands: Elsevier, 1994).
7. Philip Jenkins, "Varieties of Enlightenment Criminology," *British Journal of Criminology* 24 (1984): 112–130.
8. Cesare Beccaria, *On Crimes and Punishments,* trans. Henry Paolucci (Indianapolis: Bobbs-Merrill, 1764/1963).
9. Elio D. Monachesi, "Cesare Beccaria," *Journal of Criminal Law, Criminology, and Political Science* 46 (1955): 439–449.
10. Jeremy Bentham, "An Introduction to the Principles of Morals and Legislation," in *Classics of Criminology,* 2nd ed., ed. Joseph E. Jacoby (Prospect Heights, IL: Waveland Press, 1994), 80.
11. Frank P. Williams III and Marilyn D. McShane, *Criminological Theory,* 4th ed. (Upper Saddle River, NJ: Prentice Hall, 2004), 15–32.
12. Imogene L. Moyer, *Criminological Theories: Traditional and Nontraditional Voices and Themes* (Thousand Oaks, CA: Sage, 2001).
13. Derek B. Cornish and Ronald V. Clarke, *The Reasoning Criminal: Rational Choice Perspectives on Offending* (New York: Springer, 1986).
14. Charles Darwin, *The Origin of the Species* (Cambridge, MA: Harvard University Press, 1859/1964).
15. Deborah W. Denno, "Human Biology and Criminal Responsibility: Free Will or Free Ride," *University of Pennsylvania Law Review* 137 (1988): 615–671.
16. John van Wyhe, *The History of Phrenology on the Web,* http://pages.britishlibrary.net/phrenology/.
17. The Phrenology Page, http://134.184.33.110/phreno/.
18. Cesare Lombroso, "The Criminal Man," in *Criminological Theory: Past to Present,* 2nd ed., eds. Francis T. Cullen and Robert Agnew (Los Angeles: Roxbury, 2003), 23–25.
19. J. Robert Lilly, Francis T. Cullen, and Richard A. Ball, *Criminological Theory: Context and Consequences,* 3rd ed. (Thousand Oaks, CA: Sage, 2002).
20. Moyer, *Criminological Theories,* 39.
21. Lilly, Cullen, and Ball, *Criminological Theory,* 23.
22. Daniel J. Curran and Claire M. Renzetti, *Theories of Crime,* 2nd ed. (Boston: Allyn and Bacon, 2001), 33–35.
23. Patricia Jacobs, et al., "Aggressive Behavior, Mental Subnormality, and the XYY Male," *Nature* 208 (1965): 1351–1352.
24. Ty A. Ridenour, "Genetic Epidemiology of Antisocial Behavior," in *Theories of Crime: A Reader,* eds. Claire M. Renzetti, Daniel J. Curran, and Patrick J. Carr (Boston: Allyn and Bacon, 2003), 4–24.
25. Katharina Dalton, "Menstruation and Crime," *British Medical Journal* 2 (1961): 1752–1753.
26. Debra Niehoff, "The Biology of Violence," in *Theories of Crime: A Reader,* eds. Claire M. Renzetti, Daniel J. Curran, and Patrick J. Carr (Boston: Allyn and Bacon, 2003), 26–31.
27. Sigmund Freud, *The Ego and the Id* (London: Hogarth, 1927).
28. Sigmund Freud, *General Introduction to Psychoanalysis* (New York: Boni and Liveright, 1920).
29. G. Terence Wilson, "Behavior Therapy," in *Current Psychotherapies,* 4th ed., eds. Raymond J. Corsini and Danny Wedding (Itasca, IL: F.E. Peacock, 1989), 241–282.
30. Michael J. Lillyquist, *Understanding and Changing Criminal Behavior* (Englewood Cliffs, NJ: Prentice Hall, 1980).
31. G. David Curry and Scott H. Decker, *Confronting Gangs: Crime and Community* (Los Angeles: Roxbury, 1988).

32. Clifford R. Shaw and Henry D. McKay, *Juvenile Delinquency and Urban Areas* (Chicago: University of Chicago Press, 1942).
33. Curran and Renzetti, *Theories of Crime,* 101–102.
34. Edwin H. Sutherland, Donald R. Cressey, and David F. Luckenbill, *Principles of Criminology* (Dix Hills, NJ: General Hall, 1992).
35. Ross Matsueda, "The Current State of Differential Association Theory," *Crime and Delinquency* 34 (1988): 277–306.
36. Robert L. Burgess and Ronald L. Akers, "A Differential Association-Reinforcement Theory of Criminal Behavior," *Social Problems* 14 (1966): 128–147.
37. Ronald L. Akers, *Social Learning and Social Structure: A General Theory of Crime and Deviance* (Boston: Northeastern University Press, 1998).
38. Robert K. Merton, "Social Structure and Anomie," *American Sociological Review* 3 (1938): 672–682.
39. Robert Agnew, "The Nature and Determinants of Strain: Another Look at Durkheim and Merton," in *The Future of Anomie Theory,* eds. Nikos Passas and Robert Agnew (Boston: Northeastern University Press, 1997), 27–51.
40. Travis Hirschi, *Causes of Delinquency* (Berkeley: University of California Press, 1969).
41. Gresham M. Sykes and David Matza, "Techniques of Neutralization," *Sociological Review* 22 (1957): 644–670.
42. Curran and Renzetti, *Theories of Crime,* 167.
43. Howard Becker, *Outsiders: Studies in the Sociobiology of Deviance* (New York: The Free Press, 1963).
44. Harold Garfinkel, "Successful Degradation Ceremonies," *American Sociological Review* 61 (1956): 420–424.
45. Edwin M. Lemert, *Human Deviance, Social Problems, and Social Control,* 2nd ed. (Englewood Cliffs, NJ: Prentice Hall, 1972).
46. Edwin Schur, "Reactions to Deviance: A Critical Assessment," *American Journal of Sociology* 75 (1969): 309–322.
47. Ross L. Matsueda, "Reflected Appraisals, Parental Labeling, and Delinquency: Specifying a Symbolic Interactionist Theory," *American Journal of Sociology* 6 (1992): 1577–1611.
48. Bruce A. Arrigo, ed., *Social Justice/Criminal Justice: The Maturation of Critical Theory in Law, Crime, and Deviance* (Belmont, CA: West/Wadsworth, 1999).
49. Karl Marx, *Capital* (New York: International, 1867/1974).
50. George Orwell, *Animal Farm* (New York: Harcourt, Brace and Co., 1946).
51. Michael J. Lynch and Paul Stretesky, "Marxism and Social Justice: Thinking About Social Justice Eclipsing Criminal Justice," in *Social Justice/Criminal Justice: The Maturation of Critical Theory in Law, Crime, and Deviance,* ed. Bruce A. Arrigo (Belmont, CA: West/Wadsworth, 1999), 14–29.
52. Francis T. Cullen, William J. Maakestad, and Gray Cavender, *Corporate Crime Under Attack: The Ford Pinto Case and Beyond* (Cincinnati: Andersen, 1987).
53. Kathleen Daly and Meda Chesney-Lind, "Feminism and Criminology," *Justice Quarterly* 5 (1988): 497–535.
54. Sally Simpson, "Feminist Theory, Crime, and Justice," *Criminology* 27 (1989): 605–631.
55. Curran and Renzetti, *Theories of Crime,* 209–228.
56. Gregg Barak, Jeanne M. Flavin, and Paul S. Leighton, *Class, Race, Gender, and Crime: Social Realities of Justice in America* (Los Angeles: Roxbury, 2000).
57. Katheryn K. Russell, "Critical Race Theory and Social Justice," in *Social Justice/Criminal Justice: The Maturation of Critical Theory in Law, Crime, and Deviance,* ed. Bruce A. Arrigo (Belmont, CA: West/Wadsworth, 1999), 178–188.
58. The phrase "We are a nation of laws and not of men," originates from John Adams.
59. Francis T. Cullen, Jon Paul Wright, and Mitchell B. Chamlin, "Social Support and Social Reform: A Progressive Crime Control Agenda," *Crime and Delinquency* 45 (1999): 188–207.

outline

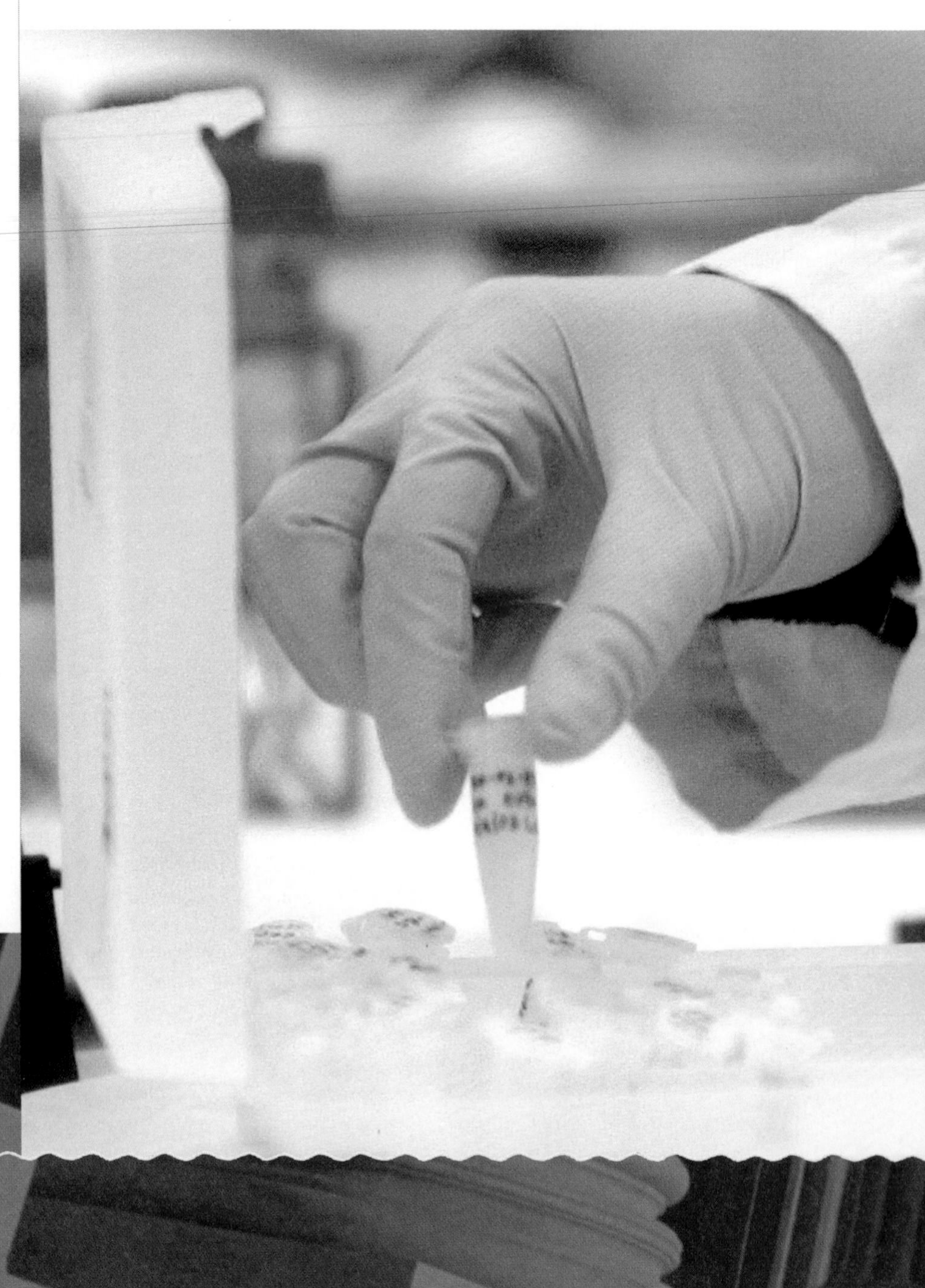

CHAPTER 4

Criminal Law

Objectives

After reading this chapter, the student should be able to:

1. Discuss where the criminal law fits into the continuum of social control.
2. Discuss the development and foundations of criminal law.
3. Discuss the role of common law in the modern criminal justice system.
4. Discuss the relationship of common law and precedent.
5. Discuss the role of the Constitution in the law and its relationship to state constitutions.
6. Discuss the role of the Bill of Rights.
7. Contrast statutes with administrative rules.
8. Discuss the differences between criminal law and civil law.
9. Discuss inchoate offenses.
10. Discuss concurrence and strict liability.

THE CRIMINAL LAW PERFORMS MANY FUNCTIONS IN SOCIETY. It details what behaviors are to be punished, as well as dictating just how governments can go about doing the punishing. The criminal law provides support for the strongly held values of citizens, and also, by omission, allows people to engage in acts that many others might find objectionable. Therefore, when we discuss criminal law, we must remember that it is not a simple concept. The criminal law is a complex, ever-changing, and highly politicized tool of government. As a form of social control, the criminal law occupies one end of a continuum.

folkways → mores → norms → laws

This continuum ranges from very mild controls, such as the table etiquette and polite manners taught to us by our parents and result in "that look from Mom" or a literal slap on the wrist, to the law that has the full force of the criminal justice system behind it and can result in incarceration or even death. In a very imperfect way, the continuum of proscribed behaviors is matched by ever-increasing sanctions. One of the principles behind social control, therefore, is proportionality: The more serious the infraction of

society's rules and sensibilities, the more severe the sanction.[1] However, as we will see throughout this chapter, one of the main crosscurrents of the criminal justice system is the variation in how similar cases are treated according to money, skin color, culture, gender, and a number of other factors that demonstrate that justice is not always blind.[2]

A democratic society has the opportunity to ensure that the criminal law reflects the values of all citizens. This is relatively easy to do when a consensus exists about which behaviors need to be outlawed. Certainly, homicide, rape, embezzlement, and carjacking are behaviors we all wish to be protected from by the criminal law. There are dangerous individuals who, we all agree, are best kept behind bars because of the harm they do. However, there are other behaviors for which there is no consensus and for which the criminal law is constantly in flux depending on which political groups are able to get their values addressed by the legislature and the court.[3]

Gambling laws are a good example of how economic and social values vie for primacy in the criminal law. In the not-too-distant past, Las Vegas and Atlantic City were the only places where legalized gambling was available in the United States. Now, many states allow casinos, and, in an in-

FOCUS ON ETHICS

Changing the Substantive Law

Laws are made by elected legislators to reflect the wishes of their constituents. In an ideal situation, communities enjoy a broad consensus as to what behaviors should be considered illegal and what the punishments should be for violating the law. However, citizens do not support a number of laws. These are broken regularly and sometimes enforced selectively.

Imagine that you are a state senator and that you have been told by the majority party leader that because of your hard work and your casting of several key votes, she can fix it with the rest of the party for you to have any law you want added to your state's criminal code. What behavior that is now legal in your state would you choose to make against the law? Does your new law address a significant social problem, or does it simply expose the rest of us to your personal aesthetic tastes, your religious sensitivities, or your individual pet peeves? For example, some people think that anyone smoking in public, even outdoors, should be arrested because of the danger of second-hand smoke.

On the other hand, what law that is currently on the books would you like to see removed? Why do you think this is a bad law, and what would be the social consequences of legalizing this behavior? For instance, if you are concerned with the right of people to choose to use drugs and decide to repeal the marijuana laws, some unanticipated consequences may accompany this change. More people may use marijuana in unsafe situations, such as while driving. Marijuana may become more easily available to children, and many people could develop health problems from long-term use.

Think through the possible ramifications of adding or deleting substantive laws. Even though no one would suggest that our system of laws is perfect as it now stands, we do need to be cautious when we change the law. One of the foundations of a democracy is the confidence of the people in the wisdom and fairness of the law. The criminal justice system cannot maintain the order of society without widespread voluntary social control. Consider how the laws that you would add to the legal code and the laws that you would delete would affect the relationship between citizens and the government.

teresting twist of the criminal law that describes the distinctions among jurisdictions, many states are forced to allow casinos on federal lands controlled by American Indians. Citizens in many states have voted to allow lotteries that produce revenue to offset taxes. It is easy to see, then, that all laws are not equally grounded in the values of all the people. Although most of us agree on laws concerning assault and rape, no such agreement exists on laws covering gambling, drug use, abortion, or pornography. All of these issues are settled by the criminal law, and that law changes depending on which groups are best able to get their concerns heard by the legislature.[4]

Sometimes the criminal law can appear discriminatory in its creation and execution. For instance, this is the case with the difference between penalties for cocaine sales and crack-cocaine sales. The punishments for selling minor amounts of crack-cocaine can be 10 times those for selling powdered cocaine. Critics of the criminal justice system contend that racism is the reason and that this disparity in punishments has caused a dramatic increase in the numbers of black males in prison. Others argue that as long as the criminal law is clear, offenders can decide to violate it or choose some other way of meeting their needs. If crack-cocaine penalties are too severe, then the offender can desist from drug use or switch to powder cocaine for which the penalties are less severe. Why the dramatic difference in laws for essentially the same drug?[5]

As covered in Chapter 3, some critical theories contend that those in power will use the criminal law to maintain and enhance their power. As the crimes of the powerful differ in kind and degree from the crimes of the powerless, we can expect the penalties to be more severe for the latter. In the case of crack-cocaine, its use has been concentrated in minority communities, and the penalties are harsh. According to some critical theories, if crack-cocaine moves into middle-class neighborhoods and schools, the penalties for its use may be relaxed.[6]

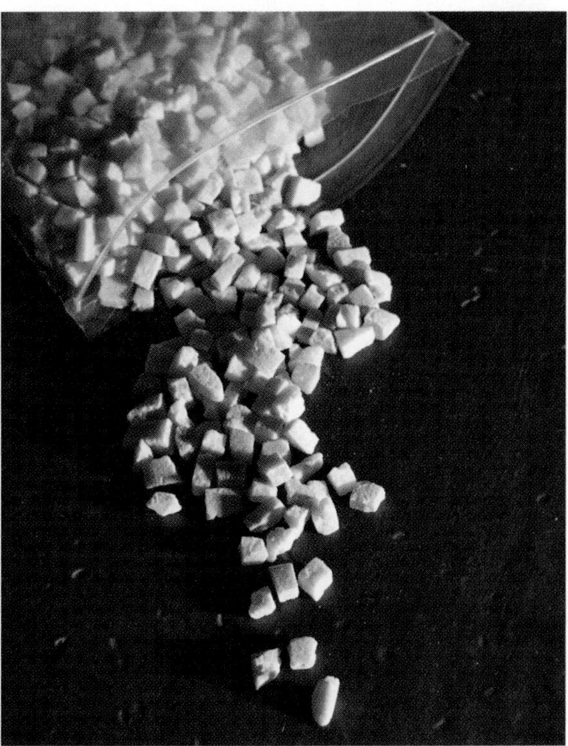

The war on drugs is in large part aimed at suppressing the availability of crack cocaine.
Courtesy of CORBIS-NY.

Development of Criminal Law

The history of the development of the criminal law is interesting because the process was episodic, uneven, and political. Societies did not systematically build on the law of previous cultures, but instead chose elements consistent with their own values, religions, and economic structures, and discarded elements that were not. Therefore, our own system is a hodgepodge of other societies' attempts to govern conduct through the criminal law.[7] A brief look at some of the previous systems of law provides insights into how our laws came to be structured as they are.

Code of Hammurabi

In 1901 a stone tablet was discovered that bore the laws of ancient Babylonia as written by its king, Hammurabi. These laws are the earliest known written laws. The 8-meter tablet, chiseled in the Akkadian language, dates to about 1780 B.C.E. and includes laws relating to a wide range of behaviors. The laws followed, literally, the "eye for an eye" philosophy, an indication that severe penalties have always been part of the history of legal codes. However, Hammurabi used this philosophy as a way of introducing some type of proportionality into the law. The **Code of Hammurabi** contained over 250 laws that covered a wide range of economic, social, and criminal issues. (For a sample of these laws, see Figure 4.1.) These laws reflect the values of the times. For instance, some of the laws make the penalties for the death or injury of slaves less severe than those for the death and injury of free people. Perhaps the most significant message to be learned from this code has nothing to do with the actual laws—which, after all, apply to a society much different from ours—but rather, that a code of laws even existed over 3,000 years ago. This tells us that the criminal law has a long and fascinating history.[8]

Code of Hammurabi
An ancient code instituted by Hammurabi, a ruler of Babylonia, dealing with criminal and civil matters.

The Code of Hammurabi is just one example of the various codes of law that were

This 7-foot stele depicts Hammurabi receiving his power to administer the law from the sun god Shamash. Carved into the black basalt underneath are Hammurabi's laws.
Photo from the Louvre, Paris, France, courtesy of SuperStock, Inc.

23. If the robber is not caught, then shall he who was robbed claim under oath the amount of his loss, then shall the community, on whose ground and territory and in whose domain it was, compensate him for the goods stolen.
109. If conspirators meet in the house of a tavern-keeper, and these conspirators are not captured and delivered to the court, the tavern-keeper shall be put to death.
135. If a man be taken prisoner in war and there be no sustenance in his house and his wife go to another house and bear children; and if later her husband return and come to his home, then this wife shall return to her husband, but the children follow their father.
148. If a man take a wife, and she be seized by disease, if he then desire to take a second wife he shall not put away his wife, who has been attacked by disease, but he shall keep her in the house which he has built and support her so long as she lives.

Figure 4.1
A Few Laws from the Code of Hammurabi

drawn up over the centuries. Figure 4.2 provides a partial list of historical documents that have influenced the development of modern laws.

The Magna Carta

A major document that contributed to U.S. law is the **Magna Carta**. The Magna Carta limited the power of the king and provided for the rights of citizens. King John signed the Magna Carta at Runneymede, England, on June 15, 1215, conceding a number of legal rights to the barons and the people. To finance his foreign wars, King John had taxed abusively. His barons threatened rebellion and coerced the king into committing to rudimentary judicial guarantees, such as freedom of the church, fair taxation, controls over imprisonment (**habeas corpus**), and the rights of all merchants to come and go freely, except in times of war. The Magna Carta has 61 clauses, the most important of which for our purposes is number 39: "No freeman shall be captured or imprisoned . . . except by lawful judgement of his peers or by the law of the land." This was the first time a king allowed that even he could be compelled to observe a law, with the barons allowed to "distrain and distress him in every possible way," just short of a legal right to rebellion. Once sworn to the document, letters were sent to all sheriffs ordering them to read the charter aloud in public. It was the first "bill of rights" that attempted to levy some kind of controls over the powers of English kings.[9]

As the law developed over the centuries, it specified not only what rulers may do, but also what they may not do. The law limited the capricious decision-making powers of kings and dictated that people had certain protections from the government. Law thus became a two-edged sword. On one hand, it delineated a vast array of behaviors that citizens were told not to engage in, and on the other hand, it granted them rights and protections.

These dual functions of the law became extremely important in the modern criminal justice system. A major factor in this system is the **common law**, which was first developed in England and brought to the North American colonies where it was modified to fit the new culture.

Common Law

Common law is different from **statutory law**. Instead of being expressly specified by a constitution or a legislature, the common law is based on the past decisions of the judiciary. Sometimes called case law, judiciary law, judge-made law, customary law, or unwritten law, common law is based on the doctrine of **precedent**. This means that judges look to previous cases with similar circumstances to see how justice was meted out. The idea behind common law is that similar cases should be treated in a similar manner. Over the decades, thousands of cases came to form the foundation of common law. As

Magna Carta
"Great Charter." A guarantee of liberties signed by King John of England in 1215 that influenced many modern legal and constitutional principles.

habeas corpus
A writ issued to bring a party before the court.

common law
Sometimes called case law, judiciary law, judge-made law, customary law, or unwritten law, common law is based on customs and general principles and is included in case law. Common law may also be used as precedent or for matters not addressed by statute.

statutory law
The type of law that is enacted by legislatures, as opposed to common law.

precedent
A prior legal decision used as a basis for deciding a later, similar case.

Figure 4.2 Important Dates in Legal History

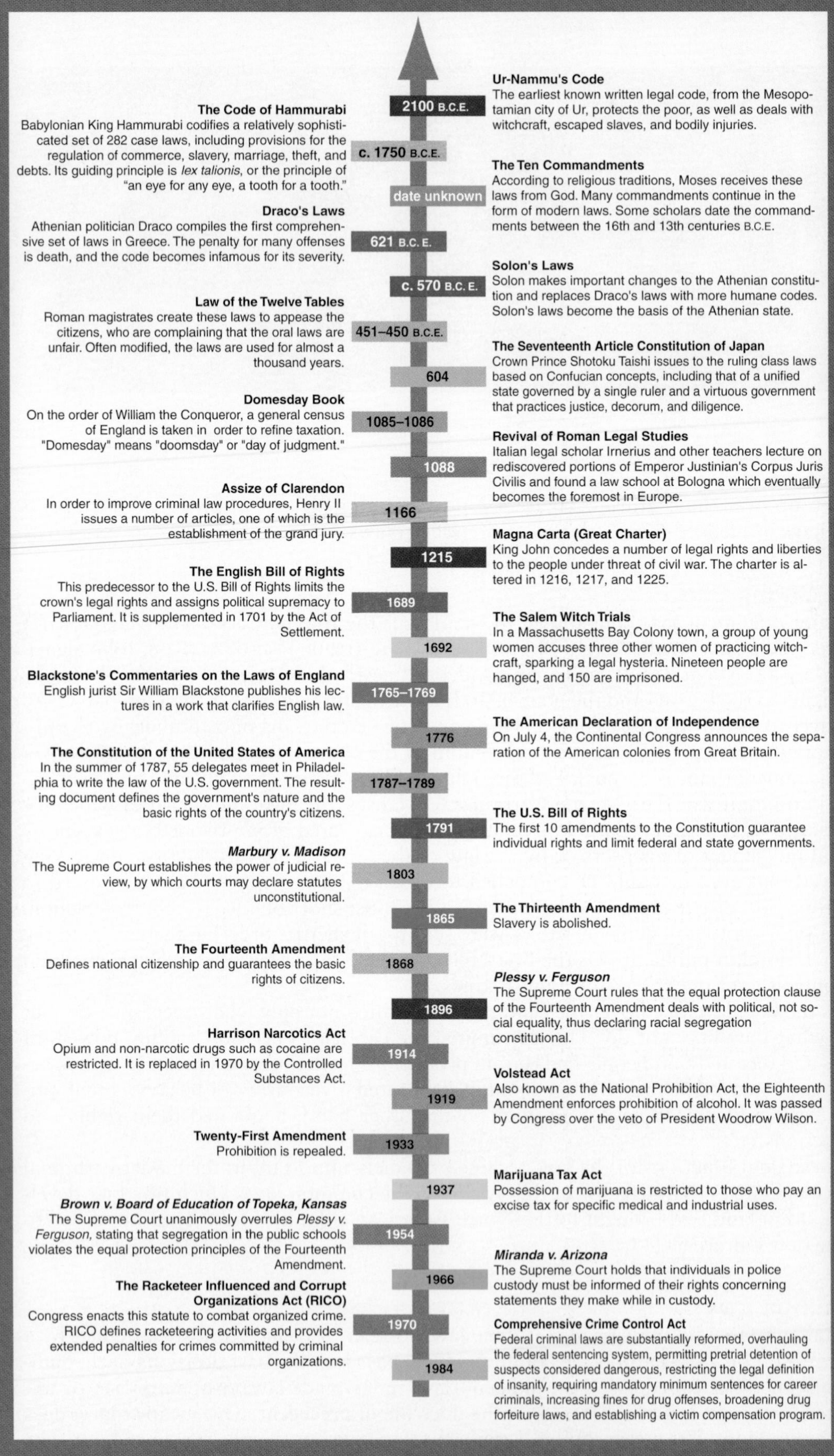

2100 B.C.E.
Ur-Nammu's Code
The earliest known written legal code, from the Mesopotamian city of Ur, protects the poor, as well as deals with witchcraft, escaped slaves, and bodily injuries.
c. 1750 B.C.E.
The Code of Hammurabi
Babylonian King Hammurabi codifies a relatively sophisticated set of 282 case laws, including provisions for the regulation of commerce, slavery, marriage, theft, and debts. Its guiding principle is lex talionis, or the principle of "an eye for any eye, a tooth for a tooth."
date unknown
The Ten Commandments
According to religious traditions, Moses receives these laws from God. Many commandments continue in the form of modern laws. Some scholars date the commandments between the 16th and 13th centuries B.C.E.
621 B.C.E.
Draco's Laws
Athenian politician Draco compiles the first comprehensive set of laws in Greece. The penalty for many offenses is death, and the code becomes infamous for its severity.
c. 570 B.C.E.
Solon's Laws
Solon makes important changes to the Athenian constitution and replaces Draco's laws with more humane codes. Solon's laws become the basis of the Athenian state.
451–450 B.C.E.
Law of the Twelve Tables
Roman magistrates create these laws to appease the citizens, who are complaining that the oral laws are unfair. Often modified, the laws are used for almost a thousand years.
604
The Seventeenth Article Constitution of Japan
Crown Prince Shotoku Taishi issues to the ruling class laws based on Confucian concepts, including that of a unified state governed by a single ruler and a virtuous government that practices justice, decorum, and diligence.
1085–1086
Domesday Book
On the order of William the Conqueror, a general census of England is taken in order to refine taxation. "Domesday" means "doomsday" or "day of judgment."
1088
Revival of Roman Legal Studies
Italian legal scholar Irnerius and other teachers lecture on rediscovered portions of Emperor Justinian's Corpus Juris Civilis and found a law school at Bologna which eventually becomes the foremost in Europe.
1166
Assize of Clarendon
In order to improve criminal law procedures, Henry II issues a number of articles, one of which is the establishment of the grand jury.
1215
Magna Carta (Great Charter)
King John concedes a number of legal rights and liberties to the people under threat of civil war. The charter is altered in 1216, 1217, and 1225.
1689
The English Bill of Rights
This predecessor to the U.S. Bill of Rights limits the crown's legal rights and assigns political supremacy to Parliament. It is supplemented in 1701 by the Act of Settlement.
1692
The Salem Witch Trials
In a Massachusetts Bay Colony town, a group of young women accuses three other women of practicing witchcraft, sparking a legal hysteria. Nineteen people are hanged, and 150 are imprisoned.
1765–1769
Blackstone's Commentaries on the Laws of England
English jurist Sir William Blackstone publishes his lectures in a work that clarifies English law.
1776
The American Declaration of Independence
On July 4, the Continental Congress announces the separation of the American colonies from Great Britain.
1787–1789
The Constitution of the United States of America
In the summer of 1787, 55 delegates meet in Philadelphia to write the law of the U.S. government. The resulting document defines the government's nature and the basic rights of the country's citizens.
1791
The U.S. Bill of Rights
The first 10 amendments to the Constitution guarantee individual rights and limit federal and state governments.
1803
Marbury v. Madison
The Supreme Court establishes the power of judicial review, by which courts may declare statutes unconstitutional.
1865
The Thirteenth Amendment
Slavery is abolished.
1868
The Fourteenth Amendment
Defines national citizenship and guarantees the basic rights of citizens.
1896
Plessy v. Ferguson
The Supreme Court rules that the equal protection clause of the Fourteenth Amendment deals with political, not social equality, thus declaring racial segregation constitutional.
1914
Harrison Narcotics Act
Opium and non-narcotic drugs such as cocaine are restricted. It is replaced in 1970 by the Controlled Substances Act.
1919
Volstead Act
Also known as the National Prohibition Act, the Eighteenth Amendment enforces prohibition of alcohol. It was passed by Congress over the veto of President Woodrow Wilson.
1933
Twenty-First Amendment
Prohibition is repealed.
1937
Marijuana Tax Act
Possession of marijuana is restricted to those who pay an excise tax for specific medical and industrial uses.
1954
Brown v. Board of Education of Topeka, Kansas
The Supreme Court unanimously overrules Plessy v. Ferguson, stating that segregation in the public schools violates the equal protection principles of the Fourteenth Amendment.
1966
Miranda v. Arizona
The Supreme Court holds that individuals in police custody must be informed of their rights concerning statements they make while in custody.
1970
The Racketeer Influenced and Corrupt Organizations Act (RICO)
Congress enacts this statute to combat organized crime. RICO defines racketeering activities and provides extended penalties for crimes committed by criminal organizations.
1984
Comprehensive Crime Control Act
Federal criminal laws are substantially reformed, overhauling the federal sentencing system, permitting pretrial detention of suspects considered dangerous, restricting the legal definition of insanity, requiring mandatory minimum sentences for career criminals, increasing fines for drug offenses, broadening drug forfeiture laws, and establishing a victim compensation program.

King John of England signed the Magna Carta in 1215 to appease the barons who demanded rights and guarantees. The document also implied the rights of the Church, towns, and the king's subjects.
Courtesy of Corbis/Bettmann.

precedents were set, lawyers and judges had to consider those precedents in the administration of cases. Today, four issues guide precedent:

1. **Predictability.** Predictability provides the concept of precedent with a certain level of order. By being consistent with the reasoning of previous cases and providing an outcome that fits with that reasoning, the common law gains legitimacy among people because they can understand on what basis judgments are determined.
2. **Reliability.** Participants in the legal system expect the court to follow precedent. Even when there is some dispute about the facts of the case, the court is obliged to consider how previous cases were decided. Reliability means that the court is using precedent as a guiding feature.
3. **Efficiency.** Participants expect cases to be resolved in a reasonable time. Common law has created an expectation of how long cases should take to resolve. Of course, there will be some extreme exceptions to the time it takes to try a sensational case, but precedent defines when the time is becoming excessive.
4. **Equality.** Similar cases are expected to be treated in similar fashion. This is the most important function of the concept of precedent. The concept of justice is dependent on the perception that the court treats individuals fairly. To have vast differences in outcome of similar cases violates the concept of equality.[10]

Courts are generally bound by the decisions of previous courts by this doctrine of precedent. This legal principle is know as **stare decisis**, whereby the precedent of a previous case become the standard by which subsequent cases are considered.[11] Part of the art of the practice of law is the attorney's skill in finding similar cases and convincing the court that the circumstances are so close to the present case that a similar decision should be imposed. The opposing attorney will dispute the similarity of the circumstances and find other similar cases with different outcomes to buttress a given position. Consequently, the law is not as cut-and-dried as sometimes believed. The law is open to interpretation, and

stare decisis
The doctrine under which courts adhere to legal precedent.

the legal reasoning, persuasive arguments, and reputation of one's attorney may play an important role in how a case is decided.

Common law is important not only for the doctrine of precedent, but also because it has informed the development of other sources of law. As legislatures developed constitutions and statutes, they used the common law as a guide. In most areas, common law has been superceded by more formal and explicit sources of law. It is worth considering these in greater detail to gain a fuller understanding on how the criminal law operates.

Sources of Law

One of the difficulties in understanding the law is keeping in mind that it is derived from no single source. Consequently, inconsistent principles, overlapping jurisdictions, and unclear nuances often appear in the criminal justice system. Considering the sources of the law can shed some light on this confusion. These sources are constitutions, statutes, and administrative rules.

Constitutions

In democracies, constitutions play a central and critical role in the development of criminal law. Constitutions express the will of the people. In a representative democracy, such as the United States, the Constitution binds elected legislators, the institutions of society, and the citizens to a system of government and laws. In the United States, the federal Constitution governs the country. Each state also has a constitution that pertains to the citizens and businesses of that state. State constitutions supplement but do not supercede the federal Constitution. This means that states cannot take away freedoms granted by the federal Constitution. Although the U.S. Constitution does not proscribe many behaviors, it sets out some broad values that cannot be abridged by the criminal law. The Constitution specifies how the government is structured and the role to be played by the various branches of government. One of the first issues the framers of the Constitution dealt with almost immediately after the Constitution was completed was specifying how citizens were to be protected from the government. The first 10 amendments to the Constitution, also known as the **Bill of Rights**, dictate the basic freedoms enjoyed by citizens (see Figure 4.3). Later legislators did not stop there. The Constitution has been amended 27 times. Emendation is a cumbersome process, requiring the ratification of state legislatures, but the important point to remember is that the Constitution is a living and changing document, not an absolute one.

Bill of Rights
The first 10 amendments to the U.S. Constitution, which guarantees fundamental rights and privileges to citizens.

Statutes

Federal and state legislative bodies have developed the common law into specific **statutes** that proscribe criminal behavior. These laws are debated and voted on by the legislative bodies and presumably represent the will of the people. For many behaviors, such as rape or homicide, a consensus exists as to what the law should cover. However, there are other crimes, such as drug use or gambling, that many citizens contend should not be against the law. Regardless of personal beliefs, however, all citizens are expected to obey the law or risk entering the criminal justice system. The advantage of statutes over the common law is that statutes are published in **penal codes** and therefore fit the principles of predictability, reliability, efficiency, and equality better than the doctrine of precedent. Statutes are easier to change than the Constitution, but new laws cannot violate rights given in the Constitution.[12] Consequently, new laws are often challenged on constitutional grounds.

statute
A law enacted by a legislature.

penal code
A code of laws that deals with crimes and the punishments for them.

Administrative Rules

A number of agencies have developed rules consistent with their responsibilities to oversee aspects of commerce and public protection. Health, environment, customs, and parole agencies all have the authority to enact rules that limit the freedoms of individuals operating within their spheres of influence. Sometimes, these administrative rules overlap with criminal statutes or constitutional rights and end up in court.[13] For instance, administrative rules about minority hiring practices or university admission policies have been found to be at

Figure 4.3
The Bill of Rights

Amendment I

Congress shall make no law respecting an establishment of religion, or prohibiting the free exercise thereof; or abridging the freedom of speech, or of the press; or the right of the people peaceably to assemble, and to petition the government for a redress of grievances.

Amendment II

A well regulated militia, being necessary to the security of a free state, the right of the people to keep and bear arms, shall not be infringed.

Amendment III

No soldier shall, in time of peace be quartered in any house, without the consent of the owner, nor in time of war, but in a manner to be prescribed by law.

Amendment IV

The right of the people to be secure in their persons, houses, papers, and effects, against unreasonable searches and seizures, shall not be violated, and no warrants shall issue, but upon probable cause, supported by oath or affirmation, and particularly describing the place to be searched, and the persons or things to be seized.

Amendment V

No person shall be held to answer for a capital, or otherwise infamous crime, unless on a presentment or indictment of a grand jury, except in cases arising in the land or naval forces, or in the militia, when in actual service in time of war or public danger; nor shall any person be subject for the same offense to be twice put in jeopardy of life or limb; nor shall be compelled in any criminal case to be a witness against himself, nor be deprived of life, liberty, or property, without due process of law; nor shall private property be taken for public use, without just compensation.

Amendment VI

In all criminal prosecutions, the accused shall enjoy the right to a speedy and public trial, by an impartial jury of the state and district wherein the crime shall have been committed, which district shall have been previously ascertained by law, and to be informed of the nature and cause of the accusation; to be confronted with the witnesses against him; to have compulsory process for obtaining witnesses in his favor, and to have the assistance of counsel for his defense.

Amendment VII

In suits at common law, where the value in controversy shall exceed twenty dollars, the right of trial by jury shall be preserved, and no fact tried by a jury, shall be otherwise reexamined in any court of the United States, than according to the rules of the common law.

Amendment VIII

Excessive bail shall not be required, nor excessive fines imposed, nor cruel and unusual punishments inflicted.

Amendment IX

The enumeration in the Constitution, of certain rights, shall not be construed to deny or disparage others retained by the people.

Amendment X

The powers not delegated to the United States by the Constitution, nor prohibited by it to the states, are reserved to the states respectively, or to the people.

The U.S. Constitution is the country's foremost source of laws. All laws must be consistent with the provisions of the Constitution.

Courtesy of CORBIS-NY.

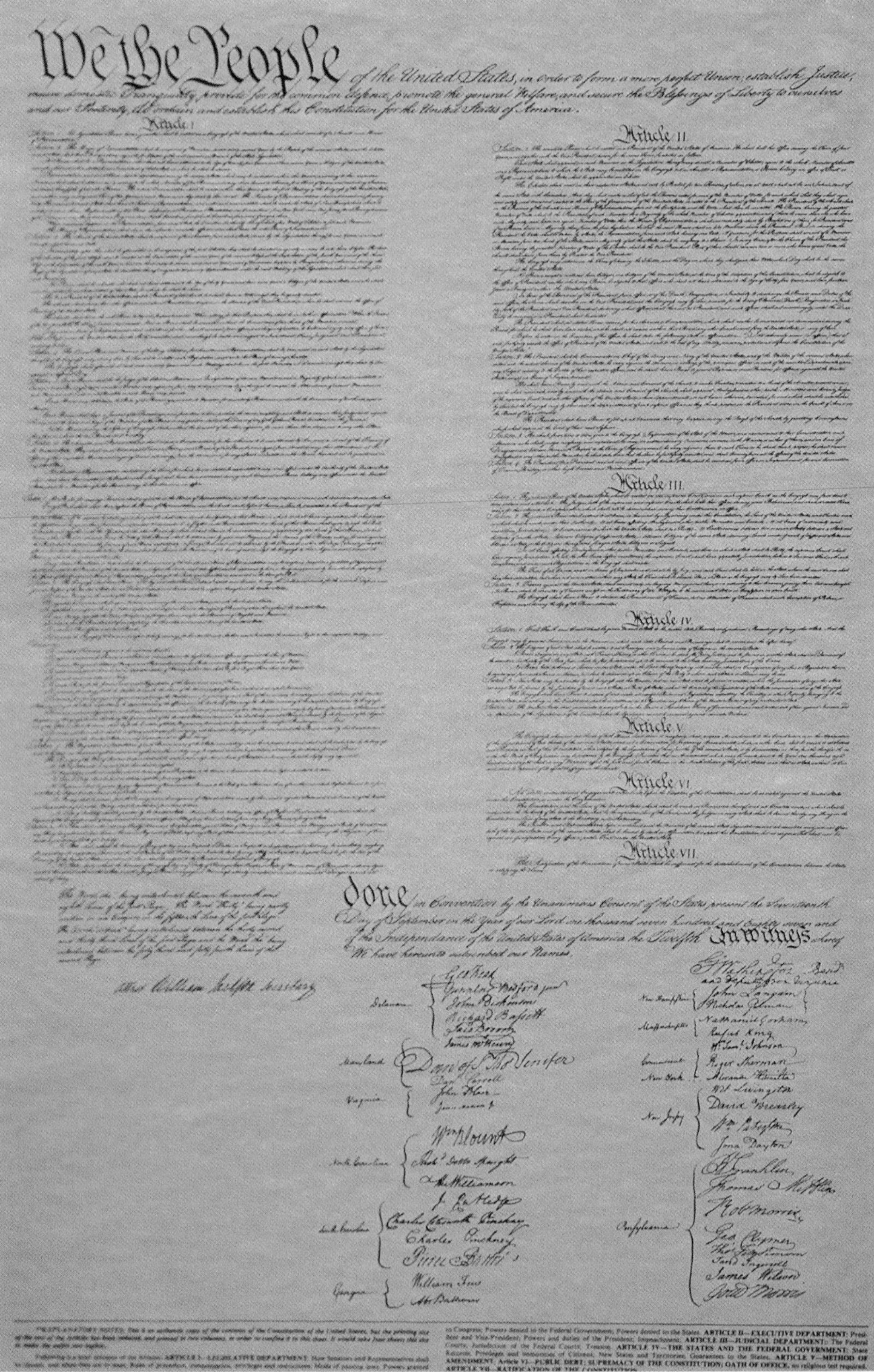

We the People of the United States, in Order to form a more perfect Union, establish Justice, insure domestic Tranquility, provide for the common defence, promote the general Welfare, and secure the Blessings of Liberty to ourselves and our Posterity, do ordain and establish this Constitution for the United States of America.

Article I

Article II

Article III

Article IV

Article V

Article VI

Article VII

done in Convention by the Unanimous Consent of the States present the Seventeenth Day of September in the Year of our Lord one thousand seven hundred and Eighty seven and of the Independance of the United States of America the Twelfth In witness whereof We have hereunto subscribed our Names.

odds with constitutional guarantees. In another example, parolees are subject to a host of conditions that require approval from one's parole officer, such as changing residences, traveling out of state, getting married, or drinking alcohol. These are all rules considered by the parole agency to be necessary to aid the parolee in the transition from incarceration to the free world. Violation of these conditions can result in the parolee returning to prison. Because these issues are administrative rules rather than legal statutes, the parolee is not accorded the full range of constitutional rights, as is the criminal defendant.

Types of Law

As a form of social control, the law is required to perform many functions. In addition to defining socially unacceptable behaviors, it also regulates the rules of social conflict, dictates how authorities control behavior and maintain public order, and regulates how behavior is punished. Different types of laws accomplish these multiple functions. The main distinction discussed here is the one between criminal law and civil law.

Criminal Law

What criteria are used to determine that a behavior is so serious that it be made a crime and specified in the criminal law? Many objectionable behaviors are not covered by criminal law. Conversely, the criminal law covers some behaviors that many people believe it should not cover. Ideally, the criminal law is the mechanism of social control used only when other mechanisms (family, church, community) have failed, and is used only on serious transgressions. Three criteria determine what behaviors are made criminal:

1. **The enforceability of the law.** Laws that cannot be enforced do little good. The prohibition of alcohol in the 1920s showed what happens when the law cannot be enforced. People continued to drink alcohol, but the government received no

Prohibition did not stop people from drinking alcohol. Because it was illegal, drinking was considered by many to be romantic and adventurous. In this 1933 photo, four young women drink to celebrate the end of Prohibition.

Courtesy of CORBIS-NY.

revenue from alcohol sales that could be used to combat the negative effects of drinking. Many critics believe that the war on drugs is another example of laws that cannot be effectively enforced. Even as prison systems are overflowing with those convicted of drug-related crimes, illegal drugs remain ample.

2. **The effects of the law.** Sometimes the cure is worse than the disease. During Prohibition, the consequences of attempting to enforce alcohol laws had a deleterious impact on society. Although alcohol was illegal, a great demand for it remained, bringing some unintended consequences in the form of organized crime and violence. Additionally, many otherwise law-abiding citizens were drawn into the criminal enterprise of alcohol production, transportation, and sales because of the lucrative alcohol trade. Perhaps even more harmful to society was the impact on the criminal justice system. Widespread corruption of judges and law enforcement officers seriously damaged the faith of citizens in the efficacy and fairness of government officials.
3. **The existence of other means to protect society against undesirable behavior.** Many people make the argument that even though drug and alcohol use have some unattractive features, the criminal justice system is not the most efficient and effective institution to control this behavior. Instead of attempting to discourage addictive behavior by punishment and deterrence, some experts contend that medical and psychological treatment would be more effective and not cause the harmful side effects of the war on drugs. Instead of using the criminal law as a weapon against drugs, the medical and mental health community could be better funded and expanded to address the problem. The repeal of Prohibition did not eliminate the problems of alcohol, but most would agree that by legalizing it, the United States dealt more effectively with its health and social problems and spared the criminal justice system the temptations of corruption.[14]

The criteria for deciding which behaviors should be made criminal are not always heeded by legislators. The making of criminal law is as much a political enterprise as it is a scientific one. Most citizens try to obey the law, but all of us are guilty of choosing to disregard some laws. Think about the last time you purposefully exceeded the legal speed limit. Was it on your way to class today? Because of people like you, the government decided to repeal the once-universal 55-miles-per-hour speed limit on the interstate highway system. The trucking industry and those who traveled routinely broke the speeding laws, and ultimately, the federal and state governments were lobbied for a more realistic speed limit. From a safety perspective, the 55-miles-per-hour limit was useful, but it was ignored by too many citizens and eventually modified.

Criminal versus Civil Law

civil law
The law that governs private rights as opposed to the law that governs criminal issues.

There is an important difference between the criminal law and another type of law called **civil law**. Both types of law try to control the behavior of people and both can impose sanctions. Also, there is some considerable overlap in the types of behavior they address, such as personal assault or environmental pollution. The important difference between them, however, concerns the identity of the aggrieved party. In civil law, the case is between two individuals. In criminal law, the case concerns the offender and the government. When someone is charged with assault, the dispute is taken away from the victim and the assailant by the court and becomes the property of the government. The victim's role is greatly reduced by the government, which prosecutes the case in the name of the state.[15] This aspect of the criminal law confuses and frustrates many victims who still consider the case as a problem between themselves and the offenders. The court, meanwhile, disposes of the case and inflicts the sentence on the offender without substantial input from the victim or often any restitution or satisfaction.[16]

At this point, the victim can invoke the civil law for redress. The victim can sue the assailant for compensation for damages. A private attorney, as opposed to the state prosecutor, represents the victim. The sentence of the court is concerned with monetary damages, not with the prospect of incarceration. Civil law covers contracts, personal

How to Read Legal Citations

Many students are perplexed by the seemingly complicated system of citations for legal cases. This figure decodes the numbers and abbreviations that go into the making of a legal citation.

CASES

United States Supreme Court

Brown v. Board of Education, 347 U.S. 483, 490 (1954).

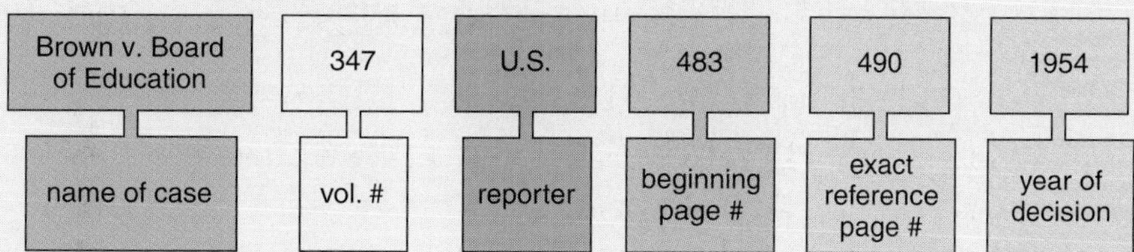

Lower Federal Court

Brown v. Board of Education, 98 F. Supp. 797 (D. Kan. 1951).

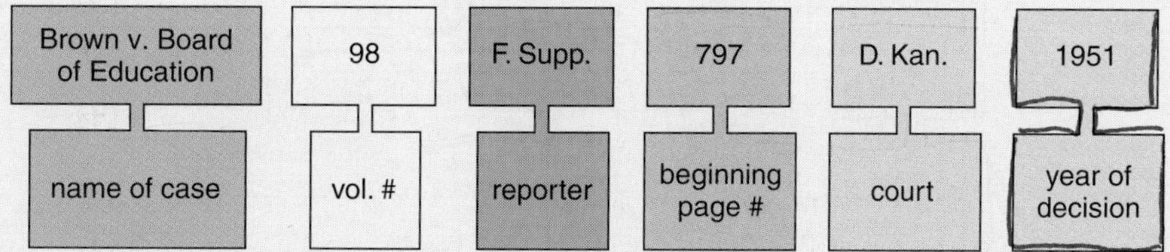

"Universal" or "Vendor-Neutral" Case Citation as adopted by the Wisconsin State Bar

Jones v. Smith, 1996 Wis 47 ¶ 15.

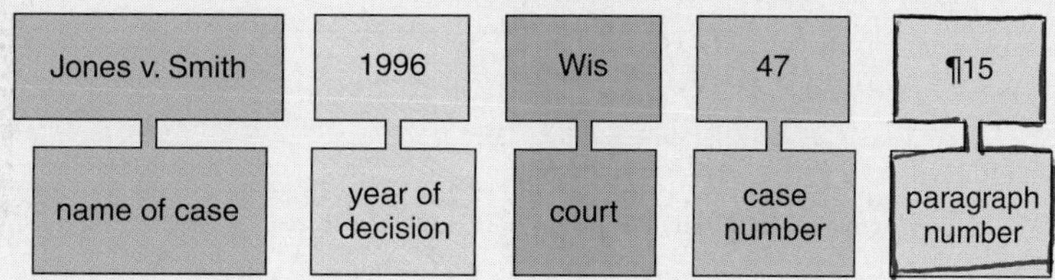

STATUTES

Session Law

Civil Rights Act of 1964, P.L. 88-353, 78 Stat. 241 (1964).

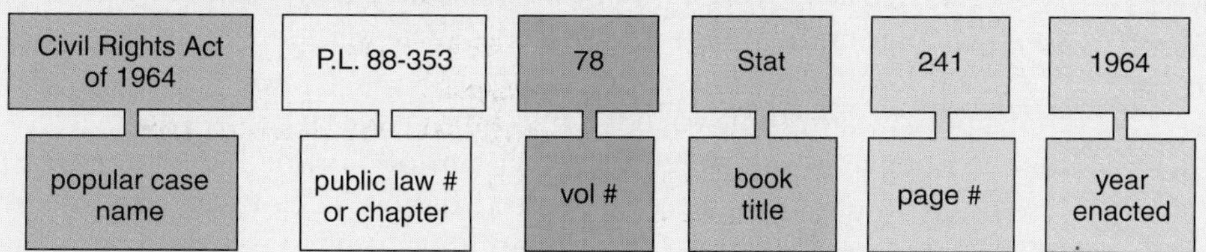

Code

Civil Rights Act of 1964, 42 U.S.C. §1971 et seq. (1988).

continued

REFERENCE (CONTINUED)

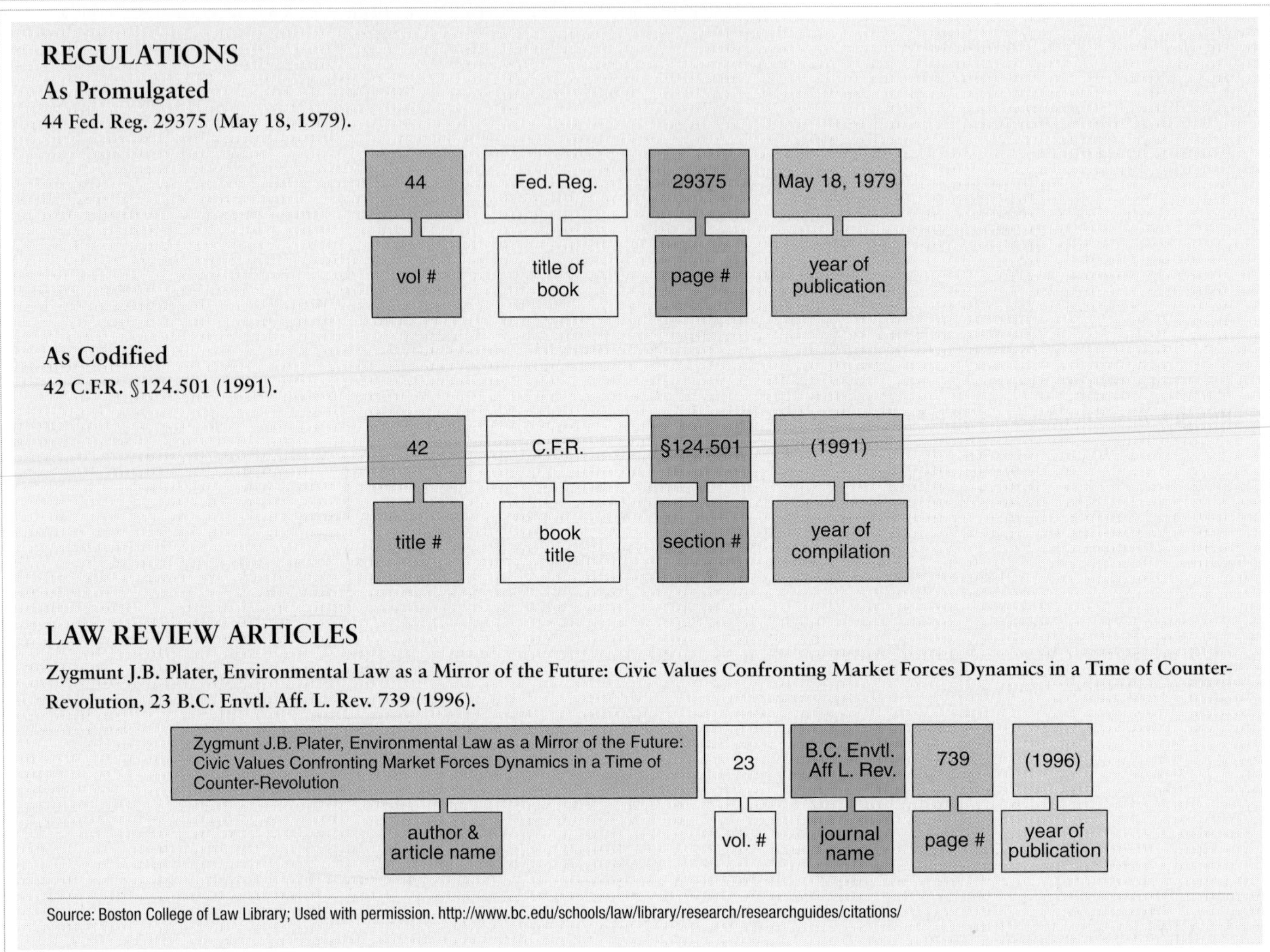

REGULATIONS

As Promulgated

44 Fed. Reg. 29375 (May 18, 1979).

As Codified

42 C.F.R. §124.501 (1991).

LAW REVIEW ARTICLES

Zygmunt J.B. Plater, Environmental Law as a Mirror of the Future: Civic Values Confronting Market Forces Dynamics in a Time of Counter-Revolution, 23 B.C. Envtl. Aff. L. Rev. 739 (1996).

Source: Boston College of Law Library; Used with permission. http://www.bc.edu/schools/law/library/research/researchguides/citations/

tort law
A large area of the law that deals with civil acts, other than breach of contract, that cause harm and injury. Tort law includes libel, slander, assault, trespass, and negligence.

double jeopardy
The prosecution in the same jurisdiction of a defendant for an offense for which the defendant has already been prosecuted and convicted or acquitted. Also refers to multiple punishments for a single offense. The Fifth Amendment states that no person will "be subject for the same offense to be twice put in jeopardy of life or limb."

property, maritime law, and commercial law. **Tort law**, a form of civil law, covers personal wrongs and damage and includes libel, slander, assault, trespass, and negligence.[17]

A well-known but misunderstood principle of law known as **double jeopardy** states that a person cannot be tried for the same crime twice.[18] This concept applies to the criminal law but does not preclude the victim of a crime from suing for private damages after the criminal trial has concluded. It was because of this distinction between the criminal law and civil law that the families of Nicole Brown Simpson and Ronald Goldman were awarded monetary damages from O. J. Simpson after he was acquitted of criminal charges. The standards of proof in a civil trial (preponderance of evidence) are not as stringent as those in a criminal trial (beyond a reasonable doubt), which may explain how two juries can consider the same case and produce such different verdicts.[19] In addition to the distinction between criminal law and civil law, an important difference within the criminal law must be appreciated. This distinction concerns **substantive law** and **procedural law**.

Substantive Law

Substantive law tells us which behaviors have been defined as crime. The "thou shall nots" of the criminal law, substantive laws are found in the criminal codes of the state

! NEWS FLASH

Rodney King and Double Jeopardy

Courtesy of CORBIS-NY.

The concept of double jeopardy is easily misunderstood. Although basically it refers to the prohibition of a defendant being tried twice for the same crime, the full definition is a bit more complicated. Take, for example, the two trials of the police officers who participated in the 1991 beating of motorist Rodney King.

On March 3, 1991, Los Angeles police officers stopped Rodney King's car after a high-speed chase and ordered him to exit the car and lie on the ground. His two passengers, both adult males, complied, but King did not leave the car immediately. King, who had been drinking, resisted arrest, behaving erratically and aggressively. Four officers, Laurence Powell, Timothy Wind, Theodore Briseno, and Stacey Koon, began beating King with their batons, fracturing his skull and causing internal injuries.

Unknown to the police, plumbing company manager George Holliday was videotaping the incident from his nearby apartment. The next day he released the tape to the media. On March 7 the Los Angeles County district attorney dismissed the charges against King. On March 15 the four officers were charged with assault.

The case went to trial in a state court, and on April 29, 1992, the officers were cleared of assault. Riots ensued and continued across Los Angeles for several days. In the end, 55 people were killed, about 2,000 were injured, and over 7,000 were arrested. The National Guard was eventually sent in to help restore order.

By February 1993 the four officers were on trial again, this time on federal charges of violating King's constitutional rights. Officers Timothy Wind and Theodore Briseno were acquitted, but the jury found Stacey Koon and Laurence Powell guilty. Koon and Powell received 30-month prison terms.

Although, at first glance, the two trials appear to violate the double jeopardy prohibition, the trials had enough differences to steer clear of double jeopardy (see table).

	First Trial	**Second Trial**
Jurisdiction	State	Federal
Offense	Assault	Violation of constitutional rights
Type of suit	Criminal	Criminal

The primary issue involves the concept of "dual sovereignty." In *U.S. v. Lanza* (1922), the Supreme Court decided that dual sovereignty permits successive state and federal prosecutions for the same crime, stating that, "an act denounced as a crime by both national and state sovereignties is an offense against the peace and dignity of both and may be punished by each." Therefore, the first trial was conducted by the State of California and the second by the federal government, each concerning a different offense. Because both cases were tried in criminal courts, the officers were eligible for incarceration in both trials.

Sources: BBC, "Flashback: Rodney King and the LA Riots," July 10, 2002, http://news.bbc.co.uk/1/hi/world/americas/2119943.stm. The Rodney King Beating Trials, *Jurist,* http://jurist.law.pitt.edu/trials24.htm. *U.S. v. Lanza,* 260 U.S. 377 (1922).

substantive law
The law that defines rights and proscribes certain actions (crimes).

procedural law
Laws that prescribe the methods for their enforcement and use.

and federal governments and are the result of generations of political and social development. Homicide, rape, assault, money laundering, and all the other behaviors that are against the law are proscribed in the substantive law. The substantive law also sets the parameters on the punishment for each type of crime. Once an offender has been convicted, the judge does not have unlimited discretion in imposing sentence. Few offenses are eligible for the death penalty. In the case of minor offenses, the judge can choose a short period of incarceration or decide that society is better served by placing the offender on probation.

Liable, but Not Guilty

Perhaps one of the most interesting demonstrations of the difference between criminal and civil law was connected to the O. J. Simpson murder case. In June 1994 Simpson was charged with murdering his former wife, Nicole Brown Simpson, and her friend, Ronald Goldman, at her Brentwood, California, home. O. J. Simpson was tried for the murders in 1995 and acquitted that October. A year later the families of Nicole Brown Simpson and Ronald Goldman sued O. J. Simpson for the victims' wrongful deaths and won an $8.5 million judgment against him. How could O. J. Simpson be acquitted of murder, yet liable for wrongful death?

The major difference between civil trials and criminal trials is the threshold of guilt. To find a defendant guilty in a criminal trial, a jury must determine whether there is proof of guilt beyond a reasonable doubt. In Simpson's criminal trial, then, doubt was all that was needed to acquit, and Simpson's attorneys were successful in introducing this doubt. However, a finding of liability in a civil trial requires a much lower threshold. A jury needs only a preponderance of evidence—not proof beyond a reasonable doubt—to find a defendant liable for a given action. The evidence that failed to bring a guilty finding in the criminal trial was enough for a liability finding in the civil trial. Another important difference is the number of jurors who must agree on a verdict. The jurors in Simpson's civil trial were unanimous, but only 9 of 12 jurors are required to agree that a defendant is responsible. In a criminal trial, unanimity is required.

Damages are not awarded in criminal trials. The plaintiff in criminal trials is the state, not the aggrieved party. Therefore, civil trials can be a way for those who believe they have been harmed by a defendant's action to recoup damages.

In August 2002 David Westerfield was found guilty of the kidnapping and murder of his seven-year-old neighbor, Danielle van Dam, and sentenced to death. In May 2003 Danielle's parents settled a wrongful death suit against Westerfield, currently on California's death row. Westerfield, who liquidated his assets to pay for his defense, did not agree to the settlement and paid no money to the van Dams. Instead, Westerfield's automotive and homeowners' insurance companies paid the van Dams an amount the family's attorney said ranged from $400,000 to $1 million.

QUESTIONS

1. Do situations such as the one in the Simpson case—with a defendant being found liable, but not guilty—make a mockery of the justice system, or is it merely a curiosity and a necessary part of the justice system?
2. In the case of the van Dams, should Westerfield's insurance company have had to pay the van Dams?

Sources: CNN, Simpson Civil Trial Special Section, http://www.cnn.com/US/OJ/simpson.civil.trial/. Harriet Ryan, "Van Dams Settle Civil Suit Against Daughter's Killer," Court TV.com, May 15, 2003, http://www.courttv.com/trials/westerfield/051403_ctv.html.

Procedural Law

Whereas the substantive law specifies what individuals are allowed to do, the procedural law specifies how the criminal justice system is allowed to deal with those who break the law (see Figure 4.4). The procedural law sets the rules by which the police and courts process cases. Based to a large degree on the rights granted to accused individuals by the Constitution, procedural law protects citizens from any arbitrary decision making of criminal justice professionals by dictating how cases are handled.[20] Procedural law specifies rules of arrest, search and seizure, rights to attorneys, and attorney/client privilege, as well as other "rules of the game." Procedural laws change with the creation of new case precedents, new laws, or new court opinions. For instance, in the wake of the terrorist attacks on New York and Washington, D.C., on September 11, 2001, the federal government decided that attorney/client privilege is not absolute and that the police may

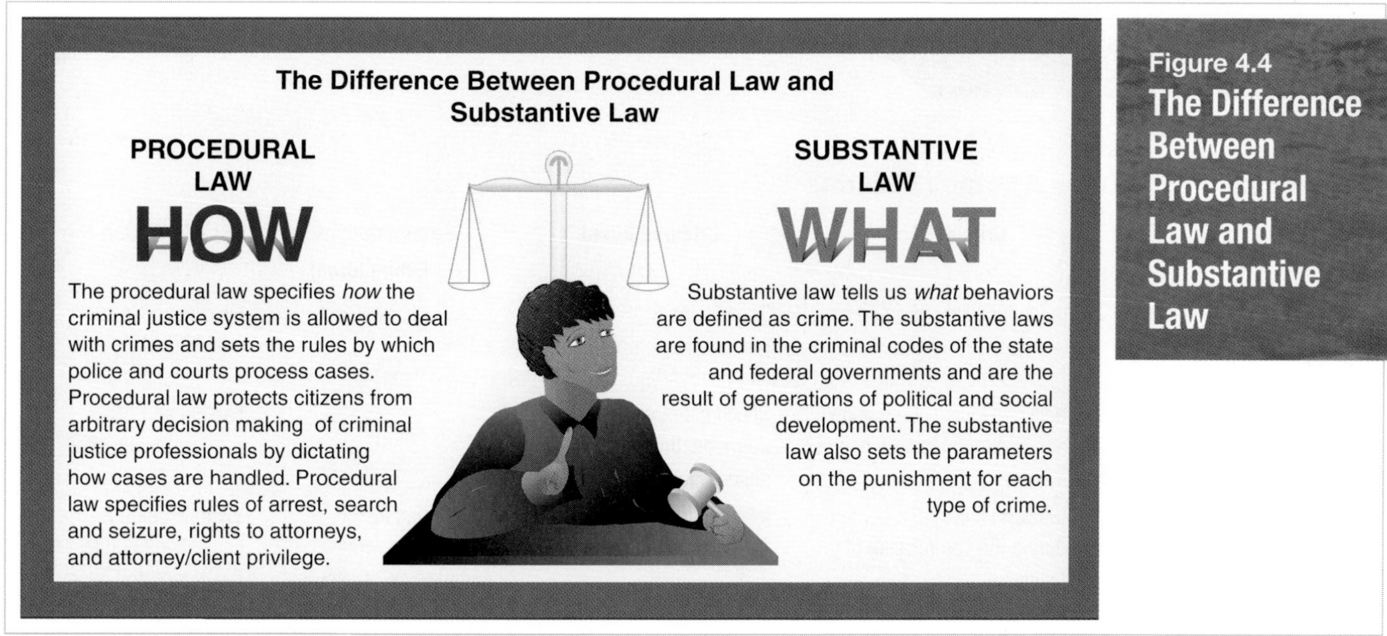
The Difference Between Procedural Law and Substantive Law
PROCEDURAL LAW
HOW
The procedural law specifies how the criminal justice system is allowed to deal with crimes and sets the rules by which police and courts process cases. Procedural law protects citizens from arbitrary decision making of criminal justice professionals by dictating how cases are handled. Procedural law specifies rules of arrest, search and seizure, rights to attorneys, and attorney/client privilege.
SUBSTANTIVE LAW
WHAT
Substantive law tells us what behaviors are defined as crime. The substantive laws are found in the criminal codes of the state and federal governments and are the result of generations of political and social development. The substantive law also sets the parameters on the punishment for each type of crime.

Figure 4.4
The Difference Between Procedural Law and Substantive Law

monitor conversations to prevent future terrorist acts. Whether this evidence could be used against an alleged terrorist in court is not clear at this time. This question will have to be decided by the courts.

Case Law

case law See *common law.*

Case law comes from judicial decisions and requires judges to consider how previous cases have dealt with similar issues. Case law enables the courts to ensure against a vast disparity in judicial outcomes and that a degree of uniformity exists across courts. Like common law, case law is dependent on the principle of precedent to ensure that cases are in line with how past cases have been decided and also serves as a guide for future cases. However, the past is not destiny. That means that case law evolves as new decisions are applied to new circumstances in each case. The legal reasoning of case law changes as appellate courts review the decisions of trial courts and note the reasons for their decisions that consequently guide future cases. The issue of jurisdiction also heavily influences case law. Cases decided in one judicial circuit might not be as influential in other circuits. Although the decisions of the U.S. Supreme Court are important to every court, a decision of a court in Seattle may be less influential on a court in New York than in another court in Seattle.[21]

Types of Crime

Many different types of crime cause a variety of problems to society and injuries to people. The criminal law has categorized crime according to a number of different features. For instance, the difference in the seriousness of crimes is captured by the felony versus misdemeanor distinction. Also, crimes are differentiated by who commits the behavior, as in the distinction of juvenile status offenses (underage drinking, for instance). Also, some statutes recognize criminal history in classifications for first-time offenders, career criminals, or sex offenders.

Felonies

Felonies are considered the most serious types of crime. They include murder, rape, assault, larceny, arson, and a host of other offenses at the state and federal level (see Tables 4.1 and 4.2). The felony distinction is important because many agencies and corporations will preclude employment to those convicted of this type of crime. Felons are also not

Table 4.1

Elements of Crimes Against Persons

Charge	Criminal Act	Criminal Intent	Circumstances (or Extenuation)	Causation
Premeditated first-degree murder	Unlawful killing of a person	Specific intent preceded by premeditation and deliberation		Factual and legal causation
Second-degree murder	Unlawful killing of a person not amounting to first-degree murder	Specific intent (without premeditation and deliberation)		Factual and proximate causation
Felony murder	Unlawful killing of a person during the commission of a felony	Intent to commit felony	Victim died in conjunction with commission of felony or flight	Victim's death is causally related to the committed felony
Voluntary manslaughter	Unlawful killing of a person	Intent to kill	Extenuation: Reasonable provocation and sudden passion or self-defense	Factual and proximate causation
Involuntary manslaughter	Unlawful killing of a person	Occurs as a result of the commission of a misdemeanor or a negligent act	Reckless or gross negligence	Factual and proximate causation
Battery	Unlawful, harmful, or offensive touching of a person	General intent		Factual and proximate causation
Attempted battery assault	Unsuccessful attempt to batter	Specific intent to batter		
Threatened battery assault	Making a person reasonably fear imminent battery	Specific intent to make a person fear imminent battery		Factual and proximate causation
Rape	Sexual penetration without consent and with use or threat of force	General intent		
Kidnapping	Seizing, detention, and hiding	Specific intent		
False imprisonment	Unlawful confinement and/or hiding of a person	Specific intent		

Source: Compiled and adapted from Frank A. Schubert, *Criminal Law* (Los Angeles: Roxbury, 2004). Used by permission.

allowed to run for public office, own a firearm, or enter certain professions, such as law enforcement or medicine. Also, the penalties for felonies are often more severe than for other types of crimes. Incarceration for felonies is usually more than one year, and life imprisonment or capital punishment are specified for some types of felonies.

Misdemeanors

Misdemeanors are less serious crimes than felonies and are subject to less severe penalties. Usually, the maximum incarceration for a misdemeanor is up to one year

Table 4.2

Elements of Property Crime

Charge	Criminal Act	Criminal Intent	Circumstances (or Extenuation)	Causation
Common larceny	Unlawful taking (caption) and carrying away	Specific intent to permanently deprive possessor of personal property	Personal property of another	
Embezzlement	Entrustment, conversion	Specific intent to defraud		
Larceny by false pretenses (theft by deceit)	Accused person has misrepresented material facts	Intent to defraud, knowledge that material facts were misrepresented	Victim relied on misrepresented facts to transfer title	
Robbery	Larceny by means of force or intimidation	Specific intent to permanently deprive possessor of property	Taken from the victim or from the victim's presence	
Extortion	Offender intimidates victim by threatening harm to victim's person, family, reputation, or property	Specific intent to permanently deprive possessor of property	Some jurisdictions require the offender to obtain the demanded property from the victim	
Forgery	Making, altering, falsifying, signing, or reproducing writing	Specific intent to defraud		
Burglary	Use of force that facilitates entry; unconsented entry (trespass)	Specific intent during trespass to commit a felony within the structure	A structure (originally a dwelling house or outbuildings) of another at night	
Arson	Burning or charring	General intent: accused person intends to commit the criminal act	A protected dwelling or structure	Factual and proximate causation
Trespass to land/premises	Entry/remaining on land or premises of another person	General intent	Entry/remaining is not without consent but after receiving written or oral notice not to enter/remain	

Source: Compiled and adapted from Frank A. Schubert, *Criminal Law* (Los Angeles: Roxbury, 2004). Used by permission.

in jail. Misdemeanants spend their time in county jails or stockades as opposed to the state prison system. More often than not, misdemeanor offenders will be placed on probation, fined, or required to do some type of community service rather than be incarcerated.

The distinction between felonies and misdemeanors can be confusing. A crime could be categorized as either, depending on the circumstances. Additionally, the prosecutor has wide discretion in deciding which type of crime to charge the offender with and may, as a result of plea bargaining, reduce the indictment from felony to misdemeanor. In some ways, this distinction gives the prosecutor immense power to coerce plea bargains from a defendant who is afraid of the vast consequence of being convicted as a felon as opposed to a misdemeanant.

Another important issue to remember about the difference between felonies and misdemeanors is that a specific behavior may be a felony in one jurisdiction and a misdemeanor in another (or maybe not even a crime at all). Gambling is a good example. Nevada has many types of legal gambling, whereas in other states most types of gambling are outlawed. For example, Georgia had no legalized gambling at all until the state decided that the revenue was so attractive that it instituted its own lottery system while continuing to prohibit other types of gambling. Additionally, the differences between felonies and misdemeanors can be observed in drug laws in which the amount of drug in possession necessary to be a felony varies widely from state to state. So although the distinction between a felony and misdemeanor is important, the actual practice in the application of the label by the criminal justice system is sometimes problematic.

Inchoate Offenses

A crime does not always have to be completed for the offender to be arrested, charged, and punished. To limit the harm caused by crime and to deter individuals from planning and attempting wrongdoing, a category of crimes was created termed **inchoate offenses.** One example of this type of offense is conspiracy. Although it is often difficult to prove, conspiracy to commit a crime is a behavior that legislators have deemed to be so serious that it needs to be discouraged and punished. For example, if Timothy McVeigh had been apprehended while collecting the materials and making the plans to bomb the Murrah Federal Building in Oklahoma City, then he could have been charged with inchoate offenses. As we move into the new millennium with a focus on terrorism, we can appreciate the need to have conspiracy laws available to incapacitate and deter individuals and groups intent on causing the type of mass destruction witnessed in the Oklahoma City bombing and the terrorist attacks on September 11, 2001.

inchoate offense
An offense comprising acts necessary to commit another crime.

Another type of inchoate offense involves attempt. An attempted rape (sexual assault) can distress a victim as much as one that is completed. Although the offender could be charged with assault, the concept of sexual assault comes closer to capturing the type of trauma done to the victim, so the punishment is more severe. The idea behind inchoate offenses is that the criminal should not have to be successful in completing the crime before the criminal justice system can successfully and severely respond. For instance, if law enforcement agents are aware of a plan to kill the president of the United States, should they have to wait until it is successfully completed before they arrest the conspirators?

Features of Crime

Not all harmful acts are considered crimes. Certainly, many automobile accidents have serious consequences for the victims, but unless the features necessary for the legal definition of a crime are present, then the accident, no matter how serious, will not be considered by the criminal court. Three elements must be present in order for an act to be labeled a crime:

1. The criminal act (***actus reus***)
2. The criminal intent (***mens rea***)
3. The relationship between *actus reus* and *mens rea* (**concurrence**)

Together, these three elements constitute ***corpus delicti*** or the "body of the crime." This does not mean an actual dead human body, as is found at the scene of a homicide, but rather, the aforementioned elements of the crime relevant to the case at hand.

actus reus
"Guilty deed." The physical action of a crime.

mens rea
"Guilty mind." Intent or knowledge to commit a crime.

concurrence
The coexistence of *actus reus* and *mens rea.*

corpus delicti
"Body of the crime." The crime itself.

Actus Reus

Actus reus or "guilty deed" occurs when an individual (whether as a principal, accessory, or accomplice) engages in a behavior specified by the criminal law. This can involve either doing something wrong (commission) or failing to do something that is legally obligated (omission). The law requires that this commission or omission be an actual behavior as opposed to a thought. Whereas some religions consider the mere thinking about prohibited behaviors to be wrong, the criminal law does not punish thoughts. Those thoughts must be translated into some type of action or intentional inaction. This is unlike inchoate offenses, which must involve something more than thoughts, even if it is only speech. For example, a bank teller is not criminally liable for considering embezzling money. However, when false accounts are created into which money is diverted, or when customers' deposited money is not recorded, then the requirements of the criminal act are met. Likewise, merely thinking about suicide is not against the law. Attempting to commit suicide by, say, taking an overdose of drugs or jumping off a tall building is a physical act that meets the definition of *actus reus.*

Actus reus does not refer to someone's status. A person who is addicted to drugs or is an alcoholic, is not considered to have met the standard of *actus reus.* However, if a person carries illegal drugs around, sells drugs, or conspires with others to sell drugs, then it is reasoned that actual criminal acts have occurred, and the person could be arrested. Additionally, drunken drivers are not punished for their consumption of alcohol, but because they committed the act of driving while impaired. To meet the test of *actus reus,* the behavior must also be voluntary. A person under the suggestion of hypnosis or some form of brainwashing is not aware of committing a crime. Similarly, liability does not extend to one who is unconscious or is having a convulsion or other reflexive reaction that causes harm.

Actus reus is sometimes more difficult to prove when it involves the act of criminal omission. Failing to act when one is legally required to report child abuse is one example. People are also expected to take steps to save the life of a victim of some trauma. Allowing someone to die—even if for logical reasons and with the consent of the person, as in cases involving the terminally ill—can sometimes be considered the basis for *actus reus.*

Mens Rea

In addition to considering the criminal act, the offender's state of mind is taken into consideration when deciding if a behavior is a crime. *Mens rea* or a "guilty mind" is considered present when a person acts purposefully, knowingly, recklessly, or negligently. The law distinguishes between general intent and specific intent when considering *mens rea.* General intent is present when the prosecution can prove that the defendant intended to do what the law forbids. Specific intent involves the intention of the defendant to accomplish a specific goal. In the case of murder, the prosecution will often say that the defendant shot the victim with the *intent* to kill. It is possible that the defendant was shooting to wound the victim or shooting warning shots in the air and struck the victim by mistake, but these conditions would need to be buttressed by other evidence to successfully circumvent specific intent. For instance, if witnesses hear me say, "Stop or I'll shoot you in the kneecap," and then I shoot you in the kneecap and the bullet ricochets into your head and kills you, my intent may not have been "to kill" but simply to do "great bodily harm." Whereas shooting someone in the head may allow the court to infer a specific intent to kill, shooting a person in the kneecap only allows the court to infer intent to injure.[22]

Concurrence

Both *actus reus* and *mens rea* must be present at the same time for a behavior to be considered a crime. If a person is killed in an automobile accident that involves another car, the driver of the other car is not charged with murder or manslaughter, because the driver did not intend to cause the accident or a death.

Strict Liability

Mens rea is not required for some statutory offenses. **Strict liability** offenses are the primary exception to the requirement of the presence of both *mens rea* and *actus reus.* Strict liability offenses tend to be crimes in which the public's welfare is at issue, such

strict liability
Responsibility for a crime without intention to commit a crime. *Mens rea* is not required in strict liability findings.

Serving alcohol to minors is against the law. Even when the servers believe the youths to be of legal age, they can be held accountable under the principle of strict liability.
Courtesy of CORBIS-NY.

as narcotics violations, health and safety violations, traffic violations, or sanitation violations. The offender need not have a guilty mind when breaking strict liability laws. For example, many bars and restaurants have a sign that reads, "We Card Everyone, Every Time." If the bartender or waiter serves alcohol to an underage person, even if that person appears to be over 21 years old, then the bartender is guilty of a crime. Because a liquor license can be crucial to a restaurant, the owners cannot afford to depend on the discretion of a bartender who works only on weekends and has no real investment in keeping the restaurant within the law. Requiring proof of age for every customer requesting an alcoholic beverage is the only way the establishment's owners can ensure that their employees do not put the business at risk of violating the strict liability rules.

Laws to protect children may also fall under the strict liability doctrine. Whereas sex between consenting adults is not considered criminal, sex between an adult and a child, even a consenting child, is a crime. Sometimes it is difficult to tell when a person is old enough to legally consent to sex, but it makes no difference to the court if an adult makes a mistake. The law is designed to protect children from predatory adults, and ignorance of a child's age is not a valid excuse.

Criminal Responsibility and Criminal Defense

The law recognizes that not all people are completely aware of the impact their behaviors have on others. Even though great physical harm or property damage may result from criminal behavior, the capacity of the offender to understand the ramifications of his or her behavior can produce mitigating reasoning that can excuse the individual from the full force of the criminal law. The defense attorney will look for reasons to justify or excuse the criminal behavior. Essentially, six arguments can be employed in the defense against a criminal indictment:

1. My client did not do it.
2. My client did it, but my client is not responsible because he or she is insane.

CASE IN POINT

Durham v. United States

The Case

Durham v. United States 214 F. 2d 862 (D.C.Cir. 1954)

The Point

The Supreme Court created a new test for insanity.

Monte Durham was convicted of breaking into a house by way of a trial without a jury. His defense at the trial was that he was of unsound mind at the time of the crime. Prior to this conviction, Durham had spent years in and out of prisons and mental institutions. He had been discharged from the navy in 1945 at the age of 17, when the navy stated that Durham suffered "from a profound personality disorder." In 1953, after the housebreaking incident, he was subjected to "subshock insulin therapy," released, and appraised by the hospital superintendent as "mentally competent to stand trial" on the housebreaking charge.

Given Durham's history, the D.C. Court of Appeals reversed the decision and remanded the case for a new trial. In setting forth a landmark new test for insanity, the court wrote that, "It is simply that an accused is not criminally responsible if his unlawful act was the product of mental disease or mental defect."

3. My client did it but has a good excuse.
4. My client did it but has a good reason.
5. My client did it but should be acquitted because the police or the prosecutor cheated.
6. My client did it but was influenced by outside forces.

My Client Did Not Do It. The best way to defend a client from a criminal charge is to show that the defendant did not do it. Unlike the rest of the defenses discussed in this section, this one claims the defendant is completely innocent of the charges. An **alibi** can be an essential part of maintaining one's innocence, demonstrating that one was not at the scene of the crime. An alibi may be established in many ways, all of which hinge on credible evidence. If other people claim you were 200 miles away in another city at the time of the crime, it is important that your witnesses be believable. Your spouse could say you were watching television together, but the court may wonder if your spouse is telling the truth. However, if your witness is the sheriff from a neighboring county who testifies that you were locked up in jail for two weeks before and after the crime, then the court is much more likely to believe the alibi. Often, dated documents such as hotel receipts, credit card purchases, and cash withdrawals from ATM machines can be used to help establish an alibi. With so many cameras around to protect establishments against robbery or other crimes, you may be able to show that you were in a store buying milk and ice cream at the time the crime took place many miles away. These cameras record the date and time of the pictures, and this evidence can be compelling in convincing the court that you have a valid alibi.

alibi
A defense that involves the defendant(s) claiming not to have been at the scene of a crime when that crime was committed.

My Client Did It, but My Client Is Not Responsible Because He or She Is Insane. The **insanity defense** is based on the concept that although the defendant did commit the criminal act, he or she is not criminally responsible because of insanity. The defendant did not appreciate that the behavior was wrong, that the behavior could hurt others, or that he or she was even committing the behavior. Because insanity is a legal term and not a medical one, this type of criminal offense sometimes elicits much confusion and bitterness.[23] Often, the public believes that the defendant is faking insanity to escape the full effects of the criminal law. Some believe that spending time in a hospital for the criminally insane would be preferable to spending time in prison and that it is easier to be released from

insanity defense
A defense that attempts to give physical or psychological reasons that a defendant cannot comprehend his or her criminal actions, their harm(s), or their punishment.

This photo shows the family of Deanna Laney (L to R)—husband Keith, Deanna, and children Joshua and Luke. Laney, 38, was charged on May 12, 2003, with killing Joshua and Luke and injuring her 14-month-old son Aaron at their home in New Chapel Hill, Texas. Authorities allege that Laney beat two of her sons to death with rocks. In April 2004 a jury found her not guilty by reason of insanity. Because Laney was not convicted of a crime, she will receive treatment for her mental illness and possibly be released if she is not considered a threat to herself or others.
Courtesy of Getty Images, Inc.

the hospital. Obviously, defendants facing the death penalty would see the value in being considered insane and therefore innocent of the guilty mind (*mens rea*) required for the state to invoke capital punishment.

How is someone determined to be insane? This question is fraught with difficulty because the legal and medical professions have different agendas. The medical profession is concerned with understanding the cause of mental illness and the best methods for treating it. The legal profession needs only to determine whether the defendant had the requisite mental capacity to have a guilty mind, so it uses standards to determine insanity (see Table 4.3).

My Client Did It but Has a Good Excuse. In addition to the insanity plea, a defense may use a number of other reasons or excuses to attempt to explain away a defendant's culpability. These include duress, age, mistake, and intoxication. An excuse contends that the defendant should not be held legally responsible for the crime because of one of these personal disabilities.

- **Duress.** Sometimes, according to the law, a person commits a crime out of fear for his or her own life or fear of bodily injury. Although not an excuse for homicide, duress or compulsion may help mitigate other types of criminal offenses as long as the defendant can show that he or she did not voluntarily join in or continue in engaging in the criminal activity. The Patty Hearst case is a good example of duress. Hearst was kidnapped by the Symbionese Liberation Army and subjected to months of abuse, isolation, and rape. She was required to participate in a robbery of a bank and was photographed holding a gun by bank cameras. Her attorneys claimed she was acting under duress in that she had been conditioned to fear her assailants. Although she could have thrown down her gun and run away from her captors during the robbery, she did not recognize this course of action as realistic. More recently, cases using the duress defense have concerned the subjugation of women. Known as the battered women's syndrome defense, this reasoning recasts the defendant into the role of a victim of a man whose power compels her to participate in crimes. This defense is sometimes used with a claim of self-defense or defense of others to mitigate a homicide charge.
- **Age.** At what age should a person be held accountable for crime? Can a five-year-old child understand the ramifications of harmful acts? Can a 15-year-old? Common law has long established that children under the age of seven are conclusively presumed to be incapable of having the necessary criminal intent for their unlawful acts to be considered a crime. For children between the ages of 7 and 14, however, this

Table 4.3

Some Legal Standards Used to Determine Insanity

M'Naghten Rule

In 1843 Daniel M'Naghten was charged with murder after he shot and killed Edward Drummond, the assistant to the prime minister of Great Britain, Sir Robert Peel. M'Naghten believed he was being persecuted by Peel, and, unfortunately for Drummond, mistook him for the prime minister. At the trial, evidence showed that M'Naghten was incapable of determining right from wrong at the time of the incident, and the jury found him not guilty. The House of Lords then produced a doctrine that the jury should acquit the defendant if it found that the accused "was laboring under such a defect of reason, from disease of the mind, as not to know the nature and quality of the act he was doing, or, if he did know it, that he did not know it was wrong." This test spread throughout the world where the British legal system had influence and became the foundation for the insanity defense. Many jurisdictions still use the M'Naghten Rule. It is up to the defense to prove that the defendant is insane.

Irresistible Impulse Rule

In some states, an additional feature has been added to the M'Naghten standards. The irresistible impulse rule states that although a defendant understands the nature and quality of the criminal act and understands that it is wrong, if he or she experiences as a result of a mental disease an irresistible impulse that makes him or her incapable of preventing himself or herself from doing the act, this is grounds for acquittal. But what constitutes an irresistible impulse? Just because the defendant failed to resist, does that make an impulse irresistible? Many of us are tempted by chocolate, beer, or pizza. Most of us are able to control our impulses and consume these products in moderation. Could a rapist use the irresistible impulse defense by claiming the victim was especially good-looking? The burden of proof for the irresistible impulse defense rests with the prosecution and is at the level of beyond a reasonable doubt.

Durham Rule

This is sometimes called the "products test." Based on a rule created in New Hampshire in 1871, it was revived in 1954 in the case *Durham v. United States.* The rule asks the jury to decide if the unlawful act was a product of the defendant's insanity. Unfortunately, very little guidance is given to the jury in making this determination, and the Durham Rule is used relatively infrequently. The Durham Rule is a legal construct, and without any clear criteria for making this determination, juries must depend on intuition rather than medical evidence or legal reasoning. The burden of proof for the Durham Rule defense rests with the prosecution and is at the level of beyond a reasonable doubt.

Guilty but Mentally Ill

This verdict says the defendant is factually guilty of the crime but was incompetent to control his or her behavior. This finding is not really a justification or an excuse for the crime, but merely reflects society's frustrations with the line of legal versus medical reasoning that underlie the insanity defense. Under the guilty-but-mentally-ill concept the judge can sentence the defendant to any sentence specified by the law. However, the judge is required to address three criteria in imposing the sentence: the protection of society, holding offenders accountable for their crimes, and making treatment available to those suffering from mental illness.

Appreciation Test

The federal government has adopted a test that in some ways is similar to the M'Naghten Rule in that it requires the defendant to be unaware of what he or she was doing or unaware that what he or she was doing was wrong. However, the defendant must show that he or she had a lack of control. The main feature of the appreciation test is that it shifts the burden of proof back to the defense, and that burden of proof need not be beyond a reasonable doubt but merely constitute "clear and convincing evidence."

Modern Penal Code Test

The Modern Penal Code provides another criterion for determining whether the defendant is mentally ill. Sometimes called the "substantial capacity test," the code is not used by many states. It attempts to determine whether the defendant, as a result of mental disease or defect, lacks the substantial capacity either to appreciate the criminality of his or her conduct or to conform his or her conduct to the requirements of the law. The burden of proof rests with the prosecution at the level of beyond a reasonable doubt.

presumption could be challenged and the prosecution could present evidence that the child had the capacity to form criminal intent.[24] This excuse of age, called **infancy**, is the foundation of the juvenile court system. With a few exceptions, young offenders are handled in the juvenile court, where the emphasis is on treatment rather than on punishment. Those 16 or older may have their cases waived to the adult court if their offenses are serious. In fact, as we will see in Chapter 14, trying juveniles in adult

infancy
In legal terminology, refers to a child who has not yet reached a specific age. Almost all states end infancy at the age of 18.

Patty Hearst participated in a bank robbery under duress from the Symbionese Liberation Army. She was later pardoned for her crimes.

Courtesy of Corbis/Bettmann. © Bettmann/CORBIS.

In 1998, Joshua Phillips, 14, beat and stabbed to death his 8-year-old neighbor, Maddie Clifton, then hid her body under his bed. He was tried as an adult and sentenced to life without parole.

Courtesy of AP Wide World Photos.

court is becoming more frequent. However, a hearing in juvenile court is required before this jurisdiction can be changed.

- **Mistake.** There is an old saying, "Ignorance of the law is no excuse." This is reasonable because it would be impossible to prove that someone knew or should have known what the law is. If when you send your taxes to the government, you claim deductions not allowed by the law, even if you do so in good faith, the government will punish you. Part of participating in a democracy is knowing and obeying the law. Although ignorance of the law is seldom an effective excuse, ignorance of facts is. For example, someone sells you a car, and you have good reason to believe that the seller actually owned the car. If it turns out when a police officer stops you that it is stolen, then you may have a valid excuse. However, if the price you paid for the car was a fraction of what it was worth, then you are considered to be responsible for suspecting deviance and investigating further. People can make honest mistakes, and the court will consider the possibility that the defendant acted honestly and in good faith.

- **Intoxication.** People who are drunk or under the influence of drugs may do things they would not normally do. Should this excuse shield them from the law? The answer is generally no. Those who use intoxicants are responsible for their behaviors. However, what if the use of intoxicants is involuntary? What if someone spikes a drink or serves marijuana brownies without the guests' knowledge? Under these circumstances, the defendant is not responsible for the circumstances that cause the crime and is unable to appreciate or control his or her behavior. Involuntary intoxication is more likely to involve drugs than alcohol. (Most people can detect the smell and taste of alcohol and are required by law to drink responsibly or face the consequences.) Sometimes voluntary intoxication can be used to reduce the level of crime. For instance, an intoxicated person could claim that he or she did not have the capacity to establish *mens rea* and ask that a murder charge be reduced to manslaughter.

My Client Did It but Has a Good Reason. Sometimes bad must be done in order for good to prevail. Justifications as criminal defenses contend that the harm caused by committing a crime was more desirable than the harm that would have been caused if one had done nothing. The justifications discussed here are self-defense, consent, and necessity.

- **Self-defense.** Law enforcement officers cannot be everywhere all the time to protect everyone. Sometimes a person faced with imminent danger is not in a position to call the police. Self-defense has long been established to be a legitimate justification for violating the law. However, to be successful, the claim of self-defense is limited to certain conditions. First, the defendant must believe that physical force is necessary for self-protection or the protection of others. Second, this belief that physical force is necessary must be based on reasonable grounds. Third, the defendant must believe that the force used is necessary to avoid imminent danger. Finally, the force used cannot be in excess of that believed necessary to repel the unlawful attack. One of the key issues in the self-defense claim is the amount of force used. The defendant is only allowed to use reasonable force for self-defense. That means that if a 250-pound linebacker is attacked by his 105-pound girlfriend, he is not justified in pulling out a gun and shooting her. The requirement of reasonable force would assume that he could protect himself without resorting to deadly force. However, if the roles were reversed, and the linebacker were beating the woman, then her use of deadly force to defend herself may be a legitimate justification. Individuals must consider other solutions before using deadly force. State laws differ on the requirement that the defendant first attempt to retreat or escape before employing deadly force. In Kentucky a person is allowed to stand his or her ground and meet the attack with deadly force. The court contends that "it is tradition that a Kentuckian never runs. He does not have to." In Florida, however, a person must use every reasonable means, including escape, before resorting to deadly force.[25] Cases involving the defense of others must follow similar criteria as cases of self-defense. Only reasonable force can be used unless there is a threat of imminent death. Likewise, a third party cannot be an aggressor in the incident. If your friend starts a barroom fight and is getting the worst of it, you are not justified in rushing to his defense. Deadly force could be used in the same circumstances as self-defense. If someone were strangling your child, you would be justified in shooting the attacker.
- **Consent.** The consent defense is often used in rape cases. For instance, the defendant claims the victim agreed to sex, whereas the victim claims there was either no consent or consent was under duress or intoxication. For the consent to be legitimate, it must be given knowingly and freely. Convincing an intoxicated person to have sex can result in a charge of rape when the intoxication wears off.

Some defendants claim they were confused when they consented, and retract their consent after the fact. In such cases the court will consider closely the circumstances to decide the verdict. Many years ago, in cases of female victims, the sexual history of the victim was examined to determine her character; however, the court now protects women from being doubly victimized.[26] If the woman is a prostitute, she still has the right to withhold consent. In cases of an adult having sex with a minor, consent is not a justification. Children are not deemed capable of giving informed consent, and such actions will invoke a charge of **statutory rape**.

statutory rape
Sexual activity conducted with a person who is younger than a specified age or incapable of valid consent because of mental illness, mental handicap, intoxication, unconsciousness, or deception.

- **Necessity.** Defense based on the principle of necessity must show that the harm that would result from compliance with the law would exceed that from its violation. For example, a man rushing his pregnant wife to the hospital is justified in exceeding the speed limit as long as he takes certain precautions such as flashing his lights and honking his horn to warn others. Campers trapped in a mountain snowstorm might use the necessity defense to justify breaking into a cabin to keep warm as long as they later notify the owner and pay for the repairs. However, a juvenile cannot claim necessity as a defense for carrying a gun to school because he or she is afraid of other students. There are other means of protecting oneself, such as informing parents, school officials, or police about the perceived dangers posed by other students. The necessity defense involves choosing the lesser of evils. It is permissible to burn some land to check a larger fire threatening a nearby town.[27]

My Client Did It but Should Be Acquitted Because the Police or the Prosecutor Cheated. A number of criminal defenses concentrate on the conduct of law enforcement authorities. Failure to follow procedural law, engaging in fraud or other misconduct, and treating defendants in a selective and discriminatory manner can all be reasons to challenge a criminal indictment. Examples of these include the following:

- **Statute of limitations.** A statute of limitations is a law applying to civil and criminal cases that specifies that prosecution must take place within a specified period. If a police officer knocked on your door and informed you that you were being arrested for a crime that happened 10 years ago, you would be hard pressed to reconstruct where you were and what you were doing at the time of the offense. Developing an alibi would be impossible because most people, unless they kept detailed diaries, would not be able to remember if they were anywhere near the scene of the crime. Depending on the jurisdiction, many offenses have statutes of limitations. Murder, however, usually does not have a statute of limitations, and suspects can be charged decades after the crime if sufficient evidence can be developed.
- **Entrapment.** Many crimes are very difficult for law enforcement agencies to respond to in a reactive manner. Prostitution, in which consenting adults exchange sex for money, is not something the police are going to be aware of if no one complains. The police must be proactive in developing prostitution cases, and in doing so, they run the risk of entrapping defendants. By posing as customers seeking the service of prostitutes, the police give the prostitute an opportunity to commit the crime in their presence. The issue is complex. Would the prostitute engage in this behavior without the inducement of the police? What has developed is an elaborate verbal dance in which the prostitute must be the first party to mention the cost of sex. Otherwise, the police cannot arrest the prostitute without risking entrapment. Entrapment has also been the defense of politicians caught accepting bribes or engaging in other illegal behavior. In the famous ABSCAM case, federal agents posing as rich Middle Eastern sheiks offered public officials, including members of Congress, money for influencing legislation. The defendants were videotaped stuffing large amounts of cash into their pockets and were subsequently prosecuted. The defendants were unable to convince the court that they were victims of entrapment.[28] Another case of a public official who claimed entrapment is

NEWS FLASH

No Pass for Murder

There is no statute of limitations for murder. Someone charged with murder can be prosecuted no matter how much time has passed after the crime. Because most murders are committed by adults, age is usually not a factor. Although time may have taken its toll, the law considers a 25-year-old man to be of the same mind as the 65-year-old man he is four decades later. However, this is not the case for juveniles. For instance, the law treats a 20-year-old woman who is caught shoplifting much differently than it treated her when she was caught at the same crime at age 10. However, if the adult woman's juvenile crime were not discovered until 10 years later, she likely would not be prosecuted. Doubtless, shoplifting in her jurisdiction would carry a statute of limitations.

The situation becomes more complicated, however, if the crime is murder.

On October 30, 1975, 15-year-old Martha Moxley was found beaten to death under a pine tree in her upper-class neighborhood of Belle Haven in Greenwich, Connecticut. She had been out early that evening with a group of teenagers who lived nearby, including two brothers from the Skakel family, Thomas, 17, and Michael, 15. By 11 P.M., when Martha had not come home, her mother, Dorothy Moxley, phoned the Skakels and spoke to Thomas, who said he had not seen her since 9:30 P.M. Around 4 A.M., Dorothy Moxley phoned the police, but they were also unable to find her. Finally, at noon the next day, Martha's body was found in a wooded area of the Moxley's backyard. Her face and hair were matted with blood and pieces of a broken golf club from a set that belonged to the Skakels lay nearby.

For a variety of reasons, the investigation dragged on for the next 25 years. In January 2000 Michael Skakel, then 39, was charged in the murder of Martha Moxley. In an interesting twist, however, the case was assigned to juvenile court because Skakel was 15 at the time of the murder. A year later a judge ruled that Skakel would be tried as an adult, partly because the state has no juvenile detention facilities for adults. In June 2002 Skakel was found guilty and sentenced to 20 years to life in prison. Had Skakel been found guilty as a juvenile—for instance, in 1976—he likely would have served no more than four years in a juvenile treatment facility.

Source: CNN, "Kennedy Nephew to Face Trial as Adult in 1975 Killing," January 31, 2001, http://www.cnn.com/2001/LAW/01/31/skakel.trial/index.html.

former Washington, D.C., mayor Marion Barry. Federal agents used a friend of Barry's to lure him to a hotel room where she gave him crack-cocaine to smoke. Barry turned down the drug several times before he decided to smoke it. He was videotaped ingesting the cocaine and immediately arrested. Given that the federal agents supplied the woman and the cocaine, Barry tried to claim entrapment, but was unsuccessful.[29]

- **Double jeopardy.** According to this defense, a defendant cannot be tried or punished twice for the same offense. Based on common law and the Fifth Amendment of the Constitution, the double jeopardy defense is designed to protect the defendant from repeated trials and excessive punishments. In a few circumstances, however, the same behavior may be considered for different purposes without violating the right against double jeopardy. Four Los Angeles police officers that were acquitted in the beating of motorist Rodney King were later tried in federal court on the charge of violating King's civil rights.[30] Two of the officers were found guilty. Another exception is found when a case is tried both in criminal court and in civil court. In criminal court, the defendant's guilt must be proved beyond a reasonable doubt, and he or she may face incarceration. In civil court, only a preponderance of evidence is required for a ruling against the defendant, and the penalty will not include prison but only monetary damages.

FOCUS ON ETHICS

A Change of Heart

You have been a judge for a very long time and have established a reputation for strictness and fairness. You plan to retire soon, but something has happened recently that has given you a new interest in your job and a new sense of the complexities of the criminal justice process. Your 18-year-old granddaughter has been convicted of selling cocaine in a neighboring state. Although you do not condone her behavior, you are concerned with the way her case was handled by the police. You learn that your granddaughter is technically guilty, but that the police came very close to using entrapment to entice her to commit the crime. An undercover officer asked her several times to help him find some cocaine, and she repeatedly told him she did not know any dealers. The officer then promised her that if she would simply introduce him to some people at her sorority party, he would leave her alone. She did know one young woman whose boyfriend had a brother who used cocaine, and a week after she made the introduction, she accompanied an undercover officer to a restaurant where the buy was made. She was arrested and charged with cocaine sales even though she did not know the boyfriend's brother, received no money from the transaction, did not use any drugs, and did not even know the undercover officer had set up the drug buy. The police contend that she was instrumental in arranging the introduction and was present at the transaction.

As a judge you are appalled by the conduct of this police officer, but because the case took place in another state, you cannot help your granddaughter. However, you are now taking a hard look at the conduct of the police officers who come before your court, and you are discovering that undercover officers who buy drugs are a creative group of people. You begin to see each case in a different light, and you do not like what you see. In your opinion, some law enforcement officers are getting a bit too proactive in developing their drug cases. They are skirting the limits of entrapment, which, although questionable from an ethical standpoint, is still legal. What concerns you most is that the officers are not using their borderline tactics to sniff out big-time drug dealers, but are instead targeting basically decent young people who are on the periphery of the drug scene. In your opinion, the problem is so acute that you are throwing some cases out of court. Although you cannot prove entrapment, you are so suspicious that you now give the benefit of the doubt to the defendant rather than the police officer in nearly every case. The chief judge has asked you if there is a problem because the word in the courthouse is that you are the judge preferred by defense attorneys in drug cases.

WHAT DO YOU DO?

1. Tell the chief judge that it is your court and you will do as you please.
2. Tell the chief judge about your granddaughter's experience. Say that you are discovering the same entrapment issues in your courtroom and that it is probably the same in every courtroom in the county.
3. Resign because you have lost your perspective.
4. Resign and run for governor and try to get laws passed that will correct this problem statewide.

- **Police fraud or prosecutor misconduct.** Law enforcement officials must play by the rules established by procedural law. Withholding evidence, making false statements, and putting forth evidence that they know is false can be grounds for a defense claim of police fraud or prosecutor misconduct.

My Client Did It but Was Influenced by Outside Forces. Some defenses for criminal acts attempt to shift the blame from the defendant to something outside his or her control. The best example of this is the alleged "Twinkie defense." The word *alleged* is used because

CROSSCURRENTS

Why the "Twinkie Defense" Gets a Bad Rap

If enough people believe in something that never happened, does that make it real?

Yes and no.

Putting aside arguments about exactly what constitutes "reality," if enough people believe in an incident that did not happen, then base their opinions and behaviors on that belief, the myth can indeed affect reality because its believers use its lessons to construct their lives and opinions. However, this does nothing to improve the myth itself. And although certain myths may be useful or instructive, they can also cause trouble.

This is the case in the infamous Twinkie defense. Here is what most people believe: A long time ago a man killed some people and blamed Twinkies for his behavior and escaped serious punishment. Although the nutshell version of the story may or may not be harmless, many people have come to base their low opinions of the "unfair" legal system, at least in part, on this story. The problem is, it never happened.

On November 10, 1978, Dan White resigned from his position as a San Francisco city supervisor, but several days later asked Mayor George Moscone to reinstate him. Moscone refused. For this, White blamed another supervisor, Harvey Milk, as well as Moscone. On November 26 White entered City Hall through a basement window (to avoid the metal detectors) and shot Mayor George Moscone twice in the body and twice in the head. He then reloaded, went to a different part of the building, and shot Supervisor Harvey Milk three times in the body and twice in the head. White then turned himself over to police.

At his trial, White's attorneys used a diminished capacity defense to explain White's actions, claiming that White had suffered severe depression in the days before the shooting. Four psychiatrists and a psychologist testified that White's decision-making ability was impaired by depression. The prosecution offered only the testimony of a psychiatrist, who found White to be "moderately depressed," but retaining the "capacity to deliberate and premeditate."

During the trial, one defense psychiatrist, Dr. Martin Blinder, mentioned that White, who was normally very health conscious, had been eating large amounts of junk food during his depression. Blinder said that this radical change of behavior was a symptom of White's depression and that eating so much junk food probably made him more depressed. Years later, Blinder said that the mention of junk food took about two minutes of the hours he spent on the stand. It is telling that in White's appeal, in which the doctors' testimony was reviewed, there is no mention of Twinkies or sugar or of any food whatsoever.

Dan White's defense, then, was that he was too depressed to make rational decisions, not that a sugar high from a Twinkie made him go nuts. In the end, a jury found White guilty of two counts of voluntary manslaughter, and White was sentenced to less than eight years in prison.*

This is how a small, relatively insignificant mention of a dessert became inflated to the point that it escaped reams of expert testimony, shrugged off almost all relationship to the truth, and mutated into an indictment of the legal system. Not only does one find the Twinkie defense still kicking around in popular opinion, but it is also proffered as truth by pundits, journalists, and scholars. What happened?

In any other trial, a brief mention of junk food may have gone unnoticed. However, the White shootings were extremely violent and unprecedented, and the victims were politically controversial. Harvey Milk was possibly the first openly homosexual elected public official. Milk, a liberal, had persuaded Mayor Moscone to replace the conservative White with another liberal. After the verdict, rioters set fire to police cars and marched on City Hall. San Francisco's volatile political situation plus the sensational crime ensured that every word said during the trial would be scrutinized. Apparently, *Twinkie* especially stood out. In a column about the situation, *San Francisco Chronicle* writer Herb Caen mentioned that an attorney had called White's plea "the Twinkie insanity defense." Weeks later, the Twinkie defense was everywhere, and the truth was rarely to be seen again.

continued

Still, "diminished capacity," the plea that had truly spared White more serious punishment, did not escape unharmed. In 1982 California voters approved a proposition to eliminate the defense.

QUESTIONS

1. What do you think of White's sentence? If he had committed the murders in 1998, what would his sentence have been?
2. Were California voters right to eliminate the diminished capacity defense?
3. Does the fact that the Twinkie defense is a myth make you think differently about this case?

Sources: Carol Pogash, "Myth of the 'Twinkie Defense,' " *San Francisco Chronicle,* November 23, 2003, http://www.sfgate.com/cgi-bin/article.cgi?file=/chronicle/archive/2003/11/23/INGRE343501.DTL. *People v. White,* 117 Cal.App.3d 270, 172 Cal.Rptr. (1981).

*White appealed and lost. He served a little over five years, leaving prison in January 1985. He committed suicide that October.

this case did not happen the way it was reported in the press and has become something of an urban legend. Although this case did not develop as many people assume, the principle is important and is used to justify a wide variety of behaviors. The central question remains: Can the diet alter body chemistry in such a way as to contribute to, or cause, someone to engage in unlawful behavior? Ask any parent who has seen their kids bouncing off the walls after consuming too much sugar, and you will get an affirmative response. However, in court this is a very tough defense to put forth successfully. The prevalence of sugar in American diets would surely demonstrate a great deal more deviant behavior and crime if it were as influential as those who support the Twinkie defense claim. The fact that most of us consume large quantities of sugar and do not commit crimes makes this defense problematic.

Another defense that has garnered its share of publicity involves premenstrual syndrome (PMS). Here, the theory is that hormonal changes to the female body during menstruation may induce some women to commit unlawful behavior. We will not deal with the scientific evidence of PMS here, but it is sufficient to say that courts in England do recognize PMS as a legitimate defense and that the issue has been addressed in U.S. courts. The difficulty with mounting such a defense rests with the task of convincing a judge and/or a jury that the client's PMS is so severe that it would cause her to break the law. When one considers the millions of women who deal with this normal human condition, it is difficult for a defense attorney to make a case that a client suffered diminished capacity to the extent that PMS contributed to, or caused, her commission of the crime.

A related defense against criminal prosecution is battered women's syndrome (BWS). The reason for criminal behavior rests on the extensive literature and experiences of women caught in domestic violence relationships. It is often difficult for women to disengage from such relationships because of economic and safety reasons. Therefore, the defense contends, the women are forced to commit what at first glance may appear to be premeditated acts of violence against their spouses or partners. These acts may include homicide in which the woman strikes at the man when he is most vulnerable, such as when he is sleeping. Because of the power imbalance (the man is physically stronger, controls the money, and is psychologically domineering), battered women act in a way that seems unfair by striking in a deliberate, but not immediately provoked, manner. The BWS defense argues that she is temporarily insane from the years of abuse and that killing her partner is an act of self-defense.[31] On the other hand, the defense could claim that the woman was sane and that she believed she was in imminent danger of bodily harm or death and that she acted in reasonable self-defense.

After the Vietnam War, a number of veterans engaged in crime and deviant behavior as well as some rather bizarre activities that caused psychologists to wonder how their

CASE IN POINT

People v. Aphaylath

The Case

People v. Aphaylath 68 N.Y.2d 945; 502 N.E.2d 998; 510 N.Y.S.2d 83; 1986

The Point

The value of expert testimony that provides evidence of a pertinent issue is not dependent on whether the witness personally knows a defendant or a defendant's particular characteristics.

May Aphaylath, a Laotian refugee who had been living in the United States for about two years, had been married for one month when he killed his wife. According to Aphaylath, she had displayed affection for an unmarried ex-boyfriend and had received telephone calls from him. Aphaylath's attorney attempted to establish that the homicide was mitigated because Aphaylath was experiencing undue pressure in trying to assimilate to American culture and had been shamed by his wife's behavior. According to the defense, in Laotian tradition, a man is shamed when his wife displays affection for another man. The combination of these factors, Aphaylath stated, caused him to "snap" and kill his wife. The defense presented evidence about Laotian culture and refugee stress by cross-examining two prosecution witnesses. The trial judge excluded this evidence because the witnesses did not personally know Aphaylath or his personal characteristics.

Later, an appeals court stated that expert witnesses do not have to personally know a defendant for their testimony to be relevant. The court ruled that Aphaylath had been denied the chance to present evidence of Laotian culture that may have been relevant to his defense and ordered a new trial.

war experiences influenced their adjustment to civilian life. Post-traumatic stress syndrome was developed as an explanation, and it was not long before this justification for crime was introduced into the criminal courts as a defense.

Finally, a related defense against criminal prosecution centers on the conflict of cultures experienced by many immigrants. In some societies, it is a matter of family honor when a woman is seduced or raped. Brothers or fathers are honor bound to avenge the insult to the family by killing the man responsible, and in some extreme cases by also killing the woman involved. Although this behavior is clearly outside the criminal law in the United States, a defense attorney can argue that the defendant was not purposely breaking the law, but was rather upholding the traditional norms of his homeland. This defense seldom works because it is unreasonable to expect the U.S. criminal justice system to grant exception for every custom that someone might bring to this country. U.S. citizens and residents are protected by U.S. law but also subject to it. However, in at least one case, *People v. Aphaylath,* a client had his homicide conviction reversed by the court of appeals and got a new trial.

Summary

The criminal justice system is governed by the criminal law. As we have seen in this chapter, the criminal law in the United States did not suddenly spring forth, fully developed and unquestioned. Rather, U.S. criminal law developed in a sporadic and uneven fashion. It can trace its influences back thousands of years to the Code of Hammurabi, which represents one of the first known attempts to put the law of the land in writing. The early North American colonies adopted the principles of English common law that called for cases to be decided on precedent. In this way, consistency in the law developed, making it less arbitrary. Common law ideals are based on predictability, reliability, efficiency, and equality.

In addition to the common law, the inspirations for U.S. criminal law can be found in other sources. The federal and state constitutions provide one foundation for criminal law. The U.S. Constitution sets out broad values that the criminal law cannot abridge or attenuate. The first 10 amendments, the Bill of Rights, are an especially important cornerstone of the criminal law.

The U.S. Congress and state legislatures provide statutes that govern the criminal law. The representatives of the people vote on these statutes, and their enactment means that everyone is bound to abide by their conditions. This is where substantive laws proscribing murder, rape, robbery, and the like originate. Each state may have slightly different statutes, but overall, there is a fairly consistent pattern of laws across the nation. Finally, the last source of the criminal law discussed in this chapter is administrative rules. A number of agencies that govern health, customs, the environment, and parole promulgate rules that are enforceable by the criminal law.

One important distinction that criminal justice students should remember is the difference between criminal law and civil law. Although both types of laws govern behavior and are subject to sanctions, the criminal law represents the state against individuals, whereas the civil law is concerned with disputes between individuals. Civil law deals with contracts, personal property, maritime law, and commercial law.

Another distinction that bears emphasis is the difference between substantive law and procedural law. Substantive law is concerned with the criminal acts committed by citizens and prescribes penalties. Procedural law, on the other hand, is concerned with how criminal justice system officials enforce substantive law. Law enforcement officers and court personnel must adhere to many laws in the course of their official duties. When the police gather evidence illegally or the defense attorney violates the principle of attorney/client privilege, the procedural law has been violated, and the case can be dismissed. In short, the procedural law ensures that the government plays fair in the criminal justice system.

The defense attorney has a number of choices to make in mounting an effective case for a client. This chapter has reviewed a few of these avenues available to the defense team, and it can be concluded that the defense can get very creative in attempting to mitigate a client's guilt or culpability. The criminal law allows for a number of defenses against the prosecutor's charges, and some are likely to be more effective than others. Of course, being able to prove that your client is innocent is better than being able to prove that even though your client committed the act, there are mitigating circumstances.

KEY TERMS

REVIEW QUESTIONS

1. What is the Code of Hammurabi? What is the Magna Carta?
2. How is common law different from statutory law?
3. What four issues guide precedent?
4. What are the three sources of law?

5. What are the first 10 amendments to the Constitution called?
6. What three criteria determine what behaviors are made criminal?
7. What effect does dual sovereignty have on the double jeopardy prohibition?
8. What is the difference between substantive law and procedural law? What is case law?
9. What three elements must be present for most acts to be labeled as crimes?
10. What six arguments can be employed in the defense against a criminal indictment?

SUGGESTED FURTHER READING

Abadinsky, Howard. *Law and Justice: An Introduction to the American Legal System.* 5th ed. Upper Saddle River, NJ: Prentice Hall, 2003.

Bazelon, David L. *Questioning Authority: Justice and Criminal Law.* New York: Knopf, 1989.

Dershowitz, Alan M. *The Abuse Excuse and Other Cop-Outs, Sob Stories, and Evasions of Responsibility.* Boston: Little, Brown, 1994.

Johnson, Herbert A., and Nancy Travis Wolfe. *History of Criminal Justice.* 3rd ed. Cincinnati, OH: Anderson, 2003.

Nolan, Joseph R., and Jacqueline M. Nolan-Haley. *Black's Law Dictionary: Definitions of the Terms and Phrases of American and English Jurisprudence, Ancient and Modern.* 6th ed. St. Paul, MN: West, 1990.

Reid, Sue Titus. *Criminal Law.* 6th ed. Boston: McGraw-Hill, 2004.

ENDNOTES

1. James Austin and John Irwin, *It's About Time: America's Imprisonment Binge,* 2nd ed. (Belmont, CA: Wadsworth, 2001).
2. Jeffrey Reiman, *The Rich Get Richer and the Poor Get Prison: Ideology, Class, and Criminal Justice* (Boston: Allyn and Bacon, 2001).
3. Samuel Walker, *Sense and Nonsense About Crime and Drugs: A Policy Guide,* 4th ed. (Belmont, CA: West/Wadsworth, 1998).
4. Robert F. Meier and Gilbert Geis, *Victimless Crime? Prostitution, Drugs, Homosexuality, and Abortion* (Los Angeles: Roxbury, 1997).
5. Katherine Beckett and Theodore Sasson, *The Politics of Injustice: Crime and Punishment in America* (Thousand Oaks, CA: Sage, 2004), 169.
6. Samuel Walker, Cassia Spohn, and Miriam DeLone, *The Color of Justice: Race, Ethnicity, and Crime in America* (Belmont, CA: Wadsworth, 1996).
7. Herbert A. Johnson and Nancy Travis Wolfe, *History of Criminal Justice,* 3rd ed. (Cincinnati: Anderson, 2003).
8. L. W. King, trans., *The Code of Hammurabi* (The Avalon Project at Yale Law School), http://www.yale.edu/lawweb/avalon/medieval/hammenu.htm.
9. The Magna Carta, The British Library, http://www.bl.uk/collections/treasures/magna.html. See also The Magna Carta (The Great Charter) at http://www.cs.indiana.edu/statecraft/magna-carta.html.
10. Richard A. Wasserstrom, *The Judicial Decision: Toward a Theory of Legal Justification* (Stanford, CA: Stanford University Press, 1961).
11. Lief H. Carter, *Reason in Law,* 4th ed. (New York: Harper Collins, 1994).
12. Kermit Hall, *The Magic Mirror: Law in American History* (New York: Oxford University Press, 1991).
13. Richard J. Pierce, Jr., Sidney A. Shapiro, and Paul R. Verkuil, *Administrative Law and Process,* 3rd ed. (New York: Foundation Press, 1999).
14. John C. Klotter, *Criminal Law,* 6th ed. (Cincinnati: Anderson, 2001), 6.
15. Nils Christi, "Conflicts as Property," *The British Journal of Criminology* 17 (1977): 1–15.
16. Jennifer Eastman, "A Constitutional Amendment for Victims: The Unexplored Possibility," in *Victimology: A Study of Crime Victims and Their Roles,* eds. Judith M. Sgarzi and Jack McDevitt (Upper Saddle River, NJ: Prentice Hall, 2003), 333–346.
17. Raymond J. Michalowski, *Order, Law, and Crime: An Introduction to Criminology.* (New York: Random House, 1985), 139–141.
18. Frank A. Schubert, *Criminal Law: The Basics* (Los Angeles: Roxbury, 2004), 101–103.
19. Ibid., 10–13.
20. James R. Acker and David C. Brody, *Criminal Procedure: A Contemporary Perspective* (Gaithersburg, MD: Aspen, 1999).
21. Charles Rembar, *The Law of the Land, The Evolution of Our Legal System* (New York: Simon & Schuster, 1980).
22. Schubert, *Criminal Law.*
23. Eric Hickey, *Serial Murderers and Their Victims* (Belmont, CA: Wadsworth, 1991), 37–45.

24. Klotter, *Criminal Law,* 514.
25. Klotter, *Criminal Law,* 547.
26. William G. Doerner and Steven P. Lab, *Victimology,* 2nd ed. (Cincinnati: Anderson, 1998), 118–119.
27. Klotter, *Criminal Law,* 540–542.
28. *Columbia Encyclopedia,* 6th ed., s.v. "Abscam." Online at Bartleby.com, http://www.bartleby.com/65/e-/E-Abscam.html.
29. Sharon LaFraniere, "Barry Arrested on Cocaine Charges in Undercover FBI, Police Operation," *The Washington Post,* January 19, 1990.
30. Jim Newton, "Koon, Powell Get 2 1/2 Years in Prison," *Los Angeles Times,* August 5, 1993.
31. Lenore E. Walker, *The Battered Woman* (New York: Harper Collins, 1979).

PART two

ENFORCING THE LAW

outline

CHAPTER 5

History and Organization of Law Enforcement

objectives

After reading this chapter, the student should be able to:

1. Understand how the history of policing can be traced to England.
2. Appreciate how the English heritage of policing produced three enduring features of American policing: limited police authority, local control, and a fragmented system.
3. Discuss how vigilante committees usurped policing in the rural South and West.
4. List several of the features of American policing that led to the professionalization of law enforcement.
5. Identify and explain how the different levels of law enforcement are problematic to policing in the United States.
6. Discuss how programs and research studies such as the Kansas City Preventive Patrol Experiment, the Rand Study of Detectives, and the DARE program have affected the practice of law enforcement in the United States.

THE INSTITUTION OF THE POLICE IS A RELATIVELY NEW PHE-nomenon. Having an agency devoted solely to maintaining order and apprehending violators of the law entails a degree of occupational specialization that is available only in highly developed societies. However, like physicians, teachers, and farmers, law enforcement officers are needed for communities to function effectively. As long as human beings have lived in large groups, there has been a need for social control. Much of this control was exerted through informal means, such as censure from families, friends, and other social institutions. However, as social groups became larger and less personally interconnected, formal means became required to deal with situations that did not respond to informal means, such as legal disputes and the control of violent people.

Although we commonly think of policing as a stable institution built on unchanging tradition, the police are, in fact, subject to rapid social change and constant challenges.[1] The way policing is done in the 21st century is the result of a long, uneven development that continues even today.

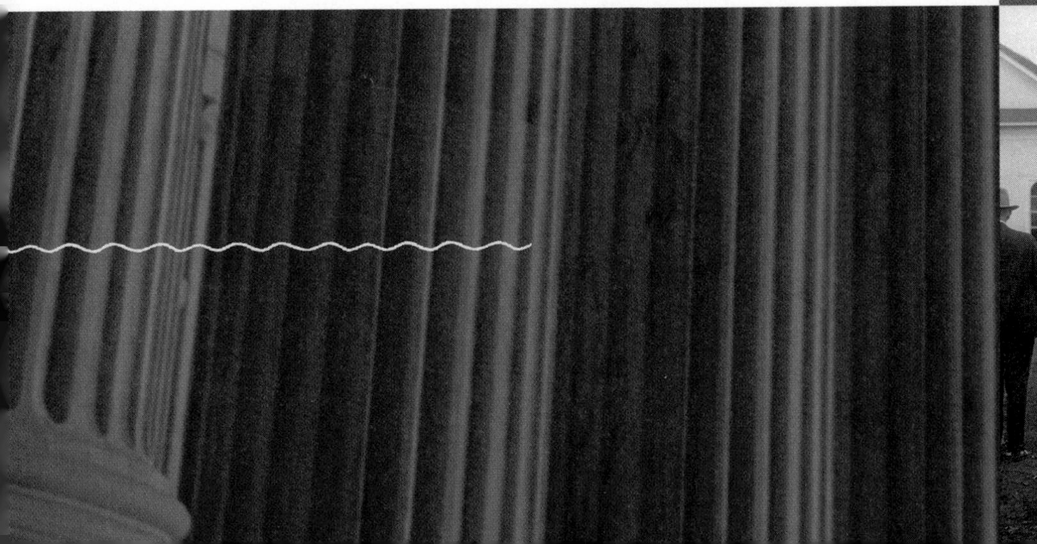

A Brief History of the Police

One function of society is the maintenance of social control. Those who break the law are subject to judgment and penalties. The police are vested with the responsibility of detecting crime and bringing lawbreakers to justice. By studying how the police have evolved through the centuries we can fully appreciate the necessary but delicate function of law enforcement.

Police in Ancient Times

The law enforcement function has existed in one form or another for thousands of years. Police in early history usually derived from the military connected with a government or ruler, or from the community when citizens joined in informal groups to protect themselves.

In the seventh century B.C.E., the Roman emperor Augustus created one of the earliest recorded organized police forces. There were three groups of police, who were part of the army and were commanded by the urban prefect. The city was divided into 14 *regiones* or wards, which in turn were divided into *vici* or precincts. Police also developed in other cultures independent of Rome. In 17th-century Japan, for example, each town had a military official, the samurai warrior, whose duties included acting as judge and chief of police. In Russia from 1881 to the revolution in 1917, the tsars' *Okhranka* was a police force that dealt with political terrorism and revolutionary matters.

frankpledge system
A form of English government that began in Anglo-Saxon England and endured until the 19th century. This system divided a community into groups of 10 men (tithings) who were responsible for the conduct of the group and ensured that a member charged with breaking the law would appear in court.

Policing in Early England

The nascent form of policing that most directly led to that of modern U.S. policing was the **frankpledge system**. The frankpledge system began in Anglo-Saxon England and continued after the Norman conquest in 1066, enduring until the 19th century. This system divided a community into tithings or groups of 10 men who were responsible for the conduct of the group and ensured that a member charged with breaking the law would show

Ancient cultures developed their own forms of policing. In 17th-century Japan, law enforcement was handled by the samurai warrior.
Courtesy of CORBIS-NY.

up in court. The tithing was supervised by a tithingman. The tithings were collected into groups of 10, or a hundred, which was headed by a **hundred-man**. The hundred-man served as an administrator and judge. The Normans updated the frankpledge system by adding the ***comes stabuli*** or **constable**. Originally part of the royal court, the constable became, by the late 13th century, an officer attached to manors and parishes. Constables oversaw the **watch-and-ward system** that guarded the city's or town's gates at night.

An office that existed before the Norman conquest was that of the **shire reeve** or **sheriff**. The person holding this office led the shire's (or county's) military forces and judged criminal and civil cases. Later, the sheriff's duties became more restricted, and his job included trying minor crimes, investigating crimes within the shire, and questioning suspects. (The office of sheriff in England continues until this day.) As for the actual nitty-gritty job of law enforcement, this was up to the citizens, who were expected to raise the alarm, or **hue and cry**, and catch the person accused of the crime. If there were no witnesses to a crime, the victim alone was responsible for identifying the perpetrator.

In 1285 these efforts were fortified and set to record by the Statute of Winchester. The statute set forth, in part, that anyone could make an arrest; that it was every citizen's duty, especially the constable's, to keep the peace; that a hue and cry must be raised to apprehend an offender and that every citizen was expected to participate; and that it was the constable's job to present the suspect in court.

Although this system lasted for hundreds of years, it had serious problems. For example, many citizens resented watchman duty, and many were not very good at it. Some were too elderly to be effective, some were drunk when standing night watch, and some were criminals themselves. In some ways, it was like asking the fox to guard the henhouse. This type of policing was riddled with inefficiencies and corruption. Likewise, it did little or nothing to prevent crime.[2] Watchmen also spent a great deal of time hiding, as it had become a common sport of rich young men to taunt and terrorize them. Consequently, the streets were dark and unsafe, and only the rich who had armed themselves or had bodyguards had any degree of safety. Those who had money were able to hire substitutes to do their watchman duties and private guards to protect their property. Those who could not recover their stolen property often hired "thieftakers," a sort of bounty hunter who went after the suspected criminal and attempted to recover the stolen property in return for a fee.

hundred-man
The head of a group of 10 tithings (men collected in groups of 10) who served as an administrator and judge.

constable (*comes stabuli*)
The head of law enforcement for large districts in early England. Constables oversaw the watch-and-ward system that guarded the city's or town's gates at night. In the modern United States, a constable serves areas such as rural townships and is usually elected. The constable is responsible for serving summonses, subpoenas, and court orders.

watch-and-ward system
An old English system overseen by the constable in which a watchman guarded a city's or town's gates at night.

sheriff (shire reeve)
The shire reeve led the shire's military forces and judged cases. Later, sheriff duties were restricted to trying minor crimes, investigating crimes within the shire, and questioning suspects.

hue and cry
In early English law, the alarm that citizens were required to raise upon the witness or discovery of a crime. The witness and all within earshot were required by law to pursue the perpetrator.

THE GIN EFFECT. A pivotal factor that advanced the development of law enforcement was the invention of gin.[3] Prior to that time, most citizens drank beer, ale, or wine. Because of a grain surplus, the agricultural interests saw the mass consumption of gin as a way to profit from their excess grain. Hard liquor had been expensive and was consumed mainly by the rich who engaged in habits of brawling and killing.[4] Gin democratized drunkenness and brought all kinds of new problems to London.

> *By 1725 there were more than seven thousand gin shops in London and drink was sold as a sideline by numerous shopkeepers and peddlers. For a penny anyone could drink all day in any "flash house" and get a straw pallet in a back room to sleep it off. The sale of gin (mainly in London) rose from three and one-half million gallons in 1727 to almost six and one-half million gallons in 1735 and then soared to over eight million in 1743. Public drunkenness became a commonplace sight, and drink-crazed mobs often roamed the city. The streets of London, never safe, were now filled with people whose behavior was unpredictable and occasionally quite violent. Not surprisingly, the gin craze was accompanied by a great rise in violent crimes and theft.*[5]

The government responded to these problems by hiring more watchmen. Unfortunately, this just fed conditions for greater corruption. As the government proceeded to get tough on criminals, the rich continued to hire "linkmen" or bodyguards, arm themselves with pistols, and move away to new parts of the city, which resulted in the type of residential segregation that we see in our major cities today.[6] The government attempted to deal with these problems by licensing the gin outlets, which proved largely ineffective

This 18th-century illustration, "Gin Lane," represents the liquor's harmful effects on society. Alcohol was popular in part because the drinking water was not safe.

Courtesy of Getty Images, Inc.-Hulton Archive Photos.

BEER STREET AND GIN LANE.

because of the further corruption it encouraged. Only after taxes made gin expensive did its consumption start to fall.

Bow Street Runners
A police organization created circa 1748 by magistrates Henry Fielding and his brother Sir John Fielding whose members went on patrol, rather than sitting at a designated post.

Thames River Police
A private police force created by the West India Trading Company in 1798 that represented the first professional, salaried police force in London.

Metropolitan Police Act
Created in 1829 by Sir Robert Peel, it was the first successful bill to create a permanent, public police force.

bobbies
A popular slang term for the police force created in 1829 by Sir Robert Peel's Metropolitan Police Act. The term is derived from the short form of Robert, Bob.

RISE OF ORGANIZED POLICING. Another tactic to combat the increase in crime was developed around 1748 by magistrates Henry Fielding and his brother Sir John Fielding with the organization of the **Bow Street Runners**. This was a more centralized system than the watch-and-ward arrangement, and the members were required to patrol their areas rather than just sit in their watch boxes. Fielding, for a brief time, even organized a mounted patrol of the highways. The Bow Street Runners did not last long after Henry Fielding died, but his innovations did signal the first time that the police were mobile.[7]

In 1798 the West India Trading Company created the first professional, salaried police force in London, the **Thames River Police**. This private police force, formed to prevent thefts from the port, was different from the frankpledge system in two major ways. First, its officers patrolled to prevent crime, and second, they were salaried and not allowed to accept any other payments. The police force worked so well that two years later the government added it to the public payroll. Still, citizens accustomed to a system in which they were basically responsible for themselves were suspicious of a standing police force.

However, social problems in London were mounting as a result of poverty and a burgeoning population. Finally, in 1829 Sir Robert Peel sponsored the **Metropolitan Police Act**, the first successful bill to create a permanent, public police force. Like the Thames River Police, these "new police" carried out preventive patrols and were paid regular salaries. They were also uniformed, and like the watchmen of old, kept a lookout for fires, called out the time, and lighted public lamps.

These police were viewed as a civilizing instrument whose effort and example would make for better civil relations in society. The police, who were nicknamed **bobbies** after

Figure 5.1
The Nine Principles of Policing

The following principles appear in the appendix of Charles Reith's *A New Study of Police History* (1956). Although popularly attributed to Sir Robert Peel, the principles were probably written by Charles Rowan and Richard Mayne, whom Peel appointed to direct and organize the newly created Metropolitan Police.

1. To prevent crime and disorder, as an alternative to their repression by military force and severity of legal punishment.
2. To recognize always that the power of the police to fulfill their functions and duties is dependent on public approval of their existence, actions, and behavior and on their ability to secure and maintain public respect.
3. To recognize always that to secure and maintain the respect and approval of the public means also the securing of the willing cooperation of the public in the task of securing observance of laws.
4. To recognize always that the extent to which the cooperation of the public can be secured diminishes proportionately the necessity of the use of physical force and compulsion for achieving police objectives.
5. To seek and preserve public favor, not by pandering to public opinion, but by constantly demonstrating absolutely impartial service to law, in complete independence of policy, and without regard to the justice or injustice of the substance of individual laws; by ready offering of individual service and friendship to all members of the public without regard to their wealth or social standing; by ready exercise of courtesy and friendly good humor; and by ready offering of individual sacrifice in protecting and preserving life.
6. To use physical force only when the exercise of persuasion, advice, and warning is found to be insufficient to obtain public cooperation to an extent necessary to secure observance of law or to restore order; and to use only the minimum degree of physical force which is necessary on any particular occasion for achieving a police objective.
7. To maintain at all times a relationship with the public that gives reality to the historic tradition that the police are the public and that the public are the police; the police being only members of the public who are paid to give full time attention to duties which are incumbent on every citizen in the interests of community welfare and existence.
8. To recognize always the need for strict adherence to police-executive functions, and to refrain from even seeming to usurp the powers of the judiciary of avenging individuals or the State, and of authoritatively judging guilt and punishing the guilt.
9. To recognize always that the test of police efficiency is the absence of crime and disorder, and not the visible evidence of police action in dealing with them.

Sources: Charles Reith, *A New Study of Police History* (Edinburgh: Oliver and Boyd, 1956), 121–142, 287–288; Civitas: The Institute for the Study of Civil Society, *Principles of Good Policing*, http://www.civitas.org.uk/pubs/policeNine.php.

their founder's nickname of Bob, were expected to adhere to a strict military-type discipline based on Peel's nine principles of policing (see Figure 5.1). The bobbies set a new standard of police professionalism; however, their jurisdiction was limited to the city of London. It was not until 1856 that the rural provinces were required to establish police forces.

Policing in the United States

Like many aspects of American culture, policing has its roots in English tradition. Although the police developed differently in England than they have here, some commonalities are worth examining. According to Samuel Walker and Charles Katz, "the English heritage contributed three enduring features to American policing":[8]

1. **Limited police authority.** As opposed to other countries in Europe, the Anglo-American tradition of policing places a good deal of emphasis on the rights and liberties of the individual.
2. **Local control.** Law enforcement agencies are, for the most part, local, city, or county institutions. The United States does not have a national police force. We do have many state and federal law enforcement agencies, but they are not like the national police forces found in many parts of the world where control is highly centralized in the federal government.

"Peel Fights Night Watchmen." A satirical English cartoon depicts Sir Robert Peel fighting a group of night watchmen.

Courtesy of CORBIS-NY.

3. **Fragmented system.** There are over 18,000 separate law enforcement agencies in the United States that range from federal (FBI, Secret Service), to state (highway patrol), to local (city police, county sheriff). These agencies are only loosely coordinated and have little oversight from the federal level.[9]

Many differences between the United States and England affected the development of their respective policing styles. One was the lack of a single, coherent philosophy. Whereas the English police were unified under the vision of Sir Robert Peel, local police organizations in the United States formed their own policies and procedures. Another factor was the large and ever-expanding political geography of the United States. As stakes were claimed and territories formed, government and law enforcement followed slowly. This led to the phenomenon of the "Wild West." The further the country developed from the cities and seats of government on the East Coast, the less controllable it became. A third factor was immigration. The constituency of the United States was (and is to this day) in constant flux, resulting in cities, states, and territories filled with people representing a vast array of cultures and languages. Conversely, the English police of the day were responsible for a static political and physical geography that had a homogeneous culture and language.

THE 19TH CENTURY. Jurisdictional difficulties and labor troubles gave rise to some of the nation's most famous private police. Laws were passed that allowed companies to maintain or contract with their own police forces and agencies. Pennsylvania's Coal and Iron Police became famous for its strong-arm antilabor activities. The Pinkerton National Detective Agency, founded in 1850 by Scottish political refugee Allan Pinkerton, was used for protection against thieves and labor activists by railroad companies and coal companies.

As the century waned, urban police became an integral part of their communities—so integral, in fact, that many police officers began to work for the political bosses of their communities. For example, officers would, through various measures, help ensure the election of "their" candidates. Or they would accept money in return for not enforcing certain laws. Two of the most important cities in which this type of activity—and its reform—occurred were New York and Chicago.

NEW YORK CITY INFLUENCE. Informal policing began in New York City in 1625 when the Dutch settlement was called New Amsterdam. There, a "schout fiscal" or "sheriff attorney" had such law enforcement duties as settling disputes and warning the colonists of fire. From 1609 to 1664 a group of men called the "Rattle Watch" patrolled at night, carrying loud rattles to raise an alarm if anything was amiss in the town. The city's first professional police force of 800 men was organized in 1845. Their badges of eight-pointed stars were made of copper and were so distinctive that civilians nicknamed the officers "coppers," which was later shortened to "cops."

LONDON VERSUS NEW YORK. Although the English police systems and those in the United States share a common heritage, some distinct differences arise from the social and political cultures of the two countries. In an article titled "Cops and Bobbies, 1830–1870," Wilber Miller compared and contrasted how policing developed along different lines in London and New York.[10] Miller argued that a major distinction between the two systems of law enforcement lay in the type of authority exercised by the patrolman. The London officer had an impersonal authority that rested on his limited discretion granted by the government. The New York patrolman, by contrast, had a much broader latitude of discretion, giving him a personal basis for his authority. For instance, by 1860 New York officers were allowed to carry revolvers to protect themselves from heavily armed criminals. Thus, the New York patrolman was a powerful force to be reckoned with and acted as a monarch on his beat with the power of life and death. The power of the London bobbie resided in the citizens' belief that the officer represented a collective power rather than an individual one.

THE CHICAGO INFLUENCE. Related to the differences in how the London police were more closely supervised than the New York police is the law enforcement environment in Chicago at the beginning of the 20th century. Chicago's official police force was created around 1855 and reorganized several times over the next six decades until 1913. The city's police officers were given no training in the law, and the criminal justice system placed little emphasis on legal procedure. Chicago police had four idiosyncratic orientations to the law:

1. Police and courts were highly decentralized and often reflected, in important ways, the values of local communities. Democratic sensitivities rather than legal norms were expected to guide police behavior and check abuses.
2. The police, as part of a larger political system, were a significant resource at the command of local organizations. Police, courts, and prosecutors provided political leaders with patronage jobs, were a source of favors for constituents, and were important agencies for collecting money that lubricated political campaigns.
3. Criminal justice institutions operated as rackets, providing the means by which police officers and other officials earned extra income.
4. Police officers and other criminal justice system personnel developed informal systems of operation that reflected their own subcultures and organizational needs. These informal methods of operation bore, at best, only an indirect relationship to the formal legal system.[11]

The political nature of the Chicago police in the early 20th century resulted in a system in which the police took bribes, solicited votes, harassed the homeless, beat suspects, and assisted gamblers. They also performed many duties now normally considered outside the responsibilities of crime control, such as taking injured people to the hospital, mediating family quarrels, rounding up stray dogs, returning lost children to their parents, and removing dead horses from city streets. One of the hallmarks of the professionalization of law enforcement that emerged over the past hundred years is the degree to which the police mission has become less informal and more legally constrained.

VIGILANTE POLICING. The development of professional police departments in large metropolitan areas is important, but it is by no means the only heritage that contributed

FOCUS ON ETHICS

Righteous Vengeance?

As a police officer you have been on the trail of a serial child molester who frequents the city's parks. You have a good idea of who it is, but this suspect has been smart enough to elude arrest and conviction for over 10 years. This morning you found your suspect dead, lying in a pool of blood with his skull crushed. Close to the body you discover a baseball bat with the name of the son of a prominent politician printed on the bat handle. You know that this 17-year-old boy was a victim of molestation 10 years ago when this problem first surfaced in the community. Your suspicion is that the boy killed the molester, but you also believe that the suspect needed killing and that the boy did the community a great service. If you hide the bat, there will be no way to trace the crime to this young man who you think had a good reason to commit this act. If you enter the bat into evidence, the boy could be convicted of murder and sent to prison for a long time. Because you have twin eight-year-old sons, you are happy this perpetrator will no longer prowl the city parks. Can you turn a blind eye to this crime? Can you protect this otherwise good boy? If you do hide the bat, should you tell his father so that he could protect you if you are found out, or maybe because you think he could help get you promoted? You know the correct procedure would be to arrest the boy, but a little voice inside your head is whispering something about a "greater justice," and you are tempted to hide the bat.

WHAT DO YOU DO?

1. Arrest the boy and let the criminal justice system take its course.
2. Hide the bat, and protect the boy.
3. Hide the bat, protect the boy, and tell his father the truth.

to the development of the police in the United States. In rural areas and small towns across the nation, particularly in the South and West, the vigilante tradition was part of American life. In the newly developed areas of the frontier, the normal mechanisms of social control emerged slowly. The normal constraints on deviant behavior exercised by churches, schools, and cohesive community life were absent, and the formal system of law enforcement was inadequate. As citizens struggled to maintain some modicum of order in newly settled areas, they took the law into their own hands by engaging in vigilante actions.

Vigilante committees were usually established by the elites of society to protect property and social order from rogues and criminals.[12] The justice meted out by the vigilantes was a rough one that included, but was not limited to, flogging, expulsion, and killing. These actions served not only as punishments, but also as a warning to others that a system of social order existed that everyone was expected to obey.[13]

However, vigilantism was a double-edged sword. On one side it was socially constructive in that it established order in the community and prevented anarchy and lawlessness whereby thieves, gamblers, drunkards, and rapists were free to commit their crimes. Social order benefited everyone, rich and poor alike, but it should be noted that the vigilante movements were concerned mostly with the interests of the rich.[14] This side of the sword was socially harmful. In some places, antivigilante movements emerged as rival local political parties or extended families vied for control of the government. Respectable men joined in fighting vigilantes, not because they had any sympathy for rogues and outlaws, but because they saw certain elements of society using the vigilantes to promote their own economic advantage rather than maintain order. Additionally, some of these vigilante movements were to become outright terrorist organizations, such as the

Ku Klux Klan. Even though these types of organizations had broad support in some segments of the community, they served to promote judicial, racial, and religious injustice in the South and West.[15]

As some of these vigilante sentiments were transformed into actual police agencies, a double standard arose that was applied to the disenfranchised in society. The Texas Rangers, organized in 1835, were among the first advanced police agencies in the United States. However, the Mexican and American Indian citizens of Texas were subject to the law being enforced to the benefit of the Anglo cattle barons. Members of these minority groups were killed with impunity because the Rangers tended to "shoot first and asked questions later."[16]

This discussion of law enforcement in U.S. history goes against many of the images we have of life on the frontier. Television and film have provided us with a highly romanticized view of law and order during this period, and the idea that the good guys always wore white hats and had to battle the "bad" American Indians and Mexicans ignores the reality of the power politics of the past. Of course, there were outlaws, criminals, and threats to the public order that required citizens to band together to protect themselves and others. What should be remembered here, however, is that vigilante groups almost always served the needs of those who had power, high positions in the social structure, and property.

Introduction of Police Professionalism

At the start of the 20th century, law enforcement in the United States was caught in a web of inefficiency, corruption, and special-interest politics.[17] The police were an arm of the interests that used the resources, budgets, labor, and authority of the city to control the lower classes and to amass power and wealth. City after city could be seen using local government institutions, such as the police, in favor of the elites.[18] Spurred by muckraking journalists, the cities began to correct some of the most obvious inequities in how citizens were treated by government and business. Politicians and heads of industry realized that to maintain the population support for the existing political and economic system, changes were required. Some scholars contend that the resulting progressive movement simply stabilized the grip of the elites on the institutions of society rather than producing fundamental changes, but it is fair to say that this period saw a surge of useful reform efforts.[19] One such effort was the Pendleton Civil Service Act of 1883. A response to public frustration with incompetence and corruption within the federal government, the purpose of the act, according to its text, was to "regulate and improve the civil service of the United States." The act basically formed a civil service system that did away with patronage and administered employment and promotions based on merit rather than political connections. This legislation shook much of the corruption out of the U.S. civil service bureaucracy, including the nation's budding police forces.

THE WICKERSHAM COMMISSION AND AUGUST VOLLMER. Reflective of the growing reform movement is the work of a police chief of Berkeley, California, August Vollmer. In 1931 he wrote the Wickersham Commission report that set the police reform agenda for the rest of the century. Vollmer is important to the movement to professionalize the police because he instituted many policies and practices that are still influencing law enforcement today. He was among the first police chiefs to recruit college graduates, and he organized the first police science courses at the University of California. Many of his students went on to become police chiefs in other cities where they extended his reform policies.

According to Samuel Walker and Charles M. Katz, Vollmer's police reform movement, which dominated the law enforcement agenda through the 1960s, focused on six issues:

1. Policing is defined as a profession in which the police serve the entire community on a nonpartisan basis.
2. Policing should be free of political influence.

CROSSCURRENTS

Frontier Justice

Courtesy of CORBIS-NY.

The western frontier of the United States confronted the new country with special challenges to its civilization. Thanks to colonization, the West also presented perhaps an unusual chapter in the history of law enforcement. Unlike the Old World, where people had divided lands and developed societies and laws over thousands of years, North America was largely a blank slate, with only a relatively vulnerable population of American Indians. As pioneers flooded into the "wide open spaces" of the West seeking land, economic opportunities, or distance from government, the frontier outgrew the ability of the young country to formally police it.

Apprehending offenders, or even awareness of crime, was much easier in the tight-knit urban East than in the expanses of the West where settlements were miles apart and criminals could simply disappear into the wilderness. Many lawless types were attracted to the frontier for its weak laws, feeble and/or corrupt governments, and engulfing vastness. Compounding law enforcement troubles were the new crimes that came with Western settlement: pilfered livestock; illegally grazed ranch lands; and racial stress among Anglos, Mexicans, and American Indians. The transportation of goods also provided new opportunities for crime. Stagecoaches and, later, trains were easy targets for outlaws, and the need for protecting these vehicles gave rise to new forms of para- and private policing. In the end, the challenge of civilizing the frontier gave the United States some of its enduring law enforcement institutions.

Private Citizens and Vigilance Committees

The first official Anglo police agency was formed in 1831 in the town of San Felipe de Austin, Texas, with the establishment of a community patrol that, much like the old English watch-and-ward system, served to alert citizens to danger.[1] In the beginning, these patrols tended to employ men who were not far from being criminals themselves; they were rough, tough, and the only ones willing to volunteer for the job. Later, however, more modern-type police organizations were formed, complete with well-paid officers and responsibilities to local governments and citizens. Still, official police often allowed ordinary citizens to expedite their own policing duties. In some areas, one private person could arrest another for a crime or might be deputized if there was a shortage of regular officers.

Vigilante groups became common, springing up in response to social undesirables from lawbreakers to labor organizers. These groups usually operated with the approval of local law enforcement—or instead of it, if no official agency existed. In Colorado, vigilantism was made law, with citizens who were appointed to "examine into . . . all criminal violations of the laws. . . ."[2] Other vigilante groups included Arizona's "Outlaw Exterminators" and Texas' "Partizan Rangers."[3] Violence in Dodge City in 1873 led to the formation of a vigilance committee that, while at first bringing peace to the town, later caused even more trouble. (The sheriffs elected in response to the vigilance committee fiasco included Bat Masterson and Wyatt Earp.)

Rangers

Although the frontier eventually became more settled, the problem of keeping the peace and ensuring some kind of justice among populations scattered across hundreds of miles of territory still existed. To address this problem, several states created early forms of state police known as "rangers." Arizona, Nevada, and New Mexico all had rangers, but the most famous of these organizations is the Texas Rangers, the oldest statewide law enforcement organization in North America.[4]

The first Rangers were assembled in 1823 by Stephen F. Austin to protect Anglo Texas colonists. In 1835 a resolution made the Rangers official. For the next 180 years, the state of Texas depended, to varying degrees, on bands of men called "rangers" for law enforcement and public safety. The first Rangers protected settlers and tracked stolen horses, cattle, and escaped slaves.[5] After 1848 the U.S. Army took over protection of the Texas frontier, and a brief resurgence of the Rangers before the Civil War was drained by that conflict as Rangers became soldiers. Not until 1874, after the Rangers had driven off the last of the American Indians and the conflict with the Mexicans had quieted, did the Rangers become a statewide police force.[6]

Hired Guns

Doing business in the Wild West was often dangerous. Merchants and corporations could not trust the uneven, sometimes corrupt law enforcement organizations to provide adequate protection. So, as the West India Trading Company had in England with the Thames River Police less than a hundred years prior, U.S. corporate interests employed their own police. These police were not confined to railroads and stagecoaches; ranchers employed range inspectors, and mining and oil companies hired their own security. In towns and villages, business owners would form special "merchants' police."[7] Later, Allan Pinkerton's private force was hired to protect railroads, conduct criminal investigations, and even guarded Buffalo Bill's Wild West Show.[8] Another famous organization, Wells Fargo, protected stagecoaches, steamboats, and railroads. Some of the agencies, through violence and corruption, eventually wore out their welcome. Pinkerton, for example, was accused of bribing juries, employing assassins, and violently breaking strikes.[9] Several states later resorted to banning the use of private police agencies. Railroads came to rely less on private agencies and directly employed their own police forces, which they employ to this day.

QUESTIONS

1. Were the various groups of rangers necessary to keep order in the Old West?
2. Are the Texas Rangers still a necessary part of law enforcement? Have they been overly romanticized or, on the other hand, not given enough credit?
3. Are private security firms a good idea for businesses and corporations, or should they rely solely on the police?

REFERENCES

1. Frank Richard Prassel, *The Western Police Officer: A Legacy of Law and Order* (Norman, OK: University of Oklahoma Press, 1981), 45.
2. Independent District, Gilpin County, Colorado, "Laws of Independent District (1861)" (University of Colorado Archives, Boulder), as quoted in Prassel, *Western Police Officer,* 130.
3. Prassel, *Western Police Officer,* 130.
4. Texas Department of Public Safety, Texas Rangers, http://www.txdps.state.tx.us/director_staff/texas_rangers/index.htm.
5. Julian Samora, Joe Bernal, and Albert Peña, *Gunpowder Justice: A Reassessment of the Texas Rangers* (Notre Dame, IN: University of Notre Dame Press, 1979), 11.
6. In 1935 Rangers were reorganized and made a unit of the state's Department of Public Safety. According to the Rangers' Web site (see note 4), this was when "the true modern-day Ranger came into being."
7. Prassel, *Western Police Officer,* 132.
8. Ibid, 134.
9. Ibid.

3. Qualified executives should lead the police. This means that the chiefs of large cities should have some experience running large organizations.
4. The standards for being a policeman should be raised. Law enforcement personnel should be screened for intelligence, health, and moral character. (Although slow in developing, this increase in the quality of personnel resulted in specialized police academies where professional training is required.)

CASE IN POINT

Miranda v. Arizona

The Case

Miranda v. Arizona, 384 U.S. 436, 86 S. Ct. 1602 (1966)

The Point

This decision set forth that confessions made by suspects who have not been advised of their due process rights cannot be used as evidence.

Ernesto Miranda was arrested in 1963 on suspicion of rape and kidnapping. Police interrogated Miranda, a Mexican immigrant, for several hours without advising him of his right to an attorney or permitting him to speak with one. Miranda signed a written confession and was later convicted and sentenced to 60 years. Miranda's case, and several others like it, were appealed, and the Supreme Court agreed with their contention that the suspects' right to due process had been violated because they had not been advised of their rights to an attorney or to remain silent. The 1966 decision set forth that confessions made by suspects who have not been advised of their due process rights cannot be used as evidence. *Miranda* was upheld by the Supreme Court in June 2000, in *Dickerson v. United States.* In that case, one of the questions considered by the court was the constitutionality of a statute enacted by Congress in 1968 that states that confessions are admissible if "voluntarily given." The court held that its constitutional decisions may not be overruled by Acts of Congress.

The Miranda warning is as follows:

1. You have the right to remain silent and refuse to answer any questions.
2. Anything you say may be used against you in a court of law.
3. As we discuss this matter, you have a right to stop answering my questions at any time you desire.
4. You have a right to a lawyer before speaking to me, to remain silent until you can talk to him or her, and to have him or her present when you are being questioned.
5. If you want a lawyer but cannot afford one, one will be provided to you without cost.
6. Do you understand each of these rights I have explained to you?
7. Now that I have advised you of your rights, are you willing to answer my questions without an attorney present?

5. Modern principles of scientific management should be introduced that involve centralizing command structures so the chief can better control officers.
6. Specialized units such as traffic, juvenile, and vice should be developed to increase the size and complexity of police agencies and allow officers to focus on particular types of crime. (This increase in complexity had the added feature of opening up law enforcement to women, who were originally hired for the juvenile units.)[20]

Other features of the progressive movement in policing included an emphasis on technology to assist the police in doing their job. Of particular importance was the introduction of the patrol car, or as Vollmer called it, "the swift angel of death."[21] Improved communications, advanced record-keeping techniques, and the creation of crime analysis laboratories were all new uses of technology that were introduced to law enforcement during this move toward professionalism.

Police professionalization included efforts at crime prevention by introducing preventive strategies that dealt with high-risk individuals such as juveniles and the unemployed before they had a chance to become criminals. The police also engaged in public relations activities to improve their image in the community. Such programs as "junior police" were instituted to give boys positive interactions with law enforcement and to provide role models.

Finally, the move toward police professionalism involved stripping away functions not normally concerned with crime control. The police had been sort of a "catch all" agency whose time was considered wasted with chasing stray dogs, licensing various enterprises, and enforcing minor morals laws such as those against kissing in public and women's wearing their skirts too short. These functions did little to protect society, and they of-

REFERENCE

Analyzing the Police

In addition to the Wickersham report, a number of other analyses of the police have led to improvements in professionalism and better use of technology. These reports include the following:

1953 The American Bar Foundation Survey.

1965 President's Commission on Law Enforcement and the Administration of Justice. From this effort, the Law Enforcement Administration Assistance program (LEAA) was established to aid criminal justice agencies in their missions to fight crime and improve the criminal justice system.

1967 The National Advisory Commission on Civil Disorders (Kerner Commission). This report had a major impact on highlighting the distrust between police agencies and minority communities, particularly those of African American citizens. It called for greater representation of minorities in police departments.

1973 The Knapp Commission. This investigation of widespread corruption in the New York City Police Department revealed systematic bribes, favors, and selective enforcement. Of particular concern was the impact of organized crime on police misconduct in protecting mob-run enterprises such as gambling; narcotics sales; loan-sharking, and illegal sex-related enterprises such as prostitution, gay after-hours bars, and pornography.

1991–1992 The Christopher and Kolts Commissions. In response to the videotaped beating of Rodney King by members of the Los Angeles Police Department and the Los Angeles County Sheriff's Department, these two commissions were created to investigate the systemic problems of the law enforcement subculture that led to complaints by many members of the metropolitan area's minority community. The Christopher Commission reported that the department had failed to control its officers and issued over 100 recommendations.

1993 The Mollen Commission in New York City found that rogue police officers extorted protection money from drug dealers and sold stolen cocaine to teenagers.*

*See, Samuel Walker and Charles M. Katz, *The Police in America: An Introduction* (Boston: McGraw Hill, 2002), 42–43. Michael D. Lyman, *The Police: An Introduction* (Upper Saddle River, NJ: Prentice Hall, 2002), 228–229. The Knapp Commission Report, "Patterns of Police Corruption," *Thinking About Police: Contemporary Readings,* ed. Carl B. Klockers (New York: McGraw-Hill, 1983), 350–353.

fered too many opportunities for selective enforcement and corruption.[22] Enforcing dress codes or purely administrative regulations was considered an inefficient use of police resources, so these activities were shifted to other means of social control, leaving the police with the sole job of maintaining public order and fighting crime.

OTHER REFORMERS. August Vollmer was not the only notable police reformer. One of his students, Orlando W. Wilson, became the police chief of Wichita, Kansas, dean of the School of Criminology at the University of California, and later the superintendent of the Chicago Police Department. Wilson made the police more efficient by using a workload formula that assigned officers based on the amount of reported crime and calls for service. He is credited with accelerating the shift from foot patrol to automobile patrol.

Perhaps the most famous of the law enforcement administrators who championed professionalism was the Federal Bureau of Investigation's J. Edgar Hoover. Hoover built the FBI into one of the premier law enforcement agencies in the world with his skillful political maneuvering, masterful public relations efforts, and surveillance of not only criminals, but also political rivals and presidents. His reputation is a mixed bag of progressive reformer and repressive tyrant. There is little doubt that the agency he created is a cornerstone of law enforcement in the United States, but the abuses of the constitutional rights

J. Edgar Hoover was the driving force behind building the FBI into a premier law enforcement agency. He was a powerful political insider who served under many presidents.
Courtesy of CORBIS-NY.

of citizens that he authorized and used as leverage to keep himself in power are as disturbing as they are legendary. Under Hoover's direction, FBI agents harassed civil rights and antiwar activists, ignored white collar crimes, and intimidated politicians.[23] Nevertheless, the FBI's crime labs, National Training Academy, Behavioral Analysis Unit (made famous by the movie *The Silence of the Lambs*), and administration of the Uniform Crime Reports all attest to its mission to bring coordination and professionalism to U.S. law enforcement.

Attempts to professionalize both police practices and police ethics have been a long-term concern for police reformers. These commissions and reports demonstrate that, as an institution, law enforcement has been historically plagued by political interference, corruption, and lack of resources. Nevertheless, police and elected officials continue in their efforts to modernize, professionalize, and humanize law enforcement agencies. There have been flagrant abuses in the past, and there will always be individual officers who exceed their authority or even behave in a criminal fashion, but it is important to keep in mind that most law enforcement officers are honest public servants who have taken on a difficult and demanding job.

Modern Police Organization

Law enforcement agencies are influenced by their structural components. By this we mean that the organization of police departments in terms of command structure, degree of centralized decision making, the expressed focus of their mission, and how success is measured all determine what type of occupational culture will exist. The potential exists for a wide range of organizational differences among police departments. However, police departments vary very little in how they are organized. With the exception of some small departments, the vast majority of law enforcement agencies hearken back to Peel's model with a structure based on a quasi-military template complete with uniforms, ranks, hierarchical chains of command, and centralized decision making. For examples of the organization of modern police departments in small and large cities, see Figures 5.2 and 5.3.

But to think of police organizations simply in terms of their military style would be a mistake. Some crucial differences between the police and the military make supervising

Figure 5.2
City of Richmond, California, Police Department, 2003

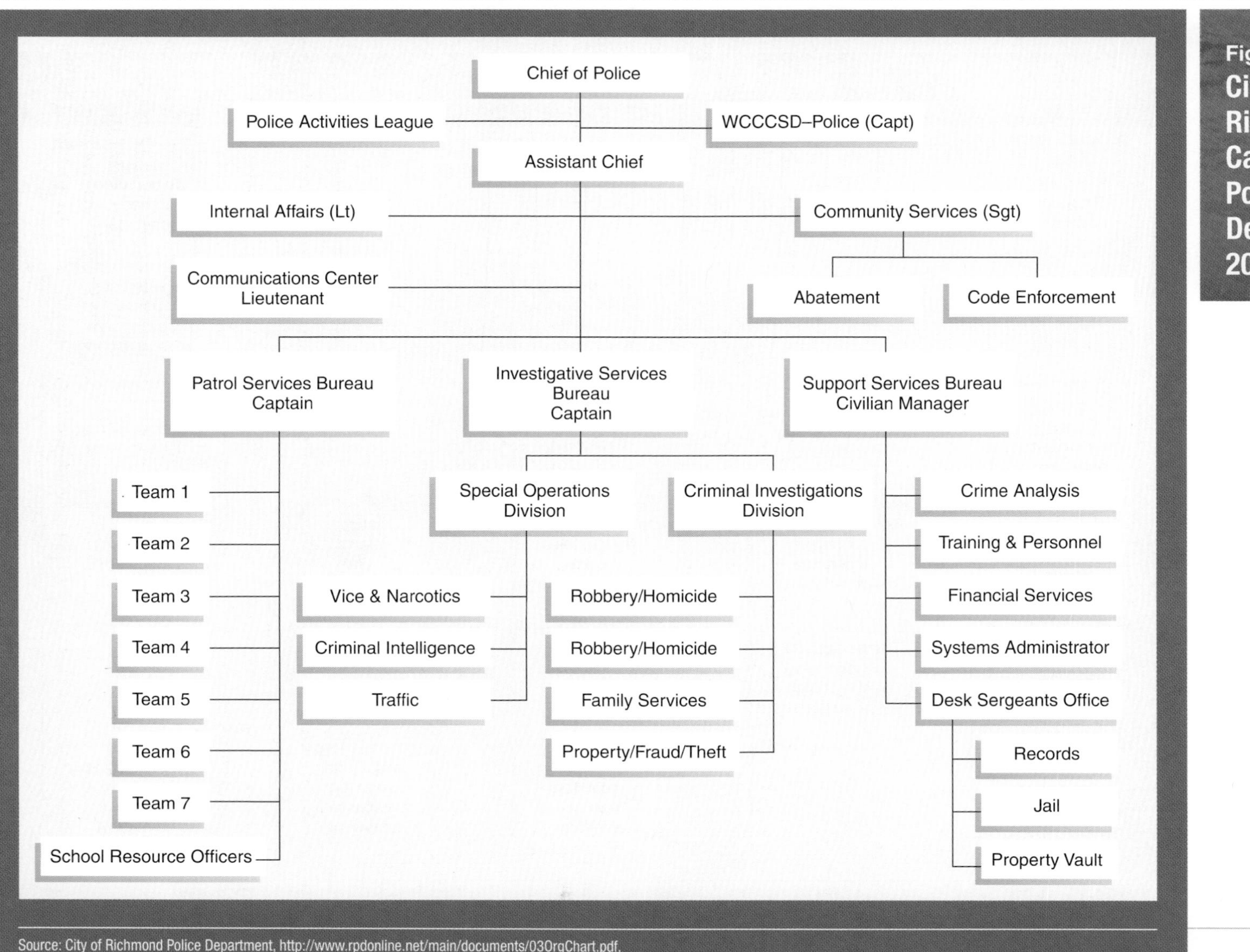

Source: City of Richmond Police Department, http://www.rpdonline.net/main/documents/03OrgChart.pdf.

Figure 5.3
Chicago Police Department Organization for Command

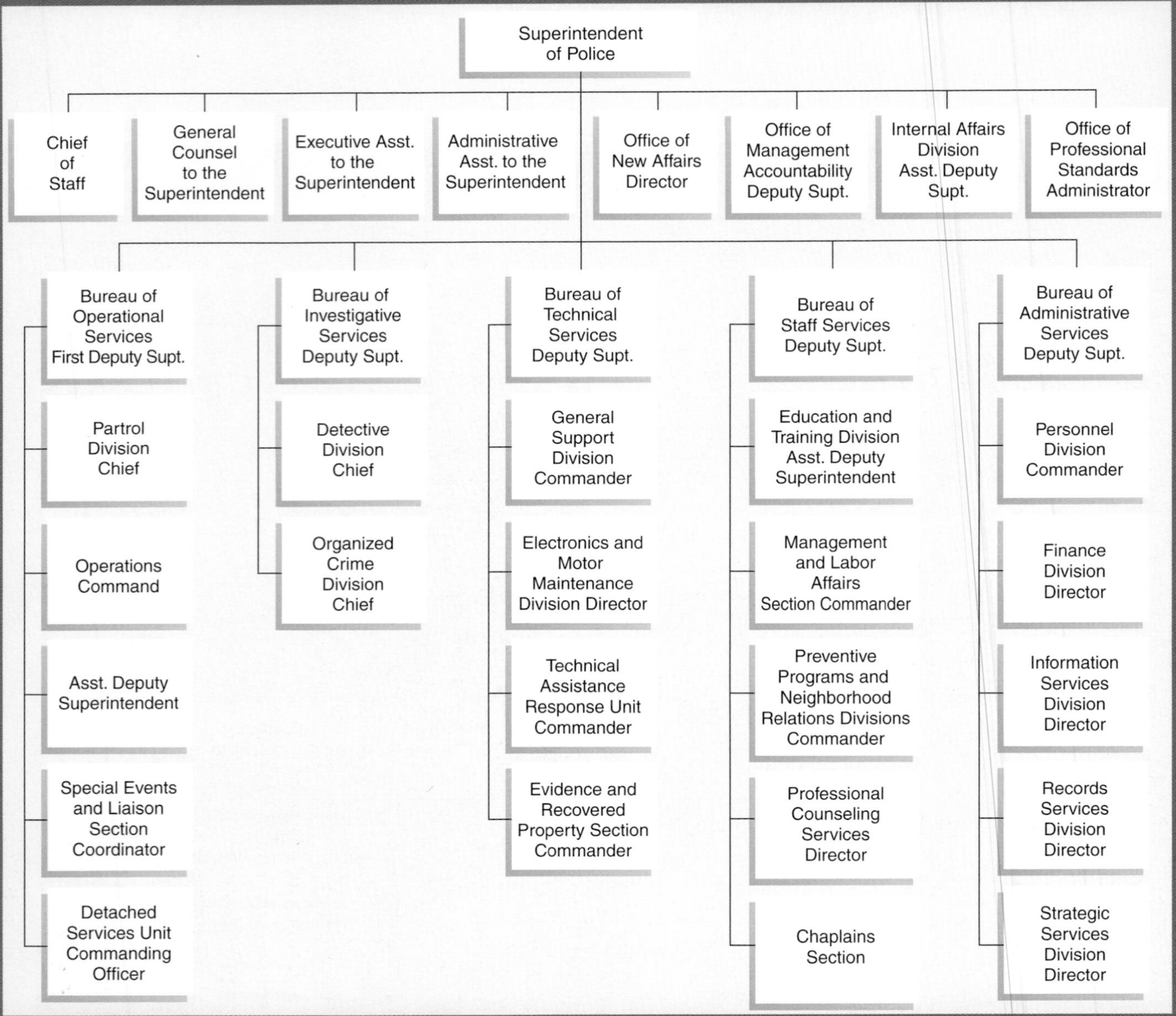

Source: Chicago Police Department, *2002 Annual Report*, http://egov.cityofchicago.org/webportal/COCWebPortal/COC_EDITORIAL/02AnnualReport.pdf, p. 38.

the police a different, and in many ways more difficult, job than supervising the military. These problems can be briefly summarized as discretion, visibility, and **authority**.

authority
The right and the power to commit an act or order others to commit an act. Permission.

1. **Discretion.** Perhaps the most fundamental difference between law enforcement and the military is the locus where discretion is exercised. In typical military units, the allowance for discretion is highest at the top, and the individual soldier makes very few decisions. There is a consistent and simple pattern of supervision in which the generals choose the battlefield strategy. The officers choose which units to commit to battle; the sergeants choose which soldiers will rush the machine-gun nest; and the soldiers do their duty, follow orders, and either succeed or die. By contrast, in law enforcement organizations, most discretion is in the hands of the individual police officer. The chief can set some broad policies, and the supervisors can require the officers to keep them apprised of situations via radio, but the individual police officer must make the important decisions. Determining whether a crime has been committed, deciding to make an arrest, and giving advice to citizens are all activities that are difficult for the command structure of law enforcement organizations to control. In effect, each police officer exercises a great deal of decision-making authority. That is one reason many individuals find police work to be rewarding.
2. **Visibility.** Police work is seen by the public on a daily basis. Law enforcement officers must interact with citizens, have their decisions second-guessed by the media, and answer to the chief for any violations of procedure and laws. The military is not exposed to the spotlight of public scrutiny. Battlefields are in other countries; the press is given extremely limited access (especially since the Vietnam War), and anonymity protects soldiers from having their actions judged by the public in all but the most egregious cases.
3. **Authority.** Military commanders have a great deal more authority over soldiers than police administrators have over police officers. If a police officer fails to follow orders, he or she may be disciplined or dismissed. If a soldier fails to follow orders, he or she may be court-martialed. Additionally, many police departments are under collective bargaining agreements that specify many of the terms of employment and disciplinary procedures. These collective bargaining agreements are much more "worker friendly" than the Uniform Code of Military Justice that spells out the rights of military personnel.

Police organizations are, first and foremost, bureaucracies. This means that they have rigid rules and procedures that work both to make policies more equitable and predictable, and to stifle quick changes and innovation. Therefore, the bureaucratic nature of police organizations acts as a double-edged sword. It protects the officers from a capricious and arbitrary chief while limiting their ability to respond to what they may determine to be preventable problems. Robert Regoli and John Hewitt suggested that the bureaucratic model inhibits police organizations in several ways:

1. Restricts personal growth and development
2. Fosters a groupthink mentality
3. Underestimates the power of the informal organization
4. Does not provide adequate due process
5. Discourages communication[24]

It is worth exploring a couple of these ways bureaucracies do not work as well in police practice as they appear to in theory. For instance, Peter Manning argued that patrolmen do not trust their supervisors because in police organizations the rules are often vague and are applied after the fact. According to Manning, some police officers remedy this by keeping information to themselves, competing with other officers for credit and prestige, and sometimes lying to escape supervision.[25]

As suggested by Regoli and Hewitt, another reason the formal police organization does not reflect the realities of police work is that there is a big difference between the organizational chart and how power is really distributed in the force. Informal power

Illustration depicting shortcomings of the police court.
Courtesy of CORBIS-NY.

structures that rival formal authority exist in all organizations. Peer pressure can exert a tremendous influence on individuals, causing them to violate rules and procedures. In law enforcement, a subculture may encourage the police officer to engage in corrupt activities. Thomas Barker argued:

> *The police occupation per se provides its members with numerous opportunities for corrupt acts and other forms of deviance. In some police departments there is a social setting where this inherent occupational structure is combined with peer group support and tolerance for certain patterns of corruption. The peer group indoctrinates and socializes the rookie into patterns of acceptable corrupt activities, sanctions deviations outside these boundaries, and sanctions officers who do not engage in any corrupt acts. The peer group can also discipline officers who report or attempt to report fellow officers.*[26]

Police organizations suffer from many of the same problems as other types of agencies that use a bureaucratic structure, and the patterning of police departments after military units may be troublesome. Police departments and military units are vastly different because of the nature of their missions, the exercise of discretion, and the visibility of their actions. We turn now to an examination of the many types of law enforcement agencies. Our goal is not to be exhaustive, but simply to demonstrate the range and complexity with which policing is organized at the federal, state, and local levels.

Problem of Jurisdiction

The development of law enforcement agencies has been a contentious one. There has been no centralized planning, and the pattern of federal, state, local, specialized, and private law enforcement agencies has developed according to historical accident, politics, special interests, and public welfare. However, what has been sacrificed in coordination and efficiency has been gained in responsiveness and accountability. One of the founding principles of the United States is that control of government should be as close to the people as possible. For that reason, local governments have been allowed to enact laws that speak to the unique needs of their citizens, and overall, an unorganized patchwork of ordinances reflects diversity instead of uniformity.

This phenomenon is extremely visible in the development of law enforcement agencies. There are over 18,000 agencies nationwide. Policing is a fragmented industry that provides differing levels of protection to citizens depending not only on geographic location, but also on social economic class, race, and gender. We will talk in greater detail about these sociological variables in Chapter 7, but we note them here because they cannot be entirely divorced from the structure and authority of law enforcement.

Levels of Law Enforcement

Federal Level

Federal law enforcement agencies have nationwide jurisdiction but concentrate on specific crimes. They are not general-service agencies that respond to 911 calls or engage in order-maintenance policing. Instead, they are special purpose agencies that concentrate on a very limited set of offenses. For instance, an FBI agent will not arrest a person in connection with a traffic violation unless it somehow relates to a case he or she is working on. Similarly, the customs officer is not concerned with prostitution activities unless they involve transnational trade.

Although there are about 60 federal law enforcement agencies, the main ones are organized under just three departments, the Department of Justice, the Department of the Treasury, and the Department of Homeland Security. (See Figure 5.4 for federal law enforcement agencies with the most officers.) Founded in 1870, the Department of Justice is responsible for enforcing federal laws. Its primary agencies are the Drug Enforcement Administration (DEA), the Federal Bureau of Investigation (FBI), the Border Patrol and Immigration and Naturalization Service (INS), and the U.S. Marshals. The Department of the Treasury, established in 1789, primarily enforces the collection of revenue. Its main agencies are the Bureau of Alcohol, Tobacco, and Firearms (BATF); the U.S. Customs Service; and the Internal Revenue Service (IRS). The Department of Homeland Security, which did not exist before the terrorist events of 2001, is the newest cabinet-level department. Under its auspices are a number of agencies that have been transferred in whole or in part to Homeland Security because their duties are related to controlling terrorism. An organizational chart of the Department of Homeland Security appears in Chapter 16. As of June 2002, more than 93,000 full-time federal agents were authorized to make arrests and carry firearms.[27] Nearly half of the duties of federal officers involve criminal investigation (See Figure 5.5). To a lesser extent, other functions may include responses to service, patrol, noncriminal investigation and inspection, and court operations.

CAREERS. Federal officers are among the best-paid law enforcement personnel, and competition for these jobs is stiff. Most federal officers are trained at the Federal Law Enforcement Training Center, which is headquartered in Glynco, Georgia. FBI and DEA agents also take some of their training at their respective academies in Quantico, Virginia. Many young people who go into law enforcement hope to advance to the federal level. One downside to this level of policing is the likelihood that employees will be transferred around the country as they advance along the career path. For this reason, some individuals who want to stay in one region will opt for jobs at the local level.

FEDERAL BUREAU OF INVESTIGATION. The FBI has nationwide jurisdiction to combat federal crimes. The emphasis on which crimes get the most attention has shifted over the years as a result of political considerations and the leadership style of its directors.

The FBI began in 1908 when President Theodore Roosevelt sent eight Secret Service agents to the Department of Justice to investigate violations of federal law. In the past century it has grown into a large organization that also provides assistance to state and local agencies with expert help in training (National FBI Academy), criminalistics (FBI Crime Laboratory), measuring crime (Uniform Crime Reports), and consultation on difficult cases (Behavior Analysis Unit).

Partial List of Federal Police Agencies

- Department of Agriculture
  - Forest Service
  - Office of the Inspector General
- Department of the Air Force
  - Office of Special Investigations
- Department of the Army
  - Armed Forces Police
  - Criminal Investigation Command
  - Provost Marshal
- Department of Commerce
  - Bureau of Industry and Security (Formerly Bureau of Export Administration)
  - National Institute of Standards and Technology Office of Security
  - National Marine Fisheries Service
- Department of Defense
  - Defense Criminal Investigative Service
  - National Security Agency (NSA)
  - Naval Criminal Investigative Service
- Department of Homeland Security
  - Border and Transportation Security
    - Animal and Plant Health Inspection Service
    - Federal Law Enforcement Training Center
    - Federal Protective Service (GSA)
    - Office for Domestic Preparedness
    - Transportation Security Administration
    - U.S. Citizenship and Immigration Services
    - U.S. Customs and Border Protection
      - Office of Border Patrol
  - Information Analysis and Infrastructure Protection
    - Federal Computer Incident Response Center
    - National Communications System
    - National Infrastructure Protection Center
    - Energy Security and Assurance Program
  - U.S. Coast Guard
  - U.S. Secret Service
- Department of the Interior
  - Bureau of Indian Affairs
    - Division of Law Enforcement
  - Bureau of Land Management
    - National Law Enforcement Security and Investigations Team
    - National Office of Fire and Aviation
  - National Park Service
    - U.S. Park Police
- Department of Justice
  - Bureau of Prisons
  - Drug Enforcement Administration (DEA)
  - Federal Bureau of Investigation (FBI)
  - U.S. Marshals
- Department of State
  - Bureau of Diplomatic Security
    - Diplomatic Security Service (United Nations)
    - Protective Liaison Division
- Department of the Treasury
  - Bureau of Alcohol, Tobacco, and Firearms (BATF)
  - Financial Crimes Enforcement Network
  - Internal Revenue Service
    - Criminal Investigation Division
    - Office of the Regional Inspector (internal investigations)
  - U.S. Mint Police
- Supreme Court Police
- Independent Agencies
  - Amtrak Police
  - Central Intelligence Agency
    - Office of Security
  - Environmental Protection Agency
    - Office of Criminal Investigations
  - Federal Emergency Management Administration
    - Security Division
  - General Services Administration (GSA)
    - Office of the Inspector General
  - Nuclear Regulatory Commission
    - Office of Enforcement
  - Securities and Exchange Commission
    - Division of Enforcement
  - Smithsonian
    - National Zoological Park Police
    - Office of Protection Services
  - Tennessee Valley Authority (TVA)
    - Office of the Inspector General
    - Police
  - U.S. Capitol Police
  - U.S. Postal Service
    - Postal Inspection Service
    - Postal Security Force

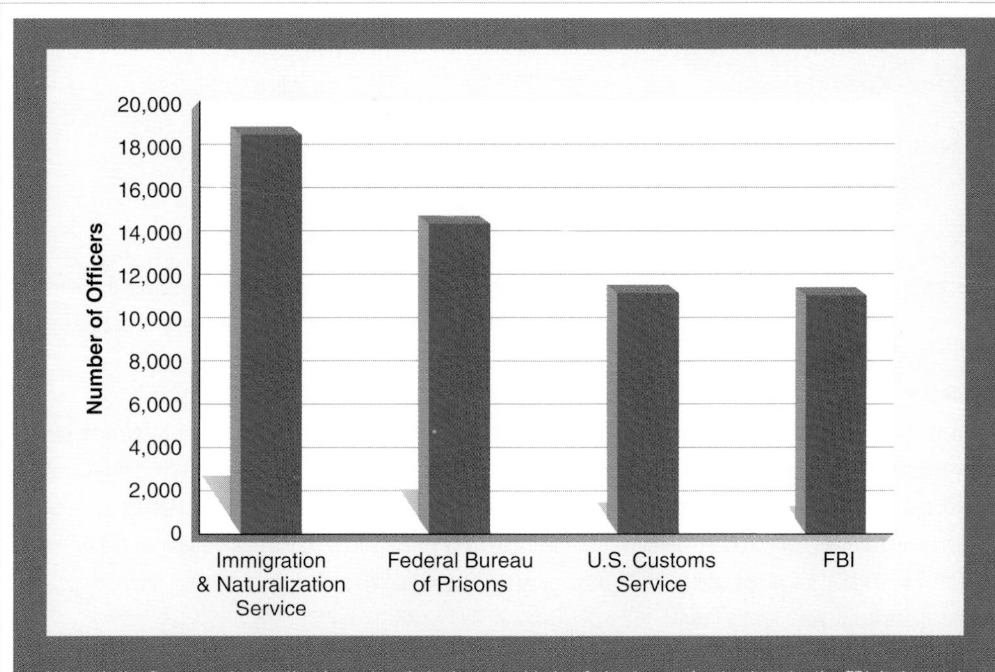

Although the first organization that leaps to mind when considering federal agencies tends to be the FBI, it does not have the most officers. According to Department of Justice statistics for 2002, the following agencies account for 60 percent of the total number of federal officers.

Source: U.S. Department of Justice, Bureau of Justice Statistics, Federal Law Enforcement Statistics, http://www.ojp.usdoj.gov/bjs/fedle.htm.

Figure 5.4
Federal Law Enforcement Agencies with the Most Officers, June 2002

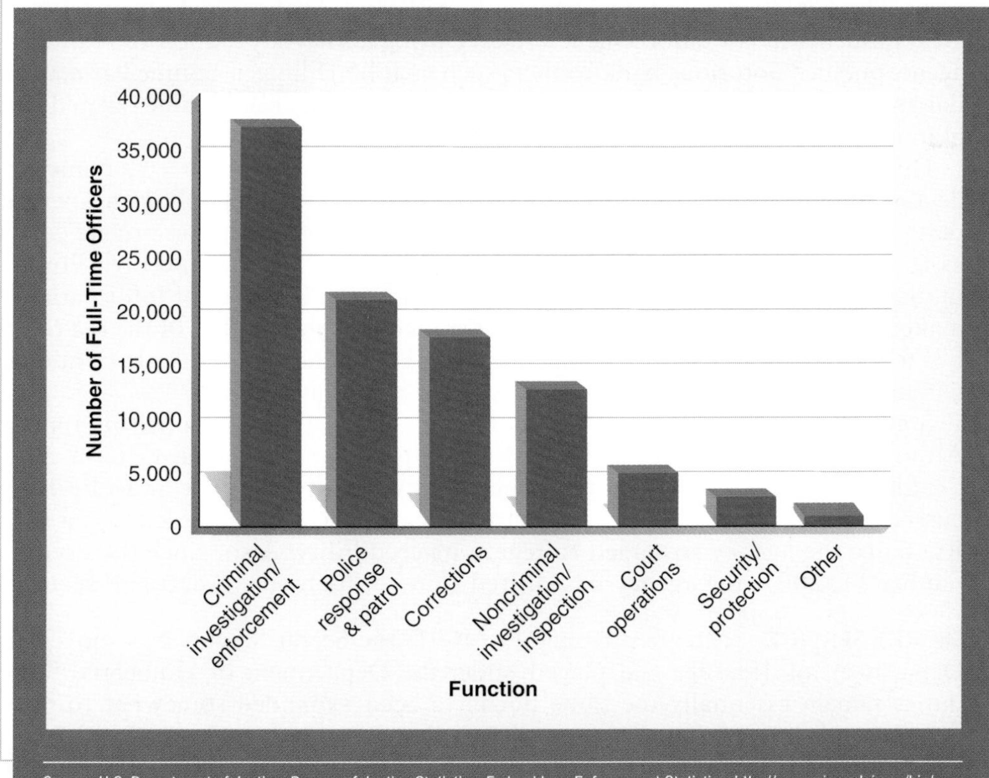

Source: U.S. Department of Justice, Bureau of Justice Statistics, Federal Law Enforcement Statistics, http://www.ojp.usdoj.gov/bjs/fedle.htm.

Figure 5.5
Functions of Full-Time Federal Officers, June 2002

CASE IN POINT

Weeks v. United States

The Case

Weeks v. United States, 232 U.S. 383, 34 S.Ct. 351 (1914)

The Point

The exclusionary rule, which states that illegally seized evidence is inadmissible in court, is applicable to federal criminal proceedings.

Kansas City police suspected that Fremont Weeks, who was employed by an express company, was sending lottery tickets through the mail, which was illegal. Without benefit of a warrant, police entered Weeks' home, searched it, and took possession of "various papers and articles," which were given to a U.S. marshal. The police returned later with the marshal and, still without a warrant, took more papers. Among these items were lottery tickets.

At his trial, Weeks was convicted of unlawful use of the mail. He appealed on grounds that the officers should not have searched his house because they had no warrant. The Supreme Court concurred. This case established that the exclusionary rule, which states that illegally seized evidence is inadmissible in court, is applicable to federal criminal proceedings.

The directorship of the FBI is one of the most prestigious positions in all of law enforcement, and a number of highly qualified and competent individuals have served in this capacity. By far the most famous and most influential is J. Edgar Hoover who was appointed in 1924 and served until his death in 1972. The legacy of Hoover is mixed. His shadow hangs over the agency like the imposing headquarters building that bears his name. He is credited with transforming the FBI into a professional organization that has great influence in law enforcement circles. During his heyday in the 1920s and 1930s, his agents pursued notorious bank robbers such as John Dillinger, Bonnie Parker, and Clyde Barrow. Hoover was a master at public relations, and the FBI became revered for its reputation of employing clean-cut, efficient agents.

Hoover built a personal empire at the FBI and was able to survive numerous presidential administrations. He is rumored to have kept records on politicians' personal lives that protected his tenure.[28] Additionally, his agents kept records on private citizens such as Dr. Martin Luther King, Jr., John Lennon, Marilyn Monroe, and Elvis Presley. (Parts of many of these records have been declassified by the Freedom of Information Act and make for fascinating reading.)[29] It can be argued that the turmoil of the era required the FBI to be vigilant in seeking out enemies, but FBI agents also broke laws in conducting wiretaps, watching citizens, and breaking into homes and offices.

Since Hoover's death in 1972, the FBI has been trying to polish its reputation.[30] Although the vast majority of its agents have performed in stellar fashion, a few high-profile cases have tarnished its image. Following the incident at Ruby Ridge (discussed in Chapter 7) and the revelation that agent Robert Hanssen was a spy for the Russians, the agency struggled to regain its credibility. Also, since the events of September 11, 2001, the agency has shifted some of its focus to national security.

SECRET SERVICE. After September 11, 2001, the Secret Service was moved from the Department of Treasury and placed under the Department of Homeland Security. Its duties remain essentially the same but have been expanded somewhat to provide for defense against terrorism. The Secret Service's original commission when it was created in 1865 was not to protect the president, but to control the proliferation of counterfeit money. Only in 1894 with President Grover Cleveland did the agency begin casual protection services. A year after the assassination of President William McKinley in 1901, the Secret Service began full-time executive protection, designating two agents to

Secret Service agents act as a team to protect those under their charge. These agents are specially trained, and those who protect the president are willing "to take a bullet" as part of their duties.
Courtesy of CORBIS-NY.

Figure 5.6
The Mission of the Secret Service

The United States Secret Service is mandated by Congress to carry out two distinct and significant missions: protection and criminal investigations. The Secret Service is responsible for: the protection of the president, the vice president, and their families, heads of state, and other designated individuals; the investigation of threats against these protectees; protection of the White House, vice president's residence, foreign missions, and other buildings within Washington, D.C.; and security design, planning, and implementation at designated National Special Security Events. The Secret Service is also responsible for the enforcement of laws relating to counterfeiting of obligations and securities of the United States, investigation of financial crimes including, but not limited to access device fraud, financial institution fraud, identity theft, computer fraud, telecommunications fraud, and computer based attacks on our nation's financial, banking, and telecommunications infrastructure.

Source: United States Secret Service, http://www.treas.gov/usss/mission.shtml.

the job. However, it was not until 1913 that Congress authorized permanent protection of the president, and it was 1917 before the president's family received protection. Security was gradually stepped up over the years, owing partly to the 1951 assassination attempt on President Harry Truman and the assassination in 1963 of President John Kennedy. Gradually, the list of protectees came to include major presidential and vice presidential candidates, presidential widows, and visiting heads of state. Former presidents and their spouses received lifetime protection in 1965, although Congress abbreviated this in 1994, giving presidents elected after 1997 protection for 10 years after leaving office. The agency's Treasury Department mission came to the fore again in 1984 when Congress authorized it to investigate credit card fraud, some types of computer fraud, and fake IDs. The protection of the president and other officials remains only part of the agency's duties (see Figure 5.6). The majority of those employed in the Secret Service, in fact, spend most of their time on duties other than executive protection.

State Level

In many ways, state law enforcement agencies are overshadowed by local and federal agencies. The state agencies do not have the numbers of officers that local agencies have, nor the visibility of federal agencies. There are as many variations in how state police are organized as there are states. Each state police system must be understood on its own terms because no two are exactly alike. This recalls the idea that the United States is a collection of united sovereign governments, with the elected government of each state deciding how that state is to be administered. Historically, three western states, Texas, Colorado, and Arizona, have police agencies called "rangers" that are over a century old and are among the first professional state/territorial law enforcement organizations in the United States. However, the Pennsylvania State Police, created in 1905, is recognized as the first uniformed, professional state police department.

Factors that may determine the simplicity or intricacy of a state police system include geography, population density, financial resources, and crime issues. Rich states with big cities may have state police agencies with special investigation units, community programs, and task forces. Poorer states may not have as many programs. A state's industry or culture can dictate the type of programs it requires. For example, New Jersey's Department of Law and Public Safety has a gaming enforcement division to regulate the casino industry, and the Alaska Department of Public Safety has its Fish and Wildlife Protection division. Some states have placed all law enforcement divisions under one organizational umbrella, such as a department of public safety, whereas in other states these programs may be discrete or lodged within different bureaus of state government. Many states also have bureaus of investigation with statewide jurisdiction for investigating crimes—such as political corruption—in which local police may not be in a position to comfortably investigate their local bosses. For example, the Georgia Bureau of Investigation provides a number of services to local law enforcement agencies such as the coordination of multijurisdictional task forces, crime laboratory services, and when requested, help in investigating crimes. Additionally, some state agencies have police training academies that provide the basic instruction that is beyond the capabilities of all but the largest local police forces.

HIGHWAY PATROL. Perhaps the most well-known of the state agencies are the highway patrol units. Many states have even organized their state law enforcement functions under their highway patrols. Regardless of how a state's police department is titled, all states have a highway patrol function, with the exception of Hawaii. These law

The highway patrol is a state-level law enforcement agency. Its officers are trained in a wide variety of duties and often aid local and federal agencies in fighting crime or responding to emergency situations.
Courtesy of CORBIS-NY.

enforcement agencies employ full-service officers who have all the responsibilities and authority of sworn police officers, but specialize in enforcing their state's traffic laws.

Law enforcement at the state level consists of a wide variety of activities. Those interested in a career in law enforcement should investigate opportunities in state agencies.

Local Level

Most of the crime in the nation is handled by local law enforcement agencies. In many ways, local policing is where the action is. Each jurisdiction, whether big city police department, county sheriff's office, or small town police department, is the first responder to the vast majority of crime. Additionally, these agencies have patrol and investigative duties in which they are often the only law enforcement agency involved in the case. Because local law enforcement officers handle most serious street-level crime, they are whom we call when we "call the cops." Most local police forces are operated by municipalities, with a few run by tribal and county governments. There are about 13,000 local police departments in the United States. The largest local police force in the country is the New York Police Department. With over 39,000 full-time officers, it is about three times the size of the next largest organization, the Chicago Police Department, which has just over 13,000 sworn officers. (See Figure 5.7 for the 10 largest police departments as of 2000.) At the other end of the spectrum, about 800 departments have just a single officer.

Full-service local law enforcement agencies perform a wide range of duties. The most labor intensive is routine patrol, in which officers travel around their assigned beats, respond to calls for service, and look for ways to keep the community safe. Some of the time that officers spend on patrol is used to interact with citizens who are not suspected of committing any crime. Officers talk to shopkeepers, watch for traffic infractions, cruise neighborhoods to show citizens they are being served, and investigate anything that looks suspicious or out of place. The business of apprehending offenders actually constitutes a small fraction of the officers' time. Local law enforcement agencies also devote resources and personnel to investigative duties, including homicide, burglary, auto

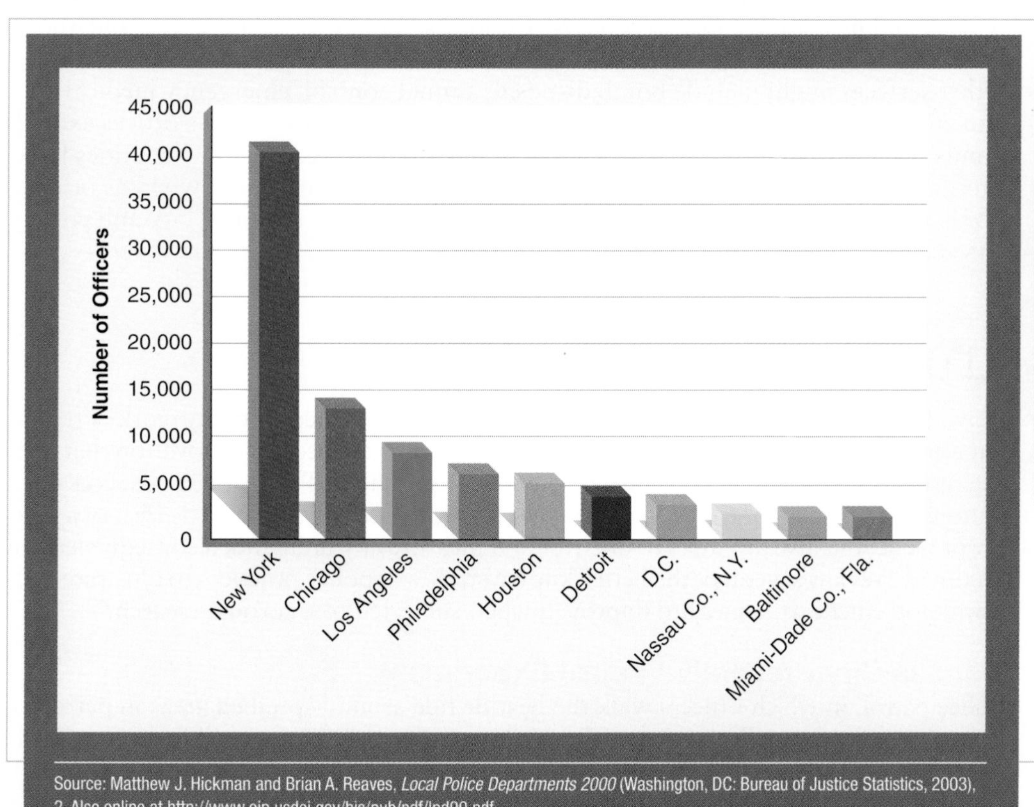

Figure 5.7 Ten Largest Local Police Departments by Total Number of Full-Time, Sworn Personnel, 2000

Source: Matthew J. Hickman and Brian A. Reaves, *Local Police Departments 2000* (Washington, DC: Bureau of Justice Statistics, 2003), 2. Also online at http://www.ojp.usdoj.gov/bjs/pub/pdf/lpd00.pdf.

theft, sex crimes, and juveniles. To a lesser degree, their duties may also include animal control, emergency medical service, and civil defense. Larger departments operate SWAT and bomb disposal teams. As of 1999 only one in 12 departments operated a jail.[31] Along with traditional car patrols, there has been a steady increase in bicycle and foot patrols. Community policing is also on the upswing, with a majority of the departments having a formal plan. Also, not all local police officers are sworn.[32] Nonsworn department employees may work in technical support, administration, and the jail. Some departments may ameliorate officer shortages with supplemental and part-time personnel such as sworn reserve officers, as well as nonsworn auxiliary officers, community service officers, police aides, and other types of volunteers. Each agency organizes its investigative duties and personnel according to its problems, resources, and needs, but each of them in some way must ensure that there is an investigative follow-up to the reported crime.

Sometimes law enforcement jurisdictions overlap. A person driving a car too fast within a city's limits may be pulled over and ticketed by a state patrol officer, a sheriff's deputy, or a city police officer. However, a murder committed within a specific jurisdiction would likely be dealt with by the police agency responsible for that jurisdiction, with rare exceptions in special cases. The state patrol or the county sheriff would be unlikely to get involved in investigating a murder committed within a city's limits. An example of such an exception would be the "Atlanta child murders." From July 1979 to May 1981, 29 young, black males were murdered in or near Atlanta, Georgia. Although the murders occurred mainly in the city of Atlanta and Fulton County, several agencies became involved in the investigation, including the local police, the sheriff's office, the Georgia Bureau of Investigation (GBI), and ultimately the FBI. (The federal agency, having no jurisdiction, only became involved by invitation from the local agencies.)

SHERIFFS' OFFICES. Sheriffs' offices are the most common form of county law enforcement in the United States, with about 3,100 offices.[33] The vast majority of sheriffs are elected officials and serve counties and municipalities without a police department. Their duties include routine patrols, crime investigation (some are responsible for crime lab services such as fingerprint and ballistics testing), executing arrest warrants, serving papers, and providing court security. Most offices operate at least one jail, and about half provide search and rescue services, as well as SWAT (Special Weapons and Tactics) teams. Other services might include bomb disposal, animal control, emergency medical services, and civil defense. Also, it should be noted that the number of sheriff's offices exceeds the number of counties (3,066) in the United States. This is because a few counties have two sheriff's offices (one for criminal matters and one for civil matters), whereas others have no sheriff's office. In cases in which a city occupies the entire county, city and county law enforcement may be combined into one department.

Innovations in Policing

How do we know whether the changes made in police practices actually work? From an occupational perspective, law enforcement agencies will embrace any innovation that provides the resources to hire new personnel or buy new equipment. The real test of successful innovations, however, is controlled research that not only looks at the desired effect of a new policy or tactic, but also attempts to uncover and measure any unintended consequences. In this section we review several of the better-known studies of police practices to illustrate just how law enforcement strategies are improved when subjected to rigorous research.

Kansas City Preventive Patrol Experiment

Police patrol, in which officers walk the beat or ride around specified areas in patrol cars, is a stable feature of police activity. The idea that officers are responsible for specified geographic areas is one of the cornerstones of law enforcement supervision. As officers have shifted away from foot patrol and into police cars, a recurring question has been how the police, citizens, and criminals have perceived the success of police patrol. In 1972 the Kansas

City Police Department and the Police Foundation designed an experiment to measure the efficacy of police patrol in terms of its impact on crime, the delivery of police services, and citizens' feelings of security. The experiment divided the city into 15 beat areas and assigned each of them one of three types of police patrol: reactive beats, control beats, or proactive beats.

1. Reactive beats did not receive regular police patrol. The police patrol cars would respond to calls for service but would otherwise stay out of the area.
2. Control beats experienced the same level of police patrol as they normally would have if there were no research experiment. For the most part, this meant a level of one car per beat.
3. Proactive beats experienced an intensified level of patrol with two to three times the number of cars passing through. These cars would normally have been in the reactive beats.

The Kansas City Preventive Patrol Experiment was impressive because of the large amount of information that was systematically collected from official police records, surveys of citizens and businesses, interviews with officers, and observations of participant-observer researchers. The bottom line from the summary report is as follows:

> *Given the large amount of data collected and the extremely diverse sources used, the overwhelming evidence is that decreasing or increasing routine preventive patrol within the range tested in this experiment had no effect on crime, citizen fear of crime, community attitudes toward the police on the delivery of police service, police response time or traffic accidents.*[34]

Does this mean that preventive patrol is a waste of time? Not really. What this study found was that the level of patrol made little difference. Even though the reactive beats, in which there was no patrol, had the same level of crime and the same level of feelings of security of citizens as the beats that had patrol, we should not be misled about the advisability of having the police on the streets. Because the beats were randomly assigned, the citizens and criminals may not have perceived any difference in the level of patrol because they could not tell where one beat ended and another began.

Do the results of this experiment suggest that the police should stay in the station house to save gasoline and simply respond when there is a crime reported or a call for service? Again the answer is no. The response time it takes to get from the station house would surely be greater than it is when the police are routinely out on the street. This experiment, done in the early 1970s, has not killed the preventive patrol concept, but it has forced police departments to assess how they can better serve their citizens. For example, focusing on "hot spots" where crimes are concentrated can be a more effective way to prevent crime.[35]

NEWS FLASH

Candid Cop Cameras

Police in Los Angeles have installed motion-sensor cameras in some of the city's garbage-filled alleys. The bulletproof cameras are designed to take a picture of people hanging around in the alleys and play a recorded warning: "Stop! This is the LAPD. We have just taken your photograph. We will use this photograph to prosecute you. Leave now."

These pictures can be used in court, and those convicted of dumping trash in an alley may receive six months in jail and a fine of $1,000.

Source: Associated Press, "Cameras to Help Keep South Los Angeles Alleys Clean," *The Sacramento Bee,* August 1, 2002, http://www.sacbee.com/state_wire/story/3804673p-4830091c.html.

Rand Study of Detectives

The Hollywood entertainment industry has given us a distorted image of what detectives do. Many students who plan to go into law enforcement would just as soon skip the years of being a street officer doing patrol, traffic, and other routine duties. They would like to skip having to wear a uniform and go immediately to becoming a detective where they believe the work will be more rewarding. They may be disappointed. Aside from the fact that experience in patrol and other uniformed duties is a requirement for becoming a detective, "detective work is neither glamorous nor exciting," according to Samuel Walker, one of the nation's leading law enforcement scholars.[36] In fact, some officers who become detectives return to patrol because detective work simply is not exciting enough.

In 1977 the Rand Corporation, a research institution, conducted a study for the National Institute of Law Enforcement and Criminal Justice in which it attempted to determine just how effective detectives are in solving crimes. The results questioned the efficacy of devoting vast resources to detective work. Rand found detective work to be superficial, routine, and nonproductive. The findings can be summarized as follows:

1. **Arrest and clearance rates.** Only 2.7 percent of the cases that are cleared can be attributed to the techniques used by investigators. These tend to be high-profile cases such as homicide, robbery, and commercial theft. For the remaining 97.3 percent of the cases cleared, the contribution of victims, witnesses, and patrol officers is more important than that of investigators.
2. **How the investigator's time is spent.** Using the Kansas City Experiment as a representative sample, the study found that most cases do not receive any investigator attention. Investigators spend 93 percent of their time on activities that do not lead directly to solving previously reported crimes. They do paperwork, survey pawnshops or junkyards, give speeches, and prepare cases for court.
3. **Collecting and processing physical evidence.** The study focused on fingerprint identification and concluded that only 4 to 9 percent of all retrieved fingerprints from four cities eventually matched those of a known suspect. They added, however, that some departments' cold searches produced more case solutions than investigators did. (It should be noted that this study was published in 1977, and that with the advancements in computer technology, fingerprint analysis has been greatly improved.)
4. **Preparing cases for prosecution.** The study looked at two prosecutors' offices in California to determine whether the quality and the amount of detail in the information supplied by the police results in successful prosecution of the case. The evidence was clear that the quality of the investigation had an impact on whether the case was dismissed. The evidence was less clear as to whether the quality of the investigation influenced plea bargaining or the severity of the sentence that was imposed.
5. **Relations between victims and police.** As detectives interact with victims of crimes, they often have to admit that there is not enough evidence to identify a suspect, make an arrest if there is a suspect, or successfully prosecute a case. The Rand study surveyed victims of crime about what kind of information they wanted from the police. The victims overwhelmingly wanted information about whether the case had been solved, a suspect arrested, a defendant tried and convicted, and to a lesser degree, whether a defendant was released from custody.
6. **Proactive investigation methods.** Police investigation is essentially a reactive practice. Once a crime has been committed, the patrol officer responds and calls in the detectives. An alternative method of detective work is to go into the community and target certain types of criminals by questioning informants about crimes committed but not yet known to the police, conducting surveillance activities, or setting up sting operations in which the detectives pose as fences to buy stolen property. The Rand study looked at such activity in two police departments and concluded that even though many of their arrests were attributable to the work of other police officers, such units can be effective for burglary and fencing arrests. The study also cautioned that such units need to be carefully monitored to ensure that officers do not become too aggressive and infringe on individual liberties.[37]

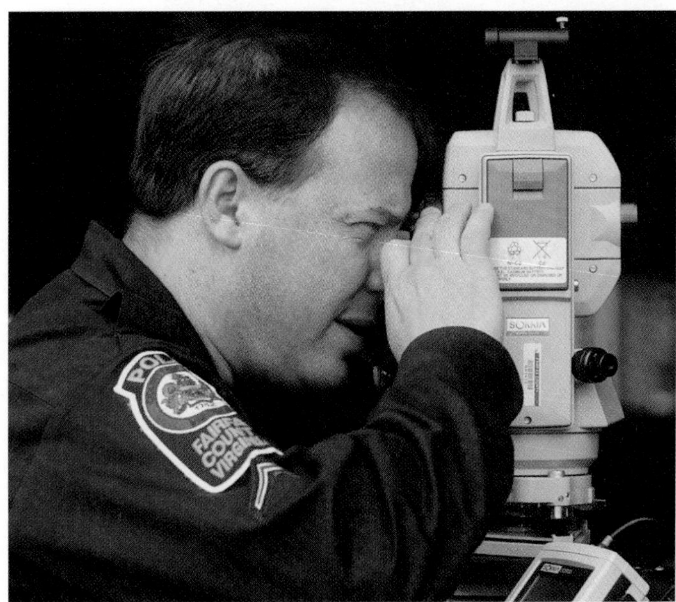

Law enforcement officers must use a wide range of technologies to investigate crimes.

Courtesy of Getty Images, Inc.

The Rand study seriously questioned the role of detectives in modern police departments and made several policy recommendations, including the following:

1. Place most postarrest investigations in the prosecutor's office.
2. Let patrol officers, not detectives, make more of the arrests of known suspects.
3. Let clerks do most of the routine investigative tasks such as tracing ownership of weapons, showing mug shots to victims, and placing reports of stolen automobiles in the "hot car" file.
4. Create investigative teams that handle crimes without suspects. These teams would include lower-paid clerical workers who are supervised by a detective. These teams could handle most of these cases more efficiently than individual officers could.
5. For proactive investigations, develop special strike forces as unique needs arise. These strike forces would be disbanded after the problem has been addressed and created again if the problem recurs.
6. Reallocate investigative duties to other parts of the police force.[38]

The Rand study did not recommend reducing total police resources. Instead, it suggested that a rethinking about the duties of detectives warrants new ways of doing this work. By creating a role of generalist-investigator whose training and experience is less than that of the detective, the study argued that much of the routine and boring work of investigations could be done at less cost and more efficiently.

DARE Program

We have looked at studies that deal with the major police functions of patrol and investigation, and now we turn our attention to a less central feature of police work: drug abuse prevention. The Drug Abuse Resistance Education program began in 1983 in Los Angeles as a cooperative effort between the Los Angeles Police Department and the Los Angeles schools. The idea behind the program was to give children information about illegal drugs, an idea about what happens when people use or sell illegal drugs, and coping mechanisms to help them avoid illegal drugs.

From its modest beginnings, the DARE program has spread across the nation and to at least 44 other countries. By 1997 it was operating in at least three-quarters of the school districts in the United States and had an annual budget of $750 million per year.[39] DARE programs are a fixture in many schools. Police cars with bumper stickers state, "DARE to keep kids off drugs." This program has enjoyed widespread popularity until

REFERENCE

Why Detectives Don't Wear Uniforms

Many criminal justice students want to become detectives. When pressed for the reason, it is often because the student wants to be a law enforcement officer but does not want to wear a uniform. Uniforms seem to be equated with blue collar occupations, whereas the suits and blazers worn by detectives are equated with white collar management. Additionally, uniforms not only identify you as a public servant of whom there are expectations, but also reveal your rank and exact status to the public.

Why do some police officers wear uniforms when others do not? Uniforms identify police officers immediately and instantly establish their authority. This is useful for patrol officers who are the first to respond to a crime in progress or a traffic accident. The officers do not have to negotiate their identity with suspects or the public. When people are running around firing guns, it is useful to know friend from foe. From time to time, mistakes are made, such as when a vice officer in civilian clothes is mistaken for a drug dealer during a gunfight. Many departments will have a "code" such a blue baseball hat that plainclothes officers can wear when situations are dangerous and they want to be sure they are recognizable as police officers to other officers.

Detectives do not usually respond immediately to a crime. They appear afterwards and gather evidence, interview witnesses, and testify in court. They generally interact with the public in ways that do not require them to be immediately recognizable as law enforcement officers. This can be advantageous when looking for suspects or dealing with the public.

A note of caution: Police uniforms are easy to obtain. Many military supply stores carry a wide variety of police uniforms and gear. Badges can be bought over the Internet. Occasionally, criminals or police-wannabes will impersonate a law enforcement officer. This is a crime.

FOCUS ON ETHICS

Do You Dare Dump DARE?

As the police chief of a large city, you instituted the DARE drug education and prevention program 15 years ago. It is a very popular program that has been adopted by 90 percent of the city's schools, and many of your best officers have rotated through the assignment and are enthusiastic about their experience. The program has become a high-profile public relations success that has earned the department a reputation for community involvement. When a team of researchers from the nearby university volunteered to evaluate the program, you eagerly accepted their offer because you were confident their report would confirm your belief that the DARE program was an unqualified success. Now the report has been completed, and it is devastating. It not only finds that those students who were exposed to the DARE program fared no better in avoiding drug use later in life than those who were not exposed to the program, but also that the students, even very young ones, think DARE is a joke. After meeting with the researchers, you are convinced that not only is the study methodologically sound, but it is consistent with the results of evaluations of other DARE programs from around the country.

WHAT DO YOU DO?

1. Suppress the results by telling the researchers they no longer have permission to use the data they have collected from your records.
2. Close down the program and reassign your officers to other duties.
3. Continue the program because even though it doesn't work, it generates good publicity and everyone (except the kids) seems to like it.

very recently when some evaluations of its effectiveness were published.[40] In fact, the evaluations say that despite widespread support for the program among schools, the public, and law enforcement agencies, the impact on preventing children from future drug use is absent. The studies contend that no measurable difference exists between students who participated in the program and those who did not.[41]

In looking at this research concerning police patrol, the use of detectives, and drug prevention activities by law enforcement officers, we have seen that controversy continues regarding how best to deploy police personnel. Clearly, these issues are only suggestive of the types of research done on police organization. Scores of other issues and hundreds of legitimate studies are conducted on police practices. What we have tried to do here is focus on three problems that illustrate the way research can inform us about how long-cherished police practices are not always as successful as we might assume.

Summary

In this chapter we have highlighted the history of law enforcement and linked that history to the way police agencies are organized today. What should be immediately apparent after reviewing this chapter is that the development of law enforcement as an institution was episodic, uneven, and fraught with issues of politics and class and racial biases, as well as a lack of consensus as to what the police were supposed to do. Consequently, we are left with a rich and colorful history of policing and, even more important, law enforcement organizations that have considerable overlapping jurisdictions, are fragmented, and vary widely in their effectiveness and resources.

U.S. law enforcement is based on the English system, as are many U.S. institutions. Although we borrowed many features of our policing from England, they were greatly modified to fit both the demands of the U.S. political structure and the national focus on individualism and less government. Over the years the United States has further modified its political institutions, and the unique historical circumstances of the country have produced a criminal justice system that is both the marvel of the rest of the world in its freedoms and oversight, and problematic in its effectiveness and fairness.

The experiences of New York and Chicago reflect the issues that confronted early law enforcement agencies, as police organizations emerged amid conditions vastly different from those in England. In short, the differences can be summarized as U.S. police having much broader latitude in the exercise of discretion than British police, and city politicians and the upper classes having much more political influence in the United States than in England. Additionally, the police were more susceptible to institutionalized corruption in the United States. In the South and the West, vigilante movements filled in where established and effective law enforcement agencies were lacking. During the early 20th century, developments in professional law enforcement were spearheaded by reformers such as August Vollmer in Berkeley, California. Vollmer advocated that the police become nonpartisan, use scientific principles, become more specialized, and be led by qualified executives who knew how to run large organizations. Despite some obvious similarities between civilian police and military organizations, individual police officers must deal with having more discretion, higher visibility, and a great deal more authority. Consequently, professionalizing the police is more difficult than simply copying the military model of administration.

Law enforcement agencies are spread across federal, state, and local levels of administration. This accounts for some problems in jurisdiction, as well as a certain amount of redundancy. The criminal justice student who wants to work in law enforcement will find a wide variety of positions that span these three levels, as well as a burgeoning private security industry. The relative merits of having so many agencies spread across the three levels of government can be debated, but it does make for an interesting and complex system of law enforcement that will continue to be tested as we enter a war against terrorism.

Finally, we looked at some recent research on police effectiveness and at some innovative strategies designed to address specific problems. The Kansas City Preventive Patrol experiment, the Rand Study of Detectives, and the DARE program all alert us not only to the difficulties of trying to effect organizational change, but also to the issues in trying to measure that change.

KEY TERMS

authority p. 161
bobbies p. 148
Bow Street Runners p. 148
constable (comes stabuli) p. 147
frankpledge system p. 146
hue and cry p. 147
hundred-man p. 147
Metropolitan Police Act p. 148
sheriff (shire reeve) p. 147
Thames River Police p. 148
watch-and-ward system p. 147

REVIEW QUESTIONS

1. How was law enforcement accomplished before the development of the first modern police force in London?
2. The Chicago Police Department of the early 20th century was considered political. Why?
3. List and discuss the six policing issues covered in the Wickersham Commission report that was written by August Vollmer.
4. Police work has been compared to military missions. Discuss how they are different by focusing on discretion, visibility, and authority.
5. Discuss the differences among law enforcement activities at the federal, state, and local levels. At which level would you most like to work? Why?
6. Do police departments really need detectives? How could a department be reorganized so that the job of detective could be eliminated? Would you like to work in such a department?

SUGGESTED FURTHER READING

Amnesty International. *United States of America: Police Brutality and Excessive Use of Force in the New York City Police Department.* New York: Amnesty International, 1996.

Center for Research on Criminal Justice. *The Iron Fist and the Velvet Glove: An Analysis of the U.S. Police.* Berkeley, CA: Center for Research on Criminal Justice, 1977.

President's Commission on Law Enforcement and the Administration of Justice. *Task Force Report: The Police.* Washington DC: U.S. Government Printing Office, 1967.

Poveda, Tony. *Lawlessness and Reform: The FBI in Transition.* Pacific Grove, CA: Brooks/Cole, 1990.

Walker, Samuel. *A Critical History of Police Reform.* Lexington, MA: Lexington Books, 1977.

Walker, Samuel, and Charles M. Katz. *The Police in America: An Introduction.* Boston: McGraw-Hill, 2002.

ENDNOTES

1. Jonathan Rubinstein, *City Police* (New York: Farrar, Straus and Giroux, 1973).
2. Center for Research on Criminal Justice, *The Iron Fist and the Velvet Glove: An Analysis of the U.S. Police* (Berkeley, CA: Center for Research on Criminal Justice, 1977), 20.
3. Rubinstein, *City Police,* 5.
4. Ibid., 6.
5. Ibid.
6. Mark Abrahamson, *Urban Enclaves: Identity and Place in America* (New York: St. Martin's Press, 1996), 11–13.
7. Rubinstein, *City Police,* 6.
8. Samuel Walker and Charles M. Katz, *The Police in America: An Introduction* (Boston: McGraw-Hill, 2002), 25.
9. Walker and Katz, *Police in America,* 25. Walker and Katz provided a nice discussion of why history is relevant to the understanding of the development of the police. They traced the political and social forces that were behind the major reforms of law enforcement.
10. Wilber R. Miller, "Cops and Bobbies, 1830–1870," in *Thinking About Police: Contemporary Readings,* ed. Carl B. Klockars (New York: McGraw-Hill, 1983), 72–87.
11. Mark H. Haller, "Chicago Cops, 1890–1925," in *Thinking About Police: Contemporary Readings,* ed. Carl B. Klockars (New York: McGraw-Hill, 1983), 87–99.
12. Richard Maxwell Brown, "Vigilante Policing," in *Thinking About Police: Contemporary Readings,* ed. Carl B. Klockars (New York: McGraw-Hill, 1983), 58.
13. Brown, "Vigilante Policing," 57–71.
14. Ibid., 69.

15. Ibid., 70–71.
16. Center for Research on Criminal Justice, *Iron Fist,* 26.
17. Samuel Walker, *A Critical History of Police Reform* (Lexington: Lexington Books, 1977).
18. Lincoln Steffens, *The Autobiography of Lincoln Steffens* (New York: Harcourt Brace Jovanovich, 1931). Lincoln Steffens was a leading muckraking journalist, and his autobiography is a fascinating and accessible account of how he exposed corruption in city and state governments across the nation.
19. Center For Research on Criminal Justice, *Iron Fist,* 32.
20. Walker and Katz, *Police in America,* 34.
21. Center for Research on Criminal Justice, *Iron Fist,* 37.
22. Ibid, 39.
23. Thomas Barker, Ronald D. Hunter, and Jeffery P. Rush, *Police Systems and Practices: An Introduction* (Englewood Cliffs, NJ: Prentice Hall, 1994), 77.
24. Robert M. Regoli and John D. Hewitt, *Criminal Justice* (New York: Prentice Hall, 1996), 259.
25. Peter K. Manning, "Lying, Secrecy, and Social Control," in *Police Deviance,* eds. Thomas Barker and David L. Carter (Cincinnati: Pilgrimage, 1986), 96–119.
26. Thomas Barker, "Peer Group Support for Police Occupational Deviance," in *Police Deviance,* eds. Thomas Barker and David L. Carter (Cincinnati: Pilgrimage, 1986), 7–19.
27. Bureau of Justice Statistics, http://www.ojp.usdoj.gov/bjs/fedle.htm.
28. Curt Gentry, *J. Edgar Hoover: The Man and His Secrets* (New York: Norton, 1991).
29. A long list of these files can be found at the FBI online Reading Room at http://foia.fbi.gov/foiaindex.htm.
30. Tony Poveda, *Lawlessness and Reform: The FBI in Transition* (Pacific Grove, CA: Brooks/Cole, 1990).
31. Bureau of Justice Law Enforcement Statistics, http://www.ojp.usdoj.gov/bjs/abstract/lpd99.htm.
32. Sworn officers are "police employees who have taken an oath and been given powers by the state to make arrests, use force, and transverse property, in accordance with their duties." Dean J. Champion, *The American Dictionary of Criminal Justice* (Los Angeles: Roxbury, 2001), 132.
33. Bureau of Justice Law Enforcement Statistics, http://www.ojp.usdoj.gov/bjs/abstract/so99.htm.
34. George L. Kelling, Tony Pate, Duane Dieckman, and Charles E. Brown, "The Kansas City Preventive Patrol Experiment," in *Thinking About Police: Contemporary Readings,* eds. Carl B. Klockars and Stephen D. Mastrofski (New York: McGraw-Hill, 1991), 163.
35. Lawrence W. Sherman and David Weisburd, "General Deterrent Effects of Police Patrol in Crime 'Hot Spots': A Randomized, Controlled Trial," *Justice Quarterly* 12 (December 1995): 5–648.
36. Walker and Katz, *Police in America,* 168.
37. Jan Chaiken, Peter Greenwood, and Joan Petersilla, "The Rand Study of Detectives," in *Thinking About Police: Contemporary Readings,* eds. Carl B. Klockars and Stephen D. Mastrofski (New York: McGraw-Hill, 1991), 170–187.
38. Ibid.
39. Walker and Katz, *Police in America,* 179.
40. Maia Szalavitz, "DARE Doesn't Work," *Gotham Gazette* (March 2001), www.gothamgazette.com/health/mar.01.shtml.
41. Susan T. Emmett et al., "How Effective Is Drug Abuse Resistance Education? A Meta-Analysis of Project DARE Outcome Evaluations," *American Journal of Public Health* (September 1994): 1394–1401.

outline

CHAPTER 6

Controlling the Police

objectives

After reading this chapter, the student should be able to:

1. Define police discretion and explain why it is important to the understanding of police behavior.
2. Evaluate how the popular expectations of the police may exceed their ability to produce effective law enforcement.
3. Discuss the advantages and disadvantages of the quasi-military nature of contemporary police departments.
4. Identify and discuss James Q. Wilson's styles of policing.
5. Explain and critique some of the pitfalls of the policing subculture.
6. Explain the difference between the Knapp Commission's types of police corruption: meat-eaters and grass-eaters.
7. Discuss the many implications of the Fourth Amendment for controlling the police.

LAW ENFORCEMENT IN A DEMOCRATIC SOCIETY IS ACCOMPLISHED with the greatest care and attention paid to how much authority is granted to the police. Although it might seem that the police simply enforce the legal statutes passed by the legislature, the reality of law enforcement in the United States is much more complicated, and for the student of criminal justice, far more interesting.

In this chapter we look at how the police are constrained in their efforts to keep order on the streets, provide services to citizens, and fight crime. These constraints include legislative mandates that limit the power of the police, court opinions that law enforcement officers must consider in their duties, and an informal subculture of policing that exerts a powerful influence on how the police conceptualize their role. By having an appreciation for how the police are controlled by forces both inside and outside of their agencies, we can begin to understand why policing is often as much an art as it is a science.

The individual law enforcement officer must make dozens of decisions each day that juggle the rights of offenders, the opinions of citizens, the

! NEWS FLASH

Police Indiscretion

In August 2002 Houston police arrested 278 people gathered in the vicinity of a 24-hour Kmart Super Center and adjacent Sonic Drive-In. The problem was, the vast majority of those arrested had committed no crime. The police, having prepared a crackdown operation on the illegal drag races that had been taking place there at night, arrived that evening to find that no drag racers were present. The officers said they were told to arrest everyone in the area regardless of what they were doing.

According to the *Houston Chronicle,* several of the officers did not want to arrest people simply for being there but had to follow orders. One officer described the arrests as "utterly, utterly senseless."

Of the 278 arrested, 42 juveniles were cited for violating Houston's midnight curfew, and 30 of them were charged with criminal trespass. Many of Houston's citizens were outraged at what appeared to be strong-arm tactics by the police. A $100 million federal lawsuit was filed against the city of Houston by one of the arrestees. The captain who ordered the arrests, Mark Aguirre, was suspended along with 12 other police supervisors pending the outcome of an investigation.

Sources: Rachel Graves, "HPD Suspends 12 More in Mass-Arrest Scandal," *Houston Chronicle,* August 28, 2002, http://www.chron.com/cs/CDA/story.hts/special/raid/1549652. S. K. Bardwell, "Raid Went to 'Hell in a Handbasket,' " *Houston Chronicle,* August 28, 2002, http://www.chron.com/cs/CDA/story.hts/special/raid/1549652.

demands of supervisors, peer pressure from fellow officers, and legal statutes against the officer's own good judgment as he or she decides how to act in what is a highly visible occupation. The first issue we will consider is police discretion. Discretion is mentioned in other chapters, but we will consider it here in more detail because it is at the core of the law enforcement officer's occupation.[1] Without the recognition of the problems and issues surrounding the exercise of discretion, a precise understanding of policing is impossible.

Police Discretion

The police do not make an arrest every time they are legally authorized to do so. Law enforcement officers turn a blind eye to many violations and never engage in full enforcement of the law. If the police attempted to enforce all the laws our legislators have passed, at least two bad things would happen. First, the criminal justice system would be swamped by the workload. The wheels of justice would simply grind to a halt under the weight of a system clogged by many times the number of cases it can reasonably process.[2]

The second problem with enforcing every law would be that the most serious offenders would be obscured by the sheer mass of cases. The police would not have the time and resources to address the cases that represent the greatest dangers to society. Therefore, it is important to appreciate that the police, both as an organization and as individual officers, decide which laws to enforce, how much to enforce them, when to let some offenses slide, and when to devote attention to truly significant crimes.[3] These decisions on differential law enforcement are referred to as discretion. The decision to investigate, arrest, charge, and incarcerate are all made by the police in the legitimate performance of their duties. It is important to understand the dynamics that structure these decisions.

Law enforcement officers have a great deal of discretion in deciding to make an arrest. However, when other officers are present, that discretion is reduced because of the visibility of the action.
Courtesy of CORBIS-NY.

Kenneth Culp Davis, in his book *Police Discretion,* argued that the fact that the police do not engage in the full enforcement of the law is positive.

> *Even though the police insist on interpreting the full enforcement legislation literally, they also insist on following what they regard as their own common sense. This means that they violate their own interpretation of the full enforcement legislation. And I regard that as an accomplishment.* The police wisdom has on a wide scale overidden the legislative unwisdom embodied in the literal terms of the full enforcement legislation. *The police are properly lenient to many offenders. They do adapt their enforcement practices to the dominant community attitudes they are able to perceive. They do often refuse to make arrests for offenses committed in their presence. They have even established many patterns of nonenforcement.*[4]

For example, consider an interstate highway on which the speed limit is posted at 55 miles per hour, but where traffic generally moves at 70 miles per hour. The police do not enforce the posted limit because to do so would mean ticketing about 90 percent of the drivers. There is an unstated understanding between the police and the public that a pattern of nonenforcement is permissible.

In some incidences the police use their discretion to engage in the nonenforcement of the law. It might be fair to argue that the more trivial the offense is, the more likely the police will be not to practice full enforcement.[5] For instance, the laws involving the possession of marijuana have long been subject to less enforcement than those involving heroin or cocaine. Additionally, the police are less likely to arrest two teenagers who fight at school than they are two adults who fight after a traffic accident. The context in which the violation occurs has a great deal to do with whether the police decide to invoke the criminal sanction.

Although we might all agree that the use of police discretion in deciding against the full enforcement of the law is desirable, another side of police discretion is troubling. Police discretion also provides an opportunity for selective enforcement.[6] When the police use their judgment in deciding which infractions to pursue, prejudice, bias, discrimination, and individual values may factor into how the law is enforced. When accusations of **racial profiling** (discussed in greater detail in Chapter 7), favoritism, corruption, or laziness accompany the selective enforcement of the law, the community begins to lose faith in the fairness of the criminal justice system.[7] Yet, the police may feel the need to enforce the law

racial profiling
Suspicion of illegal activity based on a person's race, ethnicity, or national origin rather than on actual illegal activity or evidence of illegal activity.

FOCUS ON ETHICS

It's Only Marijuana

As a city police officer, you are constantly called on to use your discretion in deciding when to invoke the criminal law. To be honest, you do not make an arrest every time you have the opportunity because you do not want to spend all your time processing petty cases. One evening you and your partner are called to a fraternity house on the local university campus after neighbors complained of loud partying at 2:00 A.M. You are admitted into the house by an obviously intoxicated fraternity president, who says, "Come on in, officers. Look around all you want. There's nobody here but us chickens." As he giggles hysterically at his joke, you realize two things. First, he has given you permission to conduct a legal search of the house, and second, there is the unmistakable smell of marijuana emanating from both the fraternity house and its president. As you and your partner conduct a cursory search, you easily find a water pipe, several half-full bags of high-grade marijuana, and about a dozen marijuana cigarettes that were tossed behind the couch, chairs, and under the rug. You are about to cobble together all the marijuana to determine whether a felony case can be made when your partner takes you aside and informs you that his wife's little sister, a high school junior, is present but passed out cold in one of the bedrooms. Your partner says his wife would kill him if her sister gets arrested, and he begs you to let everyone go with just a warning. You are concerned about the number of youths who are engaged in underage drinking and drug use, but your partner is insistent and says, "Hey, it's only marijuana."

WHAT DO YOU DO?

1. Tell your partner that "the law's the law" and arrest everyone in the house on whom you think you can make a good case, including his wife's little sister.
2. Warn everyone in the house to keep the noise down and that if the neighbors complain again and you have to come back, you will institute #1.
3. Gather up all the marijuana and alcohol and flush them down the toilet while sending everyone home, thus effectively ending the party.

selectively as a result of the inconsistencies and unpredictability of the criminal justice system. Kenneth Culp Davis listed four questions regarding selective enforcement:

1. Should the police make arrests when they know the prosecutors will not prosecute the defendants or that the court will dismiss the case?
2. Do the police violate the full enforcement legislation when a crime is committed in their presence but an arrest is (a) physically impossible, (b) less important than some other urgent duty, or (c) impossible because of limited resources?
3. Does insufficiency of police resources for full enforcement justify a system of enforcement priorities that takes into account all relevant reasons for enforcing or not enforcing, or must the police indiscriminately try to enforce on any and all occasions, so that what remains unenforced will be so due to limited resources and not policy requirements.
4. Are the police always forbidden to make enforcement decisions on individualized grounds?[8]

There are good reasons both for and against selective enforcement of the law. On one hand, it violates the idea of fair play: that everyone who commits a crime should be treated equally. When the police use discretion to decide who to arrest, it can appear discriminatory. On the other hand, there may be legitimate reasons to engage in selective enforcement, reasons that result in a community with less overall crime and with less damage to citizens and property.[9]

Take the hypothetical case of the vice officer who arrests a drug user and finds out that the offender is responsible for a number of burglaries to get money to support drug purchases. Although it might reasonably be expected that the vice officer would charge the drug user with the burglaries, the officer also has an interest in discovering the user's source of the drugs. By arresting the user, some crimes are cleared, but the vice officer is more interested in drying up the source of the drugs with the reasoning that many more drug-related burglaries will be prevented if there are fewer or no sellers to satisfy the demand for drugs. By encouraging the user to provide information on the seller in exchange for dropping the burglary charges, the vice officer can attempt to clean up the drug trade in that neighborhood. It becomes, then, a value judgment on whether this selective enforcement is a justifiable action. Certainly the owner of a home that is burglarized would want the thief arrested and prosecuted. However, if drugs were being sold to the homeowner's children, the homeowner might consider it a reasonable compromise to let the burglar go if that person could help eliminate drug sales in the homeowner's community.

Faced with these mixed messages sent by legislators, police administrators, and citizens, law enforcement officers must exercise a great deal of discretion in deciding which laws to enforce and how fully to enforce them. Certainly we do not want to give full rein to the police to completely decide how to enforce the law.

Law enforcement without boundaries is a frightening prospect and one from which we are protected by the Constitution. Later in this chapter we review how the police are constrained by the law. Suffice it to say here, however, that although the law limits the actions of the police, it also provides opportunities for the exercise of discretion on when to apply specific laws to certain situations. Consequently, even though we try to control discretion, it will always be a contested area of law enforcement.[10]

Expectations of Law Enforcement

We expect a lot from our police, maybe too much. However, the police have claimed broad powers in staking out the mandate of their occupation.[11] Like other occupations, such as physicians, lawyers, and architects, the police have established a semimonopoly on the core concerns of their profession. As the lawyer must possess certain education and training to be certified to practice law, and the physician must be qualified to practice medicine and prescribe drugs, so too the police officer has the authority to use legal force. When situations get out of hand, we "call the cops" to exercise their professional skills and judgment to maintain order and ensure justice. The alternative would be anarchy in which everyone decided for themselves what constituted reasonable force and appropriate justice. In fact, most arrests of adults do not require the police to use force (see Figure 6.1). So, for the most part, law enforcement's mandate to use force seems reasonable. Some scholars, such as Peter Manning, however, contend that when we look at what the police claim as their legitimate domain, we can appreciate how their mandate is just too broad.[12]

According to Manning, the police have been assigned the tasks of crime prevention, crime detection, and the apprehension of criminals in an efficient, apolitical, and professional manner. To respond to such an encompassing mandate, the police must develop an occupational culture that shapes their response to crime, criminals, and the criminal justice system. Manning argued that this mandate requires the police to make assumptions about everyday life that give them an occupational perspective to guide their strategies and tactics in enforcing the law. These assumptions, created historically by American non-college-educated patrol officers, define the police subculture.[13]

1. People cannot be trusted; they are dangerous.
2. Experience is better than abstract rules.
3. You must make people respect you.

CROSSCURRENTS

Life in a Police State

Courtesy of CORBIS-NY.

Our procedural law dictates the rules that the criminal justice system must adhere to in arresting, prosecuting, and imprisoning suspects. Given that some of the inefficiencies of the system allow some criminals to escape punishment, it is sometimes tempting to relax the constraints we place on law enforcement and allow the police and judges unbridled freedom in fighting crime. However, there could be negative unintended consequences to such a policy. Without any constraints on the criminal justice system, we would have a police state. What would it be like to live under such a system?

Aleksandr Solzhenitsyn gave us a good idea in his book, *The Gulag Archipelago,* in which he recounted life in the former Soviet Union where the rights of the individual were sacrificed to the unfettered discretion of the government. The result was a system of state-sponsored terror in which the criminal justice system was a tool of internal repression. Of particular interest for the study of law enforcement is Solzhenitsyn's first chapter on arrest, in which he provided multiple examples of how law enforcement, without laws for the enforcers, makes arrests in a police state.

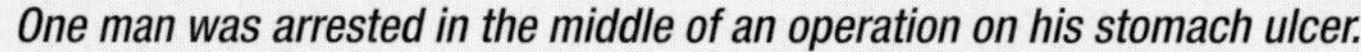

- ***One man was arrested in the middle of an operation on his stomach ulcer.***
- ***A man was with his wife at a train station when an unidentified man asked to talk to him in private. The two men stepped into an adjoining room. The woman did not see or hear from her husband again for 10 years.***
- ***After a neighbor was arrested, a woman went to the police station to inquire what she should do about the neighbor's daughter who was left behind. The police told her to sit down. They arrested her a couple of hours later solely to meet their arrest quota.***

The police do not identify themselves. According to Solzhenitsyn, "You are arrested by a meterman who has come to read your meter. You are arrested by a bicyclist who has run into you on the street, by a railway conductor, a taxi driver, a savings bank teller, the manager of a movie theater. Any one of them can arrest you, and you notice the concealed maroon-colored identification card only when it is too late" (p. 10). Solzhenitsyn, who called the police the "organs," contended that they operated with absolute authority and virtually no oversight. The criminal justice system was not only corrupt, it was surreal. There was neither rhyme nor reason to who was arrested and punished, and the courts were as ruthless and unprincipled as the police. Without the checks and balances found in democracies, a government could easily become a police state. The men who crafted the Constitution of the United States were well aware of these dangers.

QUESTIONS

1. Could the United States ever become a police state?
2. Was the Soviet Union police state a government run amok, or had there possibly been good reasons for it? What do you think?

Source: Aleksandr I. Solzhenitsyn, *The Gulag Archipelago 1918–1956* (New York: Harper and Row, 1973), 3–23.

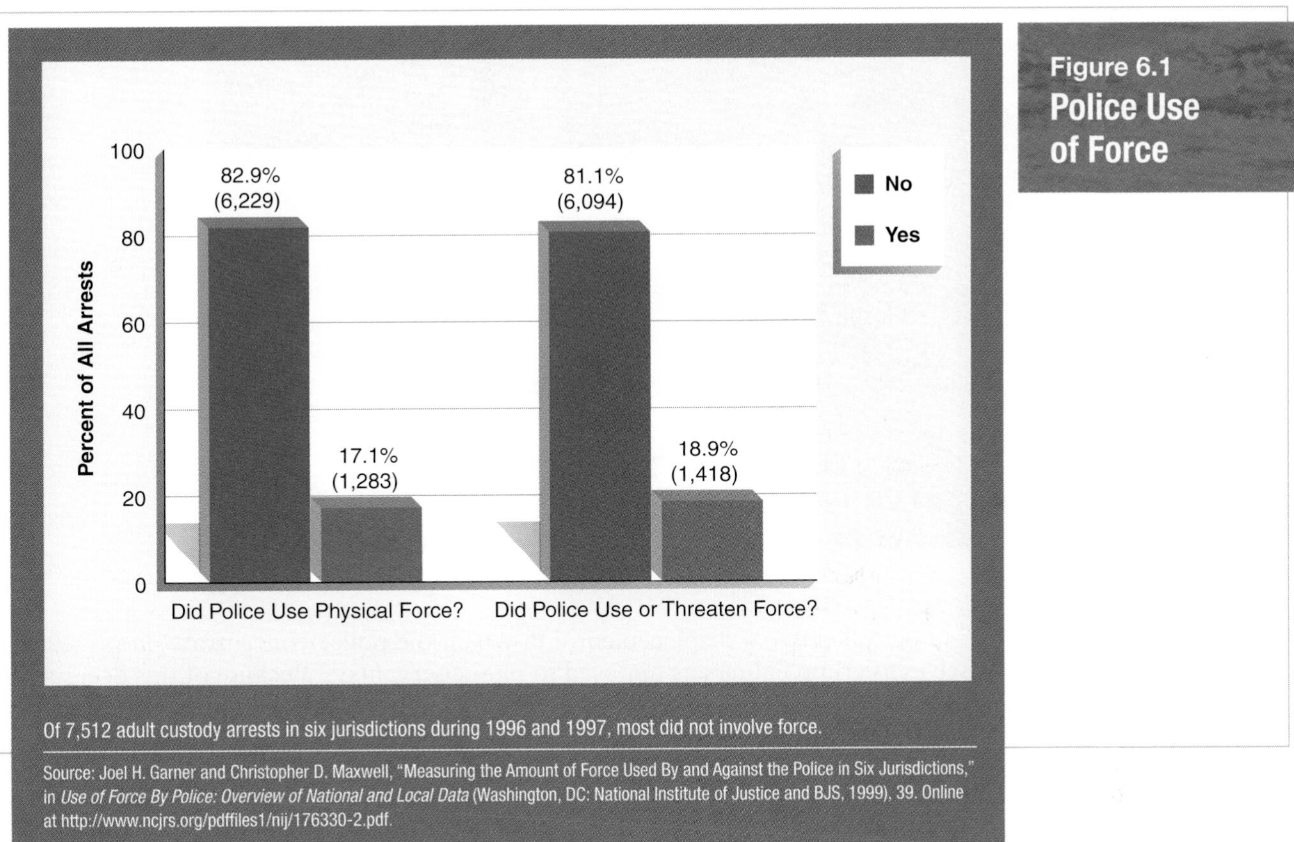

Figure 6.1 Police Use of Force

Of 7,512 adult custody arrests in six jurisdictions during 1996 and 1997, most did not involve force.

Source: Joel H. Garner and Christopher D. Maxwell, "Measuring the Amount of Force Used By and Against the Police in Six Jurisdictions," in *Use of Force By Police: Overview of National and Local Data* (Washington, DC: National Institute of Justice and BJS, 1999), 39. Online at http://www.ncjrs.org/pdffiles1/nij/176330-2.pdf.

4. Everyone hates a cop.
5. The legal system is untrustworthy; police officers make the best decisions about guilt or innocence.
6. People who are not controlled will break laws.
7. Police officers must appear respectful and be efficient.
8. Police officers can most accurately identify crime and criminals.
9. The major jobs of the policeman are to prevent crime and to enforce laws.
10. Stronger punishment will deter criminals from repeating their errors.[14]

Given this occupational perspective, it is hardly surprising that police may view their role in a highly romanticized and idealistic way that portrays them as fighting dangerous criminals and performing heroic acts. Yet, the reality of law enforcement is quite different and much more routine.

> *In an effort to gain the public's confidence in their ability, and to insure thereby the solidity of their mandate, the police have encouraged the public to continue thinking of them and their work in idealized terms, terms, that is, which grossly exaggerate the actual work done by the police. They do engage in chases, in gunfights, in careful sleuthing. But these are rare events. Most police work resembles any other kind of work: it is boring, tiresome, sometimes dirty, sometimes technically demanding, but it is rarely dangerous. Yet the occasional chase, the occasional shootout, the occasional triumph of some extraordinary detective work have been seized upon by the police and played up to the public.*[15]

The problem of projecting this unrealistic image of the nature of law enforcement to the public is that this flawed portrayal of policing becomes the standard on which the police are evaluated. Unable to live up to this idealized image, the police are forced to construct what Manning referred to as "appearances." These appearances result in what

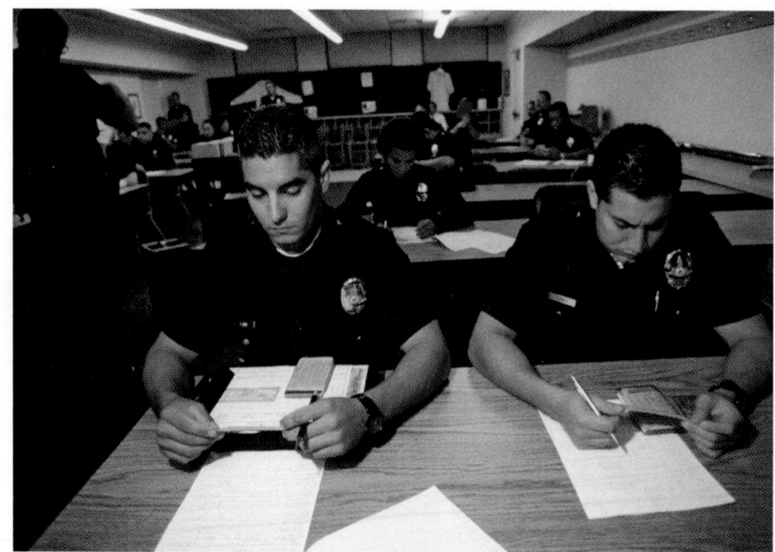

In order to prosecute cases, law enforcement officers must document their actions. Officers complain about excessive paperwork, but it is a necessary part of the law enforcement mission. Computer technology is beginning to make the paperwork less burdensome.
Photo by Kim Kulish, courtesy of Corbis/Bettmann.

can be called "goal displacement," in which the police concentrate on presenting themselves as crime fighters as opposed to public servants.[16] Because of this occupational culture of the police and the distorted view of the nature of law enforcement that the police project to the public, maintaining control of the police is a difficult issue.[17] The violent aspects of the use of force will be covered in Chapter 7, but it is useful here to consider how the military analogy affects how the police see and project themselves.

Quasi-Military Nature of Police Organizations

The structure of law enforcement agencies is similar to that of military units. A strict hierarchical chain of command accords status and responsibility according to rank, and uniforms display insignia that identify to both insiders and the public the exact social location of the officers. This quasi-military nature has some qualities that make it attractive to police organizations. Egon Bittner identified three reasons the military model is attractive to police planners.[18]

1. Both the military and the police are in the business of using force, and the occasions for employing physical force are, as Bittner put it, "unpredictably distributed." Personnel must be kept in a highly disciplined state of alert and preparedness, with reliance on "spit and polish" and obedience to superiors.
2. The introduction of military-like discipline into police agencies in the 1950s and 1960s greatly professionalized departments that had been historically plagued by corruption and political favoritism and influence.
3. The police lacked other models of organization. The military model, as primitive as it is, was easy to comprehend. Given that many officers had some sort of military background, it was easy to implement. Bittner argued that the police are the only large-scale institution that has not benefited from advances in management science.[19]

Although it is easy to understand how law enforcement organizations have evolved in this quasi-military manner, the military structure and culture result in some unintended and undesirable consequences. By having such a vast array of rules and regulations, law enforcement organizations ignore the reality that individual officers must exert a sub-

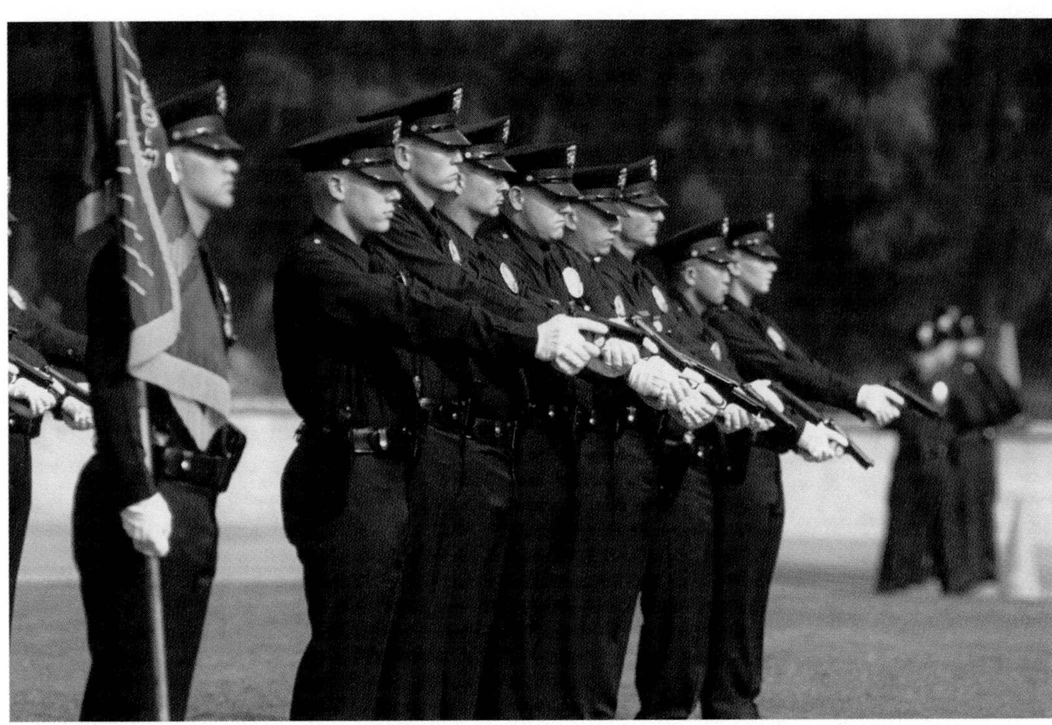

Los Angeles police officers at a graduation ceremony.
Courtesy of CORBIS-NY.

stantial amount of discretion in the everyday performance of their duties. To meet the expectations of the department, a good deal of energy is spent conforming to regulations, and creative and effective decision making is discouraged. According to Bittner, the police are beset with competing demands to stay out of trouble as far as internal regulations are concerned, while at the same time making arrests that "contain, or can be managed to contain, elements of physical danger."[20]

An important difference between law enforcement agencies and military units hampers the effectiveness of the military model in law enforcement. In the military, the superiors are expected to lead soldiers into battle. In police work, supervisory officers seldom have the chance to exert this kind of leadership and control, and are often looked upon with contempt by officers on the line. This is because the supervisors are unable to share the risks of policing but must hold the line officers accountable for decisions and behavior that are often demanded by dangerous circumstances without the luxury of a great deal of time to contemplate.[21]

Variety of Policing Styles

Not all law enforcement officers adopt the same style of interacting with the public, other members of the criminal justice system, and offenders. Each individual brings different personality traits, motivations, training, and objectives to the job. Additionally, not all law enforcement agencies are the same. The size of the community, the racial and ethnic diversity of the local population, the impact of local economic trends, and the history and political structure of the agency all exert an influence on policing styles.[22] It is easy to see the differences between big city departments and those of rural areas. The natures of the crime problems are different, and citizens have varying expectations as to what constitutes optimal policing.

One useful way to examine varieties of policing styles is to look at James Q. Wilson's classic typology from his book, *Varieties of Police Behavior.* Wilson identified three styles of policing that illustrate important differences in how the police approach their many tasks of maintaining order, fighting crime, and being of service to citizens.[23] These styles

watchman style
A mode of policing that emphasizes the maintenance of order, rather than law enforcement. Law enforcement emphasizes discovering crimes and offenders and making arrests. Order-maintenance-style policing may tolerate some illegal activity, as long as order is maintained. Discretion is a major part of the officer's job.

legalistic style
A mode of policing that emphasizes enforcement of the letter of the law. The legalistic officer will write more tickets, make more arrests, and encourage victims to sign complaints. Using little personal discretion, the legalistic officer will make arrests and allow the courts to resolve the incidents.

service style
A mode of policing that is concerned primarily with serving the community and citizens. The service-style officer will use discretion, as with the watchman style, but that discretion is visible, subject to formal review and evaluation, and can be altered when circumstances require.

of policing are termed the **watchman style, legalistic style,** and **service style.** These styles are important because they set the tone of civility between the police and the public. By looking at what the police consider their primary mandates, we can begin to appreciate the distinct differences among departments.

Watchman Style

The watchman style of policing distinguishes between two mandates of policing: order maintenance and law enforcement. Law enforcement is concerned with discovering who has violated the law and arresting that person. This mandate is the one that we usually associate with policing. There is little need to exercise discretion in the law enforcement mandate: the person either committed the crime or did not commit the crime. If he or she committed the crime, then an arrest is made.

The other mandate, order maintenance, is also a primary concern of some departments.[24] Order maintenance involves discretion. Wilson recognized that arrests are not always made even when the police discover a violation of the law and are able to identify the offender. Many times the police do not invoke the criminal sanction but instead release the offender with a warning or make an arrangement in which the offender agrees to inform on other criminals in exchange for freedom. Thus, a police officer using the watchman style might tolerate a certain amount of gambling and vice, might let minor offenders go without arrest, and may simply tell unruly teenagers to leave the area even when law violations are suspected. The key is to preserve the social order in an effort to keep citizens happy (especially powerful citizens, for whom the police officer will overlook some infractions).[25]

The watchman style is a reminder of the past when the police worked for private agencies, and the interests of those private concerns took precedence over the enforcement of the law. Under the watchman style, certain extra-legal factors such as age, race, appearance, or demeanor will be used in deciding when to arrest and when to release law violators.

Legalistic Style

Unlike the watchman style of policing, the legalistic style requires very little exercising of discretion. In many ways, this is a positive feature of policing, but it can be problematic. The legalistic style of policing concentrates on enforcing the law by writing more tickets, making more arrests, and encouraging victims to sign complaints. Whereas the watchman style of police officer might attempt to work out disputes between citizens informally, the legalistic style of officer will determine who is culpable, make the arrest, and allow the courts to resolve the incident.[26] The legalistic style is impersonal and disinterested. The focus is on treating all citizens alike and not requiring the officer to exercise discretion. The extra-legal factors of age, race, social status in the community, or appearance are much less influential in this style of policing than in the watchman style. The legalistic type of police officer is more likely to give the mayor a speeding ticket. Although it may be an oversimplification, we may think of the watchman style of police officer as walking a beat and the legalistic style of police officer as riding in a patrol car. Both of these policing styles emphasize personal interactions with citizens.

Service Style

The service style of policing shares characteristics with the other two styles but is concerned primarily with service to the community and the citizens. Like the legalistic style, it treats all law violations seriously, but the frequent result is not to arrest, as is with the watchman style. Instead, the department employs alternative strategies, such as official warnings or diversion programs. The discretion used in making these decisions is not used by the individual officer, but instead is an expressed part of the department's policy.[27] The key to the service style of policing is that discretion is widely used, but it is visible, is subject to formal review and evaluation, and can be altered when circumstances require.

Wilson's typology of policing is informative, but as with all typologies, it is not mutually exclusive and exhaustive. Other types of policing may be found in some depart-

NEWS FLASH

Seized Assets

Under asset forfeiture laws, police can take money from a suspect without making an arrest if they suspect that a crime has been committed or will be committed. These laws are specifically tools of the war on drugs.

In Houston, Texas, the police have been accused of stealing money under the guise of seizing assets. A man traveling in Houston told reporters that he and his wife were planning to buy a home from a relative and were carrying $14,000 in cash as part of the purchase. He said an officer pulled them over, explained that the man was speeding, and asked to search the car. The man consented, and when his wife was exiting the car, he said the officer told her to leave her purse in the car. The officer found the money and called for a dog to sniff for drugs. The man said the officer claimed that the dog "hit" on the money, indicating that it was money that had been in the vicinity of illegal drugs. The man had a previous drug charge for felony marijuana possession, which the officer discovered upon running a license check on the man. The man said the officer took the money, but did not charge him with a crime. Later, the man's tax returns proved that he had earned the money. Houston Police later returned to the man $13,000 of the $14,000 that had been seized.

Local attorneys have said that although they believe most police officers are honest, receipts are not always issued when assets are seized. A Houston police captain said that departmental policy requires officers to count in front of suspects the cash that has been taken from them. He admitted, however, that sometimes cash is not always counted at the scene of a seizure.

Source: Anna Werner, "Did You Know It's Legal for Police to Take Your Money?" KHOU.com, May 22, 2002, http://www.khou.com/news/defenders/investigate/khou020522_nh_DefendersPoliceMoney.1017f0e9.html.

ments, and a mixture of styles may occur within a department. A department may provide officers with very little discretion in dealing with domestic assault cases and grant wide latitude in handling drug cases. Wilson's typology, therefore, is simply a guide, and in reality we may find considerable overlap or significant gaps.

Wilson's typology is over three decades old, but the use and control of discretion remains a core issue for law enforcement scholars. What has changed is the ability of supervisors to consider the discretion of individual law enforcement officers. Primarily, because of advances in technology, the work of the officer on the street has become more ascertainable.

Police Subculture and Police Corruption

The style of policing adopted by the officer is influenced by that officer's personal characteristics in coping with the demands of the job and with family members and friends. Like many occupations, policing imposes a lifestyle that may set the police officer apart from civilians in terms of sociability, social integration, and social acceptance.[28] Many times, police officers are not invited to parties because people fear their reaction to rowdy behavior. The police often do not want to interact socially with others because their occupations tag them with a master status that causes others to treat them always as a "cop."[29] Also, the police develop what Jerome Skolnick coined the **policeman's working personality.** This term explains how law enforcement officers are drawn into a police subculture that emphasizes a different set of values from those held by mainstream society.[30]

policeman's working personality
A term coined by Jerome Skolnick to refer to the mind-set of police who must deal with danger, authority, isolation, and suspicion while appearing to be efficient. Officers may be drawn into a police subculture that emphasizes a different set of values from those of mainstream society.

Skolnick also pointed out that the particular occupational style will vary according to the demands of certain assignments.

> *A conception of "working personality" of police should be understood to suggest an analytic breadth similar to that of "style of life." That is, just as the professional behavior of military officers with similar "styles of life" may differ drastically depending upon whether they command an infantry battalion or participate in the work of an intelligence unit, so too does the professional behavior of police officers with similar "working personalities" vary with their assignments.*[31]

However, Skolnick went on to point out that all police officers begin their careers on the street in the constabulary role and that this experience tends to shape an occupational police perspective that socially isolates the officer and makes him or her suspicious of other persons. Therefore, it is useful to consider Skolnick's concept of the policeman's working personality in some detail by examining some of its key elements.

1. **The symbolic assailant.** Law enforcement officers must always be on guard. They are systematically trained and culturally reinforced to consider everyone a potential assailant until they can size up the situation and determine that an individual poses no threat. This is easy to do when confronted with a large, drunk, belligerent male wielding a knife. It is less easy when interacting with a gray-haired grandmother who seems lost and disoriented. Law enforcement officers will not relax until they are confident that the grandmother poses no harm to herself or others. They cannot assume that she is of no threat until they can independently establish that she is what she seems to be. In the grandmother's case, this is accomplished based on behavioral and contextual clues. The situation of the knife-wielding male, on the other hand, alerts officers to keep their guard up. According to Skolnick, the officer "develops a perceptual shorthand to identify certain kinds of people as symbolic assailants, that is, persons whose gestures, language, and attire may constitute a prelude to violence."[32]
2. **Danger.** Police work can be very dangerous (see Figures 6.2 and 6.3). Although death in the line of duty or serious physical injury are not everyday events, the possibility of confrontation is always there, and according to Skolnick, is part of the

Figure 6.2
Number of Law Enforcement Officers Killed during the Commission of Felonies, 1993–2002

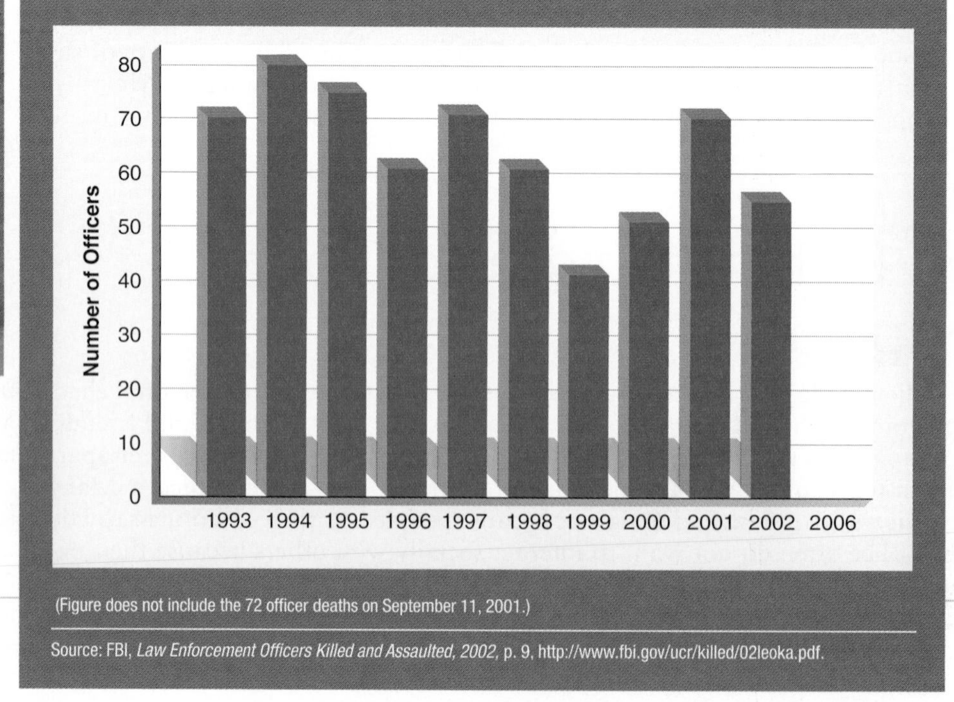

(Figure does not include the 72 officer deaths on September 11, 2001.)

Source: FBI, *Law Enforcement Officers Killed and Assaulted, 2002*, p. 9, http://www.fbi.gov/ucr/killed/02leoka.pdf.

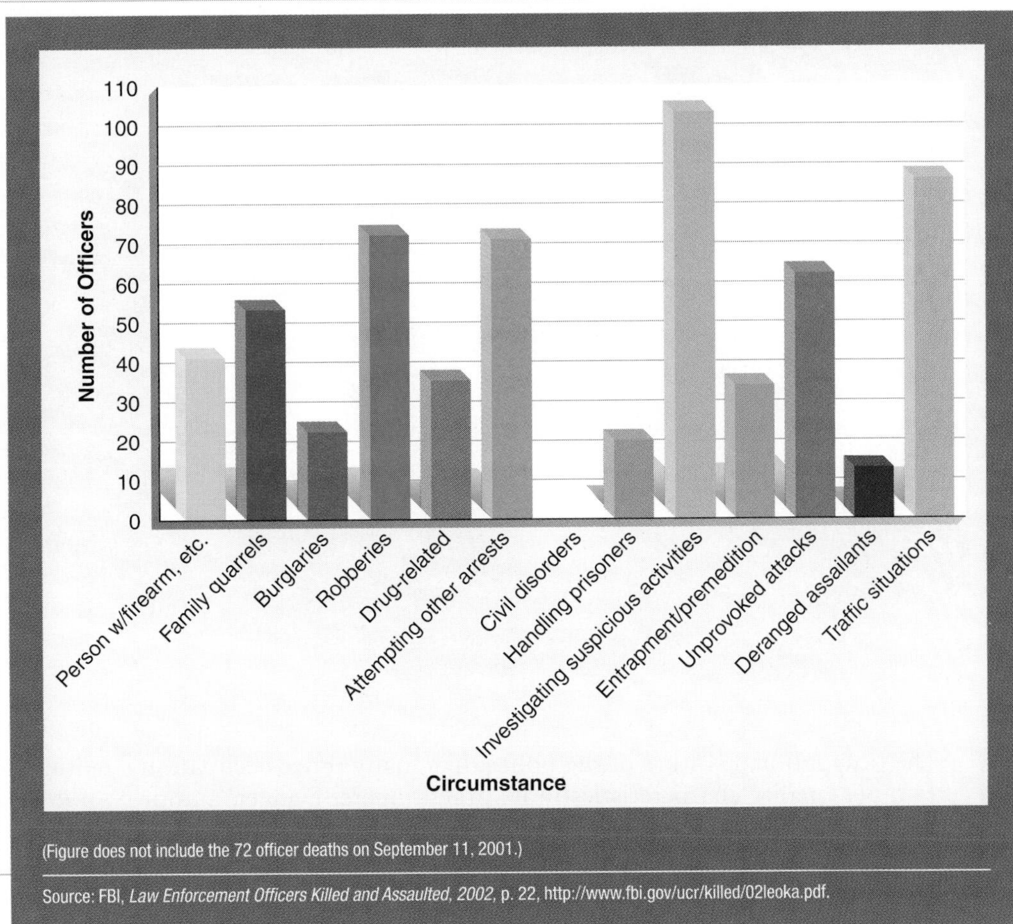

(Figure does not include the 72 officer deaths on September 11, 2001.)

Source: FBI, *Law Enforcement Officers Killed and Assaulted, 2002,* p. 22, http://www.fbi.gov/ucr/killed/02leoka.pdf.

Figure 6.3 Number of Law Enforcement Officers Killed during the Commission of Felonies, 1993–2002

makeup of the policeman's working personality. In fact, police are drawn to the more dangerous assignments, both as a function of job prestige and excitement.[33]

3. **Social isolation.** Law enforcement officers are treated differently by the public. Whereas law enforcement officers may perceive an individual as a symbolic assailant, the public sees the police officer as a symbolic authority figure. Thus, even when an individual has done nothing wrong, he or she may be wary of an officer because of the perceived power the officer has to detain, question, search, and arrest. Skolnick quoted a police officer who was at a party with his wife when someone threw a firecracker that exploded and slightly injured his wife. When the police officer confronted the man and told him to be careful, someone identified him as a police officer. What would have been a simple exchange between individuals was transformed into a situation in which a crowd of people sided against the police officer, and the officer felt unwelcome and left. Subsequently, he and his wife stopped associating with that crowd of people because his occupation of police officer was a barrier to open and honest interaction. Skolnick reported that this social isolation causes many police officers to limit their social interactions to situations in which other police officers are around.
4. **Solidarity.** The combination of danger and social isolation creates a sense of solidarity in the police subculture. An "us against them" mentality is developed to cope not only with law violators, but also with the public in general. The police, according to Skolnick, are resentful of the lack of support they perceive coming from those whom they protect and serve. The police feel as though they are taken for granted by the public and that the public does not take enough responsibility for helping to fight the war against criminals.[34]

Danger is a constant feature in police work. Officers must be periodically trained to respond to any danger or threat that might arise.
Courtesy of CORBIS-NY.

The occupational culture of the police, like many other occupational cultures, fosters certain personality characteristics in its practitioners. Danger, authority, potential symbolic assailants, and social isolation are features of the occupation that encourage the construction of the policeman's working personality. This process may have far-reaching implications for the recruitment, training, and control of law enforcement officers.[35] For example, how much money and resources should be spent on the selection and training of officers if the very nature of law enforcement occupations instills those individuals with an occupational perspective that dictates how they view the job and respond to criminals and the public? How should society address the negative features of the policeman's working personality?

Police Corruption

Although police corruption has been a significant problem for some police agencies at particular times, we do not suggest that it is as pervasive as the issues of the policeman's working personality. However, the nature and extent of police corruption are worth our attention because of the constant temptations placed before law enforcement officers and because trust in the criminal justice system is one of the cornerstones of a democratic society. Additionally, the history of policing is replete with examples of not only corruption of individual police officers, but also widespread, systemic corruption of entire departments and the municipal governments they served.[36]

meat-eaters
A slang term from the 1971 Knapp Commission report on police corruption in New York City describing officers who actively seek out situations that can produce financial gain.

grass-eaters
A slang term from the 1971 Knapp Commission report on police corruption in New York City describing officers who accept bribes but do not actively pursue them.

Knapp Commission

In 1972 the Knapp Commission issued its report on police corruption in New York City. Based on the revelations made by undercover detective Frank Serpico, 19 officers were indicted for accepting payoffs. Subsequent investigations revealed even more violators. In examining this systematic corruption, the Knapp Commission made a distinction between **meat-eaters** and **grass-eaters**.

> *Corrupt policemen have been informally described as being either* ***"grass-eaters"*** *or* ***"meat-eaters."*** *The overwhelming majority of those who do take payoffs are grass-eaters, who accept gratuities and solicit five- and ten- and twenty dollar payments from contractors, tow-truck operators, gamblers, and the like, but do not aggres-*

> *sively pursue corruption payments. "Meat-eaters," probably only a small percentage of the force, spend a good deal of their working hours aggressively seeking out situations they can exploit for financial gain, including gambling, narcotics, and other serious offenses which can yield payments of thousands of dollars.*[37]

Not all police officers have equal opportunities to engage in corruption. The nature of the department, the community, and the particular assignment all influence how much temptation is placed in the officers' paths or how fertile the situation is for the meat-eater who is aggressively seeking situations to exploit. Historically, illegal gambling, prostitution, prohibition, and other organized crime activities have been major sources of police corruption. Presently, because of the war on drugs, tremendous amounts of money are changing hands, putting narcotics officers in positions to engage in a variety of corrupt acts. According to Peter K. Manning and Lawrence John Redlinger, narcotics law enforcement can invite police corruption in at least seven principal ways.

1. **Bribes.** Officers can take bribes in a number of ways. They can provide advance warning of police raids or take bribes not to arrest those caught using or selling drugs. Additionally, police officers are reported to have testified badly in a case in exchange for a bribe. For instance, Manning and Redlinger cited the Knapp Commission's finding that an officer can admit while being questioned on the witness stand that he "lost sight" of the drugs as they fell to the ground, thus providing the defense attorney with an argument that the chain of custody was compromised.
2. **Using drugs.** On occasion, police officers may use the very drugs they are mandated to suppress. Additionally, they may use other drugs without prescription to keep themselves awake. The incidence of police officers using illegal drugs is likely not as serious a problem today as it may have been a generation ago. Now, many law enforcement agencies require random drug tests of employees that may well deter illegal drug use.
3. **Buying and selling narcotics.** It may seem incredible that narcotics officers would deal in drugs, but in some circumstances this type of corruption might seem reasonable to an officer. The testimony of addicts can be acquired by giving them drugs. Likewise, informers can be paid off by giving them a small amount of the seized drugs. Given limited budgets for operating expenditures such as "buy money," enterprising narcotics agents may use drugs to finance operations the department cannot afford. However, these activities are still considered a form of corruption and are not sanctioned by police administrators. Finally, "meat-eating" officers have been known to sell narcotics and use the money for personal gain.
4. **Arrogation of seized property.** Property relevant to a crime must be seized by the police department and held until the case is concluded, at which point the department determines whether to return it to its rightful owner, destroy it, or convert it to government use. The police must scrupulously account for all seized cash, drugs, guns, and automobiles. Although cash used by police to buy drugs is marked and the serial numbers recorded, the cash seized from drug dealers is subject to theft by the arresting officers. Some of the cash and drugs seized at a crime scene may be diverted before they are officially logged into the evidence room at the police station.
5. **Illegal searches and seizures.** Police can engage in corrupt misconduct in several ways when initiating searches and seizures on drug suspects. Lying about smelling marijuana or seeing drugs in "plain sight" is one method officers can use to claim **probable cause** to conduct a search. The planting of evidence on a suspect can happen in any of three ways. "Flaking" consists of finding evidence the officer planted on the suspect. Some officers carry a "sure-bust kit" that contains a variety of drugs that can be planted on suspects to support the type of arrest the officers desire. "Dropsey" is a variation of flaking in which the officer claims to have seen the suspect drop something and then finds drugs at the offender's feet. "Padding" refers to the practice of adding drugs to the seizure to justify a raise in the charge from misdemeanor to felony. The police can use these practices to entice drug dealers and users to offer bribes of cash or sexual favors for lenient treatment.

probable cause
A reason based on known facts to think that a crime has taken place or that a property is connected to a crime. A law enforcement officer must have probable cause to make an arrest without a warrant, to search without a warrant, or to seize property that may provide evidence of a crime.

6. **Protection of informants.** Sometimes the police are willing to tolerate a certain level of crime to battle more serious infractions. This becomes a judgment call that can lead to substantial harm to victims, the community, and the reputation of the law enforcement agencies. Both within and between criminal justice agencies there are rivalries, competition, and distrust. The narcotics division may overlook the burglaries of a confidential informant if it is receiving good information that might facilitate the bust of a big drug dealer. A federal agency may hide the crimes of a snitch from a local police department if doing so furthers its agenda. Informants may coax all kinds of rewards, such as money, drugs, or reduced charges, from several agencies at the same time based on the promise of the same information.
7. **Violence.** Finally, narcotics officers may use unwarranted violence to cope with drug dealers. They may claim the offender "went for his gun" and then kill the offender. They may threaten to tell others in the drug trade that the offender is an informant, ensuring that person's violent death at the hands of others. The police may use illegal force in a number of ways that enable them to prosecute or extort lawbreakers.[38]

These forms of police behavior all represent some type of corruption. They may sometimes be used to advance the cause of legitimate police work, but because they are illegal, they are of concern to police administrators and police scholars. A police department that allows its officers to operate in devious ways inevitably exposes itself to the scandal of corruption and the problems of litigation. Therefore, it seems prudent to consider these types of corruption and deviance as pressing issues in the control of the law enforcement profession.

Procedural Laws and Policing

In Chapter 4 we studied the distinction between substantive law and procedural law. As you may remember, substantive law delineates which behaviors are proscribed by criminal statute. Murder, rape, larceny, arson, and a wide range of other activities are defined in the substantive law, as are the penalties for committing them.

By contrast, the procedural law dictates how the government can go about discovering and prosecuting violations of the substantive law. One way to consider procedural law is to think of it as the rules by which the government must play. Some people may think of procedural law as "tying the hands of the police" or "letting criminals go free because of technicalities," but the positive aspects of this control of government actions are of extreme value in providing for a free and democratic state. Aspects of the procedural law were placed in the Constitution because its framers wanted to protect us from government abuses such as those found in the European monarchies of the time. For instance, in England, the crown used the device of general warrants to allow the king's agents to search shops and homes for whatever they wished.[39] In a famous speech before the House of Commons, William Pitt articulated the value that a person's home is private, and that the government ought not intrude.

> *The poorest may in his cottage bid defiance to all forces of the crown. It may be frail—its roof may shake—the wind may blow through it—the storm may enter—but the King of England cannot enter—all his force dares not cross the threshold of the ruined tenement.*[40]

Those who work in the criminal justice system may get frustrated by the scope and complexities of the procedural laws and will often test the interpretation with aggressive crime fighting. The law is forever in flux as new cases are brought before the courts for rulings concerning new technologies, changing community standards, evolving political pressures, and the widening of constitutional protections to more and more groups of people. Consequently, the law is a living, breathing, changing set of rules that is adjusted

CROSSCURRENTS

"We Don't Need No Stinking Fourth Amendment"

The Fourth Amendment makes the job of law enforcement officers more challenging. It strictly limits the discretion they have in searching for and seizing evidence. Furthermore, it requires the oversight of a judge to determine whether probable cause exists to obtain a search warrant. Because the police can become frustrated by procedural law, it is not surprising that they sometimes attempt to circumvent it in fulfilling their duties.

Criminologist L. Paul Sutton examined how the Fourth Amendment actually is implemented in several cities. Sutton found that the process most often appeared to operate as intended, but he also found that law enforcement officers attempt to get around the Fourth Amendment in several ways. Listed here are several strategies that are problematic:

- Consent. *Conducting a search with the consent of the subject is legal. However, that consent should be given voluntarily and intelligently. There is sometimes a question of whether a suspect actually knows that consent for a search can be denied. Law enforcement officers are not required to advise a suspect that he or she is allowed to deny consent.*
- Timing. *The police may time their arrest of the subject so that they can, for example, impound a car and conduct a legal inventory search of the contents for safekeeping. Even though the facts of the arrest may not be sufficient for a formal charge, the results of the search can be allowed. Thus, arrest can be used as a ruse to legally search the car.*
- Harassment. *Even when the police know they do not have probable cause to seek a legal search warrant, they may attempt to harass the suspects. Sutton reported some officers saying they would knock on a door and shout, "This is the police. Open up." As they listened to the toilets being repeatedly flushed, they speculated that expensive illegal drugs were being destroyed. The intent of the police was not to conduct a search but to simply scare the suspects into destroying their drugs.*
- Judge-shopping. *Some judges are more sympathetic to the concerns of law enforcement than others are. Thus, in almost every jurisdiction there are preferred judges for the police to approach with a request for a search warrant. Although Sutton did not interview any judges who admitted to being "easy," he did talk to judges who claimed that some of their brethren did not sufficiently consider the specifics of the case.*
- Falsification or misrepresentation. *Sometimes the police simply lie to the judge to obtain a search warrant. The lie may sometimes be a little "fudging" of the actual circumstances, but it may occasionally involve intentional perjury.*

Although law enforcement officers may circumvent the Fourth Amendment to be more effective in fighting crime, it is problematic for society. Violating the procedural law may not only expose the case to the potential of being thrown out of court on a technicality, but more important, it denies citizens the full protection of the law.

QUESTIONS

1. Should police try to circumvent the Fourth Amendment in order to search suspects they believe are guilty or dangerous?
2. Should search-and-seizure rules be relaxed in favor of the police? Should they be tightened in favor of citizens?

Source: L. Paul Sutton, "Getting around the Fourth Amendment," in *Thinking About Police: Contemporary Readings*, 2nd ed., eds. Carl B. Klockars and Stephen D. Mastrofski (New York: McGraw-Hill, 1991), 433–446.

to the demands of society. However, the law is based on long-held principles that limit just how far it can be stretched and dictate that the underlying values incorporated by the Constitution must either be met or the Constitution amended.

Procedural Laws and Policing: The Fourth Amendment

Procedural law controlling the activities of law enforcement is derived from the Fourth Amendment of the Constitution. Although a number of state laws, court cases, and departmental regulations specify just how the police can go about investigating crimes, interrogating suspects, and arresting criminals, all of these rules and regulations must be consistent with the Supreme Court's interpretation of the Fourth Amendment (see Figure 6.4). Even though it constitutes only one sentence, the Fourth Amendment covers a lot of territory. It specifies a wide range of protections from police activity and essentially ensures that citizens are not subject to the arbitrary actions of overzealous law enforcement officers. However, the Fourth Amendment does not completely tie the hands of the police. It is subject to interpretation by the courts, and its wording allows justices to inject into their rulings their judgment about what the framers of the Constitution intended and what contemporary society demands. For instance, the interpretation of the word *unreasonable* is fraught with difficulty. What is reasonable to one individual is unreasonable to another. Yet, the police must be given guidelines to ensure that the cases they present to the prosecutor are not considered unreasonable by the court. To appreciate the intricacies of the Fourth Amendment as a guide for procedural law, we must examine its language in greater detail.

Search

Prosecuting criminal cases depends on information. Many times, the required information is readily available to law enforcement officers, but more often they have to work hard at assembling the types of evidence necessary to secure a conviction. Suspects, especially the guilty ones, do not always cooperate fully with the law enforcement officers who are trying to implicate them. Suspects may hide, alter, or destroy evidence in their efforts to avoid detection and arrest. The police may search the suspect in a reasonable manner, but the court draws a line at the fuzzy concept of unreasonable searches, and the police must be trained in procedural law to make a judgment as to which is which. A review of some of the concerns of the court is instructive.

1. **Trespass doctrine.** The trespass doctrine defines what constitutes a search. The court says that a search requires physical intrusion into a constitutionally protected area. The Fourth Amendment specifies these areas as persons, houses, papers, and effects. Thus, any search of these areas must meet the requirements of the Fourth Amendment as being reasonable. Requiring a handwriting sample is not considered physically intrusive and is not deemed a search protected by the Fourth Amendment. However, most of us believe the government has no right to demand our bodily fluids in its search for evidence. After all, doesn't the Fourth

Figure 6.4 The Fourth Amendment

The right of the people to be secure in their persons, houses, papers, and effects, against unreasonable searches and seizures, shall not be violated, and no Warrants shall issue, but upon probable cause, supported by Oath or affirmation, and particularly describing the place to be searched, and the persons or things to be seized.

Amendment protect our person? The courts have ruled that under some circumstances, such as when you drive an automobile, participate in high school sports (or more recently, in any high school extracurricular activities), the safety of others makes taking blood or urine tests reasonable searches.[41]

2. **Privacy doctrine.** In 1967 the privacy doctrine essentially replaced the trespass doctrine in *Katz v. United States*. This case held that people, not places, are protected from government intrusion whenever they have an expectation of privacy that society recognizes as reasonable. The police are given quite a bit of latitude in dealing with citizens on the street and in public places where privacy is usually not expected. Deciding between the needs of law enforcement to maintain safety and the citizens' rights to privacy is a delicate balancing act.[42]
3. **Plain-view doctrine.** The plain-view doctrine is actually not an accurate name for the principle that officers have a lawful right to use all their senses (sight, smell, hearing, and touch) to detect evidence of unlawful action. The plain-view doctrine also stipulates that such detection of evidence does not constitute a search because the police are not searching when they merely observe what is around them. Thus, the plain-view doctrine holds that the Fourth Amendment does not protect such gathering of evidence because no search has actually occurred. Three criteria have to be met for the discovery of evidence to fall outside the Fourth Amendment's definition of a search. (a) Officers are lawfully present when and where they discover the evidence. (b) Detection occurs without advanced technology enhancing the ordinary senses. (c) Detection is inadvertent; it is not planned. Thus, when a police officer pulls a car over for speeding and sees a bag of marijuana on the passenger seat in plain view, the officer can arrest the driver for possession without the Fourth Amendment becoming an issue because no search was conducted. Conversely, if the officer stopped the car because the driver simply looked suspicious and, without asking the driver's permission, felt under the seat and found a bag

CASE IN POINT

Illinois v. Gates

The Case

Illinois v. Gates, 462 U.S. 213, 103 S.Ct. 2317 (1983)

The Point

Probable cause for a search does not demand proof beyond a reasonable doubt.

A married couple, Lance and Sue Gates of Illinois, were accused in an anonymous letter to police of buying and selling large amounts of illegal drugs. The letter contained explicit details about a complicated operation in which Mrs. Gates would drive a car down to Florida to be loaded with drugs, then Mr. Gates would fly down and drive the laden car back to Illinois, leaving Mrs. Gates to fly back alone. The letter stated that the couple had bragged about their drug-selling business. Following the details in the letter, police tracked the Gates' movements and found them to be consistent with the letter. The police obtained a warrant and searched the Gates' home, where large quantities of drugs were found. The Gates were arrested and convicted.

The couple appealed to the Supreme Court, stating that because the police could not assess the reliability of the letter's anonymous writer, no basis existed for the search warrant of their home. The court disagreed, citing that the "totality of circumstances"—meaning, in this case, how precisely the letter's specifics matched the Gates' actions—and not the letter itself justified the search warrant. As for the informant, according to the court, "[P]robable cause does not demand the certainty we associate with formal trials."

The Gates' convictions were upheld.

that was found to contain marijuana, the actions of the officer would be deemed an illegal search according to the Fourth Amendment.[43] The court does not allow law enforcement to use sophisticated technology to enhance their natural senses in discovering evidence in plain view. This does not mean that absolutely no technology can be used, but rather technology that is not available to most people. Thus, the police may use flashlights, binoculars, and even airplanes to look for unlawful activity. In a recent case, the court drew the line at the use of thermal-imaging devices. The police used such a device to measure the heat emitted by special lights used to grow marijuana in a house as probable cause to secure a search warrant. The court ruled against the government, contending that such a device was beyond the plain-view doctrine.[44]

4. **Open-fields doctrine.** The right to privacy does not extend to open fields even if the property is privately owned. The police can arrest landowners for the cultivation of marijuana on private land even if the police were trespassing on that land. The line at which the Fourth Amendment protections apply is drawn at where someone has a reasonable expectation of privacy. Thus, the open-fields doctrine does not include the curtilage of a home. One's yard, pool or patio area, and attached garage are covered by the Fourth Amendment, whereas a barn far out in a field that is not used for family purposes would fail under the open-fields doctrine.[45]
5. **Public places.** The Fourth Amendment does not protect individuals from being observed by the police using ordinary senses in public places. The street, parks, private businesses that are open to the public, and the public areas of restrooms are all outside the protection of the plain-view doctrine of the Fourth Amendment. However, employee areas of a business are protected as are the stalls of a restroom where one could reasonably expect privacy. If, however, the police officer saw smoke rising over the top of the stall and that smoke gave off the distinctive odor of marijuana, the protections of the Fourth Amendment would not apply.[46]
6. **Abandoned property.** The Fourth Amendment does not extend to abandoned property. Again, the expectation of privacy is important in concluding whether the Fourth Amendment covers the property. Abandonment requires the individual to intend to permanently discard the property. For example, turning your car over to a valet parking attendant would not constitute abandonment because you expect to get it back, and you also expect that your rights of privacy will remain intact. Putting your household trash on the curb to be picked up by the garbage collector is another matter. Because we cannot expect that our trash will be free from the prying eyes of others, we are careful (or should be) to make sure credit card numbers and other sensitive information are destroyed before putting it in the trash.[47]

We are left then with a complex pattern of the legality of law enforcement searches. The Constitution does not say the government cannot search but only that it cannot conduct unreasonable searches. Law enforcement officers must understand the parameters of lawful searching to ensure that their cases can withstand constitutional scrutiny.

We all recognize the necessity of law enforcement officers to search for evidence, but we also understand that unreasonable searches are one of the most intrusive features of the criminal justice system. No one likes to have their person, home, or "stuff" searched, and the court has tried to balance the rights of privacy of citizens with the needs of law enforcement to collect evidence of crime. The police are restrained in their searches by the requirement that they have a warrant. A valid warrant requires probable cause, a specific description of the persons and places that are going to be searched, and a description of the items that are to be seized. Furthermore, the warrant must be approved by a judge. Additionally, the law enforcement officers must knock and announce their presence and give the occupants a brief time to answer before they enter the house to search.[48]

Two considerations may exempt law enforcement providers from these Fourth Amendment provisions. The first is the problem of officer safety. If the police believe there is an armed and dangerous subject inside a home, should they be required to knock and announce their presence? To do so might invite a hail of gunfire. Second, by knock-

CASE IN POINT

Terry v. Ohio

The Case

Terry v. Ohio, 392 U.S. 1, 88 S.Ct. 1868 (1968)

The Point

Police have the right to search suspects to ensure their own safety if they think that the suspects are armed.

A Cleveland police officer who was in an area that he had patrolled for many years saw two men, John Terry and a man surnamed Chilton, walking back and forth repeatedly in front of a store and pausing to stare in the window. The officer reported that they did this about 24 times. After each pass, they met and talked on a nearby street corner. They were joined by a third man, who left the group, but met up with them again a few blocks away from the store. The officer suspected the three men of inspecting the store in order to rob it later. The officer went up to the men and identified himself as a policeman. Suspicious, he checked Terry for weapons and felt a gun concealed in his coat pocket, and, in a further search, a gun in Chilton's pocket. Terry and Chilton were charged with and convicted of carrying concealed weapons. Terry appealed, the central argument in the case being whether police have the right to search people acting suspiciously if they believe a crime is being planned. The Supreme Court upheld Terry's conviction.

ing and announcing their presence, the police may give suspects an opportunity to destroy evidence. Drugs can be flushed down the toilet or documents burned before the police have time to secure the scene. The court does not recognize any blanket exception such as a search of a dwelling where drugs may be used and sold, but it does recognize that, on a case-by-case basis, the knock-and-announce rule can be abbreviated. Anyone who has ever watched the television program *COPS* can see how the knock-and-announce rule is abbreviated in the actual practice of law enforcement.

To get a search warrant, the law enforcement officer must obtain the approval of a judge. As a practical concern, this requirement presents difficulties that can greatly hinder the case. It can take a long time to get the warrant, time in which suspects can escape or destroy evidence. Consequently, far more searches are conducted without warrants than with legally secured warrants. The court has recognized the following four major exceptions to the requirement that officers obtain warrants before conducting a search:

1. **Searches incident to arrest.** When the police arrest a suspect, it is reasonable, according to the court, for them to search that suspect for weapons and incriminating evidence. Additionally, the police may search the immediate area under control of the suspect to further ensure their safety and prevent the destruction of evidence. The legal issue of what constitutes "under immediate control" of the suspects does not allow the police to extend the search to the whole house. To do this, the police would need to secure a warrant. In the case of an arrest of an individual in an automobile, the area under the control of the offender is deemed to be the **grabbable area,** which constitutes the inside of the passenger compartment but not under the hood or in the trunk. Again, the immediate safety of the law enforcement officers at the time of arrest and the danger of escape or the destruction of evidence allow this type of warrantless search.[49]
2. **Consent searches.** Law enforcement officers may conduct a search without a warrant if they obtain the consent of the suspect. Individuals may waive their right against a search as long as the police advise them that they have the right to refuse consent and that if the officers find incriminating evidence, it will be seized and used against them. This advisement regarding the waiver of consent is like the Miranda

grabbable area
The area under the control of an individual during an arrest in an automobile. For example, the inside of the passenger compartment is considered "grabbable area," but not the space under the hood or in the trunk.

warning regarding self-incrimination. To be considered a voluntary waiver of consent, it must be given by a suspect who feels free of coercion, promise, or deception.[50]

3. **Exigent circumstances searches or emergency searches.** Sometimes events happen so quickly that it is unreasonable to expect the police to stop and get a search warrant to determine if there is a danger to their safety, a chance of suspect escape, or the likelihood of the destruction of evidence. For instance, if the police chase a suspect into a house, they are not required to get a warrant to search the immediate area, but the search would be limited to the room in which the suspect was caught. The police could not go on a fishing expedition and search the whole house.[51]
4. **Vehicle searches.** Historically, vehicles are exempt from the requirement of a search warrant. In short, a person in a vehicle has a reduced expectation of privacy as compared to someone at home. This does not mean that the police are free to search a vehicle arbitrarily. Probable cause would still be needed, but one's car is not considered as sacred as one's home. Additionally, objects in a car that could conceal items the police have probable cause to suspect, such as a purse, are also subject to a warrantless search.[52]

The procedural law attempts to strike a delicate balance between the rights of individuals to be protected from overzealous law enforcement officers and the needs of society to provide those officers with the flexibility and discretion to protect society. Although the Fourth Amendment requirement of a search warrant is highly desirable, it is not practical in all situations in which the safety of an officer or the preservation of evidence is at issue. Therefore, the court has allowed a number of exceptions. Other types of searches pose legal issues that result in the procedural law continuing to be contested. We turn now to special-needs searches.

Special-Needs Searches

So far, our review of Fourth Amendment issues has dealt with how law enforcement officers must handle cases in which a crime is thought to have occurred. In some circumstances searches are allowed in an attempt to prevent crime rather than catch criminals. This discussion of special-needs searches will demonstrate how individuals other than suspected criminals are protected by the Fourth Amendment from unreasonable searches. Although these searches can result in criminal prosecution and imprisonment, and do not require warrants of probable cause, they must meet a standard of reasonableness that balances the needs of the government against the invasion of individual privacy. For instance, the government cannot require all citizens to submit to drug testing even though many consider the drug problem in U.S. society to be extreme. In certain situations, however, individuals who are not suspected of committing crimes are subject to special-needs searches because of their special status of student, prisoner, or pilot. Examples of special-needs searches include the following:

1. **Inventory searches.** When the police impound property, they carefully inspect it and give the owner a receipt. This process protects the police from accusations of theft and ensures that drugs, guns, or explosives are not unknowingly handled in a dangerous manner while they are in police custody. If in conducting these searches, illegal drugs, weapons, or incriminating evidence are found, the police are allowed to use this information in prosecuting cases without having to meet Fourth Amendment requirements of probable cause or search warrants. For example, if your car is seized and you have your stash of drugs in a backpack in the trunk, the police may inspect the backpack and charge you with illegal possession.[53]
2. **Border searches.** The right to control what comes into or goes out of the country allows law enforcement to conduct searches at the border without probable cause or a warrant. There are some limitations, however. **Reasonable suspicion** is necessary for strip searches, and probable cause is required for body-cavity searches.[54] In addition to the problems of drug smuggling, it can be expected that increased

reasonable suspicion
A suspicion based on facts or circumstances that justifies stopping and sometimes searching an individual thought to be involved in criminal activity.

concern about terrorist attacks is going to make searches at borders more common and more rigorous.

3. **Airport searches.** Because of a wave of airplane hijackings in the 1960s, the government instituted a process of inspecting all passengers with metal detectors before allowing them to fly. After the hijacking and terrorist attacks of September 11, 2001, the security at airports has become even more stringent. Now, in addition to carry-on baggage, all checked baggage is inspected by new and powerful X-ray equipment. The searches apply to all passengers, so the court does not consider these searches to be discriminatory. Also, advance notice is posted advising everyone that they will be searched, so individuals are free to not fly and therefore not subject themselves and their luggage to intrusive inspections.
4. **Searches of prisoners.** Do those who violate the law and are sentenced to prison lose all their rights? Does the Constitution stop at the prison door? For the most part, the answer is yes. The need to maintain a safe institution where weapons and contraband are constant threats allows the prison administration to extend only a "diminished scope" of Fourth Amendment rights to prisoners. The issues of prisoner rights will be discussed in more detail in Chapter 12, but it is sufficient to say that the court allows special-needs searches in prisons and jail to circumvent the protections of the Fourth Amendment in order to ensure safe, secure, and orderly institutions.[55]
5. **Searches of probationers and parolees.** Those on probation and parole do not enjoy the same rights as those who are not under the supervision of the court or corrections department. One reason that probationers and parolees cannot expect full Fourth Amendment protections is that in order to secure their release from prison, they have signed a document waiving many of their freedoms. The court, therefore, considers any searches of probationers and parolees by a probation or parole officer to be reasonable because they have consented to the restricted terms of their liberty.
6. **Searches of students.** What level of privacy can students expect while at school? Clearly, the school administrators have a responsibility to ensure a safe and secure learning environment, but where is the line drawn when considering the students' Fourth Amendment rights? School officials do not need probable cause or a search warrant to search students. Reasonable suspicion is enough.[56] Additionally, some students such as athletes and those engaged in extracurricular activities may be subjected to random drug testing.

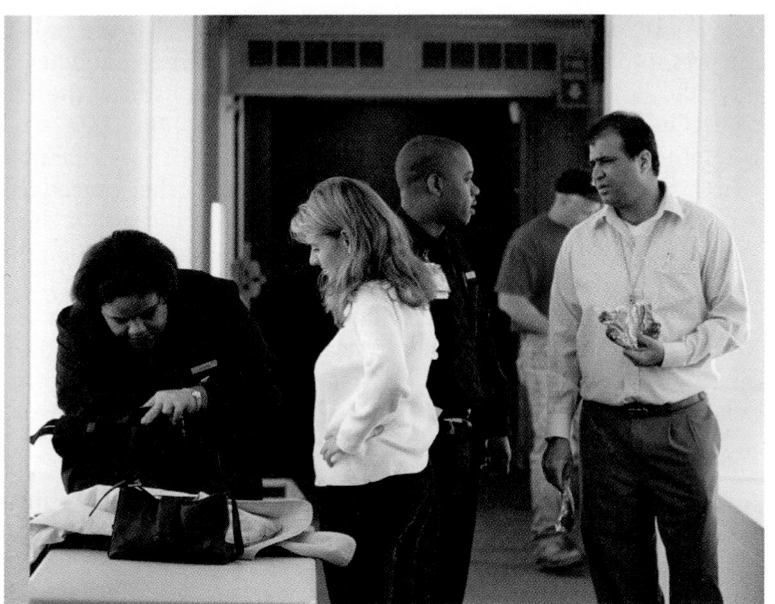

Airport searches are a routine part of air travel. With the development of the Department of Homeland Security, this function is now the responsibility of the federal government rather than private contractors.
Courtesy of CORBIS-NY.

Correctional officers must constantly search prison inmates for drugs, weapons, and contraband. While inmates do not lose all their rights, they do have greatly diminished rights against searches.
Courtesy of CORBIS-NY.

7. **Employee drug testing.** Although not strictly a law enforcement matter, the illegal use of drugs is of concern to society for a number of reasons. Drug use and abuse will be covered in greater detail in Chapter 15, but it is necessary here to point out how drug testing of employees is related to the other search-type issues that have been discussed in this chapter. With employee drug testing, the privacy of the individual from intrusion by the government must be balanced with the safety needs of society. Those who are engaged in occupations that affect the safety of others, such as pilots, bus drivers, and train engineers, can be routinely and randomly tested for drug use to ensure that they are physically competent to operate their vehicles. Additionally, those charged with maintaining order, such as law enforcement officers and correctional officers, are also tested.[57] A wide range of other employees not engaged in public safety tasks are tested by private companies. These searches do not fall under the purview of the Fourth Amendment because the government does not conduct them.

seizure
When law enforcement officers take potential evidence in a criminal case. Evidence seized without a search warrant or without probable cause may not be admitted in court.

stop
A temporary detention that legally is a seizure of an individual and must be based on reasonable suspicion.

stop and frisk
A term that describes two distinct behaviors on the part of law enforcement officers in dealing with suspects. To conduct a lawful frisk, the stop itself must meet the legal conditions of a seizure. A frisk constitutes a search.

Seizures

The Fourth Amendment does not allow evidence that the police have acquired by illegal seizures to be presented in court. **Seizures** are an interesting and complex issue. The police have the right to **stop** individuals and ask questions, and those individuals have the right to decline to answer the questions and walk away. If citizens exercise this right, the police cannot use the refusal to talk to them as probable cause that something is amiss and then search the citizen. The police need to have some other objective evidence in order to seize an individual. Citizens may feel a moral obligation or a civic duty to talk to the police, and the Fourth Amendment does not cover this. However, if the police intimidate the suspect to the point that he or she does not feel free to leave, then an illegal seizure may be deemed under the Fourth Amendment. Surrounding the suspect with several officers, a display of a weapon by an officer, some physical touching of the person of the citizen, or the use of language or tone of voice indicating that compliance with the officers request might be compelled, are the types of circumstances that could invoke a Fourth Amendment defense.[58]

Stop and Frisk

From a procedural standpoint, the term **stop and frisk** actually encompasses two distinct behaviors on the part of law enforcement officers, and they must be considered separately before we can appreciate how they are related. The most basic way to think about them is to consider stops to be seizures and frisks to be searches. To conduct a lawful

CASE IN POINT

Florida v. Bostick

The Case

Florida v. Bostick,
501 U.S. 429, 111 S.Ct. 2382 (1991)

The Point

The test of what constitutes seizure is whether the suspect is free to decline an officer's request for a search and terminate the encounter.

In Broward County, Florida, sheriff's department officers boarded a bus at a scheduled stop and asked passengers for permission to search their luggage for drugs. Two officers asked Terrance Bostick if they could search his luggage and advised him of his right to refuse. Bostick gave his permission, and the officers found cocaine in his luggage. Bostick was arrested and later convicted of cocaine possession. The Supreme Court upheld his conviction because he had allowed his luggage to be searched. The officers' actions did not constitute seizure under the Fourth Amendment because, according to the court, "taking into account all of the circumstances surrounding the encounter, a reasonable passenger would feel free to decline the officers' requests or otherwise terminate the encounter."

frisk, the stop must meet the conditions of a lawful seizure. It is useful to consider these actions individually:

1. Two types of situations in which police officers stop suspects are of concern to the student of the Fourth Amendment. These two situations are **actual-seizure stops** and **show-of-authority stops**. Actual-seizure stops involve police officers physically grabbing a person and restricting his or her freedom. Show-of-authority stops involve the officers showing their authority (such as flashing their badges) and the suspects submitting to it. The Supreme Court uses a **reasonable stop standard** that considers whether a reasonable person would feel free to terminate the encounter in deciding if the stop is constitutional. The courts have ruled on the admissibility of stops in a wide range of circumstances. Some of the issues that have been considered by the courts are as follows:
   - Whether the police officers have reasonable suspicion to stop a suspect
   - Whether an anonymous tip provides sufficient reason to make a stop
   - Whether race can be considered a valid indicator for reasonable suspicion
   - Whether preestablished profiles are valid reasons to make a stop
   - How law enforcement officers can stop individuals at international borders
   - How roadblocks can be constitutionally employed

   The legality of a stop, then, is highly contextualized and has been codified into procedural law by decisions made on a wide range of cases.[59]
2. Stops are seizures; frisks are searches. Although these two actions are closely linked, they are also quite different procedures that the law considers in great detail. Law enforcement officers may conduct a legal stop but engage in an illegal search. A frisk involves a light patting of the outer clothing of a suspect by the officer with the intent to determine if a weapon is present. However, if the officer detects contraband (such as drugs) during the frisk, then even though the frisk was initiated to detect weapons, an arrest can be made for drug possession or even intent to sell. At issue is the extent of the frisk. Frisks are considered the least invasive type of search; a full body-cavity searches are the most invasive. The court will consider evidence obtained in a frisk only if it is confident that the evidence

actual-seizure stop An incident in which police officers physically restrain a person and restrict his or her freedom.

show-of-authority stop An incident in which police show a sign of authority (such as flashing a badge), and the suspect submits.

reasonable stop standard A Supreme Court measure that considers constitutionality on whether a reasonable person would feel free to terminate an encounter with law enforcement personnel.

FOCUS ON ETHICS

Improbable Cause

As a probationary rookie police officer, you are riding with your training officer, whom you have grown to respect and like. One night he tells you that it is time to learn how to do real police work. He spots a carload of young black males cruising the local strip mall and turns his blue lights on and pulls them over to the side of the street. He cautiously approaches the car when one of the passengers says, "Hey, cop. I'm a criminal justice major in college and I want to know what your probable cause is for pulling us over. This looks like a typical case of Driving While Black. We didn't do nothing."

Your training officer, himself a black man, walks to the back of the car. Using his large flashlight, he smashes the left taillight and says, "You have a broken taillight with an inoperative turn signal. That's my probable cause. Now I want each of you to exit the car slowly and lie facedown on the street. We'll start with you, Mr. Criminal Justice Major."

A search of the youth and the car results in the discovery of nine marijuana cigarettes and an unloaded .22 caliber pistol under the front seat. Despite the protests of the youths, your training officer tells you to arrest the subjects and says, "I'm giving you the credit for this one, rookie. You get the collar and you will get to go to court and testify. It will be great experience for you."

You know you are being tested here, but you are not sure exactly what the right answer is. On one hand, your training officer may be trying to determine whether you will go along with the illegal stop and bow to his pressure. He could be seeing if you will back a fellow police officer. On the other hand, the youth with the big mouth looks uncannily like your training officer, and could even pass for his son. You wonder if you have been set up, in which case the right answer would be to challenge your training officer and refuse to make the arrest, thus showing that your first loyalty is to the law.

WHAT DO YOU DO?

1. Challenge your training officer. Insist that you do what the law requires.
2. Support your training officer. You understand that in order to be an effective police officer, you must be trusted by fellow officers even if they want you to commit minor violations.

was discovered by officers conducting the frisk with the intention of detecting weapons to ensure their own safety.[60]

Arrests

An arrest is more invasive than a stop. It involves being taken into custody, photographed, fingerprinted, interrogated, and booked (or formally charged with a crime). A suspect who is stopped and frisked may be released, but if the case proceeds to the arrest phase, then a temporary loss of liberty results. Because this loss of liberty can last anywhere from a few hours to a few days, a higher standard of suspicion of guilt is required. Although reasonable suspicion is sufficient for a stop and frisk, arrest requires the police officers to have probable cause that the suspect committed a crime.[61]

The way the police arrest suspects is also important. The amount of force used in the arrest should be consistent with maintaining the dignity of the suspects as much as circumstances allow. The court has ruled that deadly force is constitutionally unreasonable if it is used simply because the felony suspect is fleeing. In order to use deadly force, the officer must believe the suspect to be a threat to others. The court also has spoken to the need to have a warrant to arrest someone in his or her home.[62] Although a multitude of circumstances and situations complicate the sanctity-of-the-home concept (such as when the police

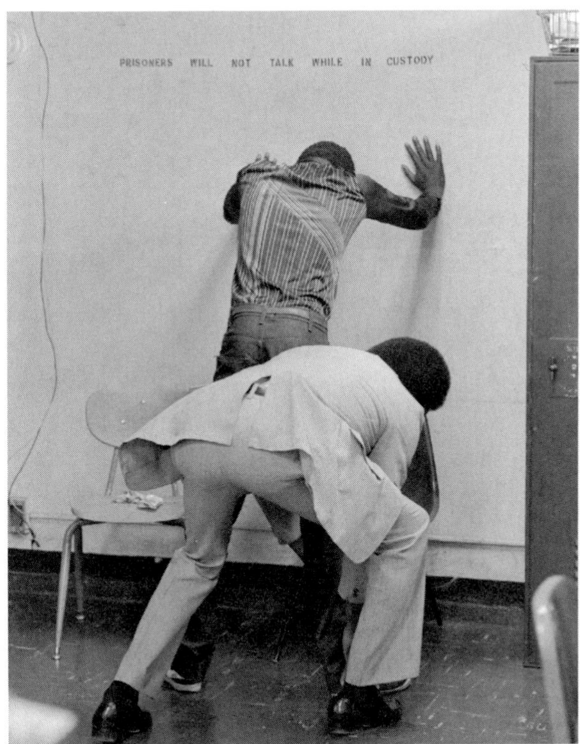

A frisk is different from a search. It is less intrusive. Here, an officer "pats down" a suspect as part of a frisk.

Courtesy of CORBIS-NY.

are chasing a suspect who runs into a residence), these exceptions must be considered in light of the language and intention of the Fourth Amendment's guarantee that people should be secure in their homes. To arrest someone at home, the court recommends four restrictions:

1. **The crime should be a felony.** This guards against arbitrary and abusive arrests and ensures that homes are invaded only for serious crimes.
2. **The police must knock and announce.** This allows the individuals to get dressed and open the front door, thus assuring them some degree of dignity.
3. **The arrest should be made in daylight.** The fear produced by someone pounding on the door in the middle of the night should be avoided.
4. **The police must meet a stringent probable-cause requirement that the suspect is in fact at home.** This guards against the police entering the home and frightening others who may live there or against them ransacking the home in their search for the suspect.[63]

Bear in mind that the four criteria listed here refer to arrests in homes, not searches. If these requirements were applied to drug busts, then the suspects would have opportunities to dispose of evidence.

Interrogation, Confessions, and the Exclusionary Rule

One of the primary ways that law enforcement officials gather information about crime is from the criminals themselves. By questioning suspects, the police can develop the required evidence to charge, prosecute, and convict lawbreakers. Although this interrogation of possible wrongdoers is exactly what we expect of the police, there are limits placed on exactly what methods can be used and on what types of help to which the suspects are entitled. Even though the police may have good reason to suspect that an individual has committed a crime, that individual has constitutional rights that must be respected in the questioning process. These rights stem from the Fifth, Sixth, and Fourteenth Amendments of the Constitution (see Table 6.1).

1. **Fifth Amendment self-incrimination clause.** "No person . . . shall be compelled in any criminal case to be a witness against himself."

NEWS FLASH

Watch Your Car

Automobile owners in many states now have the option of placing stickers on their cars allowing police to pull them over without cause between the hours of 1 A.M. and 5 A.M. Drivers who register in the "Watch Your Car" program are entered into a State Patrol database. If officers see the car on the road during the allotted hours, they may pull it over to check who is driving. The program targets not only car thieves, but teenagers who may be out without their parents' knowledge.

According to the *Seattle Times,* a local police sergeant said Texas' rate of automobile thefts dropped 50 percent in three years under the program. The U.S. Bureau of Justice Assistance says the program does not conflict with the Fourth Amendment because participation in it is voluntary.

Congress authorized the program in the 1994 Motor Vehicle Theft Prevention Act.

Source: "Decal Would Let Officers Pull Car Over," *Seattle Times,* June 5, 2001, http://seattletimes.nwsource.com/html/localnews/134303067_cartheft05m.html.

TABLE 6.1

Constitutional Amendments Related to Interrogation

Amendment	Text
Fifth Amendment	No person shall be held to answer for a capital, or otherwise infamous crime, unless on a presentment or indictment of a Grand Jury, except in cases arising in the land or naval forces, or in the Militia, when in actual service in time of War or public danger; nor shall any person be subject for the same offence to be twice put in jeopardy of life or limb; nor shall be compelled in any criminal case to be a witness against himself, nor be deprived of life, liberty, or property, without due process of law; nor shall private property be taken for public use, without just compensation.
Sixth Amendment	In all criminal prosecutions, the accused shall enjoy the right to a speedy and public trial, by an impartial jury of the State and district wherein the crime shall have been committed, which district shall have been previously ascertained by law, and to be informed of the nature and cause of the accusation; to be confronted with the witnesses against him; to have compulsory process for obtaining witnesses in his favor, and to have the Assistance of Counsel for his defence.
Fourteenth Amendment	Section 1. All persons born or naturalized in the United States and subject to the jurisdiction thereof, are citizens of the United States and of the State wherein they reside. No State shall make or enforce any law which shall abridge the privileges or immunities of citizens of the United States; nor shall any State deprive any person of life, liberty, or property, without due process of law; nor deny to any person within its jurisdiction the equal protection of the laws.

2. **Sixth Amendment right-to-counsel clause.** "In all criminal prosecutions, the accused shall . . . have the assistance of counsel for his defense."
3. **Fourteenth Amendment due process clause.** "No state shall . . . deprive any person of life, liberty, or property without due process of law."

These amendments are used by defense attorneys and the court to oversee how the police conduct interrogations, elicit confessions, and seize evidence. In some cases law enforcement officials may violate the law in conducting these activities, and the evidence gathered can be disallowed in court. We will deal with these issues in greater detail in Chapter 10 where we will examine them in the context of all the legal rights given to suspects. They are highlighted here to remind us that mistakes made at this stage by law enforcement officials will be ruled on at a later stage of the criminal justice process.[64]

Summary

In this discussion of controlling the police, we have considered the occupation as having a unique character that requires society's constant vigilance to ensure that law enforcement is conducted under lawful means. The alternative is to have a police state in which law enforcement agencies (even if they are well meaning) trample the rights of citizens and are used as a political tool of whoever happens to be in power. One of the most laudable features about policing in the United States is that the system protects the rights of even the most disenfranchised individuals such as the poor, the homeless, the incarcerated, the drunk, and the insane. The public generally has an idealized view of policing. Policing is a difficult, complex, and dangerous job. It is made even more difficult by the constraints under which law enforcement officers must pursue the goals of maintaining order, servicing citizens' needs, and detecting and apprehending offenders.

Police officers exercise a great amount of discretion in their daily routines. The police have significant decision-making authority in deciding which behaviors are labeled as crime, which behaviors are labeled as felonies or misdemeanors, and which cases are inserted into the criminal justice system. Unlike many occupations, the police officer operates outside the immediate purview of supervisors and therefore must be trained to use discretion wisely.

One of the duties of law enforcement is to secure government buildings. While it might be unexciting and uncomfortable (especially in cold weather), this function is a vital part of our collective security.

Courtesy of CORBIS-NY.

Police departments are organized like military units. Uniforms, ranks, a strict hierarchical chain of command, and daily inspection are all features of the military that have found their way into police organizations. Although going to war and patrolling a neighborhood are quite different, the quasi-military nature of police organizations exerts a profound influence on how policing is accomplished in the United States and presented to the public. James Q. Wilson provided a typology of policing styles that includes the watchman style, the legalistic style, and the service style. Most police departments may incorporate aspects of each of these styles, and the type of policing style used can have a profound influence on how the department defines and executes the law enforcement mission.

Police officers develop an occupational orientation that makes it difficult for observers to appreciate how the demands of police work affect their lives. According to Jerome Skolnick, officers develop a "policeman's working personality" around the issues of danger, isolation, and authority.

Unfortunately, some police officers cannot resist the temptation to abuse their authority. Although we can safely assume that serious corruption is confined to only a few officers, we do know that at times corruption has been widespread. From time to time, the corruption is exposed by studies such as that of the Knapp Commission, and reforms and changes are made.

The work of police officers is controlled by procedural laws. The courts have developed a wide range of guidelines governing searches and seizures and stop and frisks. The courts have attempted to strike a balance between the rights of citizens and the legitimate safety needs of society in outlining the requirements under which law enforcement officers must work.

Although this chapter focused on issues concerning controlling the police, it has not been the intention to suggest that police officers are not dedicated professionals attempting to do a difficult job under trying circumstances. Rather, the lesson the student should take from this chapter is that because of the constraints we place on the enforcement of the law, our society is stronger and more free. Do problems occur from time to time? Certainly, and the next chapter will deal with issues such as racial profiling, use of excessive force, and police officer stress. However, the strength of our democracy lies in the oversight of our institutions. Because law enforcement is such a fundamental task for any society, it will always be a controversial occupation in the United States.

KEY TERMS

actual-seizure stop p. 203
grabbable area p. 199
grass-eaters p. 192
legalistic style p. 188
meat-eaters p. 192
policeman's working personality p. 189
probable cause p. 193
racial profiling p. 181
reasonable stop standard p. 203
reasonable suspicion p. 200
seizure p. 202
service style p. 188
show-of-authority stop p. 203
stop p. 202
stop and frisk p. 202
watchman style p. 188

REVIEW QUESTIONS

1. Can discretion ever be removed from the role of the street-level police officer? What would be the likely consequences of such a change in the way laws are enforced?
2. Do we expect too much of our law enforcement officers? How does the concept that the police themselves have of their job contribute to our unrealistic expectations?
3. Why are the police patterned after the military style of organization? What are the advantages and disadvantages of this structure?
4. James Q. Wilson presented three types of policing styles. Compare and contrast these styles and tell which one you think is the most effective.

5. What is the police subculture? In what ways might it be problematic for the fair and impartial application of the law?
6. In what ways does the war on drugs contribute to police corruption?
7. What do we mean by the term *procedural law?* Where in the U.S. Constitution do we find the authority for our laws concerning searches?

SUGGESTED FURTHER READING

Atkins, Burton, and Mark Pogrebin. *The Invisible Justice System: Discretion and the Law.* Cincinnati: Anderson, 1978.

Barker, Thomas, Ronald D. Hunter, and Jeffrey P. Rush. *Police Systems and Practices: An Introduction.* Englewood Cliffs, NJ: Prentice Hall, 1994.

Davis, Kenneth Culp. *Police Discretion.* St. Paul, MN: West, 1975.

Kappler, Victor E. *The Police and Society: Touchstone Readings.* Prospect Heights, IL: Waveland Press, 1999.

Skolnick, Jerome H. *Justice Without Trial: Law Enforcement in Democratic Society.* New York: John Wiley and Sons, 1966.

Wilson, James Q. *Varieties of Police Behavior: The Management of Law and Order in Eight Communities.* New York: Atheneum, 1973.

ENDNOTES

1. Kenneth Culp Davis, *Police Discretion* (St. Paul: West, 1975).
2. Arthur Rosett, "Discretion, Severity and Legality in Criminal Justice," in *The Invisible Justice System: Discretion and the Law,* eds. Burton Atkins and Mark Pogrebin (Cincinnati: Anderson, 1978), 24–33.
3. Ibid., 25.
4. Davis, *Police Discretion,* 65-66. Davis titles Chapter 3, "The Pervasive False Pretense of Full Enforcement."
5. Albert Reiss, Jr., "Discretionary Justice in the United States," in *The Invisible Justice System: Discretion and the Law,* eds. Burton Atkins and Mark Pogrebin (Cincinnati: Anderson, 1978), 41–58.
6. Raymond Goldberg, *Drugs Across the Spectrum* (Englewood, CO: Morton, 1997), 80.
7. Jerome H. Skolnick and Elliot Currie, *Crisis in American Institutions* (Boston: Little, Brown and Company, 1973). See especially the sections on police and criminal law and corrections.
8. Davis, *Police Discretion,* 83.
9. Clearly, the police develop strategies that target high crime areas or events where crime is likely to appear. The difference between the police presence at a symphony orchestra performance and at a basketball tournament is likely to be significant even though the size of the crowd is the same.
10. American Friends Service Committee, "Discretion," in *The Invisible Justice System: Discretion and the Law,* eds. Burton Atkins and Mark Pogrebin (Cincinnati: Anderson, 1978), 35–40. This report argues that discretion should be removed from the criminal justice system so that constitutional protections of due process and equal application of the law will apply to everyone.
11. The police claim as part of their mandate the right to use force to resolve societal problems. The rest of us are mostly happy to let the police do this "dirty work" on our behalf. This relationship has been sanctioned by legislatures that pass laws giving the police their powers. Like most occupations, law enforcement officials guard their powers by forming unions, lobbying lawmakers, maintaining the image they present to the public, and ensuring that rival groups, such as the private security industry, are given only limited authority. For an excellent discussion of how occupations, especially the police, establish their mandates, see Peter K. Manning's, "The Police: Mandate, Strategies, and Appearances."
12. Peter K. Manning, "The Police: Mandate, Strategies and Appearances," in *The Police and Society: Touchstone Readings,* 2nd ed., ed. Victor E. Kappeler (Prospect Heights, IL: Waveland Press, 1999), 94–122.
13. Manning qualified these assumptions, which he drew from a number of studies conducted mainly in the 1960s, with the following paragraph, "Some qualifications about these postulates are in order. They apply primarily to the American non college-educated patrolman. They are less applicable to administrators of urban police departments and to members of minority groups within these departments. Nor do they apply accurately to non-urban, state, and federal policemen." (p. 99)
14. "The Police," Manning, 99.
15. Ibid., 100–101.
16. Jack R. Greene and Carl B. Klockars, "What Police Do," in *Thinking About Police: Contemporary Readings,* 2nd ed., eds. Carl B. Klockars and Stephen D. Mastrofski (New York: McGraw-Hill, 1991), 273–284. Greene and Klockars contended that the police do

spend more time on crime-related work than previous studies have indicated.

17. Thomas Barker, Ronald D. Hunter, and Jeffery P. Rush, *Police Systems and Practices: An Introduction* (Englewood Cliffs, NJ: Prentice Hall, 1994). These authors identified three primary roles for law enforcement: crime-fighter, order maintenance, and service. They discussed the consequences of the crime-fighter image that they contended is promoted by the public, the media, and the police themselves. These authors said of the the crime-fighter image, "in addition to creating unrealistic expectations about the police's ability to reduce crime, this narrow view prevents an informed analysis of the use of police resources." (p. 102)
18. Samuel Walker and Charles M. Katz, *The Police in America: An Introduction,* 4th ed. (Boston: McGraw-Hill, 2001), 464.
19. Egon Bittner, "The Quasi-Military Organization of the Police," in *The Police and Society: Touchstone Readings,* 2nd ed., ed. Victor E. Kappeler (Prospect Heights, IL: Waveland Press, 1999), 171.
20. Bittner, "Quasi-Military," 174–175.
21. Ibid., 176.
22. Phillip B. Taft, Jr., "Policing the New Immigrant Ghettos," in *Thinking About Police: Contemporary Readings,* 2nd ed., eds. Carl B. Klockars and Stephen D. Mastrofski (New York: McGraw-Hill, 1991), 307–315.
23. James Q. Wilson, *Varieties of Police Behavior: The Management of Law and Order in Eight Communities* (New York: Atheneum, 1968).
24. Ibid., 17–34.
25. Ibid., 140–171.
26. Ibid., 172–199.
27. Ibid., 200–226.
28. John Von Maanen, "Kinsmen in Repose: Occupational Perspectives of Patrolmen," in *The Police and Society: Touchstone Readings,* 2nd ed., ed. Victor E. Kappeler (Prospect Heights, IL: Waveland Press, 1999), 221. See also Victor E. Kappeler, Richard D. Sluder, and Geoffery P. Alpert, "Breeding Deviant Conformity: Police Ideology and Culture," in *The Police and Society: Touchstone Readings,* p. 239.
29. *Master status* is a sociological term that refers to a status or a label that dominates over all other positive or negative labels. For instance, if you introduced your boyfriend to your parents and mentioned that he had served time in prison for rape, nothing else you could say could earn their trust of him. Conversely, a label such as "Medal of Honor winner" will supercede just about any other label.
30. Jerome H. Skolnick, *Justice Without Trial: Law Enforcement in Democratic Society* (New York: John Wiley and Sons, 1966).
31. Ibid., 43.
32. Ibid., 45.
33. Ibid., 47.
34. Ibid., 42–70.
35. Michael D. Lymon, *The Police: An Introduction* (Upper Saddle River, NJ: Prentice Hall, 2002). Lyman provided an excellent chapter on the topic, Chapter 8: "Personal Administration."
36. Lawrence W. Sherman, *Police Corruption: A Sociological Perspective* (Garden City, NY: Anchor Books, 1974). See particularly Sherman's introductory chapter with its important typology of police corruption.
37. Knapp Commission, "An Example of Police Corruption: Knapp Commission Report in New York City," in *Police Deviance,* eds. Thomas Barker and David L. Carter (Cincinnati: Pilgrimage, 1986), 28.
38. Peter K. Manning and Lawrence John Redlinger, "Invitational Edges," in *Thinking About Police: Contemporary Readings,* 2nd ed., eds. Carl B. Klockars and Stephen D. Mastrofski (New York: McGraw-Hill, 1991), 398–413.
39. Joel Samaha, *Criminal Procedure,* 5th ed. (Belmont, CA: Wadsworth, 2002), 88.
40. As quoted in Samaha, *Criminal Procedure,* 88.
41. *Silverman v. United States,* 365 U.S. 505, 81 S.Ct. 679 (1961).
42. *Katz v. United States,* 389, U.S. 347, 88 S.Ct. 507 (1967).
43. Roadblocks used during DUI crackdowns are not illegal according to the Fourth Amendment because all cars are stopped. Probable cause is not an issue because no one is singled out for special treatment.
44. *California v. Ciraolo,* 476 U.S. 207, 106 S.Ct. 1809 (1986); *United States v. White,* 401 U.S. 745, 91 S.Ct. 1122 (1971).
45. *United States v. Dunn,* 480 U.S. 294, 107 S.Ct. 1134 (1987).
46. Samaha, *Criminal Procedure,* 112.
47. *Payton v. New York,* 445 U.S. 573, 100 S.Ct. 1371 (1980). White, Burger, and Rehnquist.
48. *Stanford v. Texas,* 379 U.S. 476, 85 S.Ct. 506 (1965); *Maryland v. Garrison,* 480 U.S. 79, 107 S.Ct. 1013 (1987); *Wilson v. Arkansas,* 514 U.S. 927, 115 S.Ct. 1914 (1995); *Richards v. Wisconsin,* 520 U.S. 385, 117 S.Ct. 1416 (1997).
49. *Chimel v. California,* 395 U.S. 752, 89 S.Ct. 2034 (1969), *New York v. Belton,* 453 U.S. 454, 101 S.Ct. 2860 (1981).

50. *Schneckloth v. Bustamonte,* 412 U.S. 218, 93 S.Ct. 2041, (1973); *United States v. Rodney,* 956 F.2d 295, 297 (D.C. Cir. 1992); *Illinois v. Rodriguez,* 497 U.S. 177, 110 S.Ct. 2793; (1990).
51. *United States v. Santana,* 427 U.S. 38, 96 S.Ct. 2406, (1976); *Cupp v. Murphy,* 412 U.S. 291, 93 S.Ct. 2000 (1973); *Ker v. California,* 374 U.S. 23, 83 S.Ct. 1623 (1963).
52. *Carroll v. United States,* 267 U.S. 132, 45 S.Ct. 280 (1925); *Wyoming v. Houghton,* 526 U.S. 295, 119 S.Ct. 1297 (1999).
53. *South Dakota v. Opperman,* 428 U.S. 364, 96 S.Ct. 3092 (1976).
54. *United States v. Ramsey,* 431 U.S. 606, 97 S.Ct. 1972 (1977).
55. *Hudson v. Palmer,* 468 U.S. 517, 104 S.Ct. 3194, (1984); *Bell v. Wolfish,* 441 U.S. 520, 99 S.Ct. 1861 (1979); *Mary Beth G. v. City of Chicago,* 723 F.2d, 1263 (7th cir, 1983).
56. *State v. Hunter,* 831 P.2d, 1033 (Utah Ct. App. 1992); *New Jersey v. T.L.O.,* 469 U.S. 325, 105 S.Ct. 733 (1985).
57. *Hester v. United States,* 265 U.S. 57, 44 S.Ct. 445 (1924); *Abel v. United States,* 362 U.S. 217, 80 S.Ct. 683 (1960); *California v. Greenwood,* 486 U.S. 35, 108 S.Ct. 1625 (1988).
58. Samaha, *Criminal Procedure,* 123. *California v. Hoderi* D.V, 499 U.S. 621, 111 S.Ct. 1547 (1991).
59. *Terry v. Ohio,* 392 U.S. 1, 99 S.Ct. 1868 (1968).
60. *State v. Morrison,* Ohio App. 8 Dist. (1999).
61. *Illinois v. Gates,* 462 U.S. 213, 103 S.Ct. 2317, (1983).
62. *Payton v. New York,* 445 U.S. 573, 100 S.Ct. 1371 (1980).
63. *National Treasury Employees Union v. Von Raab,* 489 U.S. 656, 109 S.Ct. 1384, (1989).
64. Samaha, *Criminal Procedure,* 355.

outline

CHAPTER 7

Issues in Policing

CHAPTER 5, DEALING WITH THE HISTORY, AND CHAPTER 6, dealing with the organization of the police, illustrated how important and difficult the law enforcement mission has become. This chapter will focus on some additional issues that police agencies continue to grapple with, although many of these issues have been at the core of law enforcement for a very long time.

1. How do we determine the correct use of force by the police? Can policies be developed that will help the police make these split-second decisions?
2. How can we ensure that police organizations recruit and promote minorities and women? How much progress has been made in diversifying law enforcement over the past 40 years?
3. How can the police be integrated more into the community? Are strategies such as community policing and problem-oriented policing effective?
4. What type of education should law enforcement officers have?
5. What are the sources and results of police stress? What reasonable policies can be enacted to reduce the social and human costs of police work?

objectives

After reading this chapter, the student should be able to:

1. Explain why, and under what circumstances, the use of force is legitimate.
2. Discuss the advantages and issues of using Special Weapons and Tactics (SWAT) teams.
3. Appreciate the special issues that face female police officers.
4. Understand how female offenders and victims present unique problems for law enforcement.
5. Appreciate the special issues faced by minority police officers.
6. Understand how racial profiling is an old practice but a new concern for law enforcement.
7. Describe how community policing differs from traditional police practices.
8. Describe how problem-oriented policing differs from traditional police practices.
9. Explain the broken windows theory and discuss why it is problematic.
10. Discuss the special police problems that cause stress.

By studying these issues, we can develop a greater appreciation for the role of the police in society. The public will better understand and support the work of law enforcement to the extent that these problems can be addressed.

Police Use of Force

use of force
The legal police use of violence to enforce the law. Excessive use of force is considered police brutality.

According to Egon Bittner, civilized society has been developing mechanisms to eliminate the legitimacy of all forms of force. From international diplomacy to the internal workings of the criminal justice system, the **use of force** has been relegated to last-resort status. Bittner contrasted this movement of the modern state with the Roman Empire, which employed "*debellare superbos,* i.e., to subdue the haughty by force."[1] Today, physical force is considered legitimate only under the following conditions:

1. **Self-defense.** Self-defense laws vary from state to state, but the generally accepted principle is that after exhausting all other means of avoiding harm, including retreat, force may be used to protect oneself or others. This means that in later court proceedings, one may be required to show how other options were ineffectively used or were unavailable when the force was employed in the name of self-defense.
2. **Specifically deputized persons against some specifically named persons.** In this case, Bittner was referring to agents such as mental hospital attendants and corrections officers. Here, the right to use force is given to those whose jobs may require them to deal with dangerous persons in a special context. What is important to remember is that the right to use force does not extend beyond the confines of the job. Their jurisdiction is limited to the hospital or the prison; the law does not recognize their actions in other parts of society.
3. **Police force.** This last legitimate use of force is much broader than the previous two. Comparatively, it appears to be almost unrestricted, but as we examine it

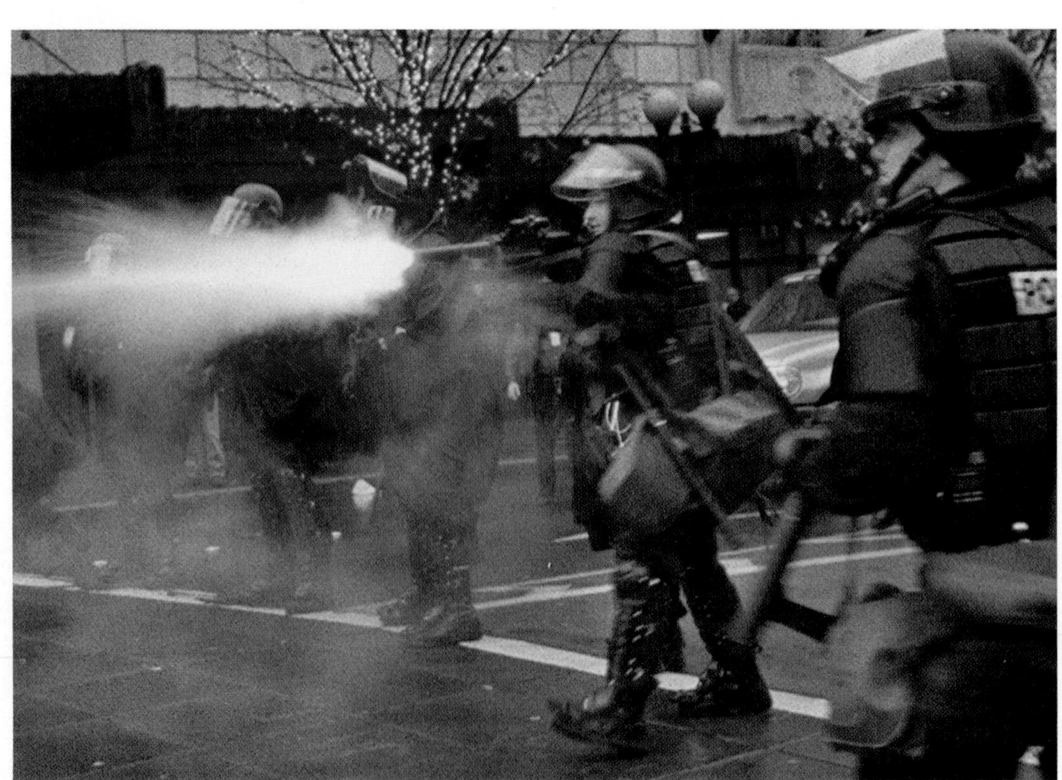

Law enforcement officers are mandated to use force in the name of society. The police are the institution that is trained and equipped to use legitimate force against lawbreakers.
Courtesy of CORBIS-NY.

more closely, we can see how it is circumscribed quite severely. According to Bittner, the restrictions of police use of force are as follows:

a. Limited to certain types of situations. In some jurisdictions, the police may shoot to kill dangerous fleeing felons, but not those who have committed misdemeanors.
b. The police may use force only in the performance of official duties and not to advance their personal interests or the private interests of other persons.
c. The police may not use force maliciously or frivolously.[2]

Although these guidelines appear to limit the use of force by police and other agents of society, Bittner said they are essentially meaningless. No one really knows what is meant by the "lawful use of force" because each incident is different, and it is impossible to cover all the circumstances in which police may use force. It is curious how society places the police in such a precarious position when it comes to using force. On one hand, we expect them to use reasonable force when our interests are at stake; on the other hand, we decide what is reasonable force only after the fact. We know that the police use force in making arrests and keeping order. The problem is that we know very little about how this force is used and how often the police decide to use force. In a review of studies about police force, Kenneth Adams summarized what we know about police use of force and where studies are still needed (see Figure 7.1).

Someone who considers calling the police into a situation spends much of that time considering the possibility that the situation may require an outside party to mediate it and possibly use force. For instance, we may be ready to use force ourselves but do not want to deal with the possibilities of lawsuits, retaliation, and the chance that someone may instead call the police on us. We call the police to use force on our behalf because they have been trained and are armed and authorized to do so. However, because the legitimate use of police force is so dependent on the context of the situation, and because the police must make decisions in the heat of the moment and often under dangerous conditions, the lawfulness of the use of force becomes problematic when considered after the fact.[3] This puts the police in a no-win situation. Failure to use appropriate force may risk injury or death to themselves or others. The use of too much force may result in

Figure 7.1
Police Use of Force

What we know with substantial confidence

Police use force infrequently.

Use of force typically occurs at the lower end of the physical spectrum, involving grabbing, pushing, or shoving.

Use of force typically occurs when a suspect resists arrest.

What we know with modest confidence

Use of force appears to be unrelated to an officer's personal characteristics, such as age, gender, and ethnicity.

Use of force is more likely to occur when police are dealing with persons under the influence of alcohol or drugs, or who are mentally ill.

A small proportion of officers are disproportionately involved in use-of-force incidents.

What we do not know

The incidence of wrongful use of force.

The impact of differences in police organizations, including administrative policies, hiring, training, discipline, and use of technology on excessive and illegal force.

The influences of situational characteristics on police use of force and the transactional nature of these events.

Source: Kenneth Adams, "What We Know About Police Use of Force," in *Use of Force by Police: Overview of National and Local Data* (Washington, DC: National Institute of Justice, NCJ 176330, October 1999).

CASE IN POINT

Tennessee v. Garner

The Case

Tennessee v. Garner, 471 U.S. 1; 105 S.Ct. 1694 (1985)

The Point

Deadly force now may only be used if the suspect(s) pose a threat to the lives of police officers or bystanders.

In 1974 Edward Garner, 15, and a friend were in a house at night at which the owners were not present. A neighbor reported to police that someone had broken into the home. When the officers arrived, they saw someone running away, shouted warnings to stop, then shot at Garner, who was climbing a fence. The officer said that he was "reasonably sure" that Garner was unarmed, but thought that once he got over the fence, he would elude capture. One of the bullets struck Garner in the back of the head, and he died later on the operating table. Because the officers suspected the boys of a felony, burglarizing the house, they believed they were justified in shooting at the boys to stop them. Garner's father filed suit, claiming that his son's constitutional rights were violated. By 1985 the Supreme Court decided that the use of deadly force was not warranted. Justice Byron White wrote, "It is no doubt unfortunate when a suspect who is in sight escapes, but the fact that the police arrive a little late or are a little slower afoot does not always justify killing the suspect. A police officer may not seize an unarmed, non-dangerous suspect by shooting him dead."

disciplinary action. According to Bittner, we ask police to make a decision requiring the exercise of two conflicting parts of the nature of police work: They must simultaneously balance their physical prowess with professional acumen.[4]

The expectation of how much and what type of force an officer will use in any given situation will vary according to a number of factors (see Table 7.1). The time of day, whether the officer is alone or working with a partner, the size and gender of the suspect, and the area of the city can all influence whether, and how much, force is used. A guide for police officers is to use only the force required to bring order to a situation and no more. This is a highly contingent judgment and one for which considerable variation can be expected. Additionally, if force is applied appropriately, we would expect to see relatively low levels of force used more often than deadly force. In one national study, Antony Pate and Lorie Fridell surveyed 1,697 law enforcement agencies and came up with a snapshot of the use of force per 1,000 officers.[5] This study showed that the rate of the use of police force declined significantly as the level of force increased. Whereas almost half the police officers (490.4 per thousand) reported using handcuffs or leg restraints during 1991, only one-tenth of one percent reported shooting and killing a civilian. In fact, the vast majority of police force was of a relatively minor type. Given that police use force routinely, it should be of some comfort to realize that they use extreme force rarely. The cases of extreme use of force that can be labeled police brutality result in the negative picture that many have of contemporary police work.

Police as Soldiers

The police and the military have a lot in common. Uniforms, classification of status by rank, the use of weapons, and chains of command are features of both organizations. The military model for the police mission, however, is problematic.[6] The analogy of the police as soldiers is inexact and faulty and creates problems when the use of police force is at issue. According to police scholars Jerome Skolnick and James Fyfe:

> *(In responding to a comparison of policing to the Gulf War) . . . it relies upon an inexact analogy and is far more likely to produce unnecessary violence and antagonism than to result in effective policing. The lines between friend and foe were*

TABLE 7.1

Reported Incidents of Police Use of Force per 1,000 Sworn Officers in City Departments during 1991

Type of Force	Rate per 1,000 Officers
Handcuff/leg restraint	490.4
Bodily force	272.2
Come-alongs	226.6
Unholstering weapon	129.9
Swarm	126.7
Twist/wrist locks	80.9
Firm grip	57.7
Chemical agents	36.2
Batons	36.0
Flashlights	21.7
Dog attack/bites	6.5
Electrical devices (TASER)	5.4
Civilians shot at, not hit	3.0
Other impact devices	2.4
Neck restraints/unconsciousness rendering holds	1.4
Vehicle rammings	1.0
Civilians shot, killed	.9
Civilians shot, wounded	.2

Source: Tom McEwen, *National Data Collection on Police Use of Force* (Washington, DC: Bureau of Justice Statistics/National Institute of Justice, 1996), 34. Online at http://www.ojp.usdoj.gov/bjs/pub/pdf/ndcopuof.pdf.

clear in the Arabian desert, but police officers on American streets too often rely on ambiguous clues and stereotypes in trying to identify the enemies in their war. When officers act on such signals and roust people who turn out to be guilty of no more than being in what officers view as the wrong place at the wrong time—young black men on inner-city streets late at night, for example—the police may create enemies where none had previously existed.[7]

There is a fundamental difference between how military organizations and police agencies deal with the issue of decision making.[8] In military organizations, the important decisions are made at the top of the chain of command and flow downward. In policing, the essential discretion is vested in the judgment of the individual police officer who determines when a crime has been committed and whether to make an arrest. Even though the police agency has a hierarchical structure that, on the surface, resembles a military organization, the nature of discretion and the authority for decision making is actually reversed.

The military overtones of police departments have become entrenched in the war-on-crime mentality that politicians and the media promote.[9] In many ways, the idea of waging war on crime is an attractive way to think about a serious social problem. Much like

The police often must act in a coordinated way. The similarity between the military and law enforcement is obvious when the police respond to mass protests.
Courtesy of CORBIS-NY.

former President Lyndon Johnson's war on poverty the war on crime implies that, finally, we are going to allocate the resources and mobilize the troops necessary to rid ourselves of the problem once and for all.[10] The war metaphor implies that sacrifices are going to be made and that a final victory over the enemy is possible. However, as Skolnick and Fyfe have already said, "police officer as soldier" is not a realistic or productive way to think about how the police do their job.

Police Use of Force and SWAT Teams

The militarization of the police and the war-on-crime analogy are the most apparent in the Special Weapons and Tactics (SWAT) divisions of law enforcement agencies. The public has a love–hate view of these units. On one hand, they are portrayed as jack-booted thugs that kick down homeowners' doors and employ police-state tactics to oppress people. On the other hand, they are sometimes viewed as professionals who must do a delicate and unpleasant job to protect the rest of us from terrorists, hostage takers, bank robbers, and mentally ill people who are violent.[11] The latter of these two characterizations is undoubtedly the more accurate portrayal of the work done by SWAT teams. In many ways, they are the elite of the police force. These officers are highly trained volunteers willing to do the more risk-laden tasks while employing the police mandate to use force. The types of situations in which a SWAT team may be used include, but are not limited to, the following:

1. Protecting police officers engaged in crowd control from sniper attack
2. Providing high-ground and perimeter security for visiting dignitaries
3. Rescuing hostages
4. Providing for the nonviolent apprehension of desperate barricaded suspects
5. Providing control-assault firepower in certain nonriot situations
6. Rescuing officers or citizens endangered by gunfire
7. Neutralizing guerrilla or terrorist operations against government personnel, property, or the general populace

Clearly, there are legitimate reasons to have SWAT teams. Law enforcement agencies are occasionally required to perform unpleasant and dangerous tasks. It makes sense to

SWAT teams are part of every major law enforcement agency. They respond to hostage situations, terrorist attacks, and other situations that may require force.

Courtesy of CORBIS-NY.

have some specially trained officers to respond to unusual situations. However, some critics are concerned that merely having a SWAT team means that it will be employed in situations that can be handled in more routine ways. A SWAT team can reduce the danger to officers and civilians during a crisis situation, but it can also use force to resolve a given situation with a quick decision. The Center for Research on Criminal Justice concluded in 1977 that, "The actual behavior of SWAT seems to contradict its avowed purpose of employing restraint in curbing incidents of urban violence. Quite the contrary, the net effect of SWAT's police-state tactics is to produce fear and outrage on the part of the community it purports to protect."[12]

It is a controversial judgment call, then, on the part of law enforcement officials as to when a SWAT response is appropriate and likely to be effective. From time to time, that judgment looks to be in error when viewed in hindsight. The federal government has received a lot of criticism for its handling of incidents in Ruby Ridge, Idaho, and Waco, Texas. In addition to the loss of life from these two incidents, they were public relation disasters for the government. Even though the agencies' use of force was upheld by the courts in both incidents, one can only wonder whether better resolutions were possible. Clearly, the actions of Randy Weaver and David Koresh were precipitating, and in some ways causative, factors. However, lessons remain to be learned about how and when to use deadly force.

In summary, it is fair to say that the police do not use excessive force as a matter of routine. Only on rare occasions is force used, and most of the time it is minimal. Most police officers are not required to use any force at all in their everyday duties. However, when force is required, it is law enforcement's responsibility to decide when and how much. One can imagine how police officers may overreact in times of fear and stress and engage in the inappropriate use of force but for the most part, we are willing to allow them to make some mistakes as long as those mistakes are made in good faith.[13]

Proactive Policing and Force

Do the police sometimes go looking for trouble? Yes, sometimes. Rather than waiting for crime to happen and then reacting to it, police will structure situations to give crime an opportunity to occur. A prostitution sting, in which police officers pose as sex workers and then arrest those who proposition them, is one example. Police units will also raid illegal gambling establishments, homes where drugs are consumed or sold, and businesses that are suspected of violating liquor laws.[14] The police cannot always predict the level of risk they will encounter when conducting proactive raids and so must be prepared for any

! NEWS FLASH

Ruby Ridge, Idaho

In August 1992, in Ruby Ridge, Idaho, six federal marshals embarked on a "reconnaissance mission" to check up on the doings of white separatist Randy Weaver. Federal law enforcement officers had been watching Weaver's cabin for a year, preparing to arrest him in connection with his indictment on the illegal sale of two sawed-off shotguns. Three of the marshals, who were in the woods near the family's mountain cabin, met up with Weaver, his 14-year-old son Sammy, family friend Kevin Harris, and their dog, Striker. Everyone, both the marshals and the Weavers, was armed. The shootout began when one of the marshals shot the dog. Less than a minute later, Sammy Weaver and U.S. Marshal William Degan were dead as well. The next day, an FBI sniper wounded Weaver and Harris and shot and killed Randy's wife Vicki while she was holding her infant. Weaver and Harris surrendered over a week later.

Weaver and Harris were acquitted by a federal jury of murdering Degan. When interviewed, most of the jurors said they believed that Harris, who had killed the marshal, had returned fire to defend Sammy Weaver. The Weaver family later filed wrongful death claims against the government, which settled with the family for $3.1 million.

Source: George Lardner, Jr., and Richard Leiby, "Standoff at Ruby Ridge," *The Washington Post*, September 3, 1995, http://www.washingtonpost.com/ac2/wp-dyn?pagename=article&node=digest&contentId=A99817-1995Sep3.

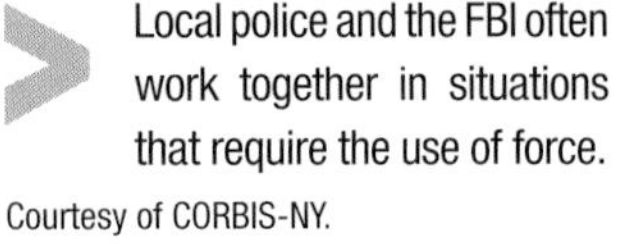
Local police and the FBI often work together in situations that require the use of force.
Courtesy of CORBIS-NY.

eventuality. Gear that includes bulletproof vests, helmets with face masks, special camouflage uniforms, and automatic weapons are precautionary measures designed to protect the police and to exceed any possible use of force by the suspects. In some incidents the police have been overzealous in their use of force and have caused injury or death to unarmed suspects. Additionally, the police have also made mistakes, such as breaking into the wrong house and using force on innocent civilians.

! NEWS FLASH

Waco, Texas

Courtesy of CORBIS-NY.

On February 28, 1993, Bureau of Alcohol, Tobacco, and Firearms agents were fired on while attempting to execute search and arrest warrants against David Koresh in his Branch Davidian compound in Waco, Texas. Four agents were killed, and 16 were wounded. Some sect members were also killed and injured. The FBI was called in, and agents were stationed in armored vehicles around the compound. Negotiations continued with Koresh by phone for the next several days and included tactical moves by the FBI such as the shining of bright lights and the playing of loud music at night to disrupt sleep. Several of the cult members left the compound during the negotiations. At one point, Koresh said he and his followers would exit the compound after their observance of Passover on April 5. However, on April 7 Koresh would not give a firm date of surrender and said he would not leave until God told him to. The FBI constructed a plan to force out the cult members with tear gas. As the FBI prepared the attack, cult members held children up in the windows, as well as a sign reading, "Flames Await." On April 19 the FBI began using its armored vehicles to insert tear gas canisters into the building and knock holes in the walls. Fires broke out. Nine cult members were arrested while fleeing as flames raced through the compound. In the end, more than 80 cult members, including 22 children, died in the fire or were found shot to death. Arson investigators concluded that the cult members started the fire.

Probes into law enforcement's handling of the siege led to the firing of two ATF supervisors who were later reinstated at a lower rank. No FBI agents were officially disciplined. Seven of the surviving Branch Davidians received 40-year prison terms, one received five years, and one received three years after testifying for the government.

Source: "Waco: The Inside Story," *PBS Frontline*, http://www.pbs.org/wgbh/pages/frontline/waco/.

The overzealous use of force has been termed the "Dirty Harry problem" by criminologist Carl B. Klockars.[15] In the film series, actor Clint Eastwood depicts a character named Harry Callahan who fights "psycho killers," corrupt police officers, and incompetent supervisors and politicians. Dirty Harry Callahan is not above bending a few procedural laws to catch the one-dimensional bad guys. Although these movies may be entertaining, they do not present the type of role model we want for our police. The Dirty Harry problem, according to Klockars, can be stated as, "When and to what extent does the morally good end warrant or justify an ethically, politically, or legally dangerous mean for its achievement?" Skolnick and Fyfe offered a further caution:

> *The Dirty Harry dilemma faces every cop in the course of his or her career, and its ultimate resolution is always problematic and subject to hindsight criticism. Extralegal resolution of the Dirty Harry dilemma is difficult enough when the "bad guy" is an identifiable and factually guilty individual. It is most problematic when the criminal is not an individual but a loosely defined gang or criminal organization, where the consequences of a mistake can be tragic for innocent individuals or bystanders, and where gut-level racism can be imputed to the officers involved.*[16]

This brings us to other issues of policing that have become increasingly problematic over the years. For the most part, police officers have been white males. This is changing rapidly in some jurisdictions and not so rapidly in others. The issues of gender and race are important to the criminal justice system, not only in terms of the demographic constitution of police departments, but also for the issues raised when women and minorities are suspected of committing crimes.

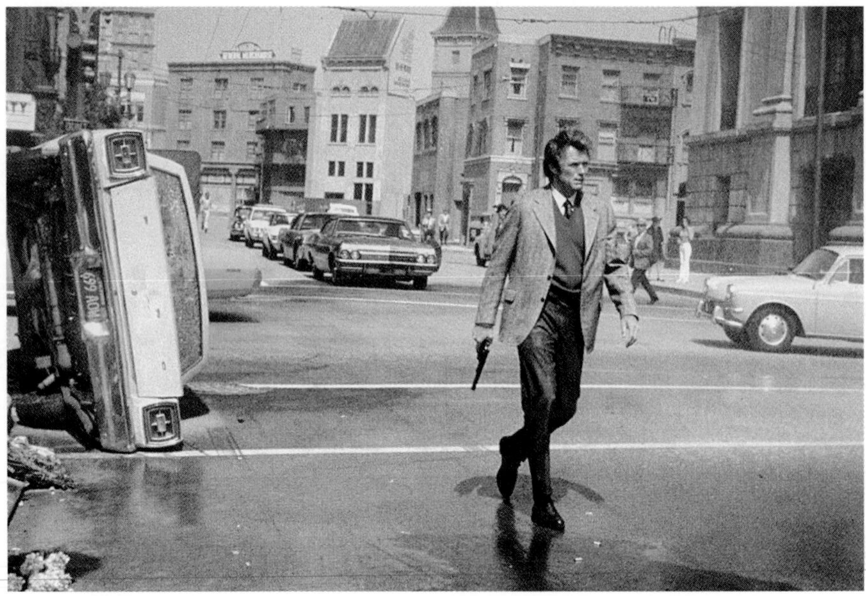

Actor Clint Eastwood made the character "Dirty Harry" a symbol of the determined law enforcement officer. In reality, the attitude and tactics of Dirty Harry would get an officer fired and possibly prosecuted.
Courtesy of Photofest.

Gender and Race

One of the basic principles advanced by critical criminologists is that social status can have a major impact on one's opportunities for pursuing a conventional lifestyle. Gender, race, and social class are considered powerful influences in determining who has access to the "American dream" and how one is treated by the institutions of society, including (and maybe especially) the criminal justice system.[17]

Gender and race are important issues in the study of law enforcement. The quality of justice and the efficiency of police work are both dependent on, and a factor in, how well the police agency is able to win the confidence of the community. When the police are viewed as promoting and protecting only the interests of certain races, genders, or social groups, then the criminal justice system is considered to be an instrument of the powerful and an oppressor of the weak.

It would be a mistake, however, to view the inclusion of women and minorities in police work as being a simple matter of politics. Diversity in criminal justice personnel adds more than the appearance of sexual or racial equity. Including women and minorities in the criminal justice system provides a broader array of tools to combat crime and develop meaningful communities. It is useful, then, to examine both gender and race as factors of both police officers and offenders.

Women as Police Officers

One of the main objectives of the move to create social and economic equality for women has been to allow them access to previously all-male occupations. In the past 50 years, women have overcome barriers to employment in private professions, the military, and the criminal justice system. Female judges, prosecutors, and corrections administrators are so commonplace in the 21st century that remarks are seldom made about their suitability for their jobs. The same is becoming true of female police officers. Women are seen on virtually every large or medium-size police force, and they have moved into positions of leadership in many of them. For instance, until recently in Atlanta, Georgia, the chief of police was Beverly Harvard, a black woman.

This road to equality for female police officers has been a rocky one, and for the most part, it is not yet complete.[18] Although the number of female officers continues to increase, the culture of the police force is still grounded in what many consider to be male values. The progress women are making in breaking down the barriers of sexism is in-

Proactive Police and Surveillance

At the 2001 Super Bowl in Tampa, Florida, each of the 100,000 fans who passed through the stadium turnstiles was photographed by a hidden video camera that the police used to check against computer files of known criminals, terrorists, and con artists. The use of this technology is becoming a fixture in public places. Police use cameras in banks, convenience stores, and malls that routinely photograph individuals to aid their search for suspects-at-large. Many times, these pictures allow the police to make arrests after crimes have been committed. What is new with the Super Bowl-type cameras, however, is that a person's photograph can be checked against photographs contained in a database of people that the police are looking for. If a match is made, then the person in the photo may be arrested. Although that person may indeed be a dangerous criminal, there is also plenty of room for error. In 2001, a picture of a man who was photographed by a surveillance camera in Ybor City, Florida, wound up in the magazine *U.S. News and World Report.* A woman in Tulsa, Oklahoma, told police that the man was her ex-husband who was wanted for felony child neglect. Police briefly questioned the man only to find out that he had never been married, had no children, and had never been to Oklahoma. The woman had identified the wrong man as her ex-husband, and police had acted on the tip all on the strength of a photograph.

This new technology gives law enforcement an additional tool to fight crime, but civil libertarians are concerned about the eroding right to privacy in the United States. They suggest that something akin to George Orwell's Big Brother is operating here.

QUESTIONS

1. Is such surveillance a good idea? Why? Why not?
2. Is such surveillance inevitable as technology improves?
3. Where do you draw the line between privacy and security?

Sources: Amy Herdy, " 'They Made Me Feel Like a Criminal,' " *St. Petersburg Times,* August 8, 2001, http://www.sptimes.com/News/080801/TampaBay/_They_made_me_feel_li.shtml. Robert Trigaux, "Cameras Scanned Fans for Criminals," *St. Petersburg Times,* January 31, 2001, http://www.sptimes.com/News/013101/TampaBay/Cameras_scanned_fans_.shtml.

cremental, sporadic, sometimes costly, and fraught with ambiguity. The resistance to women law enforcement officers from the public, male-dominated police administrations, fellow police officers, and even their own family members has caused many women to abandon their police careers.

Prior to the integration of women into police forces, law enforcement officers saw their jobs as involving danger, violence, aggression, isolation, and authority.[19] These concerns were considered exclusive to males and legitimate reasons to keep females off the force. Women were stereotyped as being physically weak and emotionally fragile, and thus ill suited for police work. The entries they did gain into police departments were as ancillary and support personnel, working as dispatchers or with juveniles.[20] The idea of women in uniform and on patrol was not seriously considered. Job qualifications for police officers stated that the applicant had to be male, or referred to police officers as "him" and "he." The concept of female police officers was not seriously considered in almost all jurisdictions.

Of course, singling out policing for being reluctant to accord women full occupational equity is unfair because this form of sexism was the norm in society until relatively recently. It is interesting, however, to look at how police have responded to the demand for women's rights because police work had been considered one of the occupations that most justified that exclusion. Arguments against women in policing included the following:

1. **Women are not physically strong enough to be police officers.** It is true that police work can sometimes require the officer to fight a large, young, strapping, intoxicated, angry male offender. This is a dangerous task that often results in physical injury to the officer. Critics of this objection point out that only a few police officers can win a street fight with young, athletically gifted males. Police officers are required to use their powers of persuasion to make arrests without fighting, to use their weapons when their safety or the safety of others is at risk, and to depend on other officers to help subdue the suspects, tasks of which women are capable. Women recruits must pass the same physical testing that male recruits do, so winning a fight really depends on which police officers maintain their readiness.
2. **Women bring different psychological attributes to police work.** Critics of women in policing contend "that women, because they are more compassionate, less aggressive, and less competitive, see their job from a different perspective and hence adopt different policing styles than do men."[21] Advocates for women in policing agree, adding that the aggressive and competitive perspective brought to the street by male police officers is appropriate for only part of the police mission, and a small part at that. The emphasis on crime control must coexist with an emphasis on order maintenance and social support. The mind-set brought by women who have been socialized into roles of caregiving and nurturing significantly expands the nature of the police role.

In summary, the increased participation of women in policing has provided some very important sociological lessons. There is more than one way to be a good police officer. According to some studies, the historically male-dominated police culture has been enriched by the infusion of women, who bring different perspectives to the job. At one time it was believed that the police subculture shaped recruits into a policeman's working personality that was determined by danger, violence, aggression, isolation, and authority.

Law enforcement is no longer an all-male occupation. Women are successfully serving in agencies across the nation.
Courtesy of CORBIS-NY.

Now the culture appears to be changing as women introduce other values into the culture of policing.

Minorities as Police

As with the section on women as police, it is unfortunate that a textbook on criminal justice in the United States has to have a section on minorities as police. This country has a checkered past in its treatment of minorities, and the criminal justice system has experienced its own stresses in accommodating the inevitable progress of opening occupations to people who have experienced prejudice and discrimination. It would be nice to say that law enforcement has led the way in providing equality to disenfranchised groups, but that has not been the case. It is fair to say, however, that some progress has been made and that the rate of improvement increases with each decade.[22]

At times in the distant past, black people worked as law enforcement officers, although these times have been rare and discontinuous. The first time black people appeared as police officers was in New Orleans in 1805. As slaves who had won their freedom because they served with the French or Spanish militia, they acted primarily to keep slaves under control and to catch runaways. The black police gradually lost their jobs to whites and did not engage in law enforcement activities again until after the Civil War. During Reconstruction, former slaves enjoyed a brief period during which they performed the same type of law enforcement duties as whites. This period of occupational equality was also quite brief, and soon, as in other aspects of politics, law enforcement was completely dominated by whites. With the exception of tokenism brought on by political patronage in northern cities, black policemen had few opportunities. Even when they were allowed into the occupation, their roles were greatly limited. Black people were responsible for policing their neighborhoods and were not allowed the full range of duties and certainly not allowed to advance into administration.[23]

A new era of opportunity for black people in all aspects of society was won during the civil rights movement in the 1950s and continues into the present day. Led by influential individuals such as Dr. Martin Luther King, Jr., the civil rights movement called attention to the problems of peoples of color in the social, economic, legal, and

People of color have been integrated into law enforcement agencies.

Courtesy of Corbis Royalty Free.

Israel Brooks, Jr.

Israel Brooks, Jr., who served with the South Carolina Highway Patrol from 1967 to 1994, was appointed in 1994 by President Bill Clinton as federal marshal for the District of South Carolina. Here, he recounts his experiences when he sought to become the state's first black highway patrolman. He was still serving as a marine when he had the following encounter.

While on leave in 1966, my Dad and I were walking down Main Street in the late morning. I decided to ask a patrolman I saw standing on the street about the process of joining the patrol. I inquired, "Sir, can you tell me how to apply for a job on the highway patrol?" His words tore through me like bayonets we used for practice in military training. "Boy, we don't have any Negras on the highway patrol, why don't you apply for the city or county." I became so furious that only my Dad's presence saved me from making a grave mistake. The Marine Corps had taught me to be aggressive and to confront anyone or anything that antagonized me, and I wanted to respond to the patrolman like the Marines had programmed me to respond to the enemy.

Source: Israel Brooks, Jr., "South Carolina's Finest," in *Critical Issues in Policing: Contemporary Readings*, 4th ed., eds. Roger G. Dunham and Geoffrey P. Alpert (Prospect Heights, IL: Waveland, 2001), 429–432.

educational arenas. Although far from complete, the civil rights movement has been successful in eliminating much of the institutional racism that had comprised the social fabric of American society. The Jim Crow laws of the South that prevented black people from going to the same schools, eating at the same lunch counters, and drinking from the same water fountains as whites are now just an ugly remembrance of the past.

Today, black officers can be found on virtually every large police force in the country. Some medium-size and small departments do not have minorities, but this has more to do with location and population than with discrimination. The law no longer allows police agencies to exclude job candidates based on race. This march toward equality has not been easy. Many black police officers met with hostility when they sought to serve their communities. As police agencies began to be integrated, black officers faced what Nicholas Alex called **double marginality**, which means that not only were they treated differently by their fellow police officers, but they were also looked on with suspicion by the black people in their communities.[24] In larger cities, with more and more black officers, the double marginality issue has decreased. However, when we look at the black female police officer, we can see a different type of marginality. These females feel the dual prejudices against women and minorities as they attempt to develop a place for themselves in the law enforcement occupation.[25]

double marginality
A term that refers to the multiple outsider status of women and minority police officers.

Black people are not the only minority group in the United States that has been historically excluded from law enforcement. Hispanics/Latinos, Asians, and American Indians have all suffered from prejudice and discrimination.[26] The effects of this racism are sometimes difficult to overcome because both whites and minorities must adjust to new ways of thinking about what police officers look like. In policing, the contributions of all Americans makes the community not only more tolerant of others but also more supportive of our institutions.

NEWS FLASH

A New Face on Racial Profiling

"Here's why profiling is so alluring: Of the suspected skyjackers responsible for upwards of 6,000 deaths on Sept. 11, 2001, 19 out of 19 were Arab. And here is why profiling is anathema to a just society: more than 3 million Arab-Americans live in the United States. Even if the government's worst fears are correct, and 50 members of terror cells remain at large, that means that more than 99.99 percent of Arab-Americans are no more connected to terrorism than is the dowager whose ancestors arrived on the Mayflower."

This quote from *Newsweek* illustrates a new development in the racial profiling controversy. Until the events of September 11, the debate centered on black and Hispanic/Latino American citizens. Now that terrorism in the United States is such a burning concern, we can expect to see those who appear to be of Middle Eastern descent experience special treatment not only from law enforcement officers, but also from other citizens. Is racial profiling motivated by terrorism different from that motivated by domestic crime? What can be done to ensure that U.S. citizens who are Arab receive the same constitutional rights as all other Americans?

Source: Sharon Begley, "What Price Security?", Newsweek, October 1, 2001, 58.

TABLE 7.2

Community Policing in Perspective

	Community Policing	Problem-Oriented Policing	Zero-Tolerance Policing
Goal	Strengthen bond between police and community	Address specific problem areas	Address specific types of offenders
Tactics	Place officers back on foot patrol or bicycles	Target situations in which crime occurs: crash houses, bars that serve minors, etc.	Make arrest for all minor violations (e.g., loitering, drinking in public, fare-jumping)
Style	Watchman style	Legalistic/service style	Legalistic style
Criticisms	Not much different from regular policing; token public relations	Discriminatory	Violates rights of those without power

Challenges to Traditional Policing

In the past 30 years, new theoretical foundations concerning how police are organized have begun to appear. In this section we will review and compare three challenges to the traditional policing model: community policing, problem-oriented policing, and zero-tolerance policing (see Table 7.2). Each of these forms of policing suggests different levels of interaction between the police and the public, and each is subject to criticism for what it fails to address as much as for what it successfully addresses.

Community Policing

community policing
A policing strategy that attempts to harness the resources and residents of a given community in stopping crime and maintaining order.

One of the major new ways of thinking about how to organize the police is the concept of **community policing**. In many ways, this idea is hardly new at all. It hearkens back to the watchman style discussed in Chapter 6, in which the police officer is integrated into the community and has the advantage of being trusted by those being policed. According to the Bureau of Justice Statistics, as of June 2000, two-thirds of U.S. local police departments and 62 percent of sheriff's departments had full-time sworn personnel doing community policing activities.[27] The concept of community policing, however, is also very different from the watchman style because both the police and the community have changed over the years. The watchman style of policing had its limitations, especially in affording equal justice to all citizens. In many cases, the watchman style simply reinforced the privileges of those in power while controlling the young and minorities. Community policing is different in content and scope, and it is worthwhile to consider its history and potential.

The term *community policing* covers a wide range of police activities and programs. Not all the practices considered to be community policing are really legitimate features of it. An exact definition is difficult to provide, but it is fair to say that community policing involves enlisting citizens to help solve law and order problems in their own communities (see Figure 7.2).[28] Good policing requires citizen cooperation. If people do not report crimes, do not provide information to the police, and are unwilling to testify in court, then the police cannot effectively fight crime. During the civil unrest of the 1960s, the police were forced to do a difficult job in controlling large groups of people. This violence revealed a deep fissure between old and young, workers and hippies, minorities and whites, and also between the police and the communities they served. Many people believed that the police were out of touch with those they served. For this and other reasons, a new approach called community policing was proposed.[29]

Chapter 6 discussed the evolution of policing styles. The professional or legalistic model emphasized efficiency and exclusivity in the mandate for crime control. This exclusivity came at a price, however, in terms of distancing the police from the communities they served. Community policing is viewed as a reform that breaks the monopoly of the police over crime-control activities and brings the citizen back into the equation as an active participant.

According to Walker and Katz, community policing represents a major change in the role of the police: "While the police have traditionally defined their primary mission in terms of crime control, community policing seeks to broaden the police role to include such issues as fear of crime, order maintenance, conflict resolution, neighborhood decay, and social and physical disorder as basic responsibilities of the police."[30] By taking an active part in improving the quality of life in the community, the police would strive not only to combat crime, but also to make other positive contributions to the everyday activities of citizens that would eventually result in a more cohesive neighborhood and better police–community relations.

Figure 7.2 The Definition of Community-Oriented Policing

The Department of Justice's Community-Oriented Policing Services (COPS) Web site defines community policing thusly:

> Community policing focuses on crime and social disorder through the delivery of police services that includes aspects of traditional law enforcement, as well as prevention, problem-solving, community engagement, and partnerships. The community policing model balances reactive responses to calls for service with proactive problem-solving centered on the causes of crime and disorder. Community policing requires police and citizens to join together as partners in the course of both identifying and effectively addressing these issues.

Source: COPS Office: Grants and Resources for Community Policing, http://www.cops.usdoj.gov/default.asp.

The goal of community policing is ambitious. It involves not only bridging the gap between the police and the citizens, but also strengthening the bond among the citizens themselves. With the realization that the police cannot be everywhere, programs such as **Neighborhood Watch** organize citizens to watch over each other's safety and property. In an article published in the *American Journal of Police,* Gordon Bazemore and Allen Cole illustrated how diverse community policing actions can be:[31]

Neighborhood Watch A community policing program that encourages residents to cooperate in providing security for the neighborhood.

1. On one street, drug dealers were escaping arrest because they hid their drugs under garbage barrels, inside fence post caps, and in mailboxes. Residents were armed with beepers and signaled police where the drugs were hidden. The police were able to find the drugs consistently, and asked if anyone wanted to claim them. No one did. The drug dealers were suspicious that there was a snitch, but because so many residents were participating in the programs, the dealers could not determine who was cooperating with the police.
2. On another street, gangs opened fire hydrants on the pretext of keeping cool and used the diversion to rob passing motorists and sell drugs. The community police officers closed the street to all traffic except those who could prove they were residents and issued $35 citations to those with no apparent reason to be on the street. In so doing, they effectively shut down the drug trade.
3. At another location, several neighborhood dealers sold drugs to individuals from outside the area. The police put up large signs reading, "Warning—area under surveillance due to illegal sale of drugs—motor vehicle registration numbers being recorded by the police." Letters were then sent to the owners of these cars informing them of the cars' presence in that location. (Presumably, many youths used their parents' cars.) According to Bazemore and Cole, the traffic reduced to a trickle in three weeks.
4. After extensively patrolling a drug-infested area, community police officers wanted to ensure that the neighborhood did not revert to its old patterns after the visible patrols ended. They invested $42 to disguise an old police special operations truck that was headed to the junkyard to look like a surveillance van (tinting the windows and installing mirrors that were thought to be two-way mirrors). They then had uniformed officers deliver empty coffee cups and pizza boxes to give the impression the van was continuously occupied. This could be called a reverse Trojan Horse tactic.
5. In one parking lot, youths would congregate to play loud music and handball. Although most of the problems were nuisances such as littering and graffiti, some of the youths were gang members and would rob passing motorists. The community police officers got the youths to agree to behave in order to be allowed to congregate and play handball. Residents of a nearby apartment building agreed to tolerate a certain level of noise in exchange for the elimination of the robbery, graffiti, and car break-ins.

In addition to these small successes, there were other positive outcomes to these community policing efforts. Residents cleaned up parks, boarded up old buildings, and participated in a variety of community programs that engendered a sense of togetherness and responsibility for each other and the youth of the community.

One strategy of community policing is to return the police to a close relationship with the public by having them patrol on foot or on bicycles. The patrol car is considered to be a barrier to communication between police and citizens. By taking the officers out of the cars and placing them in more direct contact with people, meaningful relationships are more likely. Another method of community policing is the development of Neighborhood Watch programs. By encouraging citizens to work together and cooperate with police, these programs "put more eyes on the street" to help prevent and report crime. These programs have the added feature of developing stronger community ties that can help address other neighborhood problems. When neighbors feel responsible for each others' children, property, and well-being, the job of the police becomes much easier.

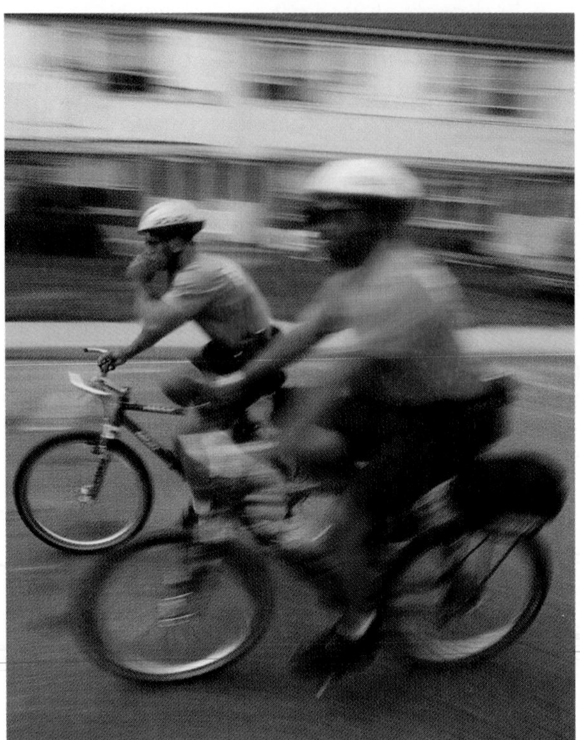

One method for getting police out of patrol cars is to put them on bicycles. This allows officers more mobility than foot patrol but still allows them to mingle with citizens.
Courtesy of Corbis Royalty Free.

One problem with community policing is that all communities are not created equal. Great variation persists among neighborhoods in terms of the socioeconomic, racial and ethnic, and age compositions of the citizens. For example, a suburb with $300,000 houses inhabited by middle-aged and elderly whites faces few crime problems compared to a neighborhood populated with transients and drug dealers. It is much easier to institute a Neighborhood Watch program in affluent suburbs where the residents' comings and goings are less frequent and easier to identify than in poor neighborhoods where the pattern of social organization and movement is less obvious. Therefore, community policing can be said to work best in the communities that need it least. Nevertheless, studies have suggested that well-planned community policing efforts can achieve at least some of their goals.[32]

A final issue in community policing is that it covers such a vast array of activities. It is hard to say (1) whether it is really any different from traditional policing and (2) whether we can declare it a success based on the limited research done on such different types of activities. Although the goal of involving communities as partners in addressing the problems of crime is laudable, getting the police to be concerned with order maintenance and community building is problematic when many officers view themselves solely as crime fighters. The inherent tension between the roles of criminal catcher and social worker limits the potential for community policing. Changing the basic orientation and occupational perspective of the police is difficult. It is like trying to get an orthopedic surgeon to "treat the whole person," when all the doctor sees is a broken leg or dislocated shoulder.

Problem-Oriented Policing

problem-oriented policing A style of policing that attempts to address the underlying social problems that contribute to crime.

A related strategy to community policing is **problem-oriented policing**. In many ways, problem-oriented policing can be thought of as simply one aspect of community policing, but it is important enough to be treated as its own topic. The reason we give special attention to problem-oriented policing is that it is designed to make more fundamental changes than community policing does. Additionally, problem-oriented policing greatly expands the role of the police officer from one of reaction to one of proactive problem solving. It allows law enforcement agencies to address crime on a more systemic level than traditional policing does.[33]

Neighborhood Watch programs enlist the support of citizens in keeping the community safe.
Courtesy of CORBIS-NY.

By way of illustration, envision a downtown business district that is experiencing a spate of robberies and muggings. In addition to responding to these crimes, a problem-oriented law enforcement agency would analyze the causative factors. Included in this analysis might be a crime-mapping effort, which would reveal that the muggings are all in close proximity to a cluster of bars. Upon surveillance of these bars, the agency may discover that the bars are staying open well past the legal closing time and serving underage patrons. Going into these bars and enforcing the existing liquor laws could affect the robbery and mugging problem. Problem-oriented policing, then, is concerned with identifying and addressing the underlying issues that contribute to crime. Within the scope of the law enforcement mission are many such opportunities that allow the police to do more than simply respond to crime. Of course, it is unrealistic to expect the police to be able to solve all the problems brought about by poverty, homelessness, and economic blight, but the police are in a position to understand the limitations in the structure of the community and design strategies to help.

Problem-oriented policing has different goals and techniques from community policing. In the long run, both types of policing may incur some of the same results, such as less crime and greater community support, but there are still important distinctions between these two styles. Problem-oriented policing is a more proactive process than community policing, and for this reason, it is more likely to appeal to police officers. Instead of responding to calls for service, the problem-oriented officer analyzes the specific trouble areas of the community and designs specific tactics to address those problems. A couple of examples may help illustrate the potential for problem-oriented policing.

1. **The Specialized Multi-Agency Response Team in Oakland, California.** The police identified a particular neighborhood that demonstrated a high level of crime and called for police service. This particular "hot spot" had a large amount of substandard housing. To address the problem, the police invited the cooperation of other city agencies to help improve the housing. Landlords were pressured to bring the houses up to housing code and fire code standards. As the housing improved, so did the overall quality of life in the neighborhood. The state government passed a law that made it a violation to maintain a dwelling where drugs were manufactured and sold. By solving the underlying problems of neighborhood neglect, the police were able to affect the crime problem. What is important to understand

about this problem-oriented policing example is that the police were not authorized to deal with all of the problems they identified, so they enlisted the help of other local government agencies that did have the authority to target specific issues, such as housing code violations.[34]

2. **The Boston Gun Project: Operation Cease Fire.** Because of a high rate of youth homicides, the Boston Police Department teamed with other agencies, including the Bureau of Alcohol, Tobacco, and Firearms; the probation department; schools; and prosecutors to crack down on youth gangs. The project put out the word to gang members that unless the gun violence stopped, full enforcement of the law for every offense, even the smallest, would be used against them. Probationers were subject to bed checks and prosecution of minor alcohol violations. Any infraction of the law was to be met with the full punishment allowed. After two years, the homicide rate had dropped by 70 percent. The program was so successful that the federal government funded 27 similar projects in other cities.[35]

Other problem-oriented policing measures might include strict enforcement of drinking ordinances in areas with a high degree of assault. By arresting store clerks for selling alcohol to minors or bartenders for continuing to serve obviously drunk patrons, the police can reduce the incidence of fighting and drunk driving. The police can work with state and city officials to terminate the liquor licenses of establishments that violate the law. By strictly enforcing the liquor laws, the police can remedy the underlying problems, such as unruly and violent behavior.

Problem-oriented policing allows law enforcement agencies broad latitude in addressing the contributing factors that cause crime. Police officers are not simply reactive, but can go into the community and enlist the support of other agencies to target problems and "hot spots" before crimes occur. In this way, problem-oriented policing has a crime-prevention mission as well as a crime-responding mission. Perhaps the most important feature of problem-oriented policing is its capacity to prevent future crime. By intervening early and effectively when patterns begin to emerge, problem-oriented policing can address the causes of crime and restore the sense of community.

broken windows theory The idea that untended property or deviant behavior will attract crime. This theory is used as a justification for clearing the streets of homeless people, drunks, and unruly teens, even when no crime has been committed.

The ways the police can engage in problem-oriented policing varies widely, from increased patrol efforts to helping communities remove abandoned cars and clean up trash-strewn vacant lots. Additionally, the police may establish substations in housing developments and assign officers on a permanent basis with the goal of creating a relationship and a partnership with the residents aimed at securing their public spaces.

As promising as problem-oriented policing appears to be, some of its implementations have been criticized. These critics are concerned with how problem-oriented policing has evolved from the controversial **broken windows theory**.

Zero-Tolerance Policing

zero-tolerance policing This form of policing punishes every infraction of the law, however minor, with an arrest, fine, or other penalty so that criminals will refrain from committing more serious crimes.

Zero-tolerance policing is a refinement of problem-oriented policing. **Zero-tolerance policing** is based on the idea that if every little infraction of the law is met with an arrest, fine, or other punishment, criminals will refrain from committing more serious crimes. James Q. Wilson and George L. Kelling developed the broken windows theory, which provides the theoretical perspective behind zero-tolerance policing.[36] The broken windows perspective is discussed in greater detail in the next section, but a brief review of it here will provide some background on zero-tolerance policing.

The central idea to the broken windows theory is that when people see a dwelling with a broken window, they are tempted to throw rocks and break the other windows. According to this theory, a broken window signals that the property is not valued. Because it has been abandoned and the owners pay little or no attention to it, it is all right to vandalize it. Property with intact windows, fresh paint, and a well-trimmed lawn sends a different signal. It says that the owners care about the property and will protect it. According to Wilson and Kelling, the broken windows theory also applies to the community and to social behavior on the streets. If the community is well kept both physically and socially, then vandals and criminals are less likely to disrupt the social order.

But what do we mean by socially well kept? According to Wilson and Kelling, it means keeping teenagers from hanging out in parking lots, shooing vagrants and homeless people, and chasing beggars and street people away from businesses and tourist locations. In this way the signal is sent that the city, the police, and the citizens care about their community and are making the streets safe. When the people of the community reclaim the streets, then a safe community is more likely. With more law-abiding people on the street, criminals will be less likely to commit crimes, and vandals will be less likely to destroy property.

The broken windows theory was the perspective behind the efforts of Mayor Rudy Giuliani's zero-tolerance policy in New York City during the early 1990s. By making misdemeanor arrests for panhandling, public drunkenness, prostitution, jumping subway turnstiles, and public urination, the New York Police Department aggressively sought to bring order and safety to the streets. In fact, serious crime did decrease, but critics point out that this was a nationwide trend and could not be attributed solely to the police department's zero-tolerance policies.[37]

Although the zero-tolerance policies suggested by the broken windows perspective are attractive to many politicians, law enforcement officials, and citizens, some important consequences remain to be considered. The main targets of zero-tolerance policies tend to be poor people. Those who are young, live on the street, look uncouth and shabby, and are drunk or mentally ill find that their minor transgressions of the law are treated much more severely than are the transgressions of others. Zero-tolerance policies aimed at reducing crime result in the unequal treatment of those without power. The civil and human rights of the least powerful in society are easy to abridge when the expressed goal is fighting crime. Given the problems of increased legal judgments against police departments for the behavior of its officers, zero-tolerance policing may be more problematic than beneficial.[38]

Perhaps the most fundamental problem with zero-tolerance policing is the adversarial relationship it seems to set up between the police and the public. By treating citizens with such a heavy hand, the police alienate the very people who could help them solve more serious crime. The marginalized street person is just as concerned with public safety as is the homeowner, maybe even more so because she or he is more vulnerable. When the police harass individuals for petty infractions, they cannot expect those people to assist them in the investigation of more serious crimes. Furthermore, zero-tolerance policies may deprive people of opportunities to eke out a living panhandling on the street and lead them to commit more serious crimes such as larceny, burglary, or robbery to survive. When people become angry and defiant, they are more likely to commit serious crimes and less likely to be of assistance to the police.[39]

! **NEWS FLASH**

Computers Add New Twist to Police Learning Curve

The investigation of computer crimes is taxing law enforcement officers' resources. With personnel already stretched thin, many officers are finding that they have to develop new investigative techniques and technological know-how to do their jobs. As budgets have not caught up with the times, many police departments must use equipment that has been donated or confiscated. However, computers also present investigators with new sources of evidence. Officers trained in computer forensics are learning to explore confiscated hard drives for clues. These skills are especially useful in white collar and financial crimes, as well as crimes involving child pornography, in which much of the evidence may be digitally stored.

Source: Amy Becker, "High-Tech Crime Challenges Law Officers," *Pioneer Press*, July 20, 2002, http://www.twincities.com/mld/pioneerpress/3703042.htm.

Broken Windows and Police Problems

Community policing and its variant, problem-oriented policing, are influenced by the broken windows theory. Law enforcement scholars James Q. Wilson and George Kelling introduced the idea in a 1982 article in the *Atlantic Monthly.* Based on the work of Stanford psychology professor Philip Zimbardo, Wilson and Kelling argued that crime follows community neglect. Zimbardo conducted a fascinating experiment in which he abandoned two cars, one in Palo Alto, California, and the other in the Bronx, New York City. Within 10 minutes the car in the Bronx was attacked, and within a few hours it was totally destroyed. Everything of value was taken from the car, and the windows were smashed (according to Zimbardo by well-dressed and clean-cut white vandals). The car in Palo Alto sat for over a week untouched until Zimbardo smashed it with a sledgehammer. Again, within a few hours the car was destroyed. Wilson and Kelling concluded:

> *Untended property becomes fair game for people out for fun or plunder, and even for people who ordinarily would not dream of doing such things, and who probably consider themselves law-abiding. Because of the nature of community life in the Bronx—its anonymity, the frequency with which cars are abandoned and things stolen or broken, the past experience of "no one caring"—vandalism begins much more quickly than it does in Palo Alto, where people have come to believe that private possessions are cared for, and that mischievous behavior is costly. But vandalism can occur anywhere once communal barriers—the sense of mutual regard and obligations of civility—are lowered by actions that seem to signal, "no one cares."*[40]

It is difficult to argue with Wilson and Kelling that untended property can draw vandals, especially when it is already damaged. We have all seen the results of such acts of vandalism (and may even have engaged in some ourselves). But Wilson and Kelling took this analogy a step further. They suggested that "untended" behavior also leads to the breakdown of community controls.

When teenagers loiter in front of a convenience store, or a drunk sleeps on the sidewalk, Wilson and Kelling believe that this signals that "no one cares," much like a broken window does. Citizens feel unsafe in their neighborhoods, and instead of being outside and involved in community activities, they hide in their homes. These actions

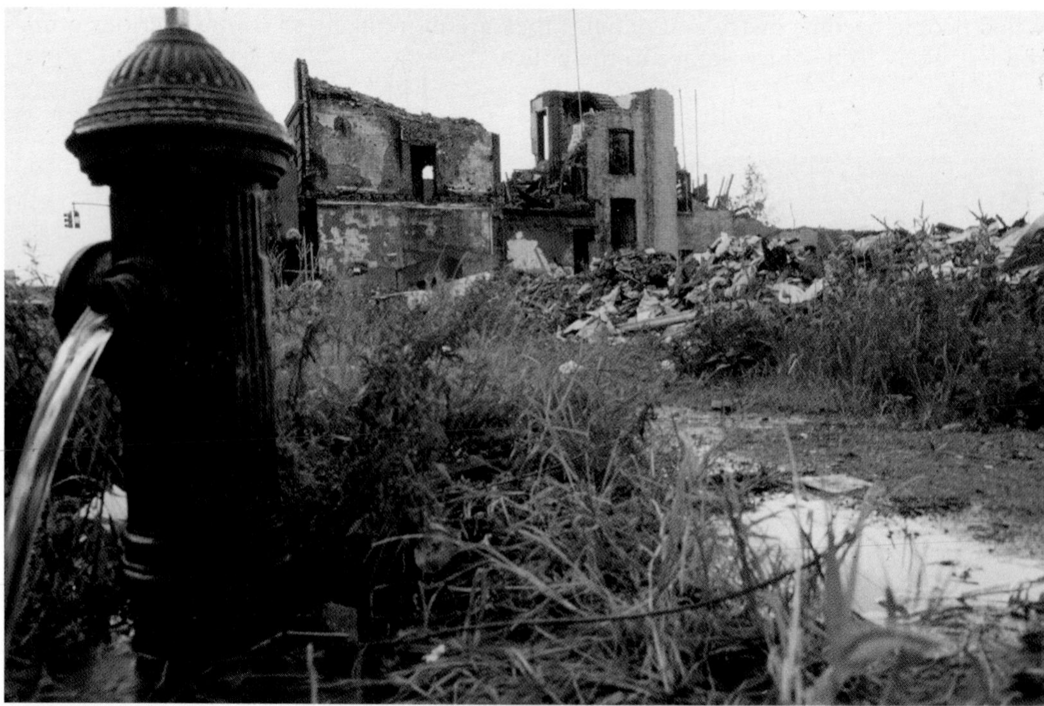

According to the broken windows theory, vandalism and criminal activity occur when it appears that no one cares about a neighborhood.
Courtesy of CORBIS-NY.

leave the streets empty of many citizens engaged in the type of everyday pursuits that signify a healthy and involved community. People are not out walking their dogs, washing their cars, talking to neighbors, or otherwise being out in the community, which suggests that the neighborhood is filled with residents who are not concerned with property or public safety. According to Wilson and Kelling, this neglect of behavior is as damaging as leaving a broken window unfixed in terms of inviting crime into the community.

The solution to this problem of the decline of the community is, according to the broken windows theory, to "fix" the "untended" behavior just as one would fix a broken window. This means arresting the public drunk, chasing the teenagers away from the store or out of the mall, and otherwise "cleaning up" the riffraff of society. This becomes problematic when we consider that these individuals have not broken any laws and have not harmed anyone. Wilson and Kelling contended, however, that to maintain meaningful communities, law enforcement officers must address the issue of street people: "Arresting a single drunk or single vagrant who has harmed no identifiable person seems unjust, and in a sense it is. But failing to do anything about a score of drunks or a hundred vagrants may destroy an entire community."[41]

In trying to balance the rights of the individual against the rights of the community, Wilson and Kelling came down solidly on the side of the community. They argued that we have let our communities slip away from the watchman style of policing in which police officers maintained order by enforcing community standards of civil behavior on the street. The broken windows theory argues that arresting or chasing away undesirable individuals will reclaim the neighborhood for citizens engaged in normal, productive activities.

Is there anything wrong with this prescription for social change? Many critics believe so. Following are three reasons to be cautious about adopting the broken windows theory:

1. **Misreading of how communities were policed in the past.** Criminologist Samuel Walker critiqued the broken windows theory in his article, " 'Broken Windows' and Fractured History: The Use and Misuse of History in Recent Patrol Analysis." Walker contended that Wilson and Kelling had misread the history of policing and that their call for an earlier model of the watchman style was misguided. In short, Walker said that there was no older tradition of policing that encompassed the principles of the broken windows theory, and that if Wilson and Kelling want to implement these ideas, they will have to start anew. Walker did say that the community-oriented policing concept is a worthy and feasible goal, but that it must be developed slowly.[42]
2. **Concern for the rights of all citizens.** Fixing a window or cleaning up a vacant lot can signal that people care about their neighborhood. Dealing with teenagers, drunks, the mentally ill, or the homeless presents a different set of problems. Wilson and Kelling erred in comparing this "untended" behavior to a broken window. They may have been right in thinking that street people affect a number of quality of life issues, such as creating excessive noise and feelings of discomfort in citizens walking the street. They were mistaken, however, in asserting that this issue can be solved by the police in a democratic country that values individual rights. The answer to the social problems presented by street people is not to arrest them or chase them to other parts of the city, but to marshal the resources of the entire community to solve the underlying problems. If the deinstitutionalization of the mentally ill means that they are in the street, then housing programs, drug treatment facilities, and a host of other social services are needed.[43]
3. **Problem of crime displacement.** Removing undesirable people from a community does not mean that the problems associated with them will disappear.[44] These people could reappear in an adjoining community with all the negative and "untended" behaviors the first community was trying to suppress. Additionally, by threatening to arrest street people and otherwise devaluing any positive contribution they may be able to make to the community, we may actually accelerate their

CASE IN POINT

Chimel v. California

The Case

Chimel v. California, 395 U.S. 752, 89 S.Ct. 2034 (1969)

The Point

An arrest warrant allows only the search of a suspect's person and the immediate vicinity. Any further searches require a search warrant.

Police officers suspected Ted Chimel of burglarizing a coin company in California. They went to his house with an arrest warrant, but not a search warrant, and were let in by Chimel's wife. The police waited for Chimel and served him with the warrant when he returned home from work. Chimel denied the officers' request to search the house. The officers searched anyway and found some of the stolen coins in Chimel's attic. The evidence was used against him in court, and he was convicted of burglary. The Supreme Court overturned the conviction on Chimel's appeal because it said the officers' search of Chimel's house went far beyond what the arrest warrant allowed.

undesirable behaviors from nuisances to crime. Our streets may be made safer by the sweeping away of what we consider the riffraff, but other communities will have to deal with these human beings who feel alienated from society and are not bound to conventional behavior.

It should be evident by now that the process of involving the police in the community is a complex task. The term *community policing* does not have a definition that is shared by everyone who advocates its use. Community policing includes a wide variety of strategies and can mean anything from a simple slogan to a definite set of programs designed to effect significant social change in how policing is done. It is important to understand how the police are connected to the community because this bond can greatly influence how the police understand their job and deal with its pressures and dangers. Police stress comes in many forms and can exert many different types of strain on officers, their families, and the police agency.

Police Stress and Burnout

Law enforcement can be a very stressful career. Unlike in many occupations, the threat of physical injury or death is a daily possibility (see Figure 7.3). Because they are the ones called when force must be used, police have the most to fear from violence. At one time in our history, there was an unwritten rule for criminals (probably a myth) that police officers should not be killed because the consequences would be severe. If that attitude ever saved a police officer's life in the past, there is little evidence that it persists today. In fact, with the vast sums of money and long prison sentences associated with some types of crime (such as drug sales), human life, even that of a police officer, is often considered expendable and treated as simply part of doing business. Additionally, as the September 11 tragedy demonstrated, the police are often called to respond to situations in which their experience and training can do little in preventing harm.

Stress for the law enforcement officer can come in many forms. It can be physical, emotional, social, marital, chemical, or occupational. At times, multiple forms of stress can be experienced simultaneously. The job of law enforcement officer invites stress, and

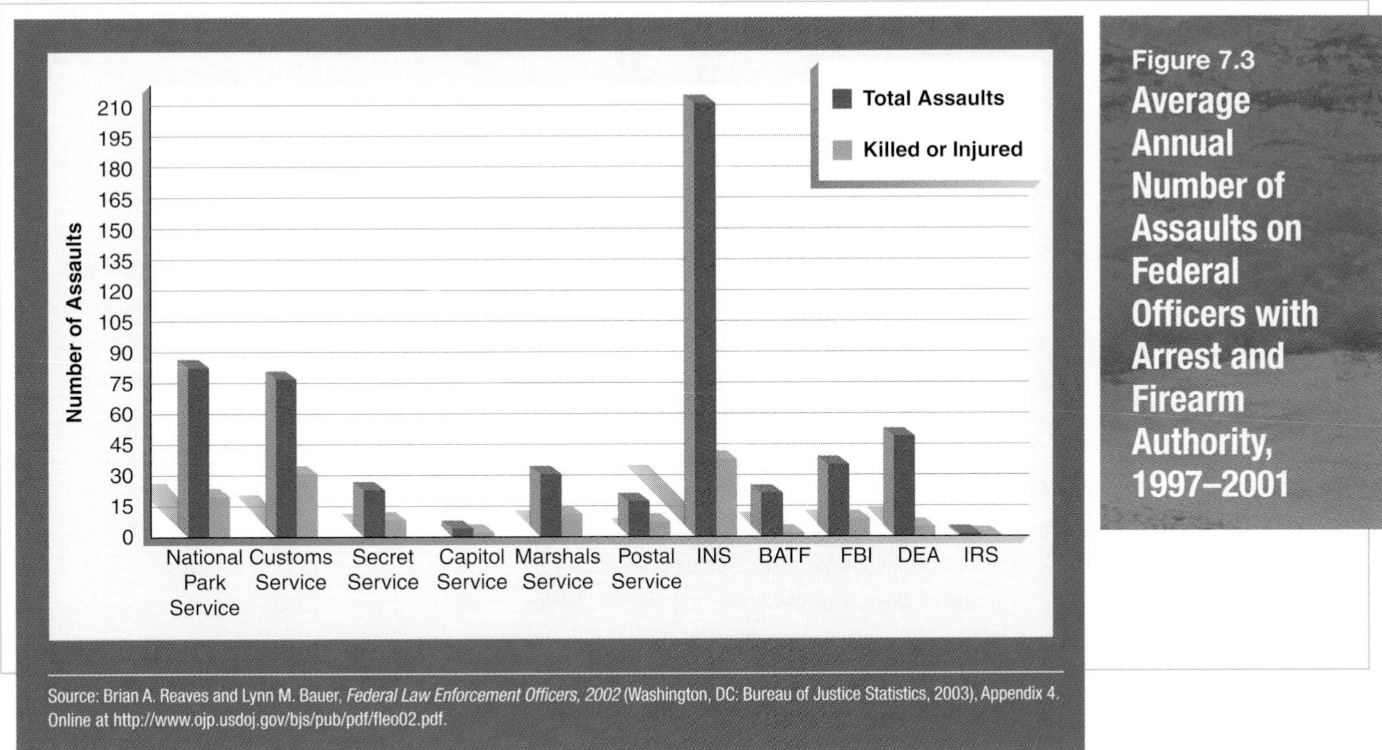

Source: Brian A. Reaves and Lynn M. Bauer, *Federal Law Enforcement Officers, 2002* (Washington, DC: Bureau of Justice Statistics, 2003), Appendix 4. Online at http://www.ojp.usdoj.gov/bjs/pub/pdf/fleo02.pdf.

Figure 7.3 Average Annual Number of Assaults on Federal Officers with Arrest and Firearm Authority, 1997–2001

the way police agencies structure assignments, shifts, support, and discipline contributes to the anxiety and strain of the job.

This section will review the literature on police stress and will offer some suggestions on how it might be alleviated. This is done with the knowledge that stress is an inevitable part of the occupation and even the reason that some people select policing as a career. Not everyone wants to sit behind a desk staring at a computer screen all day. Some people want to be out working with people in jobs that offer something different every day and have a degree of excitement. However, along with this excitement comes stress. Not everyone handles stress in the same way, and sometimes the level of stress can become so pronounced that it can overwhelm even the strongest person.

Police and Alcohol

In his 1970s novel, *The Choirboys,* former Los Angeles policeman Joseph Wambaugh portrayed the police as consuming excessive amounts of alcohol to cope with the stresses of the job.[45] After their shift ended in the early morning hours, the squad would go to what is euphemistically called "choir practice" at Los Angeles' MacArthur Park, where they would get drunk and tell each other stories about their night on patrol. Although the book can be very funny at times, there is an undercurrent of tension caused, in part, by the excessive consumption of alcohol that Wambaugh linked to the stress of policing.

This theme of policing and alcohol abuse is also present in the academic literature on the occupation. For example, one study looked at psychological stress, the demands of police work, and how police coped with these issues. The study found that the stress of police work was highly related to alcohol abuse. Other coping mechanisms such as emotional dissonance (officers learn to objectify their emotions when faced with dead or injured people, crime victims, abused children, etc.) and cynicism were found to be related either directly or indirectly to alcohol use. What is important to learn from this study is that alcohol was used as a method to relieve the inherent stress of police work 20 times more often than cynicism or emotional distancing. In fact, when those methods failed, alcohol use became more likely.[46]

Suicide by Cop

Like *road rage* and *going postal,* a new term has entered the media lexicon. *Suicide by cop* refers to suspects attempting to have themselves killed by police officers. Most of these cases involve males who are estranged from wives or girlfriends and have a history of drug or alcohol use. Feeling lost and hopeless, these suspects orchestrate events so that the police must respond to their dangerous behavior. With no real effort to resolve the conflict or escape, the suspect threatens violence, and the police are forced to kill him to protect themselves and innocent civilians. It can be a traumatic event for the police officer who seeks a peaceful means to end the case, but is left with no alternative than to end the life of a distraught and troubled individual. Los Angeles County Sheriff's Homicide Department Sergeant Jack Yarbrough doesn't like the term *suicide by cop* because it connotes that the police officer is at fault. In reality, the police officer is a victim of a purposeful act by the suspect. Yarbrough prefers the term *police-assisted suicide.*

These incidents leave the police in a no-win situation. If they kill the suspect, they can experience stress even though they had no choice. If they simply wound the suspect, then others may get shot, and the suspect could end up suing the police officer. Even the incident commanders who order the shooting may experience psychological or legal fallout.

QUESTIONS

1. What do you think of the term *suicide by cop?* Is it appropriate?
2. Do you believe there are ways for police officers to avoid shooting suspects they think may be suicidal, or are such situations unavoidable in law enforcement?

Source: Dean Scoville, "Suicide by Cop," *Police Magazine,* November 1988, 36–44.

The stress of police work may not be the only factor, however, in influencing law enforcement officers to turn to alcohol. The police subculture may also exert a powerful influence on drinking patterns as it tests trustworthiness, loyalty, and masculinity. Additionally, it may act as an obstacle to the reporting of a fellow officer with a drinking problem. Consider the following:

1. **The police subculture may socialize new officers into accepting a pattern of after-shift drinking.** New employees are anxious to fit into the group. In many occupations, the older workers want to know whether the new person can be trusted. In police work, in which the officer must depend on his or her partner, there is pressure to judge each other's reliability quickly. Learning what "makes the other person tick" through after-hours socializing is an important part of this judgment process. New officers are judged by their peers to "fit in" to the extent that they can hold their liquor; articulate the occupational worldview of the police subculture; and accept and participate in the complaining about citizens, politicians, and superiors.
2. **Socialization in the police subculture establishes that drinking is not deviant.** Because "everyone drinks after work," the consumption of alcohol is soon viewed as normal behavior. Whereas in other circumstances, consistent and excessive drinking might be viewed as a problem, in police work it just means that an officer is "one of the guys." When embarrassing incidents happen or problems with family emerge because of drinking, these issues are turned into amusing stories that are told over and over in future drinking bouts as evidence that "civilians don't understand police work."

3. **This normalization of drinking may preclude treatment because "every one of my friends drinks."** One of the issues that can lead people to seek treatment for their drug or alcohol addiction is the embarrassment it can cause in the workplace. To the extent that alcohol use is the norm among one's contemporaries, its abuse is not a cause for concern and its treatment may actually be viewed as a weakness or even a betrayal of the work group. When a fellow officer is forced to admit that drinking is a problem, other officers may feel uncomfortable in examining their own drinking patterns. A reformed drinker can sometimes help his or her friends, but often the friends continue to maintain their lifestyle, and an unspoken barrier is erected.

The impact of alcohol on the police force has not been lost on police administrators.[47] As with many other agencies and corporations, personnel policies are geared toward ensuring that the police maintain good health and do not put the force at risk of lawsuits because of unfitness for duty. In the past several years, many public safety organizations have instituted drug and alcohol testing to ensure that police officers are capable of performing their assignments.[48] Assistance is offered to those who are determined to need help, and continued failures to meet departmental standards can be cause for dismissal. This extreme remedy is more likely for those found to be using illegal drugs than it is for those who abuse alcohol, but it is fair to say that police agencies are more attuned to the impact of intoxication than they have been in the past. The police subculture that celebrates drinking as part of the job, as Joseph Wambaugh did in his novel, is coming under attack as a by-product of the war on drugs.

Family Problems and the Police

The individual police officer is not the only one affected by the stress of police work. Often, family members experience a variety of stressful concerns. The first of these is the change in the personality of the police officer and his or her relationship with spouse and/or children. Jerome Skolnick coined the term "the policeman's working personality" to explain how the police must cope with danger, isolation, authority, and suspicion.[49] Police families experience stress when the police officer brings the job home and starts to treat his or her spouse and children like potential suspects. The simple question, "Where are you going?" may be viewed as an interrogation rather than a normal concern. Children of police officers may be held to a higher standard of etiquette as the officer demands that they show proper respect and deference.[50]

The issue of isolation can take on two forms. The officer may not express the stress that comes from the job to the family, and he or she may appear withdrawn and disinterested in the family's concerns. Additionally, the family members may be treated with hostility by neighbors who believe they are being watched by the police officer. On one hand, integrating into the community is desirable; on the other hand, it may become problematic when the members of the community see the police as a threat.

The dangers associated with police work can also be a source of stress for officers' family members.[51] Knowing that one's spouse or parent is potentially just one radio call away from a deranged person with a gun can keep one in an uneasy state of mind. If each phone call could be the police commissioner calling to say there has been a shooting, it is only natural that some family members would suggest the police officer find less dangerous work. Having a spouse or parent as a police officer can be a source of pride, but it can also be a source of worry and concern.[52] Family members' pressure on the police officer about the job can create a dilemma. Feeling a loyalty to the job and responsibility to the family can result in the officer internalizing stress and, as a result, doing a bad job at both family life and policing.

Finally, the nature of police work can cause hardships in the family because of rotating shifts. Depending on the department, the nature of shift work can exert an extreme hardship on both the police officer and the family. Scheduling day care, vacations, children's after-school activities, and a host of other domestic duties is difficult when the officer's shift is always in flux.[53] Most people work best when they have a routine to which

FOCUS ON ETHICS

My Best Cop, But . . .

As a new police chief of a medium-size city, you have a variety of problems keeping up the morale in your department because of low pay, antiquated equipment, and the general resistance of the older officers to the city hiring an "outsider" to run the department. However, you have found one officer who seems to support all the improvements you are trying to make in the department. This guy is a real "hot shot." He has the highest arrest rate in the force, was cited for bravery when he rescued a baby from a burning car, and has just completed a master's degree in criminal justice at the local university. This officer is clearly "on the fast track," and you are anxious to promote him before some other department or the FBI can lure him away. Additionally, you are under pressure from the city to diversify the force, and this star happens to be black.

One morning you get a call from the deputy sheriff who runs the jail, and he tells you that your officer has brought in a youth who has been severely beaten. The deputy says that no formal complaints have been filed, but he thinks you should know what is going on because this is not the first time prisoners have complained that this officer uses excessive force.

WHAT DO YOU DO?

1. Launch an investigation into all of this officer's previous controversial arrests.
2. Informally counsel the officer on the appropriate use of force.
3. Threaten the officer with suspension if you hear of any more complaints of excessive force.
4. Tell him he is doing a great job but that he needs to be more careful in covering up his use of force.

their bodies can adjust. In police work, the routine is lost with constant changes in shifts. People become irritable when their sleeping patterns are altered and, by the time an officer adjusts to a shift, the shift changes again. Some occupations that require 24-hour/7-days-a-week coverage are able to keep stable shifts for their workers by paying a differential for the least desirable times. For example, in the medical profession, nurses who work the midnight shift are paid more than those who work the traditional 8 A.M. to 5 P.M. shift. Both are able to develop a routine that allows them to balance the demands of both work and home. The costs of illness, burnout, and stress may be higher than the cost of extra pay to individuals who are willing to work the least desirable shifts.

Police and Suicide

Suicide is an occupational hazard for police officers. A number of studies have shown that law enforcement has one of the highest suicide rates of any occupation. Given the preceding discussion about the stress of policing and its contributions to alcohol abuse and family problems, it should not be too surprising to learn that suicide also concerns the police and their families. The question is, Why would law enforcement officers resort to suicide at rates higher than those in other occupations? The answer lies in the types of stress we have already discussed and in the access the police have to handguns.

Firearms are a constant feature in the lives of police officers. They are trained in the use of guns, carry them on a daily basis, are prepared emotionally to use guns in the pursuit of lawbreakers, and have been sufficiently desensitized to the effects of guns. It is hard to think of any other occupation, including the military, in which guns are such a constant part of the job. It should come as no surprise, then, that when faced with the high levels of stress that are part of policing, some officers use firearms to take their lives. In fact, the phrase "he ate his gun" is part of the police lexicon. It is unfair, however, to argue that the gun is solely responsible for police suicide rates. Although firearms are a

Police Stress

According to the FBI, the "top ten most stressful law enforcement critical life events" are as follows:

1. The violent death of a partner in the line of duty
2. The dismissal or loss of the job
3. Taking of a life in the line of duty
4. Shooting someone in the line of duty
5. Suicide of an officer who is a close friend
6. The violent death of another officer in the line of duty
7. A murder committed by a law enforcement officer
8. A duty-related violent injury such as a shooting
9. A violent job-related injury to another officer
10. Suspension from the job

Source: Central Florida Police Stress Unit, Inc., http://www.policestress.org/busters.htm.

very efficient way to kill oneself (as opposed to a drug overdose), a determined person will find a way whether there is a convenient gun or not. It just so happens that for police officers, there is always a convenient gun.

A final source of stress may contribute to not only the high suicide rate among police officers, but also their problems with alcohol and family issues: dealing with the results of violent crime and other tragedies. Seeing human beings dead days or weeks after they are first reported missing can be very stressful. Watching families fall apart because of poverty, drugs, or marital abuse can cause some officers to become depressed. Dealing with the mentally ill offender who is armed with a gun and having to shoot to protect other people can deeply affect police officers. Finally, as demonstrated in other chapters, the vagaries of the criminal justice system can cause officers to become frustrated when they do their jobs well only to find the offender set free to victimize others. The police must deal with the underside of society, and after a time, unless officers are able to cope with the stress, the job can get so overwhelming that suicide, retirement, quitting, or engaging in deviant behavior can be considered the only ways to cope.

Dealing with the Stress of Policing

Although many occupations can cause stress to the practitioner, policing seems to have some special features that, while recognized in the literature on policing, have heretofore been neglected by police agencies. Certainly, police departments' human resources divisions have implemented policies aimed at helping individual officers, and community programs that are available to all citizens are also available to the police, but law enforcement officers often shun these resources. Within the police subculture an attitude exists that to admit stress to the administration or to outsiders is a sign of weakness. To successfully reduce police stress to manageable levels, law enforcement agencies, city or county administrations, and police officers themselves can use a variety of strategies. Bruce Arrigo and Karyn Garsky made three suggestions:[54]

1. **Stress management and stress reduction techniques.** According to Arrigo and Garsky, police academies do not provide classes on how to cope with stress. They suggested that, in addition to physical exercise, officers be given information on

A Closer Look at Police Suicide

Law enforcement can be a stressful occupation, and the perception that police officers are at risk for suicide, alcoholism, and divorce is deeply rooted in the popular culture. It is true that some studies and much anecdotal evidence support the impression of policing as an unhealthy occupation, but it is worthwhile to look more closely at what the research reveals.

Studies that show high rates of suicide for police officers include Nelson and Smith's finding of a rate of 203 suicides per 100,000 officers in Wyoming, Friedman's finding of 80 suicides per 100,000 officers in New York City, and Richard and Fell's finding of 69 suicides per 100,000 officers in Tennessee. According to Robert Loo, there are three problems with the way police suicide rates are calculated:

1. **These studies use very short time frames.** One year of a high number of police suicides can give an impression of a higher rate. Loo contended that rates of police suicide should be calculated for at least 10-year time frames.
2. **Agencies that reported no suicides were not always included in the analysis.** Had this been done, the base number would have increased, and the rate would be lower.
3. **Many studies fail to control for age, gender, and race.** To the extent that police officers tend to be young, white males, they demonstrated higher rates than the general population. In a study conducted by Aamodt and Stalnaker, these variables were statistically controlled for, and police officers were found to commit suicide 26 percent less than those of similar age, race, and gender.

Law enforcement officers endure the same pressures and limitations as those who share their social position. Young men are more likely to engage in suicide and alcoholism than the general population. To the extent that our police forces have always had an overrepresentation of males and those between 20 and 40 years of age, their rates of social problems can be expected to be at least as high. However, according to Stephen Curran, police officers are likely to be psychologically healthy, engage in exercise programs, and refrain from using tobacco or alcohol to excess. When comparing police officers to others who share their demographic characteristics, we do not necessarily find that police officers are victims of elevated occupational stress.

Sources: Michael G. Aamodt and Nicole A. Stalnaker, "Police Officer Suicide: Frequency and Officer Profiles," in *Suicide and Law Enforcement,* eds. D. C. Shehan and J. I. Warren (Washington, DC: Federal Bureau of Investigation, 2001). Also online at http://www.radford.edu/~maamodt/Police%20Research/police%20suicide.pdf. Stephen Curran, "Separating Fact from Fiction about Police Stress," *Behavioral Health Management* 23, no. 1 (2003) : 38–40. Paul Friedman, "Suicide among Police: A Study of Ninety-Three Suicides among New York Policemen, 1934–1940," in *Essays in Self-Destruction,* ed. E. Shneidman (New York: Science House, 1968), 414–419. Robert Loo, "A Meta-Analysis of Police Suicide Rates: Findings and Issues," *Suicide & Life-Threatening Behavior* 33, no. 3 (2003): 313–325. W. C. Richard and R. D. Fell, "Health Factors in Police Job Stress," in *Job Stress and the Police: Identifying Stress Reduction Techniques: Proceedings of a Symposium,* eds. W. H. Kroes and J. J. Hurrell, Jr. (Washington, DC: U.S. Government Printing Office, 1975). Z. Nelson and W. Smith, "Law Enforcement Profession: An Incident of Suicide" *Omega* 1 (1970): 293–299.

nutrition and dieting practices; physical health, fitness, and exercise routines; mental wellness, imaging, and relaxation techniques; recreational, leisure, and outdoor activities; and humor, play, and amusement strategies.

2. **Group "rap" or process sessions.** Arrigo and Garsky argued that although police agencies may have therapeutic assistance available to the officers, using this counseling is perceived as an admission of weakness, troubled conscience, or ineffectiveness. What is needed is exposure to group sessions early in the training process and regularly throughout officers' careers as a way of sharing with contemporaries

FOCUS ON ETHICS

To Trust a Partner

As a new female police officer, you have sailed through the police academy and in-service training with high marks, and you are excited to be teamed with one of the most popular and respected officers on the force. You find that the two of you work well together. He treats you with respect and increasingly gives you more authority in doing your job. You are developing mutual trust in each other, and you could not be happier with your assignment. However, in the last few weeks you have begun to become concerned about your partner's emotional stability.

When the squad goes out for a drink after the shift, you notice that your partner has been getting quite drunk. One Saturday night after a particularly stressful shift that included a high-speed chase, shots fired, and the wrestling of a suspect to the ground, your partner confides in you that he has been chronically depressed. After several beers, he admits that he and his wife are separating and that his children are the only passion he still has in life. Then the shocker comes. He looks around to make sure no other officers are listening, then tells you he has been having fantasies of "eating his gun." In the academy they told you to take all talk of suicide seriously, but you are committed to maintaining the trust you have developed with your partner.

WHAT DO YOU DO?

1. Report your partner's depression to the police psychologist and seek her advice.
2. Try to counsel your partner and tell no one about his depression.
3. Ask for a new partner.

the inevitable stress present in policing. Important issues can be discussed away from the bar and insights gained without the stimulus of alcohol that can aid the individual officer in dealing with stress. Peer support is an effective and important counseling technique that is particularly relevant to policing, and if done under the right circumstances (while not drinking), it promises to be helpful.

3. **Police mentoring.** Once out of the academy, the rookie police officer learns the job from experienced police officers. As a logical extension of the group sessions provided to new police officers, there is potential for ongoing programs in which skilled mentoring can reinforce the lessons of how to deal with stress. Arrigo and Garsky admitted that how senior officers deal with stress may be problematic and that a new orientation is needed to promote a healthy atmosphere. The idea is to provide services and mutual support for both senior and new officers.

In addition to these suggestions are some ideas that could make the very nature of policing less stressful. These ideas will require communities to put more resources into police agencies and for the police administrators to recognize that the law enforcement officers have social, family, economic, educational, and psychological needs that should be addressed.

Revisiting the impact of changing officers' shifts is a first step in reforming policing. Officers have family responsibilities that suffer when the officer has no control over his or her working hours. The problems of sleep deprivation are known, but sometimes appear to be ignored by police administrators. Making the unattractive shifts more desirable for officers can be accomplished by paying more money to those who are willing to assume the hardships. In the long run, the community will be safer, the officers will be healthier, and the city will save money with a stable and alert police force.

Another method of addressing the stress of police work is reducing the paramilitary focus that some departments have adopted. As was previously discussed, the military is a poor model on which to pattern a police department. Additionally, the police mission is considerably broader than the military mission, which concentrates on the use of force.

Finally, the move toward more community policing activities seems like a promising strategy to make police work less stressful. To the extent that the police become integrated into the community it can be expected that their work will be not only more effective, but also more socially rewarding. When the police interact with citizens on a routine and constructive basis, they can form relationships that will engender trust and reciprocal goodwill, which can make policing a more positive experience.

Summary

This chapter reviewed several selected critical issues that face law enforcement, particularly those that continue to perplex and challenge both law enforcement administrators and the public. These issues force students of criminal justice to consider some of the difficult decisions that arise when law enforcement is constrained by democracy and the rule of law.

We can argue that the single most important critical issue facing law enforcement today is to provide protection to the community while using an appropriate level of force. Because the police are authorized to use force as part of their job, we must decide what level of force is permissible, desirable, and feasible. Related to this issue is the problem of actually measuring police use of force in the community. Although the actual use of force is more infrequent than portrayed in the media, it does continue to be a constant source of tension among law enforcement agencies, the press, and the public.

At the heart of the issues concerning the police use of force is the military nature of police organization. This is most apparent in the use of Special Weapons and Tactics (SWAT) units. Additionally, overzealous police officers have also been problematic for police administrators who must carefully attempt to screen out the "Dirty Harrys" in their organizations.

Other emerging issues for law enforcement are the difficulties of integrating women and minorities into a historically white, male police profession. Although women may not be as physically strong as men, they bring other attributes to the profession, such as being less aggressive and less competitive. It could be argued that the requirement of physical force means that the optimal peaceful solution to the problem has already been compromised. Individuals who belong to racial and ethnic minorities can also bring unique experiences and viewpoints to law enforcement. A police force in which the officers reflect, at least in part, the demographic constituencies of the neighborhoods they are policing can be a benefit. Rather than looking like an invading army, the police agency appears to value the contributions that a diverse workforce can make to the fair enforcement of the law.

The issue of community policing was addressed in this chapter, as well as the tactics of problem-oriented policing and the zero-tolerance policing that flow from the broken windows theory. As a result of the the terrorist activities of September 11, 2001, the relationship of law enforcement to the public will undergo additional strains.

Finally, the chapter dealt with the human costs of being a police officer. Alcohol and drug abuse, family discord, and suicide are all critical issues that the student of law enforcement needs to consider. Only by recognizing that these issues are occupational hazards of policing can we hope to design effective programs to minimize their impact on the lives of police officers and their families.

KEY TERMS

broken windows theory p. 232
community policing p. 228
double marginality p. 226
Neighborhood Watch p. 229
problem-oriented policing p. 230
use of force p. 214
zero-tolerance policing p. 232

REVIEW QUESTIONS

1. The use of force is considered legitimate in only a few circumstances. What are they?
2. In what ways do police agencies resemble military organizations?
3. When is the use of police SWAT teams appropriate? When is their use inappropriate?
4. Have women police officers been fully integrated into the nation's law enforcement agencies? What about minorities?
5. What is community policing, and how does it differ from traditional models of law enforcement?
6. What is problem-oriented policing and how is it related to community policing?
7. What is the broken windows theory? What are this theory's implications for law enforcement? Why do some scholars see this theory as problematic?
8. Is policing more stressful than other occupations? What are the sources of police stress?
9. What problems are caused by stress in police work? What can police administrators do to make the job of policing less stressful?

SUGGESTED FURTHER READING

Alex, Nicholas. *Black in Blue*. New York: Appleton-Century-Crofts, 1969.

Chevigny, Paul. *Edge of the Knife: Police Violence in the Americas*. New York: The New Press, 1995.

Fletcher, Connie. *Breaking and Entering: Women Cops Talk about Life in the Ultimate Men's Club*. New York: Harper/Collins, 1995.

DeSantis, John. *The New Untouchables: How America Sanctions Police Violence*. Chicago: The Noble Press, 1994.

Geller, William A., and Hans Toch. *And Justice for All: Understanding and Controlling Police Abuse of Force*. Washington, DC: Police Executive Research Forum, 1995.

Skolnick, Jerome. *Justice without Trial: Law Enforcement in a Democratic Society,* 3rd ed. New York: Macmillan, 1994.

ENDNOTES

1. Egon Bittner, *The Functions of the Police in Modern Society* (Cambridge, MA: Oelgeschlager, Gumm and Hain, 1980), 36.
2. Ibid., 36–37.
3. James J. Fyfe, "The Split-Second Syndrome and Other Determinants of Police Violence," in *Critical Issues in Policing: Contemporary Readings,* 4th ed., eds. Roger G. Dunham and Geoffrey P. Alpert (Prospect Heights, IL: Waveland, 2001), 583–598.
4. Bittner, *Function of the Police.*
5. Antony M. Pate and Lorie A. Fridell, *Police Use of Force: Official Reports, Citizen Complaints, and Legal Consequences* (Washington, DC: Police Foundation, 1993), 74.
6. Peter B. Kraska and Victor E. Kappeler, "Militarizing American Police: The Rise and Normalization of Paramilitary Units," *Social Problems* (February 1997): 1–17.
7. Jerome H. Skolnick and James J. Fyfe, *Above the Law: Police and the Excessive Use of Force* (New York: The Free Press, 1993), 114.
8. Peter B. Kraska and Louise J. Cubellis, "Militarizing Mayberry and Beyond: Making Sense of American Paramilitary Policing," *Justice Quarterly* (December 1997): 607–629.
9. Peter B. Kraska and Larry K. Gaines, "Tactical Operations Units: A National Study," *Police Chief* (March 1977): 34–38.
10. In May 1964, while running for presidential office, Johnson called for a nationwide war against poverty and presented economic and social welfare legislation designed to create what he called the "Great Society." Infoplease, "Lyndon Baines Johnson," http://www.infoplease.com/ce6/people/A0859055.html.
11. Center for Research on Criminal Justice, *The Iron Fist and the Velvet Glove: An Analysis of the U.S. Police* (Berkeley, CA: Center for Research on Criminal Justice, 1977).
12. Ibid., 97.
13. Bittner, *Functions of the Police.*
14. Kraska and Gaines, "Militarizing Mayberry."
15. Carl Klockars, "The Dirty Harry Problem," *Annals of the American Academy of Political and Social Science* (November 1980).

16. Skolnick and Fyfe, *Above the Law,* 107.
17. Gregg Barak, Jeanne M. Flavin, and Paul S. Leighton, *Class Race, Gender, and Crime: Social Realities of Justice in America* (Los Angeles: Roxbury, 2001).
18. National Center for Women and Policing, "Equality Denied: The Status of Women in Policing: 2000," (National Center for Women and Policing, a division of the Feminist Majority Foundation, April 2001). http://www.womenandpolicing.org/PDF/2000%20Status%20Report.pdf
19. Jerome Skolnick, *Justice without Trial: Law Enforcement in a Democratic Society,* 3rd ed. (New York: Macmillan, 1994), 41–68.
20. Susan E. Martin, "Women Officers on the Move: An Update on Women in Policing," *Critical Issues in Policing: Contemporary Readings,* 4th ed., eds. Roger G. Dunham and Geoffrey P. Alpert (Prospect Heights, IL: Waveland Press, 2001), 401–422.
21. Alissa Pollity Worden, "The Attitudes of Women and Men in Policing: Testing Conventional and Contemporary Wisdom," *Criminology* 31, no. 2 (1993): 203–240.
22. Clemens Bartollas and Larry D. Hahn, *Policing in America* (Boston: Allyn and Bacon, 1999). See especially Chapter 12, "The Minority Police Officer," for a discussion of black, Hispanic/Latino-American, American Indian, and homosexual police officers.
23. Ibid.
24. Nicholas Alex, *Black in Blue: A Study of the Negro Policeman* (New York: Appleton-Century Crafts, 1969).
25. Susan E. Martin, "Outsider Within the Station House: The Impact of Race and Gender on Black Women Police," *Social Problems* (August 1994): 389.
26. Bartollas and Hahn, *Policing in America,* 322–330.
27. Bureau of Justice Statistics, http://www.ojp.usdoj.gov/bjs/sandlle.htm#policing.
28. Robert Trojanowicz, Victor E. Keppeler, Larry K. Gaines, and Bonnie Bucqueroux, *Community Policing: A Contemporary Perspective,* 2nd ed. (Cincinnati: Anderson, 1998).
29. Samuel Walker and Charles M. Katz, *The Police in America: An Introduction,* 4th ed. (Boston: McGraw-Hill, 2001), 202–203. Walker and Katz also stated three other reasons for this change: the police car patrol, the existing use of detectives, and the emphasis on response time. All were found wanting. Additionally, policing was recognized as a complex job that involved more than crime fighting and that citizens were coproducers of police services. Our discussion here of these alternative forms of policing is heavily influenced by their ideas in Chapter 7 of their book.
30. Walker and Katz, *The Police in America: An Introduction,* 205.
31. Gorden Bazemore and Allen W. Cole, "Police in the 'Laboratory' of the Neighborhood: Evaluating Problem-Oriented Strategies in a Medium-Sized City," *American Journal of Police* 13, no. 3 (1994): 119–147.
32. Wesley Skogan and Susan M. Hartnett, *Community Policing: Chicago Style* (New York: Oxford University Press, 1997).
33. Herman Goldstein, *Problem-Oriented Policing* (New York: McGraw-Hill, 1990).
34. Lorraine Green, "Cleaning Up Drug Hot Spots in Oakland, California: The Displacement and Diffusion Effects," *Justice Quarterly* 12 (December 1995): 737–754.
35. Walker and Katz, *The Police in America,* 226–227.
36. James Q. Wilson and George L. Kelling, "Broken Windows: Police and Neighborhood Safety," *Atlantic Monthly,* March 1982, 29–38.
37. Samuel Walker, "Broken Windows and Fractured History: The Use and Misuse of History in Recent Patrol Analysis," in *Critical Issues in Policing: Contemporary Readings,* eds. Roger G. Dunham and Geoffrey P. Alpert (Prospect Heights, IL: Waveland Press, 2001), 480–492.
38. Amnesty International, *United States of America: Police Brutality and Excessive Use of Force in the New York City Police Department* (New York: Amnesty International, 1996).
39. Lawrence Sherman, "Policing for Crime Prevention," *Preventing Crime: What Works, What Doesn't, What's Promising* (Washington, DC: National Institute of Justice, 1998). Online at http://www.ncjrs.org/works/chapter8.htm.
40. Wilson and Kelling, "Broken Windows," 29–38.
41. Ibid.
42. Walker, "Broken Windows," 480–492.
43. D. W. Mills, "Poking Holes in the Theory of 'Broken Windows,'" *The Chronicle of Higher Education* (February 9, 2001): A14.
44. Ronald V. Clarke, "Situational Crime Prevention: Its Theoretical Basis and Practical Scope," in *Crime Displacement: The Other Side of Prevention,* ed. Robert P. McNamara (East Rockaway, NY: Cummings and Hathaway, 1994), 38–70.
45. Joseph Wambaugh, *The Choirboys* (New York: Dell, 1975).
46. John M. Violanti, James R. Marshall, and Barbara Howe, "Stress, Coping, and Alcohol Use: The Police Connection," *Journal of Police*

Science and Administration 13, no. 2 (1985): 106–110.

47. Charles Unkovic and William Brown, "The Drunken Cop," *Police Chief* (April 1978): 29–20.
48. Max T. Raterman, "Substance Abuse and Police Discipline," *Police Department Disciplinary Bulletin* (December 2000): 2–4.
49. Skolnick and Fyfe, *Above the Law.*
50. Bartollas and Hahn, *Policing in America,* 199.
51. Peter E. Maynard and Nancy E. Maynard, "Stress in Police Families: Some Policy Implications," *Journal of Police Science and Administration* 10, no. 3 (1982): 302–314.
52. Mary J. C. Hageman, "Occupational Stress and Marital Relationships," *Journal of Police Science and Administration* 6, no. 4 (1978): 402–412.
53. Glory Cochrane, "The Effects of Sleep Deprivation," *FBI Law Enforcement Bulletin* (July 2001): 22–25.
54. Bruce A. Arrigo and Karyn Garsky, "Police Suicide: A Glimpse Behind the Badge," in *Critical Issues in Policing: Contemporary Readings,* 4th ed., eds. Roger G. Dunham and Geoffrey P. Alpert, (Prospect Heights, IL: Waveland Press, 2001), 664–680.

PART three

ROLE OF THE COURTS

outline

CHAPTER 8

History and Organization of Courts

COURTS PLAY A PIVOTAL ROLE IN THE U.S. CRIMINAL JUSTICE system. They are responsible for both determining the guilt or innocence of the defendant and deciding on the disposition or sentence for defendants who are found guilty. This all must be done according to a complex and ever-changing network of laws, personnel, and political pressures. The courts are besieged on all sides by those who observe an institution in crisis, such as the following:

- Law enforcement officers, who complain that offenders are treated too leniently[1]
- Corrections officials, who have no room in their prisons for new inmates and are concerned about the severe sentences that keep inmates incarcerated for many, many years[2]
- The public, who sees the court as an unfathomable machine that fails to provide justice when criminals are released because of technicalities[3]

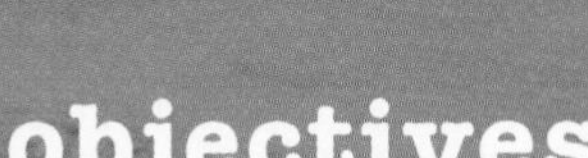

objectives

After reading this chapter the student should be able to:

1. Explain why some observers see U.S. courts as "an institution in crisis."
2. Discuss how courts are subject to outside influences.
3. Outline the history of courts.
4. Discuss trial by ordeal and trial by battle.
5. Discuss the Assize of Clarendon.
6. Discuss the beginnings of the jury trial.
7. Discuss the Magna Carta.
8. Explain the problems of early American courts.
9. Discuss U.S. slave courts.
10. Draw a connection between England's legal treatment of early American colonists and the Revolution.
11. Discuss the cases, historical events, and individuals that have affected the way the courts have evolved.
12. Explain court organization; include the federal court system and courts of appeals.
13. Discuss the role of the Supreme Court.
14. Discuss specialized federal courts and the types of cases they handle.

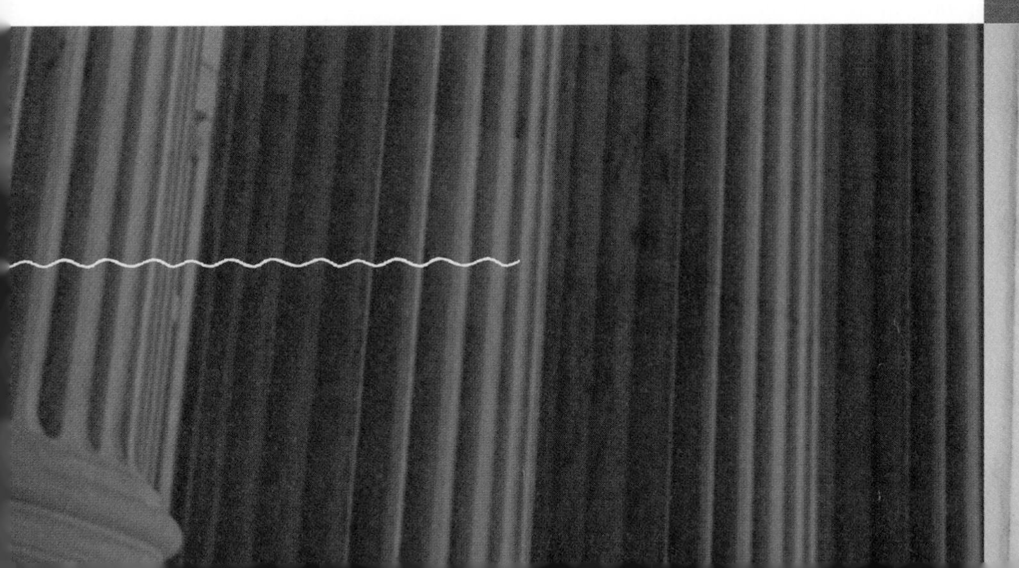

- Legislatures, which cannot provide the necessary resources to handle the huge caseloads because tax dollars must be shared with many other government functions, including law enforcement and corrections[4]
- Offenders and defendants, guilty or innocent, as well as victims, who do not believe the court is dispensing justice in an evenhanded and fair manner[5]

The court seems to be in a powerful position within the criminal justice system because it makes the important determinations of what happens to offenders. However, the court is actually at the mercy of outside forces. It does not control how it is financed; it does not control how many cases are sent to it; it cannot ensure adequate resources to carry out its sentences; and because its work is done in a courtroom open to the press, it cannot control its public image. In many ways, then, the court is an institution that takes the blame for deficiencies not of its making.[6]

Another concern of the U.S. court system also complicates its mission. The professional orientation of those who practice law affects the image and the functioning of the court. The problem is twofold:

1. **The U.S. criminal court system is an adversarial process.** The adversarial process uses defense attorneys and prosecutors to represent the positions of two opposing parties. The process places the burden on the prosecutor who must prove to a jury (or a judge, in the case of a bench trial) that the defendant is guilty beyond a reasonable doubt. The defense attorney argues for the innocence, as well as the legal protections, of the accused. The judge, a disinterested party, ensures that the two sides play by the rules. The adversarial process can sometimes seem to result in defense attorneys and prosecutors advocating for one side at the expense of the truth. The process requires lawyers to strike the most advantageous deal they can for their clients, even if they may realize that other outcomes may better reflect the goals of justice.
2. **Outsiders have difficulty understanding what is happening in the court.** Because our legal system evolved over a long period of time and because it draws its inspiration and procedures from so many sources, the process and the language of the court seem foreign to outside observers, especially to defendants. Cynical individuals might believe that the reason the courts are so unfathomable is to ensure that only those with a legal education can successfully negotiate the corridors of the courthouse.

Because of the issues of professional orientation and lack of control over funding and image, the courts seem shrouded in mystery. The result is that a rather romantic view of the courts has emerged whereby the justice that is (or is not) dispensed is more a product of the courageous attorney and less a function of the criminal justice system process. The popular image of how the courts work is informed by television programs such as *L.A. Law, Ally McBeal, The Practice,* and *Judging Amy.* A realistic image of the court is further compromised by the law-as-entertainment programs such as *Peoples' Court, Judge Mills Lane, Judge Judy,* and *Judge Hackett.* Thus, the image of our courts is either one of the good-looking defense attorney fighting valiantly against a corrupt and inefficient system or one of a short-tempered judge humiliating confused or naive people.

On the bright side, however, are the real court cases broadcast by *Court TV.* Here, much of the romanticism of the courts can be dispelled when the viewer sees the ponderous, methodical, and rule-bound process of the court. (For an example of how a state court works, see Figure 8.1.) Rather than achieving justice in a fast-paced hour (including commercials), *Court TV* reveals how cases are delayed, continued, interrupted, and even cancelled by the motions made by lawyers.

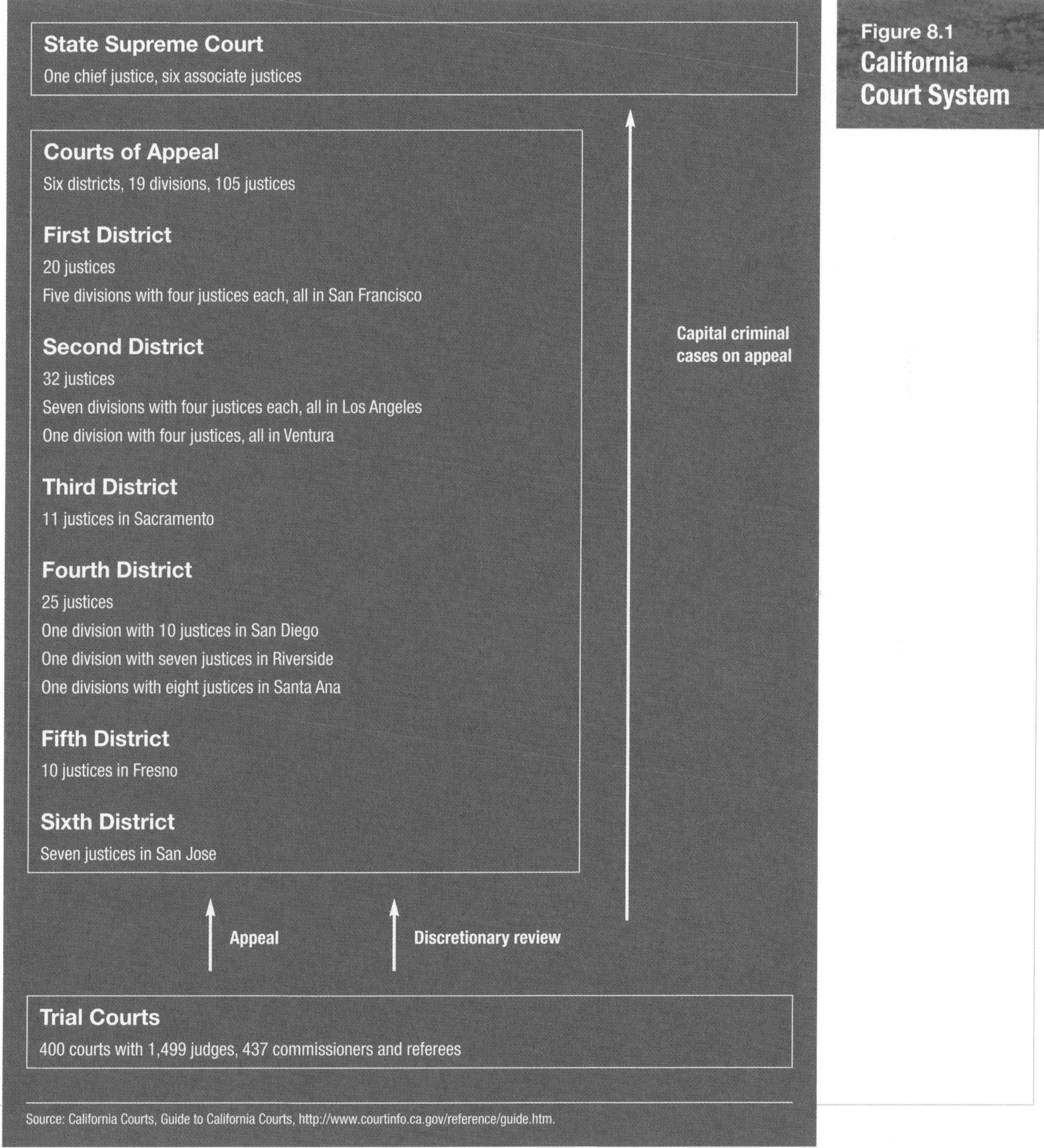

State Supreme Court
One chief justice, six associate justices
Courts of Appeal
Six districts, 19 divisions, 105 justices
First District
20 justices
Five divisions with four justices each, all in San Francisco
Second District
32 justices
Seven divisions with four justices each, all in Los Angeles
One division with four justices, all in Ventura
Third District
11 justices in Sacramento
Fourth District
25 justices
One division with 10 justices in San Diego
One division with seven justices in Riverside
One divisions with eight justices in Santa Ana
Fifth District
10 justices in Fresno
Sixth District
Seven justices in San Jose
Capital criminal cases on appeal
Appeal
Discretionary review
Trial Courts
400 courts with 1,499 judges, 437 commissioners and referees
Source: California Courts, Guide to California Courts, http://www.courtinfo.ca.gov/reference/guide.htm.

Figure 8.1 California Court System

The public gets to see real victims, witnesses, offenders, attorneys, and judges, not Hollywood actors. *Court TV,* however, does not capture the whole truth. Cases that are selected reflect only the most sensational. Most of the real work of the court, such as plea negotiations and witness preparations, is done outside the eye of the camera.

Much of the picture we have of the court is therefore an imperfect one. Like an impressionist painting, our picture is fuzzy and idealized, rather than being a clear, accurate portrait of how the court functions. Our goal in these next three chapters on the criminal courts is to paint a more realistic picture of how the courts are structured and how they operate. Our picture will reveal that courts are less sensational than the image we get from television, but they are also more fascinating. By putting courts into the larger context of how they fit into the overall governmental structure, and how they interact with the other components of the criminal justice system, we are able to appreciate how they have evolved to the critical position they hold today in the lives of so many individuals who either work as practitioners within the courts or are the victims, witnesses, and offenders circulating within the criminal justice system.

Courts in History

The concept of the court has been burned into our psyches by religion, tradition, and the media. The idea that one day we will be held accountable for our sins, transgressions of the law, and insults to others is often a worry. As the saying goes, "What goes around comes around." Each of us needs to be careful about our behavior lest we find ourselves having to explain it to the judge. Some religions evoke a Judgment Day in which a higher power will tally our good deeds and compare them to our mistakes and then make a decision about the ultimate sentence.

Courts of some type have been consistent features of many societies.[7] Although it is impossible to know for certain whether ancient peoples resolved their conflicts with processes that resemble our courts, explorers and anthropologists have found similarities between the functions of modern courts and societies that were not yet influenced by European systems of government.[8] This leads us to believe that the duties of the court satisfy universal needs in one manner or another. According to E. A. Hoebel:

> *Given such variability, we cannot assume that humans have any universal understanding of what specifically constitutes justice. We can only conclude that there appears to be a desire for some form of satisfaction,* variously construed, *that is felt to restore the balance that was disrupted by the offender's troublemaking.*[9]

Before There Were Courts: The Blood Feud

Courts are a result of the increasing sophistication of societies in which a division of labor was necessary.[10] As societies became more complex, individuals could not be the doctor, farmer, hunter, religious leader, and stockbroker all at the same time.[11] Modern courts are mechanisms for resolving disputes that have evolved from a long and uneven history of feuds, duels, wars, and other types of conflicts that often caused more problems than they solved. A peaceful way to resolve contested issues between individuals and groups was required because of the disruption to society caused by primitive methods. The **blood feud** is an example of why courts had to be invented. An example of the blood feud in primitive cultures can be found in that of the Nuer people in what is now southern Sudan.

blood feud
A disagreement, the settlement of which is based on personal vengeance and physical violence.

Disputes can often be settled on account of close kinship and other social ties, but between tribesmen as such they are either settled by the aggrieved party using force, and this may result in homicide and bloodshed, or by the debtor giving way in the knowledge that force may be used and a blood feud will result. It is the knowledge that a Nuer is brave and will stand up against aggression and enforce his rights by club and spear that ensures respect for person and property.[12]

The blood feud is based on vengeance. If an individual is killed, then it is the right, indeed the obligation, of members of the family to exact justice by revenge by killing the murderer, or lacking that, a blood member of the murderer's family. This does, of course, set off another round of violence in which the original killer's family would feel entitled to seek their own revenge. The result could be a long history of reciprocal killings based on family blood ties. It is easy to see how in times of economic hardship, in which the

FOCUS ON ETHICS

Modern Day Blood Feud

Your little brother has been dating a girl from another school for several months. Recently, while arguing with her, he got carried away and struck her. The next night he was gunned down in a drive-by shooting on the front steps of your parents' home. You are certain your brother's killers are the girl's cousins, but the police have no solid evidence and are not close to making an arrest. Although you know your brother was no saint and that striking another person deserves some punishment, his death has devastated your family and you believe that, in part, it was racially motivated. The girl's cousins are part of a white supremacy group that has continually hassled people of color in your county. Being of Hispanic origin, your family has pleaded with the sheriff's office to investigate your brother's murder again. However, the sheriff himself has commented to reporters that your brother probably deserved what he got and that his office was too busy to expend more resources on this crime unless there was further evidence.

You have lost faith in the local criminal justice system's ability and motivation to solve your brother's murder and bring his killers to justice. Meanwhile, your grandfather is mumbling that in his day the family would have avenged this death themselves. He looks at you in disgust and implies that you are a coward and a disgrace to the family. As a criminal justice major at a local university, you have hopes of one day becoming an FBI agent, but the pull of family honor has you thinking that you should make sure the killers do not get away with this crime.

WHAT DO YOU DO?

1. Do nothing. Even though you feel the local criminal justice system has failed to properly investigate your brother's murder, there is little you can do that is within the law. Besides, you have your own career to think about. Even though your family expects you to seek justice, you are unwilling to continue the cycle of violence started by your hot-headed brother.
2. Uphold your family's honor and retaliate against the cousins of your brother's girlfriend. If the local criminal justice system does not care about your community, it is your duty to seek justice through revenge. If you don't, then the Hispanic community will continue to be victimized by the powerful white majority. It is time to show the community that there will be justice for your people, one way or another.
3. Go to the FBI and make a complaint charging that this was a hate crime and that your brother's constitutional rights were violated. If the local criminal justice system refuses to act, then make a federal case out of your brother's murder.

labor of everyone is required for group subsistence, a blood feud could be devastating for a society. In lieu of violence, a payment could be made to the deceased's family to compensate for their loss and achieve a sense of justice. In the Germanic tribes of Europe this was known as a *wergeld* (which can be translated as "man-price").[13] The amount was determined by the status of the victim.[14]

Courts in England

In England, the payment to the victim's family was called a *bot* instead of a *wergeld*. An additional payment called a *wite* was also assessed against the perpetrator as compensation for

The Hatfields and the McCoys

Courtesy of Corbis/Bettmann.

Perhaps the most famous American blood feud was the one that took place in the late 1800s between two Appalachian families: the Hatfields and the McCoys. The feud grew so bloody, it attracted national attention and eventually had to be settled by the Supreme Court.

The families were headed by patriarchs William Anderson (Devil Anse) Hatfield and Randolph (Rand'l) McCoy. The two families were large, with at least 13 children each, and a host of relations and allies. They lived on opposite sides of a stream called the Tug Fork, with the Hatfields in West Virginia and the McCoys in Kentucky. The reason behind the families' animosity is vague. In some accounts, it is attributed to their being on opposite sides of the Civil War, with Hatfields being Confederates and the McCoys backing the Union. Another possible reason is that Rand'l McCoy thought a Hatfield stole one of his hogs.

The first major clash in the feud happened in 1882 when some McCoys shot and killed Ellison Hatfield during a fight. In return, the Hatfields executed three McCoy brothers: Tolbert, Phamer, and Randolph, Jr. A number of ambushes and murders followed. Although family members from either side were occasionally arrested in their home territories, they were usually released.

On January 1, 1888, a group of Hatfields attacked the home of Rand'l McCoy, shot and killed two of his children, and burned his property. Shortly thereafter, a group of McCoys and their supporters, including a deputy sheriff, crossed into West Virginia, killing at least four Hatfields. The crew took into custody nine more Hatfields to be tried in Kentucky. West Virginia filed a federal suit, and Kentucky defended the action. In May 1888 the Supreme Court ruled in *Plyant Mahon v. Abner Justice* that Kentucky had the right to try the Hatfields. In the end, one Hatfield was hanged and eight others were imprisoned.

The feud tapered off and ended by the 1920s, but a faint echo was heard again in 2002. Two McCoys filed suit against relations of the Hatfields to gain access to a Hatfield cemetery where Tolber, Phamer, and Randolph McCoy, Jr. were buried. In 2003 more than 60 descendants of the two families signed a truce during the fourth Hatfield–McCoy Festival.

QUESTIONS

1. Are blood feuds a good way to settle personal differences? Why? Why not?
2. Could the Hatfield–McCoy feud flare up again?
3. What is the likelihood that there are family blood feuds currently going on in the United States?

Source: "Hatfield, McCoy Descendants Ink Truce," *The Kansas City Star*/Associated Press, June 14, 2003, http://www.kansascity.com/mld/kansascity/news/nation/6089371.htm.

the king or the noble holding court and as a penalty for breaking the king's peace.[15] Because the royalty found these fees a convenient way to raise revenue, and one that the people did not object to, they gradually increased the fees, instituted more fines, and generally institutionalized the practice of holding court as a way of resolving conflicts in a more peaceful manner. The court did more than resolve conflicts, however. The court was usually convened to mark some celebration such as a royal birth, wedding, or religious festival. Nobles used these occasions to meet and discuss war, taxes, and other matters of government including the establishment of new laws. In many ways, the medieval court acted as both a court and a congress where a multitude of activities were accomplished. The lines between criminal and civil cases were not yet established, and the rights of the accused were absent. One important aspect of the court that needs to be emphasized is that this practice offered the king and other nobles an excellent way to raise revenues. Gradually, more and more behaviors were criminalized and made subject to fines and fees that swelled the coffers of the king. This is important because crimes were gradually redefined not so much as disputes between individuals but as crimes against the state where the king's peace represented public order.[16]

Trial by Compurgation

Compurgation involved the practice of taking an oath that one was telling the truth. Both the defense and the prosecution would present oath-takers who would swear they were telling the truth. However, many of the oath-takers could not speak to the actual crime as a witness because they had no direct knowledge. They could only swear that the defendant or victim was telling the truth. In a sense, they were character witnesses. Not all oaths were equal. The value of one's oath was pegged to one's *wergeld,* or the price that the court deemed to be the value of the person's life.[17] Consequently, the oath of a noble, whose *wergeld* was 1,000 shillings, would need to be countered by five freemen whose worths were 200 shillings each. Those who had no established value under the law, such as women or slaves, could not offer their oath and had to have others swear for them. The accuser was required to offer more oaths than the defendant, which, in a way, echoes our current notion that one is innocent until proven guilty.

compurgation
In medieval German and English law, a defendant could establish innocence by taking an oath and having a required number of people swear that they believed the oath. Also called "wager of law." Compurgation was permitted until 1833.

Finding others to take an oath swearing to one's trustworthiness was not easy. People placed a high value on the veracity of their oaths and would not swear for those whom they could not completely trust because of the prospect of eternal damnation. Consequently, thieves, pickpockets, and con artists could not convince others to stand up for them and swear an oath to their honesty. Individuals were also required to take their oaths without making mistakes. Lifting your hand off the Bible or neglecting to kiss it afterwards were considered acts against God and invalidated the value of the oath.[18]

Trial by Ordeal

When someone could not get enough people to take an oath to support him or her, or when there were enough oath-takers but the evidence was strong against the accused, **trial by ordeal** was required. There were essentially three types of trial by ordeal: trial by cold water, trial by hot water, and trial by hot iron, or as it was sometimes called, trial by fire.[19] These ordeals were, by today's scientific standards, unlikely to find the truth and obviously biased against the accused. For instance, in a trial by hot water the accused was supposed to plunge a hand into a cauldron of boiling water and pick a large stone off the bottom. Not being able to pick up the stone was evidence of guilt. If the stone was plucked from the bottom, the accused's wounded hand was bound with bandages. When examined three days later, the accused was declared innocent if the wounds were healing naturally with no signs of infection. However, if the wounds were festering and full of pus, the accused was declared guilty, and a sentence was imposed.

trial by ordeal
An ancient custom found in many cultures in which the accused was required to perform a test to prove guilt or innocence. The outcome of the test was considered to be decided by a divine authority.

These trials by ordeal depended on divine intervention to demonstrate the innocence of the accused and resulted in death or extreme pain for those whose bodies were simply following the laws of nature. Consequently, many individuals confessed to crimes they had not committed to escape the painful and unreliable trial by ordeal. The role of the judge in trial by ordeal was limited to declaring whether the accused passed the test and to imposing the sentence that was prescribed by the law.[20]

Jousting by knights is an example of trial by battle.
Courtesy of CORBIS-NY.

Trial by Battle

Trial by battle was another way to solve disputes between individuals that did not rely on religious concepts such as divine intervention. Although trial by battle could result in the same prospects of being determined guilty when in fact one was innocent, it did offer the accused a bit more control over the outcome. Although originally reserved for knights to resolve their disputes, peasants also used trial by battle. The most interesting aspect of trial by battle was that litigants could select someone else to fight their battle for them. Thus, the rich, women, and those who were not physically able to fight could have someone "champion" their cause who could stand a reasonable chance of winning the trial by battle.[21]

Development of the Jury

inquest
In archaic usage, considered to be the first type of jury. The English crown conducted proceedings to determine which lands it had conquered and who owned them. The inquest was eventually broadened to address concerns other than land ownership.

Assize of Clarendon
A 12th-century English law that established judicial procedure and the grand jury system. It also took power from the local courts and returned it to the English crown.

The **inquest** can be considered to be the first type of jury. After a war, the English crown needed to determine which lands it had conquered and so conducted an inquest in which men were summoned before the court to attest to the ownership of the land in the surrounding area. Gradually, the inquest was broadened to concerns other than land ownership, and the rudiments of a grand jury were developed whereby the crown would convene a court and individuals would be charged with committing crimes.

Grand Jury

In 1166 a law called the **Assize of Clarendon** was enacted to correct some of the problems and inefficiencies of the judicial process.[22] When the prosecution was simply an individual matter, the accuser would often fail to follow through on the complaint because of the time, expense, and difficulty of achieving a guilty verdict against the accused. This was problematic not only because the guilty would go free and the community would be left unprotected, but also because the king would not be able to collect a court fee.

The Assize of Clarendon was a series of ordinances that established the beginnings of the grand jury system. The jury, comprising 12 men from each jurisdiction, was given the duty of informing the king's judges of the most serious crimes committed in each jurisdiction. In this way, the charging decision was taken from the individual accuser and given to civic-minded citizens who performed this duty as a service to the community. Crimes, therefore, started their journey from being regarded as private wrongs to being viewed as public problems. The criminal justice system continued to become more a servant of the state than simply a mechanism in which individuals settled disputes. The Assize of Clarendon law gradually developed from a process of simply identifying and charging wrongdoers to a body that determined whether the evidence was sufficient to

The Leopard-Skin Chief

Before there were formal courts, societies had to resolve differences in other ways. One of the most prevalent was for individuals to exact justice on their own. The customs of particular peoples allowed an aggrieved party to use force to gain some measure of revenge and show others that he or she was not someone who could be taken advantage of. This revenge did not always conclude the dispute, and some form of reciprocal violence could come back to haunt the avenger. Often, this resulted in a blood feud in which members of different families continued to prey on one another long after the original violation was forgotten.

As various societies struggled to come up with alternatives to the blood feud, some interesting mechanisms for preventing violence were introduced that seem to foreshadow the role of today's court. One of the interesting developments is the mediator role of the leopard-skin chief used by the Nuer people in southern Sudan.

> *A man who has a cow stolen may ask a leopard-skin chief to go with him to request the return of the cow. The chief goes first, with several of the elders of his village, to the plaintiff's homestead, where he is given beer to drink. Later they go, with a deputation from the plaintiff's village, and here also the chief may be presented with some beer or a goat. The chief is considered to be neutral and a certain sanctity attaches to his person so that there is little likelihood of the deputation being injured. The visiting elders sit with elders of the defendant's village and the chief in one of the byres and talk about the matter in dispute. The owner of the animal gives his view and the man who has stolen it attempts to justify his action. Then the chief, and anyone else who wishes to do so, expresses an opinion on the question. When everyone has had his say the chief and elders withdraw to discuss the matter among themselves and to agree upon the decision. The disputants accept the verdict of the chief and the elders and, later, the owner of the animal gives the chief a young steer or a ram unless he is a very poor man, when he gives him nothing.*

QUESTIONS

1. What aspects of the modern court can you discern in the proceedings of the leopard-skin chief?
2. Are there any elements of due process here?
3. What hints do you see of a judge, a jury, and/or a reflection of community standards?

Source: E. E. Evans-Pritchard, *The Nuer: A Description of the Modes of Livelihood and Political Institutions of a Niotic People* (London: Oxford University Press, 1968), 162–164.

detain the accused prior to trial.[23] Today, the successor of the Assize of Clarendon, the grand jury, is primarily a check on the power of the prosecutor. The grand jury determines whether the evidence is powerful enough to charge the accused with a crime. Consequently, the grand jury has evolved into a body that protects the citizens from overzealous prosecutors.

Jury Trial

The jury trial was created to fill a vacuum in the criminal justice process. In 1215 the Fourth Lateran Council of the Roman Catholic Church forbade priests to participate in trials by ordeal. Because the trial by ordeal was determined by the divine intervention of God, and because priests not only blessed the instrument of trial by ordeal but also

A 15th-century English jury and court officials.
Courtesy of CORBIS-NY.

judged whether God did in fact provide a miracle to save the accused, the practice had to be stopped.[24] The priests had too many roles to play, creating a conflict of interest. Trial by ordeal, then, could no longer be ordained by the church.

Into this void stepped the jury trial. People had a difficult time accepting the judgment of mere men, especially when the sentence could be death. They were more comfortable letting God decide such issues with signs such as miracles. However, with the church no longer sanctioning such spectacles, the judgment of 12 "good" men was gradually accepted. At first, individuals were given the choice between being held in a dungeon indefinitely and a jury trial.[25] This choice posed an interesting dilemma, however. If the jury convicted someone of a crime, the offender's lands were forfeited to the king. If the offender died in prison, however, his lands were passed to his heirs. The type of imprisonment the accused was subjected to was called *la peine forte et dure* (strong and hard punishment). This entailed a diet of bread and water, heavy chains, and generally the worst conditions that dungeons could offer.[26] Consequently, only the most stubborn decided to perish in prison in order to bequeath their property to their heirs.[27]

For the most part, the trial jury comprised the same men who sat on the grand jury that brought the charge against the defendant. These jurors were expected to know the facts of the case, so very little testimony was required. Guilt or innocence was determined by the accused's reputation and the intimate knowledge about the facts of the case that the jurors had when they first charged the accused. This process was gradually determined to be flawed, and eventually the two juries were separated. In many places this required the use of jurors from outside the community, which resulted in the need for testimony to educate all the jurors about the facts of the case.[28]

It took the jury 250 years to develop into the powerful institution it became at the end of the 15th century. Its authority to determine the guilt or innocence of the accused was paramount, and angry judges could not change its verdict. The concept of an independent jury became firmly established in the English system and provides for us today a key check against the power of the state to prosecute citizens.

This 15th-century woodcut depicts a prisoner shackled in a dungeon.
Courtesy of CORBIS-NY.

The Magna Carta

In 1215, about the same time as the jury began to develop, the Magna Carta was signed by King John (1199–1216). He was under pressure to sign this document, which limited the power of the king and recognized the rights of nobles. Many of these rights had long been in effect, but King John was a particularly arbitrary and power-hungry ruler who had been encroaching on centuries-old legal and political customs. The Magna Carta placed the king under the rule of law. This document did little at the time for the common man because it was the nobles who forced the king to recognize their rights. However, it did set a precedent of encoding in the law limitations on the state's power. In a sense, then, it is a conservative document rather than a revolutionary one. Its effects were felt not so much immediately as over a longer period of time when the divine rights of the king were attenuated in favor of written legal rights of nobles and clergy and, eventually, through future documents patterned after the Magna Carta that called for rights for all citizens.[29]

Court of the Star Chamber

As a result of the religious strife and the power of the crown to use the courts as a tool of repression, the common law that protected the rights of the accused came under strain in the 15th century. Political crimes and treason were especially problematic, and a special judicial body, the **Court of the Star Chamber**, was established to deal with offenses such as riots, unlawful assembly, perjury, criminal libel, and conspiracy. Additionally, jurors of cases could be brought before the Star Chamber if judges felt they had violated their duties to convict the guilty.[30] The Court of the Star Chamber was notable for its abuses, such as the following:

- Interrogation of suspects in secret
- The use of torture as a fact-finding tool
- No right to a trial by jury
- Accusation brought without evidence
- The accused not informed of the identity of persons making accusations[31]

Court of the Star Chamber An ancient meeting place of the king of England's councilors in the palace of Westminster in London, so called because of stars painted on the ceiling. The court was separate from common law courts. Although its sentences included corporal punishments, convicts were never sentenced to death. It was abolished by the Long Parliament in 1641.

The Court of the Star Chamber was important because it demonstrated how a court without any sort of due process could violate the human rights of citizens. Also, it showed how unfettered power could be used to subvert the law and cause findings of guilt when in fact the suspect was innocent. Consequently, the Court of the Star Chamber had the effect of reaffirming the protections of the common law and caused citizens to become even more wary of the power of the criminal justice system. It was abolished in 1641.

By the 18th century, because of the intense reactions to the abuses of the Court of the Star Chamber, many of the essential elements of modern criminal procedure were found in some form in the courts of England. Features such as a preliminary hearing, a grand jury that determined whether evidence was sufficient to continue the case, the opportunity for the defendant to challenge jurors who might be prejudiced against the case, and the idea that the verdict of the jury is the final decision when the defendant is acquitted were added to the process.

Some aspects of modern due process that began to find their way into the 18th-century court, however, were applied in a haphazard and inconsistent fashion. Sometimes, but not always, defendants were allowed to have their own counsel. The juries were composed of "respectable" citizens who were usually of a different social class than the defendants. And finally, the concepts of probable cause and presumption of innocence were not yet fully ingrained into the criminal justice process. Nevertheless, the development of the English courts between the 11th and 18th centuries provided the foundation for the courts of the early American colonies and eventually what became the United States.

Courts in Colonial America

The migration of courts from England to the American colonies was an imperfect one. Because each of the 13 colonies was established under different motivations and conditions (for instance, Pennsylvania was founded by religious dissenters, whereas Virginia was founded by English gentry), the systems of government tended to vary widely. England made no concerted effort to develop standardized practices among the colonies, so the courts developed in response to the local economic, political, and social concerns of each colony.[32] Because many colonies were established by grants to individuals or corporations, the early governors would hold court as they saw fit, and many of the protections of the law that existed for defendants in England were absent in colonial America. Complaints about the courts were frequent, and often individuals appealed to England to send trained judges to administer the law.[33]

Slavery and the Law

The early adoption of slavery in the American colonies caused problems for the justice system. An alternative system of laws had to be created to control the slaves. Whereas England passed a tradition to the colonies on how to deal with freemen and indentured servants, the nascent United States had to develop slavery laws to protect the interests of owners of large tracts of land.[34] Slave courts put a gloss of legitimacy on the abominable practices of slave control practiced by slave owners:

> *The master himself was law, judge, and jury over most aspects of slave life: this was inherent in the system. But in North Carolina, at least as early as 1715, there were special courts for slaves who disobeyed the law. Whipping was the common mode of punishment. Serious crimes called for the death penalty; but a dead slave injured his owner's pocketbook; hence owners were repaid out of public funds. Castration was an alternative punishment for serious crimes. Happily, this punishment was eliminated in 1764.*[35]

In spite of the setbacks for legal rights of citizens that occurred during the transition of law from England to the American colonies, progress did begin to develop (except for

The Boston Tea Party is an example of the early colonists' dissatisfaction with the English government. In response to an increased tax on tea, the colonists dressed as Indians, boarded English ships, and tossed the tea into the Boston Harbor.

Courtesy of Corbis/Bettmann.

the slaves) because of the motivations of many individuals who deemed the New World a fresh start. The works of philosophers such as John Locke and Immanuel Kant inspired the Enlightenment with its values of liberty, limited government, and equality.[36]

Our Heritage of Due Process

It is fair to say that one of the primary social forces that led to the American Revolution of 1776 was the colonists' belief that the English crown was treating them unfairly. The repressive measures used by England violated the understandings many had about the rights of English subjects. These abuses of what many considered the common law included the practice of searching houses under general warrants to find untaxed items that were smuggled into the colonies, and the use of admiralty courts where trial by jury, right to counsel, and indictment by grand jury were absent. The colonists had their own interpretations about what common law, the Magna Carta, and the principles of the Enlightenment said about natural human rights. Not surprisingly, the English crown had a different interpretation about these rights, especially concerning matters of taxes and economics. Given the second-class citizenship felt by many colonists, therefore, a move for independence seemed inevitable.

One of the enduring consequences of independence from England is the documents that were created to specify the relationship between the people and the state. For our study of the courts, these documents of importance include the U.S. Constitution, particularly the first 10 amendments, called the Bill of Rights.[37] The framers of the Constitution recognized that conditions and situations change, and the process for amending the Constitution has allowed for expansion and a further delineation of rights. The courts were left to interpret how specific behaviors should be viewed. This has resulted in an important balance between the laws enacted by the legislature and how those laws are applied. In fact, although the Bill of Rights lists numerous rights concerning criminal procedure, the only one that is also included in all the state constitutions is the right to a jury trial. The other rights, such as the right against self-incrimination, were all derived from precedents established by courts. Informed by the Constitution, the courts are able to determine what constitutes cruel and unusual punishment and what is sufficient for probable cause for a defendant to be bound over for trial.

CASE IN POINT

Duncan v. Louisiana

The Case

Duncan v. Louisiana, 391 U.S. 145, 88 S.Ct. 1444 (1968)

The Point

Under the Sixth Amendment, defendants charged with serious crimes are entitled to a jury trial.

Gary Duncan was convicted of simple battery, which in Louisiana is punishable by a maximum of two years in prison and a $300 fine. Duncan requested a jury trial, but was denied this because Louisiana granted jury trials only where there was the potential of capital punishment or hard labor. In his bench trial, Duncan received 60 days in jail and a fine of $150.

Duncan's appeal eventually reached the Supreme Court, which stated that any crime that carries a potential punishment of two years in prison is not a petty offense. The Court deemed Duncan deserving of a jury trial under the Sixth Amendment.

The judgment against Duncan was reversed and remanded.

Changing Nature of the Court

Our discussion of the development of courts in England and the American colonies has demonstrated how this relatively recent institution has evolved to fit the changing social, political, and economic needs of a particular time and circumstance. Underlying the role of the court is the idea that justice should be blind to wealth, power, and social class. This idea took a long time to develop in courts in which special interests were paramount. Gradually, however, the rights given to nobles by the Magna Carta were extended to more categories of people.

A complete history of the evolution of the courts in the United States would take too much space to adequately cover here and would divert our attention from our limited concerns of the development of the criminal courts. However, some cases, historical events, and individuals had profound impacts on the way the courts have evolved that require, at the very least, a brief acknowledgement.

MARBURY V. MADISON.[38] The 1803 Supreme Court case of *Marbury v. Madison* is notable because it established the judiciary as equal to the executive and legislative branches of government. The issue in the case was a rather minor decision concerning whether William Marbury should be given a commission as a justice of the peace as President John Adams had ordered. Because of an error, Marbury did not receive his commission, and the new president, Thomas Jefferson, ordered that the commission not be delivered.[39] Marbury did not get his commission, but the case is famous because Chief Justice John Marshall established the principle of judicial review whereby the Supreme Court scrutinizes state and federal legislation and the acts of state and federal executive officers and courts to determine whether they are in conflict with the Constitution.[40] Marshall also initiated the practice of presenting the decisions as collective rather than separate opinions and providing written statements of the reasons the court reached it decisions.[41]

MCCULLOCH V. MARYLAND.[42] The 1819 case of *McCulloch v. Maryland* established that the court could find that the Constitution included implied powers that could be deduced from its nature and language. This decision is the basis for the expansion of the power of the federal government into areas such as banking and social programs aimed at the welfare of the people.[43]

SUPREMACY CLAUSE. In cases in 1816 and 1821, the Marshall court upheld the supremacy clause in Article VI of the Constitution and reaffirmed the superiority of federal law over state law. The cases concerned the sale of land and the right to conduct a lottery. The Court's decision established its power as the "final word" on all cases. The Supreme Court then became the court of last resort.[44]

RECONSTRUCTION AND THE EXPANSION OF FEDERAL AUTHORITY. The progress of the courts in granting the protections of due process to everyone was not a smooth and consistent path. The social and political issues of various places and decades had an influence on how courts ruled. This was especially evident in the South with its long history of support for slavery and the adjustment to post–Civil War reconstruction. While Congress passed laws that enfranchised the newly freed former slaves (Civil Rights Act of 1866), the Supreme Court supported the Southern courts, which had eroded the constitutional status of black people in the areas of voting, jury service, and public accommodations.[45]

BUSINESS, UNIONS, AND CIVIL LIBERTIES. The courts also used the Fourteenth Amendment, which was adopted after the Civil War to protect the rights of liberated slaves, to protect the interests of business. The courts interpreted the substantive due process language of the amendment to protect *any person* to include any corporate body, or association; and *property* to mean business or the profits of business. Thus, the conservative interpretation of law by the court served the interests of the wealthy and made suing businesses difficult in state courts. Furthermore, the issues of the workers such as safety regulations, hours, and taxation were decided in favor of corporate interests.[46]

PLESSY V. FERGUSON.[47] The 1896 Supreme Court decision of *Plessy v. Ferguson* held that a Louisiana law that mandated "equal but separate accommodations for the white and colored races" on all railroad cars was reasonable. This decision formed the basis for the Jim Crow laws of the South that treated people of color as second-class citizens and enforced a system of apartheid that did not began to change until 1954 when the Court ruled that the "equal but separate" doctrine in the public schools was unconstitutional.

THE WARREN COURT. In 1953 President Dwight Eisenhower nominated the former governor of California, Earl Warren, to be chief justice of the Supreme Court. As a Republican, Warren was expected to steer the court toward the conservative values and issues popular with the majority in the Republican Party. The Warren Court disappointed the conservatives with several decisions that expanded the rights of due process for those accused of crime. Additionally, in decisions that ruled that religious ceremonies in public schools were unconstitutional, that the right of privacy is implied in the Constitution, and that public officials must prove actual malice when suing reporters writing about public affairs, the Warren Court earned a reputation for championing the causes of the unpopular and the marginalized portions of society.[48]

As we can see from this brief review of some of the cases and issues that have confronted our courts, progress in developing protections for all citizens has not been consistent. First and foremost, we must remember that the courts are political institutions and that those with the power to influence government will use the courts to advance their own agendas. Although some justices, such as Earl Warren, surprise observers by issuing rulings that are contrary to expectations, justices may also vote in strict accordance with perceived party affiliations.

For example, in 2000 seven of the nine Supreme Court justices had been appointed by Republican presidents. In the controversial case *Bush v. Gore,* in which the Court had to decide which votes should be counted in the dead-heat presidential election in Florida, the court voted 5 to 4 in favor of Republican George W. Bush. Even though two of the four dissenting justices had been appointed by Republican presidents, the vote reflected the conservative leaning of the Supreme Court (even though the judiciary is supposed to

Former Chief Justice of the Supreme Court Earl Warren led the Supreme Court when it ruled on several cases that expanded the rights of those accused of criminal behavior.
Courtesy of CORBIS-NY.

NEWS FLASH

Capital Trials Are Costly

A judge in a tiny Ohio county ruled out a death penalty trial for a man accused of murder because it would cost too much money.

Vinton County Common Pleas Judge Jeffrey L. Simmons said the cost of Gregory McKnight's defense in a death penalty trial would drain the county's $2.7 million budget. Lawyers for McKnight said that his defense would cost more than $75,000, including fees for public defenders and investigators. Judge Simmons' ruling attracted national attention to the case, although he later reversed it. In October 2002 McKnight was convicted of the murders of Emily Murray and Gregory Julious, both 20. For the murder of Julious, he received 38 years to life in prison, and for the murder of Murray, he received the death penalty.

Murray's father argued against McKnight's execution because his daughter opposed the death penalty.

Sources: "Capital Case Too Costly for Ohio County," CNN/Associated Press, August 19, 2002, http://www.cnn.com/2002/LAW/08/19/death.penalty.courts/index.html. "McKnight Sentenced To Death," nbc4columbus.com/AP, October 25, 2002, http://www.nbc4columbus.com/news/1740819/detail.html.

be independent). With such a narrow margin between the numbers of conservative and moderate justices, the power of the president to nominate candidates for vacancies in the court is of special importance. In a sense, then, presidential politics becomes more entwined with Supreme Court politics with each passing election. This observation may alarm some of us, but we should keep in mind that, as we have seen from our selected history here, courts are, and are meant to be, political institutions.[49]

Organization of the Courts

The U.S. court system is a confusing array of organizational structures that defies quick description. Unlike other countries, the United States has no centralized court system that uses equivalent terminology, jurisdictions, and personnel. U.S. courts are the result of different developmental processes that have spawned a complex organizational structure that makes understanding how justice is meted out a difficult task. Additionally, this hodgepodge structure has the unintended consequence of subtly changing not only the style of justice, but also the quality of justice. This means that the structure of the courts plays a large part in how the courts function, which makes for an uneven system of justice and a challenge for the observer of the courts to grasp the big picture. Therefore, we will examine the organization of the courts from several different angles with the intent of demonstrating its complexity.

CIVIL COURTS AND CRIMINAL COURTS. The difference between civil courts and criminal courts lies in the types of laws they deal with: civil laws and criminal laws. Perhaps the major distinction between criminal law and civil law is that violations of criminal law are punishable by imprisonment. Criminal law concerns the major violations against society: murder, rape, robbery, theft, and so on. Civil law is often employed as a general term for anything not covered by criminal law. Civil laws govern private issues, such as breach of contract, probate, divorce, and negligence. Violations of civil law are not punishable by prison.

Nature of Jurisdiction

A good starting point to our understanding of the courts is the concept of jurisdiction. Jurisdiction simply refers to the authority of the court to hear certain cases. The jurisdiction of any court is dependent on three features: the seriousness of the case, the place the offense occurred, and whether the case is being heard for the first time or is on appeal. The three types of jurisdiction can be labeled **subject-matter jurisdiction**, **geographic jurisdiction**, and **hierarchical jurisdiction**.[50]

SUBJECT MATTER JURISDICTION. The nature of the case can determine which court will have jurisdiction. Sometimes the distinction between felonies and misdemeanors will dictate the court to which a case is sent. Courts of limited jurisdiction will tend to handle preliminary hearings and misdemeanors, whereas courts of general jurisdiction will deal with the more serious felonies. Depending on the state, tasks such as issuing warrants, establishing bail, advising defendants of their rights, and setting a date for a preliminary hearing are all handled by the limited jurisdiction court; felony criminal proceedings, including trials, are dealt with by the general jurisdiction court. A number of specialized courts handle only specific types of cases. Drug courts, traffic courts, and juvenile or family courts can be classified by subject matter jurisdiction.

GEOGRAPHIC JURISDICTION. The political boundaries of cities, counties, and states can determine the geographic jurisdiction of a court (for an example of federal court jurisdictions, see Figure 8.2). The location of a crime will dictate which court will hear the case. Depending on the state, jurisdictions may include courts in several counties that operate under the term **circuit court**. Aimed at balancing the caseload according to population, a circuit may have one densely populated county or several less populated counties. Geographic jurisdiction may also include features such as military installations, American Indian reservations, or national parks. Crimes committed in these locations can be dealt with by courts established especially for the special needs of these political structures. For instance, although a homicide on a military installation may happen within the jurisdiction of a state circuit court, it also occurred on federal land and would be handled by the federal court. Furthermore, if the defendant was military personnel, the case might be handled according to the Uniform Code of Military Justice rather than the federal court system.

subject matter jurisdiction
When the nature of the case determines which court hears it. An example would be the distinction between felonies and misdemeanors.

geographic jurisdiction
This is established when the location of a crime dictates which court will hear a case.

hierarchical jurisdiction
This is established when a case is heard by a court according to where that case is located in the system. For example, trial courts hear the facts of the case, determine guilt or innocence, and impose sentence. Appellate courts review the work of the trial court judge and determine whether the case was handled according to the Constitution.

circuit court
A court that holds sessions at intervals within different areas of a judicial district.

Figure 8.2
Federal Court Jurisdictions

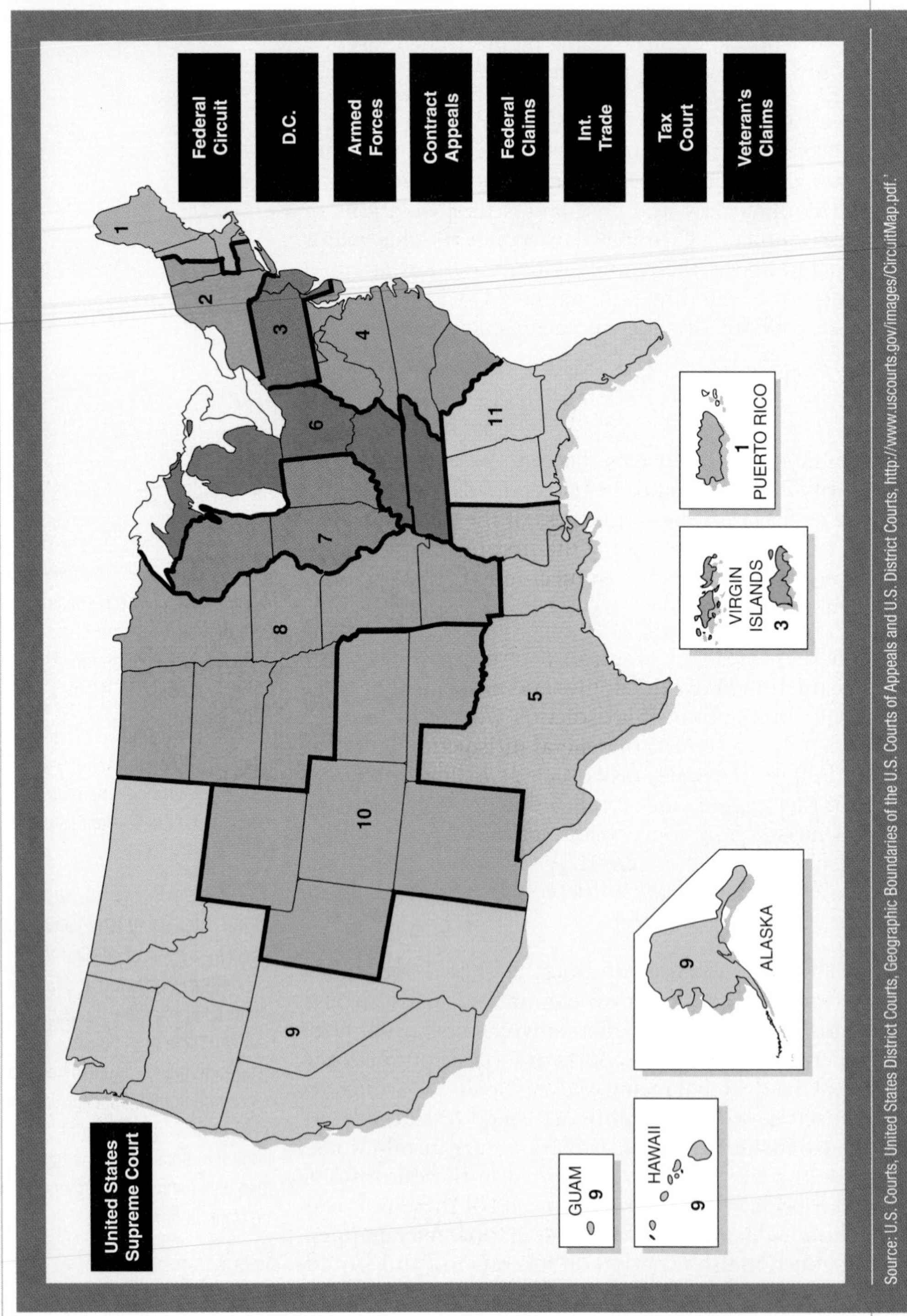

Source: U.S. Courts, United States District Courts, Geographic Boundaries of the U.S. Courts of Appeals and U.S. District Courts, http://www.uscourts.gov/images/CircuitMap.pdf.'

HIERARCHICAL JURISDICTION. An important difference between trial courts and appellate courts has to do with their placement in the court structure. Trial courts hear the facts of the case, determine guilt or innocence, and impose a sentence. Appellate courts review the work of the trial court judge and determine whether the case was handled within the constraints of the Constitution. If the trial judge allowed evidence that was illegally gathered by the police, allowed testimony of a perjured witness, or allowed the court to miss important procedural deadlines, the appellate court can overrule the verdict and set aside the sentence. Trial courts are responsible for the implementation of the substantive law, whereas appellate courts are responsible for ensuring that the procedural law is followed.

These three ways of classifying the jurisdictions of courts alert us to the various organizational structures that comprise our fragmented system of courts in the United States. As we delve deeper into the nature and structure of federal and state courts, and get confused by the complex and overlapping terminology used to identify courts, it will be useful to remember that each court is somehow classified according to each of these three measures of jurisdiction. Each court will be responsible for handling certain types of cases, according to the geographic location of the crime, and according to whether the case is being heard for the first time or is under appeal.

Structure of the Federal Courts

The court system of the United States is divided into two entities: the federal courts and the state courts. We can think of this as a dual court system in which each part is further subdivided according to subject matter, geographic, and hierarchical jurisdiction. Federal courts comprise four levels: magistrate courts, U.S. district courts, U.S. circuit courts of appeals, and the U.S. Supreme Court. Federal courts hear cases involving the following issues:

1. Cases in which the U.S. government or one of its officers is being sued
2. Cases between two or more states
3. Cases involving counsels, ambassadors, and other public ministers
4. Cases involving laws enacted by Congress, treaties and laws related to maritime jurisdiction, and commerce on the high seas

Additionally, in some cases state and federal courts may have concurrent jurisdiction. These cases may involve circumstances in which a citizen from one state sues a citizen from another state. For the most part, however, the lines between federal and state court jurisdiction are clear except in cases in which the crime is a violation of both federal and state laws, such as bank robbery or drug dealing. Another high-profile example is the D.C. sniper case in which the defendants killed a federal agent and committed murders in both the District of Columbia and other states (for more on this case, see Chapter 9, Focus on Ethics: Where to Try a Sniper?).

U.S. MAGISTRATE COURTS. The **magistrate court** is the lowest level of the federal court system. Congress created these in 1968 to ease the burdensome caseload of the U.S. district courts. The magistrate court judges are chosen by the district court judges and serve either as full-time judges (appointed to eight-year terms) or as part-time judges (appointed to four-year terms). The powers of federal magistrates are limited because their authority and independence are not explicitly delineated in the Constitution as are the roles of other federal judges. For instance, they do not serve for life and are not selected by the president and confirmed by the Senate.

magistrate court
The lowest level of the federal court system, created in 1968 to ease the caseload of the U.S. district courts.

Magistrate courts operate as courts of limited jurisdiction in that they perform many of the essential but routine tasks of the court system. For more serious felony cases that are typically handled by the district court, the magistrate court will aid by dealing with the preliminary work of sitting for initial appearances, conducting preliminary hearings, appointing counsel for those who cannot afford their own lawyer, setting bail, and issuing search warrants. This range of duties greatly relieves the workload of the district courts. Additionally, the magistrate court will handle misdemeanor cases by presiding over trials, accepting pleas, and passing sentence. In addition to their criminal case duties, the magistrate court performs a comparable set of duties for civil cases.

district courts
Courts of general jurisdiction that try felony cases involving federal laws and civil cases involving amounts of money over $75,000.

U.S. DISTRICT COURTS. The U.S. **district courts** are courts of general jurisdiction that handle cases that are more serious and involve more money than the magistrate courts. The U.S. district courts try felony cases involving federal laws and civil cases in which the amount of money in controversy exceeds $75,000. Although civil cases constitute the majority of the district courts' workload (see Figure 8.3), since 1980 drug prosecutions have gone up significantly and now comprise over 25 percent of all federal criminal cases (see Figure 8.4).[51]

Judges oversee a range of court activities. The exact authority of a judge varies according to the level of government and jurisdiction.
Courtesy of Corbis Royalty Free.

Figure 8.3
U.S. District Courts

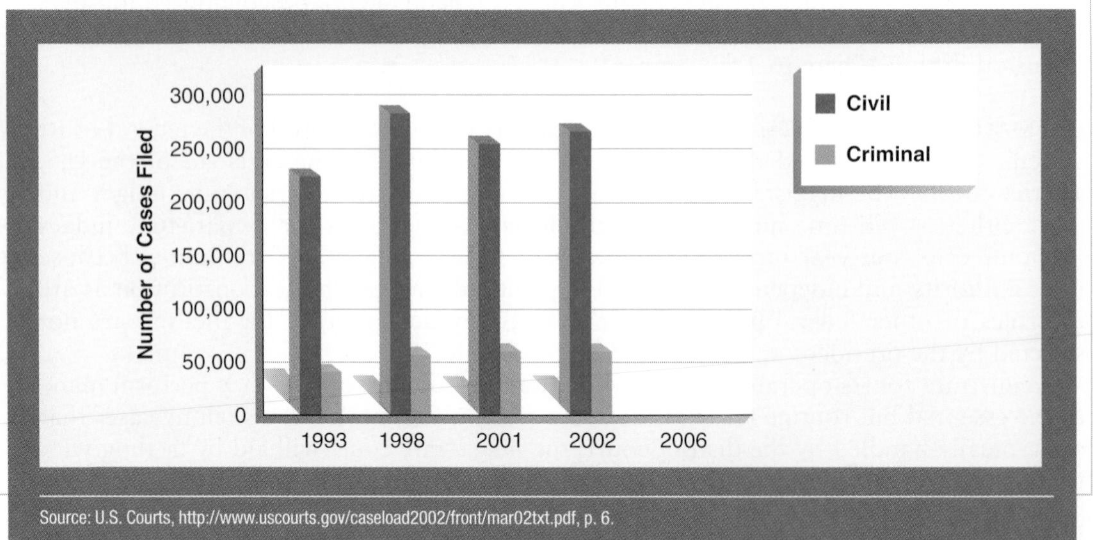

Source: U.S. Courts, http://www.uscourts.gov/caseload2002/front/mar02txt.pdf, p. 6.

Of the 94 U.S. district courts, 89 are located within the 50 states; the rest are in U.S. territories such as Puerto Rico and Guam, as well as in the District of Columbia (see Table 8.1). Each state has at least one district court, and some states, such as New York and Texas, have as many as four. No district court crosses state lines. The 94 districts have 646 district court judgeships that are distributed according to population served and the political clout of congress-members and senators. Judges are appointed to indefinite terms that depend on their good behavior, which amounts to a lifelong job unless they are caught committing crimes or bringing scandal to the court. The reason they are not given specific terms of four or six years is to allow them to be independent and objective. If they had to worry about reappointment or reelection, they might be concerned with the political impact of their rulings.

The U.S. district courts also handle bankruptcy cases, using adjunct judges to deal with the enormous caseload. Bankruptcy judges are appointed for 14-year terms and hear cases from both individuals and corporations. U.S. district courts are responsible for only a few of the types of cases that typically go to court. Most often, these are cases involving a federal question, an issue of diversity of jurisdiction, or a prisoner petition. The types of cases are as follows:

- **Federal questions.** Federal question cases involve laws that are passed by the federal government, have constitutional implications, or involve treaties with other nations. Issues such as Social Security, antitrust, and civil rights fall within the purview of the U.S. district courts.
- **Diversity of jurisdiction.** Diversity of jurisdiction involves cases between citizens of different states or with someone from another country. Although the individual has the option of suing in a state court, the opportunity to use the federal court system is attractive because of the presumed objectivity and the possibility of a greater reward. For this reason the amount of money in dispute must exceed $75,000.[52]
- **Prisoner petitions.** Prisoners in either federal or state prisons can file petitions in the U.S. district courts if they believe their rights under federal law are being violated. Typically, these cases allege violations of due process (such as lack of an effective attorney), cruel and unusual punishment (such as prison overcrowding or bad food), or inadequate medical care. Many of these cases are actually heard in the magistrate court, which then makes a recommendation to the U.S. district judge.

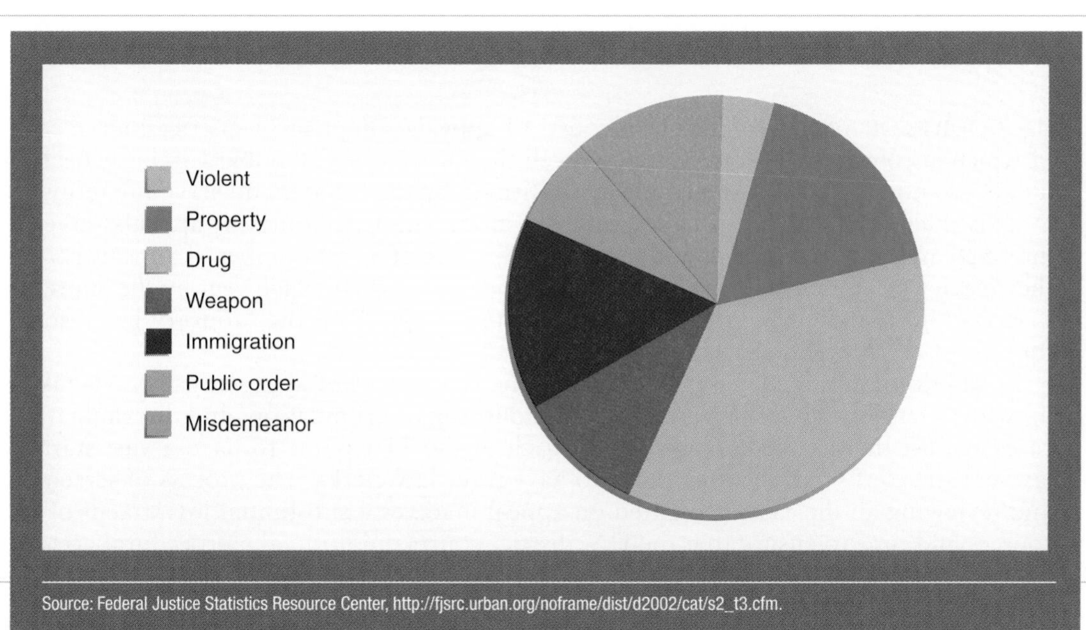

Source: Federal Justice Statistics Resource Center, http://fjsrc.urban.org/noframe/dist/d2002/cat/s2_t3.cfm.

Figure 8.4
Percent of Defendants Convicted in Federal District Courts, 2002, by Category of Offense

TABLE 8.1

U.S. District Courts			
Alabama, Middle	Illinois, Central	Nebraska	Rhode Island
Alabama, Northern	Illinois, Northern	Nevada	South Carolina
Alabama, Southern	Illinois, Southern	New Hampshire	South Dakota
Alaska	Indiana, Northern	New Jersey	Tennessee, Eastern
Arizona	Indiana, Southern	New Mexico	Tennessee, Middle
Arkansas, Eastern	Iowa, Northern	New York, Eastern	Tennessee, Western
Arkansas, Western	Iowa, Southern	New York, Northern	Texas, Eastern
California, Central	Kansas	New York, Southern	Texas, Northern
California, Eastern	Kentucky, Eastern	New York, Western	Texas, Southern
California, Northern	Kentucky, Western	North Carolina, Eastern	Texas, Western
California, Southern	Louisiana, Eastern	North Carolina, Middle	Utah
Colorado	Louisiana, Middle	North Carolina, Western	Vermont
Connecticut	Louisiana, Western	North Dakota	Virgin Islands
Delaware	Maine	Northern Mariana Islands	Virginia, Eastern
District of Columbia	Maryland	Ohio, Northern	Virginia, Western
Florida, Middle	Massachusetts	Ohio, Southern	Washington, Eastern
Florida, Northern	Michigan, Eastern	Oklahoma, Eastern	Washington, Western
Florida, Southern	Michigan, Western	Oklahoma, Northern	West Virginia, Northern
Georgia, Middle	Minnesota	Oklahoma, Western	West Virginia, Southern
Georgia, Northern	Mississippi, Northern	Oregon	Wisconsin, Eastern
Georgia, Southern	Mississippi, Southern	Pennsylvania, Eastern	Wisconsin, Western
Guam	Missouri, Eastern	Pennsylvania, Middle	Wyoming
Hawaii	Missouri, Western	Pennsylvania, Western	
Idaho	Montana	Puerto Rico	

courts of appeals
Intermediate courts that dispose of many appeals before they reach the Supreme Court.

U.S. COURTS OF APPEALS. The U.S. **courts of appeals** comprise 11 district courts, each of which encompasses several states, as well the District of Columbia Circuit. The 179 judges are nominated by the president, confirmed by the Senate, and serve life terms as long as their behavior is not called into question. The U.S. courts of appeals serve as intermediate courts of appeals and are able to dispose of a vast number of appeals before they reach the Supreme Court. Only a very few cases are heard each year by the Supreme Court, so for all practical purposes the U.S. court of appeals is the "court of last resort" for almost all federal cases.

In addition to criminal cases, the bulk of the U.S. courts of appeals caseload is taken up with cases dealing with civil rights violations, sex discrimination, and discrimination cases against the disabled. This requires each of the 11 circuits to have a vast staff of lawyers and clerks and for each judge to have three law clerks. The process of screening and reviewing all the cases presented on appeal involves a substantial investment of resources and time to ensure that the U.S. district courts did not make procedural errors.

U.S. Supreme Court
The "court of last resort." The highest court in the United States, established by Article III of the Constitution, hears only appeals, with some exceptions.

U.S. SUPREME COURT. The **U.S. Supreme Court** is at the top of the hierarchical jurisdiction for both the federal and state court systems. Even when a case has gone though the entire

CASE IN POINT

Powell v. State of Alabama

The Case

Powell v. State of Alabama, 287 U.S. 45, 53 S.Ct. 55 (1932)

The Point

This is the first case in which the U.S. Supreme Court applied the constitutional right to counsel to a specific prosecution. Powell also provides a historic look at racism within the criminal justice system.

In March 1931 nine black men were accused of raping two white women during a train trip in Alabama. The men, who became known as the Scottsboro Boys, received no legal representation until their trial dates. Their trials lasted one day each, and all were sentenced to death. The state supreme court affirmed the convictions. However, the U.S. Supreme Court overturned their convictions on appeal because of the violation of their rights to counsel.

The Supreme Court was asked to consider three specific violations of the defendants' rights. Of the following, the court only considered the second: "(1) [The defendants] were not given a fair, impartial, and deliberate trial; (2) they were denied the right of counsel, with the accustomed incidents of consultation and opportunity of preparation for trial; and (3) they were tried before juries from which qualified members of their own race were systematically excluded."

Although the judgment was eventually reversed, two justices, Mr. Butler and Mr. McReynolds, dissented.

state court process, including the state supreme court, appeal to the U.S. Supreme Court may still be a possibility, although a remote one. In truth, the U.S. Supreme Court hears only about 80 cases a year, and these cases must involve a "substantial federal question" that concerns the Constitution or a federal law. The court does not attempt to serve as a court of last resort for all federal and state cases but instead marshals its few resources to decide cases that have broad policy implications for the important questions of the day.

The U.S. Supreme Court issues a **writ of certiorari** to the lower court that orders the records of a case to be sent to the justices so that they can decide whether the case presents the type of questions that need to be decided by the Supreme Court. A **rule of four** exists whereby at least four of the nine Supreme Court justices must vote to hear a case before it is put on the docket. Cases that are heard by the U.S. Supreme Court are heard by all nine justices, as opposed to the court of appeals in which a panel of three justices hears a case. When a case is scheduled to be heard, the attorneys file written arguments, as well as briefs on behalf of other parties that are called ***amicus curiae*** meaning "friend of the court." For instance, an organization such as the American Civil Liberties Union or Amnesty International may file an *amicus curiae* brief in a case involving the death penalty for someone who is mentally retarded.

writ of certiorari
An order from a superior court calling up for review the record of a case from a lower court.

rule of four
A rule that states that at least four of the nine Supreme Court justices must vote to hear a case.

amicus curiae
Someone who is not a part of a case who gives advice or testimony. Also called "friend of the court."

SPECIALIZED FEDERAL COURTS. A number of specialized federal courts handle primarily civil cases. These include the Tax Court, the Court of Federal Claims, the Court of Veterans Appeal, the Court of International Trade, and the Court of Appeals for the federal circuit. These courts handle cases involving issues such as monetary claims against the federal government, tax disputes, trademarks, patents, and other issues in which the federal government is a party to a suit.[53] In terms of criminal cases, the federal court system has the Alien Terrorist Removal Court and the Foreign Intelligence Surveillance Court. These courts have been of greater interest to Americans since the terrorist events of September 11, 2001.

Two other specialized federal courts decide a substantial number of criminal cases. The U.S. Court of Appeals for the Armed Forces handles cases of military law in which

The number of justices on the U.S. Supreme Court changed frequently before arriving at the present total of nine in 1869. The justices of the Supreme Court are *left to right, back row:* Ruth Bader Ginsburg, David Souter, Clarence Thomas, Stephen Breyer; *front row:* Antonin Scalia, John Paul Stevens, William Rehnquist, Sandra Day O'Connor, and Anthony Kennedy.

Courtesy of Getty Images, Inc.

FOCUS ON ETHICS

Judicial Selection

As president of the United States, you have a rare opportunity to nominate a replacement for a retiring Supreme Court justice. There are many qualified candidates to choose from, but members of your political party are pressuring you to make a historic selection and pick a minority female. The individual who is being proposed is someone you believe is a person of impeccable character and unquestioned integrity. She has the backing of the American Bar Association and seems to be a candidate that even the opposing political party would not object to.

Here is the problem: The present court is divided evenly over the constitutionality of the death penalty. The person you select will become the swing vote that will decide whether the United States continues to execute murderers. You are a staunch believer in the death penalty. When you were the governor of a large southern state, you signed over 100 death warrants. The female candidate that you are being pressured to select has stated on the record that she believes the death penalty is barbaric, cruel, and unconstitutional. The two of you are like-minded on other important issues, and your party would gain a great deal of political capital from this nomination, but you are torn. Do you select this worthy candidate for this important position, or do you look for someone who shares your views on capital punishment?

QUESTIONS

1. Should a president's personal philosophy influence the Court nomination process?
2. Is a difference of opinion on a single issue enough to pass over this candidate?
3. What other single issues might be used by a president to bypass a candidate for a judicial appointment?
4. Sometimes single issues such as this are called a litmus test. What does *litmus test* mean, and where does this term come from?

questions of due process are raised in the implementation of the Uniform Code of Military Justice. Military justice imposes a broad set of rules and laws on military personnel to which civilians are not subject. Failure to follow orders or showing disrespect for an officer are violations of the Uniform Code of Military Justice and can result in punishments that include incarceration or discharge from the armed services. Armed forces personnel are not entitled to all the protections of the Constitution, and the due process afforded to violators of military law is not as extensive as that afforded by civilian courts.

The other specialized federal court that sees a good number of criminal cases is the tribal court. Indian tribes enjoy a certain level of self-determination and sovereignty on federal reservations. In many states, American Indians are able to establish gambling casinos on reservations even though the state governments do not approve. Tribal law is administered by American Indians and can be imposed in lieu of state law in some circumstances.[54] Especially for issues dealing with traditional American Indian concerns, such as hunting and fishing rights, the tribal law can take precedence over state or federal law. That is why, from time to time, the media will cover a story about a tribe in Alaska that is allowed to harvest a protected whale as part of its traditional subsistence lifestyle.

State Courts

Like federal courts, **state courts** are generally divided according to a three-tier hierarchy. At the lowest level are the state trial courts of limited and general jurisdiction. An intermediate court of appeals reviews the cases of the lower courts before the opportunity of last resort, the state supreme court, makes its final ruling. However, we use the phrase *final ruling* with caution because for a very few cases, such as those with a "substantial federal question," there is always a chance that they could be selected for review by the U.S. Supreme Court.

state courts
General courts and special courts funded and run by each state. Each state has a different system.

JUVENILE COURTS. Although juvenile courts are part of the state court system, they differ in their goals and in the way they operate. Whereas adult courts follow criminal law, juvenile courts follow civil law because the primary goal of juvenile courts is rehabilitation, not punishment. The relationship between state courts and their juvenile counterparts differs from state to state. However, only a few states operate completely

REFERENCE

State Attorneys General

Attorneys general are the primary legal authorities of the states, commonwealths, and territories of the United States. Among other duties, they serve as legal counsel to government agencies and legislatures. The authorities of the attorneys general include the following:

- Prosecuting corporations that violate antitrust laws
- Representing state agencies and addressing issues of legislative or administrative constitutionality
- Enforcing air, water, and hazardous waste laws in most states
- Conducting criminal appeals and state criminal prosecutions
- Interceding in cases involving public utility rates
- Bringing civil suits

Source: The National Association of Attorneys General, 2003, http://www.naag.org/ag/duties.php.

separate juvenile courts. Most juvenile courts are attached to family courts or trial courts. Juvenile courts will be discussed in greater detail in Chapter 14.

lower courts
Sometimes called "inferior courts," in reference to their hierarchy. These courts receive their authority and resources from local county or municipal governments.

STATE TRIAL COURTS. The trial courts of limited jurisdiction are called **lower courts** or inferior courts. This refers simply to their place on the hierarchical ladder and not to the quality of justice they dispense. Technically, they are not part of the state court system because, in most states, the lower courts of limited jurisdiction are not funded by the state but instead receive their authority and resources from local county or municipal governments. There are close to 14,000 trial courts of limited jurisdiction in the United States. They handle the vast bulk of cases either by passing sentence or holding preliminary hearings and motions.[55]

The trial courts of limited jurisdiction have a variety of names depending on the state in which they operate. They are called city magistrates, justices of the peace, county courts, or city courts. They handle over 67 million matters a year, mostly traffic cases, but also misdemeanors, small claims, and the preliminary stages of felony cases. These courts of limited jurisdiction are where most citizens will come into contact with the court system.

Trial courts of general jurisdiction are referred to as "major trial courts" and are variously named circuit courts, district courts, superior courts, or courts of common pleas. These courts handle the major cases in both the civil and criminal arenas. State trial courts of general jurisdiction hear the majority of the serious street crime cases. Whereas the federal courts deal with major white collar criminals and large-scale drug dealers, the state courts handle most rapists, murderers, thieves, and small-scale drug dealers and drug users (see Figures 8.5 and 8.6). Although this is the court that is popularly portrayed on television and in the media when there is a jury trial, the bulk of the work of the state trial court of general jurisdiction is conducted in hallways, judges' chambers, and over the telephone and via e-mail as prosecutors and defense attorneys arrange plea bargains that eliminate the need for a trial. These courts handle a wide variety of civil cases including those involving domestic relations, estate, and personal injury.

STATE INTERMEDIATE COURTS OF APPEALS. Thirty-nine states have intermediate courts of appeals that hear all properly filed appeals from the lower state courts. Only states that do not have large populations, such as Wyoming, do not have this level of courts. In most cases, the decision at the intermediate court of appeal level will be the final decision because the state supreme courts, as does the U.S. Supreme Court, select

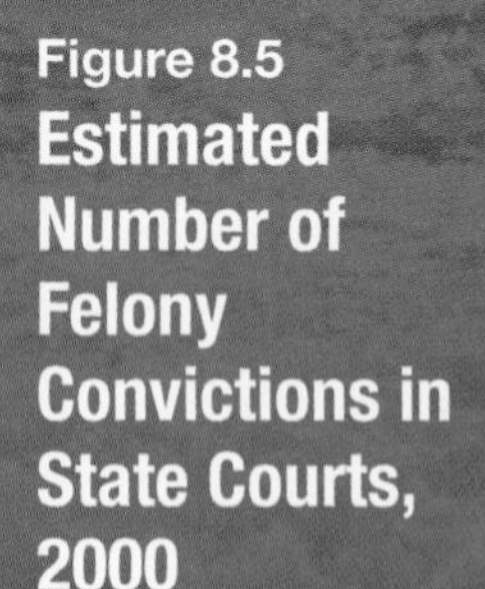

Figure 8.5
Estimated Number of Felony Convictions in State Courts, 2000

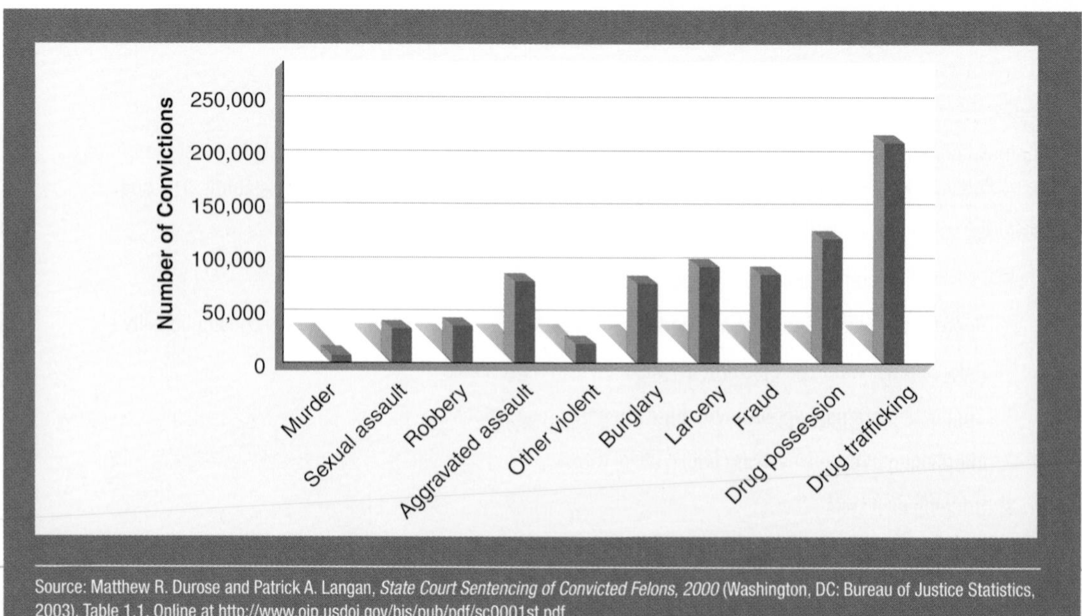

Source: Matthew R. Durose and Patrick A. Langan, *State Court Sentencing of Convicted Felons, 2000* (Washington, DC: Bureau of Justice Statistics, 2003), Table 1.1. Online at http://www.ojp.usdoj.gov/bjs/pub/pdf/sc0001st.pdf.

only a small percentage of cases to consider each year. The intermediate courts of appeals typically have three judges who hear each case. There are no jury trials at the appeal level because guilt or innocence is not the overriding issue. These courts are more concerned with the conduct of the lower court in providing the protections of due process for the defendant and ensuring that the judge followed proper procedures.

STATE SUPREME COURTS. Because court systems vary across the states, making many general statements about state supreme courts is difficult. In states that have an intermediate courts of appeals level, the state supreme court has a discretionary docket, which means they can select the cases they wish to consider. For the sparsely populated

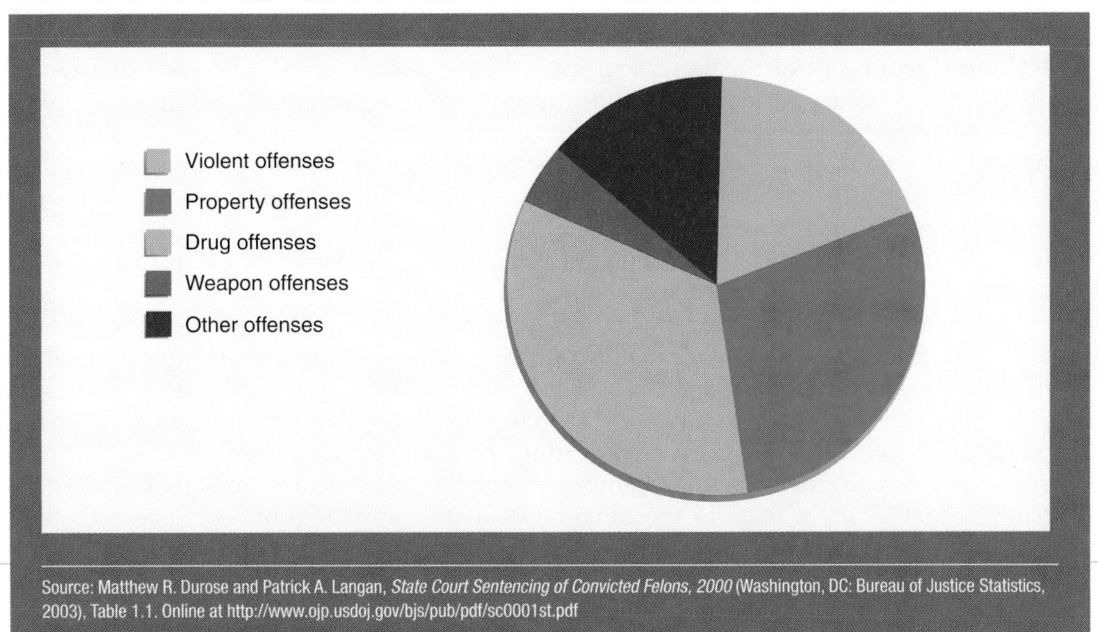

Figure 8.6 **Estimated Percent of Felony Convictions in State Courts, 2000, by Category of Offense**

Source: Matthew R. Durose and Patrick A. Langan, *State Court Sentencing of Convicted Felons, 2000* (Washington, DC: Bureau of Justice Statistics, 2003), Table 1.1. Online at http://www.ojp.usdoj.gov/bjs/pub/pdf/sc0001st.pdf

! **NEWS FLASH**

So Help Me Who?

Swearing an oath that ends in "so help me God," is probably one of the best-known rituals of U.S. courts. But what if a juror or witness is an atheist or agnostic?

In 2002 a South Carolina juror was dismissed because he said he was not religious and could not take an oath that included "so help you God." The juror, Robert Woodham, also said that he believed the phrase violated the separation of church and state. The judge said that Woodham could not serve on the jury unless he took the oath as specified by the court clerk. The case went to the state supreme court, which agreed with Woodham, referring to a nearly 300-year-old state law that allows alternative oaths.

But the court's ruling did not end with Woodham.

The two men on trial were eventually given two life sentences each after being convicted of taking hostages at a state prison where they were incarcerated. The court ruled that the two men deserved new trials because Woodham's dismissal had denied them "a fair and impartial jury."

Source: "Supreme Court: Jurors Not Required to Swear Oath to God," The State.com/Associated Press, February 11, 2003, http://www.thestate.com/mld/thestate/news/local/5155135.htm.

states that have no intermediate court of appeals, the state supreme court will hear the appeals from the lower courts. Like the U.S. Supreme Court, the state supreme courts will have all the justices hear each case instead of having rotating three-judge panels. The state supreme court is the court of last resort for all but a very few cases that bear issues of constitutional or federal law that the U.S. Supreme Court decides are of significance. The state supreme courts also have some authority to discipline lawyers and judges and will often serve as a venue for judicial training.

Summary

Underlying the role of the court is the idea that justice should be blind to wealth, power, and social class. This idea took a long time to develop, although courts of some type have been consistent features of many societies.

Courts are a result of the increasing sophistication of societies in which a division of labor was necessary. Modern courts are mechanisms for resolving disputes that have evolved from a history of blood feuds, duels, wars, and other types of conflicts. Part of the development of courts in Europe stemmed from the practice of collecting compensation from the family of the accused for the family of the victim. Courts were increasingly held to resolve disputes in a peaceful manner, and more fees were charged as more behaviors became criminalized and considered crimes against the king or state. Thus, court became an important source of revenue for the nobility.

The inquest can be considered the first type of jury. After a war, the English crown needed to determine which lands it had conquered and so conducted an inquest in which men were summoned before the court to attest to the ownership of the land in the surrounding area. In 1166 the Assize of Clarendon, which marked the beginning of the grand jury system, aimed to correct some of the problems of the judicial process. The jury trial came about in the early 13th century when trials by ordeal were halted by the Roman Catholic Church. In 1215 the Magna Carta set a precedent of encoding in the law limitations on the state's power. In the 15th century, the Court of the Star Chamber was established to deal with a variety of offenses and became known for its violations of citizens' rights.

The development of the English courts between the 11th and 18th centuries provided the foundation for the courts of the United States. Courts in colonial America also developed in response to the concerns of each colony, and many of the protections of the law that existed for defendants in England were absent in colonial America. One of the consequences of independence from England is the documents that were created to specify the relationship between the people and the state; these include the Bill of Rights and the Constitution.

Modern U.S. courts determine the guilt or innocence of the defendant and decide the disposition or sentence. As the popular image of how courts work is informed by television, much of the picture we have of the court is an imperfect one. However, the court is subject to outside forces. It does not control how it is financed; it does not control how many cases are sent to it; it cannot ensure adequate resources to carry out its sentences; and because its work is done in a courtroom open to the press, it cannot control its public image.

The modern U.S. court system is a confusing array of organizational structures that defies quick description. This structure subtly changes not only the style of justice, but also the quality of justice. The professional orientation of those who practice law also affects the functioning of the court. A good starting point to understanding U.S. courts is the concept of jurisdiction, which refers to the authority of the court to hear certain cases. The jurisdiction of any court is dependent on the gravity of the case, the place the offense occurred, and whether the case is being heard for the first time or is on appeal.

U.S. courts are divided into state and federal entities. Federal courts comprise magistrate courts, U.S. district courts, U.S. circuit courts of appeals, and the U.S. Supreme Court. The state courts are divided into the state trial courts of limited and general jurisdiction, intermediate courts of appeals, and state supreme courts.

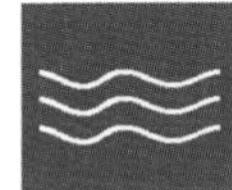

CROSSCURRENTS

Notes of a Court TV Junkie

My name is John, and I'm a professor and a *Court TV* junkie. I admit that I have a deep and perverse fascination with watching how conflicts are resolved (or not) in our courts. I admit that some afternoons I slip out of school and come home to watch the latest live trial of some celebrity, child molester, or abusive husband. I like summers when my teaching duties allow me to watch hours of courtroom action with my cat in my lap while I eat ice cream out of the carton. I tell my wife I'm doing research for my books. She knows better. She knows I'm feeding my people-watching addiction.

Court junkies are found in courtrooms across the country. Voyeurs who like to watch people in distress, busybodies who want to know other peoples' business, and law geeks who like to watch the criminal justice system in action now flock to *Court TV* to watch the high-profile trials featuring powerful judges, high-priced lawyers, nationally known technical experts, and best of all, real people in real conflict. Programs like *L.A. Law, The Practice,* and *Law and Order* are sensationalized imitations of what really happens in a trial. For those of us who like the real thing, including the tedious and boring hours of routine examination, *Court TV* offers access for our inquiring minds.

Personally, I like to watch the attorneys conduct their opening and closing arguments. Safe in my big leather chair, I critique their performances. I usually find their efforts wanting. "If that were me," I tell myself, "I would impeach that witness cold." As I shove yet another spoonful of ice cream into my mouth, I fantasize about how I would have the jury eating out of my hand. Being an armchair lawyer is easy, but it is also informative. A good bit of how the courts operate can be learned from *Court TV.* However, what is not seen, such as plea bargaining, may be even more important.

QUESTION

1. Do you watch television court and crime shows? Do you believe they are realistic? Why or why not?

KEY TERMS

amicus curiae p. 273
Assize of Clarendon p. 258
blood feud p. 254
circuit court p. 267
compurgation p. 257
Court of the Star Chamber p. 261
courts of appeals p. 272
district courts p. 270
geographic jurisdiction p. 267
hierarchical jurisdiction p. 267
inquest p. 258
lower courts p. 276
magistrate court p. 269
rule of four p. 273
state court p. 275
subject matter jurisdiction p. 267
trial by ordeal p. 257
writ of certiorari p. 273
U.S. Supreme Court p. 272

REVIEW QUESTIONS

1. What two problems affect the image and functioning of the court?
2. Are courts purely a feature of European societies?
3. What system did Europeans use in lieu of violence to settle wrongs and disputes?
4. What was the first type of jury?
5. Why were the first grand juries and trial juries flawed?
6. What was the Court of the Star Chamber?
7. What served as the foundation for U.S. courts?

8. What is the only Bill of Rights item that is also included in all the state constitutions?

9. Name the three types of court jurisdiction.

10. What types of cases do federal courts hear? What levels comprise federal courts?

11. What is an "inferior court"?

12. Discuss the differences between trial courts of limited jurisdiction and trial courts of general jurisdiction.

13. What is the purpose of state intermediate courts of appeals? Do all states have them? Why or why not?

SUGGESTED FURTHER READING

Abraham, Henry. *The Judicial Process.* 7th ed. New York: Oxford University Press, 1998.

Banks, Christopher. *Judicial Politics in the D.C. Circuit Court.* Baltimore: The John Hopkins University Press, 1999.

Rabe, Gary A., and Dean J. Champion. *Criminal Courts: Structure, Process, and Issues.* Upper Saddle River, NJ: Prentice Hall, 2002.

Smith, Christopher. *Judicial Self-Interest: Federal Judges and Court Administration.* Westport, CT: Praeger, 1995.

Stojkovic, Stan, John Klofas, and David Kalinich. *The Administration and Management of Criminal Justice Organizations: A Book of Readings.* 2nd ed. Prospect Heights, IL: Waveland Press, 1994.

Stolzenberg, Lisa, and Stewart J. D'Alessio, eds. *Criminal Courts for the 21st Century.* 2nd ed. Upper Saddle River, NJ: Prentice Hall, 2002.

ENDNOTES

1. Samuel Walker and Charles Katz, *The Police in America: An Introduction,* 4th ed. (Boston: McGraw-Hill, 2002), 41.
2. James Austin and John Irwin, *Its About Time: America's Imprisonment Binge,* 3rd ed. (Belmont, CA: Wadsworth, 2001).
3. Frances Kahn Zemans, "In the Eye of the Beholder: The Relationship between the Public and the Courts," in *Courts & Justice: A Reader,* 2nd. ed., eds. G. Larry Mays and Peter Gregware (Prospect Heights, IL: Waveland Press, 2000), 7–24.
4. David Orrick, "Court Administration in the United States: The On-Going Problems," in *Courts & Justice: A Reader,* 2nd ed., eds. G. Larry Mays and Peter Gregware (Prospect Heights, IL: Waveland Press, 2000), 207–227.
5. Stuart Nagel, "The Tipped Scales of American Justice," in *The Scales of Justice,* ed. Abraham Blumberg (New York: Transaction Books, 1970), 31–50.
6. Christopher Smith, *Courts, Politics, and the Judicial Process,* 2nd ed. (Chicago: Nelson Hall, 1997), 4–7.
7. Max Gluckman, *Politics, Law, and Ritual in Tribal Society* (Oxford: Blackwell, 1965).
8. Bronislaw Malinowski, *Crime and Custom in Savage Society* (London: Routledge and Kegan Paul, 1926).
9. E. A. Hoebel, *The Law of Primitive Man* (Cambridge, MA: Harvard University Press, 1964).
10. Raymond J. Michalowski, *Order, Law, and Crime: An Introduction to Criminology* (New York: Random House, 1985), 56.
11. Emile Durkheim, *The Division of Labor in Society* (New York: The Free Press, 1933).
12. E. E. Evans-Pritchard, *The Nuer: A Description of the Modes of Livelihood and Political Institutions of a Nilotic People* (London: Oxford, 1968), 171.
13. Bryce Lyon, *A Constitutional and Legal History of Medieval England,* 2nd ed. (New York: Norton, 1980).
14. See Janelle Brown, "The Impossible Calculus of Loss," *Salon,* January 2, 2002, http://archive.salon.com/mwt/feature/2002/01/02/fund_fairness/index.html. It is interesting to note that a victim's social status is still a factor in determining his or her monetary value. The government fund set up to compensate the families of the September 11, 2001, terrorist attacks took into account the victims' ages and future earning capacities. This caused many families anguish at the perceived unfairness of the compensation program.
15. Ellen Hochstedler Steury and Nancy Frank, *Criminal Court Process* (Minneapolis/St. Paul: West, 1996), 66.
16. Lyon, *Constitutional and Legal History,* 84.
17. Ibid.
18. John S. Beckerman, "Procedural Innovation and Institutional Change in Medieval English Manorial Courts, *Law and History Review* 10 (Fall 1992): 203–204.

19. Robert Bartlett, *Trial by Fire and Water: The Medieval Judicial Ordeal* (Oxford: Clarendon).
20. Hochstedler Steury and Frank, *Criminal Court Process,* 70–71.
21. J. H. Baker, *An Introduction to English Legal History,* 3rd. ed. (Boston: Butterworths, 1990).
22. Lyon, *Constitutional and Legal History,* 295.
23. Barbara J. Shapiro, *"Beyond Reasonable Doubt" and "Probable Cause": Historical Perspectives on the Anglo-American Laws of Evidence* (Berkeley: University of California Press, 1991), 47.
24. Hochstedler Steury and Frank, *Criminal Court Process,* 73.
25. Roger D. Groot, "The Early Thirteenth-Century Criminal Trial," in *Twelve Men Good and True: The Criminal Jury in England 1200–1800,* eds. J. S. Cockburn and Thomas A. Green (Princeton, NJ: Princeton University Press, 1988), 19–20.
26. Lyon, *Constitutional and Legal History,* 451.
27. Baker, *English Legal History,* 581.
28. Thomas Andrew Green, *Verdict According to Conscience: Perspectives on the English Criminal Jury Trial* (Chicago: University of Chicago Press, 1985).
29. Lyon, *Constitutional and Legal History,* 312–321.
30. Baker, *English Legal History,* 591.
31. Hochstedler Steury and Frank, *Criminal Court Process,* 77.
32. Edwin C. Surrency, "The Courts in the American Colonies," *American Journal of Legal History* 11 (July 1967): 252–276.
33. Ibid., 256.
34. Donna J. Spindel, *Crime and Society in North Carolina,* 1663–1776 (Baton Rouge: Louisiana State University Press, 1989), 20.
35. Lawrence M. Friedman, *A History of American Law* (New York: Simon & Schuster, 1985), 75.
36. Hochstedler Steury and Frank, *Criminal Court Process,* 84–85.
37. Robert Allen Rutland, *The Birth of the Bill of Rights* (Chapel Hill: University of North Carolina Press, 1955).
38. *Marbury v. Madison,* 1 Cranch 137 (1803), 55, 56–57, 61.
39. Mary Ann Harrell and Burnett Anderson, *Equal Justice Under the Law: The Supreme Court in American Life* (Washington DC: The Supreme Court Historical Society, 1982).
40. Mark Tushnet, "*Marbury v. Madison* and the Theory of Judicial Supremacy," in *Greatest Cases in Constitutional Law,* ed. Robert P. George (Princeton, NJ: Princeton University Press, 2000), 17–54.
41. Laurence H. Tribe, *God Save This Honorable Court: How the Choice of Supreme Court Justices Shapes Our History* (New York: Random House, 1985).
42. *McCulloch v. Maryland,* 4 Wheat. 316 (1819), 57–59, 194.
43. Harold J. Spaeth, *Supreme Court Policy Making: Explanation and Prediction* (San Francisco: Freeman, 1979).
44. Bernard Schwartz, *A History of the Supreme Court* (New York: Oxford University Press, 1993).
45. William M. Wiecek, *Liberty Under Law: The Supreme Court in American Life* (Baltimore: Johns Hopkins University Press).
46. Christopher Wolfe, *The Rise of Modern Judicial Review: From Constitutional Interpretation to Judge-Made Law* (New York: Basic Books, 1986). See also Anthony Woodiwiss, *Rights v. Conspiracy: A Sociological Essay on the History of Labor Law in the United States* (New York: Berg, 1990).
47. *Plessy v. Ferguson,* 163 U.S. 537 (1896), 68, 76, 175.
48. Howard Abadinsky, *Law and Justice: An Introduction to the American Legal System* (Upper Saddle River, NJ: Prentice Hall, 2003).
49. Alan M. Dershowitz, *Supreme Injustice: How the High Court Hijacked Election 2000* (New York: Oxford University Press, 2001).
50. Gary A. Rabe and Dean J. Champion, *Criminal Courts: Structure, Process, and Issues* (Upper Saddle River, NJ: Prentice Hall, 2002).
51. David W. Neubauer, *America's Courts and the Criminal Justice System,* 7th ed. (Belmont, CA: Wadsworth, 2002), 68.
52. Larry Kramer, "Diversity Jurisdiction," *Brigham Young University Law Review,* 1990, pp. 3–66.
53. Lawrence Baum, "Specializing the Federal Courts: Neutral Reforms or Efforts to Shape Judicial Policy?" *Judicature* 74: 217–224.
54. Judith Resnik, "Multiple Sovereignties: Indian Tribes, States, and the Federal Government," *Judicature* 79: 118–125.
55. Kathleen Maguire and Ann Pastore, *Sourcebook of Criminal Justice Statistics, 1999* (Albany, NY: Hindelang Criminal Justice Research Center, 2000).

outline

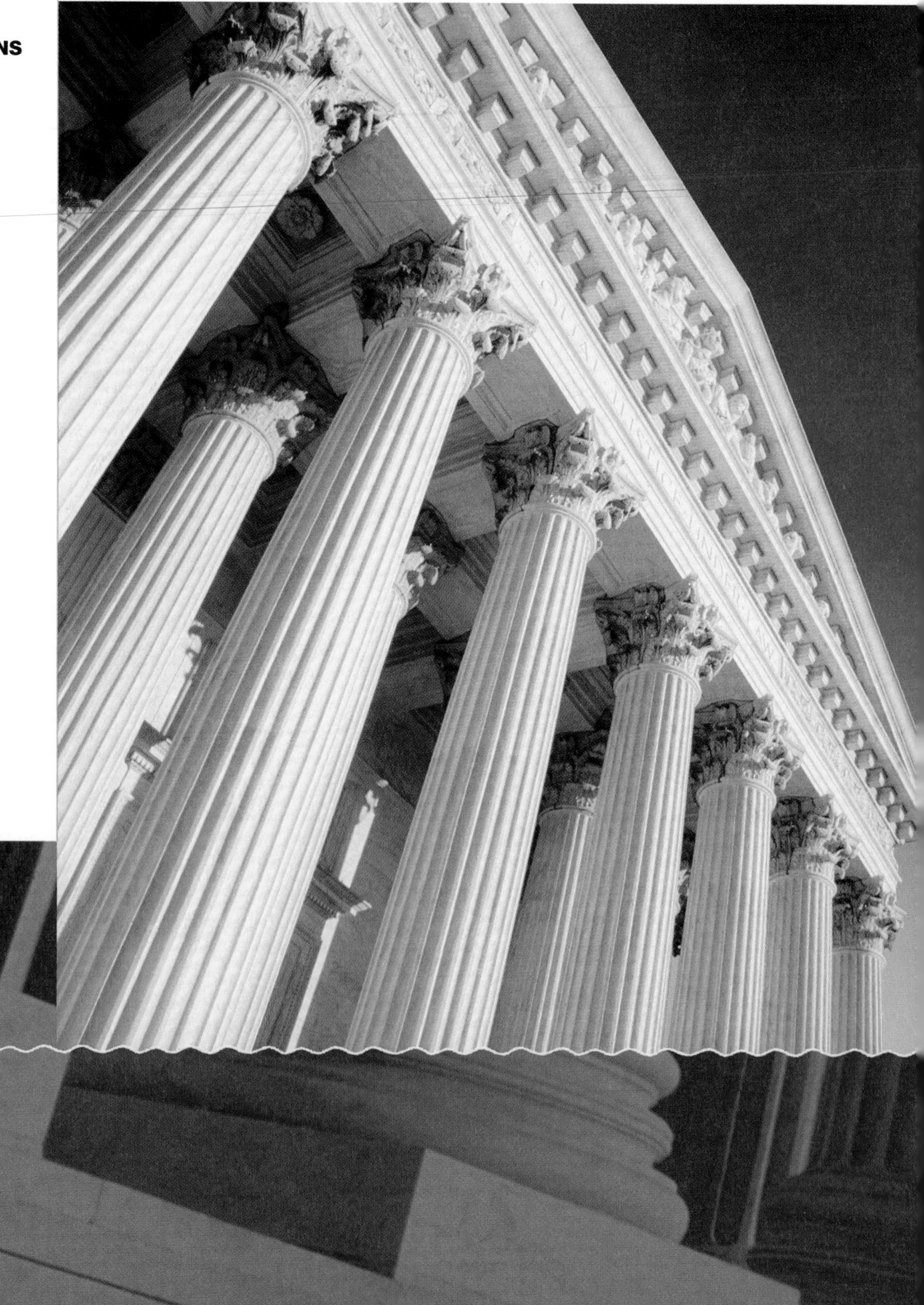

CHAPTER 9

Working in the Courtroom

objectives

After reading this chapter, the student should be able to:

1. Understand the concept of the courtroom work group.
2. List and describe the various participants in the work group.
3. Discuss the role of the prosecutor.
4. Describe the difference between the roles of federal and state prosecutors.
5. Understand how some state prosecution offices have special bureaus and programs.
6. Discuss the role of the defense attorney.
7. Describe the defense attorney's role within the courtroom work group.
8. Compare and contrast private attorneys and public defenders.
9. Describe the roles and concerns of defendants, victims, and witnesses.
10. Discuss pretrial release decisions.

THE PEOPLE WHO WORK IN THE COURTROOM FORM A complex and fascinating set of actors who work together at a variety of levels to fashion a product that is defined as "justice." On one hand, the processing of cases may look like a smoothly functioning system in which all people "get their day in court" and are assured the full range of constitutional protections, as well as the guarantee that their voices will be heard and seriously considered. On the other hand, below the surface of public scrutiny, the courtroom can be considered a chaotic place where attorneys and judges sometimes play fast and loose with the truth, individuals' rights, and justice itself. In an effort to move the docket—that is, to settle cases—justice is negotiated and bargained.

Some people are alarmed by the dynamics of the courthouse, which, in function, differ vastly from the ideal of impartial justice being dispensed by wise judges. The notion of attorneys working deals with the prosecutor to garner more lenient sentences for obviously guilty defendants violates our image of the courthouse as a place where truth prevails and the guilty get

Testifying in court is a serious endeavor because so much is at stake. Witnesses must take an oath promising to tell the truth.
Courtesy of Corbis Royalty Free.

their just deserts. However, understanding the politics of the courtroom is vital to comprehending the activities of those who comprise the courtroom work group. In this chapter we will identify the roles and responsibilities of those whose job it is to handle the vast caseload of crimes that pass through the modern courthouse. We will start with the support personnel, then turn to the prosecutor's office and the various types of defense attorneys.

The Courtroom Work Group

Not all courtrooms are the same. Different levels of jurisdiction (federal, state, and local) and different levels of responsibility (misdemeanors, felonies, and appeals) dictate different working arrangements among the participants in the courtroom work group. The following discussion of the courtroom work group is very general and refers to the typical types of issues that arise in most courts.

The Participants

Although a certain adversarial atmosphere is present in the courtroom, those in the courtroom work group also exhibit a high level of cooperation.[1] Those working in the courthouse, and, ultimately, in the courtroom, come from vastly different backgrounds, agencies, and ideologies. As in the criminal justice system in general, those who work in the courthouse have different sets of funding sources, constituents, responsibilities, and goals. These people, who sometimes seem to be working at cross-purposes, are in many other ways cooperating to dispose of cases in a timely manner.[2] Consequently, there is a certain level of expectation of how each case will be settled based on the **going rate**, or more precisely, on how other cases of a similar nature have been settled in the past by a given set of judges, prosecutors, and attorneys.[3] In sociological terms, a certain routinization of work occurs whereby everyone (except the defendant) has a good idea about the ultimate outcome of the case. Nevertheless, each actor in the drama has a vested interest in seeing cases resolved according to his or her particular social and legal location within the courthouse. It is illustrative to review this variety of courthouse actors and reflect on how they affect the daily events in the courtroom.

going rate
A term describing how similar cases have been settled by a given set of judges, prosecutors, and attorneys.

LAW ENFORCEMENT. A variety of law enforcement officers interact daily within the courtroom work group. First is the courthouse security officer, who is responsible for protecting everyone throughout the courthouse. Some jurisdictions may have metal-

Judge, attorney, and court reporter.
Courtesy of CORBIS-NY.

screening devices at the courthouse entrances to prohibit unauthorized people from carrying firearms into the courthouse. A second type of law enforcement officer working in the courthouse is the sheriff's deputy, who transports prisoners to and from jail. The courthouse will usually have a holding pen where these deputies will keep inmates until their presence is needed in the courtroom. The bailiff is a court officer responsible for maintaining order in the courtroom.[4] In some jurisdictions a bailiff will work in the courtroom of a single judge. In other jurisdictions, bailiffs will rotate from courtroom to courtroom as needed. Finally, there is a constant parade of law enforcement officers who come to the courthouse to testify in trials. Many courts have a senior law enforcement officer who coordinates with police agencies to ensure that officers do not spend all their time waiting in courthouse corridors for trials that may be cancelled.

COURT SUPPORT STAFF. A number of courtroom support staffers work behind the scenes to ensure the smooth functioning of the court. The **clerk of the court** is an administrator with a large staff who is responsible for keeping the court records and providing a sufficient pool of jurors for cases that go to trial. The **court reporter** makes a verbatim transcript of the proceedings. Given the ethnic diversity of many cities, various translators are employed by the court to ensure that defendants, victims, and witnesses can have their testimony translated into English. Finally, the **court administrator** handles a variety of administrative tasks necessary for the functioning of the court. Activities from scheduling courtrooms and procuring furniture to improving case flow, creating calendars, and managing court personnel are under the purview of the court administrator.[5]

CORRECTIONS. Probation officers perform two primary functions for the court. First, they interview offenders and write presentence investigation reports in which they review the case and make sentencing recommendations to the judge.[6] Second, for those offenders who are placed on probation, the probation officer supervises them to ensure they are following the orders of the judge and are not committing further crimes. Depending on the jurisdiction, the probation officer may be employed directly by the court via a statewide department of corrections or by a local government or private probation department. Some jurisdictions have pretrial services personnel working with the judges to help identify individuals who could be safely released from custody pending further court proceedings.[7] Finally, a number of rehabilitation specialists aid the court in identifying programs of drug and alcohol treatment for qualified offenders. Often, judges

clerk of the court
The primary administrative officer of each court who manages nonjudicial functions. Among the clerk's duties are maintaining records and dockets, paying all collected monies into the U.S. Treasury, administering the jury, providing interpreters and court reporters, and sending official notices and summonses.

court reporter
A court officer who records and transcribes an official verbatim record of the legal proceedings of the court.

court administrator
An officer responsible for the mechanical necessities of the court including, but not limited to, scheduling courtrooms, managing case flow, administering personnel, procuring furniture, and preparing budgets.

will want to know whether there is a program willing to enroll an offender before such a sentence is mandated.

bail agent
An employee of a private, for-profit company that provides money for suspects to be released from jail. Bail companies usually charge the suspect a fee of 10 percent of the amount of the bond. Also called a "bondsman."

THE PUBLIC. A number of individuals from the public sphere who have business with the court can be loosely identified as part of the courtroom work group. For-profit **bail agents** will be on hand to solicit offenders or their families to use their services. Suspects who cannot afford the entire amount of their bail may use a bail agent to get out of jail while awaiting trial. Many news agencies will have reporters covering the courthouse beat. Depending on their reputation for discretion, some of these reporters are allowed behind the scenes where they participate in the informal workings of the courtroom work group. Victim–witness program personnel, including staff members of rape crisis centers, are other informal participants in the courtroom work group.[8] These individuals advocate on behalf of victims of crime and may introduce victim impact statements to help the judge decide on an appropriate sentence.[9]

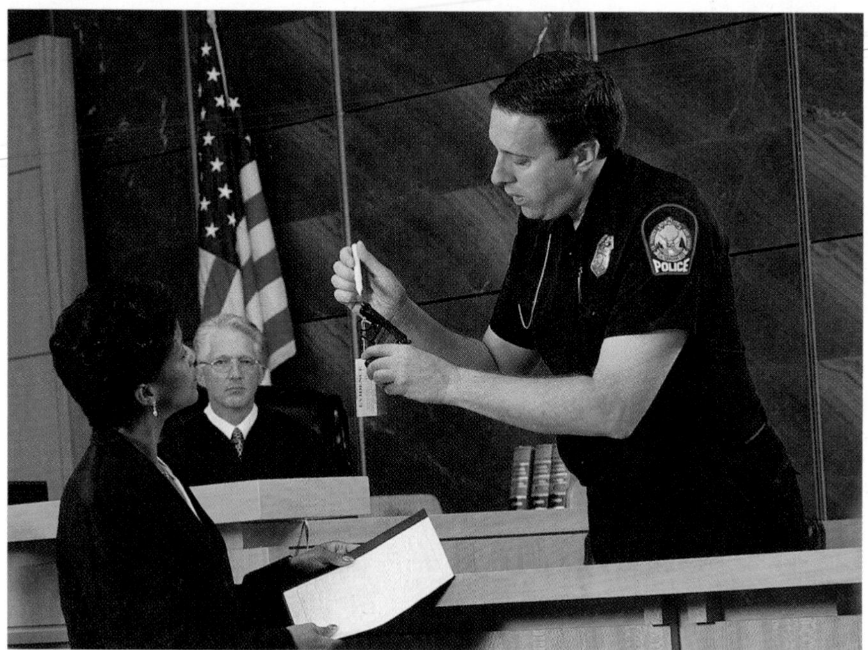

The duties of a law enforcement officer do not end with the arrest. Law enforcement officers must testify in court and defend their procedures and actions when cross-examined by the defense.
Courtesy of Corbis Royalty Free.

Bounty Hunters: A Step Ahead of the Law

Bail enforcement agents, better known as bounty hunters, carry a mysterious and somewhat romantic reputation. Generally, the profession is poorly understood, which is not surprising. Bounty hunters do a dangerous job: tracking down and bringing in bail-jumpers, while operating outside the boundaries of regular law enforcement.

Most states have few or no regulations governing bounty hunters. Thanks to an 1872 Supreme Court ruling in *Taylor v. Taintor,* bounty hunters enjoy more leeway than the police. Suspects who sign a contract with a bail-bondsman are considered to be in the custody of the bail-bondsman, and by extension, the bounty hunter. Therefore, bounty hunters are legally considered to be acting by private contract rather than enforcing government laws. Because of this extralegal status, bounty hunters are far more successful in bringing in fugitives than are law enforcement personnel. Many bounty hunters are private investigators, former police officers, or former soldiers. However, in most states, anyone can operate as a bounty hunter, free of training requirements or background checks.

This system sometimes leads to tragedy. On Christmas Eve, 2002, in Richmond, Virginia, a bounty hunter looking for a fugitive broke into the wrong home and shot and killed a man unconnected with the case. The bounty hunter was charged with second-degree murder, but breaking into what he thought was a suspect's home was not illegal. Agents in Virginia may enter a fugitive's residence without a search warrant, and are not required to announce themselves before doing so. In a 1997 incident, Martin Tong of Kansas City, Missouri, was shot three times in his apartment by two bounty hunters who thought he was a fugitive. The bounty hunters had the correct address, but the man they were looking for had moved out of the apartment six months earlier, and it had since been leased to Tong.

The most recent federal attempt to regulate the profession was in 1999 with the Bounty Hunter Responsibility Act. More states are now pursuing or have enacted legislation to regulate bounty hunters.

State Bail Enforcement Agent Requirements

License Required	Restrictions	Few or No Restrictions
Arizona	Arkansas	Alabama
California	Colorado	Alaska
Connecticut	Delaware	Hawaii
Indiana	District of Columbia	Idaho
Iowa	Florida	Kansas
Louisiana	Georgia	Maine
Mississippi	Illinois	Maryland*
Nevada	Kentucky	Massachusetts*
New York	New Hampshire	Michigan
South Dakota	North Carolina	Minnesota
Texas	Ohio	Missouri*
Utah	Oklahoma	Montana
West Virginia	Oregon	Nebraska
	South Carolina	New Jersey
	Tennessee	New Mexico
	Washington	North Dakota
	Wisconsin	Pennsylvania
		Rhode Island
		Vermont
		Virginia*
		Wyoming

*License legislation or other major regulatory legislation pending as of 2003.

Source: American Bail Coalition Compendium of State Bounty Hunter Laws, http://www.americanbailcoalition.com/new_html/compendium.htm.

QUESTIONS

1. Should bail enforcement agents be outlawed? Should they be given even more powers? Are they a "necessary evil"?
2. Would you consider working as a bail enforcement agent?
3. If you were a police officer, what view would you take of bail enforcement agents?

Sources: Timothy Dwyer, "Working Justice System's Wild Side: Clients Who 'Skip' Keep Fairfax City Bail Bond Company on the Run," *Washington Post,* February 5, 2003, http://www.washingtonpost.com/ac2/wp-dyn?pagename=article&node=&contentId=A26920-2003Feb4. Susana Vera, "Bounty Hunters," Missouri Digital News, February 10, 1997, http://www.mdn.org/1997/STORIES/HUNTER.HTM.

child advocate
An officer appointed by the court to protect the interests of the child and to act as a liaison among the child, the child's family, the court, and any other agency involved with the child. Some states have child-advocate offices.

Juvenile courts often employ a **child advocate** to ensure that the best interests of the child, and not those of the state or the parents, are considered.[10] Many courts have members of the public who act as court watchers. These individuals may represent public interest groups who advocate for better government, or they may simply be court aficionados who enjoy watching the courtroom action. Finally, perhaps the most important segment of the public that is constantly present in the courtroom are the jurors. Although no individual juror is a regular member of the courtroom work group, they are part of the proceedings and play an important role in the courts' decisions.

As we can see, the informal courtroom work group comprises a variety of individuals who represent many, and sometimes competing, interests. All are instrumental in the workings of the courts and play important roles. However, the main actors in the courtroom work group have not yet been considered. Because the prosecutor, defense attorney, and judge are such prominent players in the production of the court, we will deal with each of them in greater detail.

Prosecutor

The prosecutor has in many ways the most powerful position in the criminal justice system. The prosecutor functions as the major gatekeeper of the process and not only decides which cases are formally defined as crimes, but also argues those cases in court.[11] The position of prosecutor is powerful because the exercise of discretion (the authority to make decisions about which cases are inserted into the criminal justice system) rests with this office. With police officers pushing for harsh penalties for those they arrest, defense attorneys pleading for the best bargain they can get for their clients, and judges wanting to move the docket and dispose of cases quickly, the power of the prosecutor allows him or her to inject personal philosophy and political interests into the justice system.[12] The prosecutor has the discretion to charge the case (or not), to decide what the charge will be, and to dismiss it if he or she so chooses. This pivotal actor has the most influence in plea bargaining.

However, the discretion of the prosecutor is not completely unfettered. Even though the prosecuting attorney has sole discretion in deciding which cases to prosecute, what crimes to charge the defendant with, and what sorts of deals the government will agree to, prosecutorial behavior is limited. Especially during the trial stage of the proceedings, the prosecutor must act within firmly established parameters of procedural law. For instance, if the prosecutor knows of evidence that may show the defendant to be innocent, he or she is under obligation to share that evidence with the defense attorney.[13] The converse of this obligation is not required. Defense attorneys are not expected to share evidence of their clients' guilt. The prosecutor must prove the case without the aid of the defense attorney and the defendant. This may seem somewhat unfair, but it is important to remember that the prosecutor has the resources of the state behind his or her efforts and that the Constitution protects the individual rights of the accused. Although the prosecutor represents the interests of the state (which includes the victim, law enforcement officers, and the ideal of justice), the idea of a free society under law protects individuals from unfettered state power.[14]

Given the complexity of our court system with its various federal, state, and local jurisdictions, as well as its geographic hierarchy, it should not surprise us that the position of prosecutor also varies widely. It is useful to distinguish between prosecutors at the state and federal levels because their differences are as important as their similarities.

PROSECUTION AT THE FEDERAL LEVEL. The Department of Justice, or Justice Department, is at the top of the federal hierarchy of prosecution. The U.S. attorney general is a cabinet-level officer who is appointed by the president and confirmed by the Senate through its advise-and-consent function. Lawyers working for the Justice Department are protected from political influence by their civil service status. Because so many of them may spend their whole careers working for the government, they become

CROSSCURRENTS

How Much Justice Can You Afford?

Being accused of a crime can be expensive. Even for those who are not indigent, the expense of hiring a lawyer can seem astronomical and can place severe limits on just how effective a defense can be pursued. Attorneys cost money; this is not a surprise. Just how much money can shock even the most cynical of us.

At the extreme end of legal fees are those that resulted from the contingency fees claimed by some private attorneys who represented states in suits against the tobacco industry. According to an editorial in the *Rocky Mountain News,* "In Maryland . . . one attorney claimed his 25 percent fee entitled him to more than 1.1 billion of the state's 4.6 billion settlement. That came out to $30,000 for each hour he claimed to have worked." Of course, criminal defense attorneys do not receive that level of compensation, but even at $100 to $400 an hour, the expense of a full-blown trial with all of its preparation can run into tens of thousands of dollars. Other expenses in addition to attorney's fees may include the following:

- *Psychiatric evaluations*
- *Expert witnesses*
- *Polygraph tests*
- *Travel expenses for witnesses*
- *Expenses associated with the preparation of courtroom visual aids such as diagrams, maps, and charts*

Expenses such as these can severely deplete the savings of most people and cause them to go into debt. However, when the client is indigent and has to rely on a public defender, the expenses for the case can quickly become limited. In Bend, Oregon, a defense attorney billed the state $1,500 for plane fare for a witness from England. After interviewing the woman, the attorney decided she would not help the case. After the newspaper reported the story, the attorney paid the expense out of his own pocket. When the cost of a criminal offense soars to over $100,000, even prosperous individuals have difficulty achieving full justice. When court-appointed public defenders are compensated with as little as $65 per hour, it is understandable that each client is not going to be the beneficiary of an extensive defense.

Finally, what happens when the client runs out of money in the middle of the case or desires an appeal? Defense attorneys have the expenses of maintaining an office and paying secretaries and can afford to do only limited pro bono work. The result is that the quality of justice one receives can depend on how deep one's pockets are.

QUESTIONS

1. Should attorney's fees be capped?
2. Should the state provide the best attorneys available to defendants who cannot afford them?
3. Should all attorneys work for the state? Should they all be private?

Sources: "Put Cap on Fees From State Lawsuits," *Rocky Mountain News,* February 17, 2003, http://rockymountainnews.com/drmn/opinion/article/0,1299,DRMN_38_1749940,00.html. Charles E. Beggs, "District Attorneys Question Spending," Associated Press/The Worldlink.com, http://www.theworldlink.com/articles/2003/02/14/news/news03.txt.

REFERENCE

American Bar Association

Founded in 1878 in Saratoga Springs, New York, the American Bar Association is the world's largest voluntary professional organization. Currently, the ABA is based in Chicago, Illinois, and is operated as a private, not-for-profit corporation. With more than 400,000 members, the association represents about half of all the lawyers in the United States. Any practicing lawyer in good standing with a state or territory bar can join the ABA.

The ABA is governed by a president, a 39-member board of governors, and a 530-member house of delegates. Among other duties, the ABA accredits law schools and provides a variety of programs for lawyers and judges. The association states its mission as "to be the national representative of the legal profession, serving the public and the profession by promoting justice, professional excellence and respect for the law."

In 1995 the United States sued the ABA for violating antitrust laws. The United States accused the association of using accreditation to elevate the salaries of law school faculty members by withholding accreditation from schools that would not meet a national salary average for its faculty. In settling the case, the ABA, among other concessions, agreed it would no longer use compensation data in its accreditation process. The association currently accredits about 200 law schools in the United States and Puerto Rico.

Sources: The American Bar Association, http://www.abanet.org/. *U.S. v. American Bar Association,* U.S. Department of Justice, Antitrust Case Filings, Antitrust Division, http://www.usdoj.gov/atr/cases/americ1.htm.

experts in their particular branch of the law.[15] The attorney general's office is responsible for a range of activities not associated with the prosecution of criminal cases.

- **Executive direction and management offices.** This includes the solicitor general, who argues all the government's cases before the Supreme Court and represents the interests of the executive branch in advising Congress on the crafting of legislation.
- **Litigation.** This part of the organization handles all courtroom matters including antitrust, civil, civil rights, criminal, environmental, tax, and the oversight of the U.S. attorneys' office in all the federal districts.
- **Investigatory and law enforcement agencies.** The Justice Department is responsible for the Federal Bureau of Investigation (FBI), the Drug Enforcement Agency (DEA), the U.S. Marshals Service, and the Federal Bureau of Prisons.
- **Policy and assistance offices.** These offices include the Bureau of Justice Assistance, the Immigration and Naturalization Service (INS), and other agencies that coordinate justice interests or provide assistance to other agencies or the public.

As we can see, the Justice Department is responsible for many activities that are not concerned with the prosecution of cases. Here, the discussion will be limited to the three offices of the Justice Department that directly affect the prosecutorial aspect of the criminal justice process. The offices of the solicitor general, the criminal division of the litigation branch, and the U.S. attorneys in the federal courts are all important representatives of the federal government's interests in prosecuting cases.

Solicitor General. In addition to arguing on behalf of the federal government in proceedings before the U.S. Supreme Court, the solicitor general coordinates all the appeals of cases that went against the federal government in the lower courts. The solicitor general's office decides whether a case is important enough to the federal government to merit the time and resources required to file an appeal. The case must have a high degree of policy significance and a reasonable legal argument that will stand a good chance of success before the solicitor general's office will accept the case. The solicitor general also imposes on cases in which the federal government is not a direct participant but has some policy interest.[16] By filing an *amicus curiae* (friend of the court) brief, the position of the government can be argued in court even though neither party requests this information.[17]

Department of Justice Criminal Division. The criminal division of the Justice Department coordinates the prosecution of all federal criminal statutes. It has a wide range of sections that deal with cases spanning the spectrum from money laundering and terrorism to child exploitation and obscenity. The criminal division will prosecute cases of national significance such as the Unabomber and the Oklahoma City bombing. Headquartered in Washington, D.C., the criminal division exercises nominal supervision over the U.S. attorneys offices around the country.

U.S. Attorneys. There are 93 U.S. attorneys scattered across the country and other jurisdictions such as Guam, Puerto Rico, and countries that are considered territories of the United States. The U.S. attorneys enjoy wide latitude in deciding which criminal cases to prosecute, as well as in defending the United States in civil suits and in collection of debts owed to the federal government. There are over 4,500 assistant U.S. attorneys, and each jurisdiction handles both complex and simple cases. Some jurisdictions have higher caseloads for certain types of crimes than others. For example, jurisdictions on the U.S. border with Mexico will prosecute more cases that involve drug smuggling or illegal immigration than will jurisdictions in the midwestern United States. Although the U.S. attorneys serve at the pleasure of the president and report to the attorney general, they often owe their jobs to senators or congressional representatives who recommended them for appointment.[18] Furthermore, with so many U.S. attorneys spread across the country, the criminal division of the Department of Justice has difficulty closely supervising them all and directing their discretion.

PROSECUTION IN STATE COURTS. State court systems are highly decentralized with prosecution responsibility spread over state, county (or district), and local levels. This variety of organizational placements for prosecutors can result in an inefficient, overlapping, and often ineffective maze of responsibility for protecting the public's interests. Criminals in large metropolitan areas may be operating simultaneously in several jurisdictions, and prosecutors can be unaware of each other's efforts to bring these criminals to justice. For instance, in the greater Atlanta, Georgia, area, six counties overlap with the city limits. This results in competition, rivalries, and obstructions among law enforcement agencies and courts. Gaps may occur between jurisdictions that savvy attorneys can manipulate to broker advantageous circumstances for their clients.

Although considerable overlap in duties exists, the following three types of prosecutors are typically found in court systems across the United States.

State Attorney General. The state attorney general is the chief legal officer for a state, and the duties of this office are usually delineated in the state constitution. The state attorney general represents the state in legal actions in which the state is a party. In most states, the power of the state attorney general is limited in criminal matters. Because local prosecutors are elected by the citizens of their districts, the state prosecutor can provide only minimal supervision over their work. For the most part, the state attorney general exercises most of the office's power in the civil area of the law. A prime example of how state attorneys general prosecute civil cases on behalf of citizens is the lawsuits against the tobacco industry in the mid-1990s in which several states brought action against the major tobacco corporations.[19]

Chief Prosecutor. The chief prosecutor is the most powerful person in the criminal justice system. Depending on the state, this officer of the court is called the district attorney, the state attorney, or simply the prosecuting officer. This individual is the chief law

REFERENCE

Oath of Attorney

Attorneys in each state must take an oath of attorney in order to practice law in that state. Here is an example from the state of Washington.

Washington State Bar Association Oath of Attorney

I do solemnly declare:

1. I am fully subject to the laws of the State of Washington and the laws of the United States and will abide by the same.
2. I will support the constitution of the State of Washington and the constitution of the United States.
3. I will abide by the Rules of Professional Conduct approved by the Supreme Court of the State of Washington.
4. I will maintain the respect due to the courts of justice and judicial officers.
5. I will not counsel, or maintain any suit, or proceeding, which shall appear to me to be unjust, or any defense except as I believe to be honestly debatable under the law, unless it is in defense of a person charged with a public offense. I will employ for the purpose of maintaining the causes confided to me only those means consistent with truth and honor. I will never seek to mislead the judge or jury by any artifice or false statement.
6. I will maintain the confidence and preserve inviolate the secrets of my client, and will accept no compensation in connection with the business of my client unless this compensation is from or with the knowledge and approval of the client or with the approval of the court.
7. I will abstain from all offensive personalities, and advance no fact prejudicial to the honor or reputation of a party or witness unless required by the justice of the cause with which I am charged.
8. I will never reject, from any consideration personal to myself, the cause of the defenseless or oppressed, or delay unjustly the cause of any person.

Source: Washington State Bar Association, http://www.wsba.org/forms/oath.htm.

enforcement officer for the community and sits at the crossroads of the system between the police and the courts. There are over 2,000 chief prosecutors across the country with a combined staff of over 65,000 assistant prosecutors, investigators, secretaries, and other support staff, such as victim–witness advocates. Because chief prosecutors are elected officers in 95 percent of the districts, they are much attuned to the local political scene.[20]

Working in the office of the chief prosecutor is a very sought-after position by new lawyers. There are several advantages to securing a job as an assistant district attorney. First, the job has a salary, and for someone fresh from law school who has not had the opportunity to become established on the local legal scene, this is attractive. Even though some new attorneys can land jobs at large and prestigious law firms, the prosecutor's office carries a certain amount of status. The second reason the prosecutor's office is attractive is because it affords new attorneys ample opportunity to practice courtroom law. As opposed to working in the research department of some large law firm writing briefs for the firm's partners, the assistant district attorney will soon be in the courtroom exercising a wide range of discretion and gaining valuable experience. The third reason this is such a prized job for recent graduates is because it provides a high degree of visibility

NEWS FLASH

Whose Side Are You On?

What is the responsibility of a prosecutor? Is it to expose the truth and help the state imprison criminals? Or is it to prosecute a case to the fullest extent of his or her abilities, regardless of the truth?

In September 2002, 14-year-old Derek King and his brother Alex, 13, were convicted of beating their father to death with a baseball bat as he slept. Alex told authorities that he had been involved in an intense emotional and sexual relationship with 40-year-old convicted pedophile Ricky Chavis. Although the brothers initially confessed to the crime, they later recanted, saying that Chavis actually murdered their father and coached them to confess because, as juveniles, they would receive lighter sentences if convicted. The brothers were convicted of the murder, and Chavis was acquitted. The twist? Both were prosecuted by the same man, David Rimmer. Rimmer not only prosecuted the three defendants with equal vigor, but, as critics pointed out, with a line of reasoning that leads to a strange paradox. To Chavis' jury, he argued that the boys committed the crime. To the Kings' jury, he argued that Chavis committed the crime. When Chavis, whose murder trial came first, was acquitted, the verdict was withheld until the Kings' jury presented its verdict. The King brothers, who were tried as adults, each faced sentences of 20 years to life.

A judge later threw out the Kings' second-degree murder convictions and told prosecutors and defense attorneys that if they could not resolve the case, a new trial would be ordered for the Kings. In November 2002, in exchange for pleading guilty to arson and third-degree murder, Derek King was sentenced to eight years in state prison and Alex to seven years. Chavis was found guilty of accessory-after-the-fact to first-degree murder and evidence tampering and sentenced to 30 years in prison.

Sources: "Judge Throws Out Conviction of Two Florida Boys," AP/CourtTV.com, October 17, 2002, http://www.courttv.com/trials/king/101702_ap.html. John Springer, "Prosecutor Argues Opposing Theories of a Father's Murder," CourtTV.com, September 3, 2002, http://www.courttv.com/trials/king/090302_ctv.html. "King Brothers Guilty of Killing Their Father," AP/CNN.com, September 9, 2002, http://www.cnn.com/2002/LAW/09/07/king.trial/.

in the legal community. Assistant district attorneys are recruited into large law firms after they have established a name for themselves as effective courtroom warriors. Additionally, after prosecuting a few high-profile cases, some assistant district attorneys opt to enter politics. The exposure gained from this position can be parlayed into a political career. This is especially true in states where judges are elected, and the prosecutor can position himself or herself as someone who is tough on crime.

Additional features of the position of chief prosecutor can enhance one's career. A certain amount of patronage is available in regions in which assistant district attorneys are appointed, as well as other support staff. Political parties also like to see one of their own in such a position in the hope that their affairs will not be too closely scrutinized.[21]

Local Prosecutors. Based at the city or county level, local prosecutors perform a wide range of duties that are concerned with either misdemeanor cases or the preliminary stages of felony cases. These are important actors in the criminal justice system because the vast numbers of cases they handle concern public drunkenness, petty theft, disorderly conduct, and minor assault. Depending on the size of the local jurisdiction, some of these local prosecutors work only on a part-time basis.

THE PROSECUTOR AT WORK. Prosecutors engage in a variety of activities throughout the day. Much of the work of the prosecutor is invisible to the public, but it is precisely this invisible work that occupies the majority of the prosecutor's time and, more

CASE IN POINT

Argersinger v. Hamlin

The Case

Argersinger v. Hamlin, 407 U.S. 25, 92 S. Ct. 2006 (1972)

The Point

The accused has the right to an attorney whether the crime is a misdemeanor or a felony.

Jon Argersinger was charged in Florida with carrying a concealed weapon. With no attorney present, the indigent Argersinger was tried by a judge and sentenced to 90 days in jail. The court did not appoint an attorney for Argersinger because the crime was a misdemeanor, and the court only appointed attorneys for felony crimes. The Supreme Court later overturned Argersinger's conviction, stating that, "No accused may be deprived of his liberty as the result of any criminal prosecution, whether felony or misdemeanor, in which he was denied the assistance of counsel."

important, forms the bulk of activities that determine exactly how justice is dispensed in the courthouse. David Neubauer listed five categories of activities that divide the prosecutor's energies:[22]

1. **Fighting.** Prosecutors must struggle to get a case in shape to take to court and ultimately to trial. The efforts of the law enforcement officer must be scrutinized to determine whether the case files are complete, and more important, whether the officer followed the procedural laws in arresting and interrogating the suspect. The prosecutor plans a legal strategy to present the strongest case possible and to deflect criticism from the defense. The prosecutor must have a good sense of how the judge and jury will react to the case, and must consider the psychological and sociological dynamics of witnesses, defendants, and others affected by the cases. In short, the prosecutor must battle to ensure that the case presented by the state is strong, complete, and coherent, and satisfies the public's sense of justice.
2. **Negotiating.** Only a very small number of cases ever go to trial. Most are plea bargained, meaning that the defense attorney and the prosecutor strike a deal for a plea of guilty or no contest in return for a lighter sentence. Plea bargaining has been the subject of much controversy because it appears to the public as though defendants are able to escape the full responsibility for their actions. We will discuss plea bargaining in greater detail in Chapter 10, but it is prudent to say here that this practice is absolutely vital to the functioning of the criminal justice system. Because so many defendants are, in fact, guilty of the crimes the police charge them with, it is in their interests, as well as the interests of the state, to settle the case as quickly and as economically as possible. The state simply cannot afford the time and resources required to take every case to a jury trial, and guilty defendants cannot afford to expose themselves to the maximum sentence available under the law. Therefore, a deal is struck in which each party considers the weight of the evidence, the likelihood of a conviction, and the expenses that would be incurred by a trial, and they negotiate a settlement. The prosecutor represents the state and/or the victim in these negotiations and must make several tactical decisions to ensure that the government is getting the best deal possible and that, in a greater sense, justice is being served. Negotiating a plea is an art, and experienced prosecutors must act like poker players, sometimes revealing their evidence and sometimes attempting to bluff the defense attorney into believing that the state's or victim's case is stronger than it actually is.

3. **Drafting.** It might be the least enjoyable part of being a prosecutor, but the drafting of legal documents is a very important function for the workings of the criminal justice system. Prosecutors must be careful to lay a paper trail of their activities to ensure that cases can be upheld on appeal. Prosecutors must also prepare a number of documents that enable other actors in the criminal justice system to perform their duties. For instance, the prosecutor must draft the search warrant, specify what violations of the criminal codes defendants are charged with, and prepare documents that address motions made by the defense. The paperwork can be time consuming, distracting, and a downright pain in the neck, but for the prosecutor it is a vital part of the duties. Improperly prepared paperwork can have extremely negative ramifications that include letting obviously guilty suspects escape the clutches of justice.
4. **Counseling.** Because the prosecutor occupies such a pivotal position in the criminal justice system, he or she must contend with the emotional and psychological needs of victims, witnesses, law enforcement officers, and other officials who make up the courtroom work group. If a police officer's case is weak, the prosecutor must explain why it cannot be taken to trial, and the officer must be educated on the specific aspects of the law in which the case was inadequate. Victims may want the maximum penalty available under the law to be imposed on their assailant, but the prosecutors may be restrained by other factors and must counsel the victim on why the plea bargain was the best outcome possible given the circumstances of the case. Additionally, the prosecutor spends a considerable amount of time advising victims, witnesses, and law enforcement officers on how to testify at trial. A poorly prepared witness can be fatal to the state's case, and although the prosecutor will not advise anyone to tell a lie, he or she may advise them to answer the defense attorney's questions as succinctly as possible and not provide extra information that could be used as ammunition against the prosecution's case.
5. **Administering.** The prosecutor's office is a modern bureaucracy and suffers from the same strains as any large organization. Personnel issues include hiring, supervising, and firing assistant attorneys, secretarial staff, and investigators. The prosecutors must also play a large administrative role in keeping the cases moving by making sure victims and witnesses are interviewed, briefed, and available should they be needed to testify. Additionally, the prosecutor's office has to ensure that assistant district attorneys are available and present whenever one of the judges holds court.

Clearly, the work of the prosecutor is varied and complex. As the primary representative of the state in the courtroom, the prosecutor must fight for justice and ensure that the interests of the victim, the police, and the public are addressed. Sometimes these demands can become complicated and even conflict. For example, the prosecutor may decide that a case involving a young person charged with assault is relatively minor and that the offender would best benefit from probation and restitution, while the victim of the assault, who lost his or her front teeth, demands that the defendant be incarcerated.

Becoming an assistant district attorney can be a major step in climbing the legal career ladder. In addition to some of the features of the job that we have already mentioned, the chance to argue cases in the courtroom is especially attractive. Because of the large caseloads in many prosecutors' offices, the new district attorney, often fresh out of law school, is thrown into a position of having to exercise considerable discretion, judgment, and power in the peoples' interest. This "on the job training" can be both stimulating and intimidating for a new prosecutor who must quickly learn to swim with the sharks of the legal environment. The quick learners survive by depending on the others in the courtroom work group to educate them on courtroom etiquette, protocol, and formal as well as informal procedures for a particular judge's court.[23]

As with any occupation, certain norms emerge that guide how cases are handled in the courtroom. However, the courtroom work group has some constraints that most organizations lack, constraints that make the work of the prosecutor difficult to learn and negotiate.

disposition
The final determination of a case or other matter by a court or other judicial entity. This term can also refer to the sentence received by a convicted criminal defendant.

Although each case must be decided individually, there are shared conceptions about how any one case should be decided. These shared conceptions arise from the history of what has happened to similar cases that have been processed by the court in the past.[24] Legal variables such as the seriousness of the offense and the prior record of the defendant are factored into the **disposition**. Additionally, organizational factors of the courtroom, such as the number of cases on the docket, the experience of the defense attorney, the presence or absence of the victim, and the remaining physical capacity of the local jail and the state prison system are all ingredients that affect the shared expectations of the courtroom work group. The assistant district attorney is expected to conform to the norms of the courtroom work group with each case or have a good reason for expending extra time and effort.

What happens when the prosecutor insists on spending too much time and resources on a case? Because those who work in the courtroom work group want to maintain a regular routine in which they get to eat lunch and go home at a reasonable hour, they exert subtle influences on prosecutors who are unwilling or unable to keep the docket moving. The judge may complain about the backlog of cases that develops when the prosecutor is too stingy in the plea bargains offered to defendants. If too many cases require trials, then the court administrator must find courtroom time; the clerk of the court must empanel a jury; the court reporter must be put on standby; and attorneys, especially private attorneys, must juggle other commitments. Everyone understands that trials are sometimes required, but they also understand that there is a going rate by which each case would normally be decided. When a prosecutor violates this well-understood norm, other members of the courtroom work group will expect the case to be unique in some way; if it isn't, they will complain. Promotions and reputations are gained according to conviction rates and how promptly and efficiently prosecutors dispose of cases; their role as major gatekeepers of the criminal justice process is evaluated by others in the courtroom work group.[25]

The prosecutor's office deals with a wide variety of issues that include not only prosecuting cases in courts but also representing the interests of the state in other areas of the legal community.[26] In large jurisdictions in which the caseload is tremendous, the prosecutor's office will be divided into bureaus, special units, and programs that address specific concerns and issues that are problematic for the criminal justice system. For example, the Los Angeles County District Attorney's Office employs over a thousand deputy district attorneys and hundreds of support personnel in a vast bureaucracy that includes the following programs:[27]

- **Bad check enforcement program.** In addition to obtaining payment from individuals who write bad checks, this program counsels offenders and teaches them how to handle their personal finances. Bad check writers pay for this program themselves.
- **Hard-core gang unit.** This program works with local law enforcement officials to prosecute gang leaders and investigate serious gang-related crime.
- **Hate crimes unit.** Hate crimes are connected to the victim's race, religion, national origin, sexual orientation, gender, or disability. These crimes are given special attention and resources.
- **Insurance fraud.** Expert prosecutors and investigators pursue insurance fraud rings that operate massive workers' compensation and automobile scams.
- **Narcotics.** A special prosecution unit works with the police to arrest major drug dealers, seize narcotics and dealer assets, and get dealers off the streets.
- **Sex crimes unit.** Rape and other sex crimes are prosecuted by this special program, which also provides assistance to the victims.
- **A.C.T. (Abolish Chronic Truancy).** This program places prosecutors in schools to work with students, parents, teachers, and administrators to intervene when juveniles skip school.
- **C.A.P.O.S. (Crimes Against Police Officer Section).** This unit responds to crimes against police officers and puts special emphasis on prosecuting cases in which

officers are killed or injured. Prosecutors are called to the scene of crimes in which officers have been assaulted to ensure that proper procedures are followed so that the case will be upheld in court.

- **Speakers bureau.** This unit provides experts to meet with public groups to explain how the district attorney's office addresses criminal justice system issues. By providing this public education function, the speakers bureau is able to represent the interests of the prosecutor's office at a number of venues in which organizations and the public interact.

These are just some examples of the types of programs that can be found in a large prosecutor's office. This division of labor allows attorneys to specialize in certain types of cases and allows the prosecutor's office to ensure that competent deputy district attorneys are assigned to difficult and complicated areas of the law.

The prosecutor clearly plays an important role in the criminal justice system. As we have previously stated, the prosecutor acts as a gatekeeper in deciding which cases are inserted into the criminal justice system. Additionally, the prosecutor engages in a wide variety of other activities to ensure that the people's interests are considered. In Chapter 10 we will deal in more detail with the prosecutor's role in plea bargaining and sentencing. Now we turn our attention to the prosecutor's adversary, the defense attorney.

Defense Attorney

The defense attorney is responsible for protecting the interests of the accused and for presenting the case in the best possible light to ensure that the prosecution has adequately proved the charges. In an ideal world, the prosecutor would charge only the truly guilty, and the defense attorney would be successful in winning the cases of only the truly innocent. But alas, the world of the criminal courts is not perfect, and the struggle between the defense and prosecution too often arrives not at justice, but rather, at negotiated settlements that leave everyone feeling dissatisfied.[28]

The image of the defense attorney has two parts. On one hand, this officer of the court may be considered a valiant warrior against the injustice of the powerful and is viewed as one of the stalwarts of freedom in our country. On the other hand, the defense attorney may be viewed as a liar, a cheat, and a twister of the truth who will do anything to prevent a guilty client from facing justice. The truth is, of course, somewhere in the middle of these two extremes.[29] The defense attorney is an important part of the criminal justice system, and if his or her role did not exist, we would have to invent some mechanism to compensate for its absence. Before we examine the profession of the defense lawyer in detail, let's dispense with the most fundamental and significant issue that surrounds how legal defense is conducted in the United States. Before any intelligent and significant analysis of the defense attorney can be undertaken, we need to examine the impact of money.

Not all defense attorneys are equally competent.[30] A host of variables divide the successful from the unsuccessful, the ethical from the vile, the connected from the disenfranchised, and the one you want to argue for your life from the one you would not even let contest your parking tickets. These variables are the result of such factors as the following:

- The law school the attorney attended
- The law firm the attorney is associated with
- How long the attorney has worked in a particular jurisdiction
- How many cases the attorney has previously tried before a particular judge
- The attorney's relationship and history with the prosecutor
- Whether the attorney is a private lawyer or a public defender
- Whether the attorney has other cases to settle with this prosecutor in the near future[31]

FOCUS ON ETHICS

Difficult Decisions for the Defense

As a defense attorney you have really grown to dislike your client. He is a liar, a cheat, a drug dealer, and a drug user, and has been accused of killing a police officer. The prosecutor doesn't know about half the crimes your client has committed and has presented a case that, although convincing to many, has a major flaw that you have detected that could set your client free. You are torn about what to do.

On one hand, you believe not only that your client deserves to go to prison for a very long time, but also that your community would be a lot safer if he were taken off the streets. After all, you have a family that you want protected from this type of pathological criminal. On the other hand, you realize it is the prosecution's responsibility to make the case against your client and your obligation to provide the best defense possible.

Unfortunately, the assistant district attorney has overlooked several pieces of critical evidence that can place your client at the scene of the crime and seal his fate. To complicate matters further, your firm's founding partners have all but assured you that if you can win the case, you will jump over 10 senior associates and be made a partner next year.

WHAT DO YOU DO?

1. Win the case. It's your duty to represent your client first and foremost. It would be unethical to sabotage the case in any way or to give less than your best effort. Besides, this could be a major turning point in your career and could ensure your family's financial security.
2. Find an anonymous way of tipping the prosecutor off to the critical evidence. This man is too dangerous to be put back on the street, and your family's financial security is meaningless if dangerous criminals such as your client are roaming the streets of your community.
3. Resign from the case. Tell your senior partners that you cannot in good conscience represent such a despicable character. By making this choice, you realize not only that you risk the chance to make partner, but also that you could be fired.
4. What other options might there be?

Given this long, but not exhaustive, list of variables that may affect an attorney's effectiveness, the single most important variable may well be how much money has been invested in getting the best representation possible. This is not to say that many reasonably priced private attorneys cannot provide an excellent defense, but only to point out that assembling the witnesses and legal and technical experts and constructing elaborate exhibits can become extremely expensive, and it is the client who foots the bill for the cost of the defense.[32]

In 2000, when Baltimore Ravens linebacker Ray Lewis was tried for murder in Atlanta following a Super Bowl party in a nightclub, he was able to provide his defense team with financial resources that most individuals could not muster. When the prosecution produced a witness who claimed he saw Lewis engage in the stabbings, the defense was able to undermine the credibility of the witness by producing evidence of past lies. The hostile witness had been convicted of stealing another man's identity and running up exorbitant charges on credit cards. In a dramatic and effective courtroom maneuver, the defense attorney asked the witness if he had ever met the individual whose identity he had stolen and whose financial reputation he had besmirched, and then had that individual stand up in court to demonstrate to the jury that the witness had harmed a real person and not simply some abstraction. The Ray Lewis defense team had been

Football star Ray Lewis was able to afford a private attorney who was able to secure a dropped murder charge in exchange for a plea bargain. Here, Lewis is led from the courtroom after testifying against his co-defendant.

Courtesy of Corbis-NY.

CASE IN POINT

United States v. Leon

The Case

United States v. Leon, 468 U.S. 897, 104 S. Ct. 3405 (1984)

The Point

Evidence may be admitted if the fault for a bad warrant rests with the court and not with the police.

Police officers in Burbank, California, obtained search warrants for three residences and a number of cars owned by Alberto Leon, who was suspected of selling illegal drugs. The police seized large amounts of drug evidence, and Leon went to trial. Leon's defense argued that the poor quality of the information obtained by the police to initiate their investigation made for inadequate probable cause, thus invalidating their warrants. They argued that because the warrants were therefore invalid, the evidence against Leon should be excluded from the trial.

The state agreed that there were problems with probable cause, but it argued that the police had acted on the warrants in good faith and were unaware that the warrants were invalid. Both the district court and the California Supreme Court agreed, and the state appealed to the U.S. Supreme Court. The Supreme Court agreed that the warrants were invalid, but asserted that because the police had acted in good faith, the evidence against Leon should not be excluded.

In this case, the Supreme Court enacted a "good-faith" exception to the exclusionary rule, in which evidence may be admitted if the fault for a bad warrant rests with the court and not with the police. The exclusionary rule is designed to protect defendants against police mistakes, not judicial mistakes.

able to fly this person across the country from California to Atlanta for the purpose of standing up in court for a mere 15 seconds to hammer home a point about the trustworthiness of a witness.[33] The average defendant, who is not a multimillionaire football player, would be unable to finance such a legal tactic. Prosecutors dropped the murder and aggravated assault charges against Lewis in exchange for his plea of guilty to misdemeanor obstruction of justice charges.

THE DEFENSE ATTORNEY AND THE COURTROOM WORK GROUP. Although the defense attorney's first obligation is to provide the best defense possible for the defendant, it does not always follow that this duty will result in a full-blown jury trial in which the truth will be revealed and justice will be done to the satisfaction of all. Despite the defense attorney's commitment to the interests of the accused, other pressures mediate how aggressively the prosecutor's case is challenged.[34]

The attorney who engages in criminal defense work on a regular basis becomes part of the courtroom work group. Although ideally an adversary of the prosecutor, the defense attorney must develop a working relationship with the group to ensure that the group's goals are achieved. The wheels of justice may never function smoothly, but the obstinate defense attorney who causes them to grind to a halt by contesting and protesting every routine point of law and procedural ruling will quickly find that the judge, prosecutor, court reporter, and others in the courtroom work group will be less flexible and accommodating in their dealings with that attorney and that attorney's clients. An informal system of norms and relationships develops in the courtroom work group that works to efficiently move the docket and dispose of cases in accordance with expected outcomes. The dealings of the courtroom work group are best explained by two classic studies of the court conducted by David Sudnow and Abraham Blumberg.

David Sudnow provided us with his concept of "normal crimes," defined as cases that are considered in the context of how other, similar offenses were handled by the court.[35] Public defenders and prosecutors have a good idea what the sentence will be for a particular offense by considering how that infraction compares to the pattern of sentencing established by the court. For the offender to receive a more severe or a more lenient sentence than the going rate, the circumstances of the crime must be shown to be other than a normal crime. Given this already established norm for sentencing, the public defender will often encourage the defendant to plead guilty in return for a reduced sentence. By taking a normal crime to trial, the public defender is looked on by the others in the courtroom work group as wasting the time and resources of the court. Consequently, in the interests of conforming to the expectations of the defense of normal crimes, the public defender acts as a facilitator of the criminal prosecution process rather than a zealous advocate of the defendant. This abdication of the responsibility to protect the interests of the offender may seem wrong, but we will see in the next chapter that plea bargaining is a complicated and complex issue. In many ways, the public defender is getting the best possible deal for a client when the case is handled as a normal crime.

Part of the client's difficulty in evaluating the contributions of the defense attorney lies in determining what can be attributed to the attorney's expertise and what can be attributed simply to the normal routine of the courthouse. The attorney may be working hard for the client, doing legal research, negotiating strenuously with the prosecutors, and developing treatment plans with probation officers, but the defendant has limited opportunity to know this. In fact, according to Abraham Blumberg, the dynamics of the courtroom work group aid the defense attorney in erecting a facade of competence even when the attorney is simply "acting" in an effort to impress the client. Although Blumberg alerts us to some interesting dynamics of how courtrooms actually operate, we should be cautious about becoming too cynical. All organizations have distinctions between what Erving Goffman called front-stage and backstage behavior in which participants act one way when they are on public display and another when they are surrounded only by trusted coworkers.[36] Courts are no exception, and the defense attorney's dramatics performed for the benefit of the defendant do not differ substantially from how judges, prosecutors, or even professors or physicians may act when they are attempting to put the best face on their actions. The message of Blumberg's critique is that the defense attorney is subject to organizational pressures from the other members of the court. The defendant needs to understand that although the defense attorney negotiates with the defendant's best interests in mind, sometimes the best interests of the defense attorney differ from those of the defendants.

Cooling the Mark in the Criminal Court

In his classic article, "The Practice of Law as a Confidence Game: Organizational Cooptation of a Profession," Abraham Blumberg painted a cynical picture of the courtroom work group. Consider the following passage:

> ***The judge will help an accused's lawyer in still another way. He will lend the official aura of his office and courtroom so that a lawyer can stage manage an impression of an "all out" performance for the accused in justification of his fee. The judge and other courtroom personnel will serve as a backdrop for a scene charged with dramatic fire, in which the accused lawyer makes a stirring appeal in his behalf. With a show of restrained passion, the lawyer will intone the virtues of the accused and recite the social deprivations which have reduced him to his present state. The speech varies somewhat, depending on whether the accused has been convicted after trial or pleaded guilty. In the main, however, the incongruity, superficiality, and ritualistic character of the total performance is underscored by a visibly impassive, almost bored reaction on the part of the judge and other members of the court retinue. (p. 30)***

Blumberg went on to say that the defense attorney is acting like a double agent in representing the accused in court. On one hand, the defense attorney argues the merits of the client's case, but on the other hand, the defense attorney must convince the client that the deal offered by the court is the best that can be expected. In effect, the defense attorney must "cool out" the accused by persuading him or her that justice has been achieved. The prosecutor often has to do the same with the victim. In confidence-game parlance, by convincing the victim that the plea bargain is the best possible resolution of the case, the prosecutor also "cools the mark."

QUESTIONS

1. Do you think this is what really happens in a courtroom?
2. What does Blumberg's view of the courtroom work group say about the ideal of the adversarial system of justice?

Source: Abraham Blumberg, "The Practice of Law as a Confidence Game: Organizational Cooptation of a Profession," *Law and Society Review* 1 (1967): 15–39.

THE BEST DEFENSE: PRIVATE ATTORNEY OR PUBLIC DEFENDER? There is great variation in the quality of legal defense provided for individuals accused of committing criminal acts. An attorney's competence may depend on the level of the court, the geographic location, the resources of the client, and the way state and local governments fund indigent defense efforts. We commonly believe that private attorneys are automatically superior to those provided by the state, but in reality the issue is more complicated.[37]

Criminal defense work is not among the most lucrative specializations for private attorneys. In fact, only a small number of private attorneys can make a living doing exclusively, or even primarily, criminal defense law. Many attorneys have more comprehensive practices in which they also do tort law, family law, or business law.[38] Some of the most expensive and best attorneys confine themselves to specialties such as corporate law and seldom set foot in an actual courtroom. So although a given private attorney may look prosperous, and therefore extremely competent, he or she may not be the best one to represent a drug dealer or someone facing a capital charge of homicide.[39]

! NEWS FLASH

It's a Tough Job, but Someone Has to Do It

In January 2001 Alejandro Avila of Orange County, California, was acquitted of molesting two nine-year-old girls. His defense attorney, John Pozza, who later described the five-day trial as "difficult," said he was surprised at the verdict and that Avila broke down and cried upon hearing it. Pozza said he thought he would never hear from Avila again. Case closed? Unfortunately, no.

In July 2002 a man kidnapped five-year-old Samantha Runnion from her Orange County home. Her body was found the next day near a highway 50 miles away in the next county. Two weeks later Alejandro Avila was arrested in connection with Runnion's death and charged with kidnapping, sexual assault, and first-degree murder. On learning of Avila's acquittal, Runnion's mother said that she was angry at the jury for believing Avila over the girls. Many others, however, blamed Avila's former attorney, John Pozza. Pozza, who said he had been genuinely surprised to hear that his former client had been arrested again, wondered if he had been wrong to take the case. In an interview with CNN, Pozza said that during the time that he defended Avila, nothing about his client suggested that he would be capable of murder.

In U.S. law, anyone accused of a crime has the right to an attorney, regardless of the crime or the personal history or criminal record of the accused. The attorney is expected to defend the client as vigorously as possible. As attorneys do every day, Pozza simply presented the case of his client, an unpopular defendant, to the best of his abilities.

Defense attorneys are indispensable. Criminal justice would hardly be just without them. However, the public often perceives them as defending the "obviously" guilty for the fun of it or because the attorneys themselves are evil. For this reason, defense attorneys have a troubled reputation and a tough job. Pozza said his office received threatening e-mails and phone calls after Avila's arrest. This is not uncommon. However, the defense lawyer's job is not to determine the client's guilt, only to represent that person in court.

And, as seen in Pozza's case, the attorneys themselves are not immune from having second thoughts about their jobs.

Source: "Avila's Old Lawyer Says He's Rethinking Career," CNN, July 26, 2002, http://www.cnn.com/2002/LAW/07/26/avila.acquittal.reax/.

However, many successful private attorneys are excellent defenders for criminal defendants. Many former prosecutors or public defenders who go into private practice will regularly do criminal defense work. In this, they have an advantage in that they have been part of the criminal court's work group in the past and have already established relationships with the prosecutor's office and the judges. Depending on the reputation and experience of the private defense attorney, the cost of representation can be expensive. Because the private defense attorney is being paid by the client, the quality of the services rendered is expected to be superior to what is available from a public defender. Nevertheless, when an attorney is being paid by the hour, there is not a strong incentive to settle the case quickly. In fact, if we can believe Blumberg, the private defense attorney is likely to extend the case in order to charge a wealthy defendant as much money as possible.[40]

Public defenders have a precarious position in the criminal justice system. They are obligated to provide the best defense possible for the defendant, but the government pays their salary. Additionally, because of the large caseloads experienced by many public defender offices, the time and resources available are seldom sufficient to provide the extended defense services that the public defender would like (see Table 9.1).[41] It is difficult to generalize the work of public defenders because of the variation in how they are structured and financed. Each state has its own system for providing for the defense of indigent clients. These fall into three broad categories.[42]

TABLE 9.1

Maximum Public Defender Workload Standards in Selected States

The workload of public defenders is an important factor in the quality of defense a defendant receives. Clients of an overworked public defender may wait in jail for weeks before their first meeting with their attorney. Unlike private attorneys, public defenders have little control over how many cases they have. In some jurisdictions, public defenders receive as much as 80 percent of all criminal cases. These figures represent the maximum annual number of cases an attorney should handle if that attorney deals with only that type of case. For example, the state of Arizona suggests that a public defender handle no more than 400 misdemeanor cases a year if misdemeanors are the only type of case that attorney handles.

State	Felony	Misdemeanor	Juvenile	Appeals	Authority
Arizona	150	300	200	25	*State of Arizona v. Joe U. Smith,* 681 P. 2d 1374 (1984)
Colorado	80–241	310–598	305–310		The Spangenberg Group, *Weighted-Caseload Study for the Colorado State Public Defender,* November 1996
Florida	200	400	250	50	Florida Public Defender Association, *Comparison of Caseload Standards,* July 1986
Georgia	150	400	200	25	Georgia Indigent Defense Council, *Guidelines of the Georgia Indigent Defense Council for the Operation of Local Indigent Defense Programs,* October 1989
Indiana	200	400	250	25	Indiana Public Defender Commission, *Standards for Indigent Defense Services in Non-Capital Cases: With Commentary,* January 1995
Louisiana	200	450	250	50	Louisiana Indigent Defense Board, *Louisiana Standards on Indigent Defense,* 1995
Massachusetts	200	400	300		Committee for Public Counsel Services, *Manual for Counsel Assigned Through the Committee for Public Counsel Services: Policies and Procedures,* June 1995
Minnesota	100–120	250–400	175		Minnesota State Public Defender, *Caseload Standards for District Public Defenders in Minnesota,* October 1991
Missouri	40–180	450	280	28	Missouri State Public Defender System, *Caseload Committee Report,* September 1992
Nebraska	50			40	Nebraska Commission on Public Advocacy, *Standards for Indigent Defense Services in Capital and Non-Capital Cases,* May 1996
New York City	150	400		25	Indigent Defense Organization Oversight Committee, *General Requirements for All Organized Providers of Defense Services to Indigent Defendants,* July 1996
Oregon	240	400	480		Oregon State Bar, *Indigent Defense Task Force Report,* September 1996
Tennessee	55–302	500	273		The Spangenberg Group, *Tennessee Public Defender Case-Weighting Study,* May 1999
Vermont	150	400	200	25	Office of the Defender General, *Policy of the Defender General Concerning Excessive Workloads for Public Defenders,* October 1987
Washington	150	300	250	25	Washington Defender Association, *Standards for Public Defender Services,* October 1989

Source: The Spangenberg Group, *Keeping Defender Workloads Manageable* (Department of Justice/Office of Justice Programs/Bureau of Justice Assistance, 2001), 11–12. Online at http://www.ncjrs.org/pdffiles1/bja/185632.pdf.

Assigned Counsel. In small jurisdictions with limited resources, the judge may assign a practicing member of the bar to represent defendants who lack the financial means to hire a private lawyer. There are drawbacks to this method of assigning lawyers. One limitation in many jurisdictions is that the judge draws from a pool that consists of lawyers who volunteer. This results in a pool that consists of young lawyers developing their courtroom skills or less successful lawyers willing to take the reduced court fee just to make a living. Even in jurisdictions in which all the attorneys are in the selection pool, the defendant may end up with an excellent real estate lawyer who is not familiar with the demands of criminal defense work.

Contract Systems. In a contract system, law firms bid for the business of all indigent defense work. The advantage of this system is that the firm's lawyers quickly become proficient in dealing with the prosecutor and the courtroom work group. Opponents of this system contend that, because of the competitive bidding process, the low bidder ends up with a caseload that does not provide enough revenue for the legal support system of secretaries, investigators, and attorneys that is necessary for a vigorous defense of all cases.

Public Defender. Finally, about 37 percent of the jurisdictions have public defender systems in which a staff of full-time attorneys represents all indigent offenders. As a result of the Gideon decision, which requires states to provide for the legal defense of poor people, the public defender system has been adopted by most of the large jurisdictions and implemented statewide in 17 states. The advantages of having a full-time public defender staff are several. The attorneys who work in public defender offices quickly gain extensive experience working with the criminal law and become seasoned trial lawyers. Many attorneys like having a public defender office because it relieves their own firms of having to do pro bono work that drains their resources. Also, because of the permanence of public defender systems, the relationships with other personnel in the criminal justice system have been developed so that the attorneys enter cases at a very early stage, usually the initial hearing.[43]

The image of the public defender is sometimes cast in a negative light when compared to those of private lawyers. This image is, paradoxically, both accurate and misleading. Certainly, someone with sufficient financial resources can hire a lawyer who is experienced in criminal law and can provide the best legal defense money can buy. However, many indigent offenders also receive excellent representation from competent, experienced, and dedicated public defenders. The successes of the public defender's office are not widely publicized. As Neubauer pointed out:

> *The freedom to defend against the state cannot include the freedom to embarrass it. Hence, the complexity of the public defender's institutional role requires that the office not advertise its successes. McIntyre shows that the public defender's office deliberately retains its image of incompetency in order to guarantee its continued existence: Public defenders may practice good law, but they must do so in the darker shadows of repute.*[44]

Judge

Judges occupy a unique space in the criminal justice system. On one hand, they are looked on as the most powerful actors in the system whose scorn is to be feared and mercy courted. On the other hand, judges are viewed as impotent referees who must act with neutrality, objectivity, and impartiality. They have neither the prosecutor's power of discretion nor the prestige or salary of a successful defense attorney. The truth is that the term *judge* encompasses a range of responsibilities from the local justice of the peace to a Supreme Court justice (see Figure 9.1 for the Code of Conduct for United States Judges).

Judges perform a wide range of duties in the administration of justice. They act as a check-and-balance to the discretion of zealous prosecutors, an impartial arbiter in the

REFERENCE

American Bar Association Guidelines for Reviewing Qualifications of Candidates for State Judicial Office

These guidelines describe the minimum criteria for the evaluation of candidates for state and local judicial offices.

1. Integrity
   A candidate should be of undisputed integrity.
2. Legal Knowledge and Ability
   A candidate should possess a high degree of knowledge of established legal principles and procedures and have a high degree of ability to interpret and apply them to specific factual situations.
3. Professional Experience
   A candidate should be a licensed, experienced lawyer.
4. Judicial Temperament
   A candidate should possess a judicial temperament, which includes common sense, compassion, decisiveness, firmness, humility, open-mindedness, patience, tact and understanding.
5. Diligence
   A candidate should be diligent and punctual.
6. Health
   A candidate should be in good physical and mental health.
7. Financial Responsibility
   A candidate should be financially responsible.
8. Public Service
   Consideration should be given to a candidate's previous public service activities.

Source: American Bar Association, "Guidelines for Reviewing Qualifications of Candidates for State Judicial Office" (Judicial Administration Division Lawyers' Conference 1987, Staff: Steven Goldspiel, Chicago). Available online at: State of Nebraska Judicial Branch, http://court.nol.org/manual/aba.htm.

Figure 9.1
Code of Conduct for United States Judges

The Code of Conduct for United States Judges was initially adopted by the Judicial Conference in 1973. The code applies to U.S. circuit judges, district judges, court of international trade judges, court of federal claims judges, bankruptcy judges, and magistrate judges. The Tax Court, Court of Appeals for Veterans Claims, and Court of Appeals for the Armed Forces have also adopted this code.

The Code

Canon 1. A judge should uphold the integrity and independence of the judiciary.

Canon 2. A judge should avoid impropriety and the appearance of impropriety in all activities.

Canon 3. A judge should perform the duties of the office impartially and diligently.

Canon 4. A judge may engage in extra-judicial activities to improve the law, the legal system, and the administration of justice.

Canon 5. A judge should regulate extra-judicial activities to minimize the risk of conflict with judicial duties.

Canon 6. A judge should regularly file reports of compensation received for law-related and extra-judicial activities.

Canon 7. A judge should refrain from political activity.

Source: U.S. Courts, Code of Conduct for United States Judges, http://www.uscourts.gov/guide/vol2/ch1.html.

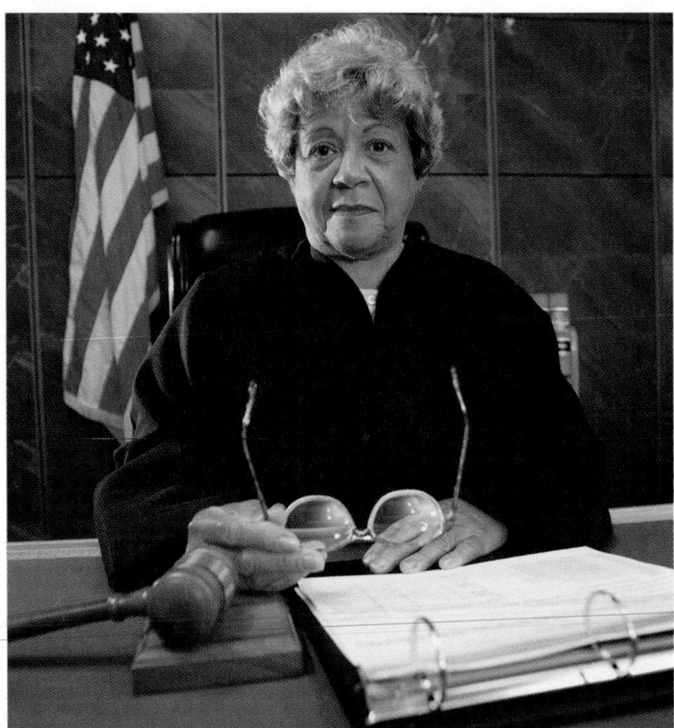

The judge is an impartial arbiter of the court proceeding. Judges are charged with many duties, the most important of which is to ensure that the proceedings are conducted in accordance with the law and are fair to both the defense and the prosecution.
Courtesy of Corbis Royalty Free.

contest between law enforcement and defendants, and a decision maker in applying punishment or treatment of the guilty. Judges have a role to play at many points in the criminal justice system, including the following:

- **Signing search warrants.** Judges ensure that law enforcement officers do not violate suspects' rights against unreasonable searches by reviewing search warrants for evidence of probable cause. Although there may be some question as to how adequately some judges actually perform these duties, their role here is to keep the police honest.
- **Informing defendants of charges.** At the initial appearance stage of the criminal justice system, the judge has the duty to inform the defendant of the charges that the law enforcement officer has filed.
- **Appointing counsel.** For indigent defendants, the judge will appoint a defense attorney. In many states, this refers to the public defender who is appointed to that judge's courtroom. But in some jurisdictions, the judge will appoint a private attorney whose turn it is to provide indigent defense.
- **Setting bail.** After hearing from the prosecutor who reviews the seriousness of the charges, the defendant's prior criminal history, and the likelihood that the defendant will appear at subsequent hearing, the judge will give the defense attorney an opportunity to rebut. The judge will either set a bail, release the defendant on recognizance, or order the defendant confined until trial.
- **Taking a plea.** At the arraignment phase of the process, the judge will once again inform the defendant of the charges and allow the defendant to enter a plea of guilty, not guilty, or no contest.
- **Ruling on motions.** The judge will rule on motions from the defense and the prosecution concerning the admissibility of evidence. These motions could be concerned with illegal search and seizure issues, the interrogation of suspects without reading them their Miranda rights, or the use of police lineups.

REFERENCE

Threats to Judicial Independence

Judges and the judicial branch of the government ideally operate unaffected by politics or ideology and thus require two types of independence. "Decisional independence" refers to a judge's making decisions without being influenced by politics or popular opinion. "Institutional independence" refers to the separation of the judicial, executive, and legislative branches of government. According to the American Judicature Society, 12 issues threaten judicial independence.

1. Threats of impeachment prompted by decisions in individual cases
2. Political threats made with the intention of influencing a judge's decision in an individual case
3. Responses to decisions that use phrases like "judicial activism"
4. Misleading criticism of decisions, compounded by the prohibition on judicial response
5. Poor relationships and communication between the judiciary and Congress
6. Line-item veto authority that allows the president to use appropriations for the judiciary in improperly influential ways
7. Congressional limits on jurisdiction or curtailment of jurisdiction
8. Requests for judicial pay increases combined with Congressional pay-increase requests; the lack of periodic, automatic judicial cost-of-living pay increases.
9. Limited public awareness of the Judicial Conduct and Disability Act as an option for addressing possible judicial misconduct
10. Underfunding and workload
11. Elections leading to concerns about and potential conflicts of interest regarding campaign contributions
12. Retention elections that pose the threat of judges being targeted by special interest groups based on legally correct but politically or socially unpopular decisions.

Source: The American Judicature Society, "What Is Judicial Independence?" http://www.ajs.org/cji/cji_whatisji.asp.

- **Participating in or ruling on plea bargaining.** Some judges will take an active role in deciding a plea bargain between the defense and the prosecution. Other judges will simply approve or disapprove the negotiated decision.
- **Presiding at trial.** The judge's role in a trial is to ensure that the defendant's due process rights are respected, to rule on the admissibility of evidence, to instruct the jury as to which laws are applicable in the case, and to ensure that all parties, including spectators, conduct themselves properly.
- **Sentencing.** Passing sentence on the guilty is one of the most difficult duties of the judge. Although many cases provide clear-cut choices between incarceration and liberty, the sad fact is that the range of options available to most judges is quite limited. Treatment options are scarce, and with prison overcrowding being so serious in many states, judges are pressured to find dispositions other than incarceration in secure institutions.

These duties illustrate the broad range of the role of the judge. In addition, there are other requirements of the job such as court administration, ceremonial duties, and in some cases, campaigning for reelection. Because the roles of the judge are so varied, it is interesting to examine what types of individuals aspire to this job and what qualifications are required.

TABLE 9.2

State Judicial Selection Methods

Each state has a unique process for selecting judges. Many states mix and match aspects of two or more methods. For example, Tennessee chooses some judges through merit selection, whereas others run in partisan elections. This table identifies each state's primary method of judicial selection.

Method	States
Nominating commission (Most states use merit selection to compile a list of nominees. Judges must stand for retention in some states.)	Colorado, Connecticut, Delaware, District of Columbia, Hawaii, Iowa, Maryland, Nebraska, New Hampshire, New Mexico, Rhode Island, Utah, Vermont, Wyoming
Gubernatorial appointment	California, Maine, Massachusetts, New Jersey
Legislative appointment	South Carolina, Virginia
Partisan election	Alabama, Illinois, Louisiana, Pennsylvania, Texas, West Virginia
Nonpartisan election	Arkansas, Georgia, Idaho, Kentucky, Michigan, Minnesota, Mississippi, Montana, Nevada, North Carolina, North Dakota, Ohio, Oregon, Washington, Wisconsin
Merit selection and mixed methods	Alaska, Arizona, Florida, Indiana, Kansas, Missouri, New York, Oklahoma, South Dakota, Tennessee

JUDICIAL SELECTION. What sorts of people become judges? Is it a job to which the best and the brightest aspire? Is the process of selecting judges adequate to weed out the incompetent, lazy, and intemperate in favor of the fair and wise? The answer to these questions is, It depends. It depends on which level of government we are referring to. It depends on which level of judgeship we are talking about. And it depends on which selection method is used. More important than the selection method, however, is the question of whether any method produces better judges than other methods. After briefly reviewing the roads to a judgeship, we will address this issue. (For a list of judicial selection methods by state, see Table 9.2.)

Executive Appointments. At the federal level, judges are nominated by the president and confirmed by the Senate according to their advise-and-consent responsibility as stated in the Constitution. For the most part, this has been a routine rubber stamp of the president's wishes, but recently it has become quite politicized.[45] Controversial cases are subjected to lengthy Senate hearings (sometimes televised) in which the nominee is grilled by senators about his or her character, legal history, and views on certain controversial issues that will likely come before the courts. For example, abortion rights are often referred to as a "litmus test" in which the nominee's views will be ascertained. Perhaps the most spectacular of these hearings occurred when Clarence Thomas was nominated, and a former subordinate, Anita Hill, accused him of sexual harassment. Although the senate eventually confirmed him and placed him on the Supreme Court, Thomas likened the experience to a "high-tech lynching." Such controversial hearings are uncomfortable

Supreme Court judges are nominated by the president and confirmed by the Senate. Occasionally this process can become contentious, such as when Anita Hill testified in 1991 before the Senate Judiciary Committee that Clarence Thomas had sexually harassed her. Thomas was eventually confirmed and took his place on the U.S. Supreme Court.
Courtesy of Mark L., Corbis/Bettmann.

for the president's party (and obviously for the nominee also). A good deal of screening takes place to find candidates who reflect the worldview of the president, yet who are not controversial. The American Bar Association plays a role in the selection process by ranking the candidates "exceptionally well qualified," "well-qualified," "qualified," or "unqualified." For U.S. district court judges, the senators of the state in which the appointment is to be made are commonly consulted as a courtesy. If the senator finds the nominee unacceptable, senators from other states (particularly those in the same party) might vote against appointment. In this way, the senators have both a formal and informal influence on the selection of judges in their state. At the state level, the legislature has no comparable advise-and-consent function, so governors have more leeway in the selection of judges. At both levels, the influence of party politics is significant.

Election of Judges. In an effort to democratize judicial selection, nearly half of the states elect judges. It is assumed that judges who must stand for reelection will conform to the wishes of the people rather than the dictates of the elites. For the most part, the campaigns for judgeships are of low visibility, and voters have very little knowledge about the qualifications or temperament of the candidates. For this reason, incumbent judges have a distinct advantage over challengers especially when the title "judge" is printed next to their names on the ballot. Some elections are hotly contested, especially state supreme court seats where decisions can affect laws concerning insurance issues. Trial lawyers will vie with insurance companies by channeling money into the campaigns of judges who will protect their interests.[46]

Merit Selection. In an effort to remove politics from the judicial selection process, court reformers have adopted a system called "merit selection," or, as it is sometimes known, the **Missouri Bar Plan.** In this type of selection process, a judicial nominating commission made up of lawyers and laypersons presents a short list of qualified candidates (usually three) to the governor, who makes the final decision. Judges are then required to face the voters after a short period of time (one year). Instead of running against another candidate, the vote is simply on whether the judge should be retained in office. Judges must stand for such reelection each term, but they are seldom removed because they essentially have no opponents and the voters seldom know of reasons why they should be removed.[47]

Missouri Bar Plan
A judicial nominating commission presents a list of candidates to the governor, who decides on a candidate. After a year in office, voters decide on whether to retain the judge. Judges must run for such re-election each term. Also called *merit selection.*

Each of the different methods of selecting judges has its merits. When judges are elected, they are considered to be more accountable to the voters and more likely to represent the interests of the average citizen rather than the elites of the legal profession. This admirable philosophy is pitted against the alternative of the appointment of judges where presumably, free from catering to the voters, the judge can enjoy judicial independence and rule on the merits of the case. Some evidence supports the idea that the type of selection method influences the decisions of judges.[48] However, in terms of personal background characteristics there is very little difference:

> *From a broader perspective, methods of judicial selection have only marginal influence on the type of lawyers who become judges. Whether elected by the voters, appointed by the governor, or selected through merit plans, state judges are more alike than different. In terms of personal background characteristics such as prior political experience, ties to the local community, political party affiliation, and quality of legal education, the systems do not appear to produce very different types of judges.*[49]

Perhaps the most important and notable change in the judicial selection process is the increase in the number of women and minorities appointed to the bench. The profile of the judge as a white male is being radically changed without affecting the other background characteristics such as judicial education. As more women go to law school and work their way up the ranks of prosecutors' offices and law firms, more of them are being elected or appointed as judges. To a large extent, the same can be said for minorities, but because of the underrepresentation of black lawyers, there are fewer black judges. In states in which judges are appointed, more minorities are on the bench than in states in which judges are elected.[50]

Defendants, Victims, and Witnesses

Those working in the criminal courts—judges, prosecutors, defense attorneys, bailiffs, clerks, and sheriff's deputies—learn the language, rituals, and protocols that dictate the pace and atmosphere of the court's daily routine.[51] These professionals must deal with civilians who are not knowledgeable about how the law is applied and how the courtroom works. Defendants, victims, and witnesses bring varying degrees of experience to the court and often leave with a sense of confusion, injustice, and bewilderment. It is useful to consider how each of these parties views the workings of the criminal court.

DEFENDANTS. Those who find themselves before a criminal court on felony charges are often the least able to understand the workings of the institution and feel powerless to affect the outcome of their case. Felony defendants are overwhelmingly male, young, poor, undereducated, and members of racial minorities.[52] Unless they are repeat offenders (and many are), they have little idea about what is happening to them as they are processed through the system. Many are illiterate and cannot comprehend even the simplest instructions or aid their attorney in preparing a defense.[53] Too many defendants come to court with problems that the criminal justice system is ill equipped to handle, such as drug addiction, mental illness, lack of education, or marital problems. Those who cannot secure bail prior to their appearance are attired in handcuffs, a jail jumpsuit, and slippers that have the effect of stigmatizing them even further.[54] The middle-class worldview of those in the courtroom work group is unsympathetic to the plight of those whose fates are being decided. The entire ritual of the courtroom serves to intimidate the defendant and impress on him or her the gravity of the situation. It is little wonder that many who experience "their day in court" often come away with a feeling of injustice and alienation.[55]

FOCUS ON ETHICS

Where to Try a Sniper?

Usually, a crime is prosecuted in the state in which it occurs, unless it is a federal crime. But what if a crime occurs in several states? And what if that crime is particularly heinous?

In October 2002 John Allen Muhammad, 41, and John Lee Malvo, 17, were arrested on suspicion of shooting and killing 10 people and wounding three with a sniper rifle. The murders were committed in Maryland, Virginia, and Washington, D.C. Authorities later discovered evidence that Muhammad and Malvo also committed murders in Washington State and Alabama. Authorities considered the evidence collected against the pair to be sound, so the question was not how to charge them, but where. The murders meant that three states and the District of Columbia could all claim jurisdiction in the case. Muhammad and Malvo were also accused of demanding a payment of $10 million to stop the shootings—considered to be extortion, a federal crime—giving federal prosecutors jurisdiction as well.

There is no law pertaining to such a situation, so the choice of where to prosecute Muhammad and Malvo fell to federal authorities, primarily because the two were in federal custody.

Other issues included the following:

- **Age.** ***Because John Lee Malvo was 17 years old at the time of the murders, he was considered a minor.***
- **The death penalty.** ***Virginia, second only to Texas in executions, condemns minors. Maryland does not execute minors, nor does the federal government. Washington, D.C., has no death penalty at all.***
- **Number and location of murders.** ***Maryland was the location of 7 of the 10 sniper shootings. Three were in Virginia. Alabama and Washington state claimed one murder each.***

Douglas Gansler, state's attorney in Montgomery County, Maryland, in which six people were murdered, said he would seek death for Muhammad and life in prison for Malvo. Virginia said it would seek execution for both.*

If you were a federal authority deciding this jurisdiction, what would you do? Here is a review: There is no law firmly governing jurisdiction in this case. The push for the death penalty is coming from all sides, and prosecutors from several states all have a rightful claim to try the accused. Some states had more evidence than others. With the exception of the District of Columbia, all have the death penalty, but not all have it for minors.

QUESTIONS

1. Is it ethical to try suspects in a jurisdiction because that jurisdiction will most likely hand down the most popular punishment?
2. What about when that punishment is execution, and one of the condemned is a minor?

Sources: "Deciding Which Jurisdiction Should Prosecute Sniper Case," *The Tampa Tribune,* October 30, 2002, http://tampatrib.com/News/MGAWJCLFW7D.html. Brandt Goldstein, "Who Gets to Prosecute the Sniper Suspects First?", *Slate,* October 29, 2002, http://slate.msn.com/?id=2073280. Laura Macinnis, "Sniper Suspect Muhammad Ordered Held Pending Trial," ABCNEWS.com/Reuters, November 5, 2002, http://abcnews.go.com/wire/us/reuters20021105_574.html. Sue Anne Pressley, "Procedural Questions Abound in Sniper Suspects' Legal Phase," *The Salt Lake Tribune/The Washington Post,* November 3, 2002, http://www.sltrib.com/11032002/nation_w/13116.htm.

*Lee Boyd Malvo was tried in Virginia and convicted of two counts of capital murder. In December 2003 he was sentenced to two life terms without parole. John Allen Muhammad, who was tried separately in Virginia, was convicted of capital murder and sentenced to death.

VICTIMS. Perhaps the only ones more disillusioned by the workings and results of the criminal court than the defendants are the victims.[56] Because the charge of a felony crime pits the defendant against the state, the role of the victim is sometimes diminished. Especially when cases are plea bargained, the interests of the victim may be slighted. Victims see their particular case as being very serious and may become disillusioned when it is treated in the routine and bureaucratic manner that is the norm of the court. Victims are perplexed when, in lieu of a trial, in which they expect to explain how they were injured by the dastardly behavior of the defendant, the prosecutor informs them that the case was settled with a disposition of probation rather than a long prison term. Many victims feel anger when they see defendants enjoying due process rights while their voices remain unheard.[57]

WITNESSES. Those who witness crime or have other relevant testimony have less attachment to the case than does the defendant or victim. Witnesses do have an important role to play, however, and they often experience frustration in dealing with the court. Being required to travel to the court to provide testimony and finding the case postponed or having to wait long periods in uncomfortable hallways can cause a good deal of distress for witnesses. Additionally, the loss of wages for time spent at court or having property that is kept for long periods of time as evidence can cause additional frustration. Perhaps the most stressful aspect of being a witness is the fear of retaliation from a defendant and the sense that criminal justice personnel are indifferent to the danger one feels.[58]

VICTIM–WITNESS PROGRAMS. The criminal justice system is not completely indifferent to the plight of victims and witnesses. Many jurisdictions have established victim–witness assistance programs to encourage cooperation in criminal cases and alleviate some of the inconvenience of appearing in court. Reducing the suffering caused by the crime and anticipating the confusion and frustration of dealing with the criminal justice system are the objectives of victim–witness programs.[59] Because each victim has different needs, programs are designed to provide a wide range of services.[60]

- **Crisis intervention.** Crime is a traumatic event for most victims. Especially in cases of violent crime, the victims and their families may need assistance in dealing with transportation to the hospital or court, notifying relatives,

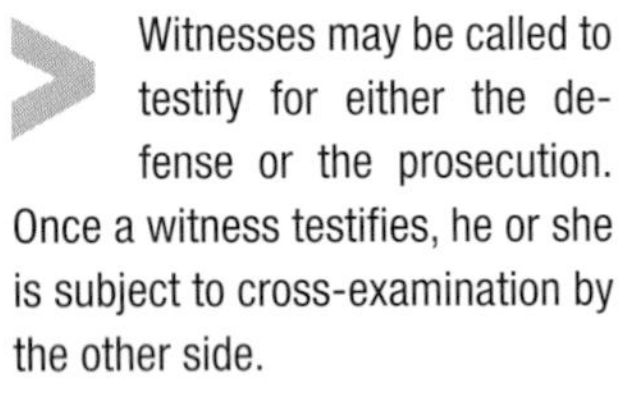

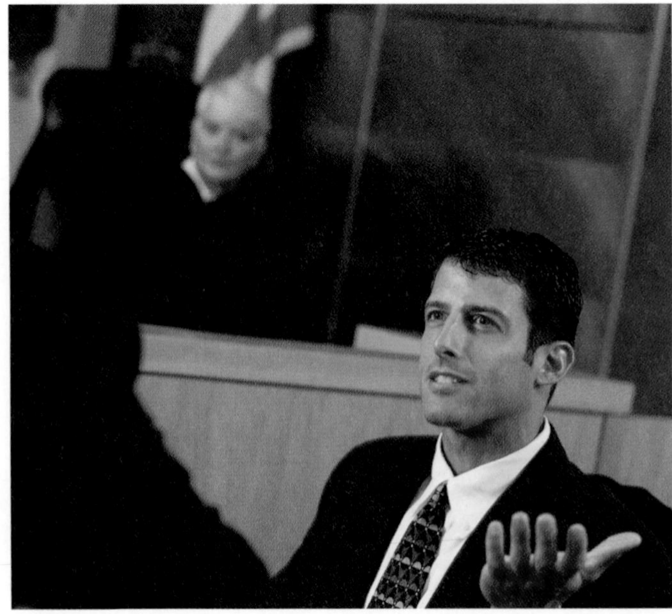

Witnesses may be called to testify for either the defense or the prosecution. Once a witness testifies, he or she is subject to cross-examination by the other side.

Courtesy of Corbis Royalty Free.

procuring money to buy meals after a robbery, and understanding how and when the criminal justice system will handle the case.

- **Follow-up counseling.** The traumatic nature of crimes such as sexual assault may require ongoing counseling until the case is brought to court and in some cases long afterward. Counseling services may be provided by victim–witness staff or by referral to a psychologist. Some programs have established support groups to help victims deal with the aftereffects of crime.
- **Personal advocacy.** Often the victim is too traumatized to effectively plead his or her side of the case to the police, prosecutor, judge, or others. The victim–witness staff member will assert the victim's interests in the repeated telling of the crime's impact on the victim. Victims can grow tired of pleading their woes and may feel that others perceive them as whining. A professional staff member, however, can advocate for the victim's best interests.
- **Employer and landlord intervention.** Victimization can have far-reaching and long-lasting effects. If the crime was committed in the workplace or apartment, the employer or landlord may see getting rid of the victim as a solution to future violence. The victim–witness staff member can intervene to convince the employer or landlord that the victim is just that, the *victim,* and that it would be morally unethical to fire or evict the victim.
- **Property return.** In cases of theft or armed robbery, the victim's stolen property can be used by the criminal justice system as evidence. Many times the property is kept for long periods of time as the case wends its way through the court process. The victim–witness staff member can sometimes expedite the return of the property to the victim when the state has concluded the case.
- **Intimidation protection.** Victims and witnesses can be subject to intimidation from offenders or their families and friends. Sitting outside a courtroom waiting to testify can be frightening for the victim when the offender, who is out on bail, or the offender's family member is pestering him or her to drop the charge. Additionally, the defense attorney may give unsolicited advice to victims or witnesses that may border on intimidation.[61] The victim–witness staff member can act as a buffer for victims and witnesses and protect them from embarrassment or intimidation.
- **Referral.** The victim–witness staff member is knowledgeable about the community resources available to the victim. Often the trauma of the crime will create problems such as excessive drinking that can be helped with counseling. The victim–witness staff member can assist in a referral.
- **Court orientation.** For many victims and witnesses, their case represents the first time they have had to go to a courthouse. Seemingly insignificant issues such as parking, finding the correct courtroom, and even what to wear are likely to be the subjects of questions for the uninitiated. Victim–witness staff members can answer questions and help prepare those who will be called to testify.
- **Court transportation and escort.** Some victims and witnesses may need transportation to the courthouse and support during the proceedings. The assistance of victim–witness program staff members may be deciding factors in getting them to court and avoiding a case dismissal.
- **Public education and legislative advocacy.** Victim–witness staff members speak to service organizations such as the Kiwanis, Rotary Club, and Chamber of Commerce to garner support for their programs and to educate the public on how the courts use victim and witness support services. Staff members may also talk to legislators about financial resources and to generate laws that support the roles of victims and witnesses in criminal proceedings.

Victim–witnesses programs provide a wide range of services to those who must help the criminal justice system by testifying in criminal trials. Unfortunately, the level of services provided varies widely across the country, especially between large urban courts and smaller ones. There is no mandate for the state or federal government to provide these services. Although everyone may agree that victim–witness programs are beneficial, they are not required in the way that legal counsel for indigent offenders is. In lean budget years, victim–witness programs are one of the "frills" for which courts can cut funding to save money.

Pretrial Release Decisions

The criminal justice system is not like a fast-food restaurant to which one can drive up and get instant justice. The process takes time, often a very long time. Those accused of crimes may be kept in jail to protect the public if they are dangerous, or released and told to come back to court when the system is ready to consider their case.[62] The court must somehow decide which option is appropriate for each offender. The pretrial release decision is one of the most important crossroads of the criminal justice system. If innocent people are jailed for months before their cases are heard, then they are being punished unnecessarily, and if dangerous criminals are released, then they may continue to murder, rape, and rob.[63] Complicating this pretrial release decision is the overcrowded condition of many of the nation's jails. Courts have developed several types of systems for making this decision that attempt to ensure that the defendant will appear. These systems all involve some sort of bail-bond alternative.

- **Cash bond.** The judge will set a bail of a certain amount of money the defendant must give to the court in exchange for release pending trial. If the defendant shows up for the future court proceedings, then the entire amount is refunded. This cash bond ensures that the defendant will come back to prevent losing the money. However, if the bail is too low or the crime is really serious with a severe punishment likely, the defendant may flee anyway or "skip bail." The court will then issue a warrant for the defendant's arrest, and the defendant will be picked up and forfeit the bail. The Eighth Amendment says that "excessive bail shall not be required," but it is still difficult for many defendants to gather a large amount of cash in a short period.[64]
- **Property bond.** By using a piece of property as collateral, defendants can avoid liquidating their assets to raise a cash bond. Property bond favors the well-off who have equity in property. Defendants who fail to appear before the court forfeit their property.
- **Release on recognizance (ROR).** The judge may release a defendant based on a promise to return to court. This is done for those accused of minor offenses and those who have ties to the community. ROR programs will evaluate defendants on how long they have lived in the community, how long they have been employed, whether they have family nearby, and other factors in an effort to determine whether they are likely to flee.[65] A South American drug lord who has no local address would not be likely to be granted ROR.
- **Bail agent.** The most common method for securing bail is to use a bail agent. A bail agent is someone who promises to pay the defendant's bail if he or she fails to appear for further court proceedings.[66] In exchange for the promise, the defendant pays the bail agent 10 percent of the bail as a fee and may put up some collateral. Thus, if the bail is $10,000, the bail agent makes $1,000. The bail agent does not give the court the bail at that time, but must pay if the defendant fails to appear. The bail agent may then hire a bail enforcement agent (or "bounty hunter") to find the defendant and bring him or her back to court. If

a bail agent thinks the suspect is likely to flee, the agent may revoke the bond and surrender the suspect to law enforcement.

Pretrial release is a controversial issue. It must balance two strongly held values: presumption of innocence and preventive detention. On one hand, we believe that someone should not be incarcerated until he or she has been found guilty by a court of law. However, given the nature of the criminal justice system and the inevitable delays caused by a crowded docket and constitutional guarantees of due process, both the guilty and the innocent may spend months in jail before a trial.[67] If the defendant is found guilty and sentenced to incarceration, the period of time spent in jail awaiting trial is credited toward the sentence. Sometimes the sentence is simply "time served," in which case the defendant is released having, in effect, served the sentence before the sentence was pronounced. In cases in which the defendant is acquitted or the charges dropped, the period spent in jail waiting for the courts to process the case is time lost. The defendant has suffered the pains of being detained and may feel a sense of injustice.

The issue of presumption of innocence must be weighed against the responsibility of the state to protect society by keeping truly dangerous people off the street while the court considers their cases. For example, in 2002 there was a case in the nation's capital in which two males, an adult and a juvenile, were arrested on suspicion of shooting and killing several people with a high-powered rifle. Referred to as the "D.C. Sniper Case," the court refused to grant any type of pretrial release because there was a reasonable fear that one of three bad things could happen.[68] First, because of the seriousness of the crimes, there was a fear that the defendants would attempt to flee the jurisdiction. Second, there was a reasonable concern that the defendants were still dangerous and could harm more citizens. Finally, because of the terror caused by the crimes, it was feared that the defendants might be injured or killed by irate individuals. In fact, these concerns are so pronounced in such cases that those who are awaiting trial on murder charges that carry the death penalty are not allowed bail.

Summary

For many, the courthouse is a frightening place. The criminal courts are viewed as something to avoid except as a form of entertainment on television. Those who work in the courts are viewed with suspicion, fear, loathing, or awe. This chapter has attempted to explain how the courts function and what roles are played by those who are responsible for processing criminal cases.

The *courtroom work group* is a term that refers to those who work in the courthouse. By viewing them as an organizational structure, we can appreciate how people from different agencies work together to do the business of the court. Although we usually think of the court as an adversarial proceeding, by considering the courtroom work group, we see that in fact a great deal of cooperation is inherent in the daily routine of the court.

The pivotal position in the criminal court is that of the prosecutor. Even more than the judge, the prosecutor can influence the environment of the criminal court. The prosecutor acts as a gatekeeper in deciding which cases are inserted into the system and which cases get dismissed.

At the top of the federal hierarchy of prosecution is the Department of Justice, or Justice Department. Three offices of the Justice Department affect the prosecutorial aspect of the criminal justice process: the offices of the solicitor general, the criminal division of the litigation branch, and the U.S. attorneys in the federal courts.

State court systems are decentralized, with prosecution responsibility distributed across state, county (or district), and local levels. Three types of prosecutors are typically found in state court systems: the state attorney general, the chief prosecutor, and local prosecutors. The state prosecutor is the primary representative of the state in the courtroom. In large jurisdictions, the prosecutor's office may be divided into bureaus, special units, and programs that address specific issues within the local criminal justice system. According to David Neubauer,[69] the prosecutor's workload can be categorized into the following: fighting, negotiating, drafting, counseling, and administering.

The defense attorney is responsible for protecting the interests of the accused and ensuring that the prosecution has adequately proved the charges. Although the defense attorneys must provide the best defense possible for their clients, they often become part of the courtroom work group. Ideally, an adversary of the prosecutor, the defense attorney develops a working relationship with the group. In this light, the defense attorney often acts as a facilitator of the disposition process rather than a zealous advocate of the defendant.

The issue of private versus public defenders is complicated, and the private attorney, although more expensive, may not always be able to offer the best defense for a client. Each state has its own system for providing for the defense of indigent clients. These fall into three broad categories: assigned counsel, contract systems, and public defenders.

Judges occupy a unique space in the criminal justice system. They act as a check-and-balance to the discretion of prosecutors, an impartial arbiter in the contest between law enforcement and defendants, and a decision maker in applying punishment or treatment to the guilty.

Because defendants, victims, and witnesses are unfamiliar with how the court works, they often find the courtrooms alienating. Many jurisdictions have therefore established victim–witness assistance programs to encourage cooperation in criminal cases.

The pretrial release decision is an important crossroads in the criminal justice system. Courts have developed several systems to help ensure the defendant's appearance: cash bond, property bond, release on recognizance (ROR), or bail agent. If concerns about public safety or the defendant's likelihood to show are pronounced, then bail may not be allowed.

KEY TERMS

bail agent p. 286
child advocate p. 288
clerk of the court p. 285
court administrator p. 285
court reporter p. 285
disposition p. 296
going rate p. 284
Missouri Bar Plan p. 309

REVIEW QUESTIONS

1. What is the "going rate"?
2. Who else may be found in courtrooms besides judges, attorneys, plaintiffs, and defendants?
3. Why is the prosecutor so powerful?
4. What else does the federal attorney general's office do besides prosecute criminal cases?
5. Do the U.S. attorneys have jurisdictions in only the 50 states?
6. What is the "invisible work" that occupies most of a prosecutor's time?
7. What are the two views the public has of defense attorneys?
8. Discuss Abraham Blumberg's critique of the courtroom work group.
9. Describe the three systems for providing legal defenses for indigent defendants.
10. What services may a victim–witness program provide?
11. Describe the systems that courts have for ensuring the appearance of a defendant.

SUGGESTED FURTHER READING

Albonetti, Celesta. "Prosecutorial Discretion: The Effects of Uncertainty." *Law and Society Review* 21 (1987): 291–313.

Baker, Mark. *D.A.: Prosecutors in Their Own Words.* New York: Simon & Schuster, 1999.

Gomme, Ian and Mary Hall. "Prosecutors at Work: Role Overload and Strain." *Journal of Criminal Justice* 23 (1995): 191–200.

Schrager, Sam. *The Trial Lawyer's Art.* Philadelphia: Temple University Press, 1999.

Walker, Samuel. *Taming the System: The Control of Discretion in Criminal Justice, 1950–1990.* New York: Oxford University Press, 1993.

Wice, Paul. *Chaos in the Courthouse: The Inner Workings of Urban Courts.* Westport, CT: Praeger, 1985.

ENDNOTES

1. Kathryn Fahnestock and Maurice Geiger, "We All Get Along Here: Case Flow in Rural Courts," *Judicature* 76 (1993): 258–263.
2. Abraham S. Blumberg, The Practice of Law as a Confidence Game," *Law and Society Review,* June 1 (1967): 15–39.
3. David Sudnow, "Normal Crimes: Sociological Features of the Penal Code in a Public Defender Office," *Social Problems* 12 (1965): 209–215.
4. N. Gary Holton and Lawson L. Lamar, *The Criminal Courts: Structures, Personnel and Processes* (New York: McGraw-Hill, 1991), 109–110.
5. Ibid., 111–112.
6. John Rosecrance, "Maintaining the Myth of the Individualized Justice: Probation Presentence Reports," *Justice Quarterly* 5 (1988): 235–256.
7. Gary H. Rabe and Dan J. Champion, *Criminal Courts: Structures, Process, and Issues* (Upper Saddle River, NJ: Prentice Hall, 2002). Chapter 7 has an excellent review of pretrial procedures.
8. Patricia Resick, "The Trauma of Rape and the Criminal Justice System," *Justice System Journal* 9 (1984): 52–61.
9. Robert Davis and Barbara Smith, "The Effects of Victim Impact Statements on Sentencing Decisions: A Test in an Urban Setting," *Justice Quarterly* 11 (1994): 453–469.
10. Ira Schwartz, *Justice for Juveniles: Rethinking the Best Interests of the Child* (New York: Lexington Books, 1989).
11. William McDonald, "The Prosecutors' Domain," in *The Prosecutor,* ed. William McDonald (Newbury Park, CA: Sage, 1979).
12. Alissa Pollitz Worden, "Policymaking by Prosecutors: The Uses of Discretion in Regulating Plea Bargaining," *Judicature* 73 (1990): 335–340.
13. *Brady v. Maryland,* 373 U.S. 83 (1963).
14. Bennett L. Gershman, "Why Prosecutors Misbehave," in *Courts and Justice: A Reader,* 2nd ed., eds. G. Larry Mays and Peter R. Gregware (Long Grove, IL: Waveland Press, 1999), 282–292.
15. Griffin Bell, "Appointing United States Attorneys," *Journal of Law and Politics* 9 (1993): 247–256.
16. Rebecca Sudokar, *The Solicitor General: The Politics of Law* (Philadelphia: Temple University Press, 1992).
17. Jeffrey Segal, "Amicus Curiae Briefs by the Solicitor General During the Warren and Burger Courts: A Research Note," *Western Political Quarterly* 41 (1988): 135–144.
18. Bell, *Appointing.*
19. "Key Events in State Suits against Tobacco Industry," CNN, http://www.cnn.com/US/9811/16/tobacco.timeline/. Nov. 16, 1998.
20. David W. Neubauer, *America's Courts and the Criminal Justice System,* 7th ed. (Belmont, CA: Wadsworth, 2002).
21. Ibid.
22. Ibid.
23. David Heilbroner, *Rough Justice: Days and Nights of a Young D.A.* (New York: Pantheon, 1990).
24. Sudnow, "Normal Crimes."
25. Pamela Utz, "Two Models of Prosecutorial Professionalism," in *The Prosecutor,* ed. William McDonald (Newbury Park, CA: Sage, 1979).
26. Joan Jacoby, "The Prosecutors' Charging Decision: A Policy Perspective," (Washington, DC: U.S. Department of Justice, 1977).
27. Los Angeles County District Attorney's Office, Office Overview, http: //da.co.la.ca.us/oview.htm.

28. David Lynch, "The Impropriety of Plea Agreements: A Tale of Two Counties," *Law and Social Inquiry* 19 (1994): 115–136.

29. Rodney Uphoff, "The Criminal Defense Lawyer: Zealous Advocate, Double Agent or Beleaguered Dealer?" *Criminal Law Bulletin* 28 (1992): 419–456.

30. Stephen Bright, "Counsel for the Poor: The Death Sentence Not for the Worst Crime, But for the Worst Lawyer," *Yale Law Journal* 103 (1994): 1835–1884.

31. Michael J. McWilliams, "The Erosion of Indigent Rights: Excessive Caseloads Resulting in Ineffective Counsel for Poor," *American Bar Association Journal* 79 (1993): 8.

32. Larry J. Cohen, Patricia P. Sample, and Robert E. Crew, Jr., "Assigned Counsel Versus Public Defender Systems in Virginia," in *The Defense Counsel*, ed. William F. McDonald (Beverly Hills, CA: Sage, 1983).

33. Laura Barandes, "Prosecutions Call Last Witness in Super Bowl Party Murder Trial," Court TV Online, June 7, 2000, http: //courttv.com/trials/raylewis/060700_ctv.html.

34. Jerome Skolnick, "Social Control in the Adversary System," *Journal of Conflict Resolution* 11 (1967): 52–70.

35. Sudnow, "Normal Crimes."

36. Erving Goffman, *The Presentation of Self in Everyday Life* (Garden City, NY: Doubleday Anchor Books, 1959).

37. Roger Hanson, William Hewitt, and Brian Ostrom, "Are the Critical Indigent Defense Counsel Correct?" *State Court Journal* (Summer 1992): 20–29.

38. Carroll Seron, *The Business of Practicing Law: The Work Lives of Solo and Small-Firm Attorneys* (Philadelphia: Temple University Press, 1996).

39. Bright, "Counsel for the Poor."

40. Blumberg, "Practice of Law." "The real key to understanding the role of a defense counsel in a criminal case is to be found in the area of the fixing of the fee to be charged and its collection. The problem of fixing and collecting the fee tends to influence to a significant degree the criminal court process itself, and not just the relationship between the lawyer and his client." (p. 24)

41. McWilliams, "Erosion of Indigent Rights."

42. Alissa Pollitz Worden, "Privatizing Due Process: Issues in the Comparison of Assigned Counsel, Public Defender, and Contracted Indigent Defense Systems," *Justice Systems Journal* 14 (1991): 390–418.

43. Neubauer, *America's Courts*, 179–182.

44. Ibid., 183.

45. Sheldon Goldman and Elliot Slotnick, "Clinton's Second Term Judiciary: Picking Judges Under Fire," *Judicature* 82, no. 6. (1999): 264–285.

46. Philip Dubois, *From Ballot to Bench: Judicial Elections and the Quest for Accountability* (Austin: University of Texas Press, 1980).

47. Richard Watson and Ronald Downing, *The Politics of the Bench and the Bar: Judicial Selection Under the Missouri Nonpartisan Court Plan* (New York: John Wiley, 1969).

48. Daniel Pinello, *The Impact of Judicial-Selection Method of State-Supreme-Court Policy: Innovation, Reaction and Atrophy* (Westwood, CT: Greenwood Press, 1995).

49. Neubauer, *America's Courts*, 202.

50. Ibid., 205.

51. Fahnestock and Geiger, "We All Get Along."

52. Marvin Free, *African Americans and the Criminal Justice System* (New York: Garland, 1997).

53. Arthur Roselt and Donald Creasey, *Justice by Consent* (Philadelphia: J.B. Lippincott, 1976).

54. John Irwin, *The Jail: Managing the Underclass in American Society* (Berkeley: University of California Press, 1985).

55. J. Dyer, *The Perpetual Incarceration Machine: How America Profits from Crime* (Boulder, CO: Westview, 1999).

56. Andrew Karnsen, *Crime Victims: An Introduction to Victimology*, 4th ed. (Belmont, CA: Wadsworth, 2001).

57. Candace McCoy, *Politics and Plea Bargaining: Victims Rights in California* (Philadelphia: University of Pennsylvania Press, 1993).

58. Kerry Healey, "Victim and Witness Intimidation: New Developments and Emerging Responses," (Washington, DC: National Institute of Justice, 1995).

59. Peter Finn and Beverley Lee, "Establishing and Expanding Victim-Witness Assistance Programs" (Washington, DC: National Institute of Justice, 1988).

60. William Doerner and Steven Lab, *Victimology* (Cincinnati: Anderson, 1995), 53–54.

61. Elizabeth Connick and Robert Davis, "Examining the Problems of Witness Intimidation," *Judicature* 66 (1983): 438–447.

62. John Goldkamp, "Danger and Detention: A Second Generation of Bail Reform," *Journal of Criminal Law and Criminology* 76 (1985): 1–74.

63. Michael Corrado, "Punishment and the Wild Beast of Prey: The Problems of Preventive Detention," *Journal of Criminal Law and Criminology* 86 (1996): 778–814.
64. Michael J. Eason, "Eighth Amendment—Pretrial Detention: What Will Become of the Innocent?" *Journal of Criminal Law and Criminology* 78 (1988): 1048–1979.
65. Tim Bynum, "Release on Recognizance: Substantive or Superficial Reform?" *Criminology* 20 (1982): 67–82.
66. Mary Toborg, "Bail Bondsmen and Criminal Courts," *Justice System Journal* 8 (1983): 141–156.
67. Keith Hansen, "When Worlds Collide: The Constitutional Politics of *United States v. Salerno*" *American Journal of Criminal Law* 14 (1987): 155–225.
68. Robert Nagel, "The Myth of the General Right to Bail," *Public Interest* 98 (1990): 4–97.
69. Neubauer, *America's Courts*.

outline

PLEA BARGAINING

- Other Benefits of Plea Bargaining
- Should Plea Bargaining Be Abolished?

THE TRIAL

- Pretrial Motions
- Opening Arguments
- Presentation of Witnesses and Evidence
- The Case Goes to the Jury
- Evidence
- The Defense Doesn't Rest

RIGHTS AND WRONGS IN THE COURTHOUSE

- "I Know My Rights"
- Victims' Rights

SENTENCING THE OFFENDER

- Indeterminate Sentencing
- Determinate Sentencing
- Mandatory Minimum Sentences

SUMMARY

CHAPTER 10

The Disposition

Plea Bargaining, Trial, and Sentencing

THE MOST DRAMATIC AND SENSATIONAL DECISION POINT IN the criminal justice system is the passing of the sentence. Rather like Judgment Day in the biblical sense, the passing of the sentence is considered the end result of a deliberation process in which the evidence of the crime, the harm done to society (or other people), and the character of the defendant are weighed, and a sentence prescribing a punishment is announced.

The road to this final disposition of a case is rocky and uncertain. Unlike the image presented by the media, the actions of the court are ponderous, fickle, and often seem unfair. Defendants (even codefendants) with identical charges, with similar prior records, appearing before the same judge, and with equal culpability may receive drastically different sentences.[1] Furthermore, sentencing disparity among judges, courts, states, or regions of the country all elicit a sense that justice is not uniform.[2] The luck of the draw in determining which judge handles a case or which prosecutor is assigned may mean the difference between incarceration and probation, a long and

objectives

After reading this chapter, the student should be able to:

1. Understand the nature of the disposition.
2. Explain plea bargaining and why it is important.
3. Understand the arguments for the abolishment of plea bargaining.
4. Discuss why a trial is a relatively rare event.
5. Explain the purpose of pretrial motions.
6. Describe the motives of the prosecutor and the defense attorney in opening arguments.
7. Understand the importance of the jury system versus government power.
8. Describe the role of the jurors.
9. Explain evidence and how it is handled.
10. Describe the stresses on victims and witnesses.
11. Explain victims' rights.
12. Describe the factors that guide sentencing.

a short prison sentence, even life and death. It is little wonder that many people are wary of the criminal justice system when they see such vast disparities in the outcomes of seemingly similar cases.[3]

This chapter will examine some of the mechanisms that the criminal justice system employs as part of its quest for justice. In part, we will argue that much of the process that many find so objectionable is required by law or is the inevitable result of funding limitations and political necessity. In turn, we look at the dynamics of the **plea bargain**, the process of the criminal trial, the concept of defendants' and victims' rights, and finally at some of the broader issues concerned with sentencing patterns. In looking at these issues, we will come to appreciate how justice is determined in the criminal court. Despite the fact that reforms are desired and needed, they are difficult to enact because of the complicated and interdependent nature of the criminal justice system. Inserting a reform in one part of the system will have ramifications and unanticipated consequences in other parts of the system. For instance, enacting the popular notion that every criminal should serve every day of the sentence would have a profound and negative effect on the prison system. There simply is not enough prison space to accommodate all the offenders serving all their time.[4] Consequently, the criminal justice system, particularly the courts, must prioritize how the precious resource of prison beds is allocated. This process of arriving at the sentence, therefore, is fraught with difficulties and dissension. Nowhere are these issues more blatant than in the practice of plea bargaining.[5]

plea bargain
A compromise reached by the defendant, the defendant's attorney, and the prosecutor in which the defendant agrees to plead guilty or no contest in return for a reduction of the charges' severity, dismissal of some charges, further information about the crime or about others involved in it, or the prosecutor's agreement to recommend a desired sentence. Plea bargains require a judge's approval.

Plea Bargaining

Plea bargaining is one of the features of the criminal justice system that most upsets the public. The prospect of a criminal escaping the full measure of punishment flies in the face of many citizens' sense of justice.[6] Yet, plea bargaining has become an essential feature of the criminal justice system.[7] If every defendant demanded a jury trial, the system

Time in the courtroom is a scarce resource. Not all cases can go to trial, so it is necessary for attorneys to engage in plea bargaining. Any plea bargains must be approved by the judge.
Courtesy of Getty Images, Inc.

! NEWS FLASH

Their Day in Court

Here is a look at a day in the life of a typical circuit court. The 14th Judicial Circuit comprises five counties and includes Beaufort County, South Carolina. (Most circuits have three or fewer counties, and three circuits have four counties.)

- *More than 4,600 new cases are filed annually in the judicial circuit.*
- *The maximum number of cases prosecutors could try each year is 235.*
- *General Sessions court is in session two weeks a month. During each of those weeks, two days are filled with court proceedings. Actual trials are held only six days a month.*
- *Since 1986 the number of cases in the circuit has risen from 2,400 cases to over 4,600. Drug cases account for over half of this increase.*
- *In early 2003 about 500 drug cases awaited trial in Beaufort County alone.*
- *Officials say the solicitor's office and the public defender's office are understaffed because of budget constraints.*
- *Family Court is struggling under an excess of cases as a result of a spike in juvenile crime in 2003.*

Source: Stephanie Broadbent, "The Trials of an Overburdened Court," *Carolina Morning News,* February 16, 2003, http://www.lowcountrynow.com/stories/021603/LOCcourts.shtml.

would quickly grind to a halt under the oppressive weight of the caseload. Defendants' right to a speedy trial would become impossible to accommodate, and the state would spend vast amounts of money on obviously guilty defendants whose cases could otherwise be quickly disposed of. Additionally, without the reduced punishments inherent in the plea bargaining process, the sentences meted out by judges would swamp the correctional system. In many ways, plea bargaining, in which the defendants plead guilty or *nolo contendere* in exchange for a lighter sentence, benefits both sides.[8] Nevertheless, politicians are constantly calling to eliminate plea bargaining.[9] Law enforcement officials, victims of crime, and the public all consider plea bargaining as thwarting justice.[10]

Not all plea bargains are the same. The prosecutors may decide that one type of bargain serves the ends of justice better than another, and the defendant may reluctantly accept one type while really desiring an alternative. Although cases are negotiated in numerous ways, the following represents a useful way to differentiate among the types of plea bargaining arrangements.[11]

1. **Vertical plea.** This is perhaps the most advantageous plea for the defendant. By pleading guilty or *nolo contendere* to a lesser included charge, the defendant can reduce the potential for a harsh sentence. For instance, a homicide charge can be pleaded vertically downward to a manslaughter charge, thereby avoiding a potential death penalty sentence and/or a longer prison term. The prosecutor may decide that the case does not have a sufficient quality of evidence to support a capital conviction and that a manslaughter plea would be better than an acquittal. Additionally, many drug cases are pleaded down to misdemeanors, which saves the offender from having a felony conviction on his or her record.
2. **Horizontal plea.** In this case, the defendant will plead guilty to a charge in exchange for other charges being dropped. It is not unusual for a burglar to be

charged with multiple counts of breaking and entering and to plead to one count in order to have the others dropped. The defendant is then vulnerable to the full penalty that one charge carries. In many cases, this arrangement is advantageous to the state because the judge may have passed concurrent sentences for the multiple charges.

3. **Reduced-sentence plea.** The prosecutor and defense attorney, in consultation with the judge, might decide on a reduced sentence. For instance, if the charge carries a maximum five-year prison sentence, the agreement might be for a three-year sentence. This way, the defendant is assured of a specific less-than-maximum sentence, and the prosecutor gets a conviction without having to go to trial.
4. **Avoidance-of-stigma plea.** One form of stigma is a legal stigma. Several types of convictions do an extra measure of damage to a defendant's chances of receiving a light sentence. For instance, several states have "habitual offender" or "three-strikes-and-you're-out" statutes that carry mandatory severe penalties. Those convicted of relatively minor felonies may find themselves facing life in prison because of offenses committed many years ago that also resulted in felony convictions. If the defendant's attorney is not successful in getting the charge reduced, the judge has no discretion in the case and must sentence the defendant according to the habitual-offender guidelines. This is a form of vertical plea, but because of the mandatory nature of these laws, the defendant has an extra incentive. Another type of avoidance-of-stigma plea concerns those facing sex crime charges. Being adjudicated a sex offender can have long-term ramifications for the defendant even after the sentence has been served. Conviction of a sex crime may lead to a defendant's identity being published in a public sex offender database.

Plea bargaining is not concerned with determining guilt or innocence. Rather, it allows the defendant and the prosecution to efficiently determine the amount of punishment without the expense of a jury trial. Although this practice initially benefits both sides, plea bargaining is criticized from a number of quarters. Some view plea bargaining as being lenient on crime, whereas others see it as a weapon the prosecution can use to circumvent the rights of the defendant. In practice, highly disparate results are obtained by plea bargaining. Individuals in similar circumstances may receive widely varying punishments, as the proportionality of punishment to offense can become distorted by overcharging, draconian legislation, and political expediency. In practice, often no bargaining occurs because the prosecutor is in the position of the landlord with the only vacant apartment in town—"take my terms or forget it." Increasingly, the prosecutor wields the sledgehammer with, for example, habitual offender laws carrying life terms for relatively minor offenses.[12]

We would be remiss in our discussion of plea bargaining if we did not examine this in the larger context of the criminal justice system.[13] Plea bargaining affects the entire system. Diverse pressure (sometimes overt, sometimes subtle) is applied to the courts by both law enforcement agencies, who want their collars to serve prison time, and correctional administrators, whose institutions are already filled to capacity. Added to these outside pressures are the dynamics of the courtroom work group, which has established patterns of plea bargaining. Finally, the peculiarities of the case will dictate just how wide a range of discretion can be applied. David Neubauer listed three fundamental issues that guide the practice of plea bargaining.[14]

1. **Presumption of factual guilt.** By the time a case gets to the trial stage of the criminal justice system, its merits have been reviewed a number of times, and it has been deemed to be a legitimate arrest with a good chance of a conviction. In other words, most cases that get to this stage have a defendant who is, in fact, guilty of some charge. The law enforcement officer believed there was reason to arrest; the prosecutor believed the case to be strong enough for a formal charge; and the judge in the preliminary hearing deemed that sufficient reason existed to move the case forward. Therefore, prosecutors and defense attorneys negotiate which level of crime the defendant will be charged with, what kind of evidence the state can

The judge must maintain control of the courtroom. Here, a judge lectures the prosecutor and defense attorney while a witness looks on.
Courtesy of Getty Images, Inc.

produce, the nature of the victim, and the character of the defendant. There is little doubt, in most cases, that the defendant is actually guilty.

2. **Costs and risks of trial.** Failing to successfully negotiate a plea is risky and costly for all involved. Trials can last days for simple cases and months for more complicated ones. During this time the judge, clerk, bailiffs, prosecutor, public defender or private defense attorney, victim(s), and witnesses are all tied to the courtroom and cannot deal with the other pressing demands of their jobs. Because trials cost money for everyone concerned, given the scarcity of courtroom time, only a few cases are actually subjected to this legal process. Another reason that plea bargains are considered preferable to trials is risk: The prosecutor risks an acquittal in which a guilty defendant might go free; the defendant risks getting a more severe sentence if convicted; and the defense attorney risks damage to his or her reputation if a guilty verdict is returned. A plea bargain may leave everyone partially unsatisfied, but losing a trial involves bigger stakes and is to be avoided if possible.
3. **What to do with the guilty.** Plea bargaining increases the discretion of the prosecutor in crafting a sentence appropriate to the offender. If a case goes to trial, the defense attorney and the prosecutor lose their ability to influence the disposition. The willingness of an offender to enter a drug treatment program or to do community service can give the prosecutor justification in the plea bargaining process to consider a full range of alternatives to incarceration. If the case goes to trial and the defendant is convicted, the courtroom work group presumes that the judge will select a more punitive disposition than would have been negotiated between the prosecutor and the defense attorney.

Other Benefits of Plea Bargaining

In addition to the previously mentioned reasons a defendant might find it desirable to engage in plea bargaining, there is the prospect of being allowed to enter a plea of *nolo contendere,* which translated from Latin means "I will not contest." In many ways, this is equivalent to entering a guilty plea in that the defendant waives the right to a jury trial and will be sentenced as though there were a determination of guilt.[15] However, there are important differences between the *nolo contendere* plea and the guilty finding. In many jurisdictions, the court will allow the offender to enter a *nolo contendere* plea and will hold the actual sentence in abeyance while the offender completes some type of diversion program, pays restitution, performs community service, or engages in some other court-ordered activity. Once this activity is successfully completed, the court will drop the criminal charges, and the offender will escape the clutches of the criminal justice system without having a criminal record. This type of plea negotiation is used extensively with young offenders who commit relatively minor crimes. It allows the defendant to avoid the negative stigma of a criminal conviction and the frequent extralegal punishments of being denied access to schools or jobs.

Another benefit of being allowed to plead *nolo contendere* is that, unlike a guilty determination, this plea does not affect future civil court proceedings. If a defendant pleaded guilty and/or were convicted, there would be little leverage available for the defendant to contest a civil case. For example, if a defendant was involved in an accident while driving under the influence of alcohol and pleaded *nolo contendere* to the criminal charge, this plea could not be used as an admission of guilt by someone who may have been injured in that accident. The civil court case would need additional evidence such as witnesses or blood alcohol tests to determine culpability.

Should Plea Bargaining Be Abolished?

Although most practitioners in the criminal justice system realize that plea bargaining is an efficient and necessary process, there is widespread opposition to this practice among the public. Many believe that offenders are cheating justice and obtaining less punishment than they deserve. Occasionally there are efforts to abolish plea bargaining and require each case to be decided on its merits. Such efforts are usually short-lived; when plea bargaining is prohibited, a number of unintended consequences arise.[16]

The first and most drastic result of eliminating plea bargaining is the increase in the number of cases that defense attorneys are willing to take to trial. When no consideration is allowed for a guilty plea, then there is no incentive for the defendant to waive the right to a jury trial. He or she might as well take a chance on acquittal before a jury if the sentence is going to be the same anyway.[17]

Another consequence of abolishing plea bargaining is that the discretion inherent in the process is moved to another part of the criminal justice system where it may not be as visible and thus subject to increased abuse or corruption. David Neubauer likened the criminal justice system to a hydraulic process in which efforts to control discretion at one stage cause it to be displaced to another stage. For instance, abolishing plea bargaining in a higher court may simply result in discretion being shifted to the charging decision made by the prosecutor at the preliminary hearing in the lower court.[18] Victims, witnesses, and the public have less opportunity to comprehend how the system is arriving at its dispositions, and consequently, may become even more disillusioned with the process.

Finally, attempts to abolish plea bargaining might simply result in squeezing the prosecutor out of the process.[19] Defense attorneys can always attempt to negotiate directly with the judge to secure the best deal for the defendant. Judges faced with an increased caseload and under pressure to keep the docket moving are approachable by defense attorneys who can offer relief. One of the roles of prosecutors in the criminal justice system is to protect the interests of society. When they are excluded from the plea bargaining process, they have more difficulty ensuring that all cases are being considered equally.

As students of the criminal justice system, we should realize that the law on the books and the law that is actually practiced in the courthouse are different. Although we tend to think that the criminal trial is the main activity of the court system, in reality, plea bargaining is the activity that is responsible for deciding the disposition of most cases.[20] In many ways, plea bargaining is considered a "necessary evil" that leaves all involved without complete satisfaction. However, as courts are faced with caseloads that outstrip their resources, plea bargaining becomes a useful way of negotiating justice.

However, calls for the reform of plea bargaining should not go unheard.[21] By opening the process to victims, law enforcement officers, and others who are affected by the sentence, plea bargaining can become a more acceptable tool.[22] Plea bargaining is not going to go away. The challenge is to harness its potential to settle cases in a way that gives voice to all concerned.

FOCUS ON ETHICS

Letting the Big Ones Get Away

As an assistant prosecutor, you are under orders from the chief to rack up drug prosecutions to help make his reputation as a drug warrior in his campaign to run for Congress. You have been successful in putting several large-scale drug dealers behind bars, and you are in line for a promotion based on your high-profile success. In fact, when the total number of years for offenders' sentences is added up, your record is tied with your only competitor for the promotion. One of your current cases promises to vault you ahead if you can secure a reasonable plea bargain from the defense attorney.

Here's the problem: The drug dealer you have in your sights is a crafty and connected criminal. He has been charged before with several crimes and has always been able to squirm out of the clutches of the law. This time he has been caught with a kilo of cocaine at his girlfriend's house, and you have a perfect case if only she will testify against him. Because love makes fools of us all, she refuses to testify. She is pregnant with his child and does not want him to go to prison. His high-priced defense attorney comes to you with a deal. If you drop the charges against him, the drug dealer will testify that the cocaine belongs to his girlfriend. Because the girlfriend has had shoplifting and bad check convictions from several years ago, the state's mandatory minimum sentence statutes will kick in, and you will be able to send her to prison for a 40-year term.

You really want to nail the drug dealer instead of the girlfriend, but she refuses to cooperate. She does not believe you when you tell her that her boyfriend has offered to roll over on her, and because the cocaine did not belong to her, she naively believes that she will not be prosecuted. Your chief prosecutor just wants a big conviction, and this one would ensure your promotion.

WHAT DO YOU DO?

1. Teach her the most painful lesson of her life. Prosecute her for the cocaine and send her to prison for 40 years.
2. Dismiss the charges on both of them.
3. Explain your problem to the judge and ask her to try to talk some sense into the girlfriend.
4. Think of another creative way to try to bring justice to this case.

For interesting further reading go on the Web to *Salon* and read "Swept Away," which details the real-life experiences of women caught in similar situations. Online at: http://dir.salon.com/mwt/feature/2000/07/20/conspirators/index.html.

The Trial

A trial of a criminal defendant is actually a rare event. Because most cases are settled in the plea bargaining process, only a few special cases actually end up in a jury trial. The question is, which ones are they? Certainly we would expect innocent defendants to assert their right to a trial. Also, sometimes the prosecution's deal is not favorable to the defendant, and the decision is made to roll the dice and go for "all or nothing." In any event, the trial, although rare, is an extremely pivotal point in the process because those cases that fail to reach a plea bargain set the parameters for how justice is negotiated by the courtroom work group.

Trials follow a very specific format that is dictated by law, custom, and the administrative procedures established by the federal government and the various states. In general, the trial process is conducted in the following steps:

1. Indictment
2. Defendant's plea

3. Prosecution opening statement
4. Defense opening statement
5. Witnesses and evidence presented
6. Defense closing arguments
7. Prosecution closing arguments
8. Judge's instructions to jurors about procedures
9. Judge's instructions to jurors about verdicts
10. Final verdict
11. Defendant released if acquitted or sentenced if convicted

Pretrial Motions

Prior to the opening statement of the prosecution and the defense, each side may file pretrial motions that seek to gain the most favorable circumstances for their side and to limit the evidence the other side can present. Often the case is won or lost based on how the judge rules on the pretrial motions. Some of the more frequent motions include the following:

- **Motion for dismissal of charges.** The defense may ask that the case be dismissed because the prosecution has failed to present a sufficient case that has all the elements necessary to charge the defendant with the crime or because the case has some critical weaknesses. This can happen at the beginning of the trial or at any point along the way. Often this motion is presented after the prosecution presents its case.
- **Motion for continuance.** This motion will delay the trial. Often the defense or prosecution needs more time to prepare the case or to interview newly discovered witnesses. The defense is more likely to be granted such a continuance because the prosecution has an obligation to provide for a speedy trial.
- **Motion for discovery.** The defense has a right to obtain documents and a list of witnesses that the prosecution plans to call.
- **Motion for severance of defendants.** When more than one defendant is charged with a crime, each has his or her own defense attorney who may wish to separate the cases so that each defendant has his or her own trial. This is often done when a conflict of interests exists in which one defendant is more culpable for the crime than the other, or when the testimony of one defendant may incriminate others.
- **Motion for severance of offenses.** Defendants charged with several crimes may ask to be tried separately on all or some of the charges. The judge usually makes this decision.
- **Motion for the suppression of evidence.** The defense will attempt to prevent incriminating evidence from being presented in the trial. If the evidence was gathered illegally or a confession coerced by the police, the judge may rule it inadmissible. The defense may raise a number of due process issues that could result in motions to suppress evidence.
- **Motion to determine competency.** The defense may request that the judge rule that the defendant is not competent to stand trial. A defendant who cannot assist in the defense and does not understand the purpose and process of the proceedings may be mentally ill. Often, the court will order that a psychiatrist examine the defendant.
- **Motion for change of venue.** In crimes that draw a good deal of media coverage, the defense may claim that finding an impartial jury would be impossible. The court can move the crime to another jurisdiction where those in the jury pool would not have heard about the case. Of course, crimes that receive national coverage make it impossible to find a jury pool anywhere in the country that has not been exposed to the case.

Evidence That Can't Be Used: The Exclusionary Rule

When a defendant is set free because of a legal technicality, the reason may be the exclusionary rule. Although the exclusionary rule dictates that the police must follow procedural law in the gathering of evidence, the issue is decided in the courts. The prosecutor is prohibited from using evidence that was illegally obtained. The Supreme Court adopted the rule for three reasons.

1. If the courts used evidence that was illegally gathered, they would be participating in this violation of the defendant's rights. The rule of law must be respected in the courts if we are to have confidence in the quality of justice.
2. The exclusionary law deters law enforcement officers from attempting to break the law. If they know their evidence will be thrown out of court, then they are less likely to try to circumvent procedural laws.
3. The alternatives to the exclusionary rule are not feasible. Although a defendant might try to sue a law enforcement officer in civil court for damages stemming from police misconduct, this is a cumbersome and expensive process that is unlikely to have the desired effect of encouraging the police to play by the rules.

The exclusionary rule covers three types of evidence: the identification of suspects, confessions in which the Miranda rules apply, and searches in which the Fourth Amendment states that "the right of the people to be secure in their persons, houses, papers, and effects against unreasonable search and seizure, shall not be violated." The law allows for the suppression of evidence that violates the exclusionary rule. This is accomplished when the defense attorney files a suppression motion if the defendant was identified in a police lineup that was conducted improperly, gave a confession as a result of police misconduct, or was subjected to an illegal search.

The exclusionary rule is a controversial issue in the criminal justice system. To many people, it seems ludicrous to equate the crimes of the defendant with the mistakes made by law enforcement officers when they gather the evidence. The court has allowed some narrow exceptions when the police make mistakes in "good faith." Proposals to eliminate the exclusionary rule have included doing away with the Miranda warning requirement.

QUESTIONS

1. Is the exclusionary rule a necessary check on overzealous law enforcement officers?
2. Do criminals enjoy too many rights and an unfair advantage because of the exclusionary rule?
3. In what ways might the exclusionary rule be modified so that defendants enjoy their constitutional rights but law enforcement officers are allowed to make reasonable mistakes without having their cases thrown out of court?

The prosecution or the defense can present other types of motions, but this list is illustrative of how motions can be used to swing the advantage to a defendant whose attorney is adept at providing an aggressive defense. These motions set the tone and the limits of the trial and are extremely important even though they do not occupy a position of high visibility in the process.

Opening Arguments

The prosecution is the first to make an opening argument, with the goal of presenting the defendant as the most likely perpetrator. The prosecution will tell why it believes that the defendant is guilty. Actual evidence will not be presented at this time, but the prosecution will outline the case and alert the jury to the types of evidence that will be forthcoming.

One of the duties of an attorney is to present evidence to the jury. Here, a prosecutor uses a computer to show how a car's skidmarks were produced by the automobile in the picture.

Courtesy of Corbis Royalty Free.

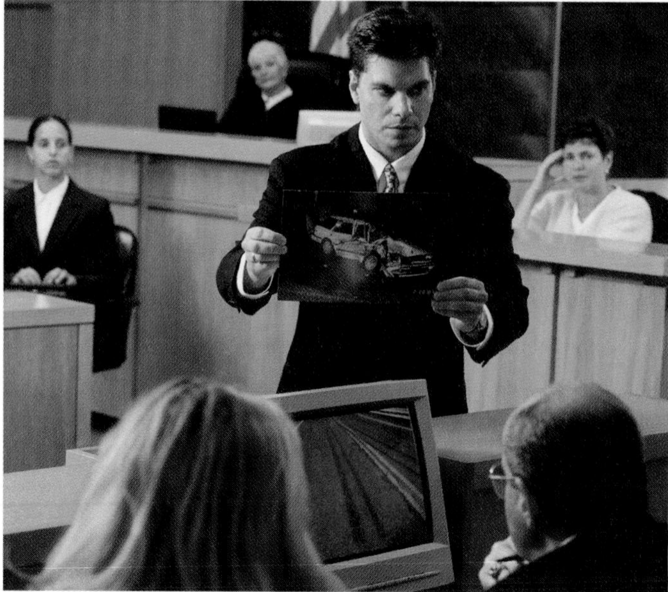

The goal of the opening statement is to convince the jury that the case against the defendant is very strong and that the prosecution can be trusted to ensure that justice is being pressed in the name of the people. The defense attorney then gets a chance to counter the outline of the case presented by the prosecution. Again, evidence is not presented, but the defense attorney will attempt to put a more favorable spin on the arguments of the prosecution and also assure the jury that once it has seen all the evidence and heard all the facts, it will want to acquit the defendant on all charges.

Presentation of Witnesses and Evidence

The prosecution begins the presentation of the case by introducing evidence and witnesses. The goal is to carefully and fully explain the defendant's motive for committing the crime and his or her capability for carrying out the action. As the prosecution presents the case, the defense attorney may raise objections to certain questions asked by the prosecutor or the answers given by a witness. The judge rules on these objections by either sustaining them or overruling them. The objections may be on points of procedural law or on the competency of a witness to answer a question. For instance, if a law enforcement officer claimed the defendant was drunk, the defense attorney would object claiming that the officer could not know for sure that this was the case. The prosecutor might then ask the police officer if a breath test was administered to the defendant and what the result of that test was. Ideally, the process is designed to present the evidence and witness testimony in a factual and fair manner so that the jury can weigh them and reach its own conclusion.

impeach
The discrediting of a witness. This may be done by proving that the witness has lied or has been inconsistent, or by producing contrary evidence.

redirect examination
The questioning of a witness about issues uncovered during cross-examination.

directed verdict of acquittal
An order from a trial judge to the jury stating that the jury must acquit the accused because the prosecution has not proved its case. A judge may not "direct a verdict of guilty," however, because such an order would violate the accused's right to a jury trial.

After the prosecution questions a witness, the defense attorney then has the opportunity to cross-examine. The right to cross-examine witnesses is derived from the Sixth Amendment of the Constitution and is one of the adversarial features of the trial. The defense attorney tries to **impeach** the witness by asking questions that help undermine the prosecution's case. Sometimes the defense attorney can be successful in soliciting information from the prosecution's witness that is favorable to the defendant. Once the defense attorney has cross-examined the witness, the prosecutor may ask additional questions under the right to **redirect examination.** In turn, the defense attorney may ask for a re-cross-examination. Often, this tactic may be used later in the trial after other witnesses reveal new evidence.

After the state has presented its case against the defendant, the defense attorney may ask the judge for a **directed verdict of acquittal**. Essentially, the defense attorney is asking the judge to rule that the prosecution has failed to present a compelling case documenting the defendant's guilt. Only in the most egregious cases would the judge be likely to make such a ruling, especially if the case is in a jury trial. However, it costs the defense nothing to make such a motion. In some cases, the judge may believe the prosecution has failed so miserably to make a logical case that issuing a directed verdict of acquittal would not circumvent justice, but save the court from having to sit through a trial with a foregone conclusion of acquittal.

Once the prosecution concludes the presentation of its evidence and witnesses, the defense is given the opportunity to present its own evidence and witnesses. Because the burden of proof rests with the prosecution, the defense attorney need only present evidence that raises a reasonable doubt about the defendant's guilt. If the prosecution had a witness from the state crime lab who testified about blood samples or hair fibers, the defense will counter with other scientists who will dispute the testimony. If the prosecution presented an eyewitness, the defense may attempt to impeach the testimony by showing that the witness's eyesight or memory is faulty. The prosecution is given the opportunity for cross-examination, and, of course, there may be redirect questions from the defense followed by re-cross-examination by the prosecutor. The intent is to give each side an equal opportunity to ask questions.

After each side has presented its evidence and witnesses, the court allows both sides to present a summation in which they attempt to account for all the facts in a closing argument designed to put the best possible spin on their case. The prosecution gets the last word before the jury because of its burden to prove the defendant's guilt beyond a reasonable doubt. New evidence may not be introduced at this stage of the trial because the opposing side does not have the opportunity to question it. Closing arguments can sometimes be very flamboyant because the attorneys are not just presenting facts; they are trying to convince the jury that the defendant is good or bad, a solid citizen or a criminal, sympathetic or disgusting, guilty or innocent. It is during the closing arguments that television dramas have the culprit blurt out a confession or the defense attorney bring the jury to tears with a dramatic and heartfelt speech. In real life, the closing arguments are not nearly so theatrical, but they can be extremely interesting and moving.

The Case Goes to the Jury

Serving on a jury allows average citizens to participate in the criminal justice system in a very important way that acts as a check-and-balance against government power. (For the requirements to be a juror on a federal case, see Figure 10.1.) The jury can prevent an overzealous prosecutor from railroading a defendant through the criminal justice system. By having a jury composed of 12 citizens (this is the ideal number, but many states allow

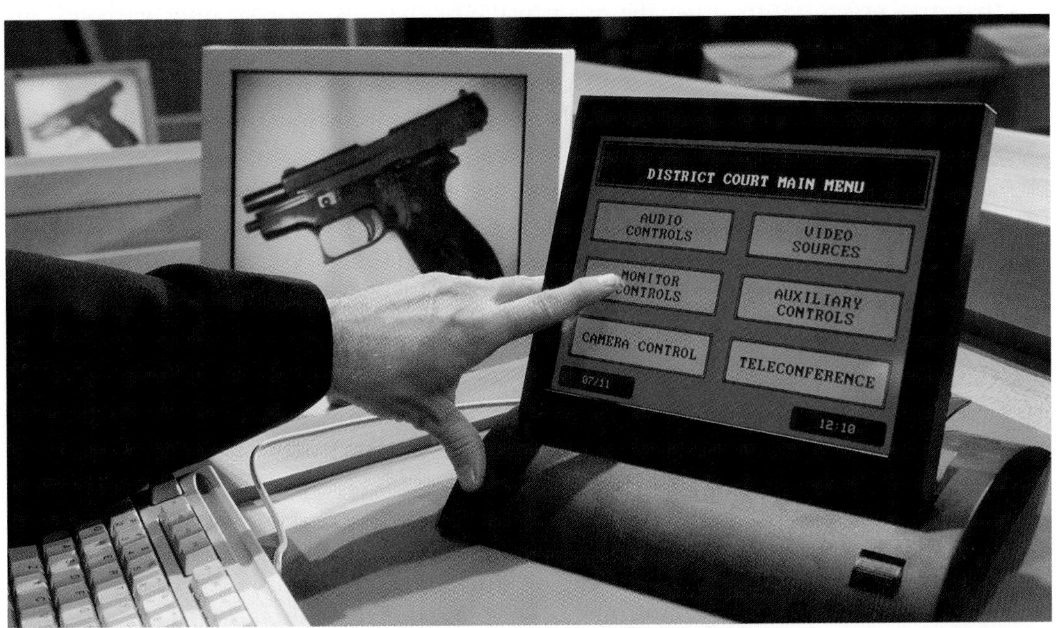

The level of technology has increased greatly in recent years. While not all courtrooms have the budgets for such technology, there are many courts that display evidence and exhibits on computers.

Courtesy of Corbis-NY.

Figure 10.1
Federal Juror Qualifications and Exemptions

To qualify as a federal juror, you must

- be a U.S. citizen,
- be at least 18 years of age,
- have resided in the judicial district for one year,
- possess adequate proficiency in English,
- bear no disqualifying mental or physical condition,
- not currently be subject to felony charges,
- never have been convicted of a felony (unless your civil rights have been legally restored).

To be exempt from service, you must be

- an active-duty member of the armed forces or
- a member of the police or fire department.

Certain public officials or others may qualify for exceptions based on individual court rules, such as members of voluntary emergency services or those who recently have served on a jury. Temporary deferrals may be granted because of hardship or extreme inconvenience.

Terms of Jury Service

Length of Service

This varies by court. Some courts require service for one day or for the duration of a single trial. Others require service for a fixed term of up to one month or more. Grand jury service may last up to 18 months.

Payment

$40 per day. In some instances, jurors receive meal and travel allowances.

Employment Protection

By law, employers must allow employees time off (paid or unpaid) for jury service. The law forbids employers from firing, intimidating, or coercing employees because of federal jury service.

Source: Understanding the Federal Courts: Administrative Office of the U.S. Courts, http://www.uscourts.gov/understand02/media/UFC99.pdf.

a jury of six for some types of cases) who decide the defendant's guilt or innocence, the dynamics of the courtroom work group are not as dominant as they would be if criminal justice practitioners decided the cases.

The jury selection process is a complicated and uncertain procedure that results in juries that may be partial to either the prosecution or the defense. Certainly, each side attempts to influence the selection of the jury to ensure that its arguments will find a sympathetic ear. The formation of a jury requires several steps.

- **Master jury list.** Each jurisdiction must develop a list of potential jurors. This list is compiled from voter registration records, driver's license lists, and utility customer lists. The goal is to develop a master jury list that is representative of the community in terms of race, gender, and social class.

venire
The list or pool from which jurors are chosen.

voir dire
French for "to see, to speak." Refers to the questioning of jurors by a judge and/or attorneys to determine whether individual jurors are appropriate for a particular jury panel. Jurors may be dismissed by the judge or attorneys.

- ***Venire.*** A list of names is randomly selected from the master jury list to form the ***venire*** or the jury pool. The sheriff's office notifies these individuals by summons to appear at the courthouse for jury duty. Not all citizens who are summoned for jury duty will report to the courthouse. In some jurisdictions, the nonresponse rate is as high as 20 percent. Furthermore, many citizens request that they be excused from jury duty because of the inconvenience and hardship it imposes. Judges vary widely in their patterns of excusing citizens from jury duty. Juries are selected from this final winnowed-down jury pool.
- ***Voir dire.*** The prosecutor and the defense attorney have some input into which members of the jury pool wind up on the jury for an actual case. The ***voir dire*** ("to see, to speak") consists of the questioning of prospective jurors to determine whether they have the necessary qualifications to serve. The questions

cover possible previous relationships potential jurors may have had with those involved in the case (this includes the attorneys—for instance, the brother-in-law of the prosecutor would not be an appropriate candidate for the jury), knowledge about the case, attitudes about certain facts that may arise in the trial, and their willingness to be fair and impartial. The defense attorney or prosecutor can attempt to exclude someone from the jury by two means:

1. **Challenge for cause.** A potential juror can be excused if it is suspected that they cannot be objective—for instance, if someone had made a statement in the newspaper about the case that clearly showed that he or she had already decided the defendant was guilty. Although challenges for cause are not often used and not often granted by the judge, this is an important safeguard against getting an obviously biased juror.
2. **Peremptory challenge.** Both the defense attorney and the prosecutor are allowed to have a certain number of potential jurors dismissed without having to provide reasons. For example, a defense attorney may decide that anyone who has experience working in the criminal justice system may not be sympathetic to the defendant and therefore may use peremptory challenges to exclude potential jurors who have been law enforcement officers, attorneys, criminology professors, or prison guards. However, using peremptory challenges to exclude individuals solely on the basis of race or gender is prohibited.

Depending on the nature of the case, serving on a jury can be satisfying, or it can turn into an arduous task. Jurors can feel proud of doing their duty as citizens, or they can feel inconvenienced by the intrusion of jury duty on their lives. For instance, some juries are sequestered, and members are forced to live in a hotel and avoid watching television or reading the local newspaper. Some complicated and high-profile cases can cause jurors to lose months of work and exert a real hardship on their employers and families.

During the trial, jurors play a passive role. They must sit and listen to the prosecutor and the defense attorney present the case. They are not allowed to ask questions of the attorneys or the witnesses. Jurors who would like to have more control over their role and are not familiar with the legal procedures that underlie the trial process may find their role frustrating. One feature that makes jury trials so interesting is that a conviction requires more than a majority vote. In fact, all the members of a jury must vote for guilt

CASE IN POINT

Batson v. Kentucky

The Case

Batson v. Kentucky, 476 U.S. 79, 106 S. Ct. 1712 (1986)

The Point

The Supreme Court established that the use of peremptory challenges to racially manipulate a jury violates the defendant's right to an impartial jury.

During James Batson's trial on burglary charges, the prosecutor used peremptory challenges to exclude the four black jurors from the jury pool. The resulting all-white jury eventually convicted Batson, who was black, of second-degree burglary. On appeal, the Supreme Court ruled that the use of peremptory challenges to racially manipulate the jury violated the equal protection rights of both Batson and the four excluded jurors. The case was remanded back to the trial court with the requirement that if "the prosecutor does not come forward with a neutral explanation for his action, our precedents require that petitioner's conviction be reversed."

Jurors are not allowed to ask questions directly to the attorneys. They must sit passively and listen to the evidence presented.

Courtesy of Getty Images, Inc.

hung jury
A term describing a jury in a criminal case that is deadlocked or that cannot produce a unanimous verdict.

bench trial
A trial that takes place before a judge, but without a jury, in which the judge makes the decision. Sometimes called a *court trial.*

or innocence or it is considered a **hung jury**. When there is a hung jury, the prosecution has the option of trying the case again.

Not all cases get a jury trial. The exceptions are those in which the possible penalty is not serious (such as six months or less in jail), those in which the defendant is a juvenile, and when the defense requests a **bench trial**. A bench trial is held before a judge who both decides on guilt or innocence and passes sentence. A defense attorney might request a bench trial when the case involves very technical or emotional issues. Some believe that the chances are better for an acquittal when a professional judge decides rather than a jury comprising ordinary citizens who might be more likely to become confused by the evidence or biased because of the nature of the case. For example, a defendant in a child abuse case might feel the chances are better in a bench trial before a judge than in a jury trial.

Evidence

beyond a reasonable doubt
Refers to the highest level of proof required to win a case. This level of proof is necessary in criminal cases to procure a guilty verdict.

To convict the defendant of a crime, the prosecutor must build a case based on evidence. Because the defendant enjoys a presumption of innocence, the prosecutor must prove **beyond a reasonable doubt** that the defendant is guilty of the crime. The term *beyond a reasonable doubt* is a legal yardstick that measures the sufficiency of the evidence. The prosecutor does not have to meet a standard of eliminating all doubt; lingering suspicions about the defendant's guilt may remain. The reasonable doubt standard works in favor of the defendant, who needs only to raise questions about the quality of the prosecutor's case and does not have to prove anything.

In building the case against the defendant, the prosecutor will use several different types of evidence. Some evidence will be more convincing to the jury than other types, but it is the prosecutor's job to weave a convincing pattern of evidence that demonstrates that the defendant is guilty as charged.

Evidence must conform to a set of rules that ensures that the rights of the defendant are respected.[23] For instance, privileged communications between a doctor and patient or lawyer and client are not admissible in court, nor is evidence that was illegally obtained by the police.[24] With these and other exceptions, however, the rules of evidence are geared toward obtaining the truth. Evidence is deemed trustworthy when every effort is made to ensure its veracity.

For example, original documents are required because copies are too easy to alter. Additionally, young children or those suffering from mental illness may be judged by the

NEWS FLASH

Seeing Things

Case I

In June 1985 Virdeen Willis, Jr., was leaving a Chicago bar with two women when someone shot and killed him. Less than a week later, police arrested Steven Smith, a convicted murderer who had once been incarcerated at the prison where Willis worked as an official. Smith insisted that he did not shoot Willis; no physical evidence connected him to the crime, and the gun could not be found. The two women with Willis could not identify Smith as the killer. Other witnesses said Smith, who had been at the bar, had left with two friends before Willis. The only strike against Smith was a woman who said she saw him shoot Willis. The woman had been smoking crack on the day of Willis' murder and had watched the crime from across the street. Her boyfriend had been a suspect before Smith's arrest, and, in contradiction of several witnesses at the bar, she claimed that Smith had left the bar alone after Willis had left. Two juries found Smith guilty of murdering Willis, and he was sentenced to death. In 1999 the Illinois Supreme Court vacated Smith's conviction for lack of evidence, and he was released.

Case II

In July 1984 in North Carolina, a man broke into two apartments, raped the women who lived in them, and robbed them. Ronald Cotton was arrested that August. His alibi was verified by his family, and one of the victims picked another man from the photo and police lineups, evidence that was withheld from the jury. The prosecution based its case, in part, on the other victim's photo and police lineup identification. Eventually, Cotton was convicted and sentenced to life plus 54 years. The state supreme court overturned the conviction, and Cotton was retried in 1987. By this time, the second victim had settled on Cotton as her assailant. Before the trial, a prison inmate convicted for comparable crimes told another inmate that he had committed the rapes and burglaries. The judge blocked this evidence, and Cotton was convicted and sentenced to life.

In 1995 samples from the victims were DNA tested. The sample from one victim was too deteriorated to be of use, but the other sample did not match Cotton. The test results were then compared with DNA samples from a state felon database. The sample matched the inmate who had confessed to the crime in 1987. After serving 10 1/2 years, Cotton was cleared of all charges, released from prison, and officially pardoned.

What's Going On Here?

Eyes and memories are famously unreliable. A few basic optical illusion tricks go far to prove that our eyes are not the most truthful reporters, and anyone who has ever played a memory game knows that the images stored in our brains are not the best records. Add these phenomena to the stress and trauma that crime causes, and it is easy to understand how eyewitnesses can be unreliable, no matter how honorable their intentions. Also, police have been known to affect lineups, whether consciously or unconsciously. For example, if a witness hesitates, an officer might encourage the witness to "closely study suspect number five" or, in a photo spread, say, "I noticed you hesitated at this photo here." With a little encouragement from authority figures, a hesitant witness can become very sure, very quickly. The Center on Wrongful Convictions at the Northwestern University School of Law studied 86 death penalty cases and found that over half were based at least partly on flawed eyewitness testimony. In 33 of those cases, eyewitness testimony alone was responsible for the conviction.

Why, then, is eyewitness testimony given so much weight in court? It is obviously moving to juries for mostly human reasons. As a juror, it can be quite powerful to see a witness on the stand point to a defendant and state, "He did it."

Sources: Northwestern University School of Law Center on Wrongful Convictions, http://www.law.northwestern.edu/depts/clinic/wrongful/History.htm. Steve Chapman, "Your Lyin' Eyes: What to Do about Eyewitnesses Who Get It Wrong," *Slate,* May 14, 2002, http://slate.msn.com/id/2065761/. "What Jennifer Saw," *PBS/Frontline,* http://www.pbs.org/wgbh/pages/frontline/shows/dna/cotton/summary.html.

court to lack competence and so their testimony would be inadmissible. This is true also for hearsay evidence. Hearsay evidence is secondhand evidence in which someone reports that they heard someone else say something. Because it can be impossible to determine whether someone actually said what is reported, hearsay evidence is, as a rule, inadmissible in court. The prosecutor presents the best evidence available to the jurors, who then decide whether to believe it. Evidence can be classified in several ways.

REAL EVIDENCE. Real evidence consists of objects that can be readily observed. For instance, fingerprints, hair fibers, or blood can all be scientifically analyzed and certified by experts. Although opinions about the quality of the evidence or the chain of custody may be conflicting, there is a standard upon which experts can agree. The courts are turning more and more to science to provide solid real evidence to determine guilt or innocence. The recent examples of death row inmates being released because of DNA evidence is a testament to how science can work both for and against the prosecution.

TESTIMONY. Testimony is statements by witnesses that are given under oath. Ideally, the prosecution will be able to present witnesses who actually saw the defendant commit the crime. Lacking that eyewitness testimony, the prosecutor may present someone who can place the defendant in the proximity of where the crime was committed at about the same time. Additionally, much of the real evidence requires the interpretation of experts. Hair fibers do not speak for themselves, so the prosecution must elicit testimony from an expert who is competent to evaluate them in relation to how the prosecutor contends they are connected to the crime.

DIRECT EVIDENCE. Both real evidence and testimony can be considered as direct evidence. Direct evidence is ascertainable by the five senses. For instance, eyewitness testimony is defined as the witness actually seeing the defendant do something. Hearing, smelling, touching, and tasting can also form the basis for direct evidence.

INDIRECT EVIDENCE. Indirect evidence can also be termed circumstantial evidence. When the prosecution fails to find the "smoking gun," then circumstantial evidence that demonstrates the defendant has bought a gun of the same caliber might be used to help establish the case. With enough circumstantial evidence, the prosecution can build a strong case. However, the defense has an easier time basing doubts on circumstantial evidence than on direct evidence.

The Defense Doesn't Rest

Once the prosecution has presented the evidence against the defendant, the defense attorney has an important decision to make. The defense can claim the prosecution has not proven beyond a reasonable doubt the guilt of the defendant and can decline to mount a defense. This is a risky gamble that defense attorney's do not often employ. The defense attorney may truly believe the prosecution's case was fatally flawed, but the jury will make its own decision, and the defense attorney will usually take the opportunity to rebut the evidence presented.[25] A defense can use a number of strategies to counter the case presented by the prosecution. According to David Neubauer, there are at least five strategies the defense might consider.[26]

REASONABLE DOUBT. The defense has the right to confront the witnesses and evidence through cross-examination and then use this opportunity to attempt to poke holes in the case, thus raising a reasonable doubt in the minds of the jury about the guilt of the defendant. By catching a witness in some contradicting testimony, or exposing how a witness might have a motivation to lie, the defense attorney attempts to weaken the prosecutor's case. When the defendant has no other plausible defense, this sometimes is the only strategy open to the defense attorney. According to Neubauer, this is the weakest type of strategy because it does not really give the jury "something to hang its hat on."

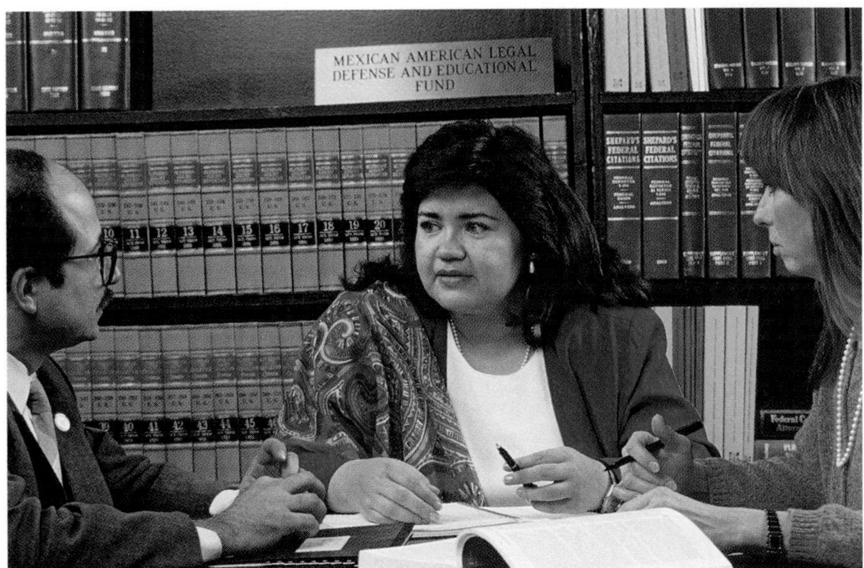

The defense attorney is responsible for presenting the defendant's case in the best possible light. While most defense lawyers are private attorneys, some of the most effective ones are public defenders.
Courtesy of Getty Images, Inc.

DEFENDANT TESTIMONY. The defendant is not required to provide testimony in the trial. Although many jurors would like to see the defendant get on the witness stand and say, "I didn't do it," this strategy would give the prosecution the right to cross-examine. The Fifth Amendment protects defendants from self-incrimination, so the defense attorney must weigh carefully the risk of subjecting the defendant to questions from the prosecution against the problem of letting the jury wonder why the defendant does not take the stand to proclaim his or her innocence.

ALIBIS. The defense can present evidence that the defendant was somewhere else at the time of the crime. Having others testify that they saw the defendant miles from the scene of the crime at the time the crime was committed can raise doubts in the minds of the jury. According to Neubauer, some states require the defense to provide a list of witnesses who are going to present alibi testimony so that the prosecution can investigate their stories before the trial. The goal of the prosecutor is to catch the witnesses in contradictory testimony or to impugn their honesty by showing that they are friends of the defendant and are likely to be untruthful.

AFFIRMATIVE DEFENSE. An affirmative defense essentially says that the defendant committed the crime but had a good reason that excuses his or her culpability. Examples of an affirmative defense are self-defense, duress, and entrapment. In each of these instances, the question of reasonable doubt is not challenged. Rather, the focus of the case shifts to the defendant's having a good reason for the actions taken. Perhaps the most recognizable affirmative defense is the insanity defense in which the defendant admits to the crime but contends that he or she should not be held responsible for the crime because of mental illness.[27]

CHALLENGING SCIENTIFIC EVIDENCE. When the prosecution presents scientific evidence, it must also summon experts to explain this evidence to the jury. Often, these experts are employees of the state or local crime laboratories that processed the evidence. The defense can present its own expert witnesses to cast doubt on the quality of the evidence or the interpretations of the prosecution's witnesses. The jury may be clueless about the issues in dispute and not really competent to distinguish which set of experts is correct. This situation favors the defense, which has only to raise a reasonable doubt in the minds of the jury to secure an acquittal.[28]

There are no right answers when it comes to picking the best tactic to defend against criminal charges. Practicing law is as much an art as it is a science, and pleading a case

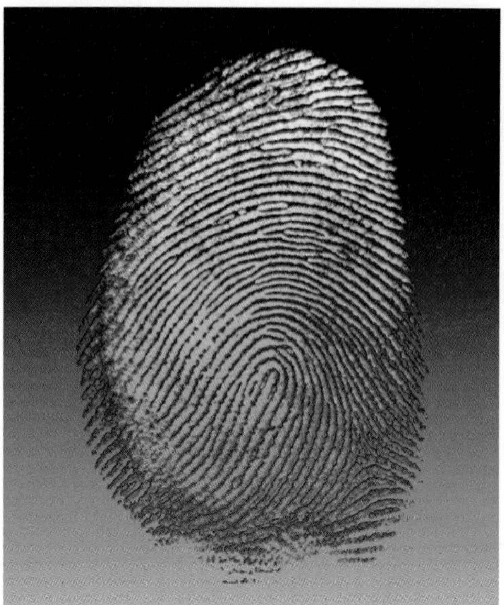

Scientific evidence has become an important factor in many cases. A fingerprint can tie a defendant to the crime scene.

Courtesy of Steven Allen, Getty Images/Photodisc.

before a jury can involve a bit of theater. Some might compare this process to a game because of its adversarial nature and because it is bound by a set of complicated rules. However, the stakes are too high to think of a trial as a game. Its impact on the lives of the offenders, the careers of those in the courtroom work group, and the public's sense of justice make this stage of the criminal justice system an extremely serious endeavor.[29]

Rights and Wrongs in the Courthouse

Thus far, we have reviewed an interesting and extensive set of decision points in which discretion is exercised by prosecutors, defense attorneys, judges, and even defendants. The administration of justice, then, is essentially the negotiation of justice. This reality leaves many observers with a negative view of the criminal justice system.[30] People want a degree of certainty in dealing with criminal offenders and often complain that the crooks have more rights than the victims. In reviewing the legal standing of defendants, victims, witnesses, and those who work in the courthouse, we should consider how the criminal justice system evolved to its present incarnation and why the legal protection of the offender seems to occupy such a prominent space in the proceedings.

"I Know My Rights"

The legal rights afforded defendants in criminal trials can be traced to the earliest codification of laws in Western societies. The Greeks and Romans developed some of the rudiments for the concept of judicial fairness, and early English common law further expanded the concept of rights of the accused. However, the rights enjoyed by defendants in criminal trials in the United States are derived directly from the Constitution, specifically from the first 10 amendments, or the Bill of Rights.

The power of the government to detain, arrest, incarcerate, or even execute must be controlled in ways that prevent overzealous criminal justice practitioners from turning the country into a police state.[31] The power of governments is immense, and documents such as the Bill of Rights help ensure that the United States remains a "government of laws, not of men."[32] Several provisions in the Bill of Rights speak directly to the rights of defendants in criminal trials.

- **Right to a speedy trial.** The Sixth Amendment guarantees that the defendant shall not languish in jail for years before the state gets around to deciding the

FOCUS ON ETHICS

Maximum Mel

You are the city's only female circuit court judge, and you are angry. Things have not been going right in your personal life or on the bench, and you have been taking out your anger on the hapless defendants who appear before you. Your daughter has married a man 20 years her senior, and your son has gone to California to become an actor but instead is a waiter. Ever since you bleached your hair, the press has referred to you as the court's "blonde bombshell," and several offenders to whom you gave probation have recently been caught running a stolen car ring.

You have decided that you have had enough of law enforcement officers who fudge the facts, lawyers who twist the truth, reporters who spin the news, and offenders who look you right in the eye and lie. For the past three months you have made your decisions based on your instincts and your gut feelings, which has resulted in your sentencing just about everyone to the longest period of incarceration possible under the law. Your nickname around the courthouse is "Maximum Mel," and defense attorneys are afraid to bring their clients before your court.

The chief judge has politely suggested that your sentencing patterns are out of step with how other judges sentence. At the local bar association annual dinner, several judges jokingly said the state's prison system would soon be called "Mel's Big House." You are feeling pressure from others in the criminal justice system, but . . . the public loves you. In fact, one of the major political parties has suggested that you might be a good candidate for attorney general and maybe even governor. In some ways, you like the attention you are getting, but your mild-mannered husband asks if you have become burned out as a judge and suggests that maybe you should consider stepping down from the bench. You become angry with him and call your daughter to complain that no one appreciates strong women these days.

QUESTIONS

1. Is it possible that you have lost your sense of perspective?
2. Is it fair to the defendants who appear before you to sentence them to long prison sentences?
3. Do you need to consider your sentencing practices in light of how other judges sentence offenders?
4. Is it ethical to use your sentencing patterns as a stepping-stone to higher political office?
5. Would anyone be asking these questions if you were a man?

case. Of course, in practice, not everyone would agree that the process results in a speedy trial. The defense can delay a trial with requests for continuances. Some detainees, such as the Al Qaeda participants captured in Afghanistan and held at the U.S. military base in Guantanamo Bay in Cuba, are not deemed by the federal government to be covered by the Constitution.

- **Right to confront witnesses.** The Sixth Amendment also says the defendant shall have the opportunity to question those called to testify against him or her. This is an important right enjoyed by U.S. citizens that prevents the government and its citizens from abusing power. In totalitarian countries, the government could simply allege that someone accused the defendant of a crime, and the defendant would have no opportunity to challenge the testimony. Related to the right to confront hostile witnesses is the right of the defendant to call witnesses on his or her behalf. This helps ensure that the court hears the defendant's side of the case.
- **Right against self-incrimination.** When someone refuses to testify and claims to "take the Fifth," they are invoking their right against self-incrimination as guaranteed by the Fifth Amendment. Although a jury may wonder why a

CASE IN POINT

United States v. Salerno

The Case

United States v. Salerno, 481 U.S. 739, 107 S. Ct. 2095 (1987)

The Point

Denying bail and pretrial release to a suspect who may be a danger to society is constitutional.

Anthony Salerno was arrested in 1986 and charged with several RICO Act violations, as well as mail and wire fraud offenses, criminal gambling violations, and extortion. He was held under the Bail Reform Act of 1984 as too dangerous to release into the community. After being convicted of the crimes and sentenced to 100 years in prison, Salerno appealed on the basis that his pretrial detention was unconstitutional. The United States Court of Appeals for the Second Circuit struck down as unconstitutional the provision of the Bail Reform Act in which a suspect may be denied bail because he or she is too dangerous to release.

Calling pretrial detention a "carefully limited exception" to the norm of liberty in U.S. society, the Supreme Court upheld Salerno's detention as constitutional, stating that it violated neither the due process clause of the Fifth Amendment nor the excessive bail clause of the Eighth Amendment.

defendant who is innocent would not testify, the refusal to take the stand is not supposed to be used against the defendant.

- **Right against excessive bail.** The Eighth Amendment provides that those accused of crimes and awaiting trial are to be allowed to post a reasonable bail unless the court finds that they are a danger to society or are likely to flee the jurisdiction and not return for further proceedings when summoned. Exactly what constitutes reasonable bail is a judgment call made by the court. For those with no financial means, any bail could be hard to secure. However, thanks to bail bond companies that can free the defendant for one-tenth the bail and courts' increased use of release on recognizance (ROR) programs, the financial status of the defendant is not as large a factor as it has been in the past.
- **Right to an impartial jury.** This right is another provision of the Sixth Amendment. In recent years, the races and genders of jurors have been attacked as not representing a jury of peers who are likely to be impartial. Defendants and their attorneys are given some discretion in challenging potentially biased jurors.

Although this list of defendants' rights is not exhaustive, it does illustrate some of the guards against abuse that are present within the criminal justice system. Courts may not be totally successful in ensuring a fair trial, but many citizens believe that the courts coddle criminal defendants and that the rights enjoyed by offenders prevent justice from being enacted. In summary, the rights given to those accused of crimes is a double-edged sword. Although these rights may protect some obviously guilty defendants from feeling the full effects of justice, they also help prevent many innocent citizens from being caught up in the gears of the system and punished for crimes they did not commit.

Victims' Rights

The victim can sometimes be the forgotten party in the criminal justice process. The rights of the offender have received substantial attention from the courts, but only relatively recently have efforts been made to empower the victim.[33] When a prosecutor charges a defendant with a crime, it is considered a crime against the state even though there is most likely a human victim as well.[34] Victims get frustrated when they are not

Figure 10.2
Victims' Rights

The California penal code has the following provisions for the rights of the victim:

1. To be notified as soon as possible when a court proceeding to which he or she has been subpoenaed as a witness will not proceed as scheduled.
2. To be informed by the prosecuting attorney of the final disposition of the case.
3. To be notified of all sentencing proceedings, and of the right to appear, to reasonably express his or her views, and to have the court consider his or her statements.
4. To be notified of all juvenile disposition hearings in which the alleged act would have been a felony if committed by an adult, and of the right to attend and to express his or her views.
5. To be notified of any parole eligibility hearing and of the right to appear, to reasonably express his or her views, and to have his or her statements considered.
6. To be notified of an inmate's placement in a re-entry or work/furlough program or of the inmate's escape.
7. To be notified that he/she may be entitled to witness-fees and mileage.
8. To be provided with information concerning the victim's right to civil recovery and the opportunity to be compensated from the restitution fund.
9. To the expeditious return of his/her property, which has allegedly been stolen or embezzled, when it is no longer needed as evidence.
10. To an expeditious disposition of the criminal action.
11. To be notified if the defendant is to be placed on parole.
12. To be notified of a pending pretrial disposition before a change of plea is entered before a judge.

Source: Frank Schmalleger, *Criminal Law Today: An Introduction with Capstone Cases,* 2nd ed. (Upper Saddle River, NJ: Prentice Hall, 2002).

notified when the court hears cases, and especially when the cases are plea bargained.[35] The prosecutor and the judge make the important decisions without the victim's input. In an effort to increase the victim's voice, many states have adopted victim rights legislation (see Figure 10.2).

Although not all states have passed such laws, the idea of treating victims and witnesses with more respect and consideration is taking hold in the criminal justice system. It would be unfair to contend that criminal justice practitioners have not always valued victims and witnesses. Certainly, they are not intentionally left out of the process because judges and prosecutors are mean-spirited or contemptuous of their input. The problems experienced by victims and witnesses are related to resources. With increased caseloads and few judges, prosecutors, secretarial support staff, and investigators, the workload of those in the courtroom work group leaves little time to ensure that victims and witnesses are being notified in a timely manner of all the changes in the docket and the status of cases and defendants. Certainly, the advent in recent years of victim–witness programs has helped alleviate some of the frustrations.[36] Laws like the ones in California, however, serve to institutionalize these reforms and ensure that decent treatment of victims and witnesses is not always relegated to the bottom of the priority list when budgets get tight.[37]

Sentencing the Offender

The criminal court process is twofold. The first part is concerned with determining the guilt or innocence of the defendant. If the defendant is found guilty, or plea bargains for a *nolo contendere* or guilty plea, the second part of the court process begins. The defendant (now the offender) must be sentenced by the judge to an appropriate disposition. A range of philosophical concerns guides the sentencing process.[38] Depending on the nature of the case and the motivations of the judge, the goal of the sentence might be treatment, punishment, incapacitation, restitution, revenge, or deterrence.[39]

CASE IN POINT

Furman v. Georgia

The Case

Furman v. Georgia, 408 U.S. 238, 92 S. Ct. 2726 (1972)

The Point

The decision set forth that the administration of the death penalty constituted cruel and unusual punishment, not the death penalty itself.

William Furman, an African American, shot and killed a homeowner through a closed door while trying to get into the house at night. Furman, 26, pleaded insanity and was committed to the Georgia Central State Hospital for a psychiatric examination. The staff who examined Furman concluded unanimously that Furman was mentally deficient with "psychotic episodes associated with Convulsive Disorder." They also said that although Furman was not currently psychotic, he also was not capable of helping his attorneys prepare his defense and needed further psychiatric treatment. Later, the hospital superintendent concluded much the same, except stated that Furman did indeed know right from wrong and was able to cooperate with his attorneys. Evidence that he was mentally unsound was presented at the trial, but Furman was convicted and sentenced to death. Furman appealed the conviction on the grounds that his Fourteenth Amendment rights were being violated. The Supreme Court concurred, saying that administration of the death penalty in Georgia was racially discriminatory and violated the Eighth and Fourteenth Amendments. In 1976 the court reversed its decision in *Gregg v. Georgia.*

The philosophical intention of the judge is not the only factor that guides the sentencing decision. The availability of prison beds or treatment programs, the demeanor or remorsefulness of the defendant, and a host of factors that should have no bearing on the sentence such as the offender's race, social and economic status, and gender, can all influence the type and severity of the disposition.[40] The judge has, therefore, considerable discretion in deciding the appropriate sentence for each offender. For the offender, then, it is a bit like gambling when he or she stands before the bench for sentencing and wonders whether the judge is in a good mood.[41]

A uniform pattern in sentencing would be comforting. If those who committed the most serious crimes and presented the greatest danger to society received the most severe sentences, the public's sense of justice would be satisfied. However, when sentences for offenders with similar crimes and prior records differ significantly, the courts appear to be arbitrary and capricious. At the heart of the matter is a long-standing debate in criminology over whether the sentence should be geared toward the crime or fashioned to fit the circumstances of the offender. This debate has spawned two types of sentences: **indeterminate sentences** and **determinate sentences.**[42]

indeterminate sentence
A prison term that does not state a specific period of time to be served or date of release. Such a sentence will specify a range of time to be served, such as 10 to 20 years.

determinate sentence
A prison term that is determined by law and states a specific period of time to be served. Sentencing grids or guidelines are usually employed in calculating the sentence. For example, an armed robbery conviction might call for a 30-year sentence in jail, regardless of the circumstances of the offender or the crime.

Indeterminate Sentencing

Is the judge the best person to decide how long an offender should spend in prison? Even when a case is plea bargained, is the courtroom work group the appropriate body to fashion a sentencing decision that affects not only the offender, but also the agencies that must carry out the sentence? Perhaps the prison is better able to decide which inmates deserve to be there and which are good probation and parole risks. Perhaps the trial, where passions are high and the details of the crime vivid, is not the time to decide how long the offender should be incarcerated. Perhaps society would be better served if the actual length of an offender's sentence were predicated on how well that offender adjusts to prison life and on how safe society would be once the offender is released.[43]

The indeterminate sentence takes these issues into consideration and leaves the discretion to the parole board to determine when the offender is ready to be released into the community. It views the judge as incapable of forecasting the future and predicting when the offender is no longer a threat to society. At its most extreme, the indeterminate sentence sends the offender to prison for somewhere between one year and life. Based on the offender's behavior in prison and his or her rehabilitation, the parole board picks a release date.

The indeterminate sentence, which is based on the medical model of corrections, considers the uniqueness of each offender's crime and social background; the sentence is fashioned to address the diagnosed problems.[44] In a hospital it would be inconceivable to handle the patient with a broken leg in the same way as the patient who experienced a heart attack. The indeterminate sentence applies the medical analogy to the criminal offender. By viewing unlawful behavior as a symptom of a social deficiency, the criminal justice system can prescribe a treatment, such as vocational training, drug or alcohol treatment, or therapeutic counseling.

The indeterminate sentence is attractive if we assume that criminal behavior is comparable to physical illness. We can prescribe individualized justice in the same way we do individualized medicine and develop a "treatment or a cure" for the antisocial behavior of the offender. The time it takes to apply a cure to each offender is different, so the prison sentences are not fixed. That way, the offender is not released too soon or kept in prison too long. The parole board, in consultation with the professional prison staff, determines when the offender has been successfully rehabilitated and is safe to return to society.[45]

The indeterminate sentence enjoyed wide popularity during the 1950s and 1960s. A progressive attitude prevalent in correctional circles advocated rehabilitation over punishment. By shifting the discretion for deciding the length of incarceration from the judge to the prison staff and the parole board, the criminal justice system based treatment on the willingness of the inmate to take advantage of the rehabilitative services available. The indeterminate sentence was predicated on three assumptions:

1. The offender is sick and the prison staff can diagnose the problem.
2. The prison can provide the necessary treatment to correct the problem.
3. The prison staff and parole board can accurately determine whether the inmate has been successfully treated and is ready to return to society.[46]

The indeterminate sentence was jettisoned in the 1970s and 1980s for four reasons. The first reason is that there was little evidence that any of the three aforementioned assumptions were warranted. Considering antisocial behavior to be analogous to physical illness and subject to diagnosis and treatment did not prove to be accurate in many cases. As offenders deemed to be rehabilitated continued to recidivate, citizens and politicians lost faith in the system.[47]

The second reason that the indeterminate sentence lost favor was the wide disparities in incarceration times. Particularly when extralegal factors such as race and social class were correlated with length of incarceration, the inexact science of indeterminate sentencing began to look like a smokescreen for discrimination and the influence of political power.[48]

The third reason the indeterminate sentence lost support concerned its impact on prison inmates. If the prison sentence were to be determined by how well inmates appeared to be rehabilitated, then it was in their interest to play the game. The inmates learned to act rehabilitated to convince prison officials they were ready to be released. They attended treatment programs, went to church, and developed the positive vocabulary of rehabilitation to attain their goal of release.[49]

Finally, the interpretations by some criminologists of the research concerning recidivism did not reveal that participation in treatment programs significantly improved the inmates' prospects for avoiding a life of crime. Although the value of rehabilitation was, and continues to be, in dispute, the prevailing attitude at the time was that it lacked evidence of effectiveness.[50] Consequently, the discretion for deciding how long the inmate would be incarcerated shifted from the prison staff and the parole board to the legislature and the prosecutor with the introduction of the determinate sentence.

Determinate Sentencing

The effectiveness of rehabilitation will be fully discussed in the chapters on corrections. For our purposes here, it is sufficient to say that there was widespread concern about its effectiveness and about the public's confidence in the criminal justice system. Although rehabilitation was considered a worthy goal, it was not deemed to be a sufficient foundation on which to base sentencing decisions. As legislators heard stories about liberal judges and parole boards, they decided to pass laws that restricted the discretion criminal justice decision makers could exercise in any individual case. Various state legislatures passed determinate or fixed sentence laws that stated that the length of time an inmate would serve would not be determined by the judge or the parole board but by the nature of the crime itself.[51] Sentencing grids or guidelines were developed that forced judges to apply sentences within a very narrow range of variability (see Table 10.1).[52] In its purest form, a determinate sentence gives a fixed sentence to each inmate convicted of a particular crime. For example, an armed robbery conviction might call for a 30-year sentence. The judge has no discretion to make the sentence longer or shorter, regardless of the circumstances of the crime or of the offender. One form of determinate sentencing, the **presumptive sentence**, allows judges limited discretion to consider aggravating or mitigating circumstances and depart from the guidelines. Some states employ voluntary guidelines, which allow judges the same departures (see Figures 10.3 and 10.4).

presumptive sentence
A sentence that may be adjusted by the judge depending on aggravating or mitigating factors.

The perceived advantage of the determinate sentence is uniformity. Similar cases are treated in the same manner and, theoretically, such factors as social class, race, and gender do not affect the sentencing equation.[53] These efforts to remove discretion from the criminal justice system have produced some unintended consequences that some consider to be detrimental to the welfare of offenders and society.

First, determinate sentencing has removed the power to make decisions from those closest to the case. These participants are often in the best position to understand a case's complexities and weigh the conflicting interests of the welfare of society and the punishment of the offender. Second, legislators who espouse a get-tough-on-crime policy are not always sensitive to the limitations of the criminal justice system to bear the demands of long prison sentences for a vast number of inmates. A primary goal of a legislator is to get elected or reelected, and the making of effective criminal justice policy is often a casualty of the demands of political expediency. Even the most mundane criminal justice resources, such as prison beds, are limited. Legislators who restrict the discretion of criminal justice administrators to allocate those resources to the most pressing cases often are the same legislators who do not allocate sufficient budgets to the criminal justice system in the first place. In many ways, correctional officials are "left holding the bag" in that they are given an unreasonable workload by the legislature and neither the resources nor the discretion to effectively handle their duties within acceptable limits.[54] The civil and human rights of inmates are infringed when prisons are overcrowded, but criminal justice decision makers, such as judges and parole board members, have little power to remedy the situation.[55]

Another detrimental effect of determinate sentencing is the shifting of power from the judge to the prosecutor.[56] By limiting the judge's discretion in imposing the sentence, determinate sentencing laws increase the impact of the prosecutor's decision as to which charges will be filed against the defendant. Defense attorneys unwilling to expose their clients to the long determinate sentences passed by the legislature are pressured to accept plea bargains to lesser included crimes or in exchange for avoiding the stigma associated with drug or sex offender convictions. The mandatory minimum sentences for these types of offenses provide the prosecutor with tremendous leverage in extracting plea bargains from defendants and their attorneys. Therefore, those in the best position to exercise discretion, the judge and the parole board, often find their hands tied by the determinate sentencing laws. Determinate sentencing reduces criminal justice decision makers to clerks without the power to apply justice to the individual case and offender.

TABLE 10.1

Minnesota Sentencing Guidelines Grid, August 2003

Presumptive Sentence Lengths in Months

Italicized numbers within the grid denote the range within which a judge may sentence without the sentence being deemed a departure. Offenders with nonimprisonment felony sentences are subject to jail time according to law.

SEVERITY LEVEL OF CONVICTION OFFENSE (Common offenses listed in italics)		CRIMINAL HISTORY SCORE 0	1	2	3	4	5	6 or more
Murder, 2nd Degree (intentional murder, drive-by-shootings)	XI	306 *299–313*	326 *319–333*	346 *339–353*	366 *359–373*	386 *379–393*	406 *399–413*	426 *419–433*
Murder, 3rd Degree Murder, 2nd Degree (unintentional murder)	X	150 *144–156*	165 *159–171*	180 *174–186*	195 *189–201*	210 *204–216*	225 *219–231*	240 *234–246*
Criminal Sexual Conduct, 1st Degree[2] *Assault, 1st Degree*	IX	86 *81–91*	98 *93–103*	110 *105–115*	122 *117–127*	134 *129–139*	146 *141–151*	158 *153–163*
Aggravated Robbery 1st Degree Criminal Sexual Conduct, 2nd Degree (c),(d),(e),(f),(h)[2]	VIII	48 *44–52*	58 *54–52*	68 *64–72*	78 *74–82*	88 *84–92*	98 *94–102*	108 *104–112*
Felony DWI	VII	36	42	48	54 51–57	60 57–63	66 63–69	72 69–75
Criminal Sexual Conduct, 2nd Degree (a) & (b)	VI	21	27	33	39 *37–41*	45 *43–47*	51 *49–53*	57 *55–59*
Residential Burglary Simple Robbery	V	18	23	28	33 *31–35*	38 *36–40*	43 *41–45*	48 *46–50*
Nonresidential Burglary	IV	12[1]	15	18	21	24 *23–25*	27 *26–28*	30 *29–31*
Theft Crimes (over $2,500)	III	12[1]	13	15	17	19 *18–20*	21 *20–22*	23 *22–24*
Theft Crimes ($2,500 or less) Check Forgery ($200–$2,500)	II	12[1]	12[1]	13	15	17	19	21 *20–22*
Sale of Simulated Controlled Substance	I	12[1]	12[1]	12[1]	13	15	17	19 *18–20*

☐ Presumptive commitment to state imprisonment. First Degree Murder is excluded from the guidelines by law and continues to have a mandatory life sentence.

☐ Presumptive stayed sentence; at the discretion of the judge, up to a year in jail and/or other non-jail sanctions can be imposed as conditions of probation. However, offenses in this section of the grid always carry a presumptive commitment to state prison. These offenses include Third Degree Controlled Crimes when the offender has a prior felony drug conviction, Burglary of an Occupied Dwelling when the offender has a prior felony burglary conviction, second and subsequent Criminal Sexual Conduct offenses and offenses carrying a mandatory minimum prison term due to the use of a dangerous weapon (e.g., Second Degree Assault).

1. One year and one day
2. Pursuant to M.S. § 609.342, subd. 2 and 609.343, subd. 2, the presumptive sentence for Criminal Sexual Conduct in the First Degree is a minimum of 144 months and the presumptive sentence for Criminal Sexual Conduct in the Second Degree—clauses c, d, e, f, and h is a minimum of 90 months.

Source: Minnesota Sentencing Guidelines Commission, http://www.msgc.state.mn.us/Guidelines/guide03aug.pdf, p. 48.

Figure 10.3
Departures from Sentencing Guidelines in Maryland, July–December 2001: Mitigating Reasons

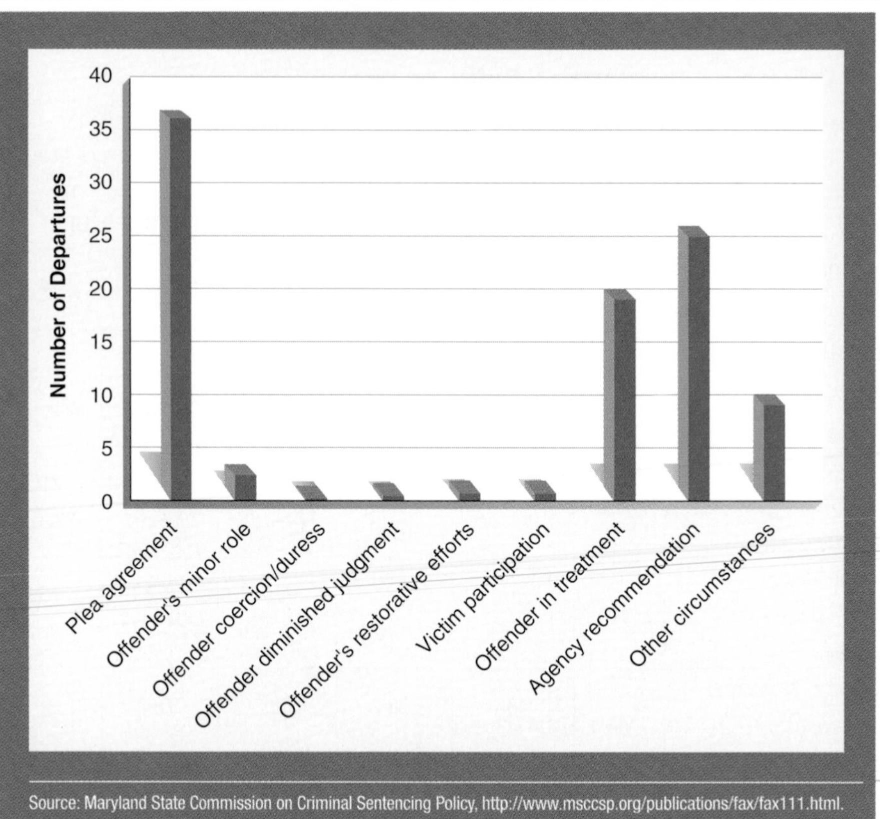

Source: Maryland State Commission on Criminal Sentencing Policy, http://www.msccsp.org/publications/fax/fax111.html.

Figure 10.4
Departures from Sentencing Guidelines in Maryland, July–December 2001: Aggravating Reasons

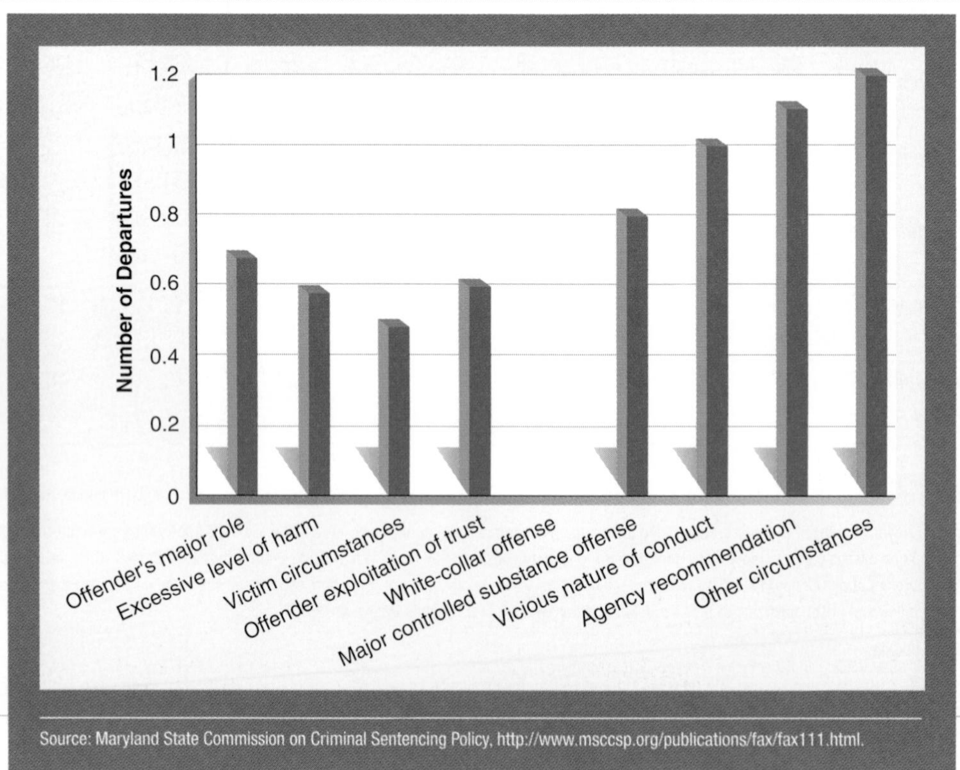

Source: Maryland State Commission on Criminal Sentencing Policy, http://www.msccsp.org/publications/fax/fax111.html.

CROSSCURRENTS

Special Interest Laws

One of the interesting aspects of living in a democracy is the ability of groups and individuals to affect the making of laws. When a number of people begin to believe that the criminal justice system does not adequately respond to the needs of public safety, they have the freedom to demand through the democratic process that government listen and respond to their concerns. Politicians who want to be reelected ignore such organized groups at their peril. These groups have the goal of educating the public about their concerns and pressuring the criminal justice system to pay special attention to the harms done by the crimes they see as problematic. A few of the most notable examples of the power of special interest groups are as follows:

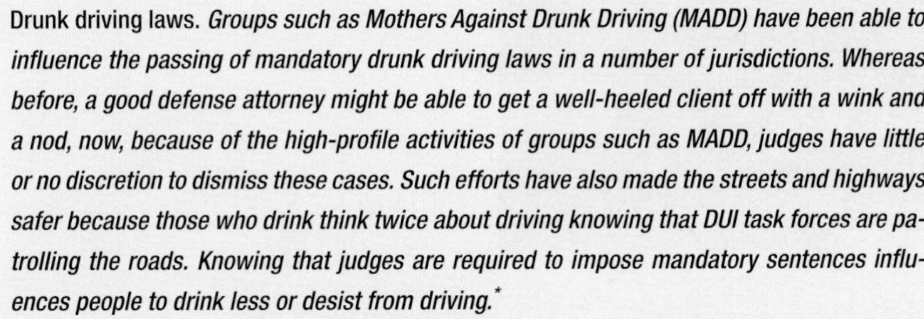

- Drunk driving laws. *Groups such as Mothers Against Drunk Driving (MADD) have been able to influence the passing of mandatory drunk driving laws in a number of jurisdictions. Whereas before, a good defense attorney might be able to get a well-heeled client off with a wink and a nod, now, because of the high-profile activities of groups such as MADD, judges have little or no discretion to dismiss these cases. Such efforts have also made the streets and highways safer because those who drink think twice about driving knowing that DUI task forces are patrolling the roads. Knowing that judges are required to impose mandatory sentences influences people to drink less or desist from driving.*[*]

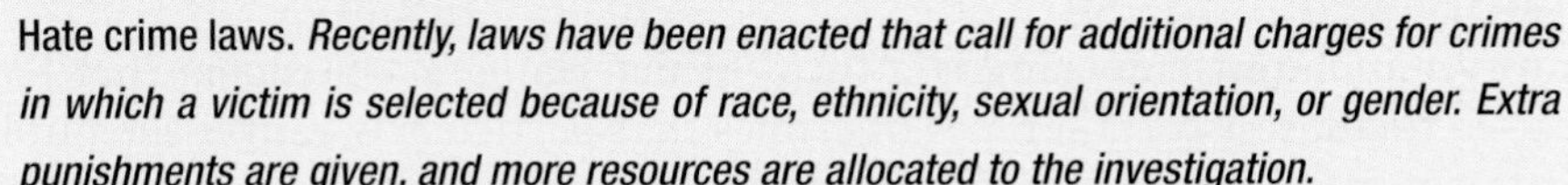

- Hate crime laws. *Recently, laws have been enacted that call for additional charges for crimes in which a victim is selected because of race, ethnicity, sexual orientation, or gender. Extra punishments are given, and more resources are allocated to the investigation.*
- Sex offender laws. *Perhaps the most feared and despised offenders are those charged with crimes of a sexual nature. Rapists, child abusers, and exhibitionists have been traditionally held in low regard by society, but recently, a number of jurisdictions have passed laws that place extra surveillance on these offenders even when they are no longer under the supervision of the court. For example, in Michigan those convicted of sex offenses have their names and addresses entered into a database that is available to the public via the Internet. Consequently, neighbors and law enforcement officials may be well aware when an offender with a history of sexual crimes moves into a community. Although parents' desire to know when a child molester moves in next door is certainly understandable some are concerned about the privacy rights of offenders who have served their prison terms and are now considered free. The stigma of "sex offender" can limit job opportunities of offenders who might very well have been successfully rehabilitated.*

QUESTIONS

1. Should some crimes require such special treatment?
2. Do these special interest laws devalue other types of crimes?
3. What other behaviors do you think warrant the enactment of special laws that call for mandatory sentences?
4. Should judges be allowed more discretion in considering the circumstances of these crimes?
5. How do mandatory sentence laws affect the ability of criminal justice practitioners to efficiently use the resources of the system?

[*] *Alcohol and Crime: An Analysis of National Data on the Prevalence of Alcohol Involvement in Crime*, Bureau of Justice Statistics, U.S. Department of Justice, Office of Justice Program, April 1998, p. 5.

Sentencing is a pivotal point in the criminal justice process. Sentencing occurs after guilt is determined in a trial or after a plea bargain is struck.
Courtesy of CORBIS-NY.

Mandatory Minimum Sentences

mandatory minimum sentence
A sentence determined by law that establishes the minimum length of prison time that may be served for a crime.

Mandatory minimum sentencing is a form of determinate sentencing that has become widely used to address certain types of crimes that particularly rankle the public and receive little sympathy from the media or criminal justice practitioners.[57] Typically, mandatory minimum laws do not allow for probation and stipulate incarceration for a term not less than a specified number of years. Following are the types of crimes that are likely to carry mandatory minimums:

- **Weapons violations.** Those who use a gun (or sometimes merely possess one) while committing a felony will find an additional prison term tacked on to the sentence. This guarantees that the case will not result in a probationary sentence.
- **Repeated drunk driving.** In some jurisdictions, those who persist in driving while intoxicated will be sentenced to mandatory prison or jail time. Groups such as Mothers Against Drunk Driving (MADD) have been effective in changing laws that they deemed too lenient on repeat offenders.[58]
- **Drug sales and drug kingpin laws.** As a result of the nation's war on drugs, many jurisdictions, including the federal government, passed laws specifying mandatory prison time for the sale of illegal drugs. Some of these laws, aimed at drug kingpins, are especially punitive.
- **Three-strikes-and-you're-out laws.** Aimed at the habitual offender, these laws result in mandatory incarceration for those who have two prior felonies. Judges are not allowed to consider the circumstances of the present offense and must sentence the offender to a prison term.
- **Truth in sentencing.** These laws specify that the offender must serve a substantial portion of the sentence before being released. These laws limit the flexibility of the parole board by ensuring that inmates spend most of the original sentence (often 85 percent) behind bars.[59]

Because the sentencing decision is such a high-profile event, it has become the primary way that citizens evaluate the quality of justice meted out by the system. This is unfortunate in many ways because sentencing is just one of many decision-making points in

CASE IN POINT

Gregg v. Georgia

The Case

Gregg v. Georgia, 428 U.S. 153, 96 S. Ct. 2909 (1976)

The Point

The Supreme Court effectively reinstated the death penalty, finding that it did not constitute cruel and unusual punishment as long as its implementation was fair.

Troy Gregg was convicted of killing and robbing two men and sentenced to death. After *Furman v. Georgia,* the state implemented bifurcated trials, in which guilt or innocence is determined in the first stage, and the penalty is determined in the second. During the penalty phase, the jury is required to consider both mitigating and aggravating circumstances, and if aggravating circumstances are overriding, then the death penalty is to be imposed. Also, the law prescribed an automatic appeal. The Supreme Court found all procedures to be correctly followed and that all were constitutional and violated neither the Eighth nor the Fourteenth Amendments. Gregg's death sentence in this case was upheld.

Four years earlier in *Furman v. Georgia,* the Supreme Court found the process by which the death penalty was imposed to be cruel and unusual. In this case, the court affirmed that the death penalty itself was not cruel and unusual, as long as its implementation was judged to be fair.

the system, and the reliance on this single event obscures the effects of the entire process. Efforts to limit the discretion of judges have been frustrated because of the inevitable shift of decision-making power to other points in the system.

Summary

This chapter has described how the courts dispose of cases. A negotiation process between the defense attorney and the prosecutor concludes the vast majority of cases. Plea bargaining has been the subject of a great deal of criticism from the public because it appears as though the offender is escaping the full impact of justice. In fact, this is true in a great many cases, but there are advantages to the state also. As we will fully discuss in the later chapters on corrections, prison sentences are available and affordable for only the most serious criminals.

The rights of defendants in criminal trials are derived from the Constitution, specifically from the first 10 amendments, or the Bill of Rights. Several provisions in the Bill of Rights directly address the rights of defendants in criminal trials. Criminal trials are actually quite rare. Most cases are settled in the plea bargaining process, so only a few cases go to a jury trial.

Prior to opening statements, each side may file pretrial motions to gain the most favorable circumstances and to limit the evidence from the other side. Cases can be won or lost given how the judge rules on the pretrial motions.

The prosecution is the first to make an opening argument, telling why it believes that the defendant is guilty. The prosecution will outline the case and tell the jury of the types of evidence to be presented. The defense attorney then counters the prosecution's version of the case. No evidence is presented during opening arguments.

The prosecution then introduces evidence and witnesses. Because the defendant enjoys a presumption of innocence, the prosecutor must prove beyond a reasonable doubt that the defendant is guilty. The prosecutor will use different types of evidence, but it all must conform to rules that ensure that the defendant's rights are respected. During this presentation, the defense may object to questions asked by the prosecutor or answers given by a witness. The defense then has the opportunity to cross-examine the witnesses. The prosecutor may then question the witness again, followed by questions from the defense. After the prosecution presents its evidence and witnesses, the defense may present its own evidence and witnesses. The prosecution may cross-examine these witnesses, followed by redirect questions from the defense and re-cross-examination by the prosecution. Closing arguments follow, and the case goes to the jury.

Jury selection is a complicated procedure subject to influence by the prosecution and defense through *voir dire* prior to the trial. The jury listens to the presentation of the case and then returns its verdict. A conviction or acquittal requires a unanimous vote. Not all cases get a jury trial. The exceptions are those in which the penalty is not serious, those in which the defendant is a juvenile, and when the defense requests a bench trial. In a bench trial, a judge decides on guilt or innocence and passes sentence.

If the defendant is found guilty, then he or she is sentenced by the judge, who has considerable discretion in deciding the appropriate sentence. There are two primary types of sentencing: indeterminate sentencing and determinate sentencing. The indeterminate sentence is fashioned to fit the offender, whereas the determinate sentence is fashioned to fit the crime. Mandatory minimum sentences, a form of determinate sentencing, do not allow probation and specify incarceration for a term not less than a certain number of years.

Finally, although the offender's rights receive substantial attention from the courts, only recently have efforts been made to empower the victim. To increase the voice and input of the victim, many states have adopted victim rights legislation.

We turn now to corrections to see how the criminal justice system punishes and treats those convicted of serious crimes.

KEY TERMS

bench trial p. 334
beyond a reasonable doubt p. 334
determinate sentence p. 342
directed verdict of acquittal p. 330
hung jury p. 334
impeach p. 330
indeterminate sentence p. 342
mandatory minimum sentence p. 348
plea bargain p. 322
presumptive sentence p. 344
redirect examination p. 330
venire p. 332
voir dire p. 332

QUESTIONS

1. What are the four types of pleas?
2. What are the steps of a trial?
3. Explain the major pretrial motions.
4. Describe the steps required in the formation of a jury.
5. What is *voir dire?*
6. What are the two means by which a prosecutor can exclude a juror?
7. How is evidence classified?
8. What five strategies might a defense use to counter the prosecution?
9. What rights do defendants have in criminal trials?
10. Give an example of a victim's right.
11. Compare and contrast determinate and indeterminate sentences.
12. What are mandatory minimum sentences?

SUGGESTED FURTHER READING

Abramson, Jeffery. *We, the Jury: The Jury System and the Ideal of Democracy.* New York: Basic Books, 1994.

Blomberg, Thomas G. and Stanley Cohen, eds. *Punishment and Social Control: Essays in Honor of Sheldon L. Messinger.* New York: Aldine De Gruyter, 1995.

Leo, Richard. "Miranda's Revenge: Police Interrogation as a Confidence Game." *Law and Society Review* 30 (1996): 259–288.

McCoy, Candace. *Politics of Plea Bargaining: Victim's Rights in California.* Philadelphia: University of Pennsylvania Press, 1993.

Miller, Kent, and Michael Radelet. *Executing the Mentally Ill: The Criminal Justice System and the Mentally Ill.* Newbury Park, CA: Sage, 1993.

Welch, Michael. *Punishment in America: Social Control and the Ironies of Imprisonment.* Thousand Oaks, CA: Sage, 1999.

ENDNOTES

1. John Hagan, "Extra-Legal Attributes and Criminal Sentencing: An Assessment of a Sociological Viewpoint," *Law and Society Review* 8 (1974): 357–381.
2. Thomas Austin, "The Influence of Court Location on Types of Criminal Sentences: The Rural-Urban Factor," *Journal of Criminal Justice* 9 (1981): 305–316.
3. Douglas Thomson and Anthony Ragona, "Popular Moderation Versus Governmental Authoritarianism: An Interactionist View of Public Sentiments Toward Criminal Sanctions," *Crime and Delinquency* 33 (1987): 337–357.
4. James Austin and John Irwin, *It's About Time: America's Imprisonment Binge,* 3rd ed. (Belmont, CA: Wadsworth, 1997).
5. Hedieh Nasheri, *Betrayal of Due Process: A Comparative Assessment of Plea Bargaining in the United States and Canada* (Lanham, MD: University Press of America, 1998).
6. Douglas Smith, "The Plea Bargaining Controversy," *Journal of Criminal Law and Criminology* 77 (1986): 949–957.
7. Arthur Rosett and Donald Cressey, *Justice by Consent* (Philadelphia: J.B. Lippincott, 1976).
8. William Rhodes, *Plea Bargaining: Who Gains? Who Loses?* (Washington, DC: Institute for Law and Social Research, 1978).
9. Michael Rubenstein and Teresa White, "Plea Bargaining: Can Alaska Live Without It?" *Judicature* 62 (1979): 266–279.
10. Jay S. Albanese, "Concern About Variation in Criminal Sentences: A Cyclical History of Reform," *Journal of Criminal Law and Criminology* 75 (1984): 260–271.
11. N. Gary Holten and Lawson L. Lamar, *The Criminal Courts: Structures Personnel and Processes* (New York: McGraw-Hill, 1991).
12. B. Grant Stite and Robert H. Chaires, "Plea Bargaining: Ethical Issues and Emerging Perspectives," *The Justice Professional* 7 (1993): 69–91.
13. Bradley S. Chilton, "Reforming Plea Bargaining to Facilitate Ethical Discourse," *Criminal Justice Policy Review* 5 (1991): 322–334.
14. David W. Neubauer, *America's Courts and the Criminal Justice System,* 7th ed. (Belmont, CA: Wadsworth, 2002).
15. Ibid.
16. David Lynch, "The Impropriety of Plea Agreements: A Tale of Two Counties," *Law and Social Inquiry* 19 (1994): 115–136.
17. Lynn Mather, *Plea Bargaining or Trial* (Lexington, MA: D.C. Heath, 1979).
18. Neubauer, *America's Courts.*
19. Thomas Church, "Plea Bargains, Concessions and the Courts: Analysis of a Quasi-Experiment," *Law and Society Review* 10 (1976): 377–389.
20. Jon'a F. Meyer and Diana R. Grant, *The Courts in Our Criminal Justice System* (Upper Saddle River, NJ: Prentice Hall, 2003).
21. Raymond Nimmer and Patricia Krauthaus, "Plea Bargaining Reform in Two Cities," *Justice System Journal* 3 (1977): 6–21.
22. Candance McCoy, *Politics and Plea Bargaining: Victims' Rights in California* (Philadelphia: University of Pennsylvania Press, 1993).
23. Henry J. Abraham, *The Judicial Process,* 7th ed. (New York: Oxford, 1998).
24. Steven Schlesinger, *Exclusionary Injustice: The Problem of Illegally Obtained Evidence* (New York: Marcel Dekker, 1977).
25. Barbara Reskin and Christine Visher, "The Impacts of Evidence and Extralegal Factors in Juror's Decisions," *Law and Society Review* 20 (1986): 423–439.
26. Neubauer, *America's Courts.*
27. Lincoln Caplan, *The Insanity Defense and the Trial of John W. Hinckley Jr.* (Boston: D.R. Godine, 1984).
28. Michael Freeman and Helen Reece, eds., *Science in Court* (Brookfield, VT: Ashgate, 1998).

29. William Brennan, "The Criminal Prosecution: Sporting Events or Quest for Truth?" *Washington University Law Review* (1963): 279–294.

30. Smith, "Plea Bargaining Controversy."

31. Richard Quinney, *Critique of Legal Order: Crime Control in Capitalist Society* (Boston: Little, Brown, 1974).

32. Chief Justice John Marshall in the Supreme Court's ruling on *Marbury vs. Madison,* 5 U.S. 137 (1803). Online at http: //caselaw.lp.findlaw.com/scripts/getcase.pl?navby=case&court=us&vol=5&page=137.

33. Mary Achilles and Howard Zehr, "Restorative Justice for Crime Victims: The Promise, The Challenge," in *Restorative Community Justice: Repairing Harm and Transforming Communities,* eds. Gordon Bazemore and Mara Schiff (Cincinnati: Anderson, 2001), 87–99.

34. Nils Christie, "Conflicts as Property," *British Journal of Criminology* 17 (1997): 1–15.

35. Valerie Finn-Deluca, "Victim Participation of Sentencing," *Criminal Law Bulletin* 30 (1994): 403–428.

36. Peter Finn and Beverley Lee, *Establishing and Expanding Victim Witness Assistance Programs* (Washington, DC: National Institute of Justice, 1988).

37. Robert Elias, *Victims Still: The Political Manipulation of Crime Victims* (Thousand Oaks, CA: Sage, 1993).

38. Andrew von Hirsch, *Doing Justice* (New York: Hill and Wang, 1976).

39. Peggy Tobolowsky, "Restitution in the Federal Criminal Justice System," *Judicature* 77 (1993): 90–95. See also Christy Visher, "Incapacitation and Crime Control: Does a 'Lock'em Up' Strategy Reduce Crime?" *Justice Quarterly* 4 (1987): 513–544.

40. Thomas Arvanites, "Increasing Imprisonment: A Function of Crime or Socioeconomic Factors?" *American Journal of Criminal Justice* 17 (1992): 19–38.

41. Elizabeth Moulds, "Chivalry and Paternalism: Disparities of Treatment in the Criminal Justice System," *Western Political Science Quarterly* 31 (1978): 416–440.

42. Tamasak Wicharaya, *Simple Theory, Hard Reality: The Impact of Sentencing Reforms on Courts, Prisons, and Crime* (Albany: State University of New York Press, 1995).

43. John Irwin, *Prisons in Turmoil* (Boston: Little, Brown, 1980). Irwin presents a scathing critique of the indeterminate sentence from a prisoner's point of view.

44. Ibid.

45. William Gaylin, *Partial Justice: A Study of Bias in Sentencing* (New York: Vintage Books, 1974).

46. Irwin, *Prisons in Turmoil.*

47. Steven P. Lab and John T. Whitehead, "From 'Nothing Works' to 'The Appropriate Works': The Latest Stop in the Search for the Secular Grail," *Criminology* 28 (1990): 405–418.

48. John Hagan, "Extra-Legal Attributes and Criminal Sentencing: An Assessment of a Sociological Viewpoint," *Law and Society Review* 8 (1974): 357–381.

49. James B. Jacobs, *Stateville: The Penitentiary in Mass Society* (Chicago: The University of Chicago Press, 1977).

50. Francis T. Cullen and Karen B. Gilbert, *Reaffirming Rehabilitation* (Cincinnati: Anderson, 1982).

51. Pamala Grie, *Determinate Sentencing: The Promise and the Reality of Retributive Justice* (Ithaca, NY: State University of New York Press, 1991).

52. Jeffery Ulner, *Social Worlds of Sentencing: Court Communities Under Sentencing Guidelines* (Albany: State University of New York Press, 1997).

53. Darrell Steffensmeier, Jeffrey Ulmer, and John Kramer, "The Interaction of Race, Gender, and Age in Criminal Sentencing: The Punishment Cost of Being Young, Black and Male," *Criminology* 36: 763–798.

54. Austin and Irwin, *It's About Time.*

55. William McDonald, Henry Rossman, and James Cramer, "The Prosecutorial Function and Its Relation to Determinate Sentencing Structures," in *The Prosecutor,* ed. William McDonald (Beverly Hills, CA: Sage, 1979).

56. John Harris and Paul Jesilow, "It's Not the Old Ball Game: Three Strikes and the Courtroom Workgroup," *Justice Quarterly* 17 (2000): 185–204.

57. Ibid.

58. Laurence H. Ross and James Foley, "Judicial Disobedience of the Mandate to Imprison Drunk Drivers," *Law and Society Review* 21 (1987): 315–323.

59. Paula Ditton and Doris Wilson, *Truth in Sentencing in State Prisons* (Washington, DC: Bureau of Justice Statistics, 1999).

PART **four**

FROM PENOLOGY TO CORRECTIONS AND BACK

outline

CHAPTER 11

History of Control

objectives

After reading this chapter, the student should be able to:

1. Describe why societies use control.
2. Compare and contrast ancient and modern methods of social control.
3. Discuss the early use of corporal punishment and the various methods used.
4. Discuss the early use of economic punishment and the various methods used.
5. Describe the means of control in colonial America.
6. Discuss the eras in the development of the penitentiary.
7. Compare and contrast the Pennsylvania and Auburn prison systems.
8. Describe the contributions of Alexander Maconochie, Sir Walter Crofton, and Zebulon Brockway.
9. Describe the history of capital punishment.
10. Discuss the arguments for and against capital punishment.

THROUGHOUT HISTORY, SOCIETIES HAVE EMPLOYED A VARIETY of means to encourage their members to adopt the socially approved standards of behavior. Sociologists and anthropologists have revealed how societies construct folkways, norms, rules, and laws. The violations of these forms of social control bring reactions from mild rebukes to extreme violence as groups struggle to make members conform. This chapter presents a brief review of the history of social control with a special emphasis on the types of behavior that are now under the purview of the criminal justice system.

This is an interesting history, not only of the wide variety of methods of control (many of them brutal by today's standards) that have been used over the centuries, but also of how some of the ancient ways of controlling deviant behavior are still used in some form today.[1] To say that the history of social control illustrates progress in changing or correcting criminal behavior would be inaccurate. At most, we can say that although science and technology have introduced new methods of punishing or correcting criminal behavior, widespread dissatisfaction exists about the humaneness of

current procedures, as well as scant evidence that they are any more or less effective than those used in earlier times.[2]

This chapter is divided into three sections. The first section covers how criminal behavior was managed before the advent of the prison. Here, the particular concern is with how society aimed to punish the offender by attacking the physical body of those who committed crimes. Flogging, branding, mutilation, and other means were used to show everyone that criminal behavior had dire consequences. The second section pertains to the history of the prison, particularly as it developed in the United States. Finally, the controversial issue of capital punishment is put into historical context, and its present day complexities are discussed. Specifically, we look at the arguments put forth by those who oppose capital punishment as well as those who defend it.

Before There Were Prisons

As we learned in our discussion of the history of the court, ancient societies did not have a well-defined criminal justice system that dealt with those who violated the law. In fact, society did not adopt the idea of a codified law until relatively recently. However, precursors of the criminal justice system developed in a patchwork fashion over time.[3]

In societies that existed before 700 C.E., justice was a private matter.[4] No criminal justice system existed to enforce societal rules, so it was up to the family, tribe, or group to enforce internal norms and to protect members from outside aggression. The blood feud, discussed in the chapters on the courts, was how justice was enforced. Retaliation for real or imagined crimes allowed aggrieved parties to settle scores with those who had offended them. Of course, the blood feud often resulted in a cycle of violence in which groups fought for years trying to balance the scales of justice. To limit the violence, societies began mandating that perpetrators compensate their victims with some type of payment.[5]

Corporal Punishment

One of the primary ways that individuals or societies extract revenge from the offender is through the use of corporal punishment. Corporal punishment entails inflicting physical harm on the body. Pain is a sensation that everyone understands, and the idea behind corporal punishment is to inflict a carefully measured amount of pain considered to be proportional to the offense.[6] Despite the fact that individuals have varying tolerances to pain, using the body as a tool of the state to inflict pain, humiliation, and suffering on an offender has had wide acceptance throughout history. The infliction of pain can be traced to the earliest of societies.[7]

TORTURE. Torture, the infliction of severe or prolonged pain, is a method of coercion, revenge and punishment used by many societies. Torture may be used by the state as a form of punishment for criminal activity. Because torture is considered inhumane by many modern societies, officials often deny that torture is used or that a certain punishment constitutes torture. However, even though some of the more gruesome forms of torture such as disembowelment or impaling are no longer used, other methods, such as long periods of solitary confinement, are common.[8] Numerous examples exist of the cruelty inflicted on individuals at the behest of the state. One of the better known and explicit depictions of torture as an act of justice is provided by Michel Foucault in *Discipline and Punish: The Birth of the Prison*. As punishment for attempting to assassinate King Louis XV in 1757, Robert-François Damiens was sentenced to be drawn and quartered. Foucault quoted the newspaper of the day thusly:

> *The flesh will be torn from his breasts, arms, thighs and calves with red-hot pincers, his right hand, holding the knife with which he committed said [homicide], burnt*

Drawing-and-quartering is an ancient form of punishment. In this 17th-century drawing, a swordsman stands ready to hack at the offender's joints to help the horses rip off his limbs.
Courtesy of CORBIS-NY.

with sulphur, and, on those places where the flesh will be torn away, poured molten lead, boiling oil, burning resin, wax and sulphur melted together and then his body drawn and quartered by four horses and his limbs and body consumed by fire, reduced to ashes and his ashes thrown to the winds.[9]

Drawing and quartering entails tying the arms and legs of the victim to four horses, which are then sent in different directions. Unfortunately for Damiens, four horses were not enough to accomplish this task, and two more horses were employed. Ultimately, his limbs were hacked apart to aid the straining horses. He remained conscious throughout this ordeal.

FLOGGING. Flogging (or whipping) is an age-old punishment. According to the Old Testament book of Deuteronomy, "If the wicked man be worthy to be beaten, that the judge shall cause him to lie down, and to be beaten before his face, according to his fault, by a certain number. Forty stripes he may give him. . . ."[10] The whips used had three separate thongs of leather, and each thong was of a different length. In effect, then, the 40 lashes actually numbered three times that. Often, the result was death.[11]

Flogging was used throughout history by the Egyptians and Romans, as well as in England, France, Germany, China, and the United States. In the slave-holding South prior to the Civil War, the whipping of slaves was a consistent form of punishment and control. The slave owner had considerable latitude in deciding how much a slave could be punished. However, the severity of the beatings was limited because a dead or disabled slave was not as valuable. Therefore, the slave owner sought methods of punishment that did not affect the slave's value:

Where any spark of leniency showed itself the motive behind it was not humanity for the sufferer, but the fear that the market value of the slave might be lowered if signs of punishment were too obvious. For the slave-owner could not have it both ways: he could not indulge his sadistic pleasures and get the top market price for the maimed or crippled slave.[12]

With flogging, the amount of pain could be precisely meted out with the number of lashes. Tied to a post or a tree, the victim would often scream in pain each time the whip struck flesh; thus, whippings were used to intimidate others who might be tempted to break the rules.

Flogging was a public form of punishment. Often, people came to witness the spectacle for entertainment.
Courtesy of CORBIS-NY.

BRANDING. In some societies, branding was used to show the community that criminals had been harshly and permanently punished. Branding identified offenders and prevented the offender from blending into the community. In colonial America, repeat offenders were branded on the forehead.[13] Females, in lieu of physical branding, were required to wear identification on their clothing that signaled their transgressions. The most visible example comes to us through literature in Nathaniel Hawthorne's novel *The Scarlet Letter,* in which Hester Prynne wears the letter *A* embroidered on her dress to announce to the community that she committed adultery.

Physical branding is a particularly extreme measure because it is a permanent stigma that forever labels the individual as an offender.[14] Today, we can see vestiges of the branding practice in prison tattoos that are proudly worn by offenders to show various aspects of their prison history. Additionally, some jurisdictions attempt to socially brand certain types of offenders (such as those accused of sexual crimes) by requiring them to have bumper stickers on their cars so police and parents can identify them when they are near schoolyards.[15]

MUTILATION. Many societies used mutilation as a form of punishment. At times, it reflected the concept of proportionality in terms of the biblical dictate of "an eye for an eye." Those who blasphemed might have their tongues cut out. Those who stole might have their hands cut off.[16] Similarly, castration was used in many societies to punish those who committed sexual crimes. According to George Ryley Scott:

> *The torture associated with castration is of two kinds. In the first place, there is the intense agony and great danger to life which are inseparable from the operation performed in the crude manner customary among savage and primitive tribes (often in-*

NEWS FLASH

Spare the Rod, Spoil the Child, Save the Inmate

Corporal punishment, one of the oldest forms of controlling criminal offenders, fell out of favor in U.S. judicial sentencing well before the 20th century. No longer are the stocks, branding, or flogging used to punish offenders. Any type of corporal punishment used on modern offenders is informal and will not be ordered by a judge, but administered suddenly by police or correctional officers. The infamous beating of Rodney King by Los Angeles police officers was captured on videotape in 1991, and as recently as 1995 the Supreme Court heard a case brought by an inmate left tied to a hitching post (see Case in Point: *Hope v. Pelzer*).

Corporal punishment is still administered, but in an unpredictable fashion that is largely frowned on by higher courts and much of society. The only population segment for which corporal punishment is generally considered to be desirable is that of children. Although punishments as extreme as observed in the Rodney-King and *Hope v. Pelzer* case are considered abuse, striking a child who has offended in some manner is not. Not only may parents strike children, but strangers may do so as well. School paddling is legal in at least 22 states. The reasons for paddling a child can vary by school and by teacher. In 2001 Jonathan Curtis, a first-grader in Alabama, was paddled twice for picking his nose. His mother agreed that paddling was fine, as long as she was notified beforehand. The next day, Jonathan picked his nose again and was paddled so severely that it left bruises. His mother filed a police report.

Since the 19th century, children have qualified for punishments not sentenced by U.S. courts, punishments that are illegal to use on adults (law-abiding or otherwise). Moreover, children are not subject to any of the legal protections guaranteed by the Bill of Rights. Children do not even get a Miranda warning before a teacher or school administrator may administer as many smacks as they wish with a wooden paddle. What separates unruly children from adult criminal offenders?

One factor could be that corporal punishment is not considered as seriously detrimental to a child as, say, prison. (Indeed, the return of corporal punishment for adults has been discussed as an alternative sentence to prison.) It does not impinge on the child offender's freedom, yet "teaches them a lesson." No one is going to send a child to jail for picking his nose, but the pain and humiliation brought by paddling is considered by many to be a great motivator. It is also immediate. Study halls, time-outs, and after-school sentences require time and attention. Paddling requires only a few minutes. Public attitudes toward corporal punishment suggest that prison inmates and arrestees will continue to successfully bring lawsuits against the authorities who inflict physical harm on them, while many schoolchildren will remain at the mercy of administrators who believe that corporal punishment keeps the peace.

QUESTIONS

1. Is it ethical to spank children and not adults? If so, why?
2. Should the justice system consider a return to corporal punishment for offenders, such as flogging, in lieu of jail or prison?

Source: Anne Cassidy, "Is Your Child at Risk?—The Scandal of Paddling in School," *Family Circle*, November 1, 2002, http://www.nospank.net/cassidy.htm.

> *volving complete ablation of the exterior genitals), where aseptic surgery is unknown and anesthetics are not employed. In the second place there is the psychological torture which cannot ever be effaced in the case of any man who is castrated against his will; so that where he succeeds in overcoming the physical dangers and suffering, he continues to suffer mentally as long as his life lasts.*[17]

Mutilation existed in the penal code of every European country and was transported to the American colonies. It is difficult to find modern remnants of mutilation, although some might contend that the suggestions that sex offenders be chemically castrated might be related.

HUMILIATION. A number of societies used public humiliation and shaming techniques to punish a variety of crimes. In colonial America, offenders were placed in stocks in the public square where they were subject to the verbal and physical ridicule of the public. On some occasions, they would be stoned while locked in these restraining devices. Some stocks required the offender to stand and support his own weight for long hours in the hot sun.[18] Humiliation techniques served a dual purpose. They exacted a degree of unpleasant punishment on the offender while serving to reinforce community norms. Those who witnessed the humiliation of the offender were presumably less likely to engage in deviant behaviors themselves. Today, although we no longer employ stocks, a number of shaming and humiliation initiatives are employed by the criminal justice system.[19] Offenders have been made to wear signs announcing their crimes, and some are required to address community groups. Others are made to do work that allows the rest of society to see them, such as picking up trash on the highways. In some jurisdictions, the names and/or pictures of drunk drivers or sex offenders are published in local newspapers or on the Internet.

SHOCK DEATH. Before the invention of the prison, societies had difficulty developing punishments that were not too severe but that got the attention of the offender. Short of actually executing a person, the amount of fear that can be instilled in an offender is difficult to measure and inflict. One ingenious colonial era method of impressing an offender with the seriousness of the offense was termed "shock death."

> *In the case of shock death, an offender would receive the sentence of death by hanging but would later be granted a reprieve. The reprieve, however, came only after the offender had proceeded through each and every ritual leading up to the execution. To elaborate, the offender would be led from the jail out to the gallows, with the mask placed over his head and the noose placed around his neck, and the wait for the trap door to open, ending his life. The sentenced offender could remain at the gallows for more than three hours, fully expecting to be executed. Finally, the noose and mask were removed and the offender was informed that his life had been spared.*[20]

Such an ordeal would likely impress upon the offender the ramifications of a life of crime. Such an extravagant charade is akin to psychological torture. It is easy to draw parallels from this account to how capital punishment is presently practiced with its multiple opportunities for appeals and stays of execution.

Economic Punishment

Although punishments on the offender's body were common before the use of prisons, a number of other dispositions featured extracting labor from the offender's body rather than pain.[21] In economic hard times, the employment of convict labor was a favorite mechanism for punishment and getting the work of society done.

THE GALLEY. Prior to the development of sophisticated sailing techniques, ships were powered by human labor. The Greeks and others used slaves or those who were captured during warfare. The French, Spanish, and Italians staffed their naval fleets with prisoners who were shackled to their oars and made to row large vessels long distances. This punishment was used primarily for those sentenced to death; however, in times of scarce labor, individuals convicted of lesser crimes would be sent to the galley ships for a specified period of years. Galley service was extremely strenuous and dangerous and was feared almost as much as execution. Many individuals died as a result of the unsanitary conditions and extreme physical exertion required.[22]

WORKHOUSES. Throughout history, prisons have had a close relationship with the economic conditions of the times.[23] When labor is abundant, the prisons are full; when labor is scarce, either fewer individuals are incarcerated or the authorities find ways to exploit the offenders. With the waning influence of feudalism in the 16th century, many people left the large estates of the wealthy landowners and migrated to the cities. This resulted in a large population of unemployed and restless individuals who threatened the cities' stability and peace. Thieves, prostitutes, and other "riffraff" needed to be brought under control, so in London, Parliament established Bridewell, a place where the poor were put to work and supposedly learned good work habits. Workhouses for the poor easily became jails for petty criminals who were a societal nuisance. Gradually, the idea of locking up the rabble led to a proliferation of jails. Because they had no organizing principles, the jails were operated in the cheapest and most squalid manner imaginable.[24]

John Howard, elected to the post of high sheriff in Bedfordshire, England, in 1773, was appalled by the local jail's inhumane conditions. He toured other jails in both England and on the European continent and discovered English jails to be inferior in terms of living conditions and the way the jailers treated the inmates. Based on his observations, Howard published *The State of Prisons in England and Wales* in 1777. Howard lobbied the House of Commons and was successful in getting Parliament to pass the Penitentiary Act of 1779, a major piece of reform legislation. This act addressed the living conditions of inmates, the need to make productive use of their labor, and humane treatment. In practice the law failed to provide many of the desired reforms, but it did subtly change the nature and status of incarceration, removing it from the purview of local authorities and establishing the idea that the federal government has a responsibility to oversee conditions.[25]

Transportation to the Fatal Shore

Australia in the early 1800s was a scary place to be sent. The British knew very little about the land when they began to transport criminals there, and many perished on the voyage or as a result of the primitive living conditions. It was a rough life for both inmates and prison officials, so much so that it was dubbed the "fatal shore." In a book by that name, Robert Hughes explained why transportation was so popular and what led to its decline:

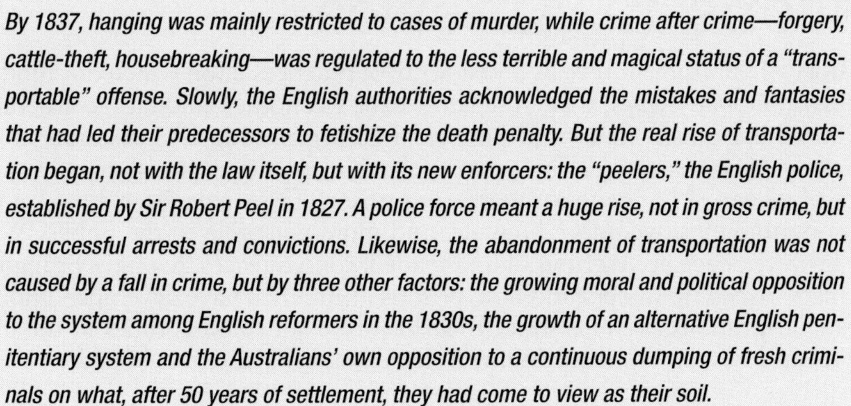

> ***By 1837, hanging was mainly restricted to cases of murder, while crime after crime—forgery, cattle-theft, housebreaking—was regulated to the less terrible and magical status of a "transportable" offense. Slowly, the English authorities acknowledged the mistakes and fantasies that had led their predecessors to fetishize the death penalty. But the real rise of transportation began, not with the law itself, but with its new enforcers: the "peelers," the English police, established by Sir Robert Peel in 1827. A police force meant a huge rise, not in gross crime, but in successful arrests and convictions. Likewise, the abandonment of transportation was not caused by a fall in crime, but by three other factors: the growing moral and political opposition to the system among English reformers in the 1830s, the growth of an alternative English penitentiary system and the Australians' own opposition to a continuous dumping of fresh criminals on what, after 50 years of settlement, they had come to view as their soil.***

QUESTIONS

1. Have other criminal justice policies been changed because of public opposition?
2. Can you think of other instances in which the police are so effective that they have a major impact on the rest of the criminal justice system?
3. Why were English prisoners not sent to the United States at this time?

Source: Robert Hughes, *The Fatal Shore: A History of the Transportation of Convicts to Australia 1787–1868* (London: Pan Books, 1988), 160.

EXILE AND TRANSPORTATION. Transportation of offenders into exile in far-flung colonies served two primary purposes. First, it rid the mother country of a good number of "ne'er-do-wells," vagabonds, and petty criminals. Second, the colonies had a significant demand for the labor of the surplus population of the mother country. European countries such as England, France, and Spain transported offenders to the colonies in the New World and Australia to serve prison sentences or to work as indentured servants.

One interesting aspect of transportation is that it was done by private contractors. The contracts of the indentured servants were sold to these private contractors, who took the responsibility and risk of transporting the offenders to the colonies where they sold the contracts to free colonists. The servants had little way of knowing what lay ahead of them. The attitudes of their owners varied widely, and some would take advantage of illiterate individuals and keep them in servitude long after their original terms had expired.[26] The American Revolution in 1776 put an end to the practice of England sending offenders to the American colonies. Instead, the English housed their prisoners in large old ships, called hulks, that were anchored in harbors. Additionally, Australia became the preferred destination for criminals. Between 1787 and 1875, over 135,000 felons were sent there.[27]

Offenders were transported to the American colonies and Australia at a high cost to their lives and health. The voyages were rigorous enough for the crew, but the offenders were locked below decks in crowded and squalid conditions. By the time they arrived at their destination, many were dead or dying. It was a difficult way to start a term of punishment, not to mention a new life. Instead of rotting in a decrepit jail cell or on one of the stinking hulks, those who survived the trip were lent out as labor to free settlers where they worked hard but had a chance for better living conditions. Those who did not get to work with free settlers were imprisoned in oppressive penal colonies such as Norfolk Island in the South Pacific.

We usually consider transportation an English idea, but other countries practiced banishment and transportation as well. Russia and the Soviet Union sent offenders to Siberia well into the 20th century.[28]

Prisons in America

The history of punishment reveals a vast array of practices upon which our modern prisons have drawn. In many ways, we can see how exile to another land has been replaced by social exile behind prison walls, and how modern prison industry programs have replaced workhouses. However, the real issues of the changing nature of punishments revolve around the idea of reform.[29] For better or worse, our prison efforts have been aimed at making the institution more effective, more humane, and more palatable to the public. What has resulted, however, have been serious, if unintended, consequences that have brought their own problematic issues. To understand how prisons in America have developed into today's bureaucratic institutions, we must trace their history from colonial times to the present with an eye toward how well-intended reforms have not worked out as hoped.

Control in the Colonies

The American colonies were faced with many of the same issues of social control as England was, but some major differences between the two led to the unique development of American incarceration. Early penal institutions were under local control and mixed a variety of types of offenders: The accused would be held with the convicted, civil violators with criminals, and so on.

The idea of incarceration as the sole punishment for convicted offenders took some time to develop. Corporal punishment, especially the stocks, or whipping were used in conjunction with jail to discourage crime. The Quakers in Pennsylvania suggested that

FOCUS ON ETHICS

Transportation in a Contemporary World

Since the fall of the Soviet Union and the closing of the remote Siberian gulags where political prisoners were sent, transportation has not been a visible feature of corrections. What if the criminal justice system were to bring it back? A host of questions would arise for which answers are difficult to formulate without considering the profound moral, legal, and political issues. How would you address the following questions?

- *Where would prisoners be sent today?*
- *Is it fair to dump our prisoners on another country?*
- *If you were an offender and told that you were to be transported and given a choice of destination, where would you most like to go? Where would you least like to go?*
- *What would be the purpose of transportation? Exile? Punishment? Deterrence? Retribution?*

Here are some recent examples of policies related to the practice of transportation:

- *U.S. judges used to routinely give young male offenders the option of going to jail or joining the military. Especially in times of war, these arrangements were seen as a way for a minor criminal to cleanse his record and get a fresh start in life. Should this practice continue? Are violent criminals the ones we want as soldiers?*
- *In the late 1970s Fidel Castro emptied the jails and mental institutions of Cuba and allowed these inmates to go to the United States in what is called the Mariel Boat Lift. Hundreds of Cubans were incarcerated in U.S. federal prisons even though they had not committed crimes on U.S. soil. What eventually happened to these inmates? Should they have been incarcerated in the first place?*
- *After the United States invaded Afghanistan, hundreds of Al-Qaeda and Taliban fighters were transported to the U.S. Naval Base in Guantanamo Bay, Cuba, and held indefinitely. Why were these prisoners not taken to the continental United States? What should have been done with them? Are they criminals or prisoners of war? What legal systems should they be held accountable to?*

Transportation today is not a viable correctional practice because of these many questions. Perhaps if we needed colonists to work on distant planets or solar systems, we might try to revive this practice. Until then, it appears that incarceration will be our primary response to the criminal offender.

incarceration and hard labor were preferable to corporal punishment. The state's penal code of 1786 allowed inmates to work on public projects while chained to cannonballs and dressed in brightly colored clothing. Because many objected to this public spectacle, the hard labor was moved behind the walls of the institution.

The Walnut Street Jail, in existence since 1776, demonstrated all the shortcomings of the early jails, such as housing men and women together and the guards selling alcohol to inmates. Used as a military prison in the Revolutionary War, it was converted in 1792 into the nation's first penitentiary in which the most hardened criminals were kept in single cells. The Walnut Street Jail did not completely accomplish its goals of solitude and hard labor, but it did set the tone for the more formal prisons that would be built in the next century.[30]

The Walnut Street Jail looms in the distance as a little church is drawn past it by a team of horses.

Courtesy of The Granger Collection, New York.

The first institution to resemble a modern penitentiary was Castle Island in Massachusetts' Boston Harbor. Established by the Massachusetts legislature in 1785, it housed only convicted offenders from the state's various jails.[31] From 1785 to 1798, about 280 prisoners served time on Castle Island, with at least 45 escaping.

The theory and practice of prisons started in the United States with the Walnut Street Jail and Castle Island, but they were only the beginning. The 19th century would bring a new era of true prisons, which would be tried and found wanting.[32]

Development of the Penitentiary: 1780–1860

Two prison systems emerged in the United States during the first half of the 19th century that attracted prison reformers across the nation and around the world. These systems, called the Pennsylvania System and the Auburn (New York) System (the names are based on their initial locations), emphasized regimens of silence and penitence.

separate-and-silent system
A method of penal control pioneered by Philadelphia's Eastern State Penitentiary in which inmates were kept from seeing or talking to one another. This method is comparable to solitary confinement in modern prisons.

PENNSYLVANIA SYSTEM. In 1829 the state of Pennsylvania opened a prison on the site of a cherry orchard outside Philadelphia. For years, the Eastern State Penitentiary, called Cherry Hill by the locals, was characterized by the **separate-and-silent system,** by which it was reasoned that inmates would reflect on their crimes and reform. By keeping the inmates from seeing and talking to each other, the state hoped they would not contaminate each other with antisocial thoughts and behavior. Kept in solitary confinement, many inmates developed severe mental problems because of the oppressive boredom and lack of human contact. The inmates developed clever means of communicating (such as tapping codes on the water pipes in the cells), but for the most part, they were kept as separate as possible by the prison's limited resources.[33] However, as the prison became more crowded, double-celling became the norm and isolation was impossible. The separate-and-silent system was very costly and soon met its demise, not only because of economics, but also because critics thought keeping anyone in isolation for so long was inhumane.

AUBURN SYSTEM. The Auburn Prison, opened in 1817 in New York, at first tried the separate-and-silent system. By 1823 it became apparent that this system caused more problems than it solved and that the mental and physical issues faced by inmates were

An interior hallway view at the Eastern State Penitentiary, built in 1822.
Courtesy of CORBIS-NY.

This 19th-century engraving depicts a silent-system workshop at London's Millbank Prison.
Courtesy of CORBIS-NY.

more than the administration thought reasonable. Therefore, although inmates were locked in separate cells each night, they were allowed to eat and work together during the day. They were forbidden to talk to each other, however. This **congregate-and-silent system** required prisoners to march in lockstep and keep their eyes downcast, and prohibited face-to-face contact.[34]

congregate-and-silent system
A style of control pioneered by the Auburn System, in which inmates were allowed to eat and work together during the day, but forbidden to speak, and locked alone in their cells at night.

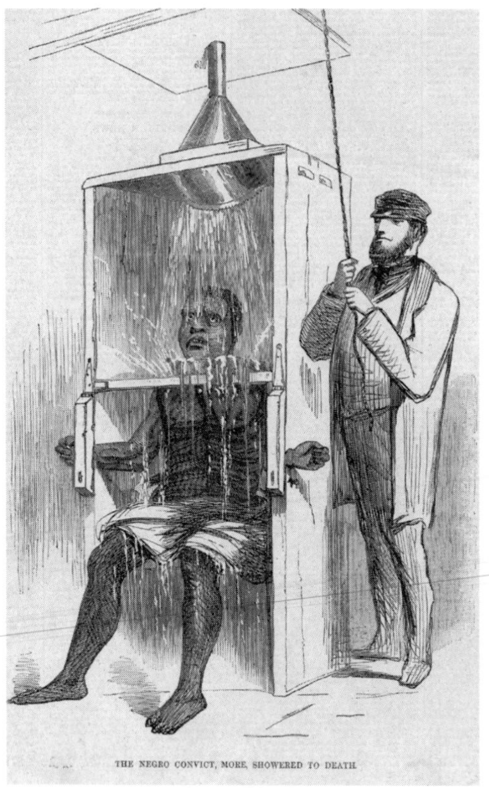
THE NEGRO CONVICT, MORE, SHOWERED TO DEATH

Punishment by the shower-bath circa the mid-19th century at New York's Auburn Prison.
Courtesy of CORBIS-NY.

Considerable debate surrounded these two prison systems. On one hand, the Pennsylvania System was touted by its supporters as superior because it was easier to control prisoners, was more conducive to meditation and repentance, and avoided the cross-contamination inherent when inmates are together. By using such extreme procedures as having inmates wear hoods when outside their cells, the Eastern State Penitentiary administration believed it was facilitating the inmates' self-reflection and eventual reform.

In contrast, proponents of the Auburn model argued that their methods and techniques of incarceration were superior because they were a great deal cheaper, could provide better vocational training, and were less harmful to the inmates' mental health. Additionally, the Auburn model used a factory-oriented labor system as opposed to the craft-oriented labor system of the Eastern State Penitentiary. Although neither of these systems was totally copied in other jurisdictions, they did serve as models for other prisons. Reformers continued to adopt aspects of the Pennsylvania and Auburn models and introduced modifications that addressed changing political, economic, and social conditions.[35]

Age of Reform: 1860–1900

As innovative and well meaning as these prison experiments were, they had their critics. Although the ideals of solitude, hard work, discipline, and reflection were attractive theoretically, in practice they produced a prison atmosphere that not only was harmful to the inmate, but also created a public relations issue. English novelist Charles Dickens, who toured the Pennsylvania prisons, wrote this:

> *In its intention, I am well convinced that it is kind, humane, and meant for reformation; but I am persuaded that those who devised this system of Prison Discipline, and those benevolent gentlemen who carry it into execution, do not know what it is that they are doing. I believe that very few men are capable of estimating the immense amount of torture and agony which this dreadful punishment, prolonged for years, inflicts upon the sufferers; and in guessing at it myself, and in reasoning from what I have seen written upon their faces, and what to my certain knowledge they feel within, I am only the more convinced that there is a terrible endurance in it*

CASE IN POINT

Hope v. Pelzer

The Case

Hope v. Pelzer, 000 U.S. 01-309 (2002)

The Point

This case helped set guidelines for what constitutes cruel and unusual punishment in prison and the circumstances under which prison officials are liable.

In 1995 Alabama inmate Larry Hope was handcuffed to a hitching post after fighting with a guard at a work site. Hope, who was ordered to remove his shirt, spent seven hours in the sun chained to the post. The guards gave him a couple of water breaks and no bathroom breaks. According to Hope, the guard gave water to some dogs, then kicked over the water cooler in sight of Hope, who watched the water spill onto the ground.

Hope filed suit against three guards.

The magistrate judge did not rule on the possibility of the Eighth Amendment violation, but ruled that the guards were immune to the suit because they were unaware of any constitutional violations. The Eleventh Circuit affirmed this judgment, but did find that the hitching post violated the Eighth Amendment.

In reversing the decision, the Supreme Court agreed with the judgment about the Eighth Amendment violation, but disagreed that the guards were not liable. Justice John Paul Stevens wrote, "A reasonable officer would have known that using a hitching post as Hope alleged was unlawful." This part of the decision allowed Hope to file suit against the guards.

which none but the sufferers can fathom, and which no man has a right to inflict upon his fellow creature.[36]

At the same time that the penitentiary was developed in the United States and copied by other nations, the practices of other nations affected U.S. corrections. While critics such as Dickens complained about the Pennsylvania and Auburn systems in the United States, European countries were experimenting with techniques designed not just to punish, but to make the inmate more likely to successfully return to free society after serving the prison sentence. This new emphasis on social reintegration was termed the *Irish System,* and, while eventually tried in the post–Civil War United States, was actually used for decades abroad. Here, we will focus on the three most well-known examples of the Irish System of reform, those developed by Alexander Maconochie, Sir Walter Crofton, and Zebulon Brockway.

ALEXANDER MACONOCHIE. Alexander Maconochie was a Scot who developed a system designed to make the inmate trustworthy, honest, and useful to society. A retired naval officer, he became superintendent of the penal colony at Van Diemen's Land (what is now called Tasmania). Here, Maconochie set about an experiment that sought to humanize prison life, but he was relieved of his duties before it could be fully implemented. In 1840 he was placed in command of another penal colony, this one on Norfolk Island off the eastern coast of Australia. Here, he imposed a system based on two fundamental beliefs:

1. Brutality and cruelty debase not only the subject, but also the society that deliberately uses or tolerates them for purposes of social control.
2. The treatment of a wrongdoer during his sentence of imprisonment should be designed to make him fit to be released into society again, purged of the tendencies that led him to his offense, and strengthened in his ability to withstand temptation again.[37]

marks-of-commendation system
An incarceration philosophy developed by Alexander Maconochie in which inmates earned the right to be released, as well as privileges, goods, and services.

Central to Maconochie's philosophy of incarceration was the indeterminate sentence, in which the offender would be released when the prison officials believed he was reformed. (As we will come to see later in the 20th century, the indeterminate sentence can work in the offender's favor or work to keep him or her imprisoned for an even longer time than a fixed term.) A **marks-of-commendation system** was instituted in which inmates earned the right to be released. Additionally, privileges, goods, and services could be purchased with marks given for good behavior. The marks system enabled inmates to progress through various stages of social control and was envisioned to give inmates a certain control over the pains of incarceration. Although many of the ideas Maconochie incorporated into the Norfolk Island system had been suggested by others, including John Howard and Jeremy Bentham, it was Maconochie's rational and systematic implementation that earned high praise from prison experts. However, the system set up on Norfolk Island was short-lived. Maconochie was recalled to England in 1844 and with him went the more humane treatment of inmates on Norfolk Island.

SIR WALTER CROFTON. In 1854, a decade after Maconochie left Norfolk Island, his progressive ways of treating inmates made an impact on Sir Walter Crofton, who was appointed director of the Irish prison system. Crofton liked both the marks system and the progressive stages of social control that Maconochie had developed. He added the concept of a completely open institution in which the inmates could gain experience in trust and avoiding temptation. Crofton is best remembered for instituting an early-release system called *ticket-of-leave,* in which inmates were given a conditional release and supervised by local police. If the inmates violated the conditions of their release, they were returned to prison.[38] (This idea will be more fully discussed in Chapter 13.)

ZEBULON BROCKWAY. The ideas developed by Maconochie and Crofton were instituted by Zebulon Brockway at the reformatory in Elmira, New York. Brockway used the 500-bed facility to house young men between the ages of 16 and 30 who were first-time offenders. A three-grade program was used in which inmates entered at the second grade. An inmate was promoted to the first grade after six months of good behavior or demoted to the third grade if he failed to conform. Only those who were in the first grade were eligible for release (they were sentenced to an indeterminate term with only the minimum amount of time being fixed). An inmate needed a year of good marks before being eligible for parole. The Elmira Reformatory used volunteers, who can be thought of as forerunners of parole officers, to keep track of the released inmates. The important distinction between this accommodation and the Irish ticket-of-leave system is that the parolees were not supervised by police officers. This separation of law enforcement and correctional activities is an enduring feature of this early program.[39]

The reform movement had its drawbacks as well as successes. Penal reform did not progress in an uninterrupted manner from brutality to humane treatment because even the reformers, such as Zebulon Brockway, had some unattractive ideas. Brockway was known as a shameless self-promoter and often hid the less desirable conditions of the reform movement. The use of corporal punishment was such a stable feature of the Elmira Reformatory that Brockway was nicknamed "Paddler Brockway." In addition, the integrity of the classification system was difficult to maintain. Designed for young first offenders, the reformatories often housed seasoned criminals, and issues of violence, revolts, rape, smuggling, and arson often arose.[40]

For those who presented significant discipline problems, a form of solitary confinement was used. Brockway called this the "rest cure," but it included being shackled and fed nothing more than bread and water for months at a time. These problems eventually led to the demise of the reform movement, but the idea of reform has become a recurring theme in corrections. Many of the ideals of the reform movement are at the foundation of modern prison systems. The repeated imperfect implementation of these reforms speaks not to the inadequacy of the reforms, but more to the economic, social, and political contexts that invariably frustrate the ideals of prison reformers.

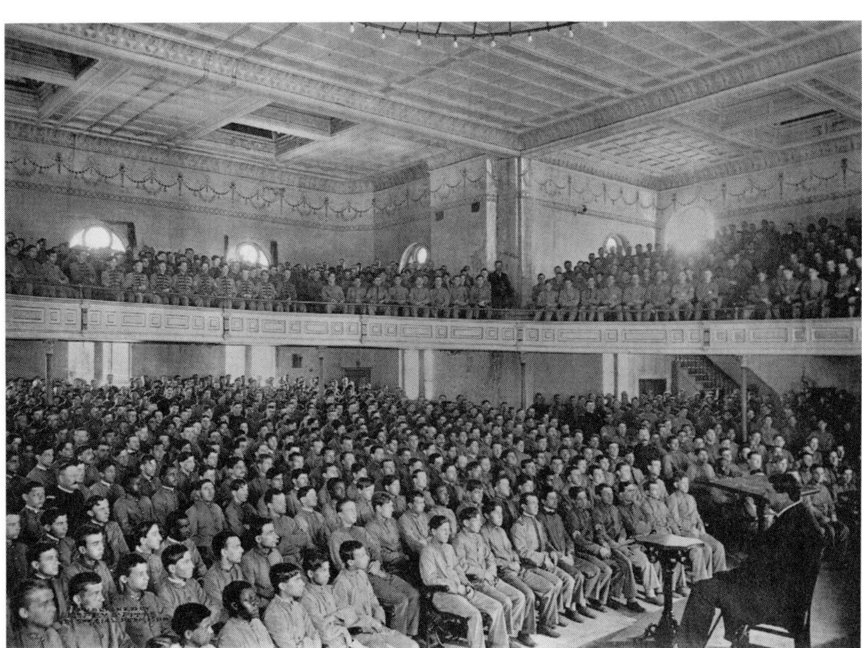

Inmates at the Elmira Reformatory during the early 1900s.

Courtesy of CORBIS-NY.

Prison Labor and Public Works: 1900–1930

The idea that work is healthy for both the inmate and society is as old as the prison. The Pennsylvania System, which viewed too much labor as interfering with rehabilitative meditation, did include a certain amount of craft work to be done by inmates in their cells. Other prison systems considered work to be wholly useful. Of particular interest is the degree to which work was viewed as a good thing in itself and when it was viewed as a means to other ends. Work was deemed beneficial in at least three ways:

1. **Work is a good way to keep inmates occupied.** By doing work (sometimes back-breaking work), the inmates have neither the time nor the energy to cause trouble.
2. **Work has a rehabilitative value.** Because most prisoners will eventually return to society, they benefit from the activities of work. They practice good work habits and sometimes learn useful skills.
3. **Inmates can offset the cost of their incarceration by work.** Inmate labor has been used to construct and maintain prisons, feed inmates, and at times make products that can be sold to other government agencies or even the outside society.

Many states currently have restrictive legislation that prevents prison labor systems from competing with businesses.[41] The advantage of free (or extremely cheap) labor gives prison labor systems an almost unbeatable competitive advantage. Therefore, many prison labor systems are restricted to making products to be used exclusively by the state government. For instance, in Georgia prisoners make office furniture that can be purchased by other state agencies. Some rural prisons grow vegetables or raise cattle that are used to feed inmates.

These examples only partially reflect the variety of ways prison labor is used. To fully appreciate the range of ways prison labor is used to produce wealth, we must consider whether the inmates are controlled and disciplined by public or private officials, who controls the sale of the products, and the size of the market. (See Reference: Prison Labor Systems.)

The distinctions among these prison labor systems may be subtle at times, but they hold important ramifications for the inmates in terms of how they are treated and fed, and what kinds of skills they may develop. The oldest of these systems are the public works systems in which inmates work on projects owned by the state. Today, the most visible examples of public works projects are the road crews that clean and maintain the

NEWS FLASH

Federal Prison Industries

Prison labor has come a long way since the days of chain gangs and license plate stamping. Although these forms of labor still exist, they have been joined by prison shops that produce clothing and textiles, office furniture, and electronics. Federal Prison Industries, or Unicor, is a government agency that trains and employs inmates to produce goods for sale to the federal government. In prisons around the country, inmates who are paid as little as 23 cents an hour produce bed linens, towels, office chairs and workstations, and filing cabinets. Unicor, established in 1934, has recently gone into the business of recycling old computer equipment and electronics.

Prison officials say this work is good for prisoners. They can earn money to buy small luxury items and pay any restitution they owe for their crimes. It also gives them something to do and makes their time pass more quickly, officials say. The inmates seem to agree. As of 2002 Unicor employed about 21,000 inmates, and there is a waiting list for jobs. The private sector takes a dim view of Unicor, however. Unicor's goods are sold at market prices, and federal agencies must first check with Unicor for products before shopping the open market. Private companies also say inmates take jobs from law-abiding workers and that it is difficult to compete with an industry that can pay its workers under a dollar an hour.

Unicor officials say their effect on private industry is negligible. Prison factories must factor in production hindrances that private industries do not. Tools and scrap materials must be tightly guarded and controlled, lest they become weapons. All outgoing vehicles must be searched, and lockdowns often halt work entirely. As a result, prison labor can't match the production of private labor. In 2000 private companies took on $456.3 million in orders that Unicor could not fill.

QUESTIONS

1. Is it ethical to pay prison inmates less than minimum wage to do factory work? What about accusations of "slave labor"?
2. Is the use of prison labor fair to workers in society who must compete with prison workers who are paid less?

Sources: Rob Kirkbride, "Prison Factory Competes against Larger Office-Furniture Makers," The Associated Press/*The Grand Rapids Press*, April 8, 2002, http://www.nj.com/newsflash/business/index.ssf?/cgi-free/getstory_ssf.cgi?g6775_BC_MI—Exchange-Inmate-M&&news&newsflash-financial. Unicor, http://www.unicor.gov/index.htm.

right-of-way on state or county roads. Some sheriffs even dress these inmates in old-style prison stripes so that they are identifiable by the public in case of escape and as a form of humiliation and shame.

The type of prison labor system that authorities choose is always subject to political and technological conditions. Decades ago in the southern states where counties rather than state governments controlled the prisons, the lease system was used extensively. Partly as a replacement for slave labor, this system allowed major landowners to employ inmates to do backbreaking work at wages that free people would not accept. Cotton in Georgia and turpentine in Florida are just two examples of crops on which prison labor was used.

Prison labor held a great appeal to both those who saw work as a form of treatment and those who saw work as a form of punishment. Today, with many prison systems experiencing overcrowding, prison labor is not used to the same degree as it was in the past. One of the by-products of overcrowding is the lack of staff to oversee the labor of prisoners. Keeping prisoners in their cells for most of the day where they cannot put other

REFERENCE

Prison Labor Systems

The use of labor in prison had many uses and stemmed from several theories of corrections. Some prison labor was deemed rehabilitative in that inmates learned work habits and kept busy; some labor was deemed punitive because the work was backbreaking; and some labor was exploitive because inmates worked hard for someone else's profit. Over the years, several labor systems were used. Here are the rudiments of six of them:

- Lease system. Some states leased inmates to private businesses as a way of offsetting the costs of crime. The inmates were worked, guarded, and cared for by the private businesses. This was a controversial system because the state no longer watched over the inmates, who were at the mercy of the private cooperation or individual who paid the lease. Inmates were leased to sugar cane plantations and turpentine camps in the South and to coal mines and railroads in other parts of the country.
- Contract system. Under the contract system, the state is responsible for feeding and guarding the prisoners, and a private company contracts for their labor. This system was accomplished in or very near the prison and had the advantage of being able to keep the machines going 24 hours as the inmates worked in shifts.
- Piece-price system. This is very similar to the contract system, but instead of paying for the labor of the inmates, the private contractor pays a set price for each piece of goods produced by the inmates. This way, the contractor pays for output rather than the number of hours worked.
- Public account system. Under the public account system, the state, rather than the private contractor, controls the sale of the products. Like the previous systems, the public account system received criticism because it competed with the work of private businesses that were required to pay the going rate for labor and were at a considerable disadvantage when competing with inmate labor.
- State use system. The goods produced by the state use system are restricted to use by state agencies. Perhaps the best example of the state use system is the manufacturing of automobile license plates. This is a business that is not found outside the prison, so there is no one to claim that the state has an unfair advantage. Some prisons grow food and raise cattle to feed inmates and other state workers, but do not sell their goods in the free marketplace.
- Public works and ways system. Much like the state use system, the public works and ways system's efforts are confined to the state and are not sold on the marketplace. With this system, inmates repair or construct public buildings, public roads, parks, and other public structures.

These various methods of employing prison labor have been subject to criticism from the outside over the centuries. However, in the hope of keeping the costs of incarceration reasonably low, states have used the labor of inmates in these various ways.

QUESTIONS

1. Which of these prison labor systems can make the most money for the state?
2. Which of these prison labor systems is most difficult for the inmates?
3. Which of these prison labor systems is most susceptible to official corruptions?
4. Can you identify any of these prison labor systems in prison movies such as *The Shawshank Redemption, Cool Hand Luke, Brubaker, Life,* or *Papillion?*

Today, some jurisdictions run high-profile inmate labor programs to prove that local law enforcement is tough on crime and that offenders are held accountable for their crimes.
Courtesy of CORBIS-NY.

inmates or staff members at risk is often easier than supervising them while they work. In many contemporary prisons, the only inmates doing any type of productive labor are those used to maintain the basic needs of the institution.

Age of Rehabilitation: 1930–1970

It can be argued that rehabilitating inmates has always been one of the goals of the criminal justice system, but it was not until around 1930 that U.S. prisons acknowledged that rehabilitation was a primary goal. Certainly as far back as Maconochie some advocated the prison's role in reforming individuals, but the responsibility of the state for changing inmates' behavior was not widely recognized. Around 1930 several influences started to coalesce that helped professionalize the field of corrections and allowed progressive reformers to advocate rehabilitation as a desirable and possible goal.[42]

A primary reason that rehabilitation became important at this time was the change in how science regarded illness. This, in turn, affected how criminologists and correctional practitioners thought about criminality. The germ theory of medicine that absolved the sick person of responsibility for contracting an illness spread to corrections. Crime was no longer simply a choice made by the offender. The idea that outside influences contribute to criminality led theorists and correctional administrators to speculate on how crime is transmitted among individuals. A medical metaphor in which criminals were viewed as "sick" developed, and rehabilitation efforts were dedicated to finding the causes of crime in the biological, psychological, and sociological deficiencies of the individual.[43] Once the cause could be diagnosed, it was a simple matter to prescribe a "cure" of drug or alcohol treatment, family or individual counseling, more education, or anger management classes. The medical model, therefore, likens crime to disease and postulates that normal (law-abiding) behavior is within reach of all offenders and that the correctional practitioner can find the optimal treatment.

Another influence that led to the era of rehabilitation was the 1931 report of the Wickersham Commission. The Wickersham Commission prescribed a wide range of criminal justice reforms, including suggestions that rehabilitation should be attempted in earnest. The commission documented the failures of prison labor systems and the idleness of inmates in most prisons in its quest to solve the penitentiary's systemic problems. The Wickersham Commission did not present particularly new information but the fact that it was a governmental fact-finding and policy-suggesting body gave its recommendations a legitimacy that previous reformers lacked.[44]

At the forefront of the prison rehabilitation movement was the Federal Bureau of Prisons, established in 1930. This agency eliminated political patronage in filling job vacancies, developed a better trained and more professional staff, and greatly improved the conditions of confinement.[45] Of particular interest to the rehabilitation movement were the new designs of prisons. Specifically, prisons were constructed with the goals of facilitating the classification and treatment of offenders. Bureau of Prison officials such as Sanford Bates, Austin MacCormick, and James V. Bennett were committed to treating offenders as individuals and keeping them occupied in productive activities, such as work and education.

Like many other prison reform movements, the rehabilitation movement in prisons was never fully accomplished. Although the theoretical foundations of treating offenders was further refined during this time, a number of features intervened to prevent it from fully taking hold in prison systems and transforming how offenders were handled. One of the first limitations of the rehabilitation movement was lack of resources. Keeping inmates confined and preventing them from hurting each other and the staff soaked up most of the time, money, and creative energies of prison officials and staff. Treatment programs were looked on as luxuries in prison systems struggling to maintain the most minimal custody standards in states that would rather spend their limited tax dollars on more popular concerns such as education, infrastructure, and health care. In most prisons, the percentage of inmates who received any significant treatment was minimal. One observer called rehabilitation efforts during this time "token treatment," designed more for public relations purposes than for producing any real change in the attitudes and behaviors of inmates.[46]

Another reason the rehabilitation era never fully developed into an effective method for changing the lives of criminals and reducing crime was the lack of consensus regarding whether it was or could ever be effective. In a major study of treatment programs, the unfortunate consensus was that "nothing works."[47] Even though this conclusion is more complex than initially reported, the correctional community jettisoned rehabilitation as an orienting perspective. Nevertheless, some claim that certain programs work for certain offenders, and that, although nothing works for everyone, rehabilitation is still a worthy and attainable goal.[48]

The final reason that rehabilitation lost favor is the belief of some scholars that the medical model was a flawed metaphor for corrections. To view offenders as "sick" and in need of a "cure" was deemed problematic by many who favored a view that placed responsibility for criminal behavior squarely on the shoulders of those who "chose" to violate the law. These scholars believed it more accurate to think of felons as lazy, unmotivated, poorly socialized, or exploitive. Their idea was that society didn't need to "cure" these individuals as much as these individuals needed to learn that their unlawful behavior would have negative consequences. Therefore, they called for deterrence rather than rehabilitation.[49]

Retributive Era: 1970s to the Present

The movement away from the rehabilitation philosophy did not occur in a social vacuum. The events of the 1960s caused a number of changes in how our social institutions operated. A backlash to the political protests, reported widespread drug use, relaxation of sexual mores, and general disrespect for authority and tradition manifested in a number of ways that affected the prison.[50] One good example of how events outside the prison found their way inside was the politicization of inmates. As minorities, youth, and women outside prison walls challenged how society treated them, inmates challenged the conditions of their confinement inside the prison.

The courts traditionally had a "hands off" policy concerning the operation of prisons, but in the 1960s they started to specify exactly which constitutional rights inmates forfeited in prison.[51] This led to major changes in areas ranging from food to disciplinary procedures. As prisoners organized to challenge the conditions of their confinement, a new racial dimension appeared in the inmates' identity. The Black Panther Party and the Black Muslims agitated to have prisons recognize them as legitimate political organizations within the prison that spoke for minority inmates. The tensions caused by this politicization of the inmates made rehabilitation efforts difficult to accomplish. When

Black Muslim inmates defined themselves as political prisoners, they became unwilling to adopt the "sick" label of rehabilitation and instead contended that it was society's institutions, particularly prisons, that were deficient. In Stateville Prison in Illinois, this politicization attracted some of the most troublesome inmates to challenge the prison authorities:

> *Whether troublemakers were attracted to Muslimism or whether attraction to Muslimism automatically defined an inmate as a troublemaker is difficult to resolve when posed in this way. The Muslims offered legitimacy and significance to the frustration, bitterness, and egotism of some of Stateville's most recalcitrant inmates. The officials countered by purging Muslims from their jobs, blocking their legitimate prison activities, and suppressing them whenever possible. Not surprisingly, many of the leaders ended up in segregation.*[52]

With inmates rebelling against the conditions of their confinement, the courts questioning how prison officials did their jobs, and society losing faith in the promises of rehabilitation, a change in the basic philosophy of incarceration was inevitable. Retribution replaced rehabilitation as the primary goal of the prison. This had significant and widespread implications for how inmates were sentenced and what happened to them in prison.[53] Some of the changes were as follows:

- **Determinate sentences.** Rehabilitation was no longer the main goal of the prison, and officials were no longer willing to certify when an inmate was safe to return to society. Therefore, indeterminate sentences were no longer desirable. In their place fixed terms of incarceration were implemented based not on the needs of the inmate but on the seriousness of the crime and the inmate's prior criminal record. In this way, the inmate would be treated for what he or she did, rather than for some perceived deficiency in psychological makeup or social conditioning.[54]
- **Voluntary treatment.** With rehabilitation no longer a primary goal of incarceration, treatment services were offered on a voluntary basis. Prison administrators believed that treatment offered to those who sought it without coercion or conditions could be more effective. When inmates engaged in treatment to impress a parole board, their motivations were suspect. Inmates learned to "play the parole game" in the rehabilitation era.[55] Inmates who entered voluntary programs were thought more likely to be sincere in their desires to learn new skills, acquire an education, or seek drug treatment. Also, there were presumably fewer "jailhouse conversions" when attendance at religious services was not considered at parole hearings.
- **Abolition of parole.** One of the logical by-products of a system that abandoned indeterminate sentencing and compulsory treatment was the elimination of parole as an early release mechanism. (Although this has not yet been accomplished, many critics want inmates to spend their entire sentences behind bars and view parole as "soft on crime." We will deal with parole issues later, but it is necessary to point out that the current retributive era in corrections has brought about a reconsideration of parole.) Coupled with a surge in prison overcrowding, the elimination of parole is problematic, but several states have eliminated discretionary parole (see Chapter 13, Reference: Discretionary Parole). However, parole's primary function, like that of the prison, has shifted from treatment to supervision.[56]

This brief history of social control highlights several themes. One is that many correctional practices that seem new and innovative are actually old gifts in new wrappers. The ideas of work as useful in reforming individuals, rehabilitation geared to the needs of the inmate, and the value of keeping prisoners busy have all been used in various eras of corrections. What has changed are not the ideas themselves, but rather the resources and political will allocated to support those ideas. One might wonder whether rehabilitation has ever been given an honest chance. No jurisdiction has ever been able to pay more than lip service to the idea of providing the counselors, modern conditions, and aftercare necessary to effectively change the behavior of criminals who have learned to survive by using a deviant lifestyle. In many ways, it is unrealistic to expect a 12-week program to overcome 25 years of poverty, discrimination, lack of education, and drug addiction. Yet, all too often a 12-week program is all society can afford to attempt to change the inmate. In a later chapter we will consider what treatment efforts in the community appear to be the most promising, but here we must recognize that rehabilitation is not a new idea and that there is still considerable room to develop and refine programs that address criminal behavior.

Capital Punishment

The history of social control requires that we consider the use of capital punishment as a method for compelling citizens to obey the law. This extreme form of control is controversial, with individuals and groups voicing impassioned opinions on both sides of the issue. Although we may debate whether the death penalty is cruel, from a historical point of view it is not unusual. Execution is much older than incarceration, and a fascinating number of ways have been devised to execute criminal offenders. We cannot do justice to all the issues and ramifications of the death penalty in the space available here, so we will content ourselves to briefly consider some of the basic arguments. Easy answers to the issues surrounding the death penalty are elusive because the research is still contested and because capital punishment is often viewed from a highly personal and subjective point of view. Therefore, the goal of this section is to simply frame the issues.

In the next two Case in Point boxes, the court limited executions by determining that mental state must be considered when imposing a death sentence. Two primary reasons for this include deterrence and the condemned's understanding of the execution and the reason for it. According to the Supreme Court, executing a mentally ill or retarded offender will not deter other offenders who suffer similar incapacities. Also, there are questions about the justice of killing those who do not understand what they are alleged to have done or that they are even being put to death.

This is Virginia's electric chair in 1990. Most states now use lethal injection for executions.

Courtesy of CORBIS-NY.

CASE IN POINT

Ford v. Wainwright

The Case

Ford v. Wainwright, 477 U.S. 399 (1986)

The Point

This decision banned the execution of the insane.

In 1974 Alvin Bernard Ford was convicted of murder in Florida and sentenced to death. Although he appeared to be mentally sound during his trial and sentencing, as well as at the time of the offense, his behavior changed while he was on death row. Suspecting mental illness, his attorney had him examined by two psychiatrists, both of whom determined that Ford was not competent to suffer execution. The governor appointed three psychiatrists, who together interviewed Ford for 30 minutes in the presence of an eight-member panel. The psychiatrists agreed that, although Ford had mental problems, he was fit for execution.

In April 1984 the governor signed Ford's death warrant without explanation or statement. A state court refused a hearing to reconsider Ford's competency. The Federal District Court denied a petition for an evidentiary hearing, and the Court of Appeals affirmed this.

The Supreme Court reversed the decision and remanded the case in June 1986. The court concluded that the Eighth Amendment prohibits the execution of the insane and that Florida's procedures in the matter were lacking.

CASE IN POINT

Atkins v. Virginia

The Case

Atkins v. Virginia, 536 U.S. 304 (2002)

The Point

This decision established limits for the execution of the mentally retarded.

On August 16, 1996, Daryl Renard Atkins and William Jones abducted Eric Nesbitt at gunpoint. They took his money, then drove him to an automatic teller machine in his truck and forced him to withdraw more. They then went to an isolated area and shot Nesbitt eight times, killing him.

Jones and Atkins both testified at Atkins' trial. Their descriptions of the incident agreed, except that each blamed the other for actually killing Nesbitt. The jury found Jones' testimony the more articulate, and credited Atkins with the murder. During the trial's penalty phase, the state introduced the testimony of four victims of Atkins' earlier robberies and assaults. Atkins' defense relied on one witness, a psychologist who said Atkins was "mildly mentally retarded," a conclusion based, in part, on a standard intelligence test that indicated Atkins had an IQ of 59.

The jury sentenced Atkins to death. At a resentencing by the Virginia Supreme Court (the trial court had used a misleading verdict form), Atkins was again sentenced to death.

The U.S. Supreme Court reversed and remanded this decision, holding that executing mentally retarded criminals violates the "cruel and unusual punishments" clause in the Eighth Amendment. According to the Court, a "significant number of states" have rejected capital punishment for mentally retarded criminals, and that "the practice is uncommon" even in states that do. Justice John Paul Stevens wrote that, "The practice, therefore, has become truly unusual, and it is fair to say that a national consensus has developed against it." The Court cited evidence that an IQ of 70 or less is the indicator of mental retardation.

Capital Punishment in Historical Perspective

Historically, death is a common form of punishment. Sometimes, however, human life was considered too valuable to sacrifice for the sake of punishing a crime.

> *The Germans, as described by Tacitus, sixty years after the death of Christ, considered only treachery, desertion, cowardice and sexual perversion to be crimes serious enough to be punished by death. In a society where every fighting man was a valuable asset, execution and mutilation could not reasonably be considered suitable punishments for lesser offenses, such as murder and theft; and so, Tacitus discovered, the German murderer or thief when convicted paid a fine 'in a stated number of oxen or cattle. Half of the fine was paid to the King, half to the person for whom justice was being obtained or to his relatives.'*[57]

Nevertheless, over the centuries, authorities used a wide variety of methods to kill offenders. Often, the executions were part of a public spectacle designed to demonstrate the consequences of violating the law. Burning at the stake, crucifixion, death by drowning, death by boiling, being skinned alive, beheading, being impaled on a sharp stick, being thrown to the lions, and an infinite variety of other creative and grotesque techniques were used to kill humans.[58] The aspect of torture is difficult to appreciate today when society takes great pains to give the appearance that executions are physically painless.

Methods of execution have changed to include more than the reduction of torture. The visibility of capital punishment has also evolved to the point that rather than have public ceremonies in which citizens can witness an execution, it is now done behind the walls of the prison with only a few corrections staff, families of the condemned and victim, and a few members of the press present.[59] See Figure 11.1 for the number of executions performed annually in the United States since 1930.

Arguments Supporting Capital Punishment

At the foundation of support for capital punishment is the deterrence argument. Two varieties of deterrence are used to justify the death penalty. Although considerable debate surrounds one of them, the other is obvious. **Specific deterrence** says that if a condemned individual is put to death, then he (most of those executed have been men) will never

specific deterrence
A method of control in which an offender is prevented from committing more crimes by either imprisonment or death.

In late 19th-century China, the head of an executed man is shown to his children to emphasize a moral lesson.
Courtesy of CORBIS-NY.

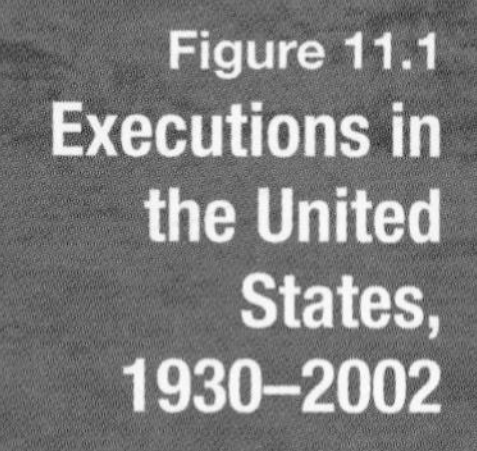

Figure 11.1
Executions in the United States, 1930–2002

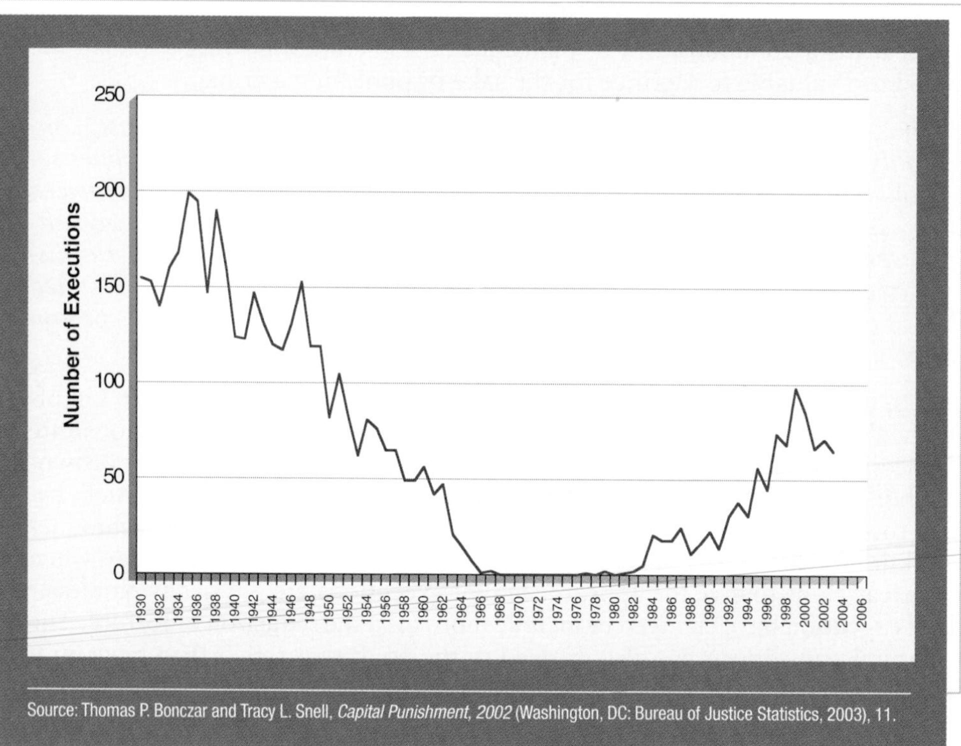

Source: Thomas P. Bonczar and Tracy L. Snell, *Capital Punishment, 2002* (Washington, DC: Bureau of Justice Statistics, 2003), 11.

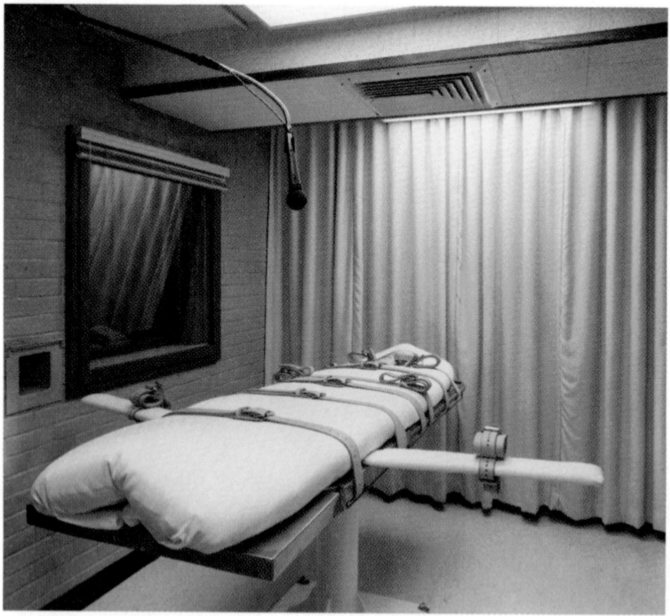

A lethal injection chamber. The curtains are opened during the execution to allow witnesses to observe the proceedings.
Courtesy of CORBIS-NY.

general deterrence
A method of control in which the punishment of a single offender sets an example for the rest of society.

commit another crime. There is no arguing with this logic. However, in practice, only a small percentage of those who commit murder are ever executed. As a policy, then, specific deterrence is of limited value. On the other hand, **general deterrence** says that if murderers are executed, the rest of us will see the ramifications of this behavior and will refrain from committing murder ourselves because we fear the consequences. General deterrence allows us to have meaningful communities. Think of how chaotic our society

CROSSCURRENTS

Killing Them Softly

The concept of killing those who offend societal norms is probably as old as humanity. For example, the book of Leviticus in the Bible states, "And he that killeth any man shall surely be put to death."[1] The reasons for such a stringent punishment are fairly clear-cut. They include retribution, revenge, and general and specific deterrence. Killing a person can be easier than expending resources to rehabilitate him or her. It is also a way for the state to show the extent of its power, organization, and control.

Prior to the 20th century, two major features of the death sentence were spectacle and pain. The spectacle aspect served many purposes, most of them related to the reasons for the sentence. Spectacle proved to the aggrieved party that justice had been done and assuaged the desire for revenge. It proved that the offender was dead, achieved specific deterrence, and provided a visual aid for general deterrence. Spectacle displayed the blunt power of the state and its willingness to see justice done. A final reason for spectacle was to entertain the masses. Although this reason may not seem related to justice, the humiliation aspect could be considered part of the offender's sentence. In many cases, the last thing an offender would see would be a jeering crowd. According to an English writer, "An Execution that is attended with more lasting Torment, may strike a far greater Awe."[2]

The other feature of pre–20th century death sentence was pain. Pain was considered to be inextricably linked to punishment. Death was not enough. The offender was required to hurt while dying and hurt publicly. This can be linked to the crowd's need for revenge fulfillment and to the desire that the offender be humiliated, as well as injured. Some means of inflicting pain were slow, and others, if the offender was lucky, were fast. Throughout the ages, the art of inflicting pain in pursuit of death became quite well developed.

Greeks and Romans

Although the death penalty and torture existed before the Greeks and Romans, these societies did much to impress their idiosyncrasies of it in Western thought. One of the most famous ancient executions was that of Socrates, who was made to drink poison. Although poisoning can be painful, torture did not seem to be a goal of Socrates' executioners. Other offenders were not so fortunate. One Roman method of execution was to tie the offender to a human corpse so that the rotting body would slowly and horribly kill the offender. The Romans are most infamous for crucifixion, a common method of execution, and forcing offenders to fight each other to the death or be killed by wild animals.

Europe

In Europe the favored methods of execution were hanging, beheading, and burning. Executions were later carried out by guillotine, a mechanized form of beheading, and firing squad. Again, pain, spectacle, and humiliation were considered important. One of the most fearsome executions was burning. Many offenders were burned alive; more fortunate ones were burned after being hanged. Burning was considered a punishment that punished beyond death because it destroyed the body, which would not receive a proper burial.

Only much later in European history did authorities seek to reduce the offender's suffering (if not the humiliation), with the executioners themselves leading the way. Prior to the 19th century, death by hanging depended on the "short drop." That is, a rope was tied to the offender's neck, and he or she was either dropped or hoisted a short distance, and death occurred by slow strangulation. In the 19th century, British hangmen discovered that a "long drop," letting the offender fall a long distance from a platform, would break the neck and cause a quicker, more humane death.[3]

In 1792 France popularized the use of the guillotine during the French Revolution. This mechanical device for lopping heads was used because it was considered humane, being quicker than hanging and less mistake-prone

continued

CROSSCURRENTS

than an executioner wielding an ax or sword. However, concerns grew that a severed head might live and consciousness might continue for several seconds or even minutes. Numerous experiments were done on severed heads, with reports of faces blushing when slapped or the victim's eyes responding to the sound of his or her name.[4] Despite the debate on this matter (which continues to this day), France continued to execute criminal offenders by guillotine until 1977. France abolished the death penalty in 1981.

Search for Humane Execution

The organized call for humane execution in the United States began in the 19th century. Although "long-drop" hangings were supposed to be less painful, they were not always carried out properly, resulting in long, painful deaths. In response, gallows were redesigned and experiments were done. One contraption, called the "upright jerker" used weights and pulleys to sharply draw the victim up, snapping the neck. The success of this method depended on the operator's skill and the condition of the machine itself. These were lacking in several cases, resulting in lingering asphyxiation and strangling rather than quick death.[5]

Electrocution

The late 19th century saw experiments with electricity move from the therapeutic to the punitive. Once it was discovered that electricity could kill, officials began searching for ways to use it to painlessly execute prisoners. Thomas Edison got in on the act in 1887, insisting that the best method of electrical execution was via alternating current, the preferred current of his chief rival, George Westinghouse. Despite Westinghouse's protests, the first electrical execution was performed with his equipment on William Kemmler at New York's Auburn Prison in August 1890. Contrary to popular hopes and expectations, this execution was worse than hanging. The science of electrocution was poorly understood, and Kemmler's execution was botched. He survived the first 17-second jolt, so the executioners, panicking and struggling with the equipment, let the second burst go for over a minute. Blood seeped through the broken capillaries on Kemmler's face, and his flesh burned, horrifying the witnesses and officials.[6]

Despite this apparent failure, officials continued to experiment until they hit on a satisfactory combination of electricity and time. Less than a year after Kemmler's execution, four inmates were executed in one day in an electrocution marathon at Sing Sing Prison. All four executions were reported to have been clean and painless. By 1937 electrocution was the preferred method of execution by the federal government and many states.

Gas

The humane execution fad continued during this era, pursued by those offended by hangings and botched electrocutions. Although it was established by 1896 that lethal gas could execute a prisoner, interest did not pick up until 1921 when the Nevada legislature passed a bill allowing execution by gas.

One of the notions held by gas advocates was that the victims did not have to know they were being executed. These advocates specified that inmates should be asleep when the sentence was carried out, never knowing the exact date and time of their executions. This proved impractical for two major reasons: Executions required witnesses, and the inmate would have to live in a special gas-ready cell for several days, thus spoiling the surprise to some degree. Officials eventually settled on something more resembling the modern gas chamber: a chair in a room with a window for spectators. In 1924 Chinese immigrant Gee Jon became the first inmate to die by gas. Unlike early episodes with the electric chair, Jon's execution went smoothly (although some later executions did not, with victims gasping and choking). By 1955 at least 11 states had gas chambers.

Lethal Injection

Despite all the developments in humane execution, society has returned to the method used to kill Socrates: poison. Although the ability to inject poison into the veins has been around for a while, doing so via syringe was developed at about the time that society became squeamish about how its condemned died. Having an executioner touch a victim while killing him or her seemed too intimate.[7] However, once the process was automated, with executioners needing only to find a vein and turn on the chemicals, the method's relative frugality, simplicity, and painlessness became apparent. In 1982 the first lethal injection execution was performed by the state of Texas on Charlie Brooks, without incident. As of 2002 lethal injection was the preferred method of execution in 37 states, plus the military and federal government.

Lethal Injection		Electrocution	Lethal Gas
Alabama	Nevada	Alabama	Arizona
Arizona	New Hampshire	Arkansas	California
Arkansas	New Jersey	Florida	Missouri
California	New Mexico	Kentucky	Wyoming
Colorado	New York	Nebraska	
Connecticut	North Carolina	Oklahoma	
Delaware	Ohio	South Carolina	
Florida	Oklahoma	Tennessee	
Georgia	Oregon	Virginia	
Idaho	Pennsylvania		
Illinois	South Carolina		
Indiana	South Dakota	**Hanging**	**Firing Squad**
Kansas	Tennessee	Delaware	Idaho
Kentucky	Texas	New Hampshire	Oklahoma
Louisiana	Utah	Washington	
Maryland	Virginia		
Mississippi	Washington		
Missouri	Wyoming		
Montana			

QUESTIONS

1. Are painless executions more palatable or ethical than those that hurt the offender?
2. Instead of abolishing execution, should efforts be made, instead, to streamline it and make it more painless and efficient?

ENDNOTES

1. Leviticus 24:17 (King James Version).
2. George Olyffe, *An Essay Humbly Offer'd, for an Act of Parliament to Prevent Capital Crimes* (London: J. Downing, 1731), 6–7, in Stuart Banner, *The Death Penalty: An American History* (Harvard University Press: Cambridge and London, 2002), 70.
3. Robert M. Bohm, *Deathquest: An Introduction to the Theory and Practice of Capital Punishment in the United States* (Cincinnati: Anderson, 1999), 73.
4. Alister Kershaw, *A History of the Guillotine* (New York: Barnes & Noble Books, 1993), 81.
5. Stuart Banner, *The Death Penalty: An American History* (Cambridge and London: Harvard University Press, 2002), 171–172.
6. Ibid., 186.
7. Ibid., 296.

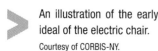

An illustration of the early ideal of the electric chair.
Courtesy of CORBIS-NY.

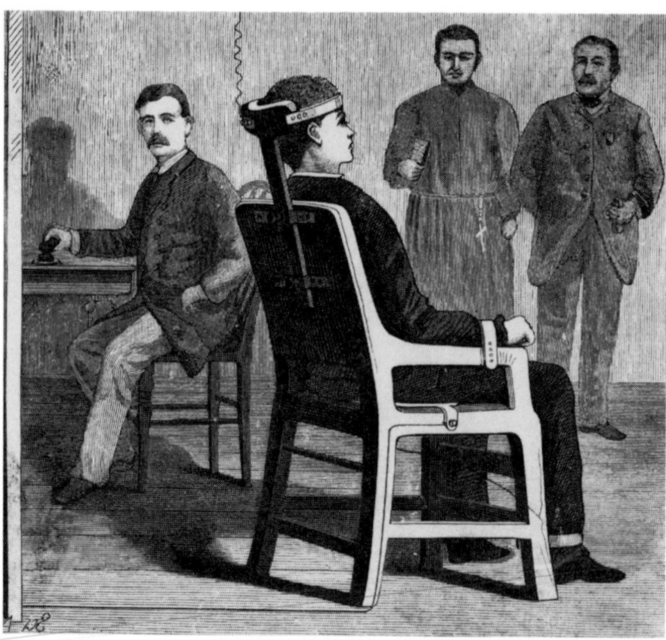

would be, according to this perspective, if each of us had to be caught at our crimes and punished before we would engage in lawful behavior. Fortunately, the vast majority of us do not commit crimes even though we may be tempted. We understand by seeing others punished that we will be held accountable for our actions.

Although embracing the deterrence argument seems logical when considering most crimes and punishments, there is considerable debate as to whether it is useful when applied to murder and capital punishment.[60] Opponents of capital punishment say the general deterrence argument is questionable for several reasons.

- Does the death penalty deter criminals to the same degree it deters the rest of us? For deterrence to be effective, we each must weigh the risks of getting caught and punished against the benefits of successfully committing the crime. Very few circumstances exist in which most citizens would risk their lives, fortunes, and reputations for the possible benefits of crime. In short, general deterrence works very well on those who have something to lose, but may not be as effective for those who have very little invested in the status quo. The idea that drug dealers who stand to gain thousands of dollars, professional assassins, young gang members, and jealous spouses rationally calculate the prospects of the death penalty is not assured.
- Does the death penalty deter better than other types of punishments? According to those who oppose the death penalty, the prospect of life in prison without parole, will, in all likelihood, deter as effectively as capital punishment.[61]
- Many murders are crimes of passion in which deterrence may not enter into the offender's motivation. Those in a blind rage may not consider the death penalty or may even reason that they are so incensed that only by exposing themselves to the ultimate punishment can they adequately express their outrage.[62]
- Deterrence is very difficult to validate empirically because it is difficult to measure something that doesn't happen. Given the multiple variables that go into someone's decision to kill another person, it is extremely difficult to isolate the deterrent effect of death penalty laws.[63]

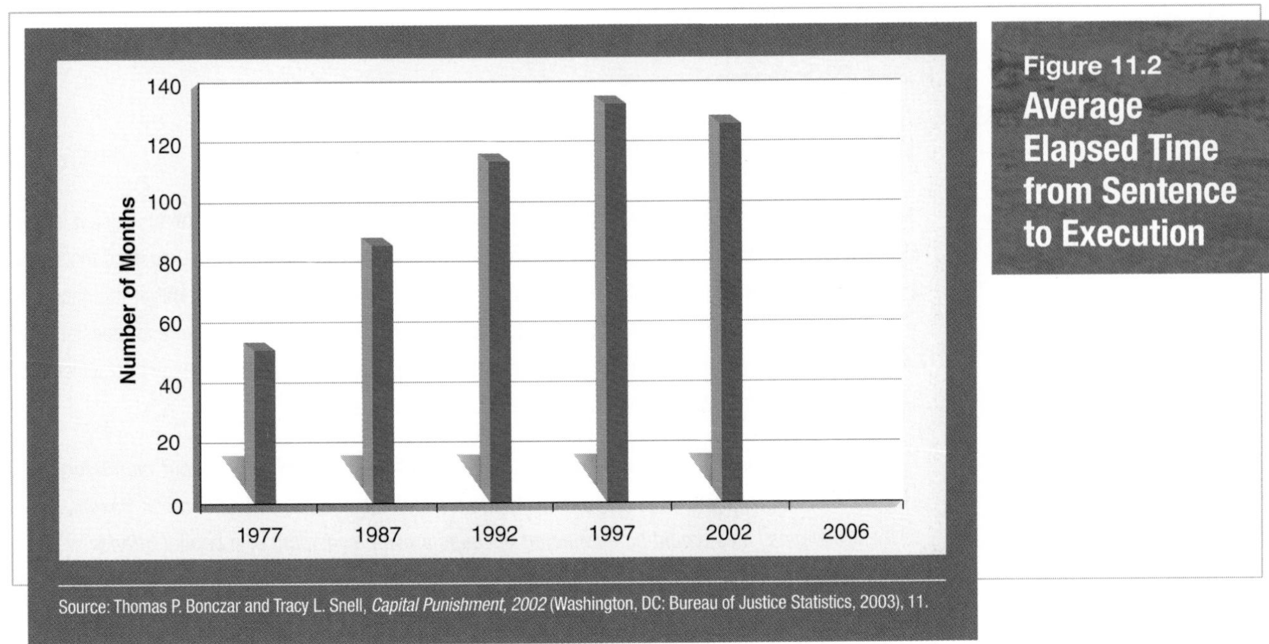

Source: Thomas P. Bonczar and Tracy L. Snell, *Capital Punishment, 2002* (Washington, DC: Bureau of Justice Statistics, 2003), 11.

Figure 11.2 Average Elapsed Time from Sentence to Execution

The deterrence argument is impossible to prove given our current laws. According to deterrence theory, we must do more than simply raise the severity of the punishment. Swiftness and certainty of punishment are also factors that criminals supposedly take into account when contemplating their crimes. In the case of the death penalty, neither swiftness nor certainty are guaranteed. Many executions occur 10 or more years after the crime (see Figure 11.2). Given the restrictive wording of statutes, plea bargaining, and the reluctance of some judges or juries to impose the death sentence, we can honestly say that, under present conditions, deterrence theory has not had a fair opportunity to demonstrate its potential. To fully assess the impact of deterrence, we would need to see some fundamental changes in the criminal justice system. By making capital punishment mandatory for some crimes, limiting the number of appeals and time allowed for appeals, and thereby executing a larger number of offenders in a swift and certain manner, capital punishment laws would be perceived as having some teeth and could possibly provide a deterrent function.

Supporters of the death penalty point to the **just deserts** argument as a justification. This argument asserts that some people commit acts so heinous that only by killing them can a society fully express its values. In a sense, this argument maintains that some people deserve to be executed because of their antisocial behavior. This is a **retribution model** that embraces the "eye for an eye" concept that many feel is the basis of justice handed down throughout history and is deeply ingrained in many religious and philosophical teachings. Not to execute killers in some way cheapens the life of the victim according to this perspective. This perspective speaks to some individuals who might take the law into their own hands if the government did not punish wrongdoers appropriately. The desire for revenge is a strong motivator for many, and the prospect of vigilante justice is always a concern. If the government fails to uphold the law and deal with offenders, then some individuals will become judge, jury, and executioner themselves. Lacking faith in the criminal justice system, the man who finds someone raping his daughter would be tempted to seek retribution by killing the rapist. Although rapists are not subject to the death penalty today, the point is that citizens must have confidence that justice will be done. For many, justice means that criminals "get what they deserve."

just deserts
A philosophy that states that an offender who commits a heinous crime deserves death.

retribution model
A style of control in which offenders are punished as severely as possible for a crime and in which rehabilitation is not attempted.

FOCUS ON ETHICS

Capital Punishment: Some Immodest Proposals

Almost everyone is dissatisfied with the death penalty for one reason or another. Liberals think it is applied in a discriminatory manner and that it fails to act as a deterrent. Conservatives say that it is used too sparingly and that the time between crime and execution is too long. Families of victims feel left out of the decision-making process, and murderers eventually believe that they are the ultimate victim. If we were to redesign how we execute people, what might we do differently? Here are some proposals that would change the face of capital punishment in the United States. How many of them would you vote for?

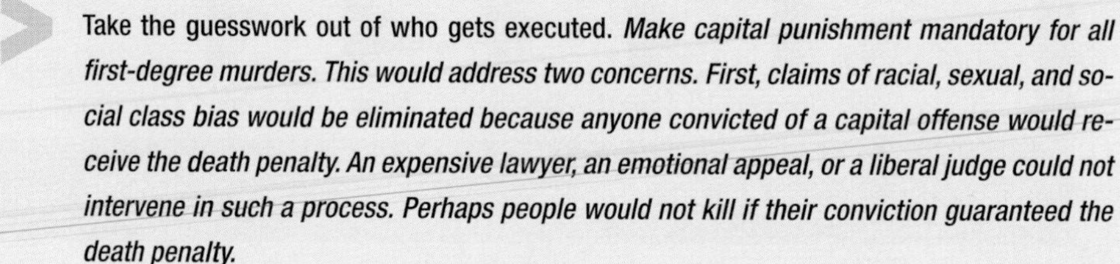

- Take the guesswork out of who gets executed. *Make capital punishment mandatory for all first-degree murders. This would address two concerns. First, claims of racial, sexual, and social class bias would be eliminated because anyone convicted of a capital offense would receive the death penalty. An expensive lawyer, an emotional appeal, or a liberal judge could not intervene in such a process. Perhaps people would not kill if their conviction guaranteed the death penalty.*

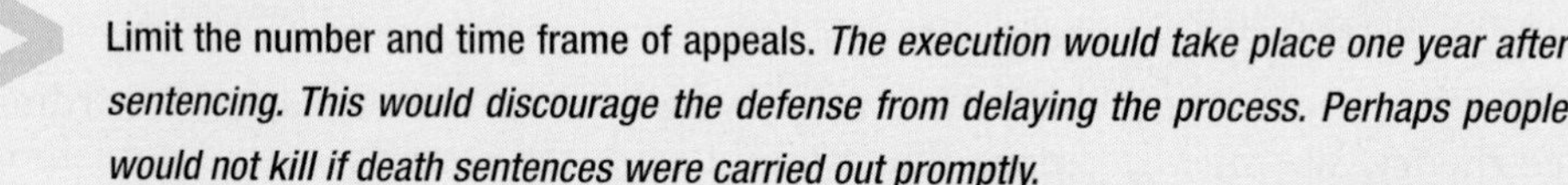

- Limit the number and time frame of appeals. *The execution would take place one year after sentencing. This would discourage the defense from delaying the process. Perhaps people would not kill if death sentences were carried out promptly.*

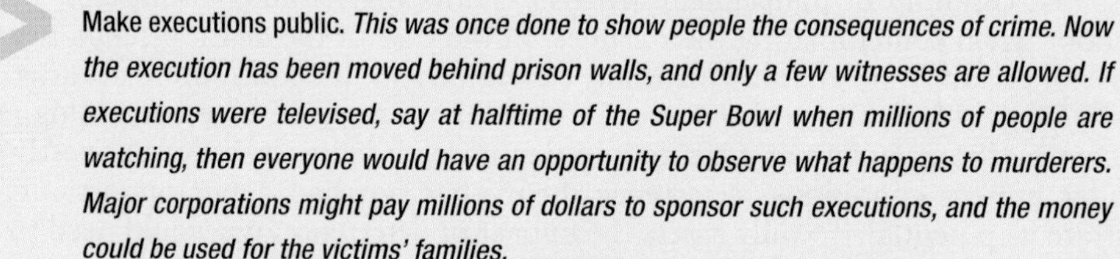

- Make executions public. *This was once done to show people the consequences of crime. Now the execution has been moved behind prison walls, and only a few witnesses are allowed. If executions were televised, say at halftime of the Super Bowl when millions of people are watching, then everyone would have an opportunity to observe what happens to murderers. Major corporations might pay millions of dollars to sponsor such executions, and the money could be used for the victims' families.*

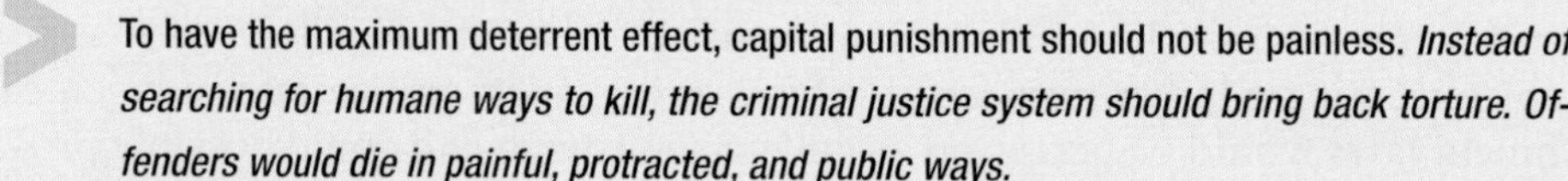

- To have the maximum deterrent effect, capital punishment should not be painless. *Instead of searching for humane ways to kill, the criminal justice system should bring back torture. Offenders would die in painful, protracted, and public ways.*

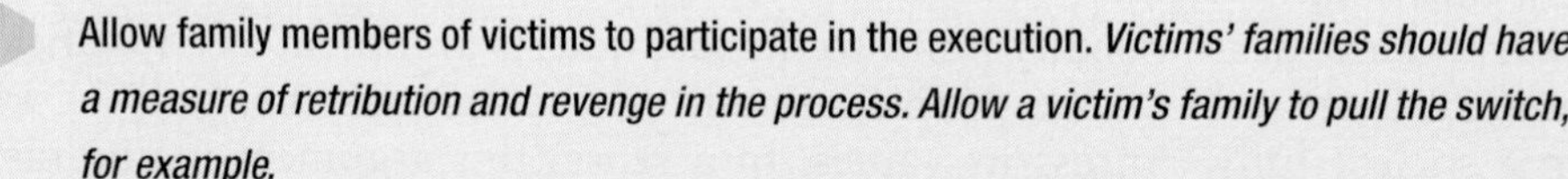

- Allow family members of victims to participate in the execution. *Victims' families should have a measure of retribution and revenge in the process. Allow a victim's family to pull the switch, for example.*

QUESTIONS

1. Are these suggestions extreme? Ask your classmates, family members, and friends what they think. Is there agreement on how offenders should be executed?
2. How far have we come from the times when these proposals were practiced? Are you willing to go back?

Arguments against Capital Punishment

Those who oppose the death penalty do so for a variety of reasons. Some religious people take to heart the Fourth Commandment found in the Old Testament of the Bible, which says, "Thou shall not kill." These individuals consider killing by the state, in the name of the people, as premeditated murder. Other capital punishment opponents point

REFERENCE

States/Jurisdictions without a Death Penalty

Alaska	Massachusetts	Vermont
District of Columbia	Michigan	West Virginia
Hawaii	Minnesota	Wisconsin
Iowa	North Dakota	
Maine	Rhode Island	

to the evidence on deterrence and conclude that capital punishment does not make society safer. Still others are concerned with the way some offenders are selected for capital punishment, while others escape it. They point to social class, race, and gender as factors that determine whether the death penalty is applied in a given case.[64] These are but a few of the concerns of those who oppose capital punishment. It is useful to explore some of these issues in more detail because they are inherently complicated and significantly important to our understanding of the criminal justice system.

An old axiom concerning capital punishment asks, "Why do we kill people to show people that killing people is wrong?" This axiom is revealing on a number of levels, not the least of which is the perceived irony of the state modeling the very type of behavior it is attempting to discourage. The Italian criminologist Cesare Beccaria expressed much the same sentiments in 1761:

> *The death penalty cannot be useful, because of the example of barbarity it gives men. . . . It seems to me absurd that the laws, which are an expression of the public will, which detest and punish homicide, should themselves commit it, and that to deter citizens from murder, they order a public one.*[65]

Despite the fact that the infliction of the death penalty has been modified over the centuries to inflict as little pain as possible, the process of execution has become so formalized, routinized, and bureaucratic that it has become a surreal procedure that some opponents consider a violation of the Eighth Amendment's proscription against cruel and unusual punishment. One vocal opponent who has studied the modern execution process is Robert Johnson, who wrote:

> *The underlying function of death row confinement, then, is to facilitate executions by dehumanizing both the prisoner and, to a lesser degree, their executioners, making it easier for both to play their roles in the execution process. The confinement that produces these results is a form of torture. Indeed, the essence of torture is the death of a person—that is, his conversion into a subhuman object, a nonperson.*[66]

Johnson is uncompromising in his condemnation of the brutal way the death penalty is applied in the United States. Its supporters, however, would contend that there is little problematic here. The death penalty, according to many, should be brutalizing to the offender just as the offender was brutalizing to the victim. To be an effective deterrent, capital punishment needs to be unpleasant, according to its proponents. In fact, there are those who would return capital punishment to the days when it was a public spectacle in order to enhance what they believe to be its deterrent effects. Taken to an extreme, the death penalty could become a form of sport to entertain the public, raise money for the state, and demonstrate what happens to lawbreakers.

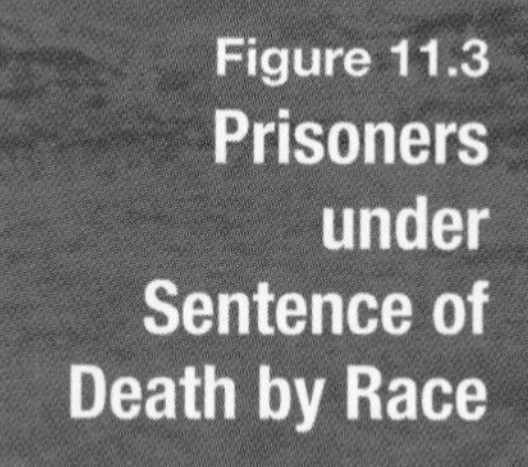

Figure 11.3
Prisoners under Sentence of Death by Race

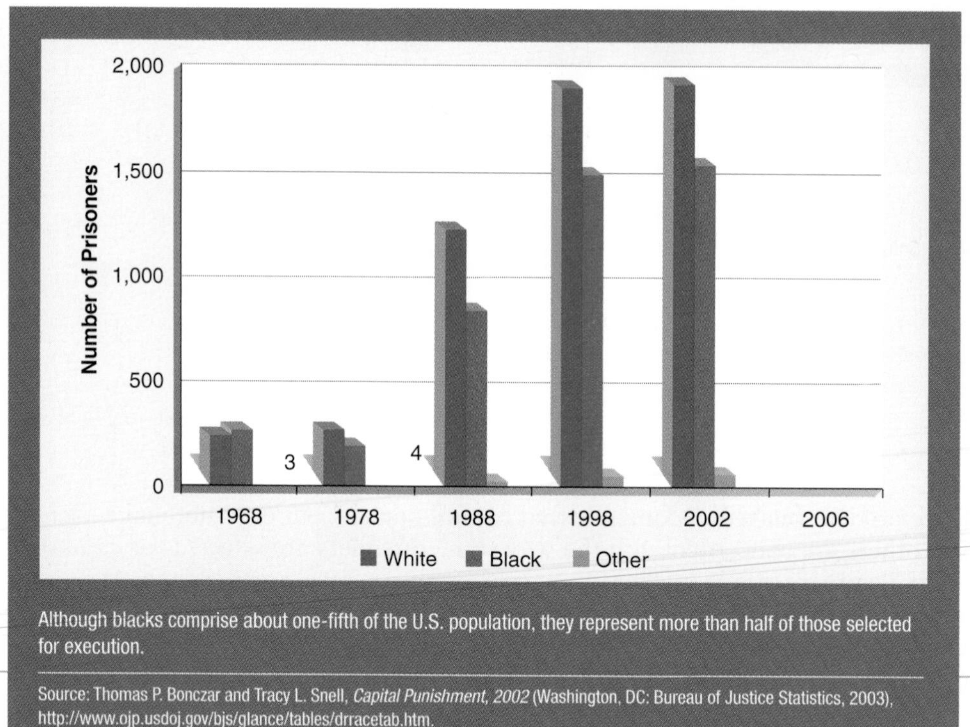

Although blacks comprise about one-fifth of the U.S. population, they represent more than half of those selected for execution.

Source: Thomas P. Bonczar and Tracy L. Snell, *Capital Punishment, 2002* (Washington, DC: Bureau of Justice Statistics, 2003), http://www.ojp.usdoj.gov/bjs/glance/tables/drracetab.htm.

Many who might support capital punishment or are neutral on the subject find themselves opposing it because of a perceived unfairness in the way certain categories of people are selected (see Figure 11.3). In other words, it is not the idea of the death penalty they oppose, but rather the state's seeming inability to impose it in a fair and impartial manner. When minorities and people of lower social classes are executed, while many whites and rich people escape with imprisonment, the procedure's fairness is called into question. If everyone is equal under the law, then there should not be patterns of discrimination in how the death penalty is administered.[67] Unfortunately, the historical evidence is unambiguous. Blacks and Latinos are executed for their crimes at a greater proportion than are whites. Another feature of racial bias is evident in how those who kill white victims are more likely to receive the ultimate sanction than are those who kill minorities.

> *A black person convicted of an aggravated murder of a white in Florida between 1973 and 1977 was more than seven times more likely to receive a death sentence than was a black who killed a black. A white person convicted of an aggravated murder of a white was almost five more times likely to receive a death sentence than was a black who killed a black. A person convicted of aggravated murder of a white, whether the killer was a black or a white, was more likely to receive the death penalty than was a person of either race convicted of aggravated murder of a black.*[68]

Is a white life more valuable than a black life? That is what the evidence on the racial bias of the death penalty suggests.[69] These kinds of patterns make those who might support the death penalty reconsider. It is important to keep in mind that the bulk of these studies that demonstrate this racial bias have controlled for other factors, such as the defendant's prior record. What these studies show is that race is a significant factor in deciding who is executed.

Social class is also an influence. Because those with financial means can afford to hire private lawyers and employ investigators, the rich have a decided advantage over the poor when charged with capital crimes. This is not to say that many public defenders cannot mount a credible defense in a capital case (in fact, in some larger jurisdictions, the public defender's office is staffed with experienced and effective attorneys), but rather that the poor often lack the financial resources necessary to provide a first-class defense.[70]

Finally, a compelling reason for many people to object to the death penalty is the problem of killing the innocent. Whereas defendants have numerous opportunities for appeal and review of their cases, condemned inmates do not. If a mistake is made in determining a defendant's guilt, a prison term, unlike death, can be rescinded. DNA evidence has proven the innocence of several individuals who were convicted of capital crimes.[71] The situation in Illinois was so problematic that in 2000 Governor George Ryan, a conservative Republican, placed a moratorium on the death penalty. Before he left office in 2002, Ryan commuted the sentences of those on death row to life imprisonment. For Ryan, who had been a supporter of capital punishment, the prospect of killing innocent offenders outweighed the death penalty's assumed benefits.

Summary

Human societies can only exist if they employ rules and if the majority of their members follow those rules. Members who do not follow the rules must be controlled for the sake of the society. Violations of the rules bring mild rebukes to extreme violence as groups seek to make members conform. Throughout history, societies have adopted a wide variety of controls.

Ancient societies did not have organized systems to deal with offenders. In many societies, justice tended to be a private matter, with the family, tribe, or group expected to enforce internal norms and to protect members from outside aggression. Corporal punishment, or inflicting physical harm on the body, was a primary means to control and extract revenge from offenders. The major formalized means of inflicting pain were torture, flogging, branding, mutilation, humiliation, and shock death.

Although corporal punishments were common before the use of prisons, other dispositions extracted labor rather than pain from the offender. These dispositions included forcing offenders to work on galley ships and in workhouses, and exiling them to foreign lands.

Our modern prisons have drawn an array of practices from the history of punishment. Early American institutions were locally controlled and imprisoned different types of offenders together. Corporal punishment was popular, and the idea of incarceration as a sole punishment took time to develop. The first institution resembling a modern penitentiary was Massachusetts's Castle Island in Boston Harbor, established in 1785. During the first half of the 19th century, two reform-type prison systems emerged: the Pennsylvania System and the Auburn System. Each emphasized regimens of silence and penitence.

Later, European countries developed the Irish System, which was designed not just to punish, but to make the inmate more likely to return successfully to free society. The three most well-known examples were those developed by Alexander Maconochie, Sir Walter Crofton, and Zebulon Brockway. Maconochie, who in 1840 ran the Australian penal colony of Norfolk Island, popularized the indeterminate sentence. Crofton, appointed director of the Irish prison system in 1854, instituted the early-release ticket-of-leave system. At the Elmira Reformatory in New York, Zebulon Brockway used volunteers, forerunners to parole officers, to keep track of released inmates.

The 20th century saw the idea that work was most useful for reforming offenders. The three major ideas were that work was a good way to occupy inmates, had rehabilitative value, and offset the cost of incarceration. These philosophies are still in force today.

Rehabilitation has probably always been a consideration, but U.S. prisons did not acknowledge it as a primary goal until around 1930. New developments in how science treated illness resulted in a renewed interest in rehabilitation. In criminal justice, a medical metaphor was developed in which "sick" criminals were to be "cured" by determining their biological, psychological, and sociological "symptoms." Another influence was the Wickersham Commission's 1931 report, which called for a wide range of reforms, including attempts at inmate rehabilitation. Like many other prison reform movements, the rehabilitation movement was never fully accomplished. Limitations included lack of resources, the lack of consensus that treatment was effective, and the idea that the medical model was a flawed metaphor for corrections.

The events of the 1960s caused a number of changes in our social institutions. Along with other social groups, inmates became politically active in demanding changes in their surroundings. The courts, which had never intervened in prison operations, started to specify exactly what rights inmates had. This led to major changes in areas ranging from food to disciplinary procedures. Circa 1970 the retributive era began in corrections, and continues to the present. This era features replacing indeterminate sentencing with determinate sentencing, making treatment voluntary, and abolishing parole.

The most extreme and controversial form of control is capital punishment. Historically, punishment by death was common, and a number of ways were devised to kill offenders. This has changed in the 20th century, with death sentences carried out with few witnesses and in the most painless way believed possible. Arguments for capital punishment include general and specific deterrence and retribution. Arguments against it include religious and spiritual concerns about killing; beliefs that it does not deter; race, gender, and class issues about who is selected for death; and fear of executing the innocent.

KEY TERMS

congregate-and-silent system p. 365
general deterrence p. 378
just deserts p. 383
marks-of-commendation system p. 368
retribution model p. 383
separate-and-silent system p. 364
specific deterrence p. 377

REVIEW QUESTIONS

1. Is it true that modern corrections no longer use any form of ancient methods of control?
2. Why did/do societies resort to corporal punishment?
3. Which economic punishment was of particular use to European colonies?
4. Has prison reform been completely successful? A complete failure?
5. What group first suggested that incarceration and hard labor were preferable to corporal punishment?
6. What were the roles of the Walnut Street jail and Castle Island in the development of U.S. penal institutions?
7. What reforms has Europe contributed to U.S. corrections?
8. What three ways has work been deemed beneficial to inmates?
9. What effect did the germ theory of medicine have on corrections?
10. What precipitated the move away from the rehabilitation philosophy?
11. What are three primary features of the retributive philosophy?
12. What are the primary differences between modern capital punishment and ancient capital punishment?

SUGGESTED FURTHER READING

Blomberg, Thomas G. and Karol Lucken. *American Penology: A History of Control.* New York: Aldine De Gruyter, 2000.

Garland, David. *Punishment and Modern Society: A Study in Social Theory.* Chicago: University of Chicago Press, 1990.

Hibbert, Christopher. *The Roots of Evil: A Social History of Crime and Punishment.* Birmingham, Ala: Minerva Press, 1963.

Hughes, Robert. *The Fatal Shore: A History of Transportation of Convicts to Australia 1787–1868.* Suffolk, Great Britain: Pan Books, 1988.

Morris, Norval, and David J. Rothman. *The Oxford History of the Prison.* New York: Oxford University Press, 1995.

Rothman, David J. *The Discovery of the Asylum: Social Order and Disorder in the New Republic.* Boston: Little, Brown, 1971.

ENDNOTES

1. Graeme Newman, *Just and Painful: A Case for the Corporal Punishment of Criminals* (New York: MacMillan, 1983). See especially Chapter 4, "The Limits of Pain: Barbarism and Civilized Punishments."
2. Karl Menningen, *The Crime of Punishment* (New York: The Viking Press, 1968).
3. David Garland, "Penal Modernism and Postmodernism," in *Punishment and Social Control: Essays in Honor of Sheldon L. Messinger,* eds. Thomas G. Blomberg and Stanley Cohen (New York: Aldine De Gruyter, 1995), 181–209.
4. Thomas G. Blomberg and Karol Lucken, *American Penology: A History of Control* (New York: Aldine De Gruyter, 2000).
5. Christopher Hibbert, *The Roots of Evil: A Social History of Crime and Punishment* (New York: Minerva Press, 1963).
6. Newman, *Just and Painful.* In Chapter 3, Newman provides a nice discussion about measuring people's thresholds of pain.
7. George Ryley Scott, *The History of Corporal Punishment* (London: Senate, 1968).
8. Rodney J. Henningsen, W. Wesley Johnson, and Terry Wells, "Supermax Prisons: Panacea or Desperation," in *Correctional Contexts: Contemporary and Classical Readings,* 2nd ed., eds. Edward J. Latessa et al. (Los Angeles: Roxbury, 2001), 143–150. These authors review the social costs of such prisons and conclude that inmates are made dysfunctional by them.
9. Michel Foucault, *Discipline and Punish: The Birth of the Prison* (New York: Pantheon Books, 1977).
10. Deuteronomy 25:1–2 King James Version.
11. Scott, *History of Corporal Punishment.*
12. Ibid., 68.
13. Erving Goffman, *Stigma: Notes on the Management of a Spoiled Identity* (Englewood Cliffs, NJ: Prentice Hall, 1963).
14. Harry Elmer Barnes and Negley K. Teeters, *New Horizons in Criminology,* 3rd ed. (Englewood Cliffs, NJ: Prentice Hall, 1959).
15. Fay Honey Knapp, "Northwest Treatment Associates: A Comprehensive Community-Based-Evaluation-and-Treatment Program for Adult Sex Offenders," in *Correctional Counseling and Treatment,* 4th ed., ed. Peter C. Kratcoski, (Prospect Heights, IL: Waveland Press, 2000), 617–633.
16. Nagaty Sanad, *The Theory of Crime and Criminal Responsibility in Islamic Law: Sharia'* (Chicago: The University of Illinois at Chicago, 1991).
17. George Ryley Scott, *A History of Torture* (London: Senate, 1994), 208–209.
18. Barnes and Teeters, *New Horizons.*
19. John Braithwaite, *Crime, Shame and Reintegration* (Cambridge: Cambridge University Press, 1989).
20. Blomberg and Lucken, *American Penology,* 31.
21. Martha H. Myers, *Race, Labor and Punishment in the New South* (Columbus: Ohio State University Press, 1998).
22. Blomberg and Lucken, *American Penology,* 18.
23. Garland, *Penal Modernism.* See especially Chapter 4, "The Political Economy of Punishment: Rusche and Kirchheimer and the Marxist Tradition," pp. 83–110.
24. Pieter Spierenburg, "The Body and the State: Early Modern Europe," in *The Oxford History of the Prison,* eds. Norval Morris and David J. Rothman (New York: Oxford University Press, 1998), pp. 44–70.
25. Barnes and Teeters, *New Horizons.*
26. Scott Christianson, *With Liberty for Some: 500 Years of Imprisonment in America* (Boston: Northeastern University Press, 1998).
27. Harry E. Allen and Clifford E. Simonsen, *Corrections in America: An Introduction,* 9th ed. (Upper Saddle River, NJ: Prentice Hall, 2001), 21.

28. Aleksandr I. Solzhenitsyn, *The Gulag Archipelago: 1918–1956* (New York: HarperCollins, 1974).
29. Alexis M. Durham III, *Crisis and Reform: Current Issues in American Punishment* (Boston: Little, Brown, 1994).
30. Harry Elmer Barnes, *The Evolution of Penology in Pennsylvania: A Study in American Social History* (Montclair, NJ: Patterson Smith, 1968).
31. Phillip L. Reichel, *Corrections: Philosophies, Practices, and Procedures,* 2nd ed. (Boston: Allyn and Bacon, 2001), 72.
32. J. Hirsch, *The Rise of the Penitentiary: Prisons and Punishments in Early America* (New Haven, CT: Yale University Press, 1992).
33. Barnes, *Evolution of Penology.*
34. Barnes and Teeters, *New Horizons.*
35. David J. Rothman, *The Discovery of the Asylum: Social Order and Disorder in the New Republic* (Boston: Little, Brown, 1971).
36. Philip Collins, *Dickens and Crime* (Bloomington: Indiana University Press, 1962), 122–123.
37. J.V. Barry, *Alexander Maconochie of Norfolk Island* (Melbourne, Australia: Oxford University Press, 1958), 72.
38. Reichel, *Corrections,* 82.
39. Barnes and Teeters, *New Horizons.*
40. Blomberg and Lucken, *American Penology* 76.
41. Glen H. Gildemeister, *Prison Labor and Convict Competition with Free Workers in Industrializing America 1840–1890* (New York: Garland, 1987).
42. Blake McKelvey, *American Prisons: A History of Good Intentions* (Montclair, NJ: Patterson Smith, 1977).
43. John Irwin, *Prisons in Turmoil* (Boston: Little, Brown, 1980). See especially Chapter 2, "The Correctional Institution."
44. Larry E. Sullivan, *The Prison Reform Movement: Forlorn Hope,* (Boston: Twayne, 1990).
45. John W. Roberts, "The Federal Bureau of Prisons: Its Mission, Its History, and Its Partnership with Probation and Pretrial Services," *Federal Probation* 61, no. 1 (1997): 53–58.
46. James B. Jacobs, *Stateville: The Penitentiary in Mass Society* (Chicago: The University of Chicago Press, 1977).
47. Robert Martinson, "What Works? Questions and Answers About Prison Reform," *The Public Interest* 42: 22–54.
48. Ted Palmer, "The 'Effectiveness' Issue Today: An Overview," in *Correctional Counseling and Treatment,* 4th ed., ed. Peter C. Kratcoski (Long Grove, IL: Waveland Press, 1999).
49. David Fogel, *We Are Living Proof: The Justice Model for Corrections* (Cincinnati: Anderson, 1975).
50. Todd Gitlin, *The Sixties: Years of Hope, Days of Rage* (New York: Bantam Books, 1993).
51. Jacobs, *Stateville.* See especially Chapter 5, "Intrusion of the Legal System and Interest Groups," pp. 105–137.
52. Ibid., 60.
53. Irwin, *Prisons in Turmoil.*
54. Pamela Griset, *Determinate Sentencing: The Promise and the Reality of Retributive Justice* (Albany: State University of New York Press, 1991). See also James Austin and John Irwin, *It's About Time: America's Imprisonment Binge,* 4th ed. (Belmont, CA: Wadsworth, 2001).
55. Irwin, *Prisons in Turmoil.*
56. Robert Martinson and Judith Wilks, "Save Parole Supervision," in *Correctional Contexts: Contemporary and Classical Readings,* 2nd ed., eds. Edward J. Latessa et al. (Los Angeles: Roxbury, 2001), 422–427.
57. Hibbert, *Roots of Evil,* 3.
58. Edward Peters, *Torture* (New York: Basil Blackwell, 1985).
59. Stuart Banner, *The Death Penalty: An American History* (Cambridge, MA: Harvard University Press, 2002).
60. Scott H. Decker and Carol W. Kohfeld, "The Deterrent Effect of Capital Punishment in the Five Most Active Execution States: A Time-Series Analysis," *Criminal Justice Review* 15 (1990): 173–191.
61. Marla Sandys and Edmund F. McGarrell, "Attitudes Toward Capital Punishment Among Indiana Legislators: Diminished Support in Light of Alternative Sentencing Options," *Justice Quarterly* 11 (1994): 651–677.
62. Robert M. Bohm, "Retribution and Capital Punishment: Toward a Better Understanding of Death Penalty Opinion," *Journal of Criminal Justice* 20 (1992): 227–236.
63. Robert M. Bohm, *Deathquest: An Introduction to the Theory and Practice of Capital Punishment in the United States* (Cincinnati: Anderson, 1999). See especially Chapter 5, "General Deterrence and the Death Penalty," pp. 83–101.
64. Samuel R. Gross and Robert Mauro, *Death and Discrimination: Racial Disparities in Capital Sentencing* (Boston: Northeastern University Press, 1989).
65. Cesare Beccaria, *On Crimes and Punishment* (New York: Macmillan, 1961/1963), 50.
66. Robert Johnson, *Deathwork: A Study of the Modern Execution Process* (Monterey, CA: Brooks/Cole, 1990), 136.

67. Elizabeth Rapaport, "The Death Penalty and Gender Discrimination," in *A Capital Punishment Anthology*, ed. Victor L. Streib (Cincinnati: Anderson, 1993), 145–152.
68. Bohm, *Retribution*, 157.
69. Raymond Paternoster, "Prosecutorial Discretion in Requesting the Death Penalty: The Case of Victim-Based Discrimination," *Law and Society Review* 18 (1984): 437–478.
70. Jeffrey Reiman, *The Rich Get Richer and the Poor Get Prison: Ideology, Class and Criminal Justice*, 6th ed. (Boston: Allyn and Bacon, 2001).
71. Michael L. Radelet, Hugo Adam Bedau, and Constance E. Putnam, *In Spite of Innocence: Erroneous Convictions in Capital Cases* (Boston: Northeastern University Press, 1992).

outline

CHAPTER 12

The Contemporary Prison

OVER THE CENTURIES, THE PRISON HAS DEVELOPED INTO A unique institution that has become a fundamental feature in our criminal justice system (see Figure 12.1). This chapter will examine the male prison in light of several important issues that illustrate how this institution affects not only the inmates, but also those who work in the prison. We will examine inmates' social roles and legal rights, the occupation of the correctional officer, the problems and dangers associated with incarceration, and finally, the move to privatize this traditionally governmental service.

objectives

After reading this chapter, the student should be able to:

1. Understand how prisons are an example of a "total institution."
2. Appreciate the ways the inmate subculture develops.
3. Discuss argot roles.
4. Compare and contrast the Attica and New Mexico prison riots.
5. Describe how civilian work roles in the prison differ from those in society.
6. List some special job functions of correctional officers.
7. Identify some aspects or themes of the correctional officer's work.
8. Discuss the "hands-off" doctrine.
9. Describe special problems or points of contention between inmate rights and institutional requirements.
10. Compare and contrast private prisons with government-run prisons.

Figure 12.1 The Increasing Imprisonment Rate

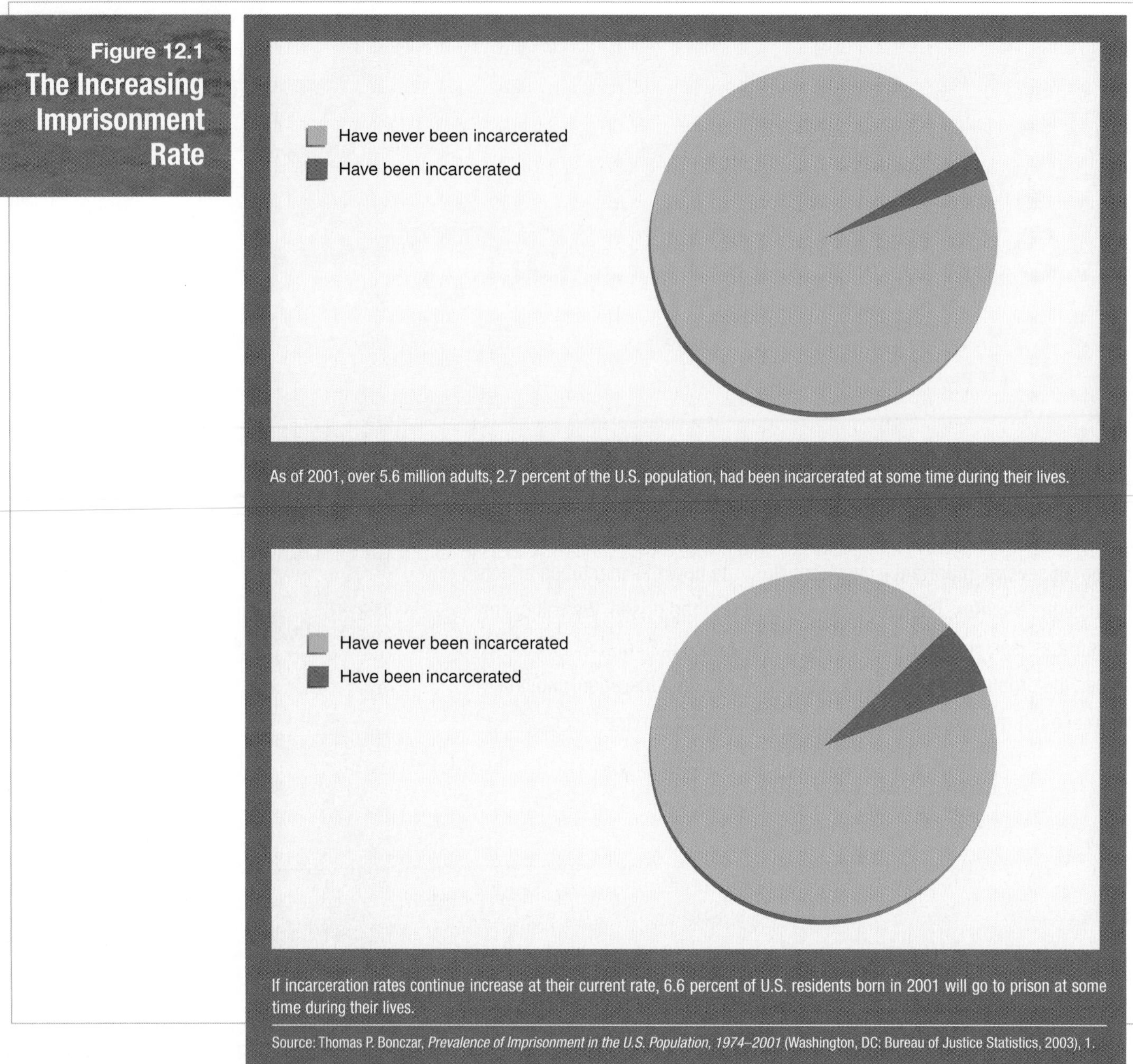

As of 2001, over 5.6 million adults, 2.7 percent of the U.S. population, had been incarcerated at some time during their lives.

If incarceration rates continue increase at their current rate, 6.6 percent of U.S. residents born in 2001 will go to prison at some time during their lives.

Source: Thomas P. Bonczar, *Prevalence of Imprisonment in the U.S. Population, 1974–2001* (Washington, DC: Bureau of Justice Statistics, 2003), 1.

Prison Life

total institution
A closed environment in which every aspect, including the movement and behavior of the people within, is controlled and structured.

The prison is what Erving Goffman called a **total institution.**[1] Much like the military, some religious monasteries, the secure mental health hospital, and tuberculosis sanatoriums, the prison is a closed institution in which everything is tightly controlled and highly structured. The inmates' ability to influence the conditions of their confinement is limited, and fleeing is almost impossible. This total control of inmates' lives, including who their cellmates are, what they eat, and when they can bathe, is designed to help the prison run efficiently, maintain order, and deprive the inmate of the discretion often taken for granted in free society. Although being confined in a small cell may be uncomfortable to many, it is not the worst thing that can happen to a person. (In fact, to many, the closeness of walls can be comforting. The first thing Defoe's Robinson Crusoe did when stranded on a deserted island was to build himself a small structure the size of a prison cell so that he would feel secure.[2]) Instead, deprivations are largely what define a prisoner's lifestyle. Gresham Sykes, in his seminal book *The Society of Captives,* argued that maximum security prisons make incarceration a painful experience by depriving inmates of some basic freedoms, stating that "the modern pains of imprisonment are often defined by society as a humane alternative to the physical brutality and the neglect which constituted the major meaning of imprisonment in the past."[3] Sykes went on to note that the pains of imprisonment can be destructive to the psyche and pose profound threats to the inmate's personality and self-worth. Because of deprivation, we have come to believe that incarceration is a sufficient punishment and that physical brutality in the form of corporal punishment is not required to achieve justice. However, this does not mean that inmates do not experience brutality at the hands of each other. Sykes described five **pains of imprisonment** in this way:

pains of imprisonment Deprivations that define the punitive nature of imprisonment.

1. **Deprivation of liberty.** The inmate is confined to an institution and then further confined within that institution. This loss of freedom is the most obvious feature of incarceration, but to adequately understand its effect on the inmate, we must appreciate that it includes not only being restricted to a small space such as a prison cell, but also that this restriction is involuntary. Because friends and family are prohibited from visiting except at very limited times, the bonds to loved ones are frayed, sometimes to the breaking point. Sykes went on to say, "What makes this pain of imprisonment bite most deeply is the fact that the confinement of the criminal represents a deliberate, moral rejection of the criminal by free society" (p. 65).
2. **Deprivation of goods and services.** Inmates do not have access to the wide range of food, entertainment, and services that free people routinely enjoy. To be sure, this deprivation is relative, and for some inmates "three hots and a cot" might be an improvement over their disadvantaged lives on the outside. Having a dry place to sleep and a government-guaranteed calorie count is something that many in this world would consider an improvement in lifestyle. However, the inmates' perception is subjective and, according to Sykes, the impoverishment incarceration brings is viewed by some inmates as the prison acting as a tyrant to deprive them of the goods and services they should reasonably have. More often, inmates may see their poverty as a consequence of their behavior and a result of their own inadequacies.

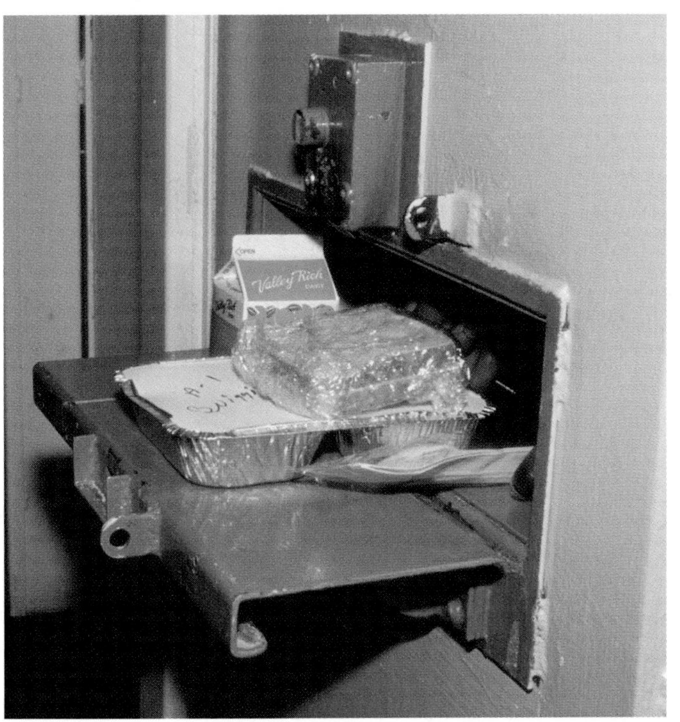

Meals are delivered through a slot in the door to inmates in solitary confinement. Often, the food is cold by the time it reaches the inmate. This is one of the deprivations that results from not being allowed to mix with the general prison population.
Courtesy of CORBIS-NY.

3. **Deprivation of heterosexual relationships.** Living in a single-sex society such as a prison imposes a variety of stresses on an individual. The deprivation of heterosexual activities is one of the most visible and controversial because it sometimes leads to sexual deviation within the prison. We will not deal with this issue here, but it is noted that homosexual activities and rape are often associated with incarceration. This is particularly true in male prisons where, as Sykes contended, the self-concept of men is bound up in their sexuality. By depriving men of the audience of females, their "self image is in danger of becoming half complete, fractured, a monochrome without the hues of reality" (p. 72). In turn, without women to provide feedback for displays of masculinity, the inmates create an atmosphere that is sexually charged and difficult to negotiate. Men do not lose their sex drive when imprisoned; it is changed into a type of hypermasculinity that demands that some men be subservient to others.
4. **Deprivation of autonomy.** The inability to make decisions about some of the most basic tasks, such as walking from one room to another, is a particularly galling deprivation. Being subject to the rules, whims, and preferences of a bureaucratic staff that makes decisions that can appear to be arbitrary or mean-spirited is a humbling experience. Having to ask for everything reduces the inmate to the status of a child. Some inmates will argue or bargain with the staff, but their position is so weak that they have little leverage in a well-run prison free of guard corruption. Finding ways to cope with this enforced lack of decision-making power occupies a good deal of the inmates' time and energy.
5. **Deprivation of security.** This is perhaps the most disturbing pain of imprisonment. Those confined to a maximum-security prison have already proven themselves to be violent, aggressive, and untrustworthy. Having to cope with such cellmates can be an extremely anxious experience, even for those who are violent themselves. There are precious few places in the prison where one can feel secure. Inmates constantly test each other for physical or emotional weaknesses. Those without the courage or nerve to protect themselves are quickly victimized by others if they cannot find a protector.[4]

These pains of imprisonment define the prison experience. Even in the best managed prisons, with well-trained guards and adequate resources, these deprivations are present. However, they are not unintended consequences. Prisons are meant to be uncomfortable for the inmates and are places that lack the niceties of home. Many people do not feel

There are multiple layers of security in a prison. Inmates are not only confined *to* the prison, but they are also confined *within* the prison. For security reasons, inmates are not allowed to roam freely within the institution.

Courtesy of CORBIS-NY.

sorry for inmates who suffer these deprivations. However, these pains of imprisonment are real to the inmates, and to understand prison dynamics, we must appreciate not only how these deprivations affect the inmates, but also how the inmates cope with this lifestyle.

NEWS FLASH

Bad Food for Bad Behavior

Baltimore's Maryland Correctional Adjustment Center has devised a way to control unruly inmates without resorting to violence or solitary confinement. They simply serve up a "special management meal," popularly known as "prison loaf." One corrections officer at a New York facility that serves the loaf claims that it is better at controlling prisoners than solitary confinement. However, inmates at some prisons are suing over the loaf, calling the baked bread-and-vegetable concoction cruel and unusual punishment, and some prison reform advocates agree, equating it to a bread-and-water diet.

Here is Baltimore's recipe for prison loaf. What do you think?

Prison Loaf

6 slices whole wheat bread, finely chopped

4 ounces imitation cheddar cheese, finely grated

4 ounces raw carrots, finely grated

12 ounces spinach, canned, drained

2 cups dried Great Northern Beans, soaked,
cooked and drained

4 tablespoons vegetable oil

6 ounces potato flakes, dehydrated

6 ounces tomato paste

8 ounces powdered skim milk

4 ounces raisins

Drain all wet items. Mix all ingredients in a 12-quart mixing bowl. Mix until stiff, just moist enough to spread. Form three loaves in glazed bread pans. Place loaf pans in the oven on a sheet pan filled with water, to keep the bottom of the loaves from burning. Bake at 325 degrees in a convection oven for approximately 45 minutes. The loaf will start to pull away from the sides of the bread pan when done.

QUESTIONS

1. Is prison loaf akin to the bread-and-water diets of old?
2. Will you attempt the recipe?
3. Some people on vegan diets say that the prison loaf recipe is not that bad and needs only a little seasoning to resemble their own recipes. In this case, does prison loaf really constitute cruel and unusual punishment?

Sources: John Stossel, "Let Them Eat Cake," ABCNEWS.com, September 13, 2002, http://abcnews.go.com/sections/2020/2020/stossel_gmab_prisonloaf020913.html. Scott Simon, "Prison Loaf: Maryland Lockup Uses Horrid Bread Dish as Disciplinary Tool," National Public Radio, April 6, 2002, http://www.npr.org/programs/wesat/features/2002/apr/loaf/index.html.

Inmate Subculture

argot roles
Specific patterns of behavior that inmates develop in prison to adjust to the environment.

According to Sykes, inmates compensate for the pains of imprisonment by adopting certain patterns of behavior called **argot roles.** An argot is a special language used by a particular group of people. Inmates have developed terms for the various roles they take on to adapt to imprisonment. According to Sykes, these names provide a map of the inmate social system and enable the inmates to engage in the "ordering and classifying of their experience within the walls in terms which deal specifically with the major problems of prison life."[5] Sykes listed and discussed these argot roles in the following manner:

- **Rats and center men.** In prison, information is a valuable commodity and one that the inmates guard jealously. Those who violate the inmate code and reveal to the administration information that can cause harm to another inmate or to the inmate population are called "rats" or "squealers." This is a serious accusation because of the physical and social consequences that can befall someone labeled in this way. There are two types of rats: those who reveal their identity in hopes of personal gain and those who remain anonymous but squeal on a competitor or to settle a grudge. A "center man" is not as vilified by the inmate population as the rat because his actions do not betray the inmate code. A center man is someone who too willingly obeys the rules, who takes the worldview of the administration or who publicly proclaims the virtue of the "rulers." The center man makes no secret of where his loyalties lie and is despised for his open disloyalty to the inmate subculture. However, inmates may adopt these roles to relieve the deprivation of autonomy and develop a way of influencing their world by squealing or ingratiating themselves to the prison administration.
- **Gorillas and merchants.** The deprivation of goods and services is partially relieved by the roles of "gorillas" and "merchants." The gorilla is the prison bully who takes what he wants from other inmates through physical force. Often, however, only the threat of force is necessary. The blatant willingness to use force can coerce other inmates to provide the gorilla with cigarettes, food, or gestures of deference, thus placing him at the top of the inmate pecking order. Gorillas can sometimes push inmates too far and find themselves stabbed for their efforts. Many inmates keep weapons as a line of last resort to protect themselves from these predators. The merchant, by contrast, does not use force to get what he wants, but rather trades for it. The merchant does not engage in the reciprocal exchange of gifts that is common in other groups and that

Inmates have a well-developed informal social system. In a situation in which resources are scarce, even the control of a basketball hoop may be a point of contention.
Courtesy of CORBIS-NY.

enhances the solidarity of equals. Rather, the merchant is concerned with his own material advantage and is willing to exploit the suffering of other inmates to advance his own standard of living. The roles of gorilla and merchant address the deprivation of goods and services.

- **Wolves, punks, and fags.** To relieve the lack of heterosexual relations, the roles of "wolves," "punks," and "fags" have emerged. A wolf is an individual who plays the masculine role in homosexual relations and uses force or the threat of force to make others submit. A wolf may or may not have been a homosexual in the free world and uses sex in the prison as a form of dominance to illustrate his masculinity. A punk is a weaker inmate who is forced to engage in homosexual relations against his will. By contrast, a fag is someone who is self-identified as a homosexual and who engages in extremely feminine patterns of behavior such as wearing makeup, walking in a feminine way, and playing games such as "stay away closer" and "hard to get but gettable." Although punks and fags differ in their motivations for homosexual activities, they are both held in low esteem by the other inmates. Inmates see the punk as lacking the inner core of toughness, whereas the fag is an overt symbol of femininity. In both cases, they are lower in the pecking order than the wolf, who exhibits masculine behavior. For the wolf, the deprivation of heterosexual relations can be substituted with the exploitation of weaker inmates and thus his manhood can be redeemed in the prison's highly artificial society.
- **Ball-busters and real men.** "Ball-busters" are inmates who give the prison administration a hard time. They are verbally abusive, defiant, and blatantly disobedient. The ball-buster refuses to see the utter hopelessness of his position and clings to the vestiges of his manhood by defying the administration at every turn. In an effort to ease the deprivation of autonomy, the ball-buster forces guards to either put up with his abusive comments or discipline him. We might expect other inmates to respect this attitude, but in fact, they look upon the ball-buster as a fool. Like a Don Quixote tilting at windmills, the ball-buster does not know when to pick his fights and ends up bringing down sanctions not only on himself, but often on the whole inmate population. For this reason, the ball-buster, although mildly amusing at times, is considered a liability by the other inmates because he can make life harder for everyone. The "real man," by contrast, is respected by the other inmates. The real man is the type of inmate most of us would like to think we would be if we were ever in prison. The real man does his time with his dignity intact. He is neither subservient nor aggressive, but "pulls his own time" with a strong and silent demeanor that suggests he is oblivious to the chaos around him. The real man refuses to let the prison strip him of his ability to control his emotions and behavior. He serves his sentence with integrity, respecting the inmate social system without exploiting others or bringing down the wrath of the administration on the general population.
- **Toughs and hipsters.** Violence is a consistent feature of the prison, and several of the argot roles we have discussed use violence or the threat of violence for various purposes. Whereas the gorilla will use it for personal gain and the wolf to get sexual favors, the "tough" will use violence simply for the sake of violence. He is a touchy individual who will fight over any real or imagined slight or insult. The other inmates tend to give him a wide berth because he fears no one and demands that others placate him with deference. He is respected more than the gorilla because he is not a coward and will fight anyone, even if he is certain to lose. By contrast, the "hipster" is someone who "talks the talk but does not walk the walk." By this, we mean the hipster will attempt to bluff and bully other inmates, but when real violence is imminent, he disappears. Each of these types is an adaptation to the deprivation of security that can exacerbate the pains of imprisonment for other inmates. While trying to maintain their own

security through violence or the threat of violence, they create an atmosphere in the prison in which everyone must be careful not to offend others.

Sykes' system of argot roles presents an interesting and informative road map of the prison subculture, but some qualifications need to be considered. First, we must recognize that Sykes wrote his book 50 years ago, and prisons have undergone substantial change in the interim. To be sure, the names of the argot roles have mutated many times over, and modern inmates might have a difficult time with the titles assigned by Sykes. However, the basic problems of the inmate social structure (security, goods and services, etc.) remain, and inmates must still adapt to imprisonment. Second, each prison will demonstrate its own variations of the inmate social structure. Sykes' argot roles, therefore, should be considered as ideal types, rather than a scheme to explain all prisons across the decades. Sykes outlined some universal truths concerning the prison; the student of today must consider how these argot roles have evolved in the contemporary prison.

Finally, there has been considerable debate as to whether these roles are actually adaptations to the new environment of the prison or whether they reflect roles that inmates occupied before they were incarcerated. John Irwin, a prominent scholar of the prison, who has the added perspective of having served five years in California's institutions, contended that inmates come to prison with their identities already developed from their criminal involvement on the street. Irwin particularly described a "thief identity" that offenders who were thieves bring with them into the prison subculture; he suggested that the student of the prison should consider Sykes' argot roles from a more holistic perspective.[6]

Irwin's concerns can be extended to include the changing nature of the prison subculture as a result of the emergence of prison gangs. Many of the argot roles identified by Sykes have been overtaken by the advent of prison gangs. Now, instead of using argot roles to respond to the pains of imprisonment, inmates join prison gangs for security and to acquire goods and services.[7] Sykes' analysis is fascinating and worth contemplating, but we should consider it in light of the changing nature of the prison subculture.

Prison Gangs

To fully appreciate how the contemporary prison's informal inmate social structure shapes the lives of inmates and staff, we must consider the impact of prison gangs. Although not all correctional systems have severe gang problems, and not all gangs are as violent as the ones we will discuss here, gangs are a concern because without proper vigilance, they can form and take partial control of any prison.

Here, we will discuss the California prison gang problem because it is the most serious in the nation and because a great deal of material has been written about it. The sig-

Gangs are a pervasive feature of the contemporary prison. Often, gang members use tattoos to signify their allegiance to a particular gang.
Courtesy of CORBIS-NY.

nature feature of the California prison gang structure is that it is based on race. Although not every inmate is affiliated with a gang, those who are stick to their own races. Christian Parenti described several gangs:[8]

- **Mexican Mafia.** The oldest of the prison gangs, the Mexican Mafia, has been traced to the 1950s when a group of Mexican juveniles from Los Angeles was incarcerated together in the Deuel Vocational Institution in Tracy, California. They began preying on white and black inmates by extorting and robbing them. They also attacked Mexican inmates from northern California, especially from cities such as Fresno and Sacramento, whom they considered to be "farmers." The prison authorities, in an effort to destabilize this cadre of troublemakers, dispersed them to prisons all across the state where, unfortunately, they recruited other Mexicans from southern California. The Mexican Mafia, or "La Eme," eventually appropriated the number 13 (*M* is the 13th letter in the alphabet). The gang became a vertically integrated organization that had considerable power not only in the prison, but also on the streets of Los Angeles. For example, according to Parenti, during the post–Rodney King gang truce in Los Angeles in 1993, La Eme ordered an end to drive-by shootings because too many innocent

FOCUS ON ETHICS

Conned by the Cons

You have known for a long time that your older brother Mike is not the brightest bulb on the Christmas tree. He always seemed to find a way to let his good intentions go astray and end up in some kind of disaster. Now it looks as though his latest scheme is going to bring you down with him unless you make a very difficult decision.

Mike has worked at the county jail for three years and has risen to the rank of sergeant and is supervisor over the visiting center. Because of his connections, you have been recently hired as a guard and work directly under him as a security officer in charge of searching visitors. Mike has wide discretion in this post in determining what types of visits are granted to inmates and is usually pretty good about making sure high-risk offenders do not get contact visits with their families. Lately, however, you have noticed that several members of a violent gang have been getting more visits than normal and that these contact visits extend well past the normal visiting hours. Furthermore, Mike has just purchased a new extended-cab pickup truck that must have cost close to $25,000, money you know he does not have because he still owes money to you. Troubled, you suspect that Mike has been taking money from inmates in exchange for letting them smuggle drugs inside the jail.

Today Mike came to you and confessed that he was in big trouble. It seems that the drugs he has allowed in the jail have become a cause for a pending all-out gang war, and he fears not only for his life but also for yours and your family's. A rival gang of the one he has been helping has put a contract out on Mike, you, and your parents. Mike says that the only way to solve this problem is to smuggle a gun inside the jail and let his gang friends "take care of business." Mike needs your cooperation in overlooking the gun, which will be carried in by a gang leader's girlfriend. She will have it hidden in a big pocketbook, and you are to do a careless search and allow her inside the jail with this loaded gun.

WHAT DO YOU DO?

1. Do you value your loyalty to your brother more than your integrity to the job?
2. Should you attempt to protect your parents by going along with Mike's plan?
3. Given Mike's limited intelligence, are you certain that even if the plan works it will solve any problems?
4. What are your other options?

civilians were getting killed. Gang members were ordered to "take care of business with honor and dignity" and not shoot regular people.

- **La Nuestra Familia.** This Mexican gang draws its members from northern California and is constantly at odds with La Eme. In recent years, some of this gang's younger members have spun off and created the Northern Structure, which, in addition to feuding with La Eme, has also clashed with the old guard of La Nuestra Familia. Together, La Nuestra Familia and the Northern Structure represent the largest prison gang in the state. It has gone to great lengths to detail its military structure and educate new gang members about its code of honor, how to identify the enemy, and how to resist interrogations. Those who are released are instructed to set up "regiments" back on the streets of their hometowns, but how successful the gang is in "calling the shots" of what happens on the outside is not really clear.
- **Black Guerrilla Family.** This gang of black inmates originates from the 1960s when members of the Black Panther Party such as Huey Newton, George Jackson, and Eldridge Cleaver were incarcerated in California prisons. Back then, the inmates were extremely political and adopted a Marxist rhetoric that cast them as political prisoners of an unjust capitalist state. They espoused revolution, but as the years passed, a number of them traded their political aspirations for more pragmatic ones. They became gangsters in their own right and instead of robbing drug dealers, they became drug dealers. Today the Black Guerrilla Family is composed of black lifers. Younger black inmates who join gangs are more likely to be affiliated with inmates who belonged to the Bloods or Crips street gangs.
- **Aryan Brotherhood.** These white gang members employ Ku Klux Klan symbols and Nazi swastikas as evidence of their racial identity. Formed partly in response to the increasing dangers posed by Chicano and black gangs, the Aryan Brotherhood is among the most violent and fights hard for its share of prison-yard drug dealing, extortion, and prostitution scams. Parenti reported that the Aryan Brotherhood has, on occasion, aligned itself with La Eme in its ongoing conflict with La Nuestra Familia to the extent of conducting assassinations. The Aryan Brotherhood has spawned franchises around the country in other prisons, but its control of these other gangs is more symbolic than real. Gangs in other states develop their own mythologies that include references to Celtic and Norse cultures in addition to the Ku Klux Klan and Nazis.

This list of gangs is incomplete, and to a great extent, already dated because of the changing nature of gang identity and the efforts of prison officials to combat gangs. Gangs mutate over time, changing their names and leadership, but racial identification is always a constant feature. One might think that the prisons could stop gang activity by isolating leaders, punishing those who display gang insignia, and transferring those who refuse to cooperate. These techniques have been partially successful in the short run, but the diffusion of gang activity to other prisons has complicated efforts at gang control.

Parenti somewhat cynically suggested that it is not entirely in the prisons' interests to eliminate gang conflict. It has been reported that prison officials keep gangs in a state of perpetual conflict by allowing rival gang members to use the exercise yard at the same time. At California's Corcoran institution, this practice was routinely a source of amusement for the guards. According to Parenti, not only would rival gang members be placed in the same yard, but when the ensuing fight took place, the guards would place bets on which inmate would win. These "gladiator fights" were videotaped:

> *At the micro-level, COs (also known as "screws" or "bulls"), were staging fights as a form of sadistic diversion, even videotaping the fights for later viewing, and gathering to watch the contests from gun towers. But this local practice, which occurred in other prisons as well, was given a veil of legitimacy by the CDC's inte-*

grated yard policy, which mandates the mixing of rival gangs and races in the name of teaching tolerance and testing prisoners' "ability to get along in a controlled setting." Not surprisingly, fist fights and stabbings were, and still are, epidemic throughout the system.[9]

For the most part, prison officials are forced to make difficult decisions in attempts to stem gang violence. On one hand, they attempt to segregate inmates from those of rival gangs and different races to avoid violence. On the other hand, they hope to allow inmates to learn to get along with one another and promote the values of diversity espoused in society. Charges of discrimination can be leveled when inmates are racially separated, but when inmates are allowed access to each other and violence ensues, there may be charges of failing to protect the weak. One solution in California was to build extremely expensive prisons where inmates are separated from each other.

Pelican Bay State Prison

Pelican Bay is a maximum-security state prison located in Crescent City, California. What makes this prison special is the way it recalls the separate-and-silent systems in the first prisons in Pennsylvania and Auburn, New York. The Pelican Bay prison architecture is designed to ensure almost total isolation of inmates as well as minimal contact with the staff. The prison itself is such a bleak, stark, and monotonous environment that inmates suffer severe disorientation, depression, and suicidal behavior.[10] High, gray concrete walls surround the exercise yards and totally block out the surrounding national forest. Inmates are confined to their cells with no work, recreation, or contact with anyone other than a cellmate who is equally deprived. When going to the shower (three times a week) or the exercise yard, the inmates are shackled and can move only with the escort of two baton-wielding correctional officers. The prison's security housing unit (SHU) is the end of the line for the state's most recalcitrant inmates. It is reserved for those who have proven unable to live in a general population prison. The majority of these inmates are gang members.

The prison at Pelican Bay is successful in a number of ways. It keeps the most dangerous offenders securely incapacitated, ensuring both their safety and the safety of the prison staff. This is a significant feat because it usually takes some degree of cooperation from the inmates to run a truly safe prison. Pelican Bay maintains order mechanically by using technology and prison design, giving inmates absolutely no opportunity to assemble outside their cells. However, this total control comes at a price. This type of prison is

The maximum-security prison is a secure institution where most inmates are placed in individual cells. Privileges are limited and boredom is constant.

Courtesy of CORBIS-NY.

extremely expensive to operate, demanding a high degree of technology. Most states could only afford to use such a specialized maximum-security institution for a small percentage of extremely dangerous offenders.[11] For the bulk of the prison population, less expensive prisons, with less control of the inmates, are the norm. Another important expense of the Pelican Bay-type prison, however, is the ultimate impact it has on the inmate who will eventually be released into society. Craig Haney finds these psychological consequences of isolation problematic:

> *My own [Haney's] review of the literature suggested these documented negative psychological consequences of long-term solitary-like confinement include: an impaired sense of identity; hypersensitivity to stimuli; cognitive dysfunction (confusion, memory loss, ruminations); irritability, anger, aggression, and/or rage; other-directed violence, such as stabbings, attacks on staff, property destruction, and collective violence; lethargy, helplessness and hopelessness; chronic depression; self-mutilation and/or suicidal ideation, impulses, and behavior; anxiety and panic attacks; emotional breakdowns and/or loss of control; hallucinations, psychosis and/or paranoia; overall deterioration of mental and physical health.*[12]

Prison Riots and Violence

The prison is a delicate social system that includes not only inmates, but also guards and administrators, and to a lesser extent, the legislators and politicians responsible for funding and personnel decisions. Although inmates are presumed to be powerless in their captivity, they may employ a number of techniques to address the conditions of their confinement. Inmates may write letters to correctional officials, complain to their congressional representatives, petition the parole board, file briefs in the courts, or shout at the top of their lungs, "I'm mad as hell, and I'm not going to take it anymore." Some of these techniques are more effective than others. The bottom line, however, is that regardless of how frustrated inmates may feel in a correctional institution, they are not able to walk away. Those of us in society can drop out of school, move out of our parents' houses, quit our jobs, or dump our significant others when we have "had enough." Inmates do not have these options. Being incarcerated means that problems and frustrations can accumulate until a breaking point is reached. This breaking point can be a mental collapse, a fight with a fellow inmate, violence against a guard, or simply retreating from prison life by being so ornery that solitary confinement is required.[13] These are daily occurrences in the prison and, for the most part, they are handled with preestablished procedures that are understood by all involved. (See Figure 12.2 for statistics on prison violence.)

On rare occasions, the inmate's frustrations are shared by others, and the authority of the institution is seriously challenged. Inmates acting together can sometimes overwhelm the guards and take over the institution in a full-scale prison riot in which people are killed and injured and property destroyed. Sociologists use the term *collective behavior* to explain how the actions of the individual are transmitted into group actions that can go well beyond what any of the individuals in the group intended.[14] This "herd mentality" can cause even law-abiding citizens to engage in destructive actions. (A good example of this would be the riots that sometimes occur after sports championships.)[15]

In the prison, collective behavior can not only have deadly consequences, but also temporarily invert the social structure and shatter the bonds of social control.[16] With the administration no longer controlling the institution, the oppressed become king, the protected become vulnerable, and anyone caught in the middle can become a victim. The prison's most antisocial individuals are, for a limited time, free to wreak havoc. A number of studies on the causes and prevention of prison riots have made it clear that despite many commonalities, each institution has its own limitations, atmosphere, and vulnerabilities.[17] Rather than attempting a comprehensive review of prison riots, we will focus on two very different but infamous examples of what can happen when things go terribly wrong in the prison.

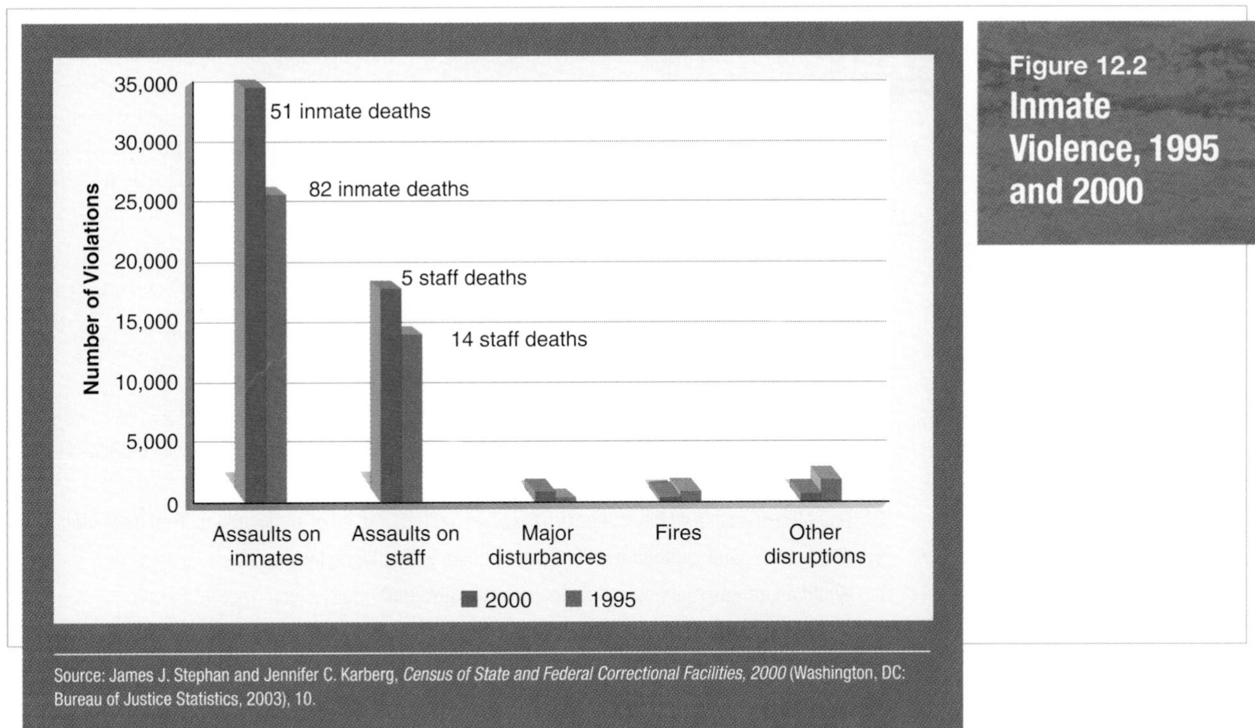

Figure 12.2 Inmate Violence, 1995 and 2000

Source: James J. Stephan and Jennifer C. Karberg, *Census of State and Federal Correctional Facilities, 2000* (Washington, DC: Bureau of Justice Statistics, 2003), 10.

At the Maricopa County Jail in Phoenix, Arizona, prisoners who refuse to cooperate or are violent are isolated and strapped into a restraining chair. The hood protects officers and staff from biting and spitting. The county has been sued by the family of a prisoner who died after being restrained in this chair.

Courtesy of Andrew Lichtenstein, CORBIS-NY.

ATTICA PRISON RIOT. The 1971 Attica prison riot may well be the most famous because so much has been written about it. It has been the subject of at least four major books, one written by the then-commissioner of corrections, one by an inmate, and two by outside observers. Additionally, it was investigated primarily by the McKay Commission, which interviewed guards, inmates, state police, national guardsmen, reporters, and former Governor Nelson Rockefeller. In total, more than 2,600 interviews were conducted. The official McKay Commission report was 500 pages long.[18]

The Attica prison opened in upstate New York in 1931. It was considered a state-of-the-art prison at the time and boasted of being both "escape-proof" and a "paradise for convicts." Neither of these proclamations turned out to be the case.[19] To understand the riot's causes, we must examine the social dynamics both inside and outside the prison as they existed in 1971. The United States was embroiled in a number of social conflicts

REFERENCE

The Demands Collected by the Inmates During the Attica Prison Riot

1. Provide adequate food and water and shelter for this group.
2. Replace Superintendent Mancusi immediately.
3. Grant complete administrative and legal amnesty to all persons associated with this matter.
4. Place this institution under federal jurisdiction.
5. Apply the New York State minimum wage law to all work done by inmates. STOP SLAVE LABOR.
6. Allow all New York State prisoners to be politically active, without intimidation or reprisal.
7. Allow true religious freedom.
8. End all censorship of newspaper, magazines, letters, and other publications from publishers.
9. Allow all inmates on their own to communicate with anyone they please.
10. When an inmate reaches conditional release, give him a full release without parole.
11. Institute realistic, effective rehabilitation programs for all inmates according to their offense and personal needs.
12. Modernize the education system.
13. Provide a narcotics treatment program that is effective.
14. Provide adequate legal assistance to all inmates requesting it.
15. Provide a healthy diet; reduce the number of pork dishes; serve fresh fruit daily.
16. Reduce cell time, increase recreation time, and provide better recreation facilities and equipment.
17. Provide adequate medical treatment for every inmate, engage either a Spanish-speaking doctor or interpreters who will accompany Spanish-speaking inmates to medical interviews.
18. Provide a complete Spanish library.

Source: Bert Useem and Peter Kimball, *States of Siege: U.S. Prison Riots 1971–1986 (New York: Oxford University Press, 1991), 236.*

during this period. Many citizens had high expectations that opportunity and social justice would be available to all and were frustrated when conditions did not improve quickly enough. Social movements concerned with civil rights, women's liberation, and opposition to the ongoing Vietnam War placed the government on the defensive and brought scrutiny to many social institutions. Universities were challenged to make their curricula more relevant; traditional family values were challenged by communal living and sexual relations without commitment; and the government's foreign policy was protested by people from a wide variety of backgrounds.

In prisons nationwide, this age of protest was embraced by inmates who thought the conditions of their incarceration were unjust, inadequate, or unconstitutional. Additionally, as John Irwin tells us, there was a major change in the collective self-concept of minorities. The "black is beautiful" idea signaled a newfound pride in racial status and convinced many to reject the second-class treatment they believed prison officials meted out to people of color.[20] Against this backdrop of challenges to institutional authority, Attica Prison imploded in 1971. Was Attica different from other prisons of the time? Probably not. But an assessment by Useem and Kimball succinctly described the state of Attica:

> *Life at Attica was terrible. The McKay Commission devoted 71 pages to discussing how bad it was and all the ways in which it was bad. The cells were cramped, the food was barely edible or nutritious, the medical care was unsatisfactory, the recre-*

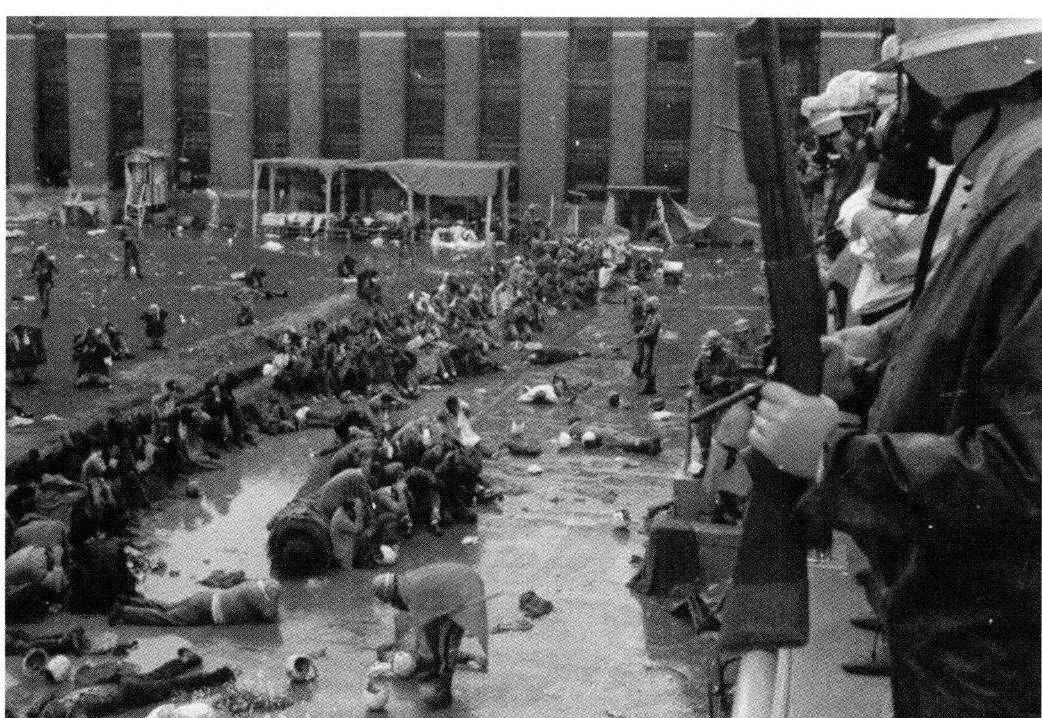

In August 1971, Attica State Prison inmates sitting under armed guard shortly after the end of the riot.
Courtesy of CORBIS-NY.

ation was minimal, the job assignments were boring and unrewarding, and the atmosphere was depressing and degrading.[21]

Yet, Useem and Kimball did not consider the prison's conditions as the major reason for the riot. Other prisons had inmate politicization and lacked an adequate physical plant like Attica, but such devastating riots did not occur at these prisons. However, the Attica administration adopted policies that exacerbated the sense of hopelessness and injustice there. For instance, the rules of the prison were mutable, unwritten, arbitrarily enforced, and frustrating to even the best behaved inmates. Usually, in such situations, the guards and the inmates negotiate which behaviors are acceptable and which are not. But at Attica, according to Useem and Kimball, the guards' job assignments were reorganized in 1970. The result was that the guards no longer had stable assignments that allowed them to get to know the inmates and work out what constituted acceptable behavior. Instead, all 400 of the guards were rotated on an apparently random basis. To avoid rule infractions, inmates would need to know the predilections of each guard. This lack of consistent rule enforcement discouraged a stable environment.

Another feature unique to Attica was the inmates' political savvy. Prior to the riot, the inmates had communicated with inmates in other New York correctional institutions, negotiated with the commissioner of correctional services, Russell Oswald, and successfully engaged in a sit-down strike in the metal shops and won a tripling of their wages. In retaliation, the prison moved the leaders of this peaceful protest to other prisons.

The Attica prison riot is instructive because the inmates were able to present a united front and negotiate as a group. The inmates established an order of discipline and formulated and presented demands to prison officials. Additionally, after the first wave of violence (in which one correctional officer and three inmates were killed), inmates protected hostages from further violence. Over 1,600 inmates took control of the prison yard, and after an initial celebration, the serious work of organizing the siege and negotiating with authorities got underway. Of particular interest was the introduction of outside observers to act as negotiators.[22] Negotiating with prisoners became problematic in that their demands would change radically and become unreasonable (some inmates wanted to be transported out of the country). With the introduction of press coverage, a circuslike atmosphere developed. Negotiations eventually broke down for a number of reasons, and the administration, using correctional officers and national guardsmen, stormed the prison and reestablished control in a violent paramilitary operation that resulted in the deaths of 29 inmates and 10 correctional officers who were being held hostage. (Autopsy reports revealed that all the hostages were killed by gunfire, which is significant because the inmates had no firearms.)

The Attica prison riot is known for the way the inmates cooperated to maintain the discipline of their social system under great stress and uncertainty. The riot is also famous for the inability of the state to bring a peaceful resolution and its botched retaking of the prison by correctional officers and national guardsmen who were not trained for such operations. In terms of brutality, however, the Attica prison riot pales in comparison to the New Mexico prison riot.

NEW MEXICO STATE PENITENTIARY RIOT. In 1980, 33 inmates died in a riot at the New Mexico State Penitentiary in Santa Fe. Although no guards were killed, 12 were severely beaten and raped. The major difference between the Attica riot and the New Mexico riot was the lack of social cohesion among the inmates. Unlike Attica, where the inmates displayed a certain amount of control and coordination, the New Mexico inmates killed with abandon and without regard for the preexisting inmate social system. According to Bert Useem:

> *No group of inmates attained clear leadership status. Control over hostages, walkie-talkies, and negotiations was fragmented, personalistic, and ephemeral. Some inmates, alone or in groups, took advantage of the situation to rape, torture, and mutilate other inmates. One inmate had his head cut off with a shovel; another died from a screw-driver driven through his head; several were immolated in their cells when inmates sprayed lighter fluid on them; and still others were tortured to death with acetylene torches. No inmate group made a serious attempt to prevent this.*[23]

The New Mexico prison riot caused great anxiety in institutions across the nation about the consequences of prison disturbances. Although the place of an inmate in the prison social structure may have prevented victimization in the past, this riot showed that when all the bonds of social control are cast aside, the prison riot can be deadly for anyone. In the few days the inmates controlled the prison, everyone lived in terror. Only the strong and the lucky escaped unscathed.

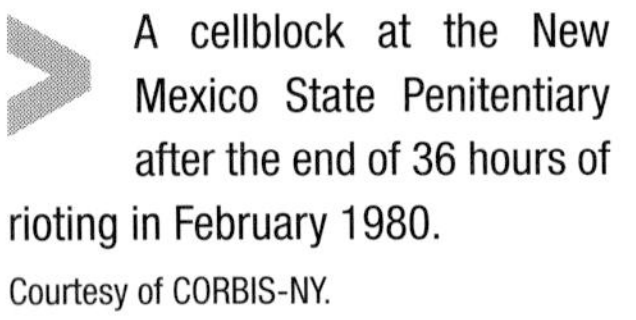

A cellblock at the New Mexico State Penitentiary after the end of 36 hours of rioting in February 1980.
Courtesy of CORBIS-NY.

CROSSCURRENTS

Stanford Prison Experiment

In 1971 Stanford psychology professor Philip Zimbardo created an experiment to test the effects of prison life on human beings. For this experiment he recruited 24 young men to act as inmates and guards in a makeshift prison. The experiment was scheduled to last two weeks. It ended in six days. Dr. Christina Maslach, who witnessed the student prison in its last stages, told a symposium of the American Psychological Association in 1996, "I was sick to my stomach. . . . I was having a hard time watching what was happening to these kids."[1]

In August 1971, in Palo Alto, California, police arrested nine young men in their homes. The men were students who had answered a newspaper ad offering to pay them $15 a day to participate in an experiment on prisons. The arrestees were part of a group of 24 men who had been randomly split into two parts: guards and inmates. Prior to the experiment, all had taken a battery of tests determining that they were in sound mental health.

The nine men who had been assigned as inmates were booked and fingerprinted at a real jail, then blindfolded and driven to the Stanford campus to a "prison" located in the basement of a school building. The students assigned as guards were given no training, only uniforms and instructions to control the prison as they saw fit without using violence. The prison cells were created by removing the doors of laboratory rooms and replacing them with steel bars and cell numbers. The prison had no windows, and no clocks were allowed. Other modifications included the addition of secret videotaping equipment and the conversion of a small closet into a solitary confinement chamber. The cells were bugged via an intercom system.

At the prison, the new inmates were greeted by the "warden," who established the seriousness of the inmates' offenses and their status as prisoners. The prisoners were strip-searched and deloused. Although the experimenters did not expect that these students would actually introduce contraband or lice, this procedure was done to imitate real prison procedures and to humiliate the student inmates. The inmates wore only dresslike smocks (no underwear) printed with their ID numbers and rubber sandals. Each inmate had a heavy chain bolted to each ankle, and his head was covered with a nylon stocking. The chain, smock, and stocking are not features in actual prisons, but they were introduced to quickly stimulate a sense of humiliation and oppression. For example, the inmates were called only by their ID numbers and could only refer to themselves by their numbers.

The experiment got underway with nine guards and nine inmates (the remaining six men remained on call if replacement guards or prisoners were needed). The guards were divided among three 8-hour shifts, overseeing the inmates, who were divided among three small cells. The guards began the simulation by counting the inmates several times a day, including waking the inmates for counts at 2:30 A.M. The guards also devised, with no input from the staff who ran the experiment, the punishment of push-ups, often placing their feet on the backs of inmates sentenced to do them.

By the second day, the prisoners staged a revolt, removing their stocking caps and numbers and barricading themselves inside their cells. The guards crushed this by calling in the three standby guards and having the night shift remain at the prison. They forced the inmates away from their cell doors with blasts from a fire extinguisher, entered the cells, and stripped the inmates. The leaders of the rebellion were forced into solitary confinement, while the remaining inmates were harassed. To break inmate solidarity, the guards set up a "privilege" cell in which the three inmates least involved in the rebellion were allowed to wash, dress, and eat a special meal in front of the other inmates who were not allowed to eat. After a few hours, the guards put the innocent inmates back in the regular cells and the scheming inmates in the privilege cell, setting up confusion and distrust among the inmates. A staff consultant who had been a former inmate in a real penitentiary confirmed that such divide-and-conquer tactics were actually used by correctional officers.

continued

According to Dr. Zimbardo, the guards continued to increase the humiliation, coercion, and dehumanization of the prisoners. For example, they would not allow any bathroom visits after 10 P.M. "lights-out," forcing the inmates to urinate and defecate in buckets in their cells. Occasionally, the guards would not allow inmates to empty these buckets. Although it might seem that the guards were overplaying their roles for the researchers, some guards were caught on videotape continuing to abuse the prisoners even when they thought the researchers were not watching.

The prisoners became so stressed that the staff released five of them early, but not easily. The staff themselves, according to Zimbardo, had already begun thinking like prison officials. When one inmate began to show signs of mental distress, they thought he was trying to "con" the staff. Instead of offering him release, the guards asked him to inform on the other inmates in exchange for better treatment. He was only released when his signs of distress increased. The staff also manipulated the inmates' parents and friends who came on visiting day. After sprucing up the prison and the inmates, they forced the visitors to comply with an assortment of rules much like those in a real prison. Although some of the parents complained, they all complied, even though some remarked that they had never seen their sons looking so stressed or fatigued.

The psychologists who ran the experiment were not immune to its effects, either. Zimbardo admitted becoming so consumed by his role as a prison official that he tried to quash a rumored mass escape plot by going to the Palo Alto police and asking to use their old jail to hold the student inmates. (The police turned down the request, much to Zimbardo's frustration.) When the escape plot did not materialize—after the prison staff had gone to a lot of trouble to thwart it—the guards and staff increased their harassment and humiliation of the inmates. Even a former prison chaplain, a Catholic priest invited in to evaluate the situation, fell completely into his role. On interviewing individual inmates, he even offered to get lawyers for them. Even more surprising was the inmates' parents' reactions. Many of them took the priest's advice and called the staff requesting attorneys to bail their sons out of jail.

According to Zimbardo, "By the end of the study, the prisoners were disintegrated, both as a group and as individuals. There was no longer any group unity; just a bunch of isolated individuals hanging on, much like prisoners of war or hospitalized mental patients. The guards had won total control of the prison, and they commanded the blind obedience of each prisoner. At this point it became clear that we had to end the study. We had created an overwhelmingly powerful situation—a situation in which prisoners were withdrawing and behaving in pathological ways, and in which some of the guards were behaving sadistically."[2]

Zimbardo's experiment became legendary, and because of the ethical questions it raised, was among the last of its kind. Not only did it shed light on human behavior, but it also raised questions of what constitutes good ethics in experiments using human subjects.

QUESTIONS

1. Did this experiment help increase our understanding of human behavior, or was it too flawed?
2. Should more experiments like this be allowed?

Sources: [1]Kathleen O'Toole, "The Stanford Prison Experiment: Still Powerful after All These Years," Stanford University News Service, January 8, 1997, http://www.stanford.edu/dept/news/relaged/970108prisonexp.html.

[2]Philip G. Zimbardo, Stanford Prison Experiment, http://www.prisonexp.org/.

A number of new features in contemporary prisons make riots less likely, and if they do happen, less deadly. Today, it is easier to segregate prisoners who cause trouble, not only because prison systems have more options in moving inmates to other prisons, but also because staffs keep better records and communicate more often about the emotional state of the inmate population.[24] Prison officials are also better at discovering and reacting to problems before they can escalate into a riot situation.

In addition to creating more professionally trained prison administrations, most prisons have developed special units to deal with explosive situations. Like the Special Weapons and Tactics (SWAT) units in law enforcement, prisons have implemented Special Operations Response Team (SORT) units to handle situations ranging from hostage taking to an inmate who refuses to leave his or her cell. Wearing helmets and protective clothing and armed with shields and batons, the team overwhelms and disarms troublesome inmates. The SORT unit marches to the cell block in double-time, chanting and banging their batons against their shields to psychologically intimidate the problem inmate and to display to other prisoners that the prison can quickly marshal sufficient force to quell any disturbance.[25]

Working in the Prison

Guards, medical technicians, treatment specialists, administrators, secretaries, and clergy all contribute to the prison dynamic. Most of these occupations are found in society, but unique demands are placed on those who serve in these positions in the prison. For instance, a secretary in most organizations is encouraged to promote good customer relations. In the prison, the consumer of the service is the inmate, and secretaries are cautioned to be wary, emotionally distant, and suspicious of every request, motive, and kindness offered by the inmate. Working in an environment in which the potential for violence, escape, and duplicity are constant is not for everyone. Those who work in the prison perform a job that, although important, is not always appreciated.

By far the most prevalent and problematic of these jobs is the correctional officer or guard (see Figure 12.3). As of 2000, there were about five inmates for every officer in state and federal facilities.[26] Lucien Lombardo, a respected scholar of the prison, has looked at the work of the correctional officer and found that, contrary to the popular media image, the job has many variations. Lombardo listed seven variations of correctional officer job assignments:[27]

1. **Block officers.** These officers not only are responsible for the security of the housing block, which may contain 300 to 400 inmates, but also must see that the daily

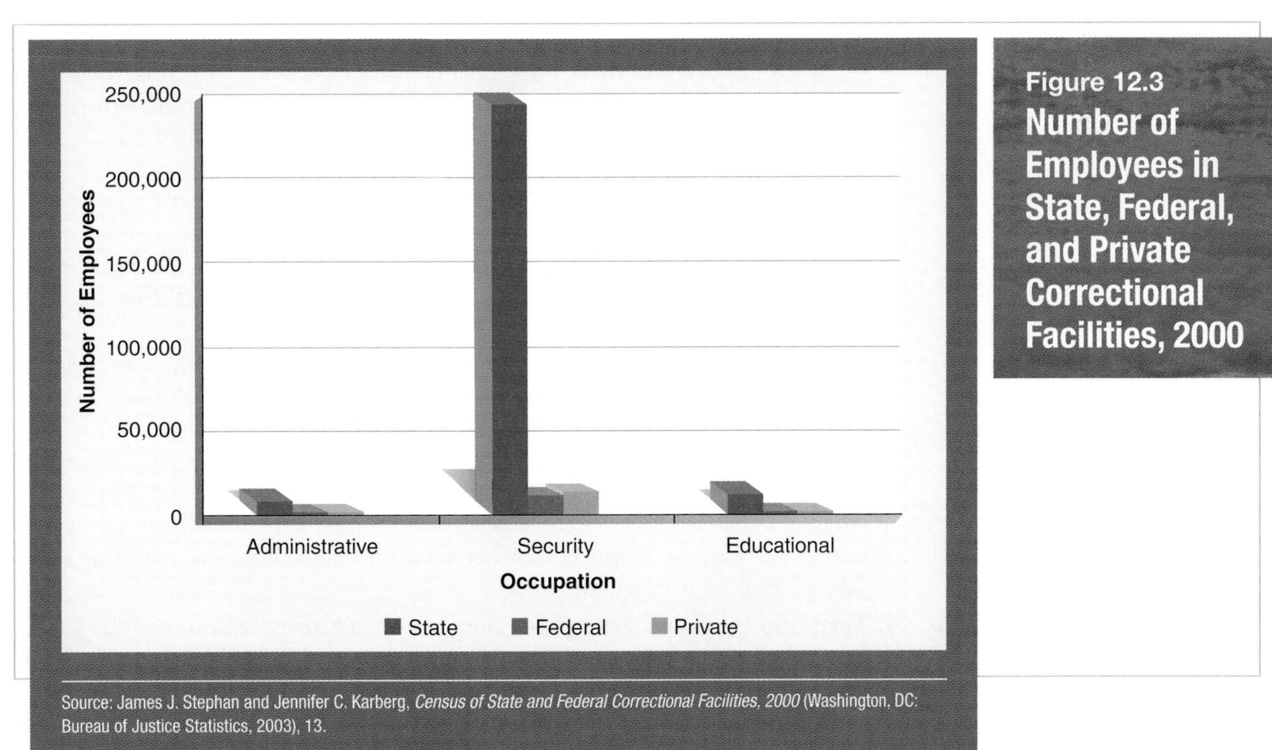

Source: James J. Stephan and Jennifer C. Karberg, *Census of State and Federal Correctional Facilities, 2000* (Washington, DC: Bureau of Justice Statistics, 2003), 13.

Figure 12.3 Number of Employees in State, Federal, and Private Correctional Facilities, 2000

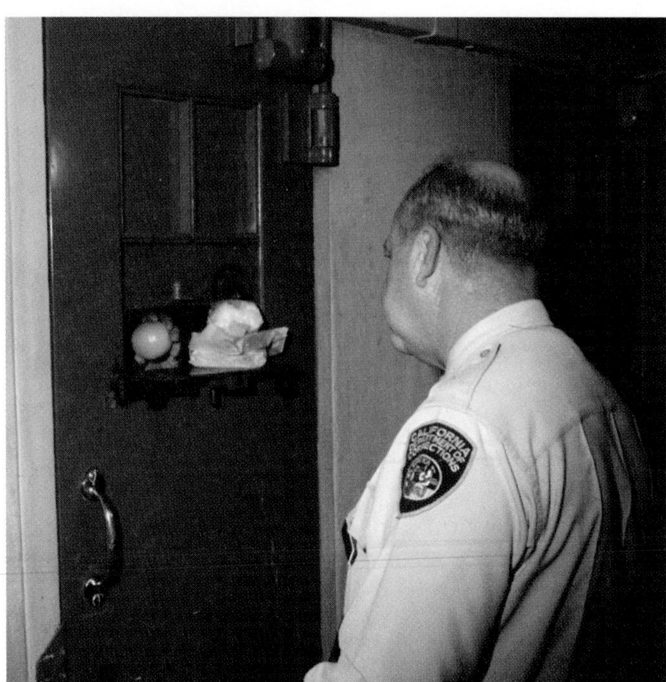

Correctional officers perform a variety of duties beyond mere security. Here, an officer delivers lunch to an inmate.
Courtesy of CORBIS-NY.

work and activities are done in an orderly way. This includes ensuring that inmates are fed, get their medical and rehabilitative treatment programs, are released into the exercise yard at the appropriate time, and get their mail. This is all done in a noisy and hectic environment in which the officer may be surrounded by inmates with varying demands. The block officer must ensure that a healthy balance of security and social services is maintained in the prison. According to Lombardo, the administration can frustrate the work of the block officer by changing the prison's rules or routine. These officers must then translate the reasoning behind the sudden changes to inmates who get upset with alterations of their routine.

2. **Work-detail supervisors.** Every function of the prison that requires inmate labor must be supervised by a correctional officer. Food, clothing, library privileges, commissary, and recreational activities all must be supervised. For the correctional officer, this job can be rewarding or frustrating. Control of scarce resources can be accompanied by pressures from inmates as well as other correctional officers to stretch the limits of discretion to do favors. Although this gives officers some bargaining power with the inmates, it also is a source of tension because the work-detail officers are accountable to the administration for getting the work of the prison done. These officers, who are evaluated on how well they are able to get 10 felons to do their work, are in a vulnerable position.
3. **Industrial shop and school officers.** These officers perform security and order-maintenance functions by supervising inmates engaged in work or school activities provided by civilians. When things go right, this can be a stable and relatively safe assignment, but if a teacher fails to show up one day, the officer may have to supervise 50 inmates who have nothing to do for two hours. The teachers get the socially rewarding tasks of educating inmates, but the school officer must maintain the discipline required for learning to occur. Imagine teaching a class of fifty 220-pound fifth-graders.
4. **Yard officers.** Lombardo made the interesting observation that the yard is the closest thing to the street in the prison environment. The block is the inmate's home, and the school or work assignment keeps the inmate busy, but the yard is where the greatest potential for trouble exists. Yard officers are often the most inexperienced, and their primary job is to be constantly alert for signs of trouble.

It is the duty of some correctional officers to stand, at post at important locations within the prison. Here, an officer is responsible for monitoring a vital prison checkpoint.
Courtesy of CORBIS-NY.

5. **Administrative building assignments.** These officers have very little contact with the inmates and perform a variety of administrative functions in the prison. They control security gates; handle the storage of weapons; field telephone calls from the outside; and supervise the visitation of friends, attorneys, and relatives.
6. **Wall posts.** Some officers watch from a tower what is going on inside the prison yard and on the outside perimeter. This duty is devoid of the anxiety of dealing with inmates at close quarters, but it can be boring. The important part of the job is to protect innocent people, especially fellow guards.
7. **Relief officers.** These officers have no steady assignment but rather fill in for other officers who take days off or go on vacation. The job can be stressful because, without a regular post, the officers have not developed working relationships with inmates. Like substitute teachers, these officers are constantly tested by inmates wanting to determine the boundaries of acceptable behavior. Written job descriptions exist for every post in the prison, but the relief officer must be able to quickly learn any of these jobs while simultaneously performing it for the first time.

Although the exact posting of the correctional officer will dictate the type of duties he or she will perform, some general functions are performed in every correctional institution. Over the years the bureaucratization of the prison has increased the number of specialist guards, but these general functions are still pertinent to the overall nature of the correctional officers' work. Lombardo identified these functions as follows:

- **Human services.** Officers perform a wide variety of services for inmates, either as a formal part of their duties or because of informal relationships they develop with certain inmates. Some officers complain about being reduced to babysitters because some inmates are incapable of dealing with these issues themselves, or as a result of their captivity, are prevented from handling the little problems they would normally deal with on the outside. Although human services work can be a headache for the officer, it can also provide a sense of satisfaction. The three aspects to human services work are providing goods and services, acting as a referral agent or advocate, and playing a role in inmates' institutional adjustment.
- **Order maintenance.** Correctional officers maintain the social order in prison by earning the inmates' trust and cooperation. By enforcing rules in a consistent and

Convict Criminology

Most of what we know about prisons is filtered through academia and reflects the views and concerns of researchers who have a variety of agendas ranging from reform to increased social control. Prisons are closed institutions that jealously guard the image they present to the public. Researchers, activists, and the media often must present the official views of the prison if they want to maintain access. Therefore, those who become experts on the prison are usually former wardens, government officials, university researchers, and members of nonprofit advocacy groups. However, an important voice is missing from the national conversation concerning prisons. This voice, that of the inmate, has some rather unflattering things to say about prisons.

"Convict criminology" is an emerging perspective in the academic study of the criminal justice system. Scholars who are sympathetic to the political, social, economic, and legal concerns of inmates promote this perspective. One of the most interesting aspects of this perspective is the handful of former inmates who are now legitimate scholars in their own right; they speak not just from their studies of the criminal justice system, but also from their experiences. These "convict criminologists" teach at universities, serve on committees that investigate prisons, sit on advisory boards, agitate in public forums, and otherwise lend the benefit of their hard-won knowledge to the way we view the criminal justice system and, most especially, the prison.

Convict criminology is a fascinating blend of autobiographical writings and traditional social-scientific research. Studies by ex-convicts and those who work closely with inmates reveal an alternative view of topics such as the development of the convict identity, problems of reentry into society, issues in prison management, the difficulties of getting an education while incarcerated, and the challenge of convincing society to allow one to use that education when one is labeled an "ex-con."

QUESTIONS

1. In what ways might a former inmate be able to shed light on the field of corrections?
2. Have former inmates forfeited their right to speak about the prison in a university setting? Is this simply a case of "the blind leading the blind"?
3. Would you feel a bias against a professor who was a former inmate?
4. With some prisoners working so hard to get an education, should you complain about taking tests and writing papers?

Source: Jeffrey Ian Ross and Stephen C. Richards, *Convict Criminology* (Belmont, CA: Wadsworth/Thomson Learning, 2003).

evenhanded manner, and showing inmates respect and allowing them a certain level of dignity, the correctional officer can help establish an atmosphere in which inmates feel not only secure, but also that their world is predictable and controllable. By maintaining order in subtle ways, as well as with the threat of punishments, the officer can reduce the level of tension in the cell block.

- **Security.** Another function officers perform is security. This is a passive function in which the officer watches to ensure that inmates are not acting out. The primary focus of the security function is to keep the inmates inside the institution.
- **Supervision.** The physical maintenance of the prison is accomplished by correctional officers' supervision of inmates. Because the inmates lack the moral obligation to do the work themselves, the officers are responsible for seeing that the work is done efficiently and safely.

Courts and the Prison

Should inmates have legal rights while they are incarcerated? This may seem like a silly question. Inmates are viewed as having forfeited their rights as citizens, and many people believe that one of the consequences of incarceration is that the inmate is stripped of the privileges and legal protections provided to citizens. Some people, however, believe that inmates should not lose all their rights. As citizens, inmates are still under the protection of the Constitution. Their legal rights, although necessarily attenuated, are not totally restricted. The rights lost by inmates should be only those consistent with their confinement and the maintenance of institutional safety. These different perspectives make for an interesting debate, but we will confine ourselves here to examining how the courts have treated this issue.

Prior to the 1960s the courts cultivated a **hands-off doctrine** toward inmates' rights.[28] It was thought that offenders had legal rights granted to them in the arrest and trial phases of the criminal justice system and that incarceration was primarily an administrative matter concerning the internal workings of the prison and not subject to a great degree of judicial oversight. There were a few significant reasons for this hands-off doctrine. First, the decisions made about the conditions of confinement were viewed as a technical matter that judges were not educationally equipped to consider. Second, because of the separation of powers, decisions about prisons were considered a matter for the executive branch of government, not the judicial branch. Third, the public did not really care about what went on in the prison and were content to allow prison administrators wide latitude in the treatment of inmates. Finally, it was thought that the treatment of prisoners was a product of privileges rather than legal rights. For these reasons, the courts were historically reluctant to involve themselves with the conditions of confinement.[29]

hands-off doctrine
The judicial attitude toward prisons prior to the 1960s in which courts did not become involved in prison affairs or inmate rights.

The social upheavals of the 1960s influenced many aspects of society. The prison felt the ramifications of the protests of marginalized people in much the same way that the rest of society was affected by the civil rights and women's movements. Inmates and those concerned with the welfare of inmates began to petition the courts to address several issues they deemed problematic. For instance, in Stateville Prison in Illinois, Christian inmates were allowed to read the Bible, but Muslim inmates were forbidden to possess the Quran.[30] Prison officials were successfully sued in *Cooper v. Pate* (1964) (see Case in Point), which began a new era in prison litigation. This new interventionist doctrine resulted in the courts considering a wide variety of issues in the prison and fundamentally changing the relationship between the courts and corrections. Inmates found the courts to be receptive to their complaints about the arbitrary ways prisons were operated. Prison administrators were forced to treat inmates in a more uniform

CASE IN POINT

Cooper v. Pate

The Case

Cooper v. Pate, 378 U.S. 546 (1964)

The Point

This case helped end the judicial "hands-off" doctrine toward prisons by allowing inmates to sue for civil rights violations.

Thomas Cooper, an inmate at the Illinois State Penitentiary, claimed that because of his religious beliefs as a Muslim he was not allowed to possess the religious literature that he wanted and was denied privileges. Two lower courts granted motions to dismiss the case. However, the Supreme Court reversed this judgment, allowing Cooper's suit to continue.

NEWS FLASH

Mentally Ill Must Go to Prison for Treatment

One of the most controversial issues in criminal justice is how to deal with mentally ill offenders. A tried-and-true method has never existed to treat mentally ill offenders or to justly punish them for the crimes they commit.

Historically, mentally ill offenders have been thrown together with healthy offenders and locked up in dungeons, jails, and dank asylums, and hanged on gibbets without cognizance of or concern for the fact that had they received the proper medical treatment, they might not have committed any crimes at all. This was especially true before the development of mental health science in the early 20th century. However, now that diseases of the mind and brain are a bit more understood, the treatment of mentally ill offenders is still much the same. They go to prisons and jails. They receive inadequate treatment or no treatment. They are executed. According to government statistics, five times as many mentally ill people are in prisons and jails than in mental hospitals, and 16 percent of all inmates are mentally ill.

In Fairfax County, Virginia, advocates say that up to 200 seriously mentally ill people are in prison at a time. Some are charged with violent offenses, and others are there for very minor things such as loitering. What they have in common is that they might not be in the lockup at all had they received the right treatment and/or medication. Paradoxically, the only way many mentally ill offenders, especially the indigent, can get treatment is by going to prison or jail where they have access to doctors and medication.

Experts say that the move toward incarceration rather than treatment began in the 1950s, when many mental institutions were closed in favor of community-based programs. Many communities, however, lack the resources or the organization to treat the mentally ill. For example, the U.S. Department of Health reported that in 1955 a total of 558,922 patients were in public mental hospitals. By 1998, with the U.S. population booming, that number had dropped to 57,151.

QUESTIONS

1. Are mentally ill offenders treated unfairly, or is a crime a crime that should be punished accordingly?
2. Should some of the funding that goes to build more prisons go to building more mental hospitals?

Source: William Branigin and Leef Smith, "Mentally Ill Need Care, Find Prison Without Treatment, Many Cycle In and Out of Jail," *The Washington Post,* November 25, 2001, http://www.washingtonpost.com/ac2/wp-dyn/A10740-2001Nov24.

manner, keep better records, and run their institutions according to well-defined and ascertainable criteria.[31]

What was the source of this newfound concern for the rights of inmates? From where did the courts draw their authority to enter into the realm of inmate rights? Inmates' lawyers turned to several places in the Constitution to convince the courts to take a closer look at prisons.

Eighth Amendment

The Eighth Amendment states, in part, ". . . nor cruel and unusual punishments be inflicted." There is considerable debate as to what should be considered cruel or unusual. The courts have ruled on thousands of cases in which prison administrators were faulted for a wide variety of policies ranging from food issues to heating to discipline. Although we cannot list and discuss all these issues, one scholar has suggested that the court has not provided a clear statement about what constitutes "cruel" or "unusual." Rather, the court has provided a general statement in which it likens a given situation to that which "amounts to torture, when it is grossly excessive in proportion to the offense for which it is imposed, or that is inherently unfair; or that is unnecessarily degrading, or is shocking or disgusting to people of reasonable sensitivity" (*Holt v. Sarver,* 309 F. Supp. 362) (ED Ark. 1970).[32]

CASE IN POINT

Wolff v. McDonnell

The Case

Wolff v. McDonnell, 418 U.S. 539, 94 S. Ct. 2963 (1974)

The Point

This case defined the processes required for prison disciplinary proceedings.

In Nebraska, prisoners earned good-time credits under a statute that granted mandatory sentence reductions for good behavior, which were revocable only for serious misconduct. In this case, inmates at a state prison challenged their institution's practice of revoking these good-time credits without adequate procedures. In Wolff, the Supreme Court set forth minimum requirements of procedural due process for prison inmates:

1. Advance written notice to the inmate of the charges
2. A written statement as to the evidence relied on and the reasons for the disciplinary action taken
3. An impartial hearing
4. An opportunity for the inmate to call witnesses and present documentary evidence in defense, as long as it does not endanger institutional security

However, Wolff does not require that the inmate be allowed to confront and cross-examine witnesses or be granted the right to counsel.

Fourteenth Amendment: Due Process

When the prison administration changes an inmate's status, such as placing him or her in segregation for disciplinary reasons, should this concern the court? On one hand, the court system is overburdened as it is and has little time to consider cases involving the internal workings of the prison. On the other hand, inmates can be abused by prison officials and need somewhere to turn to have their concerns heard. The Fourteenth Amendment says that the due process granted to citizens by the Constitution is also applicable to the states. Because of the concept of incorporation, states cannot restrict rights granted by the federal government. The courts have determined in *Wolff v. McDonnell* (1974) that inmates are allowed some level of due process.

Fourteenth Amendment: Equal Protection

The equal protection clause has also been used to help define inmates' rights. Although we might be tempted to think that equal protection means that inmates with similar circumstances are to be treated alike by the courts and the prison, we would be mistaken. Legal officials still have tremendous latitude to use discretion in fashioning punishments and rehabilitation programs to fit the perceived needs of offenders. What the Fourteenth Amendment addresses is racial and gender-based discrimination in the prison. Individuals cannot be treated differently based on their race or because they are a male or female.[33] Discrimination that is prohibited in society is not permitted in the correctional institution. Cases that involve religious freedom are also applicable here in that the prison cannot allow certain religions to be practiced while excluding others.[34] Of course, given the multiplicity of religions, there are some limits as to just how far the prison can go in accommodating inmates' needs. For security, economic, and commonsense reasons, not all inmates can practice all of their desired religious requests. For instance, the prison cannot keep kitchens open 24 hours a day to feed inmates who may have different eating concerns based on religion, nor can prisons cater to the exact requests for the specialty foods of all religions.[35] Nevertheless, prisons are obligated to make reasonable efforts to address the different legitimate religious needs of a substantial number of the inmates.

Prisons are a unique environment, and the expectations of privacy granted by the Constitution and its amendments are only partially available to inmates. For instance, the

More female correctional officers are working in prisons. Privacy issues are a concern but often are not considered as important as issues of security and workers' rights.
Courtesy of CORBIS-NY.

standards of privacy in the home do not extend to the prison cell.[36] Although the inmate lives in the cell, there is no constitutional guarantee that it cannot be searched for contraband. The prison has a security imperative to make the institution safe for other inmates and staff that overrides any demand for privacy. Cells may be searched without warning (prior notice would give the inmate time to dispose of drugs, weapons, or other contraband), as may inmates' personal effects such as books, papers, clothing, and mail.

The inmate's body is also a point of contention, according to the courts. Under what circumstances, and to what degree, can the inmate's body be searched? The inmate's body has only slightly more protection than does the cell and personal effects. The courts have deemed routine strip and body cavity searches as necessary for the institution's safety.[37] However, body cavity searches that are abusive, nonhygienic, or unreasonably degrading are prohibited. The right to privacy of the body has also been brought up as a concern where there are male guards and female inmates or female guards and males inmates. It sounds reasonable to prohibit cross-sex supervision of inmates, but the courts consider the matter in a more involved way. For instance, although modesty and privacy are important concerns, the cost of same-sex guards for the prison may be prohibitive. Additionally, male inmates may object to a homosexual guard watching them shower, or female inmates might feel uncomfortable having a lesbian guard. The courts have determined that there are simply too many such possibilities for potential embarrassment to get involved.

Courts have an additional reason to be reluctant to intervene in gender issues. To prohibit women from supervising male inmates would violate women's rights under Title VII and the equal protection clause.[38] Women cannot be excluded from large parts of the institution and from core duties of the correctional officer simply because of their gender. Certainly, institutions may establish reasonable efforts to diminish cross-sex supervision, but the legitimate demands of institutional security, efficiency, and worker rights all permit this practice.[39]

The courts have also considered the issues of what mail the inmates may receive and with whom and how they can have outside visitation. Prison officials have wide discretion in limiting the mail and publications that inmates can send and receive.[40] The institution must demonstrate how restrictions are consistent with the needs of security and efficiency of the prison. Likewise, the issue of visits from outsiders is a concern.[41] Mail from those with a personal or professional relationship with the inmate are generally allowed. Links to family, lawyers, clergy, and the like are important contacts that the court allows. However, the type of visitation that is allowed varies considerably by institution. Jails and prisons are constantly threatened by contraband that may be brought into the prison by visitors. Therefore, personal visits may be restricted by separating the visitor and

FOCUS ON ETHICS

Keeping the Condemned Alive

Horacio Alberto Reyes-Camarena needs a kidney. His dialysis treatment reportedly costs $121,000 a year, and his doctor believes he is a good candidate for a transplant. Because the state of Oregon pays for his medical care, he is at the top of the transplant list ahead of those who cannot afford a transplant. Reyes-Camarena is also on death row. He has been there since 1996, when he was convicted of repeatedly stabbing two women, one of whom died from her wounds.

Acute medical care for prisoners is a controversial subject, with many opponents citing cost as a major factor. Oregon has suffered massive budget cuts affecting such essential services as health care for the poor and education. However, even in a difficult economy, states say they are bound to provide the medical care that inmates need, regardless of the cost. A California inmate received a $1 million heart transplant, and another received a $120,000 kidney transplant. A Georgia prisoner received heart bypass surgery that cost $70,000. Because Reyes-Camarena is on death row, his case is even more complicated. Not only is the procedure he is slated for—and the drugs that follow—expensive, but he is also dipping into a highly limited resource: donated organs.

Opponents of such procedures question saving the life of a man who is going to die with an organ that could have saved someone else's life. They also point to poor, law-abiding citizens who do not even qualify for placement on organ transplant lists because they cannot afford the antirejection drugs, as well as a state already ravaged by a desperate economy. Supporters of life-saving procedures for inmates say states have a responsibility to fund the health care of those it convicts. Also, denying necessary health care to death row inmates could be construed as violating the cruel and unusual punishment provision of the Eighth Amendment. Doctors, as well, have an ethical responsibility to treat those who are sick, regardless of social status.

As of April 2004, 84,000 people were on the waiting list for an organ transplant, according to the United Network for Organ Sharing. From January to December 2003, 13,000 organs were donated.

Sources: Bryan Robinson, "Death-Row Privilege: Condemned Prisoner May Get Kidney Transplant While Law-Abiding Citizens Wait," ABCNEWS.com. May 28, 2003, http://abcnews.go.com/sections/us/GoodMorningAmerica/deathrow_transplant030528.html. United Network for Organ Sharing, http://www.unos.org/.

inmate with a glass barrier and having them communicate by telephone. Contact visits, in which inmates and visitors are allowed to touch, have been deemed problematic by the courts and not a constitutional right. There is also no right to conjugal visitation.[42] Such visitation may help maintain the marital bond while the inmate is incarcerated, but it is up to the state to allow this practice, which is usually permitted for only a few inmates.

Private Prisons

Interest in privatizing prisons began around the mid-1970s, and the first modern private prisons opened in the early 1980s.[43] A number of factors that had their roots in the social revolutions of the 1960s contributed to this trend. By the mid-1970s, the United States was reeling from the loss of the Vietnam War, economic recession, gas and oil shortages, major paradigm shifts in civil society, and a skyrocketing crime rate. All of the cures for social ills that seemed to have worked before the 1960s had become useless. To Americans, that bewildering entity known as "the government" had become very unpopular, and probably not without good reason. It had participated in an unpopular war; President Nixon had left office in disgrace, only to be pardoned by his successor; the cities were crumbling; and the country itself seemed to be at the mercy of such foreign powers

! NEWS FLASH

Tough Alabama County Stresses Prisons

Houston County, Alabama, is the state's per capita leader in convicting offenders. Although the county has succeeded in being tough on crime, critics say it's also being tough on itself. Alabama's inmate population is bursting at the seams, and taxpayers in one of the country's poorest states are faced with spending millions to house and manage those whom they send to prison.

According to the Montgomery-based Sentencing Institute, Houston County sent 1,571 people to prison between 1998 and 2002, while similarly sized Lauderdale County sent just 546. In 2001 Houston County's rate of creating inmates was nearly double the state average, according to the institute. In contrast, other counties are using alternative sentencing and work-release programs to ease the strain and provide money, which is deducted from offenders' pay. Houston County, however, has only recently embraced the concept of community corrections.

Houston County does not necessarily have more crime than other counties. FBI statistics show that Dothan, the county's biggest city, has only a typical amount of crime for an Alabama city of its size. Nevertheless, the county's courts continue to send more people to jail than any other, even though all of the prisons are overcrowded, and over a thousand state inmates are in county jails because of the lack of prison beds. Meanwhile, stressed sheriff's departments have resorted to occasionally dumping inmates unexpectedly at the gates of state prisons. The state government has had to pay extra to hasten the parole docket at Tutwiler Prison for Women and has even had some of its inmates moved to a private prison in Louisiana. In the midst of a sluggish economy, the state legislature has been pressed for an extra $25 million in 2004 to build a new women's prison and to maintain the prisons it already has but that are increasingly becoming more difficult to handle. Houston County district attorney Doug Valeska, who said he would rather try a case than plea bargain it, told the *Mobile Register,* "It's not my problem that prisons are overcrowded."

QUESTIONS

1. Is it fair for one county to overload the state's correctional system and raise taxes for everyone?
2. Would increased community corrections efforts in such a county appease its citizens' need to punish offenders as well as lower the incarceration rate?

Source: Sam Hodges, "Tough-On-Crime Counties Like Houston Contribute to Prison Crowding," *Mobile Register,* June 9, 2003, http://www.al.com/news/mobileregister/index.ssf?/xml/story.ssf/html_standard.xsl?/base/news/105516099386490.xml.

as OPEC and Iran's Ayatollah Khomeini.[44] The government, many Americans believed, could no longer do anything right, including run prisons.

As crime rates soared and states grappled with burgeoning inmate populations (see Figure 12.4), the idea grew that private firms could handle inmates more inexpensively and more efficiently. The philosophy of privatizing prisons also hewed to the tenets of a new form of political conservatism that took hold with the election of President Ronald Reagan. One of these tenets was that capitalism could solve a variety of problems because an open market forced the providers of any good or service to produce the most "bang for the buck." During the next couple of decades, three companies, the Corrections Corporation of America, Wackenhut Corrections Corporation, and Correctional Services Corporation, became the major providers of private correctional services in the United States.

- **The Corrections Corporation of America (CCA).** The Corrections Corporation of America, currently the largest provider of private prison services in the United States, was founded in 1983. Working off the idea that the government "can't do anything very well,"[45] CCA expanded quickly. As of 2003 the company operated 60 U.S. jails and prisons, housing about 53,000 inmates. Its revenues in 2002 were $962.8 million.[46]

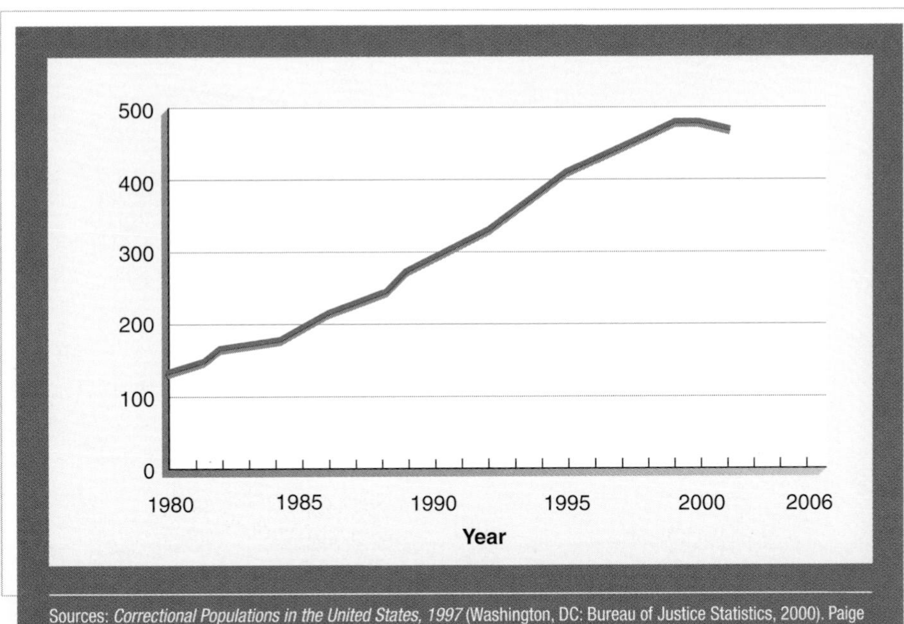

Sources: *Correctional Populations in the United States, 1997* (Washington, DC: Bureau of Justice Statistics, 2000). Paige M. Harrison and Allen J. Beck, *Prisoners in 2002* (Washington, DC: Bureau of Justice Statistics, 2003). Also online at http://www.ojp.usdoj.gov/bjs/glance/incrt.htm.

Figure 12.4 Incarceration Rate, 1980–2001: Number of Offenders per 100,000 Population

- **Wackenhut Corrections Corporation (WCC).** Wackenhut Corrections Corporation was founded as a division of the large, multinational Wackenhut Corporation in 1984. WCC, which operates facilities in Australia, Canada, New Zealand, South Africa, Scotland, and England, runs 35 facilities in the United States. Wackenhut designs, builds, finances, and manages prisons, as well as provides immigration and detention services to the U.S. Department of Homeland Security and U.S. Marshals. WCC's revenues in 2002 were $568.6 million.[47]
- **Correctional Services Corporation.** Started in 1993, Correctional Services Corporation currently operates 11 adult correctional facilities and 18 juvenile facilities in 14 states.[48] Its 2002 revenues totaled $160.4 million.[49]

Although private correctional facilities have become big business and taken in many inmates (see Figure 12.5), they have met with mixed success. According to Charles Logan, the arguments both for and against private prisons are quite numerous.[50] Following are some arguments Logan listed for private prisons:

- **Money.** According to Logan, private contracting makes "true costs highly visible." Private enterprise can run prisons more cheaply than the government can because government agencies have an incentive to grow in order to inflate their budgets. Corporations can operate a large number of prisons across several jurisdictions, which local and state agencies cannot do, allowing for economy of scale. The profit motive of private prisons demands less waste and more suppliers, which allows facilities to spend money wisely and avoid shortages.
- **Better employee control.** Workers for private enterprises are more easily hired and fired than government workers, so private prisons can adjust staff sizes more quickly when needed. Staff members are less likely to strike because they are more likely to be fired. Administration and staff have more incentive to do a good job and treat inmates fairly because their jobs are more directly at stake. Also, contracting, according to Logan, "may reduce overly generous public employee pensions and benefits," as well as promote more effective personnel management and lower absenteeism and employee turnover.

Figure 12.5 Distribution by Type of Facility

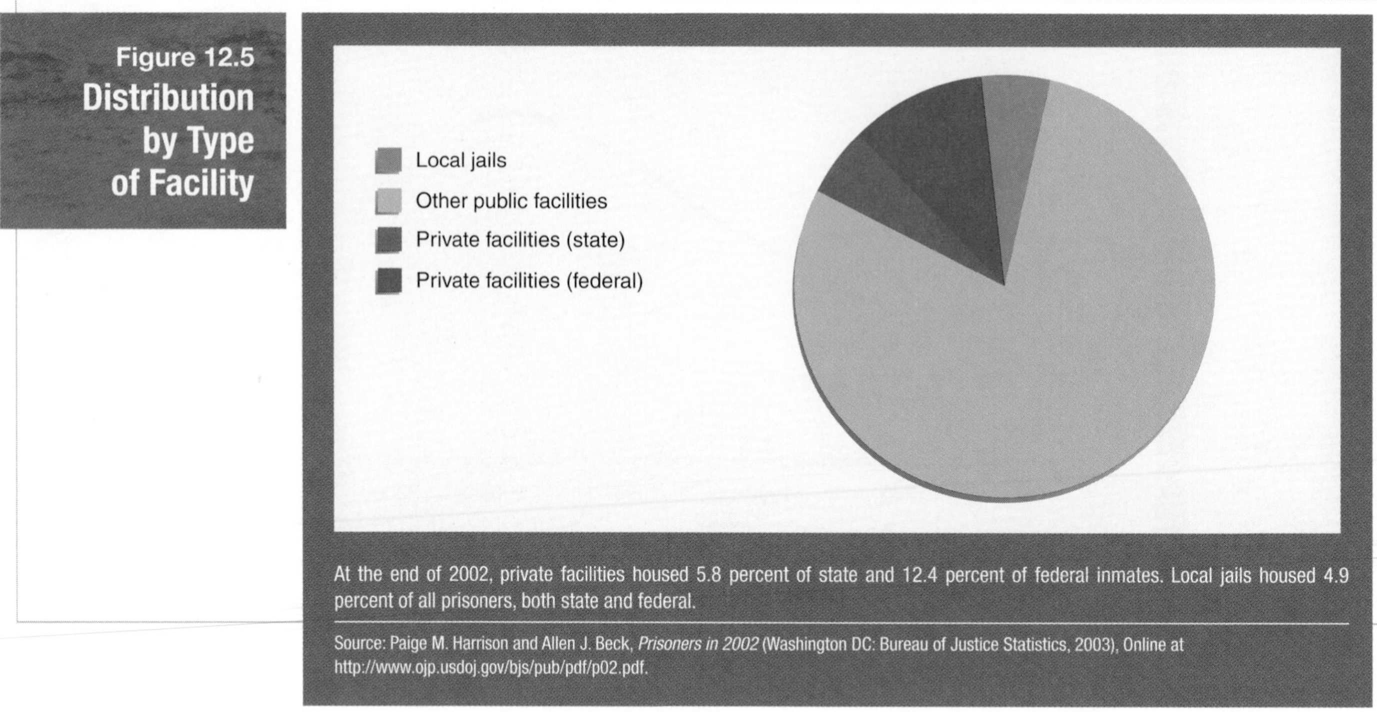

At the end of 2002, private facilities housed 5.8 percent of state and 12.4 percent of federal inmates. Local jails housed 4.9 percent of all prisoners, both state and federal.

Source: Paige M. Harrison and Allen J. Beck, *Prisoners in 2002* (Washington DC: Bureau of Justice Statistics, 2003), Online at http://www.ojp.usdoj.gov/bjs/pub/pdf/p02.pdf.

- **Flexibility and accountability.** Stockholders and corporate boards add another layer of review to decision making, while being immune to some of the political pressures inherent in governments. Prisons may be built more quickly and cheaply, and designed for more efficient operation. Competition with other private prison firms encourages higher quality and lower costs. By transferring inmates across jurisdictions, optimum residence levels may be maintained at all facilities.

Logan gave the following arguments against private prisons:

- **Money.** The first duty of a for-profit operation is to make a profit. Therefore, a private prison must necessarily put profit motives ahead of inmate welfare. Private prisons would "cut corners" to save money without concern for inmates' rights or welfare. Also, if the prison company goes bankrupt or is not meeting its profit needs in a given market, it may pull up stakes, leaving a jurisdiction without facilities. In the end, private prisons are more expensive because their profit margins are added to other costs.
- **Labor.** Private prisons threaten the jobs, benefits, professionalism, and tenure of public employees. Staff members have less incentive to do a good job because they are less secure and paid less. This increases the risk of strikes and high employee turnover.
- **Control.** Private enterprise morally should not have the degree of control over human beings that imprisonment requires. Private prisons may make government prisons more difficult to manage by housing only the best behaved offenders and refusing the difficult ones. Prison corporations may lobby to build more prisons, thus increasing society's dependence on imprisonment and weakening the use of alternatives such as parole. A poorly staffed or understaffed facility jeopardizes public safety. Private prison corporations are less accountable to the public than those governed by legislatures comprising elected officials. Lastly, another layer of managerial involvement introduces new opportunities for corruption.

The final judgment on private prisons remains to be seen. The news is rife with their failures: escapes, employee and inmate maltreatment, closings, and falling stock prices.

Some evidence even suggests that they cost only marginally less than government-run prisons.[51] However, states, as well as jurisdictions in other countries, continue to contract with private prison firms, and private facilities continue to be built.

Summary

The prison is a fundamental feature of the U.S. criminal justice system. A closed institution where everything is tightly controlled and structured, the prison dominates almost every aspect of inmates' lives. These controls help maintain efficiency and order, and deprive the inmate of discretion. Deprivations define a prisoner's lifestyle; through these deprivations we have come to consider incarceration a sufficient punishment, so that physical brutality is not required to achieve justice.

According to Gresham Sykes, inmates compensate for the pains of imprisonment by adopting argot roles. However, many of these argot roles have been overtaken by the social structure of prison gangs. Now instead of using argot roles to adapt to imprisonment, inmates join prison gangs for security and to acquire goods and services.

Without proper vigilance, gangs can take partial control of any prison. Prison officials are forced to make difficult decisions to stem gang violence. On one hand, they attempt to avoid violence by segregating inmates from rival gangs and inmates of different races. On the other hand, they hope to allow inmates to learn to get along with one another. Charges of discrimination can result when inmates are racially separated, but when inmates are allowed to mix and violence ensues, officials may be accused of failing to provide adequate security. If prison authorities are not careful, inmate rage can result in a riot. Two of the most infamous prison riots were the Attica riot of 1971 and the New Mexico riot of 1980. One recent solution has been to totally segregate the worst behaved inmates. An example of this is the security housing unit of California's Pelican Bay State Prison, where inmates are almost completely isolated.

Unique demands are placed on prison staff. Regardless of their jobs, staff members must always be on their guard because a slight amount of danger is inherent in the job. Correctional officers bear the brunt of this danger. In recent years the specialization of correctional officers has increased, but their basic function has remained the same: to control and supervise prison inmates.

Inmates are protected to some extent by the Constitution. The rights lost by inmates should be consistent with their confinement and institutional safety. Prior to the 1960s, the courts cultivated a hands-off doctrine toward inmate rights, considering incarceration as primarily a prison administrative matter. However, after the social upheavals of the 1960s, inmates and those concerned with their welfare petitioned the courts to address several issues, specifically referring to the Eighth and Fourteenth Amendments. Other points of contention include inmate privacy regarding the prison cell and physical body, the people with whom inmates may have contact, and issues concerning the genders of correctional officers.

In the early 1980s, the first modern private prisons were created. During this period, many believed that private enterprise could manage prisons more effectively and cheaply than the government. Despite criticism, over a hundred private prisons are currently operating in the United States.

KEY TERMS

argot roles p. 398
hands-off doctrine p. 415
pains of imprisonment p. 395
total institution p. 394

REVIEW QUESTIONS

1. List the five pains of imprisonment.
2. Name three general types of inmate argot roles.
3. What difficulties do prison staff and officials face in dealing with prison gangs?
4. Along what lines do prison gangs tend to be divided?
5. How is California's Pelican Bay Prison successful?

6. What are some of the causes of prison riots?
7. What are the seven variations of correctional officer job functions according to Lombardo?
8. What were the reasons for the courts' hands-off doctrine?
9. To what constitutional amendments did inmates turn to draw the courts' attention?
10. What led to the development of private prisons?
11. Give arguments for and against private prisons.

SUGGESTED FURTHER READING

Austin, James, and John Irwin. *It's About Time: America's Imprisonment Binge.* 3rd ed. Belmont, CA: Wadsworth, 2001.

Durham, Alexis M. *Crisis and Reform: Current Issues in American Punishment.* Boston: Little, Brown, 1994.

Goffman, Erving. *Asylums: Essays on the Social Situation of Mental Patients and Other Inmates.* Garden City, NY: Anchor, 1961.

Parenti, Christian. *Lockdown America: Police and Prisons in the Age of Crisis.* New York: Verso, 2000.

Silberman, Matthew. *A World of Violence: Corrections in America.* Belmont, CA: Wadsworth, 1995.

Useem, Bert, and Peter Kimball. *States of Siege: U.S. Prison Riots 1971–1986.* New York: Oxford University Press, 1991.

ENDNOTES

1. Erving Goffman, *Asylums: Essays on the Social Situation of Mental Patients and Other Inmates* (Garden City, NY: Anchor, 1961).
2. Victor H. Brombert, *The Romantic Prison: The French Traditions* (Princeton, NJ: Princeton University Press, 1978).
3. Gresham M. Sykes, *The Society of Captives: A Study of a Maximum Security Prison* (Princeton, NJ: Princeton University Press, 1974), 64.
4. Ibid. Sykes devoted his entire Chapter 4 to the pains of imprisonment.
5. Ibid. Chapter 5 is devoted to a full explication of these argot roles. A different set of roles appear in women's prisons. See Rose Giallombardo, *Society of Women: A Study of Women's Prison* (New York: John Wiley and Sons, 1966).
6. John Irwin and Donald Cressey, "Thieves, Convicts and the Inmate Culture," *Social Problems,* Fall 1962, 142–155.
7. James B. Jacobs, *Stateville: The Penitentiary in Mass Society* (Chicago: University of Chicago Press, 1977).
8. Christian Parenti, *Lockdown America: Police and Prisons in the Age of Crisis* (New York: Verso, 2000). See especially Chapter 10, "Balkan in a Box: Rape, Race War, and Other Forms of Management," pp. 182–210.
9. Ibid., p. 172.
10. Craig Haney, "Ínfamous Punishment: The Psychological Consequences of Isolation," in *Correctional Contexts: Contemporary and Classical Readings,* 2nd ed., eds. Edward J. Latessa et al. (Los Angeles: Roxbury, 2001), 172.
11. James Austin and John Irwin, *It's About Time: America's Imprisonment Binge,* 3rd ed. (Belmont, CA: Wadsworth 2001). See especially Chapter 6, "Super Max," pp. 117–137.
12. Craig Haney, "The Psychological Impact of Incarceration: Implications for Post-Prison Adjustment" (paper presented at the national policy conference of the U.S. Department of Health and Human Services: The Urban Institute, January 2002). Also online at http://aspe.hhs.gov/hsp/prison2home02/Haney.htm.
13. Ibid., 464–473.
14. Ralph S. Turner and Lewis M. Killian, *Collective Behavior,* 3rd ed. (Englewood Cliffs, NJ: Prentice Hall, 1987).
15. Gustave Le Bon, *The Crowd* (New York: The Viking Press, 1895/1960). See also Ladd Wheeler, "Toward a Theory of Behavioral Contagion," *Psychological Review* 73 (March 1966): 179–192.
16. Veron B. Fox, *Violence Behind Bars: An Explosive Report on Prison Riots in the United States* (New York: Vantage Press, 1956).
17. Randy Martin and Sherwood Zimmerman, "A Typology of the Causes of Prison Riots and an Analytical Extension to the 1986 West Virginia Riot," *Justice Quarterly* 7 (1990): 711–737. See also John Pallas and Robert Barber, "From Riots to Revolution," in *The Politics of Punishment,* ed. Erik Olin Wright (New York: Harper & Row, 1973), 237–261.
18. New York State Special Commission on Attica, *Attica: The Official Report of the New York State Special Commission on Attica* (New York: Bantam Books, 1972). This was commonly referred to as the McKay Report after its chairman, Robert B. McKay.

19. Russell Oswald, *Attica: My Story* (New York: Doubleday and Company, 1972). Richard X. Clark, *The Brothers of Attica* (New York: Links, 1973). Tom Wicker, *A Time to Die* (New York: New York Times, 1975). Herman Badillo, *A Bill of No Rights: Attica and the American Prison System* (New York: Outerbridge and Lazerd, 1972).
20. John Irwin, *Prisons in Turmoil* (Boston: Little, Brown, 1980).
21. Bert Useem and Peter Kimball, *States of Siege: U.S. Prison Riots 1971–1986* (New York: Oxford University Press, 1991).
22. Wicker, *A Time to Die.*
23. Bert Useem, "Disorganization and the New Mexico Prison Riot of 1980," *American Sociological Review,* 50 (October): 680.
24. Eliot S. Hartstone et al., "Identifying and Treating the Mentally Disordered Prison Inmate," in *Correctional Contexts: Contemporary and Classical Readings,* 2nd ed., eds. Edward J. Latessa et al. (Los Angeles: Roxbury, 2001), 380–393.
25. Matthew Silberman, *A World of Violence: Corrections in America* (Belmont, CA: Wadsworth, 1995), 122–124.
26. James J. Stephan and Jennifer C. Karberg, *Census of State and Federal Correctional Facilities, 2000* (Washington, DC: Bureau of Justice Statistics, 2003), 14.
27. Lucien X. Lombardo, "Guards Imprisoned: Correctional Officers at Work" in *Correctional Contexts: Contemporary and Classical Readings,* eds. Edward J. Latessa et al. (Los Angeles: Roxbury, 2001), 153–167.
28. Jacobs, *Stateville* 105.
29. These reasons are best articulated by Philip L. Reichel, *Corrections: Philosophies, Practices, and Procedures,* 2nd ed. (Boston: Allyn and Bacon, 2001), 517.
30. Jacobs, *Stateville,* 107.
31. James Bennett, "Who Wants to Be a Warden?" *New England Journal of Prison Law* 1 (1974): 69–79.
32. Reichel, *Corrections,* 522.
33. *Lee v. Washington,* 390 U.S. 333, 88 S. Ct. 994 (1968) and *Holt v. Sarver,* 309 F. Supp. 362 (ED Ark. 1970).
34. *Cruz v. Beto,* 405 U.S. 319, 92 S. Ct. 1079 (1972).
35. *Cooper v. Pate,* 378 U.S. 546, 84 S. Ct. 1733 (1964).
36. *Hudson v. Palmer,* 468 U.S. 517, 104 S. Ct. 3194 (1984).
37. *Bell v. Wolfish,* 441 U.S. 520, 99 S. Ct. 1861 (1979).
38. *Grummett v. Rushen,* 587 F. Supp. 913 (1984).
39. *Johnson v. Phelan,* 69 F. 3d 144 (1995).
40. *Thornburgh v. Abbot,* 490 U.S. 401, 109 S. Ct. 1874 (1989).
41. *Kentucky Department of Corrections v. Thompson,* 490 U.S. 454, 109 S. Ct. 1904 (1989).
42. *Tarlton v. Clark,* 441 F. 2d 384 (1971).
43. David Shichor, *Punishment for Profit: Private Prisons/Public Concerns* (Thousand Oaks, CA: Sage, 1995), 13–14.
44. OPEC is the Organization of the Petroleum Exporting Countries. Its current members are Algeria, Indonesia, Iran, Iraq, Kuwait, Libya, Nigeria, Qatar, Saudi Arabia, the United Arab Emirates, and Venezuela. As for the Ayatollah Khomeini, in November 1979, Iranian militants supporting Khomeini took 70 Americans captive at the U.S. embassy in Tehran. The ordeal lasted 444 days.
45. David Schichor and Michael J. Gilbert, *Privatization in Criminal Justice: Past, Present, and Future* (Cincinnati: Anderson, 2001), 209, as quoted in E. Bates, "Prisons for Profit," in *The Dilemmas of Corrections: Contemporary Readings,* 4th ed., eds. Kenneth C. Haas and Geoffrey P. Alpert (Prospect Heights, IL: Waveland, 1998).
46. Corrections Corporation of America 2002 Annual Report, http://www.shareholder.com/cxw/downloads/2002ar.pdf, p. 4.
47. Wackenhut Corrections Corporation Annual Report, March 20, 2003, Yahoo, http://biz.yahoo.com/e/030320/whc10-k.html.
48. Business Wire/Yahoo, "Correctional Services Corporation Announces Financial Results for First Quarter 2003," May 14, 2003, http://biz.yahoo.com/bw/030514/145413_1.html.
49. Correctional Services Corporation Form 10-k, Hoover's Online, March 31, 2003, http://www.hoovers.com/free/co/secdoc.xhtml?ipage=2086366&doc=0&attach=on.
50. Charles H. Logan, *Private Prisons: Cons and Pros* (New York: Oxford University Press, 1990), 41–48. Also at http://www.ucc.uconn.edu/~wwwsoci/proscons.html.
51. United States General Accounting Office, "Private and Public Prisons: Studies Comparing Operational Costs and/or Quality of Service," http://www.gao.gov/archive/1996/gg96158.pdf.

outline

CHAPTER 13

Corrections in the Community

objectives

After reading this chapter, the student should be able to:

1. Describe the four community corrections strategies.
2. Discuss the purposes of community corrections and why every offender does not go to jail or prison.
3. Discuss the purpose of diversion and arguments for and against it.
4. Discuss probation and arguments for and against it.
5. Describe how each of the participants in the criminal justice process views probation.
6. Understand the probation officer's job.
7. Discuss parole and arguments for and against it.
8. Discuss intermediate sanctions and arguments for and against using them.
9. Compare and contrast shock probation and boot camp prisons.
10. Discuss the purpose of jails.

THERE ARE MANY ALTERNATIVES TO PRISON FOR DEALING WITH criminal offenders. Some of these alternatives, such as corporal or capital punishment, are no longer used to the degree they were in the past and in many circumstances, have been abandoned altogether. Attacking the offender's body is not generally accepted as progressive or effective crime control policy. (Although a return to corporal punishment has its advocates, they are not finding an audience in the general public or legislators.)[1] Therefore, society seeks other policies and programs that provide meaningful ways to deal with offenders.

Not highly visible like prisons, community corrections account for a major portion of the correctional efforts of the contemporary criminal justice system.[2] This chapter will briefly review four interrelated community corrections strategies: diversion programs, probation, parole, and intermediate sanctions. The historical and philosophical underpinnings of attempts to reform and/or incapacitate offenders outside the prison will also be discussed.

The local jail is a primary component of the correctional system. It holds those who are awaiting trial and those sentenced to less than one year of incarceration.
Courtesy of Getty Images, Inc.

Community Corrections in Context

Why do we treat and punish offenders within the community? Why not just send them all to prison so we will not have to worry about them? The answers to these questions are both simple and complex. Simply put, we cannot afford to imprison everyone who violates the law. It is not possible to build enough prisons to house all the offenders, and, if the truth be known, there would be precious few of us not in prison who would be available to work and pay the taxes to incarcerate the majority.[3] One of the functions of the criminal justice system is to remove those offenders who pose a continued threat and place them in the relatively few prison cells.

A more complex answer to the question of why every offender is not locked up is that, for the most part, prisons work only in a limited and partial manner. As we have discussed before, the criminal justice system has multiple goals: incapacitation, retribution, and to a lesser extent, rehabilitation.

- **Incapacitation.** The prison is good at achieving the goal of incapacitation. That is, for the limited time offenders are behind bars, they are not free to commit further crimes in society. Of course, offenders may commit crimes against other inmates or correctional workers, but this depends on how effective the prison is in keeping internal order. Also, as we learned in the last chapter, prison gang members may order fellow gang members to commit crimes on the outside, but the chance of this occurring may be less than if the offender were free.
- **Retribution.** The goal of retribution is to punish the offender for transgressions of the criminal law. Prisons are somewhat successful in accomplishing this goal, but for financial reasons related to prison overcrowding, the public is generally unsatisfied with the amount of punishment they believe the offender is getting when they hear stories about country club prisons and early parole.[4]
- **Rehabilitation.** Finally, the goal of rehabilitation may not be met because of the Spartan conditions of confinement of most institutions, which seem to release

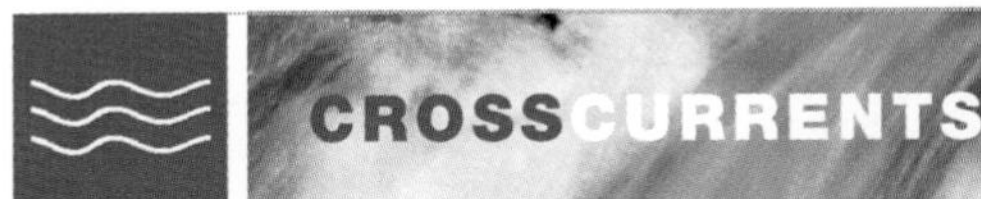

Creative Sentencing as an Alternative to Prison

Sometimes a judge does not want to send an offender to prison but instead wants to make a statement with a creative sentence that says the system takes crime seriously and that offenders can expect to pay a high price. These creative sentences can range from the commonsensical to the embarrassing, but each is a reflection of what the judge believes is an appropriate way for the offender to be held accountable for his or her transgressions of the law. Following are some examples of creative sentences:

- *In Waupaca, Wisconsin, a man who fled a hit-and-run accident in which he killed a cyclist was sentenced to spend the next five Christmases in jail. In addition, he had to take out an advertisement in the local newspaper every year on the anniversary of the death. The ad had his picture and said, "The choice I made to consume alcohol resulted in the death of another human being."*
- *In San Francisco, a man caught stealing mail from mailboxes was sentenced to two months in jail and was required to stand in front of the post office for a total of 1,000 hours wearing a sandwich board sign saying, "I have stolen mail. This is my punishment."*
- *In Athens, Ohio, two young men caught throwing beer bottles from a car and making derogatory statements to a woman were sentenced to wear dresses and walk down the main street.*
- *A municipal judge in Ohio offered Steven Thompson the choice of three days in jail or two hours standing next to a 350-pound pig with a sign saying, "This is not a police officer." Thompson, who had called an officer a "pig" during a confrontation, chose the pig option.*

These sentences are designed to either remind the offenders of the harm their actions caused or simply embarrass them. Not surprisingly, there is controversy about whether these creative sentences serve justice or make a mockery of the system.

QUESTIONS

1. Do you think any of these sentences are inappropriate?
2. Do judges give these types of sentences because it gets them in the newspapers and makes them look tough on crime?
3. If you were a judge, what types of creative sentences would you invent?
4. Would you rather go to jail or prison instead of having to serve one of these creative sentences?

Source: Dan Wilson, "Hit-and-Run Driver Gets Unusual Gift," *The Post-Crescent,* February, 15, 2003, http://www.wisinfo.com/postcrescent/news/archive/local_8703131.shtml. "Dressing as a Woman Not Punishment," November 1, 2001, *The Post,* http://thepost.baker.ohiou.edu/archives3/nov01/110101/editorial.html. "Mail Thief Ordered to Wear Sandwich Board," CNN/Reuters, February 26, 2003, http://us.cnn.com/2003/LAW/02/26/offbeat.mail.reut/. Oliver Libaw, "Courting Controversy," ABCNEWS.com, July 6, 2003, http://abcnews.go.com/sections/us/DailyNews/judicialpower020725.html.

inmates who are more antisocial than when they first went to prison.[5] In a sense, then, prisons may not enhance public safety because they act to embitter, harden, and alienate inmates.[6] Consequently, efforts are made to limit the deleterious impact of prisons by finding alternatives to incarceration for all but the most dangerous offenders.

Prisons can be boring places to spend any amount of time. Inmates may sleep for many hours during the day because they lack other activities. While many critics of prisons would like inmates to work or attend therapy programs, the most inexpensive option is simply to incarcerate offenders.
Courtesy of CORBIS-NY.

At the heart of the community corrections movement are some assumptions about the nature of crime and the benefits of using community resources to address the problems of crime. These assumptions include the following:

- Prison is a highly artificial society. Conformity in prison is not always a good indicator of the inmate's ability to conform in the free world.
- The total control of the prison does little to prepare inmates to take responsibility for their actions.
- Because the community has resources that are unavailable in the prison, the likelihood of rehabilitation is enhanced.
- The community can provide support networks to the offender that do not exist in prison. With the help of spouses, parents, children, and clergy who have already established bonds with the offender, the offender has a greater chance of leading a law-abiding life.
- The offender can contribute to the financial upkeep of his or her family and, if gainfully employed, pay taxes. Additionally, some community corrections programs require offenders to pay for the cost of their supervision.
- The state spends less money on offenders in community corrections programs than it does incarcerating them. The cost of providing prison cells is extremely high, and the state can address many more offenders by handling them outside the prison setting.
- The state can accurately identify which offenders are dangerous and need secure incarceration and which ones are safe to release into the community with supervision.
- The number of trained probation and parole officers is sufficient to adequately supervise the offenders who are selected for community corrections programs.

Is it safe to make these assumptions about the efficacy of community corrections? For the most part, the answer is yes. Millions of offenders have successfully served sentences in community corrections programs where, in addition to not committing additional crimes, they have completed treatment programs, supported their families, paid their

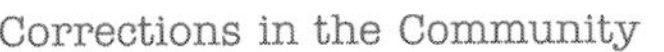

Group counseling sessions can be productive for many inmates. It is difficult to fool others who have similar experiences.
Courtesy of CORBIS-NY.

Figure 13.1
Adults Leaving Probation, 2002

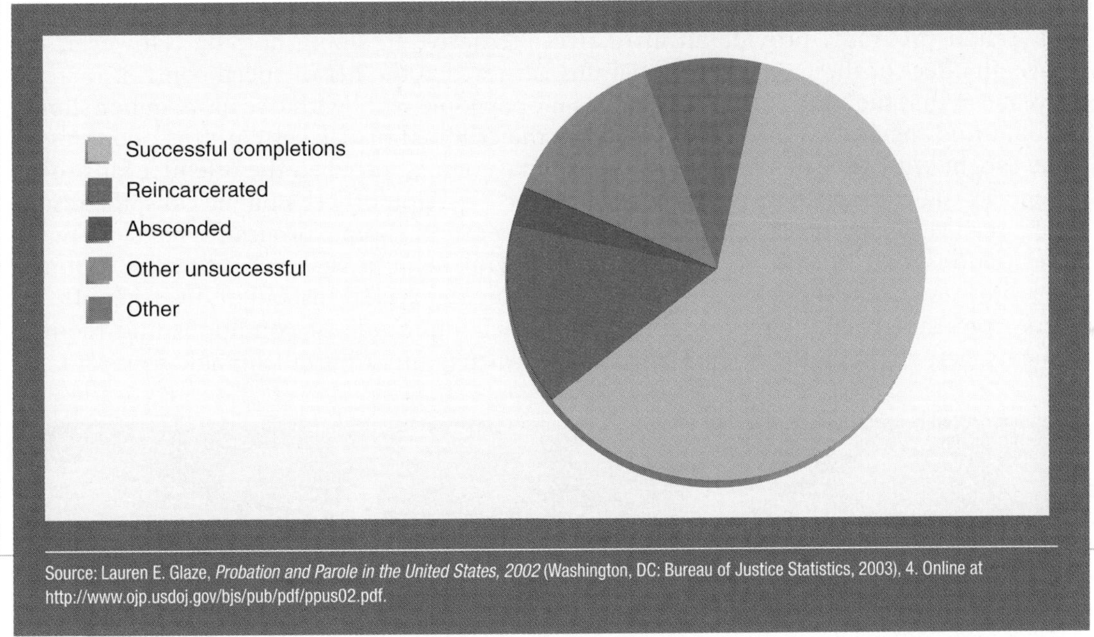

Source: Lauren E. Glaze, *Probation and Parole in the United States, 2002* (Washington, DC: Bureau of Justice Statistics, 2003), 4. Online at http://www.ojp.usdoj.gov/bjs/pub/pdf/ppus02.pdf.

taxes, and reentered societal life and made contributions to the community (see Figure 13.1 for the number of adults who have successfully completed probation).[7] Many notable failures have occurred, however, in which offenders in the community have killed, raped, or robbed and caused criminal justice officials to look incompetent and careless with whom they have allowed to go free.[8] Therefore, tension always exists about the wisdom of using community corrections. Despite this, community corrections will always be with us. Only the degree to which they are used is controversial. Which and how many inmates or offenders should be released into the community, and what level of supervision they are going to be subjected to, are the only real remaining questions. Despite calls for such radical initiatives as abolishing parole, those who understand the corrections situation in the United States appreciate that some other early-release mechanism is necessary.[9]

Diversion

Offenders may be diverted to alternative programs at a number of points in the criminal justice system. These programs are based on labeling theory, which suggests that the more limited the offender's penetration into the criminal justice system is, the less likely the offender will be to adopt a criminal self-concept and continue to commit crimes. Diversion programs are especially popular when dealing with the first-time offender who has committed a relatively minor offense.[10] Typically, the offender will have the charges held in abeyance while he or she completes some type of treatment program or community service, or simply continues to stay out of trouble for a specified period of time. Once the conditions of the diversion program are completed, the offender is released from supervision without a conviction on his or her record.

Sometimes this brief encounter with the criminal justice system is enough to get the attention of young offenders who are then successful in avoiding further contact with the law. For many young people who have college aspirations or hope for a career in law, medicine, or teaching, a clean record is crucial. Many prosecutors and judges also do not want to soil the record of young people who commit minor crimes. They see diversion programs as a method for sorting out the ones who will respond immediately and those who are going to continue to be problems for the criminal justice system.

Although diversion programs limit the number of people who enter the criminal justice system, they are not without critics. Given the present state of prison overcrowding and the heavy caseloads that probation officers carry, were it not for diversion programs, the state would dismiss the cases of many first-time offenders who commit minor crimes.[11] At a time when prosecutors must develop priorities as to what cases to pursue, diversion programs provide an attractive alternative to doing nothing. However, the overall effect of these diversion programs is to widen the net of social control. By that, we mean that the state controls more and more people who, with one more minor slipup, could find themselves inserted deeply into the criminal justice system. It is one thing to be caught with a misdemeanor quantity of marijuana, but when the offender fails to attend a drug counseling program and return the diversion officer's phone calls, the resulting revocation of diversion can mean incarceration. Some programs have so many restrictions that clients are almost sure to violate at least some of them. Thomas Blomberg and Karol Lucken called this "stacking the deck." Instead of diverting offenders from the system, some programs, with their multitude of conditions and requirements, actually suck the offender into a deeper quagmire of legal entanglements.[12]

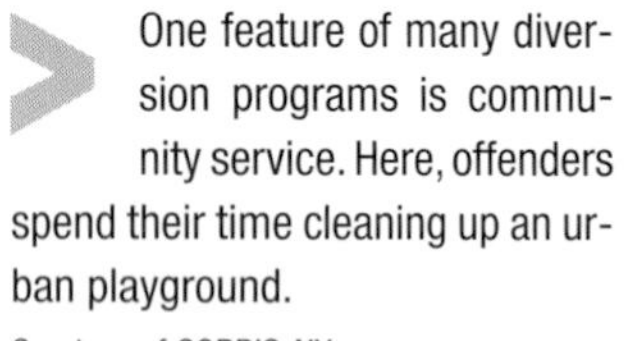

One feature of many diversion programs is community service. Here, offenders spend their time cleaning up an urban playground.

Courtesy of CORBIS-NY.

Probation

Probation is a chance for offenders to stay out of prison or jail if they promise to be good. At any given time, there are more probationers than inmates or parolees (see Figure 13.2), with state probationers far outnumbering federal probationers (see Figure 13.3). Probationers are not completely free, however. They must agree to certain terms set by the judge, such as performing public service work, refraining from alcohol, getting therapy, and reporting regularly to a probation officer. Those who violate these agreements are usually incarcerated for the term for which they were initially eligible. Probation is a widely used

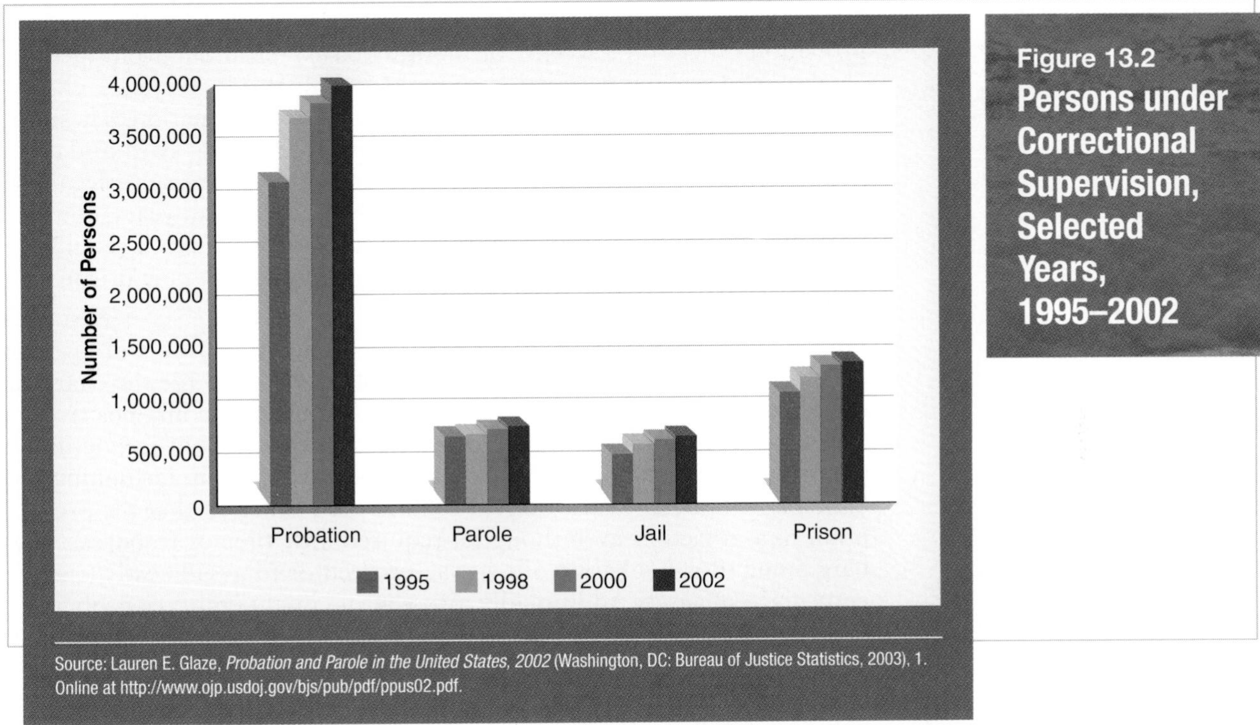

Figure 13.2 Persons under Correctional Supervision, Selected Years, 1995–2002

Source: Lauren E. Glaze, *Probation and Parole in the United States, 2002* (Washington, DC: Bureau of Justice Statistics, 2003), 1. Online at http://www.ojp.usdoj.gov/bjs/pub/pdf/ppus02.pdf.

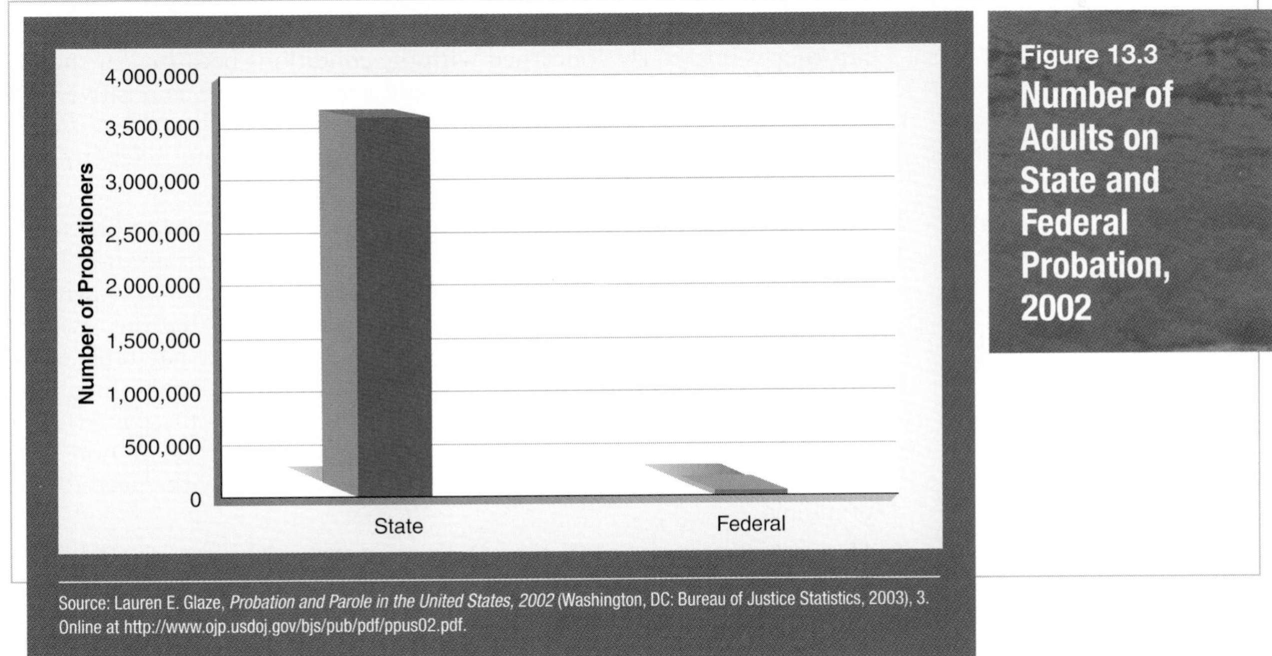

Figure 13.3 Number of Adults on State and Federal Probation, 2002

Source: Lauren E. Glaze, *Probation and Parole in the United States, 2002* (Washington, DC: Bureau of Justice Statistics, 2003), 3. Online at http://www.ojp.usdoj.gov/bjs/pub/pdf/ppus02.pdf.

sentencing alternative because it accomplishes several positive outcomes. Depending on how one views the criminal justice system, one or more of these outcomes may be more attractive than others. Here we will consider the practice of probation from the relative viewpoints of the key actors in the criminal justice system

- **How the offender views probation.** Probation can seem like a very good deal for the offender. When faced with the prospect of going to prison, many offenders embrace the prospect of probation like a lifeline. Probation allows the offender to remain in the home, at the workplace, and safe from the pains of imprisonment. Compared to life in prison, the restrictions of probation seem like a minor irritant. However, the conditions of probation do affect the offender's freedom and after a while, can seem frivolous and nitpicky. Reporting to the probation officer on a weekly or monthly basis; refraining from the use of alcohol; and seeking permission to move to a different residence, change jobs, or travel outside the county can cause resentment and alienation. These conditions must be taken seriously because their violation can bring swift and certain punishment from the state. Probationers do not enjoy the same legal rights as other citizens, and revocation, even after many successful years, could result in receiving the entire prison sentence for which one was initially eligible. Because the time served on probation does not count toward the new prison sentence, the sword of Damocles is always hanging over the probationer's head.
- **How the prosecutor views probation.** The prosecutor's first and foremost concern is to win the case. Having made the decision to file the charge against the offender, the prosecutor wants to dispose of the case in a positive way as efficiently as possible. Although often under pressure from the victim to seek prison time, the prosecutor has considerable discretion in fashioning plea bargains with defense attorneys. Probation is a sanction that the prosecutor can point to as a victory even though it required little time or resources. As a plea bargaining tool, probation allows the prosecutor to avoid costly trials for a large percentage of cases. Additionally, prosecutors might embrace probation when the facts of the case are weak and the case would likely result in a dismissal if it actually went to trial.
- **How the defense attorney views probation.** The defense attorney, just like the prosecutor, views probation as a victory. By keeping the offender out of prison, the defense attorney can claim to have preserved the offender's liberty with some reasonable compromises, such as the conditions of probation. The defense attorney is not overly concerned with the conditions because, for the most part, they will not hurt the offender and could very well serve as positive influences. Being required to get more education or alcohol counseling are not violations of fundamental human rights, and the defense attorney is not likely to object to such requirements.
- **How the judge views probation.** Judges are under tremendous pressure from the public to punish offenders despite the fact that the prisons are full. Probation allows the judge to impose a sentence that is less expensive than prison and, to some degree at least, satisfies victims and other citizens that the offender did not escape punishment. The judge can make probation more palatable to those who want punishment by adding special conditions such as drug testing, home confinement, and increased supervision. We will discuss these intermediate punishments in greater detail at the end of this chapter, but we note here that they are used to give probation more teeth and to satisfy the need to punish criminals.
- **How reformers view probation.** Probation offers the offender a variety of treatment and community service activities. Community resources such as schools, mental health centers, hospitals, and opportunities for gainful employment are offered that cannot be duplicated in the prison. If used

judiciously, these resources can provide the ingredients for the successful rehabilitation and reintegration of the offender. Perhaps the major benefit of probation as seen by reformers is the avoidance of the deleterious effects of prison. By keeping the offender away from hardened criminals, the criminal justice system can instill productive work habits and positive social skills.

- **How politicians view probation.** It should not surprise us that, as with many issues, politicians talk out of both sides of their mouths on the issue of probation. On one hand, many politicians adopt a tough-on-crime stance and advocate sending vast numbers of offenders to prison for incredibly long sentences. On the other hand, these same politicians do not provide the funds needed to build enough prisons, hire enough probation officers, or establish effective community corrections treatment services. To them, probation is a cheaper way to punish than the prison. However, politicians can be expected to condemn parole when some parolee commits a heinous crime while under supervision.

Probation means many things to many people. The emphasis of probation in any given jurisdiction may vacillate between its twin goals of supervision and treatment. Because it is such a fundamental feature of the criminal justice system, however, it will always be used in one form or another.

Probation Officers at Work

The probation officer's job requires a variety of skills, a strong sense of self-worth, and a tolerance for other people not doing what is expected of them. The probation officer spends time in the courtroom, in the office, and out in the field visiting clients where they work and live. Each probation department will have standards for monitoring offenders, and each probation officer will work out how to accomplish the job's multiple demands. Many probation officers love this work because its discretion and flexibility allow them to use their particular administrative, interpersonal, and investigative strengths to help offenders and protect society. The actual duties of the probation officer are many, but three universal functions define the occupation: investigation, supervision, and service.

INVESTIGATION. The probation officer spends a lot of time gathering information for decision makers throughout the criminal justice system. The offender's case file will contain data gleaned from police reports; prosecutors' files; and interviews with offenders, victims, witnesses, neighbors, teachers, and peers. The most time-consuming and significant report that the probation officer writes is the **presentence investigation** (PSI).[13]

presentence investigation The report prepared by a probation officer to assist a judge in sentencing. The report usually contains information about the offender's arrests, prior convictions, work history, and family. May also be called "presentencing report."

The United States has a bifurcated court process. The first goal of the proceedings is to determine the defendant's guilt or innocence. This is sometimes done by means of a criminal trial. However, the criminal trial is used sparingly; the vast majority of cases are settled through plea bargaining.[14] With plea bargaining, the judge does not have the opportunity to become familiar with the case or the defendant, so in the second part of the case proceedings, the sentencing, the judge has little information on which to base a sentence. Typically, the judge will postpone the sentencing judgment while the probation department conducts a presentence investigation.[15]

During the presentence investigation the probation officer collects information about two important aspects of the case: the legal history of the incident and the offender's social history.

- **Legal history.** The legal history offers the judge two primary items to help him or her make an informed sentencing decision. The first item is a complete report on the crime(s). The probation officer will summarize the police report, provide the offender's version of the incident, and include additional perspective(s) from the victim or other interested parties. The goal is to give the judge a good idea of the crime's impact on the victim(s) and the community.[16] This is especially useful when the case has been plea bargained because the final charge may not reflect the seriousness of the crime or the dangerousness of the offender. For example, in a case of spousal abuse, the husband may have been able to plea a savage beating down to a simple assault charge. This reduced charge will limit the sentence, but the judge is well served in knowing exactly what happened and how violent the husband can become. With this knowledge, the judge can decide to impose special conditions of probation, such as attending anger management classes. Additionally, this part of the presentence investigation will alert the judge to the dispositions of any codefendants and to any further charges that may be hanging over the offender. The second item of the legal history is the offender's prior record. Is this the first time the defendant has violated the law or the fifteenth? Has probation been attempted before, and if so, did the defendant successfully complete the probationary term without violating its conditions? Is there a pattern of increasing severity to the defendant's crimes? Did the Peeping Tom become a flasher who now is convicted of rape? Have other interventions such as alcohol and drug treatment been successful? The answers to all of these questions will help the judge determine the risk of putting this offender back on the street.

- **Social history.** The offender's social history will also help the judge craft an appropriate sentence. The probation officer will gather information on the offender's education, family, work situation and employment history, physical and mental health, and military history. If any of these factors are related to the case, the probation officer might describe in great detail how the offender might have special issues that require consideration. For example, if the offender has been convicted of child abuse, it would be important for the judge to be aware of his employment as a fourth-grade teacher and his volunteer work for the Boy Scouts. In gathering this information, the probation officer will include names, addresses, phone numbers, and other information of family members, places of employment, peers, victims, and witnesses. This information is important not only for the case at hand, but to develop a record of attachments that can be used by future probation officers to monitor the offenders. For example, sometimes the old phone number of a former girlfriend becomes the one link to a probationer who has disappeared.

The probation officer will question the client on all of these issues and then spend a great deal of time attempting to verify the truthfulness of the answers. Some clients will forget important details of their past, some will try to put a positive spin on their actions, and some will look the probation officer right in the eye and lie. A forthcoming and honest offender may find a more receptive judge than the one who continues to demonstrate that she or he cannot be trusted. The presentence investigation is the probation officer's opportunity to provide the judge not only with facts, but also with information on the offender's attitude. Because this document can determine whether the defendant goes to prison or is placed on probation, the probation officer must be fair to both the defendant and society.[17]

SUPERVISION. Once an offender is placed on probation, the probation officer will advise him or her about what is expected. Each probation system has standard conditions. Typically, these include instructions on how often to report; restrictions on changing jobs, residences, or schools without prior approval; and proscriptions on alcohol consumption, drug use, and consorting with known felons. The probationer must also cooperate with the probation officer and follow all lawful instructions. These standard conditions give the probation officer wide latitude in controlling the probationer's lifestyle. However, because of high caseloads, most officers cannot systematically ensure that all the conditions are being followed.

The judge may also apply special conditions to a particular case. For instance, in the case of a child abuser, the judge may prohibit him from loitering around schools or playgrounds.[18] Other special conditions might include community service. For example, an accountant convicted of a DUI may be required to provide free tax advice to senior citizens, or a college student involved in a hit-and-run accident may be required to speak at

FOCUS ON ETHICS

Studying for Your Drug Test

You are graduating from college next semester, and you are just starting your job search. You have an excellent résumé that includes a 3.5 grade-point average, leadership in several important campus organizations, and an honorable mention as an All-American in your favorite sport. Additionally, you have a clean criminal record and have done an internship at the local police department where your supervisor has said she would be happy to write a glowing letter of recommendation for you. In short, you are on the fast track for a good job in the criminal justice system, and you have set your sights on a federal agency such as the FBI, DEA, AFT, FBP, or one of the agencies connected with Homeland Security.

Here is the problem: Up until last year you had wanted to go to law school, so you were never worried about a history of drug use. Although you were never seriously involved with any harmful drugs such as heroin or crack-cocaine, you did smoke your share of marijuana. You justified your drug use by saying that your grades actually improved when you smoked, so there must not be that much harm in it. Now your friends and professors are telling you that to get a sensitive job in the federal government you will have to reveal your drug history on a written form, pass a polygraph test in which they will ask about drugs, and take random drug tests.

WHAT DO YOU DO?

1. Lie on the form and say that your marijuana use happened over five years ago, before you came to college.
2. Do your research and try to discover ways to successfully lie on the polygraph test.
3. Go to the local nutrition store and ask what supplements or herbal medicines they have that will help you pass a drug test.
4. Have someone else who does not have a drug history take the drug test for you.
5. Tell the truth and hope they believe that you have turned over a new leaf and will no longer be involved in drug use.
6. Stop using drugs, go to law school, and try to get the federal job after being drug-free for a few years when you have your law degree.

high schools and confess to her lack of judgment and the remorse she has for the harm she did to the victim. The probation officer must ensure that these activities are accomplished.

The supervision function of the probation officer's job accomplishes two goals. On one hand, supervision is a form of punishment in which the probationer's life is disrupted by the many conditions of probation. This disruption obviously pales in comparison to the disruption of going to prison, but still, reporting to the probation officer and asking permission for simple things such as leaving the state to go on vacation can become tiresome after a couple of years. Second, the supervision function is a form of surveillance designed to protect society by alerting the probation officer that the probationer is drifting back into unlawful behavior.[19]

Because prisons are crowded, the court must place on probation some offenders who pose a risk to society. Therefore, the surveillance function of probation is very important. To determine the level of risk for each offender, probation departments measure the type of offense, prior record, social history, and drug and alcohol use to determine the level of supervision and the frequency of probation officer contacts to require. The determination of probation risk is an internal management issue for probation departments and not a legal issue in which offenders are protected by the court. The risk assessment

REFERENCE

Probationer Risk Assessment Instrument

Georgia Department of Corrections

Please print clearly and complete each item completely

Probationer Name ____________________ **Classifier Name** ____________________

Circuit Code _____ **Probation Officer Name** ____________________

OTIS Number (10 digits) ____________________ **Date (MM/DD/YYYY)** ___ / ___ / _____

	Risk
A. Most Serious Offense Type ☐ 0 Sex Offense or Drug Sales ☐ +1 Property, Non-violent Personal, Drug Possession, Other ☐ +2 Violent or DUI/HTV	
B. Actual Age at This Sentencing ☐ 0 51 or older ☐ +1 19 to 50 ☐ +2 younger than 19	
C. Number of Felony Convictions ☐ +1 One ☐ +2 Two ☐ + 4 Three or more **(Include present offense, First Offender sentences, and juvenile convictions)**	
D. Number of Probation Revocations ☐ 0 None ☐ +8 One or two ☐ +14 Three ☐ +27 Four or more **(include juvenile offenses)**	
E. Alcohol Use (in past five years) ☐ 0 No problems encountered ☐ +1 Problems indicated – Currently in recovery – Social use – Sporadic (monthly) abuse – Level of abuse seriously interferes with lifestyle and/or work related activities – Arrest(s) for public intoxication – One or more charges of DUI – Weekly or daily abuse – Has been hospitalized for treatment or detoxification or has committed alcohol-related criminal acts (includes present offense)	
F. Illicit Drug Abuse (in past five years) ☐ 0 No use of illicit drugs ☐ +1 Problems indicated – Infrequent use – Monthly, Weekly, or Daily use – Has been or is currently in outpatient treatment – Has been hospitalized for treatment/detoxification – Current regular use of psychedelics, heroin, cocaine, amphetamines, barbiturates, or abuse of prescription medication or has committed drug-related criminal acts (includes present offense)	
G. Mental Health ☐ 0 None ☐ +1 Currently in outpatient program without medication ☐ +3 Other -In outpatient program on medication any time during past 5 years -Confined in a mental institution within past 5 years	
H. Employment (in past two years) ☐ 0 Employed ☐ +3 Not applicable (full time student, disabled, etc.) OR Period(s) of unemployment of up to six months **OR** three job changes within one year ☐ +7 Period(s) of unemployment for 6 months or longer ☐ +11 Dismissed/terminated for cause	

Up to and including 11 = Standard	**19 to and including 23 = High**	**Total Score**
12 to and including 18 = Medium	**24 and above = Maximum**	

Supervision Level: ____________________

Retain in probationer's file according to Probation Division SOPs IIIB 13-0004, IIIB 13-0005, IIB 13-0006 Rev. 4/02

Draft 4/02

Courtesy Georgia Department of Corrections.

instrument does have some built-in bias. For instance, younger offenders are automatically assigned more risk than older offenders. Similarly, juvenile crimes and adult first-offender crimes are usually treated more leniently by the courts, but in probation risk assessments, they are counted against the offender as stringently as any other crime. Probationers have reduced legal rights, and the courts have intervened only sporadically to limit the discretion of probation officers and judges.

The probationer's risk level dictates how much he or she will be watched. Typically, probation officers will allocate more attention to new offenders until they can determine that they are adjusting to their status. If the probationer follows instructions and reports when required, attends school and/or holds down a steady job, and fulfills the standard and special conditions of probation, then the supervision will be relaxed.

In an ideal world, there would be enough probation officers to ensure that every probationer was living a law-abiding life and following the conditions of probation. However, because of a lack of funding, many probationers get away with numerous minor violations, and some of them continue to maintain a criminal lifestyle. This is a precarious practice, however, because probation officers have surveillance powers that police officers lack. If the probation officer suspects that a probationer is engaged in criminal activity, then a search of the residence, car, or person can be conducted without the benefit of Fourth Amendment requirements of probable cause. When one is placed on probation, it is understood that permission is automatically given for the probation officer to conduct almost unlimited surveillance (see Figure 13.4).

When a probationer is caught committing a new crime or violating the conditions of probation, the case goes back to the judge. This is where things get dicey for the probationer. Although the court must afford the offender all the required legal rights for the new crime, this new crime will also be considered a probation violation. The legal requirements necessary to revoke the probation and sentence the offender on the old charge are far less rigorous than those needed to convict and sentence the offender on the new charge. Additionally, any plea bargaining the offender does on the new charge can affect his or her probation status. For example, suppose Joe is on probation for five years for assault and has successfully completed four years of the sentence when he is arrested for selling drugs to an undercover narcotics officer. Because he cooperated with the police by ratting out all his drug-using friends, he strikes a deal with the prosecutor on the drug charge for probation. However, Joe's prior charge of assault, because it was in another jurisdiction, has an entirely different judge who determines that his plea bargain on the drug charge is an admission of guilt and a violation of his conditions of probation. Consequently, Joe's probation is revoked, and the judge sentences him to five years in prison based on the assault charge. When Joe gets to prison, he is alarmed to find that his new cellmate is one of his friends, incarcerated as a result of his testimony. Oops.

Most violations of the technical conditions of probation do not result in revocation. Judges are reluctant to send people to jail because they failed to report to their probation officers or moved to a new apartment without prior permission. In fact, judges do not want to be bothered with minor issues and depend on the probation officer to chastise the offender. On some occasions, the probation term may be extended for an offender who cannot follow instructions, or new, more restrictive conditions may be applied until it is clear that compliance is forthcoming.[20]

The probation officer must document his or her supervision of offenders because there is always the possibility that one will commit a serious crime and not only make the officer look incompetent, but open the officer to professional liability. If the probation officer did not follow the protocols of the office and failed to require the probationer to abide by the conditions of probation, then the offender's victims might be able to sue.[21] Say, for instance, that as a probation officer, you unknowingly permitted a child molester to move to a new residence that happened to be next to an elementary school, and that for seven months you never visited the probationer, who was using a puppy to lure children into his yard where he sexually abused them. It would not be unreasonable for an attorney representing the children's parents to argue that as society's watchdog, you

Figure 13.4 Standard Conditions of Probation for Federal Offenders

(Because probation is a conditional release, the probationer must agree to limited legal rights.)

It is the order of the Court that you shall comply with the following standard conditions:

1. The defendant shall not leave the judicial district or other specific geographic area without the permission of the court or probation officer.
2. The defendant shall report to the probation officer as directed by the court or probation officer and shall submit a truthful and complete written report within the first five (5) days of each month.
3. The defendant shall answer truthfully all inquiries by the probation officer and follow the instructions of the probation officer.
4. The defendant shall support the defendant's dependents and meet other family responsibilities.
5. The defendant shall work regularly at a lawful occupation unless excused by the probation officer for schooling, training or other acceptable reasons.
6. The defendant shall notify the probation officer at least ten (10) days prior to any change of residence or employment.
7. The defendant shall refrain from excessive use of alcohol and shall not purchase, possess, use, distribute, or administer any controlled substance, or any paraphernalia related to any controlled substance, except as prescribed by a physician.
8. The defendant shall not frequent places where controlled substances are illegally sold, used, distributed, or administered, or other places specified by the court.
9. The defendant shall not associate with any persons engaged in criminal activity, and shall not associate with any person convicted of a felony unless granted permission to do so by the probation officer.
10. The defendant shall permit a probation officer to visit the defendant at any time at home or elsewhere and shall permit confiscation of any contraband observed in plain view of the probation officer.
11. The defendant shall notify the probation officer within seventy-two hours of being arrested or questioned by a law enforcement officer.
12. The defendant shall not enter into any agreement to act as an informer or special agent of a law enforcement agency without the permission of the Court.
13. As directed by the probation officer, the defendant shall notify third parties of risks that may be occasioned by the defendant's criminal record or personal history or characteristics, and shall permit the probation officer to make such notifications and to confirm the defendant's compliance with such notification requirement.
14. The defendant shall pay the special assessment imposed or adhere to a court-ordered installment schedule for the payment of the special assessment.
15. The defendant shall notify the probation officer of any material change in the defendant's economic circumstances that might affect the defendant's ability to pay any unpaid amount of restitution, fines or special assessments.

Source: U.S. Probation/Pretrial, Northern District of Indiana, http://www.innp.uscourts.gov/Forms/Standard_Conditions_for_Offenders.pdf.

should have known your probationer lived next to the school. The attorney may also examine your case records and find that you have not followed office procedures and made the required home contacts. Because you are responsible for making a reasonable effort at supervision, your case records must reflect a good-faith effort to comply with the preestablished reporting standards. In this case, losing your job may be the least of your worries.

intensive supervision probation A form of supervision that requires frequent meetings between the client and probation officer(s).

One management technique to ensure that dangerous offenders are provided with an adequate level of supervision is to give their cases to probation officers with reduced caseloads, who can then be required to make more contacts. These reduced-caseload strategies are called **intensive supervision probation** (ISP). Because this practice is similar to those used in the parole function, we will discuss them in greater detail later in this chapter.

SERVICE. One reason that individuals decide to work in corrections is to help people. Although investigation and supervision occupy most of the probation officers' time,

CASE IN POINT

Mempa v. Rhay

The Case

Mempa v. Rhay, 389 U.S. 128, 88 S. Ct. 254 (1967)

The Point

Felony defendants must be allowed to have an attorney during hearings when probation may be revoked or a deferred sentence imposed.

Jerry Mempa, an indigent, was convicted of riding around in a stolen vehicle. His sentence was deferred, and he was given two years' probation. A few months later, Mempa was accused of being involved in a burglary, and the prosecution recommended that his probation be revoked. At the hearing, Mempa was not appointed an attorney, asked about his previous court-appointed attorney, or asked if he wanted another attorney. Mempa's probation officer testified that Mempa had been involved in the burglary, but that Mempa had denied it. The probation officer was not cross-examined. Mempa then admitted to his involvement in the burglary. Without questioning Mempa further, the court revoked his probation and sentenced him to 10 years in the penitentiary as per state law, but recommended that he serve only a year.

Six years later, in 1965, Mempa, still in prison, filed a writ of habeas corpus with the Washington Supreme Court, claiming that he had been deprived of his right to counsel at the probation revocation hearing. The state court denied the petition, and he appealed to the Supreme Court. The Court agreed with Mempa and wrote that, according to the Sixth Amendment, felony defendants must be allowed counsel during hearings when probation may be revoked or a deferred sentence imposed, even if counsel had been present during the original trial at which the sentence was deferred. The decision was reversed and remanded.

they are still expected to provide some level of service to those offenders who need help. Sometimes new probation officers are disillusioned when they discover the impediments to providing the help they believe is needed. These impediments include the following:

- **High caseloads.** Because probation officers must supervise so many cases, they have little time to establish a personal rapport with each client.
- **Many offenders do not want the help and extra attention of the probation officer.** Some officers are surprised that the very clients they are trying to help are liars, cheats, and con artists. Some of these officers become cynical after being betrayed a few times and replace their naiveté with an equally ineffective bitterness.
- **Sparse resources.** Mental health centers, drug treatment institutes, and all sorts of people-helping programs have been jettisoned because of budget cuts at every level of government. This can be frustrating to both the probation officer and the probationer. Sometimes a "treatable moment" appears when the probationer is motivated to seek help; however, being placed on a six-month waiting list can mean a lost opportunity.

It is unfortunate that the service aspect of the probation officer's job is so limited. Some may argue that rehabilitation is a secondary activity, but evidence suggests that appropriate placement in a decent treatment program can have a positive effect. Although the investigation and supervision aspects of probation will always be the primary focus, the service component may well be the most important for the long-term behavior change of the offender and ultimately the protection of society.

FOCUS ON ETHICS

Going Out on a Limb

As a probation officer you have a reputation of being pretty tough with your clients. However, every once in a while, someone comes along whom you are willing to take a chance on. You have been burned a couple of times before by probationers who promised one thing and did the opposite, but this time you think you have a client who warrants your trust and help.

James is a gifted athlete who has NFL written all over him. He is a college freshman who is on scholarship but was implicated in a brawl at a rock concert where several people were brutally beaten and hospitalized. Although the degree of James' involvement is unclear, his lawyer arranged a plea bargain for probation with the stipulation that the coach would allow James to remain on scholarship and play that season. Everyone, including you when you did the presentence investigation, believed James was a worthwhile risk for probation because of his bright future.

However, as James' probation officer you have come to suspect that he is developing an entitled attitude and believes because he is a football star that he need not abide by the conditions of his probation nor listen to you when you try to give him advice. Specifically, James is missing classes, will not return your phone calls, has had beer in his dormitory refrigerator even though he is not of drinking age, and violates the court-ordered curfew of midnight on weekends. You have tried to correct the problem by contacting his coach and advising him of your concerns, but you are finding that the longer the football season goes on, the less anyone—James, his coaches, the judge, or your supervisor—cares about your complaints. Most of the issues are minor technical violations, but you have just recently noticed a hostile attitude in James both on the field and off. Today, his girlfriend shows up at your office with a black eye and a tale about violence, gunplay, and steroids. This weekend is the big game against the cross-state rival, and everyone knows that James must do well for the team to win. You are afraid he might not make it to the weekend without hurting somebody unless you take action.

WHAT DO YOU DO?

1. Go by James' dorm room and have a face-to-face, heart-to-heart talk with him.
2. Go to the coach and threaten to get the judge to revoke James' probation before the game if he doesn't shape up.
3. Go to the judge and express your concerns and essentially place the whole issue in his lap, thereby covering your own rear end.
4. Say nothing until after the game and hope that once the pressure of football is off, James will start to behave in a more appropriate way.

Parole

The origin of the word *parole* is French. *Parole d'honneur,* which means "word of honor," was used in wartime when prisoners of war were released on their promise not to engage in further fighting.[22] The practice grew from the experiences and reforms discussed in Chapter 11 on the origins of the prison. Men such as Alexander Maconochie (marks system), Sir Walter Crofton (ticket-of-leave), and Zebulon Brockway contributed to the idea that the penal system should help the offender in the transition back into society.

Many people use the terms *probation* and *parole* interchangeably. Although they do have many similarities, significant differences make these corrections practices distinct and worthy of separate consideration. Both deal with offenders in the community, but they differ in a number of distinctive ways.

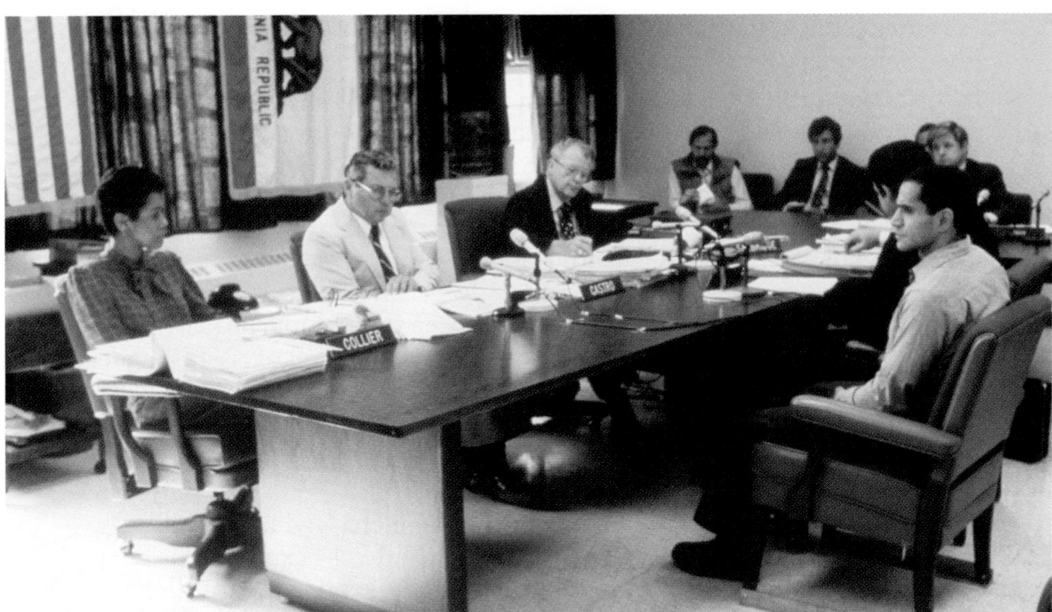

Parole board members listen to an offender explain why he should be released. Parole board members want to hear a good post-parole plan that includes a supportive residence and a viable job.
Courtesy of CORBIS-NY.

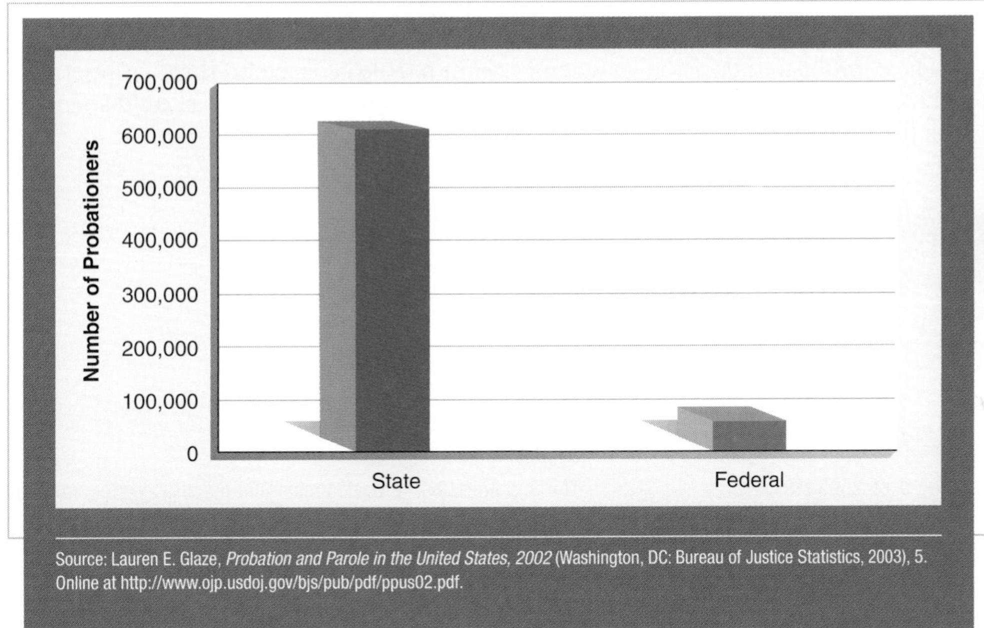

Figure 13.5 Number of Adults on State and Federal Parole, 2002

Source: Lauren E. Glaze, *Probation and Parole in the United States, 2002* (Washington, DC: Bureau of Justice Statistics, 2003), 5. Online at http://www.ojp.usdoj.gov/bjs/pub/pdf/ppus02.pdf.

- **Probation instead, parole after.** The primary difference between parole and probation is the point at which it occurs in the criminal justice process. Probation is a sentencing option that allows offenders to be placed under community corrections supervision *instead* of being placed in prison. Parole, on the other hand, is a form of early release that happens *after* the offender has served a part of the prison sentence. For a comparison of the number of state and federal parolees at the end of 2002, see Figure 13.5.
- **Governing authority.** Although there is considerable variation across the United States in the bureaucratic placement of the probation and parole functions, probation is usually attached to the judiciary, with the judge being the primary decision maker. Parole is extended by the executive branch of government and is under the auspices of the governor. Of course, there are many variations on this theme. In some jurisdictions, the agency that supervises parolees is part of the

executive branch, but the parole board is an independent decision-making panel that is presumably free of political influence.

- **Parolees and probationers are different types of clients in terms of risk factors, community ties, and social needs.** Generally, parolees have committed more serious crimes, will have readjustment issues after being incarcerated, and may not have the same support from family and friends because of weakened social bonds caused by long periods of incarceration. This may certainly be the case for many offenders; however, the truth is that whether the client is on probation or parole depends on the last crime he or she was convicted of. Many individuals, especially the most problematic ones, have been on multiple probations and paroles. Therefore, it may be misleading to judge the level of risk as higher for those on parole than for those on probation. In some ways, parolees may be more cooperative because they have already had a taste of prison life and are willing to abide by the conditions of their release in order to maintain their liberty.
- **Probation and parole officers have different mandates and responsibilities.** Again, depending on the jurisdiction, there are different expectations of probation and parole officers. In some states, parole officers carry firearms and arrest parole violators, whereas the probation officer would call a law enforcement agency to do any dangerous work.

When to Parole

The complicated decision of when to grant parole is based on three competing principles. First, there is the political issue of how much time the offender should spend in prison to satisfy the public demand for retribution and punishment. By paroling inmates too early,

CASE IN POINT

Morrissey v. Brewer

The Case

Morrissey v. Brewer, 408 U.S. 471, 92 S. Ct. 2593 (1972)

The Point

The Supreme Court provides minimum due process requirements for the revocation of parole.

John Morrissey had his parole revoked after he allegedly violated several of its conditions, including not reporting his residence to his parole officer, buying a car using a false name and driving it without permission of his parole officer, using a false name to obtain credit, and lying to police after a traffic accident. Morrissey was sent back to prison, whereupon he appealed the revocation of his parole. The Supreme Court set forth the following requirements for revocation of parole.

1. The parolee must receive written notice of the alleged violations.
2. The parolee must be advised of the evidence against him or her.
3. A preliminary hearing must be held in which a determination is made as to whether there is probable cause that the parolee has violated any parole conditions.
4. The parolee must have the chance to be heard and to present supporting witnesses and evidence.
5. The parolee may cross-examine any witnesses against him or her, unless cause is found for not allowing such confrontations.
6. A second hearing must be held in which the facts are judged by a "neutral and detached" hearing committee.
7. If parole is revoked, a written statement must be provided describing the reasons and the evidence used.

These requirements were later made applicable to both parole and probation revocation hearings.

the parole board risks losing the confidence of politicians and society, who start to question whether prison is a sufficient deterrent and punishment. In fact, some states have abolished parole and others have greatly modified the discretion of parole boards by assigning fixed sentences to several types of crimes. For an example of a state's parole process, see the Reference box "Kentucky Parole Board."

A second and competing principle when deciding whether to grant parole is the rehabilitation issue. Can a parole board accurately determine when someone is emotionally ready to be released from prison? We have already discussed indeterminate sentencing in which the offender is sentenced to serve an unspecified time; the prison officials and parole board are responsible for deciding when, based on the medical model, the inmate is "cured." However, ascertaining when an inmate is safe to release is difficult, and because of prison overcrowding, very few resources are being allocated for treatment programs.[23]

The third principle driving the parole decision is the limited number of prison beds. States simply cannot afford to keep everyone incarcerated for as long as they have been sentenced. To let new offenders in the front door of the prison, they must release others out the back door. With these complicating principles in mind, the parole board attempts to make rational, fair, and informed decisions on when to grant parole. These decisions are based on a number of factors:

1. **Time served.** The parole board does not have unlimited discretion in the release decision. The length of the imposed sentence controls, in part, when the inmate might first be eligible to be considered for parole. Another factor is the consideration of the time the inmate served in jail awaiting trial (in some cases this may be a year or more).
2. **Prison adjustment.** In many states, inmates are granted **good time** for behaving in prison, which can reduce the sentence by up to one-third. Some inmates can significantly reduce their sentence by earning **meritorious time** for completing treatment programs or educational degrees while in prison. By taking advantage of opportunities for self-betterment, inmates can demonstrate that they are able to compete for jobs or have acquired the social skills necessary to function in society.
3. **Preparole plan.** A plan is developed for the inmate's release. A parole officer (either one assigned to the institution or one in the jurisdiction where the parole will be served, or both) will develop a plan with the inmate and family members (or those who will be involved with the inmate upon release). This plan will specify where the inmate will live, how the inmate will survive financially, and what supervision level and treatment programs will be required. One reason for the denial of many paroles is an insufficient parole plan. If the parole board does not see a reasonable support network for the inmate, they will instruct all involved to develop a comprehensive plan before the next parole hearing. The longer an offender stays in prison, losing contact and trust with family and friends on the outside, the more difficult developing these plans becomes.
4. **Offender interview.** The parole board (or hearing officers acting in its name) will interview the offender prior to the parole decision to get a feel for the attitude, demeanor, preparedness, and sincerity of the offender. In these hearings, the parole board will inquire about the offender's remorse, prison experiences, parole plan, and sensitivity to criticism. The parole board will ask pointed and personal questions to see how the inmate reacts to authority figures. Some inmates will be defiant, but most will attempt to determine what the hearing officers want to hear and then provide it.
5. **Victim impact statements.** The parole staff contacts the victim(s) of the crime committed by the inmate and asks them to comment on how they suffered as a result of the inmate's actions and how the release of the inmate might now affect them. Some victims who have been especially traumatized may write impassioned statements that sink any chance of parole. On some occasions, victims—or in homicide cases, their relatives—will show up at every parole hearing to ensure that the parole board is aware of their opposition to the offender's release.

good time
The time deducted from an inmate's prison sentence for good behavior.

meritorious time
Time deducted from an inmate's sentence for doing something special or extra, such as getting a GED.

REFERENCE

Kentucky Parole Board: How the Parole Process Works

Eligibility for Parole

Parole eligibility is established by statute and regulation. Those convicted as violent offenders must serve 85 percent of their sentence before becoming eligible for parole. Many convicted of being persistent felony offenders are not eligible for parole until they have served at least 10 years of their sentences. Convicted sex offenders do not become eligible for parole until they have completed a sex offender treatment program administered by the Department of Corrections. All other incarcerated felons become eligible for parole after serving 20 percent of their sentences. Eligibility for parole in no way guarantees that an inmate will be granted parole.

Parole Board Meetings

For parole hearings at which the inmate appears, three members of the Board constitute a quorum. For all other meetings and Board business, four members are required to constitute a quorum.

With some exceptions, the Board conducts the majority of hearings through video conferencing. In these exceptions, the Board travels to the various institutions across the state to conduct face-to-face parole hearings.

Board meetings are open to the public; however, for security reasons, anyone who attends must make prior arrangements with the institution where the hearing is held. The Board makes a written record of its decision and announces the decision at the interview. If the three-member panel is not in unanimous agreement, the full Board must decide the case and a majority vote is required to make the decision.

Board Decision-Making Process

The Board has three decision options:

- Serve Out. The inmate must spend the balance of his or her sentence incarcerated.
- Deferment. The Board sets a period of months or years before the inmate will again become eligible to meet the Board.
- Parole. In all decisions, the Board considers the seriousness of the current offense, prior criminal record, institutional adjustment, attitude toward authority, history of alcohol or drug involvement, history of prior probation, shock probation or parole violation, education and job skills, employment history, emotional stability, mental capacities, health or illness, history of deviant behavior, official and community attitudes toward accepting the inmate back into the community, oral and written statements of victims, and parole plan, which includes home placement, job placement, and need for community treatment and follow up.

Parole Violations

Parolees accused of parole violations are entitled to a preliminary or probable cause hearing before an Administrative Law Judge and a final Parole Revocation Hearing before the Board. The Board employs two Administrative Law Judges who conduct probable cause hearings throughout the state. Identified victims of crimes are notified of upcoming parole hearings by the Victim Services Branch of the Parole Board and such victims may submit written statements or appear in person before the Board.

Source: Kentucky Parole Board, http://www.jus.state.ky.us/parolebd/process.htm

REFERENCE

Discretionary Parole

Discretionary parole is when a parole board has the authority to decide when an inmate is ready for release. Mandatory parole is when jurisdictions allow parole only after an inmate has served a predetermined percentage of time. As of 2000, the following states had abolished discretionary parole:

Maine
Kansas
Indiana
Illinois
Florida
Delaware
California
Arizona
Wisconsin
Washington
Virginia
Oregon
Ohio
North Carolina
Mississippi
Minnesota

For Certain Violent Offenders

Tennessee
New York
Louisiana
Alaska

Source: Timothy A. Hughes, Doris James Wilson, and Allen J. Beck, *Trends in State Parole, 1990–2000* (Washington, DC: Bureau of Justice Statistics, 2001), 2. Online at http://www.ojp.usdoj.gov/bjs/pub/pdf/tsp00.pdf.

As you can see, the decision to grant parole involves many factors and is difficult to predict in many cases. One is never sure how the hearing officer or the parole board will respond to evidence, but some established policies and a given board's track record suggest what the "going rate" is for most parole authorities.[24] Because so many cases are heard each year, patterns develop according to the length of time served and the appropriateness of the parole plan, so that even though an inmate may have a parole hearing, parole likely will not be granted until a few more years have passed.

Reentry and "Making It"

Most prison systems attempt to prepare the inmate for reentry into society. Generally, about half of inmates successfully complete parole; the other half return to prison (see Figure 13.6). Some programs may last up to a year and include mechanisms of gradual reintegration such as furloughs and work release. Other programs may last only weeks and include mock job interviews and/or studies to prepare for getting a driver's license. Regardless of how the prison prepares the inmate, at least three major adjustments stand as obstacles to successful reentry. One of these obstacles involves changes in the inmate, and the others involve changes in the world he or she is going back to.

1. **Prisonization.**[25] Life in prison is lived according to rigid rules established by both the administration and the inmate social system. The inmate quickly learns the boundaries of appropriate behavior and lives a life of predictability, routine, and boredom. The inmate is not required, or permitted, to make decisions, exercise judgment, be creative, or experiment in relationships or daily life. Some inmates find comfort in this atmosphere in which all important decisions and even most

Figure 13.6
Adults Completing Parole, 2002

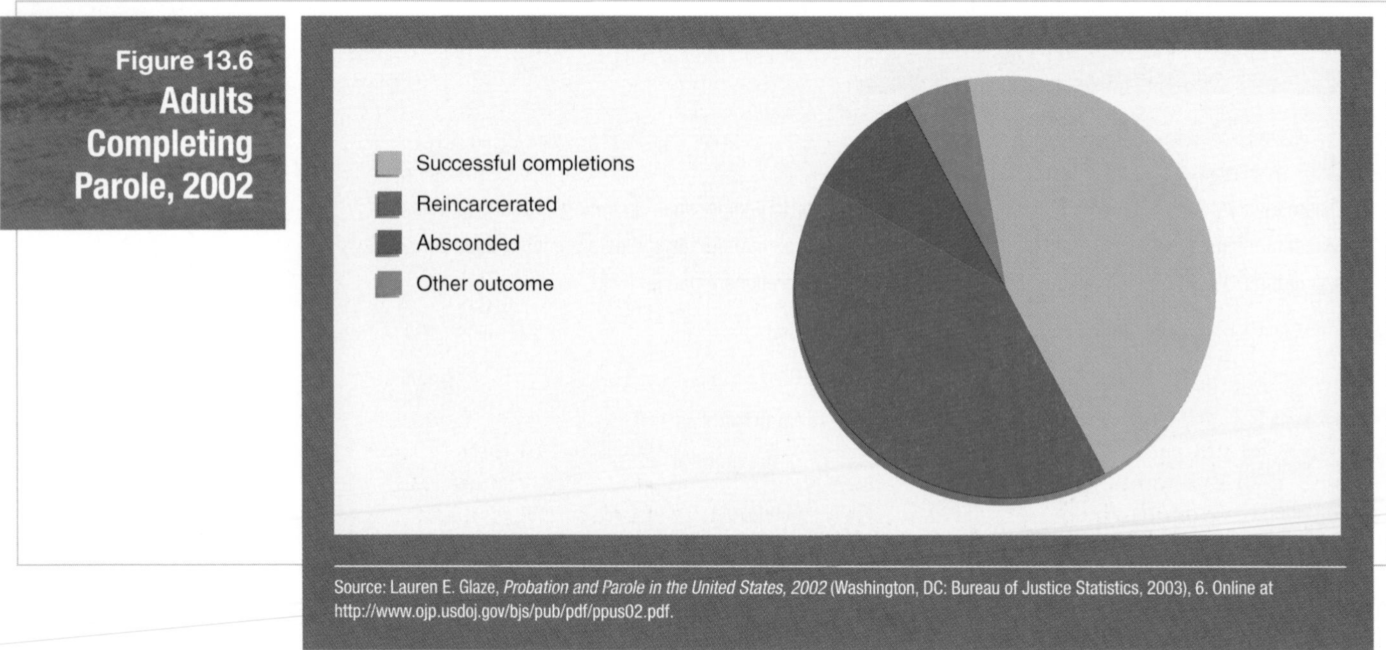

Source: Lauren E. Glaze, *Probation and Parole in the United States, 2002* (Washington, DC: Bureau of Justice Statistics, 2003), 6. Online at http://www.ojp.usdoj.gov/bjs/pub/pdf/ppus02.pdf.

unimportant decisions are made for them. When these inmates are released, they are overwhelmed by the magnitude of decisions they must make. For example, whereas in prison deciding what to eat involves sticking out a tray and assessing what is plopped on it, in the free world the menu options can be daunting. The prison has a soup of the day (sometimes it is the soup of everyday), but the grocery store has almost 100 soups of different brands, flavors, and sizes. Multiply the soup decision by the vast array of foods in the store, and the former inmate can experience decision overload. Other concerns have greater consequences than the choice of soup. The interpersonal skills needed to survive in prison are not always conducive to getting along with coworkers in society. The necessity to demonstrate a willingness to use violence that can keep one alive in prison is problematic in the workplace, where supervisors and coworkers are used to giving and taking criticism without worrying about their physical safety.

2. **Weakened social ties.** The Taoists say that you never stick your toe into the same river twice. This principle reflects a major problem of reentry. The world that the inmate left behind is not the same as the one he or she returns to. People have moved on with their lives, and the inmate must reestablish social bonds that have been weakened, twisted, or broken by incarceration.[26] Spouses, children, parents, friends, and bosses may act very differently and be wary of how the offender has been affected by prison. At its most extreme, these changes in social bonds include divorce or estrangement from spouses and rejection by children. The inmate often comes home to find that his or her former status as authority figure, breadwinner, and confidant has been usurped by someone else. While in prison, the mother might have remembered her children in a highly romanticized way, but upon release she may find them hostile, bitter, and attached to a new stepmother. The assumed social location of the inmate that was frozen in time by incarceration thaws out upon release and melts into a puddle of disillusionment, anomie, and alienation.
3. **Stigmatization.**[27] Erving Goffman defined one type of stigma as a "blemish of individual character" and included imprisonment as one of the conditions that individuals must carry around with them for a lifetime and constantly fight to overcome. This stigma is both legal and social. The legal stigma involves, depending on the jurisdiction, losing the right to vote, to parent, to hold public employment, to serve on a jury, to hold public office, and to possess a firearm, and

may mean being required to register as a felon. Perhaps these restrictions are understood by the former inmate who concedes that there is a continuous price to pay for criminal activity. However, the social stigma can be even more frustrating. The stigma of "ex-con" can be as debilitating as that of "convict." For the offender who has served a sentence and has paid for his or her crimes, the continuing discrimination and prejudice seems unjust. One is never allowed to make a fresh start and carries a **master status** that overwhelms all of the inmate's positive accomplishments.[28] Once parents hear that the new boyfriend is a convicted rapist, there is no convincing them that he has mended his ways, learned his lesson, paid his debt to society, or is in any way a suitable future son-in-law.

master status
A personal status that overwhelms all others. For example, "rapist" obliterates a positive status such as "good student" or "sports star."

Those on parole face many of the same challenges as those on probation. Being under the supervision of the state means that restrictions are placed on the offender. Conditions of parole are not significantly different from conditions of probation, but include the requirement to maintain contact with the parole officer and get permission to change residences, change employment, and travel outside the jurisdiction. For both probation and parole, a number of other tactics require examination if we are to truly appreciate how community corrections have developed over the years. Because of overcrowding in the prison systems and the concurrent heavy caseloads faced by probation and parole officers, the criminal justice system has developed intermediate sanctions designed to make probation and parole more effective, more stringent, and more palatable to the public who demand that offenders be held accountable for their actions.

Suing the Parole Board

One of the nightmares of those who work in the criminal justice system is when those offenders who have received a break commit more crimes. In the worst-case scenarios, a parolee kills while on parole. When it does happen, very little can be done to make the victim(s) or victims' families whole again. Victims and society feel an extra sense of injustice when the killer was safely confined, and the parole board decided to release the killer into society. Although this is a relatively rare occurrence, it happens enough to foster a widespread belief that the practice of parole endangers society.

In Canada at least 20 lawsuits have been filed against the Correctional Service of Canada and the National Parole Board. According to documents collected by the Canadian newspaper *The Globe and Mail,* at least 6 of the 20 known cases have been settled quietly for undisclosed amounts. Several other cases that ask for damages in the range of $10 million are still pending. In the cases that have been settled, it is rumored that the victims received six-figure sums.

QUESTIONS

1. Should victims have the right to sue the government for parole decisions that were made in good faith?
2. Are these murders the fault of the parole board for making bad decisions or the fault of citizens who refuse to pay the costs of building enough prisons to hold every inmate until his or her sentence expires?
3. Should the government be sued or just the individual parole board members who voted to release the killer?
4. Does the parole board have a duty to consider the safety of the community over the rehabilitation opportunities for offenders?

Source: Colin Freeze, "Victims Sue Ottawa for Crimes by Convicts," *The Globe and Mail,* December 26, 2001.

Intermediate Sanctions

Intermediate sanctions are sentencing alternatives available to the judge who finds regular probation too lenient and prison too severe.[29] If prisons were not so crowded, many offenders who receive intermediate sanctions may actually be incarcerated. With the pressures for parole boards to release inmates early to make room for new offenders, some of these intermediate sanctions are also employed at the parole stage of the criminal justice process.

Intermediate sanctions give the criminal justice system a broader range of mechanisms of social control and enhance the public's perception that crime does not pay. Although some of these newer intermediate sanctions are problematic, the critics' concerns are being addressed, and the courts are becoming cognizant of the issues that must be resolved. Here are some of the more notable intermediate sanctions.

Intensive Supervision Probation

Intensive supervision probation is simply what probation used to be before the advent of unreasonably high caseloads for probation officers.[30] Intensive supervision probation is actually a form of triage, whereby those offenders deemed the most problematic are allocated extra supervision. Probation officers assigned to these troublesome offenders are given small caseloads and are expected to have more frequent contact with clients. It is believed that if probation officers can concentrate on those who actually need help or really pose a threat to society, then they can recognize emerging problems and intervene quickly. A number of tools are available to the intensive supervision probation officer to aid in detecting wrongdoing. One of the most controversial of these tools is drug testing.

Drug Testing

Testing probationers or parolees for illegal drug use is a technological solution to a human problem. Rather than relying on behavioral cues or lifestyle changes to detect drug use, the officer can require that clients, either on a routine or random basis, submit a sample of urine for analysis. Because one of the conditions of freedom is to refrain from the use of illegal drugs, and because probation and parole are conditional-release practices, the client has a choice of cooperating or going to prison. Most offenders cooperate and are able to retain their liberty, live with their families, hold down a job, and escape the pains of imprisonment. Submitting a urine sample, while humiliating and insulting, seems like a small price to pay for staying out of prison. This is not to say, however, that offenders do not attempt to frustrate the system by masking their drug use. Probationers use a range of techniques to deceive authorities. These techniques include submitting someone else's urine, eating or drinking various items that mask the presence of drugs, and missing or delaying tests until drugs have been diluted in the body. Probation and parole authorities counter these deceptions by increasing the sophistication of the drug tests (for example, using hair strands instead of urine), surprising the clients with random tests, and closely monitoring the administration of the tests.

House Arrest and Electronic Monitoring

House arrest is a very old concept that has appeal today because it allows offenders to maintain family ties, work to support themselves and pay taxes, take advantage of community resources such as school and counseling services, and save the state the cost of incarceration.[31] Typically, offenders are required to stay home except when they are attending approved activities such as employment, school, treatment programs, or religious services. They are especially restricted during the evening hours when most crimes take place and when they can expect unannounced calls or visits from their probation officer. Although some citizens may be concerned about some home-confined offenders being a danger to the community, for the most part, these probationers are selected because they are low-risk and have relatively stable residences in which to be confined. Electric monitoring is often used to supplement house arrest but is also used with other programs.

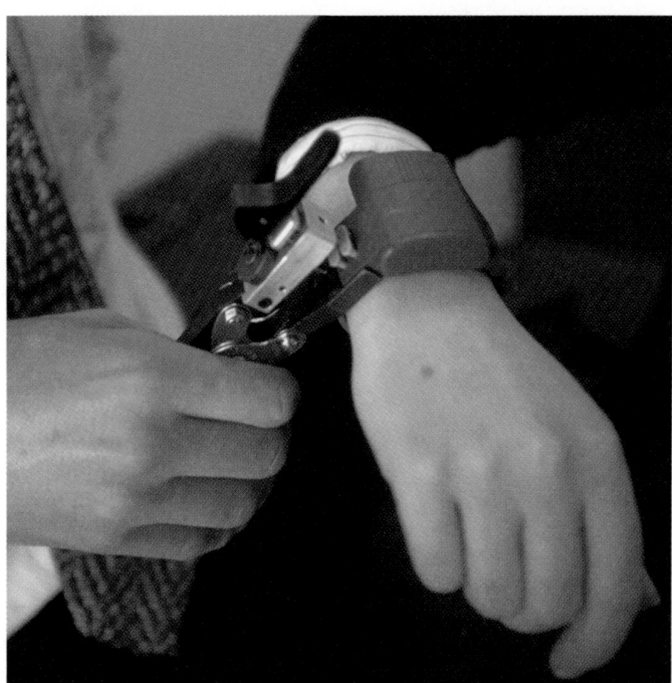

Electronic monitoring is a cost-effective method to keep track of offenders on house arrest. It allows offenders to live at home, continue employment, and stay out of prison.
Courtesy of CORBIS-NY.

Like drug testing, electric monitoring uses technology to address human concerns.[32] In this case, a device attached to the offender's ankle will alert authorities when it is moved too far from a transmitting device. If the offender can slip off the electronic bracelet and leave it next to the transmitting device, then he or she is free to roam at will, safe in the knowledge that the probation officer believes he or she is still home. Another limitation of electronic monitoring is that it can only tell the probation officer that the offender is at home, not what the offender is doing. Crimes such as child abuse, spouse battering, or drug sales could be happening, and the probation officer would have no clue.

In many ways, technological devices might lull us into thinking that offenders are adjusting to their limited freedoms when, in actuality, they are still engaging in serious crimes. Therefore, these tools should be considered merely as a supplement to face-to-face supervision, rather than as a replacement for the traditional probation or parole officer. As this type of technology becomes more sophisticated, it is interesting to speculate how it might be used to supervise the criminal offender. It is already possible to implant a small transmitter under the offender's skin and use a satellite to track his or her movements.[33] This way, probation officers are able to tell whether the offender is at home, at work, or at a bar with other offenders. Implanted monitoring devices may one day be able to report the offender's blood alcohol level or whether illegal drugs are present in the body.

Fines

Although the use of fines has been a consistent feature of the U.S. criminal justice system for a long time, other countries have used them more. For some types of crimes, especially some economic offenses, fines are an appropriate sanction. For other types of crimes, the public does not think offenders should be able to "buy their way out of trouble." In truth, fines are often used in conjunction with other types of sanctions, such as short periods of incarceration.[34]

Fines have several advantages as a criminal sanction. Fines used as an alternative to incarceration are not only less expensive to administer, but bring extra money to the criminal justice system's budgets. In fact, many probation systems require their clients to pay "cost of supervision" fines as a condition of probation, thus offsetting a major portion of the expense.[35] A final advantage of fines is the message that is sent to the public that criminals sometimes do "pay for their crimes." A large fine levied on a tax cheat or an unscrupulous businessperson gives the public a sense of justice.

Fines are an intermediate sanction that helps refill the coffers of the criminal justice system. Critics contend that excessive fines favor offenders who are financially well off and further punish those who are poor.
Courtesy of Corbis Royalty Free.

The downside of using fines as a criminal sanction involves fairness. Poor people can barely afford to support their families, and adding fines to the sentence places a hardship on them that wealthy offenders do not experience. For this reason, in addition to having fixed fines for certain offenses, some countries have instituted a "day fine" system in which the offender is fined in proportion to how much money he or she makes. The idea is that the fine would be based on how much the offender is paid for one day of work and then multiplied by the degree of punishment the court wants to administer. Consequently, someone who makes $100,000 a year would pay 10 times the fine of someone who makes $10,000 a year. Although this fine system may be more equitable than a fixed-fine system, wealth still has its advantages. Someone who makes $10,000 a year has very little discretionary money. Every dime is used for rent, food, health care, and other necessities. However, for the offenders making $100,000 a year, even though their houses may cost more and their children may go to more expensive schools, a certain economy of scale works in their favor and allows them to pay a percentage of their income without suffering as much as impoverished offenders.

Boot Camp Prisons

boot camp prison
A short-term prison that uses military boot camp training and discipline techniques to rehabilitate offenders. Often used for young offenders.

A recent addition to the intermediate arsenal of criminal sanctions is the **boot-camp prison** (see Figure 13.7). The philosophy behind boot camp prisons is that young offenders can be shocked into adopting conforming behaviors. This idea has its roots in the "scared-straight" programs of the 1970s in which young offenders were taken to adult prisons and verbally assaulted by inmates in the hope that the young offenders would be so afraid of going to prison that they would be "scared straight."[36] A documentary film entitled *Scared Straight* became the primary exposure to this policy for many politicians and decision makers. The practice spread to many states where prisoners, with good intentions, screamed at kids and made graphic suggestions about what was going to happen to them if they continued their lives of crime and landed in prison. The appeal of the scared-straight programs was the idea that an afternoon in a prison could, by fear and intimidation, overcome years of parental neglect, poor school performance, involvement in a criminal lifestyle or gang activity, social disorganization, and poverty. This quick, cheap, and highly visible program seemed almost too good to be true. It was. The shock of being yelled at by prisoners was discovered to wear off quickly. Scared-straight programs were a wonderful public relations tool for corrections but of little lasting value in changing the behavior of young offenders.

The continuing search for a correctional panacea through fear and intimidation has led to the creation of the boot camp prison. Patterned after the military boot camp ex-

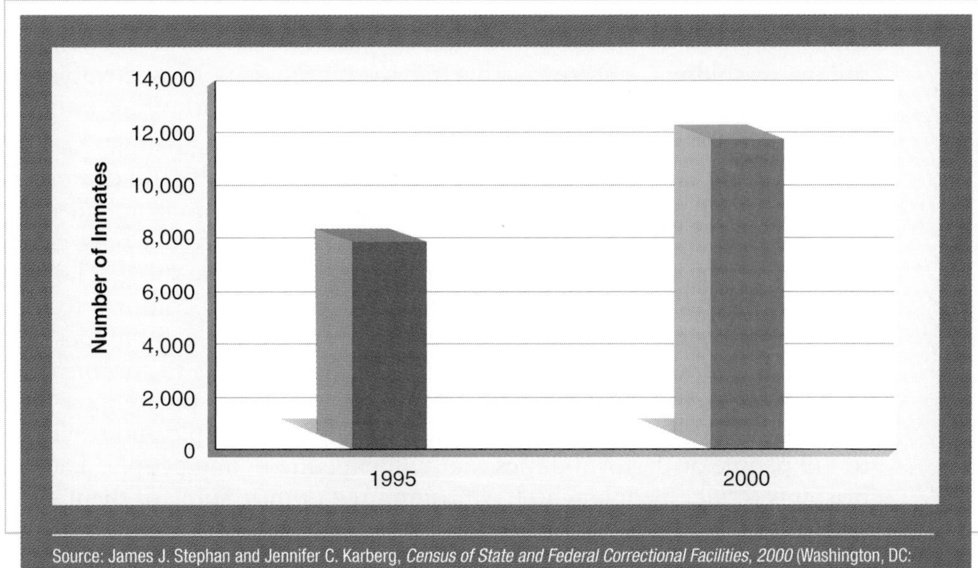

Figure 13.7 **Inmates Participating in Boot-Camp Prisons, 1995 and 2000**

Source: James J. Stephan and Jennifer C. Karberg, *Census of State and Federal Correctional Facilities, 2000* (Washington, DC: Bureau of Justice Statistics, 2003), 12.

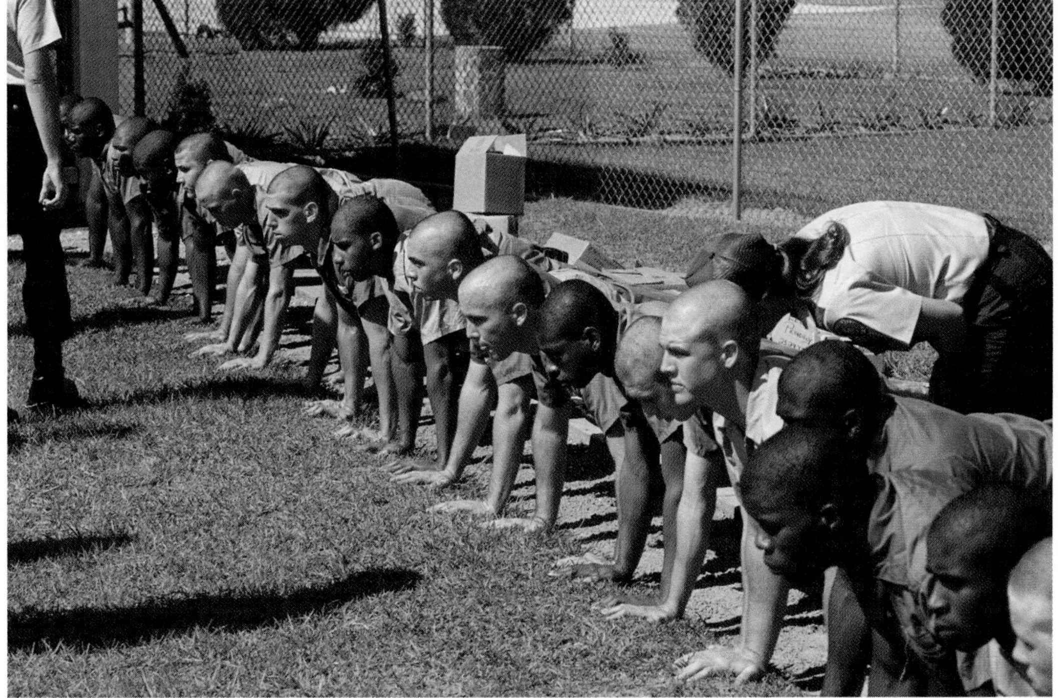

Boot-camp prisons emphasize discipline, physical conditioning, and regimentation. In theory, this provides inmates with the ability to control their behavior.

Courtesy of CORBIS-NY.

perience, these prisons are designed to address a number of issues thought to benefit the correctional mission.

- **Identity.** Erving Goffman described how each of us has an identity kit that we use to construct how we present ourselves to the outside world. How we style our hair, the clothes we wear, the makeup we apply to our faces, and the cars we drive are all selected to communicate a certain impression. Much of our identity is based on how successfully we manage that impression.[37] The purpose of the military boot camp experience is to strip its participants of their ability to project this impression and force them to conform to rules that govern not only how they look, but also how they act. A disparate group of young people enter boot camp, and by the time they graduate, they have been transformed into marines, sailors, or soldiers. The key to this transformation is not just stripping their previous identities, but also reconstructing their senses of self as military people.

- **Discipline.** Many young offenders (actually, many young people) lack self-discipline and do not work hard at school or in their jobs and cannot compete successfully in a fast-paced society. The boot camp prison is intended to instill good work habits and discipline in these offenders. Critics of boot camp prisons contend that discipline and self-discipline is not the same thing. The boot camp prison can certainly discipline offenders and make them conform to rigid supervision on the outside, but young offenders need self-discipline.[38] Although the military model looks attractive in forcing individuals to conform to a group ethos, a major distinction exists between the mission of the military and that of the prison. The military takes basically good young people and teaches them how to kill people or perform duties that will expedite killing people. The goal of the prison is to take people who have committed crimes, some of them violent, and correct this deviant behavior.
- **Cost.** Cost is the issue that drives the boot camp prison movement. With a 90-day program, each prison bed can be used for four offenders in a year, substantially reducing costs. Given the number of offenders that states are required to handle and the great expense of the traditional prison, the boot camp concept looks like an attractive alternative, even if it does not demonstrate a lower recidivism rate.[39]
- **Punishment.** Citizens do not want offenders to "get away" with committing crimes. They want to see something "done to" the prisoners, and the boot camp prison fulfills this desire in a highly visible and satisfying way.[40] The media shows "drill instructors" yelling and harassing young offenders, giving the boot camp prison an image of being a severe punishment and possibly having a deterrent effect on young people. No one can accuse the boot camp prison of being a country club. Except for its short duration, it satisfies the desires of the public that inmates serve a hard and spartan sentence devoid of frills and comforts.

Shock Probation

shock probation
The practice of sentencing offenders to prison, allowing them to serve a short time, and then granting them probation without their prior knowledge.

Another program that employs fear as a main feature is **shock probation.** In these programs, the probation officer and the judge play a confidence game on the offender. The offender receives a bogus sentence of jail or prison time, and then, after he or she has been incarcerated for 30 to 90 days, the judge converts the sentence to probation.[41] Because offenders think they are going to be imprisoned for a long time, the sudden release is presumed to encourage them to "turn over a new leaf" and to "start fresh" a new life of law-abiding and conforming behavior. There is a certain commonsense appeal to shock probation, but, on closer examination, it has some flaws that make it, like scared straight, a better public relations tool than corrections program. Incarcerating offenders for 30 to 90 days ruptures whatever stability they may have. They lose their jobs, drop out of school, and sever ties with significant social networks. However, upon release after their short stay, they're expected to instantly pick up the pieces of their shattered lives. The shock probation programs may also make the courts look hypocritical and duplicitous and further alienate and label the offender. When used sparingly with carefully selected offenders, this sanction has some corrections value, but for most offenders, probation or a short, planned incarceration is a better option.

Intermediate sanctions include several ways to make the sentence that stands between probation and prison more effective, more severe, and more politically popular. These sanctions are driven by a high crime rate with few traditional alternatives, a desire on the part of well-intentioned people to provide more effective community corrections services, and simple economics. If used intelligently, intermediate sanctions provide useful alternatives to incarceration at a low cost and without endangering the community.

NEWS FLASH

Throwing Away the Key

In the United States, the Fifth Amendment's "double jeopardy" provision states that no one may be tried twice for the same crime in criminal court and may not be punished more than once for the same offense. Convicted sex offenders, however, may find themselves serving extra time. Many states commit sex offenders to mental institutions after they have served their prison sentences because of concerns that the freed inmates may commit their crimes again. The Supreme Court has held that confinement in a mental institution does not constitute punishment and is therefore exempt from the double jeopardy rule. This trend illustrates the vague legal status of mentally ill offenders, as well as the fact that mental illness and clinical brain dysfunction are still poorly understood and often mishandled by the institutions responsible for controlling those who cannot control themselves.

In January 2002 the Supreme Court in *Kansas v. Crane* hobbled states' attempts to keep sex offenders locked up by requiring proof that the offenders have a mental illness that causes loss of self control. Prior to the case, states could confine offenders indefinitely if they had mental conditions that made them more likely to commit similar crimes if released. The Kansas statute—which the Supreme Court upheld in 1997—is called the Kansas Sexually Violent Predator Act. The following states have similar laws: Alabama, Arizona, California, Delaware, Florida, Illinois, Iowa, Maryland, Massachusetts, Mississippi, Missouri, Nebraska, New Jersey, North Dakota, Oklahoma, Pennsylvania, South Carolina, Washington, and Wisconsin.

QUESTIONS

1. Do you agree with the Supreme Court that confining offenders in mental institutions after they have served their prison sentences does not violate the double jeopardy rule?
2. Should sex offenders be confined indefinitely? What about murderers? Bank robbers? Drunk drivers?

However, intermediate sanctions are susceptible to compromise by the problem of net-widening.[42] Unless their use is monitored very closely, intermediate sanctions can be diverted from their intended targets, those who require intense supervision, and used on the trivial, frivolous, and petty offenders who would normally be released. On one hand, judges want to "teach a lesson" to small-time thieves or marijuana users and place them in programs that capture their attention and alter their lifestyles. On the other hand, because these programs are evaluated constantly and must demonstrate successful recidivism rates, judges tend to select those who are the most likely to complete the sanction successfully. The result is that a greater proportion of citizens are brought under social control by the state, and scarce resources are frittered away on petty criminals instead of being directed at those who pose a genuine threat to society.

Jails

No survey of community corrections would be complete with out a discussion of local jails. Jails, a fundamental component of the corrections system, are a vital and crucial institution. Jails are connected to the law enforcement, courts, and correctional systems and serve as a major focal point in the administration of justice. Jails are controlled by either the local sheriff or a jail administrator under the auspices of county or city administrators. Control of the jail can often be a political issue because it is such an important part of the community, the local criminal justice system, and the local power structure. How the jail is placed organizationally can have a major impact on how it is funded, who is detained there, and the quality of justice.[43]

Figure 13.8
What Jails Do

- Receive individuals pending arraignment and hold them awaiting trial, conviction, or sentencing
- Hold inmates sentenced to short terms (generally under 1 year)
- Readmit probation, parole, and bail-bond violators and absconders
- Temporarily detain juveniles pending transfer to juvenile authorities
- Hold mentally ill persons pending their movement to appropriate health facilities
- Hold individuals for the military, for protective custody, for contempt, and for the courts as witnesses
- Release convicted inmates to the community upon completion of sentence
- Transfer inmates to federal, state, or other authorities
- House inmates for federal, state, or other authorities because of crowding of their facilities
- Sometimes operate community-based programs as alternatives to incarceration

Source: Paige M. Harrison and Jennifer C. Karberg, *Prison and Jail Inmates at Midyear 2002* (Washington, DC: Bureau of Justice Statistics, 2003), 7. Online at http://www.ojp.usdoj.gov/bjs/pub/pdf/pjim02.pdf.

Offenders who cannot afford bail may spend months in jail awaiting trial. Often, the time served awaiting trial is credited toward the eventual sentence.
Courtesy of CORBIS-NY.

The jail serves two major functions (see Figure 13.8 for a complete list of functions). First, it holds suspects who have been arrested and are awaiting disposition of their cases. Judges and prosecutors decide whether suspects can be safely released prior to court hearings, so many people will spend very short periods behind bars ranging from a few hours to a few weeks. Other offenders will spend many months behind bars awaiting trial or release. The factors that determine how much time is spent in jail before trial are dependent on the crime's gravity, the offender's reputation and ties to the community, and money. The second major function of the jail is the confinement of misdemeanor offenders who have been sentenced to less than one year of incarceration. In some jurisdictions, these sentenced offenders may serve their time on weekends and live at home during the week while they maintain their employment and family ties. Sentenced offenders often act as trustees and clean the courthouse, mow the grass, shovel sidewalks, or help feed and service the inmates awaiting disposition of their cases. The local jail also

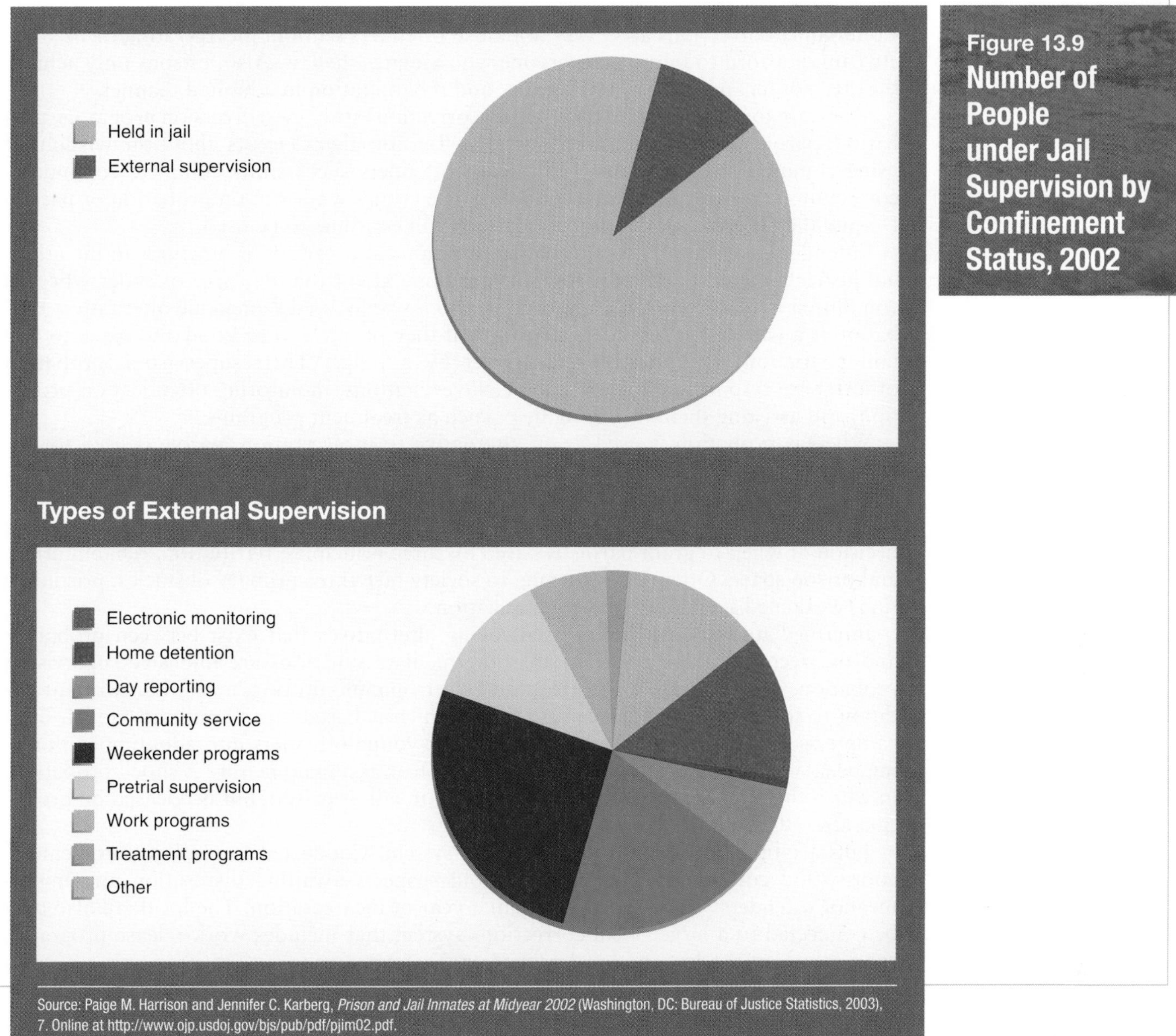

Source: Paige M. Harrison and Jennifer C. Karberg, *Prison and Jail Inmates at Midyear 2002* (Washington, DC: Bureau of Justice Statistics, 2003), 7. Online at http://www.ojp.usdoj.gov/bjs/pub/pdf/pjim02.pdf.

Figure 13.9 Number of People under Jail Supervision by Confinement Status, 2002

may be connected to a larger local corrections system that includes work-release programs (see Figure 13.9), road crews, stockades, and local probation departments. There is a wide variety of local corrections structures around the country, each with its own concerns, funding issues, and punishment philosophies.

Some see the jail as a place where society's "rabble" can be placed to improve the appearance of city streets.[44] The homeless, the drug users, the drunks, and the mentally ill are all susceptible to being swept into the jail for real or imagined infractions of the law.[45] Citizens demand that the police keep the streets safe for everyone, and those who appear to pose a security threat are quickly incarcerated in the local jail. This is not to say that jails are being used inappropriately, but rather that law enforcement is under tremendous pressure to maintain order, and jails are where those without community ties or resources often end up. Law enforcement's job would be much easier and jails less crowded if more community resources existed to help those in desperate financial or social trouble.[46]

Summary

Community corrections are a way to punish offenders without incarcerating them. Society cannot afford to imprison everyone who violates the law. Also, prisons only achieve the goals of incapacitation, retribution, and rehabilitation in a limited manner.

There are four interrelated community corrections strategies: diversion programs, probation, parole, and intermediate sanctions. Tension always exists about the wisdom of using community corrections. Millions of offenders successfully complete community corrections sentences, but some commit worse crimes while out on probation or parole. Despite the failures, community corrections will continue to be used.

Offenders may be sent to alternative programs at a variety of junctures in the criminal justice system. Diversion programs are popular for the first-time offender who has committed a minor offense. Probation is also a widely used sentencing alternative. Probation is a chance for offenders to go free if they promise to be good and agree to certain restrictions and/or requirements set by a judge. Their supervisors (probation officers) are responsible for presentence investigations, monitoring offenders on probation, and assisting them in getting help, such as treatment programs.

Whereas probation is used as an alternative to incarceration, parole is used for offenders who are leaving prison after serving a partial sentence. The idea of parole grew from the philosophy that the penal system should help the offender return to society. Parolees face much of the same restrictions and requirements as those on probation. The decision of when to grant parole is based on three principles: retribution, rehabilitation, and prison space. Offenders returning to society face three primary obstacles: prisonization, weakened social ties, and stigmatization.

Intermediate punishments are sentencing alternatives that exist between probation and incarceration. The more notable intermediate sanctions are intensive supervision probation, drug testing, house arrest and electronic monitoring, and fines. A recent addition to this list is the boot camp prison, which is based on the military model. Boot camp prisons are an attempt to literally shock young offenders into adopting conforming behaviors. Another program that employs fear as a main feature is shock probation, in which the offender receives a false sentence in jail or prison, but is released on probation after 30 to 90 days of incarceration.

Jails are fundamental to the corrections system. Connected to the law enforcement, courts, and corrections systems, jails hold suspects awaiting disposition and misdemeanor offenders sentenced to less than a year of incarceration. The local jail also may be connected to a larger local corrections system that includes work-release programs, road crews, stockades, and local probation departments.

KEY TERMS

boot camp prison p. 452
good time p. 445
intensive supervision probation p. 440
master status p. 449
meritorious time p. 445
presentence investigation p. 435
shock probation p. 454

REVIEW QUESTIONS

1. What are the three primary goals of the criminal justice system?
2. At the heart of the community corrections movement are some assumptions about the nature of crime. What are these assumptions?
3. What is the relationship between diversion and labeling theory?
4. Compare and contrast probation and parole.
5. What are the three main responsibilities of the probation/parole officer?
6. What is in the presentence investigation, and what purpose does it serve?
7. The decision concerning when to grant parole is based on what three principles?

8. What early concept of shock incarceration is the boot camp prison based on?
9. What is intensive supervision probation?
10. What two major functions do jails serve?

SUGGESTED FURTHER READING

Austin, James, and John Irwin. *It's About Time: America's Imprisonment Binge.* 3rd ed. Belmont, CA: Wadsworth, 2001.

Clear, Todd R., and Harry Dammer. *The Offender in the Community.* Belmont, CA: Wadsworth, 2000.

Cohen, Stanley. *Visions of Social Control.* Cambridge, MA: Polity, 1965.

Cullen, Francis T., and Karen Gilbert. *Reaffirming Rehabilitation.* Cincinnati: Anderson, 1982.

McCarthy, Belinda Rodgers, Bernard J. McCarthy, and Matthew C. Leone. *Community-Based Corrections.* 4th ed. Belmont, CA: Wadsworth, 2001.

Morris, Norval, and Michael Toney. *Between Prison and Probation: Intermediate Punishments in a Rational Sentencing System.* New York: Oxford University Press, 1991.

ENDNOTES

1. Graeme Newman, *Just and Painful: A Case for the Corporal Punishment of Criminals* (London: MacMillan, 1983).
2. Belinda Rodgers McCarthy, Bernard J. McCarthy, Jr., and Matthew C. Leone, *Community-Based Corrections,* 4th ed. (Belmont, CA: Wadsworth, 2001).
3. We are not suggesting that everyone is a criminal, but rather, that almost all of us have committed crimes for which we could have been brought into the criminal justice system and punished with a period of incarceration. Our drug use, DUI, and income tax creativity has largely gone undiscovered, and hence, we maintain our freedom and conventional lifestyles.
4. This is especially true of the federal prisons that incarcerate white collar offenders. Although the prisons are still uncomfortable circumstances, the media has dubbed them "Club Fed," giving federal prison a somewhat distorted view. See Jennifer Senior, "You've Got Jail," New York Metro.com, http://www.newyorkmetro.com/nymetro/news/crimelaw/features/6228/.
5. John Irwin, *Prisons in Turmoil* (Boston: Little, Brown, 1980).
6. Sasha Adamsky, "When They Got Out," *The Atlantic Online,* June 1999, http://www.Theatlantic.com/issues/99jun/9906prisoners.htm.
7. Francis T. Cullen and Karen E. Gilbert, *Reaffirming Rehabilitation* (Cincinnati: Anderson, 1982).
8. Eric W. Hickey, *Serial Murderers and Their Victims,* 3rd ed. (Belmont, CA: Wadsworth, 2002). See Hickey's profile of Henry Lee Lucas on p. 194.
9. Todd R. Clear and Harry R. Dammer, *The Offender in the Community* (Belmont, CA: Wadsworth, 2003), 226.
10. Thomas G. Blomberg, "Diversion and Social Control," *Journal of Criminal Law and Criminology* 68, no. 2 (1977): 274–282.
11. James Austin and Barry Krisberg, "Wider, Stronger, and Different Nets: The Dialectics of Criminal Justice Reform," *Journal of Research in Crime and Delinquency,* 18, no. 1 (1981): 165–196.
12. Thomas G. Blomberg and Karol Lucken, "Stacking the Deck by Piling Up Sanctions: Is Intermediate Punishment Destined to Fail?" *Howard Journal of Criminal Justice* 33, no. 1 (1994): 62–80.
13. John Rosencrans, "Maintaining the Myth of Individualized Justice: Probation, Presentence Reports," *Justice Quarterly* 5 (1988): 235–236.
14. David Sudnow, "Normal Crimes: Sociological Features of the Penal Code in a Public Defenders Office," *Social Problems* 123, no. 3 (1965): 255–276.
15. Marilyn West, "A Few Words About Interviewing in Presentence Investigations," in *Correctional Assessment, Casework and Counseling,* 3rd ed., ed. Anthony Walsh (Lanham, MD: American Correctional Association).
16. Walsh, *Correctional Assessment,* 106.
17. Anthony Walsh, "The Role of the Probation Officer in the Sentencing Process: Independent Professional or Judicial Hack?" *Criminal Justice and Behavior* 12 (1985): 289–303.
18. Fay Honey Knapp, "Northwest Treatment Associates," in *Correctional Counseling and Treatment,* 4th ed., ed. Peter C. Kratcoski, (Prospect Heights, IL: Waveland Press, 2000),

617–633. For instance, Knapp reported, "One of the most creative things we do with flashers who exhibit in their cars is to have them put their names on the front, back, and sides of the car" (p. 624).

19. Fay S. Taxman, "Dealing with Technical Violations," *Corrections Today* 57, no. 1 (1995): 46–53.
20. Ibid.
21. R. V. Del Carmen and J. A. Pilant, "The Scope of Judical Immunity for Probation and Parole Officers," *Perspectives, American Probation and Parole Association* (Summer 1994): 14–21.
22. Clear and Dammer, *Offender in the Community,* 182–183.
23. Irwin, *Prisons in Turmoil.*
24. In some states, such as Kentucky, violent offenders must serve 85 percent of their sentences.
25. Donald Clemmer, "The Prison Community," in *Correctional Contexts: Contemporary and Classical Readings,* 2nd ed., eds. Edward J. Latessa et al. (Los Angeles: Roxbury, 2001), 83–87.
26. Clear and Dammer, *Offender in the Community,* 213–214.
27. Erving Goffman, *Stigma: Notes on the Management of Spoiled Identity* (Englewood Cliffs, NJ: Prentice Hall, 1963), 4.
28. D. Stanley Eitzen and Maxine Baca Zinn, *Social Problems,* 6th ed. (Boston: Allyn and Bacon, 1992), 305.
29. Norval Morris and Michael Tonry, *Between Prison and Probation: Intermediate Punishments in a Rational Sentencing System* (New York: Oxford University Press, 1990).
30. Joan Petersilia, "Conditions That Permit Intensive Supervision Programs to Survive," *Crime and Delinquency* 36, no. 1 (1990): 126–145.
31. P. J. Hofer and B. S. Meierhoefer, *Home Confinement: An Evolving Sanction in the Federal Criminal Justice System* (Washington, DC: Federal Judicial Center, 1987).
32. A. K. Schmidt, "Electronic Monitors: Realistically, What Can Be Expected?" *Federal Probation* 55, no. 2 (1991): 47–53.
33. See "Microchips: The New Surrogate Parents?" at FoxNews.com, http://www.foxnews.com/story/0,2933,58945,00.html and "What Are Those Microchips That People Put in Their Dogs?" at Howstuffworks, http://science.howstuffworks.com/question690.htm.
34. Sally Hillsman, Barry Mahoney, George Cole, and Bernard Auchter, "Fines as Criminal Sanctions" (Washington, DC: National Institute of Justice, 1987).
35. Dale Parent, "Recovering Correctional Costs Through Offender Fees" (Washington, DC: National Institute of Justice, 1990).
36. James O. Finckenauer, *Scared Straight and the Panacea Phenomenon* (Englewood Cliffs, NJ: Prentice Hall, 1982).
37. Roberta C. Cronin, *Boot Camp Prisons for Adult and Juvenile Offenders: Overview and Update* (Washington, DC: U.S. Government Printing Office, 1994).
38. Erving Goffman, *The Presentation of Self in Everyday Life* (New York: Doubleday, 1959).
39. John R. Fuller, *Criminal Justice: A Peacemaking Perspective* (Boston: Allyn and Bacon, 1998), 136–139.
40. James Austin and John Irwin, *It's About Time: America's Imprisonment Binge,* 3rd ed. (Belmont, CA: Wadsworth, 2001), 167–169.
41. Clear and Dammer, *Offender in the Community,* 255–256.
42. Dale K. Sechrest, "Prison 'Boot Camps' Do Not Measure Up," *Federal Probation* 53, no. 3 (1989): 15–20.
43. Thomas G. Blomberg, "Beyond Metaphors: Penal Reform as Net-Widening," in *Punishment and Social Control,* eds. Thomas G. Blomberg and Stanley Cohen (New York: Aldine De Gruyter, 1995): 45–61.
44. Stan C. Proband, "Jail Populations Up-Racial Disproportions Worse," *Overcrowded Times* 4, no. 4 (1993): 4.
45. John Irwin, *The Jail: Managing the Underclass in American Society* (Berkeley: University of California Press, 1985).
46. Michael Welch, "Social Junk, Social Dynamite and the Rabble: Persons with AIDS in Jail," *American Journal of Criminal Justice* 14, no. 1 (1989): 135–147.

PART **five**

PROBLEMS IN THE CROSSCURRENTS

outline

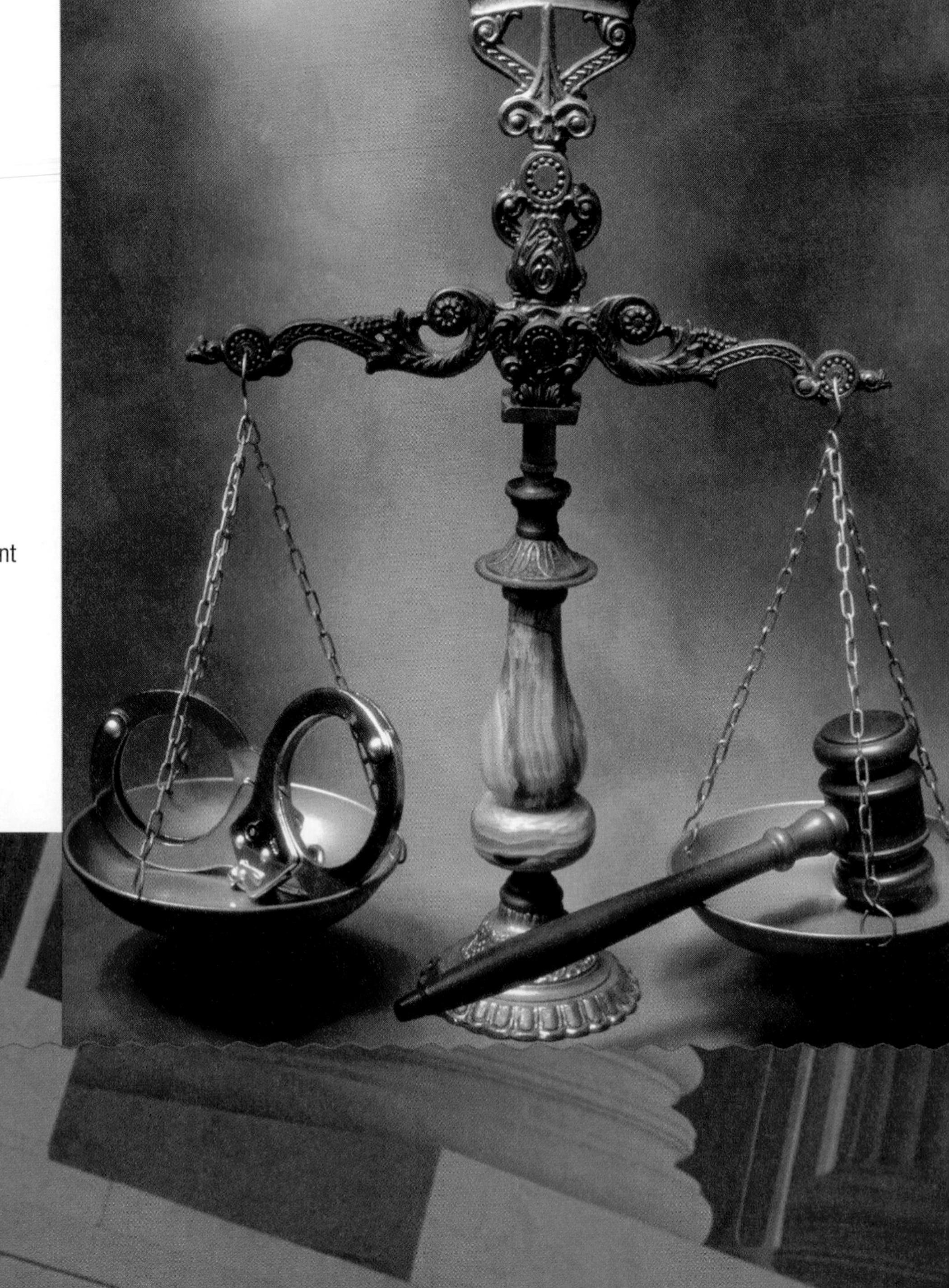

CHAPTER 14

Juvenile Delinquency and Juvenile Justice

objectives

After reading this chapter, the student should be able to:

1. Understand why the modern criminal justice system treats young offenders differently than it treats adult offenders.
2. Understand the position and role of children in pre-20th-century times.
3. Discuss the concept of *parens patriae*.
4. Describe the purpose of houses of refuge.
5. Understand the problems of the child-saving movement.
6. Describe the reforms in juvenile justice at the beginning of the 20th century.
7. Discuss the categories of children who most often come in contact with the juvenile justice system.
8. Discuss the societal issues that can cause children to come in contact with the juvenile justice system.
9. Describe the general structure of the juvenile justice system.
10. Discuss positive and negative trends that may affect the delinquency of children in the future.

IN MANY WAYS, CRIME IS A YOUNG PERSON'S GAME. ALTHOUGH crimes such as embezzlement, insider trading on stocks, and corporate malfeasance are usually committed by older offenders, much of the crime problem, especially street crime, is more likely to involve juveniles.[1] There are several commonsense reasons for the historically stable relationship between youth and crime. We will not dwell on them here—the subject is a university course in its own right—but this chapter will highlight some of the themes of youth crime. The modern criminal justice system even has a legal term for a child who has committed a crime: **juvenile delinquent**. That the term is a modern invention is important when considering the history of children. The concept of juvenile delinquency did not exist before the 20th century. As discussed later in this chapter, children who committed crimes in earlier times were punished as adults or were turned over to their parents for discipline. Of course, these days, juvenile delinquents are handled

juvenile delinquent
A person, usually under the age of 18, who is determined to have committed a crime or status offense in states in which a minor is declared to lack responsibility and cannot be sentenced as an adult.

differently than are adult offenders. It is not only a matter of degree, but rather involves a completely different system with its own philosophy, courts, and correctional system.[2] In fact, the juvenile justice system is a parallel, and sometimes competing, system of justice. Much of the dissatisfaction that many Americans have with the criminal justice system is caused by the perceived liberal tendencies of the juvenile justice system. However, although the juvenile justice system is based on a progressive philosophy, in current practice, the handling of young offenders is often punitive. Therefore, this chapter will illustrate both the promise and the problems of the juvenile justice system, with consideration toward how it contrasts with the adult criminal justice system.

Childhood and the Law

The historical treatment of children is interesting because there is still some debate as to whether young people were always "treated as children" or whether they were treated as little adults.[3] For instance, the French social historian Philippe Ariès argued that in medieval times children were treated as adults from the time they were toddlers, and adults did not make a big fuss about how little and cute children were. Although this view of European medieval childhood has been revised (medieval children, in fact, did have childhoods that we would recognize as true childhoods, and medieval parents were just as delighted by small children as we are now), young people in those societies quickly learned to pull their weight and were expected to act and behave in a responsible manner from a very early age. By today's standards, the concept of adolescence that we call "teenage" did not exist. Young men were quickly apprenticed into the workforce, and young women were often married into another family.

Before the creation of a separate juvenile justice system, parents whose children were arrested had little recourse. Placing children in the adult criminal justice system often meant they would be victimized by older offenders. In this 19th-century drawing, a mother pleads with police officers to release her son.
Courtesy of CORBIS-NY.

How did medieval laws treat children? This is difficult to answer because a great deal of variation existed. Generally, the authority for dealing with children resided with the parents, primarily the father, and not the state. In his book *Medieval Children,* Nicholas Orme reported:

> *The topic of children and the law, then, was a complicated one. It differed according to status, gender, and property. There was no single age of responsibility or majority. . . . Children . . . might suffer imprisonment, and be executed from about the age of ten in exceptional cases. The formal demarcations between childhood and adulthood were often placed lower than they are today, between the ages of twelve and fifteen.*[4]

As previously mentioned, when a child committed a crime, the courts held the parent accountable rather than the youth. This may seem like a good deal for the child, but we must remember that the child was considered to be the responsibility and property of the parent, and the state was powerless to intervene in the youth's discipline and upbringing. So, although the youth did not answer to the law, he or she did answer to the father, who wielded unlimited authority to punish the child as brutally as he wished. Thus, although the state did not recognize children as responsible, parents were not hindered by child welfare laws in how they disciplined their children.

Gradually, the status of the child began to improve in many societies. One factor was the increased availability of education. No longer only for the rich, schools became a major socializing factor.[5] Associated with schools was the apprenticeship movement, in which young people were placed in the care of craftsmen who taught them trades. This relationship was recognized by the law, and apprenticed youths were committed to work for their employers until the age of 21. For some youths, however, the apprenticeship lasted too long, and they often struck out on their own before completing their obligations. For instance, Benjamin Franklin was apprenticed to his brother to learn printing skills, but ran away from Boston to Pennsylvania because his brother treated him badly and had fewer skills as a printer.[6]

Another factor that helped the status of children in England was the establishment of the **poor laws** in the 16th century. Passed partly as a means of social control aimed at ridding the streets of destitute and homeless children, poor laws allowed for the placement of these children in the homes of the wealthy or in the shops of merchants as servants and workers. Thus, the youths learned a trade and were looked after in safe housing with

poor laws
Seventeenth-century laws that turned over vagrants and abandoned children to landowners or shopkeepers as indentured servants.

THE BRICK-YARDS OF ENGLAND—CHILDREN CARRYING THE CLAY.

In 19th-century England, poor children were put to work at an early age. Here, children carry clay in a brickyard.
Courtesy of CORBIS-NY.

adequate food rather than having to beg on the street. Those who were not placed in homes might have found themselves in a poorhouse or workhouse where they were required to work. Although this was a less attractive alternative, for the most part, these youths were separated from adult inmates and protected to a degree.[7]

A third factor in the gradual change in the legal status of children in England was the establishment of **chancery courts.** Orphans were appointed guardians to protect their inheritance rights until they reached the age of majority and could legally take care of their own affairs. The concept of ***parens patriae*** was established whereby the king could intervene in the interests of children. The term means "father of the country," but has come to refer to the right of the king (government) to take a protective role in overseeing children's welfare.[8] This important principle allows modern courts to take children away from unfit parents and to establish standards for education and welfare.

chancery court
"Court of equity." In England, these were established, in part, to assist in dispensing justice when common law courts failed to resolve a case. These courts were favorable to vulnerable individuals, especially children.

parens patriae
Latin for "father of the country." Refers to the philosophy that the government is the ultimate guardian of all children or disabled adults.

Juveniles in the Early United States

In colonial America, little distinction was made between the crimes committed by adults and those committed by children. Certainly no special mechanism was set up to handle juvenile offenders. Parents were responsible for the actions of their children, and when those actions became especially egregious, the community used the same punishments for young people as it did for adults.[9] Corporal punishments and public shaming techniques, such as confinement in stocks, were the primary means of social control for both adults and children. In some cases, banishment from the community or even capital punishment was used. The cases did not have to be especially serious.

> *Children over the age of seven were subject to the criminal law. In some colonies, children who disobeyed their parents or stole a silver spoon from their masters received the death penalty. Cases are rare, but there have been a few examples of death. As late as 1828, in New Jersey, a boy of 13 was hanged for an offense committed when he was 12.*[10]

In some colonies, such as Virginia, the exploitation of children was used to remedy periodic labor shortages. According to Barry Krisberg and James Austin, contractors in England promised young people wealth and happiness in the New World and signed them to commitments as **indentured servants.** These contracts were then sold to New World landowners, and the young people found themselves obligated to years of indentured work on large plantations with little hope of self-improvement. Some youths were kidnapped or were victims of contractual fraud. Orphans were taken from English poorhouses and shipped to the colonies to work as indentured servants. Although some did eventually achieve a viable lifestyle, many others found the arrangement to be little more than severe punishment for being young, destitute, and illiterate. Furthermore, according to Krisberg and Austin, American Indian children were kidnapped and brought into colonist households as servants and indoctrinated with the colonists' language, religion, and customs. Of course, one of the most deplorable exploitations of children happened when African children were brought to the United States as part of the slave trade.[11]

indentured servant
From the 17th to 19th centuries, a person who came to the American colonies/United States and was made to work for a period of time, usually seven years.

The Industrial Revolution of the late 18th century demanded even more from children. Because the factories required a steady stream of young and immigrant workers, little attention was focused on the social welfare of those who were brought into the labor force. In fact, many families depended on the labor of their children for their most basic needs, and the idea of child welfare was tied to his or her economic viability.

The influx of immigrants in the 19th century brought some fundamental changes in the concept of children and childhood. Waves of European immigrants flooded into the cities, each new wave challenging the customs, ideas, and practices of the ones that had come before. As immigrant adults filled the factories, their children presented challenges to the community in terms of socialization, delinquency, and schooling. New institutions were created to deal with this challenge of the "dangerous classes."[12]

REFERENCE

Juvenile Justice in the United States

Colonial period–early 19th century Juveniles are tried in adult courts as adults. There is little record-keeping, but to the extent that court records exist, they are open to the public. Many jurisdictions maintain public "shaming" policies. Delaware, for example, forces convicted thieves to wear a "T" around their neck for 6 months.

1828 12-year-old James Guild is hanged for killing a woman. Progressives agitate for a separate criminal justice system for children.

1899 Illinois establishes the first juvenile court system.

1905 Illinois enacts legislation prohibiting juvenile records from being introduced in courts or otherwise made public.

1925 All but two states have followed Illinois in establishing either a juvenile court or a juvenile probation program.

1920s The National Probation and Parole Association and the Federal Children's Bureau campaign for states to close their juvenile courts and to seal juvenile court records to foster rehabilitation.

1950s High water mark for the percentage of juveniles who are tried in juvenile courts and for the application of strict confidentiality rules for juvenile records. Very little in juvenile record-keeping is undertaken by law enforcement agencies.

1957 J. Edgar Hoover calls for reversing juvenile confidentiality policies and advocates publicizing the names and activities of juvenile felons.

1966–1967 U.S. Supreme Court decides *Kent* and *In re Gault,* holding that due process protections apply to a juvenile court proceeding.

1980s Numerous commentators and state legislators question the utility of juvenile record confidentiality. SEARCH and the Bureau of Justice Statistics (BJS) publish the comprehensive examination of juvenile record policy and practice.

1992 The FBI announces that it will accept juvenile records reported by state central repositories and will treat these records as adult records.

1992 A BJS survey of prosecutors finds that 50 percent fault the accuracy and completeness of the juvenile record information available to them.

1993 The U.S. Conference of Mayors calls for eliminating confidentiality protections for violent juvenile offenders.

1994 Illinois enacts one of the first "public release" laws requiring courts to release the addresses of juveniles convicted for serious felony offenses.

1994 Federal omnibus crime law requires selective release of juvenile record information.

1995 The *GAO Report* finds that since 1978, 44 states and the District of Columbia have amended their laws to facilitate the transfer of juveniles to adult courts.

1995 Legislatures in over a dozen states open juvenile records to schools, victims, state agencies, and others.

1995 Legislatures in 10 states amend their juvenile record law to permit public access, in certain circumstances, to juvenile records.

1995 U.S. Sen. John Ashcroft (R-Missouri) introduces a bill to require states to treat violent and hard-core juvenile offenders as adults and to make juvenile record information available on the same basis as adult information.

Source: *Privacy and Juvenile Justice Records: A Mid-Decade Status Report,* (Washington, DC: Bureau of Justice Statistics, 1997), 33-34. Online at http://www.ojp.usdoj.gov/bjs/pub/pdf/pjjr.pdf.

Houses of Refuge

The first house of refuge was established in New York City in 1825. Over the next 60 years, states designed similar types of institutions to correct the wayward habits of deviant young people. Houses of refuge were considered a major reform at the time, but the public perception and the stark reality of these institutions were often at odds. Intended as a safe haven from the life of the streets and from abusive or neglectful parents, houses of refuge were often dangerous places where older children preyed on younger children. The houses were operated by religious people who had good intentions but were also prejudiced and biased. Females were considered to be sexually promiscuous, and black youths of both sexes were treated less favorably than white youths. Although the primary mission of the houses was to provide education and training for delinquent and neglected youth, they often employed the practice of "placing out," in which boys were sent to work on farms or on dangerous sea vessels, and girls were sent into the homes of respectable ladies to serve and learn. At times, groups of children were placed on "orphan trains" (even though many were not actually orphans) and sent west to frontier families to work on their farms and ranches.[13]

The houses of refuge had the goal of improving the lives of impoverished children, but there was an underlying concern, as well, with the socialization of immigrant children. Workers in houses of refuge failed to understand the variety of cultures brought by immigrant families. They considered new customs and ideas to be deviant and sought to "rescue" the children. Unfortunately, the houses of refuge not only systematically failed to reform wayward children, but they also were such dangerous and substandard institutions that by the end of the 19th century they were abandoned as newer reforms were sought.[14]

Juvenile Court

Turning delinquent and neglected youths over to the well-meaning individuals who ran the houses of refuge eventually came to be considered ineffective and sometimes counterproductive. Clearly, the criminal law had failed to meet the needs of children and families. A new reform, in which the responsibility for children's welfare was removed from the adult criminal court, began at the dawn of the 20th century. In 1899 the first juve-

Houses of refuge had the task of helping poor children. They also helped socialize immigrant children into the language and customs of the United States. Pictured here is the House of Refuge at Randall's Island, New York.

Courtesy of CORBIS-NY.

nile court was established in Cook County, Illinois, with the mandate to process cases of children between the ages of eight and 17.

The social forces that led to the development of the juvenile court were entwined with the rapid social changes happening in the United States and the desire of many to preserve established values. Thus, the term *child savers* was attached to the civic-minded and middle-class women who extended their maternal ideas about the innocence of children into public services and carved out the role of the social worker in the juvenile court.[15] These reformers, according to C. Wright Mills, were primarily white, middle-class, Protestant, rural Americans who believed the problems of the cities were caused by social disorganization.[16] By extending the *parens patriae* philosophy, in which the state assumes the ultimate responsibility for the welfare of children, the juvenile court stripped young people of their legal rights (many of which have since been restored) and operated in what the reformers believed was the best interests of the child. This philosophy led to the development of what are today the major differences between the modern adult criminal court and juvenile court:

- **Focus on rehabilitation.** The juvenile court operates on the idea that deviant children can be redeemed. Rehabilitation instead of punishment is the primary concern. Juveniles are not subject to capital punishment unless waived to adult court, and instead of a sentence, the case receives a disposition. At the beginning of the reform movement, many believed that by keeping juveniles out of jails and reform schools, they would not be subjected to further pressures and temptations to commit crime.
- **Informal hearing.** The juvenile case is conducted as a **hearing** instead of a trial. The adversarial process is absent, and the court workers and judge determine how to best serve the needs of the child by correcting or counteracting social deficiencies such as inadequate schooling, poverty, poor neighborhoods, faulty parenting, and alcohol abuse.
- **Individualized justice.** Each juvenile case is treated according to its own merits. There is little effort to produce uniform dispositions because each child has a different set of problems and a different network of social support. The idea is to craft the disposition to the child instead of the crime.
- **Private hearings.** Juvenile hearings are closed to the public and the press, and after a period of time, juvenile court records are expunged. Deviant behavior committed as a juvenile is not to be counted against the offender when he or she becomes an adult.

hearing
A session that takes place without a jury before a judge or magistrate in which evidence and/or arguments are presented to determine some factual or legal issue.

Juvenile court has its critics. Its basis, the child-saving movement, which attempted to work for the best interests of young people, has been criticized on a number of grounds. Anthony Platt, in his examination of the history of the juvenile court, was especially harsh in his comments when he said the child savers should not be considered libertarians or humanists for the following reasons:

1. Their reforms did not herald a new system of justice but rather expedited traditional policies that had been informally developing during the 19th century.
2. They implicitly assumed the "natural" dependence of adolescents and created a special court to impose sanctions on premature independence and behavior "unbecoming" to youth.
3. Their attitudes toward delinquent youth were largely paternalistic and romantic, but their commands were backed by force. They trusted in the benevolence of government and similarly assumed a harmony of interest between delinquents and agencies of social control.
4. They promoted correctional programs requiring longer terms of imprisonment, long hours of labor and militaristic discipline, and the inculcation of middle-class values and lower-class skills.[17]

Reform schools were harsh environments where children were forced to grow up early. The faces in this picture, taken at a London reform school in 1850, show that youths were forced to take life seriously at a young age.
Courtesy of CORBIS-NY.

Widespread dissatisfaction with the juvenile courts led to a number of reforms during the 20th century. Foremost among these reforms was the move to restore some of the legal rights that had been taken from juveniles with the benign intention of doing what was best for them. Because of a number of concerns, such as law enforcement officers misleading juveniles about the consequences of admitting to crimes, perfunctory court hearings that failed to adequately consider the interests of the child, reform schools that were little better than prisons, and the public's overall impression that the juvenile justice system fostered more crime than it prevented, the courts moved to reinstate some of the **due process rights** of children. In a number of cases, such as *Kent v. United States, 1966; In re Gault, 1967; In re Winship, 1970; McKeiver v. Pennsylvania, 1971;* and *Breed v. Jones, 1975,* the courts provided that juveniles have the rights to be given notice of charges, a lawyer to represent their interests, the ability to confront and cross-examine witnesses, and the privilege against self-incrimination. Another reform that took root in the 1960s and 1970s was the move to deinstitutionalize delinquent and neglected children. Rather than incarcerate youths in prisonlike reform or training schools, community correctional practices such as foster homes, halfway houses, and extended probation-like supervision were employed.[18]

due process rights
Guarantees by the Fifth, Sixth, and Fourteenth Amendments of the U.S. Constitution establishing legal procedures that recognize the protection of an individual's life, liberty, and property.

Linked to the move to deinstitutionalize juveniles were efforts to divert them from the justice system. By referring youths to programs that addressed their educational, counseling, and drug treatment needs, diversion sought to avoid contact between casual offenders and more seriously troubled youngsters. Based on labeling theory (discussed in Chapter 3), diversion programs attempted to prevent young offenders from thinking of themselves as criminals by immersing them in conventional schools, activities, and close contact with their families.[19]

Children and Society

Each new generation of children has slightly different opportunities and faces different challenges and dangers than prior generations.[20] Although adolescence has always been a time of experimentation and boundary testing, the consequences of some of this deviant behavior today is more dangerous and is met with stiffer sanctions. Some of the most pressing and intractable issues facing young people today include the following:

CASE IN POINT

In re Winship

The Case

In re Winship, 397 U.S. 358, 90 S. Ct. 1068 (1970)

The Point

If incarceration or loss of freedom is possible, a case against a juvenile must be proved beyond a reasonable doubt.

Twelve-year-old Samuel Winship was accused of entering a locker and stealing $112 from a woman's purse in New York City in 1967. He was charged as a juvenile delinquent because, according to the New York Family Court Act, if the theft had been committed by an adult, it would have constituted larceny. The act defined a juvenile delinquent as "a person over seven and less than 16 years of age who does any act, which if done by an adult, would constitute a crime."

During the stage in which Winship was determined to be a delinquent, the judge admitted that the prosecution might have been unable to prove Winship guilty beyond a reasonable doubt. However, the judge rejected Winship's contention that the Fourteenth Amendment required such proof, even in such adjudication stages. The question was whether proof beyond a reasonable doubt of an act—which if committed by an adult would be considered a crime—was required to establish Winship as a juvenile delinquent.

Winship was adjudicated a juvenile delinquent and ordered to a training school for at least 18 months up to a maximum of six years, until he reached his 18th birthday. The Supreme Court eventually heard Winship's appeal and reversed the ruling because the reasonable doubt standard had not been considered in a case in which the defendant was subject to incarceration or loss of freedom.

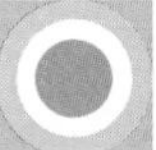

CASE IN POINT

In re Gault

The Case

In re Gault, 387 U.S. 1, 87 S. Ct. 1428 (1967)

The Point

Juveniles' right to an attorney, as well the right to confront accusers and protection from self-incrimination are established.

In 1964, 15-year-old Gerald Gault and another boy were accused of making an obscene telephone call to a female neighbor. Gault was arrested without the knowledge of his parents, who were both at work, and questioned by police at the jail. He was held in detention for four or five days, then released to his parents. In the court proceedings, Gault was not allowed to cross-examine his accuser, who was never present, or to testify in his own behalf, nor was he advised of his rights. He was sentenced to the Arizona State Industrial School until he was 21. No appeal was permitted in juvenile cases in Arizona at that time. In 1967 the Supreme Court reversed the decision on appeal and established that juveniles have a right to an attorney, as well the right to confront accusers and protection from self-incrimination.

- **Violence.** Violence has always been a feature of human societies, but it is particularly pervasive in U.S. culture today. Juveniles can be expected to commit a substantial portion of violence (see Figure 14.1). Sociologist Elijah Anderson, in his acclaimed book, *Code of the Street: Decency, Violence, and the Moral Life of the Inner City,* contended that the willingness to use violence must be

Figure 14.1
Forecast of Teen Homicide Offenders

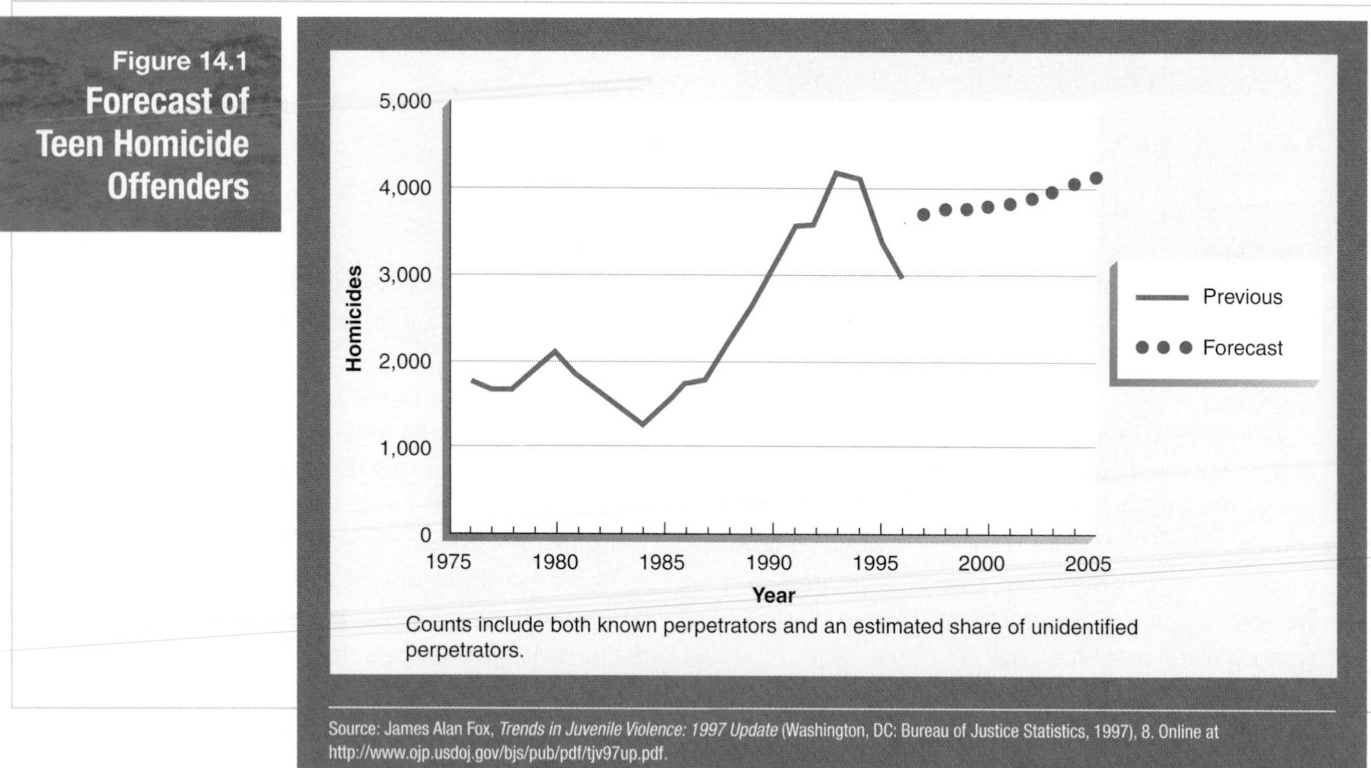

Source: James Alan Fox, *Trends in Juvenile Violence: 1997 Update* (Washington, DC: Bureau of Justice Statistics, 1997), 8. Online at http://www.ojp.usdoj.gov/bjs/pub/pdf/tjv97up.pdf.

displayed in some neighborhoods in order to be respected. Those who do not understand or employ the code of violence are likely to become victims of young people who see violence as their only method of achieving respect and self-esteem.[21] When the community is plagued by gang activity, the violence becomes even more deadly, with drive-by shootings and gang fights making death likely.[22] The streets are not the only violent threat to young people, however. As the violence at Colorado's Columbine High School in 1999 so graphically demonstrated, children are at risk in school. In reaction to Columbine and other high-profile school shootings, all schools now have specific contingency plans for dealing with disturbed students, staff members, or outside individuals who bring weapons to campus.

- **Alcohol and drug problems.** Drinking a few beers or smoking some marijuana are considered normal rites of passage for young people in many circles; however, the criminal justice system has been encouraged to severely punish these crimes as a way of deterring young people from abusing harder drugs. With the availability of cocaine (particularly crack-cocaine), heroin, methamphetamines, Ecstasy, and performance-enhancing steroids, the drug scene has become more dangerous. Additionally, because of the well-intentioned war on drugs, the violence associated with the drug trade has escalated to the point that a drug deal may get one killed more quickly than the drug itself. The problems of drug and alcohol addiction are significant, and the treatment resources are often inadequate.[23] Consequently, society's response to the drug problem often is encapsulated in Nancy Reagan's famous 1980s "Just Say No!" antidrug campaign in which abstinence was the preferred and only message given to young people.[24]
- **Sexuality and sex abuse.** Society gives children mixed messages about sexuality. Our media are saturated with messages of sexuality in both entertainment and advertising, much of it directed at teenagers, yet we restrict the pleasures and responsibilities of sex to adults. In spite of the prohibition of sex for children, we

find they are often victimized by adults, even family members.[25] It is little wonder that sexuality is one of the primary obstacles young people have in developing a healthy self-concept. Because we prohibit young people from engaging in sexual relations, and limit the amount of education we make available to them on responsible ways to engage in sex, we are finding that they are woefully ignorant of the dangers posed by HIV and other sexually transmitted diseases. Consequently, children often do not seek medical treatment for sex-associated problems, such as a pregnancy, until it is too late. On many different levels, then, children and teenagers are victims of sex-related crimes and society's response to the sexuality of children.[26]

- **Runaway and kidnapped children.** Family stress causes a number of children to lose their homes and families. For a variety of reasons, many children leave home at an early age and attempt to make their own way in the world. Sometimes this means taking a bus to a big city where adult predators called "chicken hawks" may pick them up and introduce them to a life of prostitution and drug abuse.[27] Other children live on the streets and panhandle for a living or flirt with criminal lifestyles involving larceny, burglary, and drug sales. Without the guidance of parents or responsible guardians, these children miss valuable schooling, do not learn occupational skills or good working habits, and grow up to be criminals or vagabonds. Other children are kidnapped from their homes by a parent engaged in a nasty separation or divorce. Taken to another state, forced to use a different name, and completely cut off from the parent who was awarded legal custody, these children have their lives ripped apart by a parent who believes he or she is doing the right thing.
- **Anomie and nihilism.** As adolescents bridge the span of rights and responsibilities between childhood and adult society, they are often confused about their place in the world. This is an expected, and in many ways positive,

Runaway children are vulnerable to a range of dangers, such as being exploited by those who wish to turn them into prostitutes.
Courtesy of CORBIS-NY.

> feature of adolescence. As they try on new roles and discard others, teenagers experiment with peer groups, families, and society. However, it can also be a time of great risk. Sometimes teenagers take their newfound freedoms to extremes, and in the quest to try something different, they make mistakes with irrevocable consequences. On the more innocent end of this concern is body modification: tattoos and body piercing. As a way of rebelling against conventional society, tattooing has lost much of its shock value. It has become a mainstream fashion statement embraced by movie stars and athletes. As a fad, however, tattooing has long-term implications that may restrict or affect future decisions. Tattooing the name of your boyfriend on your arm at 16 may look like a bad idea at 18 after you have broken up and gone off to separate universities. On a more serious level are those teenagers who embrace violent, racist, or nihilistic groups. When one's identity is defined by opposition to conventional values, often little positive is left on which to build an identity that has the power to withstand the passing fashion of the day. For instance, neo-Nazi or criminal lifestyles are ill equipped to provide a foundation for adulthood.[28]

These are just a few of the issues that put children at risk. The transition from childhood to adulthood in modern times is fraught with such risks, and although most young people are able to successfully navigate this passage, many others are caught in the crosscurrents of rapid social change, underfunded institutions, predatory adults, and youth-serving agencies that lack a clear vision or are politically motivated. We turn now to an examination of the juvenile justice system and how it both serves the needs of young people and produces some unintended consequences that put youth at additional risk.

Types of Youths in the Juvenile Justice System

The modern juvenile justice system is responsible for dealing with a variety of issues affecting children's lives. Controlling criminal behavior is the most visible of these duties, but it is only part of the system's mission. When controlling criminal behavior is necessary, this usually means that the other parts of the system, and indeed other institutions in society, have failed to meet the needs of youngsters.[29] The juvenile justice system is responsible for dealing with the following types of children:

- **Incorrigible children.** Some parents cannot control their children, particularly as they become teenagers and are lured by the temptations of the street. When children disobey their parents, refuse to go to school, leave home for days at a time, or physically abuse their parents and siblings, the court may remove them from their homes and find alternative living arrangements. Sometimes, parents give up on their children and ask the court to take them.
- **Dependent children.** When children are abandoned or orphaned, the state becomes responsible for their welfare. Usually, the first option is to place the child with a relative, but if no suitable relative is available, the court will seek a foster home and oversee adoption requests.
- **Neglected children.** Some parents are unconcerned, careless, or incapable of providing the physical, emotional, and economic care that children require. The juvenile justice system must ensure that neglected children are given adequate food, shelter, clothes, and schooling. Sometimes this means working with the parent(s) to monitor the family living conditions, and sometimes it means removing the child from the home and placing him or her in a more suitable environment.
- **Status offenders.** A number of behaviors are considered legitimate for adults, but deviant for children. These are known as **status offenses**. For instance, because of mandatory education laws, children are required to attend school until the age of 16, whereas there is no such requirement of those over 16 (this age may vary in some states). Underage drinking laws are another example of a status offense. Those under the age of 21 are subject to arrest for consuming alcohol, whereas

status offense
An act that is considered a legal offense only when committed by a juvenile and which can be adjudicated only in a juvenile court.

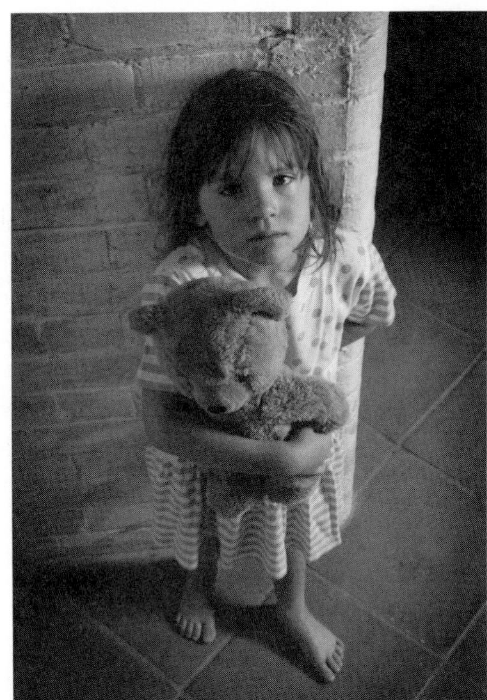

The juvenile court has jurisdiction over children who are neglected by their parents.

Courtesy of CORBIS-NY.

adults are free to drink as much as they want as long as they do not violate other laws, such as being drunk in public or driving an automobile while intoxicated. Running away from home, violating curfew, and breaking other age-determined laws make juveniles subject to a range of restrictions that do not affect adults.

- **Delinquent children.** Children must obey all the laws that apply to adults with limited exceptions.[30] As a general rule, children are subject to the same laws as adults. Upon breaking them, children are brought into the juvenile justice system, just as adults are brought into the criminal justice system. However, what happens to them once arrested can be very different. In very serious cases, the child's case may be transferred to adult court (this will be discussed in greater detail later in this chapter).

Children do not exist in a vacuum, and they are not independent. Therefore, the juvenile court has control not only over children, but also over their parents and siblings. Often, children's problems are not their own doing but are caused by parents who will not or cannot provide a suitable home. To appreciate the causes and prevention of juvenile crime, we should consider the social context of the lives of children.

Juvenile Crime in Context

One can almost predict which children will get into trouble with the law.[31] Some children exhibit early signs of maladjustment, alienation, and an inability to cope with even the minimal demands of conventional behavior. Some individual characteristics of children, such as mental illness or physical disability, are difficult to address, which makes it hard for them to successfully interact with society in a law-abiding manner. However, the state may successfully address some consistent social issues that affect the juvenile crime rate. In this section, we consider how the quality of some of society's institutions and issues might be connected to the problem of juvenile crime.

GOOD SCHOOLS, BAD SCHOOLS. Some schools are better than others. Because public school funding is dependent on local property taxes, and control of the schools is invested in local school boards, a distinct correlation between the quality of a school and

FOCUS ON ETHICS

Kids and Sex

In August 2003 the *Milwaukee Sun Journal* reported that a 14-year-old girl and her 14-year-old boyfriend were caught nude in bed by the girl's mother. The teens were not at all scared or remorseful but incensed that the mother would invade their privacy. The teens even challenged the mother to call the police, which she did. The case went to court. The boy was charged with attempted second-degree sexual assault, a felony, and the girl with fourth-degree sexual assault, a misdemeanor.

The boy's defense lawyer contended that the law prohibiting juveniles from having sex was written to protect children from being abused and exploited by adults, not to prohibit consensual sex between children. The prosecutor disagreed and said that although similar cases had been handled informally in the past, the teens' attitude dictated that they be charged with the crimes. Both youths came from troubled backgrounds and suffered from attention deficit disorder and parental abandonment. Additionally, each refused to follow the rules of a "deferred prosecution agreement"; the charges were brought because they were stubborn and uncooperative.

QUESTIONS

1. Should teenagers be allowed to have sex with other teenagers?
2. Do teenagers have the right to privacy, even from their parents?
3. Does the government have any business regulating consensual sex?
4. Should the attitude of the teenagers be held against them? If they are simply being honest and telling the court and parents to leave them alone, should they be prosecuted?
5. At what age should teenagers be allowed to engage in sexual relations without intervention by the juvenile justice system?
6. Is it possible that more damage is done to these teenagers by punishing them than by ignoring their behavior?

Source: Jamaal Abdul-Alim, "Teens Have Right to Have Sex, Lawyer Argues," August 20, 2003, JSOnline (*Milwaukee Journal Sentinel*), http://www.jsonline.com/news/metro/aug03/163688.asp.

the affluence of the community exists. This situation confronts Americans with a disturbing balance of values. On one hand, we say "no child will be left behind" and that we want to provide a quality education for all. On the other hand, we want the schools to be accountable to local authorities, not state or federal bureaucrats. However, with high dropout rates, social promotion, overcrowded classrooms, and dangerous and violent students, our schools are an institution in crisis that all too often contributes to the delinquency rate.[32] If all schools could provide academically challenging and interesting lessons in a safe and secure environment, more children would be able to take advantage of the opportunities that education provides for success in conventional society.[33]

POVERTY. Children are more likely to live in poverty than are adults, and the impact of not having health care and educational opportunities as a child are difficult to compensate for in later life. One of the most disturbing features of American society is the cycle of poverty that plagues some families and communities. Poverty is related to delinquency in two ways.[34] First, some children engage in delinquent activity to secure physical and economic needs. Stealing food, selling drugs to help support the family, or shoplifting clothes are all responses that the delinquent may believe are necessary to survival. Another category of poverty-related delinquency is related not to what the youth needs, but to what the youth wants. The idea of conspicuous consumption is not lost on young people, and although very few of them get everything they want, those in poverty have little hope of an increased allowance, significant gift, or breaking down the willpower of parents with increased whining and complaining. When all of a family's resources are devoted to maintenance, no discretionary money is available for designer clothes, musical instruments, video games, or other items that children from more affluent families may acquire.

FAULTY FAMILIES. A child's family life can affect his or her chances of delinquency. Although the ideal family structure is popularly considered to be an intact nuclear family in which both biological parents are in the home and provide the love and emotional support necessary to raise well-adjusted children, the reality in the United States is that over half of families have a different structure. Blended families, single-parent families, and foster families together outnumber traditional nuclear families, and in many instances are as successful in meeting the needs of children.[35] Family structure does not tell the whole story, however. Some intact families may be dysfunctional, in which case the children may be better off if the parents separated.[36] Although family structure might be related to economic viability, it does not reveal the interpersonal dynamics happening inside families that are more important to our understanding of delinquency. Parental drug or alcohol abuse; sexual, emotional, or physical abuse of the children; lack of positive role modeling; and a host of other problems may indicate more about family life than the convenient and easily measured factor of family structure.[37]

Today, the period of a child's dependence on parents has been extended until the completion of high school and sometimes beyond. In the tough economy of the new century, the term *rebound kids* has emerged to refer to children who return to their parents' homes after graduating from college and failing to find a job that can support them independently.

NEIGHBORHOODS. The community is one context in which juveniles develop attitudes and values that ultimately contribute to unlawful behavior. In an ideal world, the community is a supportive network of government and private organizations that provide stimulating after-school programs, healthy recreational opportunities, and a safe environment in which young people can thrive without worrying about physical violence, illegal drugs, and predatory adults. Unfortunately, not all communities can provide these safeguards. Much like our schools, our communities are a reflection of the material wealth of those who are willing to contribute to its welfare. Taxes, charitable contributions, and community fund-raising activities all work with other institutions such as schools, churches, and industry to provide the support network for young people. In many communities, opportunities are divided along socioeconomic lines.[38] As some communities can no longer afford to fund park programs, pay the liability insurance costs of organized youth activities, and ensure the safety of public functions, more and more recreational activities are being provided by private companies for profit.[39] Whereas the children of the rich attend music lessons, soccer practice, gymnastic instruction, and advanced academic tutoring sessions, the children of the less affluent often are consigned to television or the streets. Where once the community provided low-cost Little League baseball and summer camps, now these activities are expensive and, in some communities, completely absent. In difficult economic times, communities may be unable to afford many of the support activities normally associated with preventing youth crime. Cash-strapped communities must use their limited tax dollars to provide the basic services such as police and fire protection, road maintenance, hospitals, libraries, and building inspections. Everyone might agree that youth support systems are beneficial and worthy activities, but they are too low on the list of priorities to fund at an adequate level in tough economic times.

It is certainly not our intention here to indict all families, schools, and communities as neglecting children and causing delinquency. There is, of course, a wide range of quality in these institutions. Some are exemplary and provide extremely beneficial services for young people. Rather, our point here is that not all the blame can be laid at the feet of the individual youngster. Delinquency occurs in a social context, and we must understand not only the context, but also how some children through privilege, good luck, or special skills can overcome the disadvantages of deficient institutional support. We now turn to the specific types of problems that lead children to the juvenile justice system.

The Juvenile Justice System

In organizational structure, the juvenile justice system is parallel to the adult criminal justice system. This can be confusing because these two systems, although distinctly different in many of their goals, philosophies, and practices, also have points of convergence in which they share personnel, interact on certain cases, and are jointly blamed by the public for the crime rate (see Table 14.1). The cases that flow through the juvenile justice system exhibit many of the features of the cases in the adult system; however, a different vocabulary is used to signify what happens at each stage. As we consider the processing of cases in the juvenile justice system, we must be alert for these alternative

TABLE 14.1

Differences between the Adult and Juvenile Justice Systems

Issue	Adult System	Juvenile System
Status in question	The defendant's guilt in committing a crime	The child's delinquency in committing an act or violating a status offense
Searches	Rights exist against unreasonable searches of one's person, home, and possessions.	Rights against unreasonable searches are limited.
Self-incrimination	Both children and adults are protected.	
Goal of proceedings	The defendant is assumed innocent until proven guilty.	The best interests of the child, whether guilty or innocent, are paramount.
Nature of proceedings	Adversarial	Remedial
Arrests	Warrant required	Children are not arrested but taken into custody via petition or complaint.
Representation	Both children and adults have the right to an attorney.	
Trials	Open to the public	There are no trials, but closed hearings. The right to a jury trial does not exist.
Result upon conviction or finding of delinquency	Convicted adults are punished with possible rehabilitation and/or treatment.	Children are protected and rehabilitated.
Treatment	No right to treatment	Right to treatment
Release	Via bail or release-on-recognizance (ROR)	Parental or guardian custody
Public records	The results of the trial and judgment remain on public record.	Records are sealed and may be destroyed once the child reaches a certain age.
Incarceration	Prison or jail	Children are held or incarcerated in nonadult facilities.

terms. Because each state has its own structure and method of processing juvenile justice cases, the description of the system here will be a general and simplified one that highlights the common decision points and practices.

Entering the Juvenile Justice System

Cases are inserted into the juvenile justice system by a process called a **referral**. There are two types of referrals. First, referrals may come from schools, parents, or child welfare agencies that believe the child is at risk from others, as in cases of child abuse or delinquency. A parent may turn the child over to the juvenile court because of incorrigibility or because the parent lacks the necessary resources to provide an adequate home. A child welfare agency may turn the child over to the jurisdiction of the court if both parents are incarcerated and no proximate or appropriate relative is available to care for the youth. The second type of referral to the juvenile court comes from law enforcement agencies. This type of referral is the functional equivalent of an arrest. Depending on the age of the youth and the seriousness of the crime, the processing of the child may closely resemble the arrest of an adult, although the process is often very different. Based on the philosophy of doing what is best for the child, many of the larger law enforcement agencies will have specialized juvenile units that are familiar with the community resources available to treat the youth. Often, as many as one-third of the juvenile cases handled by law enforcement agencies are diverted from the juvenile justice system, and the youths are either released or funneled into alternative programs. Of the two types of referrals, the law enforcement referral is the most common by a large margin. Typically, law enforcement referrals account for up to 85 percent of the cases entered into the juvenile justice system (see Figure 14.2).[40]

referral
Similar to a "charge" in the adult system in which an authority, usually the police, parents, or the school, determines that the youth needs intervention from the juvenile court.

Prehearing Detention

Law enforcement agencies are discouraged from holding juvenile offenders in adult jails while the case is processed. Federal regulations require that youths be held no more than six hours and that they are kept out of sight and sound of adult inmates. After six hours, youths must be transferred to a juvenile agency that can provide secure detention.

Intake

The intake function is a major **gatekeeping** decision point. An intake officer, who is responsible to the juvenile probation department and/or the juvenile court judge, reviews the case to determine whether evidence is sufficient to prove the allegation. This review

gatekeeping
At several points throughout the juvenile justice process, officials make important decisions that determine what happens to the youth. Examples of these decision points or "gates" are the prosecutor's determination of whether to charge the youth with a crime and the judge's decision to sentence the youth to probation or detention.

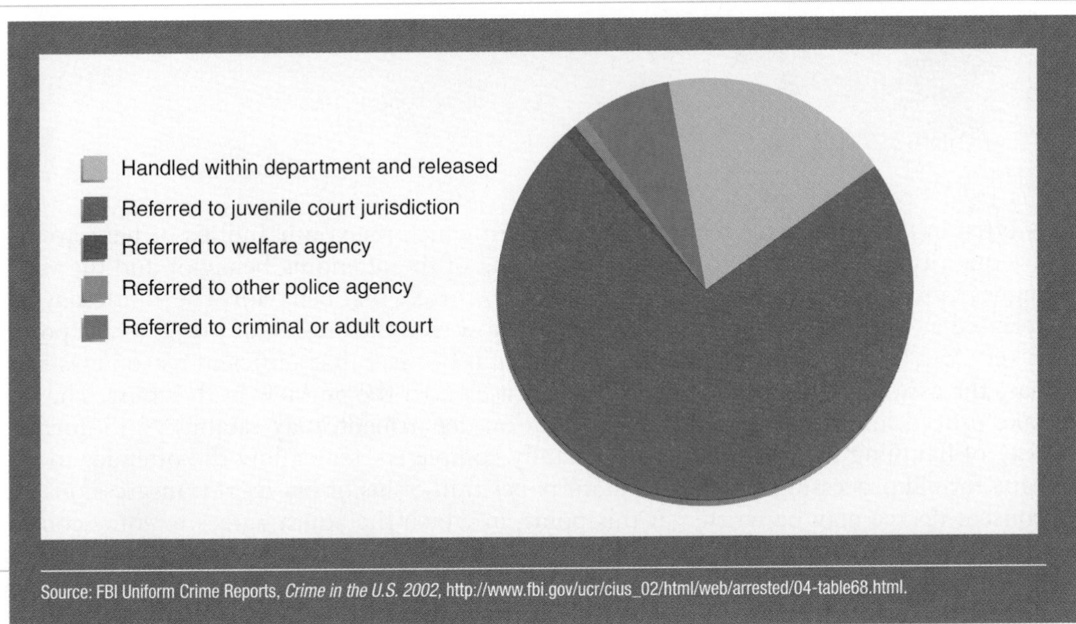

Source: FBI Uniform Crime Reports, *Crime in the U.S. 2002*, http://www.fbi.gov/ucr/cius_02/html/web/arrested/04-table68.html.

Figure 14.2 Police Disposition of Juvenile Offenders Taken into Custody, 2002

Law enforcement officers must often deal with teenage offenders. Although young people can be just as dangerous as adults, they are treated differently by the juvenile justice system.
Courtesy of CORBIS-NY.

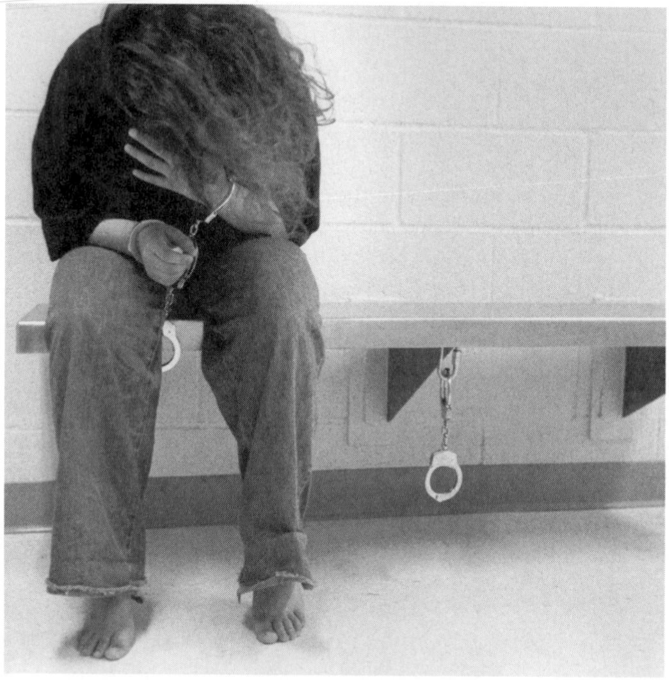

Young offenders remain in juvenile intake while authorities decide whether the case is serious enough to warrant incarceration. The juvenile intake areas in jails are separate from those used for adults.
Courtesy of CORBIS-NY.

is often in the form of a preliminary hearing in which the youth and his or her parents are questioned about the youth's understanding of the offending behavior and the willingness and ability of the parents or guardian to correct that behavior. The youth may be released at this point if the evidence is weak; however, the burden of proof at this point is very low.[41] Consequently, a finding by the intake officer that sufficient reason exists to pass the case forward is enough to keep the case under the purview of the court. The intake officer, in conjunction with the probation department, may establish an informal way of handling the case that, if successfully completed, may allow the offender to escape formal processing and the resultant paper trail of his or her legal transgressions. A **consent decree** may be written at this point, in which the youth agrees to some conditions for a specified period of time. These conditions may include restitution to a victim, drug or alcohol counseling, attendance at school, or maintaining a curfew. Once the youth successfully completes the conditions, the case is dismissed. Because these condi-

consent decree
When the parties to a lawsuit accept a judge's order that is based on an agreement made by them instead of continuing the case through a trial or hearing.

tions are often monitored by the probation department, this procedure is often called **informal probation.** This type of processing allows the case to be diverted from the system without formal charges being filed. If the youth fails to comply with the conditions, the case is reinserted into the system.[42]

informal probation
A period during which a juvenile is required to stay out of trouble or make restitution before the case is dropped.

Determining Jurisdiction

Once an intake officer decides that the case should be processed through the normal juvenile justice system and not diverted into informal probation, it is decided whether the case will remain in the juvenile court or be transferred to adult court. The states have a variety of mechanisms for making this decision. The prosecutor may decide to file the case in criminal court, or the intake officer may file a petition waiver to transfer the case.[43] The decision is based on two factors: the seriousness of the crime and the history and demeanor of the offender. Only very serious crimes such as homicide are bound over to the adult criminal court. The vast majority of cases involving youths stay under the jurisdiction of the juvenile court. If the youth has been before the court many times and has shown a disregard for the authority of the judge and probation staff, waiver to the adult criminal court may be deemed an appropriate way to handle the case. If the youth is not amenable to treatment and continues to commit criminal acts while under the juvenile court supervision, then the prosecutor may decide to kick the case up to the adult criminal court, in which the protection of society is considered as important as the welfare of the youth.

adjudicatory hearing
The process in which a juvenile court determines whether the allegations in a petition are supported by evidence.

petitioner
A person who files a lawsuit; also called a plaintiff.

commitment
An order by a judge upon conviction or before a trial that sends a person to jail or prison. Also, a judge's order that sends a mentally unstable person to a mental institution.

respondent
The party who must reply to a petitioner's complaint. Equivalent to a defendant in a lawsuit.

adversarial process
A term describing the manner in which U.S. criminal trial courts operate; a system that requires two sides, a prosecution and a defense.

Adjudicatory Hearing

Within a specified period (this varies by state), an **adjudicatory hearing** is held to determine whether the juvenile committed the crimes charged against him or her. This hearing is the equivalent of a trial in the adult criminal court but with some important differences. First, the juvenile hearing is a quasi-civil proceeding (not criminal) and therefore may be confidential. Only official and interested parties are allowed in the court. The facts of the case and most important, the names of juvenile offenders and victims may be kept from the media. Second, the adjudicatory hearing is conducted by a judge who also acts as a jury. Third, the youth, if guilty, will be adjudicated delinquent, shifting the focus of the case from the crime to the rehabilitation of the youth. Because of the legal reforms of the 1960s and 1970s, the youth enjoys many of the rights afforded adults in the criminal court, including the right to have an attorney, the right to confront and cross-examine hostile witnesses, the right to present witnesses in defense, and the right against self-incrimination. Furthermore, the standard of proof in an adjudicatory hearing is set at the highest standard: beyond a reasonable doubt. Although youths have the right to an attorney, this right can be waived by the child or the parents. This makes for a somewhat confusing situation. Attorneys are supposed to exercise independent professional judgment on behalf of their clients, but sometimes the juvenile's best interests conflict with the wishes of the parents, who pay the attorney's fee. Also, the juvenile system, to further set it apart from the adult system, has its own terminology. Therefore, in the adjudicatory hearing (trial), the **petitioner** (prosecutor) will attempt to prove the youth delinquent and in need of **commitment** (incarceration), whereas the **respondent** (defense attorney) challenges the facts of the case. Although not an **adversarial process**, the adjudicatory hearing does have many of the aspects of the trial. Because of the restored legal rights of juveniles, the case is no longer handled as juvenile cases were when the juvenile courts were originally established.[44] Remember, the welfare of the juvenile must now be balanced with his or her legal rights when the case is processed.

Disposition

The disposition of the juvenile case can be compared to the handing down of the sentence in adult criminal court. The disposition can take basically two paths: residential placement (confinement) in a secure facility or referral to probation or a similar nonresidential program (see Figure 14.3). As a rule, placement in a residential facility is

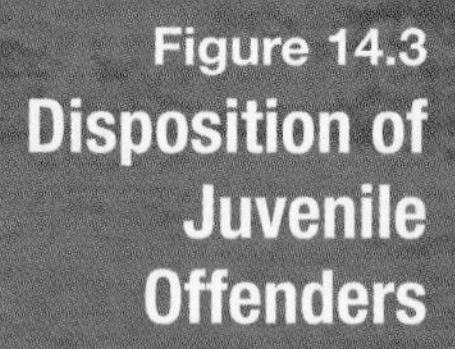

Figure 14.3
Disposition of Juvenile Offenders

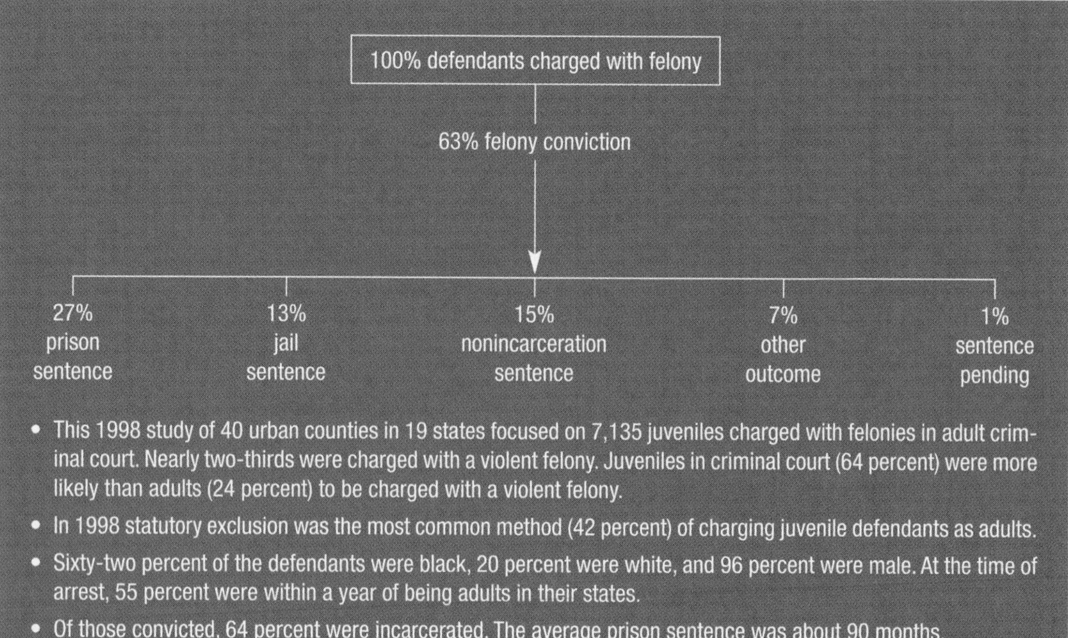

- This 1998 study of 40 urban counties in 19 states focused on 7,135 juveniles charged with felonies in adult criminal court. Nearly two-thirds were charged with a violent felony. Juveniles in criminal court (64 percent) were more likely than adults (24 percent) to be charged with a violent felony.
- In 1998 statutory exclusion was the most common method (42 percent) of charging juvenile defendants as adults.
- Sixty-two percent of the defendants were black, 20 percent were white, and 96 percent were male. At the time of arrest, 55 percent were within a year of being adults in their states.
- Of those convicted, 64 percent were incarcerated. The average prison sentence was about 90 months.

Source: Gerard A. Rainville and Steven K. Smith, *Juvenile Felony Defendants in Criminal Courts* (Washington, DC: Bureau of Justice Statistics, 2003), 1. Online at http://www.ojp.usdoj.gov/bjs/pub/pdf/jfdcc98.pdf.

residential placement
Any sentence of a juvenile offender to a halfway house or other community home in which the juvenile is closely monitored, but allowed to leave for work or school.

reserved for those adjudicated for the most serious crimes. The term **residential placement** sometimes means being placed in a community halfway house or a foster home. However, residential placement often means the juvenile is sent to a training school or reform school that is little different in appearances from a prison. Although the youth is confined with other youths, residential placement can, in many ways, be compared to "hard time" in an adult institution. A disposition of juvenile probation can be linked to a set of conditions that require the youth to participate in treatment programs, additional schooling, or public service activities.[45] Again, the philosophy of the juvenile justice system is geared toward rehabilitation, but by forcing the juvenile to engage in multiple activities, the distinction between rehabilitation and punishment can appear blurred to the offender. In some cases, youths can be sentenced to adult facilities in which relatively young adults are confined. Some youths are so advanced in their criminal lifestyles that officials believe that keeping them in institutions for juveniles would not provide the proper security and that these recalcitrant youths might provide negative examples for other young offenders.

Aftercare

To ease the transition of the youth from residential treatment back into the community, the court may order some type of aftercare. This can be thought of as similar to the parole function in the criminal court. Aftercare may consist of a number of programs designed to address the youth's problems, including drug or alcohol treatment, counseling, attending school on a regular basis, or employment. The key to aftercare programs is the ability of the court to ensure the offenders' accountability. If the youth fails to complete the aftercare requirements, the juvenile corrections worker may recommend another period of confinement.[46]

Figure 14.4 shows that juveniles may be diverted from the system at many points. However, this does not mean that they are not under some type of social control. The case is being "held in abeyance" until the youth successfully completes the diversion program or other court requirements. Sometimes this is as easy as going one year without

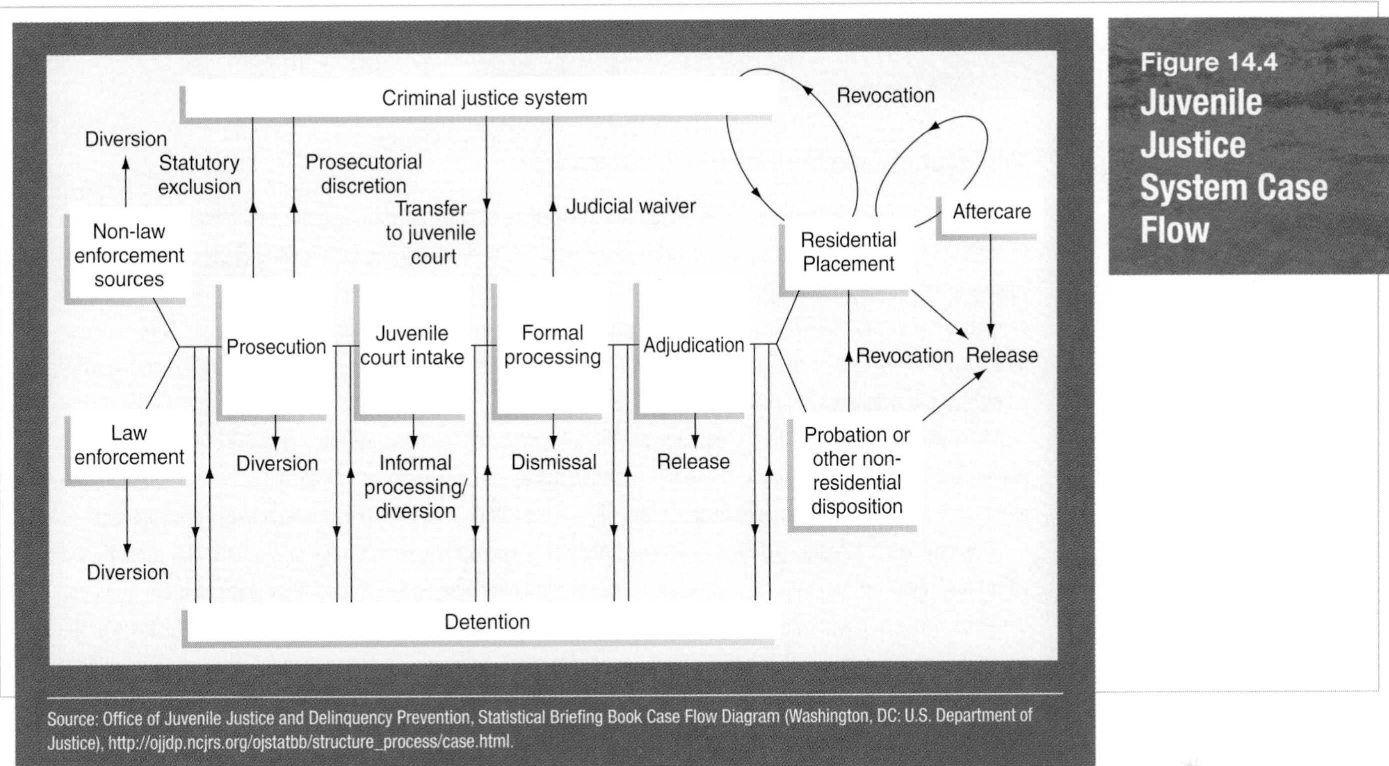

Source: Office of Juvenile Justice and Delinquency Prevention, Statistical Briefing Book Case Flow Diagram (Washington, DC: U.S. Department of Justice), http://ojjdp.ncjrs.org/ojstatbb/structure_process/case.html.

Figure 14.4 **Juvenile Justice System Case Flow**

getting into trouble again. If the court's orders are completed, the case is dismissed, but if the youth violates the law or ignores the directives of the diversion program, he or she will again face a judge who may order more draconian forms of control.

Problematic Issues in Juvenile Justice Today

Despite the good intentions and concerns of the many people working in the juvenile justice system, some issues remain that have not been resolved in a way that makes youths more controllable or society any safer. In fact, in some ways, the juvenile justice system and our society in general have not addressed delinquency in a comprehensive and effective way. All the institutions that deal with children are partially responsible for this failure. The juvenile justice system is the institution of last resort and so looks more ineffective than the school, family, or community. If those other institutions were fulfilling their missions more completely, however, there may be fewer delinquent children. Therefore, any real reform of the juvenile justice system must be linked to the way these other institutions interact with law enforcement, the juvenile court, and treatment programs. To a large extent, the solution is better funding, but other issues may be more politically feasible than raising taxes and allocating more funds to schools, recreational programs, treatment alternatives, or more law enforcement officers. To reform the juvenile justice system, the following issues should receive greater scrutiny and consideration.

Chronic Offenders

Given the broad reach of statutes criminalizing the behavior of youths, we can expect many to come in contact with the juvenile justice system as they test the boundaries of appropriate behavior, seek to establish their identities, and have a bit of fun. The "boys

FOCUS ON ETHICS

Widening the Net of Social Control

The juvenile court is responsible for safeguarding the welfare of children, including protecting them from abusive or neglectful parents. You are a juvenile court judge who has been struggling with a particularly difficult case involving a 14-year-old boy who continually smokes marijuana, shoplifts, and recently has been running with a local gang and terrorizing other children with threats of violence. The experienced caseworker who has been working hard to help this young man has told you that the source of much of the problem is his parents and his family's dynamics. The boy ignores his mother's instructions and argues with his father. You order the family to see a psychologist who specializes in family matters, but the father refuses to cooperate and contends that the problem is not himself but the "rotten" boy and has discontinued therapy. After several attempts to resolve the situation, you order the boy placed in foster care because you believe the father is an unfit parent and a negative influence.

This boy has a 12-year-old brother whose behavior is exemplary. He is an honor student, star athlete, and all-around good kid. You order the 12-year-old out of the home also because the father is recalcitrant and continues to refuse to cooperate with the courts. Your thinking is that if he is a poor father for one child, he is probably a poor father for the other and that your duty is to place both boys in foster care for their own well-being. The 14-year-old seems to be responding well to his new home, but the 12-year-old has become a problem. He runs away from home, is in danger of being dropped from the honors program because of slipping grades, and refuses to discuss his new problems with the psychologist. You are so angry with the father because of his attitude that you do not want to allow the 12-year-old to return to the home, but you are worried that your actions have resulted in a good kid going bad.

WHAT DO YOU DO?

1. Let the 12-year-old return to the home and keep pressuring the father to participate in family therapy.
2. Keep both children in foster care until the father starts to cooperate.
3. Return both boys to the home and let the situation run its course. You tried to help, but now it is the father's problem. If his sons end up in prison, it is not your fault.
4. Order the 12-year-old to live with you so that you can show the father that you care about children and are willing to go to great lengths to ensure that they are protected.

will be boys" behavior is not what concerns us most because boys (and girls) will generally outgrow much of this deviant behavior. A small percentage of youth, however, are long-term, chronic, and consistent law violators.[47] According to one landmark study, 6 percent of the juvenile offender population was responsible for 52 percent of all offenses. Furthermore, these 627 boys out of a total sample of 9,945 accounted for 71 percent of the homicides, 82 percent of the robberies, and 64 percent of the aggravated assaults. These boys were tracked from birth until their 18th birthdays, and two significant predictors of chronic offending stood out in the findings. First, the gravity of the first offense suggested that those who start with relatively major crimes are more likely to become chronically delinquent and that those who receive severe punishment are most likely to end up living a life of crime.[48] These findings are not surprising, but they do suggest that arrest and going to the juvenile court did little to deter these youths from further delinquency. Because research has shown that these youths share a number of factors such as behavior problems, poor grades, drug or alcohol use, family problems (such as criminal parents), abuse or neglect, and patterns of stealing or running away, the solution to chronic delinquency is necessarily complex, broad-based, and expensive. Although it may be tempting to identify the chronic delinquent early and implement treatment or punishment before the behavior gets deadly, there are some ethical issues with intervention based on what is expected of the youth rather than on what he or she has actually done.

Youth Gangs

Another predictor of chronic delinquency is membership in a youth gang. Gangs have become a favorite theme of the media. Much of the music of youth today is influenced by gang ideas, and even middle-class youth adopt the accoutrements of gangs in dress, tattoos, and using gang signs. Graffiti in cities and towns of all sizes across the country suggest some level of gang influence.[49] Regardless of the perceived growth and diffusion of youth gangs, they remain a particular problem in the largest cities, where there are contested neighborhoods, a critical mass of disenfranchised youth, and a long history and tradition of gang activity. There so are many types of youth gangs that it becomes difficult to construct a general definition other than that they engage in criminal or delinquent activity. This broad conception, however, would include some fraternities on college campuses. Youth gangs may be focused around drug distribution, turf protecting, robbery, extortion, or any number of other illegal behaviors. At their most extreme, gangs are highly organized, have members who remain active well into their adult years, are connected with prison gangs, and have hundreds of members.

Race is another dimension of many gangs. California has Hispanic gangs, black gangs, Asian gangs, and white gangs. This list is misleading, however, because the number and types of gangs can be subdivided in any number of ways. For instance, Asian gangs may be subdivided into Filipino, Chinese, Indochinese (Vietnamese, Cambodian, Laotian, Thai, and Hmong), Korean, Japanese, and Pacific Islander (Samoan, Fijian, Guamanian, and Hawaiian) gangs. There is a constantly shifting loyalty among gangs; sometimes certain ethnic groups will oppose each other one month and then merge to confront another group the following month. Law enforcement agencies have established gang units and have recruited as officers people from many of the nationalities that contribute to the U.S. gang problem.[50]

Although we typically think of the gang problem as being a male issue, research shows that females are also active in gangs. Previously, female gang activity was thought to be supportive of male gangs, but today, full-fledged female gangs provide many of the functions for its members that make gangs so attractive to males. From a feminist point of view, the social liberation of women and girls has enabled them to become more actively engaged in gang and criminal pursuits.[51]

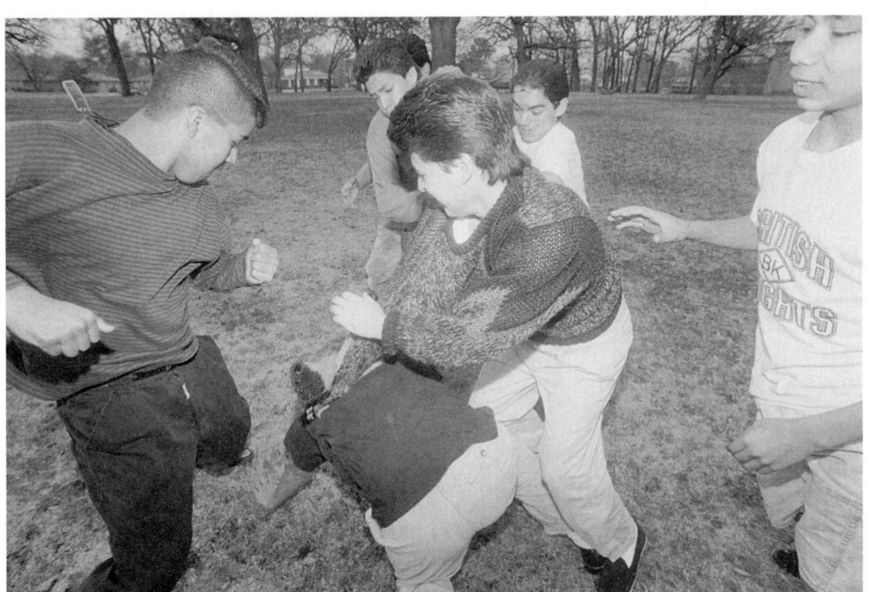

To be initiated into a gang, a new member often must suffer a "beat-down" to test his or her courage and willingness to follow gang rules.
Courtesy of CORBIS-NY.

CASE IN POINT

Schall v. Martin

The Case

Schall v. Martin, 467 U.S. 253, 104 S. Ct. 2403 (1984)

The Point

As long as procedures protect a juvenile's rights, detention of a juvenile is constitutional if it protects the juvenile and society from crimes he or she may commit pretrial.

On December 13, 1977, in New York City, 14-year-old Gregory Martin was arrested at 11:30 P.M. and charged with first-degree robbery, second-degree assault, and criminal possession of a weapon. Martin lied to the police about where he lived and was confined in jail.

Martin came under the jurisdiction of the state's family court and made his initial appearance on December 14, accompanied by his grandmother. It was determined that at the time of his arrest, Martin possessed a loaded weapon, gave a false address to police, and was away from his home at a late hour, all of which the judge cited as a lack of supervision. The New York Family Court Act allows for pretrial detention of an accused juvenile delinquent if there is a "serious risk" that the juvenile "may before the return date commit an act which if committed by an adult would constitute a crime." Because of the evidence at the time of his arrest, Martin was held until his hearing on December 27–29.

At the hearing, Martin was found guilty of the robbery and criminal possession charges. He was adjudicated a delinquent and placed on probation for two years. From the time of his arrest to the conclusion of the hearing, he had been detained for 15 full days. His attorney appealed the finding on grounds that the detention violated the due process clause of the Fourteenth Amendment. However, the Supreme Court upheld Martin's detention as constitutionally valid, stating that the New York Family Court Act provided adequate procedures to guard the juvenile's rights and that it protected "both the juvenile and society from the hazards of pretrial crime."

Finally, although youth street gangs have been involved in crime for a long time, the impact of the drug culture since the 1970s has radically changed the nature of many of these gangs and greatly increased the amount of lethal behavior associated with gang activity. Simply put, the expressive gang activities of fighting, graffiti, and turf protection have been replaced to some extent, by lucrative drug sales. Given the amount of money involved in the drug trade, neighborhood gangs are driven to act more like organized crime groups.[52]

Conditions of Youth Confinement

The types of institutions available for young offenders vary widely across the country. Even when a state has a range of sentencing options, overcrowding may mean there is no room in the most appropriate type of confinement. Four types of public facilities are available in many states.

- **Adult prisons.** Some young offenders convicted of very serious crimes may be kept here. Juvenile offenders are kept separate from the adult prisoners, but because of security risks and the harm they may cause other young offenders, they are often placed in the most restrictive confinement possible. For many of these dangerous young offenders, this means protective custody in what amounts to solitary confinement.
- **Ranches and camps.** Ranches and forestry camps enable young offenders to work outside on public lands. The intent is to provide positive work experiences so that the youth will be able to find gainful employment when released. Additionally, by being away from the temptations of urban life and the confines

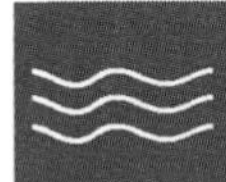
CROSSCURRENTS

Extreme Therapy

What do you do when your children simply will not behave? As a last resort, they can be turned over to the juvenile justice system where they will be placed in a foster home or secure detention. Traditionally, those affluent families that could afford it would send their sons to a military school where it was presumed they would learn discipline. Today, wealthy families have a new alternative: sending their children to alternative treatment programs that blend the discipline of military schools with the treatment strategies of drug programs, particularly behavior modification techniques. Some of these programs can cost upwards of $40,000 and include extreme tactics for uncooperative youths. Because of their draconian methods of punishment, some of these programs have moved offshore to escape the supervision of U.S. courts.

One such program as reported in *The Observer* is Tranquility Bay, in Jamaica. Here, young people are subjected to a daily regimen of exercise, study, and program propaganda. The program is designed to break the will of rebellious youths and turn them into docile teenagers who accept the program's discipline. Tranquility Bay is basically a private detention camp, but it differs in one important respect. When courts jail a juvenile, he or she has a fixed sentence and may think about whatever he or she likes while serving it. However, no child arrives at Tranquility Bay with a preset release date. Students are judged ready to leave only when they have demonstrated a sincere belief that they deserved to be sent there and that the program saved their lives. They must renounce their old selves, espouse the program's belief system, display gratitude for their salvation, and police fellow students who resist.

How does one get placed in such a program? The courts do not send young people there; parents do. In the middle of the night, guards wake and handcuff the youth and take him or her to the airport to catch the flight to Jamaica. The youths are not allowed to talk to their parents for up to six months or see them for a year.

The Tranquility Bay program is based on behavior modification principles in which students progress though six stages based on a reward-and-punishment system. Recalcitrant youths land in "observation placement," in which they are forced to lie face down and are forbidden to speak or move except for 10 minutes each hour when they may sit up and stretch. As for school, students are given books to study, but the staff is poorly trained. For those youths with severe behavioral problems that might require drug treatment, psychological counseling, or other remedial education, there is little at Tranquility Bay to help them. No long-term follow-up is done to gauge the children's progress once they return home.

QUESTIONS

1. Would you send your child to such a program?
2. The administrators of such programs may sincerely believe that their tactics save children's lives. Could this be true?
3. Are there any reasonable aspects to these programs that should be considered by U.S. institutions?
4. If you were responsible for such a program, what techniques would you employ? Remember, because your program is located offshore, you can pretty much do anything.

Source: Decca Aitkenhead, "The Last Resort," *The Observer/Guardian Unlimited,* June 29, 2003, http://observer.guardian.co.uk/magazine/story/0,11913,987172,00.html and http://observer.guardian.co.uk/magazine/story/0,11913,987168,00.html.

of a training school, the more normal summer-camp-like experience of these types of detention are thought to be less stigmatizing and deleterious to the self-concept of the youth.[53]

- **Boot camp prisons.** Patterned after military basic training camps, these short-term (usually 90-day) programs are designed to teach hard work, discipline, and

Boot camp institutions are patterned after military basic training. Critics claim that these programs are no more effective than traditional methods of reforming juvenile offenders.
Courtesy of CORBIS-NY.

obedience. They are physically and mentally rigorous and relatively inexpensive when compared with a training school. Although these programs are popular, critics point out the high potential for abuse and that the programs are no more effective in preventing recidivism than traditional programs.[54]

- **Traditional training schools.** These often overcrowded and understaffed programs are where the more serious offenders are incarcerated. Some training schools physically resemble adult prisons; and others may have the appearance of a college campus.[55]

In addition to these four types of public institutions are a number of public and private residential placement facilities, with juveniles in their mid to late teens comprising most of these placements (see Figure 14.5). These programs offer the court, the parents, and the youth an alternative to traditional types of confinement. Although the private programs can be very expensive, some can offer exceptional educational and counseling opportunities. However, some of the private programs are extremely controversial; at those located in other countries, the legal rights of young offenders can be extremely limited.

Treating Children as Adults

One of the outgrowths of the get-tough-on-crime approach has been to treat serious juvenile delinquents as adult criminals. Rather than handling these cases in juvenile courts, which are geared toward the needs of the child, these cases are waived to the criminal court where the protection of society is paramount. It is argued that the most serious juvenile offenders require a minimum criminal sentence that is not available in juvenile court. Critics of the waiver process point out that sending a juvenile to adult court does not always ensure the protection of the public because the child may serve only a fraction of the sentence imposed by the criminal court. Additionally, the criminal court may not have the treatment alternatives for young offenders that are available in juvenile court. Finally, there is evidence of a racial bias in who gets waived to criminal court, with young, black males being disproportionately selected.[56]

What is the right balance between protecting children and holding them accountable for their actions? To answer this question, we need to consider the presumed advantages

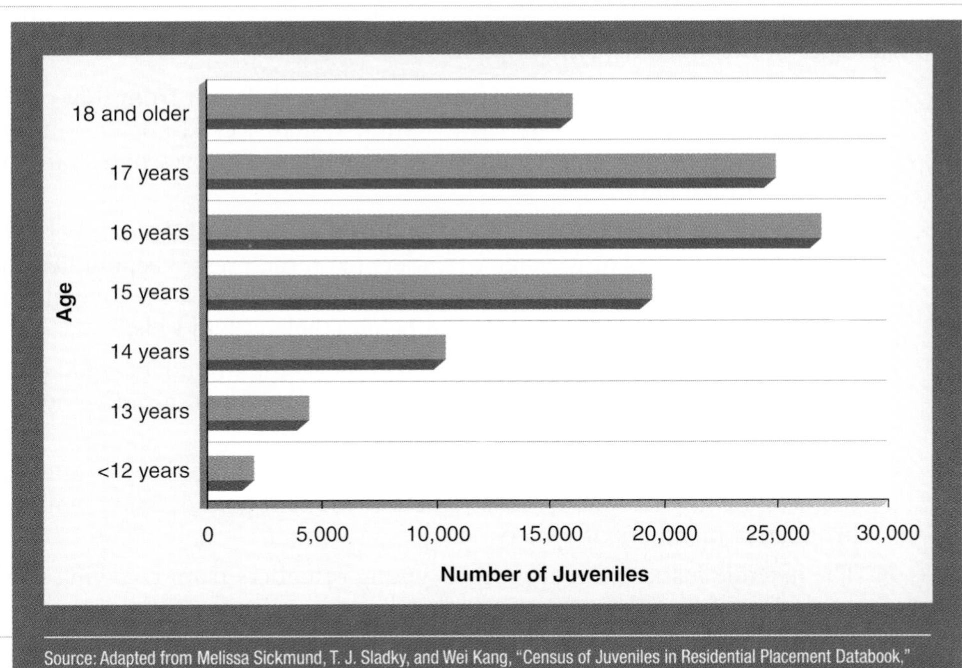

Source: Adapted from Melissa Sickmund, T. J. Sladky, and Wei Kang, "Census of Juveniles in Residential Placement Databook," 2004. Online at http://ojjdp.ncjrs.org/ojstatbb/cjrp/asp/frame.asp.

Figure 14.5
Juveniles in Public and Private Residential Placement Facilities, by Age, 2001

CASE IN POINT

Kent v. United States

The Case

Kent v. United States, 383 U.S. 541, 86 S. Ct. 1045 (1966)

The Point

In its first juvenile case, the Supreme Court ruled that a juvenile's due process rights are denied when his or her case is waived to adult criminal court without a formal hearing.

In 1961, in the District of Columbia, 16-year-old Morris Kent was charged with entering the apartment of a woman, then robbing and raping her. Kent had been judged delinquent in 1959 after being charged with a series of housebreakings and attempted purse snatchings. Kent admitted to the robbery and rape, and the juvenile court judge waived Kent to criminal court. The case went to the U.S. district court for the District of Columbia where Kent was convicted of several counts of housebreaking, but not the rape "by reason of insanity."

The Supreme Court reversed his conviction, objecting to the casual manner in which juvenile cases were waived to an adult court and the broad discretion judges had in these decisions. The Court held that for a juvenile case to be waived to an adult court a hearing must be held, with the child having access to counsel. Also, the child and/or his or her attorney must have access to the child's records on which the waiver decision is being based, and the judge must state the reasons for the waiver in writing. They ruled that, in Kent's case, his right to due process was denied when he was not allowed such a formal hearing on the waiver.

and disadvantages of having a separate juvenile justice system for young offenders. The advantages of the juvenile justice system are as follows:

- The philosophy of the juvenile justice system is different from that of the adult criminal justice system. Whereas the adult system seeks to deter crime and punish criminals to promote public safety, the juvenile justice system acts in the best interests of the child.
- The juvenile justice system seeks to reduce the stigma of deviant behavior. By shielding the names of juvenile offenders from the press, keeping hearings private, and allowing for the purging of juvenile records, the juvenile justice system seeks to prevent youths from being labeled "bad kids."
- By having a separate juvenile justice system, young offenders are kept apart from adult criminals who might abuse, exploit, or teach them negative behaviors and attitudes.
- By addressing the social, emotional, and educational needs of young offenders, the juvenile justice system seeks to help them gain the necessary skills to become productive members of society.
- The juvenile justice system protects young offenders from receiving the harsh punishments meted out by the adult criminal justice system.

Those who are dissatisfied with the juvenile justice system point to the following disadvantages:

- Youths who commit serious crimes are treated too leniently. A 17-year-old who commits murder or rape does as much harm to society as a 20-year-old and deserves to be punished as severely. Many people believe that juveniles can appreciate the consequences of their unlawful behavior and should be held accountable.
- There is a great inconsistency between the punishments meted out in the juvenile justice system and those meted out in the adult criminal justice system. For citizens to have confidence in law enforcement and the courts, the punishments need to be more uniform.
- Young offenders are not afforded all the due process rights that are available in the adult criminal justice system. Although the juvenile court is supposed to be working in the best interests of the child, some believe that certain cases are dealt with more harshly because the youth does not have the full protection of the legal rights granted to adults.

In many cases, it is a tough call as to whether the juvenile justice system promotes or hinders the application of justice and the best interests of the child. The compromise that has been crafted is that of waiving particularly serious cases to the adult court.

Zero Tolerance

Public officials and school administrators have a responsibility to ensure the safety of those entrusted to their care. However, catastrophic incidents are still possible, such as the incident at Columbine High School in which two students killed 12 students, a teacher, and themselves. Anyone in a position of responsibility must prepare policies and procedures for these infrequent but devastating incidents. Administrators looking to balance public safety with personal freedoms must always err on the side of safety. In this quest to protect those in their charge, many administrators have enacted **zero-tolerance policies** that are sometimes counterproductive to the welfare of children. In an attempt to protect young people, many have been made victims of policies that appear to be designed to eliminate judgment and discretion on the part of administrators and teachers. This is done to shield schools and administrators from legal liability should violence occur. Unfortunately, the result is that zero tolerance

zero-tolerance policies Policies of agencies in which the strict letter of the law or rule is followed without question or room for individual discretion on the part of the authority.

Tried as an Adult

All states have provisions for trying juveniles as adults. Some states lower the age for juvenile jurisdiction to 15 or 16 rather than 17 or 18. In 1996 over 200,000 cases concerning 16- or 17-year-olds went to adult criminal court because the youths were legally defined as adults by their states. Other methods by which juveniles may be sent to adult criminal court are judicial waiver, statutory exclusion, and direct filing (or concurrent jurisdiction).

Judicial Waiver

A judge sends the juvenile to adult court. The three types of judicial waiver are mandatory, presumptive, and discretionary.

- Discretionary waiver. Transfer of the juvenile to adult court is at the judge's discretion.
- Mandatory waiver. Automatic transfer to criminal court on the basis of the youth's age and the gravity of the offense.
- Presumptive waiver. The burden of proof shifts from the state to the juvenile, who must contest being transferred to adult court.

States with judicial waiver as of 1999:

No judicial waiver: Massachusetts, Nebraska, New Mexico, New York

Discretionary waiver: Alabama, Arkansas, Florida, Hawaii, Idaho, Iowa, Maryland, Michigan, Mississippi, Missouri, Montana, Oklahoma, Oregon, South Dakota, Tennessee, Texas, Vermont, Washington, Wisconsin, Wyoming

Mandatory waiver: Connecticut

Discretionary and mandatory waiver: Delaware, Georgia, Indiana, Kentucky, Louisiana, North Carolina, Ohio, South Carolina, Virginia, West Virginia

Discretionary and presumptive waiver: Alaska, Arizona, California, Colorado, Washington, D.C., Kansas, Maine, Minnesota, Nevada, New Hampshire, Pennsylvania, Utah

Discretionary, presumptive, and mandatory waiver: Illinois, New Jersey, North Dakota, Rhode Island

Direct Filing (concurrent jurisdiction)

A prosecutor has the discretion to file charges in either juvenile or adult court. States with concurrent jurisdiction as of 1999 are as follows:

Arizona
Arkansas
Colorado
Washington, D.C.
Florida
Georgia
Louisiana
Massachusetts
Michigan
Montana
Nebraska
Oklahoma
Vermont
Virginia
Wyoming

Statutory Exclusion

Also called "legislative waiver," **statutory exclusion** comes from a state's legislature and does not require a juvenile court hearing. It automatically excludes some juveniles from juvenile court, and they go directly to adult court. Criteria include age, type of offense, and prior record. Statutory exclusion is used most for particularly heinous offenses, such as murder and aggravated rape. Some states without concurrent jurisdictions may also use statutory exclusion for minor violations such as traffic, fish or game, and local ordinance. Twenty-nine states had statutory exclusion provisions as of 1999:

Alabama
Alaska
Arizona
California
Delaware
Florida
Georgia
Idaho
Illinois
Indiana
Iowa
Louisiana
Maryland
Massachusetts
Minnesota
Mississippi
Montana
Nevada
New Mexico
New York
Oklahoma
Oregon
Pennsylvania
South Carolina
South Dakota
Utah
Vermont
Washington
Wisconsin

Source: OJJDP Statistical Briefing Book, April 25, 2002, http://ojjdp.ncjrs.org/ojstatbb/.

NEWS FLASH

(Il)legal Fiction

In both society and law, fads come and go. Unfortunately, they can also take people with them.

Since the 1999 shootings at Columbine High School in Colorado, the phenomenon of extreme adolescent violence, and society's attempts to control it, has snowballed. The Columbine tragedy inspired tremendous media attention, galvanized officials to prevent another such event, and possibly gave other adolescents some terrifying ideas. Now, after several more instances of school violence, a net of regulations and procedures is in place to control teens and their worst impulses. Schools are now acting at the first signs of even remotely unusual behavior. Zero-tolerance rules leave school officials little room for decision making. A student with a Bowie knife and a student with a keychain may face the same consequences: suspension or expulsion. In that vein, a student who writes a work of fiction may find himself in a great deal of trouble.

In 2002 Oklahoma high school senior Brian Robertson wrote a short story about a school invasion based on a set of evacuation plans he found on a school computer. He wrote his story based on those plans and saved the file, showing it to no one. A few weeks later, two students found the file and showed it to their teacher. Robertson was in hot water.

Robertson, who had no history of deviant or "dark" behavior, was suspended from school for a year and charged with a felony. His parents' home was searched, and he was fired from his job. He missed graduation and had to take correspondence courses to receive his diploma. Robertson's parents had to refinance their house for the money to defend their son. Part of this troubling issue is the law itself. At the time of Robertson's case, it was new, passed in July 2001, and Robertson was its first test. Oddly, no one seems to like the law as it is currently written. Robertson's case was dismissed in December 2002 because the judge believed the law was too vague. Robertson's attorney says the young man was just being used as a test case. Even after the district attorney appealed to reinstate the case, the assistant district attorney admitted to being concerned about the way the law was written.

Sources: "ACLU of Georgia Represents Student Suspended from School for Carrying 'Tweety Bird' Key Chain," American Civil Liberties Union, October 2, 2000, http://archive.aclu.org/news/2000/n100200.html. "As Many as 25 Dead in Colorado School Attack," CNN, April 20, 1999, http://www.cnn.com/US/9904/20/school.shooting.08. Kim Zetter, "Write a Story, Go to Jail," Wired News, August 22, 2003, http://www.wired.com/news/conflict/0,2100,60144,00.html.

statutory exclusion
Provisions that exclude, without hearing or waiver, juveniles who meet certain age, offense, or past-record criteria from the jurisdiction of the juvenile court. Excluded juvenile offenders are automatically tried in adult criminal court. Crimes that may invoke statutory exclusion include murder, aggravated rape, and armed robbery.

takes the rules to extremes. For example, in Greeley, Colorado, two students were suspended from school because they were playing with a water gun, which violated the policy of having a gunlike facsimile.[57] Zero-tolerance policies rob teachers and administrators of their right to use professional judgment and can end up hurting innocent youths and lowering the respect we all have for our institutions.[58]

The Future of Juvenile Justice

What is the future of the juvenile justice system? Specifically, can we identify trends that are likely to influence how juvenile delinquents and dependent or neglected children are dealt with in the coming decades? There are reasons to be optimistic that we will become more effective in meeting the needs of youths and prevent them from becoming involved in delinquent activity. There are equally compelling reasons to be concerned that many youths will be victimized by abuse and neglect and that delinquency, and ultimately criminal behavior, will occur at relatively high levels.

- **With the graying of America, resources will be diverted from programs that serve young people to programs that serve the elderly.** This will be a factor of generational politics in which the baby boom generation will ensure by the sheer power of their voting numbers that Social Security will become a greater economic responsibility for society.
- **Programs for children will continue to become privatized.** Families with discretionary income will be able to provide the soccer camps, music instruction, extra tutoring, and/or drug treatment that their children need. Those who must rely on government programs will find these programs continuing to disappear. Small communities will not be able to afford the insurance premiums to keep parks open, cover the risks of Little League baseball or gymnastics programs, or even fund field trips for schools.
- **The juvenile justice system will continue to transfer young offenders to criminal courts.** A disproportionate number of those selected for accelerated punishment will continue to be youths who have minority status, are economically disadvantaged, and are from the inner city.
- **The age of dependency will continue to increase.** Today, the period of a child's dependence on parents has been extended until the completion of high school and sometimes beyond.
- **Technology can level the playing field.** As the price of computers decreases and a greater percentage of children are able to use them, we may witness a revolution in the way children learn. Instead of being totally dependent on their schools, now most children will be "wired to the world" and able to supplement their schoolwork and possibly compensate for inadequate home situations and exploitive media. Children will be able to find information on their own and make decisions based on a larger foundation of knowledge.
- **Trends suggest that the juvenile justice system may be shifting its emphasis away from the punish-or-treat dichotomy.** Innovative restorative justice programs are appearing in many jurisdictions. This movement toward treating crime and delinquency in a more holistic manner will be covered more comprehensively in Chapter 16.[59]

Summary

Juvenile offenders are handled differently than adult offenders are; they have an alternate, parallel, and sometimes competing criminal justice system with its own philosophy, courts, and correctional system. The juvenile justice system is based on a progressive philosophy; however, currently, the handling of young offenders is often punitive.

Not all ancient societies treated children the same way. In medieval England, the authority for dealing with children resided with the parents and not the state. In 16th-century England, the poor laws were established, which allowed poor children to be employed in homes and shops. Eventually, the legal status of children was changed with the establishment of chancery courts. The concept of *parens patriae* was established whereby the king could act to intervene in the interests of children.

In colonial America, little distinction was made between crimes committed by adults and those committed by children. Parents were responsible for their children's actions. However, when those actions became troublesome, children received the same punishments as adults, including confinement in the stocks. The Industrial Revolution of the late 18th century demanded much from children. Because the factories required a steady stream of workers, little attention was focused on the welfare of working children. The 19th-century influx of immigrants brought fundamental changes in the concept of children and childhood. While immigrant adults filled the factories, their children presented challenges to the community in terms of socialization, delinquency, and schooling.

The first house of refuge was established in New York City in 1825, and over the next 60 years states designed similar types of institutions. By the end of the 19th century, these were abandoned in favor of newer reforms. One such 20th-century reform was that the responsibility for children was removed from the adult criminal court. In 1899 the first juvenile court was established in Cook County, Illinois, with the mandate to process cases of children between the ages of 8 and 17. By extending the *parens patriae* philosophy, the juvenile court stripped young people of their legal rights. This philosophy led to the development of the major differences between the modern adult criminal court and juvenile court: a focus on rehabilitation, the informal hearing, individualized justice, and private hearings. Widespread dissatisfaction with the juvenile courts led to more reforms, among these being the restoration of some of the legal rights that had been taken from juveniles.

One reform instituted during the 1960s and 1970s was the move to deinstitutionalize delinquent and neglected children. Rather than incarcerate them in prisonlike reform or training schools, community correctional practices such as foster homes, halfway houses, and extended probation-like supervision were employed.

The modern juvenile justice system is responsible for dealing with a variety of issues affecting children's lives such as incorrigibility and neglect, as well as those who are status offenders and those who are delinquent. Connected to the problem of juvenile crime is the quality of some of society's institutions and issues such as schools, poverty, neighborhoods, and faulty families. Some of the most pressing issues facing young people include violence, alcohol and drugs, sex and sexual abuse, running away, depression, and nihilism.

The juvenile justice system is organized much like the adult criminal justice system. The stages of the juvenile justice system are entry via referral, prehearing detention, intake, determining jurisdiction, the adjudication hearing, the disposition, and aftercare. Four types of public facilities are available in many states: adult prisons, ranches and camps, boot camp prisons, and traditional training schools. A number of private facilities are also available. To reform the juvenile justice system, the following issues should receive greater scrutiny and consideration: chronic offenders, youth gangs, the conditions of youth confinement, the treatment of children as adults, and zero-tolerance policies.

Several trends are likely to influence how juvenile delinquents and dependent or neglected children are likely to be dealt with in the coming decades. These include a growing elderly population that will need increasing amounts of resources, the privatization of youth programs, the continuing transfer of juveniles to adult criminal courts, and the increasing age of child dependency.

KEY TERMS

adjudicatory hearing p. 481
adversarial process p. 481
chancery court p. 466
commitment p. 481
consent decree p. 480
due process rights p. 470
gatekeeping p. 479
hearing p. 469
indentured servant p. 466
informal probation p. 481
juvenile delinquent p. 464
parens patriae p. 466
petitioner p. 481
poor laws p. 465
referral p. 479
residential placement p. 482
respondent p. 481
status offense p. 474
statutory exclusion p. 492
zero-tolerance policies p. 490

REVIEW QUESTIONS

1. What are the four major differences between modern adult criminal courts and juvenile courts?
2. What is the significance of England's poor laws?
3. Where and under what circumstances was the first juvenile court established?
4. What is a status offense?
5. What are the most pressing issues that currently affect young people?
6. What are the four primary types of confinement for juvenile offenders?
7. What is zero tolerance? What are good reasons for its use? What are bad reasons for its use?
8. What are the juvenile system's counterpart terms to *prosecutor, defense attorney, trial,* and *incarceration?*
9. What rights do juvenile defendants have in common with adult defendants?
10. What is the driving philosophy of the juvenile justice system?

SUGGESTED FURTHER READING

Anderson, Elijah. *Code of the Street: Decency, Violence and the Moral Life of the Inner City.* New York: Norton, 1999.

Gelles, Richard Jr. *The Book of David: How Preserving Families Can Cost Children's Lives.* New York: Basic Books, 1996.

Golden, Renny. *Disposable Children: America's Child Welfare System.* Belmont, CA: Wadsworth, 1997.

Platt, Anthony. *The Child Savers: The Invention of Delinquency.* Chicago: University of Chicago Press, 1969.

Shelden, Randall G. *Controlling the Dangerous Classes: A Critical Introduction to the History of Criminal Justice.* Boston: Allyn and Bacon, 2001.

Sidel, Ruth. *Keeping Women and Children Last: America's War on the Poor.* New York: Penguin Books, 1996.

ENDNOTES

1. Howard N. Snyder and Melissa Sickmund, *Juvenile Offenders and Victims: 1999 National Report* (Washington, DC: Office of Juvenile Justice and Delinquency Prevention, 1999).
2. Mary Clement, *The Juvenile Justice System: Law and Process* (Boston: Butterworth-Heinemann, 1977).
3. Nicolas Orme, *Medieval Children* (Yale University Press: New Haven and London, 2001).
4. Ibid., 327.
5. William Glaser, *Schools Without Failure* (New York: Harper and Row, 1969).
6. H. W. Brands, *The First American: The Life and Times of Benjamin Franklin* (New York: Anchor Books, 2000).
7. Lawrence Stone, *The Family, Sex, and Marriage in England: 1500–1800* (New York: Harper and Row, 1977).
8. Larry J. Siegel, Brandon C. Welsh, and Joseph J. Senna, *Juvenile Delinquency: Theory, Practice, and Law,* 8th ed. (Belmont, CA: Wadsworth, 2003). See Chapter 1: "Childhood and Delinquency."
9. John Sutton, "Inventing the Stubborn Child" in *Juvenile Delinquency,* 2nd ed., eds. Joseph G. Weis, Robert D. Crutchfield, and George S. Bridges (Thousand Oaks, CA: Pine Force Press, 2001), 5–6. Sutton presents a 1646 law that states if the parents turn a stubborn child over to the court, the child can be put to death.
10. Clement, *Juvenile Justice System,* 9.
11. Barry Krisberg and James Austin, *Reinventing Juvenile Justice* (Newbury Park, CA: Sage, 1993).
12. Randall G. Shelden, *Controlling the Dangerous Classes: A Critical Introduction to the History of Criminal Justice* (Boston: Allyn and Bacon, 2001).
13. Leslie Wheeler, "The Orphan Trains," *American History Illustrated,* 18 (1983): 10–23.
14. David J. Rothman, *The Discovery of the Asylum* (Boston: Little, Brown, 1971).
15. Anthony Platt, *The Child Savers: The Invention of Delinquency* (Chicago: University of Chicago Press, 1969).
16. C. Wright Mills, "The Professional Ideology of Social Pathologists," *American Journal of Sociology* 49, no. 3 (1943): 165–180.

17. Platt, *Child Savers,* p. 176.
18. Clement, *Juvenile Justice System.*
19. Thomas G. Blomberg, "Diversion and Accelerated Social Control," *Journal of Criminal Law and Criminology* 68, no. 2 (1977): 274–282.
20. Neil Howe and William Strauss, *Generations : The History of America's Future, 1584 to 2069* (New York: Morrow, 1991).
21. Elijah Anderson, *Code of the Street: Decency, Violence and the Moral Life of the Inner City* (New York: Norton, 1999).
22. Randall G. Shelden, Sharon K. Tracy, and William B. Brown, *Youth Gangs in American Society,* 3rd ed. (Belmont, CA: Wadsworth, 2004), 116.
23. Alexandra Marks, "In Drug War, Treatment Is Back," *Christian Science Monitor,* July 14, 2000, http://search.csmonitor.com/durable/2000/07/14/p1s1.htm.
24. Janelle Brown, "Saying No to Propaganda," *Salon,* March 12, 2002, http://www.salon.com/mwt/feature/2002/03/12/propaganda/.
25. Cathy Spatz Widom, "Childhood Sexual Abuse and Its Criminal Consequences," *Society* 33, no. 4 (1996): 47–53.
26. Patricia Hersch, "Coming of Age on City Streets," *Psychology Today,* January 1988, 31–37.
27. Daniel J. Campagna and Donald L. Poffenberger, *The Sexual Trafficking of Children* (South Hadley, MA: Auburn House, 1988).
28. Kevin Young and Laura Craig, "Beyond White Pride: Identity, Meaning, and Contradiction in the Canadian Skinhead Subculture," in *Deviance and Deviants: An Anthology,* eds. Richard Tewksbury and Patricia Gagné (Los Angeles: Roxbury, 2000), 304–316.
29. See Jerome H. Skolnick and Elliott Currie, *Crisis in American Institutions,* 2nd ed. (Boston: Little, Brown, 1973), v. Here Skolnick and Currie "examine the roots of current social problems in the fundamental structure of American society as a whole."
30. For instance, a 15-year-old and a 14-year-old who have sex are treated much differently than is a 25-year-old who has sex with a 14-year-old.
31. Nancy Weishew and Samuel Peng, "Variables Predicting Students' Problem Behaviors," *Journal of Educational Research* 87, no. 5 (1993): 5–17.
32. Julius Menacker, Ward Weldon, and Emanuel Hurwitz, "Community Influences on School Crime and Violence," *Urban Education* 25, no. 1 (1990): 68–80.
33. Janice Joseph, "School Factors and Delinquency: A Study of African-American Youths," *Journal of Black Studies* 26, no. 3 (1996): 340–355.
34. Janet M. Fitchen, "The Single-Parent Family, Child Poverty, and Welfare Reform," *Human Organization* 54, no. 4 (1995): 355–362.
35. Judith S. Wallerstein and Sandra Blakeslee, *Second Chances: Men, Women and Children a Decade After Divorce* (New York: Ticknor & Fields, 1989).
36. Christopher R. Browning and Edward O. Laumann, "Sexual Contact Between Children and Adults: A Life Course Perspective," *American Sociological Review* 62, no. 5 (1997): 540–560.
37. James C. Howell, *Preventing and Reducing Juvenile Delinquency: A Comprehensive Framework* (Thousand Oaks, CA: Sage, 2003), 123–129.
38. Nancy Kleniewski, *Cities, Change, and Conflict with Infotrac: A Political Economy of Urban Life* (Belmont, CA: Wadsworth, 2002).
39. BBC News, "Summer Schemes Slash Youth Crime," August 21, 2001, http://news.bbc.co.uk/1/low/uk/1506876.stm.
40. Leona Lee, "Factors Influencing Intake Disposition in a Juvenile Court," *Juvenile and Family Court Journal* 46, no. 1 (1995): 43–62.
41. Douglas C. Dodge, *Due Process Advocacy.* (Washington, DC: Office of Juvenile Justice and Delinquency Prevention, 1997).
42. James Austin and Barry Krisberg, "Wider, Stronger, and Different Nets: The Dialectics of Criminal Justice Reform," *Journal of Research in Crime and Delinquency* 18, no. 1 (1981): 165–196.
43. James Howell, "Juvenile Transfers to the Criminal Justice System: State of the Art," *Law and Policy* 18, no. 1 (1996): 17–60.
44. Joseph B. Sanborn Jr., "The Right to a Public Jury Trial—A Need for Today's Juvenile Court," *Judicature* 76, no. 4 (1993): 230–238.
45. Grant Grissom, "Dispositional Authority and the Future of the Juvenile Justice System," *Juvenile and Family Court Journal* 42, no. 1 (1991): 25–34.
46. John Whitehead and Steven Lab, "Meta-Analysis of Juvenile Correctional Treatment," *Journal of Research in Crime and Delinquency* 26, no. 4 (1989): 276–295.
47. Kimberly Kempf-Leonard, Paul E. Tracy, and James C. Howell, "Serious, Violent, and Chronic Juvenile Offenders: The Relationship of Delinquency Career Types to Adult Criminality," *Justice Quarterly* 18, no. 3 (2001): 449–478.

48. Paul Tracy, Marvin Wolfgang, and Robert Figlio, *Delinquency in Two Birth Cohorts. Executive Summary* (Washington, DC: U.S. Department of Justice, 1985).

49. Wayne S. Wooden, "Tagger Crews and Members of the Posse," in *The Modern Gang Reader,* eds. Malcolm W. Klein, Cheryl L. Maxson, and Jody Miller (Los Angeles: Roxbury, 1995), 65–68.

50. Shelden et al., *Youth Gangs.*

51. Jody Miller, *One of the Guys: Girls, Gangs, and Gender* (New York: Oxford University Press, 2001).

52. Jerome H. Skolnick, "Gangs and Crime Old as Time; But Drugs Change Gang Culture," in *The Modern Gang Reader,* eds. Malcolm W. Klein, Cheryl L. Maxson, and Jody Miller (Los Angeles: Roxbury, 1995), 222–227.

53. Thomas Castellano and Irina Soderstrom, "Therapeutic Wilderness Programs and Juvenile Recidivism: A Program Evaluation," *Journal of Offender Rehabilitation* 17, no. 1 (1992): 19–46.

54. Margaret Beyer, "Juvenile Boot Camps Don't Make Sense," *American Bar Association Journal of Criminal Justice* 10, no. 1 (1996): 20–21.

55. Patricia Puritz and Mary Ann Scali, *Beyond the Walls: Improvising Conditions of Confinement for Youth in Custody* (Washington, DC: Office of Juvenile Justice and Delinquency Prevention, 1998).

56. J. Fagan, E. Slaughter, and E. Hartstone, "Blind Justice: The Impact of Race on the Juvenile Justice Process," *Crime and Delinquency* 53, no. 3 (1997): 224–258.

57. Randy Cassingham, "Losing My Tolerance for Zero Tolerance," *This is True,* http://www.thisistrue.com/zt.html.

58. Fiona Morgan, "Deadly Consequences," *Salon,* http://dir.salon.com/news/feature/2001/03/09/shooting/index.html.

59. Although some controversy exists about the restorative justice practice, it is accepted most in the juvenile justice system.

outline

CHAPTER 15

Crime and Values: Drugs, Gambling, and Sex Work

THE CRIMINAL JUSTICE SYSTEM HAS A BROAD MANDATE TO enforce all the laws passed by the legislature. The making of law is inherently a political process in which various interest groups may influence the process and have laws enacted that reflect their values. For the most part, this is not a problem because a wide consensus exists on the desirability of most laws. It would be difficult to find anyone who opposes the proscriptions on rape, murder, and robbery. Although most of us are shocked by the idea, some pedophiles believe that consensual sex between adults and children should be legalized, and they attempt to have their views considered

objectives

After reading this chapter, the student should be able to:

1. Discuss why drug use, gambling, and sex work are controversial issues.
2. Explain the concept of victimless crimes.
3. Describe a brief history of drug use in the United States.
4. Discuss why Prohibition was a failure.
5. Discuss the concept of a war on drugs.
6. Discuss the criminal justice system's attempt to treat drug addicts.
7. Compare and contrast arguments for and against drug legalization and/or decriminalization.
8. Discuss why some forms of gambling are legal and sanctioned by the state, whereas other forms are not.
9. Compare and contrast illegal prostitution and legalized prostitution.
10. Discuss the fact that gambling and prostitution exist in a legal and social gray area, in which some forms of these activities are illegal and others are not.

by lawmakers.[1] So far, the pedophiles have not been successful in normalizing this behavior and having it legalized because the vast majority of society deems it deviant and harmful to children. A number of illegal behaviors, however, do not have a strong consensus favoring their proscription. Many people knowingly and willingly break the laws prohibiting these behaviors because they believe they pose little harm or because they realize they can make money by engaging in them. This chapter will cover three of these activities: drug use, gambling, and **sex work**.[2]

sex work
The exchange of coital or sex-related activities for payment.

Drug use, gambling, and sex work are controversial issues because they challenge the values and religious beliefs of many people. Others, however, see them as consensual activities that do not harm anyone other than those who choose to engage in them. There is an old saying, "My right to wave my fist in the air ends where your nose begins." That is to say, as long as I do not harm you with my fist waving, you should not care, and you certainly should not pass a law against it. Drug use, illegal forms of gambling, and prostitution are considered by many people to be **victimless crimes** because, unlike armed robberies, these crimes have no direct victim.[3] However, not everyone agrees with the claim that these behaviors are victimless crimes, pointing to the drug addict who robs a house to pay for drugs, or the gambler who wipes out the joint checking account she has with her husband, or her husband who brings home a sexually transmitted disease he caught from a prostitute. Those in favor of legalizing these behaviors counter these claims by pointing out that burglary is already a crime and that spending money from a joint checking account is something husbands and wives do all the time. These illegal behaviors are not the problem: the wife who cannot be trusted with the checkbook, the husband who is unfaithful, or the junkie who is addicted to drugs are the problems. These people believe better ways may exist to deal with these problems than making them illegal.[4] In fact, many argue that criminalizing these behaviors is what causes social harm.[5]

victimless crimes
Behaviors such as gambling or prostitution that are deemed undesirable because they offend community standards rather than directly harm people or property.

We will not resolve these issues here because they are matters of values. Rather, we will examine the profound and wide-ranging influence that drug use, illegal gambling, and prostitution exert on the criminal justice system. These activities drain resources from the detection and prosecution of other crimes, create opportunities for selective enforcement that undermines the trust of many in the criminal justice system, and provide large amounts of cash that may be used to corrupt criminal justice officials.[6] Therefore, we examine each of these behaviors not to pass judgment on the morality of those who choose to engage in them, but merely to understand and appreciate their impact on the criminal justice system.

Drug Use and Abuse

The use and trafficking of illegal drugs is the most controversial issue facing the criminal justice system today.[7] The resources dedicated to the detection, prosecution, and punishment of the illegal drug user and seller have stretched the ability of the federal, state, and local criminal justice systems to such a point that they must establish priorities as to which crimes to pursue.[8] Simply put, drug use and drug-related crimes are so prevalent that criminal justice officials must overlook some crimes to concentrate resources on the control of other types of crime. How did the drug problem get to be this way? Can the

Drug use continues to be a problem in the United States. Pictured here is a drug user injecting heroin while in a public park.
Courtesy of CORBIS-NY.

criminal justice system solve the problems associated with illegal drug use? What alternatives are critics of the war on drugs proposing?

Drug Abuse

What do we mean by drug abuse? Drugs have a range of legitimate, beneficial uses. The pharmaceutical industry has been responsible for eradicating diseases, relieving chronic pain, and addressing a wide range of health issues. Certainly no one would advocate getting rid of all drugs. Yet, there is a problem with the use of drugs in some contexts that constitutes drug abuse. Many drugs have been made illegal because they are subject to abuse. However, other drugs, such as alcohol, tobacco, and caffeine, may be abused, yet they remain legal. Therefore, for our purposes, we will use Howard Abadinsky's definition of drug abuse: "Ingesting a psychoactive substance that is illegal to possess or that is taken in quantities that are clearly harmful."[9]

This definition is widely, although not completely, accepted. Some contend that moderate use of marijuana is not drug abuse, but it would be deemed so by this definition because marijuana is illegal. We employ Abadinsky's definition recognizing this controversy, but also understanding that if we are to consider drugs' impact on the criminal justice system, we must also recognize that illegality is an indispensable feature of a working definition of drug abuse.

A Short History of Drug Use and Drug Laws in the United States

Although patterns of drug and alcohol use have varied widely throughout history and across different societies, it is important to our understanding of the criminal justice system to consider how these patterns were established and how they changed in the United States. The large quantities of alcohol that early Americans consumed presented what we would today consider a social problem. Because it was so ingrained in colonial society, however, there was little effort to control it. Drinking alcohol was integrated into daily life because it was safer than drinking the water.[10] In his book, *The Alcoholic Republic: An American Tradition*, W. J. Rorabaugh reported that between 1790 and 1830 the United States was considered a nation of drunkards.

> *Alcohol was pervasive in American society; it crossed regional, sexual, racial, and class lines. Americans drank at home and abroad, alone and together, at work and at play, in fun and in earnest. They drank from the crack of dawn to the crack of*

Alcohol was used heavily in the American colonies and the early United States. The effect of alcohol abuse caused many citizens to worry about the safety of their communities.
Courtesy of CORBIS-NY.

dawn. At nights taverns were filled with boisterous, mirth-making tipsters. Americans drank before meals, with meals, and after meals. They drank while working in the fields and while traveling across half a continent. They drank in their youth, and, if they lived long enough, in their old age. They drank at formal events such as weddings, ministerial ordinations, and wakes, and on no occasion—by the fireside of an evening, on a hot afternoon, and when the mood called.[11]

Some groups, such as the Quakers, saw the problems associated with high levels of alcohol consumption, but the government did not take a moral stand on the issue. Instead, it adopted a laissez-faire attitude toward alcohol consumption and intervened only in taxing drugs and alcohol. In 1791 Congress passed an excise tax on whiskey that met with opposition from farmers west of the Appalachians who believed the federal government did not have the right to impose taxes on the states. In what came to be known as the Whiskey Rebellion, federal revenue agents were attacked and sometimes tarred and feathered until President George Washington was forced to call in the militia to impose the power of the government on citizens who refused to pay the tax.[12]

A good example of the government's reluctance to regulate drug use can be found in the history of opium in the United States. In the mid-1880s, many Chinese were brought to the United States for labor on large projects such as the building of the railroads. They brought with them opium, the trade of which had made many American and British merchants rich. The opium addiction of some of these Chinese was not considered a significant problem as long as it was confined to the Chinese. But when this drug use spread to other parts of society, it suddenly was deemed a serious social problem.[13] For instance, in San Francisco's Chinatown:

The practice spread rapidly and quietly among this class of gamblers and prostitutes until the later part of 1875, at which time authorities became cognizant of the fact . . . that many women and young girls, and also young men of respectable

A government inspector is tarred and feathered during the Whiskey Rebellion in 1794. Farmers objected to the government's collecting taxes on those who produced whiskey.
Courtesy of Corbis/Bettmann.

> *family, were being induced to visit the dens, where they were ruined morally and otherwise, a city ordinance was passed forbidding the practice under penalty of heavy fine or imprisonment or both.*[14]

As opium smoking decreased over the years, other drugs took its place. During the Civil War, morphine, a highly addictive opium extract, was widely used to combat pain and dysentery. Eventually, so many soldiers became physically dependent on it that its addiction earned the epithet "the army disease." Cocaine was used to treat morphine addiction, until it was realized that cocaine was just as habit forming.[15]

Because cocaine and morphine were considered legal drugs, they found their way into all sorts of patent medicines. Advertised as therapeutic medicines, these concoctions contained large percentages of alcohol and other habit-forming drugs. Although they tended to give short-term relief for a wide range of aliments, the unsuspecting public was simply getting drunk or stoned on these supposed medicines. Traveling hucksters prescribed these patent medicines for "whatever ails you" and found an especially eager audience in respectable women who, instead of going to the bar or saloon, would go home and get drunk on their "medicine."

Drug Control Legislation

In the 20th century a steady progression of laws attempted to protect people from the harmful effects of drugs. These laws, although not wholly effective, did shape and reflect the attitudes and policies that the general public developed over the years. In 1906 Upton Sinclair published his muckraking exposé of the meatpacking industry, *The Jungle.*[16] This book provided graphic descriptions of the unsanitary conditions in slaughterhouses and included stories of how dead rodents were routinely tossed into processed beef. Congress responded by passing the Pure Food and Drug Act of 1906, which required producers of food and drugs to clearly label what their products contained. Furthermore, this law made it illegal to transport across state lines mislabeled or adulterated food or drugs. This law crippled the patent medicine business. Once people could see what was in these products, they could make informed choices and avoid them.[17]

The Pure Food and Drug Act of 1906 did not criminalize drugs. Selling and consuming narcotics was still legal; they just had to be labeled accurately. The goal of this legislation was not to protect people from themselves but to ensure that incompetent or unscrupulous merchants did not take advantage of unsuspecting individuals. The next major piece of drug legislation was the Harrison Act, passed by Congress in 1914. This law was designed "to provide for the registration of, with the collectors of internal revenue, and to impose a special tax upon all persons who produce, import, manufacture, compound, deal in, dispense, or give away opium or coca leaves, their salts, derivatives, or preparations, and for other purposes."[18] The Harrison Act did not make the use and sale of narcotics illegal, but it did ensure that the government collected taxes from those who trafficked in drugs. Soon, however, the courts ruled that prescribing narcotics to addicts even to maintain their comfort was not a legitimate medical practice (*Webb v.*

CROSSCURRENTS

Flight of the Green Fairy

Absinthe, a bright green, flavored liquor, has an interesting place in the history of controlled substances and provides a good example of the role that tradition, reputation, and the durability of standing laws have in the control of drugs. Absinthe followed a tangent similar to that of marijuana, heroin, cocaine, and Ecstasy. It was legal and popular, became too popular, became associated with social upheaval, and was outlawed. The story of absinthe also proves, however, that once a substance is declared illegal, the chances of it becoming legal again are slim, regardless of how little it is used or how realistically its harms are judged. In the United States, alcohol is the single exception, with the repeal of Prohibition in 1933.

The United States' war on drugs picked up steam during the mid–20th century and became popular with legislators and the public. It continues today, with laws and penalties growing more stringent by the year. The fact that a substance is little known and little used and, when compared to substances such as crack-cocaine, is rather meek in its effects, will not get any laws reconsidered. This is the case with absinthe, which became illegal in the United States in 1912.

This 1896 advertising poster romanticizes the allure of absinthe, also known as the "green fairy."
Courtesy of CORBIS-NY.

Absinthe is a liquid made from alcohol and herbs, with wormwood (*Artemisia absinthium*) being the primary flavoring ingredient. Absinthe has a very high alcohol content, usually from 60 to 70 percent. Other ingredients include licorice, hyssop, fennel, angelica root, and anise. Absinthe was first produced commercially in the late 18th century, but only rose to overwhelming popularity in France a century later, becoming known as *la fée verte* or the "green fairy." Eventually, absinthe gained a reputation for causing insanity. The flavoring ingredient, oil of wormwood, is a poison when taken in high doses, causing seizures, convulsions, and death. Wormwood's active component, thujone, is reported to cause brain damage. Many countries, including the United States, banned absinthe between 1910 and 1915. True absinthe can still be purchased in the Czech Republic, Portugal, Spain, and the United Kingdom. Although it is possible that what was known as the "madness in a bottle" was caused as much by absinthe's high alcohol content as thujone, the absinthe of the French poets contained much more thujone, about 260 ppm, than anything available today. Modern absinthe has about 10 ppm of thujone, which is relatively safe.*

Today, absinthe is little more than a novelty. The Drug Enforcement Administration Web site has special sections on marijuana, cocaine, and heroin, but not for absinthe. There are no raids on "absinthe houses" because no such dens exist, and one is unlikely to see any absinthe busts on television shows such as *COPS.* That modern absinthe has any of the legendary druglike effects of its antique predecessor is questionable at best. Yet, anyone caught possessing absinthe could still be arrested. Is it possible that, like absinthe, drugs such as marijuana and heroin will eventually fall out of favor? It can be argued that the ban on absinthe choked off its popularity until it became little more than a footnote in the history of inebriation.

QUESTIONS

1. Is the banning of absinthe an example of a successful battle in the war on drugs?
2. Was the banning of absinthe futile because it only made room for more potent drugs?
3. If the ban on absinthe were lifted, would it become popular again? More potent?
4. Will marijuana, cocaine, and heroin ever fall out of favor as absinthe did?

Source: Richard W. Olsen, "Absinthe and γ-Aminobutyric Acid Receptors," *Proceedings of the National Academy of Sciences of the United States of America* 97, no. 9 (April 25, 2000), 4417–4418. Also online at http://www.pubmedcentral.nih.gov/articlerender.fcgi?artid=34311.

*Ji í Pato ka and Bohumil Plucar, "Pharmacology and Toxicology of Absinthe," *Journal of Applied Biomedicine* 1, no. 4 (2003), 199–205. Also online at http://www.zsf.jcu.cz/jab/1_4/patockabs.pdf.

Early efforts to demonize marijuana, such as this 1935 movie poster, were not only inaccurate but counterproductive. Those who tried the drug found their experiences differing widely from the negative propaganda.
Courtesy of CORBIS-NY.

United States [1919]), although this stance was softened somewhat in *Lindner v. United States* (1925). For the next 50 years, the United States inched toward the criminalization of narcotics and other drugs, including marijuana, through court cases and legislation. The 1951 Boggs Act increased penalties for violating drug laws and, for the first time, regulated both narcotics and marijuana in a single federal law.[19] In 1956 President Eisenhower signed into law the Narcotics Control Act, which increased both penalties and federal authority.[20] These pieces of legislation were the U.S. government's first coherent stab at criminalizing specific classes of drugs and prohibiting their sale and use. The Controlled Substances Act of 1970 set forth the drug schedules currently used to classify drugs, and the United States completed its move from allowing the use of any drug by anyone to regulating drugs for tax purposes to outlawing them completely.

To fully appreciate how drug use is a crime dictated by societal values as much as the need for the public good, we must consider the country's experience with the prohibition of alcohol in the early 20th century. On January 16, 1919, the Eighteenth Amendment was ratified, and Congress passed the National Prohibition Act (also known as the Volstead Act), which funded the Prohibition Bureau of the Treasury Department.[21] Prohibition was a monumental failure. Not only did it fail to prevent the use of alcohol, but it also provided an opportunity for corruption and organized crime. Speakeasies, bootlegging, and political payoffs became ingrained in society, and the selective enforcement of alcohol laws resulted in an overall disregard for the law. The criminal element infiltrated law enforcement agencies, and citizens became cynical not only about the liquor laws but about government in general.[22] Prohibition was regarded as a "great experiment" that not only failed to achieve its goals but produced the unintended consequences of undermining the criminal justice system by stimulating corruption, making romantic figures out of bootleggers and criminals, and straining citizens' trust in their government. Although most people may have agreed that alcohol produced problems for individuals and society, not many were prepared to give it up. Alcohol use was (and is) part of the social fabric, and a significant percentage of the population either wanted the freedom to engage in social drinking or saw an opportunity to make a great deal of money by violating the laws against smuggling, distribution, and sales.[23]

Prohibition ended in 1933, but the country was not ready to go back to the days of completely unregulated drugs and alcohol. In fact, by 1937 the Treasury Department's Bureau of Narcotics considered marijuana to be a serious problem that required national legislation. The Marijuana Tax Act resulted from a campaign by Bureau of Narcotics chief Harry Anslinger to demonize the drug by calling it the "devil drug," "assassin of youth," and the "weed of madness."[24] Whereas opium had been introduced by the Chinese, marijuana found its way to the United States by way of Mexico. Even though marijuana had been known since colonial days, particularly in the form of hemp used to make rope, the recreational use of marijuana was linked to Mexican culture and used to stigmatize Mexicans as dangerous.

When drugs affected only the marginal populations of society, such as Chinese and Mexican immigrants, they were not deemed to be serious social problems. However, as drugs moved into the middle and upper classes, they received the attention of the criminal justice system. In the 1960s rampant drug use accompanied protest movements concerned with civil rights, women's rights, and the Vietnam war.[25] Drug use was considered another repudiation of the dominant value system, and the criminal justice system reacted harshly. Although there were (and continue to be) efforts to decriminalize marijuana, people who used other drugs, particularly heroin and cocaine, were vigorously prosecuted and punished.

Government agents destroyed alcohol found during Prohibition. However, efforts to restrict the illegal use of alcohol were ultimately unsuccessful.

Courtesy of CORBIS-NY.

One might legitimately ask why recreational drugs are still demonized so long after the 1960s. Why haven't the "baby boomers" who used drugs then sought to legalize or at least greatly decriminalize drugs now that their generation is in its prime years of political and social power? The answer is extremely complex. On one hand, recreational drug use can be considered a form of youthful rebellion. As people grow older and take responsible roles in society, they no longer feel the need to act out. Furthermore, seeking to protect their own children and grandchildren, baby boomers have limited the availability of drugs. They may have enjoyed their own reckless youths, but they consider themselves lucky to have escaped the downsides of drug use: addiction, criminal records, and death.[26]

The War on Drugs

The problems of illegal drug use in the last part of the 20th century fundamentally altered the criminal justice system. Politicians, law enforcement officials, teachers, and parents developed policies that figuratively waged a "war on drugs." Although the war metaphor may be somewhat misleading, it does serve to illustrate the lengths to which our leaders are willing to go to control drug use. Few people defend the use of illegal drugs; however, a public policy debate continues about how the government should handle this problem.[27] Concerns have emerged from both conservative and liberal quarters about how the war on drugs challenges our constitutional liberties. Additionally, many believe that the war on drugs strains the trust between parents and children, alters the relationship between students and schools, and erodes the respect citizens have for the criminal justice system. The war on drugs is being waged on many fronts.[28] The following examples serve to illustrate how the criminal justice system is simply one part of the web of social control:

- **Testing children for drug use.** One of the fronts on which the war on drugs is being waged is at the consumer level. It is theorized that if the demand for drugs can be reduced, then the price of drugs will fall and fewer people will engage in drug trafficking. A vast number of prevention programs are aimed at changing the attitudes of young people who are considering drug use. One need only watch television to see public service announcements directed at children or their parents describing the dangers of drug use and how to prevent it. There are also well-meaning efforts to stem drug use by detecting it. Parents and schools are encouraged to look for signs of drug use by monitoring children's friends and the music they listen to, and by searching their children's rooms or school lockers. In extreme cases, children are actually tested for drug use. Home drug testing kits are marketed to parents who suspect drug use in their children, and some schools test athletes and anyone else who participates in official extracurricular activities.[29]
- **Increased penalties for drug use or sales.** Legislatures around the country, including Congress, have greatly increased many of the penalties for drug use or sales. These increased penalties are based on the deterrence principle—that is, individuals will eventually consider the cost (in terms of long imprisonment) to be too high when measured against the temporary pleasure associated with drug use. Debate is considerable about whether this strategy works. Certainly an increased number of inmates are serving time for drug trafficking and sales, but real questions remain about whether the streets are any safer because of these laws. Many question whether addicts can be deterred from drug use. Others examine the market dynamics of the drug trade and question whether increased penalties simply mean higher prices for drugs and greater profits for drug dealers. Finally, we may question whether the increased penalties for drug offenses make the job of law enforcement officers more dangerous. When a drug dealer is facing life in prison, is he or she more likely to attempt to resist arrest? With stakes so high, both in terms of the money to be made and freedom to be lost, one of the unintended consequences of the war on drugs has been increased violence.[30]

CROSSCURRENTS

A War on Many Fronts

The criminal justice system is not the only institution that is fighting the war on drugs. Because illegal drugs affect all aspects of society, the war is being waged on many fronts. Those who use illegal drugs, whether convicted or not, may find their lives changed in ways they never considered when they chose to get high at a party, while driving, or at home while watching cartoons. Following are some of the ways prior drug use can come back to haunt a person:

- Driver's license. *Much like driving under the influence of alcohol, driving while on drugs can be used as a reason to deprive someone of driving privileges. However, unlike in the case of alcohol, there is no test to measure the driver's impairment. The Breathalyzer can distinguish when drivers have a .08 level of alcohol in their blood, which is used as a benchmark to determine when someone is not safe to operate a motor vehicle. However, the mere presence of drugs in the body is all that is needed to make this judgment. Therefore, someone who smoked marijuana two days ago could be charged with driving under the influence even though the behavioral effects of the drug have worn off.*
- Extracurricular activities. *Some school districts test students for illegal drug use and prevent those found with drugs in their bodies from participating in sports. In addition to sports, other districts prohibit students from any type of school-sponsored activities, including cheerleading, band, and newspaper staff.*
- Military. *In the all-volunteer military, those who use drugs may be prevented from joining. This is especially true of the National Guard and the Reserves. Those already in the military will find themselves subject to the laws of the Uniform Code of Military Justice, which has broad discretion in the investigation and prosecution of drug use. Because the military has the important mission of national security, it must ensure the readiness of its personnel and take drug violations very seriously.*
- Law enforcement. *Like the military, law enforcement agencies as well as other units of the criminal justice system screen candidates and employees for drug use. If officers are going to enforce the drug laws, it seems reasonable to expect those officers to obey them, as well. Otherwise, they could have a conflict of interest, and even more important, could be susceptible to blackmail.*
- Political office. *Those who have used drugs may find their past coming back to haunt them when they run for political office. Even if they were never arrested for illegal drug use, the mere reporting of such indiscretion is something that must be explained. During the 1960s many young people used drugs, and such politicians as Al Gore, Bill Clinton, George W. Bush, and Newt Gingrich have had to explain their transgressions. Several times, candidates for appointed jobs such as the Supreme Court have withdrawn when drug use was discovered in the background check.*
- Property forfeiture. *The government has confiscated cars, boats, houses, and airplanes that have been used in the drug trade. Additionally, large amounts of cash that belonged to suspects involved in the drug business have also been taken and legally kept by law enforcement agencies.*

These examples demonstrate that the criminal justice system is not the only institution fighting the drug war. Those who use illegal drugs face consequences at a number of points in their lives. In some ways, those who make a mistake might find that society continues to persecute them long after the criminal justice system has provided its punishments. They may even have a difficult time reentering conventional society. Therefore, students, especially those who want a career in the criminal justice system, should seriously weigh any illegal drug use against the possible long-term consequences.

QUESTIONS

1. What other ways does society discourage the use of illegal drugs?
2. Has the drug war gone too far? Not far enough?
3. If you could repeal one law concerning drugs, what would it be?
4. If you could create one law concerning drugs, what would it be?

U.S. law enforcement officers are continually confronted with the sales of crack cocaine.

Courtesy of Corbis Royalty Free.

- **Drug forfeiture laws.** When law enforcement officers discover that an individual's private possessions are being used in the drug trade, those possessions may be confiscated by the state. Have you ever wondered why some DARE drug prevention law enforcement officers have sleek muscle cars? Those cars used to belong to drug dealers who were caught with drugs in their cars, and the state used drug forfeiture laws to take them. In addition to cars, the police have taken boats, airplanes, homes, and large quantities of cash from drug dealers. Although this seems to be a legitimate practice—after all, those who rob banks or embezzle money should not be able to keep their ill-gotten gains—the forfeiture laws are considerably broad enough to invite abuse. For instance, if you are stopped on the highway and you fit the profile of a drug runner, the police have the latitude to confiscate any large amount of cash you may have even if you have no drugs in your possession.[31]

These brief examples show that there is a difference of opinion about how the drug war is being prosecuted. Some people believe the war on drugs is more harmful than the drugs themselves. In critiquing the war on drugs, Elliot Currie wrote:

> *Reasonable people may debate the details. But there is no denying the fundamental realities: the American drug problem continues to tower above those of the rest of the industrial world, and it does so despite a truly extraordinary experiment in*

TABLE 15.1

Drug Schedules

Schedule 1 (no medical use; high abuse)	heroin, mescaline, psilocybin, LSD, marijuana, hashish, peyote, Ecstasy, Quaalude, synthetic heroin
Schedule II (some medical use; high abuse)	methadone, morphine, cocaine, amphetamine, methamphetamine, PCP, opium, Ritalin
Schedule III (medical use; moderate abuse)	codeine, anabolic steroids, barbiturates,
Schedule IV (medical use; low abuse)	Xanax, Valium, Darvon, Rohypnol, Halcion
Schedule V (medical use; low abuse)	cough syrups

Schedule I

1. High potential for abuse.
2. No currently accepted medical use in treatment in the United States.
3. A lack of accepted safety for use of the drug or other substance under medical supervision.

Schedule II

1. High potential for abuse.
2. Currently accepted medical use in treatment in the United States or a currently accepted medical use with severe restrictions.
3. Abuse may lead to severe psychological or physical dependence.

Schedule III

1. Potential for abuse less than the drugs or other substances in schedules I and II.
2. Currently accepted medical use in treatment in the United States.
3. Abuse may lead to moderate or low physical dependence or high psychological dependence.

Schedule IV

1. Low potential for abuse relative to the drugs or other substances in schedule III.
2. Currently accepted medical use in treatment in the United States.
3. Abuse may lead to limited physical dependence or psychological dependence relative to the drugs or other substances in schedule III.

Schedule V

1. Low potential for abuse relative to the drugs or other substances in schedule IV.
2. Currently accepted medical use in treatment in the United States.
3. Abuse may lead to limited physical dependence or psychological dependence relative to the drugs or other substances in schedule IV.

Source: U.S. Drug Enforcement Administration, http://www.usdoj.gov/dea/.

punitive control. We have unleashed the criminal-justice system against drug users and dealers with unprecedented ferocity, but drugs continue to destroy lives and shatter communities outside the Third World. And now the drug war itself contributes to that destruction—first in the incarceration of vast numbers of the young in what should be the start of their most productive years; and again in the depletion of resources that could otherwise be used to deal with the deeper problems of devastated communities.[32]

Drug Treatment

In addition to the war metaphor, the criminal justice system also addresses the problem of drugs from a medical perspective. Although it is illegal to possess and distribute certain drugs (see Table 15.1), it is not illegal to be a drug addict. Therefore, addiction is

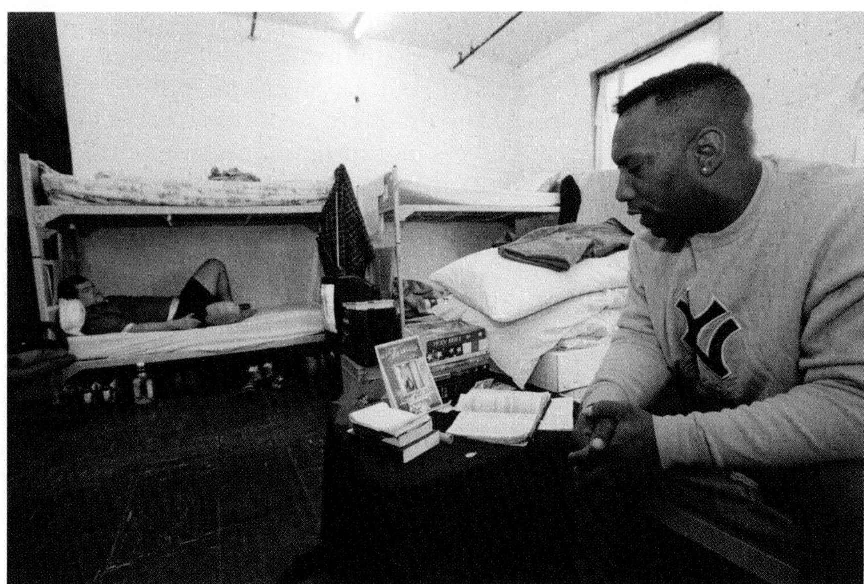

One method for combating drugs is to provide treatment for addicts. One effective technique is to place offenders in residential treatment programs where they have no opportunity to obtain illegal drugs. Courtesy of CORBIS-NY.

treated as a physical and psychological issue. If individuals are compelled to continue drug use because of addiction, then the crimes associated with that addiction will continue as long as the drug users remain trapped in the cycle of dependency. Treating the addiction is an important step in reducing the crimes associated with drug use.[33] As long as individuals physically need illegal drugs, there will always be those who are willing to engage in the highly lucrative drug trade. Few treatment programs are available for those who do not have the means to pay for private hospitalization, and government programs for the serious drug user are scarce and can have waiting lists that delay treatment until long after the user's motivation has waned. The criminal justice system is good at detecting and arresting drug users, but often fails to provide the treatment necessary to prevent recidivism.[34]

One important aspect of drug treatment is the need to consider the environment to which the client will return after the treatment. Although some users might respond to treatment in a controlled setting, such as an in-patient hospital, it is an entirely different matter when they return to their homes and neighborhoods where all the circumstances that encouraged their initial drug use still exist. For treatment to have long-term success, a number of conditions should be considered. Elliot Currie specified several goals that treatment programs should strive for:[35]

1. **Taking treatment seriously.** Many treatment programs, including those in correctional institutions and private hospitals and those connected with the courts, provide only token treatment. The resources are meager, the commitment is insufficient, and there is no realistic plan or focus. To have quality service and effective results, a certain level of funding and accountability is required. Currie advocated rigorous standards of evaluation and modification of programs based on what is found to be effective.
2. **Making treatment user-friendly.** To get addicts involved in treatment programs, the programs should regard them as partners in the treatment process rather than as criminals or deviants. Drug treatment is not something that can be imposed; rather, it needs to be accommodating to clients' social and emotional needs. The success of drug treatment is dependent on the individual client's ability to explore his or her reasons for drug use, the feelings and vulnerabilities that continue to make addiction possible, and his or her relationships and dependence on others. To be effective, drug treatment should foster a helping relationship rather than a punitive one.

3. **Linking treatment with harm reduction.** Drug treatment can be partially successful in several ways. Although the ultimate goal is to free the user from drug dependency, this should be viewed as a process, not an event. On the road to complete independence from drugs are steps that can make the drug use less deleterious to the user and others. For instance, because of the problems of HIV and AIDS, drug users can participate in educational programs that promote safe-sex practices and more sanitary drug usage. One particularly controversial harm-reduction strategy is to give addicts new syringes or bleach kits to clean their needles. Some may believe this is a tacit encouragement of drug addition by the government, but others believe it is a humane intermediate step in the treatment process. If the addict dies of AIDS and/or continues to spread the infection, the harm done by the outright prohibition policy is greater than the reduced harm of helping drug users pursue their habits in a more sanitary way.
4. **Making aftercare a priority.** When someone is locked away in a secure institution, it is not difficult to provide detoxification and counseling practices and demonstrate a healthy rate of success. The difficult part of drug treatment occurs when the user is released from custody and must return to the street where she or he is faced with the temptations that initiated the drug use. Currie advocated that addicts need to be provided with help in negotiating the "increasing inhospitable housing and labor markets, as well as the criminal justice system."[36]
5. **Linking treatment with work.** Treating the addiction is only one part of successful rehabilitation. To become a fully functioning member of society again (or sometimes for the first time), the person must have the skills to compete in the job market. This can be an awesome task because many hard-core addicts have lost their social and work skills. At the very least, they need to be retrained in such basic skills as constructing a résumé and locating employment opportunities, as well as in making themselves presentable to future employers. Such concerns as dressing appropriately, punctuality at interviews and work, and maintaining a stable residence are instrumental in maintaining long-term employment and successful drug abstinence.

The life of the hard-core drug user is a difficult one fraught with hardship, danger, loss of loved ones, poverty, and the ultimate possibility of an early death. Given a realistic choice, many addicts would like to kick their habits and return to conventional society. Unfortunately, for many, no realistic choice exists because there are not enough treatment programs available for those without the money or insurance for private hospitalization. The result of the nation's failure to provide adequate treatment for drug addiction has been a continued healthy market for illegal drugs and an overburdened criminal justice system that must divert resources from other types of offenses.[37] Is there another way for society to deal with the drug problem that will be more effective in reducing the harm done to society and those who find themselves addicted to drugs?

The Decriminalization and Legalization Debate

The war on drugs has not been effective in ridding the nation of illegal drugs. Some critics argue that the war on drugs has been such a monumental failure that the war has become a more serious problem for society than the drugs themselves.[38] We will not directly address this point here because the answer to whether "the cure is worse than the disease" is as much a political and social question as it is an empirical one. The answer is bound up in each person's value system and cannot be decided by counting the number of addicts, counting the amount of money spent on prisons, or measuring the spread of infectious diseases. It is also useful to consider carefully the terms *drug decriminalization* and *drug legalization* because they mean different things. Therefore, without advocating any of these ideas here, we simply present some of the possibilities and distinctions of drug decriminalization and **legalization**.

legalization
The total removal of legal prohibitions on specific acts that were previously proscribed and punishable by law.

LEGALIZATION AND DECRIMINALIZATION. Society has an interest in discouraging the use of recreational drugs. The lessons taught by Prohibition appear to be that the outright

FOCUS ON ETHICS

Better, but Still Bad

As a probation officer, sometimes your victories are incomplete. You have worked very hard with Winston to make sure he stays off drugs and out of trouble. You and Winston have had your moments, but you have been firm and consistent, and you seem to have won a certain amount of his respect. Winston has a long record of dealing drugs and has been in and out of treatment for his addiction to crack-cocaine. For the past several months, he has been passing his drug tests, showing up for his required appointments, and holding down the best job he has ever had as a mailroom clerk at a large publishing house. He seems to be on the right track.

On your latest home visit, you discover that Winston and his new girlfriend, Karol, have been smoking marijuana. As a matter of fact, when you walk into their living room, the pungent stench is so strong that the cats, who normally flee when they see you, only yawn. Winston cannot talk in complete sentences, and Karol plows through an entire box of cookies as you read them the riot act. It is late, and you are mad, so you order Winston to be in your office at 8:00 A.M. When Winston arrives at 9:30 the next morning, he is contrite. You are already doing the paperwork to have him arrested for violation of probation as he tries to convince you that he deserves another chance. He is very persuasive as he argues that smoking marijuana is the only way he can stay off crack. He claims he has been cheating on his drug tests to disguise his marijuana smoking, but that he has been crack-free for several months. He is convinced that if he gives up the marijuana, he will go back to smoking crack. Karol, who came with him, testifies that he is doing everything else right and that if given a chance, he will be able to eventually give up the marijuana also. Because she is a middle school English teacher, you believe she has been a good influence on Winston.

WHAT DO YOU DO?

1. Revoke his probation and take Winston back before the judge where he will face the prospect of going to prison.
2. Give him another chance and simply ignore his marijuana smoking because, in an odd way, it seems to be helping him stay off crack.
3. Give him another chance but insist that he quit smoking marijuana and double up on his drug testing to make sure he is not cheating.
4. Insist that he dump his girlfriend Karol because she smokes marijuana with him and you want to take that temptation away.
5. Report Karol to the school board because she is teaching middle school students while she is an active marijuana user.

banning of a substance demanded by the public does not work.[39] Now, although alcohol continues to cause significant social harm, it is restricted to people of a specified age, sold through a variety of controlled mechanisms depending on local and state laws, heavily taxed, and regulated in such a manner that organized crime is no longer a major factor in its sale and consumption. Alcohol is a legal but regulated substance that continues to be problematic for the criminal justice system but has generally been accepted as a moderate social risk.[40] The alcohol industry is a multi-billion-dollar enterprise that has its own lobbyists who are effective in keeping it legal.

Could the legalization of drugs follow a structure similar to that of alcohol? The answer is probably no because there are so many different drugs, and each would have to be considered according to its potential harm. Just as states have different rules for the sale of beer and wine as opposed to liquor, a variety of rules would be needed to regulate the

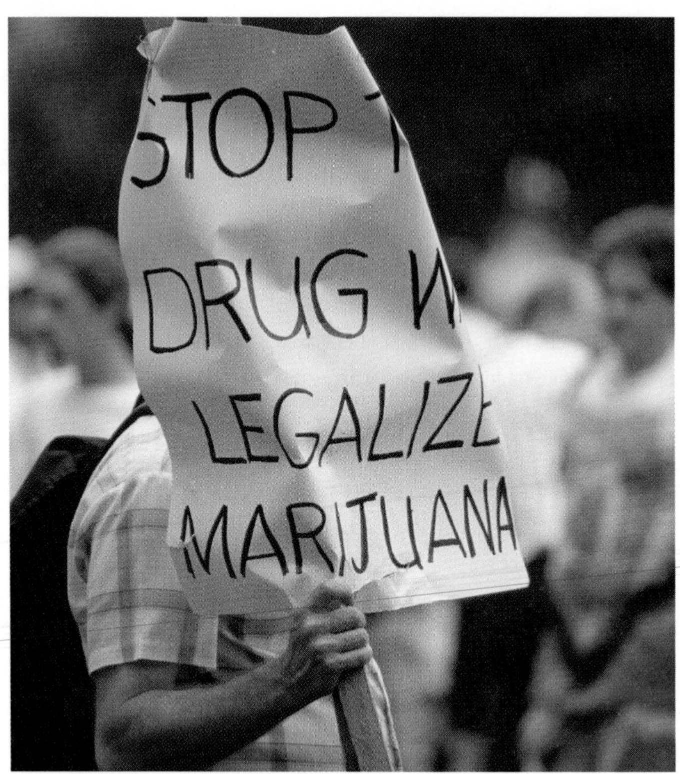

Some individuals believe the harm done by drugs could be reduced if drugs were legalized. Here, a protester carries a sign advocating the legalization of marijuana.
Courtesy of CORBIS-NY.

sale of recreational drugs. Furthermore, the legalization of drugs would probably be incremental, and some drugs would remain illegal. In the following section we consider some of the issues surrounding the legalization of drugs.

- **Marijuana.** Perhaps the drug that stands the best chance of being legalized is marijuana. It appears to be the least physically harmful of the recreational drugs and is advocated by some to be useful as a medicine. Several states, including California and Arizona, have passed laws making marijuana legal under a doctor's prescription for the treatment of some conditions such as the nausea associated with chemotherapy. The penalties for possession of marijuana vary widely from state to state (see Table 15.2). Although federal law supercedes the state laws at the present time, this issue continues to be debated. However, it is a big leap from medical marijuana to the legalization of the recreational use of marijuana. Some issues make complete legalization problematic, not the least of which is how it would be regulated. Because marijuana is grown in every state and can be grown indoors as well, it would be very difficult for the government to control its production and sale. Especially problematic would be the prospect of the government levying some sort of sales tax on marijuana that could be used to offset whatever social problems increased marijuana use might produce. One possibility would be for marijuana to be sold and taxed as are cigarettes. Presumably, individuals would be willing to pay the price for marijuana that has a consistent dose, is packaged in a safe way, and can be obtained legally.
- **Other drugs could be legalized with more stringent regulation.** For instance, heroin or cocaine could be controlled by the medical profession and given to people who had a legitimate need. If completely legalized, these drugs could be dispensed with the requirement that users be monitored and treated to control their addictions. Although the pressure to legalize these harder drugs is minimal, some claim that people should be free to use them as long as their drug use does not hurt others.
- **Drug legalization may reduce crime.** Those who are under the influence of drugs may continue to commit certain crimes as a result of their intoxication, but the

TABLE 15.2

Penalties in Selected States for Possession of Marijuana, 2003

State	Amount	Charge	Incarceration	Fine
California	28.5 g or less	Misdemeanor	None	$100
	Over 28.5 g	Misdemeanor	6 months	$500
	28.5 g or less on school grounds while school is open	Misdemeanor	10 days	$500
	Over 28.5 g on school grounds while school is open	Misdemeanor	6 months	$500
D.C.	Any amount	Misdemeanor	6 months	$1,000
Florida	20 g or less	Misdemeanor	1 year	$1,000
	Over 20 g	Felony	5 years	$5,000
Illinois	2.5 g or less	Misdemeanor	30 days	$1,500
	2.5–10 g	Misdemeanor	6 months	$1,500
	10–30 g	Misdemeanor	1 year	$2,500
	30–500 g	Felony	First offense 1–3 years; subsequent 2–5 years	$25,000
	500–2,000 g	Felony	2–5 years	$25,000
	2,000–5,000 g	Felony	3–7 years	$25,000
	Over 5,000 g	Felony	4–15 years	$25,000
Maine	Usable amount w/ proof of doctor's recommendation	None	None	None
	Less than 1.25 oz	Civil violation	None	$200–$400
	Over 1.25 oz	Misdemeanor	1 year	$2,000
Maryland	Any amount	Misdemeanor	1 year	$1,000
New York	25 g or less (first offense)	Civil citation	None	$100
	25 g or less (second offense)	Civil citation	None	$200
	25 g or less (subsequent offense)	Misdemeanor	15 days	$250
	25 g–2 oz	Misdemeanor	3 months	$500
	2–8 oz	Misdemeanor	1 year	$1,000
	8–16 oz	Felony	4 years	$5,000
	16 oz–10 lb	Felony	7 years	$5,000
	Over 10 lb	Felony	15 years	$5,000
Texas	2 oz or less	Misdemeanor	180 days	$2,000
	2–4 oz	Misdemeanor	1 year	$4,000
	4 oz–5 lb	Misdemeanor or Felony	180 days–2 years	$10,000
	5–50 lb	Felony	2–10 years	$10,000
	50–2,000 lb	Felony	2–20 years	$10,000
	Over 2,000 lb	Felony	5–99 years	$50,000

Source: California Health and Safety Code, sec. 11357-11362.9; D.C. Codes 48-904.01; Florida State Code, Title XLVI, sec. 893.13; Illinois Compiled Statutes, chpt. 720/550, sec. 4; Maine Revised Statutes, Title 22, chpt. 558, sec. 2383; Maryland Code, Title 5, sec. 601; New York State Consolidated Laws, sec. 221; Texas Statutes, chpt. 481.

crime associated with the drug trade would be eliminated because dealers would no longer be fighting over territory, and interactions between buyers and sellers would be routinized. Additionally, with the price of drugs lowered because of legalization, users would not have to rob and steal to maintain their drug habits.

- **Drug legalization may have a positive impact on the criminal justice system.** With the burden of enforcing unpopular drug laws lifted from the system's mandate, the police would be able to focus their resources on violent crime. Another expected benefit would be the reduced opportunities for corruption of criminal justice personnel with the vast amounts of money generated by the illegal drug trade.
- **Legal drugs may be more difficult for juveniles to obtain.** Presently, many juveniles are recruited into the drug trade because the juvenile justice system treats offenders more leniently than the criminal justice system. In many communities today, underage youth find obtaining marijuana easier than buying beer. Effective regulation may be a better way to separate juveniles and drugs than prohibition.
- **Respect for the law may be increased with the legalization of drugs.** Presently, thousands of people use illegal drugs in a manner that does not harm others and allows them to pursue their careers and family life without problems. The "social users" of recreational drugs develop cynical attitudes toward the criminal justice system and government in general because of the risks they must take to engage in what they believe is private behavior.

Of course, legalizing drugs would certainly have a downside. Depending on which drugs are legalized and how they are regulated, increased drug use would likely result in threats to public safety, loss of productivity, and accidental overdose cases. These are debatable concerns, but all are beyond the scope of this discussion. However, it is important to note that the harms associated with keeping drugs illegal are also of concern, and a public debate about our drug laws could be healthy for society. James

CASE IN POINT

United States v. Oakland Cannabis Buyers' Cooperative et al.

The Case

United States v. Oakland Cannabis Buyers' Cooperative et al., 000 U.S. 00-151 (2001)

The Point

The distribution of marijuana, even for medical purposes and with approval by a state's citizens, is prohibited under the Controlled Substances Act.

In 1996 voters in California approved Proposition 215, the Compassionate Use Act. The act legalized the medical use of marijuana in California for seriously ill patients who provided a doctor's recommendation. The Oakland Cannabis Buyers' Cooperative distributed marijuana to people who qualified under Prop. 215. The United States sued to stop the cooperative's activities under the Controlled Substances Act, which prohibits the distribution, manufacture, and possession with intent to distribute a controlled substance.

The district court ordered the cooperative to cease its activities and rejected its arguments of the necessity of medical marijuana. The Ninth Circuit court reversed and remanded this ruling on appeal. The case then went to the U.S. Supreme Court, which, in turn, reversed and remanded the Ninth Circuit's decision. The Court ruled in part that, "There is no medical necessity exception to the Controlled Substances Act's prohibitions on manufacturing and distributing marijuana."

The Oakland Cannabis Buyers' Cooperative is currently enjoined from dispensing medical marijuana.

Q. Wilson is one noted criminologist who argues that legalizing drugs would not accomplish all the benefits of reduced violent crime that its proponents commonly claim. Furthermore, Wilson suggested that other consequences to legalization should be considered before drug policies and laws are altered. He suggested that the number of addicts who no longer have to steal to pay black market prices for drugs would be offset by the possible increase in the total number of addicts. Because these addicts would be difficult to employ, they would still have to resort to stealing to support themselves.[41]

DECRIMINALIZATION. In the current political atmosphere, the prospect for the legalization of drugs, even marijuana, seems dim. However, another strategy could serve as a compromise between the demonization of drug use and the war on drugs. **Decriminalization** of drugs would greatly reduce the penalties for drug use. For instance, possession of small amounts of marijuana is a misdemeanor in many jurisdictions, whereas selling larger amounts remains a felony. Many consider it a waste of expensive resources to incarcerate the occasional marijuana user who is better handled by fines, probation, and community service sentencing options.[42]

decriminalization
The emendation of laws or statutes to lessen or remove penalties for specific acts subject to criminal prosecution, arrest, and imprisonment.

Decriminalization allows the criminal justice system to escape the expense of enforcing stringent drug laws and allows other institutions to help deter drug use. Schools, the workplace, and recreational programs can still prohibit drug use even though the criminal justice system no longer wages a full-scale drug war. Those who are employed in good jobs have much to lose from even a misdemeanor conviction if they work in a drug-free workplace that has the option of firing employees who consume illegal drugs. Decriminalization makes a certain amount of sense for the criminal justice system, which would be relieved of spending large amounts of money, personnel, and other resources on a drug war but at the same time need not completely surrender the moral high ground of combating drugs.[43] Decriminalization allows society to discourage illegal drug use without having to attempt to stamp it out completely.

The Police and Drugs

Until such time that U.S. policies on legalization or decriminalization of drugs change, the police will be required to deal with the laws and realities that shape the contemporary drug scene. (For arrest trends by drug type, see Figure 15.1.) This mandate for law

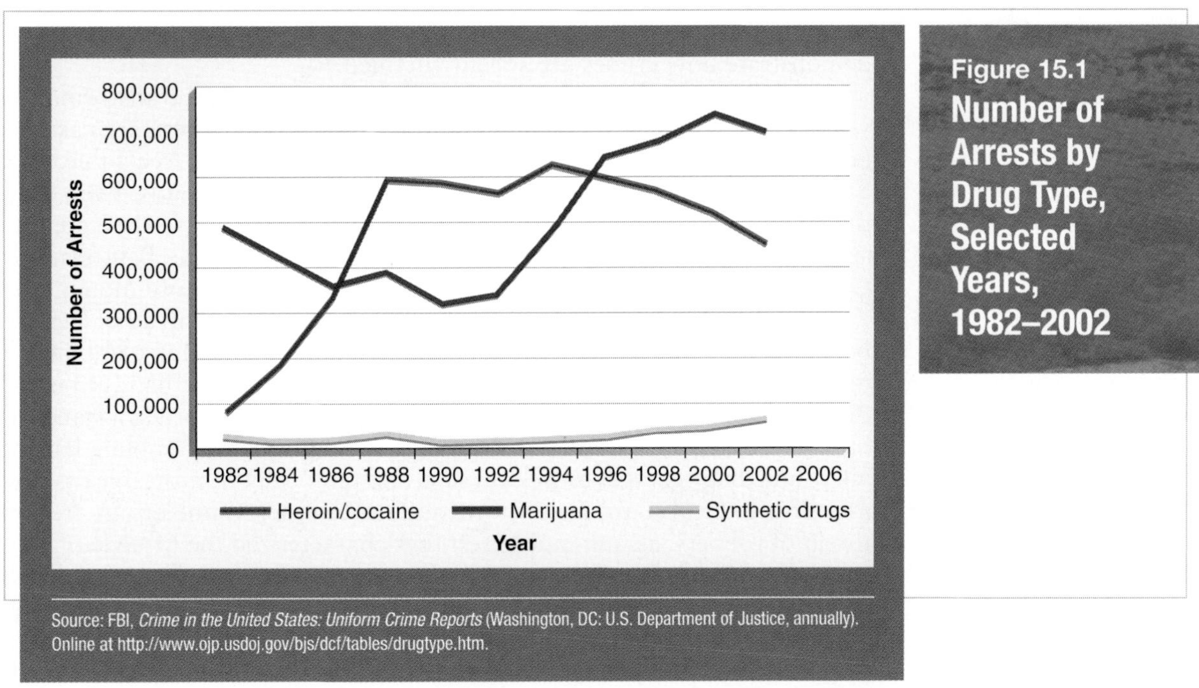

Figure 15.1 Number of Arrests by Drug Type, Selected Years, 1982–2002

Source: FBI, *Crime in the United States: Uniform Crime Reports* (Washington, DC: U.S. Department of Justice, annually). Online at http://www.ojp.usdoj.gov/bjs/dcf/tables/drugtype.htm.

enforcement is crucial in many respects because it requires the police to pursue numerous goals in controlling illegal drugs, including the following:

- Addressing the violence associated with street-level drug dealing (in many respects, pursuing this goal means dealing with gangs and preventing the emergence of powerful organized criminal groups)
- Controlling the crimes of drug users
- Addressing the health, economic, and social well-being of drug users
- Restoring the quality of life in urban communities by ending street-level dealing
- Providing programs to help keep juveniles from experimenting with drugs
- Dealing with the problems inherent with the large amount of money in the illegal drug trade, such as police corruption and the integrity of the criminal justice system[44]

These goals require that law enforcement agencies fundamentally change their structure, training, recruitment, and allocation of resources. The issues of dealing with illegal drugs mean establishing narcotics bureaus, employing community cooperation, targeting politically sensitive neighborhoods or subcultures, and convincing the citizenry that law enforcement is walking the fine line of combating drugs without violating the legal and civil rights of drug users.[45] It is probably unrealistic to expect law enforcement agencies to fulfill all of these goals alone. Other institutions such as schools, families, and human service agencies must also do their part in discouraging drug use. Unfortunately, law enforcement must deal with the problems of illegal drugs after other institutions have failed.

Gambling

Much like with drug use, Americans have ambivalent attitudes toward gambling. In a very strict and limited sense, gambling can be considered a consensual and victimless activity; however, many segments of society question the economic, moral, and social ramifications of gambling. What is particularly interesting about gambling today is the fact that our attitudes, laws, and incentives to gamble are in a state of flux.[46] Legalized gambling has spread across the country as state and local governments have tried to capitalize on the public's desire to risk a little to gain a lot even though the odds are astronomically against them. For the criminal justice system, gambling, whether legal or illegal, has important ramifications; its inclusion as a topic of interest here serves to demonstrate how crimes are socially defined.[47]

Gambling in the United States has undergone a radical transformation in the past 30 years. Once confined to Nevada and New Jersey, now there are casinos in many states and more ambiguous locations such as rivers and offshore (see Table 15.3). Additionally, a number of American Indian reservations have built casinos. Even more illustrative of the changing attitudes toward gambling in this country is the spread of government-sponsored lotteries. Even in the southern loop of the Bible Belt, states such as Florida, Georgia, and South Carolina have instituted lotteries to raise money.[48]

From the perspective of the criminal justice system, the spread of legalized gambling can be viewed as a double-edged sword. On one hand, by making gambling legal, the government has taken the management of the enterprise out of the hands of organized crime and provided a level of regulation that ensures gamblers are afforded a standard of fairness and honesty in the administration of the games. Additionally, gambling has moved from back alleys and dingy garages to well-lit, safe, and physically comfortable casinos and riverboats, as well as to local convenience stores and the Internet. Gamblers are free from the constant threat of robbery, assault, and arrest that characterized the lifestyle of illegal gambling. In short, gambling has become a much safer activity since it has been legalized, and thousands of people incorporate it into their vacations and recreational pursuits.

Gambling remains problematic for the criminal justice system in other respects, with illegal gambling requiring the attention of criminal justice agencies. Betting on sporting

TABLE 15.3

Types of Legalized Gambling

State	Charitable Bingo	Card Room Gaming	Casino Gaming	Indian Gaming	Lotteries	Pari-Mutuels	Other
Alabama	I			I		I	
Alaska	I						I
Arizona	I	I		I	I	I	I
Arkansas						I	
California	I	I	I	I	I	I	I
Colorado	I	I	I	I	I	I	I
Connecticut	I	I		I	I	I	I
Delaware	I		I		I	I	I
District of Columbia	I				I		I
Florida	I	I	I	I	I	I	I
Georgia	I		I		I		I
Hawaii							
Idaho	I			I	I	I	I
Illinois	I	I	I		I	I	I
Indiana	I	I	I		I	I	I
Iowa	I	I	I	I	I	I	I
Kansas	I		I	I	I	I	I
Kentucky	I				I	I	
Louisiana	I	I	I	I	I	I	I
Maine	I	I	I		I	I	I
Maryland	I				I	I	I
Massachusetts	I		I		I	I	I
Michigan	I	I	I	I	I	I	I
Minnesota	I	I	I	I	I	I	I
Mississippi	I	I	I	I			I
Missouri	I	I	I	I	I	I	I
Montana	I	I	I	I	I	I	I
Nebraska	I			I	I	I	I
Nevada	I	I	I	I		I	I
New Hampshire	I				I	I	I
New Jersey	I	I	I		I	I	I
New Mexico	I			I	I	I	I
New York	I		I	I	I	I	I
North Carolina	I			I			
North Dakota	I	I	I	I	I	I	I
Ohio	I				I	I	I
Oklahoma	I			I		I	
Oregon	I	I		I	I	I	I

continued

TABLE 15.3 (continued)

State	Charitable Bingo	Card Room Gaming	Casino Gaming	Indian Gaming	Lotteries	Pari-Mutuels	Other
Pennsylvania	I				I	I	
Rhode Island	I		I	I	I	I	I
South Carolina	I		I	I	I		
South Dakota	I	I	I	I	I	I	I
Tennessee					I	I	
Texas	I		I	I	I	I	I
Utah							
Vermont	I				I	I	I
Virginia	I				I	I	I
Washington	I	I	I	I	I	I	I
West Virginia	I				I	I	I
Wisconsin	I			I	I	I	I
Wyoming	I			I		I	I

Source: Compiled and adapted from U.S. General Accounting Office, *Money Laundering: Rapid Growth of Casinos Makes Them Vulnerable* (Washington, DC: GAO, 1996), 38. Online at http://www.gao.gov/archive/1996/gg96028.pdf.

Many states that once prohibited gambling have instituted lotteries to produce income for the state.
Courtesy of CORBIS-NY.

events; illegal gambling on the Internet; and privately run video poker games, numbers-running, and cock or dog fighting still exist in many parts of the country. Legalized gambling also brings some concerns to the criminal justice system. Although casinos may be well lit and have their own security, the surrounding area can be risky. According to Robert Goodman's *The Luck Business: The Devastating Consequences and Broken Promises of America's Gambling Explosion,* the neighborhoods in which casinos are located experience negative effects in terms of lower property values and urban decay. Along with the casinos come pawnshops, used car lots, bars, and other businesses that drive down property values and drive out the residents of previously stable communities.[49]

TABLE 15.4

Diagnostic Criteria for Pathological Gambling

Diagnostic Criteria	Behavior Patterns
Preoccupation	Is preoccupied with gambling (e.g., preoccupied with reliving past gambling experiences, handicapping or planning the next venture, or thinking of ways to get money with which to gamble)
Tolerance	Needs to gamble with increasing amounts of money to achieve the desired excitement
Withdrawal	Is restless or irritable when attempting to cut down or stop gambling
Escape	Gambles as a way of escaping from problems or relieving dysphoric mood (e.g., feelings of helplessness, guilt, anxiety, or depression)
Chasing	After losing money gambling, often returns another day to get even ("chasing one's losses")
Lying	Lies to family members, therapists, or others to conceal the extent of involvement with gambling
Loss of control	Has made repeated unsuccessful efforts to control, cut back, or stop gambling
Illegal acts	Has committed illegal acts (e.g., forgery, fraud, theft, or embezzlement) to finance gambling
Risked significant relationship	Has jeopardized or lost a significant relationship, job, or educational or career opportunity because of gambling
Bailout	Has relied on others to provide money to relieve a desperate financial situation caused by gambling

Source: National Gambling Impact Study Commission final report, June 1999, and American Psychiatric Association information in *Impact of Gambling: Economic Effects More Measurable than Social Effects,* United States General Accounting Office (Washington, DC: GAO, 2000), 43. Online at http://www.gao.gov/new.items/gg00078.pdf.

Perhaps the most distressing unintended consequence of legalized gambling is the increase in the number of gamblers who become addicted to the activity (see Table 15.4) and continue to gamble with money they cannot afford to lose. Problem gamblers present a number of concerns for the criminal justice system as well as society. According to Goodman, the debts of problem gamblers affect the public as a whole because these gamblers have no money to pay their bills, taxes, or other debts, and often declare bankruptcy. Other gamblers, to get the money they owe, commit crimes such as writing bad checks, fraud, embezzlement, drug dealing, and stealing.[50]

According to the Council on Compulsive Gambling of New Jersey, compulsive gamblers accrue a high level of debt with the average being around $40,000. One estimate of insurance-related fraud that could be linked to compulsive gambling was estimated at $1.3 billion a year. Additionally, those who experience problems controlling their gambling debts are reported to have a suicide rate 5 to 10 times higher than the rest of the population.[51]

An emerging issue with gambling has been the explosion of Internet sites that allow one to wager money on a wide range of activities. Many of these sites are offshore; the globalization of the Internet allows people to connect to servers in locations as far flung as the Caribbean islands, the Isle of Man, and sites in Asia. Because these offshore gambling sites are not regulated by the U.S. government, there is no way to ensure their credibility or for the U.S. government to collect taxes. For these reasons, legislation is being crafted to prohibit

! NEWS FLASH

Gambling in Your Pajamas

Until the mid-1990s, U.S. state and federal governments seemed to have gambling under control. Different forms of gambling, from casinos to lotteries, were legal in different states, and the illegal forms were relatively easy to police.

That changed once the Internet became a household service and gambling went online. Now bets on just about anything can be placed anytime from anywhere, regardless of state or federal laws. The Department of Justice says online gambling is already prohibited by the 1961 Wire Communications Act, but that law targets bookmakers, not those who place bets. Internet gambling sites have gotten around this law by locating their operations offshore, such as in the Caribbean.

According to a report in *The Tennessean,* the Interactive Gaming Council, an online gaming advocacy group, states that Internet gambling earned $1.3 billion in revenue in 2002.

As governments struggle to deal with Internet gambling, some credit card companies are already refusing some gambling transactions. One House of Representatives bill would make wagering via credit cards, checks, or other banking methods illegal. For now, the Internet gambling frontier is wide open, with no way to police the sites or gamblers. Gambling sites say they are just providing a desired service, and critics say it will simply worsen the situations of problem gamblers. Moral and mental health considerations aside, perhaps what is most upsetting to state and federal governments is their current inability to tax online gambling. Thanks to Internet gambling, dollars flow back and forth across U.S. borders and, for now, there is not much Uncle Sam can do about it.

Source: Paul Kuharsky, "Online's a Gamble: Placing Bet on Web Easy, but Can Be Addictive," *The Tennessean,* December 26, 2003, http://www.tennessean.com/sports/localsports/archives/03/12/44590693.shtml?Element_ID=44590693.

Internet gambling. For instance, the Unlawful Internet Gambling Funding Prohibition Act would make it illegal for credit card companies and other financial institutions to cooperate with offshore gambling sites by enabling the transfer of money. The impact of these coming laws is already being felt. Citibank, Bank of America, Fleet, and Chase Manhattan are some of the major credit card providers that prohibit the use of their services for betting online. E-Bay, which acquired the Internet payment company PayPal, made the banning of gambling transactions one of the terms of its purchase.[52]

Technology in gambling presents new challenges to law enforcement efforts to control the industry. With shifting attitudes toward the morality of gambling, the criminal justice system's philosophy in addressing the issue has changed from one of keeping people from harming themselves by engaging in immoral activities to one of making sure that the government gets its taxes from the gambling economy. As gambling quickly changes from a public moral issue to an economic one, the criminal justice system is being forced to modify its response. Like drug use, gambling has become a moving target for the criminal justice system. Society's attitudes change, new laws are enacted, and new technologies are introduced that alter the way the criminal justice system must respond. Overall, some positive features have accrued with the move to legalize gambling in so many states. The underworld crime and corruption generally associated with the gaming industry has been replaced by corporations that integrate gambling with hotel and entertainment concerns and provide a relatively regulated, safe, and fair product.[53]

However, even as legalized gambling has relieved the criminal justice system of some problems, it has created or exacerbated others. Robert Goodman argued that legalized gambling did not simply give those who already gambled a legitimate place to safely conduct their activities, but rather created a whole new class of gambler. In fact, governments are spending a good deal of money on promotional materials and commercials to keep gamblers interested in gaming products. Rather than protecting citizens from gambling op-

Las Vegas once was the only state in which casino gambling was legal. Today, many states offer casino gambling and other forms of wagering.
Courtesy of CORBIS-NY.

erators who might take advantage of them, the government now has a vested interest in encouraging gambling to fill the public coffers. One result of this move to promote gambling has been the trend of individuals in the lower economic brackets to use gambling as an investment rather than entertainment. Poor people spend a higher percentage of their income on gambling than do those in the middle class. The ultimate result of such patterns is a transfer of wealth from the pockets of the poor to the government.[54] In states such as Georgia, where the lottery pays for college tuition though a cleverly titled program called the Hope Scholarship, poor families are paying the college tuition for middle-class families.[55]

Sex Work

In addition to controlling illegal drug use and gambling, the criminal justice system has a mandate to enforce laws that regulate sexuality. Although most Americans would agree with the principle that the government should not be concerned with the private behavior of consenting adults, the criminal justice system still must deal with a number of behaviors that society has deemed problematic. When sexual activity is exploitive or harmful, or when sex is used as a commodity and is bought and sold, the government has a legitimate obligation and appropriate authority to intervene. We may quibble about the exact role of the government, but there is a long and well-established history of restricting sexual activity. The remainder of this chapter will review three types of sexual behaviors that are currently being contested in American society and the way the criminal justice system responds to them.[56] These crimes all revolve around the concept of selling sex. In part, they are crimes of values, and in part they are economic crimes that are committed without the government being able to set standards, regulate access, and/or impose taxes. These issues—prostitution, pornography, and exotic dancing—are termed "nuisance" sex crimes and illustrate the ambivalence on the part of society and the criminal justice system. Other serious sex crimes such as rape, child molestation, and sex-related homicide are beyond the scope of this chapter. There is little or no difference of opinion on whether society should condone or prohibit these behaviors.[57]

Prostitution

Prostitution is the practice of engaging in sexual activity in exchange for money. Although the popular concept of prostitution is that of a female prostitute and a male customer, other variations are common. Prostitution is illegal in just about every jurisdiction in United States, with the most well-known exception being Nevada, which has state-licensed

FOCUS ON ETHICS

Rolling the Dice

You are a state representative. The northeastern area of the state where your hometown is located lost its manufacturing base in the late 1980s, affecting almost everyone you know. Your friends' parents lost their jobs, and after high school, most of your friends had to leave to find work. The big textile mills moved to other countries, devastating your hometown. For the past 20 years, the town has limped along on the revenues produced by a few small businesses and fast-food outlets near the freeway.

However, things are beginning to change. Your town is only 50 miles from one of the fastest growing cities in the nation, and the city's growth is spreading toward your hometown. Even though the townsfolk never really recovered from the loss of their jobs, at least their local taxes remained low. Now, developers are plunking in high-priced subdivisions to attract people who are tired of living in the city but still work there. As a result, the cost of living in your hometown is rising quickly without new jobs. Everyone is unhappy, and the old-timers' bitterness toward the new developments and rich new neighbors is palpable.

One morning, your grandfather, who made his first million selling real estate in the county, calls you with an idea. He wants to help bring in a casino. He says it will bring money to the area through tourism and provide jobs for the locals. Casinos are not legal in your state, and he is pressuring you to sponsor legislation that will legalize casino gambling, including card rooms, slot machines, and table games. Your mother, on the other hand, is against casinos. As a paralegal, she has dealt with more than a few divorces and bankruptcies caused by gambling addictions. She is convinced that casino gambling will not only exacerbate those problems, but also bring corruption and crime to your vulnerable little town. You also know that bringing in a casino will mean that the county would have to rewrite or dispose of most of its alcohol restrictions, something that several large, influential local churches oppose. You point out to your grandfather that casino gambling is not an economic cure-all and refer him to several moribund racetracks in the next state and a struggling new lottery in another nearby state. He replies that casino gambling has done wonders for places like Branson, Missouri, and you have to agree.

Your town sorely needs jobs, and although the new housing developments have created a few, it is mostly minimum wage work at a couple of new gas stations. The commuters who live in the new developments spend most of their money in the city, not in your hometown.

WHAT DO YOU DO?

1. Tell your grandfather that you will give his plan some thought but in the meantime hope that the city's rapid economic development will eventually spread to your hometown and bring some new jobs with it.
2. Study statistics on gambling addiction and crime and tell your grandfather that you will not support casino gambling.
3. Agree with your grandfather and start pushing for laws that will allow casinos. You believe a slight rise in crime is natural in a developing area and that the increased revenues and jobs will offset any social problems.

brothels.[58] Estimating the scope of the practice of prostitution is difficult. Official arrest records show that in 2002 over 79,000 people were arrested for prostitution and commercialized vice, but this represents only a fraction of those who engage in the practice.[59] Because prostitution is essentially a consensual activity, there is no victim to alert law enforcement. Most of the arrests for prostitution are a result of proactive police stings in which law enforcement officers pose as prostitutes or customers and arrest those who express a desire to engage in the activity.[60]

Not all prostitutes are equally problematic for the criminal justice system. A hierarchy of prostitution reflects both an economic and social dimension, as well as a public safety

Prostitution is often called a victimless crime because it involves consensual behavior. However, prostitution can produce victims when juveniles are involved or when prostitutes are exploited by pimps.
Courtesy of CORBIS-NY.

dimension, to the practice of selling sex. According to N. Jane McCandless, prostitution has a four-level occupational hierarchy.[61]

1. **Call girl or male escort.** At the top of the hierarchy is the call girl or male escort who works for an escort service. These women and men command high fees, up to hundreds of dollars a night, and are able to screen their clients. Often, they have several repeat customers, and the date may include activities other than sex, such as dinner, going to plays or movies, or attending functions where presentable companions are desired. These types of prostitutes are often indistinguishable from a regular date. Occasionally, a male or female prostitute may find a rich customer who is willing to pay for exclusive access and will lease an apartment for him or her to live in that the customer can visit at will.
2. **Strippers and exotic dancers.** Next on the occupational hierarchy of prostitution are strippers or exotic dancers (this is not to imply that all dancers are prostitutes). These men and women—although they are usually women—may have some type of arrangement with the management of the bar that allows them to solicit customers in return for a financial kickback from the transaction. Additionally, the management will ensure that other prostitutes are not allowed to compete in the bar. These prostitutes have some discretion in which customers they choose.
3. **House girls.** House girls are prostitutes who work in brothels. Although brothels are legal only in Nevada, these institutions are common in many cities and are able to function because the criminal justice system turns a blind eye toward them. The brothels are run by a madam, and the girls get a percentage of the fee. The advantage of a brothel for a prostitute is that the madam recruits and screens the customers, provides the room for the tryst, provides a level of security and rules, and deals with law enforcement. The disadvantages for the prostitute include not being able to select the customer, having to give up a sizable percentage to the madam, and being told when to work and how many customers per night to see.
4. **Streetwalkers.** At the lowest end of the spectrum are "streetwalkers." These women and men publicly solicit customers on street corners, in parks, and outside bars or hotels. They command the least payment and cannot afford to be very selective in whom they choose for customers. Often they are controlled by pimps and have little control over the money they earn. Among their greatest concerns are their exposures to law enforcement officers who will continually arrest them and their customers, thus upsetting their businesses. More important, streetwalkers are at high risk for sexually transmitted disease, physical violence from customers, and abuse from pimps.

According to McCandless, a new and even lower level of prostitute works in crack houses and trades sex for drugs. This prostitute's primary goal is to stay intoxicated. While under the influence of crack, she will be extremely promiscuous in her choice of

NEWS FLASH

Police Target "Houses of Ill-Repute"

Prostitution is legal in the state of Nevada. In every other state, prostitution is a crime. Although police probably do not pursue prostitutes as fervently as they do murderers, rapists, and high-volume drug dealers, they do launch the occasional sting. These stings, even the most successful, rarely make the national headlines. For instance, in Arizona in November 2003, the Maricopa County Sheriff's Office conducted a raid that netted 45 female prostitutes and 27 male customers.

Called Operation House Call and Operation Destiny, the raids targeted not streetwalkers, but "houses of prostitution" and massage parlors. That is, the prostitutes ran their businesses out of their homes and attracted customers through advertising. The raids combed through 30 neighborhoods. In defending the sting to reporters, Sheriff Joe Arpaio said, "If you're going to have a law on the books, enforce the law." He also said that prostitution was far from being a victimless crime because it spread diseases, crime, guns, drugs, and domestic violence. To fund the sting, police used $12,000 in seized drug funds, but came away with $36,000 found in the prostitutes' homes and massage parlors.

Source: Patricia Biggs and Emily Bittner, "Prostitution Sting Nabs 72," *The Arizona Republic,* November 14, 2003, http://www.azcentral.com/php-bin/clicktrack/print.php?referer=http://www.azcentral.com/news/articles/1114raid.html

Prostitution is legal in certain parts of Nevada. However, the state has a problem with unlicensed prostitutes who work off the street in Las Vegas. Here, a prostitute works out of a state-approved brothel.
Courtesy of CORBIS-NY.

sex partners, sloppy in practicing safe sexual techniques, and likely to be the victim of rape and physical violence.

When discussing the public's ambivalence concerning prostitution, we must be careful to specify which of these strata we are considering. Many individuals consider any type of sex-for-money transaction to be morally wrong, but others are more tolerant of what consenting adults do in private. At the lower end of the prostitution hierarchy, however, are some public safety concerns that fall under the mandate of the criminal justice system.[62] Many times, the act of prostitution is not a consensual one, and the prostitute is forced by pimps, boyfriends, or organized crime to act against her or his will. On the global level young women and men are smuggled into the prostitution trade. Additionally, sex tourism has become a multi-million-dollar business in which some travel agencies sponsor tours to impoverished countries so that the tourist may engage in sex with extremely young girls or boys.[63] Many distressing issues clearly surround the practice of prostitution. Like drugs and gambling, prostitution resists efforts to suppress it. Is there another way to reduce the social harm caused by prostitution?

Thus far, we have reviewed the not-so-successful attempts to legalize drugs and the largely successful moves to legalize gambling. In that vein, a small constituency would like to see prostitution legalized. At present, the laws prohibiting prostitution seem to be ineffective, invite selective enforcement, and push the practice into the shadows where regulation is impossible and exploitation inevitable. Those who advocate the legalization or decriminalization of prostitution suggest the following benefits:

- **Women would have control over their own sexuality.** They would not be under the control of pimps or madams who take a large percentage of their earnings. They would be allowed to work out of their own homes without worrying about the police arresting them.
- **Customers would be able to find sex without worrying for their physical safety.** Sex would simply be another commodity that could be found through advertising, and the customer would not need to cruise through unsafe areas looking for sex.
- **Prostitutes could be licensed and checked for sexually transmitted diseases.** Public health could be improved by addressing the problems of unsafe sex, intravenous drug use, and violence, variables that are not measured when prostitution is illegal.
- **The government would collect taxes from legal prostitution and use that money to address the consequences that legal prostitution might bring.** Additionally, prostitutes could develop employment benefits such as unions, pension plans, health insurance, and lobbyists so that their concerns could be discussed in the open.
- **The profession would be destigmatized.** Prostitutes would be able to receive loans to finance their businesses, be able to advertise, and be free from extortion by public officials.[64]

Whether the legalization of prostitution in the United States would provide these benefits and whether either society or prostitutes would be better off with such a change is an open question. It should be noted, however, that prostitution is legal in many countries and subject to a wide variety of laws and regulatory practices. Rather than venture an opinion here, we simply suggest that, much like the case with drugs and gambling, the sale of sexual behavior is contested in our society. Additionally, prostitution continues to be a concern for the criminal justice system, and because its elimination is unlikely, selective and uneven enforcement of prostitution laws will continue to affect those with the least power in society, particularly women.

Although we typically think of prostitutes as female, some are male. These activities are almost exclusively same-sex transactions and are predominately at the lower end of the occupational hierarchy. In *The Times Square Hustler: Male Prostitution in New York City*, Robert McNamara detailed the lives of a cohort of young male prostitutes. McNamara described how these street hustlers reached a working relationship with law enforcement officers in which the officers would tell the youths to "get lost," "move it," and "hit the road." The youths would move a short distance away and then continue their hustling activities. The officers and the youths each realized that the other had a job to do and cooperated in allowing each other to pursue their occupations. The youths were respectful of officers and moved when told. The officers kept the youths from loitering in one place for too long, but did not actually make arrests, write citations, or hassle the youths too

CASE IN POINT

Nye County v. Plankinton

The Case

Nye County v. Plankinton, 94 Nev. 739, 587 P.2d 421 (1978)

The Point

This Nevada Supreme Court case demonstrates the continuing debate over the legalization of sex work in the only state where sex work is legal. It also demonstrates the movement of a controversial activity from extralegal toleration into a state's legal code.

In 1977 officials of Nye County, Nevada, tried to close a brothel, Chicken Ranch, on the basis that it constituted a public nuisance. During this period, brothels in the county—where several were already operating—were not required to be licensed. The owner of Chicken Ranch, Walter Plankinton, sued, pointing to a 1971 law prohibiting the legalization of prostitution in counties with a population above a specified limit. According to Plankinton, this law, NRS 244.345, implicitly negated the assertion that brothels are public nuisances per se. The Nevada Supreme Court agreed, and Chicken Ranch continues to operate.

much as long as they showed respect to the police officers. This accommodation is important to the appreciation of law enforcement's attitude toward sex work, as well as gambling and drug use. Certain levels of deviance are tolerated as long as the authority of the police is not directly challenged and as long as the behavior remains consensual and not exploitive.[65]

One interesting finding in McNamara's study concerned how the street hustlers viewed their sexuality. Although they engaged in homosexual activity to support themselves, most of these youths did not consider themselves to be homosexual. The viewed their behavior as "just a job" and seemed able to compartmentalize their feelings and self-concepts. Many of these youths had girlfriends, or even wives and children, and were committed to heterosexual relationships away from work.

Strippers and Exotic Dancers

Stripping and exotic dancing are other forms of sex work that operate within the purview of the criminal justice system. These activities are bound by varying sets of rules and regulations that span legal jurisdictions. Many communities pass laws that forbid establishments from offering exotic dance as entertainment, but other communities, typically ones that want to attract business conventions, permit strip clubs. For law enforcement agencies, these establishments often mean an increase in drug sales, prostitution, drunken assaults, and muggings. The activities inside the strip clubs are also monitored to ensure that the fine points of the laws, such as no touching with the hands during a lap dance, are observed.[66]

Although some strippers use exotic dancing as a way to recruit clients for prostitution, many do not engage in prostitution at all. Most strippers find that they can earn a man's (the clients are predominantly male) money without actually engaging in sex. Researchers have used the term 'counterfeit intimacy' to describe how exotic dancers provide a facsimile of sex without actually touching, caring about, or meeting the desires of strip club customers. This can cause problems when drunken clients believe they have paid a lot of money and have received "only the sizzle and not the steak."[67]

Pornography

Pornography is another form of sex work that has implications for the criminal justice system. Two issues concerning pornography are the most problematic for some people. The first concern comes from those who find pictures or descriptions of nakedness and sexual

Some jurisdictions allow strip clubs, but many do not.
Courtesy of Mark Peterson, CORBIS-NY.

activity to be immoral. Although public fashions change and partial nakedness is deemed appropriate according to context (i.e., bikinis at the beach or dresses on prom night), some individuals are offended by what appears regularly on television, in motion pictures, and in the print media. What passes as popular culture in the 21st century is considered lewd and vulgar by some. There is more consensus about what is offensive when certain "adult" magazines are considered and even more agreement regarding the content of hard-core pornographic movies. A continuum of obscenity appears to exist, and individuals might have their own opinions on what should be considered objectionable. This difference of opinion will always cause tension about what is allowed in the media, and free speech rights will continue to be a contested issue in regard to pornography.

A second concern of those who object to pornography is the link between sex and violence. Some pornography is highly sexist, racist, and homophobic. For some people, the humiliation of others (particularly women and children) is stimulating. Some feminists link pornographic objectification of women with violence against women. It is true that certain strains of pornography cater to those who find pleasure in seeing other people suffer.[68] At the extreme end of the pornographic continuum is the "snuff film," the stuff of urban legends in which a victim is allegedly killed.

The tension that exists in the policing of pornography centers on the difference between erotica and obscenity. Distinctions can be made among the following:

- Violent pornography
- Nonviolent but dehumanizing pornography
- Erotica (material that is nonsexist and nonviolent)

In attempting to regulate the types of pornography and erotica available to adults, the criminal justice system walks a fine line between enforcing laws and encroaching on citizens' legal behavior. To a large degree, the exact definition of pornography is open to interpretation. In *Jacobellis v. Ohio* (1964), Justice Potter Stewart illustrated this difficulty in defining obscenity by saying only, "I know it when I see it." If we leave the interpretation of what is obscene to each individual, we cannot have workable laws governing pornography. In some way, the criminal justice system needs guidance in defining, detecting, and enforcing these activities when there is so much difference of opinion on the part of the public.

community standards
Practices, acts, and/or media accepted by a given social group who share a geographic area and/or government.

Historically, the solution to this lack of consensus has been a reliance on **community standards.** This explains why such wide variations exist across the country in what types

Legitimizing Sex Work

Values change in societies. Many forms of gambling that were once prohibited are now not only permitted, but used by the government to generate revenue. Currently, there is also a heated debate about legalizing or decriminalizing drugs. But what about sex work? Will prostitution become legalized and regulated by the government? Many people advocate such ideas. In fact, sex workers around the world are lobbying for recognition of sex work as a legitimate occupation that should be brought into mainstream society. For example, in Australia certain forms of prostitution are legal with some restrictions. In the United States a group of exotic dancers in San Francisco won the right in 1996 to unionize and negotiate with their employer. Organizations such as the Network of Sex Work Projects focus on such issues as the following:

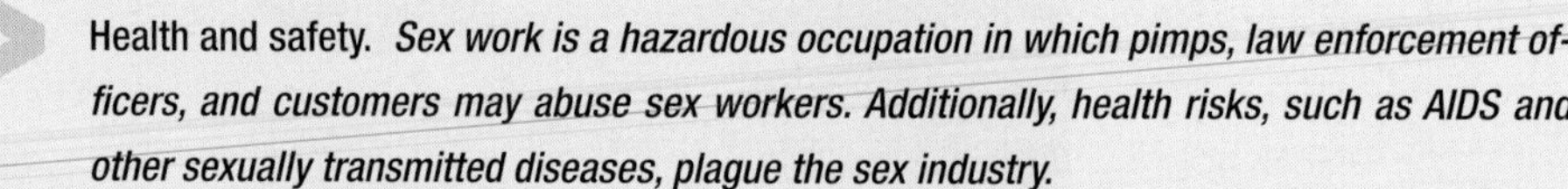

- Health and safety. *Sex work is a hazardous occupation in which pimps, law enforcement officers, and customers may abuse sex workers. Additionally, health risks, such as AIDS and other sexually transmitted diseases, plague the sex industry.*

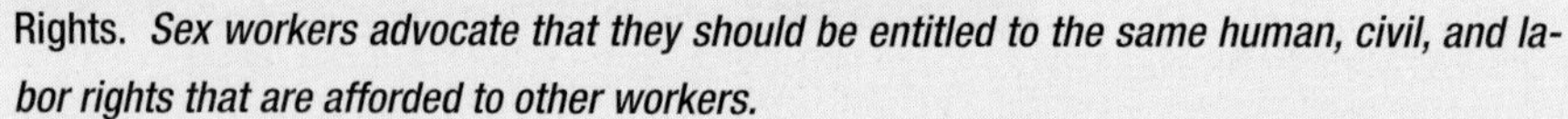

- Rights. *Sex workers advocate that they should be entitled to the same human, civil, and labor rights that are afforded to other workers.*

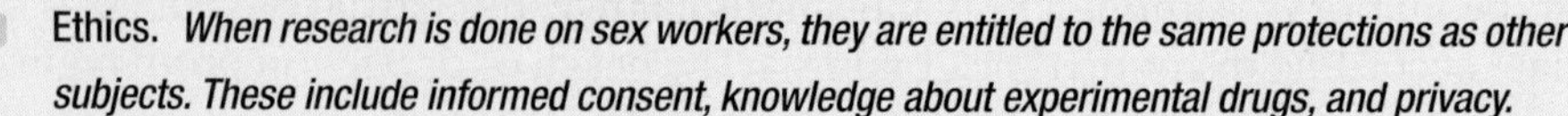

- Ethics. *When research is done on sex workers, they are entitled to the same protections as other subjects. These include informed consent, knowledge about experimental drugs, and privacy.*

Should sex workers be successful in introducing their concerns into mainstream society, many things would change. Prostitutes would be allowed to advertise their services, write legitimate business expenses off their taxes, set consistent pay rates based on objective criteria (such as amount of time or services rendered), and openly lobby legislative bodies for worker protections such as health insurance and overtime.

QUESTIONS

1. Should sex work be treated like any other occupation?
2. Are the concerns of sex workers also women's issues?
3. What do you think a feminist response would be to the proposal to legitimize sex work?
4. What unanticipated consequences might arise from such a proposal?
5. Where would the most opposition to legitimizing sex work come from? Women? Men? Religious groups? Law enforcement officials?

Source: Live Nude Girls Unite!, http://www.livenudegirlsunite.com/.

of sexually explicit material is available. When each city or small town can determine what materials can be sold in stores, then the sexual sensibilities of those residents can be respected. Sex work, such as prostitution and exotic dancing, as well as the sale of pornographic magazines, can be discouraged through arrests, fines, and the revoking of business licenses. However, in the 21st century, community standards have collided with the globalization of the media. Pornography, like many other products, is available in a variety of easily procured formats. Following are some issues the criminal justice system faces as the delivery of obscene materials matures with the overall improvement of communications:

- **Stores that sell sex.** Law enforcement has a relatively easy time dealing with business establishments that sell so-called dirty magazines or sex aids and sex toys. Local laws may require convenience stores to shield the covers of men's

CASE IN POINT

Miller v. California

The Case

Miller v. California, 413 U.S. 15 (1973)

The Point

The Supreme Court set forth a new three-part test for obscenity.

Marvin Miller sent sexually explicit advertisements for four books, *Intercourse, Man-Woman, Sex Orgies Illustrated,* and *An Illustrated History of Pornography,* and a film titled *Marital Intercourse* to addresses on a mass-mailing list. The list recipients had not specifically requested sexually explicit materials. Miller was arrested after a restaurant owner and his mother complained about receiving the advertisements in the mail. Miller was convicted under California's Obscenity Law, which made mailing obscene material a criminal offense, and his conviction was confirmed on appeal. The case went to the U.S. Supreme Court, which set forth the three-part test for obscenity that is used today:

1. Whether "the average person, applying contemporary community standards" would find that the work, taken as a whole, appeals to the prurient interest
2. Whether the work depicts or describes, in a patently offensive way, sexual conduct specifically defined by the applicable state law
3. Whether the work, taken as a whole, lacks serious literary, artistic, political, or scientific value

Two aspects of this decision are particularly important. First, it allows a jury to use community standards, not national standards, to determine obscenity. The second is that it discarded a previous requirement that obscene material be "utterly without redeeming social value" (*Memoirs v. Massachusetts,* 1966) and exchanged it for the stricter requirement that obscene material need only lack "serious literary, artistic, political, or scientific value."

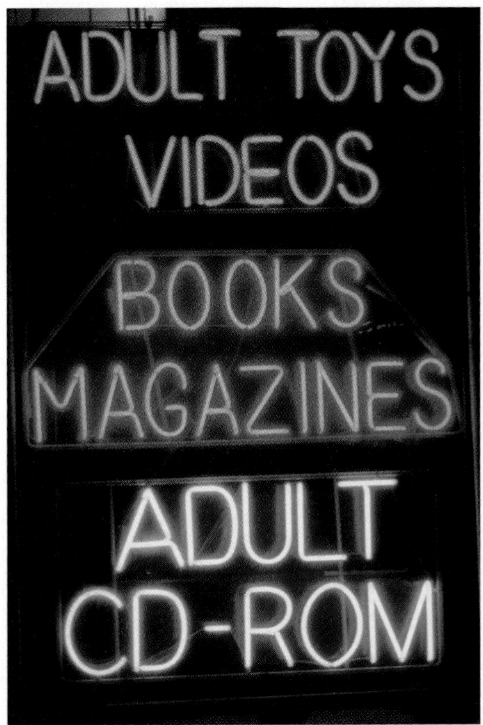

Many community members object to sex-industry advertisements. Signs like this one make the industry more high-profile than many community standards allow.

Courtesy of CORBIS-NY.

magazines, place the magazines behind the sales counter where minors cannot see them, or prohibit the sale of certain materials altogether. A visit to the store by a law enforcement officer can quickly reveal which stores are in compliance with the law and which are not. Citations can be written, arrests made, and trials held within the community. These cases can be handled without exposing the magazines' producers to state or federal courts.

- **Pornography and the mail.** Local law enforcement officials have no way of policing what is delivered to private homes in the mail. Therefore, the federal government uses the U.S. Postal Service to control some pornography. Postal inspectors investigate the illegal distribution of a wide range of products, including pornography, that is delivered via the mail. Not only can the producers and distributors of pornographic materials be arrested and fined, but so can the customers. Some people may argue that the government has no business interfering with what citizens order through the mail, but the government has a clear and compelling mandate to ensure that guns, drugs, and other items such as child pornography are not using the Postal Service to violate the law.
- **The Internet and sex.** The World Wide Web has introduced a new challenge in the law's attempt to control pornography. In what has quickly become a multimillion-dollar industry, Internet pornography is practically impossible for local law enforcement agencies to combat. They have no way of knowing if any of the citizens in their jurisdiction are actually consuming the pornography, and the producers and distributors of pornography reside in other states or countries. Although Internet filters are available for parents to control the types of sites their children can access, these filters are resisted by First Amendment advocates who believe libraries and universities should provide unfettered Internet access. The laws dealing with the Internet are evolving, and it could be several years before stable patterns of social control of online pornography emerge.[69]

Summary

The criminal justice system has a broad mandate to enforce all the laws passed by the legislature. A wide consensus exists on the desirability of most laws; however, a number of illegal behaviors do not have a strong consensus favoring their proscription. Drug use, gambling, and sex work are controversial issues because they challenge the values and religious beliefs of many people. Additionally, others see them as consensual activities that do not harm anyone other than those who choose to engage in them.

The use and trade of illegal drugs is probably the most controversial issue facing the criminal justice system today. The first popular drug in the United States was alcohol. Some groups, such as the Quakers, considered the high consumption of alcohol to be problematic, but the government intervened only to collect taxes. In the 1800s although the use of opium, morphine, and cocaine was deemed problematic, these drugs were ingredients in many patent medicines. In the 20th century, laws were passed to control these drugs. The Pure Food and Drug Act of 1906 required food and drug purveyors to label what their products contained. The 1914 Harrison Act imposed a tax on opium and cocaine. In 1919 the ratification of the Eighteenth Amendment prohibited the use and sale of alcohol. Prohibition, largely considered a failure, ended in 1933. In 1937 the government began to control the use and sale of marijuana. Although youth in the 1960s, the "baby boomers," popularized the use of illegal drugs, the 1980s brought the U.S. government's war on drugs. Some critics say this war has done more harm to society than has the use of drugs. The criminal justice system has since turned to treating drug offenders as well as punishing them. Some critics of the war on drugs suggest that taxation, decriminalization, and legalization are preferable to drug prohibition. While the war on drugs persists, law enforcement continues to pursue a variety of strategies to deal with enforcing the laws banning drugs.

Gambling, a behavior that some people find immoral, has found a place in law-abiding society. Some states and communities allow almost any form of gambling, whereas others are more restrictive. Many states operate lotteries, and casinos have also become more common. Internet-based gambling, however, has caused problems because some sites are located outside the United States, and the government cannot collect taxes or regulate it. Although many people consider gambling to be harmful, especially to those addicted to the behavior, the consumer activity it stimulates has been deemed beneficial by many communities.

The criminal justice system also enforces laws regulating sexuality. However, as with drugs, legalized prostitution has its advocates. Three types of sexual behaviors currently being contested in U.S. society involve the selling of sex: prostitution, pornography, and exotic dancing. These represent either crimes of values or economic crimes in which the government is unable to set standards, regulate access, and/or impose taxes. Prostitution, the practice of engaging in sexual activity in exchange for money, is illegal in every U.S. jurisdiction with the exception of Nevada, which has state-licensed brothels.

KEY TERMS

community standards p. 529
decriminalization p. 517
legalization p. 512
sex work p. 500
victimless crimes p. 500

REVIEW QUESTIONS

1. What is drug abuse?
2. What legislative acts and cases led to the criminalization of drugs?
3. What are some of the means of social control used in the war on drugs?
4. What goals should drug treatment programs strive for, according to Elliot Currie?
5. What are some of the arguments for legalizing and decriminalizing drugs?
6. How has legalized gambling been transformed in the last 30 years?
7. What forms of gambling remain illegal?
8. What is the occupational hierarchy of prostitution according to N. Jane McCandless?
9. What would be the possible benefits of legalizing prostitution?
10. Considering the rapid development of computers and the Internet, what challenges face the criminal justice system in controlling pornography?

SUGGESTED FURTHER READING

Albert, Alexa. *Brothel: Mustang Ranch and Its Women.* New York: Ballantine Books, 2001.

Currie, Elliot. *Reckoning: Drugs, the Cities, and the American Future.* New York: Hill and Wang, 1993.

Donziger, Steven R., ed. *The Real War on Crime: The Report of the National Criminal Justice Commission.* New York: Harper Perennial, 1996.

Gitlin, Todd. *The Sixties: Years of Hope, Days of Rage.* New York: Bantam Books, 1993.

Goodman, Robert. *The Luck Business: The Consequences and Broken Promises of America's Gambling Explosion.* New York: The Free Press, 1995.

McNamara, Robert. *The Times Square Hustler: Male Prostitution in New York City.* Westport, CT: Praeger, 1994.

ENDNOTES

1. Edward Brongersma, "Boy-Lovers and Their Influence on Boys: Distorted Research and Anecdotal Observations," in *Deviance and Deviants: An Anthology,* eds. Richard Tewksbury and Patricia Gagné (Los Angeles: Roxbury, 2000), 83–98.
2. Sex work is the behavior of engaging in the selling of sex-related behaviors as an occupation. There are many types of sex work, but we will be primarily concerned here with prostitution, exotic dancing, and pornography.
3. Robert Meier and Gilbert Geis, *Victimless Crime? Prostitution, Drugs, Homosexuality, Abortion* (Los Angeles: Roxbury, 1997).
4. Andrew Hathaway, "Marijuana and Lifestyle: Exploring Tolerable Deviance," in *Deviance and Deviants: An Anthology,* eds. Richard Tewksbury and Patricia Gagné (Los Angeles: Roxbury, 2000), 152–160.
5. Steven R. Donzigen, ed., *The Real War on Crime: The Report of the National Criminal Justice Commission* (New York: Harper Perennial, 1996).

6. Elliot Currie, *Reckoning: Drugs, the Cities, and the American Future* (New York: Hill and Wang, 1993).
7. David L. Carter, "An Overview of Drug-Related Misconduct of Police Officers: Drug Abuse Narcotic Corruption," in *Drugs, Crime and the Criminal Justice System,* ed. Ralph Weisheit (Cincinnati: Anderson, 1990), 79–109.
8. Lynn Zimmer, "Proactive Policing Against Street-Level Drug Trafficking," in *Drugs, Crime and Justice: Contemporary Perspectives,* eds. Larry K. Gaines and Peter B. Kraska (Prospect Heights, IL: Waveland Press, 1997), 249–274.
9. Howard Abadinsky, *Drug Abuse: An Introduction,* 2nd ed. (Chicago: Nelson-Hall), 3.
10. In H. W. Brands' *The First American: The Life and Times of Benjamin Franklin* (New York: Anchor Books, 2000), Brands tells of how Franklin as a young man was able to drink the water of Philadelphia without getting sick and was then able to work more efficiently than his coworkers who drank alcohol all day long (p. 71).
11. W. J. Rorabaugh, *The Alcoholic Republic: An American Tradition* (New York: Oxford University Press, 1991,) 21.
12. Oakley Ray and Charles Ksir, *Drugs, Society, and Human Behavior,* 6th ed. (St. Louis: Mosby, 1993).
13. Dean Latimer and Jeff Goldberg, *Flowers in the Blood: The Story of Opium* (New York: Franklin Watts, 1981).
14. Ray and Ksir, *Drugs, Society,* 39
15. Howard Wayne Morgan, *Drugs in America: A Social History, 1800–1980* (Syracuse, NY: Syracuse University Press, 1981).
16. Upton Sinclair, *The Jungle* (New York Bantam, 1906/1981).
17. Edward Brecher, *Licit and Illicit Drugs* (Boston: Little, Brown, 1972).
18. Ray and Ksir, *Drugs, Society,* 59.
19. Charles E. Faupel, Alan M. Horowitz, and Greg S. Weaver, *The Sociology of American Drug Use* (Boston: McGraw-Hill, 2004), 45–48.
20. Abadinsky, *Drug Abuse,* 75.
21. Edward Behr, *Prohibition: Thirteen Years That Changed America* (New York: Arcade, 1996).
22. Ibid. See especially Chapter 13, "Chicago," pp. 175–193.
23. Harvey A. Siegal and James A. Inciardi, "A Brief History of Alcohol," in *The American Drug Scene: An Anthology,* 3rd ed., eds. James A. Inciardi and Karen McElrath (Los Angeles: Roxbury, 2001), 52–57.
24. Harry J. Anslinger and Courtney Ryley Cooper, "Marijuana: Assassin of Youth," in *The American Drug Scene: An Anthology,* 3rd ed., eds. James A. Inciardi and Karen McElrath (Los Angeles: Roxbury, 2001), 89–94.
25. Todd Gitlin, *The Sixties: Years of Hope, Days of Rage* (New York: Bantam Books, 1993), 427.
26. Richard Fields, *Drugs in Perspective: A Personalized Look at Substance Use and Abuse,* 4th ed. (Boston: McGraw-Hill, 2001). See especially Chapter 5, "Substance Abuse and Family Systems," pp. 148–163.
27. Peter B. Kraska, "The Unmentionable Alternative: The Need For and the Argument Against the Decriminalization of Drugs," in *Drugs, Crime and the Criminal Justice System,* ed. Ralph Weisheit (Cincinnati: Anderson, 1990), 111–137.
28. Ralph Weisheit, "Declaring a 'Civil' War on Drugs," in *Drugs, Crime and the Criminal Justice System,* ed. Ralph Weisheit (Cincinnati: Anderson, 1990), 1–10.
29. Janelle Brown, "When the Drug War Invades the Chess Club," *Salon,* June 28, 2002, http://www.salon.com/mwt/feature/2002/06/28/boyd_interview/.
30. Peter B. Kraska and Victor E. Kappler, "Militarizing American Police: The Rise and Normalization of Paramilitary Units," in *The Police and Society: Touchstone Readings,* 2nd ed., ed. Victor E. Kappler (Prospect Heights, IL: Waveland Press, 1999), 463–479.
31. J. Mitchell Miller and Lance H. Selva, "Drug Enforcement's Double-Edged Sword: An Assessment of Asset Forfeiture Programs," in *Drugs, Crime, and Justice,* eds. Larry K. Gaines and Peter B. Kraska (Prospect Heights, IL: Waveland Press, 1997), 275–296.
32. Currie, *Reckoning,* 33–34.
33. Alexandra Marks, "In Drug War, Treatment Is Back," *The Christian Science Monitor,* July 14, 2000, http://search.csmonitor.com/durable/2000/07/14/p1s1.htm.
34. Todd R. Clear, Val B. Clear, and Anthony A. Braga, "Correctional Alternatives for Drug Offenders in an Era of Overcrowding," in *Drugs, Crime, and Justice,* eds. Larry K. Gaines and Peter B. Kraska (Prospect Heights, IL: Waveland Press, 1992), 375–395.
35. Currie, *Reckoning.* See Chapter 5, "Redefining Treatment," pp. 213–279.
36. Ibid., 253.
37. Michael Massing, *The Fix* (New York: Simon and Schuster, 1998).
38. Jerome H. Skolnick, "Rethinking the Drug Problem," in *Drugs, Crime, and Justice,* eds. Larry K. Gaines and Peter B. Kraska (Prospect Heights, IL: Waveland Press, 1997), 403–426.
39. Behr, *Prohibition.*
40. Stanton Peele and Archie Brodsky, "Gateway to Nowhere: How Alcohol Came to Be Scapegoated for Drug Abuse," in *The American Drug Scene: An Anthology,* 3rd ed., eds. James

A. Inciardi and Karen McElrath (Los Angeles: Roxbury, 2001), 58–63.

41. James Q. Wilson, "Against the Legalization of Drugs," in *The American Drug Scene: An Anthology,* 3rd ed., eds. James A. Inciardi and Karen McElrath (Los Angeles: Roxbury, 2001), 440–449.
42. Clear, Clear, and Braga, "Correctional Alternatives."
43. Faupel, Horowitz, and Weaver, *Sociology of American Drug Use,* 263.
44. Mark H. Moore and Mark A. R. Kleinman, "The Police and Drugs," in *Drugs, Crime, and Justice,* eds. Larry K. Gaines and Peter B. Kraska (Prospect Heights, IL: Waveland Press, 1997), 227–248.
45. Lynn Zimmer, "Proactive Policing Against Street-level Drug Trafficking," in *Drugs, Crime, and Justice,* eds. Larry K. Gaines and Peter B. Kraska (Prospect Heights, IL: Waveland Press, 1997), 249–274.
46. Jess Marcum and Henry Rowen, "How Many Games in Town? The Pros and Cons of Legalized Gambling," *The Public Interest* 36 (Summer, 1974).
47. Florida Department of Law Enforcement, *The Questions of Casinos in Florida—Increased Crime: Is It Worth the Gamble?* (Tallahassee, FL: Florida Department of Law Enforcement, 1994).
48. Peter Passell, "Lotto Is Financed by the Poor and Won by the States," *New York Times,* May 21, 1989.
49. Robert Goodman, *The Luck Business: The Consequences and Broken Promises of America's Gambling Explosion* (New York: The Free Press, 1995).
50. Ibid., 48.
51. Arnold Wexler and Sheila Wexler, "Compulsive Gambling: The Hidden Addiction," *The Counselor,* December 1992.
52. Margaret Kane, "eBay picks up PayPal for $1.5 billion," *CNET News,* July 8, 2002, http://news.com.com/2100-1017-941964.html.
53. John M. Findlay, *People of Chance: Gambling in American Society from Jamestown to Las Vegas* (New York: Oxford University Press, 1986).
54. Paul Della Valle and Scott Farmelant, "A Bad Bet: Who Really Pays for the Massachusetts Lottery's Success?" *Worcester Magazine,* January 27, 1993.
55. Vicki Abt, James F. Smith, and Eugene Martin Christiansen, *The Business of Risk: Commercial Gambling in Mainstream America* (Lawrence, KS: University Press of Kansas, 1985), 66.
56. Donal E. J. MacNamara and Edward Sagarin, *Sex, Crime and the Law* (New York: The Free Press, 1977).
57. Eric W. Hickey, *Serial Murderers and Their Victims,* 3rd ed. (Belmont, CA: Wadsworth, 2002).
58. Alexa Albert, *Brothel: Mustang Ranch and Its Women* (New York: Ballantine Books, 2001).
59. Uniform Crime Reports, *Crime in the United States 2002,* p. 234. Online at http://www.fbi.gov/ucr/cius_02/pdf/4sectionfour.pdf.
60. William H. Daly, "Law Enforcement in Times Square, 1970s–1990s," in *Sex, Scams, and Street Life: The Sociology of New York City's Times Square,* ed. Robert P. McNamara (Westport, CT: Praeger, 1995), 97–106.
61. N. Jane McCandless, "Prostitution as an Occupation," in *The Encyclopedia of Criminology,* ed. Richard Wright, Forthcoming.
62. Jody Miller and Martin D. Schwartz, "Rape Myths and Violence Against Street Prostitutes," in *Deviance and Deviants: An Anthology,* eds. Richard Tewksbury and Patricia Gagné (Los Angeles: Roxbury, 2000), 73–82.
63. Heather Montgomery, "Sex Tourism and Child Prostitution in Asia," in *Investigating Deviance: An Anthology,* eds. Bruce A. Jacobs and Barry Glassner (Los Angeles: Roxbury, 2002), 289–291.
64. Robert F. Meier and Gilbert Geis, "The Social Organization of Prostitution," in *Investigating Deviance: An Anthology,* ed. Bruce A. Jacobs (Los Angeles: Roxbury, 2001), 232–241.
65. Robert P. McNamara, *The Times Square Hustler: Male Prostitution in New York City* (Westport, CT: Praeger, 1994).
66. Adrienne Packer, "Critics Say Lap-Dance Law Does Not Sit Well," *Las Vegas Sun,* August 6, 2002, http://www.lasvegassun.com/sunbin/stories/sun/2002/aug/06/513814372.html.
67. Carol Rambo Ronai and Carolyn Ellis, "Turn-Ons for Money: Interactional Strategies of the Table Dancer," in *Investigating Deviance: An Anthology,* ed. Bruce A. Jacobs (Los Angeles: Roxbury, 2002), 273–288.
68. Kathleen Barry, *Female Sexual Slavery* (New York: New York University Press, 1979). See especially Chapter 9, "Pornography: The Ideology of Cultural Sadism," pp. 205–252.
69. Keith F. Durkin and Clifton D. Bryant, "Exotic Cyberspace: The Internet and 'Logging On' to Sex," in *Investigating Deviance: An Anthology,* ed. Bruce A. Jacobs (Los Angeles: Roxbury, 2001), 242–253.

outline

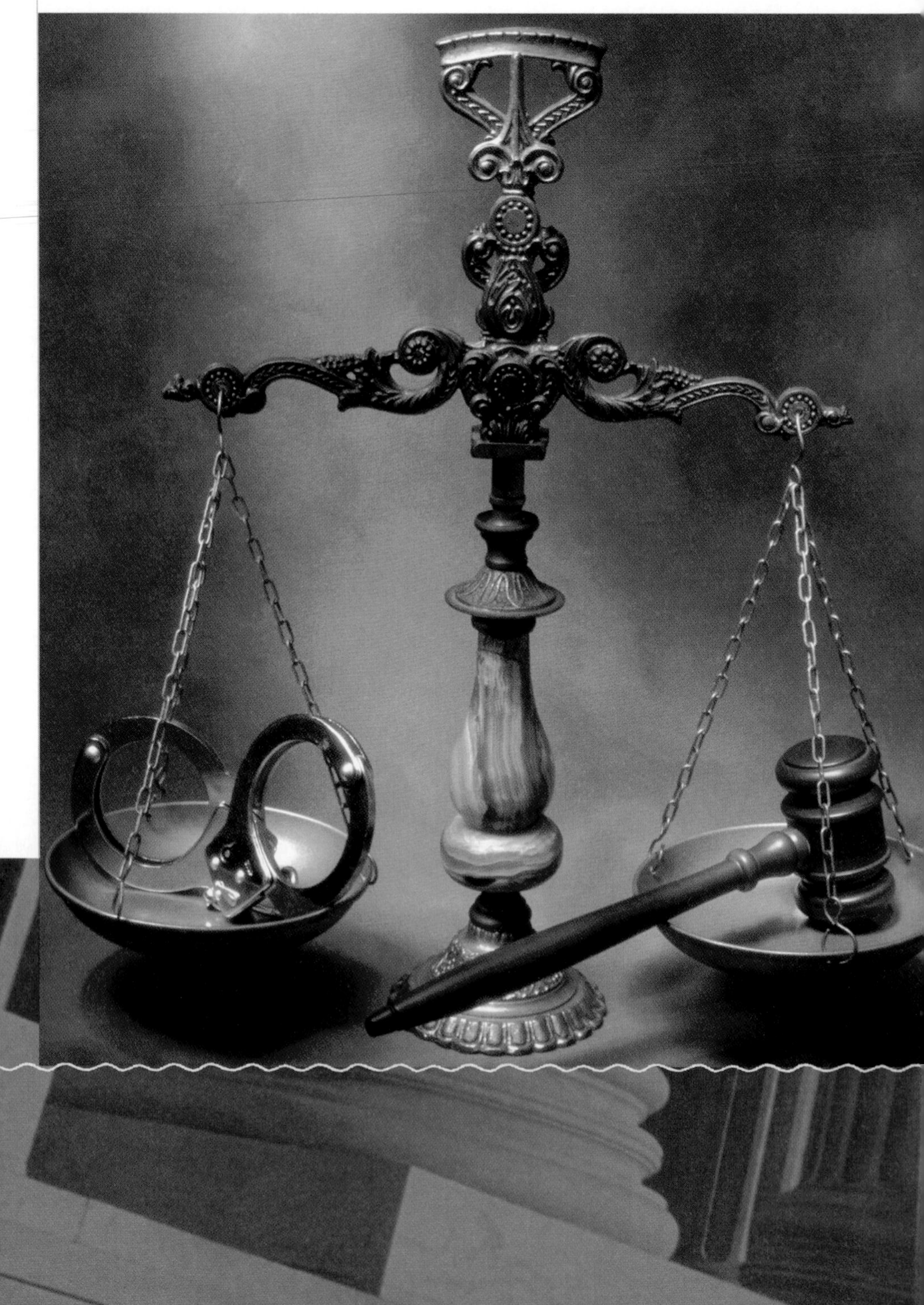

CHAPTER 16

Present and Emerging Trends: The Future of Criminal Justice

objectives

After reading this chapter, the student should be able to:

1. Discuss the significance of the war metaphor when it is applied to crime.
2. Compare and contrast the war on terrorism with the war on crime.
3. Discuss how terrorism has affected Americans' perception of civil rights.
4. Discuss the Patriot Act.
5. Discuss the Department of Homeland Security and its relationship to the criminal justice system.
6. Compare and contrast peacemaking criminology with the war metaphor for dealing with crime.
7. Discuss restorative justice and its relationship to peacemaking criminology.
8. Describe the peacemaking pyramid.
9. Discuss the principles of restorative justice.
10. Discuss why he or she may or may not want to pursue a career in criminal justice.

ONE OF THE MOST INTERESTING BY-PRODUCTS OF BEING A criminal justice major is participating in a vigorously changing discipline. As social problems wax and wane, political parties demand new programs, the economy fluctuates, and new strategies to reduce crime are implemented, the criminal justice system continues to change. The student of criminal justice can look forward to a career that will encourage innovation, reward success, recognize hard work, and foster creativity. But which of the many paths in criminal justice should one pursue? Where is the criminal justice

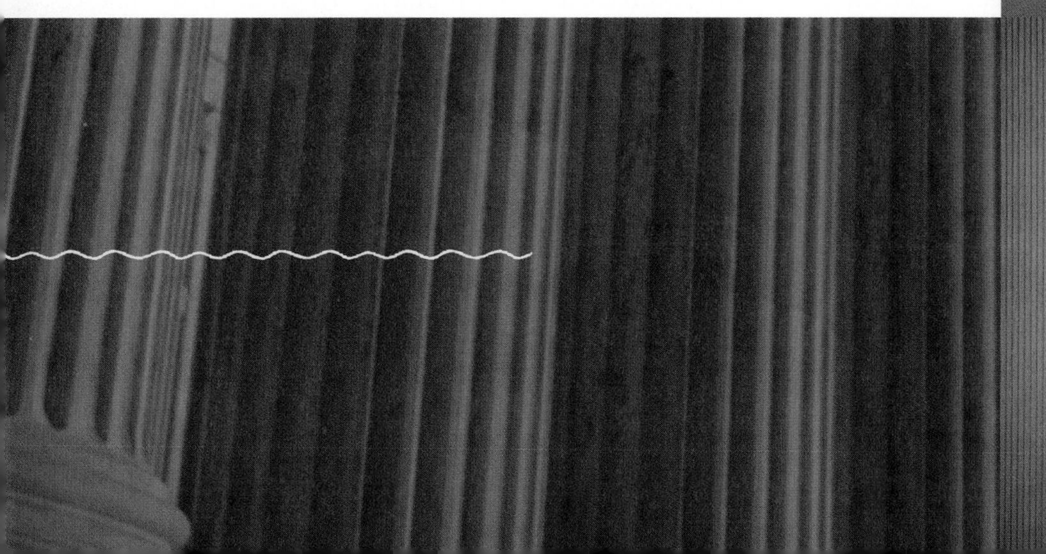

system headed, and what can the student of the discipline do to prepare for the future? This chapter will suggest that there are two emerging trends: war and peace. These two trends, however, are in competition and present a bit of a dilemma to the future criminal justice practitioner.

War and Peace in the Criminal Justice System

It is useful to think about the criminal justice system as struggling between the extremes of waging war on criminals and making peace with citizens. This view is not simply two sides of the same coin, but rather represent a fundamental difference in how the government relates to and reacts to unlawful behavior.

Without taking a stand one way or another, this chapter will introduce the history of the trends of war and peace and review several of the major initiatives pursued by each. The primary concern is to accurately and fairly reflect the promise and potential problems of each of these perspectives. Additionally, we must recognize the risk of creating a false dichotomy. We may be able to reconcile these war and peace perspectives, and in fact, the ultimate answer for developing a criminal justice system effective in reducing crime while protecting the rights of all citizens may draw from both of these perspectives. In the meantime, however, we find the criminal justice system careening into the future while simultaneously pursuing a war on crime and developing alternative approaches that emphasize mediation, reconciliation, and the preservation of individual legal, civil, and human rights.

The next generation of criminal justice practitioners—lawyers, judges, police, victim–witness program staff members, and a host of others who work in or with the criminal justice system—will be responsible for determining the nature, tone, and philosophy of how we deal with those who break the law. At another even more important level, however, the next generation of citizens will determine the nature of the substantive law. We may well find that the rules, mores, customs, expectations, and laws of tomorrow are very different from those of today.

The Wars on Crime and Drugs

War is a convenient and slippery term to use when referring to the work of the criminal justice system. It is easy to understand and easy to promote as a crime-fighting policy. Criminals are the enemy, and we should use any and all resources to defeat the enemy. Because the enemy robs, rapes, steals, and sells illegal drugs, we are justified by the principle of self-defense to use warlike strategies, tactics, and weapons to fight crime.

But is fighting crime the same as fighting a war? Are we as a nation willing to endure the consequences of treating the crime problem as a war problem? The answers to these questions are elusive because so much emotion is involved in fighting drugs and terrorism that reasoned and sober reflection on preventing crime becomes difficult. Although many citizens applaud the idea of fighting a war against criminals, the war concept becomes problematic when applied to the criminal justice system in the United States.

> *Among the characteristics implied in the notion of coping with a problem by declaring war on it are extra effort, expediency, ruthlessness, sacrifice, and subordination of the individual. It is the last mentioned characteristic that is especially troubling to students of justice and to the mind of a liberal, at least the old-fashioned liberal who regards the rights of the individual as paramount.*[1]

Before the war on terrorism, there was a war on crime, a war on drugs, and a war on poverty. These wars are still being pursued without a realistic end in sight. In fact, so much money and so many resources have been spent on these wars that it is safe to conclude that the United States has not been able to make much of a dent in these social

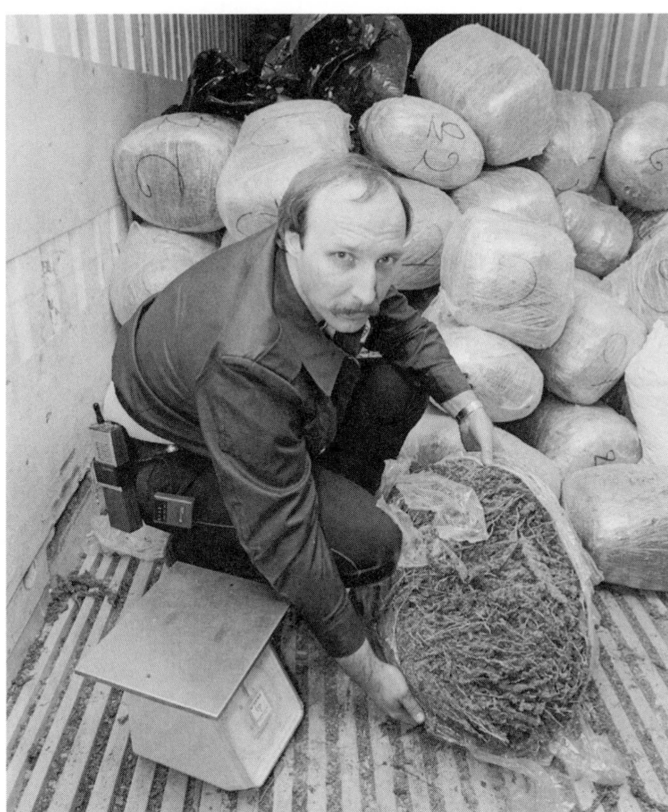

The war on drugs requires resources from law enforcement agencies. Here, a police officer displays the result of a drug bust.
Courtesy of CORBIS-NY.

problems, much less win any war against them. Although dealing with these problems is appropriate and noble, *war* is a misleading metaphor. In a traditional war between nations, national security and citizens' lives and lifestyles are at risk. For example, in World War II Americans sacrificed their fortunes, lives, and lifestyles to defeat a well-defined enemy who had committed aggressive acts against our allies and the United States. However, when we use the term *war* to describe a movement to stem crime, we mean that the government and citizenry are willing to allocate some resources to prevent or reduce a set of social problems. A war on drugs or a war on crime lacks a clear, identifiable external enemy. Hitler, the Axis, the North Vietnamese, and other peoples designated as the enemy have been relatively easy to demonize and hate. However, a war on drugs means that, in addition to attacking Colombian drug cartels, we must attack U.S. citizens who sell, buy, and consume illegal drugs. This becomes even more precarious when our children, siblings, classmates, or friends are at the business end of this declared war. The war metaphor becomes a problem when it means using military tactics, reasoning, and resources to arrest U.S. citizens for rather ordinary and conventional crimes.[2]

The Constitution has provisions to protect citizens from an overzealous criminal justice system. The Bill of Rights along with a long history of court cases interpreting the meanings of the framers of the Constitution have greatly limited what the criminal justice system can and cannot do in pursuit of criminals. Recent Supreme Court cases have illustrated that the protections of the Constitution and the law are subject to change when circumstances demand a new way of considering crime and protecting the United States. For example, during World War II, the courts allowed the internment of U.S. citizens of Japanese descent because of the perceived seriousness of the war threat. However, the question posed by wars on drugs and crime is, Are drugs and crime so harmful that Americans must give up legal and civil rights to allow the police greater flexibility in performing their duties? For the most part, the answer to this question has been no. Drugs and crime are certainly problems, and some citizens' rights have been abbreviated, but the problem does not rise to the level of war in which citizens feel so threatened that

FOCUS ON ETHICS

Could You Be a Terrorist?

Why did the terrorists of the September 11 events commit suicide by flying planes into the World Trade Center and the Pentagon? Certainly they had issues with the United States, but an almost unbelievable level of commitment is required to take one's own life to make such a political statement. Over the past 50 years a number of people have committed acts of domestic terrorism in the United States against the government or civilian targets. Under what circumstances (if any) would you resort to violence against your country? Imagine the following scenarios:

1. The government suspends the Bill of Rights and imprisons individuals for real or imagined criticisms of its policies.
2. The government declares your religion to be undesirable and forbids church attendance, the display of religious symbols, and praying. Violations are subject to fines or imprisonment.
3. The government eliminates taxes for the rich and increases them to 70 percent for the middle class.
4. The government decides that people of your religion, ethnic heritage, race, or political persuasion are no longer desirable and institutes a program to send you back to your country of origin, even though your family has been in the United States for well over a hundred years.

QUESTIONS

1. If the government treated you in such a way and abolished the traditional mechanisms for redress, such as courts and petitions, would you resort to violence to preserve your cherished values?
2. Can you understand how others might have resorted to terrorism?
3. What do you think when you see a bumper sticker that says, "You can have my gun when you pry it from my cold dead fingers"?

they would forfeit the majority of their rights. However, the events of September 11, 2001, may have changed that.

The War on Terrorism

Under normal circumstances, the police and the military are, for the most part, different. They may share such things such as organizational structures, ranks, the carrying of weapons, and the wearing of uniforms, but their goals are different. A law enforcement officer is sworn to keep the peace and protect citizens. A soldier is obligated to attack an enemy. In fact, one of the criticisms of the war-on-crime metaphor is that it puts law enforcement officers in the position of being soldiers and, therefore, citizens in the position of being enemies. Under normal circumstances, the goals and targets of the military and the police do not intersect. Terrorism has changed this, however, and the primary point of intersection, unfortunately, is citizens.

Although terrorists have always existed, this phenomenon was encountered most potently by the United States in the Vietnam war. U.S. soldiers were trained to kill an enemy, soldiers of the North Vietnamese army or the Viet Cong. However, because the war was a civil war, the enemy was often hard to discern. An enemy soldier would not necessarily be wearing a uniform, and could be an old man, woman, or child as easily as a young man. The enemy was everywhere, and that meant that all of the citizens of Vietnam, north and south, could be considered enemies.

Although in the United States, terrorists have been stereotyped as men of Middle Eastern descent, in reality, a terrorist can emerge from any political group (see Figure 16.1). (Some of the Taliban prisoners at Guantanamo Bay are Australian and British.) This poses a problem for those responsible for keeping nonviolent, law-abiding citizens safe

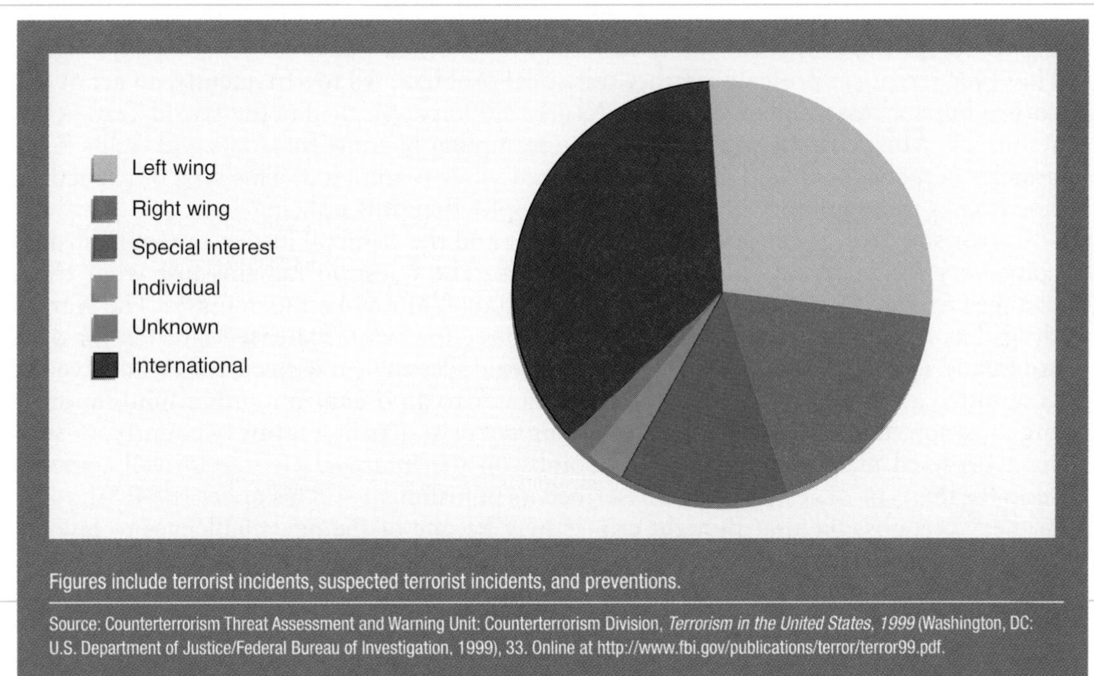

Figure 16.1
Number of Terrorist Incidents by Group Class, 1980–1999

Figures include terrorist incidents, suspected terrorist incidents, and preventions.

Source: Counterterrorism Threat Assessment and Warning Unit: Counterterrorism Division, *Terrorism in the United States, 1999* (Washington, DC: U.S. Department of Justice/Federal Bureau of Investigation, 1999), 33. Online at http://www.fbi.gov/publications/terror/terror99.pdf.

The war on terrorism has forced the government to take extraordinary strides to deal with those suspected of plotting or committing terrorist acts. Pictured here is Camp X-Ray in Guantanamo Bay, Cuba, where many of those who fought against the United States in Afghanistan are incarcerated.

Courtesy of Getty Images, Inc.

on a daily basis. Who is the enemy? This question is changing the nature of law enforcement and its relationship with government security agencies and the military.

As mentioned earlier, the police are reactive, whereas soldiers are proactive. Police respond to crimes; soldiers seek out and neutralize enemy soldiers. The criminal justice system is reactive, as well. It deals with those who are inserted into the system by way of committing a crime, and those defendants are innocent until proven guilty. A common complaint about the criminal justice system is that it cannot act until a crime is committed. For instance, a person who is suspected of being a violent sex offender cannot be arrested for thinking about attacking another person. He or she can only be arrested after the attack. Many would argue that this is too late, but from a purely statistical point of view, only a few people have been harmed by the sex offender. Currently, society is willing to accept this statistical safety in return for a set of personal freedoms and rights. However, terrorism presents another statistical problem. All too frequently, an act of terrorism hurts a vast number of people. Nearly 3,000 people died in the World Trade Center attack. Most citizens would accept the trampling of some freedoms and rights if the attack's perpetrators could have been arrested while planning it. This type of proaction, however, is more military in style and philosophy than it is policing.

Terrorism, then, is causing law enforcement and the criminal justice system to sustain some very fundamental changes and alliances. The question remains just what those changes will be. How will law enforcement become more like the military? The war on drugs has already nudged the police in that direction, with increased latitude for drug stings and search-and-seizures. How will the legal system deal with citizens who have not committed a crime but have, say, donated money to an organization that funds another organization that is suspected of committing terrorist acts in a faraway country, or who have browsed plans for making pipe bombs on the Internet? George Orwell coined a term for this type of activity—and described its punishment—in his novel *1984:* "thought crime." It is possible that thought crimes may be one of the new challenges to law enforcement, the legal system, and the civil rights of U.S. citizens.

In many ways, the war on terrorism is different from the war on crime or the war on drugs. (See Figure 16.2 for the structure of terrorist organizations.) The terrorist attacks on the Pentagon and the World Trade Center inspired a new wave of patriotism. The events of September 11 represent the greatest loss of life on U.S. soil to be caused by an

Figure 16.2 Basic Structure of Terrorist Organizations

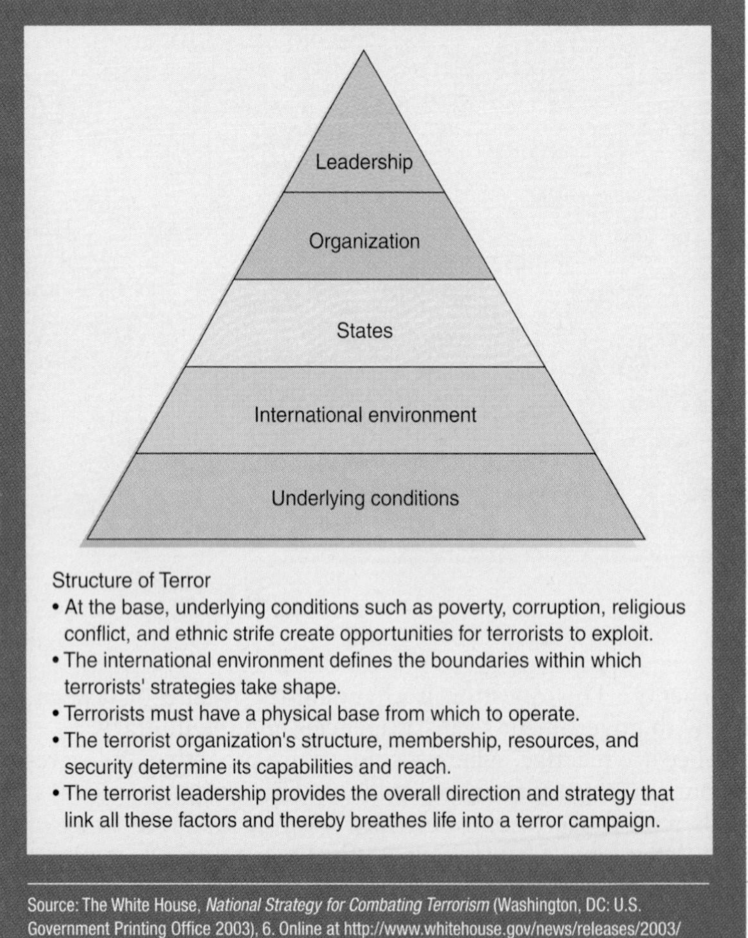

Leadership
Organization
States
International environment
Underlying conditions
Structure of Terror
• At the base, underlying conditions such as poverty, corruption, religious conflict, and ethnic strife create opportunities for terrorists to exploit.
• The international environment defines the boundaries within which terrorists' strategies take shape.
• Terrorists must have a physical base from which to operate.
• The terrorist organization's structure, membership, resources, and security determine its capabilities and reach.
• The terrorist leadership provides the overall direction and strategy that link all these factors and thereby breathes life into a terror campaign.

Source: The White House, *National Strategy for Combating Terrorism* (Washington, DC: U.S. Government Printing Office 2003), 6. Online at http://www.whitehouse.gov/news/releases/2003/02/counter_terrorism/threat.pdf.

outside aggressor since the Revolutionary War. At this point, it is worth considering some of the differences between the war on terrorism and the other social problems that we have been discussing.

- **The war on terrorism has a clear and identifiable outside enemy.** Well, sort of. This enemy is stereotyped as a Middle Eastern male of the Muslim faith. Although Osama bin Laden is the poster boy for the extreme terrorist, a popular concept in the United States is that almost anyone of Middle Eastern descent could be a terrorist.[3]
- **The war on terrorism is political rather than social.** Whereas drugs and crime may be considered social problems that can be solved by tinkering with social service agencies and the criminal justice system, terrorism occupies an international realm outside the purview of traditional U.S. state and local agencies. To effectively deal with international terrorist threats, we will have to use instruments of national defense, including the military.[4] Using the military to deal with routine, domestic drug arrests and crime is prohibited by the Constitution and takes extraordinary permissions from the courts and Congress.
- **The war on terrorism uses military weapons.** The tools of the criminal justice system are used to address drugs and crime, but terrorism requires resources not available to local and state law enforcement agencies. Although many law enforcement agencies have become more militaristic by establishing SWAT teams that wear black outfits and carry automatic weapons, the majority of police activities do not require the warlike approach and equipment needed to fight the war on terrorism.[5]
- **An outside terrorist enemy does not enjoy U.S. legal protections.** Terrorists are treated in a more efficient and determined way than are other types of criminals. They are not subject to constitutional protections, and although this is hotly debated, it would appear that they are not privileged to the protections normally afforded to prisoners of war. The over 600 members of Afghanistan's Taliban political party who are being held at the naval base at Guantanamo Bay, Cuba, are being denied basic legal rights. They are not officially charged with any crime, are not allowed to have attorneys, and have no legal recourse to protest their imprisonment. As "enemy combatants," they appear caught in a no-man's-land between being criminals and being soldiers.
- **Terrorists firmly believe their cause is just.** Most criminal and drug dealers would readily admit that their activities are legally deviant. Terrorists, on the other hand, believe their acts are justifiable, and in many cases, spiritually ordained.[6] The role of law enforcement is greatly complicated when the criminal has little regard for human life, either theirs or others, and is willing to participate in suicide bombings. The normal techniques of making targets more difficult to strike and escape do not work when the perpetrator has no intention of escaping.[7]

The war on terrorism accelerates the war metaphor of the criminal justice system's responses to crime in other ways, but these points are sufficient to illustrate how different terrorism is from conventional crime. The differences in the motivations, techniques, and consequences of terrorist crime demand that it be addressed differently. By employing the war metaphor, criminal justice practitioners can use a range of laws, equipment, surveillance techniques, and funding resources that are unavailable for combating normal crime. For better or worse, the new emphasis on terrorism will make dramatic changes in the criminal justice system that will be influential for years to come. Before we look at these changes, let us consider in greater detail just how the events of September 11 affected the resolve of Americans to fight terrorism.

THE IMPACT OF SEPTEMBER 11, 2001. Some question whether the terms *war on crime* and *war on drugs* were simply rhetorical devices created by politicians to give the illusion

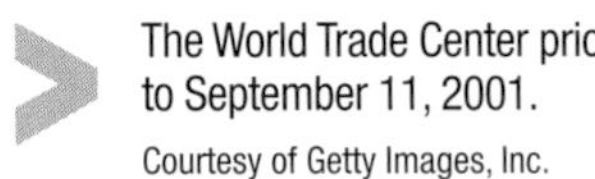

The World Trade Center prior to September 11, 2001.
Courtesy of Getty Images, Inc.

that the government took these social problems seriously. There is no such ambiguity about the war on terrorism, however. It is clear, so far, that Americans are willing to cede greater authority to government agencies to prevent terrorism.[8] The events of September 11 showed the world that large-scale terrorism can be brought anywhere, including New York City and Washington, D.C. (see Figure 16.3).

From the terrorists' point of view, September 11 was a resounding tactical success. The terrorists hijacked four planes from three airports and flew three of those planes into high-profile targets, killing thousands of people. The fourth plane crashed in a field in Pennsylvania. Officials speculate that this fourth plane was headed for Washington with a likely target of the Capitol building or the White House. The nation had not seen such a coordinated attack since Pearl Harbor. The difference with September 11, however, was that the terrorists used the nation's own airliners to wreak havoc. Looking back at September 11, we can see many issues that contributed to the tragedy.

- **Airport security.** Some airports in Europe enjoy a high degree of security, and some airlines such as Israel's El-Al are particularly vigilant; however, airport security in U.S. cities prior to September 11 was geared toward a different sort of threat. In the 1960s, there was a spat of airline hijackings in which guns were used to force planes to divert to other cities or countries. Disgruntled Cubans who wanted to go home performed several of the hijackings. The United States' response was to electronically search passengers for metal weapons. Although more drastic actions were contemplated, such as a physical search of everyone wanting to get on a plane or the use of sky marshals to ride "shotgun" on every flight, the government and the airline industry agreed to limit the public's inconvenience to walking through metal detectors. This system worked quite well in the United States for many years. Hijackings were almost nonexistent, and the public learned to accept the minimal intrusions on their privacy in exchange for safety. So what went wrong on September 11? The hijackers were able to smuggle relatively small, unobtrusive box cutters (plastic knives with razor blades) onto the planes.

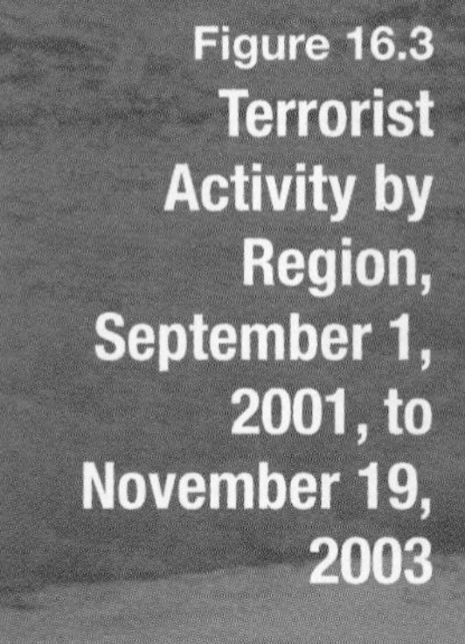

Figure 16.3
Terrorist Activity by Region, September 1, 2001, to November 19, 2003

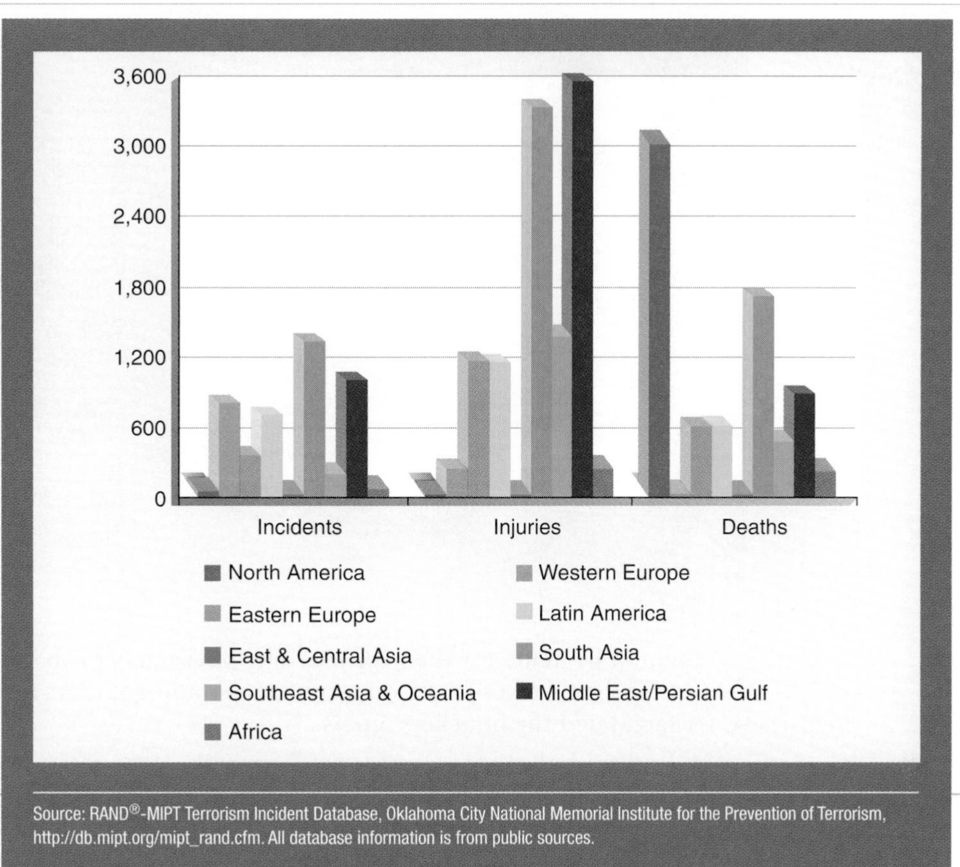

Source: RAND®-MIPT Terrorism Incident Database, Oklahoma City National Memorial Institute for the Prevention of Terrorism, http://db.mipt.org/mipt_rand.cfm. All database information is from public sources.

The hijacking of airliners for terrorist strikes surprised the United States government on September 11, 2001. Pictured here are firefighters responding to the attack on the World Trade Center in New York City.
Courtesy of CORBIS-NY.

Passengers' response. We can only speculate about the initial minutes of each of these hijackings, but clearly they were well planned and well executed. The crew was overpowered and probably killed, and the passengers were forced to the rear of the planes. Prior to September 11, the conventional wisdom was to allow professionals to handle hostage situations. Most likely the passengers expected the hijackers to make their demands known to authorities and hoped that some deal

Once passengers on United Airlines Flight 93 realized that other planes had been flown into the World Trade Center, they battled the hijackers and caused the plane to crash near Shanksville, Pennsylvania.
Courtesy of CORBIS-NY.

could be made for their release. The passengers probably did not initially realize that the hijackers were on a suicide mission and that their cooperation only facilitated the hijackers' goals.

- **Rights of aliens.** The freedoms enjoyed by Americans made us vulnerable to the September 11 attacks. It is only because of our geographic distance from those who would do us harm that we do not experience even more terrorism. One of the pressing issues that Americans face in combating terrorism is the loss of privacy. Our agencies of immigration, customs, and law enforcement did not communicate with each other very well before September 11. In fact, communications within the FBI were so compartmentalized that field agents who found suspected terrorists taking flying lessons on large jets could not get that information to other agents who were responsible for tracking terrorists.[9] It was reported that these men were not interested in learning how to take off or land the aircraft; they simply wanted to learn to control the jet in the air. In an effort to protect the privacy of citizens, and to a large extent, noncitizens, our agencies did not share vital information that would have alerted the right officials about the pending hijackings.

The events of September 11 changed the way we prepare for terrorism, and to an even greater extent, changed our criminal justice system. Several federal agencies have been reorganized into the Department of Homeland Security. Other agencies, such as the FBI, have been given increased responsibility in combating terrorism. Less visible, but more pervasive, has been the impact on local and state agencies. Because local law enforcement and emergency service agencies are likely to be the "first responders" to terrorist acts, they have taken on new responsibilities requiring additional training, improved equipment, and more money. The net effect of this new mandate has been both a blessing and a curse for local agencies.[10] On one hand, some extremely positive benefits have emerged from this new responsibility. First, the status of law enforcement officers, firefighters, and emergency service technicians has received a boost. Rather than being taken for granted, those who risk their lives on a daily basis are being recognized for the public service they perform.

A second beneficial by-product of the September 11 tragedies has been the increased attention and resources allocated to local agencies. Even though many communities are finding funding the new initiatives demanded by federal legislation difficult, there has been a substantial upgrading in the training, coordination, and equipment available to local agencies. Given that terrorist events are rare, this new level of competence can be expected to significantly address more conventional crime problems in many jurisdictions.

CROSSCURRENTS

Free Mike Hawash?

On March 20, 2003, the FBI's Joint Terrorism Task Force arrested Maher (Mike) Hawash in the parking lot of his employer, Intel Corporation, near Portland, Oregon. He was held at an Oregon medium-security prison for at least two weeks without being formally charged.

Hawash, 38, is Muslim. He was born in Nablus on the West Bank and grew up in Kuwait and Saudi Arabia before coming to the United States in 1984. He attended the University of Texas at Arlington, earning degrees in electrical engineering. Hawash became a U.S. citizen in 1988. He married a woman from Oregon, Lisa Ryan, in 1995, and the couple has three children. Hawash began working for Intel in 1992.

Those who know Hawash said that he had given about $10,000 to an Islamic charity, Global Relief Foundation, which the U.S. government asserts is linked to terrorist groups. Nevertheless, Hawash's friends and family were shocked at his arrest and his detention without charges. Initially believing his arrest to be connected to the donation, his friends established a legal defense fund and created a Web page with information about Hawash and his arrest. Senator Ron Wyden of Oregon wrote a letter to the state's U.S. attorney requesting a reason for Hawash's detention. Many Web sites picked up the story, with much of the discussion focusing on how Hawash's case was an example of the war on terrorism gone wrong. Finally, after five weeks of detention, he was charged with conspiracy to levy war against the United States with the "Portland Six." In October 2001 Hawash had tried to enter Afghanistan from China with five other Portland men, but was unable to gain entry. Hawash told authorities he was in China in search of business opportunities.

Initially, Hawash pleaded not guilty. Then, on August 6, 2003, he pleaded guilty to conspiracy to enter Afghanistan and help the Taliban fight U.S. forces and agreed to testify against the other men. In February 2004 Hawash was sentenced to seven years in prison. The Web site that Hawash's friends set up reportedly had raised $20,000 in donations for his defense.

Although Hawash's guilty plea took the wind from the sails of those who defended him, questions remain. His attorney said if Hawash had been convicted of all the charges, instead of accepting the plea agreement, he may have faced more than 20 years in prison. Other Internet pundits have speculated that Hawash pleaded guilty, possibly to something he did not do, to avoid a much longer sentence and a trial he could not possibly win. Other critics point out that the U.S. government may have gotten its man, but it did so using questionable legal means by holding Hawash for weeks without charges.

QUESTIONS

1. Did the government do the right thing by bending a few laws to stop a potential terrorist? Is this justified by the war on terrorism? Why or why not?
2. What would you have done if you had been Hawash's friend?
3. If you believe Hawash is guilty, what is your opinion of the plea agreement? What if he is innocent?

Sources: CNN, "Oregon Man Charged with Conspiracy to Levy War against U.S." April 28, 2003, http://www.cnn.com/2003/LAW/04/28/oregon.terror.charges/index.html. Dan Gillmor, "Mike Hawash Pleads Guilty," Dan Gillmor's eJournal, SiliconValley.com, http://weblog.siliconvalley.com/column/dangillmor/archives/001262.shtml. Jennifer Lin, "A Dual Image of Terror Suspect," *Philadelphia Inquirer,* April 30, 2003, http://www.philly.com/mld/inquirer/news/front/5750864.htm. Kelli Arena and Carol Cratty, "Friends of Arab-American Protest His Detention," CNN, April 4, 2003, http://www.cnn.com/2003/LAW/04/04/engineer.detained/index.html. Kristi Heim and Margaret Steen, "Ex-Intel Worker Makes Plea Deal," August 7, 2003, *The Mercury News,* http://www.siliconvalley.com/mld/siliconvalley/6477946.htm. Mike Hawash, http://www.freemikehawash.org/index.html.

A third and longer-term impact of the war on terrorism is that the criminal justice system is experiencing an influx of new and talented personnel at all levels. As an employer, the criminal justice system competes with other employers for the best talent. Prior to September 11, criminal justice salaries often were not competitive, although the work was dangerous. Now, criminal justice programs at many universities are experiencing an influx of students. There is a new urgency and status associated with serving and protecting the public, with nothing but solid support for the mission of the domestic police and fire personnel.

THE PATRIOT ACT. The response of Congress to the terrorist attacks of September 11 was to pass the Patriot Act. Officially titled "Uniting and Strengthening America by Providing Appropriate Tools Required to Intercept and Obstruct Terrorism Act," the Patriot Act gives the government greater latitude over a broad range of concerns that specify the rights of citizens, aliens, and government agents.[11] Moreover, the act toughens penalties for those who assist terrorists and provides financial relief for victims of terrorism, including public safety officers and their families. Two particularly sweeping and controversial components of the Patriot Act are of concern to students of the criminal justice system: the reorganization and retasking of federal law enforcement and the implications for civil liberties and legal rights.

Department of Homeland Security. There has been a great deal of speculation that the September 11 terrorist attacks could have been prevented if our criminal justice system had communicated more efficiently. Some people believe that enough information was in the hands of officers from different agencies and that a coordinated and centralized command structure could have collated this information and prevented the attacks. Whether this is true is not of concern here because the mere suggestion that the attacks were preventable moved the president and Congress to restructure the federal government by creating the cabinet-level Department of Homeland Security. The intent of this action was to ensure that these agencies were organizationally allied in the most efficient and productive manner to combat terrorism.

The overall impact of the creation of the Department of Homeland Security will not be known for several years, but it is interesting to observe which agencies managed to retain their independence and which ones were brought under the auspices of the new department. For instance, the two agencies that seemed to be the most likely candidates to be brought into the Department of Homeland Security were the Federal Bureau of Investigation (FBI) and the Central Intelligence Agency (CIA). Each has a mandate to protect the United States from terrorism, with the FBI being responsible for activities within our borders and the CIA being responsible for activities in other countries that may threaten the United States. Of course, the nature of the threats often overlap, and there has been considerable friction between the FBI and CIA over the years as to which agency is responsible for which threats. However, it has been suggested that these two agencies did not share vital information that could have prevented the events of September 11. Curiously, neither of these agencies was included in the reorganization. Why? There are two plausible answers, and the truth may contain elements of each. The first lies within the nature of the agencies' basic missions. Preventing terrorism is only a small (albeit significant) part of what the FBI and CIA are mandated to do. By being under the Department of Homeland Security, they could lose their authority to decide how best to deploy their resources. This is a reasonable explanation for allowing these agencies to retain their independence and their current organizational placement; however, over the next few years, it will be crucial to monitor how well each agency works with the Department of Homeland Security. The second reason the CIA and FBI have remained independent of the Department of Homeland Security is political. These are each mature agencies that, over the years, have developed networks with politicians, a large number of loyal alumni, and their own organizational culture. Placing them under the Department of Homeland Security would have required more of a political battle than was desired after September 11.

REFERENCE

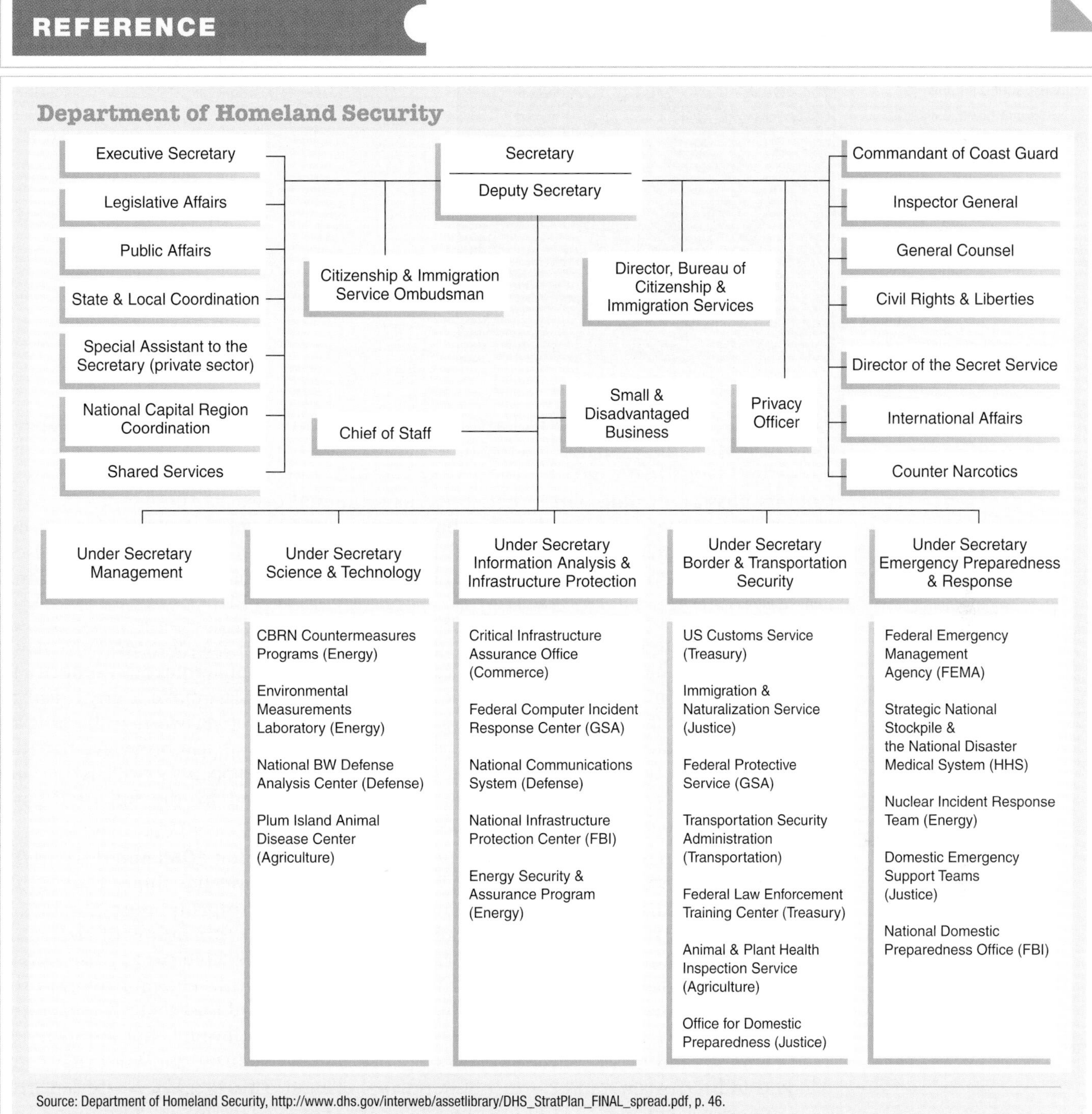

Source: Department of Homeland Security, http://www.dhs.gov/interweb/assetlibrary/DHS_StratPlan_FINAL_spread.pdf, p. 46.

The agencies that were brought into the Department of Homeland Security came from many different organizational cultures tasked with a wide range of activities only tangentially related to terrorism. The result is that the new department will need several years to design procedures and lines of communication to enable these disparate agencies to function in the coordinated manner envisioned by Congress. For instance, the Secret Service, formerly part of the Treasury Department and responsible for protecting the president and dealing with counterfeiting and other currency crimes, is now part of the Department of Homeland Security and has had to shift some of its attention to the broader issues of terrorism. Similarly, agencies such as the Plum Island Animal Disease

The FBI is one agency that was not included in the Department of Homeland Security, but the USA Patriot Act greatly expanded its powers.

Photo by Richard T. Nowitz, courtesy of Corbis/Bettmann.

Center, once attached to the Department of Agriculture, is now part of the Department of Homeland Security. It is reasonable to speculate that much of the center's emphasis will be shifted toward investigating the weaponized use of anthrax and away from its mission dealing with other concerns of animal disease. These issues of reorganization may never be problematic, but a major adjustment period of several years will be required before the formal and informal mechanisms of government are established in the way that the president and Congress envisioned when they created this new department.

Privacy Issues. The restructuring of law enforcement agencies was not the only major change made by the Patriot Act. It also greatly expanded the government's authority to gather information. In the wake of September 11, this seems to make a great deal of sense. If U.S. intelligence efforts are more efficient and effective, we may be able to prevent future attacks. However, the act has its critics, some of whom believe that the Patriot Act gives the government too much authority to snoop into citizens' private affairs and that it greatly weakens the protections provided by the Bill of Rights. Following are two of the most controversial aspects of the Patriot Act:

1. **Judicial review.** The Crime Control and Safe Streets Act of 1968 and the Foreign Intelligence Surveillance Act of 1978 limit the government's ability to conduct domestic surveillance. They provide that government agents must obtain approval from a federal judge before using wiretaps or other means of electronic eavesdropping. This may sound reasonable, but judicial review has been practiced in different ways. In criminal cases, judges are more reluctant to grant the wiretap than in foreign surveillance cases. Because the Patriot Act is concerned with terrorism, some people think the government will abuse the authority to wiretap and use it indiscriminately against U.S. citizens for activities that transcend terrorism and/or are simply normal crimes. This is particularly sensitive when we consider the links of the illegal drug trade to terrorism. Although Congress wants to fight terrorism, the Patriot Act can be used on the local level to wiretap street-level marijuana dealers without adequate judicial review. Additional surveillance issues concern the act's provisions that authorize law enforcement to check the records of bookstores and libraries to see what people are reading. For instance, this provision would allow law enforcement officers to find out who is reading library books on how to build a nuclear bomb or biological weapon. Although these provisions might seem reasonable to some, prior to the Patriot Act, the government had to convince a judge that there was probable cause to suspect an individual. Now, under the Patriot Act, government officials can go on fishing expeditions to discover what ordinary citizens

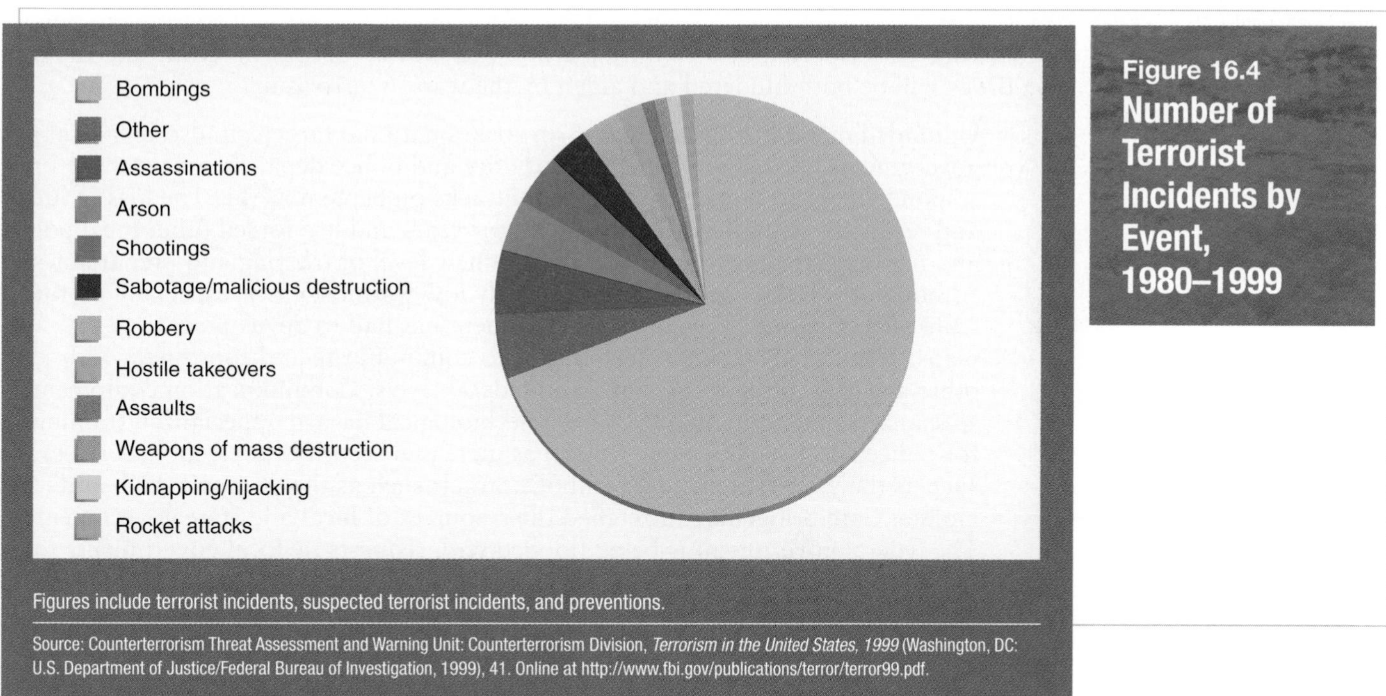

Figure 16.4 Number of Terrorist Incidents by Event, 1980–1999

Figures include terrorist incidents, suspected terrorist incidents, and preventions.

Source: Counterterrorism Threat Assessment and Warning Unit: Counterterrorism Division, *Terrorism in the United States, 1999* (Washington, DC: U.S. Department of Justice/Federal Bureau of Investigation, 1999), 41. Online at http://www.fbi.gov/publications/terror/terror99.pdf.

are reading. Other records, including financial, travel, medical, video rental, and phone records are also subject to these warrantless searches.

2. **Secret searches.** The Patriot Act authorizes government agents to search homes and property without prior or subsequent notification that the residence has been searched. This authority may be a wonderful aid to law enforcement officers in prosecuting the war against terrorism; however, it is also a threat to citizens' individual liberties. The Patriot Act is so broadly written that these powers might legitimately be used against citizens suspected not of terrorism but of regular criminal activity. These Patriot Act provisions give the appearance of creating a police state rather than protecting a free democracy. Although extreme violations of rights have not yet occurred, the legal provisions that allow for such police behavior are of concern to constitutional scholars and are being challenged in the courts.

The Patriot Act was hastily passed as a reaction to the terrorist events of September 11. Two primary motivations propelled it through Congress. The first motivation was cosmetic. Politicians were eager to demonstrate their outrage at the horrendous attacks and to demonstrate to their constituents that they had the backbone and resolve to fight terrorism. The second motivation was just as sincere but more substantive. The security of the United States was exposed as inadequate in a new age of terrorism, and Congress was anxious to shore it up. Whether the Patriot Act provisions are enough to provide this additional security or are even a step in the right direction remains to be seen. What is apparent at this juncture, however, is that controversy over how to fight terrorism without infringing on citizens' rights will continue.

HOW TERRORISM IS CHANGING THE CRIMINAL JUSTICE SYSTEM. The war on terrorism is bringing deep change to the criminal justice system. Despite the fact that terrorism has struck relatively few jurisdictions, the threat has affected the whole United States, and local criminal justice systems nationwide have had to alter their funding priorities to prepare for the day they hope will never come. (For a historical look at terrorist events in the United States before September 11, 2001, see Figure 16.4.). For the most part, however, life will go on, and law enforcement officers will continue to pursue those who are suspected of committing crimes. However, the war on crime and the war on drugs will be both hindered and aided by the war on terrorism.

- **Unfunded mandates.** When terrorism strikes national targets, it also hits local governments hard. The New York City fire and police departments were the first responders to the World Trade Center attacks on September 11. The loss of life and resources will affect these agencies for years and has forced other local police and fire departments to institute a whole new level of training and preparedness. Although the risk of terrorism is relatively low for most cities, especially on the scale of September 11, each city government has had to develop contingency plans. These plans include mechanisms to communicate and coordinate with other agencies at the local, state, and federal levels. Communication equipment, specialized suits to handle chemical and biological hazards, specialized training for police and fire personnel, as well as increased security for essential services such as the water supply and symbolic targets such as the St. Louis Arch and Golden Gate Bridge have stretched the resources of local and state governments. The federal government is being flooded with requests by local governments for more money to fund these new duties.
- **Increased capacity.** For the first time since the legislation establishing the Law Enforcement Assistance Administration in 1968, the criminal justice system has moved to the head of the line in the allocation of government resources. Because domestic terrorism is relatively rare, the personnel, equipment, and intelligence that have been established to fight it can be used to fight normal crime. Local criminal justice systems are experiencing an infusion of personnel positions, weapons, communications equipment, and training that can be used to respond to local crime concerns.[12] Furthermore, morale has improved as the contributions of local police and firefighters are reflected in the heroism of the first responders of September 11. The relatively low pay and low status of these occupations are being offset by the appreciation of citizens who are thankful for the sacrifices these public servants make.

Peacemaking Criminology and Restorative Justice

peacemaking criminology
A theoretical perspective that serves as an alternative to the war on crime. It focuses on nonviolence, social justice, and reducing the suffering of both the victim and the offender.

restorative justice
An alternative justice model that uses community programs to repair the harm done by offenders. Programs include the victim, the offender, representatives of law enforcement, and representatives of the community in attempting to craft long-lasting and satisfying solutions to the problems of crime.

The recent history of the United States' approach to dealing with crime clearly illustrates the war metaphor. Critics of this approach ask whether the war metaphor is the most effective way to address the complex problems of crime. Is the crime situation getting better? Are our communities safer? Are prisons doing their job by reducing the criminal tendencies of those they release though either deterrence or rehabilitation? The answers to these questions are mixed. Critics of the war metaphor contend that, in many ways, the tough-on-crime approach, although politically attractive, may cause even more crime. By concentrating on deterrence and incapacitation as primary crime control strategies, the United States has become a country with both a high crime rate and an expensive and punitive criminal justice system. Critics suggest that the high crime rate and the war approach are related and ask the question, What would the crime situation be like if we had a less punitive and more rehabilitative criminal justice system?

One alternative to the war metaphor is the peacemaking approach. The remainder of this chapter will detail the theoretical developments of **peacemaking criminology** and also delineate its practical applications through the **restorative justice** movement. This section will suggest that the emerging perspectives of peacemaking criminology and restorative justice provide a promising strategy for dealing with crime. The peacemaking perspective may never fully replace the war-on-crime metaphor, but it mediates some of the more destructive tactics that are the consequences of addressing crime with the war metaphor. The promise of the peacemaking perspective is that it holds out long-lasting solutions not only to the problems of crime, but also for the issues and controversies that create crime. Peacemaking criminology and restorative justice implemented in the optimal manner ease the increasing pressures on the criminal justice system by employing alternate mechanisms for resolving social conflict. The criminal justice system should be the institution of last resort for resolving social problems, and the peacemaking and restorative justice movements provide the intermediary processes that can resolve issues in ways that do not require the expense and resources of the traditional criminal justice process. We will first address the theoretical foundations of peacemaking criminology, then turn to restorative justice as a practical model for implementing peacemaking principles.

Peacemaking criminology is not a particularly new concept. In fact, many of its principles, such as social justice, nonviolence, and rehabilitation, have been advocated for centuries, and for the most part, have been discarded by the modern criminal justice system. The accuracy of this criticism is immaterial here because the foundations of peacemaking criminology have never been subjected to empirical examination or given an honest opportunity to demonstrate their promise. Although some may regard peacemaking criminology as utopian and naive, its principles are worth considering given the failure of the war metaphor to solve many of the problems of crime. Therefore, this section will present the theoretical traditions from which peacemaking criminology has developed and present some of the contributions made by current criminologists to refine the perspective to address contemporary issues of crime and justice.

In 1991 Harold Pepinsky and Richard Quinney edited a book titled *Criminology as Peacemaking*.[13] This work gathered the ideas of scholars who were concerned with developing a more effective approach to the problems of crime, an approach that was aimed at reducing the suffering of both victims and offenders. Pepinsky and Quinney gave voice to a new movement in criminology circles that rejected the violence done by the criminal justice system and sought to improve the quality of justice for society by addressing the needs of victims and offenders. Both academic criminologists and criminal justice practitioners have embraced the resulting peacemaking perspective. The Pepinsky and Quinney volume envisioned peacemaking criminology as developing from three intellectual traditions, the religious and humanist tradition, the feminist tradition, and the critical tradition.

Religious and Humanist Tradition

One of the consequences of living in such a pluralistic country as the United States is the dislocation felt by citizens from some of the ancient wisdom traditions embodied in religion. Because of the establishment clause in the Constitution dictating that there is no state religion, much of the comfort of religious teachings has been absent in civil society. This is as it should be in a pluralistic society based on the premise that each of us should be able to believe and practice in our own manner, but much has been lost as our institutions turn a blind eye to the benefits of faith.

Peacemaking criminology recognizes the contributions to meaningful communities and individual well-being that religion can supply and argues that the criminal justice system should be aware of the transformative power of religion.[14] Religious perspectives such as Buddhism, Christianity, Hinduism, Islam, Judaism, and American Indian traditions all encompass principles that are important contributions to the peacemaking perspective. The ideas of living in meaningful communities characterized by harmony, mutual cooperation, and peace is central to most major religions. Additionally, although each religion may put its own spin on the cosmic questions of why we are here and what happens after death, they all provide a prescription for following a path of kindness, respect, and healthy living.[15] The promise for reclamation of the soul is an important part of religious life and one that is often neglected or rejected by the secular criminal justice

NEWS FLASH

No Atheists in This Prison

Although religion and religious counsel have been a feature of U.S. prisons for over a hundred years, in 2003 Florida opened what Governor Jeb Bush called the first faith-based prison. The difference between the religious programs of other prisons and Lawtey Correctional Institution is that each of the nearly 800 inmates at Lawtey has the opportunity to attend prayer sessions, religious studies, counseling, and choir practice. The curriculum includes as many faiths as there are inmates. Inmates are not required to participate and are allowed to transfer to other prisons, which 111 did when the plan was announced. About 500 volunteers assist with religious instruction and act as mentors.

Source: Brendan Farrington, "Florida Faith-Based Prison Considered First in U.S.," *The Seattle Times*/The Associated Press, December 25, 2003, http://seattletimes.nwsource.com/html/nationworld/2001823149_prison25.html.

system. Some critics may contend that religious zealots have divided peoples and waged war over the centuries, but the promise of peace and individual salvation is still a powerful motivator for a great many people and something the contemporary criminal justice system can employ to help deal with the problems of criminal behavior.

Pepinsky and Quinney also recognized that humanist traditions contribute to the foundations of peacemaking criminology. Humanists believe it is possible to live a moral life without religious theory. Based on the concept that people are basically good and will cooperate for the benefit of all if society's institutions are fair, humanists embrace many of the same social concerns as do religious individuals, except without the idea of supreme guidance. Regardless of the religious or humanist particulars, Pepinsky and Quinney pointed to these intellectual traditions as being an important part of the cultural fabric by which people live their lives. By recognizing and incorporating these intellectual traditions into peacemaking criminology, its advocates believe that offenders and victims can witness how the solutions to crime are integrated into a larger pattern of righteous living.

Feminist Tradition

Feminism has a history of resisting the patriarchy in which societal rights and responsibilities are allocated according to gender roles. Feminism advocates a criminal justice system that is blind toward sex and in which women and men are treated with respect, equal opportunities and consequences, and fairness. The war metaphor, which relies on domination and power, is antithetical to the feminist perspective. The feminist model suggests that the criminal justice system's laws, biases, and personnel have been historically supportive of an unjust attitude that supports a privileged position in society for men. Feminists argue that the criminal justice system must be examined for sexist practices and chauvinistic attitudes in law enforcement, the courts, and correctional institutions. Most important, feminists want their share of the power, but contend they would exercise it differently, repudiating the culture of domination that they believe is a large part of the masculine world.[16]

Critical Traditions

In addition to critiquing the contributions of gender inequality to the dysfunctions of the criminal justice system, critical traditions consider other social characteristics such as social class, age, and race. Historically, the most pressing concern of critical criminologists has been the influence of social class on the quality of justice in society and more particularly in the criminal justice system. Karl Marx laid the groundwork for critiquing capitalist societies and their inherent contradictions in allocating wealth and power. One of the central tenets of capitalism is the prospect of upward mobility whereby

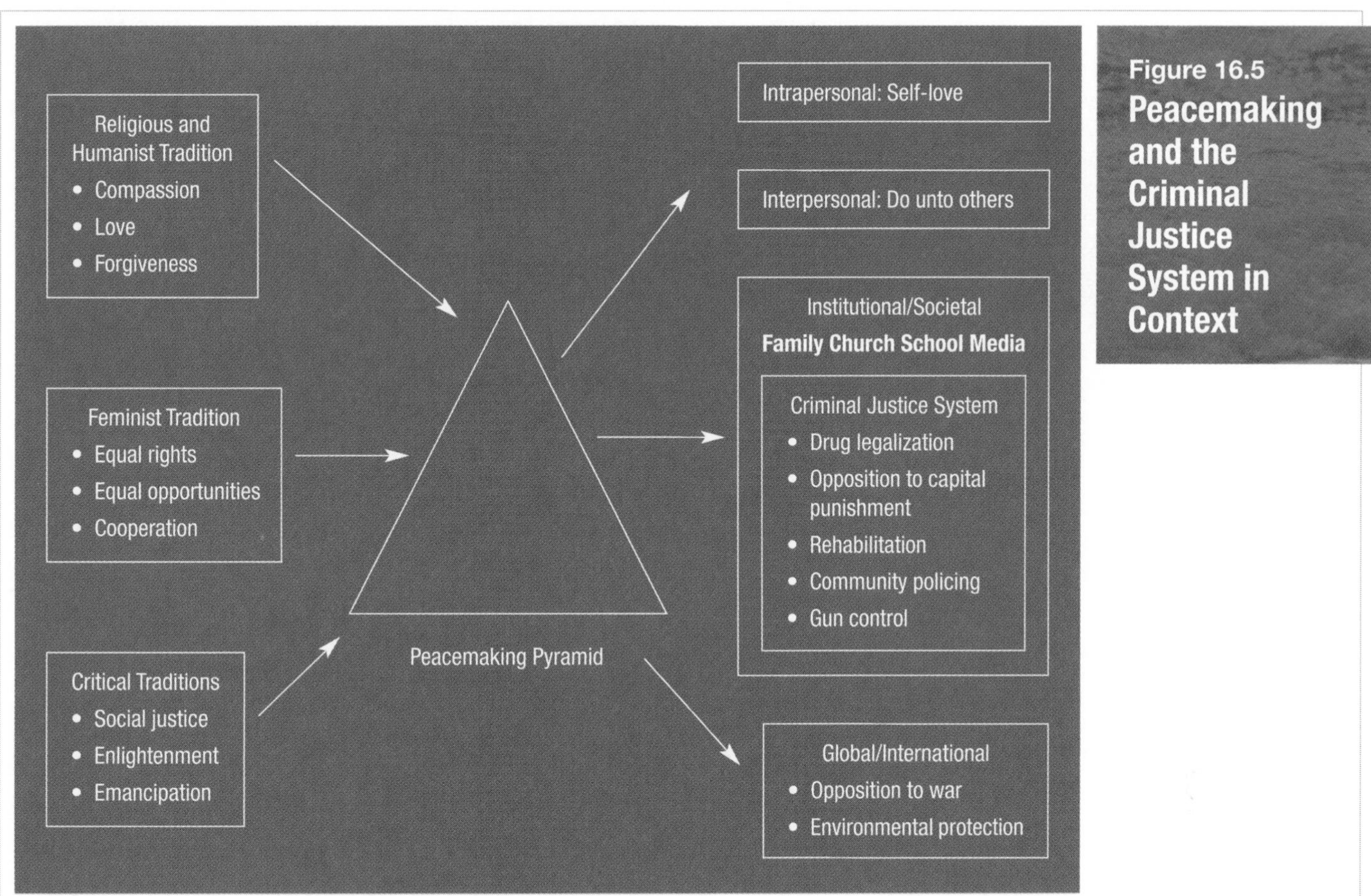

Figure 16.5 **Peacemaking and the Criminal Justice System in Context**

those willing to work hard, play by the rules, and defer gratification can "pull themselves up by their bootstraps" and realize the dream of financial independence. According to Marx, this goal is a product of false consciousness whereby the precious few who do attain the goal serve as an unrealistic example that keeps the vast majority of us slaving away at low-paying jobs that serve only the interests of those who own and control the means of production.[17]

Another characteristic that critical theorists deem problematic is that of age. Rights and responsibility in most societies are allocated according to age. This tradition may be well meaning, but it serves to reinforce the interests of those who already control society. For instance, those under 18 years of age are not allowed a voice in making the law, but are subject to a vast number of statutes that do not apply to adults. Although laws denying young people the right to drive, vote, or drink alcohol supposedly exist to protect them, they are enforced by a system that does not allow them the same constitutional guarantees afforded to the adults who passed the laws.

Each of these intellectual traditions contributes to peacemaking criminology to make it an overarching perspective that can be used not only to reform the criminal justice system but also to address problems on both the personal and social levels. The peacemaking perspective is applicable to four levels of analysis (see Figure 16.5).

- **Intrapersonal.** Religious intellectual traditions speak to the need for personal peace. The cause of much of the crime and violence in society is the torment experienced by offenders who cannot find inner peace and security and strike out at others as a way to ease their pain. Programs in prisons not only rely on religious services to attend to individuals' personal development but also encourage such activities as meditation, weightlifting, and yoga as ways for inmates to develop self-discipline and a healthy self-concept.

- **Interpersonal.** The peacemaking perspective is especially concerned with the interpersonal level of analysis in which the Golden Rule, "Do unto others as you would have others do unto you," applies.
- **Societal and institutional.** The institutional and societal level of the peacemaking perspective is where peacemaking criminology can be applied. Laws and institutions are a reflection of how people live their personal lives. According to the peacemaking perspective, people should strive to ensure that schools, families, workplaces, and especially the criminal justice system do not violate fundamental principles of living.
- **International and global.** Finally, the peacemaking perspective can be applied on the international and global level. Relationships between nations all too often erode to wars and economic sanctions. Although a strong national defense is required for protection against unstable despots, strong nations must constantly guard against the temptation to use power simply because they can.

This brief overview of the scope of the peacemaking perspective illustrates that it is more than a midlevel theory to control crime. The peacemaking perspective is a way to engage all aspects of an individual's life as well as a prescription for a society to dispense economic and social justice. We turn now to exploring the actual principles that underlie the peacemaking perspective.

The Peacemaking Pyramid

Although peacemaking can be envisioned in a number of ways, the peacemaking pyramid is intended to show that the components build on one another to form a solid and stable approach to the problems of crime (see Figure 16.6). The pyramid depicts a set of increasingly important ideas that draw from the intellectual traditions.

NONVIOLENCE. At the base of the pyramid is the principle of nonviolence. In considering the history of injustice, we can see how Jesus Christ, Leo Tolstoy, Mohandas Gandhi, and Dr. Martin Luther King, Jr., used nonviolence to confront institutional injustice in a positive way. For example, in the United States, the civil rights movement was led by King, who employed the teaching of these other peacemakers to challenge the institutionalized racism of the southern states. By not resorting to violence, King led the Southern Christian Leadership Conference in a series of demonstrations that revealed not

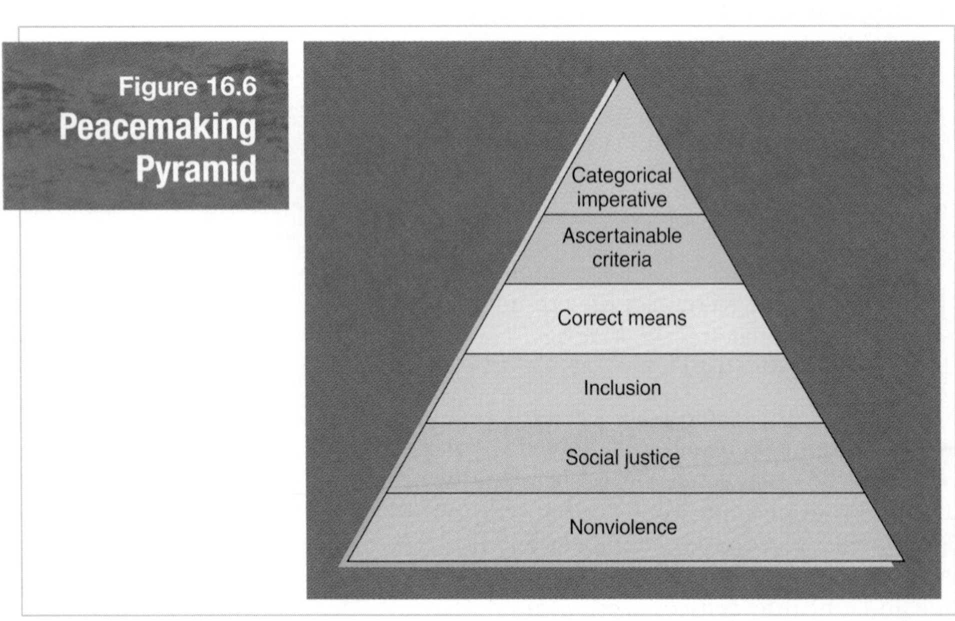

Figure 16.6 Peacemaking Pyramid

only the injustices of the law, but also how the law relied on violence for its enforcement. King used nonviolence to expose the violence inherent in the system.

Because of the unique mission of the criminal justice system, particularly that of law enforcement, a certain level of defensive violence is required. According to the principles of the peacemaking perspective, however, this violence must be proportional, used as a last resort, and continually evaluated in every situation to determine whether better alternatives were available. The goal of nonviolence as an instrument of the criminal justice system is to break the cycle of self-perpetuating violence that afflicts U.S. society.

SOCIAL JUSTICE. The criminal justice system should also strive toward social justice. A system that merely reinforces the power wielded by those who enact and enforce the laws does not serve the best interests of all citizens. When sexist or racist policies are tolerated as part of the criminal justice system, it cannot be considered peacemaking even if it is done in a nonviolent manner. For example, if police officers respond to a domestic violence complaint and are able to convince the husband to stop beating his wife and children, nonviolence has been attained. But, if that man still psychologically and economically dominates and controls the family in a manner to the detriment of the well-being of the wife and children then social justice has not been attained. The remedy for such a situation, then, is not only police response, but counseling and public education. Unfortunately, the limitations of the criminal justice system prevent it from ensuring that social justice is always considered. Criminal justice practitioners, however, can be trained to be aware of how advocating for social justice might help craft long-term solutions to problems.

Mohandas Gandhi promoted nonviolent social protest. His philosophy has inspired many peacemaking criminologists who advocate social change.

Courtesy of Hulton-Deutsch Collection, Corbis/Bettmann.

INCLUSION. In the current criminal justice system, the product of justice is imposed on the defendant with little input from the victim, the victim's family, the community, or even the defendant. As covered later in this chapter when we discuss restorative justice, a peacemaking solution to a crime often requires that the criminal justice system seek the cooperation, counsel, and commitment of all affected parties. Currently, the prosecutor represents the state, and this effectively denies the victim an opportunity to be heard. Additionally, even though most crimes reflect a dispute between the victim and the offender, the current system leaves little room for any kind of negotiation or resolution. The principle of inclusion suggests that the victim, the victim's family, the offender's family, representatives from local law enforcement, representatives of the community, and the offender work together to craft a sentence that fully resolves the dispute. In this way, the offender becomes bonded to the sentence; it is not something that is simply imposed on him or her. Moreover, because both the offender and victim have worked together to find a solution, they are more likely to be satisfied that justice has been done.

Dr. Martin Luther King, Jr., led the civil rights movement in the United States in the 1950s and 1960s. Like Gandhi, he advocated nonviolent social protest against discriminatory and racist laws.

Courtesy of CORBIS-NY.

CORRECT MEANS. *Correct means* is a term coined by Gandhi that suggests that a good solution to the problems of crime can only be attained by processes that embody the principles of peacemaking. Gandhi is reputed to have said, "There is no path to peace; peace is the path." Applied to the criminal justice system, the principle of **correct means** suggests that offenders be supplied their constitutional and civil rights. Additionally, law enforcement officers and court and correctional personnel need to abide by procedural law and institutional guidelines to ensure that offenders are treated fairly, equitably, and without rancor or deception. The intent here is not to limit the ability of law enforcement officers to pursue their duties, but to ensure that in enforcing the law, they also abide by the law. Good ends obtained by faulty means will, in the long run, only weaken the ability of the criminal justice system to achieve justice.

correct means
A peacemaking criminology term coined by Gandhi. A good solution to the problems of crime can only be attained using processes that embody peacemaking principles.

ASCERTAINABLE CRITERIA. Often, individuals caught up in the criminal justice system, whether offenders or victims, have a difficult time understanding why decisions are made, who is advocating for their best interests, or even what the legalistic language used by attorneys and judges means. As discussed in Chapter 9, the courtroom work group has an agenda of its own that often leaves the ordinary citizen confused about how and why the sentence was determined. **Ascertainable criteria** means that everyone involved should have a clear understanding of the rules and procedures employed by the criminal justice system. This may slow the court process as offenders are educated about their various options and the ramifications of accepting one plea bargain over another, but the overall result is that the offenders will feel greater accountability for the decisions they make.

ascertainable criteria
A peacemaking criminology term that states that everyone involved in a criminal justice process should understand the rules and procedures employed by the system.

CATEGORICAL IMPERATIVE. **Categorical imperative** is a term associated with the philosopher Immanuel Kant, who postulated that individuals should decide the course of their actions according to the axiom "Act only according to the maxim whereby you can at the same time will that it should become a universal law."[18] When applied to the peacemaking perspective, this means that every decision should have an underlying moral

categorical imperative
A term associated with the philosopher Immanuel Kant. When applied to peacemaking, it means that every decision should be logical enough to be applied to other cases at other times.

FOCUS ON ETHICS

How Much Could You Forgive?

One of the primary concerns of peacemaking criminology is the issue of forgiveness. To heal the harms caused by crime over the long run, the victim and the offender should reconcile. This is often difficult, especially in cases of violent injury or death. Yet, it does happen. Some of the family members of those killed in the Oklahoma City bombing did not want Timothy McVeigh executed because their religious faith(s) forbade such a policy. Through restorative justice practices, some offenders who demonstrated true remorse have been forgiven by their victims' families.

Suppose someone murdered a member of your family, and after a period of time, expressed remorse and asked for you forgiveness. Could you forgive this criminal? If you are a religious person, what does your faith have to say about forgiveness? Is forgiveness something you might be able to develop after many years?

QUESTIONS

1. Is peacemaking criminology a nice theory but something that cannot be realistically expected of victims and their families?
2. If you made a big mistake and killed someone in a car wreck while you were drunk, could you ask the forgiveness of your victim's family?
3. Does someone who is truly remorseful deserve forgiveness?

logic to it that would allow that decision to be applied to other cases at other times. This, of course, means that racial or sexist bias should be eliminated, but it does not mean that justice need be mechanical or absolutely uniform. Individualized justice allows for discretion, but the categorical imperative dictates that decisions should have a defensible reason that promotes an overarching goal of not only justice, but social justice arrived at by correct means.

Is the peacemaking perspective simply a warmed-over version of liberal philosophies? Is it unrealistic, utopian, and naive? Is it the equivalent of giving in to the criminal element and turning the asylum over to the lunatics? Actually, no. The peacemaking perspective does not excuse crime or erase the culpability of offenders. Rather, it aims to craft institutions and policies that repair the harm caused by crime and reduce the suffering of victims, families, offenders, and the greater community.

Much of what the peacemaking perspective advocates is already ingrained in the criminal justice system. What the peacemaking perspective does is to provide a philosophical foundation for practices that recognize the promise of believing that people are basically good and that our institutions can achieve better results by modeling the types of behavior we demand of our offenders. For instance, when the state kills through capital punishment, it has a brutalizing effect on society according to the peacemaking perspective. Abusive behavior by the police alienates not only the victim, but also those who witness the event. Programs that promote the rehabilitation of offenders have been a consistent feature in the criminal justice system for decades, but because of the drain of resources caused by the war on crime, they have been neglected, underfunded, and made politically unpopular. But just how has the peacemaking perspective been implemented in the criminal justice system? One major strategy for injecting the principles of peacemaking is the restorative justice movement.

Restorative Justice

Restorative justice is a way to apply peacemaking criminology to the criminal justice system and to the community.[19] Whereas peacemaking may seem theoretically vague or idealistic, restorative justice has concrete evidence that its philosophy is workable in the real world. By highlighting the principles of restorative justice and reviewing some of the types of programs in which it has been effective, our goal here is to demonstrate that restorative justice and peacemaking are serious endeavors that deserve consideration as alternatives to the war-on-crime perspective.

Restorative justice forces us to consider the problems of crime in a different manner than do the traditional methods.[20] According to the principles of restorative justice, the criminal justice system is just a small part of society's response to crime. The possibility of making substantive changes in our crime picture is limited if we depend primarily on the formal criminal justice system. Restorative justice practices involve the community and, most important, establish and strengthen programs within the community to respond not only to crime, but also to some of the underlying conditions that contribute to crime.[21] The principles of restorative justice were aptly delineated by Ron Claassen from the Center for Peacemaking and Conflict Studies at Fresno Pacific University:[22]

1. Crime is primarily an offense against human relationships and secondarily a violation of the law (since laws are written to protect public safety and fairness in human relationships).
2. Restorative justice recognizes that crime (violations of persons and relationships) is wrong and should not occur, and also recognizes that after it does, there are dangers and opportunities. The danger is that the community, victim(s), and/or offender(s) emerge from the response further alienated, more damaged, disrespected, disempowered, feeling less safe and less cooperative with society. The opportunity is that injustice is recognized; equity is restored (restitution and grace); and the future is clarified so that participants are safer, more respectful, and more empowered and cooperative with society.

NEWS FLASH

Forgiveness

Although the peacemaking perspective and restorative justice may appear to represent unattainable ideals, their principles can sometimes pop up unexpectedly with surprising results.

In Texas, in October 2001, Gregory Biggs was walking alongside the road when Chante Mallard hit him with her car. Biggs was trapped inside the car, with his broken legs lodged in the windshield. Mallard drove home and parked the car in her garage, ignoring Biggs' pleas for help. Trapped in the windshield, Biggs bled to death. Mallard was eventually sentenced to 50 years in prison. At her trial, Mallard apologized to Biggs' 20-year-old son, Brandon, who said he forgave Mallard.

In 2003 an organization of death row inmates raised $10,000 for a college scholarship for Brandon Biggs. The money was collected through donations and subscriptions to a newsletter produced by the inmates and the Roman Catholic Church's peace and justice committee.

Source: CNN/AP, "Student Gets Scholarship from Death-Row Inmates," October 23, 2003, http://www.cnn.com/2003/EDUCATION/10/23/deathrow.scholarship.ap/index.html.

3. Restorative justice is a process to "make things as right as possible," which includes: attending to needs created by the offense, such as safety and repair of injuries to relationships and physical damage resulting from the offense, and attending to needs related to the cause of the offense (addictions, lack of social or employment skills, lack of moral or ethical base, etc.).
4. The primary victim(s) of a crime is/are the one(s) most impacted by the offense. The secondary victims are others impacted by the crime and might include family members, friends, witnesses, criminal justice officials, community, etc.
5. As soon as immediate victim, community, and offender safety concerns are satisfied, restorative justice views the situation as an opportunity to teach the offender and an opportunity to encourage the offender to learn new ways of acting and being in the community.
6. Restorative justice prefers responding to the crime at the earliest point possible and with the maximum amount of voluntary cooperation and minimum coercion, since healing in relationships and new learning are voluntary and cooperative processes.
7. Restorative justice prefers that most crimes are handled using a cooperative structure, including those impacted by the offense, to provide support and accountability. This might include primary and secondary victims and family (or substitutes if they choose not to participate), the offender and family, community representatives, government representatives, faith/community representatives, school representatives, and etc.
8. Restorative justice recognizes that not all offenders will be cooperative. Therefore, an outside authority must make decisions for uncooperative offenders. The actions of the authorities and the consequences imposed should be tested by whether they are reasonable, restorative, and respectful (for victim(s), offender(s), and community).
9. Restorative justice prefers that offenders who pose significant safety risks and are uncooperative be placed in settings where the emphasis is on safety, values, ethics, responsibility, accountability, and civility. They should be exposed to the impact of their crime(s) on victim(s), invited to learn empathy, and offered learning opportunities to become better equipped with skills to be a productive member of so-

ciety. They should continually be invited (not coerced) to become cooperative with the community and be given the opportunity to demonstrate this in appropriate settings.

10. Restorative justice requires follow-up and accountability structures utilizing the natural community as much as possible, since keeping agreements is the key to building a trustful community.
11. Restorative justice recognizes and encourages the role of community institutions, including the religious/faith community, in teaching and establishing the moral and ethical standards that build up the community.

Perhaps the most distinguishing aspect of restorative justice is its goal of widening the response to crime to include the community. In our rambling, suburbanized society, much of the functions of the community have been lost. Many people are socially and emotionally closer to coworkers, old friends via cell phones and e-mail, or even strangers thousands of miles away through Internet chat rooms than to their neighbors or family members. Many of us know very little about our neighbors only a few doors away, yet these people share our concerns about safety, criminal activity, and community resources. Restorative justice establishes programs that connect the government with community programs to provide alternative mechanisms to respond to crime. Programs such as neighborhood justice centers, victim-compensation agencies, rape crisis centers, and juvenile court conferencing circles all seek to provide ways to reduce the harms caused by crime and to heal the rift between offenders and victims. Restorative justice programs include the following:

- **Victim–offender reconciliation programs (VORP).** When the traditional criminal justice system handles a case, the offender and victim sit on opposite sides of the courtroom and listen while attorneys argue about the quality of evidence, the believability of witnesses, culpability, and legal procedures. The entire trial often takes place without the victim and offender ever exchanging words. In plea bargained cases, the victim and offender may never even be in the same room. Victim–offender reconciliation programs place these parties together with a trained mediator who facilitates an interaction that allows for a more satisfying result. Victims are able to put a human face on their losses and explain to offenders the extent of their injuries. Offenders are given an opportunity to explain their motivations and mitigating circumstances. As each side learns more about the humanness and circumstances of the other, they are able to craft solutions that accomplish three goals: identifying the injustice, making things right, and establishing mechanisms for future actions. Sometimes all the victim wants is to tell his or her story to the offender and receive a sincere apology. Sometimes the offender welcomes the opportunity to confess his or her transgressions without fear that the court will use it to impose a harsh sentence. Most important, when the offender and victim are going to have an ongoing relationship, such as when they are neighbors or family members, the mediator can suggest ground rules so that the disputes are avoided or issues can be worked out before they mushroom into bad feelings.
- **Family group conferencing.** These programs, which were pioneered in New Zealand and Australia, use a mediator to enable all those connected to a crime to develop a solution that is acceptable to everyone. In addition to the victim and the offender, there is a representative of law enforcement, a representative of the community, and others with an interest in the case such as family members. Offenders are not simply sentenced; they are included in a process that works to determine an equitable solution. In this way, offenders feel accountable for carrying out the decision because they had a hand in it and were able to express their side of the story.
- **Victim–offender panels (VOPs).** Often, the victim will not want to meet with the offender. Other times, it is simply not feasible because the case has already been

CROSSCURRENTS

The Downside of Restorative Justice

We would be remiss in this chapter if we did not give voice to some of the criticism that has been leveled at peacemaking criminology and restorative justice programs. It is fair to say that these concepts, while appealing from a theoretical point of view, are little tested as public policies. They have yet to stand the test of time or be applied to multiple jurisdictions in a successful way. It has long been the experience of the criminal justice system that a good program with a dedicated staff often is less successful when transferred to another city where the staff members view it as a job as opposed to a noble experiment. Some of the concerns that will need to be rigorously considered before restorative justice and alternative conflict resolution programs become widely accepted are as follows:

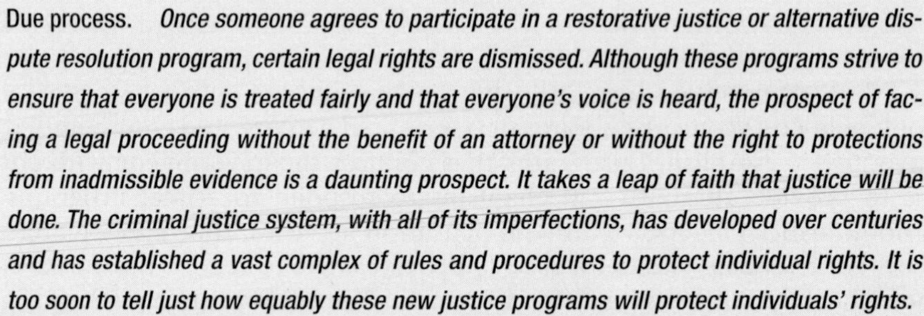

- Due process. *Once someone agrees to participate in a restorative justice or alternative dispute resolution program, certain legal rights are dismissed. Although these programs strive to ensure that everyone is treated fairly and that everyone's voice is heard, the prospect of facing a legal proceeding without the benefit of an attorney or without the right to protections from inadmissible evidence is a daunting prospect. It takes a leap of faith that justice will be done. The criminal justice system, with all of its imperfections, has developed over centuries and has established a vast complex of rules and procedures to protect individual rights. It is too soon to tell just how equably these new justice programs will protect individuals' rights.*

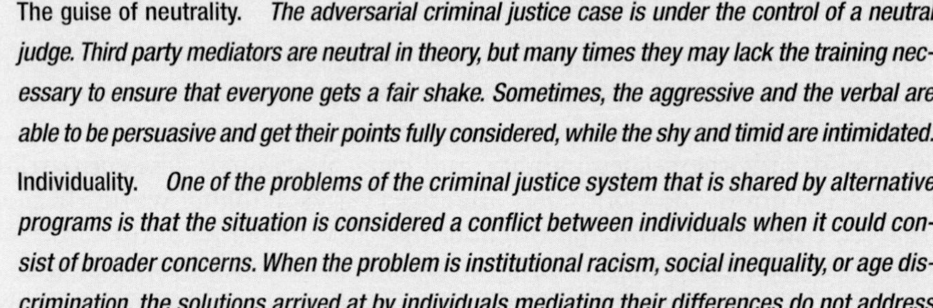

- The guise of neutrality. *The adversarial criminal justice case is under the control of a neutral judge. Third party mediators are neutral in theory, but many times they may lack the training necessary to ensure that everyone gets a fair shake. Sometimes, the aggressive and the verbal are able to be persuasive and get their points fully considered, while the shy and timid are intimidated.*
- Individuality. *One of the problems of the criminal justice system that is shared by alternative programs is that the situation is considered a conflict between individuals when it could consist of broader concerns. When the problem is institutional racism, social inequality, or age discrimination, the solutions arrived at by individuals mediating their differences do not address the underlying concerns that led to the dispute.*
- Connections to the community. *Courts have evolved over the years, and the people who work in them have a certain level of training, and in most cases are professionals. Judges and attorneys have law degrees and devote their professional lives to upholding a code of ethics that is supervised by the American Bar Association and various state bar associations. Additionally, the courts are accountable to citizens because judges are elected or appointed by others who are elected. Grassroots alternative dispute resolution programs recruit their personnel from a variety of backgrounds. Many times these well-meaning individuals have little training and may be completely ineffective in helping disputants craft reasonable solutions. There is a serious question of adequate oversight when amateurs are in charge.*

QUESTIONS

1. Are these concerns more serious than the concerns we have about the functions of the courts?
2. Is having an attorney a reasonable assurance that one's best interests will get a fair hearing in court?
3. Is abridging people's rights acceptable as long as they are happy with the solution?
4. Are judges really accountable to the community, or could the volunteers and professionals who staff restorative justice programs provide the same level of response to community needs?

Sources: Joseph A. Scimecca, "Conflict Resolution and a Critique of 'Alternative Dispute Resolution,'" In *Criminology as Peacemaking,* eds. Harold E. Pepinsky and Richard Quinney (Bloomington, IN: Indiana University Press, 1991), 263–279. Sharon Levrant, Francis T. Cullen, Betsy Fulton, and John F. Wozniak, "Reconsidering Restorative Justice: The Corruption of Benevolence Revisited," *Crime and Delinquency* 45, no. 1 (1999): 3–27.

settled and the offender is incarcerated. However, the potential still exists to educate offenders about the damage they have done through victim–offender panels. In cases such as rape or drunk driving, a victim might talk to a group of offenders who had nothing to do with his or her case. The idea is to let a victim of the type of crime committed by the offender explain how the victim has suffered, so that the offender can appreciate how angry a victim can become, and reflect on how his or her own crime might have hurt another victim. The traditional criminal justice system often does not have time for the procedures that allow offenders to understand how their actions harmed others. Especially in cases that are plea bargained, the offender misses the chance to consider the impact of his or her actions on the victim.[23]

Summary

This chapter has presented two emerging trends in the criminal justice system. On one hand, there is a serious and well-funded move to treat crimes, particularly terrorism, in a warlike manner. Given the dangers that face the United States, especially after the events of September 11, this approach to crime is understandable. Challenges to the safety of Americans come from inside our borders as well as from overseas. The government agencies that comprise our national defense and criminal justice system are beginning to coalesce in terms of mission, legal authority, and resources. The Department of Homeland Security has been created as a cabinet-level agency that oversees the protection of the United States.

Although the threats from terrorism are all too real, a number of sincere critics believe that our response has been hasty and misguided. They contend that in the rush to do something about terrorism, citizens have given the government too much authority via the Patriot Act. Americans are very possessive of their legal and privacy rights, and some are fearful that the government has been given the authority to act like a police state because of concerns about terrorism. The future will tell whether this fear is well founded. Certainly, there will be challenges to some of the provisions of the Patriot Act, and it may well be modified in the coming years.

A second trend appearing in the criminal justice system is a move to hone communities' response to crime by empowering them to take some of the responsibility of the criminal justice system. By employing a peacemaking style based on nonviolence and social justice, this trend seeks to find alternative responses to crime. Communities across the country are developing restorative justice programs in which citizens work with criminal justice officials to repair the harm done by crime. These programs seek to make offenders accountable to victims, the community, and themselves. By empowering offenders and victims to craft their own solutions, restorative justice models seek to create long-term results that satisfy all concerned.

It is too early to determine how these trends will develop. In some ways, they are so different that to support one trend is to be opposed to the other. Yet, it is not that simple. We may continue to apply the war metaphor to serious crime and terrorism, while applying a peacemaking perspective to concerns such as drug treatment and juvenile crime. In any event, the student of crime and justice in the United States can look forward to interesting times. Major challenges will continue to crop up as we seek to address the problems of crime. The real trick, and one with which our nation has always struggled, is to find ways of keeping Americans safe without abridging their legal, civil, and human rights. That is why the criminal justice system must draw from the best and brightest young people.

KEY TERMS

ascertainable criteria p. 558
categorical imperative p. 558
correct means p. 558
peacemaking criminology p. 552
restorative justice p. 552

REVIEW QUESTIONS

1. How are law enforcement officers different from soldiers? How are they alike?
2. How is terrorism changing the mission of the criminal justice system?
3. What are some of the differences between the war on terrorism and other social problems?
4. What issues contributed to the September 11 tragedy?
5. What are some of the agencies that were incorporated into the Department of Homeland Security?
6. What are some of the controversial aspects of the Patriot Act?
7. How will the war on crime and the war on drugs be hindered by the war on terrorism? How will they be helped?
8. What traditions contribute to peacemaking criminology?
9. What are the four levels of analysis to which peacemaking is applicable?
10. What are examples of restorative justice programs?

SUGGESTED FURTHER READING

Bazemore, Gordon, and Mara Schiff, eds. *Restorative Community Justice: Repairing Harm and Transforming Communities.* Cincinnati: Anderson, 2001.

Cronin, Isaac, ed. *Confronting Fear: A History of Terrorism.* New York: Thunder's Mouth Press, 2002.

Christie, Daniel J., Richard V. Wagner, and Deborah Du Nann Winter, eds. *Peace, Conflict, and Violence: Peace Psychology for the 21st Century.* Upper Saddle River, NJ: Prentice Hall, 2001.

Holmes, Robert L. *Nonviolence in Theory and Practice.* Prospect Heights, IL: Waveland Press, 1990.

Kegley, Charles W., Jr. *The New Global Terrorism: Characteristics, Causes, Controls.* Upper Saddle River, NJ: Prentice Hall, 2003.

Van Ness, Daniel W., and Karen Heetderks Strong. *Restoring Justice.* 2nd ed. Cincinnati: Anderson, 2002.

ENDNOTES

1. Eugene H. Czajkoski, "Drugs and the Warlike Administration of Justice," *Journal of Drug Issues* 20, no. 1 (1990): 125–129.
2. Eva Bertram, Morris Blackmon, Kenneth Sharpe, and Peter Andreas, *Drug War Politics: The Price of Denial* (Berkeley: University of California Press, 1996).
3. This stereotype of terrorists as being only from the Middle East is both unfair and misleading. It is unfair because only a tiny fraction of the people from Middle Eastern countries have engaged in terrorist acts. Furthermore, millions of Americans of the Islamic faith and/or of Middle Eastern descent are unjustly suspected of having terrorist tendencies. This stereotype is misleading because terrorists come from many different backgrounds. For instance, Timothy McVeigh, who blew up the Murrah Federal Building in Oklahoma City, was an army veteran who had no ties to the Middle East. In the hours after the explosion there was much speculation that it was done by Arab terrorists, and this caused great concern in the Arab community.
4. Rob de Wijk, "The Limits of Military Power," in *Terrorism and Counterterrorism,* eds. Russell D. Howard and Reid L. Sawyer (Guilford, CT: McGraw-Hill/Dushkin, 2002), 482–494.
5. Egon Bittner, *The Functions of the Police in Modern Society* (Cambridge, MA: Oelgeschlager, Gunn, and Haim, 1980).
6. Mark Juergensmeger, "The Religious Roots of Contemporary Terrorism," in *The New Global Terrorisms: Characteristics, Causes, and Controls,* ed. Charles W. Kegley (Upper Saddle River, NJ: Prentice Hall, 2003), 185–193.
7. Bruce Hoffman, "The Logic of Suicide Terrorism," in *Defeating Terrorism,* eds. Russell D. Howard and Reid L. Sawyer (Guilford, CT: McGraw-Hill/Dushkin, 2004), 103–113.
8. Patricia H. Brady, "The Impact of the September 11, 2001 Terrorist Attacks on Civil Liberties," in *Understanding Terrorism: Threats in an Uncertain World,* eds. Akorlie A. Nyatepe-Coo and Dorothy Zeisler-Vralsted (Upper Saddle River, NJ: Prentice Hall, 2004), 175–182.

9. CNN, "Senators Question 'Phoenix Memo' Author," May 21, 2002, http://www.cnn.com/2002/US/05/21/phoenix.memo/index.html.
10. Jeffrey H. Norwitz, "Combating Terrorism: With a Helmet or a Badge," in *Terrorism and Counterterrorism: Understanding the New Security Environment, Readings and Interpretations,* eds. Russell D. Howard and Reid L. Sawyer (Guilford, CT: McGraw-Hill/Dushkin, 2002), 470–481.
11. Brady, "Impact of September 11."
12. This point can be legitimately debated. The funds going to local and state law enforcement agencies are not uniformly applied. Some jurisdictions, such as Washington, D.C., and New York City, have more likely targets, whereas others have few targets of symbolic value.
13. Harold E. Pepinsky and Richard Quinney, *Peacemaking as Criminology* (Bloomington, IN: Indiana University Press, 1991).
14. Richard Quinney, "The Way of Peace: On Crime, Suffering, and Service," in *Peacemaking as Criminology,* eds. Harold E. Pepinsky and Richard Quinney (Bloomington, IN: Indiana University Press, 1991), 3–13.
15. Floyd H. Ross and Tynette Hills, *The Great Religions by Which Men Live* (Greenwich: Fawcett, 1956).
16. M. Kay Harris, "Moving into the New Millennium: Toward a Feminist Vision of Justice," in *Peacemaking as Criminology,* eds. Harold E. Pepinsky and Richard Quinney (Bloomington, IN: Indiana University Press, 1991), 83–91.
17. Ian Taylor, Paul Walton, and Jock Young, *The New Criminology: For a Social Theory of Deviance* (New York: Harper and Row, 1973).
18. Immanuel Kant, "The Categorical Imperative," in *Morality in Criminal Justice: An Introduction to Ethics,* eds. Daryl Close and Nicholas Meier (Belmont, CA: Wadsworth, 1995), 45–50.
19. David R. Karp and Todd R. Clear, eds., *What Is Community Justice: Case Studies of Restorative Justice and Community Supervision* (Thousand Oaks, CA: Sage, 2002).
20. Howard Zehr, *Changing Lenses: A New Focus for Crime and Justice* (Scottdale, PA: Herald Press, 1990).
21. Gordon Bazemore and Mara Schiff, *Restorative Community Justice: Repairing Harm and Transforming Communities* (Cincinnati: Anderson, 2001).
22. Ron Claassen, *Restorative Justice—Fundamental Principles* (paper presented May 1995 at the National Conference on Peacemaking and Conflict Resolution; revised May 1996 at the UN Alliance of NGOs Working Party on Restorative Justice, 1996). © 1996 by Ron Claassen. Printed by permission. Online at http://www.fresno.edu/pacs/docs/rjprinc.html.
23. Michael Braswell, John Fuller, and Bo Lozoff, *Corrections, Peacemaking and Restorative Justice: Transforming Individuals and Institutions* (Cincinnati: Anderson, 2001).

Glossary

Actual-seizure stop An incident in which police officers physically restrain a person and restrict his or her freedom.

Actus reus "Guilty deed." The physical action of a crime.

Adjudicatory hearing The process in which a juvenile court determines whether the allegations in a petition are supported by evidence.

Adversarial process A term describing the manner in which U.S. criminal trial courts operate; a system that requires two sides, a prosecution and a defense.

Alibi A defense that involves the defendant(s) claiming not to have been at the scene of a crime when that crime was committed.

Amicus curiae Someone who is not a part of a case who gives advice or testimony. Also called "friend of the court."

Anomie A condition in which a people or society undergoes a breakdown of social norms and values.

Argot roles Specific patterns of behavior that inmates develop in prison to adjust to the environment.

Arraignment A court appearance in which the defendant is formally charged with a crime and asked to respond by pleading guilty, not guilty, or *nolo contendere.*

Arson The act of intentionally burning a building. Any death that results from arson is murder, regardless of the arsonist's intention.

Ascertainable criteria A peacemaking criminology term that states that everyone involved in a criminal justice process should understand the rules and procedures employed by the system.

Assize of Clarendon A 12th-century English law that established judicial procedure and the grand jury system. It also took power from the local courts and returned it to the English crown.

Atavism The appearance in a person of features thought to be from earlier stages of human evolution. Popularized by Cesare Lombroso.

Authority The right and the power to commit an act or order others to commit an act. Permission.

Bail agent An employee of a private, for-profit company that provides money for suspects to be released from jail. Bail companies usually charge the suspect a fee of 10 percent of the amount of the bond. Also called a bondsman.

Bailiff An officer of the court responsible for executing writs and processes, making arrests, and keeping order in the court.

Behaviorism The assessment of human psychology via the examination of objectively observable and quantifiable actions, as opposed to subjective mental states.

Bench trial A trial that takes place before a judge, but without a jury, in which the judge makes the decision. Sometimes called a court trial.

Beyond a reasonable doubt Refers to the highest level of proof required to win a case. This level of proof is necessary in criminal cases to procure a guilty verdict.

Bill of indictment A declaration of the charges against an accused person that is presented to a grand jury to determine whether enough evidence exists for an indictment.

Bill of Rights The first 10 amendments to the U.S. Constitution, which guarantees fundamental rights and privileges to citizens.

Blood feud A disagreement, the settlement of which is based on personal vengeance and physical violence.

Bobbies A popular slang term for the police force created in 1829 by Sir Robert Peel's Metropolitan Police Act. The term is derived from the short form of Robert, Bob.

Boot camp prison A short-term prison that uses military boot camp training and discipline techniques to rehabilitate offenders. Often used for young offenders.

Bow Street Runners A police organization created circa 1748 by magistrates Henry Fielding and his brother Sir John Fielding whose members went on patrol, rather than sitting at a designated post.

Broken windows theory The idea that untended property or deviant behavior will attract crime. This theory is used as a justification for clearing the streets of homeless people, drunks, and unruly teens, even when no crime has been committed.

Bureau of Alcohol, Tobacco, Firearms, and Explosives (ATFE) A law enforcement organization within the United States Treasury that enforces federal laws and regulations relating to alcohol, tobacco, firearms, explosives, and arson.

Burglary The act of breaking into and entering a building or other structure or vehicle to commit a crime. Extreme force is not required and burglary is not restricted to theft. Any crime committed, such as assault, is considered to be burglary.

Categorical imperative A term associated with the philosopher Immanuel Kant. When applied to peacemaking, it means that every decision should be logical enough to be applied to other cases at other times.

Chancery court "Court of equity." In England, these were established, in part, to assist in dispensing justice when common law courts failed to resolve a case. These courts were favorable to vulnerable individuals, especially children.

Chemical castration Anti-androgen drugs, usually administered by injection, that have the effect of lowering the testosterone level and blunting the sex drive in males.

Chicago school Criminological theories that rely, in part, on individuals' demographics and geographic location to explain criminal behavior.

Child advocate An officer appointed by the court to protect the interests of the child and to act as a liaison among the child, the child's family, the court, and any other agency involved with the child. Some states have child-advocate offices.

Circuit court A court that holds sessions at intervals within different areas of a judicial district.

Civil law The law that governs private rights as opposed to the law that governs criminal issues.

Classical school of criminology A set of criminological theories that uses the idea of free will to explain criminal behavior.

Clearance rates The number of crimes that have been solved by the police. Often, offenders who are arrested for a crime will give information about other crimes they have committed. This allows police to "clear" those cases.

Clerk of the court The primary administrative officer of each court who manages nonjudicial functions. Among the clerk's duties are maintaining records and dockets, paying all collected monies into the U.S. Treasury, administering the jury, providing interpreters and court reporters, and sending official notices and summonses.

Code of Hammurabi An ancient code instituted by Hammurabi, a ruler of Babylonia, dealing with criminal and civil matters.

Commitment An order by a judge upon conviction or before trial that sends a person to jail or prison. Also, a judge's order that sends a mentally unstable person to a mental institution.

Common law Sometimes called case law, judiciary law, judge-made law, customary law, or unwritten law, common law is based on customs and general principles and is included in case law. Common law may also be used as precedent or for matters not addressed by statute.

Community policing A policing strategy that attempts to harness the resources and residents of a given community in stopping crime and maintaining order.

Community standards Practices, acts, and/or media accepted by a given social group who share a geographic area and/or government.

Compurgation In medieval German and English law, a defendant could establish innocence by taking an oath and having a required number of people swear that they believed the oath. Also called "wager of law." Compurgation was permitted until 1833.

Concurrence The coexistence of *actus reus* and *mens rea.*

Congregate-and-silent system A style of control pioneered by the Auburn System in which inmates were allowed to eat and work together during the day, but forbidden to speak, and locked alone in their cells at night.

Consent decree When the parties to a lawsuit accept a judge's order that is based on an agreement made by them instead of continuing the case through a trial or hearing.

Constable *(comes stabuli)* The head of law enforcement for large districts in early England. Constables oversaw the watch-and-ward system that guarded the city's or town's gates at night. In the modern United States, a constable serves areas such as rural townships and is usually elected. The constable is responsible for serving summonses, subpoenas, and court orders.

Corpus delicti "Body of the crime." The crime itself.

Correct means A peacemaking criminology term coined by Gandhi. A good solution to the problems of crime can only be attained using processes that embody peacemaking principles.

County stockade A component of a county corrections system. The stockade usually holds offenders who have already been sentenced.

Court administrator An officer responsible for the mechanical necessities of the court including, but not limited to, scheduling courtrooms, managing case flow, administering personnel, procuring furniture, and preparing budgets.

Court of the Star Chamber An ancient meeting place of the king of England's councilors in the palace of Westminster in London, so called because of stars painted on the ceiling. The court was separate from common law courts. Although its sentences included corporal punishments, convicts were never sentenced to death. It was abolished by the Long Parliament in 1641.

Court reporter A court officer who records and transcribes an official verbatim record of the legal proceedings of the court.

Courts of appeals Intermediate courts that dispose of many appeals before they reach the Supreme Court.

Crime rate The number of Crime Index offenses divided by the population of an area, usually given as a rate of crimes per 100,000 people.

Dark figure of crime A metaphor that describes crime that goes unreported to police and criminal justice officials and is never quantified.

Decriminalization The emendation of laws or statutes to lessen or remove penalties for specific acts subject to criminal prosecution, arrest, and imprisonment.

Determinate sentence A prison term that is determined by law and states a specific period of time to be served. Sentencing grids or guidelines are usually employed in calculating the sentence. For example, an armed robbery conviction might call for a 30-year sentence in jail, regardless of the circumstances of the offender or the crime.

Differential association theory A theory developed by Edwin Sutherland that states that crime is learned. Children learn crime from other children.

Directed verdict of acquittal An order from a trial judge to the jury stating that the jury must acquit the accused because the prosecution has not proved its case. A judge may not "direct a verdict of guilty," however, because such an order would violate the accused's right to a jury trial.

Discretion The power of a judge, public official, or law enforcement officer to make decisions on issues within legal guidelines. For example, a prosecutor exercises discretion about which cases are inserted into the criminal justice system.

Disposition The final determination of a case or other matter by a court or other judicial entity. This term can also refer to the sentence received by a convicted criminal defendant.

District courts Courts of general jurisdiction that try felony cases involving federal laws and civil cases involving amounts of money over $75,000.

Double jeopardy The prosecution in the same jurisdiction of a defendant for an offense for which the defendant has already been prosecuted and convicted or acquitted. Also refers to multiple punishments for a single offense. The Fifth Amendment states that no person will "be subject for the same offense to be twice put in jeopardy of life or limb."

Double marginality A term that refers to the multiple outsider status of women and/or minority police officers.

Drug Enforcement Administration (DEA) A government agency that enforces U.S. controlled substances laws and regulations. Also brings to the U.S. criminal system organizations involved in the growing, manufacture, and/or distribution of controlled substances to be trafficked in the United States.

Due process rights Guarantees by the Fifth, Sixth, and Fourteenth Amendments of the U.S. Constitution establishing legal procedures that recognize the protection of an individual's life, liberty, and property.

Electronic monitoring A form of intermediate punishment in which an offender is allowed to remain in the community but must wear an electronic device that allows the authorities to monitor his or her whereabouts. Electronic monitoring may also be done via telephone.

False consciousness An attitude held by members of a class that does not accurately reflect the reality of that class's existence. A term associated with Karl Marx.

Federal Bureau of Investigation (FBI) The principal investigative arm of the Department of Justice. It investigates the crimes assigned to it and provides cooperative services to other law enforcement agencies.

Felony A crime punishable by a term in state or federal prison and sometimes by death. In some instances, a sentence for a felony conviction may be less than one year. Felonies are sometimes called "high crimes."

Frankpledge system A form of English government that began in Anglo-Saxon England and endured until the 19th century. This system divided a community into groups of 10 men (tithings) who were responsible for the conduct of the group and ensured that a member charged with breaking the law would appear in court.

Gatekeeping At several points throughout the juvenile justice process, officials make important decisions that determine what happens to the youth. Examples of these decision points or "gates" are the prosecutor's determination of whether to charge the youth with a crime and the judge's decision to sentence the youth to probation or detention.

General deterrence A method of control in which the punishment of a single offender sets an example for the rest of society.

Geographic jurisdiction This is established when the location of a crime dictates which court will hear a case.

Going rate A term describing how similar cases have been settled by a given set of judges, prosecutors, and attorneys.

Good time The time deducted from an inmate's prison sentence for good behavior.

Grabbable area The area under the control of an individual during an arrest in an automobile. For example, the inside of the passenger compartment is considered "grabbable area," but not the space under the hood or in the trunk.

Grass-eaters A slang term from the 1971 Knapp Commission report on police corruption in New York City describing officers who accept bribes but do not actively pursue them.

Habeas corpus A writ issued to bring a party before the court.

Hands-off doctrine The judicial attitude toward prisons prior to the 1960s in which courts did not become involved in prison affairs or inmate rights.

Hearing A session that takes place without a jury before a judge or magistrate in which evidence and/or arguments are presented to determine some factual or legal issue.

Hierarchical jurisdiction This is established when a case is heard by a court according to where that case is located in the system. For example, trial courts hear the facts of the case, determine guilt or innocence, and impose sentence. Appellate courts review the work of the trial court judge and determine whether the case was handled according to the Constitution.

Hue and cry In early English law, the alarm that citizens were required to raise upon the witness or discovery of a crime. The witness and all within earshot were required by law to pursue the perpetrator.

Hundred-man The head of a group of 10 tithings (men collected in groups of 10) who served as an administrator and judge.

Hung jury A jury in a criminal case that is deadlocked or that cannot produce a unanimous verdict.

Immigration and Naturalization Service (INS) An agency of the Department of Justice responsible for enforcing the laws regulating the admission of foreigners to the United States and for administering immigration benefits, including the naturalization of applicants for U.S. citizenship.

Impeach The discrediting of a witness. This may be done by proving that the witness has lied or has been inconsistent, or by producing contrary evidence.

Inchoate offense An offense comprising acts necessary to commit another crime.

Indentured servant From the 17th to 19th centuries, a person who came to the American colonies/United States and was made to work for a period of time, usually seven years.

Indeterminate sentence A prison term that does not state a specific period of time to be served or date of release. Such a sentence will specify a range of time to be served, such as 10 to 20 years.

Infancy In legal terminology, refers to a child who has not yet reached a specific age. Almost all states end infancy at the age of 18.

Informal probation A period during which a juvenile is required to stay out of trouble or make restitution before the case is dropped.

Inquest In archaic usage, considered to be the first type of jury. The English crown conducted proceedings to determine which lands it had conquered and who owned them. The inquest was eventually broadened to address concerns other than land ownership.

Insanity defense A defense that attempts to give physical or psychological reasons that a defendant cannot comprehend his or her criminal actions, their harm(s), or their punishment.

Intensive supervision probation A form of supervision that requires frequent meetings between the client and probation officer(s).

Just deserts A philosophy that states that an offender who commits a heinous crime deserves death.

Juvenile delinquent A person, usually under the age of 18, who is determined to have committed a crime or status offense in states in which a minor is declared to lack responsibility and cannot be sentenced as an adult.

Labeling theory A perspective that considers recidivism to be a consequence, in part, of the negative labels applied to offenders.

Larceny A form of theft in which an offender takes possessions that do not belong to him or her with the intent of keeping them. Some jurisdictions specify "grand larceny" or "petty larceny" based on the value of the stolen items.

Legalistic style A mode of policing that emphasizes enforcement of the letter of the law. The legalistic officer will write more tickets, make more arrests, and encourage victims to sign complaints. Using little personal discretion, the legalistic officer will make arrests and allow the courts to resolve the incidents.

Legalization The total removal of legal prohibitions on specific acts that were previously proscribed and punishable by law.

Lower courts Sometimes called "inferior courts," in reference to their hierarchy. These courts receive their authority and resources from local county or municipal governments.

Magistrate court The lowest level of the federal court system, created in 1968 to ease the caseload of the U.S. district courts.

Magna Carta "Great charter." A guarantee of liberties signed by King John of England in 1215 that influenced many modern legal and constitutional principles.

Mandatory minimum sentence A sentence determined by law that establishes the minimum length of prison time that may be served for a crime.

Marks-of-commendation system An incarceration philosophy developed by Alexander Maconochie in which inmates earned the right to be released, as well as privileges, goods, and services.

Master status A personal status that overwhelms all others. For example, "rapist" obliterates a positive status such as "good student" or "sports star."

Meat-eaters A slang term from the 1971 Knapp Commission report on police corruption in New York City describing officers who actively seek out situations that can produce financial gain.

Mens rea "Guilty mind." Intent or knowledge to commit a crime.

Meritorious time Time deducted from an inmate's sentence for doing something special or extra, such as getting a GED.

Metropolitan Police Act Created in 1829 by Sir Robert Peel, it was the first successful bill to create a permanent, public police force.

Misdemeanor A crime considered less serious than a felony. Usually tried in the lowest local courts and punishable by no more than one year in jail.

Missouri Bar Plan A plan in which a judicial nominating commission presents a list of candidates to the governor who decides on a candidate. After a year in office, voters decide whether to retain the judge. Judges must run for such reelection each term. Also called merit selection.

National Incident-Based Reporting System (NIBRS) A crime reporting system in which each separate offense in a crime is described, including data describing the offender(s), victim(s), and property.

Neighborhood Watch A community policing program that encourages residents to cooperate in providing security for the neighborhood.

Neutralization theory A perspective that states that juvenile delinquents have feelings of guilt when involved in illegal activities. Illegal behavior is episodic and delinquents drift between legal and illegal activities. The delinquent sets aside his or her own legal and moral values to drift into illegal activities.

No-bill The decision of a grand jury not to indict an accused person because of insufficient evidence. Also called "no true bill."

Nolo contendere Latin for "I do not wish to contend." The defendant neither admits nor denies committing the crime, but agrees to be punished as if guilty. This type of plea cannot be used as an admission of guilt if a civil case is held after the criminal trial.

Operant conditioning The alteration of behavior by giving a subject rewards or punishments for a specified action until the subject associates the action with pleasure or pain.

Pains of imprisonment Deprivations that define the punitive nature of imprisonment.

Parens patriae Latin for "father of the country." Refers to the philosophy that the government is the ultimate guardian of all children or disabled adults.

Peacemaking criminology A theoretical perspective that serves as an alternative to the war on crime. It focuses on nonviolence, social justice, and reducing the suffering of both the victim and the offender.

Penal code A code of laws that deals with crimes and the punishments for them.

Petitioner A person who files a lawsuit; also called a plaintiff.

Pillory A wooden frame with holes for securing the head and hands that was used to secure and expose an offender to public derision.

Plea bargain A compromise reached by the defendant, the defendant's attorney, and the prosecutor in which the defendant agrees to plead guilty or no contest in return for a reduction of the charges' severity, dismissal of some charges, further information about the crime or about others involved in it, or the prosecutor's agreement to recommend a desired sentence. Plea bargains require a judge's approval.

Policeman's working personality A term coined by Jerome Skolnick to refer to the mind-set of police who must deal with danger, authority, isolation, and suspicion while appearing to be efficient. Officers may be drawn into a police subculture that emphasizes a different set of values from those of mainstream society.

Poor laws Seventeenth-century laws that turned over vagrants and abandoned children to landowners or shopkeepers as indentured servants.

Positivist school of criminology A set of criminological theories that uses scientific techniques to study crime and criminals.

Precedent A prior legal decision used as a basis for deciding a later, similar case.

Prejudicial error An error affecting the outcome of a trial.

Presentence report An account prepared by a probation officer that assists the sentencing court in deciding an appropriate sentence for a convicted defendant. The report includes the defendant's prior, if any, criminal history; relevant personal circumstances; the appropriate classification of the defendant and the offense under the established system; the variety of sentences and programs available; and the offense's impact on the victim.

Presumptive sentence A sentence that may be adjusted by the judge depending on aggravating or mitigating factors.

Preventive detention The jailing of a defendant awaiting trial, usually to protect an individual or the public.

***Prima facie* case** A case established by evidence sufficient enough to establish the fact in question unless it is rebutted.

Probable cause A reason based on known facts to think that a crime has taken place or that a property is connected to a crime. A law enforcement officer must have probable cause to make an arrest without a warrant, to search without a warrant, or to seize property that may provide evidence of a crime.

Problem-oriented policing A style of policing that attempts to address underlying social problems that contribute to crime.

Procedural law Laws that prescribe the methods for their enforcement and application.

Professional model of policing A policing style that emphasizes an impersonal and legalistic approach to enforcing the law.

Prohibition The period from January 29, 1920, to December 5, 1933, during which the manufacture, transportation, and sale of alcoholic beverages was made illegal in the United States by the Eighteenth Amendment. Enforcement legislation was entitled the National Prohibition Act or Volstead Act.

Racial profiling Suspicion of illegal activity based on a person's race, ethnicity, or national origin rather than on actual illegal activity or evidence of illegal activity.

Rape Sexual activity, usually sexual intercourse, that is forced on another person without his or her consent, usually under threat of harm. Sexual activity conducted with a person who is younger than a specified age or incapable of valid consent because of mental illness, mental handicap, intoxication, unconsciousness, or deception is called statutory rape.

Rational choice theory A theory that states that people choose criminal behavior consciously. The theory also states that people may choose to commit a crime upon realizing that the crime's benefits probably outweigh the consequences of breaking the law.

Reasonable stop standard A Supreme Court measure that considers constitutionality based on whether a reasonable person would feel free to terminate an encounter with law enforcement.

Reasonable suspicion A suspicion based on facts or circumstances that justifies stopping and sometimes searching an individual thought to be involved in criminal activity.

Redirect examination The questioning of a witness about issues uncovered during cross-examination.

Referral Similar to a "charge" in the adult system in which an authority, usually the police, parents, or the school, determines that the youth needs intervention from the juvenile court.

Residential placement Any sentence of a juvenile offender to a halfway house or other community home in which the juvenile is closely monitored, but allowed to leave for work or school.

Respondent The party who must reply to a petitioner's complaint. Equivalent to a defendant in a lawsuit.

Restorative justice An alternative justice model that uses community programs to repair the harm done by offenders. Programs include the victim, the offender, representatives of law enforcement, and representatives of the community in attempting to craft long-lasting and satisfying solutions to the problems of crime.

Retribution model A style of control in which offenders are punished as severely as possible for a crime and in which rehabilitation is not attempted.

Robbery The removal of property from a person by violence or by threat of violence.

Rule of four A rule that states that at least four of the nine Supreme Court justices must vote to hear a case.

Seizure When law enforcement officers take potential evidence in a criminal case. Evidence seized without a search warrant or without probable cause may not be admitted in court.

Separate-and-silent system A method of penal control pioneered by Philadelphia's Eastern State Penitentiary in which inmates were kept from seeing or talking to one another. This method is comparable to solitary confinement in modern prisons.

Serial murder Homicides of a sequence of victims committed by an offender in three or more separate events occurring over a period of time.

Service style A mode of policing that is concerned primarily with serving the community and citizens. The service-style officer will use discretion, as with the watchman style, but that discretion is visible and subject to formal review and evaluation, and can be altered when circumstances require.

Sex work The exchange of coital or sex-related activities for payment.

Sexual assault Sexual contact that is committed without the other party's consent or with a party who is not capable of giving consent (such as a child or mentally handicapped individual).

Sheriff From the English words *shire* and *reeve* (king's agent). An official of a county or parish who primarily carries out judicial duties. In early England, the shire reeve led the shire's military forces and judged cases. Later, sheriff duties were restricted to trying minor crimes, investigating crimes within the shire, and questioning suspects.

Shock probation The practice of sentencing offenders to prison, allowing them to serve a short time, and then granting them probation without their prior knowledge.

Show-of-authority stop An incident in which police show a sign of authority (such as flashing a badge), and the suspect submits.

Social control theory A theory that seeks not to explain why people break the law, but instead explores what keeps most people from breaking the law. Associated with Travis Hirschi.

Socialization A process by which individuals acquire a personal identity and learn the norms, values, behavior, and social skills appropriate to their society.

Sociological imagination Refers to the idea that we must look beyond the obvious to evaluate how our social location influences how we see society. One's race, age, gender, and socioeconomic status are thought to influence values and perspectives.

Somatotyping The use of body types and physical characteristics to classify human personalities.

Specific deterrence A method of control in which an offender is prevented from committing more crimes by either imprisonment or death.

Stare decisis The doctrine under which courts adhere to legal precedent.

State courts General courts and special courts funded and run by each state. Each state has a different system.

Status offense An act that is considered to be a legal offense only when committed by a juvenile and which can be adjudicated only in a juvenile court.

Statute A law enacted by a legislature.

Statutory exclusion Provisions that exclude, without hearing or waiver, juveniles who meet certain age, offense, or past record criteria from the jurisdiction of the juvenile court. Excluded juvenile offenders are automatically tried in adult criminal court. Crimes that may invoke statutory exclusion include murder, aggravated rape, and armed robbery.

Statutory law The type of law that is enacted by legislatures, as opposed to common law.

Statutory rape See *rape*.

Stop A temporary detention that legally is a seizure of an individual and must be based on reasonable suspicion.

Stop and frisk A term that describes two distinct behaviors on the part of law enforcement officers in dealing with suspects. To conduct a lawful frisk, the stop itself must meet the legal conditions of a seizure. A frisk constitutes a search.

Strain theory The hypothesis that the causes of crime can be connected to the pressure on culturally or materially disadvantaged groups or individuals to achieve the goals held by society, even if the means to those goals require the breaking of laws. Based on Émile Durkheim's theory of anomie.

Strict liability Responsibility for a crime without intention to commit a crime. *Mens rea* is not required in strict liability findings.

Subject matter jurisdiction This is established when the nature of the case determines which court hears it. An example would be the distinction between felonies and misdemeanors.

Substantive law The law that defines rights and proscribes certain actions (crimes).

Terrorism The use or threat of violence against a state or other political entity in order to coerce.

Thames River Police A private police force created by the West India Trading Company in 1798 that represented the first professional, salaried police force in London.

Tort law A large area of the law that deals with civil acts, other than breach of contract, that cause harm and injury. Tort law includes libel, slander, assault, trespass, and negligence.

Total institution A closed environment in which every aspect, including the movement and behavior of the people within, is controlled and structured.

Trial by ordeal An ancient custom found in many cultures in which the accused was required to perform a test to prove guilt or innocence. The outcome of the test was considered to be decided by a divine authority.

True bill The decision of grand jury that sufficient evidence exists to indict an accused person.

Uniform Crime Reports (UCR) An annual publication by the Federal Bureau of Investigation that uses data from all participating law enforcement agencies in the United States to summarize the incidence and rate of reported crime.

U.S. Border Patrol The mobile uniformed law enforcement arm of the Immigration and Naturalization Service. Its primary mission is to detect and prevent the illegal entry of foreign-born persons into the United States.

U.S. Customs Service The primary enforcement agency protecting U.S. borders and dealing with smuggling, imports, and exports.

U.S. Marshals Service (Federal Marshals) Created in 1789, the agency protects federal courts and ensures the effective operation of the judicial system. The agency also carries out fugitive investigations, custody and transportation of federal prisoners, security for government witnesses, and asset seizure in federal forfeitures.

U.S. Secret Service A federal investigative law enforcement agency authorized to protect the president and other U.S. government officials and visiting officials. The agency also investigates financial fraud and counterfeiting.

U.S. Supreme Court The "court of last resort." The highest court in the United States, established by Article III of the Constitution, hears only appeals, with some exceptions.

Use of force The legal police use of violence to enforce the law. Excessive use of force is considered police brutality.

Utilitarianism A theory associated with Jeremy Bentham that states that people will choose not to commit crime when the pain of punishment outweighs the benefit derived from the crime.

Venire The list or pool from which jurors are chosen.

Victim precipitation A situation in which a crime victim plays an active role in initiating a crime or escalating it.

Victimization surveys Surveys that attempt to measure the extent of crime by interviewing people who have suffered crime.

Victimless crimes Behaviors such as gambling or prostitution that are deemed undesirable because they offend community standards rather than directly harm people or property.

Voir dire French for "to see, to speak." Refers to the questioning of jurors by a judge and/or attorneys to determine whether individual jurors are appropriate for a particular jury panel. Jurors may be dismissed by the judge or attorneys.

War on drugs A policy aimed at reducing the sale and use of illegal drugs. The war metaphor is used to illustrate how serious the drug problem has become in the United States. The war on drugs is fought on many levels, but the criminal justice system spends enormous resources on this problem.

Warrant A writ issued by a judicial official that authorizes an officer to perform a specified act required for the administration of justice, such as an arrest or search.

Watch-and-ward system An old English system overseen by the constable in which a watchman guarded a city's or town's gates at night.

Watchman style A mode of policing that emphasizes the maintenance of order and informal intervention on the part of the police officer rather than strict enforcement of the law.

Writ of certiorari An order from a superior court calling up for review the record of a case from an lower court.

XYY syndrome A condition in which a male is born with an extra Y chromosome. Such males tend to be tall, have difficulties with language, and have relatively low IQs. The condition was once thought to cause criminal behavior.

Zero-tolerance policies Policies of schools or other agencies in which the strict letter of the law or rule is followed without question or room for individual discretion on the part of the authority.

Zero-tolerance policing This form of policing punishes every infraction of the law, however minor, with an arrest, fine, or other penalty so that criminals will refrain from committing more serious crimes.

Glosario de español

Spanish translation by
Dr. Myrna Cintrón
Prairie View A&M University

Actual-seizure stop
Aprehensión y captura Situación en la que oficiales policíacos restringen físicamente a una persona limitando así su libertad.

***Actus reus* "Guilty deed"**
***Actus reus* "conducta delictiva"** La acción por la cual se comete el delito.

Adjudicatory hearing
Vista adjudicatoria Procedimiento, en el tribunal de menores, donde se determina si hay pruebas para los cargos descritos en la petición.

Adversarial process
Sistema acusatorio Término que describe el sistema de justicia criminal de los Estados Unidos, está basado en el litigio entre dos partes, un abogado defensor (representa al acusado) y un fiscal (representa al estado).

Alibi
Cuartada Defensa en la que el acusado reclama no haber estado presente en la escena del delito cuando éste ocurrió.

Amicus curiae
Amicus curiae Persona que a pesar de no ser parte del litigio ofrece consejo o testimonio. También es conocido como "amigo del tribunal."

Anomia
Anomia Condici Condición o situación en la que una persona o sociedad pierden sus valores y normas sociales.

Argot roles
Jerga carcelaria Patrón de conducta, comportamiento, y lenguaje desarrollado por los confinados para adaptarse al ambiente carcelario.

Arraignment
Acusación Vista en la que el acusado es formalmente informado de los cargos en su contra y donde se exige se declare culpable, inocente, o que no se opone a la acusación.

Arson
Incendio provocado Acción intencional por la cual se incendia un edificio o estructura. Si alguien muere durante esta acción, el cargo criminal será homicidio, independientemente de la intención del acusado.

Ascertainable criteria
Criterios afirmables Termino usado en Criminología de la Paz, que establece que toda persona envuelta en el proceso de justicia criminal debe entender las reglas y procedimientos usados en este sistema.

Assize of Clarendon
Sesión de Clarendon Durante el siglo 12 en Inglaterra, ley que estableció el procedimiento jurídico y el sistema del gran jurado. Además removió algunos poderes de los tribunales locales y los otorgó a la corona inglesa.

Atavism
Atavismo En una persona, la apariencia de rasgos físicos que se creen son rezagos de una etapa evolucionaría anterior. Popularizado por Cesare Lombroso.

Authority
Autoridad Poder, autoridad y legitimación para realizar un acto u ordenar a otros realizar un acto. Permiso.

Bail agent
Fiador Empleado de una compañía privada (a comisión, con fines de lucro) la cual provee los medios económicos que permite que los sospechosos de actos criminales puedan ser puestos en libertad. Usualmente estas compañías recargan un 10 porciento del monto de la fianza.

Bailiff
Guardia, alguacil Oficial del tribunal responsable de ejecutar ordenes judiciales y otros procedimientos, pueden arrestar y mantienen el orden público en el tribunal.

Behaviorism
Estudio psicológico de la conducta Evaluación psicológica que usa medios objetivamente observables y acciones cuantificables, es lo opuesto al estado mental subjetivo.

Bench trial
Juicio de derecho Juicio frente a un juez, sin jurado, donde el juez hace la determinación. También se conoce como juicio.

Beyond a reasonable doubt
Mas allá de toda duda razonable Se refiere al nivel de prueba requerido para ganar un caso en un tribunal. Este nivel de prueba es necesario en casos criminales para asegurar un veredicto de culpabilidad.

Bill of Indictment
Auto de acusación Declaratoria sobre los cargos acusatorios en contra del acusado que es presentada al gran jurado para que éstos decidan si hay evidencia suficiente para la acusación.

Bill of Rights
Carta de derechos Las primeras 10 enmiendas a la Constitución de los Estados Unidos que garantizan los privilegios y derechos fundamentales de los ciudadanos.

Blood feud
Duelo a sangre Desacuerdo el cual se resuelve a través de la venganza personal y el uso de la violencia física.

Bobbies
Bobbies Jerga popular que se refiere al grupo policíaco creado in 1829 por el Caballero Inglés Robert Peel en la ley que creo la Policía Metropolitana. El termino se deriva del apodo de "Robert," "Bob."

Boot-camp prison
Campamento de re-entrenamiento Termino de reclusión a corto plazo, usando las técnicas de entrenamiento y disciplina de las fuerzas armadas de los Estados Unidos para rehabilitar a los delincuentes. Se usa con delincuentes juveniles.

Bow Street Runners
Corredores de la Calle Bow Organización policíaca creada cerca del 1748 por los magistrados Henry Fielding y su hermano el caballero inglés John Fielding, cuyos miembros patrullaban las calles y no estaban asignados a un lugar en particular.

Broken windows theory
Teoría de ventanas rotas Está basada en la idea de que la propiedad desocupada o la conducta desviada atraen el delito. Esta teoría ha sido usada para justificar el remover a los destituidos de hogar, los borrachos y gente joven de las calles aún cuando no han cometido delito alguno.

Bureau of Alcohol, Tobacco, and Firearms (ATF)
Oficina de Alcohol, Tabaco y Armas de Fuego Cuerpo policiaco del Departamento del Tesoro de los Estados Unidos que hace cumplir las leyes federales que restringen el uso de alcohol, de cigarros, las armas de fuegos, instrumentos explosivos y materiales incendiarios.

Burglary
Escalamiento o allanamiento de morada Acción por la cual se tiene acceso a un edificio u otra estructura para cometer un delito. No se requiere del uso de fuerza excesiva y no está restringido al robo. Cualquier otro delito cometido, tal como agresión, también es considerado escalamiento o allanamiento de morada.

Categorical imperative
Imperativo categórico Termino asociado con el filósofo Immanuel Kant. Cuando es usado en Criminología de la Paz (pacificación), se refiere a que cada decisión deberá ser suficientemente lógica como para ser utilizada en otros casos y en otras ocasiones.

Chancery court
Tribunal de Instancia-"tribunal de Equidad/Igualdad" Fueron establecidos en Inglaterra, en parte, para ayudar a hacer justicia en los casos donde los tribunales de derecho común no resolvían algunos casos. Estos tribunales les daban preferencia a las personas que se encontraban en situaciones vulnerables, especialmente a los niños menores de edad.

Chemical castration
Castración química Medicamento anti-andrógeno, usualmente administrado por infección intravenosa, que disminuye los niveles de testosterona y elimina el apetito sexual en los hombres.

Chicago School
Escuela de Chicago Teorías criminológicas basadas, en parte, en que las características demográficas del individuo y su localización geográfica pueden explicar el comportamiento delictivo.

Child advocate
Protector de los derechos del niño Persona designada por el tribunal para proteger los intereses y derechos legales del niño y quien actúa como enlace entre el niño, su familia, el tribunal y cualquier otra agencia de gobierno que esté interesada en el caso. Algunos estados tienen oficinas de protección al niño.

Circuit court
Tribunal de circuito Tribunal cuyos juicios se llevan a cabo a intervalos dentro de los diferentes distritos judiciales.

Civil law
Derecho civil Ley donde se aplican los derechos privados, contrario a la ley que rige los procedimientos criminales.

Classical school of criminology
Escuela clásica de criminología Grupo de teorías criminológicas que usan el libre albedrío como explicación para el comportamiento delictivo.

Clearance rates
Taza de delitos esclarecidos o aclarados Delitos resueltos por la policía. Hay ocasiones donde un sospechoso, al ser arrestado, ofrece información sobre otros actos delictivos que ha cometido. Esto ayuda a que los oficiales policíacos resuelvan otros actos delictivos.

Clerk of the court
Secretario del tribunal Oficial administrativo encargado de todas las funciones no jurídicas del tribunal. Entre sus tareas se encuentra el mantenimiento de archivos y calendarios, envio de pagos monetarios a la Oficina del Tesoro de los EEUU, organización del jurado, disponibilidad de intérpretes y estenógrafos, el envio de notificaciones oficiales y emplazamientos.

Code of Hammurabi
Código de Hammurabi Código de ley muy antiguo, escrito por Hammurabi, gobernante de Babilonia, en el que se describen los actos delictivos criminales y civiles.

Commitment
Fallo condenatorio Orden del juez, después del fallo de culpabilidad o antes del juicio, que ordena la encarcelación en cárcel o prisión. El juez también puede ordenar que personas mentalmente inestables sean enviadas a un hospital mental.

Common law
Derecho común También conocido como jurisprudencia, interpretación jurídica, leyes usuales, o ley no escrita. Este tipo de derecho está basado en costumbres y principios generales de comportamiento que han sido incluidos en jurisprudencia. El derecho común puede ser usado para sentar precedente o en hechos donde aún no se ha establecido ley alguna.

Community policing
Policía comunitaria Estrategia policíaca que intenta reunir los recursos y los residentes de las distintas comunidades para reducir el crimen y mantener el orden público.

Community standards
Estandartes comunitarios Prácticas, acciones, y/o medidas aceptadas por un grupo social quienes comparten un área geográfica y/o gobierno.

Compurgation
Compurgación En la Alemania medieval y en la ley Inglesa, donde el acusado podía declarar su inocencia haciendo un juramento y teniendo cierto número de personas quienes también juramentaban sobre la veracidad del juramento. También se le conoce como "apuesta legal." Compurgación fue permitida hasta 1833.

Concurrence
Concurrencia La coexistencia del *actus reus y mens rea.*

Congregate-and-silent system
Sistema de congregación y silencio Un estilo de control desarrollado por el Sistema de Auburn donde durante el día los confinados comían y trabajaban en grupos, pero donde estaba prohibido todo tipo de comunicación, y pasaban la noche encerrados en sus celdas.

Consent decree
Decreto de consentimiento Cuando ambas partes en una demanda aceptan el fallo del juez, quien toma su decisión basado en un acuerdo previo entre las partes y donde no hay juicio o litigio.

Constable *(comus stabuli)*
Alguacil El jefe policíaco en la cabecera de distrito en Inglaterra. El alguacil supervisaba el sistema de vigilancia y guardia que resguardaba las puertas de la ciudad o del pueblo durante la noche. Hoy día en los EEUU, el alguacil da servicio en áreas rurales y es, usualmente, elegido en elecciones populares. Es responsable de enviar citaciones, subpoena y órdenes judiciales.

Corpus delicti
Corpus delicti "Cuerpo del delito." El delito.

Correct means
Medios apropiados En criminología de Paz término usado por Gandhi. Una buena solución al problema del crimen solo puede ser adquirida a través de procedimientos que representen los principios de paz.

County stockade
Empalizada del condado Parte del sistema correccional municipal. Usado para convictos sentenciados a condena en prisión. Debido a que en muchos estados hay un número excesivo de confinados (hacinamiento), estos estados firman contratos con los condados y estas facilidades son usadas para encarcelar a personas convictas por delitos graves.

Court administrator
Administrador del tribunal Oficial responsable de las necesidades diarias del tribunal incluyendo, pero no limitado, a la planificación del uso de salas durante juicios, distribución de casos, la administración del personal, la compra de muebles y el presupuesto.

Court of the Star Chamber
Tribunal de la sala de estrellas Antiguamente, sala de reuniones de los consejeros del rey en el palacio de Westminster en Londres, llamado así por las estrellas dibujadas en el techo. Este tribunal era distinto al tribunal de derecho común. Aunque sus sentencias incluían el castigo corporal, nunca nadie fue sentenciado a muerte. Fue abolida por el Parlamento de Long en 1641.

Court reporter
Estenógrafo Oficial del tribunal que anota y transcribe verbalmente el acta en todo procedimiento legal del tribunal.

Courts of appeal
Tribunal de apelación Tribunal de segunda instancia que decide muchas de las apelaciones antes de que éstas lleguen al Tribunal Supremo.

Crime rate
Taza del crimen El número de ofensas delictivas conocidas como Índice del crimen, dividido por el número de habitantes del área, usualmente se utiliza la taza de criminalidad por cada 100,000 habitantes.

Dark figure of crime
Cifra negra del delito Metáfora que describe los delitos que no son reportados ni a la policía ni a otros oficiales del sistema de justicia criminal y que no se puede medir.

Decriminalization
Decriminalización Enmiendas a leyes o estatutos que disminuyen o remueven las penalidades de algunos comportamientos sujetos a arresto, enjuiciamiento, y encarcelación.

Determinate sentence
Sentencia determinada Sentencia que ha sido previamente determinada por acción legislativa y que especifica el término a ser servido en prisión. Usualmente se utilizan guías o modelos previamente diseñados para calcular el término a ser servido en prisión. Por ejemplo, por robo a mano armada el castigo puede ser de 30 años en prisión, independientemente de las circunstancias personales del delincuente o del delito cometido.

Differential association theory
Teoría de asociación diferencial Establece que la criminalidad es aprendida. Los niños aprenden este tipo de conducta de otros niños. Desarrollada por Edwin Sutherland.

Directed verdict of acquittal
Veredicto directo de absolución Orden dada por el juez de cargos y que ordena al jurado absolver al acusado porque el fiscal no ha comprobado los cargos. El juez no puede ordenar un "veredicto directo de culpabilidad," ya que esto violaría el derecho del acusado a un juicio por jurado.

Discretion
Discreción Poder que tiene el juez, oficial público, u oficial policíaco para tomar decisiones en asuntos legales que estén dentro de sus pautas profesionales. Por ejemplo, el fiscal puede ejercer su discreción acerca de qué casos deberán ser juzgados en el sistema de justicia criminal.

Disposition
Disposición Fallo final con relación a casos u otros hechos de naturaleza legal o judicial. Este término también se usa para referirse a la condena dada a un convicto.

District courts
Tribunal de Distrito Tribunal de jurisdicción general donde se deciden delitos graves de índole federal y casos civiles que envuelven $75,0000 o más.

Double jeopardy
Doble exposición Cuando un acusado es enjuiciado en la misma jurisdicción por una ofensa previamente juzgada y encontrado culpable o ha sido absuelto. También se usa cuando una persona recibe varias condenas por el mismo delito. La quinta enmienda a la Constitución determina que ninguna persona podrá ser "enjuiciada dos veces por la misma ofensa, ni su vida o su cuerpo puestos en peligro".

Double marginality
Marginalidad doble Término que se refiere a los diversos roles y estatus que tienen las mujeres y/u oficiales policíacos quienes por ser grupos minoritarios son vistos como fuera de grupo, que no pertenecen.

Drug Enforcement Administration (DEA)
Administración de Control de Drogas (iniciales en inglés DEA) Aplica las leyes y regulaciones sobre substancias controladas. Además se encarga de enjuiciar, en tribunales americanos, a las organizaciones envueltas en la agricultura, manufactura, y/o distribución de substancias controladas que son traficadas en los Estados Unidos.

Due process rights
Derecho a un procedimiento legal justo (debido proceso de ley) Garantías de la quinta, sexta, y 14ta Enmienda de la Constitución de EEUU donde se establecen los procedimientos legales que conceden la protección a la vida, a la libertad, y a la propiedad.

Electronic monitoring
Vigilancia electrónica Castigo de nivel intermedio donde se le permite al delincuente permanecer en su comunidad pero debe utilizar un aparato electrónico por medio del cual los funcionarios públicos responsables pueden seguir sus movimientos. Vigilancia electrónica se puede hacer a través del teléfono.

False consciousness
Concientización falsa Actitud, creencia en los miembros de una clase social que no demuestra su realidad social. Término asociado con Karl Marx.

Federal Bureau of Investigation
Oficina Federal de Investigaciones El FBI (iniciales en inglés) es la oficina principal de investigaciones del Departamento de Justicia. Investiga los delitos que le han sido propiamente designados y provee servicios en cooperación con otras agencias policíacas.

Felony
Delito grave Delitos donde el castigo conlleva condena de prisión en cárcel estatal o federal y en ocasiones la pena de muerte. La pena por un delito grave es usualmente superior a un año. También se le conoce como "delitos mayores o delito serio."

Frankpledge system
Sistema de juramento de lealtad Forma de gobierno inglés comenzado en la Inglaterra Anglo Sajona y que duró hasta el siglo 19. Este sistema dividía a las comunidades en grupos de 10 hombres (diezmeros) quienes eran responsables por la conducta del grupo y se responsabilizaban por los que habían quebrantado la ley se presentaran al tribunal para ser enjuiciados.

Gate-keeping
Porteria En el sistema de justicia juvenil hay varios momentos en el procesamiento del caso donde las decisiones importantes son hechas por funcionarios que deciden lo que puede ocurrirle a un joven. Por ejemplo dos de estos momentos decisivos o "porterias del sistema" son cuando el fiscal, determina si va a acusar al delincuente y cuando el juez, determina sentenciar a libertad condicional o reclusión.

General deterrence
Disuasión general Método de control del delito por medio del cual se castiga al acusado con el fin de dar ejemplo a toda la sociedad.

Geographic jurisdiction
Jurisdicción geográfica Cuando el lugar donde ocurrió el delito determina el tribunal competente para someter el caso.

Going rate
Precio de transacción Término que describe las situaciones y casos que han sido anteriormente transadas por jueces, fiscales, y abogado defensor.

Good time
Buena conducta Bonificación que reduce la condena de un prisionero por su buen comportamiento.

Grabbable area
Área de agarre, control En un automóvil el espacio que un individuo tiene bajo su control durante el arresto. Por

ejemplo, en el interior del vehículo el espacio del pasajero es considerado "zona de agarre," la capota y la maletera no lo son.

Grass-eaters
Hierbatero Jerga usada en el reporte de la Comisión de Knapp en 1971 sobre corrupción policíaca en Nueva York y donde se describió a los policías que aceptaban soborno pero no lo hacían activamente.

Habeas corpus
Hábeas corpus Decreto donde se ordena traer a una persona ante el tribunal.

Hands-off doctrine
Doctrina de no envolvimiento Actitud judicial hacia las cárceles antes de 1960 cuando los tribunales no se inmiscuían en asuntos carcelarios o en los derechos de los confinados.

Hearing
Audiencia/vista Procedimiento judicial sin jurado y frente a un juez o magistrado donde la prueba y/o argumento es presentado para decidir asuntos sobre los hechos u otros asuntos legales.

Hierarchical jurisdiction
Jurisdicción jerárquica Cuando un caso se juzga en un tribunal de acuerdo a donde ese caso se encuentra en ese sistema. Por ejemplo, los tribunales de primera instancia juzgan los hechos, determinan culpabilidad o inocencia, e imponen condena. El tribunal de apelaciones revisa el trabajo y la decisión del juez de primera instancia y decide si el caso fue enjuiciado de acuerdo a la Constitución.

Hue and cry
Clamor y lamento Sistema de aviso o alarma usado por los ciudadanos Ingleses cuando descubrían o eran testigos de algún delito. Los testigos, tanto el que presenciaba el delito como el que oyó algún sonido, debían perseguir al delincuente.

Hundred-man
Cien-hombres El líder de un grupo de 10 diezmeros (hombres en grupos de 10) que servían como administradores y jueces.

Hung jury
Jurado estancado por desacuerdo Término que describe un jurado cuyas opiniones se encuentran de tal forma divididas que no pueden llegar a un veredicto.

Immigration and Naturalization Service (INS)
Servicio de Inmigración y Naturalización (iniciales en inglés son INS) Agencia del Departamento de Justicia responsable de aplicar las leyes que regulan la admisión de extranjeros a los Estados Unidos y de administrar derechos de inmigración, incluyendo la naturalización de los que solicitan la ciudadanía americana.

Impeach
Impugnación La desacreditación de un testigo. Se hace para probar que el testigo mintió o es inconsistente en su testimonio o para producir pruebas contrarias.

Inchoate offense
Delito no perfeccionado Delito que requiere de la combinación de varios actos para ser realizado.

Indentured servant
Aprendiz Entre los siglos 17 y 18, persona traída a las colonias de América (Estados Unidos) y quien a cambio trabajaba por un periodo de tiempo, usualmente siete años.

Indeterminate sentence
Condena indeterminada Condena de prisión por un término no especificado. En este tipo de condena se establece un plazo de tiempo entre el máximo y el mínimo, como por ejemplo "de 10 a 20 años."

Infancy
Menor de edad, infancia Término legal que se refiere a un niño(a) quien no tiene la edad especificada en la ley para ser considerado adulto. En casi todos los estados ésta termina a los 18 años de edad.

Informal probation
Libertad condicional informal En ocasiones, se toma la decisión de continuar un caso y no se mantiene un expediente oficial que podría perjudicar al menor. Un ejemplo de libertad condicional informal es cuando al menor se le ordena evitar todo tipo de problemas o hacer restitución antes de que los cargos sean retirados.

Inquest
Inquisición Uso arcaico, considerado como el primer tipo de jurado. La corona inglesa llevaba a cabo procedimientos donde se decidía que tierras habían sido conquistadas y a quién le pertenecían. Eventualmente el uso del término se extendió y hoy es usado en otros asuntos diferentes a la adquisición de tierras.

Insanity defense
Defensa por incapacidad mental Defensa donde por razones físicas o mentales el acusado carece de culpabilidad al no entender que sus acciones son delictivas, o que causó daño, o que puede ser enviado a prisión.

Intensive supervision probation
Libertad condicional con supervisión intensiva Supervisión en la comunidad donde se requieren muchas visitas y reuniones entre el cliente y el oficial probatorio.

Just deserts
Castigo justo, Lo merecido Filosofía que sostiene que el delincuente que comete un crimen horrendo merece la pena de muerte.

Juvenile delinquent
Delincuente juvenil Persona menor de 18 años quien ha sido adjudicado por delito o falta y donde el menor carece de responsabilidad legal y no puede ser condenado como adulto.

Labeling theory
Teoría del etiquetaje Perspectiva que propone que la reincidencia delictiva es, en parte, como consecuencia del uso de las etiquetas negativas.

Larceny
Hurto Robo donde el delincuente se apropia de bienes que no le pertenecen sin tener la intención de devolverlos. En algunas jurisdicciones se especifica si es hurto mayor o hurto menor dependiendo del valor de los bienes.

Legalistic style
Estilo legalista Función policíaca donde se enfatiza la aplicación de la ley. El policía con estilo legalista escribe más boletas, hace más arrestos, y fomenta las querellas por parte de las victimas. Ejerce poca discreción personal, y al hacer arrestos asume que los tribunales van a resolver los hechos.

Legalization
Legalización Eliminación de toda prohibición jurídica de actos y conductas previamente prohibidas.

Lower court
Tribunal inferior Su nombre se refiere a su jerarquía dentro del sistema de tribunales. Estos tribunales reciben su poder jurídico y recursos económicos de las autoridades locales y municipales.

Magistrate court
Tribunal de magistrado El tribunal de nivel más bajo dentro del sistema federal, creado en 1968 con el fin de disminuir el número de casos de los Tribunales de Distrito federal.

Magna Carta
Carta Magna Salvaconducto Garantía de libertades, firmado por el rey Juan de Inglaterra en 1215, ha influenciado en muchos de los principios jurídicos y constitucionales modernos.

Mandatory minimum sentence
Condena mandatoria mínima Condena obligatoria determinada por ley y que establece el plazo mínimo a ser servido en prisión.

Marks-of-commendation system
Sistema de puntos (buena conducta) Filosofía carcelaria desarrollada por Alexander Maconochie donde los confinados tenían que ganarse el derecho a ser liberados, los privilegios obtenidos, y otros bienes y servicios.

Master status
Estatus dominante Cuando un estatus o rol opaca todos los otros roles o posiciones sociales de una persona. Por ejemplo, "violador" elimina los roles positivos como lo son el de "ser un buen estudiante" o "ser estrella del deporte".

Meat-eaters
Carniceros, comen carne Jerga usada en el reporte de la Comisión de Knapp en 1971 sobre corrupción de la policía en Nueva York donde se describió a oficiales policíacos quienes buscaban situaciones que podían producir ganancia económicas.

Mens rea
Mens rea Intencion delictiva.

Meritorious time
Conducta meritoria Bonificación que reduce la condena de un prisionero al hacer algo especial o superior a lo requerido, como el recibir su diploma de educación general (GED).

Metropolitan Police Act
Ley de la Policia Metropolitana Creada en 1929 por el caballero inglés Robert Peel, la ley que creo la primera fuerza policíaca permanente y de servicio al público.

Misdemeanor
Delito menos grave Delito considerado menos grave que un crimen grave. Usualmente se juzga en tribunales locales y que conllevan la sanción de reclusión por un término que no exceda un año.

Missouri Bar Plan
Plan del Colegio de Missouri Comisión judicial que nomina a un grupo de candidatos y los presenta al gobernador quien elige entre todos los candidatos. Al año de ejercer en el puesto, los votantes deciden si el juez retiene su escaño o no. Bajo este sistema los jueces deben ser reelegidos cada término. También se conoce como "selección meritoria."

National Incident-Based Reporting System (NIBRS)
Sistema de reporte nacional basado en Infracciones Sistema para reportar delitos donde cada infracción es descrita, incluyendo los datos que describen al delincuente(s), la victima(s), y la propiedad.

Neighborhood Watch
Programa de Observación Vecinal Programa de policía comunitaria que estimula la cooperación de los residentes en las medidas de seguridad que emplean en el vecindario.

Neutralization theory
Teoría de neutralización Perspectiva que sugiere que los delincuentes juveniles se sienten culpables al envolverse en actividades delictivas. La conducta ilícita es episódica y los delincuentes tienden tanto a la activad legal como a la ilícita. Los delincuentes ponen a un lado sus valores morales y legales con el fin de delinquir.

No Bill
Auto de No Acusación Veredicto del gran jurado denegando el procesamiento del acusado porque no hay pruebas suficientes para la acusación.

Nolo contendere
Nolo condendere Del Latín "no me opongo." El acusado no se opone, ni acepta la acusación, pero acepta el castigo, como si fuera culpable. Este tipo de admisión no puede ser usada en una acción civil posterior basada en los mismos hechos.

Operant conditioning
Condicionamiento operante Cambio en conducta donde el sujeto recibe recompensas o castigos por una conducta específica hasta que la persona asocia la conducta con placer o dolor.

Pains of imprisonment
Dolor, pena de encarcelamiento Las privaciones asociadas con las prisiones.

Parens patriae
Parens patriae (patria potestad) Del Latín "padre de la nación." Se refiere a la creencia filosófica donde el

gobierno tiene la facultad de proteger a todos los niños y minusválidos.

Peacemaking criminology
Criminología de la paz Perspectiva teorética que sirve como alternativa a la guerra contra el crimen. Enfatiza la no-violencia, justicia social, y la reducción del sufrimiento de la victima, y del delincuente.

Penal code
Código penal Código de leyes donde se describen los delitos y los castigos.

Petitioner
Peticionante, solicitante Persona que presenta la demanda. Conocido también como el "demandante."

Pillory
Picota Estructura de madera con agujeros para la cabeza y las manos, usada para aprisionar y exhibir a los delincuentes para la burla pública.

Plea bargain
Negociación Negociación entre el acusado, su abogado defensor y el fiscal en la que el acusado reconoce su culpabilidad, o no se opone a los cargos, a cambio de limitar las acusaciones en su contra, su severidad, disminución en el número de cargos, ofrecer información sobre el delito o sus cómplices, o donde el fiscal accede a recomendar la sentencia deseada. Este tipo de negociación requiere la aprobación del juez.

Policeman's working personality
Personalidad del trabajo policial Término acuñado por Jerome Skolnick que se refiere al estado mental de los policías quienes enfrentan situaciones de peligro, tiene que usar de poder y autoridad, se sienten aislados, y bajo sospecha pero tienen que ser eficientes y profesionales en la ejecución de su trabajo. A estos oficiales les atrae la subcultura policíaca que enfatiza unos valores diferentes a la de los demás ciudadanos.

Positivist School of Criminology
Escuela positivista de Criminología Grupo de teorías criminológicas que usan técnicas de investigación científicas en el estudio del delito y de los delincuentes.

Poor laws
Leyes de pobres Leyes que durante el siglo 17 entregaban los vagabundos y niños abandonados a los hacendados y mercaderes como aprendices.

Precedent
Precedente Decisión jurídica donde se usa una decisión previamente tomada para decidir casos similares.

Prejudicial error
Error prejudicial Error cometido en un acto procesal.

Pre-sentence investigation
Investigación pre-sentencia Informe preparado por un oficial de libertad a prueba y que ayuda al juez a determinar el castigo. Este informe contiene información sobre arrestos, condenas previas, historial de trabajo y familiar. También se conoce como "informe pre-sentencia."

Presumptive sentence
Condena presuntiva Castigo que puede apartarse de la pena establecida en la ley y que se basa en las circunstancias agravantes o atenuantes.

Preventive detention
Arresto preventivo El arresto de un acusado antes del juicio con el propósito de proteger a un individuo o al público.

Prima facie case
Caso a prima facie Causa donde la evidencia es suficiente para fundamentar una acción y que debe ser rebatida mediante prueba suficiente para que la acción no proceda.

Probable cause
Causa probable, razonable La existencia de suficientes elementos para creer que un delito ha sido cometido o que la propiedad esta ligada a un delito. El oficial policíaco necesita tener causa probable para arrestar sin previa orden judicial, hacer registro sin orden judicial o incautar propiedad que pueda proveer evidencia de un delito.

Problem-oriented policing
Orientación policíaca hacia el problema Estilo policíaco que intenta atacar los problemas sociales que contribuyen al delito.

Procedural law
Derecho procesal Leyes que determinan los métodos de su aplicación y su uso.

Professional model of policing
Modelo policíaco profesional Varios estilos policíacos donde se enfatiza la impersonalidad y la ley cuando se ejercen las funciones policíacas.

Prohibition
Prohibición Periodo entre el 29 de Enero de 1920 y el 5 de Diciembre de 1933, durante el cual la manufactura, transportación y venta de bebidas alcohólicas en los Estados Unidos fue prohibida por la Enmienda número 18. Esta legislación se conoce como la ley Nacional de Prohibición o la ley de Volstead.

Racial profiling
Perfil racial Cuando la sospecha de actividad ilícita está basada en la raza, grupo étnico u origen nacional, en vez de la conducta ilícita o evidencia de actividad ilícita.

Rape
Violación sexual Actividad sexual o acto sexual, que es forzado y sin consentimiento, usualmente bajo amenaza de causar daño. Si la actividad sexual se lleva a cabo con un menor o una persona que no puede dar su consentimiento debido a trastorno mental, incapacidad mental, ebriedad, inconsciencia o engaño se conoce también como "violación técnica".

Rational choice theory
Teoría de selección racional Perspectiva que señala que los delincuentes seleccionan su actividad criminal racionalmente. La teoría también señala que estos delincuentes deciden cometer el

delito al darse cuenta de que los beneficios adquiridos sobrepasan las consecuencias de quebrantar las leyes.

Reasonable stop standard
Estándar para paradas razonables por parte de la policía Regla usada por la Corte Suprema que establece que la constitucionalidad de una acción se basa en si una persona prudente se siente en libertad para dar por terminado su encuentro con un policía.

Reasonable suspicion
Sospecha razonable Sospecha justificable basada en los hechos o circunstancias que justifica parar y en ocasiones registrar a un individuo se cree esta envuelto en actividad delictiva.

Redirect examination
Interrogatorio direct Preguntas que se le hacen a un testigo sobre los hechos descubiertos durante el contrainterrogatorio.

Referral
Referido Parecido a los "cargos" en el sistema de adultos donde un funcionario público, usualmente un policía, o los padres o representante escolar, determinan que el joven necesita de la intervención del tribunal de menores.

Residential placement
Colocación residencial Tipo de sanción donde el delincuente juvenil es enviado a un hogar substituto u otro tipo de tratamiento en la comunidad donde el menor es observado pero puede ir a la escuela y al trabajo.

Respondent
Demandado Persona que deberá responder la querella del demandante.

Restorative justice
Justicia restitutiva Modelo de justicia que ofrece como alternativa el uso de programas comunitarios para ayudar a reparar los daños causados por la actividad criminal. Estos programas incluyen a la victima, al acusado, representantes policíacos y de la comunidad en sus esfuerzos de desarrollar soluciones efectivas al problema de la criminalidad.

Retribution model
Retribución Medida de control donde los delincuentes son castigados tan severamente como sea permitido por la ofensa cometida, esta medida de control se opone a la rehabilitación.

Robbery
Robo Acción por la cual se obtiene propiedad ajena por medio de la violencia o amenaza de violencia.

Rule of four
Régimen de cuatro Establece que al menos cuatro de los nueve Jueces de la Corte Suprema deben votar para reconocer una causa.

Seizure
Embargo, decomiso Cuando oficiales policíacos recogen evidencia que potencialmente puede ser usada en un caso criminal. Cualquier evidencia que a sido embargada sin orden judicial o sin causa probable no podrá ser admitida en los tribunales.

Separate-and-silent system
Sistema de silencio y separación Método de control penitenciario desarrollado en el Penitenciaria estatal del este de Philadelphia donde los confinados estaban incomunicados y sin acceso visible uno del otro. Es muy parecido al sistema de prisión solitaria usado hoy día.

Serial murder
Asesinato en serie Homicidios donde hay varias victimas y es cometido por el mismo delincuente en tres o más incidentes ocurridos a través de un periodo de tiempo.

Service style
Estilo servicial Modelo policíaco donde el servicio a la comunidad y a los ciudadanos es de primera importancia. En este estilo policíaco el agente usa su discreción, como en el sistema de vigilantes, pero su discreción es visible y es objeto de revisión formal y de evaluación, y puede cambiar de acuerdo a las circunstancias.

Sex work
Trabajo sexual Acceso carnal u otra actividad sexual por dinero.

Sexual assault
Abuso sexual Acceso carnal sin consentimiento o con una persona que no puede dar su consentimiento (como por ejemplo, un menor o persona mentalmente minusválida).

Sheriff
Alguacil Derivado de las palabras "shire" "condado" y "reeve" "administrador" (ayudante del rey). Es la persona de mayor autoridad policíaca en algunos condados y lleva a cabo labores judiciales. En Inglaterra medieval, el administrador del condado tenía poderes militares y judiciales. La labor del condado y administrador esta limitada a intervenir en delitos menores, la investigación de delitos dentro del condado, e interrogar sospechosos de delitos.

Shock probation
Libertad condicionada de shock Practica donde se sentencia a prisión donde el confinado sirve parte de la pena y luego se le otorga su libertad condicional (libertad vigilada), sin su conocimiento previo.

Show-of-authority stop
Parada demostrativa de autoridad Incidente donde el agente policíaco demuestra su autoridad (por ejemplo mostrando su placa), para que el sospechoso obedezca una orden.

Social control theory
Teoría de control social Perspectiva que no intenta explicar porque se quebranta la ley, sino que explora el por qué la mayoría de las personas no quebranta la ley. Ligada a Travis Hirschi.

Socialization
Socialización Proceso por el cual las personas adquieren su identidad y aprenden las normas, valores, conducta y destrezas sociales deseadas en su sociedad.

Sociological imagination
Imaginación sociológica La idea de que uno debe buscar mas allá de lo obvio si se quiere evaluar como nuestra posición

social influye en nuestra valoralización de nuestra sociedad. Nuestra raza, edad, sexo, y posición socioeconómica influyen nuestros valores y perspectivas.

Somatotyping
Somatotipos El uso del cuerpo y de las características físicas para clasificar la personalidad.

Specific deterrence
Disuasión especifica Método de control donde al delincuente se le impide cometer otros delitos mediante el encarcelamiento o uso de la pena de muerte.

Stare decisis
Stare decisis Principio jurídico donde los tribunales basan sus decisiones en precedentes judiciales.

State court
Tribunal estatal Sistema jerárquico de los tribunales generales y especiales, son financiados y administrados por los diferentes estados de la unión americana. Cada estado tiene su propio sistema judicial.

Status offense
Falta juvenil Conducta considerada ilegítima cuando es cometida por menores de edad y puede ser juzgada solamente en el tribunal de menores.

Statute
Estatuto Reglamento aprobado por la legislatura.

Statutory exclusion
Excepción legal Provisión que excluye de la jurisdicción del tribunal de menores y sin necesidad de audiencia o vista de renuncia, a aquellos delincuentes juveniles que son mayores de cierta edad, o que han cometido ciertas faltas o tienen expediente delictivo. Los delincuentes juveniles excluidos son automáticamente referidos al tribunal de adultos. Algunos de los delitos que conllevan esta exclusión son el homicidio, la violación agravada, y el robo a mano armada.

Statutory law
Precepto legal Tipo de ley aprobada por la legislatura, lo opuesto al derecho común, que no tiene origen legislativo.

Statutory rape
Violación técnica, ver violación.

Stop
Alto, parada policíaca Captura temporera y que legalmente es una aprehensión y debe estar fundamentada en una sospecha razonable.

Stop-and-frisk
Parada y cateo Detener y palpar con las manos- término que describe dos comportamientos por parte de oficiales policíacos cuando intervienen con personas sospechosas. Para que el cateo (palpar con las manos) sea válido, la detención debe de ser válida. El cateo es un registro.

Strain theory
Teoría de tensión, presión Hipótesis donde la causa de la criminalidad es la presión/tensión que los grupos o individuos cultural o materialmente marginados tienen de alcanzar las metas sociales, a pesar de que los medios para adquirir esas metas son ilegítimos. Basada en la teoría de Anomia de Emile Durkheim.

Strict liability
Responsabilidad objetiva Delitos donde se responsabiliza a la persona sin necesidad de probar intención criminal. No se necesita *Mens rea* en los casos de responsabilidad objetiva.

Subject matter jurisdiction
Competencia en razón de la materia Donde el tipo de caso determina el tribunal. Por ejemplo, la diferencia entre delito grave y delito menos grave.

Substantive law
Derecho sustantivo Legislación que define derechos y prohíbe cierta conducta (delitos).

Terrorism
Terrorismo El uso o la amenaza de usar violencia en contra del estado u otra entidad política con el intento de demandar alguna acción.

Thames River Police
Policía del Rio Thames Fuerza policíaca privada creada por el West India Trading Company en 1798 y que fue la primera fuerza policíaca profesional y a sueldo en Londres.

Tort law
Derecho civil Área de derecho que trata con acciones civiles, incluyendo el rompimiento de contrato, además de daños y perjuicios. Derecho civil incluye la difamación, calumnia, agresión, traspaso y negligencia.

Total institution
Institución total Ambiente físicamente restringido donde todo movimiento y comportamiento es controlado y estructurado.

Trial by ordeal
Juicio a prueba (prueba de fuego) Costumbre Antigua entre grupos culturales donde el acusado era puesto a prueba para comprobar su inocencia o culpabilidad. El resultado de la prueba era decidido por el poder divino.

True Hill
Acusación Fundada Aprobación de la acusación o procesamiento por el gran jurado porque han encontrado evidencia para la acusación.

Uniform Crime Reports
Reporte Uniforme del Delito Publicación anual de la Oficina Federal de Investigaciones que usa la información ofrecida por las agencias policíacas en los EEUU y donde se resume la incidencia y taza delictiva de los delitos reportados a la policía. También se conoce como "UCR".

United States Border Patrol
Patrulla Fronteriza Unidad del Servicio de Naturalización e Inmigración. Su misión principal es la detención y prevención de la entrada ilícita a los Estados Unidos de persona nacidas en el extranjero.

United States Customs Service
Servicio de Aduanas de los Estados Unidos Agencia encargada de proteger la frontera americana, encargada de controlar el contrabando, la importación, y exportación.

United States Marshals Service (Federal Marshals)
Servicio de Alguaciles Federales Creada en 1789, esta agencia protege los tribunales federales y se encarga de la operación del sistema judicial. También se encarga de la investigación de fugitivos, la custodia y la transportación de prisioneros federales, de proveer seguridad a testigos del gobierno, y del embargo y registro en confiscaciones federales.

United States Secret Service
Servicio Secreto Agencia investigativa federal autorizada para dar protección al Presidente, a otros oficiales del gobierno federal y a dignatarios extranjeros de visita en los EEUU. También investiga el fraude financiero y la falsificación.

United States Supreme Court
Tribunal Supremo de los Estados Unidos El "tribunal de última instancia." Corte de última instancia en los Estados Unidos, creada por el Artículo número 3 de la Constitución, con pocas excepciones, oye mayormente apelaciones.

Use of force
Uso de fuerza Se refiere al uso legal de violencia en la aplicación de la ley. Uso excesivo de fuerza se considera brutalidad policíaca.

Utilitarianism
Utilitarianismo Teoría que se asocia con Jeremy Bentham donde se propone que las personas deciden no envolverse en actos delictivos si el castigo sobrepasa los beneficios derivados del delito.

Venire
Venire Lista de donde se elige el jurado.

Victim precipitation
Instigación de la victima Situación donde la propia víctima del delito alienta o promueve activamente la comisión del delito.

Victimization studies
Estudios de victimización Encuestas donde se intenta medir la extensión del delito entrevistando a las personas que han sido victimas de delitos.

Victimless crimes
Delitos sin víctimas Se refiere a conductas tales como las apuestas de juego y la prostitución, que son indeseables porque ofenden los sentimientos comunitarios y no por los daños causados a las personas o a la propiedad.

Voir dire
Voire dire Del Francés "mirar, hablar". Se refiere al interrogatorio que hace el juez y/o los abogados cada una de las personas citadas para determinar si pueden ser miembros del jurado.

War on drugs
Guerra anti-drogas Política que intenta reducir la venta y el uso de substancias ilícitas. Esta metáfora de guerra se usa para ilustrar la gravedad del problema del crimen en los Estados Unidos. Esta guerra tiene muchos frentes de batalla pero el sistema de justicia criminal emplea muchos de sus recursos en este problema.

Warrant
Orden judicial Orden dada por un oficial judicial donde se autoriza ejecutar la acción legal especificada para hacer justicia, tal como un arresto o registro.

Watch-and-ward system
Sistema de guarda y vigilancia Sistema inglés donde el alguacil supervisaba al centinela o serenazgo que resguardaba la puerta de la ciudad o del pueblo durante la noche.

Watchman style
Centinela o serenazgo Estilo policíaco donde se enfatiza el mantenimiento del orden público y la intervención informal por parte de la policía en vez de la aplicación de la ley.

Writ of certiorari
Auto de avocación Orden de un tribunal superior solicitando al tribunal inferior correspondiente toda la documentación del caso.

XYY syndrome
Sindrome XYY Condición genética donde el hombre nace con una alteración en el patrón numérico de la cromosoma Y. Estos hombres tienden a ser de talla alta, tienen dificultades con el lenguaje, y tienden a ser poco inteligentes. Tiempo atrás se creyó estaba asociada con la conducta delictiva.

Zero-tolerance policies
Política de No tolerancia Reglas en las escuelas u otras agencias de edad y donde se aplica rígidamente la ley o donde las reglas se siguen sin cuestionamiento o lugar para usar la discreción del personal que tiene la autoridad de ejecutar la política o reglas.

Case Index

Subject Index